The Encyclopedia of Religion

The Encyclopedia of Religion

Mircea Eliade

EDITOR IN CHIEF

Volume 5

MACMILLAN PUBLISHING COMPANY
New York
Collier Macmillan Publishers
London

MACMILLAN PUBLISHING COMPANY
866 Third Avenue, New York, NY 10022

Collier Macmillan Canada, Inc.

Library of Congress Catalog Card Number: 86-5432

PRINTED IN THE UNITED STATES OF AMERICA

printing number
1 2 3 4 5 6 7 8 9 10

Library of Congress Cataloging-in-Publication Data

The Encyclopedia of religion.

Includes bibliographies and index.
1. Religion—Dictionaries. I. Eliade, Mircea, 1907–1986. II. Adams, Charles J.
BL31.#46 1986 200'.3'21 86-5432
ISBN 0-02-909480-1 (set)
ISBN 0-02-909740-1 (v. 5)

Acknowledgments of sources, copyrights, and permissions to use previously published materials are gratefully made in a special listing in volume 16.

Abbreviations and Symbols Used in This Work

abbr. abbreviated; abbreviation
abr. abridged; abridgment
AD *anno Domini*, in the year of the (our) Lord
Afrik. Afrikaans
AH *anno Hegirae*, in the year of the Hijrah
Akk. Akkadian
Ala. Alabama
Alb. Albanian
Am. *Amos*
AM *ante meridiem*, before noon
amend. amended; amendment
annot. annotated; annotation
Ap. *Apocalypse*
Apn. *Apocryphon*
app. appendix
Arab. Arabic
ʿArakh. *ʿArakhin*
Aram. Aramaic
Ariz. Arizona
Ark. Arkansas
Arm. Armenian
art. article (pl., arts.)
AS Anglo-Saxon
Asm. Mos. *Assumption of Moses*
Assyr. Assyrian
A.S.S.R. Autonomous Soviet Socialist Republic
Av. Avestan
ʿA.Z. *ʿAvodah zarah*
b. born
Bab. Babylonian
Ban. Bantu
1 Bar. *1 Baruch*
2 Bar. *2 Baruch*
3 Bar. *3 Baruch*
4 Bar. *4 Baruch*
B.B. *Bava' batra'*
BBC British Broadcasting Corporation
BC before Christ
BCE before the common era
B.D. Bachelor of Divinity
Beits. *Beitsah*
Bekh. *Bekhorot*
Beng. Bengali
Ber. *Berakhot*
Berb. Berber
Bik. *Bikkurim*
bk. book (pl., bks.)
B.M. *Bava' metsiʿa'*
BP before the present
B.Q. *Bava' qamma'*
Brāh. *Brāhmaṇa*
Bret. Breton
B.T. Babylonian Talmud
Bulg. Bulgarian
Burm. Burmese
c. *circa*, about, approximately
Calif. California
Can. Canaanite
Catal. Catalan
CE of the common era
Celt. Celtic
cf. *confer*, compare
Chald. Chaldean
chap. chapter (pl., chaps.)
Chin. Chinese
C.H.M. Community of the Holy Myrrhbearers
1 Chr. *1 Chronicles*
2 Chr. *2 Chronicles*
Ch. Slav. Church Slavic
cm centimeters
col. column (pl., cols.)
Col. *Colossians*
Colo. Colorado
comp. compiler (pl., comps.)
Conn. Connecticut
cont. continued
Copt. Coptic
1 Cor. *1 Corinthians*
2 Cor. *2 Corinthians*
corr. corrected
C.S.P. Congregatio Sancti Pauli, Congregation of Saint Paul (Paulists)
d. died
D Deuteronomic (source of the Pentateuch)
Dan. Danish
D.B. Divinitatis Baccalaureus, Bachelor of Divinity
D.C. District of Columbia
D.D. Divinitatis Doctor, Doctor of Divinity
Del. Delaware
Dem. *Demaʾi*
dim. diminutive
diss. dissertation
Dn. *Daniel*
D.Phil. Doctor of Philosophy
Dt. *Deuteronomy*
Du. Dutch
E Elohist (source of the Pentateuch)
Eccl. *Ecclesiastes*
ed. editor (pl., eds.); edition; edited by
ʿEduy. *ʿEduyyot*
e.g. *exempli gratia*, for example
Egyp. Egyptian
1 En. *1 Enoch*
2 En. *2 Enoch*
3 En. *3 Enoch*
Eng. English
enl. enlarged
Eph. *Ephesians*
ʿEruv. *ʿEruvin*
1 Esd. *1 Esdras*
2 Esd. *2 Esdras*
3 Esd. *3 Esdras*
4 Esd. *4 Esdras*
esp. especially
Est. Estonian
Est. *Esther*
et al. *et alii*, and others
etc. *et cetera*, and so forth
Eth. Ethiopic
EV English version
Ex. *Exodus*
exp. expanded
Ez. *Ezekiel*
Ezr. *Ezra*
2 Ezr. *2 Ezra*
4 Ezr. *4 Ezra*
f. feminine; and following (pl., ff.)
fasc. fascicle (pl., fascs.)
fig. figure (pl., figs.)
Finn. Finnish
fl. *floruit*, flourished
Fla. Florida
Fr. French
frag. fragment
ft. feet
Ga. Georgia
Gal. *Galatians*
Gaul. Gaulish
Ger. German
Giṭ. *Giṭṭin*
Gn. *Genesis*
Gr. Greek
Ḥag. *Ḥagigah*
Ḥal. *Ḥallah*
Hau. Hausa
Hb. *Habakkuk*
Heb. Hebrew
Heb. *Hebrews*
Hg. *Haggai*
Hitt. Hittite
Hor. *Horayot*
Hos. *Hosea*
Ḥul. *Ḥullin*
Hung. Hungarian
ibid. *ibidem*, in the same place (as the one immediately preceding)
Icel. Icelandic
i.e. *id est*, that is
IE Indo-European
Ill. Illinois
Ind. Indiana
intro. introduction
Ir. Gael. Irish Gaelic
Iran. Iranian
Is. *Isaiah*
Ital. Italian
J Yahvist (source of the Pentateuch)
Jas. *James*
Jav. Javanese
Jb. *Job*
Jdt. *Judith*
Jer. *Jeremiah*
Jgs. *Judges*
Jl. *Joel*
Jn. *John*
1 Jn. *1 John*
2 Jn. *2 John*
3 Jn. *3 John*
Jon. *Jonah*
Jos. *Joshua*
Jpn. Japanese
JPS Jewish Publication Society translation (1985) of the Hebrew Bible
J.T. Jerusalem Talmud
Jub. *Jubilees*
Kans. Kansas
Kel. *Kelim*

Ker. *Keritot*
Ket. *Ketubbot*
1 Kgs. *1 Kings*
2 Kgs. *2 Kings*
Khois. Khoisan
Kil. *Kil'ayim*
km kilometers
Kor. Korean
Ky. Kentucky
l. line (pl., ll.)
La. Louisiana
Lam. *Lamentations*
Lat. Latin
Latv. Latvian
L. en Th. Licencié en Théologie, Licentiate in Theology
L. ès L. Licencié ès Lettres, Licentiate in Literature
Let. Jer. *Letter of Jeremiah*
lit. literally
Lith. Lithuanian
Lk. *Luke*
LL Late Latin
LL.D. Legum Doctor, Doctor of Laws
Lv. *Leviticus*
m meters
m. masculine
M.A. Master of Arts
Ma'as. *Ma'aserot*
Ma'as. Sh. *Ma'aser sheni*
Mak. *Makkot*
Makh. *Makhshirin*
Mal. *Malachi*
Mar. Marathi
Mass. Massachusetts
1 Mc. *1 Maccabees*
2 Mc. *2 Maccabees*
3 Mc. *3 Maccabees*
4 Mc. *4 Maccabees*
Md. Maryland
M.D. Medicinae Doctor, Doctor of Medicine
ME Middle English
Meg. *Megillah*
Me'il. *Me'ilah*
Men. *Menaḥot*
MHG Middle High German
mi. miles
Mi. *Micah*
Mich. Michigan
Mid. *Middot*
Minn. Minnesota
Miq. *Miqva'ot*
MIran. Middle Iranian
Miss. Mississippi
Mk. *Mark*
Mo. Missouri
Mo'ed Q. *Mo'ed qaṭan*
Mont. Montana
MPers. Middle Persian
MS. *manuscriptum*, manuscript (pl., MSS)
Mt. *Matthew*
MT Masoretic text
n. note
Na. *Nahum*
Nah. Nahuatl
Naz. *Nazir*
N.B. *nota bene*, take careful note
N.C. North Carolina
n.d. no date
N.Dak. North Dakota
NEB New English Bible
Nebr. Nebraska
Ned. *Nedarim*
Neg. *Nega'im*
Neh. *Nehemiah*
Nev. Nevada
N.H. New Hampshire
Nid. *Niddah*
N.J. New Jersey
Nm. *Numbers*
N.Mex. New Mexico
no. number (pl., nos.)
Nor. Norwegian
n.p. no place
n.s. new series
N.Y. New York
Ob. *Obadiah*
O.Cist. Ordo Cisterciencium, Order of Cîteaux (Cistercians)
OCS Old Church Slavonic
OE Old English
O.F.M. Ordo Fratrum Minorum, Order of Friars Minor (Franciscans)
OFr. Old French
Ohal. *Ohalot*
OHG Old High German
OIr. Old Irish
OIran. Old Iranian
Okla. Oklahoma
ON Old Norse
O.P. Ordo Praedicatorum, Order of Preachers (Dominicans)
OPers. Old Persian
op. cit. *opere citato*, in the work cited
OPrus. Old Prussian
Oreg. Oregon
'Orl. *'Orlah*
O.S.B. Ordo Sancti Benedicti, Order of Saint Benedict (Benedictines)
p. page (pl., pp.)
P Priestly (source of the Pentateuch)
Pa. Pennsylvania
Pahl. Pahlavi
Par. *Parah*
para. paragraph (pl., paras.)
Pers. Persian
Pes. *Pesaḥim*
Ph.D. Philosophiae Doctor, Doctor of Philosophy
Phil. *Philippians*
Phlm. *Philemon*
Phoen. Phoenician
pl. plural; plate (pl., pls.)
PM *post meridiem*, after noon
Pol. Polish
pop. population
Port. Portuguese
Prv. *Proverbs*
Ps. *Psalms*
Ps. 151 *Psalm 151*
Ps. Sol. *Psalms of Solomon*
pt. part (pl., pts.)
1 Pt. *1 Peter*
2 Pt. *2 Peter*
Pth. Parthian
Q hypothetical source of the synoptic Gospels
Qid. *Qiddushin*
Qin. *Qinnim*
r. reigned; ruled
Rab. *Rabbah*
rev. revised
R. ha-Sh. *Ro'sh ha-shanah*
R.I. Rhode Island
Rom. Romanian
Rom. *Romans*
R.S.C.J. Societas Sacratissimi Cordis Jesu, Religious of the Sacred Heart
RSV Revised Standard Version of the Bible
Ru. *Ruth*
Rus. Russian
Rv. *Revelation*
Rv. Ezr. *Revelation of Ezra*
San. *Sanhedrin*
S.C. South Carolina
Scot. Gael. Scottish Gaelic
S.Dak. South Dakota
sec. section (pl., secs.)
Sem. Semitic
ser. series
sg. singular
Sg. *Song of Songs*
Sg. of 3 *Prayer of Azariah and the Song of the Three Young Men*
Shab. *Shabbat*
Shav. *Shavu'ot*
Sheq. *Sheqalim*
Sib. Or. *Sibylline Oracles*
Sind. Sindhi
Sinh. Sinhala
Sir. *Ben Sira*
S.J. Societas Jesu, Society of Jesus (Jesuits)
Skt. Sanskrit
1 Sm. *1 Samuel*
2 Sm. *2 Samuel*
Sogd. Sogdian
Soṭ *Soṭah*
sp. species (pl., spp.)
Span. Spanish
sq. square
S.S.R. Soviet Socialist Republic
st. stanza (pl., ss.)
S.T.M. Sacrae Theologiae Magister, Master of Sacred Theology
Suk. *Sukkah*
Sum. Sumerian
supp. supplement; supplementary
Sus. *Susanna*
s.v. *sub verbo*, under the word (pl., s.v.v.)
Swed. Swedish
Syr. Syriac
Syr. Men. *Syriac Menander*
Ta'an. *Ta'anit*
Tam. Tamil
Tam. *Tamid*
Tb. *Tobit*
T.D. *Taishō shinshū daizōkyō*, edited by Takakusu Junjirō et al. (Tokyo, 1922–1934)
Tem. *Temurah*
Tenn. Tennessee
Ter. *Terumot*
Ṭev. Y. *Ṭevul yom*
Tex. Texas
Th.D. Theologicae Doctor, Doctor of Theology
1 Thes. *1 Thessalonians*
2 Thes. *2 Thessalonians*
Thrac. Thracian
Ti. *Titus*
Tib. Tibetan
1 Tm. *1 Timothy*
2 Tm. *2 Timothy*
T. of 12 *Testaments of the Twelve Patriarchs*
Ṭoh. *Ṭohorot*
Tong. Tongan
trans. translator, translators; translated by; translation
Turk. Turkish
Ukr. Ukrainian
Upan. *Upaniṣad*
U.S. United States
U.S.S.R. Union of Soviet Socialist Republics
Uqts. *Uqtsin*
v. verse (pl., vv.)
Va. Virginia
var. variant; variation
Viet. Vietnamese
viz. *videlicet*, namely
vol. volume (pl., vols.)
Vt. Vermont
Wash. Washington
Wel. Welsh
Wis. Wisconsin
Wis. *Wisdom of Solomon*
W.Va. West Virginia
Wyo. Wyoming
Yad. *Yadayim*
Yev. *Yevamot*
Yi. Yiddish
Yor. Yoruba
Zav. *Zavim*
Zec. *Zechariah*
Zep. *Zephaniah*
Zev. *Zevaḥim*

* hypothetical
? uncertain; possibly; perhaps
° degrees
\+ plus
− minus
= equals; is equivalent to
× by; multiplied by
→ yields

E

(CONTINUED)

ECONOMICS AND RELIGION.

[*To explore the relations between religion and economics, this entry takes as its starting place the beginnings of modern economic theory and examines the perspectives on those relations that have developed within the sociology of religion since the late nineteenth century. For a discussion of money from a history of religions perspective, see* Money.]

A sustained scholarly interest in the relationship between religion and economics crystallized in a number of Western societies in the early years of the twentieth century. Since that time it has been a topic of considerable research and debate.

Development of Economic Analysis. The discussion of the relationship between economics and religion is plagued by a general problem having to do with how appropriate it is to speak of separate domains—such as the economic or the religious—in premodern, especially primal, societies, where such distinctions were or are not part of everyday life. Indeed, only during the last two hundred years or so have we become accustomed to speak of the *economy,* even though the term was used as long ago as the fourth century BCE by Aristotle to designate the relationships among members of the domestic household. Aristotle was particularly concerned to show, in the face of the commercial expansion of his time, that human wants and needs are not unlimited and that useful things are not, by their nature, scarce. In spite of the great expansion of trade, profit making, and eventually, price setting by market forces and the appearance of large-scale manufacture during the centuries following Aristotle, it was not until as recently as the end of the eighteenth century that "the economy" became fully thematized (and then only in the Western world) as a relatively autonomous realm of human life. That period saw the beginnings in Great Britain of the discipline that came to be called political economy and the first use of the term *économiste* by French intellectuals. The perception of the economy as a relatively autonomous realm (and, in the view of many of those who specialized in analyzing it, the most fundamental human realm) went hand-in-hand with the view that religion was of rapidly diminishing significance.

Primacy of Economic Aspect. The prevailing view among social scientists and historians has been that the economy, during the long period from ancient Greek civilization to the nineteenth century, became disembedded from the societal fabric, especially in the Western world. By the late nineteenth century, therefore, the economy was seen as standing apart from the rest of society. This move has been called the "naturalization" of the economy (in the sense that it came to be regarded as operating according to its own natural laws, particularly those issuing from the relationship between supply and demand, as expressed in monetary prices), and it constituted a crucial aspect of the nineteenth-century diagnosis of secularization (the decline in the significance of religion in modern society). The perception of the rapidly increasing autonomy of the economy inspired in Karl Marx and Friedrich Engels the idea that human history in its entirety had been motored by economic forces or, more specifically, by class conflicts centered upon economic concerns. In response to the view of the classical British political economists that the best form of society is one in which there is free competition among many private producers in line with universal economic laws, Marx argued that different modes of production have prevailed during different periods of history, and therefore the embryonic capitalist mode cannot be regarded as the paradigm of all other modes, let alone as a permanent and universal system. [*See also the biography of Marx.*]

Both the classical political economists, on the one hand, and Marx and Engels, on the other, thus saw the economy as fundamental to the operation of human societies and correspondingly regarded religion, particularly in modernizing societies, as of peripheral significance (for Marx and Engels, it was primarily an epiphenomenon), but they differed greatly with respect to the implications of the fundamentality of the economy. Religion was, according to Marx, being driven from human life by capitalist materialism and in any case impeded the realization of proletarian class consciousness, which would make possible the release of the class from the exploitative bondage of capitalism. Nevertheless, despite Marx's mainly negative assessment of the historical role of religion, he initiated an intellectual concern with the historical origins of capitalism and, more generally, with the relationship between economic matters and religion.

Primacy of Social and Moral Aspects. Classical political economy as such did not encompass the sociological and historical themes that were developed by Marx and others during the nineteenth century. For the most part, the more sociologically inclined social scientists of the period shared Marx's belief in the increasing salience of the economy but tended to view it as a threat to the social and moral integration of industrial societies. In France, for example, Saint-Simon, after having written at length about the new industrial order, came to the conclusion that a new and in a sense secular version of Christianity was necessary in order to give the new form meaningful direction.

While Marx spoke of the new industrial order as providing the opportunity for deprived, exploited classes to seize control of the mainspring of human life (that is, its productive forces) and thus bring about the religionless humanization of the species, Saint-Simon had come to the conclusion that religion in a modernized form was essential in sustaining the meaningful sociality of human life in the face of the eruption of the economic factor. For Marx, religion is the definitive form of alienation, but for those who wrote from the perspective of Saint-Simon, religion cements society and in a sense expresses the sociality of humanity. The latter view was brought to its consummation by Émile Durkheim in the early years of the twentieth century. For Durkheim religion is the serious life, as he put it, and serves, *inter alia*, so as to elevate men and women above purely material interests.

Religion and Economic Legitimation. Although the developing nineteenth-century discipline of political economy (eventually known simply as economics) did not share the concern of Marxism and non-Marxist social science with religion, religious ideas and practices emerged in the major areas of capitalism—notably Britain and the United States—that legitimated the capitalist economy and sanctioned the existing social order. Indeed, capitalists themselves quite often expressed the view that certain forms of Protestantism encouraged a dedication to industrial work. More specifically, we may point to Wesleyan Methodism in England as an important example of the way in which religion played a significant part not merely in the development of the entrepreneurial attitude but also in the acquiescence of workers to their role in the system of social stratification. (That religion could, in spite of its allegedly imminent demise, perform this service for capitalism was conceded by Marx under the rubric of "false consciousness.") The greatest degree of religious legitimation of capitalism occurred in the United States, where the predominance of a basically Calvinist form of Protestantism encouraged the view that men proved themselves before God and their fellow men and women by successful, disciplined economic striving.

German Critiques of Capitalism. By the end of the nineteenth century, intellectuals in Europe and North America had become almost obsessed by the idea that a major transformation of the West had occurred, for by that time not only had capitalistic production greatly expanded but so had bureaucracy, science and technology, and urban forms of life. Thus in the declining years of the nineteenth century theories and diagnoses proliferated concerning the causes, magnitude, and implications of what was considered a more material and less religious mode of existence. It was in Germany, however, that the particular problem of the relationship between religious and economic factors was given the most sustained initial attention, particularly as far as its history was concerned.

The fact that an interest in the connection between economic matters and religion developed so strongly among German scholars can be attributed in part to their felt need to comprehend the character and the place in the modern world of Germany, which had only recently been politically united. Although it possessed a rich culture, the area that became the German empire in the 1870s had been relatively backward in economic terms and had not developed what came to be called by Max Weber "the spirit of capitalism" to the same degree as other parts of western Europe, notably Britain and Holland, and the United States. A number of German intellectuals were thus greatly concerned (as well as ambivalent) about the origins and ramifications of the capitalist mode of production, which had in those other countries seemingly been responsible for rapid economic growth, urbanization, the increasing significance of money, and so on. They were also concerned with the problem of developing in Germany an integrated national society despite class conflicts largely produced, as they saw it, by changing economic circumstances, as well as by religious and other cleavages.

It should not be thought, however, that concern about the connection between religion and economic matters was confined to Germany, for in less self-consciously intellectual ways the link was addressed in many contexts and societies. During the rapid expansion of capitalistic forms of production, distribution, and exchange in the nineteenth century, religious leaders had responded in a variety of ways. By the 1890s the problems posed by materialism, rapid urbanization, inequality and poverty, the rise of labor unions and working-class political parties, and related conflicts between the lower and middle classes had attracted the attention of many religious leaders, organizations, and movements. Indeed the declining years of the nineteenth and early years of the twentieth centuries witnessed a spawning of movements concerned with the relationship between religion and capitalism. The most conspicuous of these movements deplored the social consequences that they attributed to the capitalist system.

Social Gospel, Christian Socialism, and Roman Catholicism. The social condition that aroused the most concern, as expressed in the Social Gospel movement in the United States and in Christian socialist movements in Britain and other predominantly Protestant societies (where capitalism had progressed the furthest), was the poverty and exploitation allegedly inherent in capitalism. In response, these movements ranged from the theological or moral denunciation of capitalism *in toto* to the more typical advocacy of methods for ameliorating the distress caused by urbanization and industrialization. Their opponents within religious organizations tended to argue either that the primary concern of religion should be with strictly spiritual matters or, as noted in the case of Calvinist Protestants, that capitalism was a God-sanctioned form of economy in the context of which individuals should strive to do their disciplined best. There were also those in American churches who were strongly opposed to anything resembling socialism, in which they saw the prospect of a world without religion, not least because of the open hostility to religion often found among secular socialists (especially those of a Marxist persuasion). Within Catholic circles and specifically in the pronouncements of the Roman Catholic church itself one did not find such conspicuous extremes. Generally speaking, what prevailed in official Catholicism was the view that capitalism contained the seeds of materialism and exploitation but that outright opposition to it in the form of socialism or labor unionism carried the potential for antireligious developments. Socialism and secular unionism were regarded as forms of attachment that rivaled commitment to the Catholic church itself. Consequently, the official Catholicism of the period expressed antagonism not only to most of the trappings of modernity but to what it saw as an ideology of modernism.

The intense religious concern with economic matters that characterized the early years of the twentieth century soon faded. While it would be an exaggeration to say that only slight concern was expressed between World War I and the 1970s, that period constituted something of a hiatus in the modern religious conciousness of the economic domain. This may be attributed in large part to the fact that during and in the aftermath of the phase of religious interest in economic matters that spanned the late nineteenth and early twentieth centuries, the modern welfare state came into being. Indeed, the concern expressed by religious leaders about poverty, health, and other issues had more than a little to do with the steps that many governments took in Europe and elsewhere to establish social welfare programs for their citizens. (Moreover, many religious organizations established their own welfare programs, partly following the lead of the Salvation Army.) During the 1970s and 1980s, however, the economic costs of maintaining the welfare state increased enormously, while serious problems of unemployment and poverty again became evident, partly due to the decline of traditional manufacturing industries in many of the more affluent societies. Meanwhile, the failure of most societies in the Third World to develop strong economies led to increasing concern about global poverty, material deprivation, and intersocietal inequalities. Against that background, there was a considerable renewal of religious interest in economic matters during the 1970s and 1980s, but this time on a much more global scale than at the beginning of the century.

Contemporary Context. One of the major sources of the revived concern with the religion-economics theme is the changed relationship between the economic and the governmental spheres. In the early decades of the nineteenth century the view developed that the economy, at least under classical capitalism, was naturelike and operated on its own terms. To that extent the government was thought to have only a small role to play in the production and distribution of wealth and material resources and that what we now call governmental intervention in the economy was inappropriate. However, thanks largely to the growth and monopolistic tendencies of industrial enterprise, governments were gradually conceded a definite role in the management of the economy. As the welfare state and strong central governments emerged, the economy was increasingly regarded as subject to state control or at least calibration rather than as an autonomous system following its own laws. The English economist John Maynard Keynes, by advocating a relatively high degree of governmental intervention in capitalist economies, did much to advance this view, which was further reinforced by the spreading influence of socialist, communist, and other conceptions of economic planning.

There has, however, been a reaction against the interventionist view, particularly in the United States, leading to a revival of the conservative idea that economic growth is best encouraged by the ethic that Max Weber considered crucial to the rapid economic growth achieved by the mainly Protestant societies of the West during the nineteenth century. On the other hand, the more recent rapid economic growth of some Asian societies, notably Japan, has further raised the possibility that it is not individualistic Protestantism as such that encourages industrial enterprise, but rather a generalized sense of sacrifice and collective involvement in work, at least in the modern corporative economy.

Max Weber's Contribution. In addressing the crystallization of scholarly interest in the relationship between religion and economics at the end of the nineteenth century it should be stressed that in the German context there was a general philosophical and sociological issue at the center of debate. In the later years of the nineteenth century Germany experienced a rapidly growing interest in the writings of Karl Marx, due both to academic engagement with them and to the growth of the German Social Democratic party, whose debates about ideology and strategy largely centered upon issues raised by Marx and Engels. For Marx and Engels and for those influenced by them, notably the historian and prominent ideologue of the Social Democratic party, Karl Kautsky, the view that the economic realm was autonomous had led to analyses which rendered religion an effect of economic factors. This view became a major ingredient in the materialist, as opposed to the idealist, perspective on human life and history. It was against this general background that Max Weber began to make his highly influential contributions to the religion-economics theme.

Economics and religion. The novelty of the argument developed by Max Weber is best indicated at the outset by the fact that his colleague Ernst Troeltsch could emphatically remark that linking the scholarly discussion of economic matters to the analysis of religion and religious change, as he himself advocated, must have seemed strange to his readers, not least in the German context. The major reason for this was that for the majority of German intellectuals (not simply those of a Marxist persuasion), the modern world was characterized by the complete triumph of material, worldly concerns over spiritual ones, and religion was therefore retreating rapidly into the background. This was widely and often pejoratively perceived to have occurred most conspicuously in Britain and North America. At the end of his most important contribution to the discussion of the relationship between economic and religious matters, Max Weber indeed expressed the view that men and women were destined to live in an "iron cage" of concern with materiality, calculation, and routine, condemned to involvement in highly structured "intramundane" matters. However, writers such as Weber, Troeltsch, and Georg Simmel took the view that this self-interested concern with worldly matters, notably those of an economic kind, had not arisen autonomously but had developed out of changes in cultural presuppositions and psychological dispositions concerning such matters as the relationship between the individual and society. More specifically, in the writings of Weber there developed a particular interest in the relationship between what he came to call material interests and ideal interests in contrast to the prevailing distinction between material, economic forces and ideas.

Max Weber began his work *The Protestant Ethic and the Spirit of Capitalism* (1904–1905) by referring to the observations and complaints in the German-Catholic press and at German-Catholic congresses about the fact that business leaders and owners of financial capital, as well as skilled laborers and commercially trained business employees, were overwhelmingly Protestant. He set out to show that this circumstance, which was duplicated on a larger scale in contrasts between whole societies (such as Britain and Italy), could be largely explained in terms of what he called the "permanent intrinsic character" of religious beliefs. Weber did not deny that such "temporary external historico-political situations" as the migration of ethnic groups to societies in which they became commercially successful had been important in effecting economic change. But he insisted that such events had occurred over a very long period of human history and in many different places, whereas his exclusive interest was in the differential development of the distinctively modern spirit of entrepreneurial capitalism.

Origins of capitalism. After the publication of *The Protestant Ethic and the Spirit of Capitalism*, Weber began to situate his inquiries into the origins of modern capitalism within a more general inquiry into the origins of the calculative, rational-instrumental, and secular spirit of the Western world. In other words, his study of the ethos of modern capitalism, with its emphasis upon disciplined work, careful calculation, a willingness to forgo short-term for long-term gains, and so on, was subsumed by a wider interest in the making of the ethos of the modern Western world.

Weber argued that the tension between religious belief and what he sometimes called the economic impulse is central to the understanding of the human condition. The economic impulse is universal. But he asked, how and in what ways has it come to be tempered by rationality? In primitive society, he argued, religion is subordinated to the economic impulse and for that reason is best described as magic. Put another way, economic and religious matters are, from our modern point of view, conflated. Rituals and myths tend to be directed toward mainly economic functions. They are relatively instrumental in the provision of economic necessities and thus more magical than religious, not least because in primitive society there is virtually no development of economic ethics. In essence, economically based magic is the embryonic form of religion.

Dualist world images. From that primitive matrix there developed, argued Weber, dualistic world images, that is, images of a cosmos divided into two relatively independent realms, such as the opposed forces of good and evil in Zoroastrianism. Dualistic images of the cosmos gave rise to the problem of the relationship between an individual's action in the mundane world and the fate of the individual in relation to the supramundane world. Given the fundamentality of the economic impulse—or, put another way, the necessity of minimum levels of material satisfaction to support human life—it was inevitable that there should have been tension between the mundane world in its economic aspect and the supramundane world as a focus of meaning. As ideas about the two domains of the cosmos crystallized, a need developed, in turn, for what Weber called an ethical interpretation of the variations and vicissitudes in human fortunes.

Theodicy. Central to Weber's analysis of the economic ethics of the major religious traditions was the concept of theodicy. First systematically used by the philosopher G. W. Leibniz, the term *theodicy* in its most circumscribed sense has to do with the existence in this world of suffering, evil, and injustice in the face of belief in an omniscient, omnipotent, and just God. Weber expanded its range of application, particularly with reference to matters concerning economic circumstances, so as to embrace not merely monotheistic religions (notably Judaism, Christianity, and Islam) but also the major religions of India, China, and Japan (notably Hinduism, Buddhism, and Confucianism). It is crucial to recognize that in loosening the concept of theodicy (illegitimately, according to some) to encompass nontheistic religions Weber had a particular, guiding purpose: his quest for the origins of the modern ethos (a central part of which was, in his view, the instrumental, calculative rationality of entrepreneurial capitalism). In other words, although Weber in one sense followed Hegel and other Germans before him, and Troeltsch in his own time, in trying to establish a framework for the comparison of the major religious traditions, his work was unique in that he was not interested (as, for example, Hegel had been) in demonstrating that Christianity carried the greatest potential for the realization of the "idea of religion." Nor was Weber concerned, as others had been, with examining the degree to which Indian religion constituted a viable metaphysical alternative to Christianity. Closer to his project was Troeltsch's attempt to demonstrate the superiority of Christianity on the grounds that it promulgated both a particularly transcendent view of the supernatural and a definite set of social teachings. Nonetheless, Weber regarded Troeltsch's work as guided too much by theological purposes and a normative commitment to maximizing the relevance of religion to the modern world, as well as by too great an emphasis upon the social teachings that were explicitly developed by the Christian churches on the basis of official doctrine. Weber was interested in what he called the "practical-ethical" applications of religious teachings, the methodical, quotidian working out of theology and religious teaching in concrete circumstances.

Spirit of capitalism. Claiming that he was attempting only to show that it was just as possible to produce an idealistic interpretation of the rise of modern capitalism centered on religious matters as a materialistic one, Weber set out to provide an account of the "spirit" of modern capitalism. In emphasizing spirit (in the sense of the ethos which animates a certain kind of economic action and sustains certain kinds of economic institutions), Weber was in effect insisting that even though much of the behavior that informs the modern world is indeed sustained by what Marx had called the dull compulsion of economics, one could not plausibly account for its emergence solely in reference to economic change as such, not least because the monetary economy had initially become much more significant in the West than in the East, and then only in certain parts of the West. Weber thus set himself the task of stipulating what aspects of Christianity in general and of Protestantism in particular encouraged the growth of a positive orientation to the economic realm.

Weber began by emphasizing Martin Luther's injunction that the world should be made into a monastery. Whereas in traditional Christian teaching a clear distinction had been made between those who were called to live a monastic life of self-sacrifice (particularly in reference to the vows of poverty and chastity) and those who lived in the world, Luther argued that all Christians should be capable of following a God-inspired way of worldly life. Thus from Weber's point of view Lutheranism constituted a crucial unfolding and further rationalization of the inherently inner-worldly attitude of Christianity. The religious calling was, in other words, considered pursuable in this world. There was no need for a separate group of exemplary religious who turned emphatically away from the everyday world. Weber argued, however, that Luther's ideas in this and other respects were not so radical as those of John Calvin. The Lutheran conception of the calling was, in spite of its greater inner-worldliness in comparison with traditional, Catholic Christianity, essentially passive. It required the typical believer to live as religious a life as possible while remaining indifferent to the wider social context. In other words, the Lutheran was to take the world as he or she found it and respect the secular authorities and institutional characteristics of the wider society. The point of the religious life was to concentrate upon one's personal and familial circumstances in intimate relationship with God.

From Weber's point of view this Lutheran ideal was not sufficient to explain the development in the Western world of an ethos which positively encouraged active involvement in worldly and particularly economic affairs, even though it opened the door to such involvement. It was thus to the rather different Protestant attitude of Calvin that he turned in his search for the most significant source of the spirit of capitalism. Before considering what Weber saw in Calvinism in this respect it is necessary to emphasize again that Weber was concerned with the capitalism of the late nineteenth and early twentieth centuries. Capitalism in the sense of profit-seeking had existed in many parts of the world for many centuries, but modern capitalism of the kind which had developed in the West since the late eighteenth century had distinctive characteristics. It was a form of economic life which involved the careful calculation of costs and profits, the borrowing and lending of money, the accumulation of capital in the form of money and material assets, investment, private property, and the employment of laborers and employees in a more or less unrestricted labor market. Given Weber's interest in the spirit, or ethos, of modern capitalism it was what we may loosely call the attitudinal aspect of capitalism and even more particularly the attitudes of businessmen which concerned him. What he was thus looking for was an image of the economic realm that emphasized the virtue of disciplined enterprise and a positive concern with economic activity as such (more or less regardless of the material riches which the successful accumulated).

The central feature of Calvinism in terms of Weber's interest in the growth of the modern monetary economy was its special emphasis upon the doctrine of predestination, the idea that the conception of God as all-powerful, all-knowing, and inscrutable led inexorably to the conclusion that the fate of the world and of human individuals was predetermined. For Weber the crucial question hinged upon the practical problem posed to those who subscribed to this doctrine. Specifically, how did Calvinistic individuals decide to act in the world when they believed that God had already determined the fate of each individual and that only a relatively small proportion of human beings could be saved? Weber argued that individuals were constrained to look for signs of having been accorded an elite salvational status. Those who were most successful would tend to regard their worldly success as an indication that they were among God's chosen. While the conviction that one had been saved was the most general indicator of being of the elect, Calvinism's emphasis upon each person having a calling in life, a calling to strive in as disciplined a manner as possible, without self-indulgence, strongly encouraged the view that worldly success was a confirmation of acting as an instrument of God's will and a sign of elect status.

Thus, in Weber's interpretation, Calvinism constituted a further evolution of the Lutheran idea that life itself could be subjected to the monastic conception of the religious calling. Whereas Luther had adumbrated the relatively passive notion of being called to be as devout as possible in the world, Calvin had articulated a more dynamic and active conception of the calling. Calvin called upon individuals to be religious by engaging with the world. And even though Calvinism as a religious doctrine did not specify how one could be supremely confident that one was acting as an instrument of God, it certainly encouraged the faithful to become actively involved in the major institutional spheres of society and, in so doing, to take individual responsibility as agents of God. Weber maintained that it was psychologically inevitable that those who were most tangibly successful as a result of disciplined, ascetic striving in the world would tend to think of themselves as chosen by God. Since worldly indulgence and luxuriating in the fruits of one's endeavors were precluded by the Calvinist ethos, the result of disciplined economic action was the accumulation of financial capital. For Weber, the process of economic investment followed by accumulation of profit and more investment was intimately related to the process of gaining confirmation of salvation, even though such a calculating attitude toward salvation was not prescribed by Calvinist theology.

Weber regarded the Calvinist doctrine of predestination (which has appeared with much less explicitness in many branches of monotheistic religions) as the extreme theological extension of the Christianity which had developed after the founding of the Christian church. It was the logical consummation of the idea of an omniscient God and the commitment to religious involvement in the world. Calvinism thus constituted a logically perfected theodicy.

In *The Protestant Ethic and the Spirit of Capitalism* Weber concentrated on showing, as he put it, that a one-sided, idealistic account of the rise of capitalism (in the sense of stressing the role of ideas) was just as plausible as the equally one-sided materialist accounts produced by Marxists. In any case, he added, a historical account of the rise of capitalism ought to acknowledge the fact that capitalism (or any other mode of production) is not merely an objective structural phenomenon but is also, at least in part, sustained by a set of presuppositions that encourage specific interests in work and industry and discourage others. Thus, contrary to some interpretations of his work, he did not seek to provide a monocausal account of the rise of modern capitalism but rather to stress the ideational factors that had encouraged the capitalist work ethic and had been neglected by the Marxists. Even though he was intent on emphasizing the critical significance of religion in the rise of modern capitalism, Weber did not simply posit Protestantism as the cause and capitalism as the effect. Rather he insisted that a vital aspect of capitalism is the "spirit," or ethos, that legitimates it, and he sought the principal origins of that spirit. In this regard it should be emphasized that Weber undoubtedly exaggerated the degree to which the affinity between certain branches of Protestantism and capitalist economic success had been overlooked prior to his writings. Nevertheless, his own attempt to provide a detailed explanation of that affinity was unique and pathbreaking. It should also be stressed that according to Weber the spirit of capitalism had gradually become self-sustaining, so that by his own time it was no longer grounded upon the "Protestant ethic."

Weber's major thesis about the link between Protestantism (particularly in its Calvinist and some other non-Lutheran forms) and capitalism was presented in the context of an expanding debate on that topic, notably, as has been emphasized, in Germany. His own ideas exacerbated the debate and have since been subjected to extensive criticism and appraisal. Indeed, the significance of his argument has probably become greater in the course of the twentieth century. This is so not merely because of the purely scholarly interest in the making of the modern world and the crucial role of the West in that regard but also because the great economic disparities between contemporary societies have become a matter of widespread concern, controversy, and conflict. Weber's major thesis about the promotion of the spirit of capitalism (and, more generally, of economic success) is thus of considerable relevance to the discussion of the making of the modern world as a whole and, more specifically, the distribution of resources and wealth within it. Before turning to such matters, however, it is necessary to indicate the ways in which Weber fleshed out his thesis about the origins of the modern Western consciousness.

Economic ethics. In the last decade of his life (1910–1920) Weber engaged in a series of studies of non-Christian civilizations with the express intent of explicating the economic ethics of their major religions. (He completed studies of India and China, as well as of the religion of ancient Israel, but not full-scale studies of medieval Christianity and Islam.) These efforts were largely guided by a general analytical contrast between Occidental and Oriental world-images, at the center of which were religious-metaphysical conceptions of the relationship between the cosmos and the world. His aim was to find out why there had arisen in the West (and more in some parts of the West than in others) the instrumental rationality which seemed to lie at the heart of not merely modern economic life but also modern science, modern forms of organization (what he called rational-legal bureaucracy), and modern life generally—or in other words, why modern capitalism and other aspects of modern life and consciousness had not arisen in Eastern civilizations.

The set of contrasts which Weber employed in his inquiries into economic ethics may be summarized as follows. The Eastern conception of the supramundane world centered upon a notion of eternal being, whereas the Western conception involved belief in a personal God. The first tended to encourage and to be consolidated by a mystical, otherworldly orientation, while the second was closely related to an ascetic, innerworldly orientation. The Eastern image was to be seen in its most acute and logically consistent form in classical Buddhism, which emphasized the basically illusory character of worldly life and regarded release from the contingencies of the everyday world as the highest religious aspiration. In contrast to Calvinism, its Western parallel and and opposite, Buddhism directed the attention of its adherents, particularly Buddhist monks, away from the conditions of everyday life and thus did not encourage the continuous application of religious ideals to the concrete circumstances of the world. More generally speaking, Weber maintained that in India, China, and Japan the dominant worldviews lacked the dynamic created in monotheistic religions, particularly in Christianity, by the conception of a demanding God who had enjoined believers to transform the world in his image. Thus in Eastern societies there was much more concern with the maintenance of an organically ordered society and the promotion of organic social ethics.

It is important to note that in his studies of Eastern societies, Weber took great pains to discuss the ways in which religious ideas and social structures were mutually reinforcing. In other words, even though he ascribed great significance to religion, he wished to demonstrate the specific links between religion and other aspects of human societies. But precisely because he did attend so closly to religion, his work has frequently been interpreted as an expression of religious determinism.

Weber's work on religion and economic life has been subject to an immense amount of exegesis and criticism, most of it centered on his thesis about the Western origins of capitalism. While much of the criticism has been well-grounded with respect to the historical record, a good deal of it has derived from tacit acceptance of the view that the modern economy is an autonomous realm lacking any kind of religious-symbolic grounding or relevance. During the 1970s and 1980s, however, renewed interest has been generated in the religious foundations of economic life. The idea of the autonomy of economic life and action, as characteristically expressed in the work of professional economists, has been strongly challenged, and religious organizations and movements have become increasingly concerned about economic issues. Weber's work hovers explicitly or implicitly in the background of much of the contemporary interest in the relationship between religion and economics.

The Modern World. While Weber was clearly conscious of the extent to which nineteenth-century entrepreneurial capitalism was itself being transformed, not least through the expansion of the modern bureaucratic state, his work on religion and economic life has primary relevance to the growth or lack of growth of classical, as opposed to what is now often called late, or advanced, capitalism. Moreover, Weber's work touched little, if at all, upon one of the most significant ingredients of modern economic life, particularly in capitalist societies—consumerism. Weber, as has been emphasized, was interested in the development of entrepreneurial asceticism (an asceticism that, for him, had become freed of its original religious mooring). In contemporary language he was concerned with the origins of the work ethic. However, a more hedonistic dimension of economic culture is to be found in the odyssey of capitalism. Certainly the value placed upon the accumulation of consumer goods is central to the modern form of capitalism. An interest in consumerism has led some social scientists—notably anthropologists—to attempt to lay bare the symbolic basis of patterns of consumption. That is, some analysts have become increasingly concerned with the underlying meanings that are produced and distributed by the advertising, purchase, and display of consumer goods. While not specifically involving the study of religion, this relatively new focus is part of a growing tendency to situate the study of economic behavior and institutions in a broader sociocultural context.

Among the more important specific developments which suggest a return to the thorough investigation of the relationship between religion and economic matters are these: the rapid economic growth in the second half of the twentieth century in societies, such as Japan, Taiwan, South Korea, and Singapore, with religious traditions—sometimes called Neo-Confucian—that do not clearly conform to the Weberian image of Calvinist Protestantism; the emergence in the same period of religious movements, many of them inspired by forms of liberation theology, which stress the importance of linking economic ideas with theological ideas and religious practices; and the general problem of the global economy.

The capitalist world system. In fact these three phenomena discussed above are closely related, with the third probably being the most important. In the tradition largely initiated by Weber, the primary concern has been to connect the comparative economic success of societies (and of groups and regions within societies) with forms of religio-cultural tradition and religious commitment. But a contrasting approach, called world-system theory, has arisen out of the increasing awareness that the world constitutes a single sociocultural system, and that the affairs of particular societies, groups, and regions are inextricably bound up with it. In one of its most influential forms, the theory maintains that the modern world system is largely the result of the growth of capitalism and that the system should be understood as a primarily economic phenomenon. According to this view, the capitalist world system, which had its earliest beginnings in Europe some five hundred years ago, has spread to the point that it now embraces the entire world.

In the version developed by Immanuel Wallerstein, who has placed himself in the Marxist tradition, world-system theory reverses the priority that Weber's work gives to religion, for Wallerstein regards the religious cleavages that occurred in sixteenth-century Europe as consequences of the placement of societies in the nascent world economy. Specifically, he argues that those societies which became predominantly Protestant were the core societies of the embryonic world capitalist system, while those that remained or became Catholic were "peripheral" societies whose major economic function was the supply of raw materials to the dominant manufacturing centers. (Subsequently, as the world system expanded so as to become literally a worldwide system, those early peripheral units of the system became semiperipheral, insofar as they were economically situated between the core capitalist centers of economic domination and the peripheral societies of the world.)

Influence of religion. Thus, in the perspective of the school of thought largely led by Wallerstein, religion has played a significant, but nonetheless epiphenomenal, part in the making of the modern global system. It has, in other words, played an important ideological role, in the Marxist sense of ideology as the form in which inequality and exploitation are presented as justified. To a considerable extent this argument constitutes the highwater mark of the economistic view that everything in human life can be reduced to and explained by economic factors. Yet, in its very extremeness, it has stimulated what promises to be a constructive reaction in the form of a reassessment of the relationship between religion and economic life. In other words, just as the view, promoted by Marx and Engels, that individual societies are driven by conflicts attendant upon economic motivations stimulated the rich, if controversial, attempts by Weber to show that under certain circumstances religion could be a critical factor in sociocultural change, so the view of the entire world as governed by the dynamics of economic motivations and relationships is stimulating new ways of thinking about the economic significance of religion.

Talcott Parsons. A major example of such thinking, although not a direct reaction to the materialist form of world-system theory, is to be found in the work of Talcott Parsons. Greatly influenced by Weber, whose *The Protestant Ethic and the Spirit of Capitalism* he translated (1930), Parsons devoted much of his academic career to the question of what others have called the degree of embeddedness of economic life. At the center of his thinking in this regard is the general proposition that while economic activity is essential to human life, it is neither fully determining nor fully determined. Nonetheless, Parsons acknowledged that at certain points in history the economic realm has appeared to be particularly significant. Thus he attended to the various ways in which this apparent significance has been interpreted. Indeed, one of his main interests was the way in which the modern discipline of economics arose as one reaction among others to the cultural thematization of the idea that the economic realm is the central and most problematic realm of human existence. Specifically, Parsons examined the relationship between the responses to this idea and the industrial revolution which began in certain Western societies in the second half of the eighteenth century.

In this regard Parsons circumvented the perennial question of whether the economic or "material" aspects of life are more or less important than the "ideal" aspects. While conceding the great importance of the economic aspects, he tried to show that the ways in which they are interpreted and symbolized are of no less importance. The perception of economic autonomy yielded a number of different religious or quasi-religious interpretations, two of which carried it to the point of economic determinism. These were classical economics as it developed in the wake of the writings of Adam Smith and the particular socialist tradition initiated by Karl Marx. Parsons regarded these economistic responses to the industrial revolution as being themselves quasi-religious in nature, for they carried with them sets of ideas concerning the nature and meaning of human existence. He proposed the important idea that nothing in social life is or can be purely economic.

Economic change. Wallerstein's world-system theory, it should be emphasized, originated as a direct response to the modernization theories of the 1950s and 1960s, which owed much to the writing of Weber on the relationship between religious and economic change. New life was given to Weber's work by the widespread concern with the economic gap between established societies, particularly those of the industrial West, and those that had won their independence during the wave of decolonization of the late 1950s and the 1960s. Many social scientists tried to account for disparities in economic circumstances and growth rates by assessing the degree to which religion encouraged or discouraged involvement in economic enterprise and the development of a work ethic.

A strong tendency among modernization theorists in the 1950s and 1960s was to maintain that cultural change, sometimes expressed more specifically as religious change, was a prerequisite of economic change, and that the mainly non-Christian societies of the world (as well as most of the Catholic Christian ones) needed either a Protestant ethic or its functional equivalent as a motivational base for engaging in economic activites which would produce economic growth. This was not at all an original idea, since, as we have seen during the nineteenth century the claim that Protestantism in its Calvinist version encouraged commitment to enterprise and work had been quite widespread. Indeed in Latin America during that period it was not uncommon for the political leaders of newly independent states to encourage the spread of Protestantism in the hope that it would yield economic growth in the face of the dominant, largely anticapitalist Catholic ethos.

World-system theory achieved prominence largely because of its opposition to the view that poor societies can achieve prosperity by their own internal efforts (even if this means the importation of new cultural and religious forms). In place of this internalist conception of societal change, the theory afforded a basically externalist conception, one that regarded the position of individual societies in the world economic system as almost entirely the consequence of the character of the system as a whole. Rather than attributing economic growth or lack of growth to indigenous, including religious, characteristics, world-system theory maintained that the economic fates of individual societies are determined by the functioning and expansion of a capitalist world system (in which even internally socialistic societies are constrained to act capitalistically in their relations with other societies).

World as whole. Even though a number of critical weaknesses have been exposed in this argument, there can be little doubt that it is to the world as a whole that we must now look in considering many of the most important questions about the relationship between economic and religious factors in modern life. One major example of this is the development of liberation theology, most conspicuously in Latin America. Latin American liberation theology, which has counterparts on all other continents, grew in part from a perspective on the world as a whole which is closely related to Marxist world-system theory. Dependency theory developed in Latin America in the 1960s in opposition to the view that the relatively backward economic state of Latin America should be attributed, *inter alia,* to its fatalistic Catholicism. Rather, it was argued, Latin America's condition was to be largely explained by its dependent status in relation to affluent countries, in particular the United States, whose very advantages were made possible by the economic underdevelopment of Third World societies. In combination with that perspective on the world system some leaders of the liberationist movement effected what during the late 1960s seemed an unlikely fusion of Christian theology and Marxist ideology, thus to a significant degree violating the traditional Marxist view that religion is, at least in the modern world, an enemy of socialist revolution. There is much debate as to the degree to which this fusion of Christian ideas concerning the achievement of the kingdom of God upon earth and the liberation of religious consciousness with Marxist ideas concerning the fundamentality of economic forces and relationships is simply a marriage of strategic convenience rather than a genuine synthesis. Nonetheless, the degree to which religion and politics, more specifically theology and ideology, have been recently combined among Marxist-tinged liberationist movements, as well as in movements often labeled as fundamentalist (ranging from Christian fundamentalism in the United States to Islamic fundamentalism in the Middle East), is very striking. Many such developments can best be understood in reference to the fact that the conspicuousness and evident fatefulness of the global economy (whether one calls it capitalistic or something else) elicits specific responses from movements, societies, regions, and so on, involving attempts to imbue the world order and its parts with some kind of symbolic meaning, such as the legitimation of privileged economic circumstances (what Weber called the theodicy of good fortune) or the attempt to overcome underprivileged conditions. In any case it is evident that the very different projections by Marx and Weber of a modern world without religion, which would allegedly yield to the force of economic interests and processes, have not yet been realized.

What thus has changed most of all since the period in which Weber wrote extensively about the economic ethics of the major religions is the highly conspicuous emergence of the global economy. This process has increasingly forced religions—more specifically, leaders of religious movements and organizations—to confront the economy and its appurtenances (such as materialism and consumerism) much more comprehensively than heretofore. Thus the original Weberian interest in the way in which religions differentially encourage or inhibit economic progress has been enlarged and refocused.

This is to be seen particularly in the case of Islam. Assisted in no small part by the economic circumstance of the world coming to depend so much, directly or indirectly, on the rich deposits of oil in a number of Islamic countries, Islam has reasserted itself in defiance of the West. In the process, many questions have been raised, both within Islamic contexts and by observers of it, as to whether the relative economic backwardness of Islamic societies in recent centuries has issued from inherent characteristics of Islam as a religious tradition, at one extreme, or from the subordinate position of Islamic societies in relation to those of West, at the other.

Weber's writings on Islam suggest strongly that it inhibited the growth of the instrumental rationality necessary for the emergence of a modern economic orientation, but that view is resisted by those who maintain that much of what appears, in Weber's terms, to be inimical to modern economic rationality is actually the consequence of Islamic culture's adaption to a subordinate politico-economic situation. Some scholars have argued that capitalism would have developed in Islamic societies but for this situation. Others have maintained that Islam is inherently more conducive to a socialist economic system, and that that is precisely what is developing in the modern period. In any case, unlike such societies as Britain and the United States, which led the way into, and in a sense created, the modern global economy, Islam, which not so many centuries ago was itself a dominant civilization, is currently engaged in a self-conscious, traumatic attempt to formulate very explicitly its economic ethics or, more generally, its economic culture. The self-conscious formulation of economic ethics or culture is also occurring to varying degrees in a number of other major religious contexts. Whether this will lead to a reunion of economics and religion of the kind that has prevailed in different patterns throughout most of human history remains to be seen.

[*For further discussion of topics treated herein, see* Bureaucracy; Modernity; Political Theology; Revolution; Secularization; *and* Wealth. *See also the biography of Troeltsch and, especially, the biography of Weber.*]

BIBLIOGRAPHY

Max Weber's major writings on religion and economic issues are available in the following English translations: *The Protestant Ethic and the Spirit of Capitalism* (1930; New York, 1977), *Economy and Society*, vol. 1 (Berkeley, 1978), *Ancient Judaism* (1952; New York, 1967), *The Religion of China* (1951; New York, 1968), *The Religion of India* (Glencoe, Ill., 1958); and *General Economic History* (1927; New Brunswick, N.J., 1981). A valuable exegesis of Weber's thesis about the economic consequences of Protestantism is Gordon Marshall's *In Search of the Spirit of Capitalism* (New York, 1982). Weber's sociology of religion in a more general sense is adumbrated, in comparison with the views of Marx and others, in my "Max Weber and German Sociology of Religion," in *Nineteenth Century Religious Thought in the West*, edited by Ninian Smart et al., vol. 3 (Cambridge, 1985), pp. 263–304. Weber's scattered writings on Islam are brought critically together in Bryan S. Turner's *Weber and Islam* (London, 1974). A very useful set of essays on Weber's ideas about economics in relation to religious change is to be found in *The Protestant Ethic and Modernization*, edited by Shmuel N. Eisenstadt (New York, 1968).

The French tradition of positive evaluation of religion in relation to economic factors is exemplified in Émile Durkheim's *Socialism*, translated by Charlotte Sattler and edited by Alvin Gouldner (New York, 1962), and in Durkheim's *The Elementary Forms of the Religious Life*, translated by Joseph Ward Swain (1915; New York, 1965). See also my essay "The Development and Modern Implications of the Classical Sociological Perspective on Religion and Revolution," in *Religion, Rebellion, Revolution*, edited by Bruce Lincoln (New York, 1985), pp. 236–265. A useful survey of Marxist theories of religions contained in Delos B. McKown's *The Classical Marxist Critiques of Religion* (The Hague, 1975). Also relevant to understanding the late nineteenth- and early twentieth-century posing of issues regarding religion and economics is Ernst Troeltsch's *The Social Teaching of the Christian Churches*, 2 vols., translated by Olive Wyon (1931; Chicago, 1981).

Talcott Parsons's important writings on economic and religious factors are exemplified by his "Christianity and Modern Industrial Society," in *Sociological Theory, Values, and Sociocultural Change: Essays in Honor of Pitirim A. Sorokin*, edited by Edward A. Tiryakian (New York, 1963), pp. 33–70, and "Religious and Economic Symbolism in the Western World," *Sociological Inquiry* 49 (1979): 1–48. Immanuel Wallerstein's basic ideas are to be encountered in his *The Modern World-System* (New York, 1974). For the relation between religion and the world system, see my chapter, "The Sacred and the World System," in *The Sacred in a Secular Age*, edited by Phillip E. Hammond (Berkeley, 1985), pp. 347–457. For liberation theology, see my essay "Liberation Theology in Latin America," in *Prophetic Religion and Politics*, edited by Jeffrey Hadden and Anton Shupe (New York, 1987), pp. 107–139.

Finally, on more general questions of the varying significance of the economic factor, see Karl Polanyi's *The Great Transformation* (New York, 1944), Marshall D. Sahlins's *Culture and Practical Reason* (Chicago, 1976), Chandra Mukerji's *From Graven Images: Patterns of Modern Materialism* (New York, 1983), and Jürgen Habermas's *Legitimation Crisis*, translated by Thomas McCarthy (Boston, 1975).

Roland Robertson

ECSTASY. The term *ecstasy* (Gr., *ekstasis*) literally means "to be placed outside," as well as, secondarily, "to be displaced." Both senses are relevant to the study of religion, the first more than the second perhaps, inasmuch as it denotes a state of exaltation in which one stands outside or transcends oneself. Transcendence has often been quintessentially associated with religion. If such an understanding of ecstasy carries the historian of religion into the hinterland of mysticism, the second sense, involving as it does spirit possession and shamanism, carries one to the borderland of anthropology and even psychiatry. The vast range of phenomena covered by the term supports the adoption of an approach toward its understanding that uses a variety of methods, one of which, the philological, has already been engaged. *Ecstasy* can thus mean both the seizure of one's body by a spirit and the seizure of man by divinity. Although seemingly in opposition, the two senses are not mutually exclusive, and between them lies the vast and diverse range of phenomena covered by the umbrella term *ecstasy*, with the magician standing at one end of the spectrum and the psychiatrist at the other. The historian of religion tries to grasp the significance of the intervening terrain with the help of historical, anthropological, phenomenological, sociological, psychological, and philosophical approaches to the study of religion.

Historical Approach. Ecstatic techniques reach back to prehistoric times; utilizing the principle of survivals, these techniques can be reconstructed through the role of shamans in modern primal societies. In the realm of history proper, the mystery religions that flourished in the Greco-Roman world, such as those celebrated at Eleusis and those centering on Orpheus, Adonis, Attis, Isis and Osiris, Mithra, and others, provide examples of the role of ecstasy in religion. The emphasis on secrecy in these cults makes it difficult to delineate the exact role played by ecstasy in their rituals, but those rituals are generally believed to have led to ecstatic states that signified salvific union with their respective cultic figures. Elements of ecstasy are not absent in Israelite religion, where groups or individuals were seized by the spirit of Yahveh; the case of Saul is often cited in this respect (*1 Sm.* 10:1–16).

It is significant that the phenomenological approach to ecstasy, though it does not divorce the ecstasy of the shaman from communion with spirits, does point out that the "specific element of shamanism is not the incorporation of spirits in the shaman, but the ecstasy provoked by the ascension to the sky or by the descent to Hell" (Eliade, cited in Lewis, 1971, p. 49); the descent of Jesus into hell and his ascent to heaven, according to the Athanasian Creed, provide a rudimentary parallel to shamanistic ecstasy. Even when spirits are associated with the work of the shaman, the parallel persists. In *Revelation*, for instance, it is ecstasy that rules from the first moment: "I was in the Spirit on the Lord's Day, and I heard behind me a loud voice like a trumpet saying, 'Write what you see in a book'" (1:10–11). John turns to "see the voice," whereupon he sees seven lampstands and, in the middle of them, "one like a son of man": "When I saw him, I fell at his feet as though dead" (1:17). Later we are told how John saw an open door in heaven, and he heard a voice saying, "Come up hither, and I will show you what must take place after this" (4:1). John responds, or something within him responds: "At once I was in the Spirit" (4:2). Again he looked, saw, and heard. Another example may be provided from a later chapter of *Revelation:* "And he carried me away in the Spirit into a wilderness, and I saw a woman sitting on a scarlet beast" (17:3). Finally there is the vision of the New Jerusalem: "And in the Spirit he carried me away to a great, high mountain, and showed me the holy city Jerusalem coming down out of heaven from God" (21:10). The role of ecstasy in other historical religions will become evident in due course.

Anthropological Approach. The anthropological approach emphasizes the role of the shaman and the phenomenon of possession in both prehistoric and contemporary preliterate societies. *Shaman* is a widely used term, the "lowest common denominator of which is that of the inspired priest" (Eliade, cited in Lewis, 1971, p. 49). In the anthropological approach, it is the shaman's role as a psychopomp that is preeminent. Through an ability to achieve a state of ecstatic exaltation, acquired after much rigorous training and careful, often painful initiation, the shaman is able to establish contact with the spirit world. In the course of this exaltation, the shaman may affect the postmortem fate of the deceased, aid or hurt the diseased in this life, as well as encounter the occupants of the spirit world, communicate with them, and then narrate the experiences of ecstatic flight on his or her return from there. [*See* Shamanism.]

Phenomenological Approach. It must be remembered, however, that while all shamans are ecstatics, all ecstatics are not shamans. Taking a broader phenomenological approach, one discovers that a variety of means, such as dancing, drugs, self-mortification, and so on, have been used across cultures, climes, and at various times to induce ecstasy and that these have generated ecstatic states ranging from the shamanistic to the mystical. If the first step of the phenomenological method is to classify, then one may employ Plato's distinction between "two types of mantic or 'prophecy', the first the *mantikē entheos*, the 'inspired madness' of the ecstatic, e.g. that of the Pythia; the second the systematic interpretation of signs, such as the augury of the flight of birds" (van der Leeuw, vol. 1, 1938, p. 225). This last category may be excluded from consideration here as a form of soothsaying. A further distinction has to be made between shamanistic and mystical ecstasy, and with the experience of someone like Saul providing a bridge between the two. As Gerardus van der Leeuw writes: "With the *Shamans*, still further, we find ourselves on the road to the prophets, but of course only in the sense in which Saul too was 'among the prophets', that is as regards the ecstatic frenzy that renders possible a superhuman development of power" (ibid., p. 218). We must therefore consider three categories of ecstasies (and accordingly, ecstatics); they may not always be separable, but they are distinct: the shamanistic ecstasy, the prophetic ecstasy, and the mystical ecstasy. The differences among the three emerge clearly when we consider the nature of ecstatic utterances.

The ecstatic utterances of the shaman relate to the

world of the spirits and to the shaman's movements in that realm. Eliade clearly distinguishes between non-shamanic, para-shamanic, and shamanic ecstasy, the characteristic feature of the last being the shaman's ability to communicate with dead or natural spirits. The ecstatic utterances of the prophet relate to God: the prophet literally speaks for God, though there are borderline cases, such as the priestess at the oracle at Delphi whose cryptic utterances had to be interpreted. These may be contrasted with the ecstatic utterances known as *shaṭḥīyāt* in Islamic mysticism; a typical example is provided by al-Ḥallāj's proclamation, "I am the Creative Truth" ("Anā al-ḥaqq"). This highly mystical utterance, which cost him his life, has been explained in later Sufism as resulting from a mistaken sense of identity with God due to God's overwhelming presence in mystical experience (as if a piece of red-hot coal in a furnace would call itself fire or a candle in the sunlight would mistake the light of the sun for its own).

Sociological Approach. The sociology of ecstasy or ecstatic religion, as explored by I. M. Lewis, provides another useful dimension to the topic. This approach relies heavily on the indirect application of the work of Émile Durkheim and Max Weber. Following Durkheim, Lewis draws attention to the socially integrative function of the shaman who, at ritual services, instills in the people a sense of solidarity by emphasizing the shunning of adultery, homicide, and other socially disruptive practices, and who often plays an active role in settling disputes.

At the same time, however, the study of ecstasy also exposes the limitations of Durkheim's approach in certain contexts: the cultivation of ecstasy, especially in mysticism, may lead to a breach within a religious tradition instead of playing an integrating role in it. Thus, Sufism was viewed with suspicion by Islamic orthodoxy until the two were reconciled by al-Ghazālī. A more Weberian approach views the shaman as discovering through his ecstatic flights the reasons for whatever may have befallen his client, providing the client with "meaning," which according to Weber is one role of religion. Moreover, a subtler application of the Weberian approach makes further generalizations possible. Thus, according to the relative-deprivation theory, secret ecstatic cults may flourish particularly among women or dispossessed groups in patriarchal or authoritarian societies. This may be as true of women dancing ecstatically in Dionysian rituals in Greece in the fifth century BCE as it is in the *zār* cult in Sudan in modern times.

Another issue raised by the sociological approach to the study of religion is the role of ecstasy in societies that are in the process of secularization. Two views seem to prevail. One is to look upon the cultivation of cultic ecstasy as possessing cathartic value in a society undergoing rapid social change. A broader view suggests that the process of secularization does not so much do away with the need for transcendence as it does provide surrogates for it. A convergence exists between the sociology of religion, which maintains that there are religious phenomena that belong to no determined religion, and the Tillichian theological viewpoint, which maintains that, though modern people think they have overcome their need for ultimate concern or transcendence, what has really happened is that they continue to seek it in secular contexts (as, for instance, in ecstatic participation in football matches). It may be further added that ecstasy is by definition an extraordinary experience that transcends routine, so that the increasing bureaucratization of modern life may impel *homo religiosus* to seek such ecstasy all the more. It has been speculatively suggested, for instance, that the evidence in Indus Valley culture of yogic practices possibly possessing an ecstatic dimension may reflect that culture's highly organized, homogeneous, even monotonous appearance.

Psychological Approach. Various approaches on ecstasy have been discussed so far but, inasmuch as ecstasy is essentially concerned with the mind or what lies beyond it, it is the psychology of religion that should prove the most illuminating. The psychology of religion, however, is a discipline with boundaries that are difficult to define strictly; this is even more true when it is brought up in relation to a subject like that of ecstasy, in regard to which approaches within the psychology of religion itself can vary from the transpersonal to the psychiatric. Thus, one must distinguish clearly among certain approaches within the psychology of religion: the psychoanalytical approach, the pharmacological approach, and the mystical approach.

The psychoanalytical approach has been applied to ecstasy at two levels, the shamanistic and the mystical. Claude Lévi-Strauss has argued that the cure administered by the shaman—who, unlike the modern analyst listening to the patient's words, speaks out on behalf of the patient—involves "the inversion of all the elements" of psychoanalysis yet retains its analogy with it. J. M. Masson, perhaps being reductionistic, sees in the ecstatic, oceanic feelings of the mystic a reversion to the experience of the fetus in the womb. Such approaches to ecstasy are difficult to assess objectively.

Modern developments in pharmacology have brought what might be called chemical ecstasy into the limelight. [*See* Psychedelic Drugs.] Drug-induced ecstasy was not unknown in ancient times. The *soma* of the Vedas, now widely identified with *Amanita muscaria,* was supposed to be one such drug; it has even been suggested that techniques of yogic ecstatic trances were developed in post-Vedic Hinduism as a substitute for the *soma*-induced trances once the Aryans moved deeper into India and lost contact with the geographical source of the mushroom. Mexico provides another example of the religious use of drug-induced ecstasy in the peyote cult, which Aldous Huxley popularized in a modern version through his experiments with mescaline. But it was the discovery of LSD (lysergic acid diethylamide) that threw the door wide open to this avenue to ecstasy, with its open advocacy by modern experimenters such as Timothy Leary and Alan Watts.

Modern psychology tends to dismiss these experiences as chemically and artifically induced and therefore not genuine. But such a dismissive approach is difficult to countenance by a historian of religion; drugs easily can be the means to, rather than the cause of, these ecstasies. However, the fact that such chemical experiences are not always ecstatic should not be overlooked; neither should the fact that drug-induced ecstasy, unlike mystical experience, is often not transformative of personality. It is also worth noting that psychedelic drugs can be used not merely to induce ecstasy but also to gain power, a fact mentioned by Patañjali in his *Yoga Sūtra* as well as illustrated in the contemporary writings of anthropologist Carlos Castaneda.

For many, the classical focus of the discussion of ecstasy is still provided by mysticism, notwithstanding the elaboration of the role of archaic and chemical techniques in this context. Mysticism, for our purposes, may be conveniently defined as the doctrine or belief that a direct knowledge or immediate perception of the ultimate reality, or God, is possible in a way different from normal sense experience and ratiocination. The two channels in which the mystical tradition of mankind has flowed are thus naturally identified by emotion and intuition. The ecstatic experience resulting from them has been distinguished accordingly as "communion" in the first case, in which the devotee, though psychologically merged in God, remains a distinct entity, and as "union" in the second case, in which the aspirant achieves an ontological identity with God. [*See* Mystical Union.] The distinction is crucial to an understanding of mystical ecstasy: in the first case, access to the ultimate reality is "gained"; that is, it is something that originally did not exist; in the second case, access to the reality is "regained"; that is, it is something that always existed but was not recognized until the moment of ecstasy. Martin Buber's distinction between I–Thou and I–It relationships is relevant here. Some traditions recognize the existence of both these types of mysticism. The Hindu mystic Ramakrishna (1836–1886) contrasts the two ecstasies as offering a choice between "tasting sugar" and "becoming sugar," without insisting that the two be viewed as mutually exclusive. In any case, many religious traditions seem to chart the path to ecstasy with precision and sophistication. Hinduism speaks of the various steps of Yoga leading to *samādhi;* Buddhism speaks of *jhānas* and *nirvāṇa;* Christianity speaks of the mystical way; and Islam speaks of the *ḥāl* and *maqām,* or states and stations en route to divine knowledge (an imagery that may be compared to the "mansions" of Teresa of Ávila), as well as of *wajd* ("ecstasy").

Ecstasy in the Hindu tradition is basically experienced in three modes: nontheistic, theistic, and transtheistic. In the nontheistic mode, it results from the suppression of all mental modifications; because of its restriction to the person of the practitioner and the absence of any outside referent, R. C. Zaehner refers to this mode as *enstasy:* "By 'enstasy' I understand that introverted mystical experience in which there is experience of nothing except an unchanging, purely static oneness. It is the exact reverse of ecstasy which means to get outside oneself and which is often characterized by a breaking down of the barriers between the individual subject and the universe around him" (*The Bhagavad-Gītā,* London, 1973, p. 143). Although the *Yoga Sūtra,* to which Zaehner's statement applies, also recognizes the existence of God, the theistic mode of ecstasy that flows from the love of God is best described in the *Bhakti Sūtra:* "It is as if a dumb man who has tasted a delicious food could not speak about it." The ecstasy experienced through the transtheistic or absolutistic mode in Hinduism is similarly considered ineffable because, in it, the distinction between the one who experiences and the experienced is annulled. Thus one is left with the Upaniṣadic paradox of the experience of the Absolute: "But where everything has become just one's own self, then whereby and whom would one see?" (*Bṛhadāraṇyaka Up.* 4.5.15). Does Meister Eckhart provide an answer to the question when he says "The eye with which I see God is the same with which God sees me"?

The Islamic mystical tradition emphasizes the passing away of individuality in God *(fanā'),* who alone represents divine unity *(tawḥīd);* this loss of self into God provides the experience of inward ecstasy. In Islamic mystical poetry wine symbolizes the "ecstatic experience due to the revelation of the True Beloved, destroying the foundations of reason" (Arberry, 1950, p. 114). It is interesting that such ecstatic experience of God constitutes the ecstatic's knowledge of God *(ma'rifah).*

In Buddhism ecstasy plays an important role in the *jhāna*s or trances, and the typical text of the first trance, for instance, runs as follows: "Detached from sensual objects, O monks, detached from unwholesome states of mind, the monk enters into the first absorption, which is accompanied by Thought-Conception [*vitakka*] and Discursive Thinking [*vicāra*], is born of Detachment [Concentration: *samādhi*] and filled with Rapture [*pīti*] and Joy [*sukha*]" (*Dīgha Nikāya* 1.182). It should be added, however, that in the fifth stage, ecstasy gives way to equanimity, and the final attainment of *nirvāṇa* is characterized not by ecstasy but by knowledge and bliss.

In Christian mysticism too, ecstasy plays a key role, as is demonstrated not only by the statement of John Cassian (360–435) that "by constant meditation on things divine and spiritual contemplation . . . the soul is caught up into . . . an ecstasy," but also by the fourteenth-century text *The Cloud of Unknowing:*

> God wishes to be served with both the body and the spirit together, as is proper, and He will give man his reward in bliss both in body and in soul. In giving that reward, He sometimes inflames the body of His devout servants with wonderful pleasures here in this life, not only once or twice, but very often in some cases as He may wish. Of these pleasures not all come into the body from outside through the windows of our senses, but come from within, rising and springing up out of an abundance of spiritual gladness and out of true devotion of spirit.
>
> (cited in Progoff, 1957, pp. 172–173)

It may be noted that, here as in other instances, ecstasy is not divorced from knowledge of God, and stages for its attainment are spelled out. In Christian mysticism, as in other forms of mysticism (especially theistic), different stages are delineated, perhaps the best known being the passage of the soul to God, first through the illuminative, second the purgative, and finally the unitive ways.

The Cross-Cultural Approach. Following Gershom Scholem's study of Jewish mysticism, we can ask why ecstatic experiences only occur in culture-bound contexts. Why, for instance, did Teresa of Ávila not have ecstatic visions of Kālī? The Hindu mystic Ramakrishna is said to have had visions of figures outside Hinduism, but he is known to have been somewhat familiar with the traditions in question. Yet evidence from C. G. Jung's clients shows that certain archetypal ecstatic visions may transcend the bounds of time and space. The role of depth psychology in uncovering the roots of ecstasy, it seems, has yet to be fully explored. The physical symptoms accompanying the states of ecstasy, at the other extreme, also stand in need of exploration. In ecstasies of the shamanistic and prophetic type the hypothalamus has been shown to become inactive so that people in trance become impervious to physical maltreatment or deprivation; they still respond to speech and social communication, however. In ecstasies of the mystical type, signs of life have been known to fade, sometimes to the point of apparent disappearance.

Humanistic psychology has taken some interest in ecstasy in its relation to the concept of peak experience, as explored in the work of Abraham H. Maslow; this interest is even more evident in Ernst Arbman's monumental work, *Ecstasy of Religious Trance* (1963–1970). In this psychological study of ecstasy, Arbman emphasizes the close relation between ecstasy and mystical experience and, within mysticism, between ecstasy and visionary experience. He classifies the latter as assuming three forms, which represents a trichotomy of medieval Christian mysticism traceable to Augustine: corporeal, imaginative, and intellectual. These three forms may be instantiated, respectively, by the experiences of the prophet Muḥammad in receiving the Qur'ān through an angel, some of the experiences of Teresa of Ávila, and the recorded experiences of Ignatius Loyola and Jakob Boehme. The distinction between these three forms of ecstatic visionary experience—the corporeal, the imaginative, and the intellectual—is said to lie in the fact that, while the first experience is felt as something actually or objectively perceived, in the second case it is something experienced only inwardly, in a psychic or spiritual sense. Regarding the third type of vision, in which sense of the word *intellectual* seems to correspond more to Platonic than to modern usage, it apprehends its object without any image or form.

A question naturally arises in relation to this classification: how is the genuineness of the experiences represented by it to be established, even if the existence of a mystical realm is granted, and even if it is further accepted that the pathological state of mind might be the most receptive for such experiences? Or, to broaden the scale of skepticism, how do we know that the shaman's journeys do in fact occur? The phenomenologist of religion is disinclined to ask such questions, as are the followers of some other disciplines, but the historian of religion cannot choose to ignore them since almost every tradition concerned with ecstatic experience has provided evaluative criteria for distinguishing between genuine and spurious experience. This provides a natural transition for assessing the role of the philosophy of religion in ecstatic experiences. It is a thorny issue, complicated by a fundamental epistemological problem: philosophers use reason in order to know, but ecstatics reason because they know. And yet a philosophical approach to ecstasy, in conclusion, still seems possible if two factors are taken into account: an ecstasy, however prolonged, is usually a temporary state, and it can be experienced by religious mystics and nonreligious mystics alike.

Duration and Efficacy. The duration of the ecstatic trance is variable. William James regarded transience as one of the four marks of the mystic state, but allowed only for "half an hour, or at most an hour or two." On the other hand, according to the Hindu mystical tradition, an ecstatic trance can be so profound that one does not recover from it at all. One reads of mystics who remained in a state of trance for six hours (Teresa of Ávila), three days (Ramakrishna), five days (Ellina von Crevelsheim), and even six months (again, Ramakrishna). It is also a point of some interest that not merely mystics per se but otherwise intellectually or aesthetically gifted persons also have experienced ecstasy. Rabindranath Tagore describes one such experience thus:

> I suddenly felt as if some ancient mist had in a moment lifted from my sight and the ultimate significance of all things was laid bare. . . . I found that facts that had been detached and dim had a great unity of meaning, as if a man groping through a fog suddenly discovers that he stands before his own house. . . . An unexpected train of thought ran across my mind like a strange caravan carrying the wealth of an unknown kingdom. . . . Immediately I found the world bathed in a wonderful radiance with waves of beauty and joy swelling on every side, and no person or thing in the world seemed to me trivial or unpleasing.
>
> (cited in Walker, 1968, p. 475)

This passage raises a vital issue: if ordinary mortals can experience ecstasy along with the great mystics, and if ecstasies are terminable, then what do the great religious traditions of the world ultimately have to offer by way of salvation? If the answer is ecstatic union and ecstasy is a temporary phenomenon, then how lasting are the results of the spiritual path? Must one tread it to experience ecstasy?

The answer is not entirely clear, but both the theistic and nontheistic mystical traditions have approached an answer by asking whether ecstasy and union (in a mystical context) are identical. For Plotinus the two are one:

> For then nothing stirred within him, neither anger, nor desire, nor even reason, nor a certain intellectual perception, nor, in short, was he himself moved, if we may assert this; but, being in an ecstasy, tranquil and alone with God, he enjoyed an unbreakable calm. (Plotinus, *Enneads* 6.9)

For Teresa of Ávila, ecstasy and union are not identical:

> I wish I could explain with the help of God wherein union differs from rapture, or from transport, or from flight of the spirit, as they call it, or from trance, which are all one. I mean that all these are only different names for that *one and the same thing, which is also called ecstasy.* It is more excellent than union, the fruits of it are much greater, and its other operations more manifold, for union is uniform in the beginning, the middle and the end, and is so also interiorly; but as raptures have ends of a much higher kind, they produce effects both within and without (i.e., both physical and psychical). . . . A rapture is absolutely irresistible; whilst union, inasmuch as we are then on our own ground, may be hindered, though that resistance be painful and violent.
>
> (Teresa of Ávila, *Life* 20.1–3)

Apart from the question of whether, in either the theistic or nontheistic context, ecstasy represents union, and if so, to what extent and degree, there is a further question: does such ecstatic union constitute the summation of religious experience? There seems to be some difference of opinion on this point. Thus, according to W. R. Inge,

> Ecstasy was for Plotinus the culminating point of religious experience, whereby the union with God and perfect knowledge of Divine truth, which are the conclusion and achievement of the dialectical process and the ultimate goal of the moral will, are realized also in direct, though ineffable, experience. Plotinus enjoyed this supreme initiation four times during the period when Porphyry was with him; Porphyry himself only once, he tells us, when he was in his 68th year. It was a vision of the Absolute, 'the One', which being above even intuitive thought, can only be apprehended passively by a sort of Divine illapse into the expectant soul. It is not properly a vision, for the seer no longer distinguishes himself from that which he sees; indeed, it is impossible to speak of them as two, for the spirit, during the ecstasy, has been completely one with the One. This 'flight of the alone to the Alone' is a rare and transient privilege, even for the greatest saint. He who enjoys it 'can only say that he has all his desire, and that he would not exchange his bliss for all the heaven of heavens'. (Inge, 1912, p. 158)

Yet when we turn to other religious traditions, the culmination of the religious life seems to be distinguished not so much by a transient, if repeatable, ecstatic union as by a blissful state of being. The final goal of a Christian existence, for example, is the "eternal life" of the beatific vision or the kingdom of God, and not transient ecstasies; and the final goal of Buddhism is the attainment of the lasting happiness of *nirvāṇa,* which is attained for good, unlike the temporary ecstasies of the trances.

> Even the word 'happiness' *(sukha)* which is used to describe Nirvāṇa has an entirely different sense here. Sāriputta once said: 'O friend, Nirvāṇa is happiness! Nirvāṇa is happiness!' Then Udāyi asked: 'But, friend Sāriputta, what happiness

> can it be if there is no sensation?' Sāriputta's reply was highly philosophical and beyond ordinary comprehension: 'That there is no sensation itself is happiness.'
>
> (Rahula, 1967, p. 43)

In the beginning of this article, it was pointed out that the most desirable approach to ecstasy, given the scope and variety characterizing the phenomenon, was one that used a variety of methods. It might then be proper to conclude by raising a methodological point: can or should one's approach to the study of ecstasy be reductionistic or nonreductionistic? A statement by Eliade provides an initial point of illumination:

> Since ecstasy (trance, losing one's soul, losing consciousness) seems to form an integral part of the human condition, just like anxiety, dreams, imagination, etc., we do not deem it necessary to look for its origin in a particular culture or a particular historical moment. As *an experience* ecstasy is a non-historical phenomenon in the sense that it is coextensive with human nature. Only the religious *interpretation* given to ecstasy and the *techniques* designed to prepare it or facilitate it are historically conditioned. That is to say, they are dependent on various cultural contexts, and they change in the course of history.
>
> (Eliade, cited in Wavell et al., 1966, p. 243)

Thus, fasting, drugs, meditation, prayer, dancing, and sex have all been used to induce ecstasy in the course of human history.

Given the current trends in the study of religion, it may be worth noting that what Charles Davis says of reductionistic explanations in general also applies to the explanations of ecstasy. In fact, his discussion is entitled "Wherein There Is No Ecstasy," a line from T. S. Eliot that refers not to the absence of ecstasy per se but to its absence in "the mystical dark night of the soul." Davis goes on to say:

> There is no difficulty in accepting reductionistic explanations of particular religious beliefs and practices, if such explanations are sufficiently grounded. Every expression of the transcendent is a particular experience. The particularity of the experience is due to non-transcendent factors. Hence, in that particularity, it is open to non-religious explanations. As for a reductionistic explanation of religious faith as such, in my judgment a reductionistic explanation is so little grounded and so patently the result of an inadequate development of the subject who offers it that I do not grant it any degree of probability. But I am not infallible. Despite the certitude of my judgment, the possibility of error and illusion remains. (Davis, 1984, p. 398)

The scholars will no doubt continue to debate the issue of ecstasy, and the shamans, the prophets, and the mystics continue to experience it—if a secularized world will let them do so.

[*See also* Enthusiasm *and* Mysticism.]

BIBLIOGRAPHY

Arberry, A. J. *Sufism: An Account of the Mystics of Islam* (1950). London, 1979.

Arbman, Ernst. *Ecstasy or Religious Trance*. 3 vols. Edited by Åke Hultkrantz. Stockholm, 1963–1970.

Davis, Charles. "Wherein There Is No Ecstasy." *Studies in Religion / Sciences religieuses* 13 (1984): 393–400.

Eliade, Mircea. *Yoga: Immortality and Freedom*. 2d ed. Princeton, 1969.

Eliade, Mircea. *Shamanism: Archaic Techniques of Ecstasy*. Rev. & enl. ed. New York, 1964.

Inge, W. R. "Ecstasy." In *Encyclopaedia of Religion and Ethics*, edited by James Hastings, vol. 5. Edinburgh, 1912.

Leeuw, Gerardus van der. *Religion in Essence and Manifestation*, vol. 1. Translated by J. E. Turner. London, 1938.

Lewis, I. M. *Ecstatic Religion: An Anthropological Study of Spirit Possession and Shamanism*. Harmondsworth, 1971.

Mahadevan, T. M. P. *Outlines of Hinduism*. Bombay, 1956.

Maslow, Abraham. *Religions, Values, and Peak-Experiences*. Columbus, Ohio, 1964.

Nyanatiloka. *Buddhist Dictionary*. Colombo, 1950.

Progoff, Ira, ed. and trans. *The Cloud of Unknowing*. New York, 1957.

Rahula, Walpola. *What the Buddha Taught*. Rev. ed. Bedford, England, 1967.

Tart, Charles T., ed. *Altered States of Consciousness: A Book of Readings*. New York, 1969.

Underhill, Evelyn. *Mysticism* (1911). 12th ed. New York, 1961.

Walker, Benjamin. *The Hindu World*, vol. 2. New York, 1968.

Wavell, Stewart, Audrey Butt, and Nina Epton. *Trances*. London, 1966.

Zaehner, R. C. *Zen, Drugs, and Mysticism*. New York, 1972.

ARVIND SHARMA

ECUMENICAL MOVEMENT. The long and varied history of Christian ecumenism is reflected in the many definitions attached to the word itself. The Greek *oikoumenē* comes from the noun *oikos* ("house, dwelling") and the verb *oikeō* ("to live, to dwell"). *Oikoumenē*, which is derived from the present passive participle of the verb, suggests the land in which people live or dwell and is usually translated "the inhabited world." The word initially had no theological implications; it was a descriptive term used by the Greeks to describe the world they knew, and later by the Romans to describe the Roman empire.

Biblical usage of the word *oikoumenē* is sparse. Eight of the fifteen references are found in *Luke* and *Acts*, and with the exception of two references that suggest the Roman empire (*Lk.* 2:1, *Acts* 17:6) and one that may have cosmic import (*Heb.* 2:5), the remaining uses are no more than descriptive references to "the inhabited world" (*Mt.* 24:14; *Lk.* 4:5, 21:26; *Acts* 11:28, 17:31, 19:27, 24:5; *Rom.* 10:18; *Heb.* 1:6; *Rv.* 3:10, 12:9, 16:14).

As the early church extended its geographical boundaries, writers begin to refer to the church throughout the *oikoumenē* as a way of distinguishing it from local assemblies. And when Christians from different locations began to meet together to discuss aspects of belief and discipline, such gatherings began to be referred to as "ecumenical councils," that is, councils having representation from all parts of the *oikoumenē*. Eastern Orthodox churches acknowledge seven ecumenical councils before the Great Schism of AD 1054, while the Roman Catholic church also claims as ecumenical subsequent councils in the West, such as the Council of Trent and the two Vatican councils. The Lutheran Formula of Concord (1577) described the early creeds (Apostles', Nicene, and Athanasian) as "ecumenical creeds" because they had been accepted by all branches of the Christian church. The meaning of the word *ecumenical* was thus extended beyond the theologically neutral notion of "the inhabited world" to include both an understanding of the church in its worldwide sense and expressions of belief that have universal ecclesiastical acceptance. [*See* Councils, *article on* Christian Councils, *and* Creeds, *article on* Christian Creeds.]

After a period of relative neglect, the word *ecumenical* reappeared in the twentieth century, with new meanings appropriate to a new situation. Many church bodies, disturbed by their divisions from one another, which were made particularly apparent by the competitive nature of nineteenth-century missionary activities, began to look for ways to overcome their diverse histories. Following a world conference of missionary societies in Edinburgh in 1910, the word *ecumenism* began to be used to signify a concern to reunite the divided Christian family. Alongside this concern for unity was a corresponding concern for mission (from *missio,* "a sending forth") to the *oikoumenē*. These twin poles of unity and mission have characterized what has come to be referred to as "the ecumenical movement." However, abroader use of the word *ecumenism* has also emerged to designate an attitude of active goodwill and concern for all peoples. Concerns about world hunger, racism, or political oppression are thus frequently described as "ecumenical concerns" and are often focal points of common action not only among Christians but in conjunction with all people of goodwill.

The Birth of Modern Ecumenism: Edinburgh, 1910. The fellowship of those who have been made "one in Christ" has almost always been marred by institutional division. In the earliest Christian literature, the letters of Paul, there are accounts of Paul's attempts to adjudicate between factions bitterly disputing with one another. The church at Corinth was particularly notorious in this regard. The creedal controversies in the early councils were attempts to set boundaries to the faith, and they provided canons for exclusion of heretics as well as inclusion of believers. In 1054 a radical division, the Great Schism, culminated the separation between Eastern and Western Christianity, and in the sixteenth century the Western church was further divided into the many separate denominations that resulted from the Reformation. [*See* Schism, *article on* Christian Schism; Reformation; *and* Denominationalism.]

It is to the credit of the groups thus divided that they continued to believe that their divisions were "sinful," but not until the nineteenth century, with its missionary advance from Europe and North America to the rest of the world, was the situation recognized as intolerable. The efforts to "make disciples of all nations" (*Mt.* 28:19) was in fact imposing divisions of European origin on newly converted Christians in Asia, Africa, and Latin America in ways that distorted the unity in Christ that the message was supposed to bestow. [*See* Missions, *article on* Christian Missions.]

It is therefore significant that the first major attempt to begin a healing of the divisions within Christianity originated in the missionary societies. In 1910, a number of missionary societies held a conference in Edinburgh, Scotland, that by common consent is described as the birth of the modern ecumenical movement. The purpose of the conference was to develop a common missionary strategy that would not only avoid the scandal of the past but provide for a more creative and collaborative use of resources in the future.

The Three Streams Flowing from Edinburgh. As delegates to the Edinburgh conference looked ahead, they saw that some kind of structure would be necessary if the goals of the conference were to be accomplished. A continuation committee was established, and by 1921 it was clear that three concerns would need attention, continuing reflection, and structural implementation: (1) the missionary task of the church, (2) the kinds of common service the churches could render to the world even in their divided state, and (3) the doctrinal issues that were responsible for the ongoing divisions.

In response to the first concern, the International Missionary Council was established in 1921 to help various mission boards coordinate their previously separate and competing activities and to hold conferences that would enable members to think in new ways about the church's mission. During its forty-year life, the council held five conferences that dealt with the impact of secularism on the life of the church (Jerusalem, 1928); the relationship of the Christian religion to other world religions (Madras, 1938); the need to see missions as a two-way street on which the so-called younger churches would now be giving as well as receiving (Whitby, 1947); the imperative need for Christian unity, if mission was to retain its credibility (Willingen, 1952); and recognition that the time had come for missionary concern to be related structurally to those Christians already grappling with questions of unity and service (Ghana, 1957). The last conference translated into a decision to merge with the already established World Council of Churches, a decision that was implemented in 1961.

The Edinburgh-inspired concern for the church's common service to the world was embodied in a second structure, called the Commission on Life and Work. Recognizing that organic reunion was years if not light-years away, members of this commission sought to develop a consensus on matters to which divided churches could relate. "Doctrine divides, service unites" became the slogan. The first Conference on Life and Work, held in Stockholm in 1925, was widely representative—over 600 delegates from 37 countries attended and discussed the church's responsibility in such areas as international relations, education, economics, and industry.

A second Conference on Life and Work, held in Oxford in 1937, drew delegates from 40 countries and 120 denominations who discussed church and state, church and community, and the church and its function in society, while small groups dealt with education, the economic order, and the world of nations. Two realities loomed behind the Oxford discussions. One was the rapid consolidation of Hitler's power in Nazi Germany and the almost "emergency" situation it created for understanding the task of the church in such a world. The other was a realization that service could not adequately be discussed apart from considerations of doctrine. Consequently, the delegates voted that the Life and Work Commission should seek to merge with the Faith and Order Commission, the third outgrowth of Edinburgh.

This third structure provided a place for the doctrinal issues that divided the churches to be explored. The members, adopting the name Faith and Order, held an initial conference in Lausanne in 1927, with over 400 delegates from 108 churches, including not only Protestants but Eastern Orthodox representatives as well. The report of the conference exemplified a descriptive process called "comparative ecclesiology," which sought to pinpoint and describe doctrinal differences as well as similarities, without as yet attempting to resolve them. However, the commonly shared conviction at Lausanne that "God wills unity" led the delegates to project a second conference, which was held at Edinburgh in 1937, with delegates from 122 participating bodies. Unanimous agreement was reached on a statement about "the grace of our Lord Jesus Christ," although in other areas, such as church, ministry, and sacraments, awesome divergences remained. The delegates did acknowledge, however, that their task was not so much to create unity, which is God's gift, as to exhibit more clearly the unity that their empirical divisions obscured.

Members of the Faith and Order Commission realized that doctrine involves action and service, and they voted at Edinburgh (in complementarity with a similar action taken by the Commission on Life and Work) that the two groups should merge. Delegates from both groups therefore met in 1938 at Utrecht to work out proposals for "a world council of churches." World War II intervened, and until 1948 the world council was "in process of formation."

Other Ecumenical Advances. From 1910 to 1948, ecumenical activity was not limited to high-level consultations. Many denominations established international bodies, such as the Lutheran World Federation and the World Alliance of Reformed and Presbyterian Churches, so that global concerns could receive greater attention. National ecumenical agencies were created, such as the British Council of Churches and the Federal Council of Churches in the United States, which later became the National Council of Churches of Christ, providing vehicles through which Protestant groups could work cooperatively on many issues.

Another ecumenical impetus reminding Christians that "the world is too strong for a divided church" was the rise to power of Adolf Hitler, whose policies were bent on the extermination of the Jews, the suppression of any Christian groups opposing Nazi claims, and the extension of racially based totalitarian rule. The Barmen Declaration (1934) of the Confessing church in Germany was a theological "no" to Hitler that brought Reformed and Lutheran groups together for the first time since the Reformation. Christians living under persecution from 1933 to 1945 discovered that in concentration camps or occupied territories their unity far outweighed their differences.

The World Council of Churches. In 1948 at Amsterdam, the World Council of Churches (WCC) became a reality, fusing the concerns of the Faith and Order and Life and Work commissions. In 1961 the International Missionary Council joined the WCC, thus completing the structural reunification of the three areas of concern originating at Edinburgh. Some 146 churches—Protestant, Anglican, and Orthodox—were the original members of the World Council. During World War II, a skeleton staff in Geneva engaged in refugee relief and found various ways for Christians to communicate across the national barriers created by the war. The person most responsible during these interim years, W. A. Visser 't Hooft, a Dutch lay theologian, was elected the first general secretary of the World Council of Churches, and permanent headquarters were established in Geneva.

At the time of its creation, the World Council of Churches defined itself as "composed of churches which acknowledge Jesus Christ as God and Savior." From the beginning the WCC has made clear (despite misunderstanding by outsiders) that its task is "to serve the churches," not to become a super-church itself or to be a Protestant/Orthodox counterpart to the Vatican.

The issue of membership in the WCC has been a delicate one. All churches accepting the basic affirmation of "Jesus Christ as God and Savior" have been welcome to apply for membership, and at each world assembly (held every five or six years) new churches have joined, so that after the Vancouver world assembly (1983) there were three hundred member churches representing around four hundred million Christians and including almost all the major Protestant and Orthodox bodies in the world. Membership in the WCC, however, does not imply that member churches believe that their own doctrine of the church is inadequate, nor does it mean acknowledging that other members are "fully" churches. At the New Delhi assembly in 1961, a more fully developed basis for membership was approved. It reads: "The World Council of Churches is a fellowship of Churches which confess the Lord Jesus Christ as God and Savior according to the Scriptures and therefore seek to fulfill together their common calling to the glory of one God, Father, Son and Holy Spirit."

Although the World Council of Churches has gone through several structural reorganizations since its inception and will continue to respond structurally to new situations, the emphases of all three Edinburgh streams have remained central throughout its history. A brief description of the structure as it existed after the Vancouver assembly will indicate the wide variety and scope of WCC commitments.

There are three major foci of concern in the World Council, identified as "program units." Program Unit I, devoted to Faith and Witness, is where the earlier Faith and Order Commission is housed. In its new guise, Faith and Order has continued to have an active history since the formation of the WCC, dealing with issues related to the visible unity of the church and preparing reports on such topics as accounts of Christian hope; the theology of baptism, eucharist, and ministry; the relationship between church and state; and the unity of the church in relation to the unity of humankind. The subunit on World Mission and Evangelism is clearly the repository of many of the concerns of the earlier International Missionary Council and deals with problems raised in proclaiming the faith today, discerning the true missionary congregation, and developing ways for churches throughout the world to share their resources, both material and spiritual.

The subunit on Church and Society is one of the continuing vehicles for the concerns of the earlier Commission on Life and Work; the World Council of Churches has held important conferences in this area, most notably a conference on "The Church in the Social and Technical Revolutions of Our Time" (Geneva, 1966), which included worldwide representation and set a new direction for Church and Society concerns. There have also been subsequent conferences on the uses of nuclear energy and issues in medical ethics. The subunit on Dialogue with People of Living Faiths and Ideologies has been a vehicle for widening contacts far beyond the Christian arena. The subunit on Theological Education seeks to make resources available for training for ministry in as ecumenical a context as possible.

Program Unit II is concerned with Justice and Service, another place where certain Life and Work emphases continue to be manifest in concrete ways. The subunit on Inter-Church Aid, Refugee and World Service has been a conduit for specific, practical, and immediate help to people in need. The subunit on Churches' Participation in Development enables churches to be involved in economic development in their own lands through grants and other acts of solidarity such as long-term low-interest loans, along with extensive educational programs and the sharing of technical services. The subunit on International Affairs calls the churches' attention to situations of injustice and conflict, particularly in such areas as the violation of human rights. The Program to Combat Racism, through separately solicited funds, gives financial support to groups of racially oppressed peoples so that they can work for their own liberation. The Christian Medical Commission engages in programs of community health care and education, particularly in areas that are without adequate hospitals or professional medical assistance.

Program Unit III is concerned with Education and Renewal and is oriented to new thinking about Christian education and its impact on parish life. The subunit on Education sponsors programs to develop leadership, educational curricula for churches, and Bible study. The subunit on Renewal and Congregational Life provides resources for local congregations and other

Christian groups. The subunit on Women is helping the entire Christian family to rethink the roles of women in both church and society. A similar subunit on Youth gives special attention to the needs of young people.

Even this cursory listing indicates the council's breadth of concern. It directs ongoing attention to theological reflection in the context of the contemporary world (Program Unit I), specific actions in various projects of service (Program Unit II), and ongoing attempts at renewing the mind for the life of the people of God (Program Unit III). In addition to a staff of about 275 persons to administer these various activities, the World Council of Churches has a Central Committee, composed of about 135 members, chosen proportionately from among the member churches, which meets annually to determine the ongoing tasks of the WCC between assemblies.

At the world assemblies, member churches meet to discuss their common task and to work on problems that have emerged since the previous assembly. The topics of the assemblies give an indication of the central themes of the WCC's ongoing life. From 1948 to 1983, six assemblies were held: "Man's Disorder and God's Design" (Amsterdam, 1948), "Jesus Christ the Hope of the World" (Evanston, 1954), "Jesus Christ the Light of the World" (New Delhi, 1961), "Behold I Make All Things New" (Uppsala, 1968), "Jesus Christ Frees and Unites" (Nairobi, 1975), and "Jesus Christ the Life of the World" (Vancouver, 1983).

The most volatile storm center of controversy in the life of the WCC has been the Program to Combat Racism. Provided for at Uppsala (1975) shortly after the murder of Martin Luther King, Jr., who was to have been the keynote speaker, the Program to Combat Racism assigns considerable sums of money each year to groups throughout the world who are victims of racism and are trying to find ways of escaping such repression. Small grants have occasionally been given to "freedom" groups, particularly in Africa, occasioning protest from others who feel that such gifts will foster violence. Although there have been no instances in which the charges have proven accurate, the issue has remained an emotionally charged one and has the effect of deflecting the public's attention from many of the other activities of the WCC.

The Development of Roman Catholic Ecumenism. During most of the developments described above, the Roman Catholic church remained uninvolved. Its posture was clear: church unity could be achieved only by the return to the Roman Catholic church of all the Christian bodies who had separated from it. Since full ecclesial reality was possible only for churches in communion with Rome, Roman Catholics were initially forbidden by Rome to participate in ecumenical activities. For example, Roman Catholic observers were not permitted to attend either the Amsterdam (1948) or Evanston (1954) assemblies of the World Council of Churches.

However, a few Roman Catholic ecumenical pioneers very cautiously began to initiate contact with non-Catholics. After World War I, Max Metzger, a German priest, founded the Una Sancta movement to foster dialogue between Protestants and Catholics. French priest Paul Couturier worked for revision of the prayers of the Christian Unity Octave of the Roman liturgy, so that Catholics and Protestants could begin to pray together. The Foyer Unitas in Rome was established for the study of non-Catholic traditions. Dominican priest Yves Congar in France, Jesuit Gustave Weigel in the United States, and other individuals trod a lonely path of seeking to put Protestants and Catholics on speaking terms with one another. After the Amsterdam assembly (1948), an "Instruction" was issued by the Holy Office in Rome in 1949, providing some cautious initial guidelines for Catholic and non-Catholic encounters; even so, an invitation to the Vatican to send Catholic observers to the Evanston assembly (1954) was declined. In 1961, however, during the pontificate of John XXIII, a similar invitation to send observers to the third assembly at New Delhi (1961) was accepted, and five priests attended.

A major ecumenical turning point occurred when John XXIII invited the major Protestant, Anglican, and Orthodox bodies to send observers to the Second Vatican Council, convened in the fall of 1962. Lasting warm and personal relationships that dissolved the frosty barriers of the centuries were established during the four sessions of the council (1962–1965).

Vatican II enhanced Catholic engagement in ecumenism in a number of ways. For one, the very calling of a council was seen as an instance of *ecclesia semper reformanda* ("the church always being reformed"), a concept Protestants had previously thought was anathema to Rome. Second, the inclusion of the observers demonstrated that Rome did not wish to continue to live in ecclesiastical isolation. Third, the influence of the "missionary bishops" who had often worked with Protestant missionaries brought fresh perspectives to other bishops trained in exclusivist patterns. Fourth, many of the council documents opened new doors of ecumenical understanding.

Of the sixteen promulgated conciliar documents, at least seven had significant ecumenical import. The document on ecumenism opened new doors for dialogue and understanding; the document on the liturgy restored the use of the vernacular and made Catholic worship less foreign to non-Catholics; the document on the church affirmed the "collegiality of the bishops," correcting certain one-sided emphases from Vatican I concerning the primacy of Peter that had been ecumenically counterproductive; the document on revelation gave scripture a greater prominence and authority in relation to tradition; the document on religious liberty dispelled fears about Catholic ecclesiastical imperialism; the document on the church and non-Christian religions created the possibility of dialogue between Roman Catholics and adherents of other world religions; and the document on the church and the world today indicated areas of concern, such as economics, labor unions, nuclear weapons, and culture, on which Catholics and non-Catholics could work together despite lack of full doctrinal consensus.

Assessments of the long-range impact of Vatican II are diverse. For many Catholics, the council brought the church into the modern world and made new levels of activity and dialogue possible. For other Catholics, the council created so many lines of rapport with modern thought and movements that the distinctiveness of the Catholic faith seemed to be placed in jeopardy. For most Protestants, the council unexpectedly legitimated Catholic attitudes that continue to enrich ecumenical life. [*For further discussion, see* Vatican Councils, *article on* Vatican II.]

In the new atmosphere created by Vatican II, the relationship of Roman Catholicism to the World Council of Churches was raised anew. There is no theological reason why the Roman Catholic church could not become a member of the WCC, since the basis of membership poses no challenge to Catholic faith. At the Uppsala assembly (1968), three years after the conclusion of Vatican II, the relations with Roman Catholic observers were so cordial that it seemed as though an application for membership might soon be possible, but by the Nairobi assembly (1975) such momentum had diminished. One important consideration, acknowledged by both sides, has been that, because of its size, the voting power of the Roman Catholic church in the WCC would be disproportionate and cause alarm to member churches that have numerically small constituencies. Nevertheless, a close working relationship has been established between Geneva and Rome, not only in areas of social service projects, such as the Commission on Society, Development, and Peace, but in the theological arena as well, and Roman Catholic theologians have for some time been full voting members on the Commission on Faith and Order, contributing to discussions and reports about ministry, baptism, and eucharist.

A further ecumenical contribution has come from Roman Catholicism. Building on the Vatican II document "The Church and the World Today," Catholics in Third World countries, particularly Latin America, have created a "theology of liberation," affirmed by the Latin American bishops in a meeting in Puebla, Mexico, in 1979, which involves committing the church to making "a preferential option for the poor." This has led to significant numbers of Catholics, frequently joined by Protestants, siding with the destitute at great personal risk in oppressive situations; Catholic-Protestant differences have paled before the awesome responsibility of ecumenical challenges to the oppressive status quo. This "practical ecumenism" provides a significant model for ecumenical involvement elsewhere. [*See* Political Theology.]

Extending Intramural Christian Activity. Within the Christian family the impetus of ecumenical concern has not only led Christian bodies to seek closer contacts with one another and to work together whenever possible, but also led many denominations to seek organic union with one another. The motivations usually include at least a desire to respond organically and structurally to Jesus' high-priestly prayer "that they all may be one" (*Jn.* 17:21); a recognition that division is a "scandal" in the sight of both Christians and non-Christians, who cannot fail to perceive the hypocrisy of those who preach unity but do not practice it; and a desire to use institutional resources with more efficient stewardship by avoiding both overlapping and competition. Although not widely heralded by the secular press, there continue to be significant numbers of mergers between denominations that are members of the World Council of Churches. While the latter body does not act as the agent or broker for such reunions, its very existence has brought diverse groups of Christians into contact with one another and thereby helped to enhance the movement toward denominational reunion.

Many of the reunions have taken place among the so-called younger churches as they have sought to overcome the legacy of divisive denominationalism that the nineteenth-century missionary enterprise bequeathed to them. Although the period is exceptional, the reunifications that took place between the years 1965 and 1972 give some indication of the intensity of the concern to heal the Christian divisions of centuries. During that period, united churches were created out of two or more confessions in Zambia, Jamaica and Grand Cayman, Madagascar, Ecuador, Papua New Guinea and the Solomon Islands, Belgium, North India, Pakistan, Zaire, and Great Britain.

Other specific steps toward organic unity will be completed only after years of further discussion and exploration. A proposal for reunification of ten denominations in the United States, the Consultation on Church Union, is now, after years of high-level ecumenical discussion, moving into a time of local denominational reacquaintance at the grass-roots level before any final decisions are made.

The tender spots in negotiating denominational mergers center less on theology than on polity. Theological agreement on most, if not all, issues is increasingly reachable, but the form and structure of new denominations is rendered difficult when any of the three major polities—congregational, presbyterian, or episcopal—are being combined. [*See* Church, *article on* Church Polity.] The Church of South India (1947) was the first such reunification to draw all three types of church government within a single new structure.

Within all denominations, and within the World Council of Churches, a new intramural issue has emerged with a vitality not anticipated even a short time ago: the role of women within the life of the church. Not only have such issues as the ordination of women and the holding of church office by women been treated very differently by the historic Christian confessions, but cultural influences, often unconsciously appropriated by various church groups and imposed on the intramural discussions, have made this a "radicalizing" issue for many women, who have been active in ecumenical affairs and have discovered that they have been the victims of conscious, or even unconscious, discrimination within the churches. The World Council of Churches has included a division within its structure to deal with the problem in an ongoing way, and a major consultation was held at Sheffield, England, in 1981; however, equality of status is far from a reality, either ecumenically or denominationally, and ongoing discussion and action on this matter will be high on the ecumenical agenda for the foreseeable future.

Extramural Ecumenical Developments. In addition to all the ecumenical concerns that center on mission and unity, there is the further meaning of *oikoumenē* that calls attention to the whole of "the inhabited world" and comprises not only service to every member of the human family but also a certain way of thinking about and relating to those who are part of the human family but not the Christian family. There are at least four areas in which the inner life of the ecumenical movement has been turning outward toward appraisal of and dialogue with groups that Christians cannot avoid confronting in an ever-shrinking world, and with whom they must seek terms of mutual understanding.

One of the most important of these areas has been the new attention accorded the relationship between Christians and Jews. Christians, born of the family of Abraham and Sarah, are beginning to acknowledge that they have been at best ungrateful heirs, and at worst despicable destroyers, of a faith apart from which they cannot truly define themselves. The ongoing history of destructive relations between Christians and Jews, frequently the result of a Christian theological imperialism, has been exacerbated in recent times by the Holocaust and the murdering by the Nazis of six million Jews, with the passive complicity and at times the active involvement of the Christian world. In the emerging ecumenical discussion, a new emphasis on the eternal nature of God's covenant with the Jews (based in large part on fresh study of *Romans* 9–11) is beginning to challenge the more traditional "supercessionist" view—that the coming of Christ superseded the divine covenant with Abraham—which has reduced the Jews living in the Christian era to objects for conversion. The World Council of Churches has sponsored several consultations on the relationship between Jews and Christians. Vatican II opened some doors for the new discussion by its clear declaration that anti-Semitism can in no way be grounded in the Christian scriptures, and many Protestant denominations, including a number in Germany, the location of Hitler's rise to power, have been exploring in fresh ways the implications of a view that Christians and Jews, who have lived in such destructive tension in the past, can create a more positive future together. [*See* Christianity and Judaism; Anti-Semitism; *and* Holocaust, The.]

A concern to understand the relationship of Christianity to other world religions is a second area that has been the object of increasing ecumenical attention. A Vatican II declaration, "The Relationship of the Church to Non-Christian Religions" (1965), began to open doors on the Roman Catholic side, and the World Council of Churches has held a series of consultations, such as one at Chiang Mai, Thailand, in April 1977, on "Faith in the Midst of Faiths," which sought to explore new ways of dealing with the many communities of faith that exist in a world where Christians have often claimed to be the unique community of faith. The discussion goes back to a meeting of the International Missionary Council in Madras in 1938 on the Christian message to a non-Christian world. The issue is to discover a *modus vivendi* for all, between an attitude of theological imperialism, which implies that if one faith is the truth no other faiths really have a right to exist, and a syncretism, which implies that there are not enough differences between the faiths to pose an issue and that some amalgamating of them all can create a new faith for the future. The unattractiveness of both options means that the discussion will continue. [*See* Faith *and* Dialogue of Religions.]

A third area of extramural ecumenical dialogue has had varying degrees of success and failure: the relationship between Christianity and Marxism. In the years immediately after World War II, an extended dialogue between Christians and Marxists flourished in Europe, since many Christians had been united with Russians and other communists in opposing the fascism of Hitler and Mussolini. However, the European dialogue was severely set back by Soviet takeovers in such places as Czechoslovakia. The issue of how Christians are to approach Marxism and communism is vitally important, as a matter of daily life as well as intellectual dialogue, because in many areas of the world Christians live under socialist or communist regimes. The entrance of the Russian Orthodox Church into the World Council of Churches at the New Delhi world assembly (1961) assured that the issue of Christian presence within a Marxist state would be under continual scrutiny. [*See* Marxism.]

The matter is rendered even more urgent in parts of the world where socialism or communism are seen as possible alternatives to oppressive governments that are perceived to be linked to imperialistic forms of capitalism. In Latin America, for example, the issue of Christian involvement in movements seeking to overthrow oppressive dictators cannot be separated from the question of the degree to which Christians are willing to work with Marxists in such situations or to accept certain elements of Marxist analysis in seeking to create a society more in keeping with their understanding of the Christian gospel. Although in the United States concern about Marxism is frequently interpreted as the camel's nose of subversion entering the tent of ecclesiology, the dialogue will remain crucial on an ecumenical level as long as Marxism represents an option for millions of people living in a world Christians are called upon to serve.

A further area of dialogical involvement centers on the appropriate relationship between Christians and those who are defined by a term such as *secularism.* A significant part of every world assembly of the WCC has addressed matters like international relations, racism, poverty, violence, and social embodiments of evil. Vatican II called attention to this new dialogue in its document "The Church and the World Today" (1965), which dealt with problems of culture, the spread of atheism (for which the church acknowledged some responsibility), the role of secular agencies in bringing about social change, and so forth.

But there is an even more fundamental issue, to which the Faith and Order division of the World Council of Churches has been directing attention and which is summarized in the title of one Faith and Order study: "Unity of the Church—Unity of Humankind." Recognizing that there is a unity that binds all people together as part of the human family, quite apart from the unity some of them have consciously chosen by their allegiance to Christ, how are those two kinds of unity to be related to one another? Does the former negate the significance of the latter, or vice versa? Can the two unities coexist? Is one too narrow, the other too broad?

The above are only a few examples of ways in which contemporary ecumenical concern is becoming broader and deeper. The original commitment to Christian cooperation has grown beyond issues of exclusive interest to Christians.

Some Unresolved Ecumenical Issues. The ecumenical movement is not so close to being successful that it will shortly render itself unnecessary. The three areas of mission, doctrine, and service still contain formidable obstacles to be overcome, though their formulation has shifted in some interesting ways since 1910.

In the area of mission the matter of "sending ambassadors of Christ" to faraway places must be viewed from a new perspective, since it now depends on who is deciding what is "far away." "Foreign missions" used to mean activities beyond the boundaries of North America and Europe. These continents constituted the "center," the rest of the world the "periphery." Mission was conceived of as a one-way street, emanating from the center toward the periphery. By the time of the Whitby conference of the International Missionary Council in 1947, it was clearly and even sternly affirmed that mission had become a two-way street and must remain that way. The new Christian vitality in the last half of the twentieth century seems to be coming from what used to be called the periphery, that is, the younger churches.

The real issue in the 1980s and 1990s and beyond maybe the degree to which the "older churches" at the "center" can have the grace to be recipients of new understandings of the gospel that will come from the "younger churches" at the "periphery." For the time being, at least, it may be more ecumenically blessed for the older churches to receive than to give. (The World Council of Churches, which at its inception was made up almost entirely of "leaders" from North America and Europe, has responded creatively to the new situation. Increasing numbers of its staff and leadership are drawn from other parts of the world.)

In the area of doctrine there have been a surprising number of theological convergences, even though certain unresolved issues remain central to the question of church reunions. There are increasing degrees of consensus on the meaning of baptism and even on eucharist, though the matter of ministry (i.e., who is properly validated to administer the sacraments) is far from resolved. [*See* Sacraments, *article on* Christian Sacraments; Eucharist; *and* Ministry.]

But Catholics and Protestants, for example, are much closer than before on such issues as the authority of scripture, the relationship of scripture to tradition, the meaning of "the priesthood of all believers," the nature of liturgy, the meaning of faith, and the necessity of social involvement on the part of Christians for the good of all. The office of the papacy naturally continues to divide Roman Catholics from the Orthodox, Anglicans, and Protestants, and the claim to infallibility of church teaching, while interpreted in different ways by the Orthodox and the Catholics, is an area where they are discernibly closer to each other than either of them is to the Protestants. The role of Mary in the economy of salvation is another unresolved area, although the Mary of the Magnificat (*Lk.* 1:46–55) is increasingly important to Protestants as well as Catholics. [*See* Mary.]

The difference of atmosphere from earlier times, however, is marked. Rather than closing off unassailable areas from discussion, there is a willingness to reexamine and even restate deeply held truths in the light of what is learned in ecumenical dialogue. Many non-Catholics, for example, could now acknowledge the possibility of some form of papacy, if defined as *primus inter pares,* the pope as a "first among equals." While this is not a definition acceptable to Roman Catholics, many Catholics are nevertheless attempting to define more precisely the meaning of papal authority, especially in the light of Vatican II's conclusion that the bishop of Rome shares teaching authority with the other bishops in the "episcopal college." [*See* Papacy.]

Another doctrinal issue, however, will be increasingly important in the life of the ecumenical movement. It has little to do with formulations of a doctrine of the papacy or eucharist or baptism, but a great deal to do with how doctrines are actually formulated. Protestant ecumenical theology has had a strong classical European stamp upon it, solidly rooted in the biblical heritage of Luther and Calvin. Roman Catholic ecumenical thought has likewise been nurtured by a European frame of reference, though, thanks to thinkers like Karl Rahner, it has been moving in new directions. Orthodox theologians have seen themselves as guarantors of past tradition, and their modes of describing that tradition have the stamp of centuries upon them.

But this is not the background from which Asians, Africans, and Latin Americans have come into the ecumenical movement. There is no reason, this new generation argues, why ways of doing theology in Europe should be normative everywhere. They are insisting that their own theology must now be done indigenously, arising out of their own cultures and using imagery appropriate to those cultures. Thus African Christians are drawing on images and experiences that maintain some continuity with their tribal pasts, to provide new metaphors to speak of the love of God in Jesus Christ. Asians are doing the same with a heritage more venerable than that of Europe, and "water-buffalo theology" (Kosuke Koyama) is more resonant for them than forensic images drawn from medieval courts of law. Latin Americans are insisting that theology must grow out of the experience of the poor, rather than being imposed on the poor by intellectuals in universities. A theological system arises out of human struggle, they are asserting, rather than being provided ahead of time by experts and then "applied" to specific situations. To the degree that the former "periphery" does begin to speak to the former "center"—and is heard—the issue of theological methodology will become an increasingly critical area of discussion. [*See* Theology, *article on* Christian Theology.]

In the third area, that of service, many difficult ecumenical issues have been posed for discussion, and the drawing of lines of difference bears little resemblance to the situation at the beginning of the modern ecumenical era. If, in the earlier period, it was true to say that "doctrine divides, service unites," the reverse has almost become the descriptive reality: service divides, doctrine unites.

A basic difference between two types of Christian approach to service seems to be part of a legacy that each era leaves to its successor. This legacy is a distinction between (1) those who see the Christian life as fundamentally an individual matter, in which, by giving sufficient attention to the personal and inner dimensions of life, a spirit is created that will transform the outer structures of society, and (2) those who believe that Christian faith is so incurably social that it is never enough just to change individuals and assume they will change society. This second view necessitates a simultaneous frontal attack on the unjust structures of society because they are causes of and manifestations of, as well as the results of, human sin. Almost all Christians, when pressed, would agree that both concerns must be present and that a theology containing one and not the other would be truncated and incorrect. But in practice, the matter of priority, or, even more, proportion, between the two is a significant cause of division.

What becomes ecumenically confusing is that divisions over such matters bear no resemblance to past denominational or confessional allegiances. For example, the lines between Roman Catholics and Protestants are not usually drawn on an issue such as the appropriateness from a Christian perspective of possessing nuclear weapons. Some Catholics will be closer to some Protestants than they will be to most other Catholics; some Presbyterians may be more at home in the company of

Methodists on this matter than with their fellow Presbyterians. Within a Catholic religious order, the most diversified opinions may be found on the ethical responsibility of multinationals, and within member churches of the World Council of Churches similar divisions occur. [*See* Christian Ethics.]

Issues of practice, then, are more often volatile sources of disagreement than issues of belief. For example, when "conservatives" attack the World Council of Churches, the issue is less likely to be a Faith and Order Commission report on baptism than the allocation of funds for the Program to Combat Racism. Some Catholics appear to be more upset with the social analysis of Catholic liberation theologians than with Protestant views of the meaning of papal infallibility. Church members in the late twentieth century are better able to tolerate doctrinal differences on the meaning of the real presence in the Eucharist than to allow for two points of view on whether or not "class struggle" is a legitimate descriptive term in Christian social analysis. So it is tensions within the realm of service—how the church is to relate to the world, what it is to do in relation to revolutionary situations, how it is to make a critique of the economic order (or whether it is even appropriate to do so)—that have become the causes of the deepest ecumenical ruptures.

Beyond the focal points of mission, doctrine, and service, other unresolved, structural issues remain. For example, what should be the relationship of world confessional bodies, which are global expressions of denominationalism, to the World Council of Churches? Is the continuation of such groups as the Lutheran World Federation or the World Alliance of Reformed Churches a contribution or a detriment to ecumenism? Do they impede the cause of Christian unity, or are they provisionally necessary for the maintenance of certain doctrinal emphases and portions of a tradition that might otherwise be lost?

Coupled with such matters is the problem of size. Is there a "critical mass" beyond which concern for the Christian message will be dissipated simply because of the need to keep the wheels of a large organization running smoothly? To the degree that ecumenical dialogue brings about new understandings that render unnecessary the ongoing life of separate denominations, will the resultant mergers necessarily be vehicles for a refining of the prophetic nature of the gospel, or will bigness breed slowness and timidity? Whatever the answers to these and yet unanticipated questions, ecumenical concerns will persist in the life of the church as long as there is a discrepancy between the actual state of the church and the will of the head of the church "that all may be one."

[*For further discussion of the varieties of Christian experience around the world, see articles on the regional dispersion of Christian religion under* Christianity. *See also* African Religions, *article on* Modern Movements; Australian Religions, *article on* Modern Movements.; North American Religions, *article on* Modern Movements; *and* Oceanic Religions, *article on* Missionary Movements.]

BIBLIOGRAPHY

For a history of the mission and expansion of Christianity, the movement out of which modern ecumenism grew, the best overall resource is still K. S. Latourette's *Christianity in a Revolutionary Age: A History of Christianity in the Nineteenth and Twentieth Centuries,* 5 vols. (New York, 1958–1962). Documents pertinent to the development of the modern ecumenical movement are conveniently collected in *Documents on Christian Unity,* 4 vols., edited by G. K. A. Bell (London, 1924–1958), which includes Protestant, Catholic, and Orthodox materials. For a full history of the ecumenical movement, with special attention to the formation of the World Council of Churches, consult *A History of the Ecumenical Movement, 1517–1948,* 2d ed., edited by Ruth Rouse and Stephen C. Neill (London, 1957), and its sequel, *The Ecumenical Advance: A History of the Ecumenical Movement,* vol. 2, *1948–1968,* edited by Harold E. Fey (Philadelphia, 1970). An interpretive account of the Faith and Order movement can be found in *A Documentary History of the Faith and Order Movement, 1927–1963,* edited by Lukas Vischer (Saint Louis, 1963), which contains excerpts from all the Faith and Order conferences through the New Delhi assembly (1961). The closest comparable volume tracing the Life and Work movement is Paul Bock's *In Search of a Responsible World Society: The Social Teachings of the World Council of Churches* (Philadelphia, 1974). The reports of all the WCC assemblies contain speeches, reports of the various commissions, and other pertinent information. These are *The First Assembly of the World Council of Churches: The Official Report* (New York, 1949), *The Second Assembly of the World Council of Churches: The Evanston Report* (New York, 1955), *The Third Assembly of the World Council of Churches: The New Delhi Report* (New York, 1962), all edited by W. A. Visser 't Hooft; *The Fourth Assembly of the World Council of Churches: The Uppsala Report,* edited by Norman Goodall (Geneva, 1968); *Breaking Barriers: Nairobi 1975,* edited by David M. Paton (London, 1975); and *Gathered for Life: Official Report, Sixth Assembly of the World Council of Churches,* edited by David Gill (Geneva, 1983). My *The Ecumenical Revolution,* rev. ed. (Garden City, N.Y., 1969), is a history of both Protestant and Catholic ecumenism through the Uppsala assembly in 1968.

For an account of the "ecumenical pioneers" who were active before Roman Catholic ecumenism was widely sanctioned, see Leonard J. Swidler's *The Ecumenical Vanguard* (Pittsburgh, 1966), which gives special attention to the Una Sancta movement. Hans Küng's *Justification: The Doctrine of Karl Barth and a Catholic Reflection* (London, 1964) is a good example of one of the earliest serious attempts to bridge the Protestant-Catholic chasm.

Two accounts of the Second Vatican Council are of special

interest: the reports from *Le monde* by the French journalist Henri Fesquet available as *The Drama of Vatican II* (New York, 1967), and Xavier Rynne's *Letters from Vatican City: Vatican Council II* (New York, 1963). The latter is an expansion of a famous series of *New Yorker* accounts, published pseudonymously throughout the council. The most easily available collection of the results of Vatican II is *Documents of Vatican II*, edited by Walter M. Abbott and Joseph Gallagher (New York, 1966). Since Vatican II, a series of volumes known as "Concilium," with more than a hundred titles, has been published by various publishers at regular intervals.

As an example of new theological and ecumenical understanding, Gustavo Gutiérrez's *A Theology of Liberation* (Maryknoll, N.Y., 1973) is the best introduction to post-Vatican II liberation theology, and Paul M. Van Buren's *Discerning the Way* (New York, 1980) and *A Christian Theology of the People Israel* (New York, 1983) represent fresh attempts to reconstitute Christian theology by taking its relationship to Judaism with new seriousness.

The most useful ecumenical periodical is *Journal of Ecumenical Studies* (Pittsburgh, 1974–), published triannually, with articles, extensive reportage on ecumenical activities throughout the world, and book reviews of new ecumenical literature. *The Ecumenical Review* (Geneva, 1948–), a quarterly publication of the World Council of Churches, contains articles, extensive journals of WCC activities, and book reviews covering ecumenical contributions from all over the world. *The Information Service of the Secretariat for Promoting Christian Unity*, published in Rome, gives papers, digests, and summaries of ecumenical activities in which the Secretariat is involved.

ROBERT MCAFEE BROWN

EDDAS. The two Icelandic works known as the Eddas form our most important source of knowledge for the northern myths. The *Poetic*, or *Elder*, *Edda* (sometimes called *Saemund's Edda* because of an Icelandic tradition that it was compiled by Saemund Sigfússon) is a collection of poems in alliterative stanzas found in a small manuscript book in an Icelandic farmhouse in 1643. Known as the Codex Regius, the original book was for many years in the Royal Library in Denmark, but has now been restored to Iceland. The book contains ten poems about the gods and eighteen about Germanic heroes. Some modern printed editions also include several poems of a similar type taken from other manuscripts, such as *Baldrs Draumar, Hyndluljóð, Rigsþula, Grógaldr*, and *Fjǫlsvinnismál.*

The book known as the *Prose Edda*, or *Snorri's Edda*, was written as a handbook for poets who needed to know the myths. Its author, the Icelandic poet, historian, and politician Snorri Sturluson, includes many excerpts from the *Poetic Edda* and other verse sources, and in fine Icelandic prose relates the myths and legends about the gods in whom his forebears believed. [*See the biography of Snorri.*] The term *Edda* is taken from a statement in one manuscript: "This book is called Edda which Snorri Sturluson composed." In Old Icelandic, the word *edda* means "great-grandmother," but in this context the term derives from *óðr* ("poetry") or from *Oddi*, the name of the place where Snorri was brought up.

The authorship, date, and place of origin of the poems of the *Poetic Edda* are unknown. The manuscript was written about 1300, but most of the poems are much earlier than this, and a number are thought to belong to pre-Christian tradition and may have originated in Norway. They give a reasonably consistent picture of the gods, who form a community in Ásgarðr, but are divided into two companies, the Æsir and the Vanir, under the leadership of Óðinn. The warlike deities such as Óðinn, Þórr, and Týr belong to the Æsir and have some connection with the sky; Njǫrð and Freyr and the goddesses come from the Vanir, the fertility deities connected with the underworld. However, the divisions are not clearly or consistently defined; Óðinn rides through the sky but rules over the dead, while Freyr has links with the sun. Some gods, like Baldr and Heimdallr, are difficult to place with certainty in either group, while Loki the trickster does not seem to be a god at all.

The myths depict nine worlds inhabited by supernatural beings and mankind, with the world tree, Yggdrasill, at their center. From a reading of the poems, a tentative list of those who dwell in the nine worlds can be drawn up as follows: (1) the Mighty Powers, the gods who rule; (2) the Æsir; (3) the Vanir; (4) the *jǫtnar* (giants); (5) the *álfar* (elves); (6) the *dvergar* (dwarfs); (7) the dead in Hel (the underworld); (8) the *einherjar* (the heroes who dwell with Óðinn); (9) mankind. But no definite, consistent picture of the supernatural world can be derived from the learned and allusive poems of the *Poetic Edda*. Certainly much interest is shown in the various worlds, their creation, and their final destruction at Ragnarǫk. The poem that presents this most effectively is the *Vǫluspá* (Prophecy of the Seeress), generally thought to have been composed about the time of the conversion of Iceland in 1000 CE. It is an impressive account of the creation of the worlds, the entry of strife into the bright realm of the gods, and the destruction of the earth by fire and water until it reemerges from the sea and a new age begins. The poet appears to be aware of the abandonment of the old religion, but even if he was a Christian, he was certainly well versed in the myths of the gods.

The Eddic poems contain much detailed information about the names of various supernatural beings and much lore about them. Three poems *(Grímnismál, Vafþruðnismál, Alvíssmál)* take the form of versified rid-

dle contests, in which Óðinn or Þórr contends with a giant or dwarf to see who has the greater knowledge of the mythological world. Defeat means death for the vanquished. Questions are asked concerning creation; the halls of the gods; the world tree, Yggdrasill, and the creatures that live on it; the life of warriors after death in the hall of Óðinn; and the events leading to Ragnarǫk. There are many complex names and terms: for instance, as many as fifty names of Óðinn are given in the *Grímnismál*. The riddle contest, a popular form of entertainment among Nordic peoples in medieval times, is used here as a method of instruction in religious lore. The detailed material in these poems was an important source of information to Snorri Sturluson when he came to compose the *Prose Edda*.

Other poems preserve complex material connected with magic and the significance of runic symbols. The *Skírnismál* gives an account of the wooing of a fair giantess, Gerðr, by the god Freyr, the leading deity of the Vanir. It is thought to have been inspired by one of the basic myths, that of the marriage of the sky god and the earth goddess. Much of the poem is in the form of a dialogue between Skírnir, Freyr's messenger, and Gerðr, whom he seeks first to persuade and then to coerce (by the use of magic runes and threatened curses) to yield to the god. The long composite poem *Hávamál* (Words of the High One), which purports to be spoken by Óðinn, lists various spells and refers to the winning of secret wisdom by the god, who is said to have hung from the World Tree in order to obtain powerful runic symbols for mankind. The *Hávamál* consists of a long series of proverbial statements offering good advice to those who want to succeed in life, get on well with their fellows, and find contentment. This is presented with wit and vivid imagery, although with little reference to Óðinn, who is traditionally supposed to have inspired it.

In other poems we have another kind of verbal contest, namely, the exchange of insults. In the *Hárbarðsljóð,* Þórr tries unsuccessfully to compel Óðinn, disguised as a ferryman, to take him across a river. When they recognize one another, they exchange vigorous insults, referring to various shameful incidents in the past. The poem containing the most spirited and elaborate collection of insults is the *Lokasenna*. Loki, the mischievous and cunning companion of the gods, comes uninvited to a feast at which all the well-known gods and goddesses are present. He insults each god in turn when they try to evict him and accuses the goddesses of infidelity toward their husbands.

Thus the majority of the Eddic poems about the gods may be seen as tests in knowledge of mythology and in verbal skills of various kinds, and some poems in the heroic section fall into a similar category. There are a few narrative poems, two concerned with the god Þórr. The *Þrymskviða* tells of the theft of his hammer, and how he recovered it from the giant Þrymr with the help of the ingenious Loki. Þórr was disguised as the goddess Freyja, wrapped in a bridal veil for her marriage with Þrymr; and he recovered his hammer when it was brought in for the ceremony. *Hymiskviða* describes how Þórr fished up Miðgarðsormr (the world serpent), the monster that lay in the depths encircling the earth. This particular myth was clearly of importance, since it was depicted on carved stones of the Viking age. Both tales are humorously told, and the first is rollicking comedy, but this does not diminish their underlying seriousness. The emergence of the monster from the depths would mean that the end of the world had come; without Þórr's hammer to protect them, the gods would be at the mercy of the giants and chaos would take over.

Two short narrative passages are also included in the *Hávamál,* and these concern exploits of Óðinn. In one we are told of his unsuccessful wooing of a resolute maiden, and in the other of his recovery of the magic mead of inspiration from the giants, with the aid of his giantess lover. These have been linked with the proverbial wisdom of the poem as examples of the difficulties of dealing with women, and it is assumed that the hearers will be familiar with the tale.

When Snorri Sturluson came to present his account of the myths in the *Prose Edda,* he made extensive use of many of the Eddic poems, and also drew on tales of the gods from other, unknown sources, thereby enlarging the canvas without creating striking contradictions to the main design. The mythology is set out in the form of answers to the questions of an imaginary Swedish king, Gylfi, who wants to learn about the gods. The information is provided by three mysterious characters in the hall of the Æsir, which puts the whole into the realm of fantasy and protects Snorri against the accusation that he is disseminating pagan lore. He gives several traditional views about the creation of the world and describes the gods and goddesses and other supernatural beings, including lists of lesser ones about which little or nothing is known. He also recounts a number of myths and legends concerning the gods and the giants. One is the tale of how a giant built the stronghold of Ásgarðr, whereupon the gods cheated him out of his wages and took his life; another relates how the god Týr bound the Fenrisúlfr (the wolf that threatened the gods) and left him in chains until Ragnarǫk, losing his hand in the process. Other tales relate how the treasures of the gods were fashioned, what befell Þórr in the land of the giants, and his duel with the giant Hrungnir; various escapades of Loki culminate in

the tale of how he caused the death of Baldr and was bound by the gods under the earth as a punishment, only to break loose at the end of all things. Finally there is a vivid account of Ragnarǫk, based on the *Vǫluspá* but also including various popular beliefs about the world's ending.

The impression given by Snorri is that he depended largely on the Eddic poems and others of the same type, although sometimes he makes it clear that he knows more than one version of a legend. However, in skaldic verse, he had one important additional source of information. This type of poetry differs from that of the *Poetic Edda* and consists of eight-line stanzas with elaborate rules of alliteration and assonance, with formal, highly figurative and obscure language, and imagery largely based on mythology. Such verses, composed by Icelandic poets, were very popular in the halls of Scandinavian kings and chiefs. A good deal of it was recorded in Iceland, together with the names of the poets, and some of the poems go back to the ninth century, predating the introduction of Christianity. Some short skaldic poems deal with myths, such as the episode in which Þórr fishes for Miðgarðsormr, while others describe the entry of kings into the hall of Óðinn after their death in battle. Snorri's extensive knowledge of such poetry thus extends our information about the myths of the Viking age.

Poems and stories provide additional information about heroes included in the two Eddas. This applies mainly to Óðinn and his interference in human affairs for his own sinister ends. There are a few stories about the gods outside the Eddas, some in the prose sagas and some (about Óðinn) included in the Latin history of the Danish historian Saxo Grammaticus, who wrote shortly before Snorri. Most of these stories, however, are late in date and doubtful in content. The material in the Eddas is mainly literary in character, and has been elaborated and worked on by poets, while in the *Prose Edda* Snorri has brought evidence together from various sources and attempted to arrange it into a consistent whole. However, the depiction of Óðinn as god of warriors, ruler of the dead, and inspirer of poetry and magic, and of Þórr as god of the sky and protector of the community and of fertility deities, corresponds to the little that is known of Wodan, Thunar, and other gods of the earlier Germanic pantheon. Few myths about the gods survive from the pre-Christian Germanic peoples on the continent or from the Anglo-Saxons, and it is to the Eddas that we must turn to make good the deficiency.

BIBLIOGRAPHY

Translations of the *Poetic Edda* can be found in Henry Adams Bellows's *The Poetic Edda* (New York, 1923) and in Lee Milton Hollander's *The Poetic Edda*, 2d ed., rev. (Austin, 1962). Unfortunately, these give little idea of the quality of the original, and the notes are limited in scope. A more attractive translation of the mythological poems only is Olive Bray's *The Elder or Poetic Edda, Commonly Known as Saemund's Edda* (London, 1908). A new translation and commentary by Ursula Dronke is in progress, but only one volume on some of the heroic poems has yet appeared: *The Poetic Edda*, vol. 1, *Heroic Poems* (Oxford, 1969). A translation of and commentary on the *Vǫluspá*, translated by B. S. Benedikz and John McKinnell, has been produced by the University of Durham (Durham and St. Andrews Medieval Texts, no. 1; Durham, 1978).

The fullest translation of the *Prose Edda*, omitting only some technical sections, is Arthur Gilchrist Brodeur's *The Prose Edda by Snorri Sturluson* (New York, 1916). An excellent translation of the material on the gods and the myths is that of Jean I. Young, *The Prose Edda of Snorri Sturluson: Tales from Norse Mythology* (Cambridge, 1954). Neither version has notes or commentary.

For the myths of the Eddas there is E. O. G. Turville-Petre's *Myth and Religion of the North* (London, 1964), which is stronger on the literary than the religious side, and my own *Gods and Myths of Northern Europe* (Harmondsworth, 1965), republished as *Gods and Myths of the Viking Age* (New York, 1981), a study of the mythology in the light of what is known of Germanic religion. Georges Dumézil, in essays translated in *Gods of the Ancient Northmen*, edited by Einar Haugen (Los Angeles, 1973), and in many other works, has dealt with the myths of the Edda in the light of other mythologies in the Indo-European tradition. A series of essays on the *Poetic Edda* was published by the University of Manitoba in 1983, under the title *Edda: A Collection of Essays*, edited by Robert J. Glendinning and Haraldur Bessason. The most helpful reference book for Germanic mythology as a whole is Jan de Vries's *Altgermanische Religionsgeschichte*, 2d ed., 2 vols. (Berlin, 1956–1957).

HILDA R. ELLIS DAVIDSON

EDDY, MARY BAKER (1821–1910), American religious leader, founder of Christian Science. Along with a growing interest in feminine spirituality within the Christian tradition, late-twentieth-century scholarship has begun to reassess the work and character of Mary Baker Eddy. Academic perceptions of her have generally been slow to catch up with insights provided by biographical studies. This is largely traceable to the persistence of one-sided portrayals, both negative and positive, going back to controversies generated in Eddy's own lifetime. Not only did she initiate a radical religious teaching that claimed to cut through centuries of orthodoxy to the living power of the gospel, but she also organized and led the Christian Science movement as a woman within a male-dominated society.

Eddy always remained a child of the American Puritan tradition in which she was raised in rural New

Hampshire. There the influence of a deep-seated Puritan piety in the theological tradition of Jonathan Edwards prevailed over the liberalizing tendencies that were shaping so much of American religious life. The toughness and resilience reflected in her leadership of the Christian Science movement were expressions of the vein of "puritan iron" in her nature.

At the same time, the independence of Eddy's nature was observable in her youthful revolt against the stark Calvinistic view of God as foredooming a major portion of the human race to eternal damnation. Later, the same tendency toward revolt was to become apparent in her rejection of the view of God as permitting any human suffering whatever. Unable to abandon her thoroughly ingrained belief in God's sovereignty or her equally strong conviction of God's goodness and love, she was to advance in Christian Science a radical interpretation of the gospel through a new concept of God's relation to humanity.

Eddy's path to what she was to call the "discovery" of Christian Science led her through twenty years of personal loss and suffering, which included the deaths of several family members (including her husband), enforced separation from her only child, an unsuccessful second marriage, and bouts of increasing nervous debility and acute, if ill-defined, physical suffering.

Through the investigation of various healing methods in her search for health, Eddy came to believe that the cause of disease lay in the mind, a belief reinforced by her contact with a Maine healer named Phineas Quimby, to whom she appealed for aid in 1862. Eddy's own thinking, however, was not basically shaped by Quimby's views, which were rooted in mesmerism, but by the New Testament Christianity to which she had always clung. She saw the gospel in a new light after a healing following a severe accident in 1866, a cure that she attributed to a moment of profound illumination upon reading an account of one of Jesus' healings in *Matthew.* That experience marked a turning point in her life. It led to nine years of scriptural study, healing activity, and teaching, culminating in 1875 with the publication of *Science and Health with Key to the Scriptures.* Eddy considered that book to contain the statement of the "science" that underlay Jesus' works and of the method that make those works repeatable.

Eddy was, however, quickly disabused of what she was to call her "sanguine hope" that the Christian churches would readily accept Christian Science. The beginnings of her pioneering efforts in the mill towns of Massachusetts were bleak and inauspicious; she attracted only a few followers during her first decade of work. In 1877 Eddy married for the third time, and relied on her husband for moral support from this time until his death five years later.

In 1879 Eddy and a small band of followers founded the Church of Christ, Scientist, which began to take shape when she moved to Boston two years later. There she continued to write, teach, and preach, and to defend the movement against both internal schism and external attack, launching Christian Science as a significant movement in American religious life.

The strong opposition she encountered, as well as the defection of followers who found the discipline of Christian Science too severe, actually brought increased authority to her leadership. This increase in authority in turn aroused charges of authoritarianism and paranoia. She herself used the image of a "lioness robbed of her young" to describe her efforts in the 1880s to prevent Christian Science from being distorted beyond recognition by those who borrowed her language to promote what she saw as an essentially non-Christian form of "mind-cure." Eddy strongly disavowed that Christian Science healing was produced in any way by mental suggestion. She did, however, insistently warn that hatred projected through mental suggestion could have destructive effects—a view that intensified the controversy she aroused.

As Christian Science gradually became a widespread religious movement, Eddy found it necessary to devise an institution effective enough to protect and perpetuate her teachings. In 1889 she suspended the operations of existing national Christian Science organizations in order to thoroughly reorganize the church, which took its present form in 1892 as the First Church of Christ, Scientist, in Boston, the "mother" church of Christian Science branch churches throughout the world. Three years later she published *Manual of The Mother Church,* a slim body of rules for governing the denomination, rules that she continued to revise to the end of her life.

Eddy was often accorded somewhat backhanded praise for displaying an organizational genius more generally associated with men. Yet her struggles to institutionalize her teaching without becoming submerged in bureaucracy were severe and were accompanied in the last two decades of her life by episodes of intense physical suffering. Her recognition of the need to relate Christian Science more effectively to the world gave impetus to her last major achievement, the founding in 1908 of the widely respected newspaper *The Christian Science Monitor.*

By the time of her death, Eddy was commanding international attention. Her view that morality was not part of God-centered reality, which is spiritual, put her thinking at variance with conventional theological formulations. This view and the healing practice that grew out of it have aroused sometimes bitter antagonism on the part of the clergy as well as the medical profession. Yet, even so strong a critic of Eddy as Oxford historian H. A. L. Fisher conceded, "When we ask what was the inner source of her power, the answer can only be that it was religion. . . . The great ideas of God, of immortality, of the soul, of a life penetrated by Christianity, were never far from her mind" (*Our New Religion*, New York, 1930, p. 61). Mary Baker Eddy's significance in the stream of Christian thought and the appeal of Christian Science itself lie in the fact that they have offered a new basis for the credibility of Christian claims to truth and have provided a new religious alternative for many people.

[*See also* Christian Science.]

BIBLIOGRAPHY

Mary Baker Eddy's major work is the "textbook" of Christian Science, *Science and Health with Key to the Scriptures* (1875; reprint, Boston, 1914). Most of her other published writings, including her autobiographical *Retrospection and Introspection*, are included in the compilation *Prose Works* (Boston, 1920). Far surpassing other biographical treatments is Robert Peel's sympathetic but exhaustively documented trilogy, *Mary Baker Eddy: The Years of Discovery, The Years of Trial*, and *The Years of Authority* (New York, 1966–1977). Extremely critical accounts include Georgine Milmine's *Mary Baker Eddy and the History of Christian Science* (New York, 1909) and Edwin F. Dakin's *Mrs. Eddy: The Biography of a Virginal Mind* (New York, 1929). In sharp contrast to these are such early "authorized" biographies as Sybil Wilbur's *The Life of Mary Baker Eddy* (New York, 1908) and Lyman P. Powell's *Mary Baker Eddy: A Life Size Portrait* (New York, 1930). In the light of Peel's more recent work, these older books have only limited biographical value but are important as documents reflecting the controversies surrounding Eddy's life and character.

STEPHEN GOTTSCHALK

EDO RELIGION.

EDO RELIGION. The Edo live in a tropical forest region of southern Nigeria. Their language belongs to the Kwa family of Niger-Congo languages. Like their linguistically and culturally related neighbors, the Yoruba and Igbo, the Edo are a population of long standing in this region. Oral traditions suggest that by the thirteenth or fourteenth century, the Edo were united into a powerful kingdom that by the fifteenth century had embarked on a course of aggressive military expansion in southern Nigeria. During this period of conquest, Portuguese explorers made contact with them, recording for the first time the name "Benin," which has been used since to refer to the kingdom (the people are sometimes referred to as the "Bini"). For four hundred years Benin traded with Portugal and other European nations until, in 1897, Benin fell to British colonial expansion and was then incorporated into the wider political framework of Nigeria. Its capital, Benin City, is now the administrative center of southern Nigeria's Bendel state. Outside the capital are numerous villages where farmers raise domestic and export crops.

In the traditional Edo view, reality is twofold: there is a visible world of ordinary human experience and an invisible world of gods, ancestors, and other supernatural beings. This spirit world is both a realm, variously located under the ground or where the sky and earth meet, and a parallel existence that constantly affects the everyday world. The rituals central to Edo religion—prayers, offerings, and sacrifices—take place at the meeting points between these realms, at shrines inside homes and villages, or at the foot of trees, crossroads, or the banks of rivers.

These two realms were created by the supreme being, Osanobua, who also established the framework of space and time and brought into being the first humans by breathing life force into molded clay images. Osanobua is envisioned as a king living in a palace, from which he presides over the spirit world, having delegated responsibility for the everyday world to his children, the other gods of the Edo pantheon. The most important of these is his senior son, Olokun, ruler of the great waters, who resides in his own palace under the Ethiope River, which the Edo believe is the source of all the waters of the world. From there he sends the blessings of wealth and children to his faithful devotees, primarily women desiring children. Olokun's wives and chiefs are the gods of the main rivers of the kingdom and are worshiped locally by villagers.

Olokun's junior brother, Ogun, is the patron deity of all who work with metal: casters, warriors, hunters, and today, drivers. Since metal enables the creation and expansion of civilization, Ogun is viewed as the god "who opens the way," that is, he enables the powers of the other deities and ancestors to be effective. Both Olokun and Ogun are vital components of contemporary Edo religious life, but some deities, such as Ogiuwu, god of death, and Obiemwen, the great mother goddess, are no longer worshiped in Benin. Religious change, however, is not just a phenomenon of contemporary times. Some of the Benin deities, such as the Yoruba-derived Eṣu, Ṣango, and Oronmila, were introduced into Benin two to four hundred years ago.

All Edo—male or female, young or old—may erect a personal shrine to Olokun, Ogun, or other gods if they have a special problem, interest, or calling. In addition, families, quarters, and villages also have communal shrines for worship of general or regional deities. Some individuals become religious specialists through apprenticeship, attainment of seniority, or a religious calling signaled by trance states. There are two main religious roles: priest or priestess and Ọsun adept. An individual becomes a priest or priestess either through seniority in a village or by being chosen by the deity. The role of the priest or priestess is to officiate at ceremonies, perform sacrifices, lead songs and prayers, and convey messages from the deity while in a state of trance. Often priests have the knowledge to cure illness, but the Ọsun specialist is the primary medical expert in traditional Edo culture. The adept of Ọsun, seeking to gain knowledge of the power inherent in leaves and herbs, undergoes an apprenticeship after which he is able to divine the cause of sickness, prescribe herbal treatments, administer poison and other ordeals, and fight the ultimate cause of illness: witchcraft. The Edo believe that witches are persons of evil intent who use their knowledge of herbalism to cause barrenness, disease, and premature death. At night witches are transformed into predatory birds and meet in trees to plot harm to their innocent victims.

Men and women who have lived a full life span and have received a proper burial after dying become personal, family, or group ancestors. Although residing in the spirit world, ancestors maintain their interest and involvement in the daily life of their descendants. The ancestral altar, located in the home of the senior male of a lineage or in a special section of a ward or a village, is the focus of sacrifices and prayers at periodic rituals and times of crisis.

The ancestors of the king of Benin (who is known as the *ọba*) are considered the protectors of the nation at large and their altars are national shrines housed in the royal palace. As the descendant of these divine kings and the possessor of vast supernatural powers, the *ọba* is a central figure in Edo religion. In Edo cosmology, the *ọba*, who is called "king of dry land," is the earthly counterpart of the great deity Olokun, "king of the waters," whose realm is the source of the *ọba*'s wealth. During the year, the king and his court are occupied with public and private rituals aimed at preserving the well-being and prosperity of the Edo nation. Although in this century some Edo influenced by Western education and mission teaching have become Christians, the traditional religion, with the *ọba* at its core, is still flourishing.

BIBLIOGRAPHY

R. E. Bradbury's *The Benin Kingdom and the Edo-Speaking Peoples of South-Western Nigeria* (London, 1957) provides a brief overview of Edo religion, and his collected essays, *Benin Studies*, edited by Peter Morton-Williams (London, 1973), explore specific issues in depth. I have discussed religious iconography in *The Art of Benin* (London, 1980) and in several articles: "Ekpo Ritual in Avbiama Village," *African Arts* 2, no. 4 (1969): 8–13, 79, written jointly with Osarenren Omoregie; "Symbolism in Olokun Mud Art," *African Arts* 6, no. 4 (1973): 28–31, 95; and "Men and Animals in Benin Art," *Man*, n.s. 2, no. 2 (1976): 243–252.

PAULA BEN-AMOS

EDUCATION, RELIGIOUS. *See* Religious Education.

EDWARDS, JONATHAN (1703–1758), American theologian and philosopher. Born in East Windsor, Connecticut, Edwards was the only son in a family of eleven children. His father, Timothy Edwards, a graduate of Harvard College, was the minister of the Congregational church in that town. His mother was the daughter of Solomon Stoddard, the minister at Northampton, Massachusetts.

Life and Work. As a youth Edwards was nurtured and instructed in the tenets of Reformed theology and the practices of Puritan piety. He entered the Collegiate School (later Yale College) in 1716; the course of study included classical and biblical languages, logic, natural philosophy, and the "new philosophy." He received the B.A. degree in 1720 and subsequently spent two additional years in New Haven studying theology. These early years, during which Edwards's inclination toward intellectual pursuits quickly became evident, were difficult but significant; the same period proved decisive religiously, too.

In August 1722 Edwards accepted his first pastorate at a Presbyterian congregation in New York City, a position he held until May of the following year. In the fall of 1723 he became the pastor at Bolton, Connecticut, but after a short time gave up the position. In May 1724 he assumed responsibilities as a tutor at Yale College. Two years later he resigned to become the ministerial colleague of his maternal grandfather in Northampton. He was ordained in February 1727 and in the same year married Sarah Pierrepont, the daughter of the Congregational minister in New Haven. Upon the death of Stoddard in 1729, Edwards became the full minister in Northampton.

The following years were times of expanding responsibilities. Edwards paid a great deal of attention to the preparation of sermons. A lecture he gave at Boston in 1731 became the first of his sermons to be published. He began to gain a reputation as a defender of Reformed doctrines. Edwards became a leading member of the Hampshire Association, an organization of clergymen in the county. His family also expanded with regularity, eventually reaching a total of eleven children.

The congregation at Northampton experienced an extraordinary manifestation of religious zeal during the winter of 1734–1735. The ferment spread to other communities in the Connecticut River valley. Accounts of these events sent by Edwards to Boston eventually circulated in expanded form throughout the American colonies and Great Britain, making him something of a celebrity. To his dismay, however, the religious fervor in Northampton proved short-lived.

In the fall of 1740 the languishing religious situation in New England changed dramatically with the arrival from England of George Whitefield, who in mid-October visited Northampton, where his preaching affected many, including Edwards. Scores of ministers adopted Whitefield's pattern of itinerancy and began to preach outside their own pulpits. In July 1741, for example, Edwards preached his now-famous sermon entitled "Sinners in the Hands of an Angry God" at Enfield, Connecticut, having delivered earlier versions at several locations. The emotional outbursts accompanying the Great Awakening became increasingly controversial, causing critics to question the legitimacy of the revivalists and of the "New Lights."

By 1742 the opponents of the revivals, led by Charles Chauncy of Boston's First Church, stepped up their attacks. Edwards answered these "Old Lights" by publishing a major defense of the revivals, declaring them the work of God's spirit and a harbinger of the millennial age. During the same period he preached a series of sermons that became the nucleus for his fullest statement on the evangelical nature of true religion, *A Treatise concerning Religious Affections.* After the revivals waned again, he sought new ways to foster religious concern: for example, he supported a plan for a worldwide concert of prayer.

Late in the 1740s Edwards was forced to turn his attention to problems in Northampton. Conflict developed with members of his congregation over questions of ministerial authority. An open rupture was provoked by Edwards's announcement that he intended to discontinue his grandfather's practice of admitting to communion those in good standing, unless they could provide evidence of a work of grace in their lives. The conflict spread into town politics and into relations with neighboring ministers; bitter factionalism prevailed. After months of controversy, a council of ministers and laity recommended a separation, and Edwards's formal dismissal followed in mid-1750.

Edwards faced uncertain prospects following his removal. After receiving several offers to settle, including one tentative proposal from Scotland, in May 1751 he accepted a pastoral call to Stockbridge in western Massachusetts, a mission outpost populated by a few whites and more than 250 Indian families. Life at Stockbridge was difficult, especially after the outbreak of warfare in the mid-1750s. Despite the circumstances, these years were perhaps Edwards's most productive. Not only did he continue his pattern of study, but he wrote several major treatises. His writings gave voice to a lifetime of reflection.

In the fall of 1757 Edwards received an invitation from the College of New Jersey (later Princeton) to become president of that young Presbyterian institution. After some reluctance, he consented and in February 1758 journeyed to New Jersey. One week after his arrival he was inoculated against smallpox; less than one month later he became a victim of that disease. Edwards was buried in the cemetery at Princeton.

Writings. The writings of Edwards fall into five categories: personal writings, sermons, occasional pieces, philosophical and theological works less directly occasional, and private notebooks. A substantial body of materials exists in each of these categories.

Edwards's most significant personal writings from the early period of his life, the "Diary" and "Resolutions," provide a contemporary record of his spiritual struggles and of his determination to pursue the religious life. The "Personal Narrative," a later recollection, records for spiritual edification his youthful experiences. Moreover, Edwards's correspondence was voluminous. He wrote to family members, students and colleagues, business associates, and evangelical leaders in America and Great Britain. His letters reveal a personal side not evident in the standard depictions of him as an intellectual, a preacher, and a polemicist.

Edwards's most pressing responsibility was preaching to his congregation. He invested heavily in the preparation of sermons, which often gave the first public expression to ideas developed in his notebooks. During his lifetime Edwards published eighteen sermons. The most famous of all, his Enfield sermon, continues to attract widespread attention today. Of greater significance, perhaps, is the "Farewell Sermon" in which he revealed his personal perspective upon the Northampton controversy. Two of Edwards's sermon series, *A History of the Work of Redemption* and *Charity and Its Fruits,* were published as treatises after his death. Today there is extant a collection of approximately thirteen hundred manuscript sermons.

A substantial number of Edwards's publications were written in response to particular circumstances. The most notable of his occasional writings describe and defend the revivals. *A Faithful Narrative* is clinically descriptive by contrast with the partisan, celebratory tone of *Some Thoughts. A Treatise concerning Religious Affections* is theologically reflective, the *Life of Brainerd* didactic, and *An Humble Attempt* guardedly optimistic. All form part of an extended apology for evangelical religion. His publications relating to the communion controversy, although polemical, reinforce the same concerns.

Nearly all of Edwards's writings are in a sense occasional. Several of his publications, however, are more programmatic, defining fundamental theological and philosophical positions. For example, in the treatises *Free Will* and *Original Sin,* Edwards addressed himself to questions regarding human nature and human capacity. But they too were written in response to Enlightenment assaults upon traditional views and are part of his defense of classic Reformed doctrines. Shorter writings, entitled *End of Creation* and *True Virtue,* have an even more abstract quality. At his death Edwards was at work on a rational defense of Christianity, a harmony of scripture, and a history of the work of redemption.

Edwards's study habits yielded an immense amount of material in his private notebooks. The notebooks "Natural Philosophy" and "The Mind" have received widespread attention, but the "Miscellanies," which contains theological, biblical, and philosophical reflections, is the most important source for tracing the development of his ideas. He also devoted separate notebooks to general biblical commentary, apocalyptic writing, typology, prophecy, history, sermon ideas, and symbolism in nature. Edwards's method of study included writing and rewriting his ideas, developing certain themes, and citing or paraphrasing works he read. The "Catalogue," a notebook referring to his reading, contains a working bibliography that documents the wide range of his interests.

Thought. Edwards's religious and philosophical ideas form a coherent body of thought, but no complete system was stated by him. Among his unfinished projects were plans for such a statement. He must be viewed as a transitional thinker, looking back to the Reformed heritage and also drawing heavily upon the Enlightenment. Edwards employed biblical concepts as well as insights from the new science. He set for himself the task of defending orthodox views against liberal assaults from the Arminian party, but he also borrowed the ideas of his contemporaries to revise and restate the tradition.

One central theme in Edwards's thought is the universal depravity of mankind. According to him, all mankind shared in the original sin of Adam whereby a supernatural gift of grace was lost. The identity of mankind with Adam was constituted by divine decree, and by virtue of that identity, the Fall condemned all to a life of certain and actual sin. Sin, in turn, merits condemnation and punishment; the greater the sin, the greater the deserved punishment. Transgressions against God are deserving of eternal retribution. Since the Fall, humans are not truly free to choose the good. Free will is a matter of semantics, for the will is free only to choose sin.

A second major theme in Edwards's thought is the sufficiency of God in the work of redemption. Mankind is totally dependent upon a gracious God who from eternity elected some for salvation. Edwards described God's nature variously. During his youth he spoke in idealistic categories, positing the necessary existence of an eternal Mind. Later he described God as the sun and the light from which everything derives its existence. He also employed the traditional language of the Trinity: the Father generates the Son from himself and is himself the source and object of his loving Spirit. In the redemptive act the Father appoints the Son as the Redeemer and accepts him as a sufficient price, and through his Spirit he communicates the good that has been purchased to those who have been chosen. The excellency of Christ is sufficient for the work of redemption. The presence of the Spirit defines a saint; only those with the indwelling divine principle are saved. The new birth signals the restoration of the supernatural gift lost with the fall into sin. Conversion is the moment when grace is infused into the life of the individual.

A third major theme is the legitimacy of the affections in true religion. Edwards believed that faith necessarily involves both the intellect or understanding and the volition or will. It is an act of affective knowledge, a sense of the heart. Belief inclines the heart toward what the understanding chooses. This holistic approach to religious experience was the linchpin for Edwards's case against both the rationalists and the enthusiasts. Against the former he held that, contrary to their belief, the emotions are legitimate in the religious life. Although he shared with John Locke a fear of the passions, he was unwilling to rule out the affections because he had investigated with great care specific cases of emotional religion and found them to be genuine. At the same time, he charged the enthusiasts with ignoring the role of the intellect in religious experience.

Edwards inherited his interest in practical religion from the Puritans, but the revivals raised the question of how to distinguish genuine religion from false. He sought to answer this question by establishing clear signs for the former. In true religion, he said, the witness of the Spirit is manifest both in the exercises of grace within the heart and in outward practice. True conversion is evident from the presence of both faith and love within the person. Self-examination is one way to test the state of grace, but the expression of holy affections in love of God and human beings is the chief means of assurance. Moreover, for Edwards conversion was never an end in itself but merely the beginning of the Christian life; the responsibility of the elect to pursue this godly life was another major theme in his thought. Sanctification, he held, follows justification as the product of the indwelling Spirit. Edwards insisted that true virtue consists in consent to or union with being in general, and that love of God for its own sake is the foundation for all other morality.

Finally, Edwards's system also embraced a vision of future glory. In his belief, the church comprises the community of the elect on earth, that is, those who have experienced grace in their lives. In covenant with others, the saints engage in the business of religion: good works, attendance at ordinances, worship, prayer, reading the Bible, and pursuit of their vocations. These activities reflect the kingdom of God in the world. Under the leadership of the ministry, the church seeks to expand and increase. Edwards's interest in missions reflected his larger understanding of history. The work of redemption, according to him, has progressed by God's direction from the time of biblical history to the contemporary moment and is moving toward a millennial climax on earth. The culmination of the Kingdom will bring the greater glory of God—the ultimate goal of creation and the purpose of the created order. Edwards looked eagerly for the fulfillment of this biblical vision.

Influence. During his lifetime Edwards achieved prominence and widespread reputation as a preacher, a leader of the revivalistic faction, and an evangelical theologian. Less than a decade after his death, Samuel Hopkins, disciple and close friend, declared that Edwards was one of the greatest theologians of the age. A school of New England theologians that emerged during the second half of the eighteenth century and that included Hopkins, Joseph Bellamy, and Jonathan Edwards, Jr., among its members held Edwards in high esteem even while beginning to depart from his specific views; that departure reflected the growing influence of the Enlightenment on American theology. Evangelicals in the first half of the nineteenth century continued this pattern of response. The publication and republication during this period of Edwards's works in collected editions is striking evidence of his stature, as is the circulation by tract societies of his works in abridged editions. On the other hand, the contrasting views of Charles Grandison Finney are a useful measure of the evangelical movement away from Edwards in antebellum America.

The second half of the nineteenth century witnessed an erosion of interest in Edwards and an increasing hostility toward his theological positions, particularly his commitment to the notion of human depravity, the doctrine of necessity, and the idea of eternal retribution. Although considerable praise was given to Edwards's skills as a metaphysician and logician, theological and cultural liberals condemned his ideas; even those who admired him and accepted his evangelical premises often viewed him as a tragic figure. The bicentennial of his birth produced only a small surge of interest in Edwards the man.

By the middle of the twentieth century, the prevailing attitude toward Edwards's work changed dramatically as a confluence of circumstances brought about a renaissance of interest in his ideas and a reassessment of his significance. This new interest, which had begun as a trickle of scholarship in the late 1930s, has in the present time risen to a flood tide. Edwards has become a major figure, a creative force, one of the most original thinkers in the American experience. Among the reasons for the change have been the new cultural climate in America following the Depression, the accompanying theological reappraisal that gave rise in American Protestantism to neoorthodoxy, and the growing concern about national origins, including the role of the Puritans in American life. An increasing number of conservative Protestants in America have also identified their thought with his evangelical views. This renewed engagement with the full range of Edwards's ideas has manifested itself among scholars in their support for a new critical edition of his writings. Today Edwards remains the object of sustained investigation by many in a variety of fields. For the moment, his place is secure within the pantheon of American thinkers.

BIBLIOGRAPHY

The works of Jonathan Edwards were collected several times in the nineteenth century. A new edition, *Works*, edited by Perry Miller and subsequently by John E. Smith, is in preparation (New Haven, 1957–). The monographic essays that constitute introductions to the volumes of this edition focus upon a range of particular religious issues relating to the life, thought, and influence of Edwards. To date seven volumes have appeared. The earliest biography of Edwards, which contains the text of the "Personal Narrative," is Samuel Hopkins's *The Life and Character of the Late Reverend Mr. Jonathan Edwards, President of the College at New-Jersey* (Boston, 1765). It has been reprinted in *Jonathan Edwards: A Profile*, edited by David Levin (New York, 1969). Numerous personal documents and items of correspondence from Edwards appear in Sereno E. Dwight's *The Life of President Edwards* (New York, 1829), the first volume of an edition of *The Works of President Edwards*, 10 vols. (New York, 1829–1830). The story of Edwards's life is told without undue concern for its intellectual dimensions in Ola E. Winslow's *Jonathan Edwards, 1703–1758* (New York, 1940), a prizewinning biography. The pastoral career of Edwards is the focus of Patricia J. Tracy's *Jonathan Edwards, Pastor: Religion and Society in Eighteenth Century Northampton* (New York, 1980). Perhaps the volume most responsible for the renaissance of scholarly interest in Edwards during the past three decades is Perry Miller's *Jonathan Edwards* (New York, 1949), a problematical interpretation focusing upon the influence of John Locke and Isaac Newton. The relationship between Edwards's thought and the tradition of Reformed theology is treated with care and precision in Conrad Cherry's *The Theology of Jonathan Edwards: A Reappraisal* (Garden City, N.Y., 1966). The influence of the English moral philosophers on Edwards is discussed in Norman Fiering's *Jonathan Edwards's Moral Thought and Its British Context* (Chapel Hill, N.C., 1981). The most comprehensive bibliography of writings about Edwards is M. X. Lesser's *Jonathan Edwards: A Reference Guide* (Boston, 1981). Lesser's volume consists of an excellent essay focusing upon the changing interpretation of Edwards and an annotated, descriptive bibliography. Three volumes that place Edwards centrally in the development of American thought and culture are Alan E. Heimert's *Religion and the American Mind* (Cambridge, Mass., 1966), Sacvan Bercovitch's *The American Jeremiad* (Madison, Wis., 1978), and Bruce Kuklick's *Churchmen and Philosophers: From Jonathan Edwards to John Dewey* (New Haven, 1985).

STEPHEN J. STEIN

EGG. The egg has aroused feelings of wonder in cultures all over the world. Its smooth, elliptical shell conceals the mystery of new life in formation. The sight of an egg hatching and a young creature bursting out from an apparently lifeless object stimulated ancient peoples to think about the creative process. It would have been difficult for early man to understand an abstraction like the creation of the world, but he could watch a similar process in the hatching of an egg. Thus the egg became an important symbol in creation stories.

The concept of a world egg that hatched the first creator appears in many early myths. The Harris Magical Papyrus, an Egyptian manuscript of the New Kingdom period (1569–1085 BCE), contains the earliest known reference to a world egg emerging from the primeval waters. Several Egyptian deities are associated with the egg: Thoth, god of the moon; the sun god, Re; the celestial goose, Seb, god of the earth; Ptah of Memphis; and Khnum, god of creation, who shaped the world egg on his potter's wheel.

The Hindu Upaniṣads (c. 600–300 BCE) describe the first act of creation as an egg breaking in two. The *Ṛgveda*, a body of Hindu hymns, sacrificial formulas, and incantations collected in the first millennium BCE, speaks of Prajāpati, Lord of Creation, who fertilizes the waters of creation, which change into a golden egg. Inside sits the golden figure of Brahmā, floating in the primeval waters for a thousand years, his golden light shining through seven shells. Land, sea, mountains, planets, gods, and mankind are all inside the egg with him.

In Chinese legend P'an Ku, the first man, emerged from the cosmic egg, as did Sun Wu-k'ung, the popular monkey king of Taoist and Buddhist legend.

Oceania has many stories of the origin of mankind from eggs. The divine bird laid one on the water, according to the Sandwich Islanders, and their islands hatched from its shell. Fijians attribute the origin of mankind to Ngendei, who nurtured the world egg, and tribes in southeastern Australia believe the sun emerged from an emu egg thrown into the air.

In the Jewish tradition, eggs are used on many ceremonial occasions. Lag ba-'Omer, a joyful festival honoring the memory of Rabbi Shim'on bar Yoḥai, falls on the thirty-third day between Passover and Pentecost. Children and their parents picnic with colored eggs. While the pious rabbi lived, God's symbolic rainbow, a sign that he would not destroy the world, was unnecessary. When he died, people needed the rainbow and hastened its coming by dyeing eggs in many colors.

The Seder, or Passover meal, always includes among its ritual foods a roasted egg. This is variously explained as a symbol of the additional sacrifice offered in the Temple at Passover, the sacrifice of travelers, or the departure from Egypt. More likely it signified rebirth, since Jewish mourners are traditionally fed baked eggs.

In the third and fourth centuries of the common era, the Christian church gradually adopted a Lenten fast of forty days commemorating the time Christ spent without food in the wilderness. Pope Gregory the Great (590–604 CE) decreed that all Christians must renounce meat, cheese, butter, milk, and eggs at this time. The Orthodox church was very strict and permitted only the consumption of fruit, vegetables, bread, honey, and nuts. Hence it is not surprising that eggs form an important part of the festival food at Easter.

Although the practice of religion is discouraged in the Soviet Union, Easter is still a major feast for Orthodox Christians, and churches are filled for the midnight Mass. On Easter Sunday the dead are remembered. Hundreds visit the cemeteries to sit by the graves of their loved ones. They consume red eggs and scatter the shells on the soil.

It is not clear when the custom of exchanging eggs at Easter was first established. In his book *Easter: Its Story and Meaning* (1950), Alan Watts suggests that there are no western European records of Easter eggs prior to the fifteenth century. But the household accounts of the English king Edward I for 1290 record that eighteeen pence was spent on decorating Easter eggs with gold leaf for presentation to members of his court. Poles were preparing Easter eggs before the eleventh century, and two goose eggs adorned with stripes and dots were found in a grave at Worms, Germany, dated 320 CE. Scholars are not sure whether this grave was the site of a Christian burial.

For Christians the Easter egg is a symbol of the resurrection of Christ. As a bird breaks out from its shell, so Christ arose from his tomb at the Resurrection. In the Middle Ages it was a usual practice to place colored eggs in the replica of the tomb during the Easter service. Sometimes the clergy laid them on the altar as they greeted each other with the words "Christ is risen." This custom was observed in parts of France until the eighteenth century.

In traditional folk religion the egg is a powerful symbol of fertility, purity, and rebirth. It is used in magical rituals to promote fertility and restore virility; to look into the future; to bring good weather; to encourage the growth of the crops and protect both cattle and children against misfortune, especially the dreaded evil eye. All over the world it represents life and creation, fertility and resurrection. It appears at all the major events in the life cycle: birth, courtship, marriage, sickness, and death, as well as during Holy Week and the Easter period. It is the bearer of strength because it contains the seeds of life. In early times eggs were interred with the dead. Later they were linked with Easter. The church did not oppose this, though many egg customs were pre-Christian in origin, because the egg provided a fresh and powerful symbol of the Resurrection and the transformation of death into life.

BIBLIOGRAPHY

Newall, Venetia. *An Egg at Easter: A Folklore Study*. Bloomington, Ind., 1971. A comparative treatment of the egg myth from the earliest recorded references until contemporary usage, and a study of the egg's symbolic role in tradition and belief.

Shoemaker, Alfred L. *Eastertide in Pennsylvania*. Kutztown, Pa., 1960. Provides information about Easter egg customs of the Pennsylvania Dutch community.

Václavík, Antonín. *Výročni obyčeje a lidové uměni*. Prague, 1959. A handsomely illustrated volume that shows examples of the ornate Easter eggs prepared in Czechoslovakia. English and Russian summaries of the text are provided.

Weinhold, Gertrud. *Das schöne Osterei in Europa*. Kassel, 1967. A well-illustrated little book that provides a brief and popularly presented overview of the Easter egg customs in Europe.

Wildhaber, Robert. *Wir färben Ostereier*. Bern, 1957. An attractive booklet by the late director of the Swiss Folklore Museum, Basel, which contains a large and famous collection of decorated Easter eggs.

VENETIA NEWALL

EGYPTIAN RELIGION.

[*This entry consists of three articles on the religious system of ancient Egypt:*

An Overview
The Literature
History of Study

The first is a multifaceted survey of Egyptian religion that emphasizes historical and social perspectives. The second article examines representative genres, works, and themes in Egyptian religious literature, and the final article traces the rise and development of modern Egyptology.]

An Overview

Before beginning to survey ancient Egyptian religion, a number of limiting factors must be considered. The data upon which this survey rests come from all periods and many different sites, but these times and places are very unevenly represented. Clearly, more data survive from the later periods, from the south of the country (Upper Egypt), and from the very highest social strata. Some cult centers were totally lost long ago. Others required periodic renovation, while the increased devotion and/or increased wealth of later generations also led to large-scale rebuilding efforts. Because of this it is often impossible to survey what went on for thousands of years at the major temples of Memphis and Heliopolis, difficult to assess the cultic changes at major sites such as the Karnak and Luxor temples, and almost impossible to reconstruct the pre-Greek beliefs and cultic practices from the largely Ptolemaic remains at the sites of Edfu, Dendera, and Philae. Material from numerous cemeteries in the deserts near town sites, sometimes on the opposite side of the Nile, provides more eschatological data than anything else, but it also occasionally provides doctrinal, devotional, ethical, or cosmological information about one or another of the creeds of ancient Egypt. Monumental architecture is often not synchronous with monumental pieces of religious literature, and some of the most commonly repeated texts are often much less insightful than some unique, fragmentary pieces.

Religious Texts and Historical Setting. Of the texts that survive from ancient Egypt, the religious literature as a whole remains the most difficult to comprehend. There are a variety of explanations for this, including the carelessness of scribes, the composite nature of the

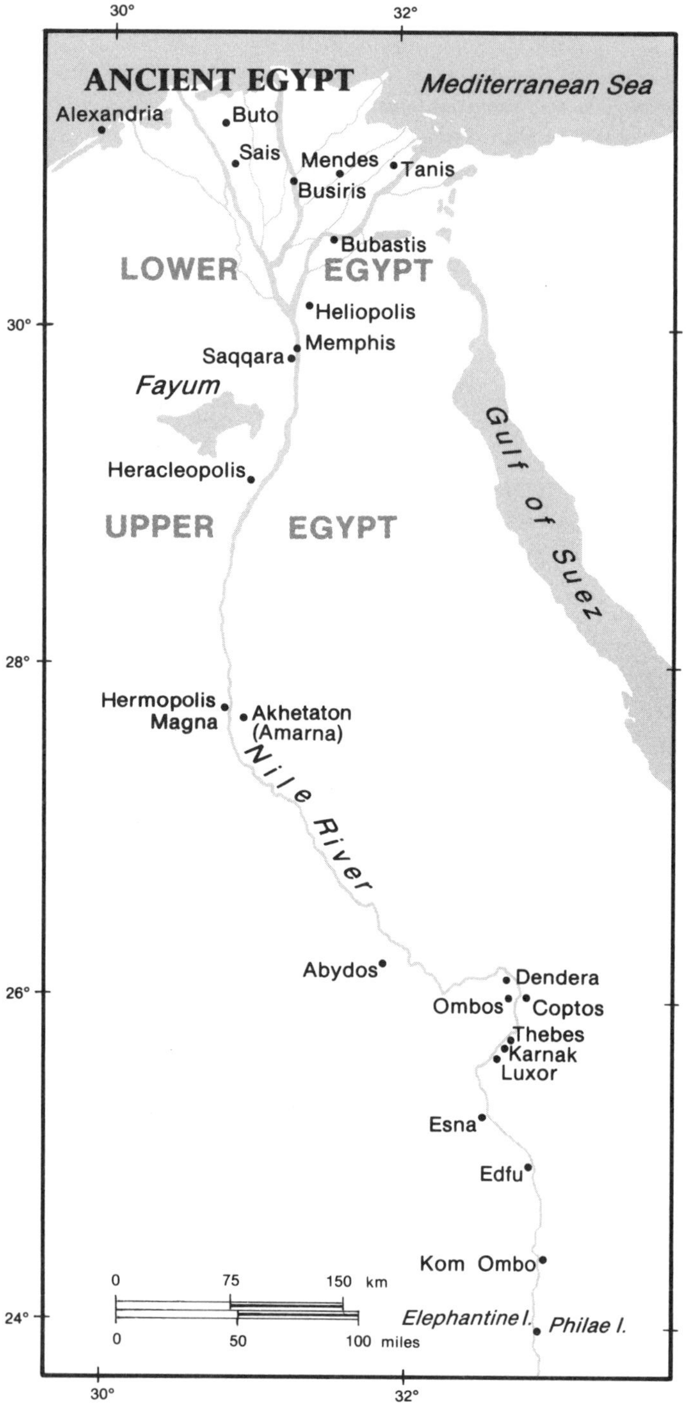

collections, efforts to keep the material esoteric or arcane, and also factors having to do with the modern editing of the texts. In examples from both temple walls and papyri, the original scribe's efforts have been mishandled by copyists and artists. Texts chosen from different sources for a new purpose were not always fully understood by the scribes, who tried to incorporate old or unfamiliar bits. For much of the religious literature we are simply not familiar enough with all the mythological allusions, the magic, the rites, and the puns, and in the case of the Ptolemaic material, efforts were made originally to encode the texts with widespread and multifold sign substitution. These Ptolemaic hieroglyphs, which contain much of the accumulated myths and rituals at several major sites, also were not completely consistent from one site to another. One problem with modern editions of the religious literature is that the major concern has been to establish the best text by assembling parallels, with the result that the individual complete manuscripts are not understood or easily compared. The order of the texts in these editions is generally not that of any individual manuscript, and the variations that occur are completely lost in them, and in the translations made directly from them.

On the positive side, it should be noted that a large quantity of texts have been published now, and these include almost all the texts on several large temples. The temple texts furnish descriptions of the deities, their mythic significance, daily rites, and festivals, and to some extent the interaction between the human and divine worlds. Not all of the texts have been translated yet, but some important ones on rites and feasts have been, and attempts based on the texts found on the temple walls to explain the function of various parts of temples are not far off the mark. The major collections of mortuary or funerary texts from tombs are also available now, and preliminary published translations at least present the different Egyptian views concerning the afterlife and provide additional information concerning almost all aspects of Egyptian religion. There have also been numerous studies dealing with individual deities or concepts based on the phenomena encountered in all sources, and while these may not accurately reflect what the religion was for any one time or place, they do provide useful references for future synchronic studies, and again are probably not terribly far from the mark. Surveys of all of ancient Egyptian religion, also for the most part phenomenological, almost always have important observations to offer, though they do tend to be much less accurate in their generalizations and their subjectivity is often too significant an ingredient. Any details from which such generalizations are made may have applied to only an individual or a small group, when many different levels of belief and devotion were possibly current at the same time. To some extent, the survey that follows indicates trends, tendencies, and what apparently was appealing or approved at the highest levels, with the political motive often as weighty as the religious.

Already in prehistoric times, burial customs indicated

a belief in life after death, which would have required that the body be preserved along with some household furnishings and food offerings. The expectation or hope was for a life after death that was not unlike human existence in this world. The locations of tombs and position of the bodies in their graves became traditional, and the traditions may have been more or less religious. Bodies were usually in a crouched position on their left sides with the head to the south and facing west, a custom that could be associated with the cult of Osiris or other gods of the dead in a western necropolis, or even with the location of the setting sun and perhaps the cult of the sun god. The exceptional site with a head to the north could also be understood in terms of an astral cult (reflected in later Pyramid Texts), with the goal of the deceased being to join the imperishable stars in the northern sky. There has been a great deal of speculation concerning the association of various cults with different localities in Egyptian prehistory, some of this based on finds but most on later evidence and claims. With the wealth of material available from historical context, it is surely best to omit speculation on undocumented origins and on the supposed interactions of the various prehistoric cult centers.

At the very beginnings of Egyptian history the slate palette of Narmer (c. 3110–3056 BCE) shows this king of Upper Egypt, who is wearing the white crown of the south, smiting a northerner, while on the reverse side of the palette Narmer is shown wearing the red crown of Lower Egypt. Whether Narmer or his son, Aha, was actually the first king (later known as Menes) of the first dynasty is still debatable, but some of the emblematic representations on the palette may have mythological significance. Both the bull and the falcon can represent aspects of the king's power, but the latter seems very likely to be associated with the identification of the king as the god Horus, a principal element in the myth of divine kingship. Since all but one king of Egypt is known to have been identified with the title "Horus," this myth is both very early and also, perhaps, one of the cornerstones of Egypt's success. There are several aspects of Horus, however, and even several Horuses, so that the full and precise meaning of this early representation could easily be overstated if it were said that all we know of the association of the king and Horus from later texts had already been formulated at this stage. Many accretions must have occurred with later explication. The divinity of the pharaoh and the notion of divine or sacred kingship have recently been challenged because of specific later references indicating that there were clear distinctions between the respect accorded the kings and the worship accorded the greatest gods. It will be seen, however, that the myth persisted, undoubtedly supported by the kings, some without doubt more vigorously than others.

Menes, besides identifying with Horus and unifying or reunifying the Two Lands, traditionally founded the capital, Memphis, and erected a temple there, presumably to the god Ptah. His civic contributions were equaled by his religious devotion, and he was thus an exemplary model for all succeeding kings. The kings of the first two dynasties probably had both tombs and cenotaphs that supported the new role of dual kingship, but their monuments at Abydos may also have had some bearing on the relationship of the living Horus to the deceased Osiris, whose cult was later at least maintained there. The fact that kings at the end of the second dynasty could take a "Seth" or a "Horus and Seth" title would indicate that the myth of the contending of Horus and Seth for the patrimony of Osiris was certainly known. But it is doubtful that this reflected a shift in religious belief; more likely a it was political move that was given a mythological framework.

For the first half of the Old Kingdom—the third and fourth dynasties—the great pyramids themselves remain, unfortunately, the principal monuments to the current beliefs. The attention given to these elaborate tombs clearly surpassed any other contemporaneous projects and would seem to show that the power of the king was reflected in the cult of his divine kingship. If the pyramids are not exclusively symbolic of royal power, they could also be symbols of divine power, either of the Horus-king or of his new father, the sun god, Re. The famous statue of Khafre with his headdress incorporating the Horus Falcon can be used to argue for the former, but the title "Son of Re," the use of *Re* in the theophoric royal names, and the true pyramid shape associated with the sun's rays and/or the Benben stone of Re point to the likelihood of either a developed or developing solar cult. In the second half of the Old Kingdom—the fifth and sixth dynasties—the central importance of the cult of Re is very well documented. The kings generally have *Re* in their name, and in addition to their smaller pyramids, they constructed substantial temples to the sun god. The story of the *Miracles That Happened in the Reign of King Khufu* (Westcar Papyrus) was probably written in the Middle Kingdom, but it reflects what was viewed as having happened earlier. The text purports to prophesy that a new dynasty will succeed Khufu's successors and that its first three new kings will be born to the wife of a priest of Re.

Much more significant for our understanding of the religion of this period and of much that had been developing and evolving before it are the Pyramid Texts, first recorded in the interior burial rooms of the pyramid of Unas, the last king of the fifth dynasty. These texts in vertical columns, lacking the illustrations and rubrics of later such mortuary or funerary literature, provided a combination of rituals, hymns, prayers, incantations, and offering lists, all designed to ensure that the king would reach his goal in the afterlife and have the information and provisions that he would need there. The texts were evidently compiled by priests connected with the temple of Re at Heliopolis. They indicate acceptance of the fact that the king is a god who ascends to the sky, joins Re on the solar bark for his voyage back and forth across the heavens, and guards Re and guides his bark past the perils, usually snakes, that threaten them. The rites, some of which may have taken place in these rooms or in the mortuary temple or valley temple to the east of the pyramid, included provision for opening the tomb, sacrificing an ox, and breaking jars for magical protection. The descriptions of the ascension in the tomb's antechamber provide alternative explanations that may have come originally from separate sources. They have the king ascending on the wings or backs of birds, on the incense wafting upward, on reed rafts, or on the outstretched arms of gods forming a ladder for him. On entering the tomb the king is still addressed as Horus; on ascension to the sky he is called Osiris. In the so-called cannibal hymn, he devours gods to acquire their attributes. He protests his guiltlessness and claims his divine perquisites. Within the burial chamber the king is presented to the great gods, and the offering-lists and spells are provided for him, while on the west gable are inscribed the serpent spells, incantations possibly intended to protect the tomb or to be used in guiding Re's bark.

Apart from the central theme of this collection, we learn much more about the religion of Egypt from these texts through the king's relationship to various deities and also through citations or mythological allusions from the texts of the other religions of the Egyptians. Here the king's genealogy is presented clearly by making him the product of the Heliopolitan Ennead. This family of nine gods represents a cosmological or cosmogonical explanation of creation by Atum (the complete one), who by himself created Shu (air) and Tefnut (moisture). From this pair, Geb (earth) and Nut (watery sky) came forth, and in the next generation they produced the two brothers Osiris and Seth and their sisters, Isis and Nephthys. Osiris, the eldest, ruled on earth in place of his father, but he was slain by his stronger brother, Seth. It fell to Osiris' son, Horus, born after his death, to avenge the slaying and assume the rule of this world.

In the form in which this genealogy survives, the significance of the Ennead is really subordinated to the son, Horus, on the one hand, and on the other to Re, who is alternately assimilated to Atum or placed before him as his creator. In the Pyramid Texts the Ennead is personified as the goddess Hathor (House of Horus), and so Re and Hathor are the parents of Horus just as surely as Osiris and Isis. Horus is also said here to be a son of Sekhmet, a statement of interest since Sekhmet was the consort of Ptah, the creator god of Memphis. According to later texts (the Shabaka Stone), Ptah sprang forth from primeval chaos conceiving the creator, Atum, in his heart and bringing him forth on his tongue by speaking his name. The chaos from which Ptah came is also known as the Hermopolitan Ogdoad: the four pairs of deities represent the different aspects of chaos from which an egg appeared as the inundation receded at Hermopolis, thus producing the creator. The names of the four pairs are not consistent in different texts, but they generally include Amun and Amaunet (hiddenness), Kuk and Kauket (darkness), Huh and Hauhet (formlessness), and Nun and Naunet (the watery abyss). The creator god of Hermopolis might well have been Thoth, the moon god of that city, but in these Heliopolitan texts the creator remains Atum, while Thoth is included as a member of the Ennead and as a companion of Re in the sky. Since the son of Ptah and Sekhmet is Nefertem, the child appearing from the lotus, the king was associated with the scions and creator gods of all three of these important and early cult centers of Egypt.

It should be noted that the roles of both Thoth and Ptah in this connection are not spelled out, but they seem to be clearly alluded to. There were thus probably some limits on how far the Heliopolitan priests would go in assimilating the doctrines and deities of their counterparts or rivals. To some extent the priests of the other temples must have approved of some such accommodation to guarantee the continuing favor and actual support of the crown, but since the formulation had been Heliopolitan, the cult of Re became preeminent, and for the most part it remained so for most of Egyptian history.

In the fifth dynasty society in general became more open, and many of the highest offices in the land could be attained by people not related to the royal family. At least a few utterances from the Pyramid Texts indicate that they were not written originally for a king, so that the goal of a blessed hereafter was not exclusively a royal prerogative. Further decentralization of power occurs in the sixth dynasty, and local nomarchs are provided with quite respectable tombs. These tombs may have been equipped with religious texts on coffins or papyri that have not survived, but certainly in the First Intermediate Period, with the breakdown of central authority, several claimants to kingship, and actual civil war, the claimants to earthly power also made claim to divinity.

The texts on the interior of the single or nested wooden coffins of nobles from many sites in Egypt are in some cases identical to the earlier royal Pyramid Texts, and in other cases are considerably expanded. The texts from different sites vary more than the texts found at each site. The local differences are not all explained as yet, but some reasonably significant collections of spells labeled "books" on the coffins from El Bersha (the necropolis of Hermopolis) have been studied. These coffins have on their fronts (the side faced by the mummy lying on its left side) a false door to facilitate the deceased's mobility; a painted table of offerings to provide sustenance; a plan and description of the Field of Hetep, which is at least one version of the paradise these Egyptians hoped for; and a list of ship's parts, information useful for the deceased, who joins the sun god in his bark and guides it through the skies.

On the inside surface of the bottom of most of the El Bersha coffins was painted an elaborate illustrated plan or map with descriptive texts known today as the Book of Two Ways. (The Book of Two Ways is a collection within the Coffin Texts.) The plans are all roughly comparable, with a blue waterway surrounded by mounds to represent the day sky, and a black land route, surrounded by water, representing the night sky. This cosmological plan provided the earliest illustrated guidebook to the beyond and attempted to locate various uncommon demons as well as some commonly known terms for places in the afterlife. Apart from the central plan, however, the book is really two different books. The earliest version was apparently written as a guide for followers of the Osirian religion, and the goal of several of its sections was to aid these followers to pass the various gates and demon keepers leading to the mansion of Osiris. The later version has the plan and one section as a guide to the route leading to the mansion of Osiris, but it also has one whole section dealing with Thoth, another dealing with Re, and a conclusion that ties together the whole in terms of knowledge of spells about the beyond. If the deceased knows the spells to the first stage, he will become a star in the sky with the moon god, Thoth. If he knows them to the next stage he will join Osiris in his mansion, and if he knows all the spells he will join Re on his bark in the sky. These goals also appear to be put in terms of social standing, commoners being associated with Thoth, great ones with Osiris, and, obviously, royalty with Re. What this does is to democratize the hereafter by making the highest goals available to anyone who has the book. It was clearly based on an original Osirian text, and in the hands of the priests of Re it would have become a good prosyletizing text for the solar religion.

The Book of Two Ways concludes with the famous statement by the All-Lord, Re, that he "made the four winds that every man might breathe," "made the great flood that the poor as well as the great might have power," "made every man like his fellow (I did not command that they do evil. It is their hearts that disobey what I have said)," and "made their hearts to cease forgetting the West, in order to make divine offerings to the gods of the nomes." The All-Lord says, "it is with my sweat that I created the gods. Mankind is from the weeping of my eye," and a little later he adds that after the deceased has spent millions of years between Re and Osiris, "we will sit together in one place. Ruins will be cities and vice versa; house will desolate house." These remarks provide rather interesting insights into the metaphysics and ethics of the Re religion as well as a noteworthy example of early ecumenism. These particular Coffin Texts came from a necropolis of Hermopolis, in middle Egypt. Whether Re priests from Hermopolis or Heliopolis were responsible is still debatable. But another text of this same chaotic period, from Heracleopolis in middle Egypt, although it is a literary text in the "instruction" genre, is actually one of the most religious documents surviving from ancient Egypt. A compact section at the end provides in capsulized form the complete philosophy and theology of the Re religion:

> One generation of men passes to another, and God, who knows characters, has hidden Himself, . . . so worship God upon his way. . . . The soul goes to the place it knows. . . . Beautify your mansion in the West, embellish your place in the necropolis with straightforwardness and just dealing; . . . more acceptable is the character of the straightforward man than the ox of the wrongdoer. Serve God, that He may do the like for you, with offerings for replenishing the altars and with carving; it is that which will show forth your name, and God is aware of whoever serves Him. Provide for men, the cattle of God, for He made heaven and earth at their desire. He suppressed the greed of the waters, he gave the breath of life to their noses, for they are likenesses of Him which issued from His flesh. He shines in the sky for the benefit of their hearts; He has made herbs, cattle, and fish to nourish them. He has killed His enemies and destroyed His own children, because they had planned to make rebellion; He makes daylight for the benefit of their hearts, and He sails around in order to see them, . . . and when they weep, He hears. . . . He has made for them magic to be weapons to ward off what may happen.

From this we see that Re is hidden, omniscient, provident, responsive and just. Men, who are created in the likeness of God, and for whom heaven and earth were created, must worship God, and provide for their fellow men. Hypocrisy is of no avail, but God gave men magic to ward off "what may happen."

This text of the instruction of a Heracleopolitan king to his son, Merikare, anticipates the fall of the tenth dynasty (2040 BCE) to the Theban family of dynasty eleven. Coffin Texts continue to be used in the Middle Kingdom, and this indicates that for the most part the religion or religions of the people did not change drastically with this change in government. The official doctrine of the state, however, had to be supported by a great deal of political propaganda literature to account for the reunification under the new Theban king, Mentuhotep II, then the apparent usurpation by his vizier, and finally the assassination of this vizier become king, Amenemhet I. Amenemhet had already returned the capital to the north and constructed defenses on Egypt's borders, but he was apparently not prepared for the threat from within his own palace. The change from dynasty eleven to dynasty twelve was also marked by a shift in the Theban's titular god and the formulation of a new national god. Previously Montu, a war god, was worshiped at perhaps four separate temples in the Theban nome, but with Amenemhet ("Amun is in front") Amun and his new cult begin a long and steady growth in the south in spite of the fact that the kings of this and succeeding dynasties ruled from the north. The new god is perhaps a conflation of Montu with Min, the ithyphallic fertility god of Coptos, which had been allied with Thebes in the war against Heracleopolis, and also, of course, with Amun, the first of the primordial gods of Hermopolis. This latter element may have provided the priority of the new god in the minds of the formulators, but the association with Re as Amun-Re was probably the significant factor in guaranteeing some continuity with the earlier dynastic gods.

The king of the twelfth dynasty was still Horus, but beginning with Senusret I (1971–1928 BCE) important new claims to kingly divinity surface. In the *Story of Sinuhe* Senusret I is called a god without peer, "no other came to be before him." In order to consolidate his power, Senusret III deposed a number of powerful nomarchs and divided the country into departments that were to be administered from the capital by his appointees. At the same time, in a cycle of songs in his honor and in a loyalist instruction he is called the "unique divine being" and is identified as Re himself. Remarkably, the propaganda literature of this dynasty remained popular for at least 900 years, and the tradition of Senusret's special position among the kings of Egypt also survived through Greek sources to the present.

The Second Intermediate Period was marked both by internal weakness eventually giving way to division and by foreign occupation of at least the major part of the delta. These Hyksos rulers were eventually driven out of their capital at Avaris by a new Theban family, which reunited the land and began the period of greatest imperialistic expansion, the New Kingdom. The new family was devoted to the cult of Amun-Re at Karnak, and also had a special interest in the moon god in several earlier forms, including Iah (the moon itself), Thoth, and Khonsu, who was now the son of Amun-Re and Mut (the mother). Thutmose I (c. 1509–1497 BCE), perhaps the first king of the eighteenth dynasty to have a palace in the north, was also responsible for leading expeditions far into Syria, perhaps to the Euphrates. His credentials as a god-king were evidently well established, but not those of his successors. His daughter by his chief wife had to become consort to his son by a lesser wife to secure that son's succession as Thutmose II. But when the latter died, handing over the throne to a son by another wife, his half sister and chief wife, Hatshepsut, took the throne for herself. There were probably very practical explanations for her success in this maneuver, but the justification she chose to propagate was her own "divine birth." She had this recorded on the walls of her mortuary temple at Deir al-Bahri, which depicted Amun-Re in the form of her father, Thutmose I, coming to her mother Ahmose, who conceived the goddess-king, the female Horus.

Hatshepsut's mythologizing goes beyond this with the commemoration of her restoration efforts since the expulsion of the Hyksos. They had "ruled without Re," and she was indeed favored by the gods of Egypt. She had extensive work done at the temple of Karnak, adding a new sanctuary, pylon gates, and very tall obelisks, monuments as much to herself as to Amun-Re, her father. Her small cult temple at Medinet Habu (ancient Djeme) probably has particular significance mythologically for the later association of the Hermopolitan Ogdoad with this sacred site. According to a Ptolemaic text in the Khonsu temple at Karnak, Amun was the father of the fathers of the Ogdoad who (as Ptah) created the egg at Hermopolis and later traveled *(khenesh)* to Thebes in his new name of Khonsu. Together with the Ogdoad, he is in the tomb chamber in the necropolis at Medinet Habu. Indeed, it seems likely that Hatshepsut and her supporters were concerned not only with her genealogy but with the genealogy of the Theban gods. Her husband's son, Thutmose III, who succeeded her and eventually tried to blot out her memory, was primarily involved with military expeditions to Syria and Palestine, and he used his additions to the Karnak temple to publicize his victories. The temple became wealthy and influential because of his generosity and devotion. His successors continued to benefit from and build upon his achievements in the international sphere; foreign alliances, foreign wives, and foreign deities were all introduced in this period, which peaked in the reign of Amenhotep III (1403–1366 BCE).

The son of Amenhotep III, who may have been his coregent for as long as ten years, changed his name from Amenhotep IV to Akhenaton by his fifth year and moved his residence to a new site, Akhetaton (modern Tell al-ʿAmarna). He devoted himself to one aspect of the solar cult, the sun disk (Aton) itself. He saw himself and perhaps his wife, Nefertiti, as the only representatives or intermediaries between the Aton and the rest of creation. Akhenaton's monolatry or henotheism, while apparently accepted by his chief officials, eventually did bring him into direct conflict with the powerful temple staff of Karnak. His supporters attacked the name "Amun" and the word *gods* throughout the Theban area. They were probably sent to eradicate the full name "Amun-Re, King of the Gods," but this attempt to erase (primarily from monuments) the term *gods* has been viewed by many as a monotheistic revolution. Later reaction to Akhenaton as a heretic is known, but what he intended or how far he went to not as clear. The Aton was not his creation either as an icon or as a deity. It had increased in significance in the early eighteenth dynasty. The emblems of almost all the gods of Egypt survive from Tell al-ʿAmarna, indicating that Akhenaton's followers either had no fear of keeping them or had greater fear of abandoning them. The fact that Akhenaton's own prenomen is Waen-Re ("the unique one of Re") is indicative of his continued acceptance of the old solar cult, or perhaps even of the Heliopolitan priests' support of the new cult. Something of Akhenaton's attitude toward the Aton in this international period can be seen in the following excerpt from his famous hymn to the Aton.

> How plentiful it is, what you have made, although they [the creatures made by Aton] are hidden from view, sole god, without another beside you; you created the earth as you wished, when you were by yourself, before mankind, all cattle and kine, all beings on land, who fare upon their feet, and all beings in the air, who fly with their wings.
>
> The lands of Khor and Kush and the land of Egypt: you have set every man in his place, you have allotted their needs, every one of them according to his diet, and his lifetime is counted out. Tongues are separate in speech, and their characters as well; their skins are different, for you have differentiated the foreigners. In the underworld you have made a Nile that you may bring it forth as you wish to feed the populace, since you made them for yourself, their utter master, growing weary on their account, lord of every land. For them the Aton of the daytime arises, great in awesomeness.
>
> All distant lands, you have made them live, for you have set a Nile in the sky that it may descend for them and make waves upon the mountains like the sea to irrigate the fields in their towns. How efficient are your designs, Lord of eternity: a Nile in the sky for foreigners and all creatures that go upon their feet, a Nile coming back from the underworld for Egypt.

Most aspects of this hymn can be found stated in almost identical terms in the universalist hymn to Amun-Re, so it cannot be regarded as totally original or epochmaking in itself. A claim in the hymn that there is no other who knows the Aton except his son, Akhenaton, is noteworthy, and the statement that the whole land was founded and its crops were raised by the Aton for Akhenaton and Nefertiti is egocentric, to say the least.

Akhenaton's coregent and short-lived successor, Semenkhkare, who some now believe may have been none other than Nefertiti herself, seems to have attempted reconciliation with the priesthood of Amun-Re. But Tutankhaton (c. 1348–1339 BCE), who next assumed the throne, changed his name to Tutankhamen, had statues of himself made both as Amun and as Osiris, and decorated the Luxor temple with scenes of the restored Opet feast. (The main feature of this feast was the procession of Amun's cult image from the Karnak temple to the Luxor temple and back.) He even had a restoration stela set up at Karnak. After his death and that of his successor, Ay, the temple reliefs and stela were usurped by his former general, Horemheb, who on becoming king began attacks on his four predecessors who were involved with the movement, now regarded as heretical.

Horemheb's successor was his vizier, who came from Tanis. As Ramses I he began the nineteenth dynasty, which for various reasons is seen as most significant in the history of Egyptian religion. On the one hand, the pharaohs of this dynasty had to indicate their continuity with the past and assure their support in all the cult centers of Egypt. They built extensively at all the old temple sites and went overboard to demonstrate their polytheism. Temples now had multiple chapels and sanctuaries dedicated to various deities, but the monuments also were used as propaganda to show the power of the kings, to depict their victories, to record their legitimate succession, and to indicate their great devotion to the gods and their munificence to both the gods and their own subjects. On the other hand, the pharaohs succeeded in reinstating their own god, Seth, whom they commemorated as having been in their new capital since the time of the Hyksos. Seth was included in the royal names now and also had one of the Egyptian armies named for him.

In the early Ramessid period the tombs of nobles had much less of the biographical material and scenes of everyday life that were common earlier. Now the emphasis was on the funerary rites and any religious offices the deceased had held. There appears to be a very conservative religious reaction to what had taken place in the eighteenth dynasty. Even the literary texts have primarily mythological settings and content for stories, but interestingly, these often make the gods look foolish and cannot be considered very pietistic. Women, even goddesses, in these texts are cast in an unflattering light, again perhaps in reaction to the powerful queens of the preceding dynasty. The long reign of Ramses II produced numerous temple constructions with colossal statues and representations of himself, but these seem to indicate that he was glorifying himself as much as any of the other gods. The group of four deities at the back of his temple at Abu Simbel shows that he was placing himself on the same level as the three earlier dynastic gods of Egypt—Ptah, Re-Harakhty, and Amun-Re.

The religious texts with which people were buried in the New Kingdom and later are now known as the *Book of Going Forth by Day* but they actually constituted at least two different collections, again emphasizing in introductions or conclusions either an Osirian or a solar afterlife, often with some elements of both in between. These papyri, illustrated with vignettes, vary greatly in length and include many interesting chapters, such as that with the servant statue or Shawabti spell (chap. 6), the heart spell (chap. 30), a spell to enable the deceased to have all requisite knowledge in one chapter (chap. 162), and the famous negative confession and judgment scene (chap. 125). The negative confession is not confession at all but rather a protestation of innocence between forty-two judges of the underworld. Following the psychostasia, or weighing of the deceased's heart, in relation to the feather of Maat, or Truth, the deceased inevitably escapes the devourer and is presented to Osiris, but most often goes forth past the gatekeepers and joins Re as well. The New Kingdom copies of the *Book of Going Forth by Day* are commonly called the Theban recension because so many copies come from Theban tombs. But the texts generally, even in the negative confession, indicate a northern origin, most likely Heliopolitan. Many texts outside of the negative confession are modifications or corruptions of the earlier Coffin Texts versions.

The negative confession, though less than ideal as a code of ethics, cannot be ignored, since it survived in thousands of copies spanning fifteen hundred years. A portion of the fuller list follows:

O Wide-of-Stride, who comes forth from Heliopolis,
  I have not committed evil.
O Embracer-of-Fire, who comes forth from Babylon,
  I have not stolen.
O Nosey, who comes forth from Hermopolis,
  I have not been covetous. . . .
O Dangerous-of-Face, who comes forth from Rosetau,
  I have not killed men.
O Ruti, who comes forth from heaven,
  I have not damaged the grain-measure. . . .
O Breaker-of-Bones, who comes forth from
  Heracleopolis,
  I have not told lies. . . .
O White-of-Teeth, who comes forth from the Fayum,
  I have not trespassed. . . .
O-Eater-of-Entrails, who comes forth from the Thirty,
  I have not practised usury. . . .
O Wanderer, who comes forth from Bubastis,
  I have not gossiped. . . .
O Wamemti-Serpent, who comes forth from the
  place of judgment,
  I have not committed adultery.
O Maa-Intef, who comes forth from the Temple of Min,
  I have not defiled myself. . . .
O Ser-Kheru, who comes forth from Wensi,
  I have not been quarrelsome.
O Bastet, who comes forth from the sanctum,
  I have not winked.
O His-Face-behind-Him, who comes forth from
  Tep-het-djat,
I have not been perverted; I have not had sexual
  relations with a boy. . . .
O Tem-sep, who comes forth from Busiris,
  I have not been abusive against a king.
O Acting-with-His-Heart, who comes forth from Tjebu,
  I have not waded in water.
O Flowing-One, who comes forth from Nun,
  My voice has not been loud. . . .

The judges and the places from which they come are not consistently prominent or frightening and cannot logically be connected with the forty-two nomes of Egypt, but while a few of the statements have uncertain meaning, the vast majority are perfectly clear and not particularly surprising.

From the beginning of the eighteenth dynasty the principal religious text selected to decorate the walls of the royal burial chambers was the so-called book of Amduat, or *That Which Is in the Netherworld.* This book, which resembles a large-scale papyrus unrolled on the walls, treats of the voyage of the solar bark through the hours of the night sky, but it involves Sokar, the god of the Memphite necropolis (Rosetau), as chief god of the underworld. The nineteenth-dynasty kings, different as they may have been from their eighteenth-dynasty counterparts, were also buried in tombs in the Theban Valley of the Kings, but their tombs were more elaborately decorated, with relief carving and paintings of the *Book of Gates* and the journey of the sun through the body of the goddess Nut.

When Ramses II made peace with the Hittites some time after the nearly disastrous battle of Kadesh, a thousand deities on either side were called to witness, and foreign deities such as Anat, Astarte, and Reshef became even more popular in Egypt. His successor, Merneptah, was beset with attacks from Libyans and the Sea Peoples. It is from his reign that the earliest surviving reference to Israel is found, but without other corroborating documentation for the story of the Exodus aside from its reasonably accurate setting.

Ramses III of the twentieth dynasty was the last great pharaonic ruler of Egypt. His building efforts included a separate small temple at Karnak, as well as a very large mortuary temple for himself at medinet Habu. This latter, which survives in very good condition, contains descriptions of the complete festivals of Min and Sokar in addition to the usual battle scenes, and it also has an elaborate calendar of feasts and offerings. The whole was surrounded by a wall with two fortifiable gateways, which probably reflect the worsening political situation of the whole country. There were strikes by the royal tomb workers, who had to be provisioned by the temple storehouses; there were attacks by a coalition of foreigners, principally Libyan; and finally, the king was slain in a harem conspiracy. In addition to punishing those responsible, his son Ramses IV recorded in a very interesting document, the great Papyrus Harris I (c. 1150 BCE), all the benefactions that his father had made to the temples of Egypt. The Wilbour Papyrus, of slightly later date (1140 BCE), confirms that the temple of Amun-Re alone controlled an exorbitant amount of land and the population of a large area in middle Egypt hundreds of miles away.

By the end of the twentieth dynasty the High Priest of Amun, Herihor, was for all practical purposes the ruler of Upper Egypt, and the twenty-first dynasty began with one of his sons assuming the kingship at Tanis in the north while another succeeded him as high priest in the south. Several of the priestly successors also claimed royal titles in the Theban area, and eventually the two offices were combined in one. Unlike the earlier usurpations of viziers or generals, who undoubtedly had a military power base, the base for the priests seems to have been primarily economic. The process can be traced back to the nineteenth dynasty, to a priestly family that gained control not only of the temple treasury but also of the royal treasury. Throughout the Ramessid period there are indications that all was not what it was supposed to be in this period of religious fervor. Banquet songs stress a *carpe diem* attitude; a workman in the royal necropolis shows no respect for his deceased king, and eventually almost all of the Theban tombs were systematically looted. Some of the robbers were accused and tried, but evidently those chiefly responsible got away with their crimes. The priests reburied the royal mummies, but with none of their original trappings or treasure. The priests apparently did not approve of the reinstatement of Seth by the Ramessid kings, and the god's name was attacked at their capital in the north.

When a Libyan family, the twenty-second dynasty, took over in the Third Intermediate Period they ruled from the north also, but controlled the south by appointing a daughter to serve as Divine Adoratress of Amun, a new position above that of high priest. The Nubian Piye (Piankhy), a very devout follower of Amun, conquered all of Egypt to set things right there but did not remain to rule himself, although he did appoint his sister (Amenirdis I) to be the successor of the current Divine Adoratress (Shepenwepet I) when she eventually died. His good intentions were not sufficient, however, and the Nubians (twenty-fifth dynasty) did return to rule the country, losing to the Assyrians, who installed the Saite (twenty-sixth) dynasty. This period marked one of the last Egyptian revivals, with a great deal of temple and tomb construction. In many respects the Saite period harked back to the Old Kingdom; several huge Theban tombs of this time had extensive collections of the Pyramid Texts.

With the Persian conquest of Egypt by Cambyses in 525 BCE, there are indications that the conquering kings had good intentions with regard to maintaining the cultural, legal, and religious traditions of the Egyptians. Although Herodotus, who was not unbiased, accused Cyrus of sacrilege in Egypt, it is known that this king dutifully performed burial rites for an Apis bull and also had small temples erected to the Egyptian gods. The Persian satraps who actually administered the country were doubtless less highly esteemed, probably deservedly so. With several native rebellions and one last gasp of independence in the thirtieth dynasty, Egypt fell again to the Persians, and in turn welcomed Alexander the Great in 332 BCE as a savior from the Persian oppressors.

Alexander was probably convinced of his own divinity on visiting the oracle of Amun at the Siwa oasis, but this was not enough to guarantee a long life. Under his successor, Philip Arrhidaeus, the sanctuary of the Karnak temple was rebuilt. When Alexander's general, Ptolemy, became king of Egypt, much new construction was begun. Alexandria, with its library, museum, and new government offices, was founded, while other Greek cities in Egypt were enlarged or planned. Under the Ptolemys truly great temples were erected at some ancient cult sites, and countless smaller temples, gates, appendages, and inscriptions were added to other places. All the main structures at the temple of Horus at Edfu are Ptolemaic. The vast main temple and its surrounding walls are covered from top to bottom with scenes and texts dealing with Horus, his myths and rituals. The texts have undergone a complicated encoding with a sixfold increase in the number of hieroglyphic signs used, and a wide range of possible substitutions for many standard signs is also encountered. The language is classical Middle Egyptian, and presumably the texts were from earlier material chosen by Egyptian priests from their own libraries, or perhaps from several sites in Egypt. The inscriptions are quite distinctive but often difficult to translate. They seem intentionally obscure despite their accessibility, and the encoding must have been used to make these texts more esoteric or arcane to their own followers and perhaps to the Greeks as well.

The temple of Hathor at Dendera has similar encoding of texts, as well as *mamisi* (birth houses) for the goddess, secret crypts, and a combined Egyptian-Greek zodiac on the ceiling of a small room on the temple's roof. The dual temple of Haroeris and Sobek (the crocodile god) at Kom Ombo may have had a crypt for oracular pronouncements. At Esna the creator god, Khnum, who fashions on the potter's wheel, is commemorated. The temple of Isis on the island of Philae had many separate buildings with inscriptions dating well into the Roman period. The cult of Isis, incorporating much of the cult of Hathor as well, is probably better known now from the Isiac temples in the rest of the Mediterranean than it is from this, the greatest center of the worship of the Egyptian goddess of love. Now that the entire temple complex has been moved to higher ground on a neighboring island, much more work will be possible here. Following construction of the old high dam at Aswan, the temple was under water for most of the year. Another major Oriental cult in the Greco-Roman world that had at least some roots in Egypt was that of Serapis, whose name comes from Osiris and the Apis bull of Ptah of Memphis. These particular sacred bulls, chosen for their markings, had been mummified and buried in large sarcophagi at the Serapium in Saqqara throughout much of the late period in Egyptian history.

Alexandria early became one of the principal centers in the world for the study of philosophy and theology, and when Egypt converted to Christianity many of the Alexandrian church fathers became deeply embroiled in controversies. Philo, Origen, Arrius, and Clement represent a few of the different positions originating in Alexandria. Traditional Greek philosophers and pagan, Jewish, Christian, orthodox, and heterodox interpretations—all had their adherents here, living virtually side by side for some time. The Septuagint and Hexapla were produced here, and the Coptic gnostic library found in Upper Egypt at Naga Hamadi probably originated here as well. The hermetic tractates may provide some link to earlier Egyptian notions, but the apocrypha and *Gospel of Thomas* preserved in this archive most likely originated elsewhere.

Monasticism in both its eremetic and cenobitic forms originated and became very popular in Egypt, partially spread by conditions in the country under the Romans, who overtaxed the people and provided them little protection from the Blemmyes' invasions. The monasteries provided food, protection, and solace. The monastic rule of Pachomius became the standard in many Egyptian monasteries, and it was introduced to the west by John Cassian, becoming the basis of Western Benedictine monasticism.

The early Christians in Egypt suffered persecution under the Romans, but after Rome converted to Christianity, the pagans suffered as well. The Neoplatonic philosopher Hypatia was stoned to death in Alexandria in AD 415, and the last outpost of paganism in the Roman empire, at the temple of Isis at Philae, was finally overcome in the late fifth century. When the Arab general ʿAmr ibn al-ʿAṣ took Egypt in 641 conversion to Islam was rapid, due as much to economic advantages as to the attractions of the Qurʾān.

Conceptions of the Universe. The ancient Egyptians conceived of their universe in a number of different ways. One view was that the firmament *(bia)* was a huge inverted metal colander, from which pieces fell; these wonders or marvels *(biau)* included meteoric iron *(biat)*, which was used in making ceremonial implements such as the adzes for the ritual of the Opening of the Mouth. This ritual was performed to give life to statues or other representations and also to revivify the mummies of the deceased. According to another view, the sky was a giant cow whose four legs were supported by four deities, while other deities (stars) on small crescent-shaped boats sailed on her belly. This heavenly cow may be associated with Hathor, who according to the Heliopolitan cosmogony was variously seen as consort of Re and mother of Horus, but also as consort of Horus and mother of Ihy, a form of the sun god to whom she gives birth. The sun god, Re, is also frequently shown being born to the goddess Nut, whose body spans the sky from east to west. According to the Heliopolitan cosmogony she should, of course, be descended from him. Nevertheless, as regularly depicted on the ceilings of royal bed chambers, the sun appears and crosses the goddess's body during the day, but is swallowed by her at night, passing through her body from west to east to be born again.

All of these concepts view the earth as quite solid, generally flat, and practically limitless in extent. The sky (Nut) receives her support from the earth (Geb), and sometimes is shown held apart from him by the air god, Shu. All that the sun encounters in its day and its night voyage is above the earth. The locations generally translated as "netherworld" or "underworld" *(imht* and *duat)* both actually appear to have been in the sky originally. Some descriptions indicate that the Egyptians also conceived of an undersky *(nenet)* and a topsy-turvy afterlife, so that one of the terms *(duat)* seems to have been relocated later. As if this were not confusing enough, another mythological cosmology would have one form of the falcon god, Horus, represent the entire sky, with his two eyes as the sun and the moon. The moon was the eye injured in the battle with his uncle, Seth, to avenge the death of his father, Osiris, in order to assume his inheritance. This great Horus would seem to be as much greater than Re, the sun, as the Heliopolitan Re of the Pyramid Texts is above his son, the Horus-king. Such seemingly incompatible cosmologies may represent either earlier separate traditions or later attempted rationalizations.

Conceptions of Human Nature and Destiny. The Egyptians' view of their own nature certainly varied in some respects from time to time, place to place, and person to person, but a few terms persisted expressing notions about their ontology that are reasonably consistent. People were created in God's image, from the weeping of his (Re's) eye, were conceived in God's heart (mind) and spoken by his tongue (Ptah), or were fashioned on the potter's wheel (Khnum). Man's body had to be preserved so that he could properly live again in the afterlife. To ensure this a replica of the body was thought to have been fashioned by the gods at birth; more were made later by sculptors and painters as stand-ins for bodies that might be lost. These *ka* figures, enlivened by the Opening of the Mouth ritual, served as second effective personalities, but they could also be protecting genii. At least by the Late Period even the great gods such as Re and Thoth have a number of these *ka*s or "attributes," including Hu (authoritative utterance), Sia (perception), Maa (sight), and Sedem (hearing).

The term most closely approximating "soul" for the Egyptians was *ba,* which was represented in hieroglyphic as a small bird and was also depicted in burial scenes departing from the body as a bird flying up to the sky. In at least one literary text, the *Dispute of a Man with His Ba,* this conscience or other self is present in life to be argued with and to help the person make up his mind after considering both sides of a question, in this case the serious question of whether to go on living. Another literary text, the *Lamentations of Khakheperreseneb,* has the scribe address his heart *(ib),* which cannot respond, rather than his *ba.* It was generally the heart that was considered the seat of both intellect and will.

Another significant aspect of man's person or personality is his *akh,* or "spirit," which is what remains apart from the body or at least is not limited by the body after death. A person wants to become an *akh aper,* an "equipped spirit" or "perfect spirit," in the afterlife, and to this end he prepares himself with the required religious spells from one or the other collections available, often including as many books and variations as possible and both full and shortened versions. The spirits in the hereafter were sometimes thought to be not content to rest in peace in a blessed state, nor were they always allowed to. Another literary text, the *Ghost Story,* tells of a long-dead spirit who appears to a priest and requests that his cracked and drafty tomb be repaired. Many letters to the dead are also found; they were left with food offerings by living relatives to urge some specific action on their behalf in the spirit world. These usually mention past favors and show confidence in the deceased's ability to effect change for righting the injustice.

Gods, Cults, and Magic. While the deceased in the necropolis were regularly called *akh*s, they were also occasionally termed *netjeru* ("gods"). A curse left on a square block at the door of a tomb threatened dire consequences to anyone who disturbed even a pebble in the tomb, and it advised finding a place that would not impinge upon the tombs of any of the gods in the necropolis. For the Egyptians the word *netjer* ("god") was used broadly to cover all levels of divinity, from the greatest gods to the justified dead (that is, those declared "true of voice" in the judgment before Osiris). Monotheism, if it ever existed in ancient Egypt, was never clearly formulated and apparently was never established as doctrine in any of the native religions. From almost all periods come texts that indicate the uniqueness of one or the other gods, usually some form of the sun god, but this monolatry or henotheism cannot be demonstrated to have the exclusivity necessary to fit the modern definition of monotheism.

There are numerous references to "god" and "the god" in Egyptian literary texts, particularly in the instructions. In some cases these may refer to a local god or to the king, but most frequently they refer to Re or

Pre (the sun). He is often called the *neb-er-djer* ("lord to the limit, universal lord"), and can indeed appear practically transcendent, as in the *Instruction for Merikare,* quoted above. The only important point lacking here is a statement that no other god exists, but of course this can also be said of the Hebrew Bible and the New Testament. Tradition is the principal source for both the Jewish and the Christian monotheistic doctrine, but it is lacking for Egyptian religion. Without this tradition the multiplicity of denominations and sects, the veneration of saints, and the loose use of "divine" and "godlike" for popular heros would all conspire to challenge the generally accepted monotheistic aspect of modern Western religions and of Western civilization. For the Atenist heresy of Akhenaton the situation is somewhat different, since the *Hymn to the Aton* states that there is no god beside (or like) Aton, there was an attack on other gods and the plural "gods," and Akhenaton was later clearly regarded as having attempted to disrupt the established religious system. Most likely the notion of monotheism was present in this period, in some minds at least, though it was harshly dispelled. By syncretizing the names and aspects of various deities into powerful new gods, the Egyptians widened the gap between the greatest god and all the rest. Re-Atum, Amun-Re, and Pre-Harakhty were unchallenged national gods each in his own time.

Probably second in importance to the great national gods was the cult of the god of the dead. This evolved very early, evidently from several separate cults. The cult of Osiris, originally from Busiris, superseded the cults of Khentyimentiu ("foremost of the westerners") and Wepwawet ("opener of the ways") from Abydos and Siut, respectively. The cults of Osiris and Re intermingle in most of the mortuary literature, and in at least one instance come close to merging. When the cult of Sokar becomes a major element in royal funerary literature and later in all the funerary literature of the New Kingdom, it leads to perhaps the ultimate syncretism in the late New Kingdom of Ptah-Sokar-Osiris-Tatenen.

The Osiris cult certainly permeated almost all aspects of Egyptian culture. Osirid statues decorated the courts of temples, and the Osiris suites are a major feature of the mortuary temples. Every owner of a book of mortuary literature is given the title "Osiris," and every deceased person named in tomb or stela has the epithet "true of voice" or "vindicated" with respect to his last judgment before this great god. The association of Osiris with death, resurrection, fertility, and the Nile touched everyone, and his cult center at Abydos, where he was supposed to have been buried, became the most important pilgrimage site in the country.

The living king is generally called the "good god," while the deceased king is the "great god." Whether death actually enhanced the king's status is debatable. As the embodiment or incarnation of the god Horus, he is already a major god on earth, and much of the doctrine of his divinity and his perquisites was widely published and accepted. Certainly the king who instructed Merikare was more aware personally of his limitations than Senusret III or Ramses II would have been. The whole concept could have been viewed in different ways at different times by different people. Based on the number of persons who had as their goal in the afterlife something approaching or equaling the goals of their kings, perhaps more would have believed in their sovereign's divinity and their own potential divinity than some modern scholars are now prepared to accept. Of course there are exceptions—the *Song of the Harper* and the story of the *Man Who Was Tired of Life* both reflect despair about the afterlife. Some kings were assassinated, and all the royal tombs were robbed. Aware of the difficulty of securing their burials, the Egyptians tried incredible masses of stone, secret hidden passages, tricks, provision of security guards, and also magic and curses. In a sense all of these would have been attempts by believers to thwart the unbelievers.

Some individuals, even nonroyal personages, attained a state of divinity far above the ordinary. The cult of deceased kings would generally not have outlived the endowment of their funerary establishment, but Amenhotep I, together with his mother, Ahmose Nefertari, continued for centuries to be venerated by the workmen of Deir al-Medineh as the great patrons or patron saints of the place. The architect of the step pyramid of Djoser at Saqqara, Imhotep, was deified, and his cult became ever more popular more than two millennia after his death. He was revered as a sage and was also identified with the Greek god Asklepios. Another architect and sage, Amenhotep Son of Hapu (the epithet is traditionally part of his name), was also exceptionally revered. In sum, the Egyptians seem to have had a number of different levels of divinity, several equivalent to different levels of sainthood, with only one word, *netjer,* to cover them all.

Worship of animals does not seem to have been a significant element in any of the religions of Egypt. The use of animals to represent some attributes of gods, or the gods themselves, is frequent, and in most religious artwork their primary importance is clearly in differentiating the principals. The conventional linking of the falcon with Horus, the falcon and disk with Re, the cow with Hathor, the baboon or ibis with Thoth, the jackal with Anubis, the crocodile with Sobek, and the ram with Amun-Re was generally recognized throughout the country and in all periods following its formulation, whereas strictly anthropomorphic representations would have been confusing. It is possible that for some ritual reenactments priests would have worn the animal masks of the gods and recited the words attributed to the gods in numerous temple reliefs. The cobra Edjo of Buto and the vulture Nekhbet of Al-Kab are usually represented in their totally animal forms, but they are protective deities for the king of Upper and Lower Egypt, and were more intimidating in this form. The often malevolent but sometimes protective deity Seth is represented as either partially or totally animal, though there was in antiquity, and there is now, little agreement as to what the animal was. Pig, hippopotamus, donkey, hound, and giraffe are all plausible in different documents or reliefs. Evil beings or demons are often composite, fanciful creations that must be armed with knives to be really threatening. The evil serpent Apophis, perhaps the greatest demon, is repulsed from attacking the sun god by means of numerous serpent spells, but it is also driven back by the spears, and bows and arrows of protecting deities such as the four sons of Horus—Imesty, Hapi, Duamutef, and Khebeksenuef—who are also the protective gods represented on the Canopic jars containing the internal organs of the mummified dead.

Although oxen and smaller cattle were among the offerings made to the gods in their temples, the Apis bull, which was emblematic of and sacred to Ptah in the New Kingdom and later, had a very special position and would have been considered by many as the embodiment of a god on earth. Burials of each successive Apis bull and its cow mother were performed with great solemnity. Later, in the Greek period, the proliferation of cemeteries for mummified cats sacred to both Bast and Paket, crocodiles sacred to Sobek, ibises sacred to Thoth and Imhotep, baboons sacred to Thoth, and falcons sacred to Horus reached all parts of Egypt, to the point that demand for some of these creatures as votive offerings began to exceed the supplies available; sometimes people who thought they had purchased jars with mummified animals actually left sealed jars of sand to be buried in the huge catacombs at sacred sites.

Magic was clearly a significant aspect of Egyptian life. Again, as noted in the *Instruction for Merikare*, magic was considered a gift of the great god, Re. There was a goddess called Weret-Hekau (Great of Magic), and several texts refer to the books containing the secret knowledge of Thoth, whom the Greeks later identified with Hermes and whose legendary knowledge is still being touted by certain groups today (e.g., the Rosicrucians). The Egyptians had magical spells believed to prolong life, to alter fate, to help in romance, and to combat any number of physical and mental afflictions. A combination of entreaty and threat is found in one type of love charm:

> Hail to you, Re-Harakhty, father of the gods!
> Hail to you, Seven Hathors, who are adorned with strings of red thread!
> Hail to you, all the gods of heaven and earth!
> Come make so-and-so [f.] born of so-and-so come after me,
> Like an ox after grass, like a nursemaid after her children, like a herdsman after his herd!
> If you do not make her come after me, then I will set fire to Busiris and burn Osiris.

Some magic spells survive in the funerary literature, some references occur in the literature, and much is found in the medical texts. The rubrics of chapters in the New Kingdom *Book of Going Forth by Day* frequently provide information about the very ancient origins of these spells for transformation and glorification, and they also provide instructions concerning the rites accompanying recitation of the spells. In some cases complete secrecy is required, and we frequently encounter the claim that a particular spell was tried and proved a million times. Chapter 64 of the *Book of Going Forth by Day* is "The Chapter for Knowing the Chapters of Coming Forth by Day in a Single Chapter." Its rubric adds:

> If this chapter is known by the deceased, he will be mighty both on earth and in the otherworld, and he will perform every act of a living person. It is a great protection that has been given by God. This chapter was found in the city of Hermopolis on a block of iron of the south, which has been inlaid with real lapis lazuli, under the feet of the god during the reign of his majesty, the king of Upper and Lower Egypt, Menkaure, justified [i.e., deceased], by Prince Hordedef, justified. He found it when he was journeying to make an inspection of the temples. One Nakht was with him who was diligent in making him understand it, and he brought it to the king as a wonderful object when he saw that it was a thing of great mystery, which had never before been seen or looked upon.
>
> This chapter shall be recited by a man who is ritually clean and pure, who has not eaten the flesh of animals or fish, and who has not had intercourse with women. And you shall make a scarab of green stone, with a rim plated with gold, which shall be placed in the heart of a man, and it shall perform for him the opening of the mouth. And you shall anoint it with *anti*-unguent, and you shall recite over it these spells . . .

The words that follow are the heart spell of chapter 30. The discovery of the text by such a famous sage in so significant a place clearly enhanced its value.

Those Egyptian medical texts that deal with surgical procedures tend to be reasonably scientific, but for the vast majority of human ailments treated in most medical texts the Egyptians relied on magic—potions, poultices, or salves applied with written or recited spells. Headaches and stomach disorders are obvious targets, and there are lengthy series of spells for hastening birth that recall the travail of Isis in giving birth to Horus.

Magic was also used in the Execration Texts, which the Egyptians devised to overcome enemies perhaps too difficult to overcome by any other means. These bowls or figurines, inscribed with a fairly standard selection of the names of Egypt's foreign and domestic enemies plus all evil thoughts, words, and deeds, were deliberately smashed to try to destroy any and all persons and things listed thereon.

The Opening of the Mouth ritual, already referred to above, was obviously a magical rite to bring to life mummies and other representations of individuals. Sculpted portraits (called reserve heads) in Old Kingdom mastaba tombs were magical stand-ins. The eradication from statues, stelae, and tomb and temple walls of names and representations of individuals was thought to be a way of eliminating those persons magically. The texts in some tombs had the animal hieroglyphs either halved or with knives in them, to prevent them from being a danger to the deceased. The names of individuals involved in the harem conspiracy against Ramses III were often changed in the records to evil-sounding names, primarily so that the evil person's memory would not live on. In this same conspiracy, magic was also apparently involved in the making of waxen images by the conspirators. Exactly how these were to be used is unclear.

In addition to reserve heads and *ka*-statues, the deceased in his tomb frequently had a supply of servant statues. In the earlier periods they were shown doing exactly what they would have done in life, but in the New Kingdom they were represented merely as mummified figures, with chapter 6 of the *Book of Going Forth by Day* written on them. This is the magic spell that says that if the deceased is called upon to do any work in the afterlife, such as moving sand from one bank to another, the "answerer" (the figurine) will respond that he is present to do it. A different type of magic is found in the *Cannibal Hymn*, in Pyramid Text utterances 273–274. Here the deceased king goes about devouring the gods, both to demonstrate that he has gained power over them in death and in order to acquire their strength and attributes.

Popular Religion and Personal Piety. Among the numerous amulets used by the Egyptians a few stand out and deserve attention. Probably the best-known amulet and symbol is the *ankh* sign, the hieroglyph for "life," which is most frequently shown being presented by the gods to men. Considerably more important for the Egyptians was the *Udjat*-eye, the eye of Horus, which symbolized the sacrifice endured by Horus in his struggle to avenge his father's murder. This eye was used to designate any offering or sacrifice and also to represent the sun and the moon gods and their barks. Similar falcon eyes are found on the fronts of Middle Kingdom coffins, presumably to enable the deceased to see; on the prows of boats and in mummy wrappings these might also have been chosen to ward off evil.

The scarab beetle was a symbol that had religious significance, but it was frequently used for the very practical purpose of identification, as a seal bearing the owner's name on its flat underside. Some scarabs have ornamental decoration and the vast majority have royal names, usually of Thutmose III or Ramses II. The scarab itself was a symbol of the sun god, apparently derived from the image of this beetle slowly pushing along a nutritious ball of dung. The Egyptian word for this beetle was *kheper,* a homonym for their word meaning "to come to be" or "to happen," and the word also became the name of the early-morning sun deity. Re, then, is the powerful and bright noonday sun, and Atum the old and worn-out evening sun.

Two symbolic figures often found on amulets seem to have been primarily associated with household deities and were particularly important for their connection with fertility and the successful conclusion of pregnancy. These are of the gods Bes, the grotesque human-faced baboon or monkey, and Taweret, the not very attractive female hippopotamus/crocodile who stands on her hind legs and holds another amulet, the "knot of Isis," in her hands. Amulets of the frog goddess, Heket, and the knot of Isis were probably used similarly by women. The feather of Maat (Truth or Justice) also symbolized order, and in those countless temple scenes showing the king presenting to various deities the small figure of the goddess wearing the feather and seated on a basket, the king is both claiming and promising to preserve order on earth on behalf of all the other gods. The plump hermaphrodite figures of Hapy are symbolic of the fertility of the Nile in flood and are frequently shown tying together the sedge plant of Upper Egypt and the papyrus of Lower Egypt.

The numerous stelae and votive offerings left at cult centers provide adequate testimony of the personal piety of the Egyptians. Many of the stelae were inscribed with a plea to the god of the place, and some had a human ear or ears carved on them as if to entreat the god to be especially attentive. Since the common people would not have had access to the god in the interior of his temple, they had their own preferred shrines, statues, or reliefs of the god (often Amun) "who hears prayers" outside the temple proper but within the sacred precincts. If they were patient they could wait to approach the god on his processions in connection with major feasts. These occasions were regularly used to make requests of the gods, and the nod of the god, perhaps aided by the shoulders of the men carrying the god, was considered a significant oracular response. The "power" or "manifestation" of a god is mentioned in several texts as punishment for an offense (e.g., being blinded for lying) or as a force compelling a person to recant earlier testimony. Some women called "knowledgeable" could use their powers for conjuring or healing. Omens were important to the Egyptians, many different dreams were interpreted as good or bad, and at least by the Late Period they had calendars of lucky and unlucky days.

One final indication of the religiosity of the Egyptians and also of their trust in magic is the very frequent occurrence, both on stelae and in graffiti, of a list of good works the writer had done, followed by his request that any passerby reading the text pronounce his name and the formula "A thousand bread, beer, oxen, and fowl," so that some day he would magically receive these stereotypical offerings. The Egyptians had a great deal of confidence in both the written and the spoken word and a proper respect for things sacred. A woman from Deir al-Medineh accused of stealing a workman's tool compounded her guilt enormously when she swore a false oath and it was discovered that she stole not only the tool but also a vessel from a temple.

Temples. The priests and priestesses of ancient Egypt included a very high percentage of the population. The king himself seems to have been the principal intermediary between gods and men. He is shown making offerings, pouring libations, and burning incense before almost all the gods in all the temples. How much of the king's time was actually spent in religious ritual is not known and probably varied from dynasty to dynasty and from one king to another. The large amount of civil authority delegated to viziers would have released time for more religious activities if that were desired. Some kings, however, seem to have preferred leading military expeditions, perhaps finding these more essential or more interesting.

The actual high priests of each temple had different titles. The word used most frequently was *hem-netjer* ("servant of the god"), which the Greeks rendered as "prophet." The great temple of Amun-Re at Karnak had four ranked prophets, and the first prophet had one of the highest positions in the land. In addition to his religious duties involving the daily temple ritual and rites connected with many special feasts, he exercised temporal power over a vast amount of landholdings and over the people who worked those lands. He also served as a judge in the tribunal headed by the vizier. Some did rise to the higher priestly offices by coming up through the ranks and being recognized for their abilities, but it was also the case that they could start at the top, apparently with the king's patronage. Royal princes frequently held the post of high priest of the temple of Ptah at Memphis. At Thebes the office of high priest often was hereditary, and it became a power base from which individuals could claim and acquire the kingship of the entire land (twenty-first dynasty).

Little is known about the lesser prophets, though the office of second prophet seems in one case to have been given over to a queen, Akhmose Nefertari of the eighteenth dynasty, either to exercise the office or to award it to another. Later a famous fourth prophet of Amun, Montuemhet (twenty-sixth dynasty), was simultaneously mayor of Thebes, and his great wealth and prestige probably accrued from that position. It is not known whether any of these figureheads and administrators were also knowledgeable theologians.

Those temple scribes who were familiar with the sacred writings were called *chery-heb* ("lector priest"). It was their responsibility to interpret omens and dreams, to know the magical spells required for any eventuality, and to read the required texts for the rituals of embalmment and burial. The scribes most likely also provided the copies of funerary texts that people wanted to be buried with, and would either have served as physicians themselves or would have provided the magical medical spells that the physicians used.

In all the temples most of the lesser tasks were in the hands of the faithful. All would be called upon to do their monthly service, and since they were regularly divided into four phylae, this meant that they alternated but served three months out of the year. These common priests (*wabu*, "pure ones") shaved their hair, washed frequently in the sacred lakes near the temples, and maintained ritual purity to enable them to serve the god in his mansion. They served as porters, watchmen, and attendants, assisted with offerings and rites, and probably did their share of cleaning, polishing, painting, and moving things around.

There was of course a major distinction between the city cult temples and the mortuary temple establishments. The great mortuary temples grew out of the smaller chapels erected above shaft tombs, and these in turn developed from the small offering niches in Old Kingdom mastaba tombs. The offerings to be left at the chapels of nobles or temples of kings were provided by endowments, and the priests who administered the endowments were called *hemu-ka* ("servants of the *ka*"). If the endowment included lands, the produce would have provided offerings as well as an income for the individual "priests." They would also benefit from the unconsumed offerings that they provided each day. These endowments became an important part of the individual's property and tended to be collected and handed on to heirs.

Women in all periods shared at least some priestly responsibilities and enjoyed priestly titles. In the Old Kingdom many women were priestesses of Hathor, Neith, or Nut. In the early New Kingdom the great royal wives were also the "god's wives of Amun" and as such bore the next divine son, but they did as well participate with male priests in temple rites. Of course Hatshepsut as king (she took the masculine title, and even wore a false beard) was also priest, but remarkably, Nefertiti appeared alone or with her daughter, making offerings to her god, Aton. The wives of nobles and even the working women of Deir al-Medineh were very frequently called songstresses of Amun and were depicted in tombs bearing two symbols of this office, the sistrum and the *menit*-necklace, with which they provided musical accompaniment for rituals at both the great and the lesser temples. Women in general also served as *ka*-priests and professional mourners. In the late New Kingdom the wives of the high priests of Amun held the title of chief concubine of Amun-Re, but while it is known that they had a great deal of influence, it is not known precisely what religious responsibilities they had. Daughters of the first prophets of Amun were given the title of "God's Wife" in the twenty-first dynasty, and then, to assume greater control of the south, the Tanite kings gave this position to their own daughters. The next step in the process is the evolution of a new position, that of Divine Adoratress, from the office of God's Wife; the new position is clearly ranked above that of the high priest. Since the Divine Adoratress remains a virgin, she adopts her successor from among the daughters of the king.

The Egyptian temple was the mansion of the god, his abode on earth or, at least, the abode of his principal cult statue. The daily ritual for a god in his temple was limited to a few priests present, and consisted of their approaching the sanctuary, opening the shrine, removing the statue, undressing it, washing it, censing it, making offerings to it, clothing it in fresh garments, replacing it, sealing the shrine, and retreating, with care taken to sweep away their footprints. Although the faithful did not have the opportunity to participate in the daily ritual, they were able to see the god during special feasts, when the statue of the god would leave the temple. For the feast of Opet the statue and shrine of the god Amun-Re was taken from its sanctuary at the Karnak temple, placed on a bark held aloft by priests with carrying poles on their shoulders, and carried to its river transport for the two-mile voyage to the Luxor temple, the southern harem, for a sojourn there before the return voyage. The Beautiful Feast of the Valley involved Amun-Re's voyage across the river to western Thebes to visit the major temples there, but numerous stops were made at small temples and way stations along the route. In addition to these great feasts of Amun-Re recorded at the Luxor and Karnak temples, the mortuary temple of Ramses III at Medinet Habu contains records of the festival processions of Min and Sokar illustrated in great detail.

Mythology. Mythology is encountered in almost everything that survives from ancient Egypt. Texts, whether religious, historical, literary, medical, or legal, or merely personal correspondence, all contain mythological allusions. Art of all kinds and on all scales, and artifacts of all types, made use of easily recognizable mythological symbols. This does not mean that everything had a ritual purpose or that the Egyptians had narrow one-track minds, but it does show how mythology and religion had permeated the culture, and also how artisans and craftsmen could capitalize on this.

It is not surprising to find that the Egyptians' mythology was not detailed and collected in any one place, but surely the various traditions were handed down by word of mouth and were generally well known. Temple libraries, known in the Late Period as "houses of life," certainly contained medico-magical texts, and also would have had many ritual, historical, and theological texts and treatises. Many of these contained mythological material, but none was entitled *Egyptian Mythology.* There may have been individual texts relating to the individual cults or sites, such as Papyrus Jumilac. The cosmogonical myths that were excerpted for use in the mortuary literature and that have been briefly summarized above were included in the Pyramid Texts to indicate the power of the king, his genealogy, or his goal, rather than to explain or justify the other gods. The temple texts of individual gods are remarkable for the little mythological information they contain and the vast amount of knowledge they presume.

Some texts, such as the *Story of the Two Brothers* and the *Blinding of Truth by Falsehood,* are in large part mythological without being mythic in purpose. The *Contendings of Horus and Seth* has a totally mythological setting, but it is a burlesque of the real myth, and perhaps a sophisticated attack on the entire pantheon as well. The *Myth of the Destruction of Mankind* is slightly more serious in intent, showing men to be totally at the mercy of the gods if they cross them. In this myth Hathor was sent to slay men because they had plotted in the presence of Re, but Re decided to save them by making bloodlike red beer to deceive and distract her. The goddess became so drunk that she could not perceive mankind, and what had begun as a story about punishment for sin becomes an etiological explanation for drinking to the point of drunkenness at the feast of Hathor. Another remarkable document from the late Ptolemaic period is Papyrus Jumilac, which provides the entire religious history, largely mythological, of the otherwise little known eighteenth nome of Upper Egypt.

Survivals. Egyptian religion does not seem to have been greatly changed by any outside influences. In the New Kingdom several Asiatic deities were introduced into the Egyptian pantheon, including Reshef, Kadesh, Anat, and Astarte. The story of *Astarte and the Insatiable Sea* has been proposed as one example of Egyptian borrowing from the Ugaritic *Poem of Baal,* but the counterargument for the indigenous nature of most of the contents of this text posits that only the names of the principals were changed to those of well-known Semitic deities. The Canaanite god Baal was regularly identified with Seth, and later many Greek gods became identified with the older Egyptian gods (e.g., Hermes-Thoth, Hephaistos-Ptah, and Min-Pan). The Isis-aretalogies that survive in Greek have a few descriptions of the goddess that may be traced back to Egyptian antecedents, but for the most part the composition appears to have been primarily Greek. Many scholars have seen similarities between the Egyptian *Hymn to the Aton* and the biblical *Psalms,* the *Instruction of Amenemope* and *Proverbs,* or the collections of Egyptian love songs and the *Song of Songs.* If there were instances of borrowing (and this is not universally accepted), they would in each case have been from the slightly earlier Egyptian texts.

Among the religious survivals from ancient Egypt, the language used in the Coptic Christian liturgy down to the present time represents the latest stage of ancient Egyptian, but it is written in the Greek alphabet. The decoration of early Coptic textiles used as vestments had incorporated *ankh* signs as well as *udjat*-eyes. As noted above, the institution of monasticism in both its eremetic and cenobitic forms, and the earliest monastic rule, can be clearly traced to Egypt. Whether the late cult of Isis had any influence on the story of the Blessed Virgin, or whether the story of the death and resurrection of Osiris influenced the gospel narrative of Christ, would be hotly contested by many Christians. In doctrinal matters it has been proposed that the Egyptian triads (such as that of Amun, Mut, and Khonsu of Thebes) influenced the concepts of the Trinity and the Holy Family, and that descriptions of the Field of Hetep (paradise) and of places of torment in the afterlife were predecessors for the concepts of heaven and hell. Slightly less controversial would be the question of Egyptian influence on the doctrines of the resurrection of the body and the communion of saints. The traditional sites for the finding of the infant Moses at the river's edge, and the places visited by the Holy Family on their sojourn in Egypt, are indeed very old, but how accurate they are historically is questionable. Surviving traditions in modern Egypt include the use of mourners at funerals, visits to tombs, the leaving of food offerings, and the burning of incense at services. Modern beliefs in afreets or ghosts certainly have ancient roots, and the modern Luxor processions carrying boats on the feast of the Muslim saint Abul Hagag are clearly reminiscent of ancient festivals.

Conclusions. In general the Egyptians seem to have been very religious, believed in an afterlife, and devoted much of their energy to preparing for this. Their preparations included both the physical burial equipment and the spiritual: rites, temple services, offerings, good works, and avoidance of evil deeds. They believed that they were destined from birth to a particular fate, but they were also optimistic that they could, perhaps with the help of a god, change an unfortunate fate. They desired a long life and eventually a proper Egyptian burial. To a great extent they wanted to continue living after death a life very like their life on earth. They were clearly optimistic about vindication in a last judgment and their ability to attain the highest goals in the afterlife.

Two characteristic features of Egyptian religious literature are syncretism and a multiplicity of approaches, and these perhaps show steps in the process of developing doctrine. In the case of the descriptions of the afterlife, the Egyptians could on the one hand place separate, mutually exclusive descriptions side by side without indicating that one is better or more accurate than another; on the other hand, they could combine in the same document aspects from different traditions in a new, apparently superior, composite, and theoretically logical entity. Perhaps this was one way of dealing with the problem of conservatively maintaining the old while also accepting the new.

The Egyptians did not believe in the transmigration of souls, but among the hymns, guidebooks, offering texts, and rituals with which the deceased were buried are many spells for transformations—often into the form of birds, perhaps because of a desire to achieve their apparent freedom. Presumably, an Egyptian purchased the texts he wanted well in advance of his death. Some manuscripts could have been read in advance by their owners, but many texts are quite flawed in extant copies and might not have been intelligible even if the person had bothered to read them. Scribes also had serious problems understanding some texts, and in at least one case (*Book of Going Forth by Day,* chap. 17) a tradition of various interpretations is handed down in the form of glosses incorporated into the text.

Hymns are probably a good gauge of the religiosity and sophistication of the priest-scribes and theologians, as well as of the believers, of ancient Egypt. The short hymns, perhaps excerpts, found in the earlier mortuary literature eventually developed into carefully constructed, easily read, edifying, and glowing tributes to the gods that spell out the gods' links with nature and their special concern for mankind. The *Hymn to the Nile,* the *Hymn to Amun-Re,* the *Hymn to the Aton,* hymns found in nobles' tombs to the rising and setting sun, and the hymns to Osiris and to Re in the *Book of Going Forth by Day* might not be as exciting and different as the so-called *Cannibal Hymn.* But these were very proper and popular works, indicating a considerable refinement in ancient Egypt that is not often recognized and appreciated by historians of religion.

BIBLIOGRAPHY

Allen, Thomas George. *The Book of the Dead or Going Forth by Day.* Chicago, 1974.

Anthes, Rudolf. "Egyptian Theology in the Third Millennium B.C." *Journal of Near Eastern Studies* 18 (1959): 170–212.

Assmann, Jan. *Ägyptische Hymnen und Gebete.* Zurich, 1975.

Bell, H. Idris. *Cults and Creeds of Graeco-Roman Egypt.* Liverpool, 1953.

Bonnet, Hans. *Reallexikon der ägyptischen Religionsgeschichte.* Berlin, 1952.

Breasted, James H. *The Development of Religion and Thought in Ancient Egypt.* New York, 1912.

Černý, Jaroslav. *Ancient Egyptian Religion.* London, 1952.

Englund, Gertie. *Akh: Une notion religieuse dans l'Égypte pharaonique.* Uppsala, 1978.

Erman, Adolf. *Die Religion der Ägypter: Ihr Werden und ihr Vergehen in vier Jahrtausenden.* Berlin, 1934.

Faulkner, Raymond. *The Ancient Egyptian Pyramid Texts.* Oxford, 1969.

Faulkner, Raymond. *The Ancient Egyptian Coffin Texts.* 3 vols. Oxford, 1973–1978.

Frankfort, Henri. *Kingship and the Gods.* Chicago, 1948.

Frankfort, Henri. *Before Philosophy.* Baltimore, 1954.

Frankfort, Henri. *Ancient Egyptian Religion.* New York, 1961.

Greven, Liselotte. *Der Ka in Theologie und Königskult der Ägypter des Alten Reiches.* Glückstadt, 1952.

Griffiths, J. Gwyn. *The Origins of Osiris and His Cult.* Leiden, 1980.

Hornung, Erik. *Altägyptische Höllenvorstellungen.* Leipzig, 1968.

Hornung, Erik. *Ägyptische Unterweltsbücher.* Zurich, 1972.

Hornung, Erik. *Conceptions of God in Ancient Egypt.* Ithaca, N.Y., 1982.

Junker, Hermann. *Die Götterlehre von Memphis (Schabaka-Inschrift).* Berlin, 1940.

Kees, Hermann. *Das Priestertum in ägyptischen Staat vom Neuen Reich bis zur Spätzeit.* Leiden, 1953.

Kees, Hermann. *Der Götterglaube im alten Ägypten.* 2d ed. Berlin, 1956.

Kees, Hermann. *Totenglauben und Jenseitsvorstellungen der alten Ägypter.* 2d ed. Berlin, 1956.

Lesko, Leonard H. "Some Observations on the Composition of the Book of Two Ways." *Journal of the American Oriental Society* 91 (1971): 30–43.

Lesko, Leonard H. "The Field of Ḥetep in Egyptian Coffin Texts." *Journal of the American Research Center in Egypt* 9 (1971–1972): 89–101.

Morenz, Siegfried. *Egyptian Religion.* Ithaca, N.Y., 1973.

Morenz, Siegfried. *Religion und Geschichte des alten Ägypten: Gesammelte Aufsätze.* Weimar, 1975.

Morenz, Siegfried, and Dieter Müller. *Untersuchungen zur Rolle des Schicksals in der ägyptischen Religion.* Berlin, 1960.

Moret, Alexandre. *Le rituel du culte divin journalier en Égypte d'après les papyrus de Berlin et les textes du temple de Séti Premier à Abydos.* Paris, 1902.

Mueller, Dieter. "An Early Egyptian Guide to the Hereafter." *Journal of Egyptian Archaeology* 58 (1972): 99–125.

Otto, Eberhard. *Das Ägyptische Mundoffnungsritual.* Wiesbaden, 1960.

Piankoff, Alexandre. *Shrines of Tut-Ankh-Amon.* Princeton, 1955.

Piankoff, Alexandre. *The Wandering of the Soul.* Princeton, 1974.

Posener, Georges. *De la divinité du Pharaon.* Paris, 1960.

Sauneron, Serge. *Les prêtres de l'ancienne Égypte.* Paris, 1957.

Sauneron, Serge. *Les fêtes religieuses d'Esna.* Cairo, 1962.

Schweitzer, Ursula. *Das Wesen des Ka im Diesseits und Jenseits der alten Ägypter.* Glückstadt, 1956.

Sethe, Kurt H. *Dramatische Texte zu den altägyptischen Mysterienspielen.* Leipzig, 1928.

Sethe, Kurt H. *Amun und die acht Urgötter von Hermopolis.* Berlin, 1929.

Sethe, Kurt H. *Urgeschichte und älteste Religion der Ägypter.* Leipzig, 1930.

Spiegel, Joachim. "Das Auferstehungsritual der Unaspyramide." *Annales du Service des Antiquités de l'Égypte* 53 (1956): 339–439.

Vandier, Jacques. *La religion égyptienne.* Paris, 1944.

Vandier, Jacques. *Le Papyrus Jumilhac.* Paris, 1961.

Westendorf, Wolfhart, ed. *Aspekte der spätägyptischen Religion.* Wiesbaden, 1979.

Wilson, John A. *The Burden of Egypt.* Chicago, 1951.

Wolf, Walther. *Das schöne Fest von Opet.* Leipzig, 1931.

Žabkar, Louis V. *A Study of the Ba Concept in Ancient Egyptian Texts.* Chicago, 1968.

Zandee, Jan. *Death as an Enemy.* Leiden, 1960.

LEONARD H. LESKO

The Literature

From the dawn of Egyptian history, and throughout the three and a half millennia of their currency, religious beliefs and practices were for practical purposes committed to written form. The singular phenomenon of the nation-state the pharaohs had created put far greater stock in the hieroglyphic script, the novel creation of a bureaucracy of wise men, than it did in any memory, individual or collective, that might serve as a repository for the important knowledge of the community. The scribal tradition, therefore, at an early date took precedence over the oral in Egypt, and the scribe became recorder and transmitter of all that was deemed important among the intellectual creations of pharaonic society. Egyptian religion was practiced according to beliefs and directives "as they were [found] in writing," and scorn was poured on anything that remained in an oral stage of transmission. The latter was "the narrative discourse of the people," and was considered to be unsophisticated, hyperbolic, and unreliable.

In the light of this it should come as no surprise to learn that the scribe in ancient Egypt was the kingpin in the running of the government, and the most respected member of the community (Williams, 1972). The "scribe of the god's book," later to become the sacred scribe, and the "lector-priest" (lit., "he who carries the book role") are found already in the Early Dynastic Period (c. 3000–2650 BCE). Precisely what kind of sacred literature such worthies wrote, copied, and guarded at this early time is difficult to ascertain. As the vast majority of texts, both originals and copies, were written on papyrus, it is scarcely to be wondered at that none has survived from the Old Kingdom (c. 3000–2200 BCE), and very few from the Middle Kingdom (c. 2134–1660 BCE). Something of the early history of the sacred library can, however, be reconstructed from hieroglyphic records and from the known exigencies of the cult. Thus, the overriding importance of sacred monarchy demanded that rites concerned with coronation and jubilee be regulated by written directories, and the remarkable uniformity of relief-scenes and texts commemorating these ceremonies over three millennia argues the presence, already in the Old Kingdom, of written prescriptions.

Of equal, if not greater, importance to the ancient Egyptian community were two rites intimately connected with the funerary cult—the offering to the ancestors and the mortuary liturgy. The former called forth at the very dawn of Egyptian history the offering-list, a formal and comprehensive listing of foodstuffs and other requirements of the dead, together with name and titles of the ancestor and occasionally a formulaic text to be used orally (Barta, 1963). The mortuary liturgy became the starting point for that ever-burgeoning body of texts known to the Egyptians as *sakhu* ("[funerary] beatifications"), pronounced by the lector-priest on the day of the obsequies to assist the deceased in securing a glorified existence in the beyond. Any person for whom offering-list and beatifications had been provided could *ipso facto* be termed "a competent and equipped spirit."

Mortuary Literature. Although we must await the twenty-fourth century BCE for the first extensive texts of funerary purport, from that point the genre rapidly becomes one of the most frequent in the repertoire of Egyptian writings.

The Pyramid Texts. The corpus of religious literature called the Pyramid Texts comprises approximately 760 individual paragraphs, or "spells," inscribed on the walls of the tomb chambers and entrance corridors of Egyptian kings (and occasionally queens) from Wenis (c. 2410–2380 BCE) to Aba (fl. c. 2185 BCE). As such it represents the earliest, and in some respects the most interesting, body of sacred literature in the ancient world (Faulkner, 1969; Barta, 1981). In later times the material was sporadically revived and recopied; but the original exemplars reflect its heyday. (Even when first seen, however, the corpus was undergoing a rapid evolution: much of the content of the Wenis texts is missing and has been replaced with additional material of like sort in the pyramid of Pepy II [c. 2290–2200 BCE].) The texts follow no special sequence, other than a general "order of service" from the arrival of the funeral cortege at the pyramid to the king's acceptance by the sun god in heaven. Broadly speaking, the intent is that of an apologia on behalf of the deceased in order to secure the gods' acquiescence to his eternal stay among them. The Pyramid Texts incorporate hymns to the gods, magical incantations, prayers for the dead, liturgical pieces, and ritual texts, and as such envisage rites of embalmment and purification, the "opening of the mouth" ceremony (to revivify the mummy and the mortuary statues), coronation, rites of passage, and the offering liturgy.

While this was not their primary intent, the Pyramid Texts introduce us to the cult and pantheon of the gods current in Egypt during the Old Kingdom. The texts were undoubtedly produced by the theologians and scribes of the great center of sun worship, Heliopolis, where lay the "great mansion" of the sun god, Re-Atum. Reflecting the amazing political unity the Egyptian state had achieved under pharaonic administration by the middle of the third millennium BCE, these Heliopolitan priests had synthesized the religion of the Nile Valley and Delta into a unified whole, and enlisted its aid in effecting the king's journey to the solar beyond (Anthes, 1959). The Pyramid Texts can, therefore, be used—with appropriate caution—as a source for Egyptian religion during the Old Kingdom.

The Coffin Texts. This body of literature, comprising over 1,150 "spells" and called in Egyptian the *Book of Justifying a Man in the Realm of the Dead,* is known in numerous copies from the ninth dynasty through the thirteenth (c. 2150–1650 BCE). Although a few extant fragments make it plain that the original was written up in papyrus copies, the vast majority of examples are found written in ink in vertical columns (in apparent imitation of the Pyramid Texts), on the insides of the large, rectangular wooden coffins that were characteristic of the period (Faulkner, 1973–1978). Unlike the Pyramid Texts, of which they could be considered a later development, the Coffin Texts often precede a spell with a rubric docket giving the purpose of the piece, and follow it with another supplying directions for use. The latter might suggest use by cult initiates during life, and indeed "the book of two ways" has been taken to be a manual of initiation. On the other hand, the rubric headings of spells most frequently point to their construing by the ancients as magical incantations designed to circumvent obstacles, combat dangers, and ensure the well-being of the deceased in the next life. Over half of the spells are concerned with mystical transformations of the deceased into animals, gods, objects, or desirable elements in nature (the Nile, grain, air, and so on), and in a large proportion of them magical effectiveness is ensured by the knowledge of esoteric mythology to which the deceased lays claim.

Much of the Coffin Texts derives from the Pyramid Texts, and belongs under the general rubric of "beatifications," but the content and atmosphere of the Coffin Texts sometimes differ markedly from the aristocratic or royal aura of the Pyramid Texts. Often a spell from the latter is distorted and misinterpreted, either to suit the new requirements of life in a different age or, more often, through ignorance of what it originally meant. Like the Pyramid Texts, the Coffin Texts come from the context of the sun cult, but yield more information on other cult centers, such as Abydos, Mendes, and Buto. For the first time in Egyptian religious literature, prominence is given to the concept of the judgment of the dead in the afterlife; and Osiris and his cycle, on the ascendant in the later versions of the Pyramid Texts, are very much to the fore in the Coffin Texts.

Book of Going Forth by Day. By the beginning of the eighteenth dynasty (c. 1569 BCE), the vast corpus of "beatifications" represented by the Coffin Texts was being pressed into service as a source for a new document of funerary use, the *Book of Going Forth by Day,* erroneously termed the *Book of the Dead* by moderns (Allen, 1974). Written most commonly on a papyrus roll that was placed in the coffin beside the mummy (of both royalty and commoners), the *Book of Going Forth by Day* derives nearly 60 percent of its material from the known Coffin Texts; but the spells were evolving under constant pressure of reinterpretation, and new incantations were being added. Their magical intent is clearer than ever: each spell has a title, and most a prescription for use. All were, as is to be expected, intended for the well-being of the deceased in the next life, although, as is the case with the Coffin Texts, use by the living is not entirely excluded. The *Book of Going Forth by Day* continues and expands a practice begun on a small scale by the Coffin Texts, that of glossing selected spells with colored vignettes showing the deceased before various gods or engaged in cultic acts. Whereas for the New Kingdom spells are treated as individual units having little connection with other material and no fixed position in a canonical order, the "archaizing" revival of the Kushite-Saite period (712–525 BCE) produced a standard sequence of spells that survived into Roman times.

The *Book of Going Forth by Day* shows us the concept of the Egyptian afterlife at a stage from which it developed little. The concept of the judgment, or psychostasia, is virtually full-blown, the trust in the efficacy of magic at its height. It now becomes standard procedure to place certain spells on "shawabtis" (servant figurines) to activate them, or on "heart scarabs" (beetle pectorals) to prevent the heart from testifying against its owner. Proper use of chapter 125 will ensure that the deceased emerges from the divine tribunal unscathed, whether he be "guilty" or not; the pious intoning of hymns to the sun at dawn and sunset will elicit divine indulgence for eternity.

Underworld literature. From the earliest period one can sense an antithesis between Re, the supernal sun god, *fons et origo* of the universe of light, and Osiris, the passive infernal hypostasis of the mystery of fertility, death, and the earth. Every night the sun passed through the perils of the infernal regions where Osiris dwelt, and it was only by magic and the prayers of the devout that it emerged whole in the morning. The "well-equipped" soul showed an ambivalence in its postmortem desires, now striving to accompany the sun boat in its eternal round through sky and the underworld for ever, now craving identity with Osiris, embedded forever in the life-giving soil. Preoccupation with these aims, ostensibly irreconcilable, conjured up in the New Kingdom (c. 1569–1085 BCE) an ever-increasing literature on the underworld and the mystery of the eventual union of Re with Osiris (Hornung, 1980). The very names of the books comprising this esoteric library reveal the nature of the realm described: the *Book of What Is in the Underworld,* the *Book of Gates,* the *Book of Caverns,* the *Litany of Re,* the *Book of Traversing Eternity.* Though they were genuine papyrus books whose origins in some cases possibly date before the New Kingdom, most of these pieces are known from hieroglyphic copies inscribed on the walls of the tombs of the kings at Thebes. They describe an underworld divided into twelve regions (corresponding to the hours of the night), peopled by fierce demons and fraught with dangers for gods and mortals alike. It is a place of punishment from which all men fervently pray to be saved. Concern for such salvation, as well as for well-being in life, led in the first millennium BCE to the practice of placing "decrees" in the mouths of the gods on behalf of other gods and individual human beings, and inscribing them on prophylactery strips of papyrus or on tablets.

The cosmic balance between Re and Osiris and the natural principles for which they stood were of great concern in the Late Period (second half of the first millennium BCE). Underworld literature envisages a union of the two at a crucial point in Re's nightly passage through the underworld. In a curious ritual called the Rite of the House of Life, designed to preserve life in the universe and prevent the sun crashing to the earth, Osiris was united with Re in the form of a mummy.

Communications between living and dead. Central to Egyptian mortuary practices was the offering to the ancestors. The entire tomb in its layout and decoration focused upon the offering station with its stone table, libation stone, and sculpted or painted representation of the deceased. Here the dead met the living, as it were, and lively "conversation" was the result. At a very early date, certainly by the close of the third dynasty (c. 2650 BCE), tomb owners had begun to use the wall space in the tomb chapel to convey messages to posterity: personal identification (name and titles), legal contracts with mortuary priests, scenes from the life of the deceased, and formal addresses to the living. The last, introduced by the heading "He [the tomb owner] says . . ." and followed by direct speech, constituted a biographical statement, and throughout Egyptian history this statement became a major source not only for history but also for personal ethics and conduct in society. Very frequently the tomb owner used it as a vehicle to cajole or harangue the passerby into either making a formal offering or (more often) pronouncing the offering formula whereby the foodstuffs named were actualized for the deceased in the next life. The tomb owner sensed that his visitor might be reluctant to comply with his request, and so he presented arguments of convenience and self-interest; at times he all but threatened. The same type of text could be used as a means of warding off would-be violators of the tomb, usually by threatening them with a lawsuit at the court of the Great God in the Beyond.

Conversation of the living with the ancestors was also possible. This took the form of "letters to the dead," written on bowls, shards, or papyrus and placed in the offering chamber of the tomb, to be seen by the spirit when it emerged to partake of the food offerings. Frequently the letters incorporated complaints that the dead relative was interfering in the writer's life.

Mythology. No myths have come down to us from ancient Egypt composed solely for the sake of the narrative itself (Schott, 1945). No practical need was felt to produce an *editio princeps.* But mythology was constantly used, so powerful were its archetypal protagonists and events felt to be as a basis for cult procedure, and mythology was drawn on as an inexhaustible source of prototypes and identifications in the realm of magic. Further, the cultic and magical act enjoyed a reciprocal influence on the myth, and we find the latter evolving and reproducing under the influence of a changing cult. This evolution, however, was not in the hands of the scribe. In the cult, indeed in everyday life, the spoken word predominated; and we often find variant forms of myth developing from like-sounding words or phrases. One senses a creative impulse here that derives from the common Egyptian belief that sound structure constitutes a powerful force throughout the elements of the created world.

Cosmogonies. There is no single text from the pharaonic period whose sole purpose is to set forth a creation myth; but allusions to creation motifs are legion in all types of religious literature. Four basic patterns manifest themselves, in all of which the act of creation is construed as the elimination of chaos and the ordering of preexistent elements: (1) the primeval ocean and the creator-god or creative element that appears within it; (2) the separation of earth from sky, both personified in a sexual union; (3) creation by means of a skilled craft (e.g., the ceramic expertise of Khnum, the plastic modeling of Ptah, or the weaving of Neith); (4) the conflict between hero-god and monster, out of whose carcass the world is created. Of the four the last is the least known, the motif in Egypt having been early carried over into a cosmic explanation of the continued integrity of creation. Thanks to its espousal by the dominant solar theology of Heliopolis, the first is by far the most common, but perhaps the most crass (expectoration, masturbation, and weeping being mechanisms involved).

A rather more sophisticated approach to the problem of creation was essayed at Hermopolis and Memphis. At the former site, the abstract qualities of the Primeval Ocean (Nun) are personified as four gods (with their consorts): Nothingness, Inertness, Limitlessness, and Darkness. At Memphis, Thought and Fiat are singled out as the essence of the divine, in this case the god

Ptah, and are made the sole elements in the creation process. Wherever rationality and the capability of enunciating thought exist in the created world, there exists Ptah, sustaining and informing his creation. This doctrine is most clearly set forth in the *Memphite Theology,* a commentary on a dramatic text, appearing under Shabaka (712–697 BCE) as an inscription on stone but purporting to have been copied from a much older document (Sethe, 1928). Although the alleged antiquity of the text has been doubted, the same concepts it sets forth are clearly alluded to in New Kingdom religious literature. The claim, often made, that it does in fact date from the late third millennium BCE may yet prove correct.

Myths of kingship and fertility. These center upon two great cycles of myths, the Horus-Seth conflict and the death of Osiris. The former describes the struggle of Order with Chaos, variously cast as an act of revenge, a fight over the right to rule, or simply a natural struggle. When linked with the Osiris myth, the fight is sharpened and humanized: it is not only a son's act of revenge upon his father's murderer, but also the son's assertion of his legal and political rights. When the king adopts the role of Horus and performs the obsequies for his deceased father, "Osiris," the whole myth takes on heightened significance as the mythological underpinning of the monarchy (Anthes, 1959).

From an early period the whole is inextricably intertwined with the myth of fertility, and Osiris and those gods with whom he is associated become hypostases of the principle of fertility. While it may well be a skewing of the evidence through the haphazard of preservation, texts pointing to Osiris and his congeners as associated with the Nile, the fertile soil, and the crops tend to become more numerous as the Late Period approaches.

Like cosmogonies, fertility myths are not in ancient Egypt accorded any special archetypal publication. There was no need for one. No canonical version existed, and constant use in the cult and in everyday life continued to produce changes in detail. Seldom is the myth of Osiris epitomized in the literature of the pharaonic period from beginning to end (cf. as exceptions the eighteenth-dynasty hymn to Osiris in Louvre stela C. 286 and the Plutarch version, the latter in Griffiths, 1970). But allusions of widely varying length to fertility myths are legion in all types of religious literature.

Myths about the destruction of mankind. Another well-defined group of myths centers upon a feline deity dispatched by the gods to punish mankind for disobedience. Identified as the sun's "eye" (i.e., the fierce heat of the sun disk, personified) or the goddess of plague, she ranges far over the earth effecting the gods' will; but soon she exhibits a mind of her own and refuses to follow the directives of the head of the pantheon. The plot turns on the means used by the gods to subdue her and bring her back into the divine fold (Hornung, 1981).

Mythological stories. Several pieces of writing exist that can be broadly characterized as elaborations on a mythological theme. Most date from the New Kingdom and are written in the Late Egyptian dialect (current as a literary medium from c. 1320 BCE to nearly 1000 BCE), but sporadic references suggest the presence of the genre already in the Middle Kingdom. These works center upon a known incident in a myth and rework it into a coherent narrative, often with dramatic overtones, lending a charming, human cast to the divine protagonists. Favorite foci around which interest gravitates are the topos of Isis and baby Horus hiding in the marshes of the Nile Delta, and the conflict/trial of Horus and Seth. Some, like the stories of Papyrus d'Orbiney, Papyrus Chester Beatty I, or the Amherst Papyrus, constitute independent works; others are found only in secondary contexts, where they are used as magic spells. Occasionally in the New Kingdom, themes of Canaanite mythology appear in Egyptian translation (Simpson, 1973; Lichtheim, 1973–1980).

Speculative Literature. The complete collapse of society and government in the obscure "revolution" that brought an end to the Old Kingdom (c. 2200 BCE) shook the Egyptians' confidence in traditional beliefs and procedures. In the literature of the First Intermediate Period that followed (c. 2200–2050 BCE) a questioning tone may be sensed: Egypt, or at least a part of it, was engaged in a fundamental reappraisal of the nation's institutions and identity. While the continuum in the mortuary cult attested by the Coffin Texts shows the presence of a traditional "mainstream" in Egyptian thought, a surprisingly large number of pieces written during the period display a questing spirit prepared to break with the past and espouse heterodox views.

Dialogues and harpers' songs. An untraditional, indeed agnostic, view of man's prospects beyond the tomb was the contribution of a very special group of texts that must have had their birth in the First Intermediate Period. In the genre of the dialogue, two proponents of differing (if not opposing) points of view engage each other in conversation, and the views expressed are startlingly heterodox. In one example, Osiris, typifying the soul on the point of entering the afterlife, gives vent to his fear of the unknown, in spite of centuries of confident mortuary practices; and Atum is obliged to offer him the assurance of eternal survival and union with the creator himself. Even more peculiar is the *Dialogue of a Man with His Soul* (a modern title—the ancient has not survived). In the sole surviving manuscript of this work, which lacks the first few pages, an unnamed man contemplates the prospect of death and declares his determination to pursue the traditional course of preparing a tomb, the funeral service, and an endowment. His soul, however, whose acquiescence in all this is crucial to the man's hope of future existence, expresses profound doubts on the efficacy of the customary procedure, on the alleged happiness of life in the beyond, and even on man's ability to attain an afterlife (Williams, 1962).

The note of doubt sounded in these works gives over into the advocacy of a hedonistic approach to life in a well-represented genre known as "harpers' songs" (Williams, 1981, pp. 4f.). Derived from the innocuous banquet song whose sole purpose is entertainment at a social event, the harpers' songs originated in the troubled times of the twenty-second century BCE as a vehicle for the expression of a profound disillusionment with traditional views of the afterlife. Recurring themes include the desuetude of tombs and mortuary installations, the impossibility of knowing what is beyond the grave, and the need to live life to the full here and now. Although most examples of the genre are today found on tomb walls in association with a scene of the harper before the deceased, there is good reason to believe that such songs enjoyed a primary *Sitz im Leben* among the living. The content of individual pieces tends to become cliché-ridden as time goes on, but the tone is always lively, with a tendency toward impiety. Harpers' songs remained popular for centuries, and their irreverent nature occasionally evoked a counterblast from the pious.

The pessimistic view of man's ability to forecast what he will meet beyond the grave leads naturally, though illogically, to the proposition that the afterlife, in pointed contrast to what we all expect, is in fact a realm of gloom and misery. A story of thirteenth-century date in which a pious priest encounters the spirit of one long departed who enlightens him on this score, sets forth this view, and a few mortuary stelae of later times elaborate on the same theme.

Discourse. The Egyptians, like many ancient peoples, identified one sort of wisdom with the ability to foretell the future under divine inspiration. The verb meaning "to foretell, to announce in advance" did not, however, give rise to a genre term. More often than not it is the wise man himself whose name is the identifying element, and the text goes under the label of "The discourse (lit., "the word") of so-and-so." Broadly speaking, such declamations are grouped by the ancients under the general rubric of "teachings."

The turbulent years of the First Intermediate Period were the heyday of the prophetic discourse, although as a "literary" phenomenon it had a longer life. In the main it constituted a lament over the sorry condition of the land, gone to ruin politically and socially, and could be cast either as a backdated prediction or a contemporary description (Junge, 1977). With the coming to power of the twelfth dynasty (c. 1991–1778 BCE) the prophecy was used as a powerful tool of propaganda to bolster the regime's claim to legitimacy; it might even be placed in the mouth of a god to support the pretensions of an individual ruler.

The discourses of the First Intermediate Period frequently reveal themselves as vehicles of heterodox messages. Ipuwer, an otherwise unknown wise man of the past, rails in a lengthy tirade against none other than the creator god himself, and lays at his feet the blame for having allowed the land to go to ruin under unjust administrators. A peasant, wrongfully deprived of his possessions, goes to lodge an official complaint before the appropriate magistrate, and the result is a series of paeons adulating justice and decrying civil corruption. The theme of the petitioner in a lawsuit robbed of a just hearing turns up in several works of the period.

Magical Texts. The Egyptians conceived of magic *(heka)* as a powerful element in the universe that, if controlled, could be employed to any end, even to the constraint of the gods themselves and the dislocation of the cosmos. So dominant was the preoccupation with this possibility that literature with magical intent constitutes the most common genre in the corpus of ancient Egyptian writings. Broadly speaking, magical texts can be divided into two subgroups on the basis of purpose, those concerned with the official cult and those for private use; but the Egyptians themselves never made this distinction. Incantations are introduced under several headings: "The protection against . . ." *(sau nu . . .)*, "The spell of . . ." *(ra n . . .)*, "The repelling of . . ." *(sehry)*, "The book of . . ." *(medjat)*, "The protection of . . ." *(meket)*, "The protection book . . ." *(nehet)* (Redford, 1985, p. 104, n. 60). As in the case of mortuary literature, rubrics specifying use are sometimes included, but stories in which magicians appear as protagonists often reflect the procedures involved.

The purpose of magic spells varied. Most often they were designed to ward off external forces of evil, whether ethereal or concrete. Temple ritual invoked magic to ensure the integrity of the rites, the cult personnel, the paraphernalia, and the installation. So closely intertwined in the ritual was the magical incantation that frequently it is difficult to distinguish cultic prescriptions, prayers, and hymns from texts with purely magical intent. A perusal of the famous Edfu library catalogue, for example, will reveal the startling fact that much of what would pass as ritual is subsumed under magic! Private use was concerned with protection from disease, bodily harm, or demons who effect harm, and thus was closely associated with medicine. Very common were spells to ward off snakes, scorpions, crocodiles, and other noisome animals, or to neutralize the evil intent of people (often foreign), of the dead, or of the evil eye. Formal execration of foreign enemies, employing the ritual smashing of pots and figurines, was well known in the sphere of pharaonic statecraft. Productive, as opposed to prophylactic, magic is not well attested.

By his thorough training in magical lore, the magician—the Egyptians used such a word *(hekay),* but magic could be learned by anyone intelligent enough—could confront the most powerful hostile force and triumph. Most often the speaker identified himself in a spell with a god, or invoked a mythological incident as precedent. Numerous myths are in fact known to us only because they were considered efficacious enough to be used as spells! Identification of celebrant or victim with a divine figure, or the extensive use of homophonous words ("pious puns"), was considered useful in ensuring the effectiveness of the spell (Borghouts, 1978).

Great compilations of magical texts were copied on papyrus and kept in temple libraries, but few of these have survived, and we are often thrown back on "unofficial" copies. Private scribal libraries have occasionally yielded magical papyri, but casual copies on ostraca are more numerous. Of special interest are the prophylactic statues of mortals or gods in various poses, covered with magical spells and provided with the means of collecting water poured over them. These usually were installed in sanatoriums attached to the temples (especially in the second half of the first millennium BCE), where sufferers from various diseases came for healing. The magical stelae and *cippi* were intended for private protection, and often show representations of the child Horus and the creatures against whom protection is sought.

Wisdom Literature. The word that in Egyptian approaches closest to the concept conveyed by the Hebrew *ḥokhmah* ("wisdom") is *sebayt* ("teaching"), but this word is so loosely used that it can scarcely point to a formal genre. Any text with broad didactic purpose could be grouped under this heading. Thus we find it used of collections of maxims (most frequently), but also of texts of occupational guidance, model letters for students, political pamphlets, word lists, and so on. Anything, in fact, within the purview of the teacher-scribe that could be used for instruction fell broadly under this rubric.

It is, however, to aphoristic literature that the term is most often applied. A piece will begin with some such introduction as "Here begins the life-teaching, the attestations to well-being, all instructions of executive deportment and the regular procedure of courtiers" or "Here begins the instruction that educates the heart and witnesses to the ignorant." The inclusion of "testimonies" and "sayings of the way of life" generally denotes the incorporation of a collection of proverbs. The usual context of wisdom literature is the father-to-son chat, in which fatherly advice is given to the young on how to win friends and influence people and, generally, how to lead a successful life. Much of the worldly wisdom set forth suggests an origin in everyday life and a primary oral transmission. Nevertheless, from the earliest period canonical versions of many books of wisdom existed, in which wording and sequence of pericopes were of paramount importance; and the motif of a wise man's words being taken down in writing at the moment of delivery is a commonplace in Egyptian literature.

Collections of wise sayings originate in all periods of Egyptian history. Purporting to be the work of a vizier of the fifth dynasty (c. twenty-fifth century BCE), the *Wisdom of Ptahhotpe* is known in a complete text, while the wisdom writings under the names of Prince Hordjedef and Vizier Kagemni, also known Old Kingdom figures, have survived in less satisfactory condition. From the First Intermediate Period comes the *Instruction for King Merikare* (c. 2075 BCE), a fascinating treatise on statecraft written by a king of the tenth dynasty for his son and successor on the throne. The twelfth dynasty has bequeathed us a wealth of wisdom literature, including the posthumous *Instruction of Amenemhet,* a political tract "written" from the grave and placed in the mouth of the assassinated founder of the house; a "loyalist" treatise supporting adherence to the pharaonic government; a "satire" of the trades, an early schoolboy text advocating the scribal calling; and several minor collections of maxims. The teachings of Ani and the thirty wise sayings of Amenemope come from the later New Kingdom; and the first millennium BCE has preserved the *Wisdom of Onkhsheshongy* and Papyrus Insinger, both of which show traces of foreign influence.

Although very much akin in form and content to its biblical or Akkadian counterparts, Egyptian wisdom literature had only limited influence abroad. The *Wisdom of Amenemope* had long been considered (rightly) the basis of *Proverbs* 30, and Psalm 104 seems to be more than an echo of Akhenaton's "teaching," as represented in his hymn to the sun disk (fourteenth century BCE). But biblical, Mesopotamian, and Greek folklore with a "wisdom" element owe more to local themes and sources than to Egypt (Williams, 1972, 1981).

Temple Libraries. While the "House of the God's Book" was originally, in the Old Kingdom, a secular registry office for royal rescripts, by the Middle Kingdom the term *god* was being construed as a reference not to the king but to a member of the pantheon, and the expression was coming to mean "temple library" (Schott, 1972, 1977). Occasionally alternating with such terms as *chamber, office,* or *hall of writings* (the last a repository of more secular documents), this department of temple administration was overseen by librarians ("keepers of the writings"), and was open to lector-priests, scribes of the god's book, and temple scribes in general. Scrolls were copied out in an adjacent scriptorium and then deposited in the library in wooden chests, less frequently in jars. Associated with the sacred library but outside the temple proper was the "House of Life," an institution open only to the highest grade of skilled scribes and to the king. Here were copied and composed the most holy rituals, hymns, commentaries, and magical texts, and here also the most esoteric rites were performed in secret.

As an archive constantly referred to in all aspects of temple life and procedure, the temple library was treated by the Egyptians as their most precious textual resource. Thoth, the inventor and master of the hieroglyphs, was the library's patron, and Seshat, the goddess of books, presided over its contents. The scribes were proud of their ability to compose, copy, and edit texts, and were strictly enjoined not to let their "fingers tamper with the god's words." One senses a continuum in the life of temple archives over many centuries in the three and a half millennia of Egyptian history. Users could ferret out scrolls of high antiquity and marvel at the difficult syntax and archaic vocabulary. The most skilled scribes boasted of their ability to restore what was lost in lacunae in moth-eaten originals. Although many such references are cliché-ridden, there is every reason to believe that a priestly scribe such as Manetho, living in the third century BCE, had access to written sources ranging back through three millennia. In our own time, although no temple library has survived intact, the contents of a typical collection are easy to reconstruct from the copious references in inscriptions and from a few papyrus caches (Reymond, 1977; Redford, 1985).

Ritual texts. Several terms designate this broad genre. The oldest, which is attested already at the dawn of Egyptian history, is *hebet* ("ritual book"), the special preserve of the *chery-hebet* (lector-priest; lit., "he who carries the ritual book"). This was a sort of breviary or missal, giving the order of service and the texts that were to be read. Occasionally the book was identified with a particular cult, as "the *hebet* of the temple of Ptah." Slightly later terms, used of documents as well as in the abstract, were *net-ʿ* ("customary procedure, ritual"; also pressed into service to render the Akkadian word for "treaty") and *iru* ("cultic forms/acts"). Sometimes "book of [such and such a rite]" is substituted for *net-ʿ*. During the Middle Kingdom a compendious order of service was referred to as "the complete [guide]," and the requirements of the ritual and, curiously, the spells to be recited were contained in the "god's offering-book." Among the few ritual papyri that have survived, one may cite a funerary ritual and a rite of succession from the Middle Kingdom, a daily offering liturgy from the New Kingdom, and rituals for various gods' festivals from the Late Period. It is important to note that, whatever mnemonic devices a priest may have employed, a ritual was always performed "in accordance with that which is in writing."

Beatifications. The category of "beatifications" (*sakhu,* from a causative root meaning "to turn someone into a glorified spirit") encompasses texts intended to "actualize" the future glorified state of the deceased in the beyond. The term is often used in captions to a scene depicting the lector-priest reading from a scroll on the day of burial. Oblique references make plain the esoteric nature of the material in their allusion to "that secret writing of the lector-priest's craft," by which beatifications are undoubtedly meant. In all probability this is the rubric under which the ancients classified such collections of mortuary spells as the Pyramid Texts and the Coffin Texts, and there can be little doubt that they were intended to be read aloud.

Hymns. In Egyptian the hymn goes under several designations. Most common is *duau* ("adoration"); less frequent, *senemehu* or *sensu* ("supplication"). Often inscribed on stelae, this adoration of the deity is sometimes explicit in its purpose, "propitiating the spirit" of the gods or goddesses addressed. Hymns are often characterized by the recurrent refrain "Hail to thee!" followed by a direct invocation of the deity, replete with epithets. Less often the key words are "Praise to thee!" The genre includes such formal hymns as cultic supplications to individual gods, litanies, and even royal apologias; but it also encompasses the popular, private hymns to the sun god at dawn and sunset, and even the inscribed "testimonies" of the semiliterate class of workers, witnessing to healing and forgiveness. By extension *duau* may also be applied to the "adorations" of Hathor, goddess of love (i.e. to love poetry). The term can refer as well to the outburst of praise, spontaneous or formal, of the king by the people.

Several longer hymns, intended for temple service, were nonetheless didactic in nature. Such were the hymns to Re-Harakhty, Amun-Re, the sun disk, and Ptah, which are known from New Kingdom exemplars. These display a sophisticated universalism, and preach (in the case of the hymn to Ptah) the same syncretistic deism as is found in the *Memphite Theology*. The monotheism of the hymn to the sun disk is well known.

Most examples imply or state directly that the hymns are to be intoned, either by private individuals as pious acts of devotion, or in a temple context by a priest or a choir. In temple ritual the papyrus containing the order of service will often give only the *incipit* of a hymn; the choristers and the celebrant undoubtedly knew it by heart.

Mythological compendiums. The Egyptians loved to compile catalogs of the salient features of the cult(s) and of the gods and their mythology for a particular nome or group of nomes. Known especially from the first millennium BCE, the genre undoubtedly has an earlier history, which is today, unfortunately, not directly attested. Late hieroglyphic texts refer to the scroll of the *Directory of Mounds of the Early Primaeval Ones* and the *Reckoning of Every Cult Seat and the Knowing of What Is in Them*. Elsewhere we hear of the *Great Plan of the Two Lands*, which contained information on Egypt and its arable land.

Chronicles and narratives. Chronicles cannot be identified as a native Egyptian genre, the form being derived from Babylonia some time in the first millennium BCE. From the early Ptolemaic period (third century BCE) comes the so-called Demotic Chronicle, in actuality a tendentious interpretation of selected events in the recent past that in form and inspiration shows strong influence from Asia. Narratives are more common. The papyrus fragments from the library of the temple of Sobek in the Fayum (the lakeland immediately west of the Nile, about fifty miles south of present-day Cairo) contained a number of quasi-legendary romances, including stories of the magician Setna, the *Romance of King Petubastis*, the story of King Djoser and his Assyrian campaign, the Amazon romance, and the *Prophecy of the Lamb*. Similar material has been unearthed in temple libraries at Saqqara, the necropolis of Memphis (Redford, 1985, chap. 8).

King-lists and offering-lists. It is most probable that temple libraries possessed historical source material in the form of king-lists and offering-lists. The offering cult of the royal ancestors had been maintained in the chief temples in the land from the earliest dynasties, and had involved an "offering invocation" in which the spirits of the deceased kings and queens were called by name to the offering table. From the twelfth dynasty at latest there had existed a formal king-list, tracing the occupancy of the pharaonic seat from the creator Ptah through an unbroken line of divine and human incumbents. Such a king-list was known to and used by Manetho, the priest-scribe who wrote a history of Egypt in Greek (third century BCE), and the relative accuracy of his *Aegyptiaca* attests to its uninterrupted and sober transmission (Waddell, 1940; Redford, 1985).

Annals of the gods. Closely allied to the compendiums mentioned above is a type of document purporting to give an account of divine acts. Derived from an old word for "annals" used originally of the yearly records of the king, the "annals of the gods" first appeared in texts of the New Kingdom and, although we lack examples, they probably contained cosmogonic and mythological material. These "mighty acts of the gods," which of course reflect the historicization of the world of the gods, were the special preserve of the House of Life. Examples are rare in the New Kingdom. The *Book of the Cow of Heaven*, though used as a set of magic spells in the extant versions, contains an etiological account of the reign of Re (Hornung, 1981). Both Ramses II (c. 1304–1237 BCE) and Ramses IV (c. 1167–1161 BCE) refer to certain books in the House of Life that contain cosmogonic material from the reigns of the gods. Late versions of well-known myths that might qualify for inclusion in this genre are the reigns of Shu and Geb from the *Wady el-Arish naos*, the myth of Horus of Edfu, and the *Expulsion of Seth*. In using these well-known pieces, however, it is well to remember that they were recast in a period of history (fourth century BCE) when xenophobia and paranoia because of foreign conquest lent a tendentious tone to theme and content.

Directories and prescriptions. Prescriptive manuals abounded, especially in the late period. One of the earliest was the *Great Inventory*, the standard compilation of directions for the manufacture of cult images and paraphernalia, the decoration of shrines, and so on. Manuals on the construction and decoration of temples were often ascribed to Imhotep, the almost-legendary savant of the reign of Djoser (twenty-seventh century BCE). Under the same heading are directories of purification, manuals of offering, and festival calendars.

Omen texts and related genres. *Omina* are not common in the Egyptian religious corpus since they are confined to the Late Period, when contact with Mesopotamia was more frequent. Hemerologies and oneiromancies, on the other hand, enjoyed native popularity and development at an early stage of Egyptian history. The former were apparently called "That Which Is in the Year," though known exemplars assign a variety of specific titles. What is important is that the explanation of why a particular day was considered propitious or inimical was always assigned a mythological context (Brunner-Traut, 1981), and in the process a myth was often adumbrated. Egyptians, like most ancient peoples, took dreams seriously, and this is reflected in the literature.

Oracle texts. The belief that a god made his will known through oracular utterances can be traced back to a relatively early period in Egypt's history, but the practice of employing oracles as an administrative and juridical mechanism dates from the nineteenth dynasty (thirteenth century BCE). Whether in the seclusion of the shrine or at the public procession of the god in his sacred bark, eliciting the god's response to solve a problem became so common that a special scribal office was called into being, that of "the scribe of oracles," to keep the records. Examples of the questions put to the god (demanding affirmative or negative responses) are extant, as are the beautiful papyrus records of the petitioner's appeal and the results. Often, especially from the twentieth to the twenty-second dynasties (c. 1200–730 BCE), a hieroglyphic record of the oracle, including a vignette showing the petitioner(s) and the divine bark, might be set up in a prominent place in the temple to serve as a legal record.

Medical texts. The writing of medical prescriptions and procedures and of the pharmacopoeia was one of the earliest acts of scribal activity in ancient Egypt. Later traditions are unanimous in ascribing certain medical books to the kings and wise men of the Old Kingdom, and in some cases the archaic syntax and vocabulary of surviving papyri bear this out. Written and edited by the sacred scribes associated with the House of Life, the papyri that have come down to us are collections of cases and recipes more or less united in common areas of interest or practice. Thus we have papyri on gynecology (P. Kahun), obstetrics and pediatrics (P. Ramesseum and P. Carlsberg), surgery (P. Edwin Smith), and veterinary medicine (P. Kahun); in some of the longest papyri (P. Ebers and the Berlin and London papyri) we have a miscellany of prescriptions and recipes. References to works now lost show specialization in diseases of the heart, eye, and abdomen, in anatomy and hygiene. While many magical incantations are found throughout these papyri in greater or smaller concentrations, there is everywhere in evidence an insight into pathology and pharmacology that is based on objective diagnosis and scientific deduction.

Administrative texts. In ancient Egypt the temple was not only the "god's mansion" where he resided and was ministered to by his servants, the priests, but also the hub of a large landowning institution comprising a number of disparate organs of production. Tenant farmers, herdsmen, artisans, and merchants all worked for their master, the god, and the revenue they raised provided a sizable income for the temple estate. The business documents that recorded this commercial aspect of temple life formed a major segment of any temple's archives. One of the oldest caches of papyri extant today, the Abusir Papyri, reflects the contents of such an archive from the pyramid-temple of Neferirkare I of the fifth dynasty, spanning a period of approximately fifty years several generations after the death of the king (c. 2370–2320 BCE). Here we find inventories of temple furniture, daily records of income, monthly accounts of food distribution and expenditures, and duty tables. In the Middle Kingdom, temple daybooks put in an appearance. These record income and disbursements, letters received in the temple office, celestial observations, work assignments, lists of personnel, records of cultic celebrations, and so on, all organized simply by calendrical notation. Throughout most periods, temple libraries contained inventories of land, personnel, and goods receivable; priestly correspondence; and account texts. Taxation documents, specifying quotas levied on sharecroppers and herdsmen on the temple estates or placed under obligation by the crown, were also to be found in the library. Moreover, during imperial times lists of booty from foreign wars were delivered to the temples and deposited in papyrus form in the archives there. Any records of special importance to the temple community, such as royal decrees, inductions and promotions of priests, and lists of royal and private bequests, were often culled from their primary locus in daybooks and the like, and inscribed in more permanent form on stelae, walls, and architraves for ease of reference (Redford, 1985; Reymond, 1977).

In addition to the above textual classifications, many of the genres already discussed, such as wisdom literature and magical texts, were also represented in temple libraries. There is every reason to believe that information on such subjects as geography, mineralogy, and biology was to be found there as well, but it is difficult to say whether any ancient categories corresponded to these modern terms of disciplinary research.

Temple Inscriptions. The wall space provided by temple construction in ancient Egypt was used as a medium for didactic, reference, and propaganda purposes. Since the source for almost all of this textual and iconographic decoration was the temple library, temples that have survived provide a most precious record of genres whose originals have perished.

For the Old Kingdom the material is limited to a handful of royal mortuary establishments (pyramid-temples). Here the range of inscriptions is wider and more varied than was later to be the case. Decorated walls display scenes and texts recounting battles, the gathering of booty, the transportation of captives, construction, and famine, as well as singing, dancing, and royal processions. The celebration of festivals (especially the jubilee) is also present in the subject matter, but purely cultic commemoration is not as common as might be thought. The listing of townships and estates as part of the record of endowment of the temple takes the form of servant personifications, arranged in rows along the bases of walls.

While little remains from the Middle Kingdom—the eleventh-dynasty temples show *mutatis mutandis* a continuation of Old Kingdom themes, while the twelfth has left virtually nothing—the New Kingdom and later periods have bequeathed us a wealth of inscriptional and iconographic evidence. As a rule, a New Kingdom "processional" (axial) temple will display on its wall surfaces texts appropriate to the status of those allowed to view them. Thus, those parts of the temple on view to the laity—external walls, pylon, and first court—are often decorated with vaguely "propagandistic" intent, and the repertoire tends toward stereotype. Here are scenes and texts of foreign wars, standard head-smiting scenes, lists of conquered places, and the welcoming of the king by the god (which continues as a major motif throughout the temple).

Most often, walls of inner courts and hypostyle hall are adorned with sequences of vignettes and accompanying texts showing the daily liturgy of waking, adorning, and offering to the god, with the king as celebrant, taken from the ritual books of the temple. Specific festivals, such as those of the jubilee, coronation, the gods Sokar and Min, the Opet feast, the foundation of the temple, and so on, are often elaborately depicted with large excerpts of accompanying texts. Processions of princes and princesses, personifications of townships, towns, and the Nile are used as decorative dadoes, or as scenes in their own right. Rooms for storage and the preparation of cult requirements are decorated with offering scenes of a "neutral" nature, which makes it difficult to ascertain the precise use of some rooms. Certain temples have preserved the records of rituals or beliefs peculiar to their localities. One may mention in this regard the Osirian rites recorded in the Sety I temple at Abydos, the Horian myths at Edfu, the ritual adapted for royal use in the Theban mortuary temples, and the jubilee rites at Soleb, Karnak, and Bubastis.

The temple courts and the immediate surroundings of the structure were deemed suitable for the display of texts set up for a variety of purposes. Prominence of place was given to royal inscriptions, either on freestanding stelae or on temple walls. These are records of royal acts or regulatory decrees affecting the temple (frequently the product of a king's speech delivered at a "royal sitting"), and often involve building inscriptions and offering endowments. The contents of such inscriptions, though rhetorically embellished for popular consumption, are usually derived from such official records as the "daybook of the king's house."

Another type of stela, set up before or just inside the temple, was inscribed with a royal encomium. Clearly associated with occasions of oral delivery, such adulations took the form either of stereotyped praise of the king in prose for his "mighty acts" or deeds, or, more often (especially in the later New Kingdom), a formal "song" to be sung to harp accompaniment, each strophe ending with the names of the king. Private individuals of high rank were allowed to set up, in an ambulatory within the temple, statues of themselves with lengthy inscriptions. Such statue inscriptions, while most often cast in the form of an address to the passerby, inevitably incorporate biographical and genealogical information of the highest importance. Citizens of low rank might, certainly in smaller temples, hope to be able to set up hymns, prayers, and testimonials to the gods on stelae where the god might see them and honor their requests.

The best-preserved temples in Egypt date from the fourth century BCE to the first century CE, and ultimately reflect the *risorgimento* of the cult during the Saite Period (664–525 BCE). In the main they follow the New Kingdom tradition, but with some modifications:

1. Offering vignettes showing king or god before the divine owner of the temple or his guests, and derived from the daily offering liturgy, are now repeated on the walls, both interior and exterior, *ad nauseam*.
2. The mystic birth of the god-child, offspring of the goddess of the temple, is given great prominence in text and iconography.
3. The stone *naos* wherein the cult image resides has become a major focus of the rites, and its sides are covered with a representative list of all the divine denizens of the temple.
4. One senses a tendency to inscribe large excerpts from ritual books, mythological compendiums, and hymns on the walls, wherever space is available, conveying a false sense of *horor vacui*.

These later temples contain a wealth of (local) mythological material, but the degree to which they reflect genuinely ancient beliefs and practices is unclear.

BIBLIOGRAPHY

Allen, Thomas George, ed. *The Book of the Dead.* Chicago, 1974. The most authoritative translation of the *Book of Going Forth by Day* in English, by a scholar who devoted his life to its study.

Anthes, Rudolf. "Egyptian Theology in the Third Millennium B.C." *Journal of Near Eastern Studies* 18 (July 1959): 169–212. The most detailed and incisive treatment of basic mythological concepts in ancient Egypt, using mainly the evidence of the Pyramid Texts.

Barta, Winfried. *Die altägyptische Opferliste von der Frühzeit bis zur griechisch-römischer Epoche.* Berlin, 1963. The standard treatment of the most common type of funerary text in ancient Egyptian tombs.

Barta, Winfried. *Die Bedeutung der Pyramidentexte für den verstorbenen König.* Munich, 1981. An excellent summary, with useful indexes and tables, of the major theories on the origins and purpose of the Pyramid Texts.

Borghouts, J. F., trans. *Ancient Egyptian Magical Texts.* Leiden, 1978. A well-written and well-translated compendium of representative incantations, with a brief but useful commentary.

Brunner-Traut, Emma. *Gelebte Mythen.* Darmstadt, 1981. A collection of five articles on specific aspects of Egyptian mythology, with a pithy introduction, useful for the student.

Faulkner, Raymond, trans. and ed. *The Ancient Egyptian Pyramid Texts.* Oxford, 1969. The most up-to-date translation into English of this early corpus of texts.

Faulkner, Raymond, trans. and ed. *The Ancient Egyptian Coffin Texts.* 3 vols. Warminster, 1973–1978. The best—and the only—comprehensive translation of the Coffin Texts available.

Griffiths, J. Gwyn, trans. *Plutarch's De Iside et Osiride.* Cardiff, 1970. There is no more authoritative treatment of the Osirian cycle of deities and their mythology in any language than this work. It is the best translation and commentary on Plutarch's *De Iside* available today.

Hornung, Erik. "Jenseitsführer." In *Lexikon der Ägyptologie,* compiled by Hans Wolfgang Helck and Eberhard Otto, vol. 3. Wiesbaden, 1980. The most recent introduction to New Kingdom literature relating to the underworld.

Hornung, Erik. *Das Buch des Himmelskuh.* Göttingen, 1981. A new publication and commentary of a long-known "underworld" book, containing the story of the destruction of mankind.

Junge, Friedrich. "Die Welt der Klagen." In *Fragen an die altägyptische Literatur,* edited by Jan Assmann et al., pp. 275–285. Wiesbaden, 1977. A study of those Middle Kingdom compositions that describe the anarchy ensuing upon the collapse of society.

Lichtheim, Miriam. *Ancient Egyptian Literature: A Book of Readings.* 3 vols. Berkeley, 1973–1980. A selection of representative texts from various genres. The translations are first-rate, and the commentary brief but very useful for the novice.

Redford, Donald B. *King-lists, Annals and Daybooks.* Toronto, 1985. A contribution to the historiography of ancient Egypt. Manetho is treated in some detail.

Reymond, Eve A. E., trans. *From Ancient Egyptian Hermetic Writings.* Vienna, 1977. Fragmentary ritual and prescriptive texts on temple buildings and cult procedure from a temple library of the Roman period. The translation is not always as reliable as one would like.

Schott, E. "Bücher und Bibliotheken im alten Ägypten." *Göttinger Miszellen* 1 (1972): 24–27 and 25 (1977): 73–75. A brief statement of work done on the study of ancient Egyptian books and libraries, an area of research in which the author's late husband excelled.

Schott, Siegfried. *Mythe und Mythenbildung im alten Ägypten.* Leipzig, 1945. A fundamental investigation of the myth-making process in ancient Egypt.

Sethe, Kurt H., ed. and trans. *Dramatische Texte zu altägyptischen Mysterienspielen.* Leipzig, 1928. A fundamental work on Egyptian religion, incorporating two studies: (1) a translation and interpretation of the *Memphite Theology;* (2) the text of a ritual papyrus of Middle Kingdom date in the British Museum.

Simpson, William K., ed. *The Literature of Ancient Egypt.* New Haven, 1973. A set of translations, by leading Egyptologists, of selected stories, wisdom texts, and poetry.

Waddell, W. G. *Manetho.* London, 1940. The only accessible translation of the history of Egypt by Manetho (third century BCE). The commentary is slim and occasionally inaccurate.

Williams, R. J. "Reflections on the Lebensmüde." *Journal of Egyptian Archaeology* 48 (1962): 49–56. Possibly the most judicious assessment of the enigmatic dialogue that goes under the title *The Man Who Was Tired of Life.*

Williams, R. J. "Scribal Training in Ancient Egypt." *Journal of the American Oriental Society* 92 (April–June 1972): 214–221.

Williams, R. J. "The Sages of Ancient Egypt in the Light of Recent Scholarship." *Journal of the American Oriental Society* 101 (January–March 1981): 1–19. An excellent summing-up of present work in the sphere of Egyptian wisdom literature, with complete bibliography.

DONALD B. REDFORD

History of Study

The classical authors Herodotus, Diodorus Siculus, and Plutarch preserved at least some useful information about both the mythology and the religion of ancient Egypt. In particular, Plutarch's work *Concerning Isis and Osiris* proves to be not far off the mark when compared with more ancient but less complete sources, and it provides the basis for our knowledge of some of the major mythological concepts, and even state doctrines, that the Egyptians produced and maintained.

The decipherment of Egyptian hieroglyphic writing and the preliminary documentation of the great temples, begun in the first half of the nineteenth century, marked the real beginning of modern Egyptology as well as the history of the study of Egyptian religion. The work of publishing the texts on temple walls is ongoing, although much progress has been made on major temples at various sites. The texts of the temple of Seti I at Abydos were largely recorded by means of reinforced photographs made by Amice M. Calverly and published in four elephant folios by the Egypt Exploration Society (London, 1933–1958). The texts in the temple of Ramses III at Medinet Habu were essentially completely recorded in facsimile drawings by the Epigraphic Survey of the Oriental Institute of the University of Chicago and published as *Medinet Habu,* 8 vols. (Chicago, 1930–

1970). Finally, the texts in the Ptolemaic temples of Edfu, Esna, and Dendera are detailed in more than two dozen volumes, published for the most part by the Institut Français d'Archéologie Orientale in Cairo between 1870 and 1985. These are as follows: *Le temple d'Édfou*, edited by Émile G. Chassinat, 14 vols. (Cairo, 1892–1934), *Le temple d'Esna*, edited by Serge Sauneron, 8 vols. (Cairo, 1959–1982), *Dendérah*, edited by Auguste Mariette, 5 vols. (Paris, 1870–1880), and *Le temple de Dendara*, edited by Émile G. Chassinat, 8 vols. (Cairo, 1934–1978).

Study of the *Book of Going Forth by Day* (also called the *Book of the Dead*) began with Karl Richard Lepsius's publication, titled *Das Todtenbuch der Ägypter* (Leipzig, 1842), of a Ptolemaic-period papyrus in the Turin collection. The major edition, *Das aegyptische Todtenbuch der XVIII. bis XX. Dynastie*, which included a good selection of the earlier New Kingdom parallels presented for easy comparison, was produced by Édouard Naville in three volumes (Berlin, 1886). This work relied on the order of the chapters in the Late Period Turin manuscript, yet despite this, the book's lack of line numbers for separate manuscripts, and its numerous errors, it remains the standard text up to the present. E. A. Wallis Budge published separately several manuscripts of the *Book of Going Forth by Day* in the British Museum collection, and also *The Chapters of Coming Forth by Day* (London, 1898), a three-volume set of text, vocabulary, and translation. This work is now dated, but it was also not up to the standards of its own time. It is, however, regularly used for *Book of Going Forth by Day* references in the relevant English-language grammars and dictionaries, which are to page and line of Budge's text volume. Since later editions and all subsequent reprints of Budge's *Book of the Dead* (first published in London in 1901) have a different pagination and layout, these cannot be used to locate such references and hence are largely useless.

While a new edition of the text of the *Book of Going Forth by Day* is sorely needed, with account taken of the order of the texts on the various manuscripts from different periods, several up-to-date translations are available, and certainly considerable effort has been expended in dealing with the formalized garbling found in this body of funerary literature. Thomas George Allen did an exemplary job in his *The Egyptian Book of the Dead: Documents in the Oriental Institute Museum* (Chicago, 1960); his translation of all the spells in his *Book of the Dead or Going Forth by Day* (Chicago, 1974) is quite adequate for the text but lacks the illustrative vignettes. Paul Barguet's translation, *Le Livre des Morts des anciens Égyptiens* (Paris, 1967) made use of the earlier Coffin Text parallels, when available, to provide less garbled versions and a more readable translation. Raymond Faulkner's literal translation, *The Book of the Dead* (New York, 1972) was reissued by Carol Andrews as *The Ancient Egyptian Book of the Dead* (London, 1985), with numerous illustrations; it probably deserves to become the most popular edition for English readers. Erik Hornung's *Das Totenbuch* (Zurich, 1979) supplies the need for an up-to-date presentation of the work in German.

After the Pyramid Texts were discovered, their publication was first begun by Gaston Maspero in five articles (in twelve parts) appearing in *Recueil de Travaux* (1882–1893). Kurt H. Sethe's *Die altägyptischen Pyramidentexte*, 4 vols. (Leipzig, 1908–1922), with paralleled versions oddly transposed to horizontal lines and with texts generally numbered proceeding from the interior rooms outward to the entrance halls, is, for all its technical flaws, a very accurate text edition and continues to be the standard text reference. Sethe's *Übersetzung und Kommentar zu den altägyptischen Pyramidentexten*, 6 vols. (Glückstadt, n.d.) has largely influenced all subsequent translations. Samuel A. B. Mercer's English translation, *The Pyramid Texts in Translation and Commentary*, 4 vols. (New York, 1952), is primarily based on Sethe's German text, but the chapters on various topics in volume 4 of this set contain many useful contributions. Raymond Faulkner's literal translation of the texts in Sethe's edition appeared as *The Ancient Egyptian Pyramid Texts* (Oxford, 1969) just after Alexandre Piankoff published the *Pyramid of Unas* for the Bollingen Foundation Series (Princeton, 1968). This last work has photographs of the original texts and proceeds more logically from the entrance to the antechamber through to the burial chamber, while Piankoff's translations are more original, although often less accurate. Thomas George Allen's *Occurrences of the Pyramid Texts* (Chicago, 1950) provided a very useful listing of the sequence of these texts on the early documents and references to later parallels, whether complete or partial, together with bibliographic references.

Pierre Lacau had already begun publishing the Coffin Texts in the Egyptian Museum at Cairo (*Sarcophages antérieurs au Nouvel Empire*, 2 vols., Cairo, 1904–1906), when James H. Breasted organized an international effort to attack the problem of editing this corpus of funerary literature. The publication of these texts, as *The Egyptian Coffin Texts*, 7 vols. (Chicago, 1935–1961), fell to Adriaan de Buck, who retained the original vertical columns and line numbers but excluded any texts paralleling what had already been published as Pyramid Texts. Louis Speleers's *Textes des cercueils du Moyen Empire égyptien* (Brussels, 1947) was a translation of the first two of de Buck's volumes, and the entire translation has now been published by Raymond Faulkner in three volumes (Oxford, 1973–1978). Reinhard Grieshammer's *Die Altägyptischen Sargtexte in der Forschung seit 1936* (Wiesbaden, 1974) is a bibliography of works dealing with the Coffin Texts, and Leonard H. Lesko's *Index of the Spells on Egyptian Middle Kingdom Coffins and Related Documents* (Berkeley, 1979) shows which texts occurred in what order on all the separate documents.

The numerous works by E. A. Wallis Budge dealing with many aspects of Egyptian religion cover so much material and have so much intuitive speculation that some of what he presented is surely correct, but his work must be dealt with by specialists with the same critical scrutiny that would be given to classical sources. In the list that follows, only those studies that still have considerable scientific merit or that have resulted in substantial progress in the field are included, and these are now practically limited to the twentieth century.

Adolf Erman's *Die Ägyptische Religion* (Berlin, 1905; 3d ed., *Die Religion der Ägypter*, Berlin, 1934) is probably the earliest general survey of the field that can still be profitably consulted. Erman's knowledge of the texts and understanding of the psychology (if not the religiosity) of the Egyptians made this a valuable contribution originally, and in many respects it is still unsurpassed.

James H. Breasted's *Development of Religion and Thought in Ancient Egypt* (New York, 1912) was remarkable for the large number of significant observations he made on the basis of a first reading of the difficult Pyramid Texts that Sethe had recently published. It also presented an explanation of the process that he saw in religion from earliest times to the New Kingdom. In the introduction to the reissue of this book (New York, 1959), John A. Wilson commented: "All subsequent studies of ancient Egyptian religion and thought have been indebted to this book. Some . . . have gone on to amplify or modify details. Others . . . have tried to remove from the story the sense of a continuous forward movement." As a matter of fact, the broad outline that Breasted presented of the osirianization of originally solar texts is probably untenable now, but the wealth of detail presented is still fascinating. His theory of the "democratization of the Hereafter" is essentially correct, although many details can be modified.

Karl Alfred Wiedemann, in his article "God (Egyptian)," and A. M. Blackman, in "Priest, Priesthood (Egyptian)," in vols. 6 and 10, respectively, of the *Encyclopaedia of Religion and Ethics*, edited by James Hastings (Edinburgh, 1913, 1919), collected their data carefully and brought considerable order to this area of the study of Egyptian religion for at least several decades. Günther Roeder provided an updated survey of Egyptian religious documents in *Urkunden zur Religion des alten Ägypten* (Jena, 1915), and Hermann Kees's *Totenbglauben und Jenseitsvorstellungen der alten Ägypter* (Leipzig, 1926) was a much-needed treatise on the early mortuary literature and the guidebooks to the beyond. This major contribution was somewhat flawed by overly subjective translations and restorations, but it was later revised for a second edition (Berlin, 1956). Kurt Sethe, besides providing so much source material in his text, translation, and commentary on the Pyramid Texts, also stirred up considerable controversy with his discussion of the gods and their cults in prehistoric Egypt in his *Urgeschichte und älteste Religion der Ägypter* (Leipzig, 1930). Even more impressive, however, was his *Amun und die acht Urgötter von Hermopolis* (Berlin, 1929), which assembled the data dealing with the Hermopolitan ogdoad from many sites and all periods in order to reconstruct what is known of this early cosmogony and its connection with later cult centers. Gustave Lefebvre's *Histoire des grands prêtres d'Amon de Karnak* (Paris, 1929) is of greater value to historians of Egypt than to historians of religion, but it does detail the growing wealth and secular power that eventually led to the regal status of the high priests at Thebes. Breasted's *Dawn of Conscience* (New York, 1933) was a rather subjective assessment of the Egyptians as biblical precursors.

In 1941 Kees brought out his *Götterglaube im alten Ägypten* (2d ed., Berlin, 1956); it is useful for its broad scope and topographical concerns, but it is also a response to Sethe's *Urgeschichte.* Gerald A. Wainright's *Sky Religion* (Cambridge, 1938) certainly took a new direction, and probably should have left a greater impression, but his case was not made convincingly enough. Jacques Vandier's *Religion égyptienne* (Paris, 1944) has become a classic of sorts, partly because of its extensive up-to-date bibliography. Henri Frankfort's *Intellectual Adventure of Ancient Man* (Chicago, 1946) is important not only for his remarks on mythopoeic thought and the idea of the Egyptians' "multiplicity of approaches" as an alternative to the "syncretism" of Breasted, but also for John A. Wilson's chapters (pp. 39–133) describing Egyptian cosmology and the cosmogonies. Frankfort's *Kingship and the Gods* (Chicago, 1948) has had great impact for many years, but it would now have to be modified to some extent to save what merit the thesis has from being discarded altogether. His *Ancient Egyptian Religion* (New York, 1948) was written from the point of view of the comparatist—a largely anthropological approach. The title was presumptuous and much of the book was speculative, but it does have a few good notions.

In 1952, Jaroslav Černý published a series of his lectures under the title *Ancient Egyptian Religion* (London, 1952). They were subjective, generalized, and not thoroughly documented, but they had some insightful observations and filled a need. While the book is far from the most important contribution to Egyptology by this great philologist, it will continue to be his most popular and widely read work. That same year appeared a very wide-ranging, practical work, Hans Bonnet's *Reallexikon der ägyptischen Religionsgeschichte* (Berlin, 1952). It covered almost all aspects of Egyptian religion in summary articles listed alphabetically and including the latest bibliography. Harold Idris Bell's *Cults and Creeds of Graeco-Roman Egypt* appeared the following year (Liverpool, 1953), and this work has continued to fill the need for something of its kind dealing with the latest periods in Egypt. It is based primarily on classical sources and has rather little about the native Egyptians.

Serge Sauneron's *Les prêtres de l'ancienne Égypte* (Paris, 1957) is a useful survey with a great deal of information not readily available elsewhere; it has also been translated into English, although this version unfortunately lacks a scholarly apparatus. In 1959, Rudolf Anthes published a remarkable article, "Egyptian Theology in the Third Millennium B.C." in the *Journal of Near Eastern Studies* 18, 1959, pp. 170–212. His approach was original, extremely objective, and unbiased, and he had managed to learn much more than was known at this time about the Egyptian gods and their relationships by carefully reexamining the earliest sources, the Pyramid Texts. A more popular version of this study appeared as the chapter "Mythology in Ancient Egypt" (pp. 15–92) in Samuel Noah Kramer's *Mythologies of the Ancient World* (New York, 1961). This too is a very fine article, although it begins with definitions that may appear disconcerting.

Siegfried Morenz's *Ägyptische Religion* (Stuttgart, 1960) has since been translated into English, as *Egyptian Religion* (Ithaca, N.Y., 1973). It is certainly the most up-to-date and complete treatment of the subject, and is most valuable for its clarity and wealth of detail. Its greatest limitation is its approach, phenomenological rather than either synchronic or diachronic, and it does show a bias for "religions of the word" over "cult religions." Jan Zandee's *Death as an Enemy* (Leiden, 1960) is a unique treatise that ties together phenomena from a wide range of Egyptian documents, apparently to provide antecedents for Christian beliefs about the afterlife. The data collected are interesting in themselves, but the link is very hypothetical.

Dieter Arnold's *Wandrelief und Raumfunktion in ägyptischen Tempeln des Neuen Reiches* (Berlin, 1962) deals systematically with the most important evidence for what took place in the Egyptian temples. M. Heerma van Voss's *De Oudste versie van Dodenboek 17a* (Leiden, 1963) is a translation and comparison of one of the most interesting Coffin Text and *Book of Going Forth by Day* spells. Following Alexandre Piankoff's preliminary work dealing with the New Kingdom guidebooks found in royal tombs, *The Tomb of Ramesses VI*, 2 vols. (Princeton, 1954), Erik Hornung produced his detailed study *Das Amduat*, 3 vols. (Wiesbaden, 1963–1967). He has continued his important work with these books by translating them in his *Ägyptische Unterweltsbücher* (Zurich, 1972) and by providing a carefully collated edition of *Das Buch von den Pforten des Jenseits* (Geneva, 1979).

The important book *A Study of the Ba Concept in Ancient Egyptian Texts* by Louis V. Žabkar (Chicago, 1968) provides not only the broad outline of what the limits of the concept often translated as "soul" were for the Egyptians, but also the specific meanings it may have had in different contexts over thousands of years. Erik Hornung's *Der Eine und die Vielen* (Darmstadt, 1971) has also been translated into English as *Conceptions of God in Ancient Egypt* (Ithaca, 1982). This outstanding work uses a wealth of detail and extensive bibliography to prove that Egyptian religion was in all periods essentially polytheistic. Leonard H. Lesko's *Ancient Egyptian Book of Two Ways* (Berkeley, 1972) presented the logic of this single lengthy composition in the Coffin Texts from El Bersha. The two different versions of the book help to explain the "democratization of the hereafter" in terms of "solarization" of the "Osirian" cult rather than vice versa. What may have taken place in the various rooms of an Egyptian temple is presented in summary fashion in A. Rosalie David's *Religious Ritual at Abydos* (Warminster, England), which uses the texts and scenes as clues and takes the mortuary temple of Seti I at Abydos as typical.

Brigitte Altenmüller's *Synkretismus in den Sargtexten* (Wiesbaden, 1975), a modern study of the term long used to describe Egyptian religion, is useful and necessary in helping us to understand this unusual ancient process. A book by Winfried Barta, *Untersuchungen zum Götterkreis der Neunheit* (Berlin, 1973) illustrates the difficulties that remain in dealing with Egyptian religion when no fewer than eighty-four different lists of the gods of the great ennead survive. Louis V. Žabkar's *Apedemak: Lion God of Meroe* (Warminster, England, 1975) shows both how much is knowable about Nubian religion and how much it has been left out of earlier discussions of Egyptian religion. Temporal and geographical considerations aside, the political and cultural links between these peoples clearly deserve more study, and Žabkar's work is a major step forward. Jan Assmann's *Liturgische Lieder an den Sonnengott* (Berlin, 1969) and his *Ägyptische Hymnen und Gebete* (Zurich, 1975) provide a detailed study of the many versions of the hymns to the rising and setting sun god that are found in nobles' tombs.

Studies dealing with individual deities have varied a great deal in their approach over the years. Some are lists of epithets, others cult studies, and still others are collections of artistic representations. Each can be quite useful for different purposes, but most of the deities are not adequately covered, nor should we expect them to be at this state of our knowledge. Among the more useful studies for this summary are J. Gwyn Griffiths's *The Origins of Osiris and His Cult* (Leiden, 1980), Maj Sandman-Holmberg's *The God Ptah* (Lund, 1946), Herman TeVelde's *Seth: God of Confusion* (Leiden, 1967), Patrick Boylan's *Thoth* (London, 1922), C. Jouco Bleeker's *Hathor and Thoth* (Leiden, 1973), Schafik Allam's *Beiträge zum Hathorkult* (Berlin, 1963), Karol Myśliwiec's *Studien zum Gott Atum* (Hildesheim, 1978–1979), and Dieter Müller's *Ägypten und die griechischen Isis-Aretalogien* (Berlin, 1961).

LEONARD H. LESKO

EIDETIC VISION. *See* Phenomenology of Religion.

EIGHTFOLD PATH. The Noble Eightfold Path (Skt., *āryāṣṭāngamārga*) was the first soteriological path enunciated by Śākyamuni Buddha. According to tradition, the Buddha preached this path immediately following his enlightenment, in his first sermon at Banaras, known as the Discourse on the Turning of the Wheel of Dharma (Pali, *Dhammacakkappavattana Sutta*). In this discourse, Śākyamuni expounded the Four Noble Truths—suffering, its cause, its cessation, and the path to cessation—and advocated the Middle Way as the basic principle of the religious life. The Middle Way avoids the extremes of hedonism and asceticism, both experienced by the Buddha as being unproductive and fruitless, as well as the dual metaphysical positions of being and nonbeing, and it affirms a critical but sensible and practical path to supreme enlightenment. This path is both a means to enlightenment and the expression of that enlightenment in daily life.

To appreciate properly the Four Noble Truths and the principle of the Middle Way in the religious history of India, it is necessary to understand the relation between the rise of Buddhism and Brahmanism, the predominant religious trend in Śākyamuni's day. The ultimate goal of Brahmanism was the realization of the unity of *ātman*, the divine personal center, and *brahman*, the divine universal center. The unity of the two led to the realization of *sat* (permanent being), *cit* (knowledge), and *ānanda* (bliss), but that insight was limited to a chosen few. What the Buddha taught, in contrast, was based on the experience of the masses of people, for whom reality was not permanent being but impermanence *(anitya)*, the common lot was not knowledge but ignorance *(avidyā)*, and life was not bliss but suffering *(duḥkha)*. He preached that the essence of a person was *anātman* (nonself), which dismantled the world view structured on the unity of *ātman* and *brahman*. This negation of the Brahmanic universe also meant the nullification of the class or caste system, which was thought to be rooted in sacred reality. Under this new dispensation, the value of a person was believed to be determined not by birth or lineage but by the conduct *(caraṇa)* that is central to the truly religious life. Thus, a low-born of noble conduct would be considered a high caste, and a person of high caste but of ignoble conduct would be regarded as low caste.

In proclaiming his revolutionary path the Buddha inherited some traditional concepts, such as *saṃsāra* and *karman*, but gave them an existential interpretation. His teachings also contained new ideas, such as the notion of *nirvāṇa*, the rejection of metaphysical speculation, and the emphasis on conduct. He also elevated the terms connoting racial or cultural superiority into words connoting high, religious ideals. Thus, the term *ārya* ("noble"), descriptive of the fair-skinned conquering race that had established the Middle Country (Madhyadeśa) in Northwest India, was appropriated by the Buddha and used to describe the nobility and truth of his teaching. Thus, it becomes an essential component in the Four Noble Truths *(catvāry āryasatyāni)* and the Noble Eightfold Path *(āryaṣṭāngamārga)*. Likewise, the term *madhyama* ("middle") was used to refer not to a sociopolitical order established by the conquering Aryan race, but to a crucial principle in the path to enlightenment, the Middle Way.

The Four Noble Truths are said to be patterned after the method of diagnosis and prognosis current in the medical science of the day. The First Noble Truth analyzes the basic human condition as suffering or dis-ease *(duḥkha)*, and the Second Noble Truth, its cause *(samudaya)*, as the insatiable thirst that drives man and keeps him within samsaric wandering. The Third Noble Truth is a prognosis of the healthy or ideal state: the extinction *(nirodha)* of thirst and the peace that ensues. The Fourth Noble Truth shows the way *(mārga)* that leads to peace, the way specifically being the Eightfold Path.

The Eightfold Path consists of right view, right thought, right speech, right conduct, right livelihood, right effort, right mindfulness, and right meditation.

While eight separate categories are listed, they are all parts of an integral discipline, and each necessarily involves the others. The adjective "right" connotes that they are all in accord with reality as it is *(yathā–bhūtaṃ)*, as opposed to the unconscious misperception and willful distortion of reality common among the unenlightened.

Right view, on an elementary level, is the appreciation of the law of *karman*, which operates through the three time worlds of past, present, and future. When one thinks according to the law of cause and effect, one is free of superstitious or irrational beliefs. On a deeper religious level it is the clear insight into the Four Noble Truths, dependent co-origination, and the understanding of life based upon these principles. Right view counteracts various kinds of beliefs that, according to the Buddha, are conducive to suffering: attachment to permanent being, whether in the external world or in the self; rejection of the law of *karman*, making claims to selfhood when there is no basis for it; eternalism, which posits a supreme being controlling human destiny; and nihilism, which holds that life is a random, haphazard event with no meaning.

When one sees life in accord with reality, then right thought, right speech, and right conduct naturally ensue. This means that our thoughts, speech, and deeds are basically free of egocentricity. In right thought we are free of the three poisons of greed, enmity, and ignorance and full of the thoughts of compassion and nonviolence. In right speech we avoid lying, slander, duplicity, careless talk, and gossip, and we speak only the truth, praise others, create harmony, and speak words that are friendly, gentle, and useful. In right conduct we avoid unnecessary injury to life, stealing, and illicit sexual contacts and strive to love all beings, give generously, preach the Dharma, and maintain proper marital relations.

All this entails right livelihood. We must secure our daily necessities of food, clothing, and shelter, but in doing so we must not become involved in professions and pastimes that hurt others, such as trading in arms, drinking, using poison, or hunting and fishing. Right livelihood, as the consequence of right thought, speech, and conduct, necessarily leads to a regulated, healthy, and productive daily regimen.

Since the maintenance of the practices described above does not come easily, right effort is stressed as central to the Eightfold Path. Effort especially is required to prevent the arising of evil, to abandon evil that has appeared, to strive for good, and to increase the good that exists. Evil here means anything that hinders the path to enlightenment, and good is that which is conducive to progression on the path. Effort is directly connected to will, patience, constancy, and courage in the face of countless obstacles we may face in life.

For effort to be properly directed it requires right mindfulness, the full awareness of everything that is happening in one's environment, including one's own body, feelings, ideas, and thought. One must remind oneself constantly of the impermanence of the world, the sufferings that abound, the nonegocentricity of self, and the impurities to which we become falsely attached. Right mindfulness is inseparable from mental alertness, vigilance, earnestness, and a sense of responsibility.

Finally, all of the above components of the Eightfold Path must be rooted in right meditation. Here meditation can refer to the various stages of meditation attained by the trained practitioner, or it can mean the single-minded concentration on the task at hand. The essential point is the unification of mind such that attention is not scattered and the mind agitated. A settled, concentrated mind is essential for success in any undertaking.

The practice of the Buddhist path is sometimes summarized as the Three Learnings: observance of precepts *(śīla)*, meditative practice *(dhyāna)*, and attainment of wisdom *(prajñā)*. When the Eightfold Path is understood in terms of the Three Learnings, right speech, right action, and right livelihood are regulated by precepts; right mindfulness and right meditation are aspects of meditative practice; and right view and right thought are related to wisdom. Right effort underlies all Three Learnings.

While the Eightfold Path is meant to lead to supreme enlightenment, it is also expressive of a sensible, practical approach to life. That is, whenever we have a goal, it is important that we have a clear understanding of what we hope to achieve, so that our thought, speech, and action coincide with the realization of that goal. This means that our entire way of living must also be conducive to that realization. And this requires constant effort, perhaps the essential component in all the different practices within Buddhism. The effort must be guided by mindfulness, so that one is constantly aware of the process leading to a fruitful end. Finally, the entire undertaking must be rooted in meditative experience, which adds clarity and power to the Eightfold Path.

In summary, the Eightfold Path was the first concrete expression of the Middle Way, a principle that is central to the subsequent developments in Buddhism. It sets the motif of Buddhist life: a practical, enlightened pursuit of daily life wherein some measure of wisdom and compassion is manifested so that all beings can manifest their full potential to create a world of equality, harmony, and peace. Whatever school one follows, such is the goal of all Buddhist undertaking.

[*See also* Four Noble Truths.]

BIBLIOGRAPHY

For the original text of the First Sermon, see the translation by C. A. F. Rhys Davids and F. L. Woodward, *The Book of the Kindred Sayings, Saṃyutta-nikāya,* vol. 5 (London, 1930), pp. 356–365. For a standard exposition of the Eightfold Path, see, for example, Walpola Rahula's *What the Buddha Taught,* 2d ed. (New York, 1974), pp. 45–50.

TAITETSU UNNO

EINSTEIN, ALBERT (1879–1955), originator of the theory of relativity and widely regarded as the greatest scientist of modern times. He was born at Ulm, Germany, of particularly loving parents who were said by friends to be "always on a honeymoon." Although Jewish by descent, the family was freethinking and cared little for religious tradition. Einstein was slow in learning to speak and was far from fluent even at age nine; his parents actually feared that he might be subnormal. Furthermore, the boy intensely disliked school and did well only in mathematics and science. He learned to play the violin in childhood and maintained a lifelong interest in music; at one point he seriously considered becoming a professional violinist.

In 1895, Einstein's plan to enroll at the Swiss Federal Polytechnic School in Zurich was frustrated when he failed the entrance examination. He managed, however, to pass the exam the following year and was graduated from the school in 1900. But formal study was so disagreeable to him that he did practically nothing for a year after graduation. He stayed in Zurich and supported himself by teaching part time, for he was unable to secure a regular academic post. In 1901 he became a Swiss citizen and also published his first scientific paper. The next year, he secured a probationary position at the Swiss patent office in Bern. There, he developed several important friendships that lasted throughout his life. Also during this period, he married a fellow student from his Zurich days.

The year 1905 was Einstein's *annus mirabilis;* while still working at the patent office, he published five papers in the *Annalen der Physik* that proved to be revolutionary. Three of the papers—among the greatest in the history of science—were, in the words of J. Robert Oppenheimer, "paralyzingly beautiful." One of them outlined Einstein's special theory of relativity, on the basis of which he derived later in the same year the well-known formula $E = mc^2$, expressing the precise quantitative relationship between a particle's energy and mass. Another of these publications was an important paper on Brownian motion, and yet another dealt with the photoelectric effect. In this work, Einstein introduced a fundamental concept of quantum physics—namely, that of quanta of light energy, which were later called photons. It was actually for his work on the photoelectric effect—not for the relativity theory—that he received the Nobel prize for physics in 1922.

Ironically, it was on the basis of Einstein's work on relativity that the University of Bern had earlier rejected him when he applied for a place on the faculty. Only in 1908, after such great physicists as Max Planck and H. A. Lorentz had recognized his genius, was he given the position at Bern. After that, academic appointments came in quick succession: in 1909, Einstein was appointed to a professorship at the university at Zurich; in 1911, to a senior professorship at the German university in Prague; and in 1912, again a position at Zurich. It was there, in 1913, that he published his first paper on the theory of general relativity. This work was brought to completion in 1916, when Einstein was a professor at the Prussian Academy and director of the Kaiser Wilhelm Institute of Physics in Berlin. Another great physicist, J. J. Thompson, called Einstein's work on the theory of general relativity "perhaps the greatest achievement in the history of human thought."

Immediately after publishing his theory of general relativity, Einstein started working out its cosmological implications, including the idea that the cosmos is, on the whole, dynamic and expanding. Back from the many travels that ensued from worldwide fame, Einstein began his last great project, the search for a unified field theory. He worked on this until the last day of his life, but the project remained unfinished. Also, by the late 1920s, the main focus of interest in physics had shifted to quantum mechanics, which proved extremely fertile in application but which lacked, as far as Einstein was concerned, philosophical rigor and aesthetic beauty. He could never accept as complete and final the probabilistic interpretation of cosmic processes offered by quantum physics, and thus he was gradually estranged from the mainstream in his field.

Einstein was always a loner, often pursuing unfashionable paths. As he, in his well-known essay "Science and Religion," wrote, "It is strange to be known so universally and yet to be so lonely." He could not accept the probabilistic interpretation of nature because of his "deep conviction of the rationality of the universe." He called this conviction a "cosmic religious feeling" and regarded it as the "strongest and noblest motive for scientific research." His intuitive feeling for this rational order was offended by quantum mechanics. He wrote to the American physicist James Franck, "I can, if the worse comes to the worst, still realize that God may have created a world in which there are no natural laws. In short, a chaos. But that there should be statistical laws with definite solutions, i.e., laws which compel God to throw the dice in each individual case, I find highly disagreeable" (*Einstein: A Centenary Volume*, p. 6).

Thoughout his life, and particularly after becoming a public figure, Einstein championed the causes of social justice, freedom of conscience, and peace. When in 1933 the political situation in Germany worsened and, as a pacifist and a Jew, Einstein became a double target for the Nazis, he decided to accept a position at the Institute for Advanced Study at Princeton, New Jersey. He retired from the institute in 1945 but stayed on in Princeton, often working at the institute. In 1952 he was offered the presidency of Israel, which he declined. Einstein was active and mentally vigorous until the end. He said, a few days before his death on 18 April 1955, "Here on earth I have done my job."

Einstein described his religious feeling as one of "rapturous amazement at the harmony of natural law." Many people who knew him personally insisted that he was the most religious person they had ever met. But Einstein was not religious in any churchly or denominational manner. As he said many times and in many ways, "My religion consists of a humble admiration of the illimitable superior spirit who reveals himself in the slight details we are able to perceive with our frail and feeble minds. That deeply emotional conviction of the presence of a superior reasoning power which is revealed in the incomprehensible universe forms my idea of God."

BIBLIOGRAPHY

There is no standard biography of Einstein; perhaps the best one available is Ronald W. Clark's *Einstein: The Life and Times* (New York, 1971). Leopold Infeld's *Albert Einstein: His Work and Its Influence on Our World* (New York, 1950) gives a good introduction to Einstein's scientific work by one of his collaborators. Carl Seelig's *Albert Einstein: A Documentary Biography* (London, 1956) gives the best account of Einstein's life in Switzerland, whereas Philipp Frank's *Einstein: His Life and Times* (New York, 1963) is the best report on Einstein's life in Prague. The biography by Banesh Hoffmann, with the collaboration of Helen Dukas, *Albert Einstein: Creator and Rebel* (New York, 1972), places much greater emphasis on Einstein's involvement in world affairs. The International Commission on Physics Education brought out *Einstein: A Centenary Volume*, edited by A. P. French (Cambridge, 1979); it is rich in reminiscences and contains some fine general-interest essays. *Albert Einstein: Philosopher-Scientist*, 2 vols., edited by Paul Arthur Schilpp (New York, 1951), contains Einstein's autobiography, descriptive and critical essays on his work, and Einstein's reply to these. Einstein's nonscientific writings are to be found at many places, particularly in his *Essays in Science* (1934; reprint, New York, 1955), *Out of My Later Years* (New York, 1950), and *Ideas and Opinions* (New York, 1954). The last two of these books contain his superb essay "Science and Religion."

RAVI RAVINDRA

EISAI (1141–1215), founder of the Rinzai (Chin., Linchi) school of Zen (Chin., Ch'an) in Japan. A scholarly monk and religious reformer, Eisai was also the popularizer of the practice of tea drinking in Japan. Although he began life in modest circumstances, he eventually gained the patronage of the shogun heading the warrior government, the *bakufu*, in Kamakura. With the shogun's backing he built monasteries in which Zen was fostered; he was also active in the rebuilding of monasteries of the older Buddhist schools. Eisai has been eclipsed in historical reputation by such later Rinzai monks as Daitō, Musō Soseki, Ikkyū Sōjun, and Hakuin, and by the Sōtō monk Dōgen Kigen. In his day, however, Eisai was an important figure and played a major role in securing at least partial acceptance for Zen in the Japanese religious world. Together with his near contemporaries Hōnen (1133–1212) and Shinran (1173–1262), the founders of popular Japanese Pure Land Buddhism, Eisai can be counted among the figures contributing to the Buddhist reformation of the thirteenth century.

Eisai's full religious name is Myōan Eisai. (The characters are sometimes read Myōan Yōsai.) He was born into the family of priests at the Kibitsu shrine in Bizen, modern Okayama Prefecture. Probably through his father's influence, he began to study Buddhist texts while still a child and took the vows of a novice in the Kyoto monastery of Enryakuji at the age of fourteen. Enryakuji was a center not only for the study of the scholastic Tendai (Chin., T'ien-t'ai) Buddhism introduced to Japan by the monk Saichō (766–822), but also for Esoteric (Taimitsu, in this case) Buddhist practices. The monastery, however, had lost the spiritual vitality evident in Saichō's day. While some Tendai monks still devoted themselves to prayer and study, others made light of their vows, engaged in political intrigue, and saw little amiss in the use of military force to promote monastic interests. In this degenerating spiritual environment some earnest young monks conceived the desire to restore Enryakuji and Tendai Buddhism to their earlier glory; Eisai too became convinced of the urgent need to revitalize Buddhism in Japan. Like many monks in the ancient period, he believed that the sources of this regeneration would be found in China.

In 1168, at the age of twenty-eight, Eisai made the first of two pilgrimages to China. In his travels he became aware of the influence of Ch'an, but as he was in China for only six months, he did not have time to delve very deeply into its teachings. On his return to Japan Eisai brought with him some sixty volumes of Tendai-related texts, gathered on Mount T'ien-t'ai and elsewhere, which he presented to the chief abbot of Enryakuji. For the next twenty years Eisai divided his time between Kyoto and Bizen. He led an active life, writing commentaries on the *sūtras*, lecturing on the *Lotus Sutra (Hokekyō)*, conducting Esoteric rituals for rain or relief from sickness, and establishing small communities of disciples. Most of this activity seems to have been devoted not to the propagation of Zen but to the reform of Tendai Buddhism.

In 1187 Eisai again set out for China. His hope was to journey on to India in pilgrimage to the sacred sites associated with the life of the Buddha, but because of disturbances on the borders, his request for a travel permit was rejected by the Chinese authorities. Frustrated, Eisai made his way to Mount T'ien-t'ai. There he met the Ch'an master Hsü-an Huai-ch'ang, under whose guidance he deepened his knowledge of the tradition. Just before returning to Japan in 1191, Eisai committed himself to the *bodhisattva* precepts and was granted a monk's robe and certificate of enlightenment by Hsü-an.

After his second visit to China, Eisai began to actively promote Zen. He established small temples on Kyushu and along the coast of the Inland Sea, where he combined the study of Zen with devotion to the *Lotus Sutra*. This activity did not go unnoticed in Tendai Buddhist circles. In 1194 monks from Enryakuji, arguing that Eisai was heretically engaged in an attempt to establish a new branch of Buddhism in Japan, persuaded the court to issue an edict proscribing Zen. In an attempt to defend himself and justify his espousal of Zen, Eisai wrote *Kōzen gokokuron* (Arguments in Favor of the Promulgation of Zen as a Defense of the Country). In this long work Eisai offered four major arguments in favor of Zen: that it was the very essence of Buddhism; that it was not a new teaching but had been accepted by Saichō and other patriarchs of Tendai Buddhism; that it was based on the disciplined observance of the Buddhist precepts; and that its sponsorship would certainly lead to the rejuvenation of Buddhism in Japan and to the prosperity and security of the nation.

The defense of Zen offered by Eisai did little to assuage the hostility of the Buddhist establishment in Kyoto. In 1199 Eisai set out for eastern Japan, where he found powerful patrons in the Kamakura warrior regime. Here Eisai was presented with an opportunity to spread Zen in the heartland of warrior power, well away from the interference of Enryakuji. But while he presumably talked privately to his patrons about Zen, the record of his public functions reveals only the conduct of Esoteric rituals and prayer ceremonies in Kamakura.

In 1202 Eisai returned to Kyoto. There, with the shogun Yoriie's backing, he established the monastery of Kenninji, in which Zen was to be practiced in concert with Tendai and Esoteric Buddhism. The writings and activities of the last twenty years of Eisai's life all reflect his conviction of the importance of renewing a broadly based Buddhism deriving its strength from the strict observance of the rules of lay and monastic life. This is the message of his *Nippon buppō chūkō ganbun* (An Appeal for the Restoration of Japanese Buddhism), written in 1204. Before his death in 1215, Eisai made one last visit to Kamakura, where he presented to the shogun Minamoto Sanetomo a treatise on the efficacy of tea drinking, the *Kissa yōjōki*.

Had Japanese knowledge of Ch'an come to an end with Eisai, it is unlikely that it would ever have taken deep root in Japan. Although Eisai provided a vigorous intellectual defense of Zen, he did not seek to put it on an independent footing. This was to be the task of his successors, monks like Dōgen, Enni of Tōfukuji, and the Chinese masters who came to Japan beginning in the mid-thirteenth century. Eisai, however, framed the terms of the debate that would continue over the acceptance of Zen, and whetted the curiosity of a small band of followers, some of whom would themselves go to China in search of a deeper understanding of Zen practice.

[*See also* Zen.]

BIBLIOGRAPHY

Collcut, Martin. *Five Mountains: The Rinzai Zen Monastic Institution in Medieval Japan.* Cambridge, Mass., 1981.

Dumoulin, Heinrich. *A History of Zen Buddhism.* Translated by Paul Peachey. New York, 1963.

Furuta Shōkin. *Eisai, Nihon no Zen goruku.* Tokyo, 1977.

MARTIN COLLCUTT

EL was the head of the Canaanite pantheon, the creator god and father of the other gods. El's consort was Athirat, and his dwelling was said to be "at the source of the two rivers, at the confluence of the two deeps," possibly a site in central Lebanon. *El* (Can., *ilu*) can also generically mean "god."

In the past thirty years, a large number of monographs have been written addressing the apparently contradictory images of El presented in the two major sources available. In the history of Phoenicia written in the sixth century BCE by Sanchuniathon (which has been partially preserved via Philo Byblius in Eusebius's *Praeparatio evangelica*), El appears as a fierce warrior god who totally dominates the pantheon. However, in the many cultic and mythic texts written in the thirteenth century BCE from Ugarit in Syria, El, while he still retains such epithets as "creator of creatures," "king," and "father," seems to play a background role, and it is Baal who is the warrior *par excellence*.

Some earlier efforts to reconcile this seeming inconsistency proposed that the Sanchuniathon account and the Ugaritic epithets are remnants of a more ancient stage of Canaanite religion, and that eventually El had in effect been dethroned by his son Baal. A parallel would be the succession in Greek mythology from Ouranos to Kronos, from Kronos to Zeus.

More recent scholarship, however, points to the different perspectives of the sources themselves. Sanchuniathon's account is theogonic; it addresses the question of the origin and relative position of the gods, and thus El's prominence. The Ugaritic myths are cosmogonic; they pertain to the process of the ordering of the world, wherein Baal fights Yamm ("sea," i.e., the primeval sea and chaos) and Mot ("death") to gain supremacy over the cosmos, but not over the pantheon. Even in these texts, El sits supremely above all this "busy work," and Baal must seek El's permission in matters pertaining to the order of the cosmos and to kingships, even Baal's own.

BIBLIOGRAPHY

The starting point for the contemporary discussion of El is Marvin H. Pope's *El in the Ugaritic Texts* (Leiden, 1955). Subsequent research can be found in four dissertations published in "Harvard Semitic Monographs," numbers 4, 5, 21, and 24, respectively: Richard J. Clifford's *The Cosmic Mountain in Canaan and the Old Testament* (Cambridge, Mass., 1972), Patrick D. Miller, Jr.'s *The Divine Warrior in Early Israel* (Cambridge, Mass., 1973), Conrad E. L'Heureux's *Rank among the Canaanite Gods* (Cambridge, Mass., 1979), and E. Theodore Mullen, Jr.'s *The Divine Council in Canaanite and Early Hebrew Literature* (Cambridge, Mass., 1980).

WILLIAM J. FULCO, S.J.

EL'AZAR BEN 'AZARYAH (late first and early second centuries CE), Palestinian tanna, a rabbinic sage of the Mishnaic period. El'azar, whose traditions are recorded in the Mishnah and related texts, is described as a wealthy priest who was a direct descendent of Ezra. It is as a result of this status that El'azar was appointed to be the head of the academy in Yavneh during the brief period that Gamli'el of Yavneh was removed from that position (J.T., *Ber.* 4.1, 7d and parallels). This event is already echoed in the Mishnah (e.g., *Yad.* chap. 4), but its full import is unclear. The Babylonian tradition claims that "on that very day [when El'azar was appointed] *'eduyyot* was taught . . ." (B.T., *Ber.* 28a). Some modern scholars have understood this tradition to mean that the Mishnaic tractate *'Eduyyot*, which they take to be the earliest tractate, was composed on that day under the direction of El'azar. Internal evidence, however, does not support this assertion. Whatever the nature of the event, it is clear that it had significant contemporary impact.

The position of honor accorded El'azar is illustrated by his frequent appearance in the company of the most respected sages of his generation. Also central to El'azar's image is his moderation. This is the ideal that he advocates in the Mishnah (*Avot* 3.17), where in a list of similar statements he suggests that "if there is no flour there can be no Torah, if no Torah, there can be no flour." Such moderate tendencies are particularly meaningful against the background of his prestige and legendary wealth; he is described as being especially sensitive to the difficulty of supporting oneself in this world (B.T., *Pes.* 118a). Moderation may have also been one of the lessons in his replacement of Gamli'el; Gamli'el was insensitive to the difficulty of making a living, and while Gamli'el restricted entrance into the academy, El'azar opened the doors to all.

El'azar contributed to both the legal and exegetical traditions. His legal record reflects no overall agenda or philosophy, although in certain notable cases moderation is evident. In exegesis he is considered to have been willing to accept the simple meaning of scripture.

[*See also* Tannaim.]

BIBLIOGRAPHY

The Traditions of Eleazar ben Azariah, by Tzvee Zahavy (Missoula, Mont., 1977), is the most comprehensive work available on El'azar. The traditions relating the ascension of El'azar to the leadership of the Yavneh academy are analyzed by Robert Goldenberg in "The Deposition of Rabban Gamaliel II: An Examination of the Sources," *Journal of Jewish Studies* 23 (Autumn 1972): 167–190. Essential contributions to understanding these traditions are also made by Louis Ginzberg in *Perushim ve-ḥiddushim bi-Yerushalmi*, vol. 4 (New York, 1961), pp. 174–220.

DAVID KRAEMER

EL'AZAR BEN PEDAT, amoraic authority of the third century. Of Babylonian origin (J.T., *Ber.* 2.1, 4b), El'azar made his career in the rabbinic academies of the Land of Israel, chiefly in Tiberias. Because both El'azar ben Pedat and the rather earlier El'azar ben Shammu'a are frequently cited without their patronymics, some uncertainty about ascription is attached to traditions bearing their names. Nevertheless, it is clear that El'azar ben Pedat left Babylonia after having studied with Rav and Shemu'el. In the Jerusalem Talmud he is once called the disciple of Ḥiyya' bar Abba' (J.T., *Qid.* 1.4, 60b), but he eventually came to be associated with Yoḥanan bar Nappaḥa' in Tiberias (J.T., *San.* 1.1, 18b). He ended his career as Yoḥanan's disciple-colleague (B.T., *B.M.* 84a) and spokesman in the academy (J.T., *Meg.* 1.11, 72b).

Possibly because of his Babylonian origins, El'azar was of great interest to the *naḥottei,* traveling scholars who went back and forth between Babylonia and the Land of Israel carrying reports of recent teachings of leading rabbis from one center to the other. (The work of these correspondents during the early generations of rabbinical activity in Babylonia was of great importance in preserving the unity and coordination of a movement that could have broken down into a number of relatively isolated national or regional branches.) El'azar's academy at Tiberias was a leading center for such exchanges of information. In the Babylonian Talmud, El'azar is called "the master of [or from] the Land of Israel" and the standard Babylonian formula "They sent from there" (i.e., from the Land of Israel) was understood by some as a reference to his teaching (B.T., *San.* 17b).

As a legal authority, El'azar was noted for his efforts to identify the masters whose teachings were incorporated without attribution in the Mishnah; he frequently sought to separate consecutive clauses of single Mishnaic pericope, saying, "Break it up; the one who taught this [part of the text] did not teach that" (B.T., *Shab.* 92b, *Ker.* 24b; see also *Bava Metsi'a'* 51a). He was the author of many *aggadot* (nonlegal rabbinic teachings) but was remembered for his aversion to the esoteric lore of *merkavah* mysticism (B.T., *Ḥag.* 13a). According to the medieval *Epistle of Rabbi Sherira' Gaon* (c. 992), El'azar died in the year 279, the same year as his master Yoḥanan.

[*For discussion of the circle of sages to which El'azar belonged, see* Amoraim.]

BIBLIOGRAPHY

Aaron Hyman's *Toledot tanna'im ve-amora'im* (1910; reprint, Jerusalem, 1964) is an altogether uncritical compendium of traditional lore concerning El'azar. It is almost useless as a tool for modern, critical biography, but it remains valuable as an encyclopedic gathering of information. The articles entitled "Eleazar ben Pedat" in the *Jewish Encyclopedia* (New York, 1906) and in the *Encyclopaedia Judaica* (Jerusalem, 1971) are also useful.

ROBERT GOLDENBERG

ELECTION.

The concept of divine election appears in a number of religious traditions that espouse belief in an omnipotent and personal God. Although not unknown among certain religious groups in ancient Greece and India, it has had particular significance in Judaism, Christianity, and Islam. In each of these faiths, one finds the claim that God, although universal, has freely elected or chosen a particular group of people for a particular destiny or relationship with him. While belief in the conditions and beneficiaries of election vary even within the traditions themselves, a common set of difficult, and in some cases, unanswered questions underlie our study. First, how can belief in the election of a particular group of people be reconciled with belief in a universal God? Second, does the concept of election necessarily imply belief in the superiority of the chosen? Third, what is the relationship between election, predestination, and free will? And finally, how, in the face of competing claims to election, can one know if one's own claim is true?

Judaism. Belief in God's having chosen Israel to be his *'am segullah* ("chosen people") has remained a central element of Jewish thought. Rooted in the biblical concept of covenant, it is developed further in the Talmud, in medieval philosophical and mystical writings, and in modern literary and theological texts. Although the concept of election is most closely associated with the Hebrew verb *baḥar* ("chose"), reference to election is often implied in other words. Indeed, belief in the election of Israel predates the introduction of the technical term *baḥar* in *Deuteronomy* (7:6, 14:2), a biblical text not written until the seventh century BCE. Underlying God's promises to Abraham and his descendants in *Genesis* 12, and those to Moses and the people of Israel in *Exodus* 19 as well, is the conviction that Yahveh has freely chosen a particular group of people to be "his people," thus making himself known as "their God." In the covenant that he establishes with Abraham, he promises to make of Abraham and his descendants a great nation, bringing them to a land that would be their own. The covenant that he establishes at Mount Sinai becomes a renewal and extension of the earlier, Abrahamic covenant. Establishing a special relationship with the Israelites as a whole, he here identifies himself not only as the "God of Abraham, Isaac, and Jacob" but also, more generally, as the "God of Israel."

The election of Israel, it seems, stems solely from God's love, not from any evidence of superiority or merit on Israel's behalf. Similarly, their election is one not of privilege but of obligation. "Let my people go," God repeatedly demands of Pharaoh, "that they may serve me" (*Ex.* 8:1ff.). In order to serve him, the Israelites are enjoined to refrain from worshiping or entering into a covenant with other gods (*Ex.* 20:3, 22:20, 23:32), and they are commanded to follow a clearly delineated code of moral and cultic behavior. Thus, by the eighth century BCE, the prophet Isaiah admonishes those who outwardly follow cultic prescriptions but fail to recognize either the proper intent with which sacrifices are to be offered or the kind of moral life that divine election entails. As a kingdom of priests and a holy nation, they, as the prophet Micah maintains, are to "do justice, and to love kindness, and to walk humbly with [their] God" (*Mi.* 6:8). They alone, the prophet Amos reminds them, have been known by God (*Am.* 3:2). Consequently, they bear a greater responsibility for their actions than do other people and will be punished by God for their transgressions. Nevertheless, as the eighth-century prophet Hosea insists, punishment does not negate their election. Comparing Israel to Gomer, the "wife of harlotry" whom the Lord commanded him to marry, he tells his listeners that while they have been "adulterous" in worshiping other gods and, like Gomer, will be punished for their actions, God will later renew his vow of betrothal, promising them, as Hosea promised Gomer, that if they return to him, he will "heal their faithfulness," turn aside his anger, and "love them freely" forever (*Hos.* 14:4).

According to the biblical view, certain Israelites are further elected for a specific role or office. Included are priests (*Dt.* 18:5, *1 Sm.* 2:28) as well as kings (*2 Sm.* 6:21, *Kgs.* 8:16). Emphasis is placed on the responsibilities that they are given. Here, as elsewhere, divine election clearly implies a setting apart for service.

In the sixth century BCE, following the capture of Jerusalem by Nebuchadrezzar, the destruction of the Temple, and the exile into Babylonia, the concept of election took on new and greater importance. Bereft of their holy sanctuary, with many exiled from their Holy Land, Israel, the people of God's promise, now known as Jews, came to identify suffering as a mark of their election. Although belief in the universality of their God, as expressed in the writings of the sixth-century "Second Isaiah," might have led them to conclude that their God, as God of the universe, had chosen another group of his creations to be his treasured people, their continued insistence that it was they alone whom God had chosen helped to create and nourish the hope that they would be redeemed in the future. In order to reconcile the particularity of Israel's election with the universality of God, prophets like "Second Isaiah" maintained that Israel had been chosen as a "light to the nations" (*Is.* 42:6). God had entered into a covenant with the people of Israel so that they might bear testimony to his reality, bringing others to recognize his greatness and to acknowledge that "besides [him] there is no god" (*Is.* 44:6).

The theme of Israel's election is reiterated throughout Jewish Hellenistic literature. In the Apocrypha, for example, *Ben Sira* describes the Lord as distinguishing between his creations, blessing and exalting some (i.e., Israel), cursing others (*Sir.* 33:12), while the author of *2 Esdras* specifically mentions Israel as the one people loved by God (*2 Esd.* 5:27). Philo Judaeus and Josephus similarly refer to the spiritual uniqueness of the Jews. As Philo writes in his *Life of Moses*, although "their bodies have been moulded from human seeds . . . their souls are sprung from Divine seeds, and therefore their stock is akin to God" (1.278–279).

A more exclusivist view of election appears in the writings of the Jewish schismatics living near the Dead Sea during the first centuries before and after the beginning of the common era. They alone, they claimed, were the true Israel. Pointing to the revelation of truth given by God to their Teacher of Righteousness, they saw themselves as the faithful remnant of Israel, the last in line of those whom God had chosen. They had been chosen, they believed, to receive both divine grace and eternal knowledge (*Rule of Community* 11). In return for these gifts and for the new covenant established with them, they were strictly to obey the teachings of Moses and the prophets and consciously to live their lives under the guidance of the spirit of truth. Members of the community identified themselves as sons of light, set apart and prepared for battle against the wicked sons of darkness. It was their contention that this battle would soon occur, in which they, as sons of light, would emerge victorious.

As Géza Vermès implies in his introduction to *The Dead Sea Scrolls in English* (1962), a predestinarian element seems to underlie the community's assertion that it was loved by God before creation, its members destined to become sons of light. Yet as Vermès further maintains, the Qumran community, like other Jewish groups, continually insisted that election was not an inherited privilege. Only through a freely taken oath of allegiance to God and to the teachings by which the community lived could one claim to be a member of the new covenant of grace that God had established. Only then could one claim to be a member of the elect, chosen by God "for an everlasting covenant" and for everlasting glory.

With the fall of the Second Temple in 70 CE and a Diaspora existence that forced Jews to live as a minority among people who often sought to oppress them, the concept of election continued to serve as a source of pride, strength, and hope for a better future. As rabbinic

Judaism developed concepts that were to become normative for Jewish life, election remained, as Solomon Schechter (1909) notes, an "unformulated dogma" running throughout rabbinic literature. Beginning in the late first century CE with the teachings of Yoḥanan ben Zakk'ai, emphasis was placed not only on the close relationship that continued to exist between God and Israel but also on the life of Torah, by which Jews, chosen for holiness by God, were to live. Holiness, as ben Zakk'ai maintained, depended on neither state nor sanctuary (*Avot* 2.8) but on the fulfillment of the Torah that alone constituted what ʿAqiva' ben Yosef identified as the essence of Jewish existence (*Sifrei Dt.* 11.22).

According to Benjamin Helfgott (1954), rabbinic emphasis on the election of Israel needs to be seen as part of a Jewish response to the Christian claim that Jews were no longer God's chosen people. While Helfgott admits that emphasis on Israel's election as a response to an anti-Jewish polemic predates the rise of Christianity and can be found as early as 300 BCE, one can justifiably argue that the Christian challenge to the Jewish concept of election was more severe than those that predated it because Christianity's identification of the church as the true Israel posed a direct challenge to the theological foundations of Judaism itself.

The rabbis of the Talmud met this challenge not by direct debate but by reasserting their own doctrine of election with renewed emphasis and vigor. They insisted that the bond between God and Israel was indissoluble (*B.T., Yev.* 102b, *Qid.* 36a). Moreover, they maintained that even the destruction of the Second Temple needed to be seen within the larger context of a universal divine plan that included the future fulfillment of those prophetic promises made to the people of Israel. Thus, even in the face of calamity, the rabbis retained an unqualified faith in God's continuing love for Israel and Israel's love for God. To underscore their contention that God's love for Israel was not arbitrary, the rabbis offered a number of explanations as to why Israel had been chosen. According to *Numbers Rabbah* 14.10, for example, Israel was chosen because no other nation, though offered God's Torah, was willing to accept its precepts, while according to *Genesis Rabbah* 1.4, Israel's election was predestined even before the world was created. Some rabbis pointed to the humility and meekness of the Israelites as making them worthy of election, while most remained silent as to the merits or attributes that might have led to Israel's becoming the treasured people of God. None, however, believed that merit alone was sufficient cause for election. Quoting scripture to support their claim, they attributed Israel's election to God's freely given act of love.

Faith in God's special love for Israel came to be expressed most clearly in daily prayer. Biblically based concepts of election were incorporated into the liturgy as expressions of gratitude to the God who had chosen Israel from all people, loved and exalted them above others, sanctified them by his commandments, and brought them "unto [his] service." One finds these ideas articulated further in the works of such medieval thinkers as Saʿadyah Gaon, Avraham ibn Daud, Ḥasdai Crescas, and Isaac Abravanel. They receive greatest attention, however, in the twelfth-century *Sefer ha-Kuzari* by Yehudah ha-Levi, a work in which the concept of chosenness plays a central role. Written as a defense of Judaism, it identifies religious truth with that that was revealed at Sinai. Consequently, it declares that the Jews, chosen to bear that truth, are alone able to grasp what transcends the limits of reason. As Henry Slonimsky writes in his introduction to *Judah Halevi: The Kuzari* (1964), the concept of Israel's election leads ha-Levi to claim, for the Jewish people and their history, a unique and supernatural character. Yet, according to Slonimsky, it is because ha-Levi wishes to eliminate from his concept of chosenness either hatred or intolerance that he assigns other historical functions to Christianity and Islam, maintaining that in the future they will be converted to religious truth.

The assigning of supernatural uniqueness to the Jewish people finds further expression in Jewish mystical works of the Middle Ages. One finds in qabbalistic literature, for example, the claim that only the souls of Israel are from God while the souls of others are base material, or *qellipot* ("shells"). Given the precarious position of the Jew in medieval Europe, such claims, it seems, became a means of making bearable, if not intelligible, the continued oppression of the Jewish people.

Yet by the eighteenth century, with the growing acceptance of Jews into European society, the question of how one could become part of the modern world while retaining belief in a concept that clearly differentiated Jews from their non-Jewish neighbors, needed new answers. Even if one could demonstrate that the traditional concept of election was intended to imply a consecration for service rather than a claim to superiority, did not the claim serve to separate the Jews from the very people of whom they wanted to be part? Although some, like the eighteenth-century philosopher Moses Mendelssohn in his *Jerusalem*, assured his non-Jewish readers that the election of Israel did not entail privilege but obligations that could not be dismissed, nineteenth-century religious reformers in Germany, America, and later in England, emphasized the universal nature of Israel's election, reiterating that the spiritual mission with which they had been entrusted would benefit humanity as a whole.

While, as Arnold M. Eisen (1983) convincingly demonstrates, the concept of election has remained a preoccupation among twentieth-century American Jewish thinkers, some, most notably Mordecai Kaplan, founder of Reconstructionism, have sought to eliminate the concept altogether. In his *Judaism as a Civilization* (1934), Kaplan suggested replacing the concept of election with that of vocation. Reflecting Kaplan's own rejection of belief in a supernatural God as well as his conviction that Jews could not hope to gain acceptance in American society as long as they maintained what, protestations notwithstanding, did seem to be a claim to superiority, his concept of vocation as the communal purpose that a specific group of people choose for themselves suggests that Jews are no more unique than others.

A number of theologians recently have sought to refute, either directly or indirectly, Kaplan's notion of Jewish "normalcy." Among them has been Michael Wyschogrod, who, in *The Body of Faith: Judaism as Corporeal Election* (New York, 1983), advances the provocative claim that in choosing Israel God chose a biological rather than an ideological people. Thus, he maintains, both religious and secular Jews are exclusively loved by God and have been chosen to enter into a covenantal relationship with him. No matter what the Jew does or believes, the fact remains that he or she has been chosen to serve as the vehicle through which God acts in history.

Christianity. The Christian concept of election is rooted in the self-identification of the early church as the true Israel. While acknowledging that the Jewish people had originally been the chosen of God, early Christian theologians insisted that those Jews refusing to acknowledge Jesus as their Messiah could no longer claim the status of divine privilege. Viewing Israel as a community of the faithful rather than as the biological descendants of Abraham, Paul declares that "not all who are descended from Israel belong to Israel" (*Rom.* 9:6). His contention here, as elsewhere, is that the concept of election, though once referring solely to the Jewish people, the Israel of the flesh, had been superseded by a new concept referring to those Jews and gentiles who, by accepting the church's teachings, can justifiably claim to be the true Israel of the spirit. Identifying the spiritual Israel with Isaiah's faithful remnant, Paul maintains that they alone are the heirs to God's promise of redemption.

Reinterpreting the biblical concept of covenant, Paul proclaims a new covenant of salvation, available to all who profess faith in the risen Christ. Given apart from the covenant with Abraham and his spiritual seed, it actually precedes the Mosaic covenant (obedience to the Torah), which, according to Paul, is a covenant of slavery (*Gal.* 4:2–31). Although Paul does not argue that Jews should no longer keep the Law, he does insist that the Law in and of itself cannot lead to salvation. Given to Israel as a means of curbing sin, the Law, Paul says, can only bring condemnation, while the new covenant of faith brings rebirth and freedom. Paul does not deny that the Jews remain chosen by God. Indeed, in *Romans* 11:29 he states that the "gifts and the call of God are irrevocable." Yet Paul equates the Mosaic covenant simply with Law, as opposed to spirit, and with privilege, as opposed to service. Given this understanding, he then distinguishes between the Law, which is irrevocable though ultimately ineffectual, and the privileged relationship between God and Israel, which, as John Gager argues in his *The Origins of Anti-Semitism* (New York, 1983), Paul believes to have been "momentarily suspended."

Paul's extension of the concept of election to include Jews and gentiles served as both a stimulus to greater missionary effort and as a didactic vehicle through which the responsibilities and privileges of the Christian life were made clear. By the second half of the first century, however, as the rift between Judaism and Christianity deepened, giving way to a predominantly gentile church, Christians focused their claim to election on the church (Gr., *ekklēsia,* "the chosen") alone, with some, like Stephen, insisting that the Israelites, in his view stiff-necked and resistant to the Holy Spirit, had actually never been God's chosen people (*Acts* 7:51). According to this view, the Mosaic covenant existed only to predict the true covenant of the future. In the Gospels and other New Testament texts, emphasis is placed not only on the elect, whose righteousness and faith reveal the workings of the Holy Spirit, but also on Christ as the elect one, the model of repentance and faith necessary to enter God's kingdom (*Lk.* 9:35, 23:35). Although election ultimately rests on an act of divine grace, proof of one's election lies in obedience to the call that Christ has issued. Indeed, as John maintains, using the image of Jesus as a shepherd gathering the elect of all nations, it is only through Christ, the "door of the sheepfold," that one gains access to the Father (*Jn.* 10:1ff.).

In the epistles of the first- and early second-century bishop Ignatius, emphasis is placed on the spiritual gifts, or privileges, that divine election entails. Although all people, he writes, enjoy such temporal blessings as food and drink, only baptism leads to the bestowal of both spiritual nourishment (i.e., the Eucharist) and eternal life. From the second through the sixth century, a number of works were written proclaiming the election of the church as a substitute for the election of Israel. Thus, for example, in his *Three Books of Testimonies against the Jews,* the third-century bishop Cyprian maintains that with the cessation of all tokens of the "old dispensation," a new law, leadership, prophecy, and election would occur, with gentiles replacing Jews as God's chosen people. Rosemary Ruether, in her *Faith and Fratricide* (New York, 1974), views this literary tradition as part of an ongoing polemic against a Judaism that by its continued and active existence seemed to challenge many of the church's teachings. Moreover, she maintains, by establishing a number of contrasting images between the synagogue and the church—carnality versus spirituality, blindness versus sight, rejection versus election—the church was better able to affirm who it was and what it hoped to be. Although the church's anti-Judaism did not always lead to a position of anti-Semitism, the use of such biblical narratives as that of the older brother Esau's forfeiting his birthright to his younger twin brother, Jacob, to convey the relationship between Judaism and Christianity powerfully underscored the church's theological claim that it alone was the true "seed of Abraham," elected by God to enter the kingdom of heaven.

The schismatic Donatist church of North Africa, originating in the early fourth century and formally denounced as heretical in the year 405, advanced its own concept of election. Formed in opposition to those bishops who, in response to the Diocletian edict of May 303, surrendered their sacred books to the civil authorities, it began to consecrate its own bishops, beginning with Majorinus as bishop of Carthage in the year 312. Claiming that the *traditores* (surrenderers) and their successors did not possess the Holy Spirit and therefore could not validly administer the rite of baptism, it maintained that it alone represented the catholic (or universal) church of Peter. Those who developed Donatist teachings, and in particular Majorinus's successor Donatus, from whom the church took its name, viewed the world as the dominion of Satan represented by the wicked "sons of *traditores.*" Forced to separate from a church that had polluted itself through its alliance with worldly powers, they insisted that only they were pure, "without spot or wrinkle." As such, they believed, they alone were the elect of God. While the opposition of Augustine and others eventually curbed its influence and growth, Donatism persisted in North Africa through the sixth century and quite probably into the seventh century and the arrival of Islam.

Between the tenth and fourteenth centuries, a number of neo-Manichaean Christian sects similarly laid claim to election. Identified by orthodox Christianity as "Manichaean" because of their dualist worldview, their identification of the God of the Hebrew Bible with Satan, and their strict asceticism—all characteristics of the Manichaean religion founded in the third century by the Persian Mani—such groups as the Armenian Paulicians, the Byzantine Bogomils, and the Latin Cathari denied that they were either heretics or Manichaeans; rather, they insisted, they alone represented true Christianity. While the label neo-Manichaean reflects the recognition by contemporary historians that Manichaean elements were present in each of these groups, scholars disagree as to whether or not a direct connection can be established between the Manichaeism of Mani and its later Christian manifestations. In either case, however, like the early Manichaeans, these medieval Christian sects divided their members into different grades or classes, including the two primary classes of the "elect" and the "hearers." Like the early gnostic pneumatics (also identified as the elect), those who were initiated into the class of the elect claimed to possess true knowledge of the self, the world, and God. Among the Cathari, the neo-Manichaean group about whom we have greatest knowledge and whose influence seemed to be most widespread, members of the elect dressed in black, carried a copy of the New Testament in a leather bag, and embraced a rigorous asceticism that was intended to free them from contact with the material world. Bound to chastity, poverty, and abstention from meat, milk, eggs, cheese, and presumably wine, they ate only one meal (of vegetables) a day, fasted several days a week and at particular seasons, regularly engaged in prayer, and yearly accepted one new piece of clothing. Prohibited from owning property, accumulating wealth, and working in any occupation, they were cared for by the hearers, whose confessions they heard and in whose religious instruction they were engaged.

For the Cathari, as for other neo-Manichaean groups, election implied purity, perfection, and knowledge. The elect saw themselves as superior to others in having nearly achieved a state of pure spirit during their lifetime; they claimed that they alone had the privilege of entering the Paradise of Light immediately after death. According to Malcolm Lambert (1977), both religious and social considerations led many to Catharism and to preparation for their future initiation as one of the elect. While some became Cathari solely out of religious conviction, many, especially among the rural aristocracy and the lower classes, turned to Catharism as a result of their rejection of what they perceived to be the growing luxury and corruption of orthodox Christianity and as a positive affirmation of self-sacrifice and poverty. In addition, Lambert maintains, the initial equality of men and women within the class of the elect attracted a significant number of women to Catharism and to the high ritual status that it alone afforded.

Within the reformed tradition, and especially within Calvinism, the concept of election came to play a particularly prominent role. Identifying the elect as those individuals predestined for salvation, John Calvin asserted that election was rooted in a divine purpose that predated the creation of the world. According to Calvin, humanity existed in a state of total depravation. Although God had sent his son to atone for human sinfulness, the efficacy of this atonement extended only to those whom God already had chosen. Rooted solely in God's love and mercy, election, in Calvin's view, was completely gratuitous, bearing no relationship to human merit. While the few who were elected into the "covenant of life" would be redeemed, the majority of humanity, rejected by God, would be condemned to eternal damnation. In his *Institutes of the Christian Religion* (1536), Calvin describes the election of Israel as a first degree of election, superseded by a second degree in which God retains some of Israel as his children and freely adopts others. Through the preaching of the gospel and an accompanying "illumination of the spirit," the elect are called to membership in Christ, bound through their election to one another. Faith, Calvin maintains, is a seal of one's election that, together with the attaining of righteousness, becomes a confirmation to the individual that he or she indeed has been chosen.

English Puritans and their American descendants similarly placed the concept of election at the heart of their theology. Sharing Calvin's belief in a double predestination consisting of the election of the few and the condemnation of the many, they described in great detail the covenant of grace into which the elect had entered. Made possible through Christ's perfect obedience, this covenant held out both the assurance of forgiveness and the promise of salvation. According to the Puritans, this covenant needed to be appropriated in faith, with salvation subsequently mediated through established laws and institutions. Great emphasis was placed on the experience of regenerating grace as a sign of one's election. By the end of the seventeenth century, this experience became a necessary requirement for membership in both American and English Puritan churches. While the later institution of the halfway covenant enabled those who had been raised as Puritans but had not undergone the personal experience of conversion to retain their membership, Puritan churches in America continued to identify themselves as congregations of visible saints, called by God to a glorious future for which they had made elaborate preparation.

Greater awareness and appreciation of the religious beliefs of others has led a number of contemporary Catholic and Protestant theologians to reassess the traditional Christian concept of election. Rosemary Ruether, for example, concludes her *Faith and Fratricide* by offering ways in which the Christian understanding of the new covenant as superseding the old might be relativized so as to acknowledge the legitimacy of ongoing Jewish claims. Similarly, Paul Van Buren, in his *Discerning the Way* (New York, 1980), suggests that Jewish and Christian concepts of election be seen as parallel claims that point toward a common hope for redemption. Sharing the concerns of both Ruether and Van Buren, Walter Bühlmann, in *God's Chosen Peoples* (Maryknoll, N.Y., 1982), suggests that chosenness be seen not as an exclusive privilege but as an inclusive model of human closeness to God. Distinguishing between a theology and an ideology of election, he warns against using religious convictions to generate and perpetuate a mentality of intolerance and supremacy.

Islam. Although the concept of election is not as fully articulated in Islam as it is in Judaism and Christianity, the Qur'ān frequently uses the word *'ahd* ("injunction, command") to convey the agreement or covenantal relationship existing between Allāh and his prophets and believers. Occasionally used as a synonym for *'aqd* ("contract"), *'ahd* implies the dynamic, religious engagement of the believer with Allāh, manifest through the obligations that the believer agrees to assume.

The Qur'ān affirms the election of both particular individuals, including Noah, Abraham, Moses, the Hebrew prophets, and Jesus, and their communities. It further affirms the election of God's last and greatest prophet, Muḥammad, and his community of believers. This community (the *ummah*) is identified in the Qur'ān with the biblical saving remnant. For the Muslims, other nations have sought after God, but it is the Islamic community alone that has drawn close to him. This community is not to be identified with any ethnic or social group but consists of all believers. While, according to John Wansbrough (1977), specific doctrines identifying Muslims as superior did not develop until later, the Qur'ān distinguishes Allāh's servants from others by identifying Muslims as the "purified ones" (surah 37:40) or, more simply, as "the elect" (38:47).

It is in Sufism, however, that the concept of election receives greatest attention. Developed during the ninth and tenth centuries CE, Sufism proclaimed that nothing exists but Allāh. The Ṣūfīs arrived at this claim not through intellectual knowledge but through mystical insight, or gnosis. The Ṣūfīs identified this insight as the inward essence of *islam*, or submission to God, an essence that, they maintained, could be penetrated only by the elect. According to the Ṣūfīs, the elect were those who not only experienced the divine directly but also, as Martin Lings (1961) notes, could pass with no transition from thought to action, from the "next world" and its mysteries to this world and all that it contained.

Believing that gnosis led one to attain the highest rank of human perfection, second only to the prophets, Ṣūfīs laid claim to sainthood. They based this claim not on personal merit but on Allāh's love or grace. To be chosen, then, was to receive the gift of sainthood, a gift that enabled one to penetrate into mysteries that could not be grasped through rational comprehension. Quoting a Ṣūfī poet, Lings describes the mystical intelligence of the Ṣūfī as a flawless jewel, an exquisitely beautiful gift that enables the elect to lift the veil from the "light of Allāh" and recognize that there is nothing but God.

The concept of election as a gift given to special souls even before their creation has led a number of scholars to associate the Ṣūfī claim to election with that of predestination. While these concepts are not identical with one another, the sense of being not merely called by God but overwhelmed by him, led early Ṣūfīs in particular to view their decision to leave the world and devote themselves to Allāh as a decision dictated or suggested to them. As Annemarie Schimmel writes in her *Mystical Dimensions of Islam* (Chapel Hill, N.C., 1975), the mystic has been chosen *(iṣṭafā)* by God for himself, not only to become a vessel of his love but also to participate in the primordial covenant established even before the creation of Adam and to remain pure through the meticulous observance of both Islamic law and Islamic tradition.

[*See* Vocation *and* Covenant *for religious phenomena closely related to election; for discussion of theological and philosophical issues involving the idea of election, see* Free Will and Determinism *and* Free Will and Predestination.]

BIBLIOGRAPHY

While most works on election have been narrowly focused, Steven T. Katz's *Jewish Ideas and Concepts* (New York, 1977) and the essay on "Chosen People" by Nelson Glueck and others in *The Universal Jewish Encyclopedia* (New York, 1941) provide good overviews of the appearance of this concept throughout Jewish history. Harold H. Rowley's *The Biblical Doctrine of Election* (London, 1950), although written from an explicitly Christian perspective, is useful in illuminating most of the major references to this concept in the Hebrew Bible, while Solomon Schechter's *Aspects of Rabbinic Theology* (1909; New York, 1961) and Benjamin Helfgott's *The Doctrine of Election in Tannaitic Literature* (New York, 1954) remain important sources of information in discovering the development of this concept in early rabbinic literature. For a detailed description of the appearance of this concept in qabbalistic literature, see Gershom Scholem's *Major Trends in Jewish Mysticism* (1941; New York, 1961). Eugene B. Borowitz's *Choices in Modern Jewish Thought* (New York, 1983) offers a clear, though brief, summary of the development or rejection of the concept of election in the works of such twentieth-century Jewish thinkers as Leo Baeck, Mordecai Kaplan, and Richard Rubenstein. Particularly noteworthy is Arnold M. Eisen's *The Chosen People in America: A Study in Jewish Religious Ideology* (Bloomington, Ind., 1983), which offers a penetrating analysis of what Israel's election has mean to American rabbis and theologians from 1930 to the present.

J. C. V. Durell, in his *The Historic Church* (1906; New York, 1969), gives an excellent summary of the concept of election in early Christianity. The Donatist claim to election is clearly detailed in W. H. C. Frend's *The Donatist Church* (1952; Oxford, 1971). Perhaps the most extensive study of neo-Manichaeanism to date is Steven Runciman's *The Medieval Manichee: A Study of the Christian Dualist Heresy* (Cambridge, 1947). Also of interest, especially in its examination of the social conditions leading to neo-Manichaean claims to election, is Malcolm D. Lambert's *Medieval Heresy* (New York, 1977). The concept of election in Calvinism and in Reformed theology as a whole is well summarized in Heinrich Heppe's *Reformed Dogmatics* (London, 1950). For a more detailed and exhaustive examination of this concept, especially in American Puritanism, see Edmund S. Morgan's *Visible Saints: The History of a Puritan Idea* (New York, 1963).

John Wansbrough's *Quranic Studies* (Oxford, 1977) provides a fine overview of the Qu'ranic concept of election, showing its relationship to themes of retribution, covenant, and exile. The development of this concept in Sufism is clearly traced by Robert C. Zaehner in his *Hindu and Muslim Mysticism* (London, 1960) and receives special attention in Martin Lings's *A Moslem Saint of the Twentieth Century: Shaikh Ahmad al-Alawi* (London, 1961).

ELLEN M. UMANSKY

ELEPHANTS. Indigenous to both Africa and India, the elephant is the largest of all living land animals. A peaceful herbivore, the adult of the species has no fear of any other animal, with the exceptions of man the hunter and small rodents that might crawl up its trunk. Because of its awesome strength and great size, the elephant—whether wild or tamed as a beast of burden—is commonly a symbol of power: both the brute force that supports the cosmos and its life forms and the majesty of royal power. At the same time, the wild elephant demonstrates numerous characteristics shared by human beings—such as longevity, social customs, and varied personality traits—which give rise to tales in which the elephant may be a companion to man or may exhibit humanlike qualities such as fearfulness, rage, and stubbornness.

In India, the elephant-headed god Gaṇeśa has been widely revered as a remover of obstacles, hence as a bringer of success, among both Hindus and Buddhists. His enormous popularity is also attested outside India. As Indian culture spread, the cult of Gaṇeśa was enthusiastically accepted in Southwest Asia, and in China and Japan, Gaṇeśa became well known through the introduction of Tantric Buddhism to these lands. [*See* Gaṇeśa.]

Since ancient times, especially in India and North Africa, the elephant has been domesticated and trained as a beast of burden. The Carthaginians, for example, rode on elephants in their war against the Romans. In Hindu mythology, elephants hold up the four quarters of the universe: the earth rests on the back of elephants, which rest, in turn, on the back of a huge tortoise. According to the *Mahābhārata,* the divine elephant Airāvata was born out of the primeval milky ocean as it was being churned by the gods and demons. This elephant was destined to be the mount of Indra, the god of thunder and battle, protector of the cosmos.

The intimate connection in Hindu mythology between Airāvata and Indra indicates that the elephant is not simply a symbol for brute force but is also most broadly associated with the powers that support and protect life. Probably because of its round shape and gray color, the elephant is regarded as a "rain cloud" that walks the earth, endowed with the magico-religious ability to produce rain clouds at will. In present-day India, the elephant plays a significant part in an annual ceremony celebrated in New Delhi for the purposes of inducing rainfall, good harvest, and the fertility of human beings and their livestock. An elephant, painted white with sandal paste, is led in solemn procession through the city. The men attending the elephant wear women's clothes and utter obscene words, as if to stimulate the dormant powers of fertility.

Although in the period of the *Ṛgveda* elephants were tamed but little used in war, by the middle of the first millennium BCE, the owning of elephants had become a prerogative of kings and chieftains, who used them in warfare and on ceremonial occasions. Elephants, particularly albino ones, became the mounts of kings and, hence, symbolic of royal power. In the mythology of kingship, the white elephant appears as one of the seven treasures of the universal monarch *(cakravartin),* who rides upon it as he sets out on his world-inspection tours.

As the embodiment of perfect wisdom and royal dignity, the Buddha himself is often referred to as an elephant. According to the older, verse version of the *Lalitavistara,* the Buddha was conceived when his mother, Maya, dreamed of his descent from heaven in the form of a white elephant. This motif is depicted in a medallion on a balustrade of the Bharhut Stupa dating from the second or first century BCE, and from that time onward, it appears repeatedly in Buddhist iconography throughout India. The later, prose version of the *Lalitavistara,* followed by the *Mahāvastu,* states more emphatically that the Buddha descended into his mother's womb in elephantine form. In subsequent centuries, the Buddhist community has generally accepted the idea that a Buddha, either of the past or of the future, must enter his mother's womb in the form of an elephant.

Many of the myths from Africa about the elephant emphasize the ways in which elephants and human beings share certain characteristics. Perhaps it is because the African elephant remained wild in comparison to its Indian cousin that its natural habits had more effect on the form of its symbolism. For instance, wild elephants are very social, living in groups with definite customs. The life expectancy of the elephant is somewhere between sixty and seventy years. It is an intelligent creature and capable of complex emotions, even neurosis and insanity. These attributes indicate ways in which human beings and elephants are similar, and therefore it is no surprise that the elephant is often regarded as a special companion of the mythical ancestors. For example, the Nandi in East Africa recount the story of how one day, when Asista, the creator, arrived on earth in order to arrange the creation, or to prepare the present condition of things, he found three beings already there, living together: the thunder, a Dorobo (a member of a hunting tribe believed by the Nandi to be their mythical ancestors), and an elephant. A similar tale is told by the Maasai. According to the Yao, the first human being emerged from the primeval wilderness carrying an elephant on his shoulders. The elephant made him a great hunter by teaching him about the natures of all the animals, granting him wild honey for food, and training him in the art of killing. Moreover, the hunter found his wife in the land of the elephants, and together they became the primordial ancestors of the Yao. In southern Africa, it is widely believed that elephants can transform themselves into human beings and vice versa.

Apparently the elephant shares with human beings the capacity for antagonizing the gods: according to the Tim in central Togo, West Africa, at the time of the beginning, the god Esso and all the animals lived together in harmony. They even shared water from the same spring. But the elephant picked a quarrel with the god, who thereupon left the earth and its inhabitants and withdrew to his heaven so that he might enjoy peace and quiet.

BIBLIOGRAPHY

The classic analysis of elephant symbolism in India remains Heinrich Zimmer's *Myths and Symbols in Indian Art and Civilization*, edited by Joseph Campbell (1946; reprint, Princeton, 1972), pp. 102ff. A more comprehensive discussion is presented by Jan Gonda in his *Change and Continuity in Indian Religion* (The Hague, 1965), pp. 90ff. On the symbolism of the elephant in Buddhism, see Alfred Foucher's *La vie du Bouddha* (Paris, 1948), translated by Simone B. Boas as *The Life of Buddha According to the Ancient Texts and Monuments of India* (Middletown, Conn., 1963), pp. 22ff. On Gaṇeśa, there is a study by Alice Getty, *Gaṇeśa: A Monograph on the Elephant-Faced God*, 2d ed. (New Delhi, 1971).

MANABU WAIDA

ELEUSINIAN MYSTERIES. The most important mystery cult of the ancient world was that connected with the sanctuary of Demeter Eleusinia on a hillside outside Eleusis, about fourteen miles northwest of Athens.

Origins and History. The ritual of initiation into the Eleusinian mysteries preserves memories of an earlier phase during which the mysteries were the initiation ritual of a political and, at an earlier stage, clan community, especially in the initiation of the *pais aph'hestias*, the "boy from the hearth," the religious center of house and state: he was an Athenian boy chosen by lot who underwent initiation at the cost and on behalf of the *polis* of Athens. Other traces are preserved in the cult of Demeter Eleusinia, which was widespread throughout Greece. On the island of Thasos, it was still a clan cult in the fourth century BCE; in Laconia, it concerned especially the initiation of women. These local variations show that cults of Demeter Eleusinia existed in Greece before the local ritual of Eleusis developed into the mysteries. Contrary to previous belief, however, the cult at Eleusis has no demonstrable Bronze Age roots; Mycenaean walls that have been discovered under the later sanctuary belong to secular structures. The first archaeologically recoverable sanctuary shows traces of an apsidal or oval cult house enclosed by a wall, both from the eighth century BCE. It is debatable when Athens took control of the cult—either in or before the time of Solon (c. 600 BCE) or, at the latest, in the time of Peisitratus (mid-sixth century BCE), when the sanctuary underwent a fundamental restructuring that gave it the plan it was to have for the rest of its existence.

At this time, a monumental new gateway was constructed, looking not toward Eleusis but toward Athens, and a square initiation hall *(telestērion)* was erected, incorporating the innermost sanctum *(anaktoron)* of a Solonian temple. In the second half of the fifth century BCE, the sanctuary was expanded by Ictinus and other architects to its final form. A new *telestērion* was built, large enough to accommodate several thousand initiands *(mustai)*, who during the initiation rites stood on steps along the four inner walls. In the center of the *telestērion* stood the *anaktoron* in its traditional location.

By the second half of the fifth century, in the Classical period of Greek culture, participation in the rites at Eleusis, previously restricted to Athenians, was open to all Greeks. In Hellenistic and imperial times, the mysteries gained even more prestige; they were now open to *mustai* from all over the Roman empire. The eschatological hopes offered by the rites attracted philosophers and emperors alike. Marcus Aurelius, who was both, rebuilt the sanctuary after a barbarian invasion in 170 CE. The Christian emperor Theodosius (r. 379–395) interdicted participation in the mysteries, as in all pagan cults, and shortly afterward, in 395 CE, the invading Goths destroyed the sanctuary.

Organization. Besides the priestess of Demeter, who lived in the sanctuary, the temple of Eleusis was attended by a host of officials, both religious and secular. The main religious official was the hierophant (Gr., *hierophantēs;* lit., "he who shows the sacred things"), chosen from the Eleusinian family of the Eumolpides to serve for life. From the family of the Kerukes came the *daidouchos* ("torchbearer") and the *hierokērux* ("sacred herald"), the two officials next in rank.

Ideology. The Homeric *Hymn to Demeter*, composed before Athenian control (between 650 and 550 BCE), narrates how Demeter's daughter, Kore ("maiden"), also called Persephone, was carried off by Hades. After an unsuccessful search for Kore, Demeter in human disguise came to Eleusis and was engaged as a nurse to the baby prince Demophon, whom she tried to make immortal by immersion in fire. Found out, she revealed her divinity, ordered a temple to be built, and, by stopping the growth of crops, blackmailed Zeus into restoring her daughter, at least for half a year; the other half Kore had to spend in the underworld with her husband Hades. [*See also* Demeter and Persephone.] Demeter then restored life to the crops and revealed the mysteries to the Eleusinian princes.

This narrative uses a traditional theme—the rape and restoration of a maiden are elements of a fertility theme that appears in various Near Eastern mythologies—to account for the origins of the Eleusinian cult. It is the central text for the mysteries. To those "who have seen these things," it promises a better fate after death (Homeric *Hymn to Demeter* 480ff.). In Peisistratean times,

Athenian mythmakers introduced an important change: Demeter was said to have given the cereal crops to the Eleusinians, who had not known them before, and Triptolemos, one of the Eleusinian heroes, was credited with teaching the art of agriculture to mankind. Vase paintings attest to the popularity of this myth from the late sixth century onward. Not much later, another change was introduced that gave more concrete forms to the vague eschatological hopes raised by the mysteries: the *mustai* could now look forward to a blessed paradise, the uninitiated to punishments after death. From the fifth century onward, both these changes are reflected in poems ascribed to Musaios (a hero related to Eumolpos, the ancestor of the Eumolpidai) and to Orpheus.

The Ritual. The initiation rites were secret. Our knowledge is restricted to scraps of information provided by those who dared to divulge them (especially converted pagans) and to those rituals that were public.

The initiation formed part of the state festival of the Musteria, or Greater Mysteries, in the Athenian month of Boedromion (September–October). Initiation at Eleusis was preceded by a preliminary ritual, at Agrai, just outside Athens, that took place in the month of Anthesterion (February–March). Pictorial sources show that this ritual, called the Lesser Mysteries, had a predominantly purificatory character: it contained the sacrifice of a piglet and purifications through fire (a burning torch) and air (by means of a fan). The Greater Mysteries themselves began with preparations in Athens: assembly of the *mustai* and formal exclusion of "murderers and barbarians" (on 15 Boedromion), a ritual bath in the sea (on 16 Boedromion), and three days of fast. On 19 Boedromion, the *mustai* marched in procession from Athens to Eleusis, guided by the statue of Iacchos, the god who impersonated the ecstatic shouts (*iacchazein*, "to shout") of the crowd and was later identified with the ecstatic Dionysos.

Toward dusk, the *mustai* entered the sanctuary at Eleusis. A secret password, known to us through a Christian source, informs us about the preliminary rites (Clement of Alexandria, *Protrepticus* 21.8): "I fasted; I drank the *kukeōn;* I took from the chest; having done my task, I placed in the basket, and from the basket into the chest." The *kukeōn* is known to have been a mixture of water, barley, and spice, taken to break the fast (*Hymn to Demeter* 206ff.), but details of the rest of the ritual are obscure. Perhaps the *mustai* took a mortar from the sacred chest and ground some grains of wheat. They also enacted the search for Kore by torchlight (ibid., 47ff.).

The central rite is clear only in its outline. Crowded in the *telestērion* for the whole night, the *mustai* underwent terrifying darkness; then came a climax full of illumination, "when the *anaktoron* was opened" (Plutarch, *Moralia* 81d–e) and a huge fire burst forth. (Note the parallel to the motif of immersion in fire to gain immortality in *Hymn to Demeter* 239f.) Details of what followed are conjectural, based largely on the account of Hippolytus (c. 170–236). "Under a huge fire," he reports, "the hierophant shouts, 'The Mistress has given birth to a sacred child, Brimo to Brimos' " (*Refutation of All Heresies* 5.8). Perhaps "the mistress" is Demeter and the "sacred child" Ploutos (Plutus), or Wealth, symbolized by an ear of wheat, for Hippolytus describes another ritual thus: "The hierophant showed the initiates the great . . . mystery, an ear cut in silence" (ibid.).

The central rite must have evoked eschatological hopes by ritual means, not by teaching. (Teaching is expressly excluded by Aristotle, *Fragment* 15.) The symbolism of the grain lends itself to such an explanation, as does the symbolism of a new birth. A year after his initiation *(muēsis)*, the *mustēs* could attain the degree of *epopteia*. The rituals of this degree are unknown; many scholars maintain that the showing of the ear belongs to this degree, on the strength of Hippolytus's terminology.

Initiation into the Eleusinian mysteries was, in historical times, an affair of individuals, as in the imperial mystery cults, but unlike them, it always remained bound to one place, Eleusis, and had presumably grown out of gentilitial cults of the Eleusinian families.

[*See also* Mystery Religions.]

BIBLIOGRAPHY

The most competent archaeological account of the Eleusinian mysteries (with a much less convincing part on the ritual) is George E. Mylonas's *Eleusis and the Eleusinian Mysteries* (Princeton, 1961). Corrections regarding the Mycenaean origin are presented by Pascal Darcque in "Les vestiges mycéniens découverts sous le Telestérion d'Eleusis," *Bulletin de correspondance hellénique* 105 (1981): 593–605. The Homeric hymn has been edited, with ample commentary, by N. J. Richardson in *The Homeric Hymn to Demeter* (Oxford, 1974); the later poems are reconstructed in my *Eleusis und die orphische Dichtung Athens in vorhellenistischer Zeit* (Berlin, 1974). The iconographical sources are collected by Ugo Bianchi in *The Greek Mysteries* (Leiden, 1976). Interesting insights, despite many debatable arguments, are given in Karóly Kerényi's *Eleusis: Archetypal Image of Mother and Daughter*, translated by Ralph Manheim (New York, 1967). Walter Burkert's *Homo Necans: The Anthropology of Ancient Greek Sacrificial Ritual and Myth*, edited and translated by Peter Bing (Berkeley, 1983), approaches the mysteries through the phenomenology of sacrificial ritual; see also his short but masterly account in *Greek Religion, Archaic and Classical* (Cambridge, Mass., 1985), pp.

285–290. Bruce M. Metzger's "Bibliography of Mystery Religions: IV, The Eleusinian Mysteries," in *Aufstieg und Niedergang der römischen Welt,* vol. 2.17.3 (Berlin and New York, 1984), pp. 1317–1329, 1407–1409, covers the years 1927–1977 and is a very thorough listing, albeit without annotation.

FRITZ GRAF

ELIADE, MIRCEA (1907–1986), Romanian-born historian of religions, humanist, Orientalist, philosopher, and creative writer. The career of Mircea Eliade, who served as editor in chief of this encyclopedia, was long and multifaceted. Since this article can give only a brief, general introduction, those who wish to know more of his life and work are referred to the works cited in the following bibliography.

Student Years. Born in Bucharest, the son of an army officer, Eliade witnessed the German occupation of his homeland when he was only nine years old. His lifelong fascination with literature, philosophy, Oriental studies, alchemy, and the history of religions began when he was still at the *lycée.* An early article entitled "The Enemy of the Silkworm" reflects the boy's intense interest in plants, animals, and insects. In fact he had already published his one hundredth article by the time he entered the University of Bucharest in 1925. At the university, he became a devoted disciple of the philosopher Nae Ionescu, who taught him the importance of life experience, commitment, intuition, and the spiritual or psychological reality of mental worlds. At the university Eliade became particularly interested in the philosophy of the Italian Renaissance, especially in Marsilio Ficino's rediscovery of Greek philosophy.

Eliade was blessed with the happy combination of an unusually keen mind, strong intuition, a fertile imagination, and the determination to work hard. Much of the structure of his later thought, and some of the paradoxes of his life, were foreshadowed during his student years. Simultaneously he was both a Romanian patriot and a world citizen. He was proud of Western civilization, although he lamented its provincial character, particularly its will to "universalize" Western ideas and values into the norm for all of humankind. Looking back, he could see that in his country previous generations had had no cause to question their historic mission to consolidate Romania's national identity. His own generation, though, had experienced World War I and seemed to have no ready-made model or mission for themselves. Eliade's plea was that his fellow countrymen should exploit this period of "creative freedom" from tradition and should try to learn from other parts of the world what possibilities for life and thought there were. His ultimate concern was the revitalization of all branches of learning and the arts, and his great hope was to decipher the message of the cosmos, which to him was a great repository of hidden meanings. Judging from his diaries and other writings, it seems that Eliade always had a strong sense of destiny, from his youth until his last day in Chicago, calling him from one phase of life to the next, though he felt he was not always conscious of what lay in store for him along the way.

Concerning his preoccupation with the Italian Renaissance in his college days, Eliade later stated, "Perhaps, without knowing it, I was in search of a new, wider humanism, bolder than the humanism of the Renaissance, which was too dependent on the models of Mediterranean classicism. . . . Ultimately, I dreamed of rediscovering the model of a 'universal man'" (*No Souvenirs: Journal, 1957–1969,* London, 1978, p.17). As though to fulfill Eliade's preordained destiny, the maharaja of Kassimbazar offered him a grant to study Indian philosophy with Surendranath Dasgupta at the University of Calcutta (1928–1932). He also spent six months in the ashram of Rishikesh in the Himalayas. To him, India was more than a place for scholarly research. He felt that a mystery was hidden somewhere in India, and deciphering it would disclose the mystery of his own existence. India indeed revealed to him the profound meaning of the freedom that can be achieved by abolishing the routine conditions of human existence, a meaning indicated in the subtitle of his book on Yoga: *Immortality and Freedom.*

The stay in India also opened his eyes to the existence of common elements in all peasant cultures—for example, in China, Southeast Asia, pre-Aryan aboriginal India, the Mediterranean world, and the Iberian Peninsula—the elements from which he would later derive the notion of "cosmic religion." In fact, the discovery of pre-Aryan aboriginal Indian spirituality (which has remained an important thread in the fabric of Hinduism to the present) led Eliade to speculate on a comparable synthesis in southeastern Europe, where the ancient culture of the Dacians formed the "autochthonous base" of present-day Romanian culture. (Dacian culture had been reconstructed by a Romanian philosopher-folklorist, B. P. Hasdeu.) Moreover, Eliade came to believe that the substratum of peasant cultures of southeastern Europe has been preserved to this day, underneath the cultural influences of the Greeks, the Romans, the Byzantines, and Christianity, and he went so far as to suggest that the peasant roots of Romanian culture could become the basis of a genuine universalism, transcending nationalism and cultural provincialism. He believed that the oppressed peoples of Asia and elsewhere might take their rightful place in world history through such universalism. "We, the people of Eastern Europe, would be able to serve as a bridge between the West and Asia." As he remarked in his autobiography, "A good part of my activity in [Romania] between 1932 and 1940 found its point of departure in these intuitions and observations" (*Autobiography: Journey East, Journey West*, vol. 1, 1981, p. 204).

Early Literary and Intellectual Activity. In 1932 Eliade returned to Romania and was appointed to assist Nae Ionescu at the University of Bucharest in the following year. His publication of *Yoga: Essai sur les origines de la mystique indienne* (1936), in which he attempted a new interpretation of the myths and symbolism of archaic and Oriental religions, attracted the attention of such eminent European scholars as Jean Przyluski, Louis de La Vallée Poussin, Heinrich Zimmer, and Giuseppe Tucci. He also plunged feverishly into literary activities. Many people were under the impression then that Eliade thought of himself primarily as a novelist, although he was strongly motivated to engage in scholarly activities as well. Eliade had made his literary debut in 1930 with *Isabel şi Apele Divolului* (Isabel and the Devil's Water), which was obviously colored by his Indian experience. According to Matei Calinescu, in his essay "'The Function of the Unreal': Reflections on Mircea Eliade's Short Fiction" (in Girardot and Ricketts, 1982), most of Eliade's fiction inspired by India was written between 1930 and 1935, and his earlier novels with Indian themes (e.g., *Maitreyi*, 1933) were strongly autobiographical. He also points out that Eliade's later novellas on these themes, such as *Secretul Doctorului Honigberger* (The Secret of Doctor Honigberger) and *Nopţi la Serampore* (Night in Serampore), both published in a single volume entitled *Secretul Doctorului Honigberger* (1940), "deal with the major problem of the fully mature Eliade, that of the ambiguities of the sacred and the profane in their characteristical relationship"; Calimescu concludes that "Eliade had discovered the 'ontological' signification of narration" by 1940 (ibid., p. 142).

Eliade once stated that young Romanians had a very short period of creative freedom, and fear that this observation might apply to himself compelled him to work against the clock. Accordingly, he published not only literary works but also a series of important scholarly studies on alchemy, mythology, Oriental studies, philosophy, symbology, metallurgy, and the history of religions. In 1938 he founded the journal *Zalmoxis: Revue des études religieuses.* (Unfortunately, circulation ceased after 1942.) Eliade was also active in the so-called Criterion group, consisting of male and female intellectuals. This group was a significant collective manifestation of the "young generation" of Romanians, which sponsored public lectures, symposia, and discussion about important contemporary intellectual issues as a new type of Socratic dialogue. "The goal we were pursuing," Eliade said, "was not only to inform people; above all, we were seeking to 'awaken' the audience, to confront them with ideas, and ultimately to modify their mode of being in the world" (*Autobiography*, vol. 1, p. 237).

Meanwhile, Romania could not help but be touched by the political whirlwind that was rising in Europe, manifested in the conflicts and tensions between communism and democracy, fascism and Nazism. Following the assassination of Romanian Prime Minister Duca in December 1933, Eliade's mentor Nae Ionescu was arrested on suspicion that he was an antiroyalist rightist. Also arrested were the leaders of the pro-Nazi Legion of the Archangel Michael, commonly known as the Legionnaires or the Iron Guard, and some of Eliade's friends in the Criterion group. Of course the Criterion experiment ceased to function because it was impossible for Legionnaires, democrats, and communists to share the same platform. Thus, Romania entered a "broken-off era," as Eliade called it with fear and trembling. The tense political atmosphere, the cruelties and excesses of all sorts, find their echoes in Eliade's *Huliganii*, 2 vols. (The Hooligans; 1935), although he explicitly said that the hooligans in the novel were very different from the actual Romanian hooligans of the 1930s—those "groups of young antisemites, ready to break windows or heads, to attack or loot synagogues" (*Autobiography*, vol. 1, p. 301). What concerned Eliade was not only the sad political reality of his homeland. He wrote, "I had had the premonition long before . . . that we would *not have time.* I sensed now not only that time was limited, but that there would come a terrifying time (the time of the 'terror of history')" (ibid., p. 292). In 1938 the royal dictatorship in Romania was proclaimed; then came World War II.

Emigration and Development. In 1940 Eliade was appointed cultural attaché at the Royal Romanian Legation in war-torn London. In the following year he became a cultural counselor in Lisbon, in neutral Portugal. When the war was over in 1945, Eliade went directly to Paris, thus starting the life of self-imposed exile. Although he could write and lecture in French, starting a new life in a foreign country at the age of thirty-eight required considerable adjustment. On the other hand, by that time he was already a highly respected, mature scholar. "It took me ten years to understand," he said, "that the Indian experience alone could not reveal to me the universal man I had been looking for" (*No Souvenirs,* p. 17). For this task he acknowledged the necessity of combining the history of religions, Orientalism, ethnology, and other disciplines. He wrote:

> The correct analyses of myths and of mythical thought, of symbols and primordial images, especially the religious creations that emerge from Oriental and "primitive" cultures, are . . . the only way to open the Western mind and to introduce a new, planetary humanism. . . . Thus, the proper procedure for grasping their meaning is not the naturalist's "objectivity," but the intelligent sympathy of the hermeneut. *It was the procedure itself that had to be changed* . . . . This conviction guided my research on the meaning and function of myths, the structure of religious symbols, and in general, of the dialectics of the sacred and the profane. (ibid., p. xii)

In 1946 Eliade was invited to serve as a visiting professor at the École des Hautes Études of the Sorbonne. He then proceeded to publish such famous works as *Techniques du Yoga* (1948), *Traité d'histoire des religions* (1949; revised translation, *Patterns in Comparative Religion,* 1958), *Le mythe de l'eternel retour* (1949; revised translation, *The Myth of the Eternal Return,* 1954), *Le chamanisme et les techniques archaiques de l'extase* (1951; revised and enlarged translation, *Shamanism: Archaic Techniques of Ecstasy,* 1964), and so on. He was also invited by many leading universities in Europe to deliver lectures, and he appeared in a number of seminars and conferences, for example, the annual meetings at Ascona, Switzerland.

In retrospect, it becomes clear that during his stay in Paris (1945–1955) Eliade solidified most of his important concepts and categories, including those of *homo religiosus, homo symbolicus,* archetypes, *coincidentia oppositorum,* hierophany, *axis mundi,* the cosmic rope, the nostalgia for Paradise, androgyny, the initiatory scenario, and so on, all of which became integral parts of a coherent outlook or system that aimed at what Eliade later called a total hermeneutics. This may account for the impossibility of isolating, or even criticizing, any part of his system without disturbing the entire framework. Side by side with this development, one notices the shift in his personal orientation. Before World War II, his scholarly and literary activities had focused very much on Romania. In those years, he affirmed that "the orthodox heritage could constitute a total conception of the world and existence, and that this synthesis, if it could be realized, would be a new phenomenon in the history of modern Romanian culture" (*Autobiography,* vol. 1, p. 132). After the war, he continued to regard himself as a Romanian writer, but something new was added. The sense that his experience suggested the paradigm of the homeless exile as a symbol of religious reality for modern, secularized humankind. In this situation, his literary works, too, took on the "coloring of a *redeeming force (forta recuperatoare),*" to quote Eugene Simon (in Girardot and Ricketts, 1982, p. 136).

Methodology and Imagination. Like many other historians of religions—for example, Raffaele Pettazzoni (1883–1959) and Joachim Wach (1898–1955)—Eliade held that the discipline of the history of religions *(Allgemeine Religionswissenschaft)* consisted of two dimensions, historical and systematic. Characteristically, he worked first on the systematic dimension (using the "morphological" method, inspired by Goethe), as exemplified by his *Traité (Patterns in Comparative Religion),* which presents an astonishing variety of religious data and their basic "patterns." The book starts with certain "cosmic" hierophanies (i.e., manifestations of the sacred), such as the sky, waters, earth, and stones. Analyses of these manifestations are based on Eliade's notion of the dialectic of the sacred, in order to show how far those hierophanies constitute autonomous forms. He goes on to discuss the "biological" hierophanies (from the rhythm of the moon to sexuality), "local" hierophanies such as consecrated places, and "myths and symbols." Throughout the book, Eliade examines both the "lower" and "higher" religious forms side by side instead of moving from lower to higher forms, as is done in evolutionary schemes. He takes pain to explain that "religious wholes are not seen in bits and pieces, for each class of hierophanies . . . forms, in its own way, a whole, both morphologically . . . and historically" (*Patterns in Comparative Religion,* New York, 1958, p. xvi).

It is not surprising that Eliade's morphology of religion, which is his version of the systematic aspect of the history of religions, has much in common with the phenomenology of religion of Gerardus van der Leeuw (1890–1950), a Dutch historian of religions, theologian, ethnologist, and phenomenologist. Eliade wrote a very positive review of van der Leeuw's *Religion in Essence and Manifestation* in *Revue d'histoire des religions* 138 (1950): 108–111. Although Eliade is uneasy with van der Leeuw's starting point, he praises the book because it shows that human beings can and do find religious meaning even in the most banal physiological activities such as eating and sexuality, and the book portrays the entire cosmos with its most humble parts serving as grounds for the manifestation of the sacred. It should be noted that religion has two dimensions in van der Leeuw's scheme, namely, "religion as experience," which can be studied phenomenologically, and "religion as revelation," which is basically incomprehensible and thus can be studied only theologically. Furthermore, van der Leeuw never claimed that his phenomenological study is empirical, because to him empirical research is needed only to control what has been understood phenomenologically. Similarly, Eliade never claimed that the history of religions, including its systematic task, is empirical in a narrow scientific sense, even though it certainly has empirical dimensions.

Eliade always felt a need for the alternating modes of the creative spirit—the "diurnal," rational mode of scholarship, which he expressed in his French writings, and the "nocturnal," mythological mode of imagination and fantasy, which he continued to express in Romanian. In 1955, the French translation of his major novel, *Forêt interdite,* appeared. According to Mac Linscott Ricketts, who with M. P. Stevenson translated this novel into English (*The Forbidden Forest,* 1978), Eliade felt it would be more for this work and other fiction that he would be remembered by later generations than for his erudite scholarly works. *The Forbidden Forest* is in a sense a historical novel, dealing with the events and activities of the protagonist and his lovers, friends, and foes during the turbulent twelve years from 1936 to 1948, in Romania, London, Lisbon, Russia, and Paris. In another sense it is an original novel. Eliade skillfully creates characters, all of whom are caught by "destiny," as people often are in his other stories. All of them try to escape from the network of historical events and from destructive "time," which is the central theme of this novel. The tangled story begins on the summer solstice in a forest near Bucharest. After twelve years, again on the summer solstice but in a French forest near the Swiss border, the protagonist encounters his long-lost girlfriend, and he finds salvation, which is "a kind of transcendental love for a girl—and death" (Ricketts, in *Imagination and Meaning,* p. 105). To be sure, the novels were not meant to be literary illustrations of Eliade's theories, but he admits there are some structural analogies between the scientific and literary imaginations, such as the structure of sacred and mythical space, and more especially "a considerable number of strange, unfamiliar, and enigmatic worlds of meaning" (*No Souvenirs,* p. ix).

Years in the United States. In 1956 Eliade was invited by the University of Chicago to deliver the Haskell Lectures, which were published under the title *Birth and Rebirth* (1958). In 1957 he joined the University of Chicago faculty and continued to live in that city after his retirement. At the time of his death in 1986, he was the Sewell L. Avery Distinguished Service Professor Emeritus.

Eliade's move to the United States at the age of forty-nine meant a second emigration for him, but he made an excellent adjustment to the new environment. The University of Chicago had traditionally been an important center for the study of the history of religions, and graduates trained by Eliade's predecessor, Joachim Wach, were scattered in many parts of North America and on other continents. Eliade's appointment at Chicago coincided with the sudden mushrooming of departments of religion or religious studies as part of the liberal arts programs of various colleges and universities in North America. Fortunately, his books and articles—mostly the scholarly ones and not his literary works—were beginning to be translated into English, and the reading public devoured them. Eliade made a deep impression on young readers with such works as *Cosmos and History* (1959), *The Sacred and the Profane* (1959), *Myths, Dreams and Mysteries* (1960), *Images and Symbols* (1969), *Myths and Reality* (1963), *Mephistopheles and the Androgyne* (1965), *Zalmoxis* (1972), *The Forge and the Crucible* (1962), *The Quest* (1975), and others. He also exerted a tremendous influence on more advanced students with *Yoga* (1958), *Shamanism* (1964), and *Australian Religions* (1973). The fact that Eliade was willing to use nonphilosophical and nontheological terms in an elegant literary style to discuss religious subjects attracted many secularized youths.

There were three new factors that helped Eliade's cause enormously. The first was the founding in the summer of 1961 of a new international journal for comparative historical studies called *History of Religion.* Wisely, Eliade suggested making it an English-language journal instead of a multilanguage one. For the opening issue, Eliade wrote the famous article entitled "History of Religions and a New Humanism" (*History of Religions* 1, Summer 1961, pp. 1–8). In it, he expressed his sympathy with young scholars who would have become historians of religions but who, in a world that exalts specialists, had resorted to becoming specialists in one religion or even in a particular period or a single aspect of that religion. Historians of religions, he said, are called to be learned generalists. He recognized the danger of "reductionism" in the history of religions as much as in the interpretation of art and literary works. He insisted that a work of art, for example, reveals its meaning only when it is seen as an autonomous artistic creation and nothing else. In the case of the history of religions he realized that the situation is complex because there is no such thing as a "pure" religious datum, and that a human datum is also a historical datum. But this does not imply that, for historians of religions, a historical datum is in any way reducible to a nonreligious, economic, social, cultural, psychological, or political meaning. And, quoting the words of Raffaele Pettazzoni, he exhorted readers to engage in the twin (systematic and historical) tasks of the history of religions. But to him, ultimately, the history of religions was more than merely an academic pursuit. He wrote:

> The History of Religions is destined to play an important role in contemporary cultural life. This is not only because an understanding of exotic and archaic religions will significantly assist in a cultural dialogue with the representatives of such religions. It is more especially because . . . the history of religions will inevitably attain to a deeper knowledge of man. It is on the basis of such knowledge that a new humanism, on a world-wide scale, could develop.
>
> (ibid., pp. 2–3)

Second, Eliade took an active part as a member (and president for a term) of a small group of North American scholars called the American Society for the Study of Religion (ASSR), established in Chicago in 1958. It was through this group that much of Eliade's personal contacts with fellow historians of religions and scholars in related fields in North America were made.

Third, Eliade, who had previously worked either on "systematic" endeavors or on studies of "particular" religious forms (e.g., yoga, shamanism, Romanian folk religion, or Australian religion) always from the perspective of the history of religions, embarked during his Chicago days on a new genre, namely, a "historical" study of the history of religions. Initially he worked on a "thematic source book" entitled *From Primitive to Zen* (1968) dealing with religious data from nonliterate, ancient, medieval, and modern religions. Then he envisaged the publication of four volumes (though his health prevented his working on the fourth volume himself) entitled *A History of Religious Ideas* (1978–1986). Although the scheme of the series follows manifestations of the sacred and the creative moments of the different traditions more or less in chronological order, readers will recognize that these books reflect faithfully his lifelong conviction about the fundamental unity of all religious phenomena. Thus, in his historical studies as much as in his systematic endeavors, he was true to his hypothesis that "every rite, every myth, every belief or divine figure reflects the experience of the sacred and hence implies the notions of *being,* of *meaning,* and of *truth*" (*A History of Religious Ideas,* vol. 1, Chicago, 1978, p. xiii).

During the latter part of his stay in Chicago, fame and honor came his way from various parts of the world. By that time, many of his books, including his literary works, had been translated into several languages. He had his share of critics. Some people thought that he was not religious enough, while others accused him of being too philosophical and not humanistic enough, historical enough, scientific enough, or empirical enough. But, as hinted earlier, he held a consistent viewpoint that penetrated all aspects of his scholarly and literary works, so that it is difficult to be for or against any part of his writings without having to judge the whole framework.

Eliade's last major undertaking in his life was the present *Encyclopedia of Religion.* As he stated himself, what he had in mind was not a dictionary but an encyclopedia—a selection of all the important ideas and beliefs, rituals and myths, symbols and persons, all that played a role in the universal history of the religious experience of humankind from the Paleolithic age to our time. It is to his credit that various scholars from every continent cooperated on the encyclopedia to produce concise, clear descriptions of a number of religious forms within the limits of our present knowledge. As soon as he had completed the major portion of his work as editor in chief of the encyclopedia, he was already thinking of several new projects, among them ones that would develop the themes of cosmos, humankind, and time. Throughout his life, Eliade never claimed that he had the answer to the riddle of life, but he was willing to advance daring hypotheses.

Once Eliade paid a high tribute to his friend and colleague, Paul Tillich, at the latter's memorial service in Chicago, and if the name of Tillich is replaced with that of Eliade, it portrays the latter admirably: "Faithful to his vocation and his destiny [Eliade] did not die at the end of his career, when he had supposedly said everything important that he could say. . . . Thus, his death is even more tragic. But it is also symbolic" (*Criterion* 5, no. 1, 1968, p. 15).

BIBLIOGRAPHY

Both as a scholar and as a writer, Eliade was prolific throughout his life, and his works have been translated into many languages. Thus, it is virtually impossible to list all his books and articles, even the major ones, although efforts were made to include the major titles in the foregoing text. Fortunately, there are some Eliade bibliographies in English that are readily available to readers, such as the one included in *Myths and Symbols: Studies in Honor of Mircea Eliade,* edited by Joseph M. Kitagawa and Charles H. Long (Chicago, 1969), and a more up-to-date one, edited by Douglas Allen and Dennis Doeing, *Mircea Eliade: An Annotated Bibliography,* (New York, 1980). One of the best introductions to Eliade's thought is his *Ordeal by Labyrinth: Conversations with Claude-Henri Rocquet* either in its French original (Paris, 1978) or in its English translation (Chicago, 1982). This book has the virtues of unfolding Eliade's own mature views about himself, and it includes "A Chronology of Mircea Eliade's Life," which calls attention to his major writings. There are also many articles and books in various languages on Eliade's scholarly and literary works, some critical, some sympathetic, and some favorable. The third section of the above-mentioned *Myths and Symbols,* as well as

Imagination and Meaning: The Scholarly and Literary Worlds of Mircea Eliade, edited by N. J. Girardot and Mac Linscott Ricketts (New York, 1982), and *Waiting for the Dawn: Mircea Eliade in Perspective,* edited by Davíd Carrasco and J. M. Swanberg (Boulder, 1985), make helpful references to his creative writing, although his scholarly side inevitably comes into the picture too.

There are many other works (mentioning only monographs) that readers should find useful. See Douglas Allen's *Structure and Creativity in Religion: Mircea Eliade's Phenomenology and New Directions* (The Hague, 1978); Thomas J. J. Altizer's *Mircea Eliade and the Dialectic of the Sacred* (Philadelphia, 1963); Guilford Dudley's *Religion on Trial: Mircea Eliade and His Critics* (Philadelphia, 1977); Jonathan Z. Smith's *Map Is Not Territory: Studies in the History of Religions* (Leiden, 1978); Ioan Petro Culianu's *Mircea Eliade* (Assisi, 1978); and Antonio B. de Silva's *The Phenomenology of Religion as a Philosophical Problem: An Analysis of the Theoretical Background of the Phenomenology of Religion, in General, and of M. Eliade's Phenomenological Approach, in Particular* (Uppsala, 1982).

JOSEPH M. KITAGAWA

ELI'EZER BEN HYRCANUS, also known as Eli'ezer the Great, but usually simply as Rabbi Eli'ezer; Jewish sage of the late first and early second centuries CE, the first generation of the tannaitic period. The legends surrounding Eli'ezer's beginnings, although contradictory, are united in seeking to create an aura of greatness. According to the dominant tradition, Eli'ezer, like 'Aqiva' ben Yosef, was an adult before he began his studies. Despite this, he was soon found to be "explicating matters that no ear had ever before heard." Elsewhere, Eli'ezer is described as a child prodigy, and those who saw him as a child predicted that he would one day be a great sage. The legends about Eli'ezer convey a close association between him and Yoḥanan ben Zakk'ai, whom Eli'ezer and his colleague Yehoshu'a ben Ḥananyah were entrusted to smuggle in a coffin from the embattled Jerusalem. The same association is emphasized in *Avot* (2.8), where Yoḥanan declares that Eli'ezer's great wisdom outweighs that of all the sages of Israel.

Eli'ezer's statements regarding himself reflect what might be termed an intense, even obsessive work ethic. He describes his extraordinary perseverance in Torah study (B.T., *Suk.* 28a), and in the same tradition he claims never to have uttered a profane word. Elsewhere Eli'ezer voices suspicion of sexuality. Most crucial, perhaps, is the claim of extreme conservatism in matters of tradition ascribed to Eli'ezer; he declares that he "never uttered a word that he did not hear from his teacher" (ibid.). Although not literally true, this accurately portrays the conservatism of Eli'ezer's legal opinions. Eli'ezer's legal concerns closely parallel those of his Pharisaic predecessors, to the extent that we can reconstruct them. His exegetical method is also often conservative, a tendency that sometimes leads him to conclusions that are harshly literal.

A picture of Eli'ezer's persona is derived to a great extent from reports of an event that led to his ban *(ḥerem)* from rabbinical circles. The traditions that describe the precipitating event (B.T., *B.M.* 59b; J.T. *Mo'ed Q.* 3.1, 81c–d), composed long after it occurred, are not unified in their description, but they agree that the immediate dispute concerned the ritual purity of a certain oven ("the oven of 'Akhn'ai"), and they appear to agree that Eli'ezer's refusal to submit to the will of the majority was the cause for his ban. This is a compelling explanation because contemporary conditions demanded cooperation with the new rabbinic center of power, the authority of which Eli'ezer was challenging. Still, other explanations for Eli'ezer's exclusion developed. One suggests that Eli'ezer's offense was his ascription to *beit Shammai* (the school of Shammai). Although widely repeated, there is no support for this conclusion in earlier sources. Another possible explanation is suggested by an enigmatic tradition that speaks of Eli'ezer's arrest for dealings with *minim* ("sectarians"; Christians?). Whatever the reason, the effect of the ban is felt in a wide variety of sources. This is particularly true in the traditions that describe Eli'ezer's death (where Yehoshu'a arose and declared "the vow is annulled"), but it extends even to the Mishnah itself, where a few of Eli'ezer's views are explicitly suppressed.

Despite this, Eli'ezer's immense contribution to the rabbinic corpus is indicative of the respect that his genius commanded. Eli'ezer is mentioned by name in the Mishnah more often than any of his contemporaries. His opinions are often debated in the Talmuds, and despite his ban, they form the basis of halakhic (legal) decisions. Legend reflects the same conclusion. Even the text that describes the ban demonstrates heavenly support for Eli'ezer's view, support that is repeated elsewhere. Much later, respect for Eli'ezer led to the pseudonymous attribution of the Midrashic work *Pirqei de-Rabbi Eli'ezer* (ninth century) to him.

Eli'ezer's contributions are particularly prevalent in the areas of purity and sacrifice, perhaps a reflection of his belief that the Temple would soon be rebuilt. He was a zealot for the circumcision ritual, preparation for which he permitted even on the Sabbath. In matters of commandment and transgression he was concerned for the act, and not the intention.

[*For discussion of the circle of sages to which Eli'ezer belonged, see* Tannaim.]

BIBLIOGRAPHY

By far the best work on Eli'ezer is *Eliezer ben Hyrcanus: The Tradition and the Man,* 2 vols. (Leiden, 1973), by Jacob Neusner. Though one might dispute individual interpretations or conclusions, Neusner's work is comprehensive and his method superior to any employed previously. A useful synthetic analysis of Eli'ezer's legal traditions is Itzchak Gilath's *Rabbi Eliezer ben Hyrcanus: A Scholar Outcast* (Ramat Gan, Israel, 1984). A full review of the literature on Eli'ezer is given in volume 2 of Neusner's book, pages 249–286.

DAVID KRAEMER

ELIJAH (mid-ninth century BCE), or, in Hebrew, Eliyyahu; a prophet of the northern kingdom of Israel during the reigns of Ahab and Ahaziah and a leader in the opposition to the worship of Baal in Israel.

Historicity of Elijah. While few scholars doubt the existence of Elijah as a religious figure of great personal dynamism and conservative zeal and as the leader of resistance to the rise of Baal worship in Israel in the ninth century BCE, the biblical presentation of the prophet cannot be taken as historical documentation of his activity. His career is presented through the eyes of popular legend and subsequent theological reflection, which consider him a personality of heroic proportions. In this process his actions and relations to the people and the king became stereotyped, and the presentation of his behavior, paradigmatic. The politics of the reign of Ahab (c. 869–850) provided an appropriate occasion for cultural and religious conflict between conservative elements in Israel and the foreign Phoenician influence at the court in Samaria. But how closely the portrayal of that controversy in the biblical story of Elijah corresponds to the actual situation is an issue that cannot be easily resolved.

Literary Sources. The reason for the difficulty in assessing the biblical figure of Elijah lies in the nature of the literary sources that are contained in *1 Kings* 17–19 and 21 and *2 Kings* 1–2. (An additional story in *2 Chronicles* 21:12–15 about a letter from Elijah to Jehoram, king of Judah, is the Chronicler's invention and cannot be taken seriously as part of the Elijah tradition.) The stories about Elijah in *Kings* do not represent a unified tradition or the work of one author. Episodes narrated in *1 Kings* 20 and 22, involving two other prophets, interrupt the account of Elijah's career and give a somewhat different view of Ahab and the court. But even when these are bracketed, the resulting presentation can hardly be derived from one literary source or author. In fact, at least three separate sources may be identified: (1) *1 Kings* 17–19, usually regarded as the oldest story and the nucleus of the Elijah tradition; (2) *1 Kings* 21 and *2 Kings* 1, stories composed by the historian of *Kings* or extensively edited by him; and (3) *2 Kings* 2, an account of the transition of the prophetic office to Elisha, which is regarded as belonging to the collection of Elisha stories.

Biblical Tradition. The historian's view of Elijah in *1 Kings* 21 and *2 Kings* 1 is stereotyped. It represents the prophet as a spokesman for the deity in issuing a reprimand and a word of judgment upon the king; Elijah's role here is similar to the role of other prophets in this source. The remarks in *2 Kings* 1:9–16 about Elijah calling down fire from heaven upon the king's soldiers present the prophet in a somewhat different role, that is, as a wonder-worker. But these verses seem superfluous; since nothing is altered by this activity, the unit has often been viewed as a later addition. Only the description of Elijah as an ascetic who wore haircloth and a leather girdle (*2 Kgs.* 1:8) suggests a distinctive tradition about an unusual personality. What is noteworthy, however, is that the historian's treatment of Elijah in *1 Kings* 21 and *2 Kings* 1 does not reflect any knowledge of the stories contained in *1 Kings* 17–19 or any suggestion of Elijah's miraculous powers.

The impression of Elijah as a major personality in Israelite history is based upon the stories in *1 Kings* 17–19. Here Elijah is a recluse and a solitary figure fed by ravens in a remote region, as well as a wonder-worker who can withhold or bring rain "by my word," who can feed a starving widow's family, and who can raise the widow's son from the dead. These stories are based upon the prophetic legend, some of them paralleling similar legends about Elisha. But all the scenes and episodes in *1 Kings* 17–19, whatever their origin, have been subordinated to the purpose of portraying the theological theme "Yahveh is God," which is also the meaning of Elijah's name.

The affirmation that Yahveh is God is demonstrated first of all by the announcement of the drought and the final coming of the rain, the events that frame and provide the background for all the scenes within chapters 17 and 18. Each episode represents a contest between Yahveh, the God of Israel, and Baal, god of the Phoenicians, whose worshipers regard him as god of the storm and the giver of rain and fertility. The contest comes to a head on Mount Carmel when the 450 prophets of Baal are unable to produce fire from heaven for their altar, while Elijah, the single prophet of Yahveh, produces fire for his altar and wins the people over. The prophets of Baal are slain, and then comes the rain. This struggle between Yahveh and Baal is not just for territory but is meant to convince Israel that Yahveh alone is God. The issue in the story is monotheism.

The flight of the prophet to Mount Horeb (*1 Kgs.* 19)

takes up the theme of the faithful remnant who remains true to Yahveh as the only God in the face of great adversity. For this purpose the fear-inspiring prophet now becomes the fearful fugitive who must learn that God is not present to his people primarily in the theophany of a storm (as with Baal) but in the quiet voice of inner conviction. The faithful remnant are ultimately vindicated by the subsequent events of history.

Many scholars regard the stories in *1 Kings* 17–19 as early, even of the ninth century, and as an independent composition prior to its incorporation into the history of *Kings*. This, however, seems unlikely, because these chapters reflect nothing of the historian's editing and seem to be unknown to him. It is more plausible to suggest that *1 Kings* 17–19 is a later addition to the history of *Kings*. In it the author has portrayed the life of the prophet in such a way as to make him the medium for a theological message, one that expresses the major concerns of the exilic period. Whatever traditions lie behind these stories, they are now so thoroughly reshaped by the writer's theological interests that they cannot be recovered by a tradition history.

The story of Elijah's ascent to heaven in a chariot of fire while Elisha looks on and receives a portion of his spirit (*2 Kgs.* 2) presupposes both the reputation of Elijah as an exceptional "man of God" and the subsequent career of Elisha as wonder-worker. It was probably composed to bridge the two bodies of tradition but belongs more closely to the Elisha stories.

The manner of Elijah's ascension is so remarkable within the biblical tradition that it calls for some comment. Scholars have been quick to note that the chariot and horses of fire are strongly reminiscent of the fiery chariot of the sun so widely attested in antiquity and even in the Hebrew scriptures (*2 Kgs.* 23:11). Does this account suggest that Elijah was transported by the deity himself to a realm beyond death? Or is this an attempt to assimilate a foreign religious symbol by association with a great figure in Israel's own tradition? Whatever the explanation, the story is so exceptional in the Bible that it sets Elijah, along with Moses and Enoch, quite apart from all other mortals as one who did not die.

Finally, in *Malachi* 3:23–24 (Eng. version 4:5–6) Elijah is viewed as returning to Israel to bring the Israelites to repentance before the day of judgment. Perhaps this return is based upon the notion that Elijah never actually experienced death.

Elijah in the New Testament. The New Testament places special emphasis upon Elijah as the forerunner of the messianic age. It seems to have regarded John the Baptist and his ministry of repentance as performing in the "spirit and power of Elijah" (*Lk.* 1:17; cf. *Mt.* 11:14, 17:10–13) and as an appropriate preparation for the ministry of Jesus as the Messiah. Yet the writer of John's gospel has John the Baptist reject his identification with Elijah (*Jn.* 1:21) so as not to detract from the importance of Jesus' ministry.

Elijah also appears in a vision together with Moses at the scene of Jesus' transfiguration to speak about Jesus' own "departure" (*Mt.* 17:3–4, *Mk.* 9:4–5, *Lk.* 9:30–31). The fact that the scene is associated with prayer and a trancelike experience suggests a connection with a mystical tradition.

Elijah in Postbiblical Judaism. The biblical tradition of Elijah received a great deal of attention in Judaism: in the apocalyptic tradition, in rabbinic *aggadah*, in Jewish mysticism, and in folklore (see Ginzberg, 1909–1938). It is remarkable how the figure of Elijah could become all things to all men.

As in Christianity, Elijah was the forerunner of the messianic age, the herald of Israel's redemption (Ginzberg, 1909–1938, pp. 233–235). He would cooperate with the Messiah as a conqueror of the world powers, he would solve all the halakhic problems that still remained to be dealt with (B.T., *Meg.* 15b; *Sheq.* 2.5; *B.M.* 3.4–5), and as the one to blow the last trumpet, he would be responsible for the resurrection of the dead. He would also restore the lost furnishings of the Temple and provide for the anointing of the Messiah (*Mekhilta' de-Rabbi Shim'on bar Yoḥ'ai* 51b).

Not only is Elijah thought of in connection with the future, but he also continues to play an active role in this present age by virtue of the fact that he never actually died. Because he ascended to heaven in a miraculous way and was translated into a realm of existence akin to that of a divine being or angel, he seems to have been regarded as a special heavenly emissary who could appear in human form to righteous persons either to instruct them or to aid them in time of trouble (see Ginzberg, 1909–1938, pp. 201–203). The mystical tradition went so far as to suggest that Elijah was not human but an angel who appeared on earth for a time in human form. Perhaps as a counter to excessive veneration of the prophet, some rabbis argued that Elijah had died (B.T., *Suk.* 5a) in spite of the biblical tradition about his ascension. They were also critical of some aspects of his ministry (B.T., *B.M.* 85b; *Sg. Rab.* 1.6.1). But any efforts to downplay the prophet's reputation seem to have had little effect.

Elijah's mediation between the heavenly realm and the mundane world expressed itself in a variety of ways. To those engrossed in the study of the law Elijah might appear in a vision or dream as their counselor or teacher because he was known for his zeal for the law and the covenant (Ginzberg, 1909–1938, pp. 217–223). He was often compared with Moses, especially as one who had also received a revelation of God at Mount Horeb. A number of sayings in the Talmud are attributed to a "school of Elijah," perhaps a school founded in his honor. But in later times this notion developed into a large collection of *midrashim, Tanna de-vei Eliyyahu* (also known as *Seder Eliyyahu Rabbah* and *Zuṭa'*), which was believed to stem in some way from Elijah himself.

To the mystics of the Qabbalah Elijah was also a mystagogue who had access to the heavenly realm and could reveal its secrets (Ginzberg, 1909–1938, pp. 229–233). To others Elijah was a psychopomp who transported the souls of the righteous to paradise and the wicked to perdition (*Pirqei de-Rabbi Eli'ezer* 15). In Jewish folklore Elijah was regarded as one who still roamed the earth in the guise of a beggar or a peasant performing wondrous deeds to help the poor and the needy (Ginzberg, 1909–1938, pp. 202–211). On this level too Elijah became associated with the veneration of a number of places, either because they were identified with events in the biblical tradition or because they were places where Elijah had appeared to later generations and performed his miracles.

A number of customs are also connected with the figure of Elijah. At the ceremony of circumcision a chair is set for him in order to invoke his presence as "angel of the covenant" of Abraham to oversee and, by proxy, to carry out the requirements of the law. Elijah was also regarded as healer and guardian of the newborn because of his care for the widow's son. In this respect amulets containing the name of the prophet were good luck charms. At the Passover Seder a cup of wine is placed on the table as the cup of Elijah and is not drunk. This was interpreted eschatologically as an anticipation of the final deliverance from bondage.

BIBLIOGRAPHY

There are few detailed monographs in English on the Elijah tradition. In German the standard treatments are Georg Fohrer's *Elia,* 2d ed. (Zurich, 1968); and Odil H. Steck's *Überlieferung und Zeitgeschichte in den Elia-Erzählungen* (Neukirchen, 1968). Two shorter essays worthy of mention are Harold H. Rowley's "Elijah on Mount Carmel," *Bulletin of the John Rylands Library* (Manchester) 43 (1960): 190–219, reprinted in his *Men of God* (New York, 1963); and Ernst Würthwein's "Elijah at Horeb: Reflections on 1 Kings 19.9–18," in *Proclamation and Presence: Old Testament Essays in Honour of Gwynne Henton Davies,* edited by John I. Durham and J. Roy Porter (London, 1970), pp. 152–166.

For a sociological approach to the tradition, see Robert R. Wilson's *Prophecy and Society in Ancient Israel* (Philadelphia, 1980), pp. 192–200. For a psychological perspective, see Aaron Wiener's *The Prophet Elijah in the Development of Judaism: A Depth-Psychological Study* (East Brunswick, N.J., 1978).

An older but very useful commentary is the one by James A. Montgomery, *A Critical and Exegetical Commentary on the Books of Kings,* edited by Henry S. Gehman (New York, 1951). Materials on the biblical tradition of Elijah are collected in Louis Ginzberg's *The Legends of the Jews,* vol. 4 (Philadelphia, 1913), pp. 189–235, with notes in vol. 6, pp. 316–342. Especially helpful for materials on the later Jewish and Christian traditions are the articles under "Elijah" in *Encyclopaedia Judaica* (Jerusalem, 1971) and those under "Elia" in *Theologische Realenzyklopädie* (New York, 1982). This last work has a very full and up-to-date bibliography.

JOHN VAN SETERS

ELIJAH BEN SOLOMON ZALMAN. *See* Eliyyahu ben Shelomoh Zalman.

ELIJAH MUHAMMAD (1897–1975), major leader of the American Black Muslim movement, the Nation of Islam, for forty-one years. Born Elijah Poole on 10 October 1897 near Sandersville, Georgia, he was one of thirteen children of an itinerant Baptist preacher. He attended rural schools but dropped out at the fourth grade to become a sharecropper in order to help his family. In 1919 Poole married Clara Evans and in 1923 his family joined the black migration from the South, moving to Detroit. For six years, until the beginning of the Great Depression, he worked at various jobs in industrial plants. From 1929 to 1931 Poole and his family survived on charity and relief, an experience that was reflected in his later hostility toward any form of public assistance and in his strong emphasis on a program of economic self-help for the Nation of Islam. "Do for self" became his rallying cry.

In 1931 Poole met Wallace D. Fard (1877?–1934?, also known, among other aliases, as Walli Farrad and Prophet Fard), who had established the first Temple of Islam in Detroit. He became a totally devoted follower of Prophet Fard and was consequently chosen by Fard as a chief aide and lieutenant. Fard named him "minister of Islam," made him drop his "slave name," Poole, and restored his "true Muslim name," Muhammad. Fard mysteriously disappeared in 1934, and, after some internal conflict among Fard's followers, Elijah Muhammad led a major faction to Chicago, where he established Temple No. 2, which became the main headquarters for the Nation of Islam. He also instituted the worship of Prophet Fard as Allah and of himself as the

Messenger of Allah. As head of the Nation of Islam, Elijah Muhammad was always addressed as "the Honorable." He built on the teachings of Fard and combined aspects of Islam and Christianity with the black nationalism of Marcus Garvey (1887–1940) into an unorthodox Islam with a strong racial slant. His message of racial separation focused on the recognition of true black identity and stressed economic independence.

Elijah Muhammad spent four years of a five-year sentence in federal prison for encouraging draft refusal during World War II. After his release in 1946 the movement spread rapidly, especially with the aid of his chief protégé, Malcolm X (1925–1965). During its peak years the Nation of Islam numbered more than half a million devoted followers, influenced millions more, and accumulated an economic empire worth an estimated eighty million dollars. Elijah Muhammad died 25 February 1975 in Chicago and was succeeded by one of his six sons, Wallace Deen Muhammad.

[*See also the biography of Malcolm X.*]

BIBLIOGRAPHY

Elijah Muhammad. *The Supreme Wisdom: Solution to the So-Called Negroe's Problem.* Chicago, 1957.

Elijah Muhammad. *Message to the Blackman in America.* Chicago, 1965.

Essien-Udom, E. U. *Black Nationalism: A Search for an Identity in America.* Chicago, 1962. A sociological study of the Nation of Islam in Chicago.

Lincoln, C. Eric. *The Black Muslims in America.* Boston, 1961. Lincoln was officially given access to the Nation of Islam by Elijah Muhammad, and his study remains the best historical overview of the development of the movement.

Mamiya, Lawrence H. "Minister Louis Farrakhan and the Final Call: Schism in the Muslim Movement." In *The Muslim Community in North America,* edited by Earle H. Waugh, Baha Abu-Laban, and Regula B. Qureshi. Edmonton, 1983. A study of Louis Farrakhan, who as successor to Malcolm X as "national representative," has sustained the black nationalist emphases and other teachings of Elijah Muhammad.

LAWRENCE H. MAMIYA

ELIMELEKH OF LIZHENSK (1717?–1787), Hasidic teacher and leading theoretician of the *tsaddiq* concept. Elimelekh and his brother, Zusya of Hanipol, who lived for some time as wandering ascetics, were both attracted to the teachings of Dov Ber of Mezhirich (Międzryzecz, Poland) and became his disciples. After his master's death, Elimelekh settled in Lizhensk (Lesajsk, Poland) and became the major disseminator of Hasidic teachings in Galicia. Most of the later schools of Polish and Galician Hasidism, including Prsyzucha, Kotsk (Kock), Ger (Góra), Sandz (Halberstadt), and Belz (Beltsy, U.S.S.R.), are ultimately derived from Elimelekh's influence, especially through his disciple and successor Ya'aqov Yitsḥaq, the "Seer" of Lublin (1744/45–1815). The collection of Elimelekh's homilies, published as *No'am Elimelekh* (1787), was one of the most popular and widely reprinted volumes of Hasidic teaching.

These homilies are primarily concerned with the promulgation of a single concept, that of the *tsaddiq.* No matter what the weekly scripture reading, Elimelekh ingeniously leads his discussion back to this theme. The *tsaddiq,* or holy man, is the necessary link between heaven and earth; the community around him is dependent upon his blessing for both spiritual and material well-being. Using strands of tradition that had a venerable history in Judaism, Elimelekh wove a picture of a universe wholly sustained by the special divine grace called forth by these few charismatic individuals. Even prayer was to be directed heavenward by means of the *tsaddiq,* since only to him were the "pathways of heaven" familiar.

An important part of the *tsaddiq* idea was the notion of his descent, usually depicted as a voluntary movement, from the heights of contemplation and absorption in God in order to raise up those more ordinary mortals who awaited his aid. Sometimes, however, this descent was also viewed as a "fall," in which the sins of the world were of such overbearing power that they caused even the *tsaddiq* to fall from his rung. In either case, this was a "descent for the sake of ascent": as he returned to his elevated state, the *tsaddiq* would carry with him those souls and sparks of holiness which had turned to him in search of redemption.

This notion of repeated descents and ascents in the life of the *tsaddiq* was adapted by Hasidism from the earlier Shabbatean movement (seventeenth century), where the "fall" or "descent" of the *tsaddiq*/messiah was used to explain Shabbetai Tsevi's bouts with depression and ultimately also to justify his seemingly treasonous act of conversion to Islam. In Hasidism the notion has been "purified" of its element of intentional sin, which was particularly prominent in the Frankist version of Shabbateanism, also current in eastern Europe. The Besht (Yisra'el ben Eli'ezer, c. 1700–1760) had spoken chiefly of the "uplifting of wayward *thoughts,*" portraying even the entry of a stray thought during prayer as sufficient taste of sin for the *tsaddiq.* In Elimelekh's work the rhythm of ascent and descent is also frequently used to assert the supremacy of the "revealed" *tsaddiq,* serving as communal leader, over the hidden one, who cultivates only his own mystical life. It is the *tsaddiq* serving as a public figure who "descends" in order to meet the people and can thus ascend to greater heights.

Elimelekh was known as a saintly and humble man who did not use his extreme views of the *tsaddiq's* powers for personal gain. Abuses of this notion by later generations have often been unfairly attributed to him. During the last years of his life he withdrew from public leadership, and his disciple Yaʿaqov Yitsḥaq began conducting himself as a Hasidic master, causing some conflict between them. Others of his disciples include Yisraʾel of Kozienice, Mendel of Rymanów, and Naftali of Ropczyce.

BIBLIOGRAPHY

No'am Elimelekh has been published in an annotated edition by Gedalyah Nigal (Jerusalem, 1978). The introduction to that work deals at length with major themes in Elimelekh's writings. The most complete legendary biography is the *Ohel Elimelekh* by A. H. Michelson (1910; reprint, Jerusalem, 1967).

ARTHUR GREEN

ELISHA (last half of the ninth century BCE), a prophet of the northern kingdom of Israel. The prophet Elisha (Heb., Elishaʿ) is presented to us in the Hebrew scriptures not primarily as a spokesman for God to king and people, as the other prophets were, but as a holy man and a wonder-worker. In a series of hagiographic tales (*2 Kgs.* 2–8), his unusual powers are portrayed by his control over nature, his multiplication of food and oil, his healing the sick or raising the dead, and his powers of extrasensory perception. Such stories are similar to the legends of Christian saints and Jewish rabbis.

Elisha is associated with prophetic guilds known as the sons of the prophets; he served as their leader, or "father." The social status and religious purpose of such communities are quite unclear from the texts, so they shed little light on the nature of Elisha's prophetic office. In some stories Elisha is an itinerant prophet, traveling from place to place with his assistant; in others, he is a city dweller and property owner. The tradition says nothing about his teaching or his social and religious concerns. Nor does it reflect any protest against political and religious authorities, such as in the case of Elijah and the eighth-century prophets.

While some scholars accept the biblical chronology and order of events, it seems more likely that the period of Elisha's activity should be placed entirely within the reigns of Jehu, Jehoahaz, and Jehoash (c. 842–786). This was a period of Syrian domination of Israel, a fact that is reflected in several of the stories. The historian of *Kings*, however, mistakenly placed the Elisha cycle in the time before the revolt of Jehu. In this way he extended Elisha's ministry back to the time of Ahab and made him a successor of Elijah (*1 Kgs.* 19:19–21, *2 Kgs.* 2), suggesting a tradition of regular prophetic succession. Thus two quite distinct prophetic traditions influenced each other in the final formation of the text.

BIBLIOGRAPHY

There are no extensive treatments of the Elisha cycle in English. For the present, therefore, see the brief discussion by Joseph Blenkinsopp, *A History of Prophecy in Israel* (Philadelphia, 1983), pp. 68–77. Two studies of special importance are J. Maxwell Miller's "The Elisha Cycle and the Accounts of the Omride Wars," *Journal of Biblical Literature* 85 (December 1966): 441–454, and Alexander Rofé's "The Classification of the Prophetical Stories," *Journal of Biblical Literature* 89 (December 1970): 427–440.

JOHN VAN SETERS

ELISHAʿ BEN AVUYAH (first half of the second century CE), also known as Aḥer (the "other"); Palestinian tanna. Elishaʿ is unique among the Jewish sages of the first centuries of the common era. Even though he was thoroughly versed in rabbinic Judaism and had been the teacher of Meʾir (one of the leading sages of the latter half of the second century), Elishaʿ eventually rejected his heritage.

There are numerous accounts of the life of Elishaʿ as a rabbi and of his eventual rejection of the rabbinic teachings (B.T., *Ḥag.* 14b–15b; J.T., *Ḥag.* 2.1, 77b–c; *Ruth Rab.* 6.4; *Eccl. Rab.* 7.8). The Tosefta names Elishaʿ, along with Ben ʿAzzʾai, Ben Zomaʾ and ʿAqivaʾ ben Yosef, as one who entered the "orchard," where he "mutilated the shoots" (Tosefta *Ḥag.* 2.3), a phrase explained in several different ways in Talmudic literature (B.T., *Ḥag.* 15a; J.T., *Ḥag.* 77b; *Sg. Rab.* 1.4; *Dt. Rab.* 1.4).

Many have attempted to explain the apostasy of Elishaʿ in terms of the philosophical schools of his time—gnosticism, Epicureanism, and the like—or have seen the story of his life as presenting an opposition between Jewish and non-Jewish thought. Talmudic sources give several reasons why Elishaʿ left Judaism. One source claims that when Elishaʿ saw that the righteous suffer while the wicked were rewarded, he decided that following the laws of the Torah was of no avail. Elsewhere the Talmud explains that while Elishaʿ was in his mother's womb, she passed by a pagan temple and the odor of the incense being burned for the idol within affected the embryo in her womb.

Elishaʿ is accused of committing a variety of sins. He is charged with killing rabbis, discouraging their disciples from continuing their studies, exacting forced labor from the Jews on the Sabbath during the persecutions of Hadrian, riding a horse on the Sabbath, and interrupting a Torah lesson on another Sabbath. The results of his actions are described in dramatic fashion. Elisha' claims to have heard a voice from heaven that proclaimed that all would be forgiven except for Elisha'. After Elisha' was buried, fire came forth from heaven and burned his grave.

Although our sources are unanimous in their picture of Elisha' as an apostate, they do not place him completely outside the rabbinical circle. Me'ir never lost respect for his teacher and continued to discuss the law with him even after his apostasy. When the daughter of Elisha' sought charity after her father's death, the sages stated, "Do not look at his deeds, look at his Torah," and allowed her to be supported by the community (J.T., *Ḥag.* 2.1, 77c). In addition, *Avot de-Rabbi Natan* contains a collection of sayings attributed to Elisha' that emphasize the value of good deeds (24).

The story of Elisha''s life, his grounding in Judaism during his youth, and his rejection of it during his adulthood resonated in the souls of a number of writers who confronted the impact of modernity following the Jewish Enlightenment. Meir Halevi Letteris (c. 1800–1871), Elisha Rodin (1888–1946), and Benjamin Silkiner (1882–1933) all utilize the image of Elisha' in their works. In addition, Milton Steinberg used the life of Elisha' as the basis for his novel *As a Driven Leaf,* in which the American rabbi raises the problem of Jewish identity in a non-Jewish environment and the importance of Jewish values in comparison with those of the secular culture.

[*For discussion of the circle of rabbinic scholars to which Elisha' belonged, see* Tannaim.]

BIBLIOGRAPHY

For traditional views of Elisha', see the *Encyclopedia of Talmudic and Geonic Literature,* edited by Mordechai Margalioth (Tel Aviv, 1945), vol. 1, pp. 105–109; Aaron Hyman's *Toledot tanna'im ve-amora'im* (1910; reprint, Jerusalem, 1964), vol. 1, pp. 155-157; and Samuel Safrai's "Elisha ben Avuyah," in *Encyclopaedia Judaica* (Jerusalem, 1971), vol. 6, cols. 668-690. Milton Steinberg's *As a Driven Leaf* (New York, 1939) is a superb novel based on the life and times of Elisha'. For a modern critical evaluation of the Elisha' material, see William S. Green's "Otherness Within: Towards a Theory of Difference in Rabbinic Judaism," in *To See Ourselves as Others See Us,* edited by Jacob Neusner and E. Frerichs (Chico, Calif., 1985).

GARY G. PORTON

ELIXIR, a latinized form of the Arabic word *al-iksīr,* is related to the Greek word *xērion* denoting a dry powder used for medicine and alchemical transmutation. Elixirs are potions believed to have restorative and curative powers. The term was first used by alchemists to describe the substance (also known as the philosopher's stone) that was believed to transmute base metal into gold, cure disease, and promise immortality. Although alchemists coined the word, belief in the existence of such a substance predates alchemy and appears throughout the history of mythology and religion.

Characteristics and Significance. In religions, myths, and fairy tales, the fantasy has prevailed that there exists, somewhere, a plant, fountain, stone, intoxicating beverage, or noxious potion brewed in a witch's caldron, that rejuvenates the old, cures the sick, and confers wealth and eternal life on those wise, lucky, or cunning enough to snatch a bite, a sip, or a sniff. In the *Epic of Gilgamesh,* the mighty king of Uruk, Gilgamesh, sets out to discover the secret of eternal life and is fortunate to find the miraculous plant of immortality growing at the bottom of the sea. He plucks it, but carelessly leaves it unguarded, and it is stolen by a water snake.

Countless others have tried to find what Gilgamesh lost. The belief that magical substances exist that can confer health, wealth, and eternal life represents a powerful example of wishful thinking that goes back to the time when men first attempted to circumvent their mortality. Far from accepting death as the natural end of life, men everywhere have considered it the unnatural consequence of ignorance and malice. The belief that man was once immortal, and should be still, is enshrined in the many myths that tell the disastrous tale of how death entered the world. Stories such as the *Epic of Gilgamesh,* in which the plant of immortality is stolen by a serpent, appear throughout the world; all are variations on the myth in which a serpent or sea monster guards a sacred spring of immortality, a tree of life, a fountain of youth, golden apples, and the like. Behind these stories lies the fear that the gods themselves are jealous and wish to keep the elixir of immortality beyond the reach of mortal hands (see *Genesis* 3:22). Men have gone to incredible lengths, both physical and spiritual, to charm or circumvent the gods and reclaim their rightful immortality. Taking their cue from the periodic regeneration in heaven and on earth, they have tried to locate the source of this eternal renewal and apply it to themselves. They have found the most potent symbols of regeneration in the sun and moon, and the "waters" associated with them.

The Water of Life. In Egyptian, Hindu, Greek, Babylonian, and Hebrew creation myths, life emerges from the waters, the primal substance containing the seeds of all things. [*See* Water.] In deluge myths, life returns to the waters (undifferentiated form), from which it can reemerge in new forms. The rite of baptism originated in the belief that water is the source of life and consequently the source of rebirth and immortality. [*See* Baptism.] As such, water becomes the supreme magical and medicinal substance. It purifies, restores youth, and ensures eternal life in this world or the next. This magical "water of life" has been given many different names—*soma, haoma,* ambrosia, wine—each one a sacred beverage with the power to confer knowledge, strength, and immortality on gods and men alike. [*See* Beverages.]

The moon is the ultimate symbol of regeneration, both because of its own monthly renewal and because of the control it exerts over the ebb and flow of water, the source of all life. The symbolism linking the moon with seawater, rain, plant life, female fertility, birth, death, initiation, and regeneration goes back to the Neolithic period, if not earlier. The sun is also a potent symbol of regeneration and immortality. The mythological and religious associations linking the sun and moon with life and rebirth explain why men have sought to concoct elixirs from the liquids, plants, animals, minerals, and metals associated with both heavenly bodies.

Ancient and Tribal Religions. In ancient and tribal religions characterized by shamanism, elixirs are available to the community at large in the form of drugs. The use of hallucinogens, intoxicants, and narcotics is extremely important for inducing the ecstatic visions that are regarded as being able to bring shamans and their followers into contact with a spiritual world more perfect and real than that in which they live. [*See* Psychedelic Drugs.] These visions reinforce (and perhaps even produce) the belief that a supernatural world exists in which poverty, disease, and death have no part. It is a short step from the vision of immortality to the quest for immortality. The substances that occasioned the vision were used in healing rituals or taken as medicines. Sometimes they were deified and worshiped in their own right, as was Soma in Vedic ritual and "Father Peyote," the hallucinogen used by the Plains Indians of North America. Men believed they had the gods within their grasp and could literally eat them and thereby absorb their power and immortality. Behind this notion lies the belief that man is what he eats and can absorb animal, human, and divine power through his digestive tract. This belief, taken literally or figuratively, provided the rationale for sacrificial meals in different religions (Dionysian, Attic, Eleusinian, Christian).

The Soma ritual described in the *Ṛgveda* is the oldest recorded religious ritual involving the preparation and use of an elixir. [*See* Soma.] Opinion varies as to what *soma* actually was. From the research of R. Gordon Wasson (1969), however, it now seems likely that *soma* was originally extracted from the mushroom *Amanita muscaria,* the juices of which are lethal at full strength but hallucinogenic when diluted. In the case of *soma,* the vision of immortality inspired by the drink became identified with the drink itself. *Soma* was deified and the men who drank it became immortal gods:

> We have drunk the *Soma* and become
> immortal;
> We have attained the light the gods discovered.
> What can hostility now do against us?
> And what, immortal God, the spite of mortals?
> (*Ṛgveda* 8.48.3)

The use of *soma* disappeared by the end of the Vedic period. Some scholars attribute this development to the migration of the Indo-Aryans away from sites where the mushrooms grew. A more compelling reason, perhaps, is the emergence of priestly religion, with its emphasis on institutionalized, nonorgiastic forms of worship.

World Religions. As shamanism gave way to more organized religious worship, the ritual use of elixirs in the form of mind-altering drugs was gradually restricted to the priestly caste. Eventually it was discontinued altogether or replaced by symbolic rituals (involving powerless substances) that were carefully controlled by the priestly hierarchy. Such was the case both in Indian worship during the post-Vedic period, when rhubarb juice and other liquids were substituted for *soma,* and in early Zoroastrianism, where the practice of drinking *haoma* was discouraged by no less a figure than Zarathushtra (Zoroaster). [*See* Haoma.] The individual ecstasy that characterizes shamanistic trance is incompatible with religious organizations based on hierarchy and the maintenance of orthodoxy. The ritual consumption of the sacred drink *kukeōn* in the Eleusinian mysteries provides an example of the way organized religion transformed individual ecstatic experience into a communal event mediated by an ordained priest.

Another example is the Christian sacrament of the Eucharist. The promise of immortality implicit in the concept of an elixir is at the very heart of this ritual. According to the *Gospel of John* (6:51ff.), the bread and wine are literally the body and blood of Christ, and the communicant receiving them is ensured eternal life. Ignatius of Antioch (d. around 113) described the bread as the medicine of immortality and the antidote against death. But Christian theologians were fully aware of the dangers of antinomianism and self-deification inherent in the eucharistic doctrine of the real presence (of Christ), and constantly warned against both. Paul's condemnation of the *agapē,* or love feast, celebrated by early Christians (see *1 Cor.* 10–11), reflects the fear that intoxication might lead to heterodoxy. As the church became more powerful, individuals who continued the older shamanistic practices were labeled heretics, and persecuted. Such was the fate of witches, magicians, and alchemists.

Alchemy. Eastern and Western alchemists alike claimed to have produced elixirs that rendered men immortal. [*See* Alchemy.] But Chinese alchemists were more single-minded in their quest for physical immortality than Indian, Greek, or Western alchemists. The Chinese never made the invidious distinction between this world and the next so characteristic of Western thought, nor did they seek eventual liberation from the cosmos like Greek and Indian alchemists. For the Chinese, matter and spirit were part of an organic continuum, and the function of elixirs was to act as a kind of permanent glue, keeping body and soul eternally united, and thus preserving "spirit" *(shen)*.

The Chinese were always interested in prolonging life, but the idea of an elixir of immortality appears to have first emerged in the fourth century BCE as a result of a literal interpretation of early Taoist philosophy. The term *tao* originally stood for the life force that makes material bodies develop and function. Over time, Taoist alchemists transformed this abstract principle into an edible elixir. The only difficulty lay in determining the material constituents of the Tao and putting them in a digestible form. The consensus was that gold and cinnabar were the two most promising ingredients because of their immutability and color, respectively. Throughout the world, men have tried to capture the perfection and indestructibility of gold and to instill it in less perfect things, including themselves. To achieve this, they ate powdered gold and drank golden brews. [*See* Gold and Silver.] (Western alchemists dubbed Moses an alchemist on the basis of *Exodus* 32:20, where it is said he forced the Israelites to drink the golden calf, ground up and mixed with water.)

The claim that cinnabar was the ideal substance for the elixir rested on its color and chemical composition. Cinnabar is red, the color of blood, and, since cinnabar is mercuric sulfide, it can be transformed into mercury (quicksilver), the most "alive" of all the metals. The problem, of course, was that cinnabar is poisonous; but immortality was a powerful vision, and alchemists, like many others, accepted suffering as the necessary price. Between 820 and 859 CE, no fewer than six emperors were poisoned by the elixirs they took in the confident expectation that they would live forever. Joseph Needham (1957) suggests that elixir poisoning was an important factor in the decline of Chinese alchemy after the ninth century.

The idea of an alchemical elixir came to the West, via Islam, in the early Middle Ages. But the Christian distinction between matter and spirit, and emphasis on the afterlife, made it more difficult for Western alchemists to accept immortality in this world. Although some alchemists did try to concoct elixirs of immortality, and in so doing contributed to medical theory and practice, the majority espoused the more limited and mercenary goal of discovering elixirs with the power to transmute base metal into gold. A select group of spiritual alchemists scorned both aims, however. They sought spiritual elixirs that would elevate the soul and enable it to reach its divine origins.

Of all those who tried to discover an elixir of immortality, no one, so far as we know, succeeded. However, the exhilarating idea that a substance exists that can free men forever from poverty, sickness, and death has provided a powerful spur to religious, philosophical, and scientific thought.

BIBLIOGRAPHY

For an excellent discussion of rebirth and regeneration and the part played in both by sun, moon, and water symbolism, see Mircea Eliade's *Patterns in Comparative Religion* (New York, 1958). On shamanism, see Eliade's *Shamanism: Archaic Techniques of Ecstasy*, rev. & enl. ed. (New York, 1964), Weston La Barre's *The Peyote Cult*, enl. ed. (New York, 1969), and *Hallucinogens and Shamanism*, edited by Michael J. Harner (Oxford, 1973). R. Gordon Wasson identifies soma and describes its effects in *Soma: Divine Mushroom of Immortality* (New York, 1968), and Joseph Needham gives a full account of Taoist elixir addicts in *Science and Civilisation in China*, vol. 5 (Cambridge, 1983). I have discussed elixirs in Eastern and Western alchemy in *Alchemy: The Philosopher's Stone* (Boulder, 1980).

ALLISON COUDERT

ELIYYAHU BEN SHELOMOH ZALMAN

(1720–1797), known as the Vilna Gaon; scholar and theologian. Born in Selets, Lithuania, to a family renowned for its Talmudic erudition, Eliyyahu became one of the major intellectual and spiritual figures in Judaism, the preeminent representative of rabbinism in the eighteenth century. At an early age he displayed both a prodigious memory and a striking aptitude for analysis, which he applied to all branches of Jewish learning—the Torah, Mishnah, Talmud, Midrash, rabbinic codes, and Qabbalah. As a youth, his authoritative knowledge was acknowledged throughout Ashkenazic Jewry, and he soon became known simply as "the Gaon," the genius (an honorific title not to be confused with the title of the heads of the Babylonian *yeshivot* a thousand years earlier). After his marriage and a tour of the Jewish communities of Poland and Germany, Eliyyahu settled in Vilnius (Vilna), where he lived for the rest of this life except for a brief, and unsuccessful, pilgrimage to Jerusalem. In Vilnius, Eliyyahu was supported by the community although he eschewed public office and formal rabbinical positions for the life of the solitary scholar. After the age of forty, he began to lecture to a small group of disciples, who subsequently broadcast his scholarly and religious teachings through a network of Talmudic academies that was established in Lithuania and continues to this day in Israel and the United States.

At the heart of the Gaon's approach was his extreme intellectuality, his determination to reach truth through a rigorous, untrammeled study of the classics of the Jewish tradition. This belief in the supreme religious worth of study was expressed in the rabbi's quasi-ascetic regimen—he was reported to sleep only two hours a night and to forbid talk not devoted to the Torah—and, perhaps more fundamentally, in his dedication to acquiring all the skills and information essential to an elucidation of the sacred texts. Thus, following the example of a small minority of Ashkenazic sages through the centuries, Eliyyahu taught himself mathematics, astronomy, geography, and anatomy through the medium of medieval Hebrew science, and, in at least one case, approved the further transmission of scientific knowledge to traditional Jews by encouraging a student to translate Euclid into Hebrew.

Equally at variance with contemporary practice, although buttressed by precedent and authority, the Gaon opposed the practice of explaining textual problems in the Talmud through an overreliance on the hermeneutic techniques of *ḥilluq* or *pilpul* (dialectic reasoning). Instead, he insisted on a thorough study of all the cognate sources and especially the Jerusalem Talmud, which had been long neglected in favor of the Babylonian Talmud. On the basis of his mastery of classic rabbinics, but without access to manuscript variants, he was able and willing to suggest a large number of emendations and corrections in the Talmudic text, many of which resulted in contradicting the interpretations of post-Talmudic masters. This approach may be dubbed critical, and indeed Eliyyahu has been called "the father of Talmud criticism." But the Gaon's source criticism, as well as his investigations into scientific teachings, were grounded in and defined by an assumption of the infallibility of tradition. Textual emendations or astronomical charts were permissible as ancillary tools in exegesis, not as competing sources of authority. The Talmud and subsequent Jewish law could only be explicated by these devices, never overruled; indeed, the point of the endeavor was to demonstrate the eternal veracity of the biblical canon and rabbinic tradition as a whole, the possibility of understanding God's purpose through a life of uninterrupted study of his words.

This basic theological stance led the Vilna Gaon to spearhead the opposition to the new form of Jewish religiosity that emerged in his time, the Hasidic movement. Regarding the anti-intellectualism and spiritualism of Hasidism as a perversion of Judaism, Eliyyahu signed a writ of excommunication against the Ḥasidim in 1772 and refused to meet with a delegation of Hasidic masters including Shne'ur Zalman of Lyady. Under the Gaon's aegis, Vilnius became the center of anti-Hasidic propaganda and activity. The venom of the opposition was heightened in response to the publication in 1781 of one of the basic tracts of Hasidic doctrine, Ya'aqov Yosef of Polonnoye's *Toledot Ya'aqov Yosef,* which severely criticized the rabbinical leadership of the age and laid out the radical new doctrine of the *tsaddiq,* or "righteous man," a term referring to the Hasidic master. The Gaon again ordered the excommunication of the new sect and called for the burning of its literature. It was only after his death in 1797 that the breach between the two camps of traditional Jewry in eastern Europe could begin to be healed.

The Vilna Gaon's denunciation of Hasidism was in no way a rejection of mysticism on the part of a rigid rationalist—as it has often been portrayed in popular literature. On the contrary, the Gaon was a consistent student of Jewish mysticism, and he had an exceptionally vivid visionary life, although he consciously constrained his mystical graces and revelations from interfering in his legal and scholarly functions. He believed that true charisma inhered only in the Torah, not in its teachers. His students reveled in his personality and produced a bountiful hagiographic literature about him, and for over a century he was revered as a saint by masses of Jews in eastern Europe.

The Gaon never published his views. His writings, including notes and jottings not intended for the public eye, were published by his disciples after his death. These include commentaries on most of the Bible, the Mishnah, the Jerusalem and Babylonian Talmuds, the *Mekhilta', Sifrei,* and *Sifra'* (three halakhic *midrashim*); glosses on the *Zohar, Sefer yetsirah,* and other qabbalistic classics; treatises on mathematics, astronomy, and Hebrew grammar; and perhaps his most important work, his commentary on the *Shulḥan 'arukh.*

BIBLIOGRAPHY

There is no full-fledged scholarly biography of the Vilna Gaon, although the literature on him is enormous. The most accessible treatments of his teachings and personality are two charming essays in works by major modern Jewish scholars: Louis Ginzberg's *Students, Scholars, and Saints* (Philadelphia, 1928), pp. 125–144, and Solomon Schechter's *Studies in Judaism,* vol. 1 (1896; Cleveland, 1958), pp. 298–320. More recent scholarship has revealed a good deal about Eliyyahu's personality and influence; particularly interesting are H. H. Ben-Sasson's "The Personality of Elijah, Gaon of Vilna, and His Historical Influence" (in Hebrew), *Zion* 31 (1966): 39–86, 197–216, and Immanuel Etkes's "The Gaon of Vilna and the Haskalah:

Image and Reality" (in Hebrew), in *Studies in the History of the Jewish Community in the Middle Ages and Modern Times Dedicated to Professor Jacob Katz,* edited by Yosef Salmon (Jerusalem, 1982), pp. 192–217. A brief but fascinating glimpse into the Gaon's mystical life can be found in R. J. Zwi Werblowsky's *Joseph Karo: Lawyer and Mystic* (London, 1962), pp. 311–316. A succinct, useful outline of his life and teachings is the Hebrew pamphlet by Israel Klausner, *The Gaon Eliyyahu of Vilna* (Tel Aviv, 1969).

MICHAEL STANISLAWSKI

EMERSON, RALPH WALDO (1803–1882), American essayist, poet, and lecturer, a leading figure among the New England Transcendentalists. Born in Boston, Emerson was descended from a long line of Christian ministers. The son of a distinguished Unitarian minister and a deeply religious mother, he was heir to the dual legacy of Boston Unitarianism: liberalism in matters of theology and Puritan piety in matters of personal devotion, morals, and manners.

Emerson himself became a Unitarian minister, and by 1829 he had secured a desirable position as pastor of the Second Church of Boston. This followed an undistinguished four years at Harvard College, from which he graduated in 1817, and a period of study at Harvard Divinity School, during which he also worked, with little satisfaction, as a schoolmaster. With the pastorate of the Second Church, Emerson for the first time felt secure both professionally and financially. During this period he married Ellen Louisa Tucker, a younger woman of a sensitive nature and delicate health. Her death from tuberculosis, less than two years after their marriage, seems to have wrought important changes in Emerson's attitudes and thought. A rebellious strain in his character was perhaps strengthened; incipient attitudes were more strongly voiced. In his solitariness he found his faith in the primacy of the individual's relation to God strengthened, so too an impatience with the theological inheritance of received religion. He wrote in his journal in June 1831:

> I suppose it is not wise, not being natural, to belong to any religious party. In the bible you are not directed to be a Unitarian or a Calvinist or an Episcopalian. . . . I am God's child, a disciple of Christ. . . . As fast as any man becomes great, that is, thinks, he becomes a new party.

Emerson eventually gave up the pastorate of the Second Church, taking issue with the congregation's customary administration of the Lord's Supper; by 1838 he stopped preaching altogether.

Though Emerson would certainly always have considered himself a "disciple of Christ," his mature thought, as expressed in his essays and poetry, was not beholden to historical Christianity. He passionately sought for the essential spirit of religion a local habitation—temporally, geographically, and in the life of the individual. In the introduction to *Nature* (1833), which came to be his most widely read essay, he wrote: "The foregoing generations beheld God and nature face to face; we, through their eyes. Why should we not also enjoy an original relation to the universe? Why should we not have . . . a religion of revelation to us and not the history of theirs?"

Emerson was not a systematic thinker, and his ideas resist any ready summation. The essays are homiletic and aphoristic and have a cumulative power not dependent on force of logic. Certain strains can be identified, however, that undermine basic Christian conceptions. Emerson's worldview is essentially nonteleological. In his radical assertion that each individual soul must remake anew an original relation to the world, he puts the perceiving self at the center of that world. To borrow the terms of German idealist philosophy, to which he was deeply indebted, Emerson took the transcendental ego, posited as a merely formal, logical entity by Kant and subsumed under the collective will by Hegel, and made it an object of experience. In this he anticipated figures as distant as the philosophers Husserl and Sartre and the poet Wallace Stevens. That the experience of this transcendental ego is akin to mysticism as it had been known even within Christianity is apparent from this famous passage from *Nature:*

> Crossing a bare common, in snow puddles, at twilight, under a clouded sky, without having in my thoughts any occurence of special good fortune, I have enjoyed a perfect exhiliration. I am glad to the brink of fear. . . . Standing on the bare ground,—my head bathed by the blithe air, and uplifted into infinite space,—all mean egotism vanishes. I become a transparent eye-ball; I am nothing; I see all; the currents of the Universal Being circulate through me; I am part or parcel of God.

Though there is an aspect of passivity in this experience that is reminiscent of an experience of divine grace, the experience proceeds upward and outward, clearly centered in the perceiver. This spatialization is telling. Often called a pantheist, Emerson repeatedly asserted the unity of all individual souls with one another and with God. With God deposed from the pinnacle of this relationship, the world becomes not hierarchical but a plurality of parts in any of which the whole might be read: "A subtle chain of countless rings / The next unto the farthest brings."

The distance between his mature views and his Christian background seems not to have troubled Emerson, perhaps because he did not see the two as incompatible.

As prophet to an age "destitute of faith, but terrified of skepticism," as his friend Thomas Carlyle characterized it, Emerson advanced his unorthodox views forthrightly and unapologetically, secure in his advocacy of "truer" religion. (We need only turn to Nietzsche, who admired the "cheerfulness" of Emerson, to be reminded of how free of anxiety the latter's writings are.) There is a consistent strain of optimism in his work that helped win him a wide audience and also has brought him some criticism, namely that he avoided any note of tragedy in his writings, even while his journal reveals that he was well acquainted with tragedy in life. Indeed his doctrine of "compensation" for evil and suffering is so philosophically ungrounded as to seem merely sentimental. But in the confidence with which Emerson forwarded his original and radical message, and in the audience he found, we see not merely evidence of an uncommonly balanced spirit and not merely the popular appeal of optimism; we see the flowering of that America seen by Hegel, where "the most unbounded license of imagination in religious matters prevails."

BIBLIOGRAPHY

The primary resources for the study of Emerson are *The Complete Works of Ralph Waldo Emerson*, 12 vols., edited by Edward W. Emerson and *The Journals and Miscellaneous Notebooks of Ralph Waldo Emerson*, 14 vols. (Cambridge, Mass, 1960–1978). The best recent biography is Gay Wilson Allen's *Waldo Emerson* (New York, 1981). Stephen E. Whicher's *Freedom and Fate: An Inner Life of Ralph Waldo Emerson*, 2d ed. (Philadelphia, 1971), is a watershed study, a point of departure for much later criticism. Jonathan Bishop's *Emerson on the Soul* (Cambridge, Mass., 1964) is another good account of Emerson's intellectual and religious development, as is Joel Porte's *Representative Man: Ralph Waldo Emerson in His Time* (New York, 1979). Two useful collections of criticism are *The Recognition of Ralph Waldo Emerson: Selected Criticism since 1837*, edited by Milton R. Konvitz (Ann Arbor, 1972) and *Critical Essays on Ralph Waldo Emerson*, edited by Robert E. Burkholder and Joel Myerson (Boston, 1983).

DAVID SASSIAN

EMPEROR'S CULT. Ruler worship was a characteristic statement of Greco-Roman paganism, reflecting its definition of godhead as a power capable of rendering benefits to the community of worshipers, and its ability to create an endless supply of cults in honor of new and specifically entitled manifestations of such beneficent divine power. The granting of cult honors to a ruler, living or deceased, was an act of homage made in return for his bestowal of specific benefits upon the community. It recognized him as the possessor of supernormal power and sought to regularize his beneficent relationship with the community by establishing the formal elements of cult, including feast days, festivals, priesthoods, and shrines.

Actual cult worship of the ruler was uncommon in pharaonic Egypt and extremely rare in ancient Mesopotamia. The Roman practice owed nothing to such Near Eastern antecedents. Rather, it was formed entirely under the impress of developments in the political and cult life of Greece. At first the Greeks offered posthumous cult honors to particular individuals distinguished for bravery or other personal prowess. Then, in the late fourth and third century BCE, it became common for individual cities to establish cults in honor of living rulers. Already in 218 BCE Roman state religion adopted the Greek practice of personifying and worshiping the collective personality of the citizen body in the cult of the Genius Populi Romani ("genius of the Roman people"). From the early second century BCE on, Rome's emergence as the dominant political force in the Greek world led individual Greek cities to establish cults in honor of Roman generals and provincial administrators who had rendered specific benefits to the community concerned. In the first century BCE, the last century of republican government at Rome, this practice of establishing municipal cults to Roman statesmen was intensified under the impact of such charismatic leaders as Pompey (d. 48 BCE) and Julius Caesar (d. 44 BCE).

After his assassination, Julius Caesar was deified. Within the context of the Roman religious mentality, this means that he was officially recognized by decree as a divine entity who had bestowed supernatural benefits upon the Roman people and in consequence had been granted immortality by the gods. Caesar was thus worthy to receive continuing cult worship from the Roman people and accordingly was adopted into the pantheon of the state religion with his own temple and feast day. With this development the imperial cult became an official part of Roman religion. The guidance and regularization of such cult expressions was a key feature in the monarchical system established during the long reign of Augustus (31 BCE–14 CE), and the forms that he established were determinative for later developments. During the first and second centuries CE, many cities throughout the empire founded cults in honor of successive emperors. The intensity of such worship began to diminish in the third century. In the fourth century, with the adoption of Christianity as the official religion and subsequent imperial prohibition of all pagan cult activity, the worship of emperors came to an end.

Under the Roman empire there was no single imperial cult. Instead, there was a wide variety of cults of the emperors, which took three main forms: the official state cult of Rome, municipal cults of cities in the empire, and private cults.

In the Roman state cult, worship of the living emperor took the indirect form of the cult of the emperor's *genius*, the divine element and creative force that resided in the emperor and guided him like a guardian angel. Following the precedent established in the case of Julius Caesar, numerous emperors, such as Augustus, Vespasian (d. 79 CE), and Trajan (d. 117 CE), were recognized as divinities *(divi)* upon their decease; a formal ceremony and a senatorial decree attested to their apotheosis and new status as immortal. Following the tenets of Stoic philosophy and popular belief, such deification was regarded as an attestation of the "virtues" of the emperor; that is, the emperor had been the vehicle for the operation of divine and beneficent qualities like Peace, Abundance, Victory, Liberty, and Security, which through his person and activities had operated for the benefit of his fellow citizens. Under such names as Pax Augusta, Abundantia Augusti, Victoria Augusti, Libertas Augusti, and Securitas Augusti, these imperial virtues were themselves the object of widespread cult activity at both the official and the private level.

Quite apart from the official pantheon of the Roman people, cities throughout the empire established cults in honor of emperors both living and deceased. Moreover, cults of particular emperors were established by private individuals and especially by corporations. The emperor himself was the main object of cult worship; but in Roman cult, municipal cults, and private worship, deification of members of the imperial family was increasingly common from the time of Augustus on.

In founding cults, building shrines, and maintaining regular worship, the imperial cult was one of the most vital features of Greco-Roman paganism in the first two centuries of the Christian era. To be sure, there were those who criticized the worship of an emperor or of any mortal as an act of impiety; moreover, there is no real evidence that men and women turned to the divine emperor as they might to Apollo or Asklepios in time of sickness or personal crisis. But it would be wrong to dismiss the imperial cult as the empty product of political sycophancy or religious decay. The function of the emperor as divinity was not to alleviate illness or to intervene in personal crisis. His divine power functioned in the sphere of material benefits, the delivery of free grain to a famine-stricken region, gifts of money to victims of earthquakes, and the general securing of peace and prosperity throughout a vast empire. In these terms he was called and genuinely regarded as "savior and benefactor of the human race." He was regarded as a divine entity who had been chosen by the supreme god Zeus/Jupiter to rule mankind with beneficence as the earthly vicegerent of the gods. His reward for fulfilling this task was immortality. From this perspective, the imperial cult was a forceful and creative response to that need for a unity of shared belief that is essential to the integration and successful functioning of a pluralistic society. Fostered by a well-orchestrated and all-pervasive system of imperial propaganda, the image of the emperor as a divine savior sent by the supreme god and triumphant over fate and death played a seminal role in the development of the terminology and content of Christian soteriology.

[*See also* Apotheosis *and* Deification.]

BIBLIOGRAPHY

For an extensive bibliography, see Peter Herz's "Bibliographie zum römischen Kaiserkult," in *Aufstieg und Niedergang der römischen Welt*, vol. 2.16.2 (Berlin and New York, 1978), pp. 833–910. Useful collections of evidence can be found in *Charisma*, 2 vols., by Fritz Taeger (Stuttgart, 1957–1960), and *The Imperial Cult in the Latin West* by Duncan Fishwick (Leiden, 1985). For interpretive studies that treat the imperial cult as a religious as well as historical phenomenon, see my *Princeps a Diis Electus: The Divine Election of the Emperor as a Political Concept at Rome* (Rome, 1977); "The Cult of Jupiter and Roman Imperial Ideology" and "The Cult of Virtues and Roman Ideology," in *Aufstieg und Niedergang der römischen Welt*, vol. 2.17.2 (Berlin and New York, 1981), pp. 3–141, 827–948; and "Gottesgnadentum," in *Reallexikon für Antike und Christentum*, vol. 11, (Stuttgart, 1950).

J. RUFUS FEARS

EMPIRICISM is best understood not as a single doctrine but as a cluster of theses, each of which affirms the primacy of human experience in the general area of epistemology. As used here, the term *experience* refers primarily to sense experience, but it must also be extended to cover introspective experience. Insofar as other types of awarenesses, such as feeling states, pains, pangs, and so forth, are not already included in one of these categories, they too should be separately included in the general class of experiences. Following are discussions of three theses usually associated with empiricism. The first two have had considerable impact on the history of Christian theology; the third has not.

The first thesis is that ideas are derived entirely from experience. For example, the idea of red is derived entirely from experiences of red things—in this case visual sense perceptions or impressions of red objects. A complex idea such as the idea of a desk or of a unicorn may be derived directly from complex sense impressions (e.g., perceptions of desks), or may be constructed out of other ideas that are, in turn, derived entirely from sense impressions. Assuming, for instance, that no one has ever seen (i.e., had a complex sense impression of) a unicorn, still there are no elements of this idea that are not themselves derived from sense impressions.

That ideas have their origin in perception is a view worked out in some detail by Epicurus (341–270 BCE) in his work *On Nature.* It is also a thesis held by Thomas Aquinas (*Summa theologiae* 1.84.3, 6, 7) who in turn claimed to find it in Aristotle. As a doctrine of importance in modern philosophy, however, it is identified primarily with the classical British empirical tradition of the seventeenth and eighteenth centuries, as represented in the epistemological writings of Locke, Berkeley, and Hume. In contrast to the doctrine of innate ideas held by Descartes and other so-called rationalists, such as Leibniz, Locke insisted that all ideas are derived from experience. In its original state, Locke said, the mind is a blank tablet *(tabula rasa)* and, as such, does not possess ideas. Ideas are acquired either as a result of the operation of the sense faculties (the idea of red); or as a result of the mind's operation on the data supplied by the sense faculties (the idea of a unicorn); or as a result of introspection (what Locke called "inner sense"), observing the mind as it operates on materials supplied by the sense faculties (for instance, the idea of mind).

In Hume, the claim that all ideas are derived entirely from impressions served as the cornerstone of his empirical theory of meaning. Hume held that a word has meaning only when it is (to use his phrase) "annexed" to an idea. A term's specific meaning can be decided only by consulting the content of the idea annexed to it. But since, as Hume claimed, the content of any given idea is completely determined by the impressions from which it is derived, the meaning of a given word can be exhaustively analyzed by itemizing the impressions from which the idea annexed to that word is derived. Hume relied on this theory of meaning when he dismissed as meaningless a host of traditional metaphysical items such as the Aristotelian doctrine of substratum. With respect to the latter, Hume argued that since we have no impression of substratum, we have no such idea; thus the operative term used by metaphysicians when formulating this doctrine is without meaning. An argument of this sort was used to establish virtually all the doctrines usually associated with Hume's "skeptical" philosophy—for instance, his well-known analysis of "causation" and his highly controversial analysis of "mind."

In *Alciphron,* one of his last major works, Berkeley reviewed with approval a theory concerning the origin of the idea of God. According to the theory in question, the idea of God is a complex having as ingredients ideas generated from our experience of creatures. Thus, for example, the idea of a being who has knowledge is derived from our experience of finite beings like ourselves. Though we do not have any direct experience of the perfect case, we can construct the idea of perfect knowledge by imagining away the imperfections (e.g., limited scope) that invariably attach to knowledge in imperfect cases. This gives us the idea of omniscience, the exemplary version of knowledge. Ideas of the other so-called perfections standardly attributed to God (omnipotence, eternity, etc.) are derived by a similar process from the ideas we have of attributes possessed by finite beings. Berkeley said that this account of the idea of God is precisely the one given by Thomas Aquinas and developed by the Schoolmen under the title "analogy by proportionality." This interpretation of Thomas's doctrine of analogy is supported by a number of contemporary commentators as well (e.g., Copleston, *History of Philosophy,* vol. 2, chap. 38). It is an account that fits well both with Berkeley's and with Thomas's general empiricist stance concerning the origin of ideas.

Perhaps the most provocative empiricist account of the ideas operative in the area of religion is the one advanced by Friedrich Schleiermacher in *The Christian Faith* (1830) and subsequently expanded by his student Rudolf Otto in *The Idea of the Holy* (1917), which no doubt is the most influential study in the phenomenology of religion published in the twentieth century. According to Otto, the idea of God is derived from a complex "nonrational" (i.e., preconceptual) awareness that he referred to as "the experience of the Numen." Otto undertook to show how this primitive awareness is (as he said) "schematized" (i.e., conceptualized) in standard theological doctrines that give expression to its various ingredient feelings. Following Schleiermacher, Otto insisted that the content of the concept of God is determined by the preconceptual religious phenomena of which that concept is the schematization. Although this theory differs from the one given by Berkeley, it clearly reflects the influence of classical empiricist thought. Framed in the language of Locke or Hume, the claim is made that the idea of God comes directly from religious experiences. Berkeley (and Thomas) would disagree only with respect to the claim that the experiences in question are of a specifically religious nature.

The second thesis associated with empiricism is that human knowledge concerning matters of fact is grounded ultimately in experience. Since there is a distinction between an idea (e.g., the idea of red) and a statement (e.g., "Apples are red"), and since knowledge is formulated in statements, we must distinguish a theory concerning the origin of ideas from a theory concerning the source of knowledge. Unlike the former, the latter specifies conditions under which it can be legitimately claimed that a statement is true. These are conditions under which a knowledge claim is warranted. According to this second thesis, whatever may be the origin of our ideas, our knowledge of facts about the world is formulated in statements supported entirely by empirical evidence. This claim stands opposed to one made by Kant (and a number of other modern and medieval thinkers such as Descartes and Thomas Aquinas), namely, that some statements that describe facts about the world (e.g., "Every event has a cause") are known to be true *a priori,* that is, prior to or independent of experience. Such statements are sometimes described as self-evident. The empiricist's claim is that all factual knowledge is, by contrast, *a posteriori,* that is, posterior to and consequent upon experience. No factual statement is self-evident, if this means that the statement in question can be known to be true without consulting observational evidence.

It is important to note that the thesis just reviewed is explicitly restricted to knowledge about the world, that is, to knowledge of what Hume called "matters of fact." It is thus not extended to knowledge formulated in what Kant labeled "analytic" statements, that is, to statements whose truth values depend entirely on word meanings. As regards these latter statements, empiricists acknowledge that they are *a priori.* They add, however, that such statements are empty of factual content. This is to say that, while *a priori* statements may reveal something about the way we use words or about what Hume referred to as "relations between ideas," they tell us nothing about the objects or circumstances to which our words presumably refer or to which our ideas presumably correspond. This dichotomy between the factual *a posteriori* and the analytic *a priori* remains to this day a point of embarrassment for empiricists. The problem is not that the distinction is unintelligible or inapplicable, but rather that some knowledge statements do not fit comfortably into either class. As mentioned above, Kant thought that the statement "Every event has a cause" is of the kind last mentioned. He also thought that mathematical knowledge such as that formulated in the statement "2 + 3 = 5" defies classification in either of these categories.

The idea that knowledge about the world is grounded in experience is the hallmark of what is usually thought of as the "scientific" mentality. As such, it is antithetical to the traditional Christian insistence that revelation is the ultimate source of the factual knowledge codified in theological doctrine. Still, in the three centuries that have elapsed since the publication of Newton's *Principles,* Christian theology has exhibited some affection for the scientific style of theory construction. Largely inspired by the theological writings of Newton, eighteenth-century England was crowded with advocates of what Hume called "experimental theism," that is, theism entertained as a hypothesis and supported by reference to evidence provided by the appearance of design in nature. This trend stood in contrast to medieval methods for proving the existence of God by purely *a priori* considerations, as in Anselm's ontological argument, or by arguments making use of *a priori* (self-evident) factual premises such as the first three of Thomas's five proofs for the existence of God. Theism cast as a scientific theory and supported by the abductive logical procedures characteristic of the natural sciences reached its climax in the nineteenth century in William Paley's monumental work *Natural Theology* (1825). Although this approach to Christian apologetics is still practiced (witness Robert Clark's *The Universe: Plan or Accident,* Oxford, 1961), it is not widely held to be effective. A great many contemporary philosophers of religion think that Hume's *Dialogues concerning Natural Religion* (1779) constitutes the definitive critique of theism as an explanatory hypothesis.

The third thesis associated with empiricism is that factual statements are meaningful only insofar as they are verifiable. If we assume that all knowledge concerning matters of fact is ultimately grounded in experience, it follows that, except for statements whose truth values can be determined by reference to the meanings of the terms they employ, any statement known to be true is so only because it has been verified by experience. Given the same exclusion, it follows that, insofar as a statement affirms something knowable, to that extent it affirms something verifiable. Anything that cannot be verified cannot be known. Let us now make a second assumption, namely, that a statement is meaningful insofar, but only insofar, as it has a discoverable truth value. Restricting attention to statements whose truth values cannot be determined by reference to the meanings of their constituent words, this second assumption tells us that all meaningful statements affirm something that is knowable. This is so because, for any meaningful statement that is not contradictory (in which case its truth value can indeed be determined by reference to the meanings of its constituent words), there is some possible world in which it is true and in which it has been discovered (i.e., is known) to be true. It is, then, in principle knowable. But if a given statement is in principle knowable, then, by our first assumption, it is also in principle verifiable. By this sequence of reasonings, the second empiricist thesis discussed above yields the following theory: the meaning of any statement whose truth value cannot be determined by reference to the meanings of its constituent words consists entirely of its empirically verifiable content. Of course, given this theory, any statement about the world for which no verifying observations could in principle be specified would not count as a genuine statement: it would be devoid of meaning. This is because according to the principle before us, any purported statement about the world is meaningful only to the extent that it is empirically verifiable.

This last principle, usually referred to as the verifiability principle, became the centerpiece of empiricism—called logical empiricism or more often logical positivism—during the second quarter of the twentieth century. [*See* Logical Positivism.] It is important to see that it connects not only with the second of the empiricist theses treated above (as indicated in the last paragraph), but with the first as well. Here, for the second time, we are confronted with a theory of meaning. Of course the verifiability principle is not the same as the theory used by Hume. In fact, it differs on two counts: (1) it takes statements rather than individual words as the meaningful units; and (2) it requires empirical consequences rather than antecedently acquired empirical ideas as the conditions of meaning. Still, the verifiability principle is a recognizable cousin of Hume's empirical theory of meaning. It was also utilized by positivists such as A. J. Ayer, in a characteristically Humean program, to dismiss as meaningless a whole range of traditional metaphysical doctrines. At its height, positivism dominated the philosophical community, influencing as well trends in psychology (behaviorism) and in the physical sciences (operationalism). Burdened, however, by its own inability to provide a version of the verifiability principle acceptable to philosophers of science, at the end of the 1950s this theory vanished quite abruptly from the philosophical scene. It is now dead—or at least as dead as any philosophical theory can be.

As for the impact of logical positivism on theology or on religious studies more generally, there is little to say. That there exists a transcendent being who created the universe is one of the metaphysical doctrines that positivists typically dismissed as meaningless. Of course this was not atheism, if one understands atheism to be the view that God does not exist, that is, that the statement "God exists" is false. To have a truth value—that is, to be either true or false—a statement must have meaning. For positivists, the words "God exists"—being, as A. J. Ayer used to say "nonsensical"—simply did not have credentials enough to be false. As yet few (if any) religious thinkers have found this position worthy of serious attention.

[*See also the biographies of philosophers mentioned herein.*]

BIBLIOGRAPHY

Ayer, A. J. *Language, Truth and Logic.* 2d ed. London, 1946. See also *Logical Positivism* (Glencoe, Ill., 1959), edited by Ayer, which contains essays by most leading positivists such as Carnap, Neurath, Schlick, and Ayer himself. It also contains essays by other important twentieth-century empiricists such as Russell and Stevenson. The bibliography is amazingly complete.

Epicurus. *On Nature.* In *Epicurus: The Extant Remains,* translated by Cyril Bailey. Oxford, 1926.

Paley, William. *Natural Theology* (1802). Edited by Frederick Ferré. Indianapolis, 1963.

Schleiermacher, Friedrich. *The Christian Faith.* Translated from the second German edition. New York, 1963. Schleiermacher's best-known student and disciple was Rudolf Otto, whose study of the nature of religious experience in *Das Heilige* (Breslau, 1917), translated by John W. Harvey as *The Idea of the Holy,* 2d ed. (1950; New York, 1970), is a modern classic in religious studies.

Taylor, Richard, ed. *The Empiricists.* Garden City, N.Y., 1974. Contains a handy collection of the writings of Locke, Berkeley, and Hume. Unfortunately, Taylor's text does not include Hume's *Treatise,* which is available in *Enquiries concerning Human Understanding and concerning the Principles of Morals,* 3d ed., edited by L. A. Selby-Bigge (Oxford, 1975).

Thomas Aquinas. "Treatise on Man," *Summa theologiae* 1.75–89. In *Basic Writings of Saint Thomas Aquinas,* vol. 1, edited by Anton C. Pegis. New York, 1945. Helpful studies of Thomas's theory of knowledge and philosophy of mind can be found in Frederick C. Copleston's *History of Philosophy,* vol. 2 (Westminster, Md., 1952), chapter 38; and in chapter 4 of Copleston's *Aquinas* (Baltimore, 1967).

NELSON PIKE

EMPTINESS. *For discussion of the Buddhist concept of emptiness, see* Śūnyam and Śūnyatā.

EMRE, YUNUS. *See* Yunus Emre.

ENCHIN (814/5–891/2), posthumously known as Chishō Daishi; sixth patriarch *(zasu)* of the Tendai school of Japanese Buddhism and one of the so-called *nittō-hakke,* or "eight (Esoteric) masters who studied in China." Enchin, a distant cousin of Kūkai (Kōbō Daishi, 774–835), founder of the Shingon sect, was born on the island of Shikoku. From the age of fifteen he studied under Gishin, a direct disciple of Saichō (Dengyō Daishi, 767–822), founder of the Tendai sect, at the Enryakuji on Mount Hiei, the center of the Tendai monastic establishment.

Enchin was sent by the government to China, where he studied from 853 to 859, first on Mount T'ien-t'ai (center of the T'ien-t'ai sect), and then at the Ch'ing-lung Monastery in the capital, Ch'ang-an, thus absorbing the teachings and practices of both Tendai and Esoteric Buddhism. Upon his return to Japan he was sponsored by the court (he established an initiation hall within the precincts of the imperial palace) and by the leaders of the Fujiwara clan, and took up residence in the Onjōji in Shiga Prefecture, at the foot of Mount Hiei. In 868 he became *zasu* of the Tendai sect, a position he held until his death. Together with Ennin (Jikaku Daishi, 794–864), he was a central figure in the development of classical Japanese Tendai Buddhism.

Enchin's contributions gave rise to a movement that resulted in the complete esotericization of Tendai thought and practice, leading to the creation of "Tendai Esotericism" (Taimitsu, as opposed to "Shingon Esotericism," or Tōmitsu). Enchin believed that the teachings of Tendai and Shingon were of equal value (in contradistinction to various hierarchical gradings fashionable at the time), but he also believed that the praxis of Shingon was superior *(ridō-jishō).* He also stated that the transcendental Buddha appearing in Tendai's major scripture, the *Lotus Sutra,* was the same as Mahāvairocana, the main figure of the pantheon of Shingon Buddhism. Enchin was also the first proponent of the *hongaku* ("original enlightenment") theory, according to which all sentient and nonsentient beings are from the outset fully endowed with complete awakening. This theory played a central function in the evolution of Tendai doctrine and Buddhism at large, and was also instrumental in the theoretical interpretations of the associations between Shintō and Buddhist divinities *(shinbutsu-shūgō).* Finally, Enchin was also, according to the tradition, a key figure in the development of the Tendai branch of mountain asceticism (Shugendō), especially in the Kumano region. [*See* Shugendō *and* Shingonshū.]

In the generation after Enchin, the Onjōji came to be known as the Jimon branch of the Tendai sect, in opposition to the Sanmon branch located in Enryakuji. The Jimon branch was run by the disciples of Enchin, the Sanmon branch by Ennin's disciples. The patriarchs of the Tendai sect were to be chosen from either Ennin's or Enchin's lineage. This and other questions ultimately led to friction between the two institutions, and then to armed attacks, provoked largely by political considerations. During the late Heian period the so-called warrior monks *(sōhei)* of these great monasteries battled the government and each other mercilessly in a quest for privileges, land, domains, and power. This situation resulted in the demise of the Tendai institutions at the end of the medieval period, and in the total destruction of the monasteries by Oda Nobunaga in 1571.

Enchin had many disciples and composed a large number of doctrinal treatises, among which the *Dainichikyō-shiiki* (The Final Truth of the Mahāvairocana Sūtra) and the *Kōen-hokke-gi* (Lectures on the Rites of the Lotus Blossom) are noteworthy. After his death, Enchin became the object of a cult centered around a sculptured representation holding his ashes.

[*See also* Tendaishū.]

BIBLIOGRAPHY

Chishō Daishi. Ōtsu, 1937. Published under the auspices of the Onjōji (Miidera).

Murayama Shūichi. *Hieizan to Tendai bukkyō no kenkyū.* Tokyo, 1975.

Tsuji Zennosuke. *Nihon bukkyōshi; jōsei-hen,* vol. 1. Tokyo, 1944.

ALLAN G. GRAPARD

ENDOWMENTS, MUSLIM.

See Waqf.

END TIME.

See Eschatology.

ENKI is the Sumerian name of the Mesopotamian god of wisdom, incantation, and groundwaters; his Akkadian name is Ea. Enki was one of the four great cosmic gods, the others being the sky god, An; the earth god, Enlil; and the mother goddess, Ninhursaga (Ninmah). Enki was the ruler not only of fresh waters on the earth but of those under the earth as well. Hence he was also the god of springs dispensing fresh water and its accompanying fertility. He was considered a master craftsman, patron of all the arts and crafts, and endowed with a wisdom and cunning that the myths, hymns, and prayers never tired of praising.

Enki was originally the local deity of Eridu (modern-day Abu Shahrein), a southern city where his main temple was called Eabzu ("deepwater house"). However, he was venerated throughout the region. His spouse was variously known as Ninki, Ninhursaga, and Damkina. The city god of Babylon, Marduk, who shared many of Enki's attributes, was later identified as his son. In some myths, such as *Enki and the World Order,* Enki was regarded as a god of creation, and this is reflected in one of his epithets, Nindimmud ("begetter of mankind"). According to the myth *Enki and Ninmah,* Enki bestowed on the mother goddess the secret of making the first man from clay. In the *Enuma elish* myth, it is Enki himself who creates man, probably originally at Enlil's directions.

As god of wisdom, Enki was known as Ninigiku ("lord of the bright eye [intelligence]") or as *bel nemeqi* ("lord of wisdom"), and it is in this capacity that gods and mortals turned to him for help and advice in difficult situations. Generally, Enki was very favorably disposed toward men. For example, in the Sumerian and Akkadian flood stories, it is he who informs the heroes Ziusudra, Atrahasis, and Utanapishtim of the impending flood. However, in the myth *Adapa* he plays the role of a divine deceiver, since he counsels Adapa, the protagonist, not to accept any food or drink offered him at the heavenly court. Enki knows well that the food of the gods imparts immortality, and by this false counsel he prevents Adapa from becoming immortal.

Since water plays a large role in incantation ritual and Enki was the god of water, he was also the god of magic and incantations. Holy water from his temple at Eridu was sought after for use in magical rites, whether therapeutic or prophylactic. His "water of life" *(me balati)* was thought to have the power to cure sickness and disease, and did so effectively for Ishtar in the myth *Descent of Ishtar*. On an Old Akkadian seal, Enki is represented as sitting on his throne encircled by streams of water. He is such a source of water that streams of it even flow out from his shoulders. His emblem, as befits a god of the waters, is a fish, the mullet.

[*See also* Mesopotamian Religions, *overview article*.]

BIBLIOGRAPHY

There is at present no full-length treatment of Enki. The best surveys are those by Erich Ebeling in *Reallexikon der Assyriologie*, edited by Erich Ebeling and Bruno Meissner, vol. 2 (Berlin, 1938), pp. 374–379; by Édouard Dhorme, *Les religions de Babylonie et d'Assyrie* (Paris, 1945), pp. 31–38, 50–51; and by D. O. Edzard in *Wörterbuch der Mythologie*, edited by Hans Wilhelm Haussig, vol. 1, *Götter und Mythen im Vorderen Orient* (Stuttgart, 1965), pp. 56–57.

DAVID MARCUS

ENLIGHTENMENT. In the context of Asian religious traditions, especially of Buddhism, the term *enlightenment* typically refers to that existentially transformative experience in which one reaches complete and thorough understanding of the nature of reality and gains control over those psychic proclivities that determine the apparent structures and dynamics of the world. As is consistent with a general South and East Asian notion that final truth is apprehended through extraordinary "sight" (hence, religious "insight" or "vision"), enlightenment is often depicted as an experience in which one is said to "see" things as they really are, rather than as they merely appear to be. To have gained enlightenment is to have seen through the misleading textures of illusion and ignorance, through the dark veils of habitual comprehension, to the light and clarity of truth itself. [*See* Truth.]

The English word *enlightenment* usually translates the Sanskrit, Pali, and Prakrit term *bodhi*, meaning in a general sense "wise, intelligent, fully aware." Thus, *bodhi* signifies a certain "brightness" (again, a visual theme) to one's consciousness. The term *bodhi* is built on the same verbal root—Sanskrit *budh* ("awaken, become conscious")—as that from which derives the adjective *buddha* ("awakened one"). Thus, an enlightened being, a Buddha, is one who has dispelled all of the personal and cosmic effects of ignorance and has become fully awake to reality as it truly is. From the word *bodhi* come also the terms *sambodhi* and *sambodha*, the "highest" or "most complete enlightenment." [*See* Buddha.]

The word *enlightenment* also, yet less often, translates other Sanskrit and Sanskrit-related terms from a variety of religious traditions other than Buddhism. The Jain notion of *kevalajñāna* (omniscience, knowledge unhindered by the karmic residues of former modes of understanding the world) describes in part the quality of an *arhat*, a person worthy of highest respect. The paradigmatic *arhat*s in the Jain context are the twenty-four *tīrthaṅkara*s, those "ford-crossers" (the most recent being Vardhamāna Mahāvīra in the sixth century BCE) whose experiences of such enlightenment stand at the center of Jain religious history. Similarly, yogic Hindu traditions teach of the experience of *samādhi* ("absolute equanimity") and of *kaivalya* ("the supreme autonomous state of being free of ignorance"), both of which lead the yogin to the experience of *mokṣa*, the release from the hitherto ceaseless and painful cycle of transmigration. [*See* Samādhi *and* Mokṣa.]

But it is to Buddhist traditions that the experience of enlightenment is most pertinent. Although Buddhist lessons regarding enlightenment *(bodhi* and its correlatives, Chinese *p'u-t'i*, *wu*, or *chüeh*, Tibetan *byaṅ chub*, and Japanese *satori)* vary somewhat, Buddhism in general has stressed the key significance of that experience in which one fully and compassionately understands the world without discoloring or disfiguring it according to one's desires, expectations, or habits. The Buddhist insight into the nature of pain and suffering, of fear and doubt, of the feelings of insecurity and hopelessness, is that these states arise in one's ignorant mind as one selfishly tries to have reality the way one wants it rather than to know it as it is. The Buddhist way to freedom from the suffering these states cause, therefore, is to remove—usually through the practice of meditation or through the development of compassion—the conditions one places on the world, on other people, and on oneself. Thus, Buddhist enlightenment constitutes an experiential transforming and normative "deconditioning" of the self and of the world.

And what does a person "see" when he or she has so deconditioned his or her response to, and analysis of, the world? Sanskrit and Pali accounts of Siddhartha Gautama's enlightenment at the age of thirty-five as he sat under a tree near what is now the North Indian town of Bodh Gayā through the night of the full moon in the spring of 538 BCE might well serve to summarize the elements early South Asian Buddhists felt would comprise such an experience.

That person would first have to confront and defeat, as Gautama is reported to have done, all of the various temptations, selfish desires, and fears (sexual lust, faint-heartedness, physical weakness, passion, laziness, cowardice, doubt, hypocrisy, pride, and self-aggrandizement) that usually define and delimit his or her identity, an exceedingly difficult task represented in Buddhist myth and iconography as Gautama's struggle in the late afternoon with the demonic and tempting Māra, the evil one.

Second—still following hagiographical accounts and traditional teachings as the paradigm—the aspirant would enter into four levels of meditative absorption (Skt., *dhyāna;* Pali, *jhāna.* Technical terms will hereafter be given first in the Sanskrit, with Pali and other terms following when appropriate.) At the first level he would detach his attention from the objects of the senses to look inward into his own mind. His thoughts would be discursive in nature, and he would feel relaxed but energetic. Entering the second level, his thoughts would no longer be discursive, but he would still feel great energy, comfort, and trust. At the third level the feeling of zest would give way to a sense of dispassionate bliss, and at the fourth level he would feel free of all opposites such as pleasure and pain, euphoria and anxiety. This fourth level of meditation would be characterized by pure and absolute awareness and complete calmness.

Gautama is said to have mastered all four of these stages of meditative concentration and could move from one to the other with ease. This was to be of central importance to his subsequent series of insights gained through the night, for through them he perceived what are known as the six types of extraordinary knowledge *(abhijñā; abhiññā):* magical physical powers, the ability to hear voices and sounds from all parts of the universe, the ability to know other people's thoughts, memory of his former lives, the ability to see all creatures in the world, and the extinction of all harmful psychological states. One would have to use these skills in order to understand the nature of suffering in the world, for not to do so would mean that one were merely a wizard or magician rather than a healer.

Third, having gained control over one's entrapping emotions, and having mastered the four levels of contemplation, the seeker would endeavor through meditative analysis of his life to comprehend how the present is determined by the sum total of his past actions. One would see that each person is responsible for his or her own personality and that others cannot be blamed for one's psychological predicament. This third stage of enlightenment finds narrative representation in traditional accounts of Gautama's ability to remember, in order, all of his former lives *(pūrvanivāsanusmṛti-jñāna; pubbenivāsanussati-ñāṇa)* and to understand how all of those lives led to the present one. Gautama is said to have gained this insight during the first watch of the night (from 6:00 PM to 10:00 PM).

Fourth, he would develop his ability to understand other people's idiosyncratic psychological and existential predicaments in the same manner as one has understood one's own. That is, he would be able to see how people have got where they are and how they have created their own problems, even though they may not know it. He or she would then be able to respond fully and compassionately to any given situation with other people. Buddhist hagiographies say that Gautama gained such a skill during the second watch of the night (from 10:00 PM to 2:00 AM), a time in which he attained the "divine vision" *(divyacakṣu; dibbacakkhu)* to see all of the former lives of all beings in the universe.

Finally, he would comprehend and destroy the source of all psychological "poison" (*āsrava; āsava:* "befuddling discharge") and come to realize what are known as the Four Noble Truths: (1) that conditioned existence is permeated by suffering *(duḥkha; dukkha);* (2) that this suffering comes from somewhere *(samudāya);* (3) that this suffering, therefore, can come to an end *(nirodha);* and (4) that the way one brings an end to all suffering is to follow the Buddhist way of life, known as the Noble Eightfold Path. To tread this path, one practices (1) the "right view" *(dṛṣṭi; ditthi)* of the true nature of things; (2) "right thought"; (3) "right speech"; (4) "right action"; (5) "right livelihood"; (6) "right effort"; (7) "right mindfulness"; and (8) "right concentration."

Gautama is said to have realized the Four Noble Truths during the third watch of the night, in the dark hours before dawn. [*See* Four Noble Truths.] Gaining these insights, he saw that one's ignorance of the fact that it is the thirst *(tṛṣṇā; taṇhā)* for sensual, emotional, or personal gratification that leads one to think and act in certain ways, and that those thoughts and actions then determine how one understands and lives one's life. In other words, it is people's desire to have the world the way they want it to be rather than to know it as it is, free of their preconceptions and demands, that leads to suffering. The cure for this dis-ease, according to Buddhist tradition, is to relinquish one's attachment to the world as one thinks it is, or should be, so that one can be free to see it as it really is. One has to blow out the flames of one's unquenchable desires in order to know the cool waters of truth, of *dharma.*

This "blowing out" of conditioned existence, this *nirvāṇa,* is enlightenment. Gautama is said to have attained *nirvāṇa* as the sun came up, an appropriate time to be "awakened" to the nature of reality. Standing up from his place under the tree, Gautama then walked forth as the Buddha.

Theravāda Buddhism recognizes three different types of people who have gained enlightenment. *Sāvakabodhi* ("enlightenment gained by one who has heard [the Buddha's lessons]") applies to the disciples of the Buddha. *Paccekabodhi* ("enlightenment in solitude") refers to the enlightenment experienced by a person who has never actually heard the Buddha's teachings but, nevertheless, has understood in full the nature of reality. The Theravāda tradition does not recognize the teachings of a *paccekabuddha* but does not dispute the validity of his or her experience. *Sammā-sambodhi* is the complete and absolute enlightenment known by Gotama (Gautama) and other Buddhas in other world cycles.

Recognizing the important link between ignorance *(avidyā; avijjā)* of the way things are and the craving *(tṛṣṇā; taṇhā)* to have them otherwise, Theravāda Buddhist commentatorial tradition has tended to equate the experience of enlightenment with that of the extinction of desire *(tṛṣṇakṣaya; taṅhākkhaya),* and thus not only to *nirvāṇa* but also to the third of the Four Noble Truths (*nirodha,* "cessation"). Other near-synonyms appear throughout the earliest Pali texts: the abolition of passion *(rāgakṣaya; rāgakkhaya),* the cessation of hatred *(dośakṣaya; dosakkhaya),* the extinction of illusion *(mohakṣaya; mohakkhaya),* and uncompounded or unconditioned existence *(asamskṛta; asamkhata)* all restate the general connotations of the enlightenment experience.

The Mahāyāna tradition, too, has understood enlightenment to include the direct perception of things-as-they-are. According to the Mahāyāna, the enlightened being sees all beings in their uncategorical integrity, their "suchness" (Skt., *tathatā, yathābhūta;* Tib., *yaṅ dag pa ji lta ba bźin du*) or their "thatness" (*tattva;* Tib., *de kho na* [*ñid*]). Mādhyamika Buddhist tracts hold that to perceive all things in their suchness is to see that they are empty *(śūnya)* of any substantial or essential being and thus cannot be characterized. They are what they are, nothing more and nothing less. The Prajñāpāramitā (Perfection of Wisdom) school of the Mahāyāna holds that a person who is to understand the "emptiness" *(śūnyatā)* of the world as it truly is must cultivate wisdom *(prajñā),* a wisdom that is identical with awareness of all things *(sarvajñātā)* and perfect enlightenment *(sambodhi).* [*See* Śūnyam and Śūnyatā.]

Despite the many and long discourses on the subject, Buddhism in general, particularly the various schools of the Mahāyāna, holds that the experience of enlightenment is an ineffable one, for what lies beyond all categories cannot itself be expressed in words. That it cannot be expressed, however, is part of its experience. The *Mumonkan,* a Zen Buddhist chronicle, recounts a story purported to appear in an as yet undiscovered *sūtra* that would exemplify this point: When asked about the nature of truth, the Buddha silently held up a flower in front of his followers. Nobody understood his point—except for the venerable Kaśyapa, who smiled softly. Knowing that Kaśyapa understood, the Buddha declared his disciple to be enlightened.

BIBLIOGRAPHY

The most accessible Sanskrit account of Gautama Buddha's enlightenment is the *Buddhacarita,* Aśvaghoṣa's poem written in the first century CE. English translations of the sections on the temptation by Māra and the enlightenment appear in *The Buddhacarita, or Acts of the Buddha,* translated and edited by Edward H. Johnston (1935–1936; reprint, Delhi, 1972), pp. 188–217, and in *Buddhist Scriptures,* translated and edited by Edward Conze (Harmondsworth, 1959), pp. 48–53. Translations from selected Pali literatures pertinent to the enlightenment appear in Henry Clark Warren's *Buddhism in Translations* (1896; reprint, New York, 1976), pp. 129–159. Historical and analytical discussions of the Buddha's enlightenment appear in Edward J. Thomas's *The Life of Buddha as Legend and History,* 3d ed. (1949; reprint, London, 1969), pp. 61–80: Bhikkhu Ñāṇamoli's *The Life of the Buddha* (Kandy, 1972); Richard H. Robinson and Willard L. Johnson's *The Buddhist Religion,* 3d ed. (Belmont, Calif., 1982), pp. 5–20; Hajime Nakamura's *Gōtama Buddha* (Los Angeles and Tokyo, 1972), pp. 57–65; and Winston L. King's *Theravāda Meditation* (University Park, Pa., 1980), pp. 1–17.

WILLIAM K. MAHONY

ENLIGHTENMENT, THE. The eighteenth-century European intellectual movement known as the Enlightenment was affiliated with the rise of the bourgeoisie and the influence of modern science; it promoted the values of intellectual and material progress, toleration, and critical reason as opposed to authority and tradition in matters of politics and religion. The eighteenth century itself is sometimes referred to as "the Enlightenment," but this appellation is highly misleading. For despite the patronage of a few powerful individuals (Frederick the Great of Prussia, Catherine the Great of Russia, Josef II of Austria, and Pope Boniface XIV), the Enlightenment was always a critical and often a subversive movement in relation to the established political and religious order. Its values may have dominated certain intellectual circles in the eighteenth century, especially in France, but they did not dominate the political structures or the religious life of eighteenth-century people generally; and though many political goals of the Enlightenment were largely achieved in the nineteenth century, few of them were achieved in the eighteenth. In the eighteenth century, moreover, there were other powerful movements, particularly religious ones, that diverged from and were sometimes decidedly hostile to the Enlightenment (among them, Pietism, Jansenism, and Methodism). [*See* Pietism; Methodist Churches; *and the biography of Descartes.*] It is also a mistake to suggest that the ideas and values of the Enlightenment were limited to eighteenth-century thinkers, for these values have had a prominent place in European thought down to the present day.

The Enlightenment has always been regarded as predominantly a French movement, but its influence was certainly felt elsewhere, chiefly in Germany, England, and the American colonies. The terms *éclaircissement* and *Aufklärung* were generally used by its proponents, but the English term *enlightenment* does not appear to have been widely used until the nineteenth century, when it had largely derogatory connotations associated with the continent. In Germany too, the movement's opponents frequently played on anti-French sentiments.

The way was paved for the French Enlightenment by the wide influence of Cartesian philosophy and science in the latter half of the seventeenth century. But it also took stimulus from philosophical and scientific advances elsewhere, particularly in England. Within France, the principal forerunner of the Enlightenment was Pierre Bayle (1647–1706), whose *Historical and Critical Dictionary* (1697) combined sharp wit, copious historical learning, and dialectical skill with a skeptical temper and a deep commitment to the values of intellectual openness and toleration, especially in religious matters. In the sciences, the Enlightenment owed much to the publicist Bernard Le Bovier de Fontenelle (1657–1757), whose long and active career brought the ideas of scientific philosophers, especially Descartes, Leibniz, and Newton, into currency in France. But the chief philosophical inspiration for the French Enlightenment was provided by John Locke (1632–1704), whose epistemology, political theory, and conception of the relation of reason to religion became models for French Enlightenment thinkers. [*See the biography of Locke.*]

We may distinguish two generations of French Enlightenment thinkers, with the transition occurring around 1750. The principal representatives of the first generation were Voltaire (François-Marie Arouet, 1694–1778) and the Baron de Montesquieu (Charles-Louis de Secondat, 1689–1755). Montesquieu's chief writings were in social theory, political theory, and history. His *Persian Letters* (1721) and *The Spirit of the Laws* (1748) give the lie to the common charge that the Enlightenment perspective on society and history was shallow, naive, reductionistic, and ethnocentric. Voltaire's massive oeuvre includes poetry, plays, and novels, as well as philosophical treatises and innumerable essays on the most varied subjects. His interests were exceptionally broad, but perhaps his chief concern was with religion. Voltaire's famous motto *Écrasez l'infâme!* ("Crush the infamous thing!") accurately portrays his hostility toward the Roman Catholic church and toward clericalism in all forms. His writings contain many eloquent pleas for religious toleration and numberless irreverent satires on the narrowness, irrationality, and superstition of traditional Christianity. Voltaire was characteristic of Enlightenment thinkers in that he was uncompromisingly anticlerical, but it would be wholly incorrect to describe him as an atheist and inaccurate to call him an irreligious man. His writings bear witness to a lifelong struggle to achieve a rational piety that might sustain a person of moral disposition in a world full of monstrous human crimes and terrible human sufferings.

The younger generation of French Enlightenment thinkers (or *philosophes*) represents a considerable variety of viewpoints, some of them far more radical politically and more antireligious than those of Voltaire and Montesquieu. The leading French philosopher of this generation was Denis Diderot (1713–1784), a versatile and gifted writer, and the principal editor of the massive *Encyclopedia,* unquestionably the greatest scholarly and literary achievement of the French Enlightenment. Diderot left no finished philosophical system, but rather a variety of writings that expressed an ever-changing point of view and covered many subjects—metaphysics, natural science, psychology, aesthetics, criticism, society, politics, morality, and religion. In religion, Diderot began as a Deist, but later abandoned this position as an unworthy compromise with religious superstition. Yet even as an atheist, he retained great sympathy for many aspects of religion, especially for the religious predicament of the conscientious individual moral agent. His atheism has sometimes been accurately (if anachronistically) described as existentialist in character. In his later years, he occasionally flirted with some form of theism, especially with a sort of naturalistic pantheism. Like Voltaire, he was adamantly opposed to the simpler and more direct atheism of materialists such as d'Holbach.

The first volume of Diderot's *Encyclopedia* was published in 1751, prefaced by the famous "Preliminary Discourse" by the scientist Jean Le Rond d'Alembert (1717–1783). Seven volumes were published by 1759, when the work was suppressed by royal decree as causing "irreparable damage to morality and religion." In the same year, Pope Clement XIII threatened those who read it or possessed copies of it with excommunication. Six years later, with tacit permission of the government, Diderot managed to publish the remaining ten volumes. The *Encyclopedia* contained articles by many distinguished French intellectuals: Voltaire and Montesquieu, Rousseau and Condorcet, Quesnay and Turgot. [*See the biography of Rousseau.*] Some of the articles are anonymous, perhaps written by Diderot himself, or taken by him from other sources. (The article "Reason," for instance, is a close paraphrase of Coste's translation of Locke's *Essay concerning Human Understanding* [4.18.10–11], an eloquent part of Locke's treatment of the relation of reason to faith.) The *Encyclopedia* by no means disseminated a single "party line" on moral, political, or religious questions. Many of the articles on theological subjects, for instance, were by Abbé Claude Yvon (1714–1791), who, in his article "Atheists," attacks Bayle's view that atheism should be tolerated and that the morals of atheists are as high as those of believers. The real ideology behind the *Encyclopedia* is its confidence that moral, political, and religious progress can be achieved in society by the simple means of "raising the level of debate" on these matters. It was precisely this, and not immoralist or antireligious propaganda, that aroused the fear of Louis XV and Pope Clement XIII.

The most important epistemologist and psychologist of the second-generation *philosophes* was Étienne Bonnot, abbé de Condillac (1715–1780), whose *Treatise on Systems* (1749) and *Treatise on Sensations* (1754) developed a theory of human knowledge grounded wholly on sense experience. It is probably in Condillac, in fact, together with David Hume, that we find the true beginnings of modern empiricism.

The *philosophes* also included some infamous philosophical radicals, particularly Julien Offray de La Mettrie (1709–1751), Claude-Adrien Helvétius (1715–1771), and Paul-Henri Thiry, baron d'Holbach (1723–1789). La Mettrie expounded an openly materialist theory of the soul in *Man a Machine* (1748) and a blatantly hedonist ethics in *Discourse on Happiness* (1750). Helvétius's *On the Mind* (published posthumously, 1772) presents a thoroughgoing determinist and environmentalist psychology, together with a utilitarian ethical theory. D'Holbach's attack on religion was begun in his *Christianisme dévoilé* (1761; the title is cleverly ambiguous: "revealed Christianity" or "Christianity exposed"); it was continued in his materialistic, deterministic, and atheistic *System of Nature* (1770).

Elsewhere in Europe, the Enlightenment took more moderate forms. In Germany, the alleged religious unorthodoxy of the *Aufklärung*'s representatives often made them objects of controversy, sometimes victims of persecution. But in fact there was nothing more radical among them than a rather conservative form of Deism. The founder of the German Enlightenment was Christian Wolff (1679–1754). He was possessed of an unoriginal but encyclopedic mind suited to the task of exercising a dominant influence on German academic philosophy. And this he did during the whole of the eighteenth century, at least until its last two decades. Although Wolff's theology was orthodox to the point of scholasticism, his rationalistic approach to theology brought upon him the wrath of the German Pietists, who had him dismissed from his professorship at Halle in 1723. (He was reinstated by Frederick the Great, however, on the latter's accession in 1740.) Among the influential exponents of Wolffianism in the *Aufklärung* were the metaphysician and aesthetician Alexander Gottlieb Baumgarten (1714–1762), the first to describe philosophy of art as "aesthetics"; the "neologist" theologian Johann Salamo Semler (1725–1791); and the controversial early biblical critic Hermann Samuel Reimarus (1694–1768). [*See the biographies of Wolffe and Reimarus.*]

The *Aufklärung* flourished during the reign of Frederick the Great (r. 1740–1786). Himself a Deist and an admirer of the *philosophes*, Frederick refounded the Berlin Academy in 1744 and brought the distinguished French scientist Pierre-Louis Moreau de Maupertuis (1698–1759) to Berlin as its head, along with Voltaire, La Mettrie, and d'Alembert. The Academy's nonresident members included Wolff, Baumgarten, Fontenelle, Helvétius, and d'Holbach. Beyond (or beneath) the patronage of Frederick, there were also the so-called popular Enlightenment thinkers, such as Christoph Friedrich Nicolai (1733–1811) and Christian Garve (1742–1798). By far their most distinguished representative, however, was the Jewish Deist Moses Mendelssohn (1729–1786), a gifted German prose stylist, an early advocate of the disestablishment of religion, and the grandfather of composer Felix Mendelssohn. [*See the biography of Mendelssohn.*]

One of the most independent and influential voices of the German Enlightenment was that of Mendelssohn's close friend Gotthold Ephraim Lessing (1729–1781), a dramatist, critic, theologian, and admirer of Spinoza and Leibniz. Lessing's theological writings are powerful but enigmatic in content, perhaps because his aim was simultaneously to criticize the arid rationalism of Wolffian theology and to reject the irrationalism and bibliolatry of Pietism. (The term *bibliolatry* as an epithet of opprobrium was coined by him.) [*See the biographies of Lessing, Leibniz, and Spinoza.*]

In the second half of the eighteenth century, there arose several empiricist critics of Wolffianism in Germany, notably Johann Heinrich Lambert (1728–1777) and Johann Nikolaus Tetens (1736–1807). But towering over them, and indeed over all other philosophers of the German Enlightenment, is the foremost critic of Wolffian philosophy, Immanuel Kant (1724–1804). [*See the biography of Kant.*] It is often said that Kant's ethics displays signs of his Pietist upbringing. In fact, however, Kant's specific references to Pietist forms of religiosity (emphasis on devotional reading of the Bible and on prayer as means of raising oneself to an actual experience of grace and justification) harshly criticize them as fanaticism *(Schwärmerei)* subversive of moral autonomy. Kant's theology was always a form of Wolffian rationalism, his moral religion a form of Enlightenment Deism. Kant's famous avowal that he "limits knowledge in order to make room for faith" makes reference not to a voluntarist or irrationalist "leap," still less to a biblical faith. Kantian moral faith is a form of rational belief, justified by a subtle (and usually underrated) philosophical argument. Throughout his maturity, and even during his term as rector of the University of Königsberg, Kant refused on principle to participate in religious services (which he condemned as "superstitious pseudo-service" [*Afterdienst*] of God). His uncompromising anticlericalism and deep suspicion of popular religion ("vulgar superstition") are characteristic French Enlightenment attitudes. Kant's 1784 essay "What Is Enlightenment?" expressed wholehearted support for the movement and for the policies of academic openness, religious toleration, and anticlericalism pursued by Frederick the Great.

The Enlightenment in Britain is represented in theology by the tradition of British Deism (the position of such men as John Toland and Matthew Tindal) and in politics by Whig liberalism. Representative of both trends was the philosopher, scientist, and Presbyterian (and Unitarian) cleric Joseph Priestley (1733–1804). Other Britons displaying the impact of the Enlightenment included the utilitarian Jeremy Bentham (1748–1832), the economist and moral theorist Adam Smith (1723–1790), the historian Edward Gibbon (1737–1794), and the radical political thinker William Godwin (1756–1836). David Hume (1711–1776) is often regarded as an opponent, even a great subverter, of the Enlightenment, partly because of his political conservatism, but chiefly because of his skeptical attack on the pretensions of human reason. [*See* Empiricism *and the biography of Hume.*] Hume was, however, personally on good terms with many of the *philosophes* and at one with their views on religious matters. To see Hume's attack on reason as anti-Enlightenment is to ignore the fact that it is carried on in the name of the other important Enlightenment ideal, nature. Along with Condillac and the *philosophes,* Hume views our cognitive powers as part of our natural equipment as living organisms and urges us to view our use of them as bound up with our practical needs. His skeptical attack on reason is an attack not on the faculty praised by the Enlightenment, but rather on that appealed to by vain scholastic metaphysicians and crafty sophists hoping to provide "shelter to popular superstitions" by "raising entangling brambles to cover their weakness." Far from being a critic of the Enlightenment, Hume is one of its most characteristic and articulate voices.

The founding fathers of the United States included prominent Enlightenment figures: Thomas Paine, Benjamin Franklin, and Thomas Jefferson. The Federalist suspicion of centralized state power and the hostility to clericalism motivating the complete separation of church and state in the new republic both reflect the influence of Enlightenment ideas.

Even today we still tend to view the Enlightenment through the distorting lens of nineteenth-century romanticism and its reactionary preconceptions. Enlightenment thought is still accused of being ahistorical and ethnocentric, when (as Ernst Cassirer has shown) the conceptual tools used by post-Enlightenment historians and anthropologists were all forged by the Enlightenment itself. [*See the biography of Cassirer.*] Enlightenment thought is charged with naive optimism, despite the fact that some of the most characteristic Enlightenment thinkers (Voltaire, Mendelssohn) were historical pessimists. It is said that the Enlightenment had too much confidence in human reason, despite its preoccupation with the limits of human cognitive powers. Moreover, many of the Enlightenment thinkers who were most hopeful of salutary social change because of the progress of reason also expressed profound doubts about this (witness Diderot's posthumously published masterpiece *Rameau's Nephew*).

On the subject of religion, the common twentieth-century view—inherited from nineteenth-century romanticism—is that Enlightenment thinkers were shallow and arrogant, showing an irreverence and contempt for tradition and authority. Of course, any movement that (like the Enlightenment) sets out to deflate the pretensions of pseudo-profundity will naturally be accused of shallowness by those it makes its targets. It is equally natural that people who are outraged by crimes and hypocrisy carried on under the protection of an attitude of reverence for tradition and authority should choose irreverent wit and satire as appropriate vehicles for their criticism. In fact, the Enlightenment attack on religious authority and tradition was motivated by a profound concern for what it conceived to be the most essential values of the human spirit, the foundations of any true religion.

Kant defines "enlightenment" as "the human being's release from self-imposed tutelage"; by "tutelage," he means the inability to use one's understanding without guidance from another, the state of a child whose spiritual life is still held in benevolent bondage by his parents. Tutelage is self-imposed when it results not from immaturity or inability to think for oneself, but rather from a lack of courage to do so. Thus enlightenment is the process by which human individuals receive the courage to think for themselves about morality, religion, and politics, instead of having their opinions dictated to them by political, ecclesiastical, or scriptural authorities.

The battle cry of the Enlightenment in religious matters was toleration. The cry now sounds faint and irrelevant to us, partly because we flatter ourselves that we long ago achieved what it demands, and partly because toleration itself appears to be a value that is bloodless and without specific content. But on both counts we seriously misconceive the meaning the Enlightenment attached to toleration. Toleration is the beginning of enlightenment as Europe in the eighteenth century conceived it because it is the necessary social condition for people to use their own intellects to decide what they will believe. The Enlightenment's demand for toleration is thus the demand that people be given the opportunity to fulfill their deepest spiritual vocation: that of using their intellects to determine the faith they will live by. People miss this vocation whenever "faith" for them ceases to be a belief founded on their own evaluation of the evidence before them and becomes the submission of their intellect to some unquestioned authority. The Enlightenment's judgment on such a spiritually crippling, unenlightened "faith" was pronounced most eloquently by the father of Enlightenment thought, John Locke.

> There is a use of the word *Reason,* wherein it is opposed to *Faith.* . . . Only . . . *Faith* is nothing but a firm Assent of the Mind: which if it be regulated as is our Duty, cannot be afforded to any thing, but upon good Reason. . . . He that believes, without having any reason for believing . . . neither seeks Truth as he ought, nor pays the Obedience due to his Maker, who would have him use those discerning Faculties he has given him.
>
> (*Essay concerning Human Understanding* 4.17.24)

Enlightenment is release from tutelage. It is not surprising that a person who subjects himself to the authority of church or scripture or to his own fancies should be intolerant of others' beliefs and should attempt to impose his own upon them. "For," asks Locke, "how almost can it be otherwise, but that he should be ready to impose on others Belief, who has already imposed on his own?"

Kant, writing in 1784, did not claim to be living in an enlightened age, an age in which people had come to intellectual maturity and governed their own beliefs through reason; but he did claim to be living in an age of enlightenment, an age in which people were gaining the courage to free themselves from the spiritual oppression of tradition and authority. Before we dismiss Enlightenment thought as shallow or as irrelevant to our time, we should ask ourselves whether we can say even as much for our age as Kant was willing to say for his.

[*See also* Deism; Theism; Atheism; Doubt and Belief; Reason; Truth; *and* Faith.]

BIBLIOGRAPHY

The best general study of Enlightenment thought is Ernst Cassirer's *The Philosophy of Enlightenment* (Boston, 1951). Also valuable are Paul Hazard's *European Thought in the Eighteenth Century* (New Haven, 1954) and Frederick C. Copleston's *A History of Philosophy,* vol. 6, *Wolff to Kant* (Westminster, Md., 1963), parts 1 and 2. Carl Becker's *The Heavenly City of the Eighteenth-Century Philosophers* (New Haven, 1932) is a famous and paradoxical defense of the continuity between Enlightenment thinkers and the Christian tradition they criticized. The best known of many replies to it is Peter Gay's *The Enlightenment,* 2 vols. (New York, 1966), especially volume 1, *The Rise of Modern Paganism.*

On the French Enlightenment, see Frank E. Manuel's *The Prophets of Paris* (Cambridge, Mass., 1962); on England, see John Plamenatz's *The English Utilitarians,* 2d ed. (Oxford, 1958). An excellent treatment of the German Enlightenment can be found in chapters 10–17 of Lewis White Beck's *Early German Philosophy: Kant and His Predecessors* (Cambridge, Mass., 1969). Studies emphasizing the religious thought of the four most important Enlightenment thinkers are Norman L. Torrey's *Voltaire and the English Deists* (1930; reprint, Hamden, Conn., 1967); Aram Vartanian's *Diderot and Descartes* (Princeton, 1953); *Hume on Religion* (New York, 1963), edited by Richard Wollheim; and my book *Kant's Moral Religion* (Ithaca, N.Y., 1970).

Allen W. Wood

ENLIL (Sum., "lord; gust of wind") was, with An, Enki, and sometimes Ninhursaga, one of the chief Mesopotamian cosmic deities; his provenance was the atmosphere and the earth. Enlil was the tutelary deity of Nippur, the religious center of the ancient Sumerians. His temple, Ekur ("mountain house"), was considered the link between heaven and earth. His consort was Ninlil, and the story of the birth of four of their children, including the moon god, Nanna (Sin), is related in the myth *Enlil and Ninlil.* Other children attributed to Enlil were the gods Nergal, Shamash, Ninurta (Ningirsu), and Adad.

Enlil was the most powerful and dynamic god of the entire Mesopotamian pantheon. He often took over from the nominal chief god, An, as the real head of the gods. Among his epithets were "father of the gods," "king of the gods," and "he whose lordship among the gods is supreme." When the Akkadian abstract element *utu* is added to his name, the resultant form *(enlil + utu = ellilutu)* signifies "supreme power." In the prologue to his code of laws, Hammurabi records that An and Enlil had extended to Marduk, the city god of Babylon, the supreme power. One of Marduk's titles was "Enlil of the gods," that is, the highest-ranking god; similarly, in Assyria, Ashur was the Assyrian "Enlil," and he too had the title "Enlil of the gods." Apart from extending power to gods and men, Enlil was also possessor of the tablets of destiny by means of which the fates of men and gods were decreed on the first month of the year. According to the myth of Anzu, these tablets were stolen from Enlil by the storm bird Anzu, and Enlil's son Ninurta was dispatched to recover them.

Enlil was generally perceived as a most beneficent and fatherly deity. He was the recipient of numerous hymns and prayers, and his approval was held to be the prerequisite for a good life in the land. Even the gods were eager for his blessing. Various gods had the habit of traveling each year to Nippur to ask Enlil's blessing for the ruler of their cities and for general prosperity. One of the most famous of such journeys is that related in the myth *Journey of Nanna to Nippur,* where the moon god, Nanna, travels to Nippur on a boat loaded with many gifts to obtain his father Enlil's blessing. Enlil accedes to his son's request: "In the river he gave him overflow, in the field he gave him much grain. . . . In the palm grove and vineyard he gave him honey and wine, in the palace he gave him long life."

Enlil was extolled in the hymns as a nature god who brings abundance and prosperity, "who holds the rains of heaven and waters of earth," and "who makes the barley and vines grow." The great *Hymn to Enlil* is a paean in his honor: without Enlil "no city could be built, no population settled, no cattle pen built, its sheepfold not set up, no king could be raised to office." Nothing, in fact, could exist or function without Enlil; he was essential to man and nature.

Enlil, though, is not always totally beneficent to man. The storm he embodies is potentially destructive. In the *Lament for Ur,* the destruction of the city Ur is attributed to Enlil's storm "that annihilated the land." One petitioner bemoans in a prayer the fact that Enlil is "the storm destroying the cattle pen, uprooting the sheepfold; my roots are torn up, my forests denuded." In the *Epic of Atrahasis* Enlil is portrayed in this destructive capacity, as one who, alarmed by the rapid growth of the human race (whose noise disturbs his sleep), attempts to reduce and eventually destroy mankind by plague, by drought, and finally by flood.

Commencing with the Old Babylonian period, Enlil occupied a less exalted position in the pantheon. Many of his attributes were assumed by Marduk in Babylonia and by Ashur in Assyria. Indeed, it is likely that Marduk's and Ashur's prominent roles in the great Mesopotamian national epic, *Enuma elish* (in the extant Babylonian and Assyrian recensions, respectively), originally belonged to Enlil.

The emblem of Enlil, as depicted on Middle Babylonian boundary stones, was the same as that of An—a horned tiara. In recognition of the fact that Enlil's actual rank was lower than An's, however, his designated symbolic number was only fifty, as compared with An's sixty—the highest number in the Mesopotamian sexagesimal system.

[*See also* Mesopotamian Religions.]

BIBLIOGRAPHY

There has been no full-length treatment of Enlil since Friedrich Nötscher's *Ellil in Sumer und Akkad* (Hannover, 1927), a condensation of which appeared in *Reallexikon der Assyriologie,* edited by Erich Ebeling and Bruno Meissner, vol. 2 (Berlin, 1938), pp. 382–387. The best surveys since then are D. O. Edzard's "Enlil," in *Wörterbuch der Mythologie,* edited by Hans Wilhelm Haussig, vol. 1, *Götter und Mythen im Vorderen Orient* (Stuttgart, 1965), pp. 59–61; W. H. P. Römer's "Religion of Ancient Mesopotamia," in *Historia Religionum: Handbook for the History of Religions,* edited by C. Jouco Bleeker and Geo Widengren, vol. 1, *Religions of the Past* (Leiden, 1969), pp. 128–129; and Thorkild Jacobsen's *The Treasures of Darkness: A History of Mesopotamian Religion* (New Haven, 1976), pp. 98–104.

David Marcus

ENNIN (794–864), posthumous title, Jikaku Daishi; Japanese Buddhist monk of the Tendai school. Ennin was born in north-central Japan. At fifteen he entered the monastic center on Mount Hiei, the headquarters of the Tendai school, where he soon became a favorite disciple of Saichō (767–822), the Japanese monk who transmitted the Tendai (Chin., T'ien-t'ai) teachings to Japan from China. In 814 Ennin became a full-fledged monk, after which he studied the Buddhist precepts at Tōdaiji in Nara for seven years. Eventually, a physical ailment forced him to retire to a hut at Yokawa in the northern part of Mount Hiei, where he waited quietly for death. According to legend, Ennin devoted himself to copying the *Lotus Sutra* (Jpn. *Hokekyō*; Skt., *Saddharmapuṇḍarīka Sūtra*) for three years, and miraculously regained his health after experiencing a vision of the Buddha in a dream. The next year (835) Ennin petitioned the court for permission to visit China. He left Japan in 838 with the last official Japanese embassy to the T'ang court. Unable to gain permission to visit Mount T'ien-t'ai, eponymous headquarters of the Chinese T'ien-t'ai school, he studied Sanskrit and received initiation into the Vajradhātu Maṇḍala and the Garbhakośadhātu Maṇḍala and other Esoteric (Mikkyō) doctrines and practices.

The following year he made a pilgrimage to Mount Wu-t'ai in northern China, a center of Pure Land practices. Here, Ennin studied T'ien-t'ai texts and Mikkyō, and participated in Pure Land practices. In 840 he went to the capital, Ch'ang-an, where for six years he deepened his knowledge and added expertise in the *susiddhi*, an Esoteric tradition as yet unknown in Japan. Ennin survived the persecution of Buddhism under Emperor Wu-tsung and finally returned to Japan in 847 with hundreds of Buddhist scriptures from the T'ien-t'ai, Esoteric, Ch'an, and Pure Land traditions, as well as treatises on Sanskrit, Buddhist images, assorted ceremonial objects, and even rocks from Mount Wu-t'ai. These are listed in the *Nittō shingu shōgyō mokuroku*, a catalogue Ennin submitted to the court. Ennin also returned with a diary, the *Nittō guhō junrei kōki*, a scrupulously accurate account of his travels and of the China of T'ang times, and with new knowledge and experience to lead the Japanese Tendai school to social and doctrinal preeminence in Japan.

His busy career after returning to Japan was a combination of hectic activity and prestigious official recognition. On Mount Hiei he founded centers for Pure Land and *Lotus Sutra* practices. He presided over an initiation for a thousand people in 849, an initiation for Emperor Montoku and the crown prince in 855, and bestowed the Mahāyāna precepts on Emperor Seiwa in 859. Incumbency of the office of *zasu*, or abbot, of the Tendai school was granted him by the court in 853. Ennin died in 864 (some sources have 866). In 866 he was granted the exalted title Jikaku Daishi ("master of compassionate awakening"); Saichō was (posthumously) given the title Dengyō Daishi ("master of the transmission of the teachings") at the same time. This was the first use of the title Daishi in Japan.

The contributions of Ennin to Japanese Buddhism are as follows:

1. The transmission of Pure Land practices from Mount Wu-t'ai. Although Saichō had already introduced a type of Pure Land practice, the verbal Nembutsu introduced by Ennin provided the foundation for the later independent Pure Land schools of the Kamakura period (1185–1333).
2. Compilation of his diary of his journey to China, an extremely valuable and unique record of T'ang China.
3. Consolidation of Tendai Mikkyō. Ennin completed Saichō's limited transmission of Mikkyō so that the Tendai Mikkyō tradition, known as Taimitsu, could successfully compete with the Tōmitsu Mikkyō of the Shingon school transmitted and founded by Kūkai (774–835). [*See the biography of Kūkai.*]
4. Introduction of *shōmyō*, a melodious method of chanting the scriptures, and transmission of new Pure Land, Mikkyō, confessional, and memorial ceremonies; construction of many important buildings on Mount Hiei; and development of the Yokawa area of Mount Hiei.
5. Strengthening of the position of the Mahāyāna precepts platform on Mount Hiei through his contacts with the imperial court. Ennin's *Kenyō daikai ron*, an important treatise on the subject, further contributed to the power and influence of the ordination center on Mount Hiei.
6. Cultivation of many important disciples. Ennin's lineage, called the Sanmon-ha, although in competition with the Jimon-ha of Enchin (814–891), dominated the Tendai hierarchy for centuries.

Ennin's legacy thus includes the development of the doctrine, practices, and social prestige of the Japanese Tendai school to the point where it dominated the Japanese Buddhist world of the later Heian period (866–1185) and provided the basis for the Pure Land, Zen, and Nichiren schools. Ennin's meticulous diary is also our best source of information on the daily life and times of T'ang China.

[*See also* Tendaishū.]

BIBLIOGRAPHY

The only English-language work on Ennin is Edwin O. Reischauer's pioneering study, *Ennin's Travels in T'ang China*, and his translation of Ennin's diary, *Ennin's Diary: The Record of a*

Pilgrimage to China in Search of the Law (New York, 1955). This work is widely recognized as authoritative, but its approach is historical rather than religious and does not cover Ennin's life and contributions after his return to Japan. The most detailed study and translation of Ennin's diary in Japanese is Ono Katsutoshi's four-volume *Nittō guhō junrei kōki no kenkyū* (Tokyo, 1964–1969). There are two volumes of collected essays concerning Ennin, *Jikaku Daishi sangōshū*, edited by Yamada Etai (Kyoto, 1963), and the more scholarly *Jikaku Daishi kenkyū*, edited by Fukui Kōjun (1964; reprint, Tokyo 1980), first published on the eleven hundredth anniversary of Ennin's death. There is no single collection of Ennin's works, which are instead scattered throughout various collections of Buddhist texts.

PAUL L. SWANSON

EN NO GYŌJA (634?–701), literally, "En the ascetic *(ācārya)*"; famous Japanese mountain ascetic and *hijiri*. Details of his life have been recorded, *inter alia*, in the *Nihon ryōiki* (820) and in his biography, *En no Gyōja hongi* (724). He is also known as En no Ozunu, En no Shōzunu, Shōkaku, or simply as the Master En.

En no Gyōja was born to a family of Shintō priests in the village of Kuwahara in Yamato Province (Nara Prefecture). Although he converted to Buddhism as a youth, he decided to forgo ordination as a monk and to remain a layman. As a result, he is often referred to as En no Ubasoku, "the layman En," after the Japanese transcription of the Sanskrit *upāsaka* ("layman"). At the age of thirty-two he retreated to Mount Katsuragi (Nara Prefecture) and adopted the severe life of a mountain ascetic, clothing himself in grasses and living on the bark of trees. In a cave on the mountainside he installed a copper statue of his patron the *bodhisattva* Kujaku Myō-ō (Skt., Mayūrīrāja), who is believed to assume the shape of a bird in order to dispense his mercies. For more than thirty years En no Gyōja practiced austerities and meditation in front of this statue. During this period he also forayed to other famous peaks, including the Ōmine range and Mount Kimbusen, which later became important centers of *yamabushi* activity. His experience of enlightenment, the culmination of years of ascetic practice, he recorded in this way:

> Long ago I listened to Shaka (i.e., Śākyamuni Buddha) himself as he was preaching on the Eagle mountain [Gṛdhrakūṭa]. Later I became an emperor of Japan and ruled the empire. Here I am now on this mountain in a different body, to engage in the work of saving sentient being.
>
> (Coates and Ishizuka, 1949, p. 18)

Tradition relates that with the attainment of enlightenment En no Gyōja became endowed with miraculous powers, including command of the winds and clouds and even of the indigenous *kami;* his use of a Buddhist spell *(dhāraṇī)* to exorcise the god Hitokotonushi offered vivid proof of the superior magical power available to the practitioner of Buddhism and went far to establish his reputation. Such episodes, however, brought him the disfavor of the public officials, who were chary of the potential for political and social disruption presented by such episodes, and so in the year 700 he was exiled to the island of Izu. The account in the *Nihon ryōiki* reports that during his exile he walked nightly from Izu to the mainland in order to ascend Mount Fuji. In 701 he was allowed to return to Kyoto, after which he traveled to Kyushu to continue his ascetic practices until his death later that year.

En no Gyōja's reputation as the prototypical mountain wizard, who commands the powers of nature and engages in prolific displays of magical prowess gained through his ascetic activities, led him to be canonized as the founder of the Shugendō sect of mountain ascetics. In his doctrines, En no Gyōja is recorded to have attempted to harmonize the Japanese respect for nature and belief in the sacrality of mountain precincts with the teachings of Buddhism. His followers in later generations came to recognize in certain mountain peaks and caves the indigenous equivalents of the Kongōkai (Diamond Realm) and Taizōkai (Womb Realm) *maṇḍalas* of the Tendai and Shingon esoteric traditions in Japan. En no Gyōja's legacy continued to inform the mind of Heian Japan (794–1185): instances of his legend may be found in the *Makurazōshi* (Pillow Sketches) of Sei Shōnagon and in the *Konjaku monogatari* (Narratives of Past and Present). As late as 1799 he was awarded the honorary title Daibosatsu Shimben, "Great Bodhisattva of Divine Change."

[*See also* Shugendō.]

BIBLIOGRAPHY

Coates, H. H., and Ryūgaku Ishizuka. *Honen the Buddhist Saint.* 5 vols. Kyoto, 1949.

Hori Ichirō. *Folk Religion in Japan.* Edited and translated by Joseph M. Kitagawa and Alan L. Miller. Chicago, 1968.

J. H. KAMSTRA

ENOCH, or, in Hebrew, Ḥanokh (from a Hebrew root meaning "consecrate, initiate"); son of Jared, according to biblical tradition, righteous antediluvian, and the subject of substantial hagiography in the Jewish and Christian traditions.

In the Hebrew Bible. *Genesis,* in listing the descendants of Adam until Noah and his sons, mentions Enoch, the seventh, in ways distinct from the others: Enoch "walked with God"; he lived only 365 years, a considerably shorter time than the others; and at the end of his life he "was no more, for God took him" (*Gn.* 5:21–24). Modern scholars agree that a fuller tradition about Enoch lies behind the preserved fragment. They disagree however, on whether that tradition can be recovered from depictions of Enoch in postbiblical Jewish literature of Hellenistic times and from parallel depictions of antediluvian kings, sages, and flood heroes in ancient Mesopotamian literature.

In Jewish Literature of Second Temple Times. The Septuagint (the Greek translation of the Bible, c. 250 BCE), *Ben Sira* (c. 190 BCE), and the *Jewish Antiquities* by Josephus Flavius (37/8–c. 100 CE) all state that Enoch was taken by or returned to the deity. The *Wisdom of Solomon* (first century BCE) explains that God prematurely terminated Enoch's life on earth so that wickedness would not infect his perfect saintliness. Philo Judaeus (d. 45–50 CE) allegorizes Enoch so as to represent the person who is ecstatically transported (echoing the Septuagint) from perishable (physical) to imperishable (spiritual and intellectual) aspects of existence, and from mortality to (spiritual) immortality. Like the Greek version of *Ben Sira,* Philo describes Enoch as a sign of repentance for having changed from the "worse life to the better." Enoch is not found among the sinful multitude but in solitude. Philo contrasts Enoch's piety with that of Abraham, which is exercised within society rather than in isolation.

The portrayals of Enoch in contemporary writings displaying apocalyptic interests are considerably more laudatory of him and expansive of the underlying biblical text. Here Enoch is depicted as a medium for the revelation of heavenly secrets to humanity: secrets of cosmology, sacred history, and eschatology. The principal sources for these traditions are *1* and *2 Enoch, Jubilees, Pseudo-Eupolemus,* and previously unknown writings among the Dead Sea Scrolls. They span a period from the third century BCE to the first century CE.

Enoch's "life" and the secrets revealed to him are summarized in *Jubilees* 4:16–26 and detailed in the *Books of Enoch.* Enoch receives these revelations first in nocturnal visions, and then in a heavenly journey lasting three hundred years, during which he dwells with angels and is instructed by them in hidden cosmological and historical knowledge. After a brief return to earth to transmit a record of his witness to his descendants, he is removed to the garden of Eden, where he continues to testify to humanity's sins and to record God's judgments of these sins until the final judgment. Enoch is also said to officiate in paradise at the sanctuary before God. Elsewhere, certain religious laws are said to have originated with Enoch and his books. In some later parts of this literature, Enoch himself becomes a divine figure who dwells in heaven and executes justice. In most traditions, however, he is an intermediary between the divine and human, even after his transfer to paradise. Thus, Enoch combines the functions of prophet, priest, scribe, lawgiver, sage, and judge.

Ancient Near Eastern Parallels. For over a century, scholars have argued that the biblical Enoch has his roots in Mesopotamian lore about similar antediluvian figures, and that the likenesses between Enoch and such figures reemerge in the depictions of Enoch in Jewish literature of Hellenistic times. Such parallels have most frequently been drawn with the seventh (or sixth or eighth) member of the Sumerian antediluvian king-list, Enmeduranna. According to some versions of this tradition, the king, associated with the city of the sun god Shamash, is received into fellowship with the gods and is initiated into the secrets of heaven and earth, including the art of divination, knowledge of which he passes on to his son. Other scholars, noting that no mention is made of Enmeduranna's transcendence of death, find Enoch's antecedents in the wise flood heroes Ziusudra and Utnapishtim, who are said to have been rewarded with eternal life in paradise. Most recently, scholars have argued that Enoch is modeled after the *apkallu* sages, who reveal wisdom and the civilized arts to antediluvian humanity, the seventh *(utuabzu)* of whom is said to have ascended to heaven.

In Christianity. The church fathers exhibit considerable interest in Enoch's transcendence of death as a paradigm for Jesus and the Christian elect. However, some stress that it was only with Jesus' resurrection that Enoch's ascension was consummated. In the second and third centuries, Christian writers (among them, Tertullian and Irenaeus) place particular emphasis on Enoch's bodily assumption in support of belief in physical resurrection. Some (Tertullian, Hippolytus, and Jerome) identify him as one of the two witnesses of *Revelations* 11:3–13 who battle and are killed by the Antichrist, are resurrected a few days later, and are taken to heaven. Ephraem of Syria (fourth century) stresses that Enoch, like Jesus, in conquering sin and death and in regaining paradise in spirit as well as body, is the antipode of Adam. Because Enoch precedes the covenant of law (he is said to be uncircumcised and unobservant of the Sabbath), his faith and reward are of particular importance to Christianity in its polemic against Judaism and in its mission to the gentiles.

In Rabbinic Judaism. Rabbinic exegesis is concerned less with Enoch's righteousness during life, questioned by some early rabbis, than with the nature of his end. The main issue of dispute is whether he died like other righteous people, his soul returning to God, or whether he was transported, body and soul (like Elijah), to heaven or paradise.

Some rabbinical circles, initially those responsible for the mystical, theosophical literature of Merkavah (divine chariot) speculation (our earliest texts are from the fifth to sixth centuries), adapted prerabbinic traditions of Enoch's transformation into an angel. This angel (now identified with the archangel Metatron) is said to rule the heavenly "palace," to have a role in the revelation of Torah and its teaching on high, and to guide the righteous in their tours of heaven. The tension between the mystical exaltation of Enoch and the more qualified praise of him and denial of his assumption continues through medieval Jewish literature.

In Islam. In the Qur'ān (19:57–58, 21:85), Idrīs is said to have been an "upright man and a prophet," who was "raised to a high place." While Idrīs's identity within the Qur'ān is uncertain, Muslim writers, drawing upon Jewish sources that venerate him, have regularly identified him with Enoch (Arab., Akhnūkh). He is said to have introduced several sciences and arts, practiced ascetic piety, received revelation, and entered paradise while still alive.

[*For related discussion of the* Books of Enoch, *see* Apocalypse, *article on* Jewish Apocalypticism to the Rabbinic Period.]

BIBLIOGRAPHY

There is no comprehensive work on the figure of Enoch in biblical and postbiblical religious traditions. For a thorough treatment of the biblical, Mesopotamian, and apocalyptic sources, see James C. Vanderkam's *Enoch and the Growth of an Apocalyptic Tradition,* "Catholic Biblical Quarterly Monograph Series," no. 18 (Washington, D.C., 1984). For a pastiche of some of the Jewish traditions with notes referring to most of the others, see Louis Ginzberg's *Legends of the Jews,* 7 vols., translated by Henrietta Szold et al. (1909–1938; reprint, Philadelphia, 1946–1955), vol. 1, pp. 125–140, and vol. 5, pp. 156–164. His notes, while comprehensive, are not always sufficiently critical. A collection of short treatments of Enoch in Jewish and Christian primary sources can be found in *Society of Biblical Literature 1978 Seminar Papers,* edited by Paul J. Achtemeier (Missoula, Mont., 1978), vol. 1. pp. 229–276.

On the biblical tradition of Enoch, see, in addition to Vanderkam's book, the following representative commentaries: John Skinner's *A Critical and Exegetical Commentary on Genesis,* 2d ed. (Edinburgh, 1930), pp. 131–132; Umberto Cassuto's *A Commentary on the Book of Genesis,* vol. 1, *From Adam to Noah,* translated by Israel Abrahams (Jerusalem, 1961), pp. 263, 281–286; and Claus Westermann's *Genesis (1–11),* "Biblischer Kommentar Altes Testament," vol. 1.1 (Neukirchen-Vluyn, 1974), pp. 464–486. The last is particularly good, includes a bibliography, and will soon be available in English.

For a comprehensive bibliographical review of recent scholarship on the *Books of Enoch,* see George W. E. Nickelsburg's "The Books of Enoch in Recent Research," *Religious Studies Review* 7 (1981): 210–217. Important additions to that bibliography are Devorah Dimant's "The Biography of Enoch and the Books of Enoch," *Vetus Testamentum* 33 (January 1983): 14–29, and Moshe Gil's "Ḥanokh be-erets he-ḥayyim" (Enoch in the Land of Eternal Life), *Tarbiz* 38 (June 1969): 322–327 (with an English summary, pp. I–III). On the significance of the Enochic literature for the history of Judaism, see, besides Vanderkam's work, Michael Edward Stone's essay "The Book of Enoch and Judaism in the Third Century B.C.E.," *Catholic Biblical Quarterly* 40 (October 1978): 479–492.

On the ancient Near Eastern background to the biblical Enoch and his postbiblical depictions, see Pierre Grelot's "La légende d'Hénoch dans les apocryphes et dans la Bible: Origine et signification," *Recherches de science religieuse* 46 (1958): 5–26, and Rykle Borger's "Die Beschwörungsserie *Bīt Mēseri* und die Himmelfahrt Henochs," *Journal of Near Eastern Studies* 33 (April 1974): 183–196. Both refer extensively to earlier scholarship.

On Enoch in Merkavah and related traditions, see Jonas C. Greenfield's prolegomenon to *3 Enoch, or The Hebrew Book of Enoch,* edited by Hugo Odeberg (New York, 1973), pp. xi–xlvii. For a Christian treatment of Enoch, see Jean Daniélou's *Holy Pagans in the Old Testament,* translated by Felix Faber (Baltimore, 1957), pp. 42–56. For Idrīs in post-Qur'anic Islamic literature, see Georges Vajda's "Idrīs," in *The Encyclopaedia of Islam,* new ed. (Leiden, 1960–).

STEVEN D. FRAADE

ENTHUSIASM.

The history of enthusiasm is as much the history of the word as of the phenomenon it signifies. In the English-speaking world, the word came to prominence as a technical religious term in the seventeenth century, used always in reference to religious experience, and, for the most part, as a term of denigration. For about two hundred years, the usual usage was to denote ill-regulated religious emotion or, more specifically, fancied inspiration, the false or deluded claim to have received divine communications or private revelations. In the course of the last hundred years the technical religious meaning has been almost completely superseded by the more positive meaning now current (ardent zeal for a person, principle, or cause), though unfavorable overtones still cling to the derivative term, *enthusiast,* as connoting an impractical visionary or self-deluded person. It is, however, the technical religious term with which we are here concerned.

A discussion of enthusiasm is also a discussion of the word, in the important sense that disputes over its applicability were also disputes over the propriety and validity of any claims to divine inspiration and revelation. For those hostile to religion as such—or to any save a strictly rational religion—enthusiasm was no different from superstition, a charge which could be brought against the Jewish prophets of old, the apostle Paul, or Muḥammad with as much justice as against John Wesley. For members of the established church who were fearful of schism, *enthusiasm* was another name for sectarianism, and as such could be used of Francis of Assisi or Dominic, or "papists" in general, as well as the followers of George Fox or Madame Guyon. For those suspicious of any display of emotion, particularly in religion, enthusiasm was synonymous with fanaticism. Only in the nineteenth century, under the influence of the Romantic revival, did a more positive sense of enthusiasm—as emotion deeply felt or the heightened perception of poetic inspiration—begin to free the word from the negative overtones of religious disapproval.

In a strict sense, then, the study of enthusiasm is the study of seventeenth- and eighteenth-century Christianity, understood as the study of movements within Christianity that were regarded by their critics as peripheral and as threatening to the integrity of Christianity, although perhaps it could more properly be understood as the study of the attitudes of those who condemned such movements as "enthusiastic." In addition, it should be borne in mind that *enthusiast* was used as a translation of the German *Schwärmer,* a term used by Martin Luther to describe such radical reformers as Andreas Karlstadt, Thomas Müntzer, and the Anabaptists. Like the English "enthusiasts," the German Schwärmer pretended to divine inspirations and revelations and could be classed as fanatics and sectarians. As a technical religious term, therefore, *enthusiasm* denotes the diverse expressions of radical, spiritualist, or sectarian Christianity, particularly in Europe, during the three hundred years from the beginning of the Reformation to the nineteenth century.

Ronald Knox's Enthusiasm. It is this narrowly defined enthusiasm which Ronald Knox describes in his classic study *Enthusiasm.* "Enthusiasm did not really begin to take shape until the moment when Luther shook up the whole pattern of European theology" (Knox, 1950, p. 4). "Enthusiasm in the religious sense belongs to the seventeenth and eighteenth centuries; it hardly reappears without inverted commas after 1823" (p. 6). To be sure, Knox notes that the pattern of enthusiasm is one which recurs spontaneously throughout church history, and he presents brief studies of the Corinthian church, the Montanists, the Donatists, and some medieval sects, particularly the Waldensians and the Cathari. But Donatists are hardly a good example of enthusiasm, despite their zeal for martyrdom. Knox dismisses Montanism as "naked fanaticism" (p. 49) and the medieval movements as fed by an inspiration "alien to the genius of Europe" or as "sporadic and unimportant, freaks of religious history" (p. 4). All these are brought into the picture less as examples of enthusiasm requiring analysis in their own right than as foils to the subsequent descriptions of enthusiasm proper. Even the Anabaptists, the Schwärmer themselves, are given scant treatment and serve largely as a vehicle for Knox's Roman Catholic disapproval of Luther and the Reformation. In all this, it is clear that Knox's chief objection to enthusiastic movements is their tendency to schismatic sectarianism. "The enthusiast always begins by trying to form a church within the Church, always ends by finding himself committed to sectarian opposition" (p. 109).

Knox's somewhat more sympathetic depiction of enthusiasm begins with his treatment of George Fox (1624–1691), the founder of the Society of Friends (Quakers). His attention naturally focuses on Fox's belief in "the inner light," as illustrated by Fox's interruption of a preacher at Nottingham: "It is not the Scripture, it is the Holy Spirit by which holy men of old gave forth the Scripture, by which religions . . . are to be tried" (p. 152, note 3). In the twofold implication of this assertion, the marks of the enthusiast are clearly evident: the claim to an immediacy of inspiration (comparable to that elsewhere readily acknowledged in, but otherwise confined to, the biblical writers) not to be confused with reason or conscience; and the claim that this inner illumination is the true source of authority above the letter of scripture, the creeds, and the ordinances of church and state. The violent tremblings which often accompanied and were thought to attest to the movement of the Holy Spirit, and from which the nickname "Quakers" was derived, apparently occurred only in the very early days. [*See* Quakers.]

The central section of Knox's monograph is given over to a treatment of Jansenism (mid-seventeenth to mid-eighteenth centuries) and Quietism (latter half of the seventeenth century). Significant certainly for their challenge to the mainstream of Roman Catholic tradition, these movements should probably not be classified as examples of enthusiasm, at least in the technical sense of the word as used by Knox. Jansenism stressed the corruption of human nature by original sin and the power of divine grace. Rigorist in character—a kind of Roman Catholic Puritanism—it came closest to enthusiasm in the degree to which it understood grace in terms of experiences of "sensible devotion" (pp. 224–

225). Quietism was a doctrine of Christian spirituality which sought to suppress all human effort, so that divine action might have full sway over the passive soul. It emphasized the immediacy of contact between the soul and God, but since it also denied that such contact need be a matter of conscious experience, Quietism is better studied in connection with Christian mysticism than (Christian) enthusiasm. [*See* Quietism.]

The real targets of Knox's critique at this point are Madame Guyon and the convulsionaries at Saint Médard. Madame Guyon (1648–1717), who did much to promote Quietism, evidently epitomizes a good deal of what Knox regarded as detestable in enthusiasm: particularly her spiritual "smugness" and, not least, the prominent role of influential women in supporting enthusiastic movements. The convulsions at the Paris cemetery of Saint Médard in the early 1730s (including ecstatic dancing, many alleged cures, and speaking in unknown languages) were regarded by participants as the outpouring of the Holy Spirit expected in the last days. But for Knox they are a fitting expression of popular Jansenism and a terrible warning of what can happen to a movement which sits too loose to ecclesiastical authority. Similar to the Jansenist Catholic convulsionaries were the Huguenot Camisards in southern France (late seventeenth to early eighteenth centuries), among whom a form of ecstatic prophecy, involving prostrations, trancelike states, and glossolalia, was prominent, and who in exile in Britain (where they were known as "the French Prophets") converted Ann Lee, the subsequent founder of the North American Shakers. [*See* Shakers.]

The other main object of Knox's analysis is John Wesley (1730–1791). Here Knox's critique focuses on the religion of experience. An initial chapter examines the Moravian piety inculcated in Germany by Count Nikolaus Zinzendorf (1700–1760). Like the Quietists, the Moravians practiced a piety of stillness. But unlike the Quietists, Zinzendorf preached religion as felt experience and salvation "as an immediate and joyful apprehension of a loving Father" (Knox, 1950, p. 410), assurance not merely as a doctrine believed but as something felt, the sense of God's protective love. It was the importance of such experience which Wesley learned from the Moravians and emphasized in his own doctrine of assurance—assurance of present pardon, the inner witness of the Spirit of God. Wesley never abandoned this belief in the importance of feelings, of "heart-religion," though he did subsequently concede that the consciousness of God's acceptance was not an invariable or essential concomitant of that acceptance (p. 539). [*See* Moravians *and* Wesley Brothers.]

These examples might seem to have represented relatively mild forms of enthusiasm. But it is the consequences of such emphases, when freed from the constraints of traditional discipline and ecclesiastical authority, which concern Knox. It was the place given to the nonrational in Wesley's scheme of things which incited the famous remark of Bishop Butler to Wesley: "Sir, the pretending to extraordinary revelations and gifts of the Holy Ghost is a horrid thing, a very horrid thing" (p. 450). So, too, under the heading "Wesley and the religion of experience," Knox describes the convulsions, weeping, and crying out which often accompanied Wesley's preaching. Wesley's willingness to recognize the work of God in such paroxysms and to defend their occurrence makes the charge of enthusiast harder for him to escape, though Wesley himself resisted the charge, was never carried away with such enthusiasm, and clearly perceived its dangers. The other aspect of his teaching which might seem to merit the accusation was his view of Christian perfection, since a belief in the possibility of achieving sinless perfection results inevitably in spiritual elitism and claims of special revelation. However, "sinless perfection" was never Wesley's own phrase: what he encouraged his followers to seek was renewal in love or entire sanctification; nor did he indulge in or encourage the more extreme ideas which his teaching sometimes precipitated.

Knox's survey concludes with a brief foray into the nineteenth century and a reference to the Irvingites, the Shakers, and Perfectionism. Under the ministry of Edward Irving in London in the 1830s, prophecy and speaking in tongues became prominent, understood as utterances in the vernacular and in unknown languages prompted by the Holy Spirit, comparable to the first Christian Pentecost. [*See* Glossolalia.] For Irving, these manifestations confirmed his belief that the second coming of Christ was imminent. The Shakers emerged in the second half of the eighteenth century from a branch of English Quakers who adopted the Camisards' ritual practice of devotional dance to induce states of inspiration (the "shaking Quakers"). Under Ann Lee, who was convinced by revelation that the millennium had already dawned, the movement was transplanted to North America in 1774. "Perfectionism" is identified by Knox with three roughly contemporaneous movements in the first half of the nineteenth century—one in Prussia, one in England, and one in North America (the only other example of North American enthusiasm that Knox really considers). All three shared the belief that the experience of conversion made sin an impossibility.

From all this it is possible to derive a thumbnail sketch of the typical enthusiast in classical terms. The fundamental belief of the enthusiast is in the immediacy and directness of his experience of God. For the enthusiast, as distinct from the Quietist, this experience is self-evident and self-authenticating: self-evident, because it will be marked by distinct inward impressions (a clear sense of God's presence or acceptance, and inspiration or particular revelations, including visions) or by outward bodily manifestations (trembling or prostration, inspired utterance, or miraculous healings); self-authenticating, because it bears greater authority than scripture (as usually interpreted), ecclesiastical creed, rite, or office—greater, even, than reason itself. The enthusiast knows God's will and acts as his agent, accountable only and directly to him. Such experiences will regularly lead the enthusiast to conclude (1) that he is more spiritual than other believers, or that he has reached a higher stage in the Christian life; (2) that a less restrained form of worship should be permitted or encouraged, one in which the outward manifestations of the Holy Spirit have proper place; and (3) that any forms and structures of traditional Christianity which stifle the Holy Spirit should be dispensed with. Not untypically, such convictions can have a strong eschatological tinge—a belief that the millennium has dawned or that Christ's second coming is imminent—which invests the enthusiastic individual or sect with universal significance and can thus justify strongly antisocial or revolutionary action.

Toward a Broader Evaluation of Enthusiasm. Obviously, then, the classic view of enthusiasm has to a considerable extent been determined by the negative connotations attached to the word. Within Christianity, because of fear of superstition, fanaticism, and sectarianism, claims to inspiration and fresh revelation have repeatedly been labeled as "enthusiastic" without more ado. Even Knox, in this love-hate fascination with the subject, regularly allows his account of enthusiastic eccentricities to color the total picture. However, the very evolution in the meaning of the word itself, from censure to approbation, invites a broader evaluation of the subject matter, regarding both the range of phenomena covered (outside as well as inside historical Christianity) and the possibility of a less negative appraisal. In particular, a less value-laden approach to enthusiasm must view more objectively the fact that claims to inspiration and fresh revelation are a fundamental feature of most religions, not least of all Christianity itself. Such an approach should therefore include a fuller analysis of why some such claims are acceptable and others are not.

Outside Christianity. A history of religions approach, which looks beyond the traditional intra-Christian critique of enthusiasm, broadens the range of the phenomena studied and of the tools used in evaluation.

An obvious starting point is the context of Greek thought and religion, from which the word *enthusiasm* comes, and in which one could regard enthusiasm as something positive without being uncritical. According to Plato's Socrates, "our greatest blessings come to us by way of madness, provided the madness is given us by divine gift" (*Phaedrus* 244a). Socrates proceeded to distinguish four types of this "divine madness"—as E. R. Dodds has shown in his concise summary (1951): (1) prophetic madness, whose patron god is Apollo; (2) telestic or ritual madness, whose patron is Dionysos; (3) poetic madness, inspired by the Muses; and (4) erotic madness, inspired by Aphrodite and Eros. Madness *(mania)* is not synonymous with enthusiasm (*entheos*, "full of or inspired by the god"; *enthousiasmos*, "inspiration, frenzy"), but there is considerable overlap in meaning, since *enthusiasm* also designated the classic examples of the first two kinds of madness: the Pythia of the Delphic oracle, who prophesied in a state of possession, speaking in the first person as Apollo's voice, and the frenzied dancing of the Dionysian cult, through which the devotees sought the release of ecstasy. This early recognition of a dimension of experience beyond control of the human mind—of an inspiration experienced as coming from without, to which one must yield in order to experience its full benefit—is of lasting relevance in any critique of enthusiasm, as is the recognition of a continuity or similarity between poetic inspiration and sexual ecstasy on the one hand and enthusiasm on the other. And, while Christianity looks more to the Hebrew idea of prophecy than to the ecstatic prophecy of the Hellenistic world, the phenomenology of Hebrew inspiration is not so very different, as the visions and first-person oracles of the major prophets of the Hebrew scriptures clearly testify. [*See* Oracles *and* Prophecy.]

The association of enthusiasm with the ancient Bacchanalia was well known by those who first used the term in the seventeenth century, which explains their heavy note of disapproval. In the past hundred years, however, documentation of similar phenomena from other cultures has grown apace. Most striking of these is shamanism, defined by Mircea Eliade as a "technique of ecstasy."

By examining the religious interpretations and intentions of shamans who communicate directly with the supernatural world, Eliade argues for a more precise distinction between ecstasy and enthusiasm. In ecstasy, the soul is believed to leave the body during a trance in order to ascend to the sky or descend to the underworld, where it may retrieve the soul of sick persons and restore them to health. [*See* Ecstasy.] Enthusiasm, on the other hand, is a term more suitably applied to cases in which a supernatural being (divinity, ancestor, or demon) inhabits or possesses an individual's body or personality. As in the many instances already mentioned, the indwelling spirit is recognized by some unusual behavior, sentiments, or especially sounds. For a parallel to the group ecstasy of the Camisards or the Shakers, we need look no further than the Muslim fraternity known as the dervishes, who since the twelfth century have sought clearer apprehension of God and greater spiritual illumination through hypnotic-like trance culminating often in a whirling dance.

A further advantage enjoyed by present-day students of enthusiasm over their predecessors is the availability of developed analyses of the social functions and psychological mechanisms of enthusiasm: for example, the shaman's role in enabling a community to cope with the unknown or with sickness and death; the techniques by which ecstasy can be induced; or the way in which ecstasy can be manipulated to strengthen and legitimize a leader's authority or to voice the protest of a deprived section of society. It would be unfortunate, however, if such analyses were confined to the field of abnormal psychology or subordinated to theories of social and economic deprivation, as has often been the case. Enthusiasm in itself deserves neither praise nor blame; it can be as integrative for some individuals and communities as it is disintegrative for others. The extreme forms of enthusiasm are just that, extreme forms, and may be as much due to the hostility of those who feel threatened by any expression of enthusiasm as to the enthusiast's own lack of control. We can speak of the cathartic benefit of phenomena such as a Dionysian ritual (and not only for the less articulate) and compare it to the temporarily inhibition-loosening benefits of a festival like the Mardi Gras. Enthusiasm can bring to expression nonrational and unconscious aspects of the personality and thus provide both release and stimulus for the individual and the community if sympathetically handled. In a fully rounded assessment of enthusiasm, psychological and sociological categories should not be permitted to squeeze out the more theological categories of symbol and sacrament.

Christian enthusiasm. A broader evaluation of enthusiasm must also take full account of the extent of enthusiasm within the Christian tradition itself. Not least in importance is the fact that Christianity in its beginnings can properly be described as an enthusiastic sect within first-century Judaism. Jesus himself can hardly be called an ecstatic, but the immediacy of his experience of God as Father and of the power of the Holy Spirit, not to mention his healings and claims to eschatological finality, are clearly attested in Christian sources and have left their mark on subsequent spirituality as well as doctrine. However, so far as enthusiasm is concerned, much more influential has been the record, given in the *Acts of the Apostles,* of the Christian movement itself, from the first Christian Pentecost onward. According to this account, ecstatic visions (described on two occasions precisely in those terms) played a significant part in directing the course of the earliest Christian expansion. Regular reports are given of miracles, including healings effected by Peter's shadow or handkerchiefs touched by Paul. The Holy Spirit was understood to come upon, enter, and fill the individual Christian with a clear physical impact which included glossolalia. Experiences of inspired utterances were evidently prized, not least as evidence that the long withdrawn spirit of prophecy had been poured out in eschatological fullness. All this is the stuff of enthusiasm throughout the history of Christianity, so it is hardly surprising that the desire to recover or experience again the Pentecostal spirit of the primitive church is one of the most recurrent features of enthusiasm from the radical Reformation onward. Similarly, it should occasion little surprise that the canonical *Revelation to John* has provided a ready source of inspiration for apocalyptic and millenarian movements within Christianity down through the centuries.

Paul was no stranger to enthusiastic phenomena, including the ascent to heaven and speaking in tongues. But his approach to excessive enthusiasm, particularly in the church at Corinth, is marked by a rare balance of sympathy and firmness. In Paul, the older Jewish recognition of the need to "test the spirits" in cases of claimed inspiration achieves a degree of sophistication seldom matched before or since. To be accepted as a manifestation of the Holy Spirit, inspiration (1) must be in accord with the gospel, whose power constituted them as Christians, (2) must be consistent with and expressive of love for fellow Christians, and (3) should aim to provide beneficial service to the community. In short, Paul viewed enthusiasm as an aberrant phenomenon only when it offended the love of neighbor which Jesus so completely embodied.

A broader critique of enthusiasm, less dominated by Western rationalist perspectives, would also take fuller account of the whole phenomenon of Eastern Christian spirituality, including such early writings as the *Odes of Solomon* and the homilies of Makarios of Egypt, and such early movements as that of the Desert Fathers and Messalianism, the latter the only Christian sect to be explicitly called "enthusiast" by the church fathers. In the medieval period, mysticism as well as millenarianism provide overlapping phenomena, and with the fuller documentation now available, it is possible to achieve a more balanced view than that attained by Knox of both the prophetic impact of Joachim of Fiore

(1145–1202) and the character of the radical Reformation.

Most striking of all, for an author writing in the mid-twentieth century, was Knox's neglect of enthusiastic features of North American Christianity during the nineteenth century, particularly camp meetings, revivalism, and the holiness movement, as well as his neglect of the emergence in Britain of primitive Methodism and "higher life" teaching. Nor should the role of claimed revelations and prophecies in the beginnings of the Church of Latter-Day Saints (Mormons) and of the Seventh-day Adventists be ignored.

A prime example of enthusiastic Christianity is the twentieth-century Pentecostal movement, with its special emphasis on a second experience of the Holy Spirit distinct from and subsequent to conversion, on continued bestowal of spiritual gifts, and particularly on speaking in tongues. Within the history of Christian enthusiasm, the importance of Pentecostalism can hardly be overestimated. It is the form of Western Christianity which has been least influenced by the traditions of Western rationalism and most conducive to the emergence of indigenous forms of Christianity in Africa and South America, as illustrated especially by the profusion of independent African churches which are Pentecostal (i.e., enthusiastic) in character. This suggests, once again, that European antipathy to enthusiasm reflects as much the culture patterns particularly of northern Europe as it does the emphasis of enthusiasm on experience and emotion. Furthermore, since the 1950s, Pentecostalism has been increasingly recognized as a valid and vital expression of Christianity—the first formal recognition from within mainstream Western Christianity that the enthusiastic dimension should have a place within a fully rounded Christianity. Finally, while classical Pentecostalism was largely vulnerable to reductive psychological and sociological analyses, the spread of Pentecostal emphases into the older Christian denominations with the charismatic renewal which began in the 1960s has embraced a much broader range of society and undermined many analytic stereotypes. [*See* Pentecostal and Charismatic Christianity.]

Concluding Reflections. Enthusiasm should not be dismissed as a primitive throwback or marginal movement, whether in religion in general or in Christianity in particular. It expresses a fundamental aspect, an experiential dimension, of religion. Within the Judeo-Christian tradition, especially, it forms a strand as important as scripture, creed, or priesthood—an experience of the Spirit of God not restricted to mediation by holy book or holy ritual. The history of enthusiasm within Christianity strongly suggests that, unless given adequate expression within Christian worship and spirituality, it will burst forth sooner or later outside organized structures, often in exotic forms. This further suggests that, without checks such as those counseled by Paul, enthusiasm all too soon becomes the *reductio ad absurdum* of the religion of the Spirit. Here, too, the words of Jonathan Edwards on the similar theme of "religious affections" have continued application. "As there is no true religion where there is nothing else but affection, so there is no true religion where there is no religious affection" ([1746] 1959, p. 120).

[*See also* Spirit Possession; Inspiration; *and* Frenzy.]

BIBLIOGRAPHY

Given the ambiguity of the word *enthusiasm*, the reader should consult Susie I. Tucker's *Enthusiasm: A Study in Semantic Change* (Cambridge, 1972), which traces the evolution of the meaning of the word.

For the background in Greek thought, see E. R. Dodds's *The Greeks and the Irrational* (Berkeley, 1951), especially chapter 3, and Walter F. Otto's *Dionysus: Myth and Cult* (Bloomington, Ind., 1973). Alfred Guillaume's 1938 Bampton Lectures, *Prophecy and Divination among the Hebrews and Other Semites* (London, 1938), treats enthusiasm in Jewish and Muslim tradition. Mircea Eliade's classic history of religions study, *Shamanism: Archaic Techniques of Ecstasy* (1951; rev. & enl. ed., London, 1964), examines shamanism in Siberia and elsewhere. Eliade's study is complemented by I. M. Lewis's *Ecstatic Religion: An Anthropological Study of Spirit Possession and Shamanism* (Harmondsworth, 1971). Still valuable are the psychological observations of William James's *The Varieties of Religious Experience: A Study in Human Nature* (New York, 1902).

For enthusiasm within Christianity, the period of Christian beginnings is covered in P. G. S. Hopwood's *The Religious Experience of the Primitive Church* (New York, 1937) and in my *Jesus and the Spirit: A Study of the Religious and Charismatic Experience of Jesus and the First Christians as Reflected in the New Testament* (Philadelphia, 1975). Simon Tugwell provides a light introduction to the enthusiasm of Eastern Christian spirituality in his *Did You Receive the Spirit?* (London, 1972). For the medieval period, see the fascinating account of the revolutionary millenarian sects in Norman R. C. Cohn's *The Pursuit of the Millennium*, 3d ed. (New York, 1970). For one of several specialist studies of Joachim of Fiore and his influence, see Marjorie E. Reeves's *The Influence of Prophecy in the Later Middle Ages: A Study of Joachimism* (Oxford, 1969). Equally fascinating is Herbert Thurston's *The Physical Phenomena of Mysticism* (London, 1952). George H. Williams's *The Radical Reformation* (Philadelphia, 1962) corrects the traditional "bad press" given to the most enthusiastic strand of the Reformation.

Any enquiry into the Christian phenomena must begin with Ronald Knox's *Enthusiasm: A Chapter in the History of Religion with Special Reference to the Seventeenth and Eighteenth Centuries* (Oxford, 1950), which, despite the deficiencies noted above, remains a magnificent and magisterial study. From the period treated by Knox, two contributions from men of stature who knew enthusiastic movements from the inside are still worth considering: John Wesley's sermon *The Nature of Enthusiasm* (1750), usually printed as sermon 32 in standard collections of Wesley's forty-four sermons; and Jonathan Edwards's *A Treatise concerning Religious Affections* (Boston, 1746), which is reproduced in volume 2 of *The Works of Jonathan Edwards*, edited by John E. Smith (New Haven, 1959).

For the modern period, Timothy L. Smith provides a balanced view in his *Revivalism and Social Reform in Mid-Nineteenth-Century America* (New York, 1957). The compendious study by Walter J. Hollenweger, *The Pentecostals* (London, 1972), is the standard work on the subject. Kilian McDonnell provides a countercritique of the wide range of psychological and sociological analyses of Pentecostal phenomena in *Charismatic Renewal and the Churches* (New York, 1976).

JAMES D. G. DUNN

ENUMA ELISH is a major seven-tablet Babylonian literary myth that relates the beginning of the gods, the rise of the god Marduk, the battle between Marduk and Tiamat, and the creation of the universe and of mankind. *Enuma elish* was one of the earliest Mesopotamian literary creations discovered, and since its first publication, in 1876, new editions and translations have come out as new texts were discovered.

The text is often called "the creation epic," but it is more properly named "the exaltation of Marduk." Its purpose is to relate how Marduk became king of the gods, and its epilogue calls the work "the song of Marduk, [who] vanquished Ti[amat] and achieved the kingship." The text was probably composed in the period when Marduk became the supreme god of the pantheon, that is, the latter half of the second millennium BCE. The most probable time is during the reign of Nebuchadrezzar I (twelfth century BCE), when there was a nationalistic revival in Babylon and the cult statue of Marduk was brought back to Babylon from Assyria.

The Plot. *Enuma elish* ("when above") begins at a time when nothing existed in the world but the primordial waters, Apsu (the sweet-water abyss), and Tiamat, the salt seas. From their intermingling grew first Lahmu and Lahamu, then Anshar and Kishar, and then Anu (An), first to be called "born." Anu's son Nudimmud (another name for Ea) was begotten in his image, marking the final stage in divine evolution. The activity of Anu and his sons prompted Apsu to try to restore the earlier quiet. He was encouraged in this by Mummu ("form"?), his vizier, but not by the motherly Tiamat, who did not want to destroy what she had created. When Apsu went to fight against the gods, Ea killed him and bound Mummu. Ea thereby became "lord of the Apsu," established his home in the depersonalized sweet waters, and there engendered Marduk, a young supergod.

Anu then created the winds, which further disturbed the ocean, and the "non-Anu," possibly oceanic, gods, appealing to Tiamat to grant them rest and to avenge Apsu. Tiamat thereupon created eleven monsters, established an army, and elevated Kingu to be her consort and head of the army. When the gods heard of Tiamat's plan they were frightened: Anshar turned to Ea and then Anu, but neither dared face Tiamat. Upon Ea's advice, Marduk offered to fight Tiamat, but on the proviso that the gods make him their king and let his word, rather than theirs, determine destinies. The gods agreed and signaled this by setting out a constellation that Marduk's creative word could make disappear and reappear, a power restricted to fate-determining gods. Marduk then went to battle Tiamat arrayed as a storm god, with a bow (of lightning) and with the winds. He met Tiamat in single combat and defeated her by blowing the winds into her as she opened her mouth to swallow him and by piercing her distended belly. He then captured Tiamat's fleeing army and took the tablets of destiny from the captured Kingu.

After his military victory, Marduk turned back to crush Tiamat and create the universe. He divided Tiamat's body in two, separating the two halves with the sky, and created the heavenly bodies, the mountains, and the springs. He then brought Tiamat's monsters and the tablets of destiny back to the gods, who again declared him king. Marduk proposed to build Babylon as a place where the gods could come to assemble, and the gods offered to do the building according to his specifications. In response, Marduk had Ea create man out of the blood of the slain Kingu so that man could do the work of the gods, and he organized the world of the gods, assigning to each god his function. The gods built the temple of Marduk in Babylon and then gathered to celebrate his kingship. They awarded him fifty great names, each bearing its own powers, thus "making his way supreme." The epic ends with an injunction that all should tell this story and rejoice in Marduk.

Interpretation. The text may be interpreted on several levels. The first, and probably most important, is the political level. *Enuma elish* is fundamentally a political document. It not only describes the rise of Marduk to kingship of the gods but also sees the cosmos as a political organization. The text begins in an atmosphere of watery chaos, and describes the first beings as "formed" within these waters. The introduction of activity by Anu and his children produced tension and a reaction to restore the former status; at this early stage, however, both the threat of Apsu and his defeat by Ea were accomplished by individual action. The next step in political evolution is marked by the attack of Tiamat, who organized an army and appointed a general. The threat posed by this could no longer be met by any individual god, even Ea, and therefore the gods had to appoint a leader-king to meet the emergency, much as the Greeks and Romans appointed "tyrants" and "dictators" in times of war. Marduk went to fight Tiamat as the champion of the council of the gods, who marched behind him. His mandate could have been considered ended after the defeat of Tiamat. He, however, extended it, not by brute force but by showing, through his creation of the world, that his leadership had positive value, even in peacetime. Then, when he brought the tablets of destiny and Tiamat's monsters to the council, the gods reaffirmed his kingship and offered him obedience. Marduk suggested that Babylon be built as a center to which all the gods could come, and when the gods offered to do the building, he increased the benefits of his rule by creating humanity to do the manual labor of the universe and by granting the gods "portions" in the universe, assigning to each one his proper functions. It is through these kingly acts that Marduk consolidated his rule and became the true monarch of the gods and the universe. Kingship among the gods and its reflection, kingship among mortals, rests not only on the ability to achieve military victory but on the benefits the people receive by obeying a king.

The political sense of this myth was clearly felt by the Babylonians. They read the story at the annual Akitu festival, which celebrated the rule of Marduk and at which the king played a prominent role, "taking the hand" of Marduk and possibly identifying his kingship with the god's. There are, however, additional layers in this text. One prominent one involves the element of theomachy, in that the two ancestor gods, Apsu and Tiamat, are both killed. This motif, known to us from classical mythology, is found in Mesopotamia only in the theogony of Dunnu, an obscure city. The theomachy in *Enuma elish* is integrated into a plot that centers on other themes. The parricide of Apsu paves the way for Ea to become lord of the Apsu; the matricide of Tiamat is more complicated in that it is from her body that the world is created. If the abyss is the depersonalized body of Apsu, then our universe is the depersonalized body of Tiamat. It is not the killing of Apsu and Tiamat that is emphasized in this composition, but rather their defeat—a defeat necessary to the survival of the gods and the destiny of Marduk. It is also worth noting that the role of the mother as one who must be defeated before the son can fulfill his destiny is the only role that females play in *Enuma elish.* In the cosmos organized as a state, females are not found at center stage.

The defeat of Tiamat is depicted as a battle between the storm god and the primeval sea. This motif is found elsewhere in the ancient Near East (see below). However, it is not found in earlier Mesopotamian sources, and does not seem to be indigenous to Mesopotamia, where the sea is not the immediate presence and threat that it is along the Mediterranean littoral. The motif may have come into Mesopotamia with the West Semites, who immigrated in vast numbers during the period between 2000 BCE and 1850 BCE. It may therefore seem surprising to find it the fulcrum of the Babylonian state myth. Thorkild Jacobsen (1976) has suggested that the motif became important because of the identification of Tiamat with Mat Tamtim, the "Sea Land," which was an independent state downriver from Babylonia on the site of ancient Sumer. This state was a threat and an antagonist to Babylonia from the Old Babylonian period until its defeat and absorption in Kassite times. The Sea Land considered itself the heir to the Sumerian mother-culture, and could thus embody the figure of mother Tiamat. The myth of the sea's defeat could serve as a mythological representation of the defeat of the Sea Land and the unification of Sumer and Babylonia, and on this level *Enuma elish* can be read as a mythologized account of Marduk's and Babylon's reign over a unified Babylonia.

Enuma Elish and the Bible. Ever since the first publication of the work's text, comparisons have been drawn between it and the Bible, particularly the first chapter of *Genesis.* Attention has been drawn to the parallels between the seven tablets of *Enuma elish* and the biblical seven days of creation. Both stories begin with primeval water, which in the Bible is called *tehom,* the Hebrew cognate of Tiamat; the biblical spirit (or wind) of God that hovered over the waters bears some similarity to the winds of Anu that roiled Tiamat. Both stories contain the notion of creative work; the biblical sky divides the waters above from the waters below, as the upper half of Tiamat's body is divided from her lower half by the sky; both stories depict in the same way the origin and function of the sun and the moon. However, the differences between *Genesis* 1 and *Enuma elish* are so vast that there is no reason to talk of mythological similarity or literary dependence. The similarities are evidence only of a shared cosmology, a shared "science" that saw our world as beginning in water and surrounded by it, a concept also found in early Greece. The importance of *Enuma elish* to the study of *Genesis* 1 is that it demonstrates that these concepts were in fact (and were almost certainly perceived to be) common Near Eastern lore rather than data of Israel's revelation, and that Israel used this lore to convey its own independent message.

The most striking parallels between *Enuma elish* and

the Bible are not to *Genesis* but to the scattered poetic passages that allude to the Lord's defeat of the sea in primordial times. This defeat of the sea is often accompanied by mention of the kingship of God, of the creation of the world, and sometimes of the Temple. These themes present a fundamental biblical cluster of ideas, one that has striking similarities with ideas in *Enuma elish*. This does not mean that the motifs have a Babylonian origin. The defeat of the sea, kingship of the god, and the building of the god's palace (but not the theme of creation) are also found together in the Ugaritic Baal epic, written circa 1500 BCE and therefore (we believe) earlier than *Enuma elish*. This cluster is not found in earlier Mesopotamian sources; most probably it was an ancient West Semitic collection of ideas that found expression in Ugaritic literary works and the Bible, and that at some point was brought into Mesopotamia.

BIBLIOGRAPHY

Enuma elish was first published by George Smith, in *The Chaldean Account of Genesis* (London, 1876). The most recent English editions are those by Alexander Heidel, in *The Babylonian Genesis* (Chicago, 1942), and E. A. Speiser, in "The Creation Epic," in *Ancient Near Eastern Texts relating to the Old Testament*, 3d ed., edited by James Pritchard (Princeton, 1969), pp. 60–72; additions are given by A. K. Grayson on pages 501–503. A composite cuneiform text has been published by W. G. Lambert and Simon Parker in *Enuma Eliš* (Oxford, 1966), and a new edition has been promised by Lambert.

For analytic studies of *Enuma elish*, see Heidel's *The Babylonian Genesis* and Thorkild Jacobsen's *The Treasures of Darkness* (New Haven, 1976), pp. 167–191. The West Semitic origin of the battle with Tiamat is discussed in Jacobsen's article "The Battle between Marduk and Tiamat," *Journal of the American Oriental Society* 88 (January–March 1968): 104–108. For the biblical allusions to the defeat of the sea, consult Bernhard W. Anderson's *Creation versus Chaos: The Reinterpretation of Mythical Symbolism in the Bible* (New York, 1967) and the articles collected in Anderson's *Creation in the Old Testament* (Philadelphia, 1984).

TIKVA FRYMER-KENSKY

EPHESUS, COUNCIL OF. *See* Councils, *article on* Christian Councils.

EPHRAEM OF SYRIA (c. 306–373), theologian, biblical interpreter, teacher, poet, and hymnographer whose teaching activity and prolific writings have had lasting influence on the Christian tradition. Renowned for his hymns and poetic homilies, he is regarded as the preeminent Syrian father, a doctor of the universal church, and, according to Robert Murray, "the greatest poet of the patristic age . . . perhaps, the only theologian-poet to rank beside Dante" ("Ephrem Syrus, St.," in *Catholic Dictionary of Theology*, vol. 2, London, 1967, p. 222).

Born in Edessa (present-day Urfa, Turkey) in a Christian family (not a pagan household as some sources would have it), Ephraem lived for many years in Nisibis and taught at the catechetical school there. A town on the eastern Roman frontier, Nisibis was frequently pressed by the Persians. It was finally ceded to them in 363, at which time Ephraem, with the larger part of the Christian population, fled westward to Edessa, a partially hellenized cultural center still in Roman hands. Ephraem's hymns on Nisibis reflect the vicissitudes of the Christian community there.

Edessa was a hotbed of heresies, where Arians, Manichaeans, Marcionites, and the followers of the famous Bardaisan (Bardesanes)—many of whom successfully spread their teachings through poems and songs—had confused and divided the Christians. It was here that Ephraem, perhaps ordained a deacon by this time, flourished as an orthodox teacher, effective apologist, and unifying leader.

Ephraem was called "the harp of the Spirit" by his contemporaries. His fame spread after his death, and he came to be venerated as a saint. His ancient biographers embellished his life with many accounts emphasizing his apologetic work against the Arians and highlighting the traditional view of Ephraem as father of Syrian monasticism. He is said to have visited the great monastic centers in Egypt; it is also told that upon his return he met with Basil of Caesarea, in whose presence he miraculously spoke Greek. Although Ephraem no doubt led a celibate life of evangelical fervor and simplicity and greatly admired contemporary ascetics, the traditional image of him as a monk does not fit his actual intense activity as a Christian teacher, public defender of the faith, and inspired poet who led people in song.

An immense legacy of writings in Syriac, Armenian, Greek, and Latin has been preserved under Ephraem's name, but much of it is spurious, especially the materials in Greek and Latin. Nevertheless, scholarship after World War II has uncovered an impressive body of authentic works in the original Syriac and also in Armenian versions.

Ephraem's writings consist of prose works, poetic homilies, and hymns. Of his prose works the most numerous are biblical commentaries (on *Genesis*, *Exodus*, the letters of Paul, and Tatian's *Diatessaron*). He also wrote prose refutations against Mani, Marcion, and Bardaisan, as well as a number of prose sermons and ascetical works the authenticity of which is disputed.

Ephraem's poetical homilies are metrical sermons intended for recitation rather than singing. Among them are the six *Sermons on Faith* deriving from the Nisibine period and containing references to the Persian danger. Many other similar metrical sermons on various topics attributed to him are of doubtful authenticity.

Ephraem's fame justly rests on hundreds of exquisite poetic hymns that interpret, defend, and celebrate the basic mysteries of the Christian faith: creation, incarnation, redemption, Christ, the Holy Spirit, Mary, the church, sacraments, and the kingdom of God. They are preserved in individual collections under such titles as *Hymns on Faith, Hymns against Heresies, Hymns on the Crucifixion, Hymns on Paradise,* and *Hymns on the Church.* Acknowledged as jewels of Semitic poetry, these hymns reflect Ephraem's superb talents in their diverse symmetrical forms, cascades of imagery, breathtaking parallelisms, and artistic wordplays, all extremely difficult to render in English. Although many are composed of multiple stanzas accompanied by refrains, others are cast in the form of dramatic disputations, for example, between Death and Christ or Death and Satan, a style with Mesopotamian precedents.

Although Ephraem used traditional Christian themes and known Semitic literary forms, his originality and freshness are striking. Some examples may indicate why he is hailed as one of the world's greatest religious poets. In one hymn to Christ, translated by Robert Murray in *Eastern Churches Review* 3 (1970), Ephraem vividly associates images of the Holy Spirit's descent on Mary, Jesus' baptism, Christian baptism, and the Eucharist:

> See, Fire and Spirit in the womb that bore You!
> See, Fire and Spirit in the river where you were baptized!
> Fire and Spirit in our Baptism;
> in the Bread and the Cup, Fire and Holy Spirit!

In another incarnational hymn, Ephraem fashions extended imagery of Christ as the pearl. This hymn plays on the words *amoda* ("diver") and *amida* ("baptized"). The pearl is found by plunging into the water, but it must be pierced (a reference to Christ's suffering) before it can be set in its place of honor.

The form of the dramatic disputation is exemplified by several hymns on Christ's descent into hell that celebrate his cosmic victory over Death. In one such hymn, Death addresses Christ on the cross, challenging and taunting him in his apparent weakness. Then Jesus signals his own death with a loud cry ("Our Lord's voice rang out thunderously in Sheol"), and angels of light illumine the darkness of hell. Seized by terrible fear, Death repents of its prideful words, confesses Jesus as king, and submissively hands over Adam as the first fruits of death with the words: "As first hostage I give you Adam's body. Ascend now and reign over all, and when I hear your trumpet call, with my own hands I will bring forth the dead at your coming" (Brock, 1983, p. 44). The hymn ends in a crescendo of praise to Christ that is typical of Ephraem's poetry.

BIBLIOGRAPHY

The following sources and studies can be recommended for further reading. A systematic study of Ephraem's theology is yet to be written.

Beck, Edmund, ed. Corpus Scriptorum Christianorum Orientalium, Scriptores Syri. Louvain, 1955–1975. The standard editions of the hymns and homilies of Ephraem, with German translations, are available in different volumes in this series.

Brock, Sebastian, trans. *The Harp of the Spirit.* Studies Supplementary to Sobornost, no. 4. San Bernardino, Calif., 1983. The best collection of English translations of seventeen of Ephraem's hymns and the *Homily on the Nativity.*

Gwynn, John, ed. *Selections from the Hymns and Homilies of Ephraim the Syrian.* Select Library of Nicene and Post-Nicene Fathers, second series, vol. 8, pt. 2. Grand Rapids, Mich., 1969. English translations of the hymns on nativity, Epiphany, faith, and Nisibis, as well as of the homilies on the Lord, repentance, and the Sinful Woman.

Murray, Robert. *Symbols of Church and Kingdom: A Study in Early Syriac Tradition.* London, 1975. A pioneering exploration of sources and themes of early Syrian writers, especially Aphraates and Ephraem, dealing with Christ and the church.

Vööbus, Arthur. *Literary, Critical and Historical Studies in Ephrem the Syrian.* Uppsala, 1958. An analysis of the sources, life, thought, and role of Ephraem in the tradition of Syrian monasticism.

THEODORE STYLIANOPOULOS

EPICS are extended narrative poems that establish for their hearers and/or readers a particular universe of the imagination by means of cosmogonic and sacrificial mythologies, chronicles of kings and nobles, religious and philosophical teachings, and, above all, the heroic exploits of a past age. Where a living oral tradition persists, this bygone age of gods, goddesses, and heroes may be reactualized and experienced anew each time an epic is recited or sung and performed in ritual, festival, or secular contexts. The capacity of an oral epic to change is definitive, for it is continually recreated by singers, actors, audiences, and environments, and the sequence and length of its episodes remain fluid. By contrast, epics that have passed from oral to written poetry or heightened prose with no surviving performance traditions, and epics such as Vergil's *Aeneid* that were first composed in writing, have become records of particular worldviews, histories, and religious attitudes that now are modified only by our interpretations of them.

Since they are indeed "epic" in scope, there is scarcely a dimension of human experience that may be excluded from these versified repositories. The Sanskrit *Mahābhārata,* longest of oral-literary epics with its one hundred thousand verses in eighteen books, serves as a vast library of mythology, folklore, religion, and philosophy, compiled from oral traditions during a period of eight centuries in the formative age of classical Hinduism. Major narrative portions are still recited in Sanskrit all over India, and various regions have vernacular versions, as is the case also with the other great Sanskrit epic, the *Rāmāyaṇa.* In the nearly sixty thousand verses of the Persian *Shāh-nāmah,* the poet Firdawsī, working from older sources, undertook nothing less than the history of Iran from creation to the Arab conquest in the seventh century. The effort required thirty-five years, but one poet produced the Persian national epic. Even the shortest of epics, folk or classical, oral or literary, suspends in its episodes the details of a worldview. A worldview may be articulated directly or obliquely, within the context of individual heroic quests or in the intricate relations of a diverse range of characters and subcultures, in a close-knit set of episodes and locales or on a heterogeneous scale that spans generations of time and worlds of space. Some epics speak directly from living religious traditions, although the faith of contemporary singers and audiences may vary markedly from that of distant epic origins. Other epics are cryptic memorials or vague signposts to religious traditions only dimly apprehended in their narratives, as is the case with suspected Anatolian expressions fossilized, but still undeciphered, in the linguistic, folkloric, and symbolic strata of Homer's *Iliad.*

Oral epics emergent to literary forms have almost everywhere been influenced and more or less reshaped by new religions, as well as by new literary tastes and conventions. Certain themes in ancient India persisted in oral form side by side with, but unrepresented in, the thousand-year textual production of Vedic religion, then surfaced in classical Sanskrit and Tamil epics, where they were given structure and redefinition by sectarian Hinduism. Similarly, mythic themes of Iran's ancient heritage, disguised by the monotheistic reforms of Zoroaster, found new expression in the epic of Firdawsī and other Persian narrative poetry, although this time within an Islamic ethos. And as Christian tradition rides lightly on the surface of the ancient heroic mythology preserved in *Beowulf,* so too does Muslim tradition appear only marginally in the Mandingo (Malinke) epic *Sundiata* of the Mali empire.

Some epics, such as the vast Kirghiz cycle known as *Manas,* declare mythicized history, while others, such as the *Aeneid,* display cores that are historicized myths. But almost every epic immerses its hearers and readers in the largest of human questions: human nature and its destiny; the structure of society with its hierarchies and tensions; the character of supernatural beings and powers, of gods, goddesses, demons, and of the proper human response to each of them in ritual, devotion, propitiation, or defiance; the problems of evil and good, insurrection and authority, guilt and innocence, cowardice and valor, suffering and reward. Since epics are frequently dramas of great migrations and violent conflicts in the divine and human worlds, questions of theology and history, eschatology and fate, death, regeneration, and salvation are often posed in the context of cosmic warfare (the Akkadian epic *Enuma elish*), or cultural confrontations (the *Iliad*), or dynastic strife (the Japanese *Heike monogatari*), or a melding of all of these, as in the *Mahābhārata,* where the complex destinies of the heroes are assumed into the sacrifice and regeneration of the cosmos itself.

The great majority of known epics, whether oral in composition, oral-literary, or solely literary, have been heroic ones. They are dominated by heroes (rarely heroines) whose actions and fates not only dramatize particular human emotions, predicaments, and responses, but whose destinies reinforce essential religious statements and paradigms. Among these paradigms are certain roles of the hero as shaman, sorcerer, or warrior (or combinations of these); certain concepts of space, order, time, and deity; as well as all-important expressions of the meaning of death and salvation.

Shamans and Journeys of the Soul. The hero as shaman-sorcerer and the religious significance of the journey of the soul are well known in the oral epics of northern and central Asia and appear in such diverse characters as Grandfather Qorqut in the oldest epic of the Oghuz Turks, the *Kitab-i Dedem Qorqut;* Volkh or Vseslav in the epic song form known to Russian singers as starina (bylina); and Gesar in the Tibetan epic that bears his name. The sage Väinämöinen journeys as a serpent to Tuonela, the nether world, and this magical transformation in a northern Eurasian shamanic episode survives into the late compilation of the Finnish national epic, the *Kalevala.*

Several scholars have noted that sources of epic poetry may in part be sought in the narratives of shamanic visions, ecstatic journeys, and initiatory ordeals. As Mircea Eliade has shown in *The History of Religious Ideas* (vol. 1, Chicago, 1978, p. 80), Gilgamesh undergoes several ordeals of an initiatory type, and the *Epic of Gilgamesh,* "the first masterpiece of universal literature," may be understood from one perspective as the dramatization of a failed initiation. His journey to the bottom of the sea to find the plant that restores youth, a plant he then loses to a serpent in the discovery of his mortal destiny, has numerous parallels in other epics in which heroes learn of their fates in descents to the underworld and combats with chthonic powers, or in magical flights to celestial realms. The popularity of such motifs in the epic genre has carried them far from the traditional loci of Asian shamanism.

Despite reworking in the direction of medieval romance conventions, the Germanic epic *Nibelungenlied* retains such a quest in narratives of Siegfried, better known as a warrior-hero, and one with older analogues in the Scandinavian Eddas and sagas. Siegfried journeys to the land of the Nibelungen and there discovers the sword and treasure that, like Gilgamesh's plant, hold not immortality but his fate. He also gains a magic cape, as well as invulnerability, from bathing in the blood of the dragon he has dispatched in combat. And in one of South India's great store of living folk epics, the Telugu *Epic of Palnāḍu*, a performance tradition eight centuries old, continues to dramatize with a mélange of shamanic motifs the heroes' prescient skills, their ascents by magical beasts, cosmic trees, or turbans; initiatory dismemberment and reconstitution by healing; descent to the underworld; combat with monsters; trance states; nurturance by and guises as animals. These motifs in the *Palnāḍu* and certain other South Asian and Southeast Asian oral epics and songs are all the more arresting in the context of contemporary performances in which individuals emulating the heroes undergo spirit possession and séances of self-immolation and regeneration. In a word, their ancient heroes, in roles as either shaman-redeemers or warriors, are alive today in ritualized epic time.

Warriors and Decisive Battles. More common in epic narrative than the high calling of the shaman who journeys to the other world and establishes defenses against demons, diseases, and death is the role of warrior in this world, often a hero of "outsiderhood" who must overcome great odds to gain or regain a heritage or position denied him or stolen from him. Strength, courage, and personal honor are his major assets. While the resourceful shamanic hero engages in fabulous struggles with death, the warrior hero stands up to its blood-red realities. At times the warrior seems to be locked in combat with himself as well as designated demons and enemies. This-worldly aspirations, the ambiguities of his morals and actions, limitations placed upon him by nature, fate, divine or human treachery, all balance out his superhuman traits and heroic pedigree (semidivine or miraculous birth, surrogate parenting by animals, discovery by shepherds or fisherfolk, precocious skills and strengths), and render him more accessible to the epic audience. There is a recognizable trajectory to his career after his astonishing youth, including confrontation with established authority, exile, return and conquest, heroic status, frequently an early death, and apotheosis. The popularity of the cult that succeeds this life cycle proves the value of his tragic death and the repeated singing of it.

It is sometimes stated that violent cultural changes and social upheavals attendant upon warfare and great migrations were productive of epic themes in a "heroic age." The history of China, however, as turbulent and war-scarred as that of any long, cumulative civilization, produced no surviving epic tradition, and only a few lines of the classic *Shih ching* (Book of Poetry) recall the exploits of heroic ancestors. By contrast, a brief period of epics in the thirteenth century emerged directly from the brutal succession of wars that devastated early medieval Japan. These poetic-prose war tales *(gunki monogatari)*, a genre with no counterpart in Chinese literature, were composed in the same period as the *chansons de geste* of medieval Europe and various regional battle epics of South Asia. More important than the common factor of war may have been a particular cultural glorification of the warrior. While China gave him little recognition in a social hierarchy that established the scholar-bureaucrat above peasants, artisans, and merchants, it was the epic age of medieval Japan that produced a warrior aristocracy, the samurai, and an elaborate warrior code eventually known as Bushidō.

The best known of warrior cults, and prolonged epics in which their traditions are displayed, remain the Indo-European ones, and these derive from a deep and complex mythological base. Comparative studies, in particular those of Georges Dumézil and Stig Wikander, have revealed the religious significance of a Proto-Indo-European warrior tradition. Reconstruction from mythic and epic details dispersed from Iceland to India permits a vision of the parent culture as it may have existed six or seven thousand years ago, a culture in which the warrior occupied a key median position in a three-class hierarchy between the dominant priestly-sovereign class and that great bulk of society in the third estate, the producers.

Continuities between a divine tripartite trifunctional hierarchy and this human social hierarchy allowed for homologies between gods and heroes and, later, between mythic and epic themes. The fact that both the mythic human heroes and the epic warrior heroes are narrative continuations of the mythic warrior god is significant and enables us to understand certain configurations of the Proto-Indo-European warrior cult and mythology. The warrior enters, for example, a state of intoxication or heated fury, becoming invincible like fire, or he terrorizes enemies by assuming the form of a wolf or a bear, subsequent to initiatory ordeals undergone for acceptance into the warrior society. Combat with a three-headed monster, first sacrifice, and ritualized cattle raids are a part of this myth-ritual complex, as Bruce Lincoln has demonstrated for the Proto-Indo-Iranian tradition that is the backdrop to many themes of the later epics in India and Iran.

Many important themes have moved with the currents from Indo-European mythic to epic genres and surfaced in diverse regional literatures and languages (including some non-Indo-European ones), from the twelfth-century Danish historian Saxo Grammaticus's *Gesta Danorum* to Russian, Rajasthani, or Tamil oral poetry. One of Dumézil's special contributions to an ongoing profile of the warrior's "destiny" has been his study of the hero's programmatically untoward behavior that leads to self-destruction. The warrior may commit three successive sins against the three functional classes: betrayal of sovereign trust, strikingly uncharacteristic acts of cowardice within his own echelon, and crimes of avarice or rape. As a consequence he suffers successive losses of his spirituality, force of arms, and beauty or form, and dies the warrior's typical early, tragic death. Another recurrent theme is a tension between two types of warrior figures, one superhuman and aristocratic, a warrior who fights with proper weapons and, ideally, a code of chivalry (Arjuna, Sigurd, Aeneas), the other a subhuman, animalistic or monstrous hero who fights brutal, solitary battles without standard weapons or code (Bhīma, Starkad, Turnus). Still another characteristic Indo-European theme is the special relationship that may develop between the warrior and a goddess or heroine-goddess. Herakles and Hera or Athena, Camillus and Matuta, Arjuna and Draupadī (Śrī) have all provided complex illustrations of this liaison.

Divine warrior heroes such as Marduk in the Akkadian epic *Enuma elish*, the Canaanite Baal, the Hittite Taru, Zeus of the *Theogony*, or Indra of the *Ṛgveda* are all, in their respective single combats with Tiamat, Yamm, Illuyanka, Typhon, and Vṛtra, involved variously in cosmogonic acts or paradigmatic contests for celestial sovereignty. Human warrior heroes, by contrast, are most often revealed in epic action *in medias res*, preparing to defend a tribe or a nation in jeopardy. Such epics program their episodes toward decisive battles in which warrior heroes are driven to fulfill their destinies. Necessity becomes a standard impulse, as in Diomedes' terse proclamation in the *Iliad* when he and the Achaeans are backed up to the sea, their best warriors and leader Agamemnon disabled: "Let us return to the battle, wounded as we are. We must." This necessity bears the stamp of the mythic heritage: the hero, semidivine or blessed by divine guidance and the powers of order and justice, opposes an enemy, semidemonic or impelled by a hand from the powers of evil and chaos, and the tribe or nation defended represents the created world.

Spaces, Times, and Authority. The notion of founding the world anew, reestablishing world space, time, and order through the holocaust of battle, is a widespread epic theme. Numerous cycles have been labeled "national epics," for they are the songs of peoples establishing identities, legitimizing traditions of particular places and events, and carrying an authority, certified by the blood of heroes, from past to present. In the singing of the epic, episode by episode, all of the true points of the world are connected once again. As Gene Roghair has said of the people who preserve the Palnāḍu epic, it "is the history of their land" and "seems largely sufficient to satisfy the local need for knowledge of the past" (Roghair, 1982, p. 70). All the features of the local villages, temples, crop fields, rivers, and roads have epic associations, and a rock inscription, for example, may be ascribed to a particular Palnāḍu hero, or to something done, quite simply, in "that time."

The recognition of the local region or kingdom as ordered space, and local history as ultimate time, leads also to the designation of outside space and time as disordered, wild, threatening. W. T. H. Jackson has considered the inside-outside dichotomy in European epics from Homer to *The Cid* as a theme of paradigmatic conflict between the intruder hero as mobile, active, unpredictable outsider and challenger, and the older, established king as settled, passive, predictable insider. Achilles and Agamemnon, Beowulf and Hrothgar, Siegfried and Gunther are among his examples, to which could be added for an enriched set of subthemes Arjuna and Yudhiṣṭhira, Rostam and Shāh Kāvus, the legendary Cyrus and Astyages, and others, as well as discussion of that seminal tension in Proto-Indo-European mythology between the sovereign and warrior ethos. Much of this conflict, according to Jackson, turns on the movement from an ageing king who upholds the social order to a challenger hero whose aims are personal honor and glory. What seems equally important in the structure of Indo-European epic tradition is the alliance of both ruler and heroes over against the agriculturalist-producers, and the resultant hierarchy of three ranked estates in interdependence under an ideal hero-king and divine mandate.

One of the richest themes concerning the values of space and time is that of the epic hero or heroine in exile. Banished to the wilderness or the seas, deprived of lands, family, status, and pride, the hero in exile is literally outside, in nature apart from culture. Gilgamesh as questing hero journeys outside purposefully, but the hero in exile is a wanderer. Rāma and Sītā, the Pāṇḍavas in their forest exile, and Odysseus during his nineteen years on the seas are such wanderers. The Bible, too, has been discussed in themes of exile (slavery in Egypt, the Babylonian captivity, Jesus in the wilderness or the tomb) and restoration (delivery, return, resurrection), occurring in what some have seen as a grand epic cycle of narratives moving from creation to apocalypse, and including the quest of the hero (Messiah-Christ), his early death, and apotheosis.

The importance of remembering exemplary events of the past was no doubt of central importance in the creation and preservation of epics. The compilation of the *Mahābhārata* was to some extent furthered by the demand for great cycles of songs in which local kings, performing Vedic royal sacrifices such as the Aśvamedha or the Rājasūya, were equated with victorious heroes and kings of past ages. Albert Lord's hypothesis that "the special, peculiar purpose of oral epic song at its origin . . . was magical and ritual before it became heroic" (Lord, 1960, p. 66) may not be provable, but nevertheless is cogent. In many regions of Africa and Asia today, particular epics are linked to seasonal festivals such as sowing or harvesting. Others involve not cosmic but personal time, such as those performed at life-cycle rites, in which births, puberty ceremonies or initiations, marriages, and deaths become the foci for narratives culled from mirror episodes in the life cycles of epic heroes and heroines.

Deaths and Regenerations. It is India once again that provides the strongest drama of epic warfare as sacrifice, even cosmic destruction and renewal, although several sacred texts from Scandinavia and Iran also reveal the theme of final cataclysm. Behind them, as Wikander has shown, is a Proto-Indo-European eschatological myth in which the forces of evil and good confront one another in the decisive time. The Battle of Brávellir, an episode in Icelandic sagas and in Saxo's narratives, is the Scandinavian heroic parallel to the *Mahābhārata* eschaton.

And it is Kṛṣṇa in the *Mahābhārata*, sometimes the detached, transcendent deity Viṣṇu, beyond the tensions of battle and reconciliation, sometimes imminent counselor, involved in human time and space, who reminds us of the broad range of roles taken by deities in epics, from distant observers to randomly intrusive actors, and to immediate saviors and redeemers. Apollo moves once to restore the fallen Hektor, but cannot deter the moment of his fate. The Kirghiz Manas is in the act of prayer when his destiny traces him and, armorless, he is dispatched. Once served by fate, however, heroes may, like the world itself, be regenerated, and this is the special talent of Hindu gods and goddesses in both classical and regional epics. In the best known of Tamil literary epics, the *Cilappatikāram*, the heroine-become-goddess Kaṇṇaki restores her wrongfully executed husband, the hero Kōvalaṉ, by destroying the city (world) of injustice.

This sacrificial regeneration is perhaps the strongest of many links between classical and folk epics of South Asia and is reinforced by numerous active cults of heroes and heroines from the Sanskrit epics and uncounted regional ones. These include the enshrinement and ritual use of heroes' weapons and the sacrality of spirit residences such as caves and are reminiscent of ancient cults of heroes in Greece in which relic bones, weapons, and ships were preserved in sanctuaries, as the bones and weapons of medieval heroes and saints were kept in the churches of Europe. Unlike immortal gods, the heroes have died significant deaths and then have conquered time; their weapons are still a vivid point of contact for the religious experience of their return and, in the case of several oral epics of South India, spontaneous possession of members of the audience, whose dramatic "deaths" and revivifications while the epic is under way are undeniable proof of the living presence of the heroes.

The nearly universal appeal of the epic must reside in the charisma of an old and much-loved tale well told and the glimpse it provides into definitions of human existence. During its performance, the channels are open to a time and space that remain powerful, accessible, and paradigmatic. Heroes and heroines challenge, and thereby define, limitations placed by gods, fate, or self-absorption, as well as those social, political, economic, religious, and sexual roles by which humans divide themselves. To the audience the resolution may be clear at the outset, but the telling of the drama of transformation, sung now as it was in "that time," is itself a powerful form of renewal.

[*See also* Flight; Heroes; Quests; Shamanism; War and Warriors; *and discussions of particular epics in various entries such as* Enuma Elish; Gilgamesh; Mahābhārata; *and* Rāmāyaṇa.]

BIBLIOGRAPHY

Brief surveys by fifteen specialists and bibliographies for major epic traditions, including texts, translations, and studies, may be found in *Heroic Epic and Saga*, edited by Felix J. Oinas (Bloomington, Ind., 1978). Discussions of background traditions by twelve other specialists in epics are in *Traditions of Heroic and Epic Poetry*, vol. 1, *The Traditions*, presented by Robert Auty and others under the editorship of A. T. Hatto (London, 1980). Jan de Vries's *Heroic Song and Heroic Legend* (London, 1963) is a short, readable overview. *The Growth of Literature*, 3 vols. (Cambridge, 1932–1940), by H. Munro Chadwick and Nora Kershaw Chadwick remains a valuable resource despite sections now dated; particularly useful are chapters on Turkic, Russian, and Yugoslav epics.

Where comparative studies of epics are concerned it is largely the Indo-Europeanists who have been productive for the history of religions. All of the many works of Georges Dumézil have relevance for epic research. Parts of *Mythe et épopée*, 3 vols. (Paris, 1968–1973), have appeared in English translation as *The Destiny of a King* (Chicago, 1973); *Camillus: A Study of Indo-European Religion as Roman History*, edited by Udo Strutynski (Berkeley, 1980); and *The Stakes of the Warrior*, edited by Jaan Puhvel (Berkeley, 1983). See also the untranslated first volume of *Mythe et épopée* and *The Destiny of the Warrior* (Chicago, 1970). Bruce Lincoln has summarized the Indo-Iranian warrior and priestly traditions that provide much of the background to the Sanskrit and Persian epics in *Priests, Warriors, and Cattle* (Berkeley, 1981). Alf Hiltebeitel, in *The Ritual of Battle: Krishna in the Mahābhārata* (Ithaca, N.Y., 1976), has continued the pioneering efforts of Dumézil, Stig Wikander, and Madeleine Biardeau in relating the *Mahābhārata* to other Indo-European mythic and epic narratives.

An older effort accomplished in the myth-ritual context is Gertrude R. Levy's *The Sword from the Rock* (London, 1953), a broad comparative discussion of the Mesopotamian, Sanskrit, and Homeric epics. Although lacking attention to mythic themes or Indo-European studies on kingship and warrior traditions, W. T. H. Jackson provides a suggestive analysis of the confrontation between intruder-hero (individual) and establishment-king (society) in the works of Homer and Vergil and in the medieval European epics in his *The Hero and the King: An Epic Theme* (New York, 1982).

A basic discussion of epic poetry in oral composition is the work of Milman Parry and Albert B. Lord, summarized in Lord's *The Singer of Tales* (Cambridge, Mass., 1960). Theories generated by their studies of epic singers in Yugoslavia are applied to the *Iliad* and the *Odyssey*. Among recent studies of South Asian oral epics, the most complete is that of Gene H. Roghair, *The Epic of Palnāḍu* (Oxford, 1982), a translation and study of a recitation of a Telugu epic in Andhra. Farther south in India, Brenda E. F. Beck has investigated a Tamil epic in *The Three Twins: The Telling of a South Indian Folk Epic* (Bloomington, Ind., 1982). The image of the hero in a dozen sub-Saharan oral epics, and the usefulness of the Parry-Lord hypothesis, are the subjects of Isidore Okpewho in *The Epic in Africa: Toward a Poetics of the Oral Performance* (New York, 1979).

Jeffrey H. Tigay's *The Evolution of the Gilgamesh Epic* (Philadelphia, 1982) is a study of the Old Babylonian epic as it emerged from older Sumerian tales, myths, and folklore. On folkloric motifs in the *Iliad* and the *Odyssey*, see Rhys Carpenter's *Folk Tale, Fiction and Saga in the Homeric Epics* (Berkeley, 1946). Despite a Frazerian style of compilation, Martti Haavio provides important shamanic-folkloric backgrounds to themes in the *Kalevala* in *Väinämöinen, Eternal Sage* (Helsinki, 1952).

David M. Knipe

EPIPHANY is the Christian feast of the manifestation of Jesus Christ. Traditionally celebrated on 6 January, it is also celebrated by the Roman rite in some places on the Sunday following the octave of Christmas. The feast is called Epiphania ("manifestation") among Western Christians and Theophaneia ("manifestation of God") among Eastern Christians. That the feast is of Eastern origin is indicated by the Greek origin of both names. Epiphany is one of the twelve major feasts of the Orthodox church year.

The origins of Epiphany are obscure and much debated. It was originally either a feast of Christ's baptism in the Jordan or of his birth at Bethlehem. The theory that the date of 6 January corresponded to an old date for the Egyptian winter solstice has been largely discredited. The date may have at first been observed as a feast of the baptism of Christ among the second-century Basilidian gnostics. In the fourth century it was certainly a feast of the nativity of Christ, celebrated with an octave, or eight days of celebration, at Bethlehem and all the holy places of Jerusalem.

At the end of the fourth century, when the Western feast of the nativity of Christ came to be observed in the East on 25 December, 6 January came to be widely celebrated as the feast of Christ's baptism, although among the Armenians Epiphany is the only nativity feast celebrated to this day. As the feast of Christ's baptism, Epiphany became for Eastern Christians a major baptismal day, and hence it was given the Greek name Ta Phōta ("the lights"); baptism itself was called *phōtismos* ("enlightenment").

At the same time as the East was accepting the Western Christmas, the Feast of Epiphany was being adopted in the West. Outside of Rome it was celebrated as the Feast of the Three Miracles, comprising the visit of the Magi, the baptism of Christ, and the miracle of changing water into wine at the wedding feast of Cana. In Rome, however, the feast concentrated solely on the visit of the Magi, connoting Christ's manifestation to the gentiles. With their adoption of the Roman liturgy all other Western Christians eventually came to observe Epiphany as the Feast of the Magi.

Among Eastern Christians the celebration of Epiphany is notable for several reasons. At Alexandria the patriarch would solemnly announce the date of Easter for the current year on 6 January. Throughout the East, Epiphany, together with Easter, was a special day for performing baptisms. The most enduring custom, however, has been the blessing of the waters on Epiphany. There are two blessings. The first takes place during the vigil of Epiphany in the evening and is followed by the priest's sprinkling of the town or village with the blessed water. The second blessing takes place on the day of Epiphany itself, when the local waters of stream, lake, or sea are blessed by having a cross thrown into them, after which young men dive into the waters to retrieve it. [*See* Baptism.]

The Western observance of Epiphany has centered on the figures of the Magi, popularly called the Three Kings. Their cult was especially strong at Cologne in the Middle Ages, for their supposed relics had been brought there in the twelfth century. The idea that the Magi were kings was derived from several verses of scripture (*Ps.* 71:10, *Is.* 60:3–6). The tradition that there were three of them was probably derived from the number of gifts mentioned in the biblical account of their visit (*Mt.* 2:1–12). The account of the visit of the Magi and of the miraculous star that guided them inspired several mystery plays during the Middle Ages. The story of their visit also gave rise to the custom of gift giving on Epiphany: in Italy gifts are given on that day by an old woman named Befana, and the feast is also an occasion for gift giving in Spanish cultures. [*See* Gift Giving.]

BIBLIOGRAPHY

For a survey of the development of Epiphany and associated customs, see Francis X. Weiser's *Handbook of Christian Feasts and Customs* (New York, 1958). For a view of Epiphany from the perspective of the history of religions, see E. O. James's *Seasonal Feasts and Festivals* (New York, 1961). For Greek customs associated with Epiphany, see George A. Megas's *Greek Calendar Customs*, 2d ed. (Athens, 1963).

JOHN F. BALDOVIN, S.J.

EPISCOPALIANISM. *See* Anglicanism.

EPISTEMOLOGY. This branch of philosophy studies the nature, origin, and validity of knowledge; it is sometimes called "theory of knowledge." Epistemology has been central to modern philosophy since the sixteenth century, although it originally developed in Greek philosophy in close relation to ontology (theory of being) and metaphysics. (It is an open question whether epistemology can be completely disentangled from metaphysics.) [*See* Metaphysics.]

In Greek philosophy, and especially in Plato and Aristotle, the two words used to mean "knowledge" are *epistēmē* and *gnōsis*, the former having the narrower, more scientific connotation in opposition to *doxa* ("belief"), the latter the wider one, covering also perception, memory, and experience. Plato and Aristotle relate these two conceptions to the terms *noēsis* ("thinking, intuition") and *sophia* ("wisdom"). The Western Christian tradition, however, has paid more attention to epistemology than to gnoseology; the latter plays a greater role in Eastern Christian philosophy and theology, and, it goes without saying, among the gnostics.

Among the various epistemological positions (that is, theories of knowledge in the narrower sense), realism, which is the claim—deriving from Plato and Aristotle—that forms and universals are objectively real (whether *ante rem*, "before things," as in Plato or *in re*, "in things," as in Aristotle) has had by far the longest tenure. In modern times, at least since William of Ockham in the fourteenth century, nominalism, or the view that forms and universals are only in language and in the mind, has held the field. The issue, however, is by no means dead and, oddly enough, returns in connection with modern philosophies of mathematics and even in the understanding of information theory.

A second, equally important epistemological question has been whether universal ideas are innate or only obtained through the senses. The two positions on this question were staked out by Plato and Aristotle respectively, the controversy continuing through the Middle Ages, with Augustine on the Platonic side and Thomas Aquinas on the Aristotelian. Modern philosophy begins with Descartes's emphatic support for the Platonic-Augustinian position. His contention that clear and distinct ideas are innate (a view often called epistemological idealism, to distinguish it from Plato's joint ontological and epistemological idealism) was challenged in turn by the British empiricists (Locke, Berkeley, and Hume), who sought to show that all ideas derive from the senses. Kant defined a new position by arguing the so-called presuppositional character of the "forms of perception" and "categories of understanding."

These epistemological controversies (which find remarkable—although still insufficiently studied—parallels in the histories of both Hindu and Buddhist philosophies) have had a close relation to religious practices and doctrines, not only among Christians, but also among Jews and Muslims. Thus, for example, realism appears to support the theological doctrine concerning the real presence of the body and blood of Christ in the Mass, while nominalism is more congruent with the Protestant idea of the Last Supper, or "meal of remembrance." Similarly, realism is helpful in harmonizing revealed and natural theology, while voluntarism and fideism are more naturally related to nominalism.

Christianity, like the other monotheistic religions, cannot submit knowledge about God to ordinary epistemic criteria. Nor can it, without abjuring the biblical conception of faith, accept the pretensions of unrestrained gnosis or esoteric accretions. The resultant difficulties have given rise to such theological maneuvers as the Averroistic "double truth" (one for the natural, the other for the revealed) and the Thomistic "analogy of being" (in which the possibility of a single univocal meaning for the word *being* is renounced). In attempting to escape the Scylla of fideism, in which knowledge ultimately has no place at all in religion, Western religions have always been in danger of running afoul of the Charybdis of gnosticism, in which there is no need or room for faith. And behind these doctrines lurk the still greater dangers of atheism and pantheism, as well as gnostic dualism.

Epistemological issues in modern times have tended to revolve around the question of the existence of God and whether it is possible to know this or to establish it by some kind of "proof." Thus Anselm's purely *a priori* "ontological proof" vies with Thomas Aquinas's "five ways," which allegedly derive from empirical experience. All such "proofs" were rejected by Kant in favor of a moral argument that finds God a necessary presupposition of the moral, or practical reason. Here epistemology once again is closely related to ethics, as it had been in a different way in Greek and medieval philosophy. If the medieval world culminated in Dante's visionary belief that knowledge is love, the modern world has been working out the quite different formula of Francis Bacon that knowledge is power. The limits of this power, now coming into view, suggest the limits of our conception of knowledge and perhaps the limits of the epistemological enterprise as a whole.

A word must be said also about mysticism as a way of knowing in religion, apart from both reason and ordinary experience. When, for example, the poet Henry Vaughan says, "I saw eternity the other night," or an otherwise normal and ordinary person reports, "In one moment I was liberated and knew the purpose of life," we do not have criteria for judging the validity of the "knowledge" involved. Epistemology tends to look at such matters in terms of psychology and ethics, rather than ontology and metaphysics.

In the twentieth century there have been signs that the three-hundred-year-old predominance of epistemology in philosophy is giving way to a concern with semantics, semiology, and meaning. If epistemology cannot find its way out of either subjectivism (Cartesianism, psychologism, psychoanalysis) or objectivism (materialism, positivism, Marxism), it is perhaps because these are simply two faces of the epistemological attitude itself, which, because it begins with the separation of knower and known (and, as it were, makes this central), cannot get them back together except in these unsatisfactory ways. Seen in this light, epistemology may lose its central role in philosophy. Other ways of conceiving human involvement in the world may turn out to be more sensible and useful.

If religion has been on the defensive against science in the modern era, the difficulty may turn out to lie not so much in the differences between religious and scientific ways of knowing as in the epistemological stance itself. Important modern philosophers, particularly Martin Heidegger and Ludwig Wittgenstein, abandoned the epistemological or "representational" point of view itself in their later philosophies. And this is very likely to be the direction in which philosophy itself will go in the future.

BIBLIOGRAPHY

No outstanding survey history of epistemology exists. The most important works on the subject are the classic sources themselves.

Aristotle. *Posterior Analytics*. In *The Basic Works of Aristotle*, edited by Richard McKeon. New York, 1941.

Augustine. *Concerning the Teacher*. Translated by G. C. Leckie. In *Basic Writings of Saint Augustine*, edited by Whitney J. Oates, vol. 1, pp. 361–389. New York, 1948.

Berkeley, George. *A Treatise concerning the Principles of Human Knowledge*. Edited by A. C. Frazer. London, 1901.

Descartes, René. *Meditations*. In *Philosophical Works of Descartes*, edited by Elizabeth S. Haldane and G. R. T. Ross. Cambridge, 1911.

Hegel, G. W. F. *The Phenomenology of Mind*. Translated by J. B. Baillie. New York, 1910.

Kant, Immanuel. *Critique of Human Reason*. Translated by Norman Kemp Smith. London, 1950.

Leibniz, G. W. *New Essays on Human Understanding*. Edited by A. G. Langley. La Salle, Ill., 1949.

Locke, John. *An Essay concerning Human Understanding*. 2 vols. Edited by A. C. Frazer. Oxford, 1894.

Plato. *Theaetetus*. In *Plato's Theory of Knowledge: The Theaetetus and the Sophist of Plato*, edited by Francis M. Cornford. London, 1935.

Russell, Bertrand. *Human Knowledge, Its Scope and Limits.* New York, 1948.

Thomas Aquinas. *Truth.* 3 vols. Translated by R. W. Mulligan, J. V. McGlynn, and R. W. Schmidt. Chicago, 1952–1954.

HENRY LE ROY FINCH

EPOCHĒ. *See* Phenomenology of Religion.

EPONA is a Celtic goddess associated with horses. Her name is attested in Gaul and throughout the Roman empire of the first three centuries CE by about 250 figurative monuments and more than 60 votive inscriptions. In fact, she is the Celtic divinity whose name, if not whose cult, appears beyond the Gaulish borders. It is also exceptional that her name has been retained by several Latin writers.

Her Celtic name is related to the general designation for the horse, *epo-s* (Irish, *ech;* Welsh, *ebol;* Breton, *ebeul,* "foal," from **epalo-s*), and a suffix of theonymic derivation, *-ona,* suggests that Epona was the goddess of horses, if not of stables. Actually, the Gallo-Roman iconography of Epona is divided into two main types of depictions: Epona on horseback and Epona between two facing horses. It is very likely that Epona represents a Celtic transposition and interpretation of the Hellenistic theme of the "lady of horses." The images are foreign, but the name is Celtic and has been applied to the great sovereign feminine divinity (often called Augusta and Regina in the Celtic-Roman inscriptions). There is no correspondence in the insular Celtic cultures.

Care must be taken not to see Epona as a hippomorphic divinity, that is, as one possessing equine attributes. Henri Hubert and Jean Gricourt have made comparisons—all fallacious—to insular deities, the Welsh Rhiannon ("great queen") and the Irish Macha ("plain"), eponym for Emhain Mhacha, residence of King Conchobhar in the tales from the Ulster Cycle, but neither of these mythic figures is any more hippomorphic than Epona herself. In the *Mabinogion* Rhiannon is the wife of Pwyll, and after being falsely accused of slaying her newborn son she is condemned to carry on her back the visitors to her husband's court for seven years. Macha is a war goddess of Irish tradition; after some imprudent bragging on the part of her husband, Crunnchu, Macha is forced, despite her advanced pregnancy, to run a race on a solemn feast day against the king's horses. She wins the race and then dies giving birth to twins, a boy and a girl. But before dying she hurls a cry to punish Ulates, and all the men of Ulster who hear her (and all their descendants for nine generations) are condemned not to have more strength during military encounters than a woman in childbed.

It is difficult to view Rhiannon as anything other than a queen or sovereign deity. As to Macha, she is a trifunctional divinity who also goes by the names of Bodb and Morríghan, warrior goddess of Ireland. The problem posed by Epona's plurality must be reexamined in light of these facts about Rhiannon and Macha.

[*See also* Horses.]

BIBLIOGRAPHY

Benoit, Fernand. *Les mythes de l'Outre-Tombe, le cavalier à l'anguipède et l'écuyère Epona.* Brussels, 1950.

Le Roux, Françoise. "Epona." Ph.D. diss., École Pratique des Hautes Études, Paris, 1955.

Le Roux, Françoise, and Christian-J. Guyonvarc'h."Morrigan-Bodb-Macha: La souveraineté guerrière de l'Irlande." *Celticum* (Rennes), no. 25 (1984).

Magnen, René, and Émile Thevenot. *Epona, déesse gauloise des chevaux, protectrice des cavaliers.* Bordeaux, 1953.

FRANÇOISE LE ROUX AND CHRISTIAN-J. GUYONVARC'H
Translated from French by Erica Meltzer

EQBAL, MUHAMMAD. *See* Iqbal, Muhammad.

ERASMUS, DESIDERIUS (1469?–1536), Dutch scholar, "prince of humanists." Neither the date nor the place of Erasmus's birth is known with certainty; he was probably born in 1469 in Rotterdam (he styled himself Roterodamus).

Life and Works. Erasmus's life was wholly dedicated to scholarship. After his early education, mainly in the school of the Brethren of the Common Life at Deventer (1475–1483), his guardians sent him to the monastery of the Augustinian canons at Steyn. Ordained to the priesthood in 1492, he entered the service of Henry of Bergen, bishop of Cambrai, who gave him leave to study theology at the University of Paris (1495–1498). A visit to Oxford (1499–1500) brought him into the company of such kindred spirits as John Colet (1466?–1519) and Thomas More (1478–1535). Later he visited the cradle of the Renaissance, Italy (1506–1509), and made further journeys to England, including Cambridge, before settling in the Netherlands, at Louvain (1517–1521). There, at the height of his fame, he intended to devote himself quietly to the cause of classical and sacred literature.

But from 1518, Erasmus's labors were increasingly overshadowed by the Lutheran Reformation. He could not but welcome the addition of Martin Luther's voice to his own outspoken criticisms of ecclesiastical abuses, yet he distrusted Luther's aggressive manner, which he feared could only harm the cause of learning and piety. His friends and patrons finally induced him to challenge Luther in print. The ostensible theme of his *De libero arbitrio* (On Free Choice; 1524) was the freedom denied by Luther's necessitarianism, but more fundamentally the book was a warning against theological contentiousness.

In 1521, driven from Louvain by the hostility of the Dominicans to the new learning, Erasmus moved to Basel, home of publisher Johann Froben (c. 1460–1527). When Basel turned Protestant, he moved to Freiburg im Breisgau (1529–1535), but it was in Protestant Basel that he died without the ministrations of the old church, which later placed his books on the Index.

In response to the requests of his friends, Erasmus himself drew up a "catalog" of his numerous writings in nine divisions. The items vary widely in literary form, from letters to treatises, and in readership intended, from schoolboys to princes. But many of them can be distinguished by certain dominant themes. Some embody Erasmus's research on the language, literature, and wisdom of classical antiquity. Others apply the tools of classical scholarship to the original sources of Christianity, this being what is generally meant by "Christian humanism." In 1516, Erasmus brought out the first published edition of the Greek New Testament, which he furnished with a new Latin translation, notes, and prefaces, including the famous *Paraclesis* (a prefatory "exhortation" to study the philosophy of Christ). In the succeeding two decades, his series of editions of Greek and Latin fathers appeared, beginning with Jerome (1516) and ending with Origen (1536), his two favorites.

In a third group of writings, Erasmus exposed to mockery the moral failures and religious abuses of the day, notably, in his *Moriae encomium* (Praise of Folly; 1511), some of the *Colloquia familiaria* (Familiar Colloquies; 1st ed., 1518) and, if he did indeed write it, the anonymous pamphlet *Julius exclusus e coelis* (Julius [the warrior pope] Shut Out of Heaven; 1517). Finally, to a fourth group of writings, which present Erasmus's own Christian vision, may be assigned the *Enchiridion militis Christiani* (Handbook [or Weapon] for the Christian Soldier; 1503), a powerful plea for an inward, spiritual, and moral piety that does not lean on outward religious observances. The strongly pacifist vein in Erasmus's piety is reflected in his *Institutio principis Christiani* (Instruction for a Christian Prince; 1516) and especially in *Querela pacis* (The Complaint of Peace; 1517).

The Erasmian Program. A consistent humanistic program, in which learning assumes a moral and religious character, lends unity to Erasmus's many writings. The study of ancient languages and literature is propaedeutic to following the philosophy of Christ, which can be recovered in its purity only if the theologians will leave, or at least moderate, their endless squabbles and turn back to the sources of the faith equipped with the tools of the new learning. The program is not antitheological, but it is antischolastic: moral utility, rather than dialectical subtlety and metaphysical speculation, becomes the test of genuine theology. Erasmus proposed a new ideal of the theologian as more a scholar than a schoolman, an ideal that made a profound impact on many who did not share the Erasmian view of the gospel, including the Protestants.

What Erasmus discovered in the New Testament was, above all, the precepts and example of Christ. To be a Christian is to enlist under Christ's banner. The philosophy of Christ is not speculation or disputation, but the good life—a philosophy not essentially different from the teaching of the best classical moralists, only conveyed with unique authority and made accessible to all. It would be a mistake, however, to reduce the Erasmian imitation of Christ to mere copying of an external model; in the scriptures, as Erasmus reads them, the Savior comes alive, and Christ's philosophy is nothing less than a dying and living in him.

The work of Erasmus marked an important stage in the course of biblical and patristic scholarship. It is true that his New Testament text rested on inferior manuscripts and had no lasting usefulness, but his biblical studies, even when vitiated by overeagerness to extract an edifying lesson from the text by means of spiritual exegesis, established a new emphasis on the human and historical character of the sacred text. No less historically important is the fact that he arrived, through his study of the Gospels, at a distinctive interpretation of Christianity and of religion generally.

Stormier religious personalities, such as Luther, have found the Erasmian outlook bland. They have judged Christian existence to be neither as simple nor as placid as Erasmus supposed, since God makes a Christian not by gently strengthening a feeble will but by putting to death a vigorous, arrogant will. But the recall of Christians to a simpler, more practical ideal of discipleship has continued to win friends for Erasmus among those who doubt the usefulness of the constant refinement of dogma.

Some have hailed the Erasmian dislike of dogmatism as one source of modern undogmatic Christianity, or even of religious skepticism. Historically, that is a correct estimate of his actual influence, or at least of one strand of it. No doubt, it must be qualified by Erasmus's own professed submission to the decrees of the church. But nothing he says has quite laid to rest the suspicion that, for him, the institutional church was not so much directly salvific as a condition of that outward order and peace without which scholarship and the gospel cannot flourish.

BIBLIOGRAPHY

Erasmus published about one hundred writings, some of which were very popular and went through several editions. Many have been translated into English. An English translation of his voluminous correspondence and all the major writings is being published as *Collected Works of Erasmus*, 40–45 vols. projected (Toronto, 1974–). Erasmus samplers are *The Essential Erasmus*, translated and edited by John P. Dolan (New York, 1964), and *Christian Humanism and the Reformation: Selected Writings of Erasmus with the Life of Erasmus by Beatus Rhenanus*, rev. ed., edited by John C. Olin (New York, 1975). Dolan has the *Enchiridion*, *Moriae encomium*, and *Querela pacis;* Olin includes the *Paraclesis*, perhaps the best statement of the Erasmian program. Other translations are *Ten Colloquies of Erasmus* (New York, 1957) and *The Colloquies of Erasmus* (Chicago, 1965), both translated and edited by Craig R. Thompson; *The Education of a Christian Prince*, translated and edited by Lester K. Born (New York, 1936); *The Julius Exclusus of Erasmus*, translated by Paul Pascal, edited by J. Kelley Sowards (Bloomington, Ind., 1968); and *Erasmus-Luther: Discourse on Free Will*, translated and edited by Ernst F. Winter (New York, 1961). An excellent biographical study is Roland H. Bainton's *Erasmus of Christendom* (New York, 1969), and a useful companion to Erasmus's writings is *Essays on the Works of Erasmus*, edited by Richard L. DeMolen (New Haven, 1978).

B. A. Gerrish

EREMITISM is a form of monastic life characterized by solitariness. (The term derives from the Greek *erēmos*, "wilderness, uninhabited regions," whence comes the English *eremite*, "solitary.") In this type of life, the social dimension of human existence is totally or largely sacrificed to the primacy of religious experience. It is thus understandable that Christianity has traditionally regarded eremitism as the purest and most perfect form of a life consecrated to God. While other forms of monasticism or of the religious life have striven to bring religious experience to bear on human relationships (Western Christianity especially emphasizes external service), eremitism has always been purely contemplative in thrust. Hermits live only in order to cultivate their spiritual life in prayer, meditation, reading, silence, asceticism, manual work, and, perhaps, in intellectual pursuits. In eremitism, the celibacy characteristically practiced in monachism extends to the suppression of all social relationships. While Christian monks have always stressed charity in relationships within the monastic group and, in the Middle Ages especially, written treatises on Christian friendship, Buddhist monks have emphasized the necessity for freedom from every affective relationship that might hinder the achievement of enlightenment.

While isolation for a limited period of time is common in many religions, especially as part of a process of initiation or as a special time dedicated to prayer and reflection, eremitism as a permanent vocation or prolonged phase of asceticism is found only in those religions that grant monasticism an established and determinative role. The religions in question are salvation religions, whether in the sense of self-liberation or of redemption. In Buddhism, Jainism, and Christianity religiosity has a personal character as opposed to a merely societal character (religion as a series of beliefs and rites of a tribe, *polis*, or state). Buddhism, Jainism, and Manichaeism are essentially monastic religions, owing to the importance they attach to the pursuit of the self-liberation of the human being. Christian hermits, too, often went into the wilderness in hopes of finding there the answer to the all-absorbing question: "How can I attain salvation?"

However, the theme of personal salvation does not seem to be the deepest and most constant motive behind the eremitical vocation. The Ṣūfī mystics, as well as many Christian monks and nuns, have gone primarily in pursuit of union with God. Some of them, such as Teresa of Ávila or Thérèse of Lisieux, have consecrated their lives to interceding for the world. Monks who, like Thomas Merton, distance themselves even from their own monastery, do so not to assure their own salvation but rather to devote themselves to constant prayer. In the early Christian world it was commonly said that solitaries pursued an angelic life, because they wished to be, like the angels, always in the presence of God. It can be legitimately affirmed, then, that what really permits the birth of monasticism in general and of eremitism in particular is the desire to consecrate one's whole life to religious experience.

Historically, there have been two forms of eremitism. The more common form is that of the anchorite, a term derived from the Greek verb *anachōrein*, originally used to designate the act of draft dodging or tax evasion by fleeing to out-of-the-way places. In Hellenistic times, the word came to refer generally to those who moved far away from towns and particularly to sages who withdrew in order to devote themselves to contemplation. The less common type of eremitism is that of the recluse, who often remained in town but enclosed himself in a cell, communicating with the outside world only through a small window. In the Middle East during the early Christian period there were anchorites (male and female) who not only went into the wilderness but also became recluses, in a spirit of penitence. In their different ways both anchorites and recluses profess a life of solitude as a privileged situation for personal growth.

Eremitism in the Ancient World. Eremitism first appeared as a lifelong vocation in India among the numerous ascetics on the margin of Aryan society. The ascetics stood out from the general population by their long hair and distinctive dress, or by their wearing no clothes at all. Some lived in tombs, while others, the "ascetics of the forest," lived in the woods. From them we derive the most archaic strata of the Upaniṣads and the Āraṇyakas, dating from the eighth century BCE. The Aryan ascetics withdrew from society in order to pursue individual religious experiences that were fostered by a series of extraordinary renunciations. Their ascetical discipline was aimed to induce a state characterized by illumination and by the attainment of supernatural powers. The withdrawal of these ascetics seems to have involved a rejection of priestly mediation and can be interpreted as reflecting a crisis in a ritual system that had become somewhat fossilized.

The life of Siddhartha Gautama, called the Buddha (the Enlightened One), established the paradigm for eremitism in Indian culture. After his conversion experience, Gautama determined to become a truth-seeker and placed himself under the direction of some famous sages. After this period of discipleship, Gautama withdrew to a lovely woodland grove, where he gave himself over to the practice of extreme asceticism and came to be surrounded by a small group of disciples. One day, Gautama observed to a certain adept that physical asceticism had not led him where he wished to go and that he had therefore given it up. Upon hearing this, his disciples, bound to the ascetical tradition, abandoned him. So Gautama remained alone, and alone he ultimately reached Enlightenment. After attaining this fulfillment, the Buddha went forth to preach his message. His spiritual itinerary is an exemplary instance of the four stages (*āśramas*) into which Hindu tradition divides the journey of a brahman: student, father of a family, forest dweller or solitary *(vānaprasthin)*, and, finally, renouncer *(saṃnyāsin)*, follower of an itinerant and often mendicant life. The withdrawal into solitude for a certain time is, thus, an integral part not only of Buddhist spirituality but of various forms of Hindu spirituality as well.

Withdrawal into solitude is likewise observable in other types of monastic movements that appeared in India from the sixth century BCE onward. It may also be observed in Jainism, begun by Pārśvanātha in the eighth century BCE and reformed by Mahāvīra in the sixth century BCE. Jainism aims at a life of communion with nature in places removed from the social mainstream. Both of the original great heroes of Jainism lived largely eremitical lives. Gosāla, the founder of the Ājīvikas in the sixth century BCE, began his ascetical life by withdrawing naked into the forest.

In the fourth century BCE, the conquests of Alexander the Great in the Middle East and his expeditions into India brought the Greek world into contact with Hindu philosophy and religion. Pyrrho of Elis, who took part in the Indian expedition, displayed afterward a strong inclination toward tranquil solitude, so much so, in fact, that he rarely presented himself even to the members of his household. It is said that he did so because he had heard a Hindu admonish Anaxarchos that the latter could hardly pretend to be good, let alone instruct others, because he frequented the court. Philostratus and Hippolytus later praised the asceticism of the Hindu philosophers. From about the first century BCE to the second century CE there arose in Hellenism the ideal of the sage as one who had achieved a personal contemplative relationship with the divine through the practice of solitude and certain ascetical techniques. Seneca recommended that Lucilius live a quiet and retiring life ("consistere et secum morari"). Thus the way was paved for the emergence of the figure of the hermit. Plutarch in the first century CE speaks of a famous solitary who lived on the shore of the Eritrean Sea and communicated with others only once a year. Lucian tells of a recluse who had remained for twenty-three years in a subterranean temple, where he was instructed by Isis. Around the second century CE the verb *anachōrein* and the noun *anachōrēsis* underwent an evolution of meaning and came to indicate a withdrawal from social commitments in order to pursue inner wisdom.

The influence of these tendencies is observable also in Hellenistic Judaism. In Palestine, the Essenes withdrew from the sway of normative Judaism and created their own community of salvation with a strict, ritualized life. In Egypt, the Therapeutae mentioned by Philo Judaeus followed a predominantly eremitical form of life. They confined themselves to individual cells, where they devoted themselves to asceticism and meditation, coming together only on the Sabbath for community worship.

Ascetical renunciation became central to Manichaeism, the religion founded in Babylonia by Mani in the third century CE. Asceticism became so important because Mani attributed the material world to the workings of the principle of evil. Since the material world was thus to be shunned, this doctrine implied almost necessarily a monastic conception of life. There seems to have been some Hindu influence on the group, for its members were divided into the elect (monks) and the "hearers" (laity); the latter received the same name as was given to the laity in Jainism. The elect professed a radical poverty and sexual continence, which some carried to the point of castration. Among the elect, many were itinerant ascetics, although some of them withdrew into solitude.

Primitive Christian Eremitism. Tertullian, the celebrated African writer, stated in the second century CE that among Christians there were no naked philosophers, brahmans, or forest dwellers, but that all lived in moderation among the rest of those devoted to family and public life (*Apologeticum* 42.1). A century later eremitism launched a veritable invasion of Christian churches. What, one may ask, had happened to bring about this apparent reversal?

The radical commitment that Jesus asked of his disciples, involving faith, conversion, and suffering, was lived by his first followers within the context of a prophetic mission organized around the announcement of the imminence of the kingdom of God. This mission necessarily led them to involve themselves with society, and especially with those on its margins. In contrast to John the Baptist and his followers, Jesus neither practiced asceticism as a preparation for the judgment of God nor had recourse to solitude, except in decisive moments requiring prayer and reflection. It is significant, then, that the first Christian ascetics frequently invoked, not the example of Jesus, but rather that of Elijah or of John the Baptist. Early on, a group of wandering prophets who preached the imminent return of the Son of man seem to have taken quite literally the recommendations of Jesus on the need to abandon all things (*Didachē* 11.8). Their asceticism developed in the context of a prophetic mission, sustained by their hope in the end of the present world.

Only at a later date did this radical discipleship transform into an asceticism aimed at personal perfection or salvation. This step from commitment as a prophet to pursuit of individual asceticism—both expressions of Christian radicalism—came about simultaneously with the step from the eschatological dualism of Jesus (the "already" and the "not yet" of the kingdom of God) to the static dualism of the Hellenistic world (the world above versus the world below, spirit and body). The number of ascetics seems to have increased considerably throughout the third century. While some practiced asceticism in the cities, numerous others built cells near towns or villages and committed themselves to prayer in an early attempt at the solitary life. There were a few cases of ascetics seeking a more total isolation in the desert. Eusebius relates that Narcissus, bishop of Jerusalem, weary of slanders against him and eager to embrace a philosophical life, retired to the wilderness around 212. The ecclesiastical writer Socrates mentions a certain Eutychianus, a hermit living in Asia Minor around 310.

But it was only toward the end of the third century in Egypt that Christian eremitism appeared in a definitive and exemplary manner. Once martyrdom, as an extreme test of fidelity to the gospel, ceased to occur and once the church with its bishops became recognized as part of the urban establishment, numerous men and some women fled to the solitude of the desert in search of God. There they defiantly faced the demons whom popular belief assigned to such solitary places. Thus arose a type of Christian life characterized by solitude, constant prayer, radical poverty, manual labor, and practices of mortification.

It should be noted that, since the time of Tertullian and Origen, the two great Christian writers of the third century, the idea of retreat to the desert had become emblematic of a new religious attitude. The gospel accounts of the time Jesus spent in the desert lent a profound significance to the biblical traditions of Israel's wanderings through the wilderness and the withdrawal of some of the Israelite prophets into solitude. Tertullian wrote to the Christian martyrs that their isolation from the rest of the world during their imprisonment might well engender the spiritual benefits that the desert or solitude had given the prophets and the apostles: a lively experience of the glory of God. Origen used the desert as a symbol of spiritual progress and also transformed it into an emblem of the solitude and peace that are necessary to encounter the word and wisdom of God. It is significant that the first translators of the Greek Bible into Latin coined the noun *eremus* ("desert"), which did not exist in profane Latin. Thus the desert, the *eremus*, had been converted into a symbol of a spiritual attitude, a reliving of certain incidents in the Christ event foreshadowed by the passage of Israel through the wilderness. [*See* Deserts.]

These precedents must be considered in any account of the origins of Christian eremitism. The first influential Christian eremite is Anthony, a Coptic Christian born around 250. Anthony was early converted to asceticism and then retired to the desert at about age thirty-five; he enclosed himself for the next twenty years in a small, ruined fortress. Athanasius describes this period of reclusion as the phase of Anthony's mystical initiation. At the end of this period, Anthony accepted a few disciples. Toward the end of his life, he withdrew alone to a place near the Gulf of Suez, although he continued to make periodic visits to some of his anchorite followers who dwelt nearby. He died in 356, his fame widespread. His biography, written a few years after his death by Athanasius and twice translated into Latin, enjoyed a remarkable success and inaugurated a new Christian literary genre. Jerome later used Athanasius's work as a model for his lives of Paul, Malchus, and Hilarion.

Very early on, even during the lifetime of Anthony, Egypt had a large number of anchorites. Paul of Thebes, the hero whose novelistic life was written by Jerome, lived as a solitary on Mount Colzim, near the Gulf of Suez. Amun of Nitria, who like Paul was a disciple of Anthony, began a colony of hermits in the Nitrian desert (today's Wadi el Natrun) to the east of the Nile Delta. There were also the two great hermits named Makarios: Makarios of Egypt and Makarios of Alexandria, both of whom died around 390. In the desert of Scete, forty miles beyond the Wadi el Natrun, lived the celebrated Arsenius (354–449), his contemporary Agathon (a disciple of the first abbot, Daniel), and later Isaias. The sayings of the principal solitaries were gathered into popular collections called *Apophthegmata Patrum* (lit., "sayings of the fathers," but referring specifically to the Desert Fathers). The collections were first set in alphabetical order according to author by compilers writing in Greek around 450. Not long after this an excellent collection was drawn up arranged according to subject matter.

There were as well three famous women who were desert solitaries, Theodora, Sarah, and Syncletica. From the beginning of Christian monasticism, there were anchoresses, although it is impossible to accurately assess their number. That the *Apophthegmata Patrum* include the sayings of some women, and that the lives of certain spiritual women were written, suggests that any apparent silence on women is most likely due to the fact that a relatively small number settled in the wilderness. One obvious reason for a relative dearth of anchoritic women would be the frequency with which bands of robbers and highwaymen attacked isolates in the desert; women were presumably in greater danger than men. It must be acknowledged, however, that the spirituality of the first Christian anchorites had a very masculine slant, for athletic and military terminology abounds in their biographies and writings. It is not surprising, then, that this quality influenced the anchoresses, who affirmed their spiritual masculinity. Sarah stated a number of times that although she was a woman as to her sex, she was not so in spirit and resolve. Syncletica also used terminology drawn from military life and athletic contests. The practice of some anchoresses of disguising themselves as men probably arose from their concern for personal security in a time and place that was extremely hazardous for all travelers.

The most celebrated anchoress was undoubtedly Mary of Egypt (344–421), who underwent a conversion while on pilgrimage to the Holy Land and went to live in solitude on the other side of the Jordan River, where she spent the next forty-seven years. Her life, first alluded to by Cyril of Scythopolis in his sixth-century *Life of Cyriacus*, became a legend. Alexandra, a serving girl who enclosed herself in a funeral grotto, receives mention in Palladius's *Historia Lausiaca*. Another legendary figure is Theodora, a married woman who abandoned her husband and, fearing that she might be recognized by him if she entered a nunnery, decided to disguise herself as a man and managed to enter instead a monastery outside Alexandria. In time the monks accused her of being the father of a baby boy whom an unhappy young woman had left at her doorstep and expelled her from the community. She was obliged to live with the boy in the wilderness for seven years. After that time she was readmitted to the monastery, where she became a recluse in a cell apart from the rest. Syncletica (sixth century), too, withdrew to a tomb not far from Alexandria; she has the distinction of being the first Christian heroine to be the subject of a biography. Sarah lived a solitary life for some seventy years on the eastern branch of the Nile. The sayings of Theodora, Syncletica, and Sarah may be found in the *Apophthegmata Patrum*.

These anchorites and anchoresses were not the only Christians to practice the eremitical life. Alongside them, from the beginning, existed another group of solitaries: the recluses. The latter separated themselves from the world not by going to some far-off place but by enclosing or immuring themselves in cells. The great Anthony spent his first twenty years of solitude as a recluse. The famous John of Nicopolis (fourth century) lived in the same manner. Likewise, the solitaries of the Desert of Cells, east of the Nile near Cairo, preferred to live a life of withdrawal in their caves, which were "like hyenas' dens."

Anchorites and recluses held one basic attitude in common: a radical lack of interest in the world, that is, in human society and history. They called this attitude *xenoteia* (from Gr. *xenos*), the condition of being a stranger, an alien, a passerby. Their disinterest was motivated by a desire for total self-commitment to God in contemplative quiet. The Christian anchorite was at the same time in pursuit of interior peace, which could be attained only through *apatheia*, or detachment from the passions. The experience of God in his mystical fullness was for the anchorite a return to the primordial condition of the human being. One could not return to this lost paradise except by way of a continual struggle with the demons that populate society, allusions to which appear in many personal accounts. The hermits often acquired a great analytical acuteness, yet numerous allusions to dreams and visions show some of the negative effects of a life of pure interiority. Although the dialectical orientation of human nature was safeguarded by the constant dialogue with God, the fact that this dialogue was almost completely interior may well have overintensified psychic activity.

It should be remembered that at the outset hermits could not count on the help of the Christian community. They were laypersons, who had separated themselves even from ecclesiastical society and were unable to participate in the common liturgy or the sacraments. The life of Anthony makes no allusion to the Eucharist. Soon the solitaries discovered the need to consult those who were more experienced and began to make visits to them, which began with a customary greeting, "Give me a word." They also felt the need of listening to the exhortations of the most famous holy men and of celebrating the liturgy together. This gave rise to colonies of hermits who gathered together on certain days of the week for the liturgy and conferences. Anchorites who periodically went to churches for worship (this became common at an early date) were allowed to bring the Eucharist with them to their retreats, so that they could receive daily Communion alone. From the beginning, however, it was the Bible that occupied the central position in the spiritual life of the Christian hermit. Even those who did not know how to read customarily memorized psalms and New Testament passages for recitation and meditation. They turned to the Bible whenever they needed a standard for conduct. Nevertheless, the anti-intellectualism of the majority led them to oppose all theological reflection on the sacred book.

Basil of Caesarea (329?–379) is the only father of the church who ruled out the possibility of a solitary life, basing his reasoning on both anthropological (the social dimension of the human being) and religious (the Christian vocation to communion) insights. Augustine also expressed reservations regarding the eremitical life, believing that Christian charity can never prescind from the neighbor. In general, however, the church continued to regard eremitism as the highest, though most difficult, vocation, one meant only for the strongest and best-formed personalities. The vast majority of the early anchorites were simple folk with little education. Many of those of Coptic origin were ignorant of Greek; indeed, many were illiterate. Early on, it became requisite that candidates for eremitism place themselves under the direction of an experienced anchorite before undertaking the solitary life. Later, once cenobitical monasticism (monks and nuns living in community) spread, a consensus arose that subjection to the discipline of a community was the best preparation for the eremitical life. The Palestinian laura, made up of a central monastery surrounded by a scattering of eremitical cells, is based on this idea. The Council of Trullo (692) decreed that future recluses should submit to at least three years of community discipline before going into reclusion. The canonists eventually extended this norm to all solitaries.

Although the first solitaries in Egypt and Syria were for the most part unlettered countryfolk, they developed a rich spiritual doctrine. Drawing on their own experience, their prayers and their temptations, they developed and orally transmitted the first art of spiritual direction, as well as the first analyses in Christianity of interior states. Toward the end of the fourth century, a number of scholars educated in Greek culture went to listen and learn from the solitaries. Rufinus of Aquileia, a famous sage at first admired but later attacked by Jerome, arrived in Egypt in 371. Evagrios of Pontus began his apprenticeship around 383. Palladius, the future historian of the desert, arrived there around 389. John Cassian spent ten years in Egypt toward the end of the fourth century. Later, he founded two monasteries, one for men and the other for women, in Marseilles. His *Monastic Institutions* (twelve books) and his *Conferences* exercised a lasting influence on Western spirituality.

Historical Development and Spread of Eremitism. Eremitism spread rapidly throughout the Middle East. It was also developing, contemporaneously and independently, in Syro-Mesopotamian Christianity, where it assumed some quite original forms. Some eremites, the Dendrites, lived in trees or in hollow tree trunks; others lived always in the open air, either on a rocky height or in groves, while still others lived in huts. The celebrated Simeon (390?–459) mounted a pillar in order to escape the importunities of people who sought his prayers, inspiring numerous imitators (the Stylites). There were a great number of recluses who, like James and Sisinnius, dwelt in tombs or, like Thalalaeus, in hovels with roofs built so low that it was impossible to stand inside. Marana and Cyriaca loaded themselves with heavy chains. All the hermits practiced great mortifications. Some of their actions and words seem inspired by a Manichaean worldview, while others resemble the feats attributed to the Indian fakirs. Toward the middle of the fourth century, many hermits lived in the mountains near Nisibus, on Mount Gaugal in Mesopotamia, and in the mountainous region around Antioch. The origins of eremitism in Palestine are unknown; we know only that around 330 Hilarion began a form of eremitism similar to that of the Egyptian anchorites. Throughout the fourth and fifth centuries, hermits were very common in Palestine. Around 390, the well-publicized pilgrim Egeria found them nearly everywhere.

In the West, the Latin translation of the life of Anthony seems to have given rise not only to numerous admirers but also to some imitators. Already in the second half of the fourth century, numerous hermitages appeared on the islands and islets surrounding Italy (Gallinaria, Noli, Montecristo), and a colony of Syrian hermits settled near Spoleto. By his own example Eusebius of Vercelli gave rise to a group in the mountains of Oropa. Somewhat later, there were hermitages on the hills about Rome. Ascetics had lived in France since the second half of the second century. One of the early martyrs of Lyon and Vienne had sustained himself on bread and water. But it was Martin of Tours (316?–397) who truly propagated eremitism in Gaul. His life, written by Sulpicius Severus, contributed effectively to the movement. Converted to the monastic life in Milan, Martin underwent his first anchoritic experience on the island of Gallinaria and later settled at Ligugé. There a number of disciples established their cells near his. Made bishop of Tours in 371 by popular acclamation, he alternated the exercise of his pastoral office with the life of a hermit, and in these solitary periods he was again joined by numerous disciples.

Between the fifth and eighth centuries, hermits abounded in Ireland, Scotland, and Wales. In Spain, however, solitaries were not established until the sixth century. The bishops of the Iberian Peninsula took a dim view of asceticism as a result of their struggle with the ascetic rigorism of the monk Priscillian (340?–385) and his followers, who are said to have felt the greatest scorn for those Christians who would not embrace their austerities.

In the Eastern churches, eremitism has always enjoyed great prestige, although the spread of monachism in community (cenobitism) considerably reduced the number. Periodic reactions against cenobitism, in part inspired by Basil of Caesarea, have promoted a type of monastic life focused on contemplative quiet and personal prayer, rather than on liturgical worship. Among the proponents of hesychasm (cultivators of inner peace, or *hēsuchia*) were the Sinaitic school of the seventh century and Symeon the New Theologian (949?–1022). The laura of Mount Athos was founded in 963 by Athanasius, although solitaries had already been living on the mountain. Another famous laura is the Monastery of Saint John, founded in 1068 on the island of Patmos. Both still exist today. At almost the same time, monachism was introduced into Russia by Anthony of Kiev, who had formerly been a monk at Mount Athos. When he returned to Russia, he chose as his dwelling a cave on the side of a hill that faced the city of Kiev. Numerous disciples joined him there, thus giving rise to the Pecherskaia Laura, the Monastery of the Caves. Sergii of Radonezh (1314–1392), saint-protector of Moscow and all Russia, spent several years in complete solitude. Nil Sorskii (1433?–1508) spent a great part of his life in complete solitude, developing his version of the hesychasm he had learned during a stay at Mount Athos. Cornelius of Komel shared his love of poverty and solitude. In the nineteenth century the eremitic ideal held a strong attraction for a significant group of Russian personages who spent the last stages of their lives in solitude. From this time date Feofan the Recluse (1815–1894), translator of the *Philokalia,* who remained in strict enclosure from 1872 until his death, and Serafim of Sarov (1759–1833).

The Maronite church, founded by the Syrian monk Maron (fourth century), has always professed a particular devotion to monachism. Among the Maronites, too, has arisen the practice of solitaries situating themselves in the neighborhood of its monasteries. Two Maronite hermits, the brothers Michael and Sergius ar-Rizzi, became patriarchs toward the end of the sixteenth century. The last illustrious example of this tradition is Charbel Maklouf, a popular thaumaturge of the nineteenth century.

In the West, eremites were always less numerous than in the Middle East. The teaching of Augustine on the central value of fraternal communion in the service of Christ, the preference of John Cassian for cenobitism, and, above all, the gradual conquest of the West by the *Rule of Saint Benedict* all converged to impose community monasticism as the common form. Nevertheless, even in the European West there have always been hermits. The fact that the councils of Vannes (463), Agde (506), and Toledo VI (648) all gave rules for recluses indicates that they were not a rare phenomenon. In the days of the French queen and saint Radegunda (518–587), a liturgical ceremony celebrated the entry of recluses into their cells. Grimlac, a tenth-century hermit of Lorraine, wrote the first *regula solitariorum* known in the West. Further such rules were written in the twelfth century by Ethelred of York and, for the recluses of Cluny, by Peter the Venerable. Even in a community as well organized as that of Cluny, some monks were permitted to go into reclusion and separate themselves from community life after a certain number of years. The same practice was in effect in the Cistercian monasteries, despite the communitarian spirituality that had developed at Cîteaux.

These developments were varied manifestations of a tendency toward solitude that had been growing since the tenth century. The early eleventh century saw the founding in Italy of the monastic congregations of Fuente Avellana by Peter Damian and of Camaldoli by Romuald. These monastic congregations were made up of groups of mutually independent hermitages or monasteries, or of a monastery and a colony of hermitages united under the prior of the colony. Silence and individual solitude predominated. (These congregations were joined in 1569.) In 1084, Bruno of Cologne settled in Chartreuse, France, and established there a monastery where monks lived separately in small hermitages situated around a cloister and met only for liturgical prayer in the church. Around 1090, Stephen of Muret founded the Order of Hermits of Grandmont at Haute-Vienne, France. In a short time the order had spread widely. Small groups of solitaries began to multiply in Italy and became more common in the west of France during the twelfth century. Others appeared in Italy in the thirteenth century. Francis of Assisi, for example, was strongly attracted to the eremitical life and wrote a rule for it and for his disciples.

But there were also instances of an opposite phenomenon—groups of hermits who gave rise to orders characterized by a more communal way of life. The Carmelite order, for example, was started by hermits from the West who settled at Mount Carmel in Palestine during the twelfth century; as the order spread in the West it evolved into a conventual order. Something similar happened to the Servites, founded near Florence, and to the Hermits of Saint Augustine, an order formed by the coming together of various eremitic and semi-eremitic Italian groups.

Alongside the eremitic life organized within an institutional framework, the individual eremitic life has persisted sporadically. Instances from twelfth-century England include the solitaries Henry, Caradoc, Wilfrid, and Godric. Richard Rolle de Hampole, a hermit and director of recluses, was a spiritual master and esteemed writer of the fourteenth century. The most celebrated English anchoress was Julian of Norwich, whose *Revelations of Divine Love* remains a spiritual classic. In fourteenth-century Spain, John de la Pena was the founder of a colony of hermitages. In Switzerland, there is the celebrated case of Nicholas of Flüe (1417–1487), a layman who at the age of fifty left his wife and children to go into solitude, where he spent the last twenty years of his life. "Bruder Klaus," as he is affectionately known in Switzerland, was canonized in 1947 and is venerated there by both Catholics and Protestants because of the ecumenical guidance he gave from his hermitage.

In sixteenth-century Spain, the noblewoman Catalina of Cardona escaped from the ducal palace to take refuge as a hermitess on the banks of the river Júcar. Later she founded a convent of Carmelite nuns and then spent the rest of her life in a nearby cave. In the fifteenth century an unnamed woman supposedly lived disguised as a friar in the Franciscan hermitage of the Carceri near Assisi. Another woman, who died around 1225, lived in the same manner in Burgundy. Perhaps these women were imitating the legend of the desert eremite Theodora. Some scholars have suspected that the stories of these women are fictional legends that arose in the exclusively masculine environment of the monastery, where the presence of a woman disguised as a monk could easily have been felt as a threat to the monastic vocation. Another type of mitigated feminine eremitism was initiated by Teresa of Ávila (1515–1582) under the influence of the primitive ideal of the monastery of Mount Carmel and the example of her confessor and spiritual adviser, Peter of Alcántara (1499–1562), who built a separate hut for himself in the monastery garden. Something similar happened in a number of Poor Clare convents in Spain, again under the influence of Peter of Alcántara.

In the seventeenth century, there was a new flowering of eremitical spirituality. New editions of various writings of the Desert Fathers, as well as numerous paintings of the saints Anthony and Jerome and the penitent Mary Magdalene, reflect this interest. Notable among other eremitical foundations in Spain at the time was the hillside colony at Cordova, which continued to exist until the mid-twentieth century. In the eighteenth century there were still some hermits living in the vicinity of Rome, and some new groupings of hermits arose in Germany. In the history of Christian eremitism in the West, the nineteenth century was one of the most desolate periods. Significantly, in the 1917 Code of Canon Law for the Roman Catholic church, pure eremitism disappeared as an officially recognized form of monastic life because of the code's insistence on community life as an essential element of all monastic life.

In contrast, the twentieth century has witnessed a reflourishing of the eremitical life, beginning with the withdrawal of Charles-Eugène Foucauld (1858–1916), a French cavalry officer, to the Sahara. He spent the last fifteen years of his life as a hermit. John C. Hawes (d. 1956), an Anglican missionary who later joined the Roman Catholic church, spent the last years of his life as a hermit on Cat Island in the Bahamas. Foundations of eremitical groups have been established in Germany, France, and Canada. The phenomenon seems to have been particularly intense in the United States. A strong current of mystical spirituality, together with a certain disenchantment with the life of many apostolic communities, has led a certain number of religious, especially women, to seek the solitary life. The Trappist monk Thomas Merton (1915–1968) influenced this movement to a great extent. After spending twenty years at the Abbey of Gethsemani in Kentucky in an atmosphere combining total silence and intense group life, Merton arrived at a paradoxical state: he had a keen and very open awareness of a pressing need for dialogue with the contemporary world, yet he withdrew for some time into profound solitude. In 1963, he obtained permission to withdraw periodically to a small hut on a hillside near the abbey. In October 1964, thanks to his efforts, a meeting of Trappist abbots modified the order's official attitude toward eremitism. The order now regards eremitism as a possible option for monks who have spent a certain number of years in community. As he grew older, Merton's recourse to solitude became increasingly continuous. At present, a certain number of Trappists follow the eremitical life.

The Church of England has also witnessed a revival of one of its ancient traditions, in a number of women solitaries. Prayer and silence predominate in the first purely contemplative Anglican community, the Sisters of the Love of God, founded by Father Hollings in 1906. In response to this strong trend the Roman Catholic church revised its official attitude toward eremitism, as stated in the 1917 Code of Canon Law. The new code (canon 603) officially recognizes the eremitical state, even among those who do not belong to any monastic institute.

Eremitism in Islam. In Islam, eremitism is regarded as an exceptional type of life. In general, the religious life is lived either in the bosom of the family or in a community made up of a master and a number of disciples. However, a radical form of Sufism is found among itinerant monks, who express their estrangement from the world in a manner somewhat reminiscent of Hindu or Syrian practitioners of pilgrimage. Many Ṣūfīs, even if they do not fully profess this type of life, spend a certain number of years traveling throughout the Muslim world in search of a spiritual master. The ideal of the Muslim spiritual masters is "solitude in the midst of the multitude" *(kalwat dar anjuman),* that is, a state of remaining habitually in the presence of God without being touched by the tumult of one's surroundings. As means for achieving this state spiritual masters recommend detachment, silence, and interior peace. Some Ṣūfī orders insist on both material and spiritual withdrawal or retreat.

Nevertheless, a commitment to serving God while remaining in his presence has led more than a few Muslim spiritual adepts to seek material solitude. In contradistinction to the *khalwah* ("retreat," i.e., the house of a man or woman of God), *rābiṭah* designates an isolated dwelling for a person committed to the cultivation of his or her spiritual life, that is, a hermitage. Ibn al-ʿArabī tells of an Andalusian mystic, Abū Yaḥyā al-Sunhājī, who often traveled along the coast looking for solitary places in which he could live. He also tells of a holy woman of Seville who lived in a hut built so low to the ground that she could hardly stand up straight within it. Although Muslims have always professed a lively devotion toward these servants of God, there has always been also a certain opposition to what is regarded as an extreme way of life. This ambivalence is expressed in the following story. One day, a Ṣūfī who lived in a city received a visit from a pilgrim who brought him greetings from a man who had fled to the mountains. The Ṣūfī replied, "A person should live with God in the bazaar, not in the mountains" (Javād Nurbakhash, *Masters of the Path,* New York, 1980, p. 80).

Eremitism and Communion. Eremitism in its pure form is beset with a few serious difficulties, because the solitary life projects an image of spirituality exclusively in terms of interiority, an image involving individual prayer or meditation, intense inner struggles, and so on. What role does the believing community play in this conception of spirituality? Not surprisingly, the Buddha provided certain community horizons for the individual search for salvation in order to mitigate the extremes of ascetic traditions of his day. Nor is it surprising that many Muslim teachers note that materially suppressing outward "noise" is far less important than remaining open to inner silence, even amid the bustle of the marketplace. Pure eremitism encounters insuperable objections in relation to the Christian concept of community as the vehicle of salvation. What role do the sacraments play in such a scheme? Are rites of all sorts only for "beginners," with the more developed not in need of such props? It is easy to discern in these questions a potential for gnostic aberrations, such as were possible in the context of the total isolation of the primitive Christian anchorites. Understandably, total and sustained isolation soon disappeared in Christianity, and the eremitical life became limited to colonies or lauras, where adherents listened to the word and participated in the sacraments. Today Christian churches would not accept any form of total isolation.

In reality, the difficulties come not only from the communitarian vocation of the believer but also from the basic social orientation of human beings. We need others, with both their experience and their limitations, in order to grow. After nine years of austere solitude, Pachomius (290?–346) reacted angrily to a slight disagreement. Seven years of fasts and vigils had not taught him patience. Here, for the first time in the history of Christian monasticism, interpersonal relationship appears as a form of mutual purification. Dorotheus of Gaza (sixth century) affirmed: "The cell exalts us, the neighbor puts us to the test." The praxis of charity shows whether personal progress has been real or illusory, but interpersonal relationships are also a source of enrichment. Dorotheus repeats a traditional saying when he states, "To stay in one's cell is one half, and to go and see the elders is the other half."

Eremitism and Human Solidarity. The quest for personal salvation, carried out in a type of life withdrawn from society and history, does not seem to leave room for solidarity with the rest of humanity. Today, when human communion and interdependence are so strongly felt, eremitism might seem like little more than a form of solitary egoism, giving rise to serious doubts as to its basic morality. The Buddhist vision of history as pure illusion presents a different perspective. From the Buddhist point of view, no good results from immersing oneself in this illusion, in this flux of sorrows and joys. On the contrary, one would do better to put oneself beyond the contingent and illusory, thus giving others the testimony of one's victory and wisdom. It is significant that in the life of the Buddha, as well as in the Hindu tradition generally, a phase of itinerant monasticism follows the period of eremitism.

Christian anchorites, too, often consider themselves alien travelers who cannot afford to be concerned with earthly affairs. [*See* Exile.] But Christian eremitism constantly encounters a serious difficulty. If the transcendent God of the Bible reveals himself in the often tortuous and painful history of the human race, can any Christian turn away from history in order to encounter God? Would this God really be the God of the Bible, or would he not be some remote god encountered only in a flight from the world? Many Christian anchorites reveal the tensive pull of this implicit dualism. Nevertheless, their deep sense of being pilgrims and exiles has not prevented many of them from feeling and identifying with the problems of their contemporaries. Athanasius left his solitude and went to Alexandria in order to defend the orthodox cause against the Arians. The church meant more to him than a quest for pure interiority. Other solitaries sold their produce at market, bought what they needed for survival, and distributed among the poor any surplus before returning to their hermitages. Anthony worked not only for his maintenance but also for the needy. Poemen recommended that the brethren work as much as possible so that they could give alms.

A famous saying of Evagrios of Pontus is often quoted: "The monk lives separate from all and united to all." Significantly, he places this saying in the context of a group of sayings that stress the solitary's communion with other human beings, rejoicing in their joys, seeing God and himself in them. This meant not simply that the solitary, in finding God, finds all good things, rather that through solitude he learns to see God in his neighbor. Peter Damian explains that hermits, although they celebrate the Eucharist alone, should always use the greeting "The Lord be with you," because the solitude of the hermit is a *solitudo pluralis,* a corporate solitude, and his cell is a miniature church. The whole church is present in the solitary, and the solitary is most present to the whole church. Teresa of Ávila would invite her daughters to pray for the divided church and to respond to the division among Christians (of the Reformation and the Counter-Reformation) by intensifying their own fidelity to the gospel.

In the present era Thomas Merton has exemplified the possible ambiguity latent in the relationship between the hermit and the exterior world. Merton, who desired to devote his life to prayer in solitude, regarded the Trappist Abbey of Gethsemani as "the only real city in America" (*Secular Journal,* New York, 1959, p. 183). For years, his life involved total silence (the monks communicated their needs only by signs), common and individual prayer, and agricultural work. His first writings reflect an elitist view of contemplative monachism and a negative view of the secular milieu. In *Seeds of Contemplation* (1949) he said that whoever wanted to develop the interior life had no recourse other than to withdraw, to shun theaters, television, and the news media, and to retreat periodically from the city. In *New Seeds of Contemplation* (1979), however, he wrote that "solitude is not separation" and revealed total openness to the world. More paradoxically, during these years of growing openness he increasingly distanced himself from his community, becoming a virtual hermit.

[*For the practice of eremitism in South Asia, see* Saṃnyāsa; *see also* Retreat; Silence; *and, for a discussion of monks living in community,* Monasticism.]

BIBLIOGRAPHY

General information on eremitism can be found in most encyclopedia articles on monasticism; see, for example, "Mönchtum," in *Die Religion in Geschichte und Gegenwart,* 3d ed., vol. 4 (Tübingen, 1960); "Monachismo," in *Enciclopedia delle religioni,* vol. 4 (Florence, 1972); and "Monasticism," in *Encyclopaedia Britannica,* vol. 12 (Chicago, 1982). On eremitism in Buddhism and Hinduism, see A. S. Geden's "Monasticism, Buddhist" and "Monasticism, Hindu" in the *Encyclopaedia of Religion and Ethics,* edited by James Hastings, vol. 8 (Edinburgh, 1915). For the Hellenic tradition, see A. J. Festugière's *Personal Religion among the Greeks* (Berkeley, 1954). On Christian eremitism, see Clément Lialine and Pierre Doyère's "Eremitisme," in the *Dictionnaire de spiritualité,* vol. 4 (Paris, 1960); Jean Leclercq's "Eremus et eremita," *Collectanae Ordinis Cisterciensium Reformatorum* (Rome) 25 (1963): 8–30; and Louis Bouyer and others' *A History of Christian Spirituality,* 3 vols. (New York, 1963–1969). On Muslim practices, see A. J. Wensink's "Rahbānīya" and "Rāhib" in the *Shorter Encyclopaedia of Islam* (Leiden, 1974) and Hermann Landolt's "Khalwa" in *The Encyclopaedia of Islam,* new ed., vol. 4 (Leiden, 1978);

see also René Brunel's *Le monachisme errant dans l'Islam* (Paris, 1955) and J. Spencer Trimingham's *The Sufi Orders in Islam* (New York, 1971).

JUAN MANUEL LOZANO

ERIUGENA, JOHN SCOTTUS (fl. 847–877), Christian theologian and philosopher. Eriugena was born in Ireland in the first quarter of the ninth century, and there he received his early education (which probably included some Greek). He appeared around 847 in France at the itinerant court of Charles the Bald. Later, in Laon, he found himself in the company of a number of Irish scholars who were distinguished for their knowledge of Greek, the most important of whom was Martin Scottus. Although a teacher, Eriugena may not have been a cleric. He was invited by Archbishop Hincmar of Reims and Pardulus of Laon to refute the predestinarian errors of the theologian Gottschalk of Orbais. In so doing, he produced his first work, *On Predestination*, which did not meet with the approval of Hincmar and Pardulus and which was condemned by the councils of Valence (855) and Langres (859). Nevertheless, he was invited sometime before 859 by Charles the Bald to attempt a new translation of the writings of Dionysius the Areopagite. This work, *Translation of the Works of Saint Dionysius the Areopagite*, he completed in the years 860 to 862. Subsequently, he translated into Latin *Matters of Question* and *Questions to Thalassios* of Maximos the Confessor (862–864), *On the Making of Man* of Gregory of Nyssa, and possibly some other Greek theological texts. The effect on him of such an immersion in Greek theology was profound and abiding. From then on his compositions, despite his dependence on and reverence for Augustine of Hippo, show a strong Neoplatonic influence. Apart from his writings we know little more of Eriugena, and we lose track of him altogether around 877. There remain, however, a number of well-known legends about him.

From 859 to 860 Eriugena composed a commentary on Martianus Capella's *On the Marriage of Philology and Mercury*. This was followed by the translations mentioned above. From 864 to 866 Eriugena wrote his great original work, *Periphyseon*, also known as *De divisione naturae* (The Division of Nature). This was followed between 865 and 870 by *Expositiones*, or *Commentary on the Celestial Hierarchy of Dionysius the Areopagite*, and by a homily and a commentary on the *Gospel of John*. Finally, he composed some verses of only moderate poetical quality. Other works are also attributed to him. The body of his works is to be found in the edition of H. J. Floss in J.-P. Migne's *Patrologia Latina* (vol. 122).

The theology of Eriugena may be seen most clearly in his *Periphyseon*, a work of some quarter of a million words divided into five books. Nature, or all existing things, is divided or distinguished into four parts: that which creates but is not created (God as source, book 1); that which is created and creates (the Word and the primordial causes, book 2); that which is created but does not create (the created universe, book 3); and that which does not create and is not created (God as end, books 4 and 5). The work therefore takes the Neoplatonic approach of the progression from and regression of all things to the Father. The primary division of nature, however, is into being and nonbeing, both of which can be considered in five different modes: according to the perceptibility of the object; according to its order or place on the descending and ascending scale between the creator and the creature; according to its actualization (as against mere possibility); according to its perceptibility by intellect or sense; and according to its realization as the image of God.

God does not come within any of the categories of nature. He cannot be seen, although the divine nature does appear to angels and has appeared and will appear to human beings in theophanies, or appearances. We cannot know what God is, only that he is. We know more about him through negative rather than affirmative theology: one can more truly say what God is not than what he is. The primordial causes, also called divine ideas or volitions, remain invisible in the Word. In these are established the unchangeable "reasons" of all things to be made. The biblical *Book of Genesis* gives the account of how creatures, and especially human beings, were made. One can say that all things always were, are, and always will be because they always had being in God's wisdom through the primordial causes: "We should not understand God and the creature as two things removed from one another, but as one and the same thing. For the creature subsists in God, and God is created in the creature in a wonderful and ineffable way, making Himself manifest, invisible making Himself visible."

The divine nature, however, is above being and is different from what it creates within itself: in this way pantheism is avoided. The return of all things to God is best seen in the human creature, who, being body, living, sensible, rational, and intellectual, is a harmony of all things. Originally, humankind was simple, spiritual, celestial, and individual. The division into male and female was caused by sin; it was something added to true human nature. Humanity will return by stages to become intellect (here Eriugena follows Gregory of Nyssa); the body will resolve into its physical elements;

the human person in the Resurrection shall recover the body from these elements; the body will be changed into spirit; that spirit will return to the primordial causes. Finally, all nature and its causes will be moved toward God; there will be nothing but God alone.

The influence of Eriugena has been important and continuous in philosophy and theology. Remigius and Heiric of Auxerre and Pope Sylvester II were his early followers. Those of a mystical disposition made great use of him: the school of Saint Victor, Meister Eckhart, Johannes Tauler, Jan van Ruusbroec, Nicholas of Cusa, and Giordano Bruno. His reputation, however, suffered from the enthusiasm of Berengar of Tours, Gilbert of Poitiers, Almaric of Bena, and David of Dinant, all of whose espousal of his doctrine led to its condemnation by the councils of Vercelli (1050) and Rome (1059) and in a bull of Honorius III (1225). His ideas, nevertheless, have persisted, especially among German philosophers, and a reawakening of interest in him and his thought has begun.

BIBLIOGRAPHY

Brennan, Mary. *A Bibliography of Publications in the Field of Eriugenian Studies, 1800–1975.* Estratto degli Studi Medievali, third series, vol. 18, no. 1. Spoleto, 1977.

Cappuyns, Maieul. *Jean Scot Érigène* (1933). Reprint, Brussels, 1969. By far the best book on Eriugena's life, works, and thought.

Contreni, John J. *The Cathedral School of Laon from 850 to 930: Its Manuscripts and Masters.* Munich, 1978. Gives the context of Eriugena's life.

O'Meara, John J. *Eriugena.* Cork, 1969. A brief introduction.

O'Meara, John J., and Ludwig Bieler, eds. *The Mind of Eriugena.* Dublin, 1973. Papers of a colloquium held in Dublin (1970) by the Society for the Promotion of Eriugenian Studies. Subsequent papers from Laon (1975) and Freiburg im Breisgau (1979) were published, respectively, in *Jean Scot Érigène et l'histoire de la philosophie,* edited by René Roques (Paris, 1977), and *Eriugena: Studien zu seinen Quellen,* edited by Werner Beierwaltes (Heidelberg, 1980).

Sheldon-Williams, I. P., ed. *Iohannis Scotti Eriugenae Periphyseon.* 3 vols. to date. Dublin, 1968–1981. Two more volumes of this modern edition of the *Periphyseon,* which includes an English translation, are projected.

JOHN J. O'MEARA

ERLIK, or Erlik Khan ("King Erlik"), is a deity of the Turkic peoples of Siberia (Yakuts, Altai-Sayan Turkic tribes, Tuvin) and of the Mongolian tribes (Mongols, Buriats, Oirats/Kalmucks). Generally, Erlik is considered to be lord of the lower world and judge of the dead.

It seems, however, that Erlik (possibly meaning "the mighty one," from the Old Turkic term *erklig*) originally was a celestial god. This role can be surmised from Erlik's character as Lord Spirit of the Blue Boundlessness in the religion of the Yakuts of northeastern Siberia, who separated from their Turkic and Mongolian kinsmen in early times. Erlik's heavenly origin is also attested by Altai-Sayan Turkic tradition. Here, however, he has already been degraded to a position second to Ülgen (Kudai), their supreme deity. He is the first man, Ülgen's brother or created by him, assisting him in the creation of the earth. Erlik wants to become equal to Ülgen, however; he wants to create land himself. He also tries to seize all human beings created by Ülgen, seducing them to take forbidden food from the first tree. As a result, Erlik is banished from the celestial realm.

Thus Erlik becomes the ruler of the lower world, the king of the realm of darkness, which is opposed to the upper world, the realm of light. Erlik, his sons and daughters, and a host of other mischievous spirits created by him cause all kinds of misfortune, sickness, and death. Animals must be sacrificed to pacify the evil forces, sometimes with the help of shamans who risk the dangerous descent into Erlik's world. Specific sites in this place of horror, such as the lake of tears and the bridge of one hair that must be crossed, as well as details of Erlik's sanguinary appearance, are vividly described in various myths.

Heavenly origin is also attributed to Erlik in Buriat, Tuvin, and Mongol traditions. In Buriat shamanism, Erlen (i.e., Erlik) Khan leads the cruel black or eastern spirits against the friendly white or western spirits. At the same time he is the king of the lower world.

Erlik's role, however, has not become completely negative, as can be seen from the special relationship between him and the souls of humans. In Altai-Sayan tradition Ülgen makes the body from soil and stone, and Erlik blows in the soul. When Erlik became the devil, he remained as subject to Ülgen as he had been when he assisted him in creation. Of course, he tries to force the souls of the deceased into his realm in order to make them his servants. Soon he becomes an agent of divine justice, however, the judge of the dead who administers his office by order of Ülgen. His judgment is not arbitrary, but just.

Erlik remained a figure in the religious thought of the christianized Turkic peoples, and he became identified with the Mongolian Buddhist judge of the dead, the Tibetan Gśin-rje, and the Indian Hindu-Buddhist Yama. Erlik, the bull-headed, dreadful "protector of the [Buddhist] religion" *(nom-un sakighulsun)* and "king of Dharma" *(nom-un khan),* judges the dead using his mirror and the count of white and black pebbles representing good and evil deeds. Those condemned to hellish punishments are tortured by Erlik's executioners. There can be no doubt that Erlik also preserves traits of the Indian Yama's Iranian counterpart Yima, who is regarded as primordial man and primordial king.

[*See also* Ülgen.]

BIBLIOGRAPHY

Erlik's character in the religion of the Altai-Sayan Turkic peoples has been discussed by Wilhelm Schmidt in volume 9 of his *Der Ursprung der Gottesidee* (Münster, 1949). Erlik's fall is impressively related in an Altai Turkic myth translated by V. V. Radlov in his *Proben der Volkslitteratur der türkischen Stämme,* vol. 1 (Saint Petersburg, 1866), pp. 175–184. Erlen Khan of the Buriats is described in Garma Sandschejew's "Weltanschauung und Schamanismus der Alaren-Burjaten," *Anthropos* 23 (1928): 538–560, 967–986. Notes about Erlik Khan and his cult among the Mongols can be found in Aleksei M. Pozdneyev's *Religion and Ritual in Society: Lamaist Buddhism in Late Nineteenth-Century Mongolia,* edited by John R. Krueger, translated from the Russian by Alo Raun and Linda Raun (Bloomington, Ind., 1978), pp. 122–123. Important additional information about Erlik can be found in recent Soviet publications, for example, see T. M. Mikhailov's *Iz istorii buriatskogo shamanizma* (Novosibirsk, 1980), pp. 168–169, which also examines divergent opinions about the etymology and character of Erlik/Erlen.

KLAUS SAGASTER

EROS was the ancient Greek god of sexual (either homosexual or heterosexual) love or desire. The word *erōs* is the ordinary noun denoting that emotion; it could be personified and treated as an external being because of its unfathomable and irresistible power over humans (and animals, and gods). This was, however, a sophisticated, largely literary phenomenon without roots in popular religion. At Thespiae (Boeotia) a sacred stone, perhaps a menhir, was venerated as Eros, but it is doubtful how old the identification was. Otherwise cults of Eros do not seem to have been established before the Classical period. He was often honored in the gymnasia (sports centers), where adolescent males were constant objects of attraction for older men. The Spartans and Cretans are said to have sacrificed to Eros before battles, because the soldiers' personal devotion to one another was recognized as an important military factor. [*See* Agōgē *and* Homosexuality.]

Eros is not mentioned as a deity in the Homeric poems but appears frequently in the works of other poets. He is represented as a beautiful youth, or, later, as a young boy, and as the son or attendant of Aphrodite, the goddess who presided over sexual union. He is sportive and mischievous: he plays roughly with men; he shoots arrows into them (this first in the dramas of Euripides, c. 480–406 BCE). Poetic conceit may predicate of him whatever is appropriate to the effects he produces. He can be called blind, for instance, because he chooses his victims so indiscriminately. Sometimes, in and after the fifth century BCE, poets speak of plural *erōtes,* corresponding to the many separate loves that are always flaring up.

Eros appears in art from the sixth century BCE but becomes much more common in that of the fifth. He is usually shown as winged and carrying a lyre and a garland, both appropriate to the symposium, at which he was always active. Often he hovers above scenes of amorous import. In the fourth century the sculptors Praxiteles and Scopas portrayed him in celebrated statues. (Praxiteles' mistress donated one of these to the sanctuary at Thespiae.)

Eros had a special significance in cosmogonic myth. Hesiod (c. 730–700 BCE) places him among the first gods to come into being, and several later poets echo this. As they saw cosmic evolution in terms of sexual reproduction of divine entities, Eros was needed from the start to provide the impulse. In a cosmogony composed under the name of Orpheus about 500 BCE, Eros (also called Protogonos, "firstborn," and Phanes, "manifest") came out of a shining egg created by Time; he fertilized the cosmic darkness, and Heaven and Earth were born. This account has connections with Semitic, Iranian, and Indian cosmogonies.

Plato gives Eros another serious role, as the craving for the beautiful that is capable of leading the soul upward to a philosophical appreciation of ideal beauty. In poetry and art of the Hellenistic period the association of Eros and Psyche is variously represented. It finds its most famous expression in the story of Cupid and Psyche (the Latin *Cupido* is equivalent to the Greek *Erōs*) in Apuleius's *Metamorphoses,* or *The Golden Ass* (second century CE).

BIBLIOGRAPHY

Two scarce dissertations contain the main accounts of Eros in poetry and art respectively: François Lasserre's *La figure d'Eros dans la poésie grecque* (Lausanne, 1946) and Werner Strobel's *Eros: Versuch einer Geschichte seiner bildlichen Darstellung* (Erlangen, 1952). For the Orphic Eros and his affinities, see my own work, *The Orphic Poems* (Oxford, 1983).

M. L. WEST

ESCHATOLOGY. [*This entry comprises two articles. The first,* An Overview, *provides a cross-cultural discussion of beliefs about an end time. The second,* Islamic Eschatology, *examines Qur'anic and later views of the final reckoning and future dispensation. For discussion of*

Jewish eschatology, see Apocalypse, *articles on* Jewish Apocalypticism to the Rabbinic Period *and* Medieval Jewish Apocalyptic Literature. *For discussion of Christian eschatology, see* History, *article on* Christian Views; Jesus; *and* Antichrist.]

An Overview

The term *eschatology* means "the science or teachings concerning the last things." Derived from the Greek *eschatos* ("last") and *eschata* ("the last things"), the term does not seem to have been in use in English before the nineteenth century, but since then it has become a major concept, especially in Christian theology.

Most religions entertain ideas, teachings, or mythologies concerning the beginnings of things: the gods, the world, the human race. [*See* Cosmogony *and* Cosmology.] Parallel to these are accounts of the end of things, which do not necessarily deal with the absolute and final end or with the consummation of all things. The end may be conceived positively, as the kingdom of God, a "new heaven and a new earth," and the like, or negatively, for instance as the "twilight of the gods." Sometimes these accounts refer to events expected to take place in a more or less distant future. There is considerable overlap with messianism, which may, therefore, be considered as one form of eschatology. [*See* Messianism *and* Millenarianism.]

An important distinction has to be drawn between individual and general, or cosmic, eschatology. Individual eschatology deals with the fate of the individual person, that is, the fate of the soul after death. This may be seen in terms of the judgment of the dead, the transmigration of the soul to other existences, or an afterlife in some spiritual realm. Cosmic eschatology envisages more general transformations or the end of the present world. The eschatological consummation can be conceived as restorative in character, for example as the *Endzeit* that restores the lost perfection of a primordial *Urzeit*, or as more utopian, that is, the transformation and inauguration of a state of perfection the like of which never existed before.

Asian Religions. Cultures that view time as an endless succession of repetitive cycles (as in the Indian notions of *yuga* and *kalpa*) develop only "relative eschatologies," since the concept of an ultimate consummation of history is alien to them. Individual eschatology means liberation from the endless, weary wheel of death and rebirth by escaping into an eternal, or rather timeless, transmundane reality that is referred to as *mokṣa* in Hinduism and *nirvāṇa* in Buddhism. Within the cosmic cycles there are periods of rise and decline. According to Indian perceptions of time, our present age is the *kaliyuga*, the last of the four great *yugas*, or world epochs. In various traditions these periods often end in a universal catastrophe, conflagration, or cataclysmic annihilation, to be followed by a new beginning inaugurated by the appearance of a savior figure, such as the *avatāra* (incarnation) of a deity or the manifestation of a new Buddha.

Chinese Buddhism developed the idea of periods of successive, inexorable decline (Chin., *mo-fa;* Jpn., *mappō*), at the end of which the future Buddha Maitreya (Chin., Mi-lo-fo; Jpn., Miroku), who is currently biding his time in the Tuṣita Heaven, will appear and establish a kind of millennial kingdom and inaugurate a new era of bliss and salvation for all. "Messianic" and "millennial" movements in China and Southeast Asia, some of which became social revolts and peasant rebellions, have often been associated with expectations of the coming of Maitreya. Occasionally political agitation and ideologies of rebellion developed without Buddhist influences on the basis of purely Taoist or even Confucian ideas. But in these cases the ideology was "restorative" rather than eschatological in character; it announced the restoration of the lost original "great peace" (T'ai-p'ing)—as, for example, at the end of the Han dynasty or in the fourth-century Mao-shan sect—or propagated the message that the mandate of Heaven had been withdrawn from the reigning dynasty.

Taoism, like Buddhism, entertained notions concerning a postmortem judgment. According to Taoist belief, the judgment took place before a tribunal of judges of the dead who decided the subsequent fate of the soul and assigned it to one of the many hells or heavens that figured in the popular mythologies. Confucianism, however, has no eschatology in the narrow sense of the term; it has no doctrines concerning a day of judgment, a catastrophic end of this world, or a messianic millennium. Other Chinese ideas of individual eschatology were in part drawn from ancient lore and were later amalgamated with Buddhist and Taoist elements. Japanese Shintō has no cosmic eschatology and only vague ideas concerning the state of the dead. It is precisely this vacuum that was filled by Buddhism in the history of Japanese religion.

Zoroastrianism. Individual and universal, or cosmic, eschatology merge when the ultimate fate of the individual is related to that of the world. In such a case the individual is believed to remain in a kind of "provisional state" (which may be heaven or hell, a state of bliss or one of suffering) pending the final denouement of the historical cosmic process. One religion of this eschatological type is Zoroastrianism, a religion in which world history is seen as a cosmic struggle between the forces of light led by Ahura Mazdā (Pahl., Ōhrmazd) and the forces of darkness led by Angra Mainyu (Pahl., Ahriman). This struggle will end with the victory of light, the resurrection of the dead, a general judgment in the form of an ordeal of molten metal (similar to the individual postmortem ordeal when the soul has to cross the Chinvat Bridge), and the final destruction of evil. Some of these Iranian beliefs, especially those concerning the resurrection of the dead, seem to have influenced Jewish and, subsequently, Christian eschatology.

Biblical Religions. In the Hebrew Bible the terms *aḥarit* ("end") and *aḥarit yamim* ("end of days") originally referred to a more or less distant future and not to the cosmic and final end of days, that is, of history. Nevertheless, in due course eschatological ideas and beliefs developed, especially as a result of disappointment with the moral failings of the Jewish kings, who theoretically were "the Lord's anointed" of the House of David. In addition, a series of misfortunes led to the further development of these ideas: the incursions and devastations by enemy armies; the fall of Jerusalem and the destruction of the Temple in 587/6 BCE; the Babylonian exile; the failure of the "return to Zion" to usher in the expected golden age so rhapsodically prophesied by the "Second Isaiah"; the persecutions (e.g., under the Seleucid rulers and reflected in the *Book of Daniel*); the disappointments suffered under the Hasmonean kings; Roman rule and oppression; and finally the second destruction of Jerusalem by the Romans in 70 CE, which, after the failure of subsequent revolts, initiated a long period of exile, tribulation, and "waiting for redemption."

The predictions of the Old Testament prophets regarding the restoration of a golden age, which could be perceived as the renewal of an idealized past or the inauguration of a utopian future, subsequently merged with Persian and Hellenistic influences and ideas. Prophecy gave way to apocalypse, and eschatological and messianic ideas of diverse kinds developed. As a result, alternative and even mutually exclusive ideas and beliefs existed side by side; only at a much later stage did theologians try to harmonize these in a consistent system. Thus there were hopes and expectations concerning a worldly, glorious, national restoration under a Davidic king or victorious military leader, or through miraculous intervention from above. The ideal redeemer would be either a scion of the House of David or a supernatural celestial being referred to as the "Son of man." Significantly, Jesus, who seems to have avoided the term *messiah*, possibly because of its political overtones, and preferred the appellation *Son of man*, nevertheless was subsequently identified by the early church as the Messiah ("the Lord's anointed"; in Greek, *christos*, hence *Christ*) and was provided with a genealogy (see *Mt.* 1) that legitimated this claim through his descent from David.

Redemption could thus mean a better and more peaceful world (the wolf lying down with the lamb) or the utter end and annihilation of this age, the ushering in, amid catastrophe and judgment, of a "new heaven and a new earth," as in the later Christian beliefs concerning a last judgment, Armageddon, and so on. The doctrine of the resurrection of the dead played a major role in the eschatological beliefs held by the Pharisees and was also shared by Jesus. The chaotic welter of these ideas is visible not only in the so-called apocryphal books of the Old Testament, many of which are apocalypses (i.e., compositions recounting the revelations concerning the final events allegedly granted to certain visionaries), but also in the New Testament.

Christianity. The message and teachings of the "historical Jesus" (as distinct from those of the Christ of the early church) are considered by most historians as beyond recovery. There has been, however, a wide scholarly consensus, especially at the turn of the century, that Jesus can be interpreted correctly only in terms of the eschatological beliefs and expectations current in the Judaism of his time. The Qumran sect (also known as the Dead Sea sect) was perhaps one of the most eschatologically radical groups at the time. In other words, he preached and expected the end of this world and age, and its replacement in the immediate future, after judgment, by the "kingdom of God." Early Christianity was thus presented as an eschatological message of judgment and salvation that, after the crucifixion and resurrection, emphasized the expectation of the imminent Second Coming. The subsequent history of the church was explained by these scholars as a result of the crisis of eschatology caused by the continued delay of the Second Coming. Some modern theologians have taken up the idea of eschatology as the essence of the Christian message, though interpreting it in a less literal-historical and more spiritual or existential manner. Karl Barth, for example, has portrayed the life of the individual Christian, as well as that of the church, as a series of decisions to be apprehended in an eschatological perspective. C. H. Dodd, in his conception of "realized eschatology," has stressed the present significance of future eschatology. Christian history has been punctuated throughout by movements of a millenarian, chiliastic, and eschatological character. Certain modern movements (e.g., Marxism) are interpreted by some thinkers as secularized versions of traditional utopian eschatologies.

Islam. The tradition of Islam absorbed so many Jewish and Christian influences in its formative period that it is usually counted among the biblical (or "biblical type") religions. While the eschatological aspects of these traditions were deemphasized in later Islamic doctrines, they undoubtedly played a major role in the original religious experience of the prophet Muḥammad, for whom the end of the historical process and God's final judgment were a central concern. The notion of "the hour," that is, the day of judgment and the final catastrophe, the exact time of which was known to God alone, looms large in his message and is vividly portrayed in the Qur'ān (see surahs 7:187, 18:50, 36:81, and 78:17ff.). As in the Jewish and Christian traditions on which Muḥammad drew, God will judge the living and the dead on a day of judgment that will be preceded by a general resurrection (surah 75). The agents of the final hour will be Gog and Magog (surahs 18:95ff. and 21:96), led, according to some sources, by the Antichrist.

There is also a messianic figure, the Mahdi (the "rightly guided one"), and Mahdist, or messianic, movements have not been infrequent in Muslim history. The eschatological Mahdi is more prominent in Shīʿah than in Sunnī Islam. In the latter, belief in the Mahdi is a matter of popular religion rather than official dogma. As regards individual eschatology, Muslim belief in Paradise and Hell, in spite of much variation in detail, is essentially analogous to that of Judaism and Christianity.

Primal Religions. In most primal religions eschatology plays no major role, since they are generally based on the notion of cyclical renewal rather than on a movement toward a final consummation or end. While it is hazardous to generalize on the subject, in such traditions eschatological or messianic beliefs and expectations are often due to direct or indirect Christian or Western influences, whether relayed through missionaries or through more general cultural contact. These influences can precipitate crises that result in so-called crisis cults (many of which are of a markedly messianic character); they can also introduce eschatological notions concerning conceptions of time and history.

For example, according to the ancient Germanic myths recounted in the Eddas and the *Vǫluspa*, in the fullness of time all things are doomed to final destruction in a universal cataclysm called Ragnarǫk, the "doom of the gods." During this cataclysm there will be a succession of terrible winters accompanied by moral disintegration, at the end of which the Fenrisúlfr (Fenriswolf) will swallow the sun and then run wild; the heavens will split, the cosmic tree Yggdrasill will shake, the gods will go forth to their last battle, and finally a fire will consume all things. There are some vague but inconclusive indications that this total doom may be followed by a new beginning. Scholars are at variance on the question of possible Christian influences on Germanic mythology. Of greater methodological relevance to our present considerations is the question as to what extent this mythology was a response to a crisis. In other words, we may have to consider Christianity not as a hypothetical source of "influences" but as the cause of crises within the non-Christian cultures it confronted. Thus the "doom of the gods" mythology may have developed as an expression of the sense of doom that engulfed the original Nordic culture as a result of its disintegration under the impact of triumphant Christianity.

The contemporary sense of crisis and fear aroused by expectations of imminent nuclear catastrophe and cosmic destruction has reawakened an apocalyptic-eschatological mood in many circles. Some Christian groups, especially those in the United States, calling upon their particular interpretations of biblical prophecies, are "waiting for the end"—it being understood that the believing elect will somehow be saved from the universal holocaust, possibly by being "rapt up" and transferred to other spheres. This phenomenon is not, however, confined to the Christian West. Some of the so-called new religions in Japan and elsewhere similarly exhibit millenarian and even eschatological characteristics, often related to the figure of Maitreya, the Buddha of the future.

[*See also* Afterlife; Death; Heaven and Hell; Judgment of the Dead; Paradise; *and* Resurrection.]

BIBLIOGRAPHY

Since Judaism and Christianity possess the most highly developed eschatological doctrines, most of the relevant literature has been produced by theologians and students of these religions. In addition to the works of Albert Schweitzer, Johannes Weiss, and, in the first half of the twentieth century, the Protestant theologians Karl Barth and Emil Brunner, the following should be noted: R. H. Charles's *Eschatology*, 2d ed. (London, 1913); Hermann Gunkel's *Schöpfung und Chaos in Urzeit und Endzeit* (Göttingen, 1895); F. Holstrom's *Das eschatologische Denken der Gegenwart* (1936); Rudolf Bultmann's *History and Eschatology* (Edinburgh, 1957); C. H. Dodds's "Eschatology and History," in his *The Apostolic Preaching and Its Developments*, 2d ed. (New York, 1951); W. O. E. Oesterley's *The Doctrine of the Last Things: Jewish and Christian* (London, 1908); Paul Volz's *Die Eschatologie der jüdischen Gemeinde im neutestamentlichen Zeitalter* (Tübingen, 1934); Roman Guardini's *Die letzten Dinge*, 2d ed. (Würzburg, 1949); Norman Perrin's *The Kingdom of God in the Teaching of Jesus* (Philadelphia, 1963); and Reinhold Niebuhr's *The Nature and Destiny of Man*, vol. 2, *Human Destiny* (New York, 1943), pp. 287ff. For a review of the current interest in apocalyptic prophecy, see William Martin's journalistic but instructive report, "Waiting for the End," *Atlantic Monthly* (June 1982), pp. 31–37.

R. J. Zwi Werblowsky

Islamic Eschatology

In every area of religious life, the scriptural religions have developed along courses charted between the constraints and potentialities of their sacred texts and the expectations of the popular imagination. Nowhere has this process been more evident than in the development of Islamic eschatology, which has never been completely systematized. Many intertwining factors account for this situation. Like all scriptures, the Muslim sacred book is elliptical. The Qur'ān may hammer away at the inevitability of resurrection and the rewards and punishments of the afterlife, but of the period between death and resurrection, the topography of heaven and hell, the possibility of intercession, or the nature of redemption it says little indeed.

Furthermore, the otherworldly, radical dualism of the monotheistic scriptures has rarely existed in pure form; it has usually been blurred through interaction with popular ideas and practices. Special tensions arise in the handling of death, where this world meets the next; thus eschatology becomes particularly complex. Of the monotheistic faiths, Islam had perhaps the richest backdrop and the widest cross-cultural stage. Preceded by a rich pagan heritage, the pioneers of Islam also worked within a larger monotheistic environment: some actually entered Islam from Judaism, Christianity, or Zoroastrianism; others came into contact with the practitioners of those religions. The impact of Islamic eschatology on this and other types of exposure was particularly pronounced, as was the Islamic cast given even to the most closely shared elements. Finally, the natural temporal, geographical, and ideological variations of the first thirteen centuries of an expanding Islam have been joined in its fourteenth and fifteenth centuries by modernist rethinkings.

The Qur'anic Foundation. Not even a casual reader could miss the Qur'ān's emphasis on the final reckoning and dispensation, or its parallel concentration on the homiletic and hortatory dimensions of the prophetic role itself; almost every surah refers to eschatology, particularly to the physical rewards and punishments of heaven and hell. However, one must always keep in view the larger ethical and monotheistic context that surrounds the Qur'ān's insistence on physical resurrection and consignment; taking this insistence out of context has led many modern Western scholars to confuse the sensuous with the sensual while they ignore the equally sensuous treatments of a Dante or a Bosch.

The Qur'ān's pervasive appeal to the senses—the concrete, graphic presentation of the two dispensations and most other matters as well—is consistent not only with its oral nature but also with its need for reiterated proof of the most persuasive kind. As a didactic as well as apocalyptic work, it must argue against an archaic Arabian cosmos in which fateful time determined the course of life and assured the finality of death, neither of which depended on the creator's intentions:

> And when they see a sign [from God], they would scoff. And they say, "This is nothing but manifest sorcery. What! when we are dead and become dust and bones, shall we indeed be raised up?" (37:14–16)

In contrast, the Qur'ān's caring creator, Allāh, is also the annihilating judge who will end the human world at his chosen time (Yawm al-Qiyāmah, the Day of Resurrection; al-Sā'ah, the Hour); resurrect humans, body and soul; judge them according to their acceptance or rejection of his clear signs as elucidated by the many messengers he has sent; and consign them to their eternal reward—the fiery suffering of Jahannam (Hell, Gehenna) or the easeful pleasure of Jannah (Garden, Paradise):

> And they [the unbelievers] say, "Woe, alas for us! This is the Day of Doom. This is the Day of Decision, even that you cried lies to." (37:20–21)

The distinction between these two is stark and unequivocal, much like the distinction between desert and oasis. Fire and the Garden are a pair of polar opposites, each being everything the other is not (dead/living, shady/hot, shadowy/light), just as the inhabitants of one are everything the inhabitants of the other are not (bestial/human, deaf/hearing, ignorant/understanding, blind/sighted, living/dead, dumb/speaking, ungrateful/grateful, neglectful/mindful, uncharitable/charitable, indecent/chaste, faithful/idolatrous, prideful/humble):

> The unbelievers . . . shall be in the fire of Gehenna, therein dwelling forever; those are the worst of creatures. But those who believe, and do righteous deeds, those are the best of creatures. (98:6–7)

Jahannam is, like the desert, hot and dry, its inhabitants always thirsty; Jannah is cool and moist, its inhabitants never wanting. Irony informs the contrast. The denizens of Hell are given "drinks," but of molten metal or oozing pus that melts the contents of their stomachs; they are "cooled" by boiling water poured over their heads, new skins replacing the burned ones; and they are "sheltered" by columns of fire over their heads. They are "clothed," but in garments of pitch or fire; they eat, but like cattle:

> As for the unbelievers, for them garments of fire shall be cut, and there shall be poured over their heads boiling water whereby whatsoever is in their bellies and their skins shall be melted. . . . (22:19–20)

The Garden has rivers flowing underneath and fountains; its inhabitants recline on cushioned couches, clothed in brocade garments, peaceful, never fatigued, sheltered, eating fruits in a refined way, drinking a musk-perfumed wine that produces no sickness or intoxication, and enjoying the presence of the *ḥūr*, "wives" made pure and untouched. (Although the Qur'ān says that women gain entrance to the Garden, too, it describes no pleasure for women equivalent to the *ḥūr*.)

> See, the inhabitants of Paradise today are busy in their rejoicing, they and their spouses, reclining upon couches in the shade; therein they have fruits, and they have all that they call for. (36:55–57)

This marvelously wrought dichotomy underscores the need for humans to choose. Fire and Garden appear not for their own sake but as signs of God's mercy or wrath. Belief in the last day is only a small part of the total challenge (see, for example, surah 2:172–173). Although Adam's expulsion from the original Garden is acknowledged, it produced no original sin that must be redeemed, even if Iblīs, the fallen angel, does constantly tempt humans to wrongdoing. One earns one's fate by choosing to adhere or not adhere to clearly specified spiritual and behavioral norms. Judgment is as fair as a business transaction: one's deeds are weighed in the balance, neither wealth nor kin availing. If one has been faithful and grateful, accepted his signs and messengers as true, prayed, and given charity, one is rewarded. If one has been faithless and ungrateful, given the lie to the signs and messengers, given God partners, prayed insincerely or not at all, and been selfish with and prideful of one's material goods, one is punished. In this instance of the radical transvaluation common to the monotheistic religions, what one valued is taken away, and what one did not value becomes an eternal reward.

The signs of the advent of the Day are equally frequent and graphic: people scattered like moths, mountains plucked like wool tufts and turned to sand, earth shaken and ground to powder, heavens split and rolled back, stars scattered, seas boiling over, and sun darkened. However, not every question is anticipated, and little attention is paid to the period between revelation and eschaton, even less to the time between death and resurrection, except to say that it will seem like nothing. As later Muslims took the Qur'anic eschatological drama to heart, they interpreted it where is was specific and elaborated it where is was not.

Post-Qur'anic Variations. This process of elaboration produced considerable variation, in scholarly discourse as well as in the popular imagination, where the rich folklore of millennia was enriched by the new religion and transmitted in elaborate detail.

Sunnī variations. The Sunnī majority turned to the elaboration of the Qur'anic eschatological schema as soon as the *ḥadīth* (reports about the exemplary deeds, utterances, and unspoken approval of the Prophet) began to form; significant developments continued for centuries, especially in three topic areas: (1) the period between death and resurrection; (2) the role of eschatological figures; and (3) judgment, afterlife, and the mitigation of punishment.

1. In classical thought, the word *barzakh* came to stand for both the time and place of waiting between death and resurrection, even though the Qur'ān uses the word rarely and only in the sense of a barrier. By the time of the famous theologian al-Ghazālī (d. 1111), who wrote in detail about the *barzakh*, a clearer picture had emerged. At the moment of death, 'Izrā'īl, the angel of death, appears; then the soul slips easily from the body, borne upward by other angels. Subsequently, the angelic pair Munkar and Nakīr question the dead in their graves about their deeds. The interrogation is followed by pressure on all grave-dwellers and punishment of some. Whether this punishment prefigures or mitigates later punishment is unclear. According to some, the dead may interact with the living during the *barzakh*, particularly in their dreams.

2. The period between revelation of the Qur'ān and the Day of Judgment, as well as the eschatological figures who function therein, also received further attention. Key figures include al-Dajjāl, the false savior or "Antichrist," and the Mahdi, the divinely guided one. Al-Dajjāl, who appears in the *ḥadīth* but not in the Qur'ān, will emerge toward the end of time after a long period of social and natural disintegration, and he will conquer the earth until killed either by the returned Jesus or the Mahdi, another non-Qur'anic figure. The latter, in this sense, is an unnamed reforming member of the family of the Prophet who will be sent to restore peace and justice on earth for a period of time before the end and to fulfill the mission of Muḥammad as his last temporal successor (caliph), as interpreter of his revelation, and as enforcer of Islamic law *(sharī'ah)*.

However, not all Sunnī Muslims expect such a figure and the term has often been used more like the related *mujaddid*, that is, a divinely guided renewer who at any point may bring the Muslim community from deviation back onto God's straight path through intellectual, spiritual, or temporal leadership. Unlike *mahdī, mujaddid* has cyclical connotations; it has been applied to figures at the turn of each Muslim century, from the first to the most recent. Since the eschaton failed to arrive, and since Muḥammad was believed to have purified and sealed off revelation for all time, not to reappear until the Day of Judgment, other figures could frequently rise to importance. [*See* Messianism, *article on* Islamic Messianism.]

3. According to many post-Qur'anic commentaries, the Day of Judgment will be announced by two blasts from the trumpet of the archangel Isrāfīl, whereupon souls will be reunited with bodies in the graves, resurrected, and assembled, perhaps to wait for an extended period of time. Their deeds will be read out of the heavenly books and weighed in the balance. When they cross the bridge over the Fire, the reckoning will be verified: sinning believers will fall into the Fire temporarily; sinning nonbelievers, permanently. Saved believers will cross safely into the Garden, where some kind of "vision" of God may await them. According to many writers, each prophet will lead his own community, with the whole procession led in turn by Muḥammad and the Muslim community. At the pool or pond *(ḥawḍ)*, the Prophet may intercede for some of the Muslim faithful in the Fire. However, some authors even argued that the Fire was a kind of purgatory for not only some but all its inhabitants.

The structure of Fire and Garden was delineated, too, with architectural models preferred, as in the Qur'ān. The Fire has seven concentric circles or layers, representing hierarchically arranged levels of punishment; the Garden has seven or eight layers, perhaps pyramidal, with the throne of God at the top. This kind of elaboration was promoted by the concomitant development of several genres of literature that detailed the Prophet's famous night journey to Jerusalem and ascension from there through the seven heavens. [*See* Mi'rāj.]

Shī'ī variations. The informal structure of Sunnī eschatological figures has a formal analog in the Shī'ī imamate. Among the Twelver Shī'ah, the cosmic order and the eschaton's arrival depend absolutely on a line of descendants of the Prophet through his daughter Fāṭimah and cousin 'Alī. These imams, as they are called, are understood to have been conceived in God's mind from one beginning as the principle of good, to have been transmitted for centuries as light in the loins of the prophets and the wombs of holy women, and to have emerged in human form as the twelve vicegerents of Muḥammad (like the twelve assistants of all previous prophets).

They suffered, as had all the prophets, and their suffering and that of all previous and subsequent humanity culminated in the martyrdom of the third of their line, Ḥusayn, at the hands of the sixth caliph, Yazīd (680–683). Ḥusayn's suffering was the central redemptive act in the cosmic drama, shared in and made visible to all previous prophets and identified with by later followers. Its final avenging on the Day of Judgment will symbolize the triumph of good over evil, justice over injustice. The followers of the imams will be redeemed not only through Ḥusayn's actions but also by the identification with his suffering they demonstrate when they weep and when they visit Karbala, the site of his martyrdom, reenacting its drama *(ta'ziyah)*, and reciting poetic laments.

Before the Day, the twelfth and absent imam, al-Qā'im, will have returned as Mahdi to prepare the way. The Mahdi will arrive at the end of a long period of disintegration culminating in the appearance of al-Dajjāl, whom he will kill, just as he will kill all the enemies of the family of the Prophet. By then Jesus will have returned and will rule for a time, after which the Mahdi (and perhaps Ḥusayn himself) will reign in peace and justice, fulfilling the mission of all the prophets. The family of the Prophet will participate not only in intercession but in judgment as well, in the persons of 'Alī or Fāṭimah or Ḥusayn. [*See also* Imamate.]

Ṣūfī Variations. Muslims who adopted a Ṣūfī orientation were led to special eschatological views as a result of their asceticism, their search for union with God in this life, and their extreme love of God. Early ascetics such as Ḥasan al-Baṣrī (d. 728) stressed their fear of Hell and their desire for Paradise because they were ultrasensitive to their human sinfulness; they tended to seek the otherworld because they so strongly rejected this one. In Ḥasan's words, "Be with this world as if you had never been there, and with the otherworld as if you would never leave it." However, when love of God became a key element in Sufism, new views of the otherworld began to appear. For the earliest Muslim love mystic, the Arab poetess Rābi'ah al-'Adawīyah (d. 801), selfless love of God required the Ṣūfī to be veiled from both this world and the other by her vision of God, whom the Ṣūfī must love so much that Paradise and Hell are both forgotten. Ṣūfīs such as Yaḥyā ibn Mu'ādh al-Rāzī (d. 871) replaced fear of punishment and hope of reward with complete trust in God's mercy and found death beautiful because it joined friend with friend. Others went much further. The Turkish poet Yunus Emre (d. 1321?) argued that the Ṣūfī must reject not only this world but also the next; some of his poems ridiculed a literal interpretation of the Qur'ān's eschatological details.

Among those Ṣūfīs who sought union with God and a vision of him in this life, that experience transformed conventional notions of Paradise and Hell. For them, the perfect Ṣūfī was not subject to changing states, including death, or concerned about created states, such as the otherworld. Some came to believe that having been touched by the primordial fire and light of God's love made them impervious to the fires of Hell, and that Paradise would provide pure experience of God, not the sensuous delights described in the Qur'ān. In the words of Shiblī (d. 945), "the fire of Hell will not touch me; I can extinguish it." Ṣūfī enlargements of Muslim eschatological thinking was not without its ironies: while popular Ṣūfī practice encouraged rituals that might increase the joys of Paradise, cultivated Ṣūfī thought discouraged hoping for Paradise even for the vision of God it might provide.

Modern Responses. Many modern Sunnī thinkers do not discuss the eschaton at all, apparently finding it too difficult to rationalize. The concerns of those who do treat the eschaton are unusually continuous with those of their premodern counterparts, but modern thinkers have also developed new emphases and rediscovered old ones.

Along the traditionalist end of the spectrum, thinkers such as Aḥmad Fā'iz (d. 1918), Muḥammad 'Awwād (d. 1980), Shaykh al-Islām Ibrāhīm al-Bayjūrī, Muḥammad Khalīfah, Muṣṭafā al-Ṭayr, and Ahmad Galwash tend toward various kinds of literalism, reiterating in modern language such concerns as the agony of death, questioning and punishment/reward in the grave, the awareness of the dead, and the physicality of resurrection and afterlife. At the other end of the spectrum are those, such as M. Sadeddin Evrin, who attempt to verify the Qur'ān with scientific research (the description of the signs of the eschaton, for example). Some, such as Ṭanṭāwī Jawharī (d. 1940) Muḥammad Farīd Wajdī (d. 1954), lean toward a kind of European-inspired spiritualism that posits a world from which the spirits of the dead think about and help the living. In between the two poles are various modernists who tend to downplay the traditional eschatological specifics in favor of a stress on the continuity between this life and the next, the naturalness of death and the likeness of the *barzakh* to sleep or semiconsciousness, and the nature of human responsibility and accountability. Many practice allegorical interpretations of the Qur'ān. For example, Syed Ameer Ali (d. 1928) sees a spiritual meaning in the Qur'ān's sensuous descriptions of Paradise and Gehenna. Abū al-A'lā al-Mawdūdī (d. 1979) stresses the practical value of Islamic eschatology in helping human beings deal with death and mortality. Muḥammad Iqbal (d. 1938), in *The Reconstruction of Religious Thought in Islam,* describes Paradise and Gehenna as states rather than localities.

Modernist thought has also taken forms much less consistent with received eschatological thinking. The founder of the Aḥmadīyah sect, Mirza Ghulam Ahmad of Punjab (d. 1908), made eschatological claims of his own, asserting in 1880 that he was the Mahdi, at once the incarnation of Jesus, Muḥammad, and Kṛṣṇa. Aḥmadī Qur'ān commentaries, such as that of Maulana Muḥammad Ali (d. 1951), have continued to develop unusual eschatological views. For example, the opening of the graves is said to be prefigured by the opening of the earth to the mining of precious metals; the afterlife is seen as an example of the unceasing progress that also takes place on earth; the resurrection is presented as a new manifestation of hidden realities; and a heaven on earth is anticipated as well as a heaven after death.

The use of allegorical interpretation in the service of modernist rationalization has not been universal. Important modernists such as Muḥammad al-Mubārak, Sayyid Quṭb, Muṣṭafā Maḥmūd, and Muḥammad 'Abduh have remained loyal to Qur'ān and *ḥadīth* in their rejection of allegorical interpretation but have also argued against literalism, finding both of them inadequate means of expressing the realities of the next world. Others have established a relationship between the eschaton and the widely perceived need for social reconstruction. For them, death and resurrection are most meaningful in the context of living an ethical life. They emphasize human accountability and focus on the ways in which considerations of the next world can promote morality in this one. These approaches have their parallel among those Shī'ī Muslims who, embarrassed by the supernaturalism of traditional eschatology, deny the return of the last imam and yet find meaning and a redemptive quality in Ḥusayn's death when it is understood as a protest against injustice and oppression. Such thinkers seem to have rediscovered ancient Qur'anic priorities in their pursuit of modernization.

[*See also* Nubūwah.]

BIBLIOGRAPHY

The only comprehensive study of Islamic eschatology is Jane I. Smith's and Yvonne Y. Haddad's *The Islamic Understanding of Death and Resurrection* (Albany, N.Y., 1981), an unprecedented survey, largely of Sunnī thought, clearly and simply organized and concisely presented, with unusual attention given to modern thinkers of several kinds. Fritz Meier's "The Ultimate Origin and the Hereafter in Islam," in *Islam and Its Cultural Divergence: Studies in Honor of Gustave E. von Grunebaum,* edited by Girdhari L. Tikku, (Urbana, Ill., 1971), pp. 96–112, is an awkwardly translated general survey with a useful comparison of Sunnī and Shī'ī concepts of revelation, their relationship to other forms of divinely inspired knowledge and leadership, and their place in eschatology. Annemarie Schimmel's *Mystical Dimensions of Islam* (Chapel Hill, N.C., 1975) contains fascinating material on Ṣūfī eschatology throughout.

Works that address the issue of eschatology in the Shī'ī tradition in particular include S. Husain M. Jafri's *Origins and Early Development of Shī'a Islam* (London, 1979), a straightforward, narrative, chronological account that stresses the ways in which pre-Islamic views of leadership informed various Shīʿī constituencies, concentrating on the centrist, legitimist Twelver Shīʿah and the contributions of Jaʿfar al-Ṣādiq to their institutionalization. Mahmoud Ayoub's *Redemptive Suffering in Islam: A Study of the Devotional Aspects of ʿĀshūrāʾ in Twelver Shīʿism* (The Hague, 1978) is a moving and deeply felt rendering of eschatologically relevant piety, with suggestive comparative comments. A. A. Sachedina's *Islamic Messianism: The Idea of the Mahdi in Twelver Shīʿism* (Albany, N.Y., 1981) is a clear interpretive account of an important topic, with a particularly important analysis of the relationship between imam and prophet.

An important case study is Ignácz Goldziher's "Zur Charakteristik Gelâl ud-dîn us-Sujûtʿî's und seiner literarischen Thätigkeit," *Sitzungsberichte der kaiserlichen Akademie der Wissenschaften in Wien* 69 (1871): 7–28, a rare history and analysis of the concept of *mujaddid*, with an emphasis on one important thinker's identification with the role. John B. Taylor's "Some Aspects of Islamic Eschatology," *Religious Studies* 4 (October, 1968): 57–76, is a selective comparison of Qurʾanic and Mongol-period views, with eschatological thought divided into three categories: didactic, apocalyptic, and mystical. Taylor's references to modern Muslim responses to the topic are unfortunately seriously outdated.

Useful information can be found also in the *Shorter Encyclopaedia of Islam* (Leiden, 1974), in the following articles in particular: "Barzakh," "al-Dadjdjāl," "Djahannam," "Djanna," "Firdaws," "Ḥawḍ," "Iblīs," "ʿĪsā," "Isrāfīl," "ʿIzrāʾīl," "ak-Ḳiyāma," "al-Mahdī," "Malāʾika," "Munkar wa-Nakīr," "Shafāʿa," and "Yādjūj wa-Mādjūj." However, the articles are sometimes unclearly or elliptically presented or marred by the open display or subtle influence of many of the ethnocentric biases of earlier generations of scholars, especially as regards the allegedly derivative, irrational nature of Islam.

MARILYN ROBINSON WALDMAN

ESHMUN was a Phoenician healer god, later identified with Asklepios, the patron of medicine, by the Greeks and Romans. Although not a major god, Eshmun enjoyed widespread popularity, especially in the Hellenistic period. The etymology of his name is not clear.

Eshmun had an important shrine at Berytos (modern-day Beirut), and as late as the rule of the Roman emperor Elagabalus (218–222 CE) coins of Berytos depict Eshmun on their reverse, usually with a caduceus or a border of snakes. (Snakes had long been a symbol of healing, even to the times of ancient Sumer.) At Sidon, King Eshmunazar II ("Eshmun has saved"), about 475 BCE, boasted that he had built "a temple for Eshmun on the mountain, established him in high heaven." This temple was excavated in 1963–1964, and among the finds were votive statues dedicated to Eshmun, apparently on behalf of sick children.

Eshmun was also worshiped in the Phoenician colonies on Cyprus, and here his popularity is reflected in the common choice of personal names meaning "Eshmun is lord," "Eshmun prospers," "servant of Eshmun," and the like. He was identified with the Phoenician god Melqart, apparently as a god of youthful vitality.

At Carthage there was a temple of Eshmun on the Byrsa acropolis, and his name was combined with that of Astarte, perhaps to represent a compound, sexually ambiguous god of life-giving. Some Greek sources preserve the tradition that Eshmun was killed at the height of his youth and was brought back to life by Astronomē (Phoen., Ashtartnaama; i.e., Ashtart the Gracious). From Carthage the cult of Eshmun spread to Sardinia and westward.

In Greece Eshmun was evidently also identified with the healer god Apollo, as well as with Asklepios. Apollo was sometimes called Apollo Ismenios, and a river in Thebes sacred to him was named Ismēnos, both names surely based on that of Eshmun. There is also evidence that Eshmun was associated with Adonis, another god who was killed in his youth.

The noun *eshmun* in the plural occurs in *Isaiah* 59:10, where from context the meaning seems to be "those in vigorous health": "Among the *ashmannim* we are like dead men."

BIBLIOGRAPHY

The best source of materials concerning Eshmun, particularly in regard to Phoenician-Greek religious syncretism, is Michael C. Astour's *Hellenosemitica: An Ethnic and Cultural Study of West Semitic Impact on Mycenaean Greece* (Leiden, 1967). On Eshmunazar, Sidon, and the temple there, see John C. L. Gibson's *Phoenician Inscriptions*, vol. 3 of *Textbook of Syrian Semitic Inscriptions* (Oxford, 1982).

WILLIAM J. FULCO, S.J.

ESKIMO RELIGION. *See* Inuit Religion; *see also* Arctic Religions.

ESOTERICISM. Prior to the mid-nineteenth century there was no single name for the body of ideas that we today refer to as esotericism, although one often spoke of "occult philosophy." We owe the word *esotericism* itself to a nineteenth-century "occultist," Eliphas Lévi. By whatever name it appears, however, esotericism has had a long history. It has been composed of a collection of ideas, each with its own character, but is, as a whole, remarkably coherent. Initially, the need to conceptualize the phenomenon as a single concept was barely felt; it was enough to name its constituents (theosophy, theurgy, astrology, alchemy) and each of its many traditions or schools as branches of the esoteric tree. Until around the fourteenth century this tree was integrated rather well into the surrounding cultural landscape and drew a heightened beauty and majesty from certain very widespread philosophical doctrines, such as Neoplatonism.

Considered in a very general way, the situation was changed by what may be called the secularization of the cosmos. This secularization began in the fourteenth century, when official thought began to adopt a kind of formal Aristotelianism and to reject the belief in a series of living relationships uniting God or the divine world, man, and the universe, relationships that had been fundamental to esotericism. The technical sciences profited greatly from this epistemological rupture, but the mind found itself impoverished by it, and philosophy was cut off from some of its most enriching sources. Modern esoteric currents—that is to say, those that have appeared since the Renaissance—have defined themselves as a reaction against this rupture and as the continuation of the earlier intellectual tradition, preserving or reestablishing a sense of the relationships that unite man, the world, and the divine. The definitions of esotericism that can be given vary according to broader or narrower conceptions of these relationships.

General Characteristics. In its narrower sense, the word *esotericism* has a meaning that is apparent from its etymology (Gr., *esōteros,* "inner"), which refers to an "interiorism," an entry into the self through a special knowledge or gnosis, in order to attain a form of enlightenment and individual salvation. This special knowledge concerns the relationships that unite us to God or to the divine world and may also include a knowledge of the mysteries inherent to God himself (in which case it is, strictly speaking, theosophy). To learn these relationships, the individual must enter, or "descend," into himself by means of an initiatory process, progressing along a path that is hierarchically structured by a series of intermediaries.

According to the particular form an esoteric tradition takes, these intermediaries may be known as angels or spiritual entities, sometimes called Agent Intellects or *animae coelestes.* They may be more or less numerous, and more or less personalized. In all cases, however, they have something common in essence with the initiate, since otherwise the necessary relationships could not be established. Each of them must be known if the initiate is to progress successfully through the initiatory steps. The procedure requires total commitment, whether the initiate progresses alone, aided by the intentionally obscure texts that provide the keys to the mysteries, or whether with the aid of an initiator, who may be an isolated master or a member of an initiatory school. The function of the initiation is to regenerate consciousness through the reappropriation of primal knowledge that was lost to man after the Fall. Once attained, this knowledge makes possible a new experience in our relations with the sacred and the universe. Whether or not the initiate has a master, it is finally up to him to realize the knowledge of the bonds that unite him to superior entities (theosophy in the narrow sense) and to cosmic forces and living nature (theosophy in the broad sense).

Success on the initiatory path requires what is traditionally known as "active imagination," an essential key to esoteric knowledge. It is the active imagination that permits one to escape both the sterility of purely discursive logic and the disorder of fancy and sentimentality. In this way the initiate prevails against the dangers of the lower, less spiritual imagination, which, as Pascal says, is the mistress of errors and falseness. The active imagination, which is the real organ of the soul, puts us in contact with the *mundus imaginalis,* with what Henry Corbin has called the "imaginal" world, the place of intermediary beings, the mesocosm possessing a geography of its own and perceptible to each of us according to our respective cultural images. [*See* Images, *article on* The Imaginal.]

Understood in this way, esotericism corresponds to what is generally referred to as gnosis (knowledge), of which the gnosticism of the first centuries of our own era is but a particular case. It is, in fact, appropriate to distinguish the gnostic movement from gnosis in general, since the teachings of gnosticism can hardly be equated with those of the later esoteric traditions of the Middle Ages and of modern times. Gnosticism in most of its forms taught an absolute dualism, according an equal ontological footing to the powers of good and the powers of evil. The God of the Old Testament, for example, was presented as an evil demiurge. Gnosis, by contrast, should be understood more generally. [*See* Gnosticism, *article on* Gnosticism from the Middle Ages to the Present.] The Greek word *gnōsis,* as also the related Sanskrit *jñāna,* means both "learning" and "sapiential wisdom," a double meaning that it tended to lose in late Greek thought and in patristic Christianity. Its root, which also appears in the word *genesis,* in fact implies both learning and coming into being. Thus it was possible for the most important German theosophist of the nineteenth century, Franz Xaver von Baader, to devote part of his work to the ontological identity of knowing and begetting. By giving birth to us—or rather rebirth—gnosis unifies and liberates us. To know is to be liberated. It is not enough to know symbols and dogmas in a merely external fashion; one must be engendered by them.

Gnosis is thus not mere knowledge; between believing and knowing there is the knowledge of interior vision proper to the *mundus imaginalis*, or "imaginal" world, mentioned above. These various types of knowledge have been clearly distinguished within Islamic gnosis as intellectual knowledge *('aql)*, knowledge of traditional facts that are the object of faith *(naql)*, and knowledge through inner vision or intuitive revelation *(kashf)*. It is this last that opens up the world of the imaginal. As Corbin says, gnosis is an inner vision, a recital, whose mode of exposition is narrative. Insofar as it believes, it knows, but inasmuch as what it believes does not give positive, empirical, or historical evidence, it believes. Gnosis is wisdom and faith; it is *Pistis Sophia*. According to Pierre Deghaye's elegant definition, the idea of gnosis is therefore the foundation of the idea of esotericism, if one understands gnosis in its primary sense of "superior knowledge which is added to the common truths of objective Revelation, or the deepening of that Revelation rendered possible by a particular Grace." It is what the eighteenth-century theosophist Friedrich Christoph Oetinger called the *philosophia sacra*. It is a sacred, saving philosophy, soteriological because it effects the inner transformation of man, not through discursive thought but, according to Corbin, through a narrative revelation of hidden things, a saving light that itself brings life and joy, a divine grace that operates and assures salvation. For the esotericist, to know what one is and where one comes from is already to be saved. It is not a theoretical but a practical knowledge which, for that reason, transforms the knowing subject.

Mysticism, Gnosis, and Theosophy. Esotericism thus permits access to a higher level of understanding where dualities of all kinds are transcended in a unity that is not to be grasped in a purely conceptual fashion but is to be experienced by one's whole being. Various words have been used to refer to this higher level: "the inner man" (Saint Paul), "the supramental" (Aurobindo Ghose), "illuminative intuition" (René Guénon), "the transcendental ego" (Edmund Husserl), "enstasy" (Mircea Eliade). Raymond Abellio, who has drawn up a list of these terms, speaks of "infusion," and of a "concrete and permanent participation in universal interdependence," aimed at the fulfillment in man of the mystery of incarnation. Such infusion or enstasy aspires to express itself, to spread and communicate itself, not, however, merely in the form of emotional effusions, but in the form of oral or written traditions that speak through a veil of symbols.

Strickly speaking, gnosis should be distinguished from mysticism, even though they are usually found together. Mysticism, which is more "feminine," more nocturnal, voluntarily cultivates renunciation, although this does not exclude a taste for symbolism. Gnosis, more "masculine," more solar, cultivates detachment and is more attentive to structures. In his own journey, the mystic discovers the same intermediate entities as the gnostic. But while the gnostic views such entities as a source of enlightening and saving knowledge, the mystic limits their numbers as much as he can and aspires to pass beyond them and be united directly with his God.

The properly esoteric or gnostic attitude can thus be seen as a mystical experience in which intelligence and memory come to participate, expressing themselves in a symbolic form that reflects the different levels of reality. Or gnosis may be described, with the theosophist Valentin Tomberg, as the expression of a form of intelligence and memory that has effected a passage through mystical experience. In a sense, then, a gnostic is a mystic who is capable of communicating his own experiences to others in a manner that conveys the impact of the revelations he has received while passing through different levels of the imaginal world (the mirror of the spiritual world). Whereas the mystic proclaims his personal union with God, the gnostic formulates a doctrine. The mystic contemplates; the gnostic learns through revelation.

In addition to this gnostic side of esotericism, esotericism in the broad sense includes a theosophical dimension as well. Here gnosis is no longer restricted to the individual's relationship to the divine world, but pertains as well to the nature of God himself, or to the nature of divine personages and to the origin and hidden structure of the natural universe, its relation to man, and its ultimate ends. [*See* Theosophy.] It is in this general sense that one traditionally speaks of theosophy. Theosophy adds to esotericism in its restricted sense that cosmic or cosmosophic dimension that prevents the gnostic from falling into solipsism. It opens esotericism up to the whole universe, making possible a philosophy of nature. Occultism, in all its forms, draws or can draw its heuristic foundations from esotericism and from a philosophy of nature.

Universality and Secrecy; Esotericism and Exotericism. Esotericism thus is shown to be a way of life and an exercise of vision. The dangers of subjectivism are overcome by the presence of the world (when gnosis is combined with theosophy) and by the historical density of esotericism itself, which is dependent upon specific, revealed religious traditions. Every esotericist reinterprets his own tradition, adding his own personal commentary, and it can undoubtedly be said that active esotericism is the privileged form of hermeneutics. Esotericism presupposes that an esoteric tradition originally accompanies all revealed religions, even if this tradition becomes explicit only later, through commentaries such as the major texts of Jewish Qabbalah, for example, which are a theosophy of the Old Testament. These new interpretations do not exclude the preceding ones; rather, they extend and enrich them. Thus the Christian Qabbalah is a hermeneutic variation on the Jewish. In the same vein, Louis-Claude de Saint-Martin commented on the work of Jakob Boehme, who himself had commented on the book of *Genesis*. [*See* Qabbalah.]

Here we are far from the historicizing tendency that confuses historical truth with the truth of the sacred origins of each revelation, a tendency that is as well represented by the supporters of *Formgeschichte* as it is by the demythologizing orientation of Rudolf Bultmann and his followers. On the contrary, the esotericist begins with the assumption that these origins go beyond the human. He seeks to recapture both the structure and the living meaning of the language of symbols and myths, first in his own culture, but eventually in other cultures as well. Here we encounter what Seyyed Hossein Nasr has called the "relatively absolute." In reaching beyond his own tradition, the esotericist is not seeking to relativize his own faith. Rather he attempts to see, in the foundations of each religion, one of the many possible manifestations of the supreme Logos, and in each sacred book a manifestation of the supreme book—what Muslims call "the mother of the book" *(umm al-kitāb)*. He does this even if he believes that the whole truth was revealed in a privileged fashion in his own tradition. Consequently, esoteric activity is intent upon detecting the trace of the Absolute in all of its diverse manifestations. This makes esoteric literature as a whole a particularly rich resource for the spiritual needs of today's pluralistic world.

Esoteric traditions can be especially valuable in suggesting ways of thinking beyond the closed systems, abstract terms, and dehumanizing ideologies that characterize so much of modern life. They offer the immense depths of a traditional wisdom and hermeneutics, which are becoming progressively more accessible thanks to the progress of historical research and publication. Esotericism presents us with a form of nonreductive thought that reveals the richness of the correspondences uniting God, man, and the universe in the play of its reflecting mirrors. Its potential value for a renewal of the human sciences has yet to be realized.

The relation of esotericism to exotericism is a question often posed, along with its corollary: whether the idea of secrecy is the same as the idea of esotericism. Esotericism is, in fact, opposed to exotericism in the same way that what is reserved for an elite is opposed to what is addressed to all. The distinction remains valuable and fruitful as long as two mistakes are avoided. First, one must not believe them to be incompatible. In fact, exotericism and esotericism mutually qualify one another, as though they were two sides of the same coin.

Second, it is a mistake to believe that all esotericism is necessarily connected with the idea of secrecy and composed of elements that it is forbidden to divulge, whereas exotericism is a discourse intended for the public. Esotericism is not simply a *disciplina arcani*, a discipline of the arcane. Although the arcane sometimes plays a role, especially in certain initiation societies, to reduce esotericism to this single dimension can only be the result of bad faith, ignorance, or the desire to limit greatly the subject of one's research. In most cases, there is no conscious desire for secrecy. What the term *disciplina arcani* suggests (for example, in reference to a "secret" teaching that Jesus is said to have offered his apostles, or a certain ritual that an initiation society treasures and hides) is above all the fact that the mysteries of religion, the ultimate nature of reality, the hidden forces of cosmic order, and the hieroglyphs of the visible world do not lend themselves to immediate comprehension or to a didactic or univocal explanation, but must be the object of a progressive penetration at several levels by each seeker of knowledge.

In an essay published in 1906, Georg Simmel identified the essential elements of the sociology of secrecy and its function in constituting social structure and facilitating interaction. We may add that a "secret society" is not created with the intention to hide something, but, as Raymond Abellio has rightly reminded us, in order to make a small group of people "transparent" to one another; for the world at large, taken as a whole, is opaque. It is not doctrine that the initiate is supposed to keep secret, but, at the very most, the details of a ritual. Thus, for example, the fact that almost all the rituals of Freemasonry were published long ago is not at all a betrayal of the Masonic "secret." If a Freemason, or any member of an esoteric society, must keep the names of his affiliated brothers quiet, it is essentially a discretionary measure. A comparable situation existed in the religions of Hellenism; the "mystical" secret not to be revealed was not a piece of ineffable religious knowledge, but only the knowledge of a rite in its purely material aspect. The sacred, that which is set apart, requires a slender partition between itself and the secular world. One feels obliged to prevent the desecration of that which one values most highly and which was obtained only with difficulty through submitting to diverse trials. Finally, the apparent opposition between the hermeneutic activity (linked to speech, logos, endless "interpretation," etc., proper to esotericism) and the discipline of silence is more a dynamic and creative paradox—a hermeneutic tension—than a contradiction in the strict sense. It is best illustrated in a drawing printed in Achilles Bocchi's *Symbolicae questiones* (1555) that represents Hermes, the god of speech and of esoteric sciences, lifting a forefinger to his lips—a typical gesture of Harpocrates, interestingly transferred to Hermes by Bocchi. [*See also* Silence.]

Historical Overview. In the intellectual currents of the late Roman empire (Neo-Pythagoreanism and Stoicism, Alexandrian Hermetism, pagan Neoplatonism, and the work of Philo Judaeus), Western esotericism found the themes and elements that were to inspire it up to our own day. After Origen and Clement of Alexandria, theosophical speculation incorporated the angelic hierarchies and divine names established by Dionysius the Areopagite; it was further enriched by the work of Maximus the Confessor and reached a high point in the ninth century with the work of John Scottus Eriugena. Meanwhile, Greek Hermetism maintained a discreet presence. The Jewish Qabbalah of the period is known to us through the *Sefer Yetsirah.* At the dawn of the Middle Ages, the Arabs played the important role of preservers and translators, restoring to the Christian world some of the ancient traditions that had been forgotten.

Roman art and thought were dominated by images of the cosmos, the temple, and man. Alain of Lille, Hildegarde von Bingen, and Honorius were the bards of a symbolic universe in which both Hermetism and alchemy blossomed forth in new forms. The myth of Alexander, a movement known as the Fedeli d'Amore, ("devotees of love"), myths of chivalry, and, above all, the work of Joachim of Fiore also left their permanent mark on a Europe, which, during its thirteenth century, avid for new forms of spirituality, discovered the Franciscan spirit. The genius of this spirit was Bonaventure, whose work contained many theosophical themes; many spiritual alchemists were also to be found in the Franciscan milieu. The School of Oxford, with Robert Grosseteste and Roger Bacon, followed a similar path, while the great *summae* of Vincent of Beauvais, Bartholomew the Englishman, and William of Auvergne developed a foretaste of the *philosophia perennis* that would be so dear to the Renaissance. Theurgy, astrology, and medicine also headed in this direction, in an epoch that witnessed not only the works of Arnau de Villanova but also the *Roman de la rose,* the *Zohar,* and a form of Gothic sculpture connected with the "Great Work" and the earliest forms of Freemasonry.

Nevertheless, as early as the twelfth century a tendency best represented by the Salernitan School (School of Salerno) spread that was intent upon developing the *artes mechanicae* at the expense of the *artes liberales,* hence a secularization of space and time that entailed a "mechanization" of the image of the world. This tendency can be seen in the work and influence of the mathematician Jordanus Nemorarius, who flourished in the thirteenth century. Moreover, in the theology of the fourteenth century the influence of the Aristotelianism originally championed by Ibn Rushd (Averroës) led to the progressive disappearance of angelology, or the notion of intermediary worlds that had given the *mundus imaginalis* its specific character. Consequently, esotericism became marginal. At the same time there was a rapid development of Rhenish mysticism. This was also the age of Rulman Merswin, with his Fidèles de l'Île Verte ("devotees of the Green Isle"), who were spiritual cavaliers. The imagery of chivalry was more present than ever. Ramón Lull and Peter of Abano wrote their great works. Alchemy, well represented by John Dastin, Petrus Bonus, John of Rupescissa, and Nicolas Flamel, also influenced literature. Dante's *Commedia* became a source of inspiration for esoteric exegesis in the following centuries. So did the work of Nicholas of Cusa, which burst forth in the fourteenth century, the age of the initiatory romance as well as of a pervasive interest in astrology and alchemy, present even in book illumination and the plastic arts. The end of the century saw the conceptualization and systematization of esotericism and what would later be called "occultism." This was the work in large part of Marsilio Ficino of the Florentine Academy, whose "occult philosophy" was based on his studies of Plato and his translation of the texts of Alexandrian Hermetism into Latin. [*See* Occultism.] Indeed, thanks to Ficino's translations, nearly all of the Hermetic corpus became well known in Europe. At the same time, Pico della Mirandola introduced Christian Europe to the Jewish Qabbalah, maintaining that nothing proved the truth of Christianity more than the Qabbalah and magic.

In the sixteenth century esotericism appeared as a form of counterculture, even while appropriating a good number of the characteristic values and ideas of the Renaissance. It stood almost entirely under the triple sign of the Hermetism rediscovered by Ficino, the Christian Qabbalah, and Paracelsus. Ludovico Lazarelli, Giordano Bruno, and many others came under the influence of that renewed Hermetism, whose Alexandrian texts were considered a sort of new gospel coming to complete the gospel of Christianity. These were thought to be contemporary with Moses, when in fact they date from the second and third centuries of our own era.

If the presence of Hermetism was diffuse, the christianized Qabbalah was presented as a body of doctrine, and was elaborated little by little throughout the Renaissance and up to the middle of the seventeenth century. Especially after the expulsion of the Jews from Spain in 1492, people sought to "qabbalize" in a Christian context. The cardinal Egidio da Viterbo translated the principal texts of the Qabbalah into Latin, and the German humanist Johannes Reuchlin made them known by christianizing them. Heinrich Corneliius Agrippa, in his *De occulta philosophia,* a work characteristic of the literature on magic at the beginning of the Renaissance, studied the Qabbalah along with alchemy and astrology. Perhaps the most widespread work on the Qabbalah during the Renaissance was Galatin's *De arcanis catholicae veritatis.* The *De harmonia mundi* of Francesco Giorgi of Venice became, along with the works of Pico, Reuchlin, and Pietro Galatino, one of the principal sources for later Qabbalah. In France, the most celebrated name in this domain was Guillaume Postel.

Paracelsus initiated yet another movement. In his works, magic, medicine, an alchemical conception of the world, and a philosophy of nature are brought together on the unifying canvas of Christian Neoplatonism, in order to depict a universe throbbing with Germanic inspiration and poetry. In his wake, but in the margins and as if in contrast, we find the silhouette of the legendary Johann Faust, the black magician. The true disciples of Paracelsus, however, were Leonard Thurneysser, Leonard Fioravanti, and Gerard Dorn.

The seventeenth century was the recipient of this diverse heritage. It opened with the publication of the *Amphitheatrum sapientiae aeternae* by Heinrich Khunrath, a major book of Western esotericism that included alchemical and qabbalistic materials. The most outstanding qabbalistic work of the century, the famous *Cabala denudata* by Christian Knorr von Rosenroth, appeared somewhat later. Although there were other works on the Qabbalah produced at this time, such as the writings of Athanasius Kircher and Robert Fludd, who made the science known in England, the innovations of this period lie elsewhere: on the one hand, in the appearance of the myth of the "Rosy Cross" during the first half of the century; on the other, in the work of Jakob Boehme. Joannes Andreae, with his manifestos *(Fama* and *Confessio)* and his initiatory and alchemical novel *(Chymische Hochzeit des Christian Rosenkreuz),* inaugurated the tradition called Rosicrucianism, which immediately inspired Robert Fludd and the "Great Hermeticizer," Michael Maier. [*See* Rosicrucians.]

Alchemy and Rosicrucianism were happily married in a golden age of esoteric iconography, when an alchemist could be sure of finding welcome at the court of the emperor Rudolf II. Jakob Boehme, the prince of Christian esotericists, inaugurated the rapid development of the great age of European theosophy, prefigured in the preceding century by the work of Valentin Weigel. In Boehme can be found all the theosophical themes that were to follow: the Fall of Lucifer and Adam, sophiology (prefigured in the work of Khunrath), androgyny, and so on. The poetry of the mystic Angelus Silesius, as well as of other Baroque authors, was inspired by Boehme. In the second half of the century, Johann Georg Gichtel became his great disciple. Pierre Poiret, Antoinette Bourignon, and Gottfried Arnold also left original work in Boehme's wake. In England, Boehme's works were translated and popularized by John Pordage and Jane Lead. Under the influence of Paracelsus and Boehme, faith and knowledge were increasingly unified, especially among the Neoplatonists of Cambridge, of whom Henry More is the most eloquent representative. But it was also during this period that esotericism became a marginal phenomenon. The scientific community's break with esotericism is symbolized by the exclusion of astrology in 1666 from the new Academy of Sciences founded in Paris.

At the beginning of the eighteenth century, Andreas Freher gave England one of the clearest and most faithful expositions of Boehme. At the dawn of the century of Enlightenment, the theosophy of Georg von Welling and Sincerus Renatus also revived esoteric thought in Germany, while Saint-Georges of Marsais and the authors of the Bible of Berlebourg in France mixed elements borrowed from the mysticism of Madame Guyon du Chesnoy with Boehmean teachings. New editions of alchemical and theosophical works multiplied, and little by little a form of esotericism that came to be called Illuminism emerged. Johann Kaspar Lavater, the pastor of Zurich, joined this trend, as did Heinrich Jung-Stilling and William Law. The most famous of the Illuminati was Emanuel Swedenborg, less a theosophist than a visionary and rather marginal to European Illuminism despite the considerable influence that his work continues to exercise. Friedrich Christoph Oetinger publicized him, but was himself more interested in Boehme and the Qabbalah.

If Oetinger was the greatest German theosophist of the eighteenth century, the most important in Europe generally was Louis-Claude de Saint-Martin, whose influence was the most profound and the most durable. Joseph de Maistre, whose work is colored by his teachings, saw him as "the most learned, the wisest, and the most elegant of theosophists."

The influence of Illuminism can be seen in early German Romanticism, in the writings of Novalis, Karl von Eckartshausen, and the first works of Franz Xaver von Baader. Freemasonry was also touched by it, and initiatory obedience, rites, and systems proliferated. Thus emerged such traditions and movements as the Strict Templar Observance, the Illuminati of Avignon (Dom Pernéty's system), the "Egyptian" Freemasonry of Cagliostro (pseudonym of Giuseppe Balsamo), the Chevaliers Bienfaisants of the Holy City (the system of Jean-Baptiste Willermoz), the Rose-Croix d'Or, and many others. Willermoz owes the essence of his Masonic inspiration to Martínez Pasqualis, the founder of the theosophical and theurgical order called the Elus-Cohens, and secondarily to Saint-Martin. "Martinism," a rather vague esoteric current constructed out of elements borrowed from the ideas of Martínez, Saint-Martin, and Willermozian Masonry, spread through Russia, where the names of Nikolai Novikov, A. F. Labizine, and I. V. Lopuchin grew famous. Literature felt the effects of such esoteric societies, especially in Germany, where initiatory novels proliferated.

German Romanticism after 1800 gathered together a large part of this heritage and used it to develop a philosophy of nature. [*See* Nature, *article on* Religious and Philosophical Speculations.] Theosophizing philosophy appeared in the works of G. H. von Schubert, A. K. A. von Eschenmayer, Justinus Kerner, and later in Carl Gustav Carus. Theosophical philosophy appeared in the works of J. J. Wirz, Michael Hahn, and especially von Baader, the greatest of them all. In France, Antoine Fabre d'Olivet and Pierre-Simon Ballanche each developed a very personal work, while Swedenborgianism and Martinism became the subjects of commentaries and exegesis, and even influenced the writings of Honoré de Balzac. Also in the early nineteenth century, England experienced a renewal of interest in Boehme and, even more, in Swedenborg. German philosophy came increasingly under the influence of esotericism, an influence that extended beyond *Naturphilosophie.* Ernst Benz has shown the importance of esoteric sources and a secularized form of mysticism for Hegelian Marxism. In the ideology of modernism one can discern the influence of a distorted esotericism, which is translated into the expectation of a new universal order.

Occultism in its present-day sense appeared at this time, with Eliphas Lévi, the "New Agrippa" and a talented popularizer. As the offspring of the naturalistic magic of the Middle Ages and the occult philosophy of the Renaissance, occultism in general had no specifically Christian elements. Christianity, esotericism, and occultism nevertheless blended together well in the works of Papus (pseudonym of Géraud Encausse), the founder of the Martinist order and the most famous French magus of the *fin de siècle,* a time that also witnessed the flourishing of the works of Joséphin Péladan, Edouard Schuré, Saint-Yves d'Alveydre, Stanislas de Guaita, and Paul Sédir. Richard Wagner and the Symbolists also have roots in the esoteric tradition.

In the twentieth century esotericism scatters in different directions, mainly because of the decline of faith, the confusion with occultism, a growing infatuation with often badly assimilated Eastern doctrines, and the miracles achieved by science. On bookstore shelves labeled "esotericism" it is not unusual to see works dealing with unidentified flying objects, parapsychology, fakirs, and healers. The mysteries of religion are readily presented as problems to be solved scientifically, and scientific problems are presented as religious enigmas. People tend to confuse the psychic and the spiritual. Or they proceed to hasty syncretisms, mixing a poorly understood Western esotericism with a debased orientalism of the bazaar. The Theosophical Society, founded in 1875 by H. P. Blavatsky and still flourishing throughout the world, has not always been exempt from such doubtful syncretisms, despite much doctrine that is undeniably valuable. As René Guénon pointed out, even its title is a usurpation of the word *theosophy,* and *theosophism* would be a more accurate term. For the rest, traditional theosophical thought remains alive among certain Orthodox thinkers such as Vladimir Solov'ev and, closer to us, Sergi Bulgakov and Nikolai Berdiaev in Paris, and Leopold Ziegler in Germany. There is a little of it among most editors and commentators on Western esotericism of the past. Alchemy, both spiritual and practical, still has numerous followers, who readily quote Fulcanelli, a cryptologist inspired by the symbolism of cathedrals. Fulcanelli (a pseudonym) has found a disciple in Eugéne Canseliet.

Esotericism has colored the work of Czeslaw Milosz, Gustav Meyrink, William Butler Yeats, Thomas Mann, and many other writers. Its influence on literature is facilitated by the existence of numerous initiatory societies, many of which maintain the venerable title "Rosy Cross" (e.g., the Lectorium Rosicrucianum and especially AMORC, or the Ancient and Mystical Order of Rosae Crucis), but these do not always have a sufficiently specific body of doctrine and tradition. A small and very traditional element of present-day Freemasonry still continues the Illuminism of the eighteenth century. Also still alive, but divided into several branches, is the Martinism that continues the teachings of Papus. The Astrum Argentinum, an anti-Christian society emerging from the Golden Dawn, founded by Aleister Crowley, contains as much occultism as esotericism. The teaching of G. I. Gurdjieff rallies some of the better spirits, but without drawing much inspiration from the traditional currents of Western gnosticism. Nor has it exerted much influence on the most prominent esotericist of our time, René Guénon, who has been affected mainly by India and Islam. Guénon made himself the commanding and uncompromising defender of the idea of tradition; his merit in this domain is mainly in having recalled to intellectual rigor and a form of metaphysical precision many students of esotericism who had been content to leave things vague. Besides Guénon, two great names have marked the esotericism of our century: Rudolf Steiner, whose "anthroposophy" revived the tradition of Romantic *Naturphilosophie*, and C. G. Jung, the last representative of the latter school. Unlike Steiner, Jung never presented himself as a spiritual master, and he rarely made any kind of profession of religious faith. But his scientific work renewed psychoanalysis by exploring the visionary, or imaginal, dimensions of the psyche, which had previously been virtually ignored. He also contributed to a rediscovery of the treasures of alchemical thought by applying alchemical symbolism to the process of psychological integration, which he called "individuation."

Evidently less popular than Jung's work, but more and more numerous, are the scholarly works that have been appearing since the 1930s. Translations, new editions, critical apparatuses, monographs, and university dissertations have all improved our knowledge of the history of esotericism. Arthur E. Waite and Paul Vulliaud were pioneers; Gershom Scholem, Ernst Benz, Frances A. Yates, Henry Corbin, and many others are nearer to us. Mircea Eliade, Joseph Campbell, Gilbert Durand, and others reveal to specialists, as well as to a large cultivated public, anthropological dimensions of the subject whose existence had barely been considered. They restore esotericism to its rightful place in the study of myth, symbols, and the sacred. To be sure, we witness the most diverse tendencies in exegesis and interpretation, and interpretations that are often reductive. Nevertheless, thanks to the cross-disciplinary breadth of research in the human sciences, esotericism is currently being taken seriously, even if largely as a subject for historical research.

[*See also articles on specific esoteric traditions:* Astrology; Theurgy; Hermetism; *and* Alchemy.]

BIBLIOGRAPHY

There is no single book on the history of esotericism. An interesting general reflection on esotericism and tradition can be found in Seyyed Hossein Nasr's *Knowledge and the Sacred* (New York, 1981). On Islamic esotericism, see Henry Corbin's *En Islam iranien*, 4 vols. (Paris, 1971–1972). A philosophical approach is to be found in Raymond Abellio's *La fin de l'ésotérisme* (Paris, 1973). On esotericism in the eighteenth century, see my *L'esotérisme au XVIIIe siècle* (Paris, 1973) and *Mystiques, théosophes et illuminés au siècle des lumières* (Hildesheim and New York, 1976); for a more general encompassing approach see my *Accès de l'esotérisme* (Paris, 1986). The classic work on the theosophy of Jacob Boehme is Alexandre Koyré's *La philosophie de Jacob Boehme* (1929; Paris, 1979). Well-documented studies on Christian theosophy include Will-Erich Peuckert's *Pansophie*, rev. ed. (Berlin, 1956); the commentaries on the works of Friedrich Christoph Oetinger published by Walter de Gruyter in Berlin from 1977 onward; the studies by Bernard Gorceix, *Flambée et agonie: Mystiques du XVIIe siècle allemand* (Sisteron, 1977) and *Johann Georg Gichtel, théosophe d'Amsterdam* (Lausanne, 1975); and articles by Pierre Deghaye and many others, some of them authors referred to above, that have appeared in *Cahiers de l'hermétisme* (Paris, 1977–) and *Cahiers de l'Université Saint-Jean de Jérusalem* (Paris, 1975–).

ANTOINE FAIVRE
Translated from French by Kristine Anderson

ESSENES. The Essenes were a sect of Jews during the Hasmonean and Roman periods of Jewish history (c. 150 BCE–74 CE). This group was noted for its piety and distinctive theology. The Essenes were known in Greek as Essenoi or Essaioi. Numerous suggestions have been made regarding the etymology of the name, among which are derivation from Syriac *ḥase'* ("pious"), Aramaic *asayya'* ("healers"), Greek *hosios* ("holy"), and Hebrew *ḥasha'im* ("silent ones"). The very fact that so many suggestions as to etymology have been made and that none has carried a scholarly consensus shows that the derivation of the term cannot be established with certainty. No Hebrew cognate appears either in the Dead Sea Scrolls, taken by many scholars to be the writings of this sect, or in rabbinic literature (the Talmuds and *midrashim*). Only with the Jewish rediscovery of Philo Judaeus (d. 45–50 CE) and Josephus Flavius (d. 100 CE?) in the Renaissance was the Hebrew word *issiyyim* (Essenes) coined.

Historical Sources. Until the twentieth century, the Essenes were known only from Greek sources. They are described twice by Philo, in *Hypothetica* (11.1–18) and *Every Good Man Is Free* (12.75–13.91). Both of these accounts were written by 50 CE and, in turn, drew on a common, earlier source. (Philo also described a similar sect, the Therapeutae, in *On the Contemplative Life*.)

Josephus describes the Essenes in passages of several of his books. In *The Jewish War*, written around 75–79 CE, there is a detailed account (2.119–161). *Jewish Antiquities* contains a shorter account (18.18–22). In his autobiography, written about 100 CE, Josephus tells us that he investigated the Essenes, among other Jewish sects, in his youth (*The Life* 2.9–11). Scattered references to the Essenes occur elsewhere in the works of Josephus.

Pliny the Elder wrote about the Essenes in his *Natural History* (5.73), completed in 77 CE. *Philosophumena* (9.18–30), considered to have been written by Hippolytus, a third-century bishop, contains a description of the Essenes that, in part, is drawn from a no longer extant source that was also used by Josephus.

Since the discovery of the Dead Sea Scrolls at Qumran in 1947, a consensus has developed that identifies the sect of the scrolls with the Essenes described by Philo and Josephus. This view has led many scholars to interpret the Greek texts describing the Essenes in light of the scrolls from Qumran, and the scrolls in light of the Greek texts, although the term *Essene* is absent from the Qumran scrolls. To avoid this methodological pitfall, evidence for the Essenes will first be presented and then compared with the corpus of the Dead Sea Scrolls.

History. No solution to the question of the origins of Essenism is likely to emerge from our sources. Suggestions of Iranian and Hellenistic influence are possible but cannot be documented.

Josephus (*Antiquities* 13.171–173) first mentions the Essenes in his account of the reign of Jonathan the Hasmonean (r. 161–143/2 BCE). There he briefly describes the Pharisees, Sadducees, and Essenes. He himself claims to have known of the three sects through "personal experience" (*Life* 2.10–11) in the mid-first century CE. He then mentions Judas, an Essene prophet, who was instructing his disciples in fortune-telling during the reign of Judah Aristobulus I in 104 and 103 BCE (*Antiquities* 13.311–313). Herod excused the Essenes from swearing a loyalty oath because, in the view of Josephus (or his source), Menahem the Essene had foretold a lengthy reign for Herod (*Antiquities* 15.371–378). A certain Simeon the Essene predicted dire circumstances for Archelaus, the son of Herod and ethnarch of Judah (4 BCE–c. 6 CE; *Antiquities* 17.345–348); clearly, the Essenes were known for their prediction of the future.

John the Essene was one of the Jewish generals in the great revolt against Rome in 66–74 CE (*War* 2.567). Josephus tells us that the Essenes were tortured by the Romans during the great revolt (*War* 2.152–153); this may indicate further their participation in the war against the Romans. An entrance through the south wall of Jerusalem was called the "gate of the Essenes" (*War* 5.145). With the destruction of the province of Judaea following in the wake of the unsuccessful uprising against Rome in 66–74 CE, the Essenes disappear from the stage of history.

The Essene Way of Life. There were about four thousand Essenes, according to the testimony of Philo and Josephus. They apparently were scattered in communities throughout Palestine, although some evidence exists that they avoided the larger cities. According to Pliny, there was an Essene settlement between Jericho and 'Ein Gedi on the western shore of the Dead Sea. This description has been taken by many scholars as indicating that the Qumran sect whose library was found at the shore of the Dead Sea is to be identified with the Essenes of Philo and Josephus. [*See map accompanying* Judaism, *overview article.*]

Membership and initiation. Only adult males could enter the Essene sect. Our sources tell of both married and celibate Essenes. We can assume that in the case of married Essenes, full membership was not extended to women. Rather, their status was determined by their being wives or daughters of members. Children were educated in the ways of the community.

The Essenes were organized under officials to whom obedience was required. Members who transgressed could be expelled from the community by the Essene court of one hundred. Aspiring members received three items—a hatchet, an apron, and a white garment—and had to undergo a detailed initiation process that included a year of probation. An initiate was then eligible for the ritual ablutions. Subsequently, he had to undergo a further two years of probation, after which time he was to swear an oath, the only oath the Essenes permitted. In this oath the candidate bound himself to piety toward God, justice to men, honesty with his fellow Essenes, the proper transmission of the teachings of the sect, and the preservation of the secrecy by which the sect's doctrines were guarded from outsiders. Among the teachings to be kept secret were the Essenes' traditions concerning the names of the angels. The candidate was now able to participate in the communal meals of the sect and was a full-fledged member.

Social system. The Essenes practiced community of property. Upon admission, new members turned their property over to the group, whose elected officials administered it for the benefit of all. Hence, all members shared wealth equally, with no distinctions between rich and poor. Members earned income for the group through various occupations, including agriculture and trades. (The Essenes avoided commerce and the manufacture of weapons.) All earnings were turned over to the officials, who distributed funds for purchasing necessities and for taking care of older or ill members of the community. In addition, the Essenes dispensed charity throughout the country, much of it to those outside their group. Traveling members were taken care of by special officers in each town.

Characteristic of the Essenes was their moderation and avoidance of luxury, as evidenced in their eating and drinking habits, their clothing, and the fact that they did not anoint themselves with oil, a practice common among the Jews of the Greco-Roman period. For them, wealth was only a means to provide the necessities of life. This asceticism also manifested itself among those Essenes who were celibate. On the other hand, it appears that in many cases this celibacy was embarked on later in life, after having had children, so that it was not absolute.

Religious life. The Essenes had an ambivalent relationship with the Jerusalem Temple. While they sent voluntary offerings to the Temple, they themselves did not participate in the sacrificial worship there.

The members of the sect began their day with prayer. After prayer, they worked at their occupations. Later, they assembled for purification rituals and a communal meal that was prepared by priests and eaten while wearing special garments. After the members took their places at the table in silence, the baker and cook distributed the food to each in order of his status. A priest recited a short prayer before and after the meal. The community then returned to work and came together once again in the evening for another meal. At the setting of the sun they recited prayers to God. (These prayers cannot have been directed to the sun, as some scholars suggest, in view of the Essenes' close adherence to basic Jewish theology, that is, to a biblical conception of God.)

Ritual purity was greatly emphasized. Not only were ablutions required before the communal meals, but they were also performed after relieving oneself, or after coming in contact with a nonmember or novice. Members were extremely careful in attending to natural functions, and in bathing and expectorating. The Essenes were accustomed to wearing white garments, and rules of modesty were very important.

Theology. The Essenes are said to have believed in absolute predestination. Probably related to this doctrine was their gift of prophecy. Josephus asserts that the Essenes seldom erred in their predictions. The name of Moses was held in high esteem, and the Essenes saw blasphemy of it as a capital crime. They studied the Torah and its ethics, and interpreted the scriptures allegorically. They were extremely strict in observing the Sabbath. Their teachings were recorded in books that the members were required to pass on with great care. The Essenes were experts in medicinal roots and the properties of stones, the healing powers of which they claimed to have derived from ancient writings.

Most notable among the doctrines of the Essenes was their belief in the immortality of the soul. According to Josephus, they believed that only the soul survived after death, a concept of Hellenistic origin. However, according to the *Philosophumena* (c. 225; generally ascribed to Hippolytus of Rome), the Essenes believed that the body survived as well and would eventually be revived.

The Dead Sea Scrolls. Since the discovery of the Dead Sea Scrolls, the majority of scholars have taken the view that these documents were the library of the Essenes who, accordingly, were settled at Qumran. Indeed, many parallels do exist between the sect described by the Greek sources and the sect of the scrolls from Qumran. Similar initiation ceremonies exist for both groups, although the procedure described in the classical sources diverges in some respects from that of the Qumran texts. The Essenes seem to have eaten communal meals regularly. The Qumran texts, however, envisage only occasional communal meals. For the Essenes all property was held in common, whereas at Qumran private ownership prevailed, and only the use of property was common. The Essenes' observances of ritual purity, although paralleled at Qumran, were not uncommon among the sects of this period.

The main weakness of the identification of these two groups is the fact that the word *Essene* or its equivalent is not present in the Qumran scrolls. In addition, the texts have many small discrepancies. There is no evidence that the Essenes had the apocalyptic dreams of the Dead Sea sect. Nor do we know that they adhered to a calendar of solar months such as that which the Qumran sect followed. Scholars usually account for these minor differences by saying that the classical sources, especially Josephus, were written with a Greek-speaking audience in mind and, therefore, described the sect in terms that would be understandable to such readers. [*For further discussion of the Qumran material, see* Dead Sea Scrolls.]

If, indeed, the Essenes are to be identified with the sect of the Dead Sea Scrolls, then the Qumran evidence may be used to fill in the picture derived from the classical sources. If not, we would have to reckon with two sects having similar teachings and similar ways of life. As a matter of fact, Palestine in the Second Commonwealth period was replete with various sects and movements, each contributing to the religious ferment of the times.

Judaism and Christianity. Although the Essenes are nowhere mentioned in the New Testament, certain parallels may indicate an indirect influence of this sect on nascent Christianity. It may be generally stated that the various sects of Second Temple Judaism provide important background material for understanding the rise of the new faith.

The end product of the ferment mentioned above, combined with the great revolt of the Jews against Rome and the resulting destruction of the land, was rabbinic Judaism. Some scholars have claimed that Talmudic sources refer to the Essenes; however, the term *Essene* is not mentioned. While definite evidence is lacking, we can speculate that Essene teachings must have contributed, at least indirectly, to the subsequent development of Jewish tradition regarding such topics as purity, cult, angelology, and the division of body and soul.

BIBLIOGRAPHY

An excellent introduction is found in volume 2 of Emil Schürer's *The History of the Jewish People in the Age of Jesus Christ, 175 B.C.–A.D. 135,* revised and edited by Géza Vermès, Fergus Millar, and Matthew Black and translated by T. A. Burkill et al. (Edinburgh, 1979), pp. 555–597. Extremely important is Morton Smith's "The Description of the Essenes in Josephus and the Philosophumena," *Hebrew Union College Annual* 29 (1958): 273–313. Frank Moore Cross's *The Ancient Library of Qumrân and Modern Biblical Studies,* rev. ed. (Garden City, N.Y., 1961), pp. 70–106, argues for the identification of the Essenes with the Dead Sea sect. The treatment in Martin Hengel's *Judaism and Hellenism,* vol. 1, translated by John Bowden (Philadelphia, 1974), pp. 218–247, accepts this identification yet discusses at length the problem of Hellenistic influence. For the phenomenon of Jewish sectarianism in the Greco-Roman period, see my "Jewish Sectarianism in Second Temple Times," in *Great Schisms in Jewish History,* edited by Raphael Jospe and Stanley M. Wagner (New York, 1981), pp. 1–46.

LAWRENCE H. SCHIFFMAN

ESTHER, or, in Hebrew, Ester; the daughter of Abiḥail, also called Hadassah; heroine of the biblical book that bears her name. Adopted and raised by her cousin Mordecai, Esther, whose name is derived from the Persian *stara,* "star," plays a crucial role in the event of persecution and deliverance of the Jews in the ancient Persian empire that the late biblical *Book* (or *Scroll*) *of Esther* purports to record. The story of this deliverance, which draws on ancient Near Eastern courtier motifs, wisdom themes, and, quite possibly, topoi from Mesopotamian and Persian New Year festivals, serves as a festal legend for the Jewish holiday of Purim.

The main outline of the *Book of Esther* is as follows. At the outset, the Persian ruler Ahasuerus has a grand feast that is spoiled when his wife, Vashti, refuses his demand that she perform before the assembled males. Vashti is banished, a decree is issued that all wives must honor their husbands, and the stage is set for a search to replace the defiant queen. The choice is Esther, a Jewess, who follows Mordecai's counsel not to reveal her ethnic-religious origins (*Est.* 2:1–18). While Esther keeps her secret at the court, Mordecai uncovers a plot to kill the king. Meanwhile, one of the viziers, Haman, is elevated to a position of high power. Piqued by the refusal of Mordecai to bow down in homage to him, Haman slanders the Jews to the king and, with the use of lots (Heb., *purim*), sets a date for their annihilation (*Est.* 3). Mordecai now enlists the help of Esther on behalf of her people (*Est.* 4:1–17). An initial soiree between the king and queen passes successfully. Several minor scenes follow dealing with Haman's plot to hang Mordecai (*Est.* 5:9–14) and Ahasuerus's insomnia, during which he learns of Mordecai's role in saving his life and determines to reward him, an event that provokes Haman's shame (*Est.* 6:1–14). A second soiree leads to the disgrace of Haman, the elevation of Mordecai, the disclosure of the plot against the Jews, and, finally, royal permission for the Jews to protect themselves on the day of the planned uprising (*Est.* 7:1–8:17), so that a day of national fasting and sorrow is turned into a time of joy and gladness (*Est.* 9–10).

Mordecai is presented as descended from Saul, the Benjaminite, and Haman, from Agag, the Amalekite; in this way, the novella dramatizes a typological repetition of the episode reported in *1 Samuel* 15 and recalls the divine exhortation never to forget the destructive deeds of Amalek (*Dt.* 24:17–19).

Various additions to *Esther* have been incorporated into the Apocrypha and Septuagint, and there are numerous expansions in the Aramaic *Targum sheni.* In the Middle Ages, the role of Esther took on powerful symbolic dimensions among Jews for at least three reasons. First, Esther came to symbolize the court Jew who risked everything to defend the nation so often slandered, despised, and threatened. Second, Esther, as a "hidden" Jew (together with the frequently noted absence of an explicit reference to God in the scroll), symbolized in mystical circles the hiddenness of the Shekhinah (divine feminine presence) in the world and in the Jewish exile. And finally, Esther (and the festival of Purim) was a great favorite of the Marranos in Spain and in their far-flung dispersion; they saw in her disguised condition the factual and psychological prototype of their own disguised condition.

[*See also* Purim.]

BIBLIOGRAPHY

Bickerman, Elias J. *Four Strange Books of the Bible: Jonah, Daniel, Koheleth, Esther.* New York, 1967. See pages 171–240.

Gaster, Theodor H. *Purim and Hanukkah in Custom and Tradition.* New York, 1950.

Ginzberg, Louis. *The Legends of the Jews* (1909–1938). 7 vols. Translated by Henrietta Szold et al. Reprint, Philadelphia, 1937–1966. See the index, s.v. *Esther.*

Moore, Carey A. *Esther.* Anchor Bible, vol. 7B. Garden City, N.Y., 1971.

Réau, Louis. *Iconographie de l'art chrétien,* vol. 2. Paris, 1956. See pages 335–342.

MICHAEL FISHBANE

ESTONIAN RELIGION.

See Finnic Religions.

ESUS, a Celtic deity of uncertain attributes, was variously identified by the Romans with Mars and with Mercury. As a theonym *Esus* is unknown in Gallo-Roman writing except for a single inscription from the first century CE on the Altar of the Nautae of Paris, currently preserved at the Musée de Cluny (*Corpus inscriptionum Latinarum*, Berlin, 1863, vol. 13, no. 3026). But the name is indirectly attested in several godlike anthroponyms: *Esumagius* ("he who is as powerful as Esus"), *Esugenus* ("son of Esus"), and *Esunertus* ("he who has the strength of Esus"). There are also several ethnic names with related etymologies, such as *Esuvii, Esubii, Esuii,* and *Esubiani (Vesubiani).*

The name *Esus* appears in the *Pharsalia* of Lucan (1.444–446), at the center of the "Jupiterean" triad: "Et quibus inmitis placatur sanguine diro, / Teutates horrensque feris altaribus Esus / Et Taranis Scythicae non mitior ara Dianae . . . ("And those who appease ferocious Teutates with horrible bloodletting, hideous Esus in his savage sanctuaries, and Taranis, whose altars are no less cruel than those of Scythian Diana . . ."). Esus is also mentioned much later in the Bernese Scholia, which propose two successive interpretations of him. One reads: "Hesus Mars sic placatur: homo in arbore suspenditur usque donec per cruorem membra digesserit" ("Hesus-Mars is appeased in this mannner: they hang a man from a tree until his members fall off from the loss of blood"). The other reads: "Hesum Mercurium credunt, siquidem a mercatoribus colitur, et praesidem bellorum et caelestium deorum maximum Taranin Iovem adsuetum olim humanis placari capitibus" ("They think that Esus is Mercury, although he is honored by the merchants, and as war leader and great god of the heavens they have Taranis-Jupiter, who was once appeased by human heads but who is now content with herds").

The sculpture from the Altar of the Nautae shows him felling or pruning a tree, and he has often been called "woodcutter god," which is a rather dubious interpretation. It is much more likely that the pruning or lopping off of the tree is associated with the birds of Tarvos Trigaranus ("bull of the three cranes") depicted on the same monument. Esus also shows up on a monument in Treves, although here too one cannot be sure of a sound interpretation.

The etymology of *Esus* has for a long time been subject to doubt, and parallels from Sanskrit or Latin (e.g., *herus*, "master") have been sought. But it would appear that the etymology is simply a case of the evolution of the stem **veso-s* through the disappearance of the initial *v-*, as frequently happened in all the Celtic languages. In any case, the etymology is proved by the coexistence of the ethnic names *Esubiani* and *Vesubiani*. **Veso-s* denotes "better, excellent," and *Esus* is thus the Celtic semantic equivalent of the Latin *Optimus*, an epithet for Jupiter that also resembles the Irish *Daghdha*.

BIBLIOGRAPHY

Deonna, Waldemar. "Les victimes d'Esus." *Ogam* 10 (1958): 3–29.

Guyonvarc'h, Christian-J. "Der Göttername Esus." *Die Sprache* (Vienna) 15 (1969): 172–174.

Holder, Alfred. *Alt-celtischer Sprachschatz,* vol. 1. Leipzig, 1896.

Le Roux, Françoise. "Des chaudrons celtiques à l'arbre d'Esus: Lucien et les Scholies Bernoises." *Ogam* 7 (1955): 33–58.

FRANÇOISE LE ROUX and CHRISTIAN-J. GUYONVARC'H
Translated from French by Erica Meltzer

ETERNITY is the condition or attribute of divine life by which it relates with equal immediacy and potency to all times. The notion emerges at the point of contact of three distinct religious concerns. The oldest of these is the question of the state of life after death, especially in light of the continuing presence of the dead among the living as acknowledged in the various forms of the cult of the dead. A later-developing speculative concern is the question about divine creation, especially when creative power is seen as the production in a divine mind of a world of ideas, a *logos* or paradigm made present in this world as in an image. Finally, there is the concern with contemplative or mystical experience, especially when regarded as a way of partaking of the divine life within the conditions of present existence. Reflection on these themes converges upon the notion of a dimension of life that is "vertically" related to the "horizontal" flowing of time, that transcends time without being apart from it.

Because eternity touches each and every time, it is easily confused with the closely related concept of what "always was, is, and will be," or, in a word, the everlasting. But in its own proper concept, the eternal only "is"; only in the present tense can it be said to be or act in any way. Exempted from all having-been and going-to-be, eternity is familiarly defined as timelessness, in distinction from the everlasting (sometimes also called the sempiternal). The everlasting antecedes and outlasts everything that begins and ends in time, but because it is just as much given over to being partly past, partly future as are things that come to be and perish, it is therefore just as much in time. Eternity, on the other hand, does not transcend finite spans of time extensively, but intensively. It draws the multiplicity of times into a unity no longer mediated by relations of precedence and posteriority and therefore, at least in this specific sense, no longer timelike.

Yet it oversimplifies to call eternity timelessness. Though eternity excludes pastness and futurity, it remains correct to speak of it as presence, which after all is one of the three fundamental determinations of time. In the Platonic tradition, which gave the concept its classical development and passed it on through Muslim and Christian theology to modern European philosophy, the present tense retains its temporal sense in affirmations concerning eternity. In this way the Western notion of eternity differs from some Buddhist accounts of *nirvāṇa,* into which not just pastness and futurity but presence as well are dissolved. Platonic eternity by contrast is a paradigmatic presence, and the present in time is its partial but authentic image.

The present is called the "now." Latin metaphysics spoke therefore of eternity as *nunc stans,* a "standing now," and of time as *nunc fluens,* a "flowing now." Since the now of time, which is always experienced as having a certain duration, converges under logical analysis toward the limiting concept of the instantaneous, the dimensionless moment of transition, the problem arises whether the eternal Now is itself a kind of frozen instant, a durationless simplicity about which no experiences of life in time are instructive. Remarkably, the single feature most vividly affirmed of eternity by its classic expositors is that it is life, and not just life but divine life, "a god, manifesting himself as he is," as the third-century CE Neoplatonist mystic Plotinus says in one place (see the following). How does one incorporate a religious discourse in which eternity is divine life into the stark conceptual analyses of pure metaphysics, which seem to lead to a static, almost mathematical abstraction?

The synthesis of logical, psychological, and theological analyses into a rigorous conception of eternity is proprietary to the Platonic philosophical tradition, and is in many ways the single-handed achievement of Plotinus. There are rather complete analogies to the concept in some of the Upaniṣads in India, but in Asia one finds in the main only partial parallels; the metaphysical cake that is the complex Western idea is there cut apart in different ways, so to speak. Pending the outcome of more penetrating philosophical study than the Asian texts have so far received from Western translators and historians, the story of eternity remains at present the story of the Plotinian synthesis, its sources and its influences. The discussion that follows reflects this situation. It reviews, in decreasing detail (1) the classic Platonic conception of eternity as Plotinus understands it, (2) the place of this conception in its own, mainly European, spiritual history, and (3) those points in Indian and Asian philosophy where search for analogous intuitions most plausibly might begin.

Platonic Eternity in Plotinus. In the Platonic tradition, eternity and time are regularly considered together. They make up in fact a single topic, in the old literary sense of the Greek term *topos* ("place"), where it refers to a particular place in a canonical text. The discussion of eternity invariably proceeds among Platonists as a meditation on the place in the *Timaeus* of Plato where eternity is described as "abiding in unity" and time as an "eternal image of eternity, moving according to number" (37d). At a minimum, this passage imposes the idea that eternity and time are in some respect comparable to one another. But Neoplatonism makes a stronger claim for a vision of eternity and time as extremes of a continuum. Life itself, the interior life of the soul, bridges the gap according to Plotinus, and this makes possible an account of the experience of eternity itself.

In some ways it is an extremely familiar experience. Consider reading a book that one finds completely compelling, that draws one along in apparently inexhaustible attentiveness and interest. Hours can pass unregistered; it can be shocking to discover how much time has passed, and how meaningless that fact seems compared with the inner composure and vividness of the interval. Any activity that is intensely self-collected, full of purposiveness and power, can generate this effect—not just intellectual but also aesthetic, even physical activity like dancing or athletics.

Experiences of this kind are a threshold for the pure experience of eternity, contemplation. It is important to notice that they are not without duration, indeed they are rich in inner activity and movement. One experiences something like time in them, but a time that arises more than passes, that gives rather than takes. An inexhaustible power seems to well up within oneself. When, as is inevitable, the spell is broken, one speaks of having fallen away from that power, not of the power itself having lapsed.

Plotinus calls this power the life of the Mind, and in order to express its inexhaustibility says that it is infinite, limitless. In earlier Greek philosophy, to be infinite was to be indefinite, without form or intelligibility, wholly a negative condition. Plotinus too portrays the intelligible world of Platonic Ideas as finite, formally and structurally. But grasped within the living Mind that is its origin and substrate, it is limitlessly vivacious, a world "boiling with life" (6.7.12). The living and dynamic quality of eternal Mind is as central a theme in Plotinus as its simplicity and composure, and is expressed in a remarkable passage where he says that "its nature is to become other in every way," accomplished in a "wandering" (*planē*, as of the planets) within itself that is like a ceaseless adventure on the "plain of truth" (6.7.13).

For the soul that awakens to this presence of mind, the experience is like a homecoming, a coming into oneself rather than a journey to another self or state of existence. The old Platonic image of this movement as an *anamnēsis*, an unforgetting, depended on the Orphic mythical theme of the preexistence of the soul and was therefore easily understood to be a recollection from elsewhere and elsewhen, so to speak. But in Plotinus *anamnēsis* is altogether what it is in Augustine also, an interior conversion of the soul completed in contemplative immediacy—conversion both in the sense of a turning, from distracting cares to tranquil insight, and of a transformation, from the condition of life that is soul to that of pure intellectual apprehension or Mind. [*See* Anamnesis.]

Because the condition of the life of the soul is time, humans fall away from presence of mind in a recurrent downward movement that makes our encounter with eternity multiple and episodic. Yet, "if you look attentively at it again, you will find it as it was" (3.7.5). In that contemplation we will be ourselves again, self-possessed and self-contained, puzzled by the vulnerability to scatteredness and confusion into which the soul falls in time. A traditional term for the self-possession of eternal life is *stasis*, still used in English, and especially in the familiar complaint that the eternity of Greek metaphysics is "static." This is a fundamental misunderstanding.

Stasis means "staying, standing rather than falling, holding together rather than lapsing into dispersion." One can get the sense of eternal stasis best from the English word *homeostasis*, as used in biology to name the dynamic composure that the very diverse movements of metabolism and organic activity maintain within a living system. The simplicity and unity of eternal life is that of a homeostasis, a self-enveloping completion that is at the same time the space for an unlimited enjoyment of activity, purpose, and power.

"Hence," Plotinus writes, "eternity is a majestic thing, and thought declares it identical with the god." He goes on: "Eternity could be well described as a god proclaiming and manifesting himself as he is, that is, as being which is unshakeable and self-identical and always as it is, and firmly grounded in life." From this follows the definition: eternity is "life that is here and now endless because it is total and expends nothing of itself" (3.7.5).

Familiar in the Latin West through the paraphrase of Boethius, "interminabilis vitae tota simul et perfecta possessio" ("the all-at-once total and perfect possession of endless life," *The Consolation of Philosophy* 5.6), the Plotinian experience of eternity marks the divine life as a presence and opens the route of human approach to this life through contemplative mysticism. [*See* Plotinus.]

Historical Background and Consequence. The Greek term we translate as "eternity" in Plato and Plotinus is *aiōn*, and this has given many students of the history of the notion pause. *Aiōn* survives in English in the latinized spelling *aeon*, and here retains much of its original meaning. *Aiōn* means "life, span of life, lifetime; epoch, aeon." While it never suggests duration simply on the level of measure or standard interval, even the Homeric places where it comes closest to meaning "inner life force" include strongly the suggestion of power to perdure, of life reaching out to take up its proper span of time. It seems a very timelike term, not only because of its connotation of span or duration, but because beginning, middle, and end belong so much to the kind of totality or completion it expresses still in English.

The term first occurs in surviving fragments of early Greek philosophy in the fifth-century BCE writer Heraclitus, in the gnome "*Aiōn* is a child playing a board game; the kingly power is a child's" (Heraclitus, B52). The translation "eternity" is clearly inadmissible; those translators who instead supply "time" have good cause. Heraclitus's theme is the spontaneity and immanence of the laws or patterns manifest in the give-and-take of natural processes; the intelligibility of constant change is not outside nature like a god, but the cosmos is in and by itself an "Everliving Fire, flaring up by measure, dying down by measure" (B30). Under the control of this ruling image, *aiōn* again means a form of completion embracing birth and death and the process that weaves them together.

It is not at all clear to what degree Plato distinguishes between the adjectival form *aiōnios*, "eternal," and another term *aïdios*, "everlasting." Because in fact he inclines to the (false) etymology that takes *aiōn* from *aei ōn*, "always being," he gives place to the very confusion the Neoplatonists are most concerned to prevent. In the very text in *Timaeus* that becomes decisive, he says of *aiōn* that "its nature is everlasting [*aïdios*]" (37d).

Among consequences of this situation is a protracted controversy among the Hellenistic Platonists of the centuries around the beginning of the common era concerning what is called "the eternity of the world." The question was whether, as Aristotle argues in the *Metaphysics* (12.6), the world is everlasting and has no beginning in time or whether, as *Timaeus* would suggest if its mythical form were given substantive import, the world began to be at some definite time. Alexandrian Jewish and later Christian Platonists tended to join the argument on the latter side, partly through their effort to coordinate the story in *Timaeus* with that of *Genesis*. It should be clear that once the rigorous nontemporal concept of eternity had been established, it was a mistake to call this question the question of the "eternity" of the world, but only Augustine (*Confessions* 11) diagnoses the category mistake with full philosophical precision.

The antecedents of the Neoplatonic conception of eternity lie not in the lexicography of the term's classical philosophical usage, but in the associations it takes on through the constant interaction of Platonic image and argument with popular religious consciousness. This includes first of all the concern with immortality and afterlife, the context for talk of the eternal life of the soul. Because this concern is profoundly rooted in the archaic, mythological sensibility and its experience of the structure that Mircea Eliade has called "eternal return," it made available the notion of another time, a transcending and divine time that could intersect with mundane time, embedding life in a dimension that surpasses birth and death. The eternity that can be abstracted from this archaic experience is an eternal past more than the eternal present of the proper concept; fundamental imaginative possibilities were appropriated from this origin. The mediating religious context was in large measure the emergence of the mystery religions in the Greco-Roman world, among them the mysteries of baptism and of table blessing central to Christianity.

Aiōn in the New Testament is principally an apocalyptic term, qualified as "this aeon" as against "the aeon to come" (synoptic Gospels, Paul). It shares with the rest of the apocalyptic scenario a Persian, Zoroastrian background, and in a few Pauline or deutero-Pauline places (e.g., *Col.* 1:26, *Eph.* 3:9) seems to be personified in the sense of an equation of Aion with Zurwān, an equation that sets the stage for the florid multiplication of such personified aions in the gnostic literature of the second century CE. Though there has been speculation that this kind of connection between Mediterranean and Near Eastern symbolism contributed to the emergence of the novel Neoplatonic sense of *aiōn*, it seems preferable to portray this as a digression.

A richer question is whether "eternal life" in the *Gospel of John* is consonant with the radical Platonic idea, or already on common ground with it. The predominance of present-tense statements by the glorified Son in that text ("Before Abraham was, I am," *Jn.* 8:58, et al.), its transformation of apocalyptic into realized eschatology, and its eucharist of epiphany and participation ("He who eats my flesh and drinks my blood abides in me, and I in him," *Jn.* 6:56) made it possible for Christian Neoplatonism of the Augustinian type to embrace the strict nontemporal eternity without sensing any violence in its interpretation of scripture.

The story of the appropriation of Plotinian contemplative mysticism by later Christian and Muslim theology defeats summary. Suffice it to say that the Neoplatonic system was adapted to biblical monotheism with considerable penetration and accuracy, especially by Augustine and the Latin tradition through Boethius and Bonaventure, by the apophatic tradition from Dionysius the Areopagite through John Scottus Eriugena to Meister Eckhart, and by Ṣūfī philosophy. The close connection between the theoretical role of eternity as an attribute or name of God and its experiential richness as an element of contemplative spirituality remained characteristic of these traditions.

A certain purely logical interest in the eternity/time contrast, detectable already in Boethius (responding more to Porphyry than Plotinus) and Thomas Aquinas, was amplified by the new mathematical spirit of the metaphysics of the seventeenth century, resulting in the reduction of eternal presence to a kind of schematic simplicity illustrated particularly clearly in the system of Spinoza. The effect was to dissociate the speculative notion from its experiential basis, producing in the end the degraded conception of eternity as lifeless stasis or logical tenselessness that has been the target of complaint in historicist, existentialist, and process theologies of the past century.

Eternity in Non-Western Thought. It is a commonplace that the religious themes of afterlife, divine creation, and the nature of the soul are drawn together in different patterns by non-Western traditions. The Buddha is represented as holding that speculation on none of these furthers one toward enlightenment. It is no surprise to find that a concept like eternity, which emerges at the intersection of these themes in Platonism and then becomes influential precisely through its adaptability to biblical theology, does not always have strict analogies in other religious discourse.

The exegetical and hermeneutical complications that derive from this situation have not always been registered in the translations of non-Western sources. Only some preliminary pointers about other treatments of eternity are here appropriate.

The striking parallels that are being discovered between Neoplatonism and Vedānta philosophy appear to hold also in the case of eternity. The Sanskrit *nitya* can be translated "eternity" with some confidence already in Upaniṣads, especially at the point where "immortality," *amṛta*, is pressed beyond the popular image of outliving death, or life after death, to the radical notion of *mokṣa*, "liberation," deliverance from the cycle of birth and death itself. The fundamental conception in the Upaniṣads that the authentic self, the *ātman,* gathered into its own interior unity from the levels of psychic life, is one with *brahman,* the universal spirit, is developed in ways that regularly parallel the account of the authentic self on the level of the *Nous,* or divine Mind, in Plotinus. It is less clear, however, whether the eternal present, self-consolidated beyond all passage through birth and death, is to be found in the Vedas.

Buddhism presents a much more complex situation. The negative assessment of timelike continuity and the rejection of substantiality and causality that are frequent in Buddhist philosophy lead to descriptions of enlightenment that often have a Platonic ring. In Buddhism, the parallels are particularly pronounced in the meditative traditions that emphasize "sudden enlightenment," where the unconditioned and spontaneous quality of transcendental insight (Skt., *prajñā*) is stressed. In the Mahāyāna Pure Land tradition, the paradisical Sukhāvatī ("land of bliss") of the Buddha Amitābha is sometimes developed in ways reminiscent of the Platonic world of ideal presences, pervaded by divine mentality. If there is an authentic parallel here to the notion of eternity, this will have to be tested by careful analysis of the account of temporal presence itself, for it is this that is ascribed to eternity by Platonism, and in turn made the image of eternity and mark of authentic being for life in time. In those radical portrayals of nirvana as release from all forms of temporal conditioning, not just pastness and futurity, but presence itself sometimes seems to be denied of awakened mind.

A focal problem in the search for analogy to eternity in Chinese thought is the proper account of the first line of the *Tao-te ching,* often translated, "The Tao that can be spoken is not the eternal Tao [*ch'ang tao*]." "Eternal" may overtranslate *ch'ang;* the core meaning is closer to "steadfast," "constant," "abiding." The parallel seems strongest to *aiōn* at the stage it had reached in Heraclitus. It needs study whether the idealization found in the Vedānta or late Platonic pattern is appropriate for interpretation of this text.

Special wariness should be reserved for the use of the phrase "eternal life" in describing prephilosophical doctrines of immortality and afterlife, or "eternal return" for the transcendental relation of divine life to mundane in the experience of cyclical time that is fundamental in myth-using cultures. Most commonly what is meant by "eternal" in this context is "perpetual" or "everlasting." Whether the primordial time of beginnings, the transcendent past of divine creative action, is a predecessor of the eternal present is a separate question that needs careful consideration. While the proper notion of eternity may be very near the surface in Egypt, it is much less likely to exist in the preliterate cultures for which the cycle of death and rebirth is a naturalistic image more than a philosophical idealization.

[*See also* Sacred Time.]

BIBLIOGRAPHY

The concept of eternity is still most accessible from primary sources, notably the treatise "On Eternity and Time" of Plotinus, *Enneads* 3.7.45, in *Plotinus,* translated by A. Hilary Armstrong, "Loeb Classical Library," vol. 3 (Cambridge, Mass., 1966), and book 11 of the *Confessions* of Augustine, for which there are many suitable editions. An instructive summary of the concept in the full technical development it received in medieval theology can be found in the article by Adolf Darlap and Joseph de Finance, "Eternity," in *Sacramentum Mundi,* edited by Karl Rahner (New York, 1968), vol. 2. Mircea Eliade's *Cosmos and History: The Myth of Eternal Return* (New York, 1954) remains a standard introduction to the role of a transcending divine time in the religious experience of myth-using cultures. A very helpful account of eternity is incorporated into a sketch of the history of the idea of immortality in the ancient Near East and Christian Europe by John S. Dunne, *The City of the Gods* (Notre Dame, Ind., 1978). The classic exposition of the interior experience of eternity in Western mysticism is Bonaventure's "The Soul's Journey into God," in *Bonaventure,* edited and translated by Ewert Cousins (New York, 1978). For eternity in Indian thought, the edition of *The Principal Upaniṣads* by Sarvepalli Radhakrishnan (New York, 1953) is especially useful, both for its extensive introduction and its very rich annotations, which include frequent citation of Western parallels.

PETER MANCHESTER

ETHICAL CULTURE, a movement dedicated to the ethical improvement of society and the ethical growth of the individual, was inaugurated with the founding of the New York Society for Ethical Culture in May 1876 by Felix Adler and a group of his Jewish supporters. Adler was the son of Rabbi Samuel Adler of New York's Temple Emanu-El, and he was expected to succeed his father in this cathedral pulpit of American Reform Judaism. But having been exposed in German universities to nineteenth-century science, Kantian philosophy, and historical criticism of religion, he came to reject theism and the finality of Jewish theology even in its most liberal form. His new faith consisted of a passionate belief in the inviolability and power of the moral law and the duty to apply it to society, especially to the problems of industrialization, urbanization, and the working poor.

What initially began as a Sunday lecture movement, somewhat patterned after the Independent Church movement and free religious societies such as those of

O. B. Frothingham, grew under Adler's leadership to become a vital organization spearheading social reforms and social reconstruction. Adler's personal magnetism drew a membership of well over one thousand to the society by the early 1880s, mostly but not exclusively people of Jewish origin. He also attracted ethically idealistic and socially committed people of liberal Christian background whom he helped groom to be leaders of other Ethical Culture societies. The Ethical Culture movement took on a national flavor as Adler's apprentices organized new societies in other cities: William M. Salter, Chicago, 1883; S. Burns Weston, Philadelphia, 1885; Walter L. Sheldon, Saint Louis, 1886. The American societies federated as a national organization in 1889, the American Ethical Union, and over the years, new societies springing up in urban and suburban areas across the country (Brooklyn, Westchester County, Washington, Baltimore, Pittsburgh, Los Angeles, Cleveland, Essex County, N.J.) were added to its roster. By 1930, membership in American Ethical Culture societies numbered about 3,500, and by the mid-1980s, membership in the more than twenty societies totaled approximately 5,000. (The largest society remains the New York branch, at about 1,000.)

Ethical Culture became truly international in scope in the 1890s. The London Ethical Society had been founded in 1886, with such distinguished thinkers participating as Bernard Bosanquet, Edward Caird, and Leslie Stephen, and British interest had been spurred when Stanton Coit, another Adler apprentice, arrived in 1887 and led London's South Place Chapel into the Ethical Culture movement. Coit subsequently created a British Ethical Union in 1896. The movement reached Germany, where a society was founded in Berlin in 1892, and societies also appeared in France, Austria, Italy, Switzerland, and Japan in this new decade. The various societies, each with its own nuanced organizational goals and ethical approaches, were in contact and quite cognizant of each other's activities. At a Zurich meeting in 1896 they created an international confederation, the International Ethical Union, which kept member organizations in touch with each other and which also convened world congresses devoted to specific themes, such as those in London (1908) and the Hague (1912). In the wake of World War II the union became moribund, but in 1952 humanist organizations joined with Ethical Culture societies led by the American Ethical Union to found the International Humanist and Ethical Union with member groups in North and Latin America, Europe, Africa, Asia, and Australia.

Whether or not Ethical Culture is judged a religion depends on one's definition of *religion* and one's inclination either to use or not use the word to designate an ethical humanist posture. Felix Adler did regard Ethical Culture to be a religion and in his later years tried to work out a metaphysic to express it. Still, he adamantly insisted that Ethical Culture embraced all in ethical fellowship regardless of diverse approaches and different names given to the quest for meaning in life. This openness has clearly persisted to this day. Nonetheless, the societies do assume the guise of a religious organization to some extent. (In the United States, many are incorporated as "religious and educational" institutions in their respective states.) A weekly meeting is usually held on Sunday morning or evening (in Germany, during the weekdays), consisting of music, an inspirational reading, and a major address on a topical issue, usually with an eye to its ethical implications. There are no symbols or ritual acts, although the English societies tend to be a bit more ceremonial. Ethical leaders officiate at life-cycle events such as marriage and funerals; they come individually from a variety of social and intellectual backgrounds and may have previous religious affiliations. There is no Ethical Culture seminary, but each prospective leader undertakes a personally tailored training program administered by the Leadership Training Committee of the American Ethical Union.

No established Ethical Culture ideology exists, although general principles certainly have been articulated. To a large extent, Adler's early motto, "Not the creed, but the deed," still serves as the unifying theoretical orientation of Ethical Culture, although with a deepened and richer meaning than Adler himself provided. Members are free to believe what they wish on all issues, including religion, but they generally subscribe to the following ideals: (1) the intrinsic worth of each human being, (2) the importance of seeking ethical principles as a guide to all aspects of life, and (3) the need to work for the material and spiritual betterment of society and humanity.

This last commitment to applied social ethics rather than to any theoretical formulation of an ethical approach has been the quintessential characteristic of Ethical Culture from its inception. In this regard, the Ethical Culture movement, particularly in the United States, has been quite successful, far beyond its limited membership. Its leaders in the first four to five decades—Adler, Salter, Weston, Coit, John L. Elliott, Alfred Martin, David Muzzey, Henry Newman, Algernon D. Black, among others—were actively involved in most of the progressive causes of social welfare and reform. They and their societies were pioneers in the areas of education for young and old, tenement reforms, settlement work, legal aid societies, boys' clubs, good government clubs, and visiting nursing associations. Many of their ventures—free kindergarten (1877), district visiting nursing (1877), the Neighborhood Guild (1886), the Bureau of Justice (1888), the Arts High School (1913)—served as models for similar undertakings by urban communities. In more recent decades, Ethical Culture, while not a leader as it once was, has nevertheless been involved with significant programs supporting liberal social causes, such as prison reform, drug rehabilitation, the right to abortion. The movement has also sponsored journals of popular and scholarly nature to reflect on the ethical domain as it relates to public policy and philosophy: *Ethical Record* (1888); *International Journal of Ethics* (1890); *Ethical Addresses* (1895); *The Standard* (1914); *Ethical Outlook* (1956); *Ethical Forum* (1965).

[*See also the biography of Adler and, for a broader context,* Morality and Religion.]

BIBLIOGRAPHY

The most comprehensive one-volume history of Ethical Culture is Howard B. Radest's *Toward Common Ground: The Story of the Ethical Societies in the United States* (New York, 1969), which deals with the origins and evolution of the movement through the 1960s. Although written by an insider, the book is not unwilling to take a critical look at the movement and its leaders. My book *From Reform Judaism to Ethical Culture: The Religious Evolution of Felix Adler* (Cincinnati, 1979) gives a detailed institutional history of the founding of the New York Society for Ethical Culture and forwards a careful analysis of Adler's early ideological postures. Important evaluations of the meaning of Ethical Culture can be found in Horace L. Friess's *Felix Adler and Ethical Culture* (New York, 1981), which traces the development of Adler's own thinking on the subject, from initial conceptions to mature reformulations. Robert S. Guttchen's *Felix Adler* (New York, 1974) analyzes Adler's concept of human worth, which remains vital to Ethical Culture's own self-understanding. Another important analysis of Ethical Culture has been made by David S. Muzzey in *Ethics as a Religion*, 2d ed. (New York, 1967). A second-generation leader in the movement, and distinguished professor of American history, Muzzey argues for the religious nature of Ethical Culture. The book contains a brief, useful epilogue on the founding of the movement by Adler.

BENNY KRAUT

ETHICS. *See* Morality and Religion; *see also* Buddhist Ethics; Christian Ethics; *and* Jewish Thought and Philosophy, *article on* Jewish Ethical Literature.

ETHIOPIAN CHURCH.

The Ethiopian or Abyssinian church, on the Horn of Africa, is one of the five so-called monophysite churches that reject the Council of Chalcedon (451) and its formula of faith. The church does not call itself monophysite but rather Tawāḥedo ("Unionite"), a word expressing the union in Christ of the human and divine natures, to distinguish itself from the Eastern Orthodox churches, which accept the formulas accepted at Chalcedon. For the Tawāḥedo Orthodox Church of Ethiopia, both Nestorius and Eutyches are heretics. Although formally under the jurisdiction of the Coptic church of Alexandria until 1950, the Ethiopian Orthodox church has managed to retain its indigenous language, literature, art, and music. It expects its faithful to practice circumcision, observe the food prescriptions set forth in the Hebrew scriptures (Old Testament), and honor Saturday as the Sabbath. The church has its own liturgy, including an horologion (initially for each of the twenty-four hours of the day), a missal of over fourteen anaphoras, the Deggwā (an antiphonary for each day of the year), doxologies (various collections of *nagś* hymns), and homiliaries in honor of the angels, saints, and martyrs. The most innovative aspect of this church is the provision in the Deggwā for the chanting of *qenē* (poetic hymns) in the liturgy. There are several types of *qenē* varying in number of lines from two to eleven, which one of the clergy usually improvises during the service in keeping with the spirit of *Psalms* 149:1, "Sing unto the Lord a new song."

Until the Ethiopian revolution of 1974, the Ethiopian Orthodox church (which in the mid-1980s had a membership of about twenty million people, or about half of the population) had been a national church defended by the political leader of the country. The monarch's reign had to be legitimized by the church at a religious ceremony where the new king swore allegiance to the church and committed himself to defend the Christian kingdom.

Early History. Historians disagree in assigning a date to the introduction of Christianity into Ethiopia, depending upon which Ethiopian king they think first adopted the faith. The conversion of the monarch, however, is a poor indication of the date of that introduction because not only was he by no means among the country's first converts, but also because until about 960, the monarchy changed hands so frequently that the ruler was not as consistently Christian as were certain segments of the population. We should also be wary of using the local tradition that the Ethiopian eunuch Qināqis (*Acts* 8:26–39) was martyred teaching Christianity in Ethiopia as evidence of the country's conversion. However, we do know that Adulis, the famous port of Ethiopia, and Aksum, the capital, were frequented by Christian traders from the Hellenistic world since the early history of Christianity. Some of these settled there, forming Christian communities and attracting to their religion those with whom they interacted daily. [*See* Aksumite Religion.]

Ethiopia officially joined the Christian world when Frumentius was consecrated its first bishop by Athanasius of Alexandria in about 347. The contemporary historian Rufinus (*Ecclesiastical History* 1.9) tells us how this came about. A certain ship was attacked while calling on one of the Ethiopian ports. Of the voyagers, only two Syrian boys from Tyre (modern-day south Lebanon), Frumentius and Aedesius, escaped death. The boys were taken to the palace, where the king made Frumentius his secretary and Aedesius his cupbearer. Frumentius used his influence in the palace to facilitate the building of an oratory by the Christians in the city. This center was also used as a school where children, even those from non-Christian families, came to receive religious instruction. As soon as the two foreigners received their freedom, Frumentius went to Alexandria to ask the archbishop there to consecrate a bishop for the Christians in Ethiopia. Athanasius thereupon chose Frumentius to be the bishop of Aksum. Rufinus says that he received this story "from the mouth of Aedesius himself," who became a priest in Tyre. Even though Rufinus, like some other historians, calls the country "India," there is no doubt that the story deals with Ethiopia. A letter from the Arian emperor, Constantius II (r. 337–361), to the rulers of Ethiopia, Ezana (ʿĒzānā) and Sazana, concerning Frumentius is extant in Athanasius's *Apology to Constantine* (*Patrologia Graeca*, ed. by J.-P. Migne, 25. 636–637). From Ezana's rule to the middle of the twentieth century, the head of the Ethiopian church remained a Copt. It was only in the twentieth century that an Ethiopian, Bāsleyos (1951–1970), was consecrated patriarch. It must be noted, however, that the Coptic metropolitan was in charge primarily of spiritual and theological matters. The administration of other church affairs was the responsibility of a native official with the title of *ʿaqqābē saʿāt* and subsequently *echagē*.

Medieval Period. The Ethiopian church took many significant steps forward between the fourth and the seventh century. It vigorously translated a great deal of Christian literature from Greek. This included the Old Testament from the Septuagint and the New Testament from the Lucianic recension (the Greek Bible revised by Lucian of Antioch, d. 312) used in the Syrian church. The Ethiopian Bible of eighty-one books includes the *Book of Jubilees* and the *Book of Enoch*, two books which have been preserved in their entirety only in Ethiopic. The *Synodicon* (a collection of canon law), the *Didascalia Apostolorum* (a church order), the *Testament of Our Lord*, and the *Qalēmenṭos* (an apocalyptic writing ascribed to Clement of Rome) are also part of the Ethiopian canonical scriptures. The number of churches and monasteries also grew quickly. Traveling through Ethiopian territories in the sixth century, a Greek monk, Cosmas Indicopleustes, was impressed to see churches everywhere.

It has been suggested that the *Rule of Pachomius* and the theological writings of the Fathers in the *Qērelos* (including writings from Cyril of Alexandria, Epiphanius, et al.) were brought to Ethiopia by the so-called Nine Saints who came from the Hellenistic or Mediterranean world, including Egypt, in the sixth or seventh century. But any of the many travelers and anchorites (such as Abbā Yoḥannes Kamā) who came to Ethiopia much earlier than the Nine Saints might have brought them along with several other works. Our historical knowledge about the Nine Saints is not firmly based even though they are highly revered in the church as the founders of monasticism in Ethiopia.

Unfortunately for the faithful, the young church suffered encroachment and harassment by Islam, starting in the eighth century. Locally, too, a vassal queen of one of the provinces, Gudit, revolted and devastated the Christian civilization, paving the way for another dynasty, the Zāgwē (1137–1270).

The Zāgwē kings were more interested in religion than in politics. Many of them were priests as well as rulers, and the last four of the dynasty are, in fact, among the saints of the church. The building of the several rock-hewn churches in Lāstā (central Ethiopia) is ascribed to them. The so-called Solomonic dynasty, which was to overthrow them, would boast of its alleged descendance from Solomon of Israel, while the Zāgwē attempted to reproduce the holy places in their own land, calling their capital Roha (after Edessa), their river Yordanos (after Jordan), and so on.

In 1270 the clergy, led by Takla Hāymānot, the founder of the Monastery of Dabra Libanos (in Shewa), and Iyyasus Mo'a, the founder of the Monastery of Ḥayq Esṭifānos (in Amhara), collaborated with Yekunno Amlāk to overthrow the Zāgwē and to found the Solomonic dynasty. Although the Solomonic kings did not always observe the church's teaching, it was nonetheless during this period that indigenous religious literature flourished, and Christianity spread into the south and west through the efforts of the monks of Dabra Libanos of Shewa, the twelve *neburāna ed*, chosen by the metropolitan according to the number of the apostles.

Religious Controversies. Late in the medieval period and afterward, religious controversies arose because of objections by some to the tradition of undue reverence for the Cross, icons of the Madonna and Child, and the king. We hear of these disputes during the reign of Yāqbe'a Ṣeyon (r. 1285–1294), and they appear again in the days of Sayfa Arʿada (r. 1344–1372). The controversies became serious during the reign of Zar'a Yāʿeqob (1434–1468), when an anchorite, Esṭifānos, succeeded in attracting to his teaching of rejection of the tradition many monks who, like him, refused to be shaken by the dreadful persecution that ensued. Another controversy, this time involving the Coptic church also, centered around the Sabbath observance of Saturday in addition to Sunday. Several monasteries, led by the monk Ēwosṭātēwos (d. 1369), successfully defied the decree of the king and the Coptic metropolitan that sought to abolish the practice of observing the "first Sabbath" (Saturday). But the most serious controversy dealt with the concept of the unity and trinity of God. The church taught that each person in the Trinity (three suns with one light) has a form or image, *malke'*, which must look like that of man because man was created in God's image (*Gn.* 1:27). The "heretics," followers of Zamikā'ēl, while admitting that God has an image, refused to define his form, quoting *John* 1:18—"No one has seen God." They also maintained a different theology of the unity and trinity of God (one sun with three attributes—disc, light, and heat). Another dispute developed when some monasteries objected to the use of the Deggwā in the liturgy; this intricate collection of antiphonary hymns recommends dancing while chanting during service (*Ps.* 150:4). The number of canonical books and the inclusion of the pseudepigrapha and the pseudoapostolic writings in the canon were also challenged.

Religious Civil War of the Sixteenth Century. The chronic skirmishes between the Christians and the Muslims in Ethiopia took a different form in the sixteenth century when the latter, led by Imam Aḥmad ibn Ibrāhīm al-Ghāzī or Grāññ Maḥammad, sought and received help from the Turks. By this time also the astounding wealth of the individual churches in solid gold, silver, and precious clothes had become an irresistible booty and the grāññ sacked the monasteries and burned the churches of the empire for about fifteen years (1527–1542). The Christians turned to Portugal for help. The army of the imam collapsed when he was killed in early 1543. But it was about this time that the Cushitic people the Galla, who call themselves Oromo, migrated into Ethiopia en masse, destroying a great part of the Christian heritage that had escaped the grāññ's devastation.

The Jesuits' Enterprise. The Portuguese came to help the church in her war against Islam with the assumption that "the lost flock," the church of Ethiopia, would come back to the Roman Catholic church. The Ethiopians, however, were never ready to abandon their faith. The pressure of the Jesuits, however, which started with missionaries sent by Pope Julius III (1487–1555), continued until the seventeenth century, when they succeeded in converting Emperor Suseneyos (r. 1607–1632) to Catholicism. In 1626 a Catholic patriarch, Alphonsus Mendez, came from Rome, and the emperor issued a decree that his subjects should follow his own example. However, the sweeping change that Mendez attempted to introduce into the age-old religious traditions of the nation met with stiff resistance. Led by the monastic leaders, tens of thousands of the faithful were martyred. The Catholic missionaries were finally asked to leave, and the emperor was assassinated, even though he had abdicated the throne to his son Fāsiladas (r. 1632–1667). Fāsiladas was magnanimous with the Jesuits despite the fact that they had attempted to overthrow him by courting one of his brothers.

Even though the Jesuits left, the controversy stemming from their theology of the two natures of Christ continues to the present, taking a local character and creating schism in the Ethiopian church. Overtly, this controversy is centered on the theological significance of *qeb'at*, "unction" (*Acts* 10:38), and *bakwr*, "firstborn" (*Rom.* 8:29), when applied to Christ the Messiah, the only Son of God. But those who raised these questions were clearly attempting to show the "monophysites" the implication of a theology of one nature in Christ, by drawing their attention to the distinct presence of the human nature in him and its inferior position vis-à-vis his divinity. For one group, the Kārroch, or Tawāḥedo (the "Unionists" of Tegrāy), whose position the church has held officially since 1878, *unction* means the union of divinity with humanity: Christ, who is the ointment and the anointed, became the natural Son of God in his humanity through this union. For the Qebatoch ("unctionists" of Gonder and Gojam), *unction* means that Christ in his humanity became the natural Son of God through the unction of the Holy Spirit: God the Father is the anointer, the Son the anointed, and the Holy Spirit the ointment. The third group, the Ṣaggoch ("adoptionists" of Shewa), who are accused of tending toward Catholicism, believe that Christ in his humanity became the Son of God by grace through the unction of the Holy Spirit either in Mary's womb at the Annunciation or at the baptism. They call the occasion when he became the Son of God by grace a third birth for Christ, in relation to the eternal birth from the Father and the temporal birth from Mary, hence the heresy of the "three births" condemned at the Council of Boru Mēdā in Welo (central Ethiopia) in 1878. The Ṣaggoch vehemently oppose the notion that Christ became the natural Son of God in his humanity. They are, however, in the minority.

The Church outside Africa. Designed to express its spiritual message and to perform the services in the local culture, the Ethiopian church is strictly local and national. In its history it has not engaged in any missionary activities beyond the frontiers that political leaders claimed to be territories of their ancestors. King Kālēb's expedition to Najrān (southern Arabia) in about 525, to rescue the Christians from the persecution of a Jewish ruler and to reorganize the Christian communities there, may not be considered sustained activity by the church outside Ethiopia. Even the Ethiopian churches in the Holy Land could not be exceptions to this historical fact, since they were built to serve Ethiopian nationals who visited the holy places in Palestine and Egypt. Ethiopian monastic communities have lived in Jerusalem since the Middle Ages, and they were Ethiopia's main window to the outside world. In modern times, there were also Ethiopian churches in the former British Somaliland, Kenya, and the Sudan, but they too were serving Ethiopian nationals, refugees who fled the 1936–1941 Italian occupation of Ethiopia.

In the 1950s the Ethiopian church was faced with a most unusual challenge. The local church was called upon to respond to the need for cultural and racial identity of the oppressed black people in Africa and the Americas. Churches with the term *Abyssinian* as part of their name started to emerge in these continents. Although the historical link between the Ethiopian church and these churches is lacking, and the Ethiopian church was not economically, educationally, and politically up to the challenge, delegates consisting of clergymen were sent from Ethiopia to East Africa (still under British rule), the Caribbean region, and North America. The inevitable problems were how to attract the middle class to an African church and how to adapt the culturally alien church services to English-speaking communities in Africa and the Americas, not to mention the question of rebaptism. The compromise reached was to retain some parts of the liturgy in Geʿez and conduct the rest in English. This compromise was not only unsatisfactory to both the church authorities and congregations, but it also meant training the clergy, Ethiopians and non-Ethiopians alike, in Geʿez and English. In spite of several problems, the church is gaining strength, especially in the West Indies and the Carribean (e.g., Jamaica, Guyana, Trinidad, and Tobago). The number of the faithful in the United States (New York, Washington, D.C., and Los Angeles) is growing because of the influx of Ethiopian refugees fleeing the military Marxist repression that started with the overthrow of the monarchy in 1974. It is not clear how they will solve their problem of allegiance to the mother church in Ethiopia, which is controlled by the Marxist government.

BIBLIOGRAPHY

For the history of both the church and the country, Jean Doresse's *Ethiopia* (London, 1959) is a good introduction even though it lacks annotation to the sources. Carlo Conti Rossini's *Storia d'Etiopia*, vol. 1, *Dalle origini all' avvento della dinastia Salomonide* (Bergamo, 1928), remains the standard reference for the early history. Unfortunately, however, this book too has neither adequate annotation to sources nor a bibliography. An index for it has been prepared by Edward Ullendorff in *Rassegna di studi etiopici* 18 (1962): 97–141.

The only book that examines many aspects of the Ethiopian Bible is Edward Ullendorff's *Ethiopia and the Bible* (Oxford, 1968). This book also contains an excellent bibliography. See also Roger W. Cowley's *The Traditional Interpretation of the Apocalypse of St. John in the Ethiopian Orthodox Church* (Cambridge, 1983). The introduction to this work offers more than the title suggests. The history of Geʿez (Ethiopic) literature has been ably surveyed in Enrico Cerulli's *La letteratura etiopica*, 3d ed. (Florence, 1968). Ernst Hammerschmidt's *Studies in the Ethiopic Anaphoras* (Berlin, 1961) summarizes the different studies of the anaphoras in one small volume. For an English version of the anaphoras themselves, see Marcos Daoud and Marsie Hazen's *The Liturgy of the Ethiopian Church* (Cairo, 1959). The most comprehensive study thus far on *qenē* hymns is Anton Schall's *Zur äthiopischen Verskunst* (Wiesbaden, 1961).

The period of the Zāgwē dynasty and the rock-hewn churches of Lāstā are well treated in Georg Gerster's *Churches in Rock* (London, 1970), with many large and impressive photographs and an adequate bibliography. The history of the church from the beginning of the Solomonic dynasty to the Islamic invasion of the sixteenth century has been uniquely treated in Taddesse Tamrat's *Church and State in Ethiopia, 1270–1527* (Oxford, 1972). Francisco Alvarez's *Narrative of the Portuguese Embassy to Abyssinia during the Years 1520–1527*, translated by Lord Stanley of Alderley (London, 1881), is a rare description of church and secular life immediately before the war with the *grāññ*. The translation was revised by C. F. Beckingham and G. W. B. Huntingford and published under the title *The Prester John of the Indies*, 2 vols. (Cambridge, 1961).

Some of the sources for the religious controversies of the late medieval period were edited and translated in Enrico Cerulli's *Il libro etiopico dei miracoli di Maria e le sue fonti nelle letterature del medio evo latino* (Rome, 1943) and *Scritti teologici etiopici dei secoli XVI-XVII*, 2 vols., "Studi e testi," no. 198 (Rome, 1958).

The unique source for the destruction of the churches by the forces of the *grāññ* in the sixteenth century is *Futūḥ al-Ḥabashah*, composed by ʿArab Faqīh, the chronicler of the imam, edited and translated in René Basset's *Histoire de la conquête de l'Abyssinie (seizième siècle) par Chihab ed-Din Aḥmed ben ʿAbd el-Qâder surnommé Arab-Faqih*, 2 vols. (Paris, 1898–1901). The Portuguese, too, have left invaluable though sometimes exaggerated and conflicting reports of the campaign. See *The Portuguese Expedition to Abyssinia in 1541–1543, as Narrated by Castanhoso, with Some Letters, the Short Account of Bermudez, and Certain Extracts from Correa* (London, 1902).

The best work on the religious controversies that started in the seventeenth century is Friedrich Heyer's *Die Kirche Äthiopiens: Eine Bestandsaufnahme* (Berlin and New York, 1971). This book is also the best description of the church in its present setting. The history of the religious controversy caused particularly by the Portuguese has been ably and succinctly presented in Germa Beshah and Merid Wolde Aregay's *The Question of the Union of the Churches in Luso-Ethiopian Relations (1500–1632)* (Lisbon, 1964). See also Donald Crummey's *Priests and Politicians: Protestant and Catholic Missions in Orthodox Ethiopia, 1830–1868* (Oxford, 1972). The book has an excellent bibliography with useful comments on some of the works.

Questions about the church that are of interest to Western Christians are answered in *The Teaching of the Abyssinian Church as Set forth by the Doctors of the Same,* translated from Amharic, the vernacular of Ethiopia, by A. F. Matthew (London, 1936). See also Harry Middleton Hyatt's *The Church of Abyssinia* (London, 1928). This work describes in detail the religious practices of the church.

Kirsten Pedersen's *The History of the Ethiopian Community in the Holy Land from the Time of Emperor Tewodros II till 1974* (Jerusalem, 1983) is a result of several years of study of the original and secondary sources on the subject. The minor mistakes pertaining to modern history of Ethiopia do not in any way minimize the usefulness of this work. The major English sources on all aspects of the church are surveyed in Jon Bonk's *An Annotated and Classified Bibliography of English Literature Pertaining to the Ethiopian Orthodox Church* (Metuchen, N.J., 1984).

GETATCHEW HAILE

ETHNOASTRONOMY. [*This entry is limited to discussion of the ethnoastronomies of native South America because of their primary importance in the development of this area of study.*]

Patterns. In the ethnographic literature on indigenous South American Indian populations, there is a considerable body of evidence attesting to the importance of ethnoastronomical beliefs. These beliefs, expressed with varying degrees of emphasis in mythology and ritual, bear witness to long-standing traditions of astronomical observations undertaken for a variety of purposes, ranging from the construction of precise calendar systems to the production of symbols and metaphors for expressing enduring relationships that characterize interactions between men and women, social groups, humans and animals, and so forth. While there are no universally shared astronomical symbols, several recurrent thematic patterns emerge from a comparative study of the ways in which different groupings of celestial bodies are interrelated in the mythology and ritualism of the Andean and Tropical Forest (Amazonian and Orinocoan) religious traditions.

Sun and Moon. A clear expression of the notion of the thematic patterning of relations in an astronomical mode is found in a number of origin myths, especially those in which the origin of humans is thought to have occurred virtually simultaneously with their separation into different—but complementary—kinship or social categories (e.g., siblings, spouses, clans, or moieties). The Apinagé of the Araguaya River of Brazil hold that Sun created the two moieties and localized one (the Kolti moiety) in his own northern half of the circular villages while leaving the other (the Kolre) with his sister, Moon, in the south. The Apinagé held ceremonies directed to Sun during the planting and harvesting periods, while they invoked Moon to help the crops mature (Nimuendajú, 1967, p. 164).

The pairing of Sun and Moon as, respectively, brother and sister is also found among the Tapirapé (Wagley, 1940, p. 256) and the Conibo *(Handbook of South American Indians,* 1948, p. 595; hereafter referred to as *H.S.A.I.).* Among the Chiriguano (*H.S.A.I.*, 1948, pp. 483–484), the Koghi (Reichel-Dolmatoff, 1982, p. 178), and the Inca, Sun and Moon are simultaneously brother and sister and husband and wife. For the Xerente, who once occupied several villages southeast of the Apinagé along the Tocantins River, Sun and Moon are "companions" (i.e., neither siblings nor spouses), although each is associated with one of the two moieties. Sun, who is referred to by all Xerente regardless of their moiety affiliation as "Our Creator," communicated with the Siptato moiety through a group of intermediaries, including Venus, Jupiter, the Belt of Orion, and κ Orionis; the intermediaries between Moon and the people of the Sdakra moiety are Mars, Carrion Vultures, and Seven Stars (probably the Pleiades; Nimuendajú, 1942, pp. 84–85).

Through the association of Sun and Moon with linked pairs of complementary, yet often asymmetric and hierarchical, social categories (e.g., husband and wife, brother and sister, and the moieties), astronomical phenomena are made to participate in the process of classifying human society on the basis of fundamental dichotomies and processes (e.g., alliance and reproduction) that occur throughout the natural world. The relations between Sun and Moon serve as the "charter" for cosmic and social order throughout the succession of the generations.

Yet just as inevitably as social order is established and maintained within each society by rules governing relations among different groups of people, the rules are forever being broken and the right order of things momentarily threatened. The inevitability of disorder arising from the violation of rules and prohibitions has its celestial reminder in the spots besmirching the face of the full moon. Throughout the mythological traditions of the tropical forest, the spots on the moon are commonly associated with incestuous relations, especially between brothers and sisters. In a typical example of this theme, the Záparoan-speaking tribes of the Marañón, Napo, and Pastaza rivers say that Moon was formerly a man who, in the dark of night, had sexual intercourse with his sister. In order to identify her lover, the girl one night smeared his face with *genipa* (a blue-black vegetable dye). Out of shame, the man went away to the sky and became the moon, his *genipa*-covered face being reexposed to the Záparo every month (*H.S.A.I.*, 1948, p. 649; cf. Roth, 1908–1909, p. 255; Wagley, 1940, p. 256). Asocial (incestuous) sexual relations may generally be compared with unproductive sexual encounters, which are everywhere signaled by menstruation. Among the contemporary Quechua of the Peruvian highlands, Sun (Inti) is male and Moon (Killa) is female; menses is referred to as *killa chayamushan* ("moon coming, or arriving").

Sun and Moon are also often associated with brightly colored birds or with the plumage of such birds. For example, the Trumai and the Paresí (*H.S.A.I.*, 1948, pp. 348, 360) say that Sun is a ball or headdress of red parrot feathers, while they identify Moon as a collection of yellow feathers. In the Záparo myth discussed above, the wife of the incestuous man who became the moon was herself simultaneously transformed into a night bird. And in a congeries of these various bird images and relations, the Tapirapé of central Brazil, west of the Araguaya River, say that Moon was the sister of Sun and that the latter wears a headdress of red parrot feathers. Sun is said to have slapped Moon's face with his *genipa*-covered hand because of her sexual misbehavior. Moon was married to a culture hero who divided all birds into two groups. Among the Tapirapé, the two men's moities are subdivided into three age grades, each of which carries the name of a bird (Wagley, 1940, p. 256).

The Milky Way. Aside from the sun and the moon, one other celestial phenomenon is important throughout the ethnoastronomies of South America: the Milky Way. The Milky Way serves as a means for organizing and orienting the celestial sphere in the spatial, temporal, and mythological dimensions. The Quechua-speakers of the Peruvian Andes refer to the Milky Way as a river *(mayu)* composed of two branches. The branches originate in the north within the cosmic sea that encircles the earth. Water is taken into the Milky Way, and the two branches separate, flowing away from each other toward the south, where they collide in the heavens near the Southern Cross. The foam *(posuqu)* stirred up by their collision is seen in the bright clouds of the southern Milky Way from the Southern Triangle to the False Cross in Carina. The two branches of the celestial river alternately rise, pass through the zenith, and set; one branch, when it stands in the zenith, passes from the northeast to the southwest, while the other branch passes from the northwest through the zenith to the southeast (Urton, 1981, pp. 54–63).

The Barasana, a Tucanoan-speaking group on the Vaupés River in Colombia, conceive of the Milky Way as divided into two "star paths"; one, called New Path, is oriented southeast-northwest, while the other, Old Path, is oriented northeast-southwest. New Path and Old Path are the sites of most of the constellations recognized by the Barasana (Hugh-Jones, 1982, p. 182). For the Desána, another Tucanoan-speaking group of the Vaupés region, the Milky Way, as a single construct, is likened to a river, a trail in the forest, an immense cortege of people, a cast-off snake skin, and a fertilizing stream of semen. In a dualistic image focusing on its cyclical, alternating axes, the Milky Way is imagined as two huge snakes: the starry, luminous part is a rainbow boa, a male principle; the dark part is an anaconda, a female principle. The shifting of the Milky Way, seen as a swinging motion made by the two snakes, punctuates the cycle of fertilizing forces emanating from the sky (Reichel-Dolmatoff, 1982, pp. 170–171).

Using metaphors of human sexuality that recall the menstrual cycle of the moon, the Barasana, like the Desána, conceive of the Milky Way as participating in a cycle of fertilizing forces. The connection between the principle of fertility, the Milky Way, and the flow of menses is occasioned by the comparison of the menstrual and seasonal cycles. The rainy season is the menstrual period of the sky, which is personified by Woman Shaman, a creator who has a gourd of wax identified with the Pleiades, which are called Star Thing and are the principal aspect of the New Path of the Milky Way. The gourd is Woman Shaman's vagina; the wax, her menstrual blood; and the melting of the wax, her menstrual period, which is compared, as an internal, rejuvenating "skin change," to the rainy season, which begins in the Vaupés in April, as the stars of the Pleiades set. In Barasana cosmology, the internal skin change of Woman Shaman, associated with Star Thing (the gourd of melting wax), is contrasted with the external skin change of the constellation called Caterpillar Jaguar (Scorpius), which stands opposed to, and alternates with, Star Thing (Hugh-Jones, 1982, pp. 196–197).

Bright-star and dark-cloud constellations. Data from the Barasana and Desána introduce a final and far more complex recurrent theme, one that forms perhaps the core of ethnoastronomical symbolism among South American Indian societies. This theme concerns groups of interrelated metaphorical images built up out of animals, anthropomorphic beings, and constellations stretched along the bright path or paths of the Milky Way.

The theme of animals and humans as constellations concerns a group of celestial phenomena located principally along, or within, the path of the Milky Way. In order to understand many of the references discussed below, it is necessary to see the Milky Way as visually composed of two distinct but interconnected elements: first, it appears in its overall form as a wide, bright band of stars; and second, it contains several dark spots and streaks formed by fixed clouds of interstellar gas that cut through the central path. Both of these galactic phenomena, the bright band of stars against the dark background of the night sky and the dark clouds cutting through the bright path of stars, are recognized as named celestial constructs in South American ethnoastronomical traditions.

When viewed as a path, the Milky Way is often considered to be a road along which animals, humans, and spirits move. The Indians of Guiana refer to the Milky Way as both the "path of the tapir" and the path that is walked upon by a group of people bearing white clay, the type used for making pottery (Roth, 1908–1909, p. 260). The Chiriguano (*H.S.A.I.*, 1948, p. 483) know the Milky Way as the "path of the rhea"; they identify the head of the rhea either with the Southern Cross or with the Coalsack, the dark spot at the foot of the Southern Cross. The Amahuaca say that the Milky Way is the trail or path of the sun, formed when a jaguar dragged a manatee across the sky. For the Trumai, the Milky Way is like a drum containing animals; it is the road to the afterworld and the abode of jaguars (*H.S.A.I.*, 1948, p. 348). Finally, the Tapirapé see in the Milky Way the "path of the shamans," by which shamans travel to the sky to visit celestial bodies (Wagley, 1940, p. 257).

That many of the characters who move along the celestial path (or river) are animals reinforces the observation that the most common identifications of the dark clouds that cut through the Milky Way are with animals, birds, or fish. As mentioned earlier, among the Quechua of Peru the Milky Way is seen as two interconnected branches of a river. Within the river, in the southern skies, are several animals, each identified as one of the dark clouds *(yana phuyu);* these include a snake, a toad, a tinamou, a mother llama with her baby, and a fox that pursues the llamas (Urton, 1981, p. 170). The pursuit of a herbivore by a carnivore, as in the pursuit of the llamas by the fox, is a common element in the South American ethnoastronomical symbolism of the dark spots. Within the tropical forest, however, the carnivore is most often a jaguar rather than a fox. For instance, the Paresí and Conibo see a jaguar pursuing a deer in some dark spots in the southern Milky Way (*H.S.A.I.*, 1948, pp. 360, 595). Certain tribes of Guiana see, in the same general area, a tapir being chased by a dog, which in turn is pursued by a jaguar (Roth, 1908–1909, p. 260). The Tukuna locate the bodies of a jaguar and an anteater in dark clouds in the southern skies near the constellation of Centaurus; the two animals are locked in a nightly struggle, although in a Takuna myth that describes a similar fight the anteater defeats the jaguar, rips open his stomach, and sucks out his liver (Nimuendajú, 1952, p. 143). The Campa say that a dark streak near Antares (in the constellation of Scorpius) is a digging stick and that the Coalsack below the Southern Cross is a bees' nest (Weiss, 1972, p. 160). The Múra, however, see in the Coalsack a manatee carrying a fisherman on its back (*H.S.A.I.*, 1948, p. 265).

As is clear from the illustrations above, the identification of the dark clouds of the Milky Way with animals is a widely shared feature in South American Indian ethnoastronomies. Although the specific animals vary from tradition to tradition (as one would expect, given that the various ethnoastronomical data derive from societies in widely differing environmental settings), it is reasonable to suppose that the animals may be identified and interrelated according to similar classificatory principles and symbolic interests as one moves from one society to the next. That this may be so, in at least one respect, is suggested by the fact that the ethnographic literature contains several references to the belief that there is a conceived (if not perceived) relationship between an animal's reproductive cycle and the first appearance of that animal's celestial counterpart in the early morning (Urton, 1981, pp. 176–189). In addition, there are suggestions that the rising of the celestial representation of an animal or bird serves as an indication that the season to hunt the terrestrial version of that same animal or bird has arrived (Roth, 1908–1909, p. 261). These data suggest that in the process of establishing local calendar systems there is considered to be a temporal correlation between the appearance of a particular dark-cloud animal and the biological periodicity of, or the cycles of human activity in the exploitation of, its terrestrial counterpart.

Classification and Symbolism. Such a purely calendrically oriented interpretation of the significance of the animals located in the dark spots of the Milky Way should be augmented by two other considerations, one classificatory, the other symbolic. In relation to the former, the animals of the Milky Way may represent those forms considered to be classificatorily "prototypical," the most representative members of particular classes of animals. Alternatively, they may represent "marked" animals, ones that do not fit comfortably into a single class but that rather bridge two or more classes. That one or the other of these considerations may be significant in Quechua astronomy is suggested by the fact that the sequence of animals that stretches along, and within, the Milky Way includes a reptile (snake), an amphibian (toad), a bird (tinamou), a herbivorous mammal (llama), and a carnivorous mammal (fox). The classificatory significance of these life forms would therefore rest not only on the particular characteristics of each individual animal in turn but also on the relations between and among the various types as they are projected into the sky in a particular sequence (i.e., from a reptile to a mammal).

Another classificatory factor that may be important throughout the various ethnoastronomical traditions is a consideration of the color of the animals in question. That is, many of the animals have either a dull, dark coloring (e.g., fox, deer, anteater), or else they are spotted or mottled (e.g., tinamou, toad, anaconda, rainbow boa, jaguar). The dark spots along the "body" of the Milky Way recall the dark or mottled coloring of the terrestrial animals. In this regard, there may also be a conceptual similarity between the dark spots of the Milky Way and the spots on the moon. The latter, as mentioned earlier, are typically associated with asocial (e.g., incestuous) relationships.

Mythic oppositions. The symbolic significance of the dark-cloud animals will vary considerably from one ethnoastronomical tradition to another and can be understood only on the basis of a careful consideration of the particular characteristics of the celestial animals as they are portrayed in the mythology of each culture. In considering the mythological descriptions of celestial phenomena, however, it is essential first to turn to the material referring to those constellations that are composed of clusters or groupings of stars, since the mythological data for stellar constellations are more abundant, and explicit, than those for the dark spots of the Milky Way.

The principal stellar constellations recognized in South American ethnoastronomies are, for the most part, also located near or within the Milky Way; these include the Pleiades, the Hyades, the Belt (and Sword) of Orion, Scorpius, the Southern Cross, and α and β Centauri. By far the richest ethnoastronomical material concerns the Pleiades, a small cluster of some six to ten stars (visible with the naked eye) in the constellation of Taurus. The Pleiades are referred to in a variety of ways, many of which emphasize the visual appearance of this cluster of stars as a group or "bunch" of things. In the tropical forest, the Pleiades are variously referred to as bees, wasps, a handful of flour spilled on the ground, parrots, white down, a bunch of flowers, and so forth (Lévi-Strauss, 1969, p. 222). Claude Lévi-Strauss pointed out an important principle in Tropical Forest ethnoastronomies when he argued that the Pleiades are typically classed together with, while at the same time opposed to, the nearby constellation of the Belt and Sword of Orion. The latter is referred to as a tortoise shell, a bird, a stick, and a leg (or a one-legged man; Lévi-Strauss, 1969, pp. 222–223; cf. Reichel-Dolmatoff, 1982, pp. 173–174). Lévi-Strauss's argument is that the Pleiades and Orion are diachronically associated, since they rise within a few days of each other, but that they are synchronically opposed, since the Pleiades represent, or are in the category of, the continuous, whereas Orion is in that of the discontinuous. For the Pleiades and Orion, respectively, he notes that "we have names that boil down to collective terms describing a chance distribution of . . . related elements: and on the other, analytical terms describing a systematic arrangement of clearly individualized elements" (Lévi-Strauss, 1969, pp. 222–223; cf. 1973, pp. 268–270).

Throughout South America, it can be shown that the Pleiades are contrasted in various ways with other nearby star groupings (e.g., Orion and the Hyades), whereas, on another level, they are grouped together with these same nearby stars and contrasted with other constellations (e.g., Coma Berenices, Corvus, Scorpius, the Southern Cross, and α and β Centauri). These two groupings of stars are contrasted or deemed complementary in terms of their symbolic characteristics, and they are coincidental or alternating in terms of the phasing of the dates of their rising and setting (cf. Hugh-Jones, 1982; Zuidema, 1982; Wilbert, 1975). The questions to be addressed with regard to these observations are "On what bases are the Pleiades contrasted with other, nearby constellations?" and "On what bases are the Pleiades grouped together with these nearby constellations and contrasted with another, more distant group of constellations?" I suggest that the first question may be approached primarily through a consideration of the mythological data referring to social relations and social organization, whereas the second question can best be addressed on the basis of data referring to meteorological, seasonal, and, ultimately, economic concerns.

As for the contrast between the Pleiades, the Hyades, and Orion, there are several myths that mention these three constellations in related mythological contexts. For instance, among certain Carib-speaking tribes there are myths of a woman (the Pleiades) who cuts off her husband's leg (Orion's Belt and Sword) and runs away with a tapir (the Hyades; Jara and Magaña, 1983, p. 125; cf. Roth, 1908–1909, p. 262). The Amahuaca of eastern Peru say that the V-shaped Hyades represent the jaw of a caiman that bit off the leg of a man who mistook it for a canoe; the leg is seen in the Pleiades, while Orion's Belt and Sword represent the man's brother holding the lance with which he killed the caiman (cf. Reichel-Dolmatoff, 1982, pp. 173–174). The Campa see in the Pleiades a Campa man and his family; the man's brother-in-law is the Belt and Sword of Orion. They also say that Orion is a Campa man who is being pursued by a warrior wasp and has received an arrow in his leg (Weiss, 1972, p. 160).

The various myths that deal with the Pleiades, the Hyades, and Orion are centered on animals and people (or their body parts) who are related by ties of blood or, more commonly, marriage. In many cases, there are also characters present who are implicated in the violation of these kinship and marriage ties (e.g., the tapir who seduces and runs away with a man's wife). In this regard, it should be recalled that among the Xerente, who practice moiety exogamy, the belt of Orion and κ Orionis are related to one moiety, while Seven Stars (the Pleiades?) are related to the other (Nimuendajú, 1942, pp. 25, 85).

In addition to the "local" contrast between the Pleiades and the neighboring constellations of the Hyades and Orion, there are several references to the contrast between the Pleiades and constellations farther removed. In Barasana cosmology, the Pleiades (Star Thing) are associated with the dry season and opposed to Scorpius (Caterpillar Jaguar), which is associated with the wet season (Hugh-Jones, 1982, p. 197). The Pleiades and Scorpius are similarly opposed, and each is related to either the dry or the wet season, or to planting or harvest, in the cosmology of the Quechua (Urton, 1981, pp. 122–125) and the Chiriguano (*H.S.A.I.*, 1948, p. 483).

Similar examples of the opposition of the Pleiades to other constellations (e.g., Corvus and Coma Berenices) appear in the timing of fishing cycles (Lévi-Strauss, 1978, pp. 36–40), honey availability (Lévi-Strauss, 1973, pp. 57–58, 268–272, 282–285), or both fishing cycles and honey availability (Lévi-Strauss, 1973, p. 114). The evening rising and setting of the Pleiades (which occur at different times of the year) are associated by the Barasana and the Desána with the fruiting periods of trees (Hugh-Jones, 1982, p. 190; Reichel-Dolmatoff, 1982, p. 173). R. Tom Zuidema has shown that the critical dates in the Inca calendar system, a system that coordinated political, ritual, and agricultural events throughout the year, were determined by the times of the rising, setting, and the upper and lower culminations of the Pleiades in opposition to the Southern Cross and α and β Centauri. In Inca and contemporary Quechua astronomy, the Pleiades represent (among other things) a storehouse; the Southern Cross is important, as it stands just above the dark-cloud constellation of the tinamou; and α and β Centauri are the eyes of the dark-cloud constellation of the llama (Zuidema, 1982, pp. 221–224; Urton, 1981, pp. 181–188).

Mythic similarities. While particular contrasts between (1) the Pleiades, the Hyades, and Orion and (2) the Southern Cross, α and β Centauri, Corvus, Coma Berenices, and Scorpius vary over different parts of South America, the temporal relations between the two groups of constellations represent essentially similar seasonal oppositions regardless of which particular members of the two sets are contrasted. In terms of their celestial locations, the constellations in group 1 are located between right ascension three to six hours, while those of group 2 are between right ascension twelve to sixteen hours. Therefore, the members of one group will rise as the members of the other set. This temporal opposition, and its attendant symbolic and mythological associations, is one other important feature shared by the ethnoastronomies of South American Indians.

Although the various Indian tribes of South America are situated in extremely diverse environmental regions, from the dense tropical forests of the Amazon and Orinoco basins to the high Andean mountains along the western side of the continent, there are a number of similarities in the ethnoastronomical traditions of these various groups. One source of similarities may lie in the fact that these cultures are all located within the tropics (see Aveni, 1981): the Amazon River is roughly coincident with the line of the equator. But beyond the similarities that are encountered in the observational phenomena viewed by these cultures, there are perhaps more fundamental similarities in the way in which the celestial bodies are described and interrelated in their mythological and religious traditions. There are fundamental principles that give meaning and coherence to ethnoastronomical beliefs concerning the sun and the moon, the Milky Way, and the two types of constellations. These are the same conceptual foundations that ground the various religious traditions. These basic premises revolve around relations between and among men and women, humans and animals, and beings on earth and those in the sky.

BIBLIOGRAPHY

For an excellent discussion of naked-eye observational astronomy in the tropics, see Anthony F. Aveni's "Tropical Archaeoastronomy," *Science* 213 (July 1981): 161–171. Separate ethnographic descriptions, many of which include ethnoastronomical material for a variety of Tropical Forest tribes, can be found in *The Tropical Forest Tribes*, vol. 3 of the *Handbook of South American Indians*, edited by Julian H. Steward (Washington, D.C., 1948). Excellent collections of Tropical Forest Indian myths are included in the following three books by the

French anthropologist Claude Lévi-Strauss: *The Raw and the Cooked* (New York, 1969), *From Honey to Ashes* (New York, 1973), and *The Origin of Table Manners* (New York, 1978), all translated by John Weightman and Doreen Weightman. The ethnoastronomies of various tribes in northeastern South America are described in Fabiola Jara and Edmundo Magaña's "Astronomy of the Coastal Caribs of Surinam," *L'homme* 23 (1983): 111–133; Walter E. Roth's "An Inquiry into the Animism and Folk-lore of the Guiana Indians," in the *Thirtieth Annual Report of the Bureau of American Ethnology* (Washington, D.C., 1908–1909); and Johannes Wilbert's "Eschatology in a Participatory Universe: Destinies of the Soul among the Warao Indians of Venezuela," in *Death and the Afterlife in Pre-Columbian America*, edited by Elizabeth P. Benson (Washington, D.C., 1975). Ethnoastronomies of the Indians of the Colombian rain forest are discussed in Stephen Hugh-Jones's "The Pleiades and Scorpius in Barasana Cosmology" and in Gerardo Reichel-Dolmatoff's "Astronomical Models of Social Behavior among Some Indians of Colombia," both of which can be found in *Ethnoastronomy and Archaeoastronomy in the American Tropics*, edited by Anthony F. Aveni and Gary Urton (New York, 1982). The ethnoastronomies of Tropical Forest tribes in eastern Peru are discussed in Gerald Weiss's "Campa Cosmology," *Ethnology* 11 (April 1972): 157–172. Some of the best descriptions of the astronomy and cosmology of the tribes of the southern Amazon basin are to be found in three works by Curt Nimuendajú: *The Sherente*, translated by Robert H. Lowie (Los Angeles, 1942); *The Tukuna*, translated by William D. Hohenthal, edited by Robert H. Lowie (Berkeley, 1952); and *The Apinayé*, translated by Robert H. Lowie, edited by John M. Cooper and Robert H. Lowie (Oosterhout, The Netherlands, 1967). Another interesting discussion of southern Amazonian ethnoastronomy is Charles Wagley's "World View of the Tapirape Indians," *Journal of American Folklore* 53 (1940): 252–260. For descriptions and analyses of Inca and contemporary Quechua ethnoastronomy, see R. Tom Zuidema's article "Catachillay: The Role of the Pleiades and of the Southern Cross and α and β Centauri in the Calendar of the Incas,"in *Ethnoastronomy and Archaeoastronomy in the American Tropics*, mentioned above; and my book, *At the Crossroads of the Earth and the Sky: An Andean Cosmology* (Austin, 1981). For an example of astronomic configurations in the religious life of hunters, see Otto Zerries's "Sternbilder als Audruck Jägerischer Geisteshaltung in Südamerika," *Paideuma* 5 (1952): 220–235.

GARY URTON

ETHNOLOGY. *See* Anthropology, Ethnology, and Religion; *see also* Study of Religion.

ETRUSCAN RELIGION. From about the eighth to the fourth century BCE, the inhabitants of Etruria, a country occupying what is now Tuscany and part of Umbria in west-central Italy, achieved the highest civilization on the Italian Peninsula before the rise of Rome. In ancient times the Etruscans were considered to be more attached to their religious beliefs than any other people and more proficient in the practice of their ceremonies of worship. In modern times, from the various sources of information available for studying Etruscan religion, the impression is no different.

Sources of Information. The direct sources are literary, epigraphic, and archaeological. A single literary text has come down to us. Discovered on an Egyptian mummy that today is in the Zagreb Museum, this is a linen scroll nearly fourteen meters long on which a lengthy ritual calendar is written. This is undoubtedly a description of the ceremonies to be carried out on different days of the year in honor of several gods. But even today the Etruscan language is very problematical to interpret, and the precise meaning of this miraculously preserved book still resists, for the most part, scholarly efforts. Such is also the case with epigraphic religious texts of any length like the one engraved on the famous Tile of Capua. However, we should emphasize the importance of the discovery in 1964, at Pyrgi, a port of ancient Caere, of three gold plates, the first two bearing Etruscan inscriptions and the third, a Carthaginian inscription. These are not bilingual texts, properly speaking, but rather parallel texts manifesting a religious assimilation of the highest significance. In 500 BCE the ruler of Caere declared himself a follower of Astarte, the great Phoenician-Punic goddess, and simultaneously a follower of the Etruscan guardian divinity Uni (since for him she was the same goddess bearing different names); Uni was herself a homologue of the Greek Hera and the Roman Juno.

The pieces of archaeological evidence instructing us on the Etruscan religious life are in themselves extremely numerous and varied. They come either from fortuitous discoveries or from organized excavations in the earth of the Etruscan cities and necropolises in Tuscany itself and also in the plains of the Po and in Latium and Campania. In the urban areas, numerous remains of sacred buildings, temples, and altars with their rich architectonic decorative style have come to light and continue to do so. As for the necropolises themselves, spread out over vast areas, they too continue to reveal their treasures. The architecture of the tombs themselves, often built in rooms modeled on the homes of the living; the paintings decorating their walls and ceilings in several sites in southern Etruria; the sculptures; the reliefs; and the documents from minor arts of all types that the tombs contain: these are all precious elements for our knowledge of the life of the Etruscan people and of their religious customs especially. From this perspective, our study is far from complete.

Finally, the importance of indirect literary sources should be mentioned. These consist of numerous writings by Latin and Greek authors who at various times directed their attention to one or another aspect of the religion of ancient Tuscany. To be sure, the texts most often come several centuries after the realities they describe. But nothing is more tenacious in human memory than recollections of important religious traditions, and romanized Etruscans at the end of the republic and the beginning of the empire still kept alive in their minds the rules and doctrines of a nation they were proud to claim their own. Moreover, they had at their disposition sacred Etruscan books of a later date that they had no trouble translating into Latin and hence made accessible to all. Such was the case of Caecina and Lucius Tarquinius Priscus. Thus later Latin and Greek authors could in turn use these faithful transpositions of works that survived in this way long after the destruction of Etruria itself.

Etruscan Revelation and Religious Doctrine. If the ancients were already studying attentively the religion of a people who had lost their independence long before, it was because they were confronting a world of ideas and beliefs truly quite removed from their own. Greco-Roman polytheism did not admit of revelation brought to men by prophets. The Etruscan religion, on the contrary, was a revealed religion, and a prophet, Tages, presumably taught the principles and rules at Tarquinia to a crowd gathered around him, following his miraculous appearance in the furrow of a plowed field. Cicero narrates this fable in his treatise on divination (2.23). Tages had the body and face of a child, but the gray hair and wisdom of an old man. Perhaps he was the son of Jupiter himself, that is, of the Etruscan Tinia. After revealing the rules of wisdom and religion, Tages disappeared.

According to another tradition, the primordial revelation was due in part to a woman prophet or sibyl called Begoia or Begoé. The transcription of Etruscan names in Latin or Greek is naturally subject to many uncertainties (as is the Etruscan adaptation of Greek and Latin names). Begoia also bore a divine message and delivered it to an Etruscan of her own choice, a man named Arruns Velthumnus, a native of Clusium. Matching the diversity of the large Etruscan cities was a variety of legendary narratives concerning the contacts between man and the divinity through an intermediary sent from heaven.

The books of Tages stating the principles of the Etruscan religion kept their renown under the Roman empire. The books of Begoia contained "the decisions of Jupiter and Justice" and concerned the art of interpreting and also that of attracting flashes of lightning, the *fulguratura*. Her books likewise taught the rules for land divisions and boundaries. The Etruscans placed the greatest importance on the inviolability of properties and boundaries. Their proven technique of land measurement passed into the hands of the Romans, who applied it first in Italy and then in various parts of the world that they ruled.

Etrusca disciplina, the Etruscan religious doctrine, thus conveyed regulations made by one or another divine messenger to a people whose attitude toward the sacred was, in my opinion, unparalleled in classical antiquity. In Greece and Rome, the gods and human society always instituted and pursued a dialogue. But in Etruria men who were seemingly seized with fright kept still and listened to a divine monologue with fear and respect. We must look to the Near East for valuable parallels in a comparable situation. In the West, in this respect as in others, Etruria is unique.

According to the ancients, the sacred Etruscan books were divided into three groups. The first concerned haruspicy, that is, properly speaking, the art of studying and interpreting the entrails of victims in order to infer warnings and omens for the future. True specialists, the priests applied this technique of divination with unequaled science and earned the title of haruspices. They developed this art of exegesis as highly as had the Babylonian priest, the *baru* of the third millennium BCE. A particular anatomical observation would result in a particular warning or prediction.

A large number of terra-cotta maquettes discovered in various regions of the Near East represent the viscera of sacrificial sheep and contain inscriptions stating the predictions resulting from their conformation. In Etruria a massive bronze maquette discovered about a century ago south of Piacenza likewise represents a sheep's liver and indicates the numerous divinities that occupy, so to speak, the various parts. It is at present the only known object of its kind in the world, and it illustrates strikingly the major principle of all divination and in particular that of the Etruscans: the close interdependence between the different parts of the world. The Etruscans' faith is not to be doubted: at the moment of the sacrifice the victim's liver was like a mirror of the universe, and this strict parallelism bestowed upon it its eminent instructional value.

The second group of books treated lightning flashes, their origin, value, and significance. The extreme importance of this fulgural divination was emphasized by ancient authors such as Pliny the Elder and Seneca, who in celebrated passages convey the originality of the Etruscan interpretation. The latter has no parallel elsewhere and is no doubt explained by the frequency and violence of storms and lightning in a region as volcanic as Tuscany.

The third group of books, called *libri rituales,* had a vast field of application and detailed the most diverse rituals bearing on the life of men and states. Included here were the *libri Acheruntici* ("Acherontic books") or books of the dead, and the *ostentaria,* compendia of rules relative to exegesis and to the expiation of prodigies.

The Gods of the Etruscan Pantheon: Temples and Tombs. The Etruscan pantheon is problematical. It shows great diversity, if we can believe the archaeological sources and documents at our disposition. A council of gods, anonymous and mysterious, had to give its consent to Jupiter-Tinia before the latter launched his most destructive flashes, which would strike and destroy cities and states. Beneath these secret powers we encounter a whole series of Etruscan divinities. Some have names that are theirs alone, such as Turan, goddess of love, the homologue of Aphrodite-Venus. Others have names borrowed from Greek gods, as for instance *Aplu,* which comes from *Apollo,* and *Artumes,* which comes from *Artemis.* Finally there are others who borrow their names from the Italian languages, such as *Ani,* derived from *Janus; Selvans,* derived from *Silvanus;* and *Maris,* derived from *Mars.* Thus everything proceeds as if, in contrast to the solid body of Etruscan doctrine concerning different mantic modes, the world of the Etruscan gods and heroes demonstrated great plasticity and could easily be assimilated with gods of foreign countries, notably Greece. The gold plates of Pyrgi, mentioned earlier, prove that around 500 BCE a similar assimilation could be effected between an Etruscan goddess and a great Semitic divinity.

It is difficult for us to grasp what compelled the Etruscans to create certain groupings of gods. However, many literary or archaeological sources prove incontestably that Etruria tended to form divine triads. The most famous among them is the Capitoline triad formed by Jupiter, Juno, and Minerva, whose names translate those of Tinia, Uni, and Menerva. The temple that the Tarquin dynasty constructed at great expense was dedicated to this triad; it later became the religious center of Rome, then of the whole Roman world. According to tradition, Etruscan cities, which, once good omens were secured, were laid out in the form of a checkerboard and respected strict rules of cardinal orientation, all had to include a tripartite temple, or capitol. This temple was placed at the north of each city, so the major gods could keep the urban space under protective surveillance.

The prominence of the funerary cult for the Etruscans indicates the importance they attached to the destiny of the deceased in the hereafter. The *libri fatales,* which are lost to us completely, dealt with human destiny and contained a doctrine concerning *saecula* ("centuries"). These books fixed the term the gods set to the life of individuals and states, a term that was inescapable. The *libri Acheruntici,* treating the passage to death, apparently indicated the rites permitting access to immortality.

Scholars and tourists have always been struck by the extreme care the Etruscans took in furnishing the dwellings of the dead. They accorded no less importance to all other aspects of the funerary cult. For them, only the wine of libations and the blood of sacrifices could give back to the dead a little of the life they had lost. The frescoes covering the walls of the funerary chambers of southern Etruria helped restore for the deceased the framework of their life on earth. But with the passing centuries, the tomb decoration underwent modifications. As Etruscan power declined, demons with frightening faces like Charun and Tuchulcha multiplied, and the view of the world of the dead became as a result more gloomy and threatening.

Thus at the end of its history Etruscan religion showed somber traits, as if the rigorous application of its necessary rituals, carried out by a clergy of proven specialists, had not sufficed to ward off the implacable judgments of destiny. Yet the prestige of the haruspices did not disappear along with the independence of Etruria. Emperor Claudius in 47 CE reorganized their order, and their fame as thaumaturgists lasted as long as the Roman empire itself. In 408 CE, they pretended to call down lightning on the hordes of the Visigothic king Alaric. It is an astonishing destiny for the prestige of priests to survive the disappearance of their own people. From the beginning to the end of its history, Italy, despite some misgivings, showed a degree of trust in the Etruscan priesthood.

BIBLIOGRAPHY

Bloch, Raymond. *Les prodiges dans l'antiquité classique: Grèce, Étrurie et Rome.* Paris, 1963.

Bloch, Raymond, et al. *Recherches sur les religions de l'Italie antique: Interpretatio.* Geneva, 1976. See pages 1–45.

Bouché-Leclercq, Auguste. *Histoire de la divination dans l'antiquité,* vol. 4 (1889). New York, 1975.

Die Göttin von Pyrgi. Florence, 1981. Proceedings of an international colloquy organized by the Istituto di Studi Etruschi ed Italici at Tübingen, January 1979.

Grant, Michael. *The Etruscans.* New York, 1981.
Grenier, Albert. *Les religions étrusque et romaine.* Paris, 1948.
Heurgon, Jacques. *La vie quotidienne chez les Étrusques.* Paris, 1961.
Pallottino, Massimo. *Saggi di antichitá.* 3 vols. Rome, 1979.
Pfiffig, Ambros J. *Religio etrusca.* Graz, 1975.
Richardson, Emeline. *The Etruscans: Their Art and Civilization.* Chicago, 1964.
Thulin, Carl O. *Die etruskische Disciplin.* 2 vols. Göteborg, 1906–1909.

RAYMOND BLOCH

Translated from French by Carol Dean-Nassau and Marilyn Gaddis Rose

EUCHARIST. The Eucharist, also known as the Mass, Communion service, Lord's Supper, and Divine Liturgy, among other names, is the central act of Christian worship, practiced by almost all denominations of Christians. Though varying in form from the very austere to the very elaborate, the Eucharist has as its essential elements the breaking and sharing of bread and the pouring and sharing of wine (in some Protestant churches, unfermented grape juice) among the worshipers in commemoration of the actions of Jesus Christ on the eve of his death.

The word *eucharist* is taken from the Greek *eucharistia,* which means "thanksgiving" or "gratitude" and which was used by the early Christians for the Hebrew *berakhah,* meaning "a blessing" such as a table grace. When Christians adopted the word from the Greek into other languages, the meaning was narrowed to the specific designation of the ritual of the bread and wine.

History. The ritual attributed to Jesus by the writers of the New Testament is portrayed as a Jewish Passover Seder meal in which Jesus reinterprets the symbolism of the traditional celebration (Paul in *1 Cor.* 11:23–26, *Mk.* 14:22–25, *Mt.* 26:26–29, and *Lk.* 22:14–20). Passover commemorates the liberation of the Hebrews from slavery in Egypt, which was the first step in their becoming a people in covenant with God. It is celebrated to this day by a lengthy ceremonial meal with prescribed foods, in which the story of the deliverance is symbolically reenacted (see *Ex.* 12:1–28). Selecting from the many symbolic foods customary in his time, Jesus takes only the unleavened bread (the bread of emergency or affliction) and the wine. The tradition of the early witnesses is that Jesus asks the traditional questions about the meaning of the ritual and answers, first about the bread he is breaking, "This is my body, broken for you," and then about the wine, "This is my blood, the blood of the covenant, which is to be poured out for many." It is clear that Jesus refers to his death and is interpreting the significance of that death in terms of the symbolism of the Exodus story and the Passover ritual. He invites the disciples to repeat the action frequently and thus enter into his death and the outcome of that death. By placing his death in the context of Passover, Jesus interprets it as a liberation bringing his followers into community as one people in covenant with God (see *1 Cor.* 11:17–34). [*See* Passover. *For discussion, in broad religious perspective, of related topics, see* Food; Beverages; Bread; *and* Leaven.]

In the earliest Christian times, eucharist was celebrated rather spontaneously as part of an ordinary meal for which the local followers of Jesus were gathered in his name in a private home. By the second century it is clear that there were strong efforts to regulate it under the authority and supervision of the local church leaders known as bishops. By the fourth century, eucharist was celebrated with great pomp and ceremony in public buildings, and the meal was no longer in evidence. At that time, solemn processions emphasized the role of a clergy arrayed in special vestments. The form of the celebration included several readings from the Bible, prayers, chants, a homily, and the great prayer of thanksgiving, in the course of which the words and actions of Jesus at his farewell supper were recited, followed by the distribution of the consecrated bread and wine to the participants.

The Orthodox and other Eastern churches retained this general format with some variations. The liturgy of the Western churches, however, went through a long period of accretion and elaboration of secondary symbolism which obscured the meaning of the action and tended to leave the congregation passive spectators of what the clergy were doing. During the Middle Ages there also emerged the private Mass, a Eucharist celebrated by a priest without a congregation of worshipers present.

The sixteenth-century reformers took action to strip away all accretions and elements that did not seem to be in accord with the text of the Bible. Zwingli and Calvin were more radical in this than Luther. The Roman Catholic church also instituted extensive reforms of the rite in the sixteenth century, leaving a uniform pattern later known as the Tridentine Mass. This, however, was very substantially revised after the Second Vatican Council (1962–1965), allowing more spontaneity and congregational participation as well as offering more variety.

Theology. Eucharist is understood by all Christians to commemorate the saving death and resurrection of Jesus, and to mediate communion with God and community among the worshipers. Beyond this basic concept, the theology of the Eucharist varies very widely among the Christian denominations and has often been a cause of bitter dispute between them.

Both Orthodox and Roman Catholic Christians understand the presence of Christ very concretely, taking seriously the so-called words of institution, "This is my body . . . this is my blood." However, the Orthodox insist that while there is an actual change in the bread and wine that justifies these words, the manner of the change is a mystery not to be analyzed or explained rationally. Since medieval times Catholic Christians have attempted to give an intellectually satisfying explanation, focusing on the notion of a transubstantiation of bread and wine. While the eucharistic theology of the various Protestant churches varies widely, they are united in finding a theology of transubstantiation not in harmony with their interpretation of scripture.

The meaning and effect of the Eucharist have also been discussed in Catholic theology under the term *real presence.* This emphasizes that the presence of Christ mediated by the bread and wine is prior to the faith of the congregation. Protestant theology has generally rejected the term *real presence* as one liable to superstitious interpretation.

Orthodox and Catholic Christians also agree on an interpretation of the Eucharist in terms of sacrifice; that is, a renewed offering by Christ himself of his immolation in death. Again, there have been determined efforts in the Catholic theological tradition to give intellectually satisfying explanations of this, while Orthodox theology tends to tolerate a variety of explanations at the same time as it insists on fidelity to the words of the liturgy itself. Protestants believe the theology of sacrifice lacks biblical foundation and doctrinal validity, and prefer to emphasize the role of the Eucharist as a memorial.

It is paradoxical that the Eucharist is the sacrament of unity for Christians yet is a sign and cause of disunity among denominations. In general denominations exclude others from their eucharistic table, usually on account of theological differences. Contemporary initiatives reflect attempts to reconcile some of these differences and to experiment cautiously with "intercommunion" among the churches. Such initiatives appear to be far more extensive among laity than in the official legislation of the churches.

BIBLIOGRAPHY

The texts of the eucharistic celebrations of the various Western churches are given in *Liturgies of the Western Church,* selected and introduced by Bard Thompson (1961; reprint, Philadelphia, 1980). An account of the Orthodox Divine Liturgy and its theology is given in Alexander Schmemann's *Introduction to Liturgical Theology* (London, 1966). A description of the early Christians' Eucharist and eucharistic theology, with identification of sources, is presented in *The Eucharist of the Early Christians,* by Willy Rordorf and others (New York, 1978). More specifically concerned with the theology of the Eucharist are Joseph M. Powers's *Eucharistic Theology* (New York, 1967), from a Catholic perspective, and Geoffrey Wainwright's *Eucharist and Eschatology* (1971; reprint, New York, 1981), from a Protestant, particularly a Methodist, perspective. A discussion of the social implications of eucharistic celebration can be found in my own book, *The Eucharist and the Hunger of the World* (New York, 1976).

MONIKA K. HELLWIG

EUCLID (c. 300 BCE), Greek mathematician. Plato described mathematics as a discipline that turns one's gaze from the Becoming of the sensible world to the Being of the intelligible. The great value of mathematics is to prepare the mind for the apprehension of pure ideas. After Plato's death, geometry flourished among his students. One of the few details we know about Euclid's life is that he studied under Plato's followers. Subsequently he founded the great school of mathematics at Alexandria, Egypt. He wrote on mathematics, optics, and astronomy.

Euclid's *Elements* is the most influential work in all of mathematics. Though other "Elements" were produced before Euclid, his work organized and completed that of his predecessors, whom we now know chiefly by reference. As the letters (Gr., *stoikheia;* "elements") of the alphabet are to language, so are the *Elements* to mathematics, wrote the Neoplatonist Proclus in the fifth century CE. The analogy is apt. In thirteen books Euclid goes from the most elementary definitions and assumptions about points, lines, and angles all the way to the geometry of solids, and he includes a theory of the proportions of magnitudes, number theory, and geometric algebra. His procedure epitomized the axiomatic-deductive method and became a paradigm for philosophical and scientific reasoning. The greatest works in the history of astronomy imitate the *Elements:* Ptolemy's *Almagest* (c. 150 CE), Copernicus's *De revolutionibus* (1543), and Newton's *Principia* (1686). There is no greater example of Euclid's influence in philosophy than Spinoza's *Ethics* (1675), which scrupulously reproduced Euclid's method of definitions, axioms, and propositions.

The *Elements* became the elementary introduction to mathematics in Hellenistic civilization. Translated into Arabic in the ninth century and into Latin in the thirteenth, it became the foundation of Islamic, medieval, and Renaissance mathematics. It standardized the body of mathematical knowledge well into the twentieth century. The *Elements* was not translated into Sanskrit until the 1720s, though there is evidence of some prior knowledge. The Chinese may have known Euclid in the thirteenth century, but it did not affect the development of their mathematics until 1607, when the Jesuit Matteo Ricci produced a highly praised translation of the first six books of the *Elements* as part of the Jesuit missionary strategy in China. The use of the *Elements* as *the* textbook of mathematics over millennia is the source of the often repeated claim that, second only to the Bible, the *Elements* is the most widely circulated book in human history.

Euclid's religious significance can be seen in two ways. First, Euclid fulfilled the value Plato saw in mathematics. Euclid's masterpiece remains the enduring testament of the human capacity to construct a transparently intelligible system of relations grounded in logic and capable of extension to the physical world, though not derived from it. He demonstrates with lucid brevity how reason can successfully operate with purely intelligible objects such as points, lines, and triangles, and discover new and unforeseen truths with them. Such exercise frees the mind from the appearances of the senses and initiates it into an intellectual realm that Plato referred to as the realm of Being. In Neoplatonism such exercise had a paramount spiritual value. Augustine of Hippo, in his *Soliloquies* (386), written the year before his baptism, esteemed mathematics as a preparation for the soul's ascent to God. The mind perceives necessary truths first in mathematics and is then prepared to pursue eternal, divine truth. Having tasted the sweetness and splendor of truth in mathematics and the liberal arts, the mind actively seeks the divine. A millennium later, the Christian mystic Nicholas of Cusa wrote in his *Of Learned Ignorance* (1440) that the most fitting approach to knowledge of divine things is through symbols. Therefore he uses mathematical images because of their "indestructible certitude" (bk. 1, chap. 11).

Second, Euclid's geometry implicitly defined the nature of space for Western civilizations up to the nineteenth century. That "a straight line is drawn between two points," Euclid's first postulate, is also a statement about the space that makes it possible. Conceptions of space have religious repercussions because they involve matters of orientation. Isaac Newton (1642–1727) reified Euclidean space in his physics. He identified absolute space and absolute time, which together constitute the ultimate frame of reference for cosmic phenomena, with God's ubiquity and eternity. Euclid's fifth postulate stipulated the conditions under which straight lines intersect, and, by implication, when they are parallel. To his continuing credit, Euclid presented the conditions as assumptions. For millennia mathematicians tried unsuccessfully to prove them. But, because Euclid's postulates were only assumptions, other conditions were possible. Thus in the nineteenth century Nikolai Lobachevskii, Farkas Bolyai, and Georg Riemann were inspired to develop non-Euclidean geometries. These were crucial to Einstein's theories of special and general relativity (1905, 1913) and, hence, to our present cosmology, wherein a straight line cannot be drawn between two points. The conclusion that space and time are inseparable in the mathematical and physical theories of the nineteenth and twentieth centuries owes its existence to the force of the Euclidean tradition.

BIBLIOGRAPHY

The classic English translation of the *Elements* is Thomas L. Heath's *The Thirteen Books of Euclid's Elements*, 2d ed. (New York, 1956). It includes an introduction to Euclid's place in the history of mathematics and a thorough commentary on the text. A more recent account of Euclid and his achievement, as well as the history of the *Elements*, with comprehensive bibliographies, is found in Ivor Bulmer-Thomas's "Euclid" and John Murdoch's "Euclid: Transmission of the *Elements*," in the *Dictionary of Scientific Biography* (New York, 1970–1980). A discussion of the historical and philosophical antecedents to Euclid and how his methods incorporate Platonic and Aristotelian developments in the philosophy of mathematics is provided in Edward A. Maziarz and Thomas Greenwood's *Greek Mathematical Philosophy* (New York, 1968). The importance of mathematics in the education of the philosopher is addressed in Werner Jaeger's *Paideia: The Ideals of Greek Culture*, 3 vols., translated by Gilbert Highet (Oxford, 1939–1944).

MICHAEL A. KERZE

EUHEMERISM. *See* Apotheosis; Historiography; *and* Manism; *see also* Chinese Religion, *article on* Mythic Themes.

EUSEBIUS (c. 260/70–c. 339), Christian bishop of Caesarea in Palestine from 314, a leading early Christian historian, exegete, and apologist. Eusebius was a disciple of Pamphilus at Caesarea; he wrote a life of his master and called himself "of Pamphilus." He traced his intellectual descent to Origen, and with Pamphilus wrote a defense of Origen against the theological and personal criticisms current during the persecution of 303–313. Little is known of Eusebius's early life, but it seems clear that he wrote his *Historia ecclesiastica* (History of the Church) at Caesarea during the persecution, possibly though not certainly after composing at a slightly earlier date a first draft of it as well as a first draft of his *Chronicon* (Chronicle). At the end of the persecution, in spite of occasional slanders concerning apostasy spread by his enemies, he became bishop of Caesarea. During this time he continued to update his *History* and composed other significant works, such as the *Demonstratio evangelica* and *Praeparatio evangelica.* He gradually became involved in the Arian controversy; his defense of a traditional subordinationist Christology partly resembling Origen's was criticized by many fellow bishops. Indeed, a synod held at Antioch in 324 or 325 condemned him and a few others, though he was given the right of later appeal. At the synod held at Nicaea Eusebius set forth the local creed of Caesarea but accepted the Alexandrian term *homoousios* ("of the same substance"), which transformed the creed's meaning. Thereafter he helped drive the pro-Nicene bishop Eustathius out of Antioch, acted as a judge when Athanasius was brought before several synods, and attacked Marcellus of Ancyra as a Sabellian. At the celebration of Constantine's thirtieth anniversary Eusebius delivered a panegyric on the emperor and his divinely inspired deeds. Similar themes appear in his *Life of Constantine,* written after 337. Eusebius died before the synod of Antioch in 341.

Eusebius is known less for his deeds than for his multitudinous writings, some of which are lost. Constant revision and the transfer of materials from one work to another make his development as a writer difficult to assess. He was an exegete, an apologist, a historian, and a panegyrist, but his various roles cannot be completely separated.

As exegete he followed the example of Origen in his textual criticism and made some use of the latter's works in his commentaries on *Isaiah* and *Psalms.* In addition, he produced "canons" for finding gospel parallels and wrote an introduction to theology (*General Elementary Introduction,* of which parts survive in his *Eclogae propheticae*). Biblical exegesis recurs throughout the *Demonstratio,* primarily in regard to Old Testament prophecies of Christ and the church.

Eusebius's apologetic is implicit throughout the *History* and explicit in the *Praeparatio* (sages and seers anticipated Christianity, although inadequately), the treatise *Against Hierocles* (Christ superior to Apollonius of Tyana, a first-century wonder-worker), and the twenty-five lost books against the Neoplatonist philosopher Porphyry, who had written against Christians and criticized Origen. A treatise that survived only in a Syriac version is entitled *On the Theophany;* it combines materials from other books.

As historian, Eusebius is best known for his ten books on the history of the church from its divine origin to Constantine's defeat of the pagan emperor Licinius in 324. The work does not discuss the later conflicts over Arianism, Melitianism, and Donatism, or the synods of 324 and 325. A late edition deletes Eusebius's expectation that Constantine's son Crispus would be the emperor's heir; the deletion must have been made after Crispus's execution in 326. The main sources of the *History* lay in the church archives and libraries at Caesarea and Jerusalem, where there was no documentation for the churches of the West or for many churches of the East. Eusebius seems to have known little about the church of Antioch and had the good sense to refuse translation there in about 330. His strong emphasis on Alexandrian Christianity results from his love for the school of Origen.

Eusebius's panegyrics usually start from his own experiences. Thus his work *The Martyrs of Palestine* (two editions) was based largely on his own acquaintance with the persecution in 303–313; he visited Egypt perhaps in 312, where he witnessed mass executions of Christians. He praised also other martyrs (especially of Gaul), the benefactors who rebuilt the ruined church at Tyre, and above all the emperor Constantine as the divinely appointed champion of Christianity.

It may be that Eusebius's major contribution was as librarian or bibliographer. To him is owed the collections of Origen's letters and the stories of "ancient martyrdoms." The *Chronicle, History, Praeparatio,* and *Demonstratio* are essentially collections of collections or even source books without very full annotation. In other words, his materials may be more important than what he did with them. Although one has to watch for deletions, misconceptions, and other errors, Eusebius does not usually falsify his materials, but his changing attitudes have left strange juxtapositions in the text of the *History.*

He was conciliatory toward pagan philosophy and politics but hostile toward pagan religion, in which he could see a main cause of the Great Persecution. In this regard he was aligned with Origen, but he underestimated the ultimate force of the newer Alexandrian theology and its preference for orthodoxy over the harmony that Eusebius, like Constantine, had supported. During his lifetime he enjoyed good fortune. He was in imperial favor at least during his last decade, and by 340 his opponent Eustathius was dead, Athanasius in exile, and Marcellus about to be deposed. The question of his supposed Arianism has agitated historians of doctrine for centuries, but it cannot be answered without greater knowledge of the theology of the early fourth century.

His place in the history of Christian learning and literature was high during his lifetime and continued so for centuries. Those who wrote the history of the Eastern church in the fifth and sixth centuries invariably refered to his work as basic and irrefutable. Less innovative or skilled in philosophy than Origen, he was more concerned with tradition, and this concern led him to an exegesis often more sober and literal. It was this concern, also, that led to his search for early Christian documents. Perhaps he succeeded to the headship of Origen's school at Caesarea. It is possible that the lost life of Eusebius by his successor Acacius resembled the panegyric that a disciple, probably Gregory Thaumaturgus, addressed to Origen. If so, there must have been significant differences. A disciple of Eusebius would have insisted on the importance of history, not philosophical theology, as the key to exegesis and apologetics.

BIBLIOGRAPHY

Most of Eusebius's works have been critically edited by Ivar A. Heikel and others in *Eusebius Werke: Die griechischen christlichen Schriftsteller der ersten drei Jahrhunderte* (Berlin, 1902–1975). Most important in this collection is the three-volume *Kirchengeschichte*, edited by Eduard Schwartz (Leipzig, 1908). Other texts can be located through Johannes Quasten's *Patrology*, vol. 3 (Utrecht and Westminster, Md., 1960), pp. 309–345. Quasten also takes note of the modern literature. Important secondary sources include Glenn F. Chesnut's *The First Christian Histories* (Paris, 1977), Pierre Nautin's *Origène: Sa vie et son œuvre* (Paris, 1977), Robert M. Grant's *Eusebius as Church Historian* (Oxford, 1980), and Timothy D. Barnes's *Constantine and Eusebius* (Cambridge, Mass., and London, 1981).

ROBERT M. GRANT

EUTYCHES (c. 378–454), archimandrite and founder of the monophysite heresy. Eutyches was born in Constantinople and was archimandrite of a monastery near there. As sponsor of the eunuch Chrysaphius, Eutyches was very influential in the imperial court. Chrysaphius was one of the more powerful counselors of the emperor Theodosius II.

Eutyches was the originator of an extreme form of monophysitism that came to be called Eutychianism. In reaction to the separationist Christology of Nestorius (who accepted two distinct natures in Christ), Eutyches concluded that there was in Christ a single nature. When Theodoret of Cyrrhus wrote the *Eranistes* against Eutyches' opinions, Flavian, the patriarch of Constantinople (446–449), sent Eutyches to the Council of Constantinople (448) for judgment.

Eutyches appeared at the council but refused to accept the existence of two natures in Christ and was on that account condemned and deposed. Flavian's successor on the throne of Constantinople, Cyril, was, however, sympathetic to Eutyches' teaching, which corresponded to the general framework of the teaching of the Alexandrian school, rather than that of the Antiochene school. Since Cyril assumed that Flavian was a representative of the Antiochene school, he opposed the measures taken against Eutyches. Cyril promoted the convocation of a synod that later became known as the Robber Synod (449), which restored Eutyches and condemned and deposed Eusebius of Dorylaeum—who also opposed the heresy of Nestorius—as well as Flavian. Despite this, and on account of the loss of imperial favor because of the death of Theodosius II (450), Eutyches was expelled from his monastery. The new emperors, Pulcheria and her consort Marcian, convoked an ecumenical council at Chalcedon in 451, which denounced the Robber Synod, excommunicated Dioscorus (patriarch of Alexandria who had presided over the synod), restored the expelled bishops, and condemned Nestorianism, as well as Eutyches along with his teachings.

Eutyches believed that after the union of the divine and the human in Christ, there were no longer two natures but one, and this one nature was a mingling of the two. After this blending, only the divine nature remained, because the human nature was absorbed by the divine. The Council of Chalcedon, by contrast, affirmed that within Christ there are united, without confusion or division, two natures that are wholly God and wholly man.

BIBLIOGRAPHY

The texts of Eutyches' *Confessions of Faith* and several of his letters can be found, along with notes and commentary, in Eduard Schwartz's *Der Prozess des Eutyches* (Munich, 1929). See also W. H. C. Frend's *The Rise of the Monophysite Movement* (Cambridge, 1979), which includes sources and a bibliography.

THEODORE ZISSIS
Translated from Greek by Philip M. McGhee

EVAGRIOS OF PONTUS (345–399), also known as Evagrios Pontikos; Greek theologian and mystic. Evagrios was surnamed Pontikos because he was a native of Pontus, in Asia Minor. He was born to a prosperous, educated family. His father was a *chorepiskopos*, a bishop, of an area adjacent to the family estates of Basil of Caesarea. Evagrios studied under Basil, who ordained him a reader. When Basil died in 379, Evagrios became a disciple of Gregory of Nazianzus, who ordained him deacon and took him under his aegis. Under the Cappadocian fathers, Evagrios became a skilled theologian. Directly or indirectly influenced by the thought of Origen and Gregory of Nyssa, he viewed Hellenism as an enrichment rather than as a corruption of Christianity.

When Gregory of Nazianzus moved to Constantinople

as patriarch, Evagrios was invited along. There he participated in the deliberations of the Council of Constantinople (381), which brought the Arian controversy to an end and established the Nicene Creed in its final form. The young deacon impressed many in the council with his brilliant mind and skillful debating.

When Evagrios fell in love with a married woman, he decided to leave the capital and seek peace and salvation in the monastic life. He traveled to centers of monasticism in Egypt and Palestine, where he was the guest of Melania, the Roman aristocrat who ran a hospice on the Mount of Olives for Christian pilgrims. He also became acquainted with Rufinus, who had founded a monastery near the Mount of Olives. Later he moved to Egypt, where he spent two years in the mountains of Nitria and fourteen in the nearby Desert of the Cells (a settlement where six hundred anchorites lived). In Egypt, he came under the influence of the Macarii monks, known as the Makroi Adelphoi (Long Brothers), champions of Origenism. Early in his life among the Egyptian monks he encountered their hostility. They did not like "the cultured Greek living in their midst." Still the Desert Fathers exerted a significant influence on Evagrios's spirituality. He was to live among these monks until his death.

Evagrios was a prolific author of theological and ascetic essays, biblical commentaries, and letters. Some of his writings survive in the original Greek but most have survived only in Syriac, Armenian, or Latin translations. His writings reveal his indebtedness to Origen, the Desert and the Cappadocian fathers (Gregory of Nyssa in particular), and his concern with mystical and ascetic theology.

Among some fourteen authentic works by Evagrios is a trilogy: the *Praktikos*, the *Gnostikos*, and the *Kefalaia gnostika*. The first is a comprehensive exposition of his ascetic philosophy in short chapters intended for simple monks; the second is a continuation of the *Praktikos* for educated monks; and the third, the most important, known also as the *Problemata gnostika*, develops his cosmological, anthropological, and philosophical thought. It is here that Origen's influence on Evagrios is most apparent. This work was used for Evagrios's condemnation by the Second Council of Constantinople (553). Evagrios's most important essay, known as "Chapters on Prayer," is preserved in its original Greek under the name of Nilos of Ancyra.

Evagrios is acknowledged as an important spiritual influence on Christian spirituality and Islamic Sufism. He influenced Maximos the Confessor, Dionysius the Areopagite, and John of Klimakos (John Climacus) and became the forerunner of the hesychasts of later Byzantium. Through Rufinus and John Cassian, Evagrios's ascetic and mystical theology influenced John Scottus Eriugena as well as Bernard of Clairvaux and other Cistercian mystics.

BIBLIOGRAPHY

Primary Sources. Evagrios's works (including fragments) in their original Greek can be found in *Patrologia Graeca*, edited by J.-P. Migne, vols. 40 and 79 (Paris, 1858–1860)—in volume 79, s.v. *Nilus Ancyranus*—and in *Nonnenspiegel und Mönchsspiegel des Euagrios Pontikos*, edited by Hugo Gressmann (Leipzig, 1913). Sources in other languages include *The Praktikos: Chapters on Prayer*, translated and edited by John Eudes Bamberger (Spencer, Mass., 1970); *The Ecclesiastical History* by Socrates Scholasticus (London, 1884), bk. 4, pt. 23; *Evagriana Syriaca: Textes inédits du British Museum et de la Vatican*, edited and translated by Joseph Muyldermans (Louvain, 1952); and *The Lausiac History* by Palladios, edited and translated by Robert T. Meyer (Westminster, Md., 1965).

Secondary Sources. Works about Evagrios and the milieu in which he flourished include Ioustinou I. Mouseskou's *Euagrios ho Pontikos* (Athens, 1937); Hrothrd Glotobdky's "Euagrios ho Pontikos," in *Ethikē kai threskeutikē enkyklopaideia*, vol. 5 (Athens, 1964); and Derwas J. Chitty's *The Desert a City* (Crestwood, N.Y., 1977).

DEMETRIOS J. CONSTANTELOS

EVANGELICAL AND FUNDAMENTAL CHRISTIANITY.

The term *evangelicalism* usually refers to a largely Protestant movement that emphasizes (1) the Bible as authoritative and reliable; (2) eternal salvation as possible only by regeneration (being "born again"), involving personal trust in Christ and in his atoning work; and (3) a spiritually transformed life marked by moral conduct, personal devotion such as Bible reading and prayer, and zeal for evangelism and missions. Among Lutherans the term *evangelical* has long had a more general usage, roughly equivalent to *Protestant*, and some neoorthodox theologians have used the term in its broad sense of "gospel-believer." In the English-speaking world, however, *evangelical* designates a distinct movement that emerged from the religious awakenings of the eighteenth century and that by the early nineteenth century had taken clear shape in America, in England and the British empire, and in many mission fields.

"Fundamentalism" is a subspecies of evangelicalism. The term originated in America in 1920 and refers to evangelicals who consider it a chief Christian duty to combat uncompromisingly "modernist" theology and certain secularizing cultural trends. Organized militancy is the feature that most clearly distinguishes fundamentalists from other evangelicals. Fundamentalism is primarily an American phenomenon, although it has British and British empire counterparts, is paralleled by some militant groups in other traditions, and has been exported worldwide through missions.

Both evangelicalism and fundamentalism are complex coalitions reflecting the convergences of a number of traditions.

Although evangelicalism is largely an Anglo-American phenomenon, its origins give it ties with European Protestantism. The central evangelical doctrines, especially the sole authority of the Bible and the necessity of personal trust in Christ, reflect Reformation teachings. Seventeenth-century Puritanism solidly implanted these emphases in a part of the British Protestant psyche, especially in the North American colonies. In the eighteenth century this heritage merged with parallel trends in continental pietism. The influence of the Moravians on John Wesley best exemplifies this convergence. Wesley's Methodist movement in the mid-eighteenth century was part of a wider series of awakenings and pietist renewal movements appearing in Protestant countries from the late seventeenth century through much of the nineteenth century. In England the awakenings were manifested in Methodism, in evangelical renewals among nonconformists, and in the rise of a notable evangelical party in the Church of England. By the mid-nineteenth century evangelicalism was the most typical form of Protestantism in Great Britain.

In America, evangelicalism was even more influential. Evangelical religion had fewer well-established competitors than in the Old World. The rise of the United States as a new nation and the rise of evangelicalism coincided, so that the religion often assumed a quasi-official status. Evangelical emphasis on voluntary acceptance of Christianity also was well matched to American ideas of individual freedom.

The character of American evangelicalism began to take shape during the Great Awakening of the eighteenth century. This movement, really a series of revivals throughout the middle decades of the century, brought together several movements. These included New England Puritanism, continental pietism, revivalist Presbyterianism, Baptist antiestablishment democratic impulses, the Calvinist revivalism of the Englishman George Whitefield (1714–1770), and Methodism (which surpassed all the others after the Revolutionary era). During the first half of the nineteenth century, "evangelicalism" and "Protestantism" were almost synonymous in America. Evangelicalism had many denominational varieties but tended to blend Calvinist and Methodist theologies, to emphasize conversion experiences evidenced by lives freed from bar-room vices, to vigorously promote revivals and missions, and to view the church as a voluntary association of believers founded on the authority of the Bible alone.

By the early nineteenth century, evangelicals in Great Britain and America had established a formidable network of nonsectarian "voluntary societies" to promote their causes. Of these the various missionary societies, founded around the beginning of the century, were the most prominent, providing, together with denominational agencies, the home support for the most massive worldwide missionary effort ever seen. Home missionary endeavors were comparably vigorous, supported by a host of agencies for promoting evangelism, founding Sunday schools, distributing Bibles and religious tracts, establishing schools and colleges, and bringing the gospel to various needy groups. Revivalism spearheaded such efforts, exemplified best in the extensive campaigns of Charles Finney (1792–1875) both in America and England. These mission and evangelistic efforts were accompanied by campaigns, organized by voluntary societies, for charity and social reform. On both sides of the Atlantic, evangelicals played leading roles in combating slavery; in Great Britain, especially under the leadership of William Wilberforce (1759–1833), they were influential in bringing about its abolition throughout the empire. Evangelicals promoted other reforms, including Sabbatarian and temperance legislation, prison reform, and the establishment of private charities. Such reforming spirit was usually part of a postmillennial vision of steady spiritual and moral progress leading to a millennial age of the triumph of the gospel throughout the world, after which Christ himself would return. Especially in America, such millennialism was often tied to strong patriotism and anti-Catholicism.

In the latter half of the nineteenth century, the vigorous evangelicalism that had grown so successfully in the early industrial era found itself in a new world. The concentrated new industrialism and the massively crowded cities tended to overwhelm the individualistic and voluntaristic evangelical programs. Conceptions of dominating the culture became more difficult to maintain. Evangelicals, accordingly, increasingly stressed those aspects of their message that involved personal commitment to Christ and personal holiness rather than social programs, although aspirations to be a major moral influence on the culture never entirely disappeared. The evangelicalism of Dwight L. Moody (1837–1899) exemplified this trend. Moody, like Finney before him, had great successes in both America and Great Britain. He omitted entirely, however, Finney's postmillennial emphases on social reform, stressing instead the importance of rescuing the perishing from the sinking ship that was the condemned world. This increasing sense of evangelical alienation from Anglo-American culture was reflected in Moody's premillennialism and in the growth of premillennialism among most of the newer evangelical movements of the day. Premillennialists looked to the second coming of Christ as the only cure for the world's social and political woes. New emphases on personal holiness, notably exemplified in the rise of the British Keswick holiness movement after 1875, reflected similar tendencies. Keswick teaching, which spread widely among American evangelical and later fundamentalist followers of Moody, stressed personal victory over sin, personal witnessing about the gospel, and support of missions as chief among Christian duties. Keswick was only one of several new holiness movements that flourished among evangelicals in the mid- and later nineteenth century. Most of these movements had generic ties with Methodism and John Wesley's teachings concerning Christian perfection. Some holiness groups, most notably the Salvation Army, founded in England in 1865, combined their evangelism with extensive charitable work among the needy. Others among an emerging number of holiness denominations emphasized more the personal experience of being filled by the Holy Spirit. Such emphases in heightened forms were apparent in the rise in America after 1900 of Pentecostalism, which also brought separate denominations and almost exclusive emphasis on intense personal spiritual experience. By the early twentieth century, evangelicalism was thus subdivided into a variety of camps on questions of personal holiness and the nature of spiritual experience.

Equally important during this same era, from the latter decades of the nineteenth century to World War I, was that evangelicals were finding themselves in a new world intellectually. Darwinism became the focal symbol of a many-faceted revolution in assumptions dominating the culture. Some of the early debates over Darwinism left an impression, damaging to evangelicalism, that modern science and biblical Christianity were inherently opposed. A deeper issue, however, was a broader revolution in conceptions of reality and truth. Rather than seeing truth as fixed and absolute, Western people were more and more viewing it as a changing function of human cultural evolution. Religion in such a view was not absolute truth revealed by the deity, but the record of developing human conceptions about God and morality. Such conceptions were devastating when applied to the Bible, which in the higher criticism of the late nineteenth century often was regarded as simply the record of Hebrew religious experience. The widespread evangelical consensus was shaken to its foundations. The absolute authority of the Bible as the source of the doctrine of salvation was widely questioned, even within the churches. Moral absolutes based on scripture were also questioned; again, the questioning was often from within the churches. The result was a profound split in most of the denominations that had been at the center of the mid-nineteenth-century evangelical alliance. Liberals, sometimes called "modernists" in the early twentieth century, adjusted Christian doctrine to fit the temper of the times. God's revelation of his kingdom was not so much in startling supernatural interventions as in working through the best in the natural processes of the growth of civilization and morality. Essentially, Christianity was not so much a doctrine of eternal salvation for another world as a divine revelation of a humane way of life for this world. Sometimes liberals advocated a "social gospel," based on the progressive politics of the early twentieth century, to replace the individualism of older evangelicalism's conceptions of salvation. Many traditionalist evangelicals, on the other hand, resisted these trends toward more naturalistic, relativistic, and modern conceptions of the heart of the gospel, continuing rather to preach traditional evangelical doctrine of a miraculous Bible whose revelation centered on describing the means of divine rescue from sin, death, and hell.

Fundamentalism arose in this context. It combined an organized militant defense of most traditional evangelical doctrines with some of the revivalist evangelical innovations of the nineteenth century. Most important of these innovations, eventually accepted by most fundamentalists, was the elaborate system of biblical interpretation known as dispensationalism. Dispensationalism was a version of the premillennialism popularized among revivalists in the later nineteenth century. Originated in England especially by the Plymouth Brethren leader John Nelson Darby (1800–1882), dispensationalism was developed and promoted in America principally by Bible teacher associates of Dwight L. Moody, such as Reuben A. Torrey (1856–1928), James M. Gray (1851–1935), and C. I. Scofield (1843–1921), editor of the famous dispensationalist *Scofield Reference Bible*, published in 1909. Dispensationalism is a systematic scheme for interpreting all of history on the basis of the Bible, following the principle of "literal where possible"; biblical prophecies, especially, are taken to refer to real historical events. This approach yields a rather detailed account of all human history, which is divided into seven dispensations, or eras of differing relationships between God and humanity (such as the Dispensation of Innocence in Eden or the Dispensation of Law, from Moses to Christ). The last of these eras is the millennium, which will be preceded by the personal return of Jesus, the secret "rapture" of believers who are to "meet him in the air," a seven-year period of wars among those who remain on earth (resulting in the victory of Christ), the conversion of the Jews, and the establishment of a kingdom in Jerusalem where Jesus will reign for exactly one thousand years before the Last Judgment. Such exact interpretations of prophecy committed dispensationalists firmly to a view of the Bible as divinely inspired and without error in any detail. The "inerrancy" of scripture in scientific and historical detail accordingly became the key test of faith for fundamentalists. This doctrine, while not entirely novel in the history of the church, was also given a new and especially forceful articulation by nondispensationalist Presbyterian traditionalists at Princeton Theological Seminary, especially Benjamin B. Warfield (1851–1921), who for a time was allied with dispensationalists in battles against liberal theology and higher criticism of the Bible.

The other major innovation widely accepted by fundamentalists was the Keswick holiness teaching. The same groups of Bible teachers who taught dispensationalism widely promoted Keswick doctrine as well. These leaders established regular summer Bible conferences and, more important, founded a network of Bible institutes for training lay workers in evangelism. These institutes, together with local churches and agencies directly promoting revivalism, such as those of Billy Sunday (1862–1935), provided the principal institutional base for fundamentalism.

Fundamentalism was also a mood as much as a set of doctrines and institutions. It was a mood of militancy in opposition to modernist theology and to some of the relativistic cultural changes that modernism embraced. This militancy provided the basis for a wider antimodernist coalition that emerged as a distinct movement in America during the 1920s. The immediate occasion for the appearance of fundamentalism was the sense of cultural crisis that gripped America after World War I. Reflecting this mood, fundamentalism gave focus to the anxieties of Protestant traditionalists. This focus was directed first of all against the modernists in major denominations, most notably the major Baptist and Presbyterian churches in the northern United States. Especially in the years from 1920 to 1925, fundamentalists led major efforts to expel such liberals from their denominations, but these efforts met with little success. The other focus was American culture itself. America seemed to many evangelicals to have lost its Christian and biblical moorings. World War I precipitated this sense of alarm, for the war sped up a revolution in morals that, despite the rearguard action of Prohibition legislation, replaced Victorian evangelical standards with the public morals of the jazz age. The international crisis also generated fears of social upheaval at home, particularly alarm about the rise of Bolshevism and atheism in America during the "Red Scare" of 1919 and 1920. Many Protestants also remained concerned about the social and moral impact of the immense immigration of the preceding half-century and were antagonistic to the spread of Roman Catholic influences.

Fundamentalists saw all these factors as signs of the end of a Bible-based civilization in America. Their chief social anxieties, however, centered on the question of evolution. During the war extreme propaganda had convinced most Americans that Germany, the homeland of the Reformation, had lapsed into barbarism. The same thing might happen in America. The "will to power" philosophy of Friedrich Nietzsche, said the propagandists, had destroyed German morals. Fundamentalists contended that this was an evolutionary philosophy and that evolutionary and relativistic ideas had long been incorporated into German theology, now taught by liberals in America's churches. Under the leadership of William Jennings Bryan (1860–1925), fundamentalists campaigned to bring America back to the Bible by banning the teaching of biological evolution in public schools. This crusade brought fundamentalism, which had been largely northern, into the American South, where homegrown Protestant antimodernist tendencies had been strong since the Civil War. The fundamentalist antievolution campaign reached its peak in the 1925 trial of John Scopes in Dayton, Tennessee, for teaching biological evolution in a high school. At the highly publicized proceedings, Bryan debated lawyer Clarence Darrow concerning the authenticity of biblical miracles. Bryan was ridiculed in the world press, and his death shortly after the trial signaled the beginning of a decline of early fundamentalist efforts to control American culture. During the later 1920s the strength of fundamentalist efforts to purge major northern denominations also declined dramatically. During this era, organized fundamentalism had some branches in Canada and some relatively small counterparts in Great Britain.

In America, fundamentalism was only the prominent fighting edge of the larger evangelical movement. During the decades from 1925 to 1945 the public press paid less attention to fundamentalist complaints, but the movement itself was regrouping rather than retreating. During this time fundamentalism developed a firmer institutional base, especially in independent local churches and in some smaller denominations, although considerable numbers of fundamentalists remained in major denominations. The revivalist heritage of the movement was especially apparent in this era, as it turned its strongest efforts toward winning America through evangelization. In addition to traditional means for evangelization, fundamentalists developed effective radio ministries. Particularly prominent was Charles E. Fuller's "Old-Fashioned Revival Hour," which by 1942 had a larger audience than any other radio program in America.

Fundamentalist-evangelicals were also founding new sorts of ministries, such as Youth for Christ, begun in 1942, which soon had hundreds of chapters across the country. Bible institutes, such as Moody Bible Institute in Chicago, the Bible Institute of Los Angeles, and many others, remained important centers for the movement, training and sending out evangelists and missionaries, conducting Bible conferences, establishing effective radio ministries, and publishing many books and periodicals.

A sharp tension was developing in the fundamentalist-evangelical movement that survived the controversies of the 1920s. This tension led eventually to a deep split between "fundamentalists" and "evangelicals." The fundamentalists kept in the forefront the militancy that had characterized the movement in the 1920s. Furthermore, they followed the logic of their military metaphors by adding ecclesiastical separatism as a test of true commitment. This separatist stance sometimes reflected also the influence of dispensationalism, which taught that the Bible prophesied the decline and apostasy of the major churches during the present era.

Another element in the generation that had been raised on the fundamentalist controversies of the 1920s sought to bring the movement back toward a broader evangelicalism. Without rejecting entirely their fundamentalist heritage, they nonetheless softened the militancy and often moved away from dispensationalism. Repudiating separatism as a test of the faith, they especially emphasized positive evangelism. By the early 1940s a distinct movement with these emphases was apparent, signaled by the founding of the National Association of Evangelicals (NAE) in 1942. In contrast to the smaller, militantly separatist American Council of Christian Churches, founded in 1941 by the fundamentalist Carl McIntire, the NAE included Pentecostal and holiness denominations, as well as individual members who remained in major American denominations.

Following World War II some younger leaders, notably Harold John Ockenga, Carl F. H. Henry, and Edward J. Carnell, organized a "neoevangelical" movement with the explicit purpose of moderating and broadening fundamentalist-evangelicalism. Joined by Charles E. Fuller, they organized the Fuller Theological Seminary in Pasadena, California, in 1947. Their efforts were vastly aided by the emergence of Billy Graham as America's leading evangelist after 1949. This group in 1956 also founded *Christianity Today* to provide a solid periodical base for the movement.

The final break in the fundamentalist-evangelical movement came with Billy Graham's New York crusade in 1957. Graham accepted the cooperation of some prominent liberal church leaders. Separatist fundamentalists such as Bob Jones, Sr. (1883–1968), founder of Bob Jones University; John R. Rice (1895–1980), editor of the influential *Sword of the Lord;* and Carl McIntire anathematized Graham and the neoevangelicals as traitors from within. Neoevangelicals in turn soon ceased altogether to call themselves fundamentalists, preferring the designation "evangelical."

In the meantime, Graham's crusade in Great Britain in 1954 set off a small flurry of ecclesiastical debate known as the "fundamentalist controversy" in England. This designation confused the terminological issue, since in England the friends of Graham, rather than just his more conservative enemies, were called fundamentalists. (British parlance still often lacks the distinction between *fundamentalist* and *evangelical* that has developed in America since the late 1950s.) In any case, conservative evangelicalism remained strong in British church life, especially in the evangelical party in the Church of England. Influenced considerably by the longstanding university ministry of the Inter-Varsity Fellowship, and less a product of the sensational promotional competitions that characterized American revivalism, British evangelicalism was often more sophisticated than its American counterpart and played an important role in the intellectual leadership of the international movement. Throughout the English-speaking world there are also counterparts to the more strictly fundamentalist, holiness, and Pentecostal groups found in America.

Evangelicalism was indeed a widespread international phenomenon, even if its Anglo-American manifestations gave it its most focused identity as a distinct movement. The pietist varieties of worldwide Protestantism were scarcely distinguishable from Anglo-American evangelicalism. Moreover, nearly two centuries of massive missionary efforts had planted evangelical communities in most of the nations of the world. The sense of identity of an international evangelicalism was evidenced in world conferences, notably the 1966 World Congress on Evangelism in Berlin and the 1974 International Congress on World Evangelization at Lausanne. Such gatherings were initially organized primarily by Anglo-American friends of Billy Graham, but they also marked the emergence among evangelicals of significant voices and leadership from developing nations. The Lausanne congress, for instance, included over two thousand participants from 150 countries. Traditional evangelical emphases on the reliability and authority of scripture and on the urgency for world evangelization were apparent, but so were emphases on the necessity of social and political concern for aiding the poor and victims of injustice.

The United States, however, remained the place where evangelicalism had its greatest impact. During the 1970s the American media suddenly discovered that evangelicalism was a major force in American life. Evangelicalism had in fact been growing steadily for many years, so that the numbers of evangelicals had grown to forty or fifty million, while other Protestants and Roman Catholics were declining in numbers. Once evangelicals were discovered, they became conspicuous in the media, boasting many sports and entertainment stars. Being "born again" suddenly became a political asset, evidenced in 1976 by the victorious presidential campaign of Jimmy Carter, and evangelicalism was reckoned as a powerful, if mysterious, political force.

The discovery of evangelicalism reflected not only real growth and change in the movement but also the power of a concept. Numerous strands in American religious life were now viewed as part of a more-or-less unified "evangelicalism." Such a perception was at once helpful and deceptive. It was helpful in pointing to a very large phenomenon: Christians who shared fundamental evangelical beliefs. It was deceptive, however, in its implication that their movement was more unified than it actually was. Certainly evangelicalism as a movement that could claim forty or fifty million adherents was much larger than the consciously organized evangelical movement that had grown out of fundamentalist-evangelicalism and that was led by associates of Billy Graham. For instance, black evangelicals, including most of black Protestantism, had had very little to do with that fundamentalist-evangelicalism, even though most of their beliefs and emphases were closely parallel. The same was true, but to a lesser degree, of much of the Southern Baptist Convention, the largest of American evangelical groups. Most holiness denominations and evangelical Methodists were only tangentially related to the organized fundamentalist-evangelical movement. So also were most Pentecostals and charismatics, who sponsored some of the largest television ministries and set the tone for much of the evangelical resurgence. Peace churches were generally evangelical in doctrine but preserved a heritage distinct from fundamentalist-evangelicalism. Confessional denominations, such as the Missouri Synod Lutheran and the Christian Reformed church, were close allies of evangelicals but always kept enough distance to preserve distinct doctrinal heritages. Many evangelicals were in major American denominations, such as Baptist, Presbyterian, Methodist, Disciples of Christ, or Episcopal, but might be as much shaped by the distinctives of their denomination's history as by a conscious evangelical identity. Others in such denominations might identify closely with the doctrines and emphases of a parachurch evangelistic agency, such as Campus Crusade, founded by Bill Bright in 1951. Such variety within evangelicalism, compounded by many denominational and regional differences, suggests that generalization about the movement is hazardous.

Such hazards are especially great concerning evangelicals' political stances. Whereas an important strand of nineteenth-century American evangelicalism was politically progressive and reformist, in the twentieth century most fundamentalist-evangelicals and other white evangelicals have been politically conservative. Since the 1960s, however, much more variety has appeared, especially among spokespersons of the sort who hold conferences and issue declarations. Evangelical voices have been heard across the spectrum of political options, although most of the evangelical constituency is probably at least moderately conservative.

Most hard-line fundamentalists went their separate ways after about 1950, reorganizing themselves loosely in a number of fellowships or smaller denominations. The largest fellowship was the Baptist Bible Fellowship, founded by fundamentalists who split with the volatile Texas fundamentalist F. Frank Norris. By the early 1980s this fellowship claimed to represent two to three million members. During this era some local fundamentalist pastors built huge churches, claiming both membership and Sunday-school attendance of over ten thousand each by the 1970s. Prominent among these were First Baptist of Hammond, Indiana, pastored by Jack Hyles, Lee Roberson's Highland Park Baptist Church in Chattanooga, Tennessee, and Jerry Falwell's Thomas Road Baptist Church in Lynchburg, Virginia. Typically, such ministries were structured as small, individually run empires including branch chapels, a college, publications, radio and television broadcasts, missionary work, and specialized ministries. The total number of members of strictly separatist fundamentalist churches in the United States by 1980 was perhaps around five million, although the number of evangelicals leaning toward fundamentalism is probably much greater. Moreover, such militant fundamentalism has spread throughout the English-speaking world, and active missions have carried its doctrines to every nation where Christian missions are permitted.

Soul winning and church growth are the fundamentalist's first concerns, as they are for most evangelicals. In addition, extreme militancy against theological liberalism has led them to emphasize separation even from other evangelicals, especially neoevangelicals, charismatics, and members of large groups such as the Southern Baptist Convention. The question of separation has also divided fundamentalists among themselves. Some fundamentalist leaders, especially those associated with Bob Jones University, have advocated "second-degree separation," that is, separation even from fellow fundamentalists who are not strict fundamentalists. In the 1970s, for instance, Bob Jones III attacked the noted fundamentalist evangelist John R. Rice for publishing materials by Southern Baptists in his widely read paper *The Sword of the Lord.*

Fundamentalists have also drawn strict lines for personal separation from worldliness. Not only do they forbid drinking, smoking, card playing, theater attendance, and dancing, as do many evangelicals, but they often also have made strict rules against fashion trends: slacks for women, long hair, beards or mustaches for men, flared pants, and wire-rimmed glasses. Some fundamentalists have also marked their separation by promoting such teachings as the necessity not only of believing the inerrancy of the Bible but also of insisting on the King James Version.

Most fundamentalists are militant dispensationalists, usually claiming that the signs of the times indicate that within a few years the dramatic events surrounding the return of Christ will bring the present era to a violent end. The dispensationalist heritage has made most fundamentalist-evangelicals sympathetic to the state of Israel, whose existence is viewed as the fulfillment of prophecy. During the 1970s, dispensationalist prophetic views attracted wide interest, as indicated by the popularity of Hal Lindsey's book *The Late Great Planet Earth* (1970), of which some ten million copies were printed during the decade.

Until the later 1970s, most separatist fundamentalists were not active politically. Some prominent fundamentalist leaders, such as Carl McIntire and Billy James Hargis, were in the forefront of anticommunist crusades during the decades following World War II, but such activists probably did not represent the majority of the movement. Fundamentalists emerged as a considerable force in American political life with the formation of the Moral Majority in 1979. This political coalition of fundamentalists and some other political conservatives was led by Jerry Falwell and benefited from his large television ministry. Some strict fundamentalists condemned such efforts since they involved cooperation with Roman Catholics, Orthodox Jews, neoevangelicals, and other alleged apostates. Nonetheless, the Moral Majority brought together several longstanding fundamentalist concerns and some recent political issues. Most evangelicals and almost all fundamentalists, for instance, had long held conservative views on the role of women, on the family, and on questions related to sexuality. Sparked by the legalization of abortion in 1973, the women's movement and the proposed Equal Rights Amendment, legislation favoring homosexuals, and general permissiveness, many fundamentalist and conservative evangelicals expressed alarm. The Moral Majority focused such sentiments and organized them politically. Reaching a constituency well beyond fundamentalists and fundamentalist evangelicals, its program included endorsement of American conservative political ideals: smaller government, larger military, patriotism, and freedom for businesses. Fundamentalists, supported by the Moral Majority, also successfully revived the antievolution crusade, introducing legislation into a number of states that would require the teaching of fundamentalist "creation science" (arguments that the earth is no more than ten thousand years old) whenever biological evolution is taught in public schools.

Perhaps the closest parallel to such American political fundamentalism has been the militant Protestantism in Northern Ireland led by Ian Paisley. Paisley, an avowed fundamentalist with connections to American leaders such as Bob Jones and Carl McIntire, has mixed conservative Protestantism with aggressive political anti-Catholicism. The long history of the Irish conflict, however, has given Irish fundamentalism a character more violent than its American counterparts. A far more genteel political action movement with some evangelical leadership is England's Festival of Light, an organization prominent in the 1970s and 1980s in its efforts to maintain public decency, particularly in matters concerning sexuality.

[*For discussion of related Christian phenomena, see* Pentecostal and Charismatic Christianity; Modernism, *article on* Christian Modernism; *and* Christian Social Movements. *See also* Protestantism. *For discussion of related notions in broader religious perspective, see* Millenarianism]

BIBLIOGRAPHY

Sydney E. Ahlstrom's *A Religious History of the American People* (New Haven, 1972) contains solid introductory surveys of American evangelicalism and fundamentalism. *The Eerdman's Handbook to the History of Christianity in America*, edited by Mark A. Noll and Nathan O. Hatch (Grand Rapids, Mich., 1983), is a valuable survey by evangelical authors. Of the more specific studies, Ernest R. Sandeen's *The Roots of Fundamentalism: British and American Millenarianism, 1800–1930* (Chicago, 1970) is an outstanding study of the role of dispensational premillennialism in shaping fundamentalism. George M. Marsden's *Fundamentalism and American Culture:*

The Shaping of Twentieth-Century Evangelicalism 1870–1925 (New York, 1980) looks at the subject in terms of both cultural and religious history. Ferenc M. Szasz's *The Divided Mind of Protestant America, 1880–1930* (University, Ala., 1982) provides additional insights on the same period. A very readable survey of an important aspect of the movement is William G. McLoughlin, Jr.'s *Modern Revivalism: Charles Grandison Finney to Billy Graham* (New York, 1959). Richard Hofstadter's *Anti-intellectualism in American Life* (New York, 1963) draws heavily on McLoughlin but adds some brilliant observations. A valuable biographical treatment of some early twentieth-century fundamentalist leaders is C. Allyn Russell's *Voices of American Fundamentalism* (Philadelphia, 1976). George W. Dollar's *A History of Fundamentalism in America* (Greenville, S.C., 1973) offers a hard-line fundamentalist perspective and some information not found elsewhere. *Aspects of Pentecostal-Charismatic Origins*, edited by Vinson Synan (South Plainfield, N.J., 1975), is valuable on a related movement often confused with fundamentalism. Richard Quebedeaux's *The Worldly Evangelicals* (San Francisco, 1978) provides an impressionistic but informative survey of the American movement in the 1970s. *Varieties of Southern Evangelicalism*, edited by David E. Harrell, Jr. (Macon, Ga., 1981), deals with a major part of American evangelicalism that has not received proportionate scholarly attention. British evangelicalism as a distinct phenomenon has received even less attention. One can gain initial impressions of the dimensions of the movement from surveys such as Owen Chadwick's *The Victorian Church*, 2 vols. (London, 1966–1970), David A. Martin's *A Sociology of English Religion* (London, 1967), and Alan D. Gilbert's *The Making of Post-Christian Britain: A History of the Secularization of Modern Society* (London, 1980). James Barr's *Fundamentalism* (Philadelphia, 1977) is an antifundamentalist polemic with some valuable theological insights, although it confuses fundamentalism with evangelicalism generally.

George M. Marsden

EVANGELIZATION. *See* Missions, *article on* Missionary Activity.

EVANS, ARTHUR (1851–1941), English archaeologist who excavated the ruins of Knossos in Crete, center of an early civilization he called Minoan. Son of Sir John Evans, a wealthy Victorian polymath and active amateur archaeologist, Arthur Evans began his work at Knossos, which established his fame and for which he was knighted in 1911, in 1899. Seeking evidence for an early system of writing, Evans uncovered an inscribed clay tablet in his first week of excavation and soon amassed a large archive written in two syllabic scripts now known as Linear A and Linear B. (The latter was deciphered as an early form of Greek by Michael Ventris and John Chadwick in 1952.) The treasures of the palace at Knossos, which Evans named for the legendary King Minos, included many objects that he interpreted as possessing religious significance. In the palace, a building of great size and complex plan, images of bulls' horns, the motif of the double ax, and depictions of young men and women performing acrobatic feats with bulls furnished attractive parallels with Greek legend: *labrus* means "ax," so that *labyrinthos* suggests "the place of the ax," to which, according to legend, seven young men and seven young women were sent from Athens each year to encounter the Minotaur. Evans interpreted the double ax as symbolizing, or marking the presence of, the Cretan Zeus, a deity of quite different type from the Indo-European sky god of the same name with whom he became identified. The Cretan Zeus died and was reborn in an annual cycle. Also important in Minoan religion was the association of trees and pillars as cult objects, a theme Evans discussed in works published in 1900, in the earliest days of the excavation, and in 1931.

Evans faced the usual difficulties of interpreting religious objects in the absence of verbal evidence. (The Linear B tablets, which proved to be records of tribute paid and other stocktaking records, have added very little.) In the manner of his day, Evans was an evolutionist and comparatist, and he drew heavily on the folklore and practice of other cultures. Evaluations of his interpretations vary, but in the field of Greek religion, as in other branches of classical studies, his importance rests on the abundance of material he excavated and assiduously published.

BIBLIOGRAPHY

Evans's views on Minoan-Mycenaean religion are to be found in *The Mycenaean Tree and Pillar Cult and Its Mediterranean Relations* (London, 1901) and *The Earlier Religion of Greece in the Light of Cretan Discoveries* (London, 1931); the latter was Evans's Frazer Lecture for 1931 at the University of Cambridge. The full account of the Knossos excavation is contained in *The Palace of Minos*, 4 vols. in 6 (London, 1921–1935).

A. W. H. Adkins

EVANS-PRITCHARD, E. E. (1902–1973), English anthropologist. Edward Evan Evans-Pritchard was the son of a clergyman of the Church of England. He took a degree in history at the University of Oxford and in 1927 a doctorate in anthropology at the University of London, where he was supervised by C. G. Seligman. His thesis was based on field research undertaken from 1926 to 1930 among the Azande of the Sudan. He carried out research among the Nuer, another Sudanese people, intermittently between 1930 and 1935 and also for brief periods among the Anuak, the Luo, and other East African peoples. During World War II he worked at intervals, when free from military service, among the bedouin of Cyrenaica. In 1944 he joined the Roman Catholic church. He taught at the University of London, Fuad I University in Cairo, Cambridge University, and finally Oxford, where in 1946 he succeeded A. R. Radcliffe-Brown as professor of social anthropology. He retired in 1970, was knighted in 1971, and died in Oxford in September 1973.

Evans-Pritchard's work in religion is unique. It is based on brilliant, sensitive, and meticulous field research, on his mastery of languages (he was fluent in Arabic, Zande, and Nuer), and on his deep knowledge and understanding of the work of his predecessors, in particular those sociologists (Durkheim et al.) associated with *L'année sociologique.* Most of his writings on religion fall into one of four main categories: works on the Azande, the Nuer, the Sanusi, and comparative and theoretical topics.

Each piece of Evans-Pritchard's research and writing is based on certain central problems in anthropology, although never limited to them in a narrow sense. His work among the Azande, a cluster of kingdoms of the southwestern Sudan, led to the publication of *Witchcraft, Oracles, and Magic among the Azande* (1937), perhaps the outstanding work of anthropology published in this century. It is concerned essentially with questions asked, although hardly answered in any convincing manner, by Lucien Lévy-Bruhl in his writings on "primitive" and "scientific" modes of thought. The questions as to whether there are differences between these two modes of thought and, if so, what they are and how they might function in social contexts are basic to anthropology, and Evans-Pritchard's discussion of them has changed the nature of anthropological inquiry. He writes about Zande notions of magic, witchcraft, and divination, that is, their notions of natural and supernatural causation and interference in people's everyday lives. He shows that Zande ideas are rational and systematic; given certain premises of knowledge they are closed and self-perpetuating, and they are not held in isolation but are consistent with forms of authority and power found in Zande society. This is essentially a study of rationality and corrects all earlier views about the "irrationality" of so-called primitive peoples. Later Evans-Pritchard published an immense number of Zande texts, in both Zande and English, with commentaries. This work is probably the greatest single corpus of the myths and tales of an African culture that has yet been published and confirms one of his strongest beliefs: that "primitive" texts are not quaint "folkloristic" stories but are as worthy of careful analysis as those of literate cultures.

Evans-Pritchard's *Nuer Religion* (1956) is the final volume of a trilogy on the Nuer of the southern Sudan (the others are *The Nuer,* 1940, and *Kinship and Marriage among the Nuer,* 1951). In this book he presents Nuer religious thought and ritual as a system of theology that has a subtlety and profundity comparable to those of literate cultures. Here he takes up another basic problem raised by Lévy-Bruhl, that of "mystical participation" between men and what in ethnocentric terms are called the supernatural and the natural. This problem is examined within the context of a series of related aspects of Nuer religion: conceptions of God, spirits, the soul, and ghosts; symbolism; sin and sacrifice; and priesthood and prophecy. Because of Evans-Pritchard's great skill in unfolding the complexity of Nuer religious thought, never since has it been possible for scholars of comparative religion to dismiss a nonliterate religion as "primitive" or as a form of "animism." Throughout this work, as in that on the Azande, Evans-Pritchard stresses what he considered to be the central problem of anthropology, that of translation—not the simple problem of translation of words and phrases in a narrow linguistic sense, but the far more complex question of translation of one culture's experience into the terms of another's.

Evans-Pritchard's other "ethnographic" work on religion is rather different, taking as its basic problem the relationship between prophets (a topic raised earlier in his work on the Nuer) and forms of religious and political authority as exemplified in the history of the Muslim Sanusi order in Cyrenaica (*The Sanusi of Cyrenaica,* 1951). Here he was able to use written records as well as his own field research, and he produces a model account of religious history and change.

Evans-Pritchard's last achievement in the study of religion is his many critical writings on the history of the anthropology of religion, of which the best known is *Theories of Primitive Religion* (1965). It is a superb and sophisticated study of the relations between thought, ideology, and society.

The influence of E. E. Evans-Pritchard's writings in the anthropological study of religion has been immense. There has been little later analysis made of modes of thought, systems of causation, witch beliefs, sacrifice, notions of sin, and ritual symbolism that has not been influenced by, if not based upon, his work. In addition, much recent research on the philosophy of knowledge has leaned heavily on his book on the Azande. Evans-Pritchard's influence upon younger anthropologists has been great. The anthropological, historical, and comparative study of religions owes more to him than to any other anthropologist.

BIBLIOGRAPHY

The main works of Evans-Pritchard are cited in the article. The most insightful view of his work, in the form of an obituary, is by T. O. Beidelman, "Sir Edward Evan Evans-Pritchard, 1902–1973: An Appreciation," *Anthropos* 69 (1974): 553–567. Beidelman is also the editor of *A Bibliography of the Writings of E. E. Evans-Pritchard* (London, 1974). Mary Douglas's *Edward Evans-Pritchard* (New York, 1980) is a fuller but rather uneven account.

JOHN MIDDLETON

EVE, or, in Hebrew, Ḥavvah; the first woman in the creation narratives of the Hebrew Bible, according to which she was formed from one of the ribs of Adam, the first man (*Gn.* 2:21–23). In this account the creator god wished for Adam to have a mate and so brought all the beasts of the fold and birds of the sky before him to see what he would call each one (*Gn.* 2:19). However, among these creatures the man found no one to be his companion (*Gn.* 2:20). Accordingly, this episode is not solely an etiology of the primal naming of all creatures by the male ancestor of the human race but an account of how this man *(ish)* found no helpmeet until a woman was formed from one of his ribs, whom he named "woman" (*ishshah; Gn.* 2:23). This account is juxtaposed with a comment that serves etiologically to establish the social institution of marriage wherein a male leaves his father and mother and cleaves to his wife so that they become "one flesh" together (*Gn.* 2:24). The matrimonial union is thus a re-union of a primordial situation when the woman was, literally and figuratively, flesh of man's flesh.

Such a version of the origin of the woman, as a special creation from Adam's body, stands in marked contrast to the creation tradition found in *Genesis* 1:27b, where there is a hint that the primordial person *(adam)* was in fact an androgyne. Alternatively, this latter half-verse may have been concerned with correcting a tradition of an originally lone male by the statement that both male and female were simultaneously created as the first "Adam." [*See* Adam.]

This mythic image of a male as the source of all human life (*Gn.* 2:21–22) reflects a male fantasy of self-sufficiency. The subsequent narrative introduces a more realistic perspective. Thus, after the woman has succumbed to the wiles of the snake, eaten of the tree of the knowledge of good and evil, and shared it with her husband, she is acknowledged as a source of new life—albeit with negative overtones, since the narrative stresses the punishment of pain that must be borne by Adam's mate and all her female descendants during pregnancy and childbirth. In token of her role as human genetrix, the man gave to the woman a new name: she was thenceforth called Eve—"for she was the mother of all life" (*Gn.* 2:19).

This new name, *Eve* (Heb., *Ḥavvah*), is in fact a pun on the noun for "life" (Heb., *ḥay*), since both *ḥavvah* and *ḥay* allude to old Semitic words (in Aramaic, Phoenician, and Arabic) for "serpent," as the ancient rabbis noted. Another intriguing cross-cultural pun should be recalled, insofar as it may also underlie the key motifs of the biblical narrative. Thus, in a Sumerian myth it is told that when Enki had a pain in his rib, Ninhursaga caused Nin-ti ("woman of the rib") to be created from him. Strikingly, the Sumerian logogram *ti* (in the goddess's name) stands for both "rib" and "life."

According to one rabbinic *midrash,* Eve was taken from the thirteenth rib of Adam's right side after Lilith, his first wife, had left him (*Pirqei de-Rabbi Eli'ezer* 20). [*See* Lilith.] Other legends emphasize Eve's susceptibility to guile and persuasion. Christian traditions use the episode of Eve to encourage the submission of women to their husbands (cf. *2 Cor.* 11:3, *1 Tm.* 2:22–25). Several church fathers typologically compared Eve with Mary, the "new Eve" and mother of Jesus: the sinfulness and disobedience of the former were specifically contrasted with the latter. The temptation motif and the banishment of Eve and Adam are frequently found in medieval Jewish and Christian illuminated manuscripts and in Persian iconography. The theme is also found in medieval morality plays and in the apocalyptic tract *Life of Adam and Eve.*

BIBLIOGRAPHY

Ginzberg, Louis. *The Legends of the Jews* (1909–1938). 7 vols. Translated by Henrietta Szold et al. Reprint, Philadelphia, 1937–1966. See the index, s.v. *Eve.*

Mangenot, Eugène. "Eve." In *Dictionnaire de théologie catholique,* vol. 5, cols. 1640–1655. Paris, 1913.

Speiser, E. A. *Genesis.* Anchor Bible, vol. 1. Garden City, N.Y., 1964.

MICHAEL FISHBANE

EVIL. If there is one human experience ruled by myth, it is certainly that of evil. One can understand why: the two major forms of this experience—moral evil and physical evil—both contain an enigmatic element in whose shadows the difference between them tends to vanish.

On the one hand, it is only at the conclusion of a thoroughgoing critique of mythical representations that moral evil could be conceived of as the product of a free act involving human responsibility alone. Social blame, interiorized as guilt, is in fact a response to an existential quality that was initially represented as a stain infecting the human heart as if from outside. And even when this quasi-magical representation of a contamination by an external or superior power is replaced by the feeling of a sin of which we are the authors, we can feel that we have been seduced by overwhelming powers. Moreover, each of us finds evil already present in the world; no one initiates evil but everyone has the feeling of belonging to a history of evil more ancient than any individual evil act. This strange experience of passivity, which is at the very heart of evildoing, makes us feel ourselves to be the victims in the very act that makes us guilty.

On the other hand, it is also only at the conclusion of a comparable critique of mythical representations that physical evil is recognized as the effect of natural causes of a physical, biological, and even social nature: sickness, which often takes the form of great epidemics ravaging entire populations, simultaneously attacks each person in the very depths of his existence by making him suffer and is spontaneously experienced as an aggression, at once external and internal, coming from maleficent powers that are easily confused with those that seduce the human heart and persuade it to do evil. Moreover, the sort of fate that seems to lead the sick and aging to the threshold of death tends to make mortality the very emblem of the human condition. From this, it is easy to take the next step and consider suffering and death as punishments. Do not guilt and mortality constitute the same enigma?

The persistence of mythical representations of evil can be explained by a third phenomenon, namely the extraordinary way in which guilt and suffering remain intertwined with a stage of development in which the human mind believes it has freed itself from the realm of mythical representations. To declare someone guilty is to declare that person deserving of punishment. And punishment is, in its turn, a suffering, both physical and moral, inflicted by someone other than the guilty party. Punishment, as suffering, therefore bridges the gap between the evil committed and the evil suffered. This same boundary is crossed in the other direction by the fact that a major cause of suffering lies in the violence that human beings exercise on one another. In fact, to do evil is always, directly or indirectly, to make someone else suffer. This mutual overlapping of evil done and evil suffered prevents the two major forms of evil from ever being entirely separate and, in particular, from ever being entirely stripped of their enigmatic character. An essential opaqueness in the human condition is therefore bound up with the experience of evil, which is continually carried back to its darkness, its obscurity, by the exercise of violence, always unjust, and of punishment, even when it is held to be just.

This invincible connection of moral evil and physical evil is expressed on the level of language in the specific "language game" designated by the general term *lamentation*. Lamentation, indeed, is not confined to the moanings rising up from the abyss of suffering, announcing the coming of death. It encompasses the guilty and the victims, for the guilty suffer twice over, first by blame, which states their unworthiness, and then by punishment, which holds them under the reign of violence. With lamentation, the experience of evil becomes heard. The cry becomes a voice, the voice of the undivided enigma of evil. Lamentation forms a bridge between the evil committed or suffered and the myth. And indeed it connects suffering to language only by joining a question to its moaning. "Why evil?" "Why do children die?" "Why me?" In turning itself into a question, lamentation itself appeals to myth.

Myths of Evil. How does myth reply to the enigma of evil? It provides the first explanatory schema available to humanity. Myth replies to "why?" with "because"—which claims to fulfill the request for sense that is the mediation of lamentation. We shall discuss, in conclusion, why this claim is doomed to fail. But first we must discuss the power of myth.

Before stressing the fantastic, legendary, and even delirious side of myths, three features must be noted that define myth, at least provisionally, as an appropriate response to the "why?" that rises up from lamentation. The first characteristic of myth is to state an order indivisibly uniting ethos and cosmos. By encompassing in a single configuration celestial and terrestial phenomena, inanimate and animate nature, seasons and festivals, labors and days, myth offers a privileged framework of thought within which to link together moral evil and physical evil, guilt and mortality, violence and punishment: in short, a framework that preserves, in its answer, the unity of the enigma of evil as a question.

Next, the ambivalence of the sacred, as Rudolf Otto describes it, confers upon myth the power of taking on both the dark and the luminous sides of human existence. Many myths point to a primordial sphere of existence that can be said to be beyond good and evil. Finally, myth incorporates our fragmentary experience of evil within great narratives of origin, as Mircea Eliade has stressed in his many works on this topic. By recounting how the world began, myth recounts how the human condition reached the wretched and miserable form that we know it to take. Theogony, cosmogony, and anthropogenesis therefore form a single narrative chain that scans the "great time" of origin. Order, ambivalence, and omnitemporality are thus the major features of myth, owing to which the mythical explanation can claim to provide an all-encompassing framework for evil.

This is all we can say about myth in general, however, without running the risk of applying to one precise category of myth characters belonging solely to another. This is not to imply that we must cease to speak of myth in general: the case of myths of evil is exemplary in this respect. It appears, in fact, that myth, considered as a type of discourse, draws a certain unity from the place it assumes in a hierarchy of levels of discourse that can be organized according to stages of increasing rationality. Myth constitutes in this regard the lowest level, coming before wisdom and gnosis, which leads to the threshold of the rationalizing theodicies of philosophy and theology. One must be aware, however, that the ordering principle thus alleged is the offshoot of a certain idea of reason that was, in the West, born with philosophy itself. A purely comparativist approach could never assume unreservedly this "prejudice of reason." On the other hand, if we bracket it completely—and doubtless this must be the case in a purely descriptive history of religions—then we expose ourselves to the inverse danger, which is that the universe of myths will splinter into an infinite number of parts.

It is precisely this feature that prevails in the case of myths of evil when we bracket, at least for a while, the question of the place of myth in an ordered series of levels of discourse. Order, ambivalence, and omnitemporality then appear only as inconsequential abstract and formal elements in relation to the explanatory schemas that mythical thought has produced throughout space and time. Nowhere else as much as in the area of the explanation of evil does myth reveal itself to be this vast field of experimentation, which is unfolded in the literature of the ancient Near East, India, and the Far East. In this immense laboratory everything occurs as if there were no conceivable solution that had not been tried at one point or another as a reply to the enigma of evil. It is precisely here that the myth forms the great matrix in which are rooted the sapiential, gnostic, and properly speculative modes of the great discourse proffered by men in the space opened up by lamentation between the cry and utter silence. In this sense, myth remains the schema for all subsequent speculation. The question then arises whether, outside any hierarchical order of discourses, this great phantasmagoria of evil lends itself to some typology that will not do violence to its proliferating diversity.

A prudent reply is needed to this methodological question: on the one hand, myths of evil lend themselves to classification by virtue of their narrative character, mentioned above as the third general feature of the mythical universe. Narratives of origin are presented as dramas recounting how evil began; it is therefore possible to apply a structural analysis to them that reduces them to a relatively limited number of ideal types, in Max Weber's sense—that is, of paradigms constructed by comparative science midway between the clearly transcendental *a priori* and empirical proliferation. The ideal types are those of an exemplary story, organizing segments of action, characters, fortunate and unfortunate events, as in the great epics that take place in our time, after the beginning.

The proliferation of myths can thus be mastered to a relative degree by a typology of dramatic paradigms. On the other hand, individual myths contain so many inconsistent elements, which convey a desperate attempt to explain the unexplainable in order to give an account of what is inscrutable, that they prove to be in large part hostile to all classification. At the most they present "family resemblances" that cause a number of overlaps between types of myth. There is no myth that, in some way or other, does not coincide with another myth. In this way we are prevented from working out a table of the strict play of differences and combinations among myths. In *The Symbolism of Evil,* I proposed a typology limited to the ancient Near East and to archaic Greece, that is, to the cultural memory of European man. (I shall discuss below a vaster typology that will take into account Indian and Buddhist mythology.)

The ancient Near East and Archaic Greece. The restricted typology of *The Symbolism of Evil* verifies the two opposing characteristics mentioned above. On the one hand, the attempt to classify myths in terms of a limited number of paradigms is relatively successful; on the other, the overlapping that occurs shows that every paradigm implies in some aspect or another a very different paradigm.

For a static analysis of the myths of evil, the myths of the cultural sphere considered can be divided fairly easily into four great paradigms.

1. In the myths of chaos, illustrated most strikingly by the Sumerian-Akkadian theogonic myths but also by the Homeric and Hesiodic theogonies, the origin of evil that strikes humans is included within the larger narrative of the final victory of order over chaos in the common genesis of the gods, the cosmos, and humanity. [*See* Chaos.] The great creation epic, *Enuma elish,* makes the appearance of man the final act in a drama that begins with the generation of the gods. One can truly speak in this connection of an epical ontogenesis to describe this sort of total narrative. As regards evil in particular, it is noteworthy that chaos precedes order and that the principle of evil is coextensive here with the generation of the divine. The poem does not hesitate to characterize as evil the hates, the plotting, and the murders that mark not only the primitive struggles among the most ancient gods but also the victory of the younger gods—Marduk, for example, in the Babylonian version of the myth.

Evil therefore precedes man, who finds it already present and merely continues it. Evil, in other words, belongs to the very origin of all things; it is what has been overcome in setting up the world as it now is, but it, too, contributed to this state of affairs. This is why order is precarious and its genesis must continually be reenacted by cultic rites. If, in this family of myths, the fall of man is mentioned, it is never in the sense of the unprecedented emergence of an evil that would be simply "human, all too human," but as an episode in the drama of creation. [*See* Fall, The.] In the same way, the failure of the quest for immortality, recounted in the famous *Epic of Gilgamesh,* is tied up with the jealousy of the gods, who trace out the boundary between the sphere of mortals and that of immortals by an act of violence placed beyond good and evil.

2. An evil god and a tragic vision of existence are depicted in the second paradigm of evil in the culture of European man. Here, evil is in a way shared by man and gods. It calls, on the one hand, for a figure with the stature of a hero, possessing higher qualities than ordinary men like ourselves but who commits a grave error, which can be said to be neither the effect of mere ignorance, in the Socratic sense, nor the result of a deliberately bad choice, in the Hebraic sense. Moreover, the overwhelming error that precipitates his fall is deplored by the tragic chorus and by the hero himself as a blindness that has crept over him as a result of the jealousy of the gods; thus the hubris of the tragic hero is at once the cause and the effect of the wickedness belonging to the plane of the divinities. Aeschylus's *Prometheus Bound* is the frightening document of this tragic theology and this tragic anthropology in which the hero in a sense cooperates in a loss, the origin of which is superhuman. It is important to note that the tragic myth produced a spectacle, rather than a speculation, a spectacle that makes the spectators participate in the tragic drama through the catharsis of the emotions of terror and pity.

3. The third type is illustrated by Archaic Orphic myths, which are continued in Platonism and Neoplatonism. This can be termed the myth of the exiled soul, imprisoned in a foreign body. It assumes a radical distinction between a soul, akin to the gods, and a body, perceived as a prison or a tomb. Life itself appears as a punishment, possibly for some fault committed in a previous life. Evil is therefore identified with incarnation itself and even, in certain Far Eastern mythologies, with reincarnation. The model of the body-as-prison, extended by that of the repetition of reincarnations, is further darkened by the model of infernal punishment, as if life in the body were the image of hell. Life is then a death, which calls for a death that will be true life. Only through purification, at once ethical, ritual, and meditative, can the soul be delivered from this quagmire of bodily existence, which itself mirrors hell. In a sense, this myth alone can properly be termed a myth of the fall, for the incarnation itself marks the loss of an infinitely superior condition and so a loss of height, of altitude, which is precisely what the word *fall* signifies.

4. Compared with these three paradigms, the biblical myth of paradise lost differs in three ways. First, the Adamic myth is purely anthropological, excluding any drama of creation in which evil would originally be included: creation is good, very good; man alone initiates evil, although he is tempted, to be sure, by the serpent (an important feature discussed below); but the serpent too is a creature. Next, evil is clearly ethical, in the sense that it results from an act of disobedience. It therefore cannot be a matter of hubris, which like disobedience would represent a blindness sent down by jealous gods, although "Second Isaiah" does not hesitate, after the difficulties of exile, to make his confession in the form of God's own self-presentation, as in prophesy: "I form light and create darkness, I make weal and create war, I am the Lord, who does all these things" (*Is.* 45:7). Finally, evil is not the result of the fall of the soul into a body; it consists of a gap, a deviation of man as a whole, of the flesh, which is unaware of the body-soul dualism.

The Adamic myth is therefore anthropological in the strongest sense of the term, to the extent that Adam is Man, neither a Titan nor a captive soul but the ancestor of all mankind, of the same nature as all the generations springing from him. If the Adamic myth nevertheless deserves the title of myth, this is inasmuch as the narrative in which it consists is incommensurate to the historical time in which the exemplary adventure of the people of Israel takes place. The myth elevates to the level of exemplary and universal history the penitential experience of one particular people, the Jewish people. All the later speculations about the supernatural perfection of Adam before the Fall are adventitious interpretations that profoundly alter the original meaning; they tend to make Adam a superior being and so foreign to our own condition. Hence the confusion over the idea of the Fall.

The intention of the Adamic myth is to separate the origin of evil from that of good, in other words, to posit a radical origin of evil distinct from the more primordial origin of the goodness of all created things; man commences evil but does not commence creation. However, it is in the form of a story that the myth accounts for this catastrophe at the heart of the goodness of creation; the passage from innocence to sin is narrated as something that took place. That is why the explanation given here of the origin of evil is not yet elevated to the plane of speculation, as will later happen with the dogma of original sin, but remains an etiological myth involving legendary characters and fabulous events.

With respect to its structure, the myth takes on the form of a twofold conflict: on the one hand, that between the central figure, Adam, and the Adversary, represented by the serpent, who will later become the Devil, and on the other hand, that between the two halves of a split figure, Adam and Eve. From this complex configuration the Adamic myth receives an enigmatic depth, the second pair adding a subtle psychological dimension and an internal density that would not have been attained by the confrontation between Man and his Other alone. In this way the myth universalizes the penitential experience of the Jewish people, but the concrete universal that it forges remains caught up in the gangue of the narrative and the symbolic.

The protohistorical myth is the only vehicle for a speculation akin to sapiential literature. In order to state the discordance between a creation that is fundamentally good and a historical condition that is already bad, the myth has no other resources than to concentrate the origin of evil in a single instant, in a leap, even if it stretches out this instant in a drama that takes time, introduces a series of events, and involves several characters. In this way the myth reflects in its very structure, in which the concentrated instant and the extended drama confront one another, the structure of the phenomenon of evil as such, which at one and the same time commences with each evil act and continues an immemorial tradition.

The etiological character of the myth is further reinforced by the narrative of the maledictions that ensue, following the initial act of disobedience: every human dimension—language, work, institutions, sexuality—is stamped with the twofold mark of being destined for the good and inclined toward evil. The power of naming all beings is so deeply perverted that we no longer recognize it except in reference to the division of speech into different tongues. Work ceases to be a sort of peaceful gardening and becomes hard labor that places man in a hostile relation to nature. The nakedness of innocence is replaced by the shame that casts the shadow of concealment over all aspects of communication. The pain of childbirth tarnishes the joy of procreation; death itself is afflicted by the malediction of the awareness of its immanence. In short, what the myth recounts is how it happened that man is obliged to suffer the rule of hardship as we know it in our present condition. The myth's "method" is always the same: stretching out in the time of a narrated drama the paradoxical—because simultaneous—aspects of the present human condition.

This is the restricted typology that we can construct in the limited sphere of the archaic state of European man. Before attempting to move into other cultural spheres, it is important to do justice to the contrary aspect stressed above concerning the level of the typology of myths of evil: the paradigms, we said, are not simply distinct from one another in the sense of Weberian ideal types but they overlap with one another to such an extent that we can discover in each one some aspect that lends it a family resemblance to the others. The danger of the structural approach we have followed up to now lies in giving an exaggerated cohesiveness to narratives of origin that also possess a composite, paradoxical, even extravagant character, well suited to the heuristic function of myth, when myth is considered as a thought experiment that unfolds in the region of the collective imagination. This is why the static analysis of myths, governed by the search for and the description of ideal types, must be completed by the addition of a dynamic approach to myths, attentive to the internal discordances that make them overlap in places and in this way outline a vast narrative and symbolic cycle. [*See* Myth.]

If we take the Adamic myth as a point of reference, we find in it the muted echo of all the others and vice versa. We can therefore speak of a tragic aspect in the Adamic myth, expressed in the deep and shadowy psychology of temptation. There is a sort of fatalistic side of the ethical confession of sins. But there is also an irreducible remainder of the theogonic combat, which can be seen in the figure of the serpent and in other biblical figures related to the primordial chaos. What is more, the essentially ethical affirmation of God's saintliness can never entirely rid us of the suspicion that God is somehow beyond good and evil and that for this very reason he sends evil as well as good.

This is why later speculation will continually return to what is at once an unthinkable and an invincible possibility, namely that the deity has a dark and terrible side, in which something of the tragic vision and also something of the myth of chaos is preserved and even reaffirmed. If this admission shows itself to be so persistent it is precisely because the human experience of evil itself contains the admission that, in positing the existence of evil, man discovers the other side of evil, namely that it has always existed, in a paradoxical exteriority that, as stated above, relates sin to suffering within the undivided mystery of iniquity. The acknowledgment of a nonhuman source of evil is what continually gives new life to theogony and to tragedy alongside an ethical vision of the world.

The same thing should be said with respect to the typological distance between the Adamic myth and the myth of the exiled soul. It is not by sheer chance that, under the influence of Platonism and of Neoplatonism, the Adamic myth has almost fused with the myth of the Fall. There was most likely in the original myth a tendency that led it to confuse the quasi-external character of evil as already present with the body, understood as the sole root of evil. In the same way, the Babylonian exile provided the model of banishment, which continues with that of the expulsion from the garden of paradise. The symbols of captivity and of exodus that underlie the Adamic myth thus lend themselves to contamination by the symbolism, coming from another source, of a fallen "soul." Elevating the figure of Adam above the condition of ordinary mortals doubtless facilitated the reinterpretation of the myth of disobedience in terms of a myth of the Fall: when Adam is represented as a sort of superman endowed with all knowledge, beatitude, and immortality, his degradation could be represented in no other way than as a fall.

This play of overlappings could be considered from the perspective of each of the four myths that structure the symbolic imagination in the Western world: there is no myth of chaos that, at one moment or another, does not include the confession of sins by a repentant sinner; there is no tragic myth that does not admit the deep fault tied to a hubris for which man recognizes himself to be guilty. And would the fall of the soul be such a misfortune if man did not contribute to it at least through his consent?

Hindu and Buddhist mythologies. The division into four great paradigms that we apply to the vast—although restricted—domain of Semitic archaism and Hellenic archaism, which, together, structure the cultural memory of Western man, itself constitutes only a restricted typology. What happens when Western man attempts to extend his vision to a wider field? Does the typology offer the same features of relative order and of multiple overlappings when we try to pass from the restricted form to a generalized form? For anyone who undertakes the perilous task of incorporating into his own vision the universes of thought that entertain complex relations of distance and proximity with one's own cultural memory, two warnings should be taken into consideration: first, it is senseless to seek to be exhaustive; there is no Archimedes point from which one could attempt to raise the totality of mythical universes. We must always confine ourselves to limited incursions into the regions that we intuitively suspect will contain treasures likely to enrich our cultural memory, and from this results the unavoidably selective nature of the itinerary of these incursions.

Second, we must give up the hope of any simple taxonomy, such as a distribution into monisms, dualisms, and mixed forms of these. These distinctions are practically useless on the mythical level itself, assuming they have a less debatable validity on the level of more speculative discourse. The two examples we have chosen, Hindu mythology and Buddhist mythology, taking into account the first warning, also raise issues related to the second warning: Hindu mythology perhaps more than Buddhist mythology confronts us with a profusion of explanatory frameworks requiring a taxonomical refinement that challenges any classificatory principle. Buddhist mythology, perhaps more than Hindu mythology, shows us how the same "solution" can oscillate among several planes of expression, from the level of legend and folklore to that of a metaphysical speculation. This profusion and this variation of levels constitute fearsome challenges for any attempt at typology.

If we admit that theodicy is not restricted to monotheism but forms the touchstone of all religions, when the existential need to explain suffering and moral evil is brought to the level of language, then we can seek and find theodicies in all of them. If, moreover, we admit that Vedantic Hinduism, in which the problem of evil is dismissed rather than resolved by a refined speculation on the relation between suffering and ignorance, is not the same as all systems placed under the vast heading of Hinduism, we can, following Wendy Doniger O'Flaherty in *The Origin of Evil in Hindu Mythology* (Berkeley, 1976), class the expression of theodicies on the clearly mythological level as Puranic Hinduism. These figurative and narrative theodicies lend themselves to a certain classification of different conceptual attitudes toward evil, a classification that struggles with the proliferation of myths to the point of succumbing under their weight.

O'Flaherty, our guide through this labyrinth, observes that four characters can assume the role of the villain in the drama: man, fate, demons, and gods. The first type of myth, which recalls the Adamic myth, seems surprising if one considers the doctrine of *karman*, according to which our present experience is the direct result of the good or bad actions of previous existences to be the Indian solution to the problem of evil. Neither gods or demons are then to blame, and even blame itself is obliterated by the recognition of an eternal cycle in which everything is justified and finds its recompense. The paradox lies in the fact that the feeling generated by rumination on past faults opens the way for all sorts of speculation on the moral responsibility of man for the origin of evil, nuanced by the attitude that man is always as much a victim as a guilty party (as we see in the myths of the loss of a golden age).

After all, the very doctrine of *karman* posits that the links in the endless chain of evil are our desires and our sins; Buddhism takes this as its starting point. The paradox, however, is reversed when a primordial fall is evoked; then it is fate rather than man that is to blame. This forms a second cycle of myths, where we see God or a god create evil as a positive element in the universe, whether he acts as a willing or unwilling instrument of fate or whether he himself decides that evil must come to be. Logical thought tends to see a contradiction here between being constrained or deciding freely to create an ambivalent universe; Hindu thought, however, moves effortlessly between what ultimately appears to be two variants of a *dharma* that abolishes the distinction between what is and what ought to be.

The opposite is no less true: it is because a doctrine like that of *karman* proves to be emotionally unsatisfactory in certain ways while remaining valid in the eyes of the wise that mythology continually reworks the variants, producing new divergences. It is then not surprising that mythical speculation turns toward gods and demons. Myths placing guilt on the shoulders of gods or demons proliferate, all the more so as ethical and cosmic dualism, illustrated in its purest and most coherent form by Manichaeism, was never victorious in India: the ambiguous nature of the demons, and even of the gods, served to thwart this clear and radical distinction. India prefered to struggle with the paradox of superhuman entities, which are almost all of the same nature and which are distinguished and opposed to another only by their combat. Those who always win are gods, but because their adversaries are never really eliminated, the kinship of the gods and the demons always resurfaces.

Here the guide we have chosen to follow remarks with irony that as a consequence of these reversals the gods reputed to be good are more wicked than we might expect and that the demons reputed to be evil prove to be good demons. This gives rise to a reflection on the demonic as such, in which power overrides benevolence, thus verifying the extent to which myths operate as depth probes sounding the ambivalence of the human condition itself, while on the surface they seem to operate as explanations. By recounting our origins, where we come from, myths describe in a symbolic way what we are: the paradox of the good demon and that of the evil god are not merely playful fantasies but the privileged means of unraveling the tangled skein of passions belonging to the human heart. When the myth tells, for example, how the gods corrupted the demons, something is said about the hidden perversity of the "higher" part of ourselves. When the myth recounts the birth of death, it touches the secret thread of our fright in the face of death, a fright that in fact closely links together evil and death and confronts death as a personified demon.

The fact that myths are indifferent to logical coherence is attested to by another cycle of myths, characteristic of *bhakti* spirituality, where we see a god create evil (for example, a fallacious heresy) for the good of humanity, a lesser malediction freeing a graver one. The cycle is then complete: submitted to this stringent economy, man is carried back to the problem of his own evil, as in the theory of *karman*. This cycle, however, is considerably vaster than that of the restricted typology with which we began. It is also more loosely knit. And it is truly in the mythic theodicies of India that we see verified the notion suggested at the beginning of this article, namely that the mythical world is an immense laboratory in which all imaginable solutions are tried.

This acceptance of multiplicity by the same culture confirms one of the conclusions arrived at by our restricted typology (restricted to the archaic Semitic and Greek worlds)—namely, that in every myth, owing to its own incoherence, we discover a sketch in miniature that another myth will develop on a much larger scale. The feature that has not received sufficient attention, however, has to do with the difference in level that allows us to go beyond a lower truth (for example, the struggle between gods and demons or the corruption of demons and men by the gods) by means of a higher truth (for example, *karman*), which, far from eliminating the prior truth, confirms it in its subordinate place. This is what Buddhism forcefully demonstrates.

Buddhism poses a singular problem for any careful investigation, not only with respect to the multitude of mythical figures of evil, but also to the oscillation between different levels of discourse. On the one hand, indeed, no religion has gone so far toward a speculation stripped of any narrative or figurative element on behalf of a doctrine of inner illumination. On the other hand, Buddhism seldom appears in a form completely cut off from popular beliefs and from their characteristic demonology, especially in the cultural universes previously shaped by Hinduism. What is more, Buddhism has generated within its own midst, if not a new demonology, at least a mythical figure of evil, Māra, somewhat comparable to Satan in late Judaism and in early Christianity. Buddhism reinforces in this respect the hypothesis according to which one can speak of the origin of evil only by way of myths. At the same time it appears to constitute a counterexample to this hypothesis, because mythology seems at first to be so incompatible with the purified form of spirituality characteristic of Buddhism. It is, to be sure, in the Pali canon and not in the Mahāyāna documents that T. O. Ling, in his *Buddhism and the Mythology of Evil* (London, 1962), finds the most striking illustration of this phenomenon, which at first sight seems paradoxical.

To begin with, one must admit that a wide gap exists between pure Buddhist doctrine and popular mythologies concerning the origin of evil. The latter are characterized basically by the radically external nature they attribute to demonic powers, represented as threatening, terrifying, devouring creatures. In addition, as is not the case in Iranian dualism, these demons form a swarm in which it is difficult to distinguish the forces of evil from the forces of good. Finally, the principal resource of men in defending themselves against these external forces is an action itself turned toward the outside, whether this is a propitiatory sacrifice, an invocation addressed to higher powers or the manipulation of hostile forces through magical actions, or even the constraint that is supposed to be exerted on the gods by self-mortification.

On the other hand, if, following T. R. V. Murti in *The Central Philosophy of Buddhism* (Calcutta, 1955), we take as our criterion for Buddhism the "philosophical" section of the canon, that is the Abhidhamma Piṭaka and, more precisely, Buddhaghosa's *Visuddhimagga* (Path of Purification), which in the Theravāda school is at once its conclusion and compendium, then we are correct in speaking of a Buddhism without mythology, as Ling does. The thinking behind this radical position is easy to understand. In the first place, the doctrine is entirely directed toward the purely mental conditions of the evils of existence. These conditions are analyzed, catalogued, and hierarchized with the most extraordinary care; they are also submitted to an exploration of the "dependent origination" of the lines of interdependence, which allows the sources of evil to be tracked down in their deepest hiding places. What the analysis exposes are not external forces but, basically, ignorance, which itself results from false views of the world, generated in their turn by an overestimation of the self. Popular demonologies are precisely the crudest sort of expression of these false points of view.

The second reason for incompatibility with mythology is that the analysis itself, in certain schools, is confined to scholasticism, due to the subtlety of its distinctions and derivations, and is placed in the service of a wisdom aimed at establishing a state of emptiness, a void. This state is entirely separate from the familiar realities of everyday existence and wholly unrelated to the fantastic creatures produced by desire and, even more so, by fear. Demons vanish along with all external reality as a result of the purifying meditation that deserves the name of enlightenment.

And yet, it is not simply a matter of making concessions to popular beliefs if the Pali canon assigns a place in its teachings to the Evil One and gives him the name of Māra. This entity can be termed mythical due to his resemblance to the demons of popular belief and, more precisely, due to his personification of original evil. Ling confirms here the earlier analysis of Ernst W. Windisch in *Māra und Buddha* (Leipzig, 1895). According to both of them, this figure is finally not foreign to the central core of Buddhism to the extent that it is part of the very experience of the Buddha's enlightenment, as a force that threatens, attacks, and seeks to distract the individual from contemplation—a force that the wise man must address, confront, and finally conquer.

Specialists in this field argue whether this confrontation with the threat of distraction is characteristic only of the first stage in the spiritual adventure or whether it is present up to the end; they argue whether the proliferation of legends that attribute to this figure of evil the status of a demon result from subsequent contamination by the surrounding demonologies or whether they develop a mythical core inherent in the pure doctrine. The essential point is that the figure of Māra in its barest signification is the product of Buddhism. Ignorance driven out by knowledge; shadows dissipated by that enlightenment, are experienced as an inner adversity that is spontaneously personified in the figure of an adversary. As is not the case in popular demonology, however, Māra is personified by a single figure, symbolizing the internal enemy, namely the adversary of meditation.

If Buddhism seems to confirm in such a paradoxical fashion the thesis that one can speak only in mythical terms of the origin of evil, this is because the source of evil, however much it may be interiorized, retains a certain hostile nature that calls for a figurative approximation in terms of externality. Expressed in external terms, the myth gives a symbolic expression to the interior experience of evil.

Beyond Myth? Myth, however, is not alone in using language to deal with the enigma of evil. I mentioned above that there exists a hierarchy of different levels of discourse within which myth takes its place. We can go beyond myth in two directions, that of theodicy and that of wisdom. These two paths often intersect but they conform to two distinct series of requirements.

The path of theodicy. Theodicy replies to a demand for rational coherence. [*See* Theodicy.] This requirement stems from lamentation itself, inasmuch as it carries within it an interrogation: "Why? Why must my child die? Why must there be suffering and death? How long, O Lord?" But it also stems from myth itself, inasmuch as it brings the reply of a vaster and more ancient order than the miserable condition of man. This reply, however, suffers at once from an excess and from a defect: an excess resulting from a proliferation that staggers the imagination (the mythical world, Lévi-Strauss observes, is a world that is too full); its defect is due to the mutual incompatibility of myths, to their internal contradictions, and, finally, to their narrative form itself: to tell a story is not to explain. Rationalization has taken a number of different forms: in India, this involves the grand speculations on *karman*, on the degrees of being, on the order of things placed beyond good and evil. In Buddhism, this concerns speculation on the tie between ignorance and suffering and, above all, on the tie between wisdom, which I shall discuss below, and suffering. In Greece, myth was surpassed by philosophy, which essentially separates the question of origin in the sense of foundation from the question of the beginning in the sense of theogonies and genealogies. By virtue of this fundamental clarification, Plato prefers to say that God is the cause of good alone rather than to say, along with myth, that the gods are bad or that they are beyond good and evil.

In the Christian sphere, rationalization takes place within theology, mainly at the time of the confrontation with gnosis, which is still no more than a rationalized myth, and in connection with an overall hellenization of speculation. In this regard, the doctrine of original sin in Augustine offers at once the features of an antignosis as a result of what its conceptual framework borrows from Neoplatonism (being, nothingness, substance, etc.) and the features of a quasi gnosis, and hence of a rationalized myth, due to the way it mixes together the legal model of individual guilt and a biological model of contamination at birth and of hereditary transmission. This is why such rationalization was continued beyond this quasi gnosis in onto-theologies to which we owe the theodicies as such, in Leibniz and, finally, in Hegel. To these theodicies we owe, if not a solution to the enigma of evil, at least the transformation of the enigma into a problem, namely whether or not we can maintain the following three propositions at once: God is all-powerful. God is absolutely good. Evil exists. This is not the place, however, to weigh the success or failure of rational theodicies.

The path of Wisdom. Assuming that a coherent reply could be given to the enigma that has been raised in this way to the level of a rational problem, there could still be no exclusive means for explaining it. The question of evil, indeed, is not simply "Why does evil exist?" but also "Why is evil greater than man can bear?" and, along with this, "Why this particular evil? Why must my child die? Why me?" The question is also posed, then, to wisdom. [*See* Wisdom.]

It is Wisdom's task first to develop an argument on the basis of this personal and intimate question that myth does not treat, since it invokes an order that does not concern individual suffering. Wisdom thus forces myth to shift levels. It must not simply tell of the origin in such a way as to explain how the human condition reached its present miserable state; it must also justify the distribution of good and evil to every individual. Myth recounts a story, Wisdom argues. It is in this sense that we see the *Book of Job* question explanation in terms of retribution in the name of the just man who suffers. If the *Book of Job* occupies a primary place in world literature, it does so first because it is a classic of Wisdom's argumentative mode. But it is so because of the enigmatic and even perhaps deliberately ambiguous character of its conclusion. The final theophany gives no direct reply to Job's personal suffering, and speculation must be made in more than one direction. The vision of a creator whose designs are unfathomable may suggest either consolation that has to be deferred until the eschaton, or that Job's complaint is displaced, even set aside, in the eyes of God, the master of good and evil, or that perhaps the complaint has to stand one of the purificatory tests to which Wisdom, itself grafted on a certain *docta ignorantia,* must submit so that Job can love God "for nought" in response to Satan's wager at the beginning of the tale.

This final suggestion reveals the second function of Wisdom, which is no longer to develop arguments or even to accuse God but to transform, practically and emotionally, the nature of the desire that is at the base of the request for explanation. To transform desire practically means to leave behind the question of origins, toward which myth stubbornly carries speculative thought, and to substitute for it the question of the future and the end of evil. For practice, evil is simply what should not but does exist, hence what must be combated. This practical attitude concerns principally that immense share of suffering resulting from violence, that is, from the evil that man inflicts on his fellow man. To transform desire emotionally is to give up any consolation, at least for oneself, by giving up the complaint itself. It is perhaps at this point that Job's wisdom coincides with that of Buddhism. Whatever can be said of this meeting of two such remote traditions of wisdom, it is only at this point that myth can be surpassed. But it is not easy to give up the question "why?" to which myth attempts—and fails—to reply.

[*Other entries dealing with the origins and consequences of evil include* Suffering; Sin and Guilt; *and* Devils.]

BIBLIOGRAPHY

Davis, Stephen T., ed. *Encountering Evil: Live Options in Theodicy.* Edinburgh, 1981.

Ling, T. O. *Buddhism and the Mythology of Evil.* London, 1962.

Murti, T. R. V. *The Central Philosophy of Buddhism.* 2d ed. London, 1955.

O'Flaherty, Wendy Doniger. *The Origins of Evil in Hindu Mythology.* Berkeley, 1976.

Ricoeur, Paul. *The Symbolism of Evil.* Boston, 1967.

Windish, Ernst W. *Māra und Buddha.* Leipzig, 1895.

PAUL RICOEUR

EVOLUTION. The story of Charles Darwin's struggle against the benighted religious authorities of his day has become part of the folklore of science. It ranks alongside the Catholic church's persecution of Galileo as a classic example of the war between reason and superstition. But like most legends, the image of the father of modern biology hounded by Bible-thumping fanatics dramatizes at the expense of gross distortion. It obscures how rapidly Darwin's theory of evolution achieved not merely acceptance but resounding acclaim, even from many religious leaders. After all, Darwin, never a crusading agnostic, was finally laid to rest with full national honors beside Isaac Newton at Westminster Abbey; eulogies on the great man were preached there and at Saint Paul's Cathedral. By the time of his death in 1883, most thoughtful and articulate clergy had worked their way to the conclusion that evolution was wholly compatible with an enlightened understanding of scripture. Before the century was out, there was a sizable body of Christian Darwinist literature (the works bore such titles as *The Religion of Evolution, The Theology of an Evolutionist, The Religious Aspects of Evolution*) whose purpose was to prove the harmony between Darwinism and the gospel.

Early Religious Responses to Darwin. Even the famous first review of *The Origin of Species,* written by the Anglican bishop of Oxford Samuel Wilberforce for *The Quarterly Review* in 1860, has far more to do with pure science than with matters of faith. Though Wilberforce is remembered as the most notorious of Darwin's clerical foes and as the main antagonist of "Darwin's bulldog" Thomas Huxley, his review is a model of competence and courtesy. It poses only a few modest theological objections toward the end; the bulk of the piece is devoted to studied scientific criticism. This is hardly remarkable, since the review was prepared in consultation with Sir Richard Owen, Britain's foremost paleontologist and an adamant, lifelong anti-Darwinist. That fact should serve to remind that, as Darwin had expected, his main critics were to be found not among the clergy but among his fellow scientists, many of whom were professionally committed either to the concept of special creation (the immutability of species) or to alternative theories of evolution. Darwin candidly admitted that his scientific opponents found many troubling gaps and inconsistencies in his original theory, more than enough to call his work into reasonable question, and many of which he was unable to make good in later editions of the *Origin.* The clergy who resisted Darwin, therefore, were simply defending the prevailing view of nature among educated people of the day and enjoyed ample scientific support in doing so. As that support dwindled among the scientists with steady conversions to the Darwinian party, the clergy also lowered its resistance and set about assimilating evolution to received religious teachings. This did not prove difficult to do; hence the fact that, throughout the later nineteenth century, not a single Christian congregation went on record as officially rejecting evolution. Even the then highly conservative Roman Catholic papacy did not see fit to place any of Darwin's works on the *Index of Forbidden Books,* and evolution was not mentioned in Pius IX's *Syllabus of Errors* (1864). Where the church did express reservations about Darwin, as in the first edition of *The Catholic Encyclopedia* (1909), the doubts were raised on purely scientific, not theological grounds. Provided it did not presume to explain the nature of the soul, his theory was treated as a reasonable but as yet unproven hypothesis.

From the viewpoint of well-informed religious thinkers, Darwin's theory was but one more aspect of a challenge that had been under discussion throughout the nineteenth century and with which many had long since made their peace. This was the "higher criticism," the scholarly reinterpretation of scripture that had been developed primarily in the German universities. Together with ancient and biblical archaeology, these critical philological studies had been steadily replacing a naive scriptural literalism with a richer, more rational approach to the Bible. It should be remembered that one effect of the Romantic movement, with its fascination for exotic times and places, had been to make nineteenth-century Europe very historically minded. This was the great age of classical and medieval scholarship; the higher criticism arose in part as an expression of this taste for well-documented historical knowledge.

The first of the exact sciences to become involved in this critical reexamination of the scriptural past was not biology, but geology. Well before the *Origin* was published, James Hutton's *Theory of the Earth* (1795) and Charles Lyell's *Principles of Geology* (1830–1833) had already made the case that the earth was far older than a literal reading of the Bible would suggest. For those liberal clergy who had come to terms with the new geology and with the findings of scriptural scholarship, it was hardly difficult to accommodate what Darwin had to say about the prehistory of life on the planet. They needed simply to reinterpret the fabulous material in the first few chapters of *Genesis* within a sounder historical framework. Little more than a decade after the publication of the *Origin*, there were religious thinkers who had gone to remarkable lengths to prove the compatibility of evolution and Christian teachings. Among the more prominent of these was the Christian Darwinist St. George Jackson Mivart, a biologist who had been born an evangelical and later converted to Catholicism. In his book *On the Genesis of Species* (1871), Mivart sought to demonstrate that the theory of evolution was harmonious with "ancient and most venerable authorities" reaching as far back as Augustine.

At first glance, this might seem like a great and welcome gain for Darwin. But he soon came to regard evolutionary enthusiasts like Mivart as a thorn in his side. While biblical literalists might summarily reject evolution, Darwin's Christian supporters frequently insisted upon reading evidence of divine supervision into the process. This radically violated the spirit of scientific objectivity that Darwin wished to claim for his theory. The "providential evolutionists" argued that if selection takes place in nature, then there must be an intelligent selector behind the scenes. Thus, the theologian James McCosh, one of Darwin's earliest American converts, hastened to assure the devout that "supernatural design produces natural selection." For many Christian thinkers, Darwin's religious credentials were enhanced by the fact that he had based so much of his work on the population theories of the dour cleric Thomas Malthus. One can indeed read *The Origin of Species* as a general biological extension of Malthus's *Essay on the Principle of Population* (1798), a work that had long since imbued Christian moral theology with ideas of providential selection, extinction, and moral fitness. By way of that connection, even the most orthodox were able to discern traces of the divine will in Darwin's vision of nature.

Fundamentalism versus Darwinism. Given the possibility of such religiously skewed readings of Darwin, it is not surprising to learn from one historian of the period, James R. Moore in his *Post-Darwinian Controversies* (1979), that by the end of the century "with few exceptions, the leading Christian thinkers in Great Britain and America came to terms quite readily with Darwinism and evolution" (p. 92). This conclusion, of course, leaves the rank-and-file majority of Christians unaccounted for. How palatable did they find Darwin? We have no way of knowing with any exactness, but certainly there existed among them a residue of bewilderment, if not hostility toward Darwin, especially in the English evangelical and nonconformist congregations, where biblical literalism lingered. It was not, however, until the early twentieth century that an aggressively outspoken anti-Darwinist position—biblical fundamentalism—achieved any organized standing in religious circles. Fundamentalism, which takes its name from the twelve-volume polemical work *The Fundamentals* (published through the Moody Bible Institute of Chicago between 1909 and 1912), found its adherents mainly within the American Protestant churches of the Far West and in the Southern Baptist congregations of the "Bible belt."

It should be emphasized that Darwin (even science as a whole) was only a secondary and indirect target of the fundamentalists. Their primary grievance was moral, and it was addressed to the dominant liberals or "modernists" of the major congregations, whose intellectual pluralism and more compliant ethical standards were viewed as a compromise of traditional Christian teachings. In effect, fundamentalism may be seen as a backlash within the Christian community on the part of those in all the Protestant churches—but mostly the rural, the economically insecure, and meagerly educated—who felt most threatened by the increasing pressures of the surrounding secular civilization. But until well after World War II, the fundamentalists were no more than a beleaguered fringe even within the religious community. An event like the famous Scopes "monkey trial" in Dayton, Tennessee, in 1925 may have made for a journalistic sensation, but its significance in the mainstream of Western intellectual and religious history should not be exaggerated. In America, fundamentalism, in the form of well-organized and well-financed groups like the Moral Majority, was to find its most potent expression only much later, during the 1970s and 1980s. Then, the rising political and economic status of the Sunbelt states was to give the evangelical congregations of that region an unprecedented prominence. Hence the assertiveness during this period of the "scientific creationism" movement, with its demand that the public schools grant *Genesis* parity with evolution in biology classes.

Ironically, it is the scientific community itself that has done the most to grant fundamentalism an inordinate importance in the discussion of evolution. The legend of Darwin persecuted by what Thomas Huxley called "the mistaken zeal of the Bibliolaters" has enhanced the heroic self-image of science. It has also given the Darwinians the advantage of a patently vulnerable opposition by creating the misleading impression that the only alternative to Darwin is fundamentalism. This not only obscures the fact that the religious response to evolution has included much more than the doctrinaire hostility of the evangelical Christians; it also contributes to a narrow, defensive Darwinian orthodoxy that eclipses the historic truth that major elements of Darwin's theory have been under dispute among scientists themselves since *The Origin of Species* was first published. As Brian Leith observes in his *Descent of Darwin* (1982), "Since the days of Darwin . . . any attack on evolutionary theory has been treated rather like flat-earthism: evidence of mental aberration due to religious mania or political fanaticism." Some of the reservations about Darwin that have been expressed by religious thinkers who accept the concept of evolution echo the doubts that dissenting scientists have raised regarding standard evolutionary theory.

If fundamentalism represents what might be called the "right wing" religious reaction to Darwin, then we can also identify a liberal "center" and a radical "left wing" whose views of evolution carry much greater intellectual weight.

Liberal and Left-Wing Responses. The response of the religious center to evolution has been part of a general adaptation by liberal Christians and Jews to the intellectual standards of a scientific and humanistic culture. In making that adaptation, liberal religious thought has tried to draw a significant line of demarcation between itself and science. Its main concession to science has been to withdraw the authority of the scriptures from the areas of history, anthropology, and the physical sciences. As Raymond J. Nogar puts it in *The Wisdom of Evolution*, "The Bible is not a scientific textbook but a book that sets forth religious truths designed to manifest to man the path to eternal salvation" (p. 296). If this represents a retreat by religion, the withdrawal may be viewed as an honorable and orderly one that relinquishes ground improperly occupied or held only by default during the prescientific era. It has also worked to strengthen appreciation of the ethical and existential aspects of the Bible and of theological thought generally. It is surely significant that in the post-Darwinian period, when liberal Christian leaders were busily stripping scripture of its scientific authority, their commitment to the Social Gospel was rapidly expanding. What the Bible was losing as a biological treatise and a historical text, it was gaining as a work of moral wisdom and spiritual counsel.

Boundaries of scientific inquiry. At the same time, an important limitation was being imposed upon evolutionary theory. While granting that Darwin's work adequately explains the development of the human body from earlier ("lower") animals, most liberal Christians and Jews have argued that natural selection cannot account for the emergence or the nature of the soul. Thus, the liberal Catholic Robert W. Gleason, writing in *Darwin's Vision and Christian Perspectives*, edited by Walter J. Ong (1960), insists that "there is an essential difference between matter and spirit," and goes on to suggest that in the course of evolution "an animal body evolved and was slowly formed under the direction of God to that point where it was suitable for the infusion of the spiritual soul" (p. 110). This has become the position officially enunciated for the guidance of Roman Catholics in Pius XII's encyclical letter *Humani generis* (1950).

To approach evolution along these lines involves placing certain nonphysical aspects of human nature beyond the logic and methodology of science. The object is to achieve a state of peaceful coexistence with the scientists by marking out distinct spheres of influence. Since the 1960s, this adjustment of biblical authority has proved acceptable even to some elements within the evangelical churches, where the doctrine of "limited inerrancy" tends to restrict the infallibility of scripture to matters of faith and practice—a marked departure from fundamentalism. Thus, the neoevangelical theologian Jack Rogers, writing in *Biblical Authority* (1977), concludes that "it is historically irresponsible to claim that for two thousand years Christians have believed that the authority of the Bible entails a modern concept of inerrancy in scientific and historical details" (pp. 44, 46).

Metaphysical evolutionism. The radical left-wing response to Darwin is far more complex than that of the liberal center. It embraces the many efforts of "metaphysical evolutionists" to assimilate Darwin to a spiritual worldview. In contrast to the liberal position, the metaphysical evolutionists do not simply accept the idea of evolution as received from the biologists; rather, they insist upon extending the idea to include the mind, the soul, and the entire universe. Rather than taking its place as a scientific discovery outside the perimeter of religion, evolution becomes the essential content of religion within a universe that is seen as a drama of progressively unfolding consciousness. This inevitably involves reading notions of purpose and value into evolution that are no part of the strict scientific formulation.

Evolution viewed in this way, as a comprehensive

metaphysical system, actually predates *The Origin of Species* by at least a generation. It is important to realize that Darwin's work appeared within a cultural climate that was already saturated with evolutionary philosophies like those of Herbert Spencer and Robert Chambers. Indeed, Chambers's book *Vestiges of the Natural History of Creation* (1844) was among the greatest of all Victorian best-sellers. In it, Chambers, like Spencer, elaborated a cosmic vision of evolution (which he called "development") that was deeply imbued with the popular ideal of progress. Under divine direction, Chambers claimed, the universe was developing steadily toward greater complexity and perfection. Man takes his place in this scheme as "the type of all types of the animal kingdom, the true and unmistakable head of animated nature upon this earth." Chambers's book, though roundly condemned by scientists as the speculation of a rank amateur, became an overnight sensation that made the concept of evolution part of the popular culture of its day. Darwin studied it closely, as he did the evolutionary system of Herbert Spencer, his generation's most celebrated philosopher. (It was from Spencer that he borrowed the morally pregnant phrase "survival of the fittest.") With speculation of this kind so well and widely installed upon the scene, it was inevitable that the metaphysical evolutionists should seize upon *The Origin of Species* as soon as it reached print, lending it ethical and religious implications with which Darwin was never comfortable.

The earliest of these efforts to spiritualize Darwinian evolution appeared in the 1870s, soon after *The Descent of Man* was published (1871). They include the writings of the American philosopher John Fiske and the occult leader H. P. Blavatsky, founder of the then prominent Theosophical Society. Shortly afterward (in the 1880s) the highly influential *Übermensch* philosophy of Friedrich Nietzsche appeared. All these enthusiastically embrace the evolutionary paradigm, but then insist upon expanding it beyond the physical. In their hands, evolution becomes a cosmic phenomenon shaped either by divine forces or by mysterious emergent tendencies that operate from within the process itself: Fiske calls these "psychical variations"; Nietzsche, "the will to power." Human intention and effort play a central role in furthering this cosmic process; they become the forward edge of evolutionary development. Thus, human beings, displaced from the center of the universe by modern astronomy, gain a new centrality from modern biology. They are cast as the leading participants in evolution, striving toward ever higher levels of consciousness that reach ultimately to divinization. Quite simply, evolution is destiny—the destiny of the human race if not of nature as a whole. In the words of Fiske, from his book *Through Nature to God* (1899): "Spiritual perfection is the true goal of evolution, the divine end that was involved in the beginning."

Obviously, natural selection, the key mechanism of evolution for Darwin, cannot account for developments of this magnitude. In standard biology, natural selection is conceived to operate blindly, without plan or goal; it does not move in a uniform direction. This is the point at which the metaphysical evolutionists and the scientists part company. Since Darwin, mainstream evolutionary theory has been adamantly opposed to teleology or orthogenesis in any form. For Darwin, evolution is a random and mindless process that operates independently of any human or divine agency, and without recourse to inherent, emergent tendencies. Though it may, by selective pressure, improve the various organs and structures of living things, it does not *aim* at doing so. The process is therefore as capable of producing regression and extinction as it is of achieving steady improvement by adaptation. There is no overall trend, no intended goal, no guarantee of progress. One must recall that, in fashioning his theory, Darwin's main objective was to overthrow Lamarck's conception of evolution in which the urge to perfection and the will to improve were principal factors. To one degree or another, all forms of metaphysical evolution hark back to Lamarck, and for this reason have proved to be unacceptable to orthodox biology.

In the twentieth century, theories of metaphysical evolution have included a range of philosophies and occult systems. Among the latter, the most noteworthy have included the work of the Christian visionary Rudolf Steiner (originally a founding member of the Theosophical Society) and the esoteric teacher G. I. Gurdjieff, some of whose principles were later elaborated by P. D. Ouspensky. [*See the biographies of Steiner, Gurdjieff, and Ouspensky.*] Gurdjieff's spiritual disciplines have been particularly influential; along various routes, they have contributed to the numerous "human potential" psychotherapies that have risen to prominence in the post–World War II period, many of which are based on an evolutionary image of human nature.

Bergson and Teilhard. But of all those who have sought to extend evolution beyond its Darwinian limits, none has proved more provocative than the vitalist philosopher Henri Bergson and the Jesuit theologian Pierre Teilhard de Chardin. Only the biblical fundamentalists have succeeded in drawing more critical fire from the scientific community.

Like all metaphysical evolutionists, Bergson relegates natural selection to the status of a narrow, purely mechanistic conception that, at best, explains some aspects of physical adaptation. In contrast, what Bergson calls "creative evolution" draws its driving energy from an indwelling *élan vital,* a vital impulse whose nature can only be grasped by direct intuition, and which he characterizes as being "either God or of God." Bergson, whose literary eloquence earned him the Nobel prize for literature in 1927, describes the course of evolution in terms that are poetically evocative, but deliberately clouded. The future, he held, was an open adventure, an uncertain struggle between the life force and dead matter. Born a Jew but later converted to Catholicism, the most Bergson would suggest concerning the future was that the Christian saints prefigured the next upward thrust of the *élan vital* in its insistent quest for higher consciousness.

His disciple, Teilhard de Chardin, was, however, prepared to go into much greater detail in predicting the forward course of evolution. His system, which is densely couched in a vocabulary of quasi-scientific neologisms, foresees a cosmic terminus for evolution called "the Omega Point," where all being will be apocalyptically gathered into a final divine union. Despite the mystical texture of his thought, Teilhard insisted that his principal work *The Phenomenon of Man* (written in the late 1930s but published posthumously in 1955) was to be read "purely and simply as a scientific treatise." The book has, however, been as harshly criticized by scientists as was Bergson's philosophy a generation before. The biologist P. B. Medawar has called it "nonsense, tricked out by a variety of tedious metaphysical conceits." Unfortunately, Teilhard's effort to integrate Christian theology and evolutionary science has fared no better at the hands of the Roman Catholic church, which censored his philosophical writings during his lifetime. While the strongest adherents to vitalist theories of evolution have been found among philosophers and artists, the school has found at least a few champions among the scientists, most notably the biologists Pierre Lecomte de Noüy (in his *Human Destiny,* 1947) and Edmund W. Sinnott (in his *Biology of the Spirit,* 1955).

Religious Contributions to Evolutionary Theory. It is important to emphasize that the various religious responses to evolution dealt with here do not stand on the same footing with respect to science. Biblical fundamentalism appeared as an openly declared enemy of science, which it correctly perceived as a challenge to the literal inerrancy of scripture. Even in its updated and refurbished form of "scientific creationism," fundamentalism remains profoundly estranged from scientific standards of logic and evidence. It continues to insist that the *Book of Genesis* contains a valid account of how the physical universe and life began. It cannot accept the age of the universe as this is now known from numerous empirical sources ranging from astronomical observations to radioactive dating methods; it cannot accept fossil evidence for the history of life on earth. This places fundamentalism at odds not only with biology and geology, as it was in the time of Darwin, but with astronomy, chemistry, physics, physical anthropology, archaeology, and paleontology, all of which directly contradict creationist cosmology.

On the other hand, both religious liberals and metaphysical evolutionists have sought to remain on speaking terms with science and may even have something of value to offer theoretical biology. While scientists may not be able to endorse the more speculative flights of the metaphysical evolutionists, there are at least a few important issues that have emerged from the center-left religious response to Darwin. Two points in particular deserve attention.

1. *Increasing complexity.* Insofar as evolution describes a steady, overall increase in the complexity of living forms (including the complexity of human sentience and human culture), might this not reasonably be identified as the direction in which nature is moving? To that degree, the process is not formless or haphazard but may be said to have a favored tendency. This is not quite the same as teleology; no specific goal need be named, only a net gain in intricacy over time. But this may be enough to serve as a way of finding human meaning in the universe.

To be sure, this is not how mainstream biology views the evolutionary record, but, at the same time, such a reading seems to do no violence to the empirical evidence. What is at question here is how the fact of increasing complexity is to be interpreted. Metaphysical evolutionists choose to see that increase as something special added to the course of evolution, lending it a vertical dimension that requires independent explanation. *Is* increasing complexity a special feature of evolution or its normal characteristic? Obviously, there is no way to answer such a question since we know of only one evolutionary process—the one we find recorded in the history of the earth. We can, however, *imagine* an evolution in which no ascending order of complexity appears: an evolution limited to the endless adaptation of primitive microorganisms. While such a natural history could be accommodated by Darwinian theory, it would be a very different evolutionary pattern than has occurred on earth, where life has taken a riskier, more adventurous course. It was precisely this aspect of evolution that persuaded even the inveterate agnostic Thomas Huxley to allow for the possibility of "a wider teleology" in nature that he felt was compatible with

Darwinian theory: "The whole world, living and not living, is the result of the mutual interaction . . . of the forces possessed by the molecules of which the primitive nebulosity of the universe was composed." This universal tendency of raw matter to assume rational form and complex structure, Huxley admitted, "may be the result of mechanical dispositions fixed beforehand by intelligent appointment and kept in action by a power at the center." This is a considerable concession for religious thinkers, who will readily identify the "power at the center" as God.

2. *Human transcendence.* Insofar as no obvious selective advantage can be adduced for such cultural creations as art, music, higher mathematics, philosophy, or religion, might the human mind not be reasonably regarded as a special element in nature that escapes, perhaps transcends, the forces that determine physical evolution?

In striking such a distinction between the human and subhuman levels of evolution, theologians and philosophers have enjoyed the support of no less an authority than Alfred Russel Wallace, cofounder with Darwin of the theory of natural selection. In his later years, Wallace formed strong doubts that the theory could be applied to the mind and so to human nature generally. He observed that natural selection operates upon marginal advantages that are directly related to survival. But, he argued, the cultural creativity of the human species has evolved so far beyond what survival requires that the mind seems to have developed (and to be developing still) in obedience to needs wholly different from utilitarian advantage in the struggle for existence. In his book *Darwinism* (1891), Wallace remarks, "Because man's physical structure has been developed from an animal form by natural selection, it does not necessarily follow that his mental nature . . . has been developed by the same causes only." He goes on to conclude, as have many religious thinkers since his time, that in the development of human consciousness, we see evolution cross from simple, practical intelligence into "an unseen universe—a world of spirit, to which the world of matter is altogether subordinate." Where this transition occurs, natural selection loses its explanatory power and science is left behind.

This seems to be a graceful compromise between the claims of religion and the claims of science, one which, indeed, uses the facts of evolution itself to segregate the one from the other. That distinction, of course, leaves militant agnostics free to argue that what religion retains for itself—the realm of soul or spirit—is a meaningless figment whose erratic influence over human conduct can be accounted for only by certain unfortunate excesses in the evolution of the human brain. But this line of argument leads to a strange and somewhat uncomfortable conclusion. After all, science, including Darwin's own magnificent work, also emerges from that realm of mental excess. It is a quest for truth, often pursued with religious dedication by those who have no practical goal in mind. It would be ironic in the extreme if evolutionary biology, one of the glories of the human intellect, should finish by writing off intellect itself as nothing but a fortuitous overdevelopment of the mammalian nervous system.

[*See also the biographies of Bergson and Teilhard de Chardin. For discussion of the influence of Darwin's theory on the study of religion, see* Evolutionism.]

BIBLIOGRAPHY

Benz, Ernst. *Evolution and Christian Hope: Man's Concept of the Future from the Early Fathers to Teilhard de Chardin.* Garden City, N.Y., 1966. Includes chapters on evolution in works of Nietzsche, Marx, and Aurobindo Ghose.

Bergson, Henri. *L'évolution créatrice.* Paris, 1907. Translated as *Creative Evolution* (New York, 1911). The basic text for all vitalist theories of evolution.

Bergson, Henri. *Les deux sources de la morale et de la religion.* Paris, 1932. Translated as *The Two Sources of Morality and Religion* (Notre Dame, Ind., 1977). A more extensive discussion of the relationship of evolution to religion.

Deely, John N., and Raymond J. Nogar, eds. *The Problem of Evolution: A Study of the Philosophical Repercussions of Evolutionary Science.* New York, 1973. A valuable collection of essays. See especially Nogar's own contributions.

Eldredge, Niles. *The Monkey Business: A Scientist Looks at Creationism.* New York, 1982. A critique of creationism by a leading American paleontologist.

Gillespie, Neal C. *Charles Darwin and the Problem of Creation.* Chicago, 1979. Reviews doctrine of special creation and pro- and anti-Darwinian theories of evolution.

Himmelfarb, Gertrude. *Darwin and the Darwinian Revolution.* New York, 1968. Gives special attention to religious responses to Darwin, both pro and contra.

Irvine, William. *Apes, Angels, and Victorians: Darwin, Huxley, and Evolution.* New York, 1955. A study of the religious and scientific debates over evolution in Victorian England.

Kitcher, Philip. *Abusing Science: The Case against Creationism.* Cambridge, Mass., 1982. A "manual for self-defense" designed by a philosopher of science to be used by teachers and school administrators under pressure from creationist groups.

Lecomte de Noüy, Pierre. *Human Destiny.* New York, 1947. A theory of metaphysical evolution by a leading vitalist biologist.

Leith, Brian. *The Descent of Darwin.* London, 1982. Reviews scientific criticism of Darwinian evolution to the present day.

Mayr, Ernst. *The Growth of Biological Thought: Diversity, Evolution, and Inheritance.* Cambridge, Mass., 1982. The definitive statement to date of mainstream evolutionary theory.

Also deals with issues of teleology and orthogenesis as these relate to metaphysical theories of evolution.

Moore, James R. *The Post-Darwinian Controversies: A Study of the Protestant Struggle to Come to Terms with Darwinism in Great Britain and America, 1870–1900*. London, 1970. A thorough survey.

Morris, Henry M. *The Scientific Case for Creationism*. San Diego, 1977. Christian creationist response to evolution by a leading proponent.

Nogar, Raymond J. *The Wisdom of Evolution*. Garden City, N.Y., 1963. An examination of evolutionary theory by a liberal Roman Catholic theologian.

Ong, Walter J., ed. *Darwin's Vision and Christian Perspectives*. New York, 1960. Essays by liberal Catholics on evolution.

Rogers, Jack B., ed. *Biblical Authority*. Waco, Texas, 1977. Neoevangelical essays revising the doctrine of biblical inerrancy.

Roszak, Theodore. *Unfinished Animal: The Aquarian Frontier and the Evolution of Consciousness*. New York, 1975. Deals with occult and metaphysical evolutionary systems of Blavatsky, Steiner, and Gurdjieff.

Teilhard de Chardin, Pierre. *Le phénomène humain*. Paris, 1955. Translated as *The Phenomenon of Man* (New York, 1959). The major statement of Teilhard's evolutionary theology.

THEODORE ROSZAK

EVOLUTIONISM is a term commonly employed to designate a number of similar, usually nineteenth-century anthropological theories that attempt to account for the genesis and development of religion. Although the term *evolutionism* is also used to name a brand of theological speculation chiefly associated, in the twentieth century, with the work of the French theologian Pierre Teilhard de Chardin, this article will focus strictly on the uses of the term within the development of anthropological science. [*For discussion of theological evolutionism, see* Evolution *and the biography of Teilhard de Chardin.*]

Evolutionist theories of religion's origin hold in common a presupposed "psychic unity of mankind"; that is, they assume that all human groups are possessed of a more or less common developmental pattern (though the shape of this pattern differs from theorist to theorist) and that, therefore, significant clues as to how religion originated—and, in turn, as to what religion essentially is—can be detected through a study of the religious life of the world's "primitive" peoples. If evolutionist assumptions are correct, it should follow that commonalities displayed among groups at each level of development will reveal, when set in diachronic order, a necessary "psychic history" of the human race.

Influences on Evolutionist Thought. Evolutionist anthropological theories represent one manifestation of the nineteenth century's enthusiasm for developmental schema that find their bases in what might loosely be called a philosophy of history. This philosophy of history declares that human development is rectilinear and progressive and that mind tends necessarily toward greater and greater rationality and complexity. The idea of progress, especially in its component notion that history is unidirectional and proceeds by way of identifiable stages, is older, certainly, than the beginning of the nineteenth century. Indeed, we may speculate that there is a nascent "evolutionism" at work already in the Pauline formulation that, with the appearance of the Christ, an age of grace has supplanted and rendered obsolete an earlier age of law. (To trace "scientific" evolutionism's origins to the beginnings of Christian historiography provides some insight regarding the apologetic purposes that evolutionist thinking seems always to serve.) But for convenience we may point to the philosophical work of G. W. F. Hegel (1770–1831) as having planted the seed that led, by the nineteenth century's close, to the full flowering of the evolutionist creed among those who considered themselves the first truly scientific investigators of the phenomenon of man.

In his *Phenomenology of Spirit* (1807), Hegel launched a revolution in thinking about the human past. Put simply, the Hegelian system declares that history (by which Hegel and his followers mean the history of the world as a whole) reveals the progressive manifestation of *Geist* ("spirit") in the world: a process that leads, eventually, to Spirit's self-actualization and to human self-understanding. History, according to Hegel, propels itself forward through a dynamic process within which each successive age "resolves and synthesizes" the antagonisms of earlier eras. Each historical period, therefore, not only results from what has gone before but also in some sense contains within itself the self-understanding of earlier eras. Locating anthropological evolutionism's foundation in Hegelian philosophy may therefore help us to comprehend what amounts to a "genetic obsession" on the parts of the participants in the debates that raged during the latter part of the nineteenth century, debates that had as their crux a question concerning what constitutes the essential—that is, the originary—form of the religious consciousness. To identify this originary form would be to uncover an essential element of human being, for it was generally held among evolutionist theorists that religious belief was the distinguishing characteristic setting the human apart from the animal. This endeavor may seem odd, given much of the later history of scientific anthropology, but it makes sense when placed within the context of a fledgling scientific discipline that had not yet weaned itself of philosophical anthropology.

More directly influential than Hegelian philosophy

upon the development of scientific anthropological evolutionism, however, is the work of Herbert Spencer (1820–1903), English polymath and, with the Frenchman Auguste Comte, the cofounder of the discipline of sociology. Even before Charles Darwin's *The Origin of Species* (1859) revolutionized biological science, Spencer had landed on evolution as the principle that accounts for all change, whether inorganic, organic, or mental (if we may so characterize the quality that separates the development of human societies and individuals from mere organic growth). In his essay "Progress: Its Law and Cause" (1857), Spencer first gave voice to what may be called the essential element of anthropological evolutionist dogma:

> The advance from the simple to the complex, through a process of successive differentiations, is seen . . . in the evolution of Humanity, whether contemplated in the civilized individual, or in the aggregate of races; it is seen in the evolution of Society in respect alike of its political, its religious, and its economical organization; and it is seen in the evolution of all those endless concrete and abstract products of human activity. (*Essays: Scientific, Political, and Speculative*, New York, 1915, p. 35)

Having thus laid the theoretical groundwork for his never-to-be-completed "natural history of society," Spencer nevertheless managed to construct the first systematic sociology of religion in English (one of the tasks undertaken in his three-volume *Principles of Sociology*, 1876–1896). In this work, he identifies the origin of religion (which, Spencer says, supplanted an aboriginal atheism) in what he perceives to be the universal practice among primitive peoples of worshiping the ghosts of their ancestors. He then goes on to trace the further evolution of religious consciousness through polytheism and monotheism. According to Spencer, religion culminates in agnosticism, a metaphysical position girded by the "positivist" epistemological principles that are the earmarks of the scientific age and of the scientific historiography, epitomized in Spencerian sociology, that helps to inaugurate this new era of human development. That Spencer considered agnosticism to be a genuinely religious position bears noting insofar as we may be tempted to see the work of Spencer and other evolutionists as being antagonistic toward religion; it is nearer the case to say that at least some of these thinkers sought, among other agenda, to defend what they found to be the "spiritual maturity" of the age of science to which they belonged.

Tylor and His Critics. Among theorists of religion, E. B. Tylor (1832–1917) perhaps best deserves the name "evolutionist." It is Tylor's work more than that of any other scholar that invites us to identify evolutionism with British "armchair" anthropology of the late nineteenth century. Among influences on Tylor we may list, first, Spencer (whose "ghost theory" of the origin of religion closely resembles the animistic hypothesis forwarded by Tylor), then F. Max Müller, the German-English philologist whose etymological investigations helped to inspire Tylor's researches into the *Urgrund* of religious consciousness. [*See the biography of F. Max Müller.*]

Before proceeding to a description of the theory of religion's origin advanced by Tylor, let us note what is perhaps the most significant characteristic of Tylor's (and, indeed, of other evolutionist theorists') manner of thinking about religion. That "religion" is, for these writers, at root *one* thing goes without saying. But, beyond this, it is worth emphasizing that the one thing that religion is, is essentially of an intellectual, or cognitive, kind. Evolutionist theories of religious development proffer histories of religions within which religion is singlemindedly construed as *belief;* the affective dimensions of religious experience are simply elided or are written off as so much superstructure. This intellectualist approach to anthropological research is clearly to be seen in Tylor's famous "minimum definition of Religion" as "belief in Spiritual Beings." Tylor's intellectualism—and that of his contemporaries—has been harshly derided and largely superseded by twentieth-century anthropologists. And yet this, at least, ought to be said in its favor: for all their concern to distinguish between modern, Western rationality and the "primitive" mentality of "savage" or "low" races, it is yet the case that the nineteenth-century initiators of anthropological discourse were the first Europeans to conceive of the human race as a single entity; they were the first, that is, to accord to "savages" human minds. Though they were termed "primitive," the religions of "low races" were recognized as religions. (It is clearly a part of Tylor's purpose to put the lie to what he considered the slanderous reports of missionaries and adventurers concerning the godlessness of the tribal peoples they encountered.) Moreover, in so doing, the evolutionists—who, through their examinations of "primitive" men, hoped to uncover keys to human nature per se—helped to overturn the privileged position of the European scientific observer, no matter how far such an outcome may have been from their intention. Certainly, the work of Tylor and others (especially James G. Frazer) was instrumental in revolutionizing classical studies and thus in altering forever our picture of antiquity and, hence, of the West's own intellectual heritage.

E. B. Tylor's name has come to be identified with the term *animism* or, as he also called it, "the doctrine of souls." He first proposed this as the most rudimentary stage of religious belief in a paper entitled "The Religion of Savages," published in the *Fortnightly Review* in 1866. Tylor's monumental influence upon succeeding generations of students of religion can be measured by the fact that, although Tylor's theory of religion's origin has long ago been discredited, the term *animism* is still widely used to describe the religious beliefs of those peoples who have, as yet, resisted conversion to one or another of the "great" missionary religions. In articulating the concept and the conceptual basis of animism, however, Tylor did not mean to describe an obsolescent form of religious consciousness but rather to identify the constant center, or core, of religious belief. The following passage, extracted from Tylor's masterwork *Primitive Culture* (1871), both points up the universality of animistic belief and identifies the conceptual maneuver responsible for engendering the animistic hypothesis.

> At the lowest levels of culture of which we have clear knowledge, the notion of a ghost-soul animating man while in the body, and appearing in dream and vision out of the body, is found deeply ingrained. . . . Among races within the limits of savagery, the general doctrine of souls is found worked out with remarkable breadth and consistency. The souls of animals are recognized by a natural extension from the theory of human souls; the souls of trees and plants follow in some vague partial way; and the souls of inanimate objects expand the general category to its extremest boundary. . . . Far on into civilization, men still act as though in some half-meant way they believed in souls or ghosts of objects.
>
> (quoted in Jacques Waardenburg, *Classical Approaches to the Study of Religion*, vol. 1, *Introduction and Anthology*, The Hague, 1973, pp. 216–217)

Tylor's doctrine of "survivals"—that is, his claim that, although they may over the course of time lose much or even most of their original meaning, elements of the primitive worldview perdure within, and continue to exercise influence upon, the mind-sets of more advanced cultures—is also hinted at in the foregoing passage. For Tylor, as for perhaps the latest of his heritors, Sigmund Freud, the child is truly father to the man. Both of these thinkers depended, whether consciously or not, upon the Hegelian principle that "ontogeny recapitulates phylogeny"; for Tylor as well as, decades later, for Freud, the investigation of the mental life of primitive races provided insight into the psychic infancy of mankind and so to the inevitable hurdles that must be overcome in order for the human species to achieve psychic adulthood. [*See* Animism and Animatism.]

Within British anthropological circles, criticism of Tylor's animistic hypothesis came from two corners. The first of Tylor's critics was the Scottish folklorist Andrew Lang (1844–1912). Though Lang's constructive contributions to anthropological science were minimal, he dealt a devastating blow to the notion that animism represented the earliest stage of religious consciousness. In his book *Myth, Ritual, and Religion* (1887), he pointed to the overwhelming evidence of what he termed "high gods" among many of those peoples who, until then, had been characterized by anthropologists as being too primitive to be able to conceptualize so abstractly as to arrive at any notion resembling that of an omnipotent, creative deity. Though Lang turned his attention toward other interests during the remainder of his career, his critique of Tylor laid the foundation for the massive researches into the topic of "primitive monotheism" that were later to be conducted by Wilhelm Schmidt. [*See* Supreme Beings *and the biography of Schmidt.*]

The second blow to the animistic hypothesis was struck by R. R. Marett (1866–1943), Tylor's disciple, biographer, and successor to the position of reader in social anthropology at Oxford University. In an essay entitled "Preanimistic Religion," published by the journal *Folklore* in 1900, Marett, drawing on the ethnographic data compiled in Melanesia by the Anglican missionary R. H. Codrington, advanced the claim that animism had been preceded by a preanimistic stage of religious consciousness characterized by belief in an impersonal force, or power, that invests persons and objects, rendering them sacred. Marett, borrowing from the Melanesian vocabulary supplied by Codrington, termed this "electric" force *mana*. In accord with the evolutionist principles outlined earlier, belief in *mana* possesses, for Marett, both diachronic and ontological priority. One hears an echo of Tylor in Marett's proposition, contained in the article "Mana" that he contributed to James Hastings's *Encyclopaedia of Religion and Ethics*, that *mana* and *tabu* (which Marett conceives of as *mana*'s "negative" complement) together constitute "a minimum definition of the magico-religious." [*For further discussion, see* Power.] While neither Lang nor Marett disavowed evolutionist principles, it is worth noting that the criticisms leveled against Tylor by these writers had the effect, eventually, of helping to undermine the cogency of evolutionist explanations of the origin and development of religion, insofar as the work of each served to invite anthropologists to closer examination of actual ethnographic data. [*See* Dynamism.]

Further History of Evolutionist Theories. The early twentieth century saw the demise of "armchair" approaches to anthropological research as anthropologists began to conduct detailed, long-term studies of tribal peoples within the contexts of these peoples' actual habitats. One effect of this focus on field research was the production, especially during the middle decades of the twentieth century and within the Anglo-American anthropological tradition, of great numbers of immensely detailed monographs on the day-to-day life of primitive societies. The quest for a comprehensive and systematic natural history of mankind came gradually to be abandoned.

This abandonment undoubtedly found one of its sources in an awakening to the theoretical inadequacies of the evolutionist approach to human culture. It began to become clear to anthropological researchers that the systematic theoreticians of humankind's development employed, in their search for the unvarying laws underlying what they perceived to be the relentless progress of human societies toward ever more complex and rational forms, a logic that was wholly circular: in the mere designation of some societies as "primitive" and others as "advanced," a host of culturally engendered presuppositions were employed, and a host of significant theoretical questions were begged. Another inadequacy of evolutionist thinking that began forcibly to strike the notice of scholars of religion was the fact that this mode of explanation ignores the trading of cultural elements, which so evidently has always figured importantly in the change, and especially the complexification, of human societies. (It should be noted that few evolutionists adhered strictly to a doctrine of absolute rectilinear evolution; Spencer admitted the possibility that racial differences accounted for the multiple and apparently irreconcilable directions taken by different cultures, and even the archevolutionist Tylor in his early work proposed "diffusionist" explanations for the puzzling appearance of "high" cultures among the Indians of Mesoamerica.) This insight alone was responsible for the instigation of what we may loosely term a school of thought regarding the origins and development of religious phenomena: that of the so-called diffusionists. [*See, especially,* Kulturkreiselehre.]

Twentieth-century anthropological science also saw a falling out of fashion of interest in religion as an (or *the*) essential element in the life of human societies. From the 1920s through the 1960s, many anthropologists, especially those who received training in England or America, focused their attention on kinship relations, economic arrangements, and the like: aspects of society, that is, that they considered more tractable to the "hard," objective studies that they were intent upon pursuing. (There were, of course, exceptions to this trend—E. E. Evans-Pritchard and Raymond Firth stand as two of the more important—but even these scientists concentrated their efforts on conducting meticulous examinations of the religious life of particular societies.) It may not be too inaccurate to generalize to the effect that the nineteenth-century obsession with origins (as a concomitant of the grandiose quest to discover the foundational design of human progress) was replaced in the twentieth century, at least among Anglophone anthropologists, by an obsession with "objectivity."

But to generalize in this manner is dangerous insofar as it ignores, first, the continuing influence of evolutionist anthropological theory on continental anthropological science and, second, the powerful, hardly diminishing influence of evolutionist theory upon Western culture generally. Though there is too little space in this brief treatment to do more than to mention them, we may list Émile Durkheim and Lucien Lévy-Bruhl as among the continental heritors of evolutionist theory. The debate concerning the nature of "primitive" as opposed to "civilized" (or rational) forms of mentation that was refueled by Lévy-Bruhl continues, though in different, structuralist guise even to the present day. [*See* Structuralism *and the biographies of Durkheim and Lévy-Bruhl.*]

Though his work represents what many consider a dead end in terms of continuing influence on anthropological thought, James G. Frazer (1854–1941) produced what must count as the single most imposing monument of evolutionist theory, *The Golden Bough* (1890), which in its third edition (1911–1915) ran to twelve volumes. Not only the most prolix of evolutionist theorists, Frazer was also the most doctrinaire, convinced as he was that human culture's development is governed by unvarying natural laws and that the human race has evolved, mentally and physically, in uniform fashion. Frazer's temper was utterly intellectualist; his evolutionary scheme, which posits the successive replacement of an aboriginal magical mode of thought by, first, a religious and, then, a scientific mode, finds its basis in Frazer's conviction that human culture's development is effected as later generations of human beings awaken to the errors and the resultant practical inefficacy of their predecessors' worldviews. (A reading of *The Golden Bough* prompted Ludwig Wittgenstein's trenchant remark to the effect that, when Frazer reports on a primitive European peasant woman pulling a doll from beneath her skirt during a fertility rite, he seems to think that she is making some sort of mistake and actually believes the puppet to be a child!)

The influence of Frazer's work on later anthropological theory has been negligible, aside perhaps from the significant impact it had on classical studies. Yet Frazer's *Golden Bough* rates as one of the century's most celebrated books, because of its profound effect on the literary and artistic dimensions of Western culture, and because of its formative influence on psychoanalytic theory, which, with Marxism (itself utterly dependent upon evolutionist assumptions regarding history), stands as a ruling ideology of the twentieth century. Though the axioms of the psychoanalytic model for understanding the human mind and its cultural products probably owe more to evolutionist biology and its philosophical antecedents than they do to British anthropological theory, it is nevertheless the case that especially the late work of Sigmund Freud (1856–1939) drew heavily upon that of Frazer. Frazer's *Totemism and Exogamy* (1910) was a direct influence upon Freud's *Totem and Taboo* (1913), which together with *The Future of an Illusion* (1927) and *Civilization and Its Discontents* (1930) constitute Freud's contribution to evolutionist theory. Seeking to demonstrate the logical coincidence of the behavior of neurotics with the "obsessional" practices of primitive peoples, Freud aimed to map a theory of culture whose purposes are both descriptive and prophylactic, insofar as (in the manner of clinical psychoanalytic method) to understand past conflicts that live on within an unconscious realm whence they continue to exert control over human destiny is to take a sure step toward resolving these conflicts and thereby achieving psychic health, or emotional (and, by implication, political) maturity. It may need no pointing out that Freud identifies the coming of the race's adulthood with the waning of religious belief. [*See the biography of Freud.*]

Freud's influence on anthropological science during the middle decades of this century was minimal, but Freudian-based anthropological theory seems lately to be experiencing a rejuvenescence, as a work such as Melford E. Spiro's *Oedipus in the Trobriands* (1984) demonstrates. As for the medical import of Freud's program for human destiny, it again is instructive to observe that evolutionist theory has consistently coupled a descriptive aim with an apologetic and heuristic intention. This has remained true of evolutionism from its modern origins in the thought of Hegel and Spencer down through its modern embodiments both in Marxist historiography and political practice and in Freudian theory and psychoanalytic technique.

BIBLIOGRAPHY

The best introduction, for the layperson, to the impact on Western thought of various ideas of history is R. G. Collingwood's *The Idea of History* (Oxford, 1946). Good surveys of the evolutionist movement in anthropology (and its decline) can be found in Eric J. Sharpe's *Comparative Religion* (London, 1975) and Jan de Vries's *The Study of Religion* (New York, 1967). E. E. Evans-Pritchard's insightful and amusing critique of "intellectualist" theories of religion, among which he includes the evolutionist mode, appears in his *Theories of Primitive Religion* (Oxford, 1965).

JAMES WALLER and MARY EDWARDSEN

EXCOMMUNICATION.

To excommunicate means "to cut off from communion" or "to exclude from fellowship in a community." In a Christian setting, the term *excommunication* also applies to exclusion from Holy Communion, or the Eucharist.

Historically, religious practice admitted some form of putting a person outside the community. Any community claims the right to protect itself against nonconforming members who may threaten the common welfare. In a religious setting this right has often been reinforced by the belief that the sanction affects one's standing before God, inasmuch as it entails being cut off from the community of the saved. In religious traditions in which nonconformity was punishable by death, excommunication was introduced as a mitigation of the death penalty. In medieval Christendom and during the early years of the Reformation, excommunicated persons were turned over to civil authorities, who could inflict the death penalty upon them.

With the shift in modern times to considering religious affiliation a matter of free choice, doubts have been expressed about the meaning and value of excommunication. Although practiced less frequently today, some current examples include the *ḥerem* in Orthodox Judaism, "shunning" among some traditional Christian bodies, withdrawal of membership by congregation-based communities, and "excommunication" as practiced by Mormons, Roman Catholics, and some other mainline Christian churches.

In the Western Christian tradition, excommunication is seen as based on practice reflected in scripture, especially Paul (see, for example, *1 Cor.* 5:1–13, *2 Cor.* 2:5–11, *2 Thes.* 3:14–15). Theoretical justification is taken from the command to bind and loose (*Mt.* 18:15–18). This same passage supplies key elements of procedure, including advance warning and attempts to lead the delinquent to conversion.

Early Christian practice mixed liturgical excommunications, which were part of the nonrepeatable public penitential practices, with disciplinary ones that could culminate in a person being declared anathema. In the thirteenth century Innocent III specified excommunication as a disciplinary penalty distinct from other punishments, characterizing it as specifically medicinal, intended to heal the delinquent. The number of crimes for which excommunication could be incurred increased steadily through the eighteenth century, but a marked reduction in their number began with the reforms of Pius IX in 1869 and continued with the promulgation of the Code of Canon Law in 1917.

As a medicinal, or healing, penalty, excommunication under Roman Catholic law may be incurred only if a serious sin has been committed, or if the person is obstinate in a position after being given formal warnings and time to repent. Reflecting medieval and later developments, some excommunications are automatic *(latae sententiae)*, incurred by committing a specified act, such as abortion or physically striking the pope. Other excommunications are imposed *(ferendae sententiae)* after an administrative or judicial investigation. Excommunication must always be lifted as soon as the delinquent repents and seeks peace with the church.

A distinction used to be drawn between major excommunications, which cut a person off from all participation in community life, and minor ones, which prohibited participation in the sacraments, especially the Eucharist. Current canon law has dropped this distinction, although the 1917 code did characterize some excommunicates as *vitandi*, with whom contact must be completely avoided. Under the 1917 code all others were *tolerati*, and contact with them could be permitted.

An excommunicated person loses basic rights in the church, but not the effects of baptism, which can never be lost. In the revision of the code carried out after Vatican II the effects of excommunication were clarified, and the distinction of *vitandi* and *tolerati* was dropped. Instead, all are treated as *tolerati* so far as the effects are concerned. These depend on whether the excommunication was imposed by a public declaration or sentence of condemnation, or was incurred automatically but without much public notice.

Generally, a person who is excommunicated is denied any role in administering the sacraments, especially the Eucharist. He may not receive any of the sacraments or administer sacramentals, such as burials, and he is forbidden to exercise any church offices or functions. If the penalty has been declared or imposed by a sentence, any liturgical actions the excommunicate attempts are to be suspended until he leaves; he loses any offices or other functions in the church; and he may make no claim for income or other benefits from the church.

Under the reform of the law, automatic excommunication can be incurred in only six instances, including abortion. It may be imposed for a limited number of other crimes against faith, the Eucharist, or the seal of the confessional in the sacrament of penance. If imposed by a sentence or public declaration, excommunication can be lifted only by a public authority in the church, usually the local diocesan bishop. Otherwise, it can be lifted by a priest during the sacrament of penance, but unlike the 1917 code the revised rules require that in all cases the bishop be contacted afterward for the reconciliation to remain in effect.

BIBLIOGRAPHY

Recommended studies of early Christian practice are Kenneth Helm's *Eucharist and Excommunication: A Study in Early Christian Doctrine and Discipline* (Frankfurt, 1973) and John E. Lynch's "The Limits of *Communio* in the Pre-Constantinian Church," *The Jurist* 36 (1976): 159–190. For historical background and detailed commentary on Roman Catholic canon law through the 1917 Code of Canon Law, see Francis Edward Hyland's *Excommunication: Its Nature, Historical Development and Effects* (Washington, D.C., 1928), and for an overview of efforts to reform Roman Catholic law on this subject, see Thomas J. Green's "Future of Penal Law in the Church," *The Jurist* 35 (1975): 212–275, which includes a bibliography. Both the *Dictionnaire de droit canonique* (Paris, 1953) and the *Lexikon für Theologie und Kirche*, 2d ed. (Freiburg, 1957–1968), offer extensive articles, under the terms *Excommunication* and *Bann*, respectively.

James H. Provost

EXEGESIS. *For discussion of traditional disciplines of interpretation of particular sacred literatures, see* Biblical Exegesis; Buddhist Literature, *article on* Exegesis and Hermeneutics; *and* Tafsīr. *For discussion of the intellectual discipline concerned with the nature and presuppositions of interpretation, see* Hermeneutics.

EXILE. Often prompted by historical conditions, the concept of exile appears in various religious traditions as a symbol of separation, alienation, and that which is unredeemed.

In Judaism. With the Babylonian invasion of Judah and the subsequent destruction of the Jerusalem Temple in 587/6 BCE, the concept of exile (Heb., *golah* or *galut*) came to reflect both a historical reality and a communal perception. Forced into exile in Babylonia, members of the upper classes found themselves uprooted from their national and spiritual homeland. Literally, then, the term *exile* came to describe the forced dispersion of the Jewish people and their subjugation under alien rule. Although according to Jewish tradition (*Jer.* 29:10) the Babylonian exile was only seventy years in duration, the destruction of the Second Temple in 70 CE and the triumph of Rome caused a national uprootedness that lasted for almost two thousand years. Historically, one can thus maintain that the exile of the Jewish people from Palestine began in the sixth century BCE and came to an end in 1948 with the establishment of the state of Israel and the restoration of Jewish political independence.

Metaphorically, however, the term *exile* was and is still used as a symbol of alienation, reflecting the

Jews' separation from the land of Israel, the Torah by which God commanded them to live, from God himself, and from the non-Jew and the non-Jewish world in general.

To the biblical prophets, exile was a symbol of divine retribution. As Isaiah makes clear (44:9–20), in worshiping other deities the people of Israel revealed a lack of fidelity to their God and to the covenant that he had established with them. Their punishment, then, was the destruction of their spiritual center, Jerusalem, as well as of the Temple in which sacrifices were offered; and the forced removal of many from the land that had been promised to them. At the same time, however, exile became a symbol of judgment. Those who remained religiously faithful, becoming, in Isaiah's words, God's "suffering servants" (43:10), would reap the rewards of righteousness and ultimately be redeemed.

According to the prophet Ezekiel (14:3ff., 21:31ff.), exile was a trial through which God tested his people's faithfulness to him and his teachings. It was also a symbol of Israel's election, with the Babylonians, and later the Romans and all those under whose rule the Jewish people were subjugated, acting as instruments of a divine schema through which, as Isaiah writes, God's "faithful remnant" (27:31ff.) would be redeemed. Exile thus became a metaphor of separation not only from God but also from righteousness. As such, it was associated with a premessianic, preredemptive era. In exile, as John Bright (1981) maintains, one was to purge oneself of sin in order to prepare for the future. To "return," that is, to remember that God, the creator of the world, chose Israel to be his people and to obey his commandments, was therefore a way out of exile both historically and spiritually. On a historical level, the Jewish people would be led back to the Land of Israel, with the Temple rebuilt and political independence restored, while on a spiritual level, as Isaiah writes (51:6), the righteous would attain eternal salvation.

Throughout the Middle Ages, the concept of exile gave theological significance to the continued political, social, and economic oppression of the Jewish people. The tenth-century philosopher Sa'adyah Gaon, in his *Book of Beliefs and Opinions*, emphasized the importance of exile as a trial and as a means of purification, while according to an anonymous contemporary, exile, as a divine gift and a "blessing of Abraham," served as a mark of Israel's election. According to this view, exile was not a punishment for sin but an opportunity given by God to bring his teachings to all of humanity.

To many medieval Jewish mystics, exile took on additional significance as a metaphor describing on the divine level what historically had befallen the Jewish people. One finds in the thirteenth-century *Zohar*, for example, the claim that with the destruction of the Second Temple both the Jewish people and the tenth emanation of God, identified as *shekhinah* (God's visible presence in the world), went into exile. Thus, the separation of the Jewish people from the Land of Israel became mirrored in the alienation of God from a part of himself. This idea is reiterated and broadened in the writings of the sixteenth-century mystic Isaac Luria, in which the exile of the *shekhinah* is said to reflect the exile or "fall" of humanity as a whole into the domination of demonic powers. [*See* Shekhinah.]

Finally, on a psychological level, the concept of exile served to reinforce the national self-consciousness among a people who no longer shared a common culture, language, or land. Exclusion from non-Jewish society, coupled with a Jewish liturgy and calendar that reinforced the notion of Palestine as home, underscored the alien nature of the Jew in the non-Jewish world. After the seventeenth century, however, as European emancipation came to afford growing numbers of Jews the opportunity to participate more fully in non-Jewish society, many began to feel that the Diaspora did not necessarily have to be equated with exile. One sees this most clearly in the writings of nineteenth-century religious reformers who, insisting that Jews were members of a religious community but not of a specific nation, maintained that it was possible for Jews to view any country as home.

Since 1948, it is debatable whether Jews choosing to live outside the state of Israel historically are still in exile. Yet one can argue, as does Arthur Hertzberg in *Being Jewish in America* (New York, 1975), that on a psychological level the concept of exile remains a compelling symbol. Hertzberg maintains that even in America, where Jews have gained great acceptance and freedom, the Jew continues to be an alien. As an externally and internally imposed sense of self-identification, exile thus reflects the conviction of many Jews that the Diaspora can never truly be seen as "home."

In Christianity. The metaphor of exile appears in Christianity in two separate ways: (1) as that reflecting the historical and spiritual conditions under which the Jewish people have lived since the fall of the Second Temple and (2) as descriptive of life in this world as opposed to life in the kingdom of heaven.

Like their Jewish contemporaries, the Fathers of the early church attached theological significance to the destruction of the Jerusalem Temple in 70 CE. They maintained, however, that its destruction was not caused by sinfulness in general but by one particular sin, namely the rejection by most of the Jewish community in Palestine of Jesus as the Messiah for whom they had been waiting. Thus, the historical exile of the Jewish people was seen to mirror the spiritual exile—or alienation—of the Jews from God. To "return" in the Christian sense came to imply not only repentance but also an acknowledgment of Jesus as savior.

In the New Testament *Gospel of John,* one sees that which is usually identified as a more gnostic understanding of exile. Jesus here identifies himself as one who is "not of the world." Those who are "of the world," he says (*Jn.* 17:16), are those who have not acknowledged that he is the Christ (Messiah), sent by his father, the one true God, in order to redeem his people. To be "not of the world," he continues, is to be with God in his spiritual kingdom, possible even before death. Exile thus functions here as an individual rather than a collective metaphor of alienation or separation from God. Not surprisingly, John's understanding of "return," rooted in an individual declaration of faith, is also personal in nature.

In Gnosticism. The concept of exile comes to play a central role in a number of early gnostic texts. Set within a dualistic framework of spirit versus matter, light versus darkness, goodness versus evil, exile again functions as a symbol of alienation. Here, however, it is not a particular people who are said to be in exile or the nonbeliever per se but the human soul. Belonging to the spiritual realm of light but trapped in the world of matter or darkness, it depends upon the "saving knowledge" of the gnostic to begin its journey home.

The *Apocryphon of John,* written probably in the late second century CE, the third-century *Gospel of Thomas,* and the fourth-century *Pistis Sophia* are among several gnostic Christian texts that depict Jesus as having been sent down to earth to impart this saving knowledge to others. Reminding his listeners of their heavenly origin, he tells them that the soul can be set free only through this insight, or *gnōsis.* To be in exile is to be unredeemed, ignorant of one's origins and of the nature of the human soul. In these and other texts, knowledge thus becomes the necessary key to salvation.

Yet having attained this knowledge, the gnostic cannot help but experience life in this world as "alien." Hans Jonas (1963) maintains that this experience serves as the primary symbol not just of Christian gnosticism but of other forms of gnosticism as well. Life in this world is depicted as a descent into darkness and captivity, a life of exile for which, as the Mandaeans claimed, the only "day of escape" is death. As a metaphor, then, exile takes on personal rather than communal significance, reflecting the experience of the gnostic who, alienated from and in revolt against the cosmos, longs to return home.

Among the Ismā'īlīyah, an Islamic movement of radical Shī'ah founded in the late third century AH (ninth century CE), one again finds the concept of exile serving as a central symbol of alienation. Here, it is the imam who leads the gnostic away from the world of darkness. Possessing the esoteric knowledge of the soul's true spiritual birth, the imam offers this knowledge to his disciple as a "salvatory revelation." Having attained this revelation, the disciple is freed from exile and reborn as a "being of light."

The Ishrāqīyah. Revealing the influences of Zoroastrianism, gnosticism, Persian mysticism, and Neoplatonism, the illuminative philosophy of the twelfth-century thinker Shihābal-dīn Yaḥyā Suhrawardī uses exile as a symbol of ignorance of one's true spiritual nature and of reality in general. "Home," in the Ishrāqī school, is metaphorically identified with the world of light, while exile is described as entrapment within the realm of darkness. In order to journey homeward, the Ishrāqīyūn need to move beyond rational inquiry to the imaginal world and illumination *(ishrāq).* Only then can the souls of the Ishrāqīyah attain mystical union with the inner divine presence, experiencing an ecstatic separation from the physical body and an anticipation of death. Thus, to journey out of exile is to overcome the separation of the soul from the divine and to become inflamed by what Henry Corbin (1971) labels the "divine fire."

Suhrawardī's understanding of exile is developed most fully in his *Recital of the Western Exile,* a spiritual autobiography that describes the struggles of the "man of light" to free himself from darkness. Associating ignorance with the West and illumination with the East, Suhrawardī begins his tale with the exile of the soul to the western city of Kairouan. Forgetting his origins and eventually taken captive, the man of light slowly comes to an awareness of his true identity and sets out on the long journey home. Though at first he is forced to return to the West, he is finally set free. Stripped of the "fetters of matter," his soul becomes possessed by an angel who helps it return to its celestial condition. Thus beginning its heavenly ascent, it leaves the world of exile forever.

[*See also* Gnosticism; Ishrāqīyah; *and* Soul.]

BIBLIOGRAPHY

Excellent summaries of the early historical development of the concept of exile in Judaism can be found in John Bright's *A History of Israel,* 3d ed. (Philadelphia, 1981), and William F. Albright's essay on "The Biblical Period" in *The Jews,* vol. 1, edited by Louis Finkelstein (Philadelphia, 1949), pp. 3–69. For a discussion of the significance of this concept in medieval Jewish mysticism, see Gershom Scholem's *Major Trends in Jewish Mysticism* (1941; New York, 1961), especially lectures two, six, and seven. Finally, Michael A. Meyer's *The Origins of the Modern Jew* (Detroit, 1967) provides insight into the relationship between European emancipation and the later Jewish reevaluation of exile as a meaningful theological symbol.

The best study of exile as metaphor in Christian and Hellenistic gnosticism remains Hans Jonas's second revised edition of *The Gnostic Religion* (Boston, 1963). For a comparison between these ideas and those found in the New Testament gospel of John, see James M. Robinson's "Gnosticism and the New Testament," in *Gnosis: Festschrift für Hans Jonas*, edited by Barbara Aland (Göttingen, 1978), pp. 125–157. Bernard Lewis's *The Origins of Ismāʿīlism* (1940; New York, 1975) provides a good overview of this concept among the Ismāʿīlīyah, while Henry Corbin's *En Islam iranien: Aspects spirituels et philosophiques*, vol. 2 (Paris, 1971), and *Spiritual Body and Celestial Earth* (Princeton, 1977) offer cogent accounts of exile as metaphor in Suhrawardī's theosophy of light.

ELLEN M. UMANSKY

EXISTENTIALISM is a type of philosophy difficult to define because it does not have any agreed body of doctrine; it is rather a way of doing philosophy in which life and thought are closely related to each other. Thus, while some existentialists have been theists and others atheists, they have arrived at their different results by rather similar processes of thought. The existentialist who believes in God does so not as a result of intellectual demonstration—he is more likely to say that the attempts to prove God's existence are a waste of time, or even harmful—but on the grounds of passionate inward conviction; likewise the atheistic existentialist rejects God not because he has been persuaded by argument but because the very idea of God poses a threat to the freedom and autonomy of the human being, and so to the integrity of humanity. But if such nonrational factors are allowed their say, have we not departed from philosophy altogether? Perhaps not, if one thinks that reason has become so ambitious that it ceases to perceive its own limitations and so becomes misleading. The all-embracing rational system of Hegel provoked not only Kierkegaard's existentialism but also the skepticism of the left-wing Hegelians and Neo-Kantian positivism. The existentialists of the twentieth century emerged about the same time as the logical positivists, and both groups shared doubts about the omnicompetence of reason. The existentialist would still claim to be a philosopher, in the sense of a thinker, but, in Kierkegaard's expression, an "existing thinker," that is, a thinker who is always involved in the reality he is thinking about, so that he cannot take up the purely objective attitude of a spectator; also, he is always on his way from one matter to another, so that as long as he exists he never has a complete picture. So existentialism stands opposed to all those grand metaphysical systems that profess to give a comprehensive and objective account of all that is. Significantly, Kierkegaard entitles two of his most important writings *Philosophical Fragments* and *Concluding Unscientific Postscript*, and these titles implicitly contrast his work with that of philosophers who aim at a comprehensive system.

Though some earlier writers, such as Blaise Pascal (1623–1662), who criticized the theistic proofs and contrasted the God of the philosophers with the living God of Abraham, Isaac, and Jacob, have been seen in retrospect as forerunners of existentialism, the movement belongs essentially to the nineteenth and twentieth centuries. Søren Kierkegaard (1813–1855) is usually regarded as its founder. His philosophy is inextricably entangled with his struggle over what it means to become a Christian. Friedrich Nietzsche (1844–1900) is in many ways at the opposite extreme from Kierkegaard, but his proclamation of the death of God was just as passionate as Kierkegaard's fascination with the God-man paradox. Some Russian thinkers of the same period showed similar existentialist tendencies, notably Fedor Dostoevskii (1821–1881) and Vladimir Solov'ev (1853–1900). All of these profoundly influenced the existentialists of the twentieth century, among whom may be counted Miguel de Unamuno (1864–1936), Karl Jaspers (1883–1969), Martin Heidegger (1889–1976), and Jean-Paul Sartre (1905–1980), though it should be noted that the term *existentialist* had, in popular usage, become so widely applied and covered so many differences that most of the philosophers mentioned were unwilling to accept it. The Jewish thinker Martin Buber (1878–1965) had existentialist affinities but criticized the individualism of the typical existentialist. Nevertheless, all the philosophers mentioned above share a number of "family resemblances" that make them existentialists in a broad sense.

It is sometimes suggested that existentialism is a thing of the past, that it was a phenomenon called into being by the specific events of the times in which these thinkers lived but that we have now moved into new times with new problems. Up to a point, this may be true. The very fact that the existentialist is an *existing* thinker means that he has a concrete relation to the events of his own time. Yet there are some characteristics of the human condition that seem to belong to all times or to recur at different times, and some of the insights of the existential philosophers into what it means to be human have a permanent value and are likely to provoke new thought and new investigations in the future.

Some Distinguishing Characteristics. As the name implies, existentialism is a philosophy of existence. It should be noted, however, that the word *existence* is used in a restricted sense. In ordinary speech, we say that stars exist, trees exist, cows exist, men and women exist, and so on of everything that has a place in the spatiotemporal world. The existentialist restricts the term to the human existent. By doing this, he does not intend for a moment to suggest that stars, trees, cows and the like are unreal. He only wants to draw attention to the fact that their being is quite different from the being of a human person. When he speaks of a human being as "existing," he is taking the word in what may be supposed to be the original etymological sense of "standing out." Stars and the like have their being simply by lying around, so to speak. Their nature or essence is already given to them. The human being exists actively, by standing out or emerging through the decisions and acts that make this person the unique being that he or she is. In Sartre's famous definition, *existence* means that the human person begins as nothing, and only afterward does that being become something and form its essence through its chosen policies of action.

Although existentialists use the word *existence* in the sense just explained, it retains something of its traditional meaning. In the history of philosophy, existence (referring to the fact *that* something is) has usually been contrasted with essence (referring to *what* something is or the basic properties of that thing). Philosophies of essence (Platonism is the great example) concentrate attention on the universal properties of things, properties which remain the same in all circumstances and at all times. These universals are amenable to the operations of thinking, so that the essentialist tends to end up as an idealist, holding that thought and reality coincide. The philosopher of existence, on the other hand, concentrates attention on the concrete, individually existing reality, but this has a particularity and contingency that make it much more resistant to the systematizing tendencies of thought, so that, for such a thinker, reality does not conform to thought, and there are always loose ends that refuse to be accommodated in some tidy intellectual construction.

We should notice too that the existentialist finds room for dimensions of human existence other than thinking. For several centuries, Western philosophy has been deeply influenced by Descartes's famous pronouncement, "I think, therefore I am." The existentialist would claim that this accords too much preeminence to thinking. We are also beings who experience emotion, and our emotions are not just transient inner moods but rather ways of relating to the world and becoming aware of some of its properties that do not reveal themselves to rational observation. Equally important is the will. We learn about the world not just by beholding it and reflecting upon it but rather by acting in it and encountering its resistances.

It follows from this that existentialism is also a philosophy of the subject. Kierkegaard declared that truth is subjectivity. At first sight, this seems a subversive statement, one which might even imply the abolition of truth. But what Kierkegaard meant was that the most important truths of life are not to be achieved by observation and cannot be set down in textbooks to be looked up when required. They are the kind of truths that can be won only through inward and perhaps painful appropriation. The truths of religion are the most obvious case—they cannot be learned from books of theology but only by following the way of faith that is one with the truth and the life (*John* 14:6).

Implications for Religion. The existentialist recognition of the distinctiveness of human existence as over against the world of nature, together with the claim that the truth of human existence is to be reached by the way of subjectivity, is significant for the philosophy of religion. The tendency in modern times has been to treat the human person as one more natural phenomenon, to be understood objectively through human sciences which model their methods on that of the natural sciences. Existentialists, however, believe that human nature can be understood only from the inside, as it were, through our own participation in it. The phenomenological analysis of consciousness, developed by Husserl, has been adopted by existentialist philosophers, but long before Husserl similar methods were being used, for instance, by Kierkegaard in *The Concept of Anxiety*.

One obvious result of the application of such methods of inquiry to the human person is the claim that freedom is essential to being human. Decision, conscience, and responsibility are major themes in existentialist writers, in opposition to the determinism or near-determinism characteristic of supposedly scientific views of man. Perhaps it would not be going too far to say that freedom is the supreme value among the existentialists. Human existence is said to be "authentic" when the individual freely chooses who and what he will become. The freedom to choose and decide is, of course, never absolute. The human being is finite, inserted at a given position in space and time and therefore subject to all the constraints and influences that operate at that point. Thus his freedom is always threatened. He may simply reflect the values of his culture, without ever deciding for himself his relation to those values, or he may be caught up in the race for money or pleasure, though these may be inimical to the development of his finest potentialities.

Thus all human existence is lived in the tension between finitude and freedom. This tension can also be expressed as that between freedom (the areas that are still open for choice) and facticity (those elements in existence which are simply given and reduce the area of free decision). It is because of this tension that freedom is always accompanied by anxiety. Existentialists, from Kierkegaard on, have laid great stress on anxiety as a basic emotion or state of mind which illuminates the human condition. In the case of Kierkegaard and other Christian existentialists, the experience of anxiety may predispose toward the life of faith by awakening the need for salvation; but among atheistic existentialists, anxiety points rather to despair, for the inner contradiction in the human being is taken to be incapable of resolution, so that human existence is always on the verge of absurdity. Part of human finitude is the fact that existence will in any case come to an end in death. But here too there are differences in interpretation. Heidegger believes that the fact of death, by closing off the future of existence, makes it possible to achieve a unifying and meaningful pattern in that existence. Sartre, on the other hand, thinks that death, by canceling out all achievement, is the ultimate indication of the absurdity of existence.

The criticism is sometimes made that there is something morbid in the existentialists' preoccupation with anxiety and death, and this criticism also impinges on those Christian theologians who have used these ideas to urge the need for faith and dependence on God. But it should be noted that there is another and more affirmative side to existentialism. Many writers of the school speak also of "transcendence," and by this they do not mean the transcendence of God, as commmonly understood in theology, but the transcendence of the human existent as he moves constantly beyond himself into new situations. Those who stress transcendence believe that the goal of human life is to realize more and more one's authentic possibilities. Whereas the early Heidegger believed that this is to be achieved by human effort, by a steady "resoluteness" in the face of facticity and death, Christian writers such as Gabriel Marcel have thought of human transcendence as a transcendence toward God, and have taught that this is to be achieved not just through human effort but through the assistance of divine grace.

Most existentialists have had a bias toward individualism. This was true of Kierkegaard, who was alarmed by the tendencies toward collectivism in Hegel's philosophy. It is also true of Sartre, who depicts interpersonal relations as essentially frustrating. On the other hand, Marcel claims that a relation to others is essential to an authentic human existence, while Heidegger sees "being-with-others" as an inescapable dimension of the human being. Critics of existentialism have reckoned its individualism as a defect, on the ground that it prevents the development of a political philosophy, but others have praised the stress on the individual as a defense of human freedom in face of the totalitarian pretensions of the modern state. Nietzsche and Heidegger have both sought to go beyond the biography of the individual to the outlines of a philosophy of history. In this, they oppose the so-called scientific history that seeks to establish objective facts. Nietzsche speaks scornfully of the "antiquarian" type of historian who seeks to reconstruct the past. He prefers the "monumental" historian who goes to some great creative event of the past in order to discover its power and to learn its lessons for the present and future. Heidegger likewise is uninterested in the history that confines itself to the analysis of past events. History, he claims, is oriented to the future. The historian goes to the past only in order to learn about such authentic possibilities of human existence as may be repeatable in the present. This view of history was very influential for Rudolf Bultmann's existential interpretation of the "saving events" of the New Testament, an interpretation succinctly expressed as "making Christ's cross one's own."

The stress on human freedom together with the bias toward individualism raises the question of the significance of existentialism for ethics. The existentialist has no use for an ethic of law, for the requirement of a universal law ignores the unique individual and conforms everyone to the same pattern. So we find Kierkegaard defending Abraham's decision to sacrifice Isaac, for although this meant the "suspension" of ethics, only so could Abraham be true to his own self and be "authentic." We similarly find Nietzsche claiming that the "superman" must create his own values to supersede traditional values, while Heidegger claims that what is ordinarily called "conscience" is only the voice of the mediocre values of society and that the true conscience is the deep inward summons of the authentic self. In each case, the value of an action is judged not by its content but by the intensity and freedom with which it is done. Such an ethic is too formless for human society as we know it and represents an overreaction against the cramping restraints of legalism. Nevertheless, this extremely permissive ethic has seemed to some Christian thinkers to be compatible with Jesus' teaching that love rather than law must guide our conduct, and it is reflected in the various types of "situation ethics" that flourished for a short time.

Finally, although existentialism turns away from the attempt to formulate any detailed and inclusive metaphysic, its adherents seem to find it impossible to avoid assenting to some ontology or theory of being. Kierkegaard and other Christian existentialists assume (but do not seek to prove) a theistic view of the world as the setting of human existence; Sartre is frankly dualistic in opposing the free but fragile being of man (the *pour soi*) to the massive unintelligent being (the *en soi*) of the physical world; there are mystical elements both in Heidegger's talk of "being" and Jaspers's of "transcendence." Existentialist theologians have also found that the reconstruction of Christian theology in terms of human possibilities is inadequate and needs the supplementation of a theistic philosophy.

[*See also the biographies of philosophers mentioned herein.*]

BIBLIOGRAPHY

An introduction to existentialism is provided in my book *Existentialism* (Baltimore, 1973). Major existentialist texts include Søren Kierkegaard's *Philosophical Fragments*, translated by David F. Swenson (Princeton, 1936); Martin Heidegger's *Being and Time*, translated by me and Edward Robinson (New York, 1962); Jean-Paul Sartre's *Being and Nothingness*, translated by Hazel E. Barnes (New York, 1956); and Fritz Buri's *Theology of Existence*, translated by Harold H. Oliver and Gerhard Onder (Greenwood, S.C., 1965).

JOHN MACQUARRIE

EXORCISM. The Greek root of *exorcism, exorkōsis* ("out-oath"), implies the driving out of evil powers or spirits by solemn adjuration or the performance of rituals. Such practices are worldwide, present in archaic as well as modern societies.

Ancient and Modern Japan. Some of the most striking descriptions of exorcisms in past and present times have come from Japan. The thirty-fifth and thirty-sixth chapters of the famous *Tale of Genji*, written by the court lady Murasaki Shikibu in the eleventh century CE, give lengthy accounts of possessions and exorcisms. The work describes Murasaki being taken ill with violent chest pains and high fever, both generalized and acute. Many prayers were said for her, and Buddhist priests performed esoteric rites. Soothsayers drew up diets and lists of abstinences, but there was no improvement for months. Finally, after their spells and fire rituals had failed, the priests said that Murasaki was dead, and they packed up their altars. But Prince Genji made more vows and summoned more powerful ascetics, who made such intense efforts that clouds of black smoke seemed to hang over their heads. Then the evil spirit suddenly passed from Murasaki to a little girl who was acting as a medium, and the girl began to weep and fling her hair about. She identified herself as the spirit which had caused all the trouble and asked for prayer, that her sins be forgiven. She said that the chanted holy texts were smoke and flames in whose crackle she could not hear the holy word. She advised Murasaki to atone for her sins and concentrate upon the Good Law.

Then Prince Kashiwagi was taken ill. His head ached, though he was not drinking, and he grew worse every day. He had no wish to live but rejected suicide because of the need to care for his parents. Soothsayers agreed that a jealous woman had taken possession of him, and mountain ascetics *(yamabushi)* of repulsive and fierce aspect flocked to his bedside. One ascetic with cold and forbidding eyes intoned mystic spells in a threatening voice. Kashiwagi implored the holy man to send away the spirit, the angry lady possessing him, but to no avail. Kashiwagi died while his wife gave birth to a son.

Murasaki's diary describes another exorcism. The empress Akiko had such a difficult labor that possession was suspected. Buddhist priests and exorcists as well as mountain ascetics were called. Some recited texts, some shouted spells in loud voices. Several court ladies offered to act as mediums. Each lay on a couch attended by an exorcist, and the night passed in a frightful clamor of chanting. When the empress was delivered of a son toward morning, the screams of the spirits were acute. One spirit threw an exorcist to the ground, though the ladies were not molested, and the exorcists lamented that they had not been more effective.

The *Pillow Book* of Sei Shōnagon, written during the same period, presents another vivid picture of exorcism. In a house surrounded by tall pine trees and with a spacious courtyard a young, handsome Buddhist priest, in gray robe and fine silk stole, knelt on a round hassock fanning himself with a scented fan while he recited the *Senju Darani*, a section of the *Thousand Hand Sutra*. This was used especially by Shingon Buddhists to avert all manner of evils. In an inner room invisible to the writer lay someone afflicted by an evil spirit. A medium was brought, a heavily built girl with a fine head of hair, dressed in a long stiff robe and light trousers. The girl sat next to the priest, who gave her a thin, polished wand. With eyes shut the priest recited the sacred syllables, and after a time the medium trembled and went into a trance, while her young brother stood behind fanning her. The medium wailed and groaned in a terrible way as friends rearranged her disordered clothing. After a while the patient began to improve, and attendants brought her hot water. By afternoon the priest had brought the spirit under control, forced it to beg for mercy, and then dismissed it. When the medium came to herself she was filled with embarrassment but was encouraged by the priest with a few more incantations. He was thanked by the lady of the house and offered gifts, but he excused himself, as it was time for evening prayers. It was a very obstinate spirit, he explained, and we must not be off our guard. He left with such dignity that everyone felt that the Buddha himself had appeared on earth. Such an elegant priest at an exorcism may well have been an exception.

Linking such classical examples to modern times, Carmen Blacker (1975) has given accounts of present-day exorcisms, as revealed by her own research among Nichiren Buddhist priests in Japan. Four kinds of possession are distinguished. The first kind, when only the body is affected by mysterious pains, frequently is attributed to an angry spirit. The second kind consists of hallucinations; the third, of an altered personality which could be blamed on possession by an animal such as a fox. The fourth kind consists of more rare cases when different voices and personalities appear and indicate possession. Blacker notes that the Roman Catholic church now recognizes only cases in the fourth category as true possession.

Any of these afflictions may be treated in Nichiren Buddhist temples. There, exorcisms are based on the teachings of the *Lotus Sutra*. Methods of prayer spells with the help of a medium are used in some temples, but in others, mediums have been generally abandoned "in favour of a direct confrontation between exorcist and patient" (Blacker, 1975, p. 302).

In preparation for exorcisms, Nichiren priests undergo a very severe training in austerities, consisting of a hundred of the coldest days of winter spent on mountaintops or in temples. The training comprises brief periods of sleep, repeated cold baths, two meals a day of thin rice gruel, chants of the *Lotus Sutra*, and practice in the use of magic castanets *(bokken)*. The sharp click of the castanets is thought to have a powerful effect on the spirits.

In exorcisms witnessed by Blacker at a temple in Kanazawa in 1967, the priest's mother acted as a medium. One morning a fox, three snakes, a jealous woman, a frantic man, and a cat spoke through her mouth. During each morning's service of exorcism the priest, dressed in white, sat in front of the altar chanting verses from the *Lotus Sutra* and sharply tapping a shelf with a wooden mallet. When the medium entered and knelt at the foot of the dais on which the priest sat, he "turned to face the room with a rosary in his hand" (Blacker, 1975, p. 303). A pile of papers at his side contained problems given by patients and petitioners. As the priest read them aloud in a firm voice, the medium gave answers which were said to come from the guardian deity of the temple. The deity diagnosed the patient's trouble and declared whether it came from simple tiredness or from a possessing spirit, such as a fox, a snake, or a neglected ghost. Cases of general illness were given instructions and reassurance, but in cases of possession the spirit would be forced to name itself, leave the body of the patient, and speak through the medium. The priest read out the name and age of the patient, recited verses from the *Lotus Sutra* in nasal tones, struck sparks from a flint, and made sharp clicks on the *bokken*, all of which were intended to force the spirit into the medium so that it could be brought into submission. When a fox spoke through the medium's mouth, she crouched in a position like a fox, begged forgiveness of the priest, and joined him in singsong recitations of sacred passages. More simple cases of possession, where snakes and a cat were identified, were dealt with by scriptural recitations repeated to lay the spirits to rest.

In another temple of the Nakayama branch of the Nichiren sect, the use of mediums had been abandoned about a century ago. In 1963 Blacker there witnessed exorcisms in which there was direct confrontation between the exorcising priest and the patient. At this temple the patients could stay days or weeks until they were completely cured. The patients were obliged to cooperate fully with the priest, reciting nearly all day long, with only brief intervals for rest and food, repeating the powerful formula, "Hail to the Lotus of the Wonderful Law." This was believed to convince the evil spirit that it was in the wrong abode, cause it to change its nature, and make it wish to leave.

The priest, in a cape of white muslin and a cope of red brocade, recited verses from the *Lotus Sutra* in stern tones for ten minutes. Wheeling around to face the patients, his right hand raised the wooden *bokken* and flashed it to and fro with sharp clacks. At this, some of the patients began to shake and twist about, and one woman who jumped up and down on her heels was sternly addressed by the priest. He shook the *bokken* at her and told her fiercely to change for the better, addressing the spirit inside her. He asked how many years it had possessed the woman and where, what ward, what street, and why. When the spirit confessed that it had possessed the woman out of spite, it was told to leave her and agreed to go at once. The promise to leave was repeated three times, as the woman shrieked and then collapsed on the floor, before the priest turned to the next sufferer. People came to congratulate the exorcised woman, who sat limp and dazed on the floor, and then they continued their recitations. The priest later explained that he always began by demanding a change from the possessing entity, after detailing the symptoms and the time of suffering. After the exorcism it was always necessary to set up a small shrine to the spirit and give daily offerings to keep the spirit in peace.

The majority of patients were women, and Blacker suggests that "symptoms of malevolent spirit possession are an unconscious attempt by women to protest against neglect and oppression in a society largely dominated by men" (Blacker, 1975, p. 312). In this way these possessions may parallel spirit possessions in Africa, notably Somalia. However, Blacker notes that the Japanese possessions are not public, in the sense of seeking to draw attention to women's lot. The exorcisms take place in temples or even in private houses. The results are not material gains but spiritual rewards like peace of mind. There are mental hospitals in Japan, but many people prefer the exorcisms to be conducted in religious terms by priests initiated into the sacred life.

China and North Asia. Doctrines and practices used in Japanese Buddhist exorcisms were partly brought from China, usually by Tendai and Shingon sects, and introduced to Japan by the eminent monks Kūkai and Ennin about the ninth century CE. The Nichiren school, after the thirteenth-century reformer of that name, was a Japanese development and no doubt, like the Tendai and Shingon sects, incorporated Shintō and nature beliefs.

The use of small children as mediums for divining the future and for serving as mouthpieces for gods and spirits is said to have been brought from China and ultimately from India. In Japan such rituals were called *abisha no hō*, a term derived from the Sanskrit word *āveśa*, signifying possession by a spiritual entity or its entry into a medium. Unblemished children were selected, bathed, dressed, purified, and anointed in order to reveal hidden or future things. At times they served as organs of prophecy, and more often as mediums for exorcists or as vessels for the subjection of malignant spirits.

The activities of shamans in ancient China may be gathered from the *Nine Songs* of the fourth century BCE. These intermediaries in the cult of spirits were called *wu*. Experts in exorcism, predictions, rainmaking, and healing, they were men and women whose services seem to have been widely available. Like Siberian shamans, they went into ecstatic states, descending into the underworld and propitiating evil powers.

There were many Chinese religious officials of various ranks and grades who maintained local or state rites and ceremonies, but the *wu* of both sexes belonged to lower classes of officials, though they were probably the most ancient priests in China. Male *wu* were said to call spirits from all directions by exclaiming and waving long grasses. In winter they ejected evil from halls, and in spring they warded off disease by averting the demons. Female *wu* performed exorcisms at fixed times annually, using ablutions with aromatics, dancing during sacrifices for rain, and chanting and wailing at times of natural calamities.

The *wu* specialists who acted as exorcists, seers, and soothsayers either were possessed by spirits themselves or employed mediums who were so possessed. In times of epidemics they joined in processions, stripped to the waist, dancing frantically, pricking themselves with knives and swords, thrusting needles through their tongues, or carrying heavy lamps from hooks thrust through their arms like the ecstatics in some Hindu and Sinhalese temples. Their aim was to frighten evil spirits away by displays of power, slashing the air with double-edged swords to drive off demons or wounding themselves with swords or with balls studded with sharp iron points. J. J. M. de Groot describes the *wu* in great detail in *The Religious System of China* (6 vols., 1892–1910).

In China down to modern times exorcisms are held more frequently on behalf of the sick than for any other purpose. De Groot describes a typical healing exorcism. After reciting spells, burning papers of incantations, and offering incense, the shaman began his or her "communication with the medium" (de Groot, 1892–1910, vol. 6, p. 1274). The medium shivered and yawned, but as incantations became louder to the accompaniment of drums and as "eye-opening papers" were burnt in quick succession, he or she began to jump about. Assistants forced the medium to a seat, his limbs shaking, his head and shoulders jerking from side to side, and his eyes staring as if into the invisible world. The consultant (the sufferer or the shaman) put questions to the medium, who replied with incoherent sounds which were interpreted as a divine language and were written down on paper. When the spirit announced its intention to depart, drums were beaten, water and ashes were spurted over the medium, and gold paper money was burned for the spirit. The medium swooned, and when he revived he declared that he had no recollection of the event.

De Groot also describes a more direct exorcism of the demon of sickness. The medium was stripped of most of his clothes, and on his stomach was placed a piece of red cloth or silk with two embroidered dragons, emblems of the Emperor of Heaven. His hair was unbraided and a sword placed in his hand. In this dress the exorcist yelled and jumped through the room, brandishing his sword over the patient and even beating him with the flat of the blade, knocking the sword against the bed and the door. If the patient panted and groaned, that was a sign of the dismay of the possessing spirit. The exorcist waved a whip, strewed uncooked rice and salt about the room, and wounded his own body with the sword or with a prick-ball. After a short time, or after many dances and woundings, the medium might declare which spirit was the author of the illness, how it had been offended unwittingly by the patient, and what sacrifice would pacify it. To drive the evil spirit away dances were sometimes taken into the streets, with mock fights and the burning of incense sticks and paper money. If the patient recovered, the family god was thanked, but if he did not get better, further expensive exorcisms were required.

Exorcism was practiced both by Taoist priests and by esoteric Buddhist sects. They performed before altars, surrounded by candles, incense, long scrolls with painted figures, and the accompaniment of drums. Reciting texts from the *Shih ching* (Book of Odes) and later writings, they expelled demons by making noise, striking out at the demons with clubs, and spitting water from the mouth in the four cardinal directions. The educated, however, came to dislike such practices. These opponents of shamanism and exorcisms quoted a saying attributed to Confucius that one should "revere spirits, but keep them at a distance."

Opposition to shamanism seems to have grown along with the spread of Confucianism. When the shamans' performances were abolished at the Chinese court in 32 BCE, the minister who sponsored the reform quoted Confucius as justification. Other commentators of the time noted that when rulers encouraged shamanism cases of haunting became more frequent. With the establishment of Confucianism as state religion in the first century BCE, the ruling classes more and more looked down on the *wu,* putting them on the same low level as professional entertainers and musicians. From the point of view of the elite, even if the *wu* were not impostors, they certainly were not gentlemen either.

In the Han dynasty Wang Ch'ung wrote a short dissertation refuting the necessity of exorcism. His work provides a good picture of contemporary beliefs about the spirit world, revealing that exorcism was widely practiced. He acknowledges that his contemporaries trust the power of sacrifices and exorcisms to remove evil. They first hospitably set out sacrifices for the entertainment of the spirits, then chase them away with swords and sticks after they have enjoyed the sacrifice. According to Wan Ch'ung's account, if these spirits have any sense, they will refuse to go but stand and fight, causing more misfortune. On the other hand, if the spirits have no knowledge they cannot cause any evil. Therefore exorcism represents meaningless labor and no harm is caused by its omission.

Further, if spirits have no material shape, they are like vapor or clouds and cannot be chased away. If we do not know their shape, we cannot guess their feelings, and if they are disposed to murder, they will hide and come back again after exorcism. The most elaborate system of exorcism can no more ensure the banishment of misfortune than the killing of tigers and wolves can undo the effects of misgovernment. Exorcism has no use, therefore, since the spirits either do not leave the house or will return to it. "The conclusion is, that man has his own happiness in his own hands, and that it is not in the hands of specters, being determined by his virtues, not by his sacrifices" (de Groot, 1892–1910, vol. 6, pp. 938f.).

Despite this criticism, exorcisms continued, and Confucians found approval for some of the rituals in Confucian texts. In the *Analects* of Confucius (10.10), it is said that when the men of the village hold their expulsion rite, the gentleman puts on his court dress and stands on the eastern steps. The expulsion rite, called No, was performed by an exorcist and four wild assistants, "inspectors or rescuers of the country to the four quarters" (de Groot, 1892–1910, vol. 6, p. 974). Over their heads they wore bears' skins decorated with four eyes of yellow metal. Dressed in black coats and red skirts and grasping halberds and shields, they led the house servants on a search through the buildings in order to drive out evil influences. It is said in the *Lun-yü* that Confucius stood at the east of the ancestral shrine in order to reassure the ancestral spirits so that they would not take flight along with other spirits and noxious influences. This No ritual was later stylized as a court dance, and the Son of Heaven performed the No to give succor against disease, ordering his officers to offer sacrifices at the same time.

Popular No ceremonies were performed in China in many places down to this century not only at the end of the year but also at times when there was high mortality from the demons of cholera. Through a medium, the god of the temple gave orders for a procession in which his image and a board bearing his name and titles were to be carried through the town so that the environs might be purified by the god's presence. Male and female *wu* were possessed by the divinity, dancing about with drums and cymbals. Other participants in specter masks, or in brilliantly colored dresses, armed with spears and banners, represented good powers suitably attired to terrify demons.

Siberian techniques of exorcism, at least in their modern forms, appear to have been strongly influenced by Chinese and Tibetan techniques and ideas. The Tunguz reindeer herders believe that sickness and misfortune come from the malice of the protective spirits of other clans or from the neglect of their own clan spirits. Shamans, as described by Soviet ethnographers, exorcise the foreign demons by driving them into the lower world. In retaliation, they then seek to send out their own guardian spirits in monstrous forms to fight the invading spirits.

Séances are undertaken in order to know and master the spirits by means of sacrifices. Disease may be attributed to the soul staying away from the body, or to its being stolen, or to its possession by evil spirits. The expulsion of the demons can only be undertaken by the shaman, for he alone can perceive the spirits and know how to exorcise them. Only he recognizes that the soul has disappeared, and only he, in his ecstatic state, can overtake the soul and return it to its body.

Séances described among the Yakut usually include four stages: the evocation of the helping spirits, the discovery of the cause of illness (generally thought to come from an evil spirit), the expulsion of this evil spirit, and finally the shaman's ascent to the sky. The shaman summons the clan spirits to help fight the invading evil; he goes into a trance and chants solemn verses to the rhythm of a drum, calling on the highest powers to prepare his way. He invokes the help of his tutelary spirit as well as other familiar spirits, who can arrive so violently as to throw him over backward. Finally, drumming and dancing, jumping in the air, chanting and shrieking, he goes to the patient and commands the cause of the illness to depart, "or he lays hold of the trouble, carries it to the middle of the room and, never stopping his imprecations, chases it away, spits it from his mouth, kicks it, drives it with his hands and breath" (account recorded by W. Sieroszewski and quoted in Eliade, 1964, pp. 231f.).

The shamanistic tradition of the ancient Bon religion of Tibet was preserved almost in its entirety in Buddhist Lamaism. The most famous Tibetan Buddhist monks were said to have performed miracles and exorcisms like other shamans. In one Tibetan legend a notable lama expelled the spirit of sickness in the form of a black pin from a queen, and his fellow worker flew through the air and danced on the roof of a house. However, not a great deal has been done to investigate the shamanistic elements in Bon and Lamaism.

In Tibet and Sikkim, demons who had caused death were exorcised within two days of the removal of the corpse. This ritual was called "turning away the face of the destroying devil" (Waddell, 1895, p. 494). The head lama, invoking his tutelary deity, blew upon human and animal images while assistants beat drums and cried "Begone." The chief lama then ordered the death demon to leave the house and sent it away to oppress his enemies. The images were deposited at crossroads while the lama uttered spells and made passes with a bell and a model thunderbolt *(rdo rje)* to ensure that no evil lurked behind.

In an example recorded in Tibet in 1940, an exorcist of demons was called from Lhasa to summon back the soul of a woman. After using magical devices and burning twigs, he went into a trance, first staring fixedly and then dancing wildly. By so doing, he called up the spirit, who demanded through a medium, "Who called me?" The spirit, through the medium, was then required to identify the sickness and indicate the means by which life could be restored to the woman. Once a sacrificial ceremomy was arranged and gifts offered, the woman recovered (Hoffmann, 1961, p. 26).

India and South Asia. Parallels to shamanistic techniques and exorcisms are found in Indian classical texts. The *Atharvaveda* (5.15–16) gives spells for exorcising, "speaking away " *(apa-vaktri),* warding off or averting pests and their leaders, as well as rites against demons. "O Agni, burn against the demons. . . . Let Rudra crush the ribs of sorcerers . . . Mitra-Varuṇa drive back the devourers" (6.32). Charms were recommended for the expulsion of adversaries, rivals, wizards, and assorted demons (2.18). In particular, the fire god, Agni, was offered sacrifice so that he would slay the demons and touch sorcerers with his flame. Agni would pierce the demons with arrows and thunderbolts or shut them up in his mouth, grind them with his teeth, split their skin, and crush their joints (8.3).

Āyurveda ("science of life, health") was closely associated with the *Artharvaveda.* One of its eight departments was *bhūta-vidyā* ("knowledge of evil beings"), which was demonology, or the treatment of diseases produced by evil influences. After describing how spirits are sent by sorcerers to plague individuals, Āyurveda recommends employing an exorcist who by means of spells and propitiatory formulas can send the malady back to its author or transfer it to a tree, animal, or human being. More philosophically, the *Chāndogya Upaniṣad* (7.7) affirms that understanding *(vijñāna)* gives knowledge of the Vedas and sciences, including *bhūta-vidyā,* and that therefore *vijñāna* should be revered as *brahman.*

In Indian village religion the activities of professional exorcisers ranged from warding off hailstorms to expelling evil spirits from those possessed by them. L. S. S. O'Malley (1935) describes an exorcism during an epidemic in the sub-Himalayan districts of Uttar Pradesh. The exorcist was simply carried outside the village tied upside down on a bedstead. Driving a wooden peg into the ground, he assured the villagers that the evil spirit had been tied up. Spirits that possessed men or women might be induced by the exorcist to leave by offerings of sweetmeats or sacrifices of goats. If this persuasion failed, harsher methods were used: beating the sufferer, applying red pepper to his nose, or undertaking the fire-walking ceremony. "Only those possessed by an evil spirit are affected by the fire, and, if their skin is burnt, it is a sign of deliverance from demonical possession" (O'Malley, 1935, p. 160).

In South India and in Sri Lanka professional exorcisers paint their faces, put on hideous masks, dress in gaudy costumes, arm themselves with symbolic weapons, and take to dancing in order to impersonate particular demons. In this way they induce evil spirits to leave the persons they have possessed. Sinhala exorcism has been described in detail by Paul Wirz (1954).

The Sinhala exorcist (*ẹdura* or *kattadiya*, "devil-charmer") is distinct from the general medical practitioner or natural healer. He usually comes from a lower caste, though he is just as prominent in his social activities. Exorcists preserve the ancient folk religion's belief in demons, spirits, and the occult powers needed in dealing with them. But the exorcists also link their practices to Hinduism and Buddhism. Like Āyurveda, medical science in Sri Lanka includes a section on *bhūta-viya*, those illnesses *(viya)* believed to be caused by demons or ghosts. They include epidemics sent by the gods in response to human offenses, illnesses caused by the unfavorable conjunctions of the planets and constellations, and sicknesses caused by the human "evil eye" or "evil talk." The demons may be appeased by the presentation of offerings or driven away by exorcists.

In addition to the Sinhala *ẹdura*, devil-charmer or exorcist, there is a *bandhanaya*, whose task it is to "bind" *(bandhana)* or confine evil beings and render them harmless. There are also astrologers, though the three professions are difficult to separate. The *ẹdura* is one of the best-known figures in Sinhala villages, making offerings to spirits and demons, persuading them to release the persons they have made sick and make them healthy again. Most *ẹdura* belong to the low castes of fishermen, land workers, drummers, or chair carriers. They are trained through a long apprenticeship to a teacher *(guru)*, often in their own family, learning *mantras* that eventually enable them to perform ceremonies independently.

When a person is ill in Sri Lanka, he sends first for the general medical practitioner, but if the practitioner's remedies do not help the invalid, a soothsayer is called in to determine the cause of the sickness. The soothsayer may suggest an astrologer, who is cheaper, or an exorcist. The exorcist makes his diagnosis by asking where the patient has stayed, whether he has come into contact with harmful spirits, eaten food that attracted them, or lived in a haunted house. He ties a charm on the patient to prevent the sickness from getting worse and to show the demons that a fuller ritual offering will be made.

Wirz gives several detailed descriptions of exorcism ceremonies, including the following account (Wirz, 1954, pp. 41ff.). For every great ceremony an auspicious day must be selected by consulting the patient's horoscope and noting, above all, the quarter of the compass where Mārea is to be found. Mārea or Māraya (Skt., Māra, "death, the evil one") is the mischievous and evil being, the leader of the demons, the personification of death, and the great adversary of the Buddha in mythology. Mārea changes his place in the sky each day. The exorcist and his assistants must never face in his direction lest their spells be rendered useless. Their spells would also be ineffective on the four days of the moon's phases that are Buddhist holidays. Saturdays and Wednesdays are the most auspicious days, other things being equal, because demons are hungry then and most likely to obey a summons.

The patient's relatives are told by the exorcist to procure certain herbs and roots, especially a large number of small lemons or limes, palm leaves, and banana stems. Other herbs and leaves are brought by the exorcist himself. Although the fee for the ceremony is fixed according to how elaborate it is to be, the exorcist must have at least one drummer and one or two assistants who help with arrangements and participate in dances. The ritual must always take place at night and continue until dawn, because that is the only time the spirit *(yakku;* Skt., *yakṣa)* may be called up. Ceremonies and dances are performed in front of the house where the patient is seated. From a small leaf hut to one side the dancers emerge. On the other sides of the house are another hut, stands for offerings and branches, and chairs for water, flowers, and roots.

The ceremony begins with a dance "by three or four persons who are supposed to represent the *yakku* at their evening-dance or their assembly" (Wirz, 1954, p. 52). A dialogue between a *yakku* and a drummer reveals that somebody has fallen ill and has been prescribed certain medicines. The *yakku* says that the medicines are no good, but that if he is given twelve presents, he will cure the patient. After two or three hours of dancing, herbs are placed at the patient's feet. Then the chief exorcist dances, utters spells, passes a mat through smoke, and lies on it in front of the patient. At the same time incense is carried around the exorcist.

After further dances and offerings, the *yakku* severally promise to restore the patient to health. The climax of the ceremony is a dance by a *yakku* with double torches in his mouth, which builds to a peak of intensity until he collapses in exhaustion. The patient is paraded round the hut and the stands of offerings and then gives gifts to the chief *yakku*, who promises recovery and health in words such as these: "Om, honour to Buddha, honour to Shiva, the eighteen mental disorders, the eighteen convulsion diseases, the eighteen fevers . . . may they be put to an end by the help of the deities and of glorious Buddha" (Wirz, 1954, p. 61).

At last the exorcist sings a magic word or exclamation *(dehena)* which assures the patient of his recovery. He passes a ritual brush over the patient's head and body, and all the *yakku* and bystanders join in the exclamation to confirm that the exorcism has been successful.

Such famous "devil dances," elaborate exorcisms of the demons of disease, take place in southern and western provinces of Sri Lanka, but these performances are not practiced everywhere in the rural highlands. However, Richard F. Gombrich (1971) has described more simple forms of exorcism in the highlands. Gombrich recounts how a sick patient believed that he had been plagued by an evil spirit sent by malicious neighbors and called in an exorcist to nullify the spell by performing a lime-cutting ceremony. The exorcist prepared offerings of five kinds of grain and meat. The offerings were placed at a crossroads so that when the spirit *(yakku)* had left the patient it would be unable to find its way back. Incense sticks were burned before pictures of the Buddha and the gods which were hanging on the wall of the patient's house. Twenty-one limes were placed at crucial points on the patient's body, then they were cut and thrown into sizzling oil. Finally, an egg was passed down the sufferer's body from head to feet, then broken and thrown into the pot along with the limes and the cutters that had sliced them. This indicated that all the evil influence *(dosa)* had been drained out of the patient and burned (Gombrich, 1971, p. 199).

Other sufferers from evil spirits go to popular shrines, such as the famous center of Kataragama in southeastern Sri Lanka, named after a god who is the second son of the Hindu god Śiva. Although primarily a Hindu center for the Tamils, this shrine attracts members of other religions. Enthusiastic devotees have become notorious for walking on fire or hanging in the air by means of skewers through their back muscles. At Kataragama are claimed cures of physical, mental, and spiritual possession. More simply, Buddhists may claim that evil spirits can be exorcised by recitation of the Three Refuges, which causes spirits and ghosts to flee.

In Burma and other countries of Southeast Asia, Buddhist sects practice exorcism for diseases believed to be caused by witchcraft or demonic possession. Combining ancient indigenous beliefs in spirits with faith in the Buddha and his attendants, some monks exorcise evil spirits by enlisting both traditional esoteric skills and the powers of benign Buddhist gods.

In Thailand the concept of *phii* includes a wide range of spirits. The *phii paub* is a particularly malevolent type of spirit whose removal requires the services of an exorcist. Women, married and single, are the most common victims of this kind of possession. Children also are affected, but very rarely adult men. Symptoms of hysteria—crying out, laughing loudly, hiding the face, and general depression—are diagnosed as possession.

Stanley J. Tambiah argues that the Thai exorcist is "an inversion of the orthodox Buddhist monk" (Tambiah, 1970, p. 322). The Thai exorcist uses Buddhist texts, but in diametrically opposed ways to those of the monk who uses these texts to teach morality and transfer blessings. The exorcist uses "the sacred words to frighten the spirits and drive them away," and he treats diseases of women, whereas the monk keeps his distance from women.

The Thai exorcist *(mau tham)* is an expert in reciting the Buddhist sacred texts (Dhamma), for they are considered to have great power. At the beginning of a séance the exorcist sits facing the propitious east and first worships the Buddha, the Sangha, the Dhamma—the Three Refuges. Then he invokes the powers of his teacher and other benevolent spirits to come wage war against the evil. He goes into a trance, trembling, waving his arms, shaking his body, gabbling magical spells, rushing to confront the patient. To make the spirit reveal itself, the exorcist may attack the patient, beating her with a whip or a fern, even scratching her with a tiger's tooth.

Once the spirit is identified, the exorcist and patient quiet down and proceed to the phase of purification. By reciting charms, washing with and drinking charmed water, and chanting outside and inside the house, the patient is purified. Her neck, wrists, and ankles are bound with cord to prevent the spirit from entering her body again. The exorcist teaches her the five Buddhist precepts of morality, usually recited only by monks. Lastly, she is given five pairs of flowers and candles to place by her bed until she is fully cured. To help toward this end the patient may visit the exorcist several times more to receive further washings with sacred water.

Africa and Islamic Lands. In Africa, belief in possession by good or evil spirits flourished in ancient indigenous religions and has survived in modern Islamic and Christian contexts. Such beliefs have been noted in northern desert regions—Egypt, Arabia, and Ethiopia—as well as in tropical regions where both Islam and Christianity have flourished in modern times.

In Somalia a victim is said to have been entered or seized by spirits. When this happens, both the spirits and the resulting illness are called *sar* (*zār* in Ethiopia). Somalians believe that these evil spirits are consumed with greed and lust after luxurious food, clothing, jewelry, and perfume. Women, especially married women, are particularly vulnerable to such possession. I. M. Lewis (1971) suggests that this results from women's depressed social status, for divorce and absent husbands are common. Speaking through the lips of the possessed woman, the spirits demand fine clothes, perfumes, and dainties with an authority that the women rarely achieve in ordinary life. When a *sar* specialist recognizes this possession, the woman's husband pays large sums of money for dances for "beating the *sar*" to bring relief and recovery. Some men are skeptical of this possession, regarding it as female trickery, noting that it occurs more often among the wives of the wealthy than among the poor. The women retort that some *sar* spirits attack the wealthy and others molest the poor, but that in any case the *sar* spirits hate men.

In Tanzania a similar "devil's disease" reveals its presence by hysterical symptoms of craving for food and presents. The exorcism includes not only cathartic dances but also the continuing presence of the exorcist in the house of the possessed woman. The exorcist's presence makes the woman feel like the center of attention and persuades her husband to show kindness. Similarly possessed women of the Luo in Kenya are treated by female exorcisers, who summon up the possessing spirits, find out their requirements, and expel them with dancing and feasting. The victim may be taken to the exorciser's home in order to find relief from the drudgery of her own household. Some possessed women dress in male clothing, and by so doing perhaps show their envy of the higher status of men. When they have undergone exorcism they return to a more respected position in their own home.

The Hausa cult of spirit possession is widely distributed in West Africa. The cult includes some two hundred spirits (*bori*), many of which are named and characterized by a specific behavior. These spirits are also called by words related to Arabic, for example *iblisi* ("devil") or *aljannu* (related to the Arabic word for Gehenna). Such spirits are believed to control different illnesses. Each spirit requires an appropriate type of sacrifice to propitiate it, such as a white sheep or a red cock. The "children of the *bori*" is the Hausa term for members of the cult of spirit possession. Dancers are referred to as "mares," and possession is described as "the spirit mounted her" or "she mounted the spirit." The spirit indicates its name and nature by distinctive behavior and gestures. At its departure the medium sneezes and recovers from trance. Interpreters believe that women accept the afflictions caused by the spirits as release from situations of domestic conflict. After their cure they are treated with deference.

In West Africa evil may also be expelled or transferred in a manner reminiscent of the ancient Hebrew practice of transferring a social evil to a scapegoat who carries it away into the wilderness. In ancient Dahomey the mother of twins that had died knelt in front of a priest. The priest proceeded to dust her chest, brow, knees, and feet with a fowl that she had brought. She was then instructed to take a goat by the horns and place her forehead three times against it in order to transfer her evil. The fowl and goat were then set loose to wander away from the village, while the woman was dusted with powdered clay in order to prevent a return of the evil.

The Islamic world tolerates the belief in witchcraft and possession. Although such beliefs at times are condemned, their prevalence is not questioned. *Siḥr* ("glamour, magic") is based upon belief in a world of spirits. Magicians claim that they can control the spirits by obeying Allāh and using his name in exorcisms. Illicit magicians are believed to enslave spirits for evil purposes and do so by performing deeds displeasing to God.

A crucial verse in the Qur'ān states that unbelievers "follow what the devils used to recite in the reign of Solomon. Solomon did not disbelieve, but the devils disbelieved, teaching the people magic . . . and they learn what injures them and does not profit" (2:96–102). Later Islam traced all good magic back to Solomon, and the devils listened at the walls of heaven and added lies to what they heard. In the traditions it is said that Muḥammad permitted the use of spells to counteract the effects of the evil eye or to remove the yellowness which came from a malignant eye.

Exorcism was *da'wah,* a call or invocation, interpreted by the orthodox as permissible only through the invocation of God himself. A further tradition said, "There is nothing wrong in using spells as long as you do not associate anything with God." Exorcists and licit magicians claim that they control the spirits by supplicating God and bringing adjurations to bear on the spirits. Illicit magicians are said to enslave spirits by making evil offerings and by performing deeds displeasing to God. Incantations used by exorcists consist of the recital of the names and attributes of God, either "amiable attributes" or "terrible attributes." The name and initials of the person to be influenced are also considered by many popular exorcists to be connected with the twelve signs of the zodiac, the seven planets, and the four elements. Books on exorcism correlate these signs with types of incense and with the names of presiding spirits which make other souls obedient to the will of the exorcist.

The *jinn,* or genies, of Islamic belief are fiery spirits, some of whom are believers and will enter paradise, while others will go to the fire of hell. They appear in many popular stories, as in the *Thousand and One Nights.* Solomon had great power over the *jinn* by means of his seal or ring, on which was engraved "the most great name" of God. He built the Temple at Jerusalem with the help of thousands of *jinn.* But the relation of the *jinn* to the evil spirits or *shayṭāns* is obscure, for Iblīs, the devil *(diabolos),* is said to be both a *jinnī* and an angel. The presence of the *jinn* in many strange events leads people to invoke the name of God against possession by them. Mental and physical illnesses are often ascribed to *jinn,* and prayers for protection against them are uttered on entering a house or taking a bath. *Jinn* are frightened away by strong smells or sounds, by salt or water or smoke, but only with the help of the invocation of God.

In Morocco the *jinn* were exorcised from sick people by persons who had plenty of *jinn* themselves and never ate salted food. The exorcist required that the sick person bring clothes of a certain color and a cock or hen of the same color. The exorcist then dressed in the clothes brought by the patient and killed the fowl over a vessel held above the patient's head. The fowl was boiled and eaten by the exorcist and the patient, while a company of dancers played music, sang, and invoked various saints. If the patient was seriously ill, he might remain with the exorcist for seven days and nights. During this time they both ate only unsalted food. Other exorcists also sacrificed fowls and performed dances so that the *jinn* afflicting the patients would be identified. The dances continued up to seven days, during which time the house was fumigated.

Some other Semitic exorcisms are illustrated in the Old Testament Apocrypha, the writings of Josephus, and the New Testament. Generally these exorcisms use no magic rituals or mediums to contact or contain the possessing spirits but rely on powerful words in the name of God.

[*See also* Healing; Diseases and Cures; Shamanism; *and* Spirit Possession. *For discussion of exorcism in specific contexts, see* Drums; Folk Religion, *article on* Folk Judaism; *and* Affliction.]

BIBLIOGRAPHY

For general studies of exorcism and its practitioners, see Traugott K. Oesterreich's *Possession, Demoniacal and Other* (New York, 1930) and Mircea Eliade's *Shamanism: Archaic Techniques of Ecstasy,* rev. & enl. ed. (New York, 1964). Arthur Waley's translation of *The Tale of Genji* (London, 1925) was long the standard version, but Edward G. Seidensticker's translation under the same title (New York, 1978) is complete and beautifully done. Carmen Blacker's *The Catalpa Bow* (London, 1975)—the title taken from an instrument used by a Japanese exorcist—is an invaluable study of popular religion past and present based on firsthand experience. *The Pillow Book of Sei Shōnagon* has been translated and annotated by Ivan I. Morris (Baltimore, 1970). *The Religious System of China,* 6 vols., by J. J. M. de Groot (1892–1910; Taipei, 1967), is full of detail on traditional beliefs and practices, as is L. Austine Waddell's *The Buddhism of Tibet* (1895; Cambridge, 1971). Helmut Hoffmann outlines more modern practices in *The Religions of Tibet* (New York, 1961). *Popular Hinduism* by L. S. S. O'Malley (New York, 1935) provides brief studies. *Exorcism and the Art of Healing in Ceylon* by Paul Wirz (Leiden, 1954) is more detailed and analytical. Stanley J. Tambiah's *Buddhism and the Spirit Cults in North-East Thailand* (Cambridge, 1970) is a more anthropological study. Richard F. Gombrich examines the relationship between "cognitive" and practiced religion in Sri Lanka in *Precept and Practice* (Oxford, 1971). An anthropological study of possession and exorcism with special reference to Africa is found in I. M. Lewis's *Ecstatic Religion* (Harmondsworth, 1971). For a comparative study of beliefs see my *West African Psychology* (London, 1951). On exorcism in popular Islam, see Edward A. Westermarck's *Ritual and Belief in Morocco,* 2 vols. (1926; New Hyde Park, N.Y., 1968).

GEOFFREY PARRINDER

EXPERIENCE, RELIGIOUS.

See Religious Experience.

EXPIATION.

See Atonement *and* Confession of Sins.

EXPULSION.

Religious expulsion ranges from temporary ostracism to more extreme forms of banishment or exile. The practice of expulsion was widespread in ancient Greek, Roman, and Middle Eastern cultures. It was also practiced as a form of social control farther east, particularly in India. Although not all forms of banishment can be classified under the rubric of religious expulsion, it is difficult in many instances to separate religion from society, especially in those societies where religion permeates all aspects of human life.

A distinction should be drawn between individual and corporate types of expulsion. In most cases, offenses like adultery or murder result in either the expulsion or ostracism of the individuals who have participated in the act itself. In some cases, an entire group of people is punished by exile or excommunication. This form of corporate expulsion, while not widely practiced, results in the alienation, sometimes permanently, of a lineage or class of persons, who lose all rights and privileges they formerly enjoyed. Corporate religious expulsion is best known in the case of the untouchable outcastes of India. It is also a key theme in Judaism, beginning with the banishment of Adam and Eve from the Garden of Eden and continuing throughout Jewish history in the recurring pattern of captivity, enslavement, and deliverance.

The most common social crimes that result in expulsion include murder, adultery, and deliberate recalcitrant breaking of social rules. Religious offenses ending in expulsion include various forms of sacrilege, such as blasphemy, disrespect against the person of priest or king, violation of rules associated with holy days, and disregard for pollution/purity norms.

Religions vary widely regarding reasons for expulsion. Some religions expel only those guilty of the most extreme offenses; others may banish anyone who deviates from community norms. Even within a single religious tradition, there may be several different degrees of expulsion. The first stage may be termed "exclusion," where the individual is left out of mainstream activities, either voluntarily or by force of law, but still retains other rights and privileges. In more advanced degrees of expulsion there is a stripping of identity, then excommunication, along with various restrictions placed on the person's behavior and freedom of movement. The most severe form of religious expulsion is forced exile, particularly when it is permanent.

The intensity of an act of religious expulsion is further determined by whether it is meant to be temporary or permanent. The latter is more rare, while the former is widespread. Temporary expulsion, sometimes called "ostracism," is an effective means of social control that assists in the maintenance of religious norms. Only large social units can engage in banishment or exile with any frequency, since small religious communities would be decimated rapidly if they invoked exile as an ordinary method to punish offenses. Permanent expulsion is a form of "social death" because the banished person is cut off from the lifeline supplied by his or her religious community.

Expulsion is closely entwined with two significant survival values operative in religious groups: (1) sacred purity and (2) social boundaries. These two dimensions of religious community are inseparably bound together. Thus, sacred texts, rites, and sanctuaries must be kept "pure" if they are to retain their religious efficacy from one generation to another. Also, the social norms that demarcate the boundaries of the religious community need to be reinforced and protected if the group is to survive, particularly under conditions of conflict, austerity, or attack from enemies. Expulsion is one means for protecting both sacerdotal and social boundaries. It is not always possible, or even useful, to consider these two types of boundaries separately; the sacred is often the religious community itself. Thus, anyone who violates social rules automatically commits a sacred crime, requiring extreme action to protect the integrity and continuity of the religious tradition.

Religious boundaries are particularly stressed under conditions where small religious groups attempt to survive in larger, more powerful communities. The Amish, and the other Mennonite groups in America, have stressed rules of boundary maintenance by their exclusive use of High German, their special clothing, and avoidance of "modern" customs from the surrounding culture. In these small religious communities expulsion remains, even today, an important mechanism for retaining religious and social purity.

In general, the larger and more diffuse the religious group, the less it relies on exclusion or expulsion as a means for establishing religious control. Also, in the context of the contemporary heterogeneity of world civilization, religious communities have increasingly abandoned formal expulsion as a means to punish or bring censure for religious transgressions. Even in the late nineteenth century historical records of some mainline Protestant churches reveal that expulsion was practiced for transgressions like drinking, violating the Sabbath, acts of adultery, or extramarital sexual encounters. In small, closely knit, agriculturally based village communities, where the church community played a central role in virtually all aspects of life, punishment by expulsion was a serious form of censure. Today, particularly in complex industrial societies, expulsion by religious communities rarely holds the same awesome power over individual adherents.

Special Cases of Expulsion. Different degrees of expulsion were practiced in ancient Greece. In the case of homicide, exile was usually voluntary, since it was a means of escaping the death sentence. Punishment for other offenses involved either temporary or permanent exile. Banishment was usually reserved for serious crimes of sacrilege or murder. In Athens, and other Greek city-states, individuals judged as being tyrants by popular majority vote (through the accumulation of power or wealth) were banished for a period of ten years. This custom was practiced for only a brief period in Greek history during the fourth century BCE.

The Hindu caste system provides a classic example of highly institutionalized religious expulsion. In the first place, the hierarchical structure of caste, with its multiplicity of subcastes and its complex pollution/purity norms, is founded on a scriptural tradition that expels large segments of population considered to be in a state of permanent, irreversible pollution. These outcastes, sometimes referred to as "untouchables," are exiled by their low place of birth in the hierarchical system. They retain a level of social servitude that, until recent years, has placed them at the bottom of a rigid system of social conformity.

In a more general sense, religious expulsion may be applied to individuals of all Hindu castes as a form of punishment for religious or social transgressions. In the past anyone who violated caste rules could be cast out by either the raja or the *pañcāyat* (caste council). The guilty party could move to a new place of domicile. Or he might be severely ostracized within his own community. In these cases, the individual (and sometimes even his close relatives) suffered a kind of "social death" (Dumont, 1970). He was treated as though he were one of the living dead.

In the ancient Hindu system the king or caste council had the power to excommunicate and reintegrate either an individual or a whole group. This punishment was rendered for eating cow meat, for cohabitation with members of a lower caste, and for committing murder, adultery, or another serious offense. Reintegration was possible if the transgression were relatively minor. Restoration to caste privileges involved abject submission to the king or the *pañcāyat*, along with ritual cleansing with the five purificatory products of the cow: dung, urine, milk, curds, and clarified butter. A penitential pilgrimage to the Ganges River was another rite of reconciliation. In some cases, the individual needed to make payment in grain or money as reparation for his offenses. Once all these rites were performed, individuals (or groups) who had been exiled or ostracized could be reinstated. Such severe religious expulsion is rare in contemporary India, but despite a general weakening of caste norms, more subtle types of ostracism continue to be practiced in the Indian subcontinent.

Religious expulsion is still extant among the Mennonite, Amish, Hutterite, and Bruderhof communities of North America. A moral principle activated among the Amish is the practice of *Bann* ("excommunication") and *Meidung* ("shunning"). The purity of the Amish church is maintained by excommunicating sinners, then shunning them. Thus, a person who has broken the religious code must be expelled in a formal ceremony. This rule of expulsion applies particularly to church members who leave the Amish to join other religious groups and to those who marry outside the brotherhood. One cannot eat at the same table as an excommunicated person, nor buy or sell from him, and in the case of a husband and wife, marital relations must be suspended (Hostetler, 1963). The purpose of expulsion among the Amish is to teach the person his error and to help him repent.

In the Bruderhof communities of New York State, Pennsylvania, and Connecticut, various levels of exclusion are enacted as punishment for offenders against community rules. Social control is articulated in an elaborate system of ostracism. The sanctions range from mild admonitions through various types of exclusion from communal life, culminating in the most severe punishment, banishment. In the case of admonishment, the individual is told that his behavior is offensive. If this does not help him to change his behavior, he is excluded from meetings, allowed only minimal contact with other community members, or isolated from the daily life of the Bruderhof. The most extreme form of exclusion is to be sent away into the outside world (Zablocki, 1971).

Expiation and Renewal. Most theories that explain expulsion are rudimentary and unsophisticated. Expulsion is usually attributed either to the maintenance of social boundaries or to the protection of religious purity. Mircea Eliade (1954) offers an intriguing alternate view. He asserts that the act of expulsion, often an annual event in historical religions, was a ceremony of expiation and renewal. Demons, diseases, sins were all periodically removed from the religious community as a means of revitalizing it.

In Eliade's view, ritual purification is not the main purpose of expulsion. The purpose is rather one of regeneration—to restore mythical or primordial time. This repetition of the cosmogony, a reenactment of the original creation, places the act of expulsion in the role of sweeping away the old to make room for the new. Thus, expulsion is a supreme act of expiation for the purpose of spiritual renewal. Unfortunately, Eliade's bold thesis has received little attention among religion scholars. Nor has expulsion been given the attention it deserves in the more general study of religion. There has been no book-length treatise on the topic, and whatever work has been done is embedded in other topics, such as the Hindu caste system, scapegoating more generally, or the Roman Catholic tradition of excommunication.

It is erroneous to think that expulsion is confined to antiquity. Today, in even the most modern forms of Protestantism, subtle pressures of shunning or ostracism are at work. Although in many religious communities formal rites of expulsion may be rare (or even absent), pressures for conformity continue to be strong enough to exclude individuals or groups who break religious codes. This should not be surprising in the Western religions, where the archetype of banishment is articulated in the first pages of the *Book of Genesis*. [*See* Fall, The.] Here, not only is there a fall from paradise—a universal theme in world mythic systems—there is also an active and deliberate expulsion of mankind from the garden of Eden. This archetype of expulsion continues to reverberate even today in Western religions. Ironically, expulsion, with its exclusiveness, is a difficult religious principle to reconcile with the popular, opposite, inclusive thrust of modern religions that claim a universal appeal, embracing all people and dissolving social as well as religious boundaries.

[*See also* Excommunication *and* Scapegoat.]

BIBLIOGRAPHY

Dumont, Louis. *Homo Hierarchicus: An Essay on the Caste System.* Rev. ed. Chicago, 1980.

Eliade, Mircea. *Cosmos and History: The Myth of the Eternal Return.* New York, 1954.

Hostetler, John A. *Amish Society.* Rev. ed. Baltimore, 1963.

Zablocki, Benjamin. *The Joyful Community: An Account of the Bruderhof.* Baltimore, 1971.

JAMES J. PRESTON

EYE. The eye is one of the most widespread symbols in all religious representation. As the active organ of visual perception, it is closely linked with light. Without light, the eye could neither see nor discern clearly. It is therefore only natural that in most cultures the eye is the symbol of intellectual perception and the discovery of truth. The eye knows because it sees. As early as the fifth century BCE, Democrites thought that certain images exist already in the body and that they emerge from the gaze of certain persons. Pliny the Elder explained that the small image inscribed in the pupil is a sort of miniature soul (*Natural History* 21.12.51). Similarly, the Bambara of West Africa say that the image perceived by the eye is, in fact, the double of the object or being that is seen: "Man's world is his eye." Thus the eye is often considered the mirror of the soul, the body's window, which reveals each person's deep thoughts by means of his gaze. As the mirror of the interior, the eye is the place where the mysterious life of the soul is glimpsed. In seeking to discover the reality behind the physical appearances it perceives, the eye becomes the locus of inner revelation. The expression "His eyes were opened" means that a rational or religious truth has been unveiled.

According to the symbolic conception of man as microcosm, which is found in the most ancient cultures, the eye is likened to the sun. Like the luminous star, it sees all, shines, and sparkles. Its glances are rays that pierce like arrows. Among the Semang, the Boshiman, and the Fuegians, the sun is the eye of the supreme god. This isomorphism of the eye and the sun reveals moral and religious values according to which all vision introduces clairvoyance, justice, and righteousness. Just as the sun illuminates by projecting its light everywhere, the eye seeks to discover and see everything, even faults and crimes. It thus becomes the emblem of a superior being who punishes and takes vengeance. To be all-seeing is to become omnipotent. Such valorization of the eye sometimes leads to its sacrificial oblation, which results in a supernatural second sight that replaces and sublimates simple, corporeal vision. This second sight is like the inner eye, or the "eye of the heart," so common among mystics who perceive the divine light. [*See* Sun.]

The Eye as Divine Attribute. In Egypt, as in the most ancient cultures of the eastern Mediterranean Basin, the presence of a symbolic eye signifies the power of the supreme divinity to see and know everything. Thus "the eye of Horus" appears on the stelae of Memphis, and eyes are engraved on a Cretan ring in the Ashmolean Museum (Oxford University), the symbol of an anonymous divinity who looks at and listens to men. The sacerdotal myths and traditions of ancient Egypt testify that the eye has a solar nature and is the fiery source of light and knowledge. Re, the sun god, is endowed with a burning eye and appears in the form of a rearing cobra with dilated eyes. In the cult of Harmerti, Re and Thoth are the two eyes of Horus, the god of the sky. One Harmerti story relates the struggle between Horus and Seth; Seth pokes out the eye of Horus, who is later cured by Thoth. The healed, healthy eye is the *oudjat* eye that shines in the dark and vanquishes death. *The Book of Going Forth by Day* (17.29ff.) recapitulates that mythical episode in a formula that is said to the dead person by the one playing the role of Thoth: "I restore to the eye the fullness it possessed on the day of the fight between the two adversaries." This means that light and darkness, life and death, are reconciled in the beyond. This *oudjat* eye was painted on the inner sides of the coffin, on each side of the head, and an inscription affirmed that they were hereafter the eyes by which the dead person would see in the afterlife and which would permit him to follow the spectacle of the exterior world while remaining in his tomb. The *oudjat* eye was provided for the dead person "in order that he be animated by it" (Pyramid Texts 578). This is why Horus's eye made an excellent amulet.

At Tell Brak in eastern Syria, the excavation of a sanctuary going back to 2500 BCE has revealed the worship of a divinity with a thousand eyes. In this temple consecrated to Inanna (Ishtar), hundreds of statuettes with multiple eyes have been found, votive offerings or apotropaic images attesting that the eye was the emblem of that all-seeing and omnipresent feminine divinity. Analogous finds have been made at Ur, Lagash, and Mari. Inanna's brother Shamash is the sun god, whose eye sees everything and who knows the most secret thoughts. He can reward or punish deliberately. In Babylon, Shamash was invoked before every divination, for he was the one who wrote the signs in the entrails of sacrificial victims. Without his help, the diviner could not see them.

The Indo-European world attached the same value to the eye as to the sun and to the gods, that is, the quality of being able to see everything. In the *Ṛgveda,* the god Sūrya, son of Dyaus, is called "the eye of the sky" (10.37.2) and "the eye of Mithra and of Varuṇa" (1.115.1, 7.61.1, 10.37.1). He sees from afar and everywhere, and spies on the whole world. Varuṇa, the celestial god, is described as *sahasrāta,* god of a thousand eyes, for he sees everything. According to the hymn of Puruṣa (*Ṛgveda* 10.90), the sun was born from the eye of the cosmic giant Puruṣa so that at death, when a man's soul and body return to the cosmic primordial man, his eye will go back to the sun. It is understandable why, in the *Bhagavadgītā* as well as in certain Upaniṣads, eyes are identified with the two celestial lights, the sun and moon, which are the eyes of Viśvakarman, the divine architect with multiple eyes who ordained everything. The Tamil caste of the Kammalans, who claim to descend from him, have as their main task painting the eyes of divine statues according to a ritual as sacred as that of the *oudjat* eye, the eye of Horus, in Egypt. In Iranian tradition, the sun is also the eye of Ahura Mazdā (*Yasna* 1.11), whereas in the tenth *Yasht* of the Avesta, Mithra is called the "master of vast plains who has a thousand ears and ten thousand eyes," thus assimilating him to the sun.

For the Greeks, the gods "with piercing gaze" saw everything belonging to the past, present, and future in a single, unified vision. This *panopteia* is the very mark of their divinity. Thus there is Kronos, who has four eyes, two in front and two in back; Zeus, whose "vast gaze" pierces through to the most secret things (Hesiod, *Works and Days* 240, 265); Apollo, the solar god, who sees everything (*Iliad* 3.277, *Odyssey* 11.109); and Dionysos, whose Bacchic hymn repeats that he "shines like a star with his eye of fire that darts its rays over the whole earth" (Diodorus of Sicily, 1.11.3). All the Greek gods cast a sovereign and pure gaze on man. The gaze of Athena Glaukopis shines and fascinates; the eye she fixes on her enemies is "a sharp one, an eye of bronze." When Achilles, driven by rage, tries to kill Agamemnon, Athena seizes him by his hair and forces him to look at her. The hero cries out, "It is terrifying to see the light of your eyes" (*Iliad* 1.200), for the light in her eyes is the light of reason. In Greek poetry, the image of the eye or the pupil is used to mark the quality of a person and the affection one feels for him: "Where is the eye of my beloved Amphiaraos, this hero who was both a seer and a valiant warrior?" (Pindar, *Olympian Odes* 6.16.7). The Greek religious experience consisted primarily of a vision. Since Homeric times, an indissoluble relationship has existed between knowing and seeing: knowledge is based on sight, on an optical intuition. In his *Metaphysics,* Aristotle speaks of that joy of seeing, which makes a better basis for knowing than any other perception. The joy of sensitive contemplation is the climax of the initiation into the great mysteries of Eleusis, the *epopteia,* and the very source of all philosophy, repeats Plato (*Timaeus* 47a). For the knowledge of truth rests on a vision that moves upward from tangible realities to timeless and eternal things: "Holy is the man who has the gods before his eyes" (scholium on Pindar, *Pythian Odes* 4.151b).

The Germanic and Celtic worlds also valued the magical power of the eye. Óðinn (Odin), god of war and magic, is a one-eyed god, for he voluntarily gave an eye in payment to the sorcerer-giant Mímir, or Memory. In return, Óðinn was permitted to drink every day at the spring of knowledge and thus to learn the science of the runes. The loss of an eye is therefore the means of acquiring superior vision and the supernatural powers that flow from it. After the Vanir killed Mímir, Óðinn practiced divination by interrogating the head, which he succeeded in preserving (*Ynglingasaga* 4, 7). This theme of knowledge acquired as a result of blindness—even ocular mutilation—is found elsewhere in other Indo-European traditions. Thus, the Greek diviner Tiresias attains the ability to see the future by becoming blind; Oedipus learns the will of the gods by blinding himself; and the blind king Dhṛtarāṣṭra in the *Mahābhārata* has special powers. Blindness, or voluntary mutilation of the eyes, becomes the sign of the superior sight possessed by the druids and the diviners. Indeed, this quasi-magical power of the eye is found again in Celtic myths. The god Lugh keeps only one eye open. He makes a tour of the enemies' camp, hopping and singing in an act similar to Óðinn's during the battle between the Æsir and the Vanir. The same attitude is found in the Celtic hero Cú Chulainn, who, when seized by furor, closes one eye and enlarges the other, or sometimes swallows one eye and places the other on his cheek to frighten his adversary. Many Gallic coins show a hero's head with an eye disproportionately enlarged.

Other myths also valorize the magical power of the one-eyed person, as if the reduction of vision to a single eye increased the intensity of the gaze. Thus a glance from Medusa's single eye petrifies anyone who crosses its path, for it is the glance of death that leads to Hades. To overcome it, Perseus must first escape the other two Gorgons and hide the one eye they share between them. He conquers Medusa only by making use of Athena's mirror, which allows him to see the monster without being seen by her.

The Evil Eye and Magic. The belief in the unlucky influence of the evil eye is universal. It rests on a valorization of the gaze reputed to be harmful because the eye is abnormal (eyes of different colors, double pupils, squinting); such a gaze magically reveals the malevolent intention of the soul whose window the eye is. The evil eye, cast for vengeance or out of envy, is an invisible threat against which one must protect oneself with countermagic, as, for example, in this Babylonian incantation: "Take the eye, attach its feet to a bush in the desert, then take the eye and break it like a pottery vase!" In Egypt it was common practice to bear apotropaic names, wear amulets, and recite formulas. In the Roman world, fear of the *fascinum* was constant. Many mosaics have as a central motif a dangerous eye pierced by an arrow, surrounded by animals, and defended by an owl (the bird of evil omen) perched on its eyelid. Against this danger, people resorted to amulets picturing an eye or a phallus. Eyes were even painted on the prows of boats.

Ever since the time of the apostle Paul (*Gal.* 3:1), Christian preachers never ceased to raise their voices, in vain, against the belief in the evil eye. Some rituals of the Greek Orthodox church as found in the *Mikron Euchologion* contain a formula for exorcism against *baskania* ("witchcraft") similar to that found in certain Babylonian curses. The same belief is found in pre-Islamic Arabia and in the Muslim world. Muḥammad himself recited incantations to preserve his grandson from the evil eye, reviving the formulas that Abraham made use of in order to protect Ishmael and Isaac, the legend says. One Arabic proverb states that "the evil eye empties houses and fills tombs." The eye frequently occurs in the magical preparations of certain African ethnic groups as well as in the Eastern Orthodox world, where the eyes of the figures in icons were poked out and crushed and then made into a magical powder.

Religious and Mystical Values of the Eye. The word *eye* recurs 675 times in the Hebrew scriptures (Old Testament) and 137 times in the New Testament; this indicates the richness of its symbolic meanings. It designates, first, the organ of vision fashioned by the creator for the good of man (*Ps.* 94:9, *Prv.* 20:12), for "it is a joy for the eye to see the sun" (*Eccl.* 11:7). But the eye is also a privileged organ of knowledge that scripture always associates with the characteristics of the wise and learned: for example, Balaam, the diviner whose eye is closed to the terrestrial realities that surround him but is open to the hidden and the invisible once he meets the All-Powerful (*Nm.* 23–24). The Targum Yerushalmi makes Balaam a one-eyed seer, thus taking up again the theme of a second sight superior to normal corporeal vision. Symbolically, the eye designates the consciousness of man that Yahveh opens to the knowledge of his law and therefore of good and evil (*Dt.* 29:3, *Is.* 6:10). For Yahveh sees all (*Ps.* 14:2); he is the witnessing God from whom nothing escapes (*Ps.* 139:7–8). This ability to see all is an essential characteristic of his transcendent sovereignty, and the divine eye is the administrator of justice: before it the just man can find grace (*Dt.* 31:29, *Jb.* 11:4). But it is also the paternal eye of Providence, "who turns toward those who fear him" (*Ps.* 33:18), like Nehemiah praying night and day for the people of Israel (*Neh.* 1:6, *Lv.* 16:2, *Nm.* 4:20).

But however great his desire, man may not see God face to face (*Ps.* 42:3), for no one can see Yahveh without dying (*Ex.* 19:21, *Lv.* 16:2, *Nm.* 4:20). Even Moses saw only the back of the glory of God (*Ex.* 33:20–23). If some prophets have had a vision of divine glory, it is in a fugitive and symbolic fashion, through a cloud or in human shape. Thus Zachariah (c. 520 BCE) saw Yahveh put before the high priest "a single stone decorated with seven eyes," symbol of God's vigilant presence in his temple. They are the seven planets, or seven divine eyes that sweep over the earth without resting. Likewise Ezekiel, in his vision of the chariot evoking Yahveh's throne, sees wheels whose rims are decorated with open eyes (*Ez.* 1:18), signs of Yahveh's omniscience.

Although, as the apostle John says, "No one has ever seen God" (*1 Jn.* 4:12), Jesus promised the pure in heart that they shall see God (*Mt.* 5:8). This beatitude makes of the eye a symbol of inner purity (*Mt.* 6:22–23); otherwise the eye, as the opportunity for scandal, ought to be plucked out and thrown far away. Early Christian preaching insists on the opposition between the eyes of flesh and those of the spirit; in Paul's case, physical blinding symbolically preceded the opening of the eyes of the heart (*Acts* 9:18). Furthermore, the function of the Son is to render visible his Father: "Whoever sees me has seen the Father," says Jesus to Philip (*Jn.* 14:9). But at the end of time, full vision will be given to everyone and "man's eyes will contemplate the glory of God just as he is" (*1 Jn.* 3:2). Gnosticism especially retains the Pauline theme of "the eye of the heart," an image already frequent in the writings of the Greek philosophers and the Hebrew rabbis. For the gnostic, "the eye is the inner light to the man of light" (*Gospel of Thomas*, logion 24), and the prototype of the man of light is "the eye of light" *(Sophia of Jesus Christ).*

In numerous philosophical and religious traditions, the inner eye allows access to wisdom. Plotinus explains that the eye of the soul dazzled by the light of understanding is fixed on pure transparency; the soul therefore sees the light found at the interior of his own gaze, and the eye of understanding contemplates the light of *nous* by participating in the very light of this sun-spirit (*Enneads* 5.3[17].28). Recalling that the wise man is he who sees and that the fool is blind, Philo Judaeus explained that formerly the prophets were called "seers" (*1 Sm.* 9:8). For him, wisdom is not only what is obtained by the vision of the inner eye, just as light is perceived by the carnal eye; but wisdom also sees itself, and this is the splendor of God, who, in opening the soul's eye to wisdom, shows himself to man (*De migratione Abraham* 38).

In Hinduism, the god Śiva is endowed with a third eye, the frontal eye that gives him a unifying vision. His look of fire expresses the pureness of the present without any other temporal dimension, as well as the simultaneity of beings and events, which he reduces to ashes in revelation of the all. Likewise Buddha, the "awakened one," received inner enlightenment through the celestial eye, which permitted him to see the life of all beings simultaneously and gave him the knowledge of the chain of the fundamental forces of existence as well as its previous forms. This eye of wisdom, *prajñācakṣus*, is found at the limit of unity and multiplicity, of emptiness and creation; it permits the wise man to grasp them simultaneously. The organ of inner vision, it is the very sign of Buddhist wisdom.

But the inner eye is the organ of wisdom only because it is capable of actually experiencing the divine. Every revelation presents itself as a veil that has been pulled back before the gaze of religious man, for whom the beatific vision and the contemplation of God are the very essence of eternal life. The eye of the heart is thus a frequent theme in spiritual and mystical literature. Just as the eye can neither see nor discern its object without light, so the soul cannot contemplate God without the light of faith, which alone opens the eyes of the heart. "Man must therefore become entirely eye"; such is the teaching of the Desert Fathers reiterated by Symeon the New Theologian (*Hymns of the Divine Loves* 45), for the soul's eye, relieved of carnal passions, can perceive the divine light that opens up on the heavens. Following Origen and his theory of spiritual senses, Gregory of Nyssa, Augustine, Bernard of Clairvaux, and all the Fathers state that it is God who, by opening the heart's eye, makes one see. Meister Eckhart again picks up this teaching *(Sermons)*, and Teresa of Ávila specifies that what we know otherwise than by faith, the soul recognizes at sight, although not by eyesight. Leon Bloy writes in his *Journal* (6 June 1894) that "we must turn our eyes inward" in order to speak our desire for a vision of truth, for the carnal eye only allows us to see "in enigma and as in a mirror." The eye of the heart is therefore man seeing God and, at the same time, God looking at man; it is the instrument of enlightenment and inner unification: "We shall find the pearl of the kingdom of heaven inside our hearts if we first purify the eye of our spirit" (Philotheus of Sinai, *Forty Chapters on Spiritual Sobriety* 23).

[*See also* Visions.]

BIBLIOGRAPHY

Bleeker, C. Jouco. *The Sacred Bridge.* Leiden, 1963.

Boyer, Régis. *La religion des anciens scandinaves.* Paris, 1981.

Crawford, O. G. S. *The Eye Goddess.* London, 1957.

Durand, Gilbert. *Les structures anthropologiques de l'imaginaire.* 3d ed. Paris, 1969.

Hocart, Arthur M. "The Mechanism of the Evil Eye." *Folk-Lore* 49 (June 1938): 156–157.

Pettazzoni, Raffaele. *The All-Knowing God.* Translated by H. J. Rose. London, 1956.

Seligman, Siegfried. *Der böse Blick.* Berlin, 1910.

Vries, Jan de. *Altgermanische Religionsgeschichte.* 2d ed. 2 vols. Berlin, 1956–1957.

Vries, Jan de. *Keltische Religion.* Stuttgart, 1961.

MICHEL MESLIN
Translated from French by Kristine Anderson

EZEKIEL (sixth century BCE), or, in Hebrew, Yeḥezqe'l; Hebrew prophet. A hereditary priest, Ezekiel is known primarily from the biblical book of prophecy named after him that contains first-person reports of revelations made to him. For example, the opening verse of *Ezekiel* reads: "In the thirtieth year, in the fourth month, on the fifth of the month, when I was among the exiles on the Chebar canal [in the vicinity of the Babylonian city of Nippur], the heavens opened and I saw a divine vision" (a description of God's majesty borne on the divine "chariot" follows). The time of his prophesying is fixed by some fifteen dates scattered through the book, which, apart from the obscure first one cited above, belong to the era of "our exile"—that is, the exile of King Jehoiachin of Judah, his courtiers, and his administrative staff, in 597 BCE); it may be inferred that Ezekiel was among those deported to Babylon with the king. The dates fall between 593 and 571, all within the reign of the Babylonian king Nebuchadrezzar II (605–562), who is mentioned several times in the book as a world conqueror. No references to events subsequent to the reign of that king are made, nor does the editorial work on the book necessitate assumption of later hands, so that its contents—internally consistent though literarily varied—may be considered the record of a single author's career. The only personal details given of Ezekiel's life are his priestly descent and the death of his wife in exile. That the enigmatic "thirtieth year" of the opening verse (cited above) alludes to the prophet's age at the start of his vocation is an unsupported guess that goes back at least as far as Origen.

Two determinants of the prophet's outlook stand out in his prophecies: his priesthood and his exile. The former is reflected in his schooling in the full range of Israel's literary traditions (legal, prophetic, historiographic), his manner of expression (echoing the Priestly writings of the Pentateuch), and his preoccupations (the Temple, God's holiness, offenses against his worship). The response to exile is reflected in Ezekiel's anguish and rage at what he perceives as God's rejection of his apostate people. Ezekiel's prophecy is characterized by a leaning toward systematization; he propounds doctrines permeated by a severe logic that centers on the injury Israel inflicted on the majesty of God and its reparation rather than on the piteous situation of the people.

The *Book of Ezekiel* may be divided into three sections:

- Chapters 1–24 are composed mostly of dooms against Jerusalem that date before its fall in 587/6 BCE. (Chapter 33 is an appendix related to this section.)
- Chapters 34–48 contain prophecies of the restoration of Israel, composed, presumably, after the city's fall. The first six of these chapters are rhapsodic, the latter nine legislative.
- Chapters 25–32 link the two main divisions in the form of prophecies against Israel's neighbors, settling accounts with them for their exploitation of, or participation in the collapse of Judah.

No other prophetic book shows so thorough a working through of principles in its arrangement, pointing to the hand of this prophet.

Main Themes of Ezekiel's Prophecy. The chief burden of Ezekiel's pre-586 prophecies (chaps. 2–24) was that Jerusalem was inevitably doomed to destruction by Nebuchadrezzar. This contradicted the mood both of the exiles and of the homelanders, among whom prophets of good tidings were at work (chap. 13). Patriotism, faith in the security offered by God's presence in the Jerusalem Temple, and the encouragement by Egypt of anti-Babylonian forces in Judah combined to rouse the people's hopes, indeed their expectation that subjection to Babylonia was ephemeral; that the exiles would shortly return home; and that resistance to the overlord, supported by Egypt, would be successful. Like Jeremiah, his contemporary in Jerusalem, Ezekiel regarded such hopes as illusory; worse, they revealed spiritual obtuseness in their blindness to the divine purpose realizing itself in Judah's plight. As Jeremiah and Ezekiel saw it, the people's idolatrous infidelity to their covenant with God, reaching back to the beginnings of their history and peaking during the reign of King Manasseh of Judah (*2 Kgs.* 21), had finally outrun God's patience. And alongside apostasy was the corruption of the social order (idolatry and immorality were bound together in the minds of biblical authors): the oppression of the governed by their rulers, the trampling of the poor, the unfortunate, and the aliens by the people at large, until not one righteous man could be found in Jerusalem to stem the onset of God's retributive fury (*Ez.* 22). Another form of infidelity to God that Ezekiel denounced with particular vehemence was the resort of Judah's kings to Egypt for help against Mesopotamian powers (Assyria, Babylonia), instead of trusting in divine protection. These offenses are set out in bills of indictment ending in sentences of doom: God had resolved to abandon his Temple (desecrated by the people) and to deliver his city and land to be ravaged by the Babylonians (chaps. 8–11, 16, 23). In listing the evidences of Jerusalem's guilt and stressing the unavoidability of its fall, Ezekiel sought to disabuse his fellow exiles of their misplaced hopes, turn their minds to consider their evil ways, and lead them to repentance. (Since his dooms are addressed rhetorically to Jerusalem, it has been thought that they were intended to dissuade the Judahite court from pursuing its rebellious policy against Babylonia, but their emphatic unconditionality could hardly serve that end.)

Ezekiel conveyed his messages in deeds as well as words, making much use of dramatic and symbolic acts. He arrayed toy siege works against a representation of Jerusalem drawn on a brick; he lay on his side eating scant siege rations for many days; carrying an exile's pack on his shoulder, he acted out the clandestine flight of the king from the fallen city; he repressed his sighs of mourning for his dead wife to presage the stupefaction of those who would live through the coming carnage (chaps. 4–5, 12, 24)—all these and more. No prophet went to such lengths to impress his audience because none was so convinced of their imperviousness to his message (chaps. 2–3). Still, although at his commissioning he was forewarned of his audience's adamant hostility, in actuality he became the cynosure of exiles in his hometown, Tel Abib: indeed, he complains that they flock to him as to an entertainment but fail to act on his admonitions (chap. 33).

To the exiles he addressed calls for repentance. For their conversion he propounded the doctrine of the eternal availability of divine forgiveness, thus countering the despair that was bound to follow on acceptance of his interpretation of events. For if Israel indeed lay under a generations-long accumulation of guilt—Ezekiel once went so far as to describe Jerusalem as congenitally depraved (*Ez.* 16:3–45)—so overwhelming it caused God to forsake his Temple and his land, what future had they to look forward to? Ezekiel met despair with the twin doctrines of the moral autonomy of each generation—that is, the nonbequeathal of guilt from fathers to sons and God's ever-readiness to accept the penitent wicked. God judges each according to his own ways, not those of his ancestors, and he judges him as he is now, not as he was yesterday. Hence each generation may hope for reconciliation with God, and anyone can unburden himself of his guilty past by renouncing it and turning a new leaf. God does not desire the death of the wicked man but his repentance, so that he may live (chaps. 18, 33).

As Jerusalem suffered under the protracted siege that was to end in its fall (in 587/6), Ezekiel began to deliver his oracles against foreign nations; the first is dated in 587, the last in 585 (except for an appendix dated to 571, in chap. 29). Judah's small neighbors, formerly corebels with it, abandoned it in the crisis. Some gloated over its fall; Edom seized the occasion to appropriate some of Judah's territory. These countries are denounced for their hubris and their show of contempt toward their downfallen neighbor, and their own ruin is predicted (chaps. 25–28). On the other hand, Egypt, which had encouraged Judah to revolt, is condemned to temporary exile and permanent degradation for having proven to be a "reedy staff" in the hour of need, collapsing when Judah leaned on it (chaps. 29–32). When God punishes his own so ruthlessly, the perfidy and contemptuousness of their neighbors will not be ignored. Some of the most vivid passages in the book occur in these prophecies: a unique list of the Phoenecian trade (Tyre's imports and exports and the nations with which it traded); a mythical depiction of the king of Tyre as the denizen of Paradise, expelled from it for his sin; and a picture of the underworld realm of the dead receiving Pharaoh and his defeated army.

The fall of Jerusalem gave rise to a new concern: the only nation on earth that acknowledged the one true God (however imperfectly) had suffered a crushing defeat on the field and the cream of its population had, for a second time, been deported. However justified these punishments were in terms of Israel's covenant with God, to the world they could only signify the humiliation of Israel's God—or so at least Ezekiel portrayed it in chapter 36. The extreme measures taken to punish Israel for flouting God (in Ezekiel's words, for "profaning God's name") resulted in a still greater "profanation": the nations pointed to the exiles and jeered, "These are the Lord's people and from his land they have come forth!" It followed as an ironbound consequence that God must now vindicate his authority by restoring Israel to its homeland and so redeem his reputation. This key idea of chapter 36 is the motive of the rhapsodic restoration prophecies of chapters 34–39. All is done for the greater glory of God: Israel's "dry bones" are vivified and the miraculously recreated people are gathered into their land; the former two kingdoms (Israel and Judah) are united under the rule of a new David; the land is blessed with peace and unprecedented fertility. The crowning transformation is in the very nature of the Israelites: their "heart of stone" will be replaced with a "heart of flesh." God's spirit will animate them to observe his laws effortlessly, thus averting forever the recurrence of the terrible cycle of sin, punishment, exile, and profanation of God's name among men. Moreover, since the restoration of Israel will not be for their sake, but for the sake of God's name (reputation), it will not depend on Israel's taking the initiative to reform itself but will happen at God's initiative. Israel's self-recrimination and remorse over its evil past will follow, not precede, its salvation (chap. 36).

To impress his sovereignty finally on the minds of all men, God will, after restoring Israel, engineer an attack on them by the barbarian Gog of Magog. Attracted by the prospect of plundering the prospering, undefended cities of Israel, Gog and the armies mustered from the far north under his banner will descend on them, only to be miraculously routed and massacred. Then all will realize that the misfortune that befell Israel was punishment for their sins (not a sign of God's weakness!), and their restoration, a "sanctification of God's name" in the sight of all mankind (chaps. 38–39).

The last major section of the book is legislative and prescriptive: a unique series of revisions of certain Israelite institutions designed to maintain the sanctity of the Temple precinct. The section consists of a vision of the future Temple climaxed by God's return to it (chaps. 41–43:12), and instructions for righting past misconduct in relation to it so that it would never again be abandoned (chaps. 43:13–48).

The future Temple is envisaged as laid out with a well-defined gradation of sacred areas, access to which is rigorously controlled in accordance with grades of personal holiness. The corps of Temple servants is restructured, with a sharp division between priests and nonpriests, the latter being strictly excluded from access to the highest grades of holy space. The role that the future king (archaically entitled "chief") is to play in worship is so defined as to prevent him, a layman, from trespassing on the areas of highest sanctity (as preexilic kings were accustomed to do), while at the same time making allowances for his superior dignity. New periodic sacrifices of purgation are instituted to keep the inevitable contamination of the sanctuary by the natural impurities and inadvertencies of the people from accumulating dangerously. Finally, the land is redistributed among the ingathered population, archaically defined as the twelve tribes, with boundaries derived from the ancient idea of the promised "land of Canaan" rather than from the actual boundaries of the land under the monarchy. The disposition of the tribes is such as to isolate the Temple from contact with the profane by cordons of sacred personnel surrounding it. God will dwell forever in his holy city, renamed accordingly *YHVH Shammah,* "The Lord is there" (replacing *Yerushalayim,* "Jerusalem").

Later Influences. In later times, Ezekiel's justification of the collapse of Israel influenced the revision of the old history of the monarchy (the *Book of Kings*) undertaken under Persian rule embodied in the *Book of Chronicles.* The Chronicler's story of the conduct of the last Judahite kings (from Manasseh on) shows the effect of Ezekiel's doctrines with particular clarity. On the other hand, Ezekiel's rhapsodic descriptions of restoration were far removed from the modest dimensions and achievements of returned exiles. And their mood of repentance (surely owing at least in part to Ezekiel's teachings) kindled in them a resolve to adhere scrupulously to the ancient covenant laws of Moses rather than to Ezekiel's newfangled revisions (which anyway supposed a very different geodemographic reality from that of the postexilic community). Ezekiel had to give way before Moses, and his program was relegated to messianic utopia. His vision of the divine "chariot" (chaps. 7, 10) was to play a decisive role in Jewish mystical experience from Second Temple times onward.

BIBLIOGRAPHY

A number of commentaries on *Ezekiel* may be consulted, among which the following, listed chronologically, are recommended.

Herrmann, Johannes. *Ezechiel, übersetzt und erklärt.* Kommentar zum Alten Testament. Leipzig, 1924.

Cooke, G. A. *A Critical and Exegetical Commentary on the Book of Ezekiel.* 2 vols. New York, 1937.

Fohrer, Georg. *Ezechiel.* Handbuch zum Alten Testament, vol. 13. Tübingen, 1955.

Eichrodt, Walther. *Der Prophet Hesekiel.* Das Alte Testament Deutsch. Göttingen, 1965–1966. Translated into English as *Ezekiel: A Commentary,* "Old Testament Library" (Philadelphia, 1970).

Wevers, John W. *Ezekiel.* Century Bible, n.s., pt. 1, vol. 26. London, 1969.

Zimmerli, Walther. *Ezechiel (1–48).* 2 vols. Biblischer Kommentar Alter Testament, vol. 13, nos. 1–2. Neunkirchen, 1969. Translated into English in two parts: *Ezekiel 1,* by R. E. Clements (Philadelphia, 1979), and *Ezekiel 2,* by James D. Martin (Philadelphia, 1983).

Greenberg, Moshe. *Ezekiel 1–20.* Anchor Bible, vol. 22. Garden City, N.Y., 1983.

For general surveys, consult Walther Zimmerli's "The Message of the Prophet Ezekiel," *Interpretation* 23 (1969): 131–157, and my own article "Ezekiel" in the *Encyclopaedia Judaica* (Jerusalem, 1971). Bernhard Lang's *Ezechiel: Der Prophet und das Buch,* "Erträge der Forschung," no. 153 (Darmstadt, 1981), is a good review of modern scholarship on Ezekiel. The influence of Ezekiel on Jewish mysticism is treated in David J. Halperin's *The Merkabah in Rabbinic Literature,* "American Oriental Series," no. 62 (New Haven, 1980).

MOSHE GREENBERG

EZRA (late fifth and early fourth centuries BCE), known for his restoration of the Law of Moses in the postexilic period and generally regarded as the founder of Judaism.

Literary Sources. The account of Ezra's activity is contained in *Ezra* and in *Nehemiah* 8–9. The history covered by *Ezra* is a continuation from *2 Chronicles* and is probably by the same author. It begins with the edict of Cyrus (538 BCE), which permitted the return of exiles from Babylonia to their homeland and the chance to rebuild the Temple. Using some independent sources whose chronology is not clearly understood, the author attempts to trace the history of the Jerusalem community down to the time of Ezra (Heb., 'Ezra'), which begins only in chapter 7. Within chapters 7 to 9 there is a first-person narration by Ezra, often considered to be a separate source, "the memoirs of Ezra," although it cannot easily be separated from its context in 7:1–26 and chapter 10, where Ezra is referred to in the third person. It appears to have been composed after the style of the so-called Nehemiah memoirs.

On the basis of the Greek version *(1 Esd.)* it appears that *Nehemiah* 8 originally followed and was a part of *Ezra,* so that the climax of the history was Ezra's reading of the law book to the Jerusalem community. A later editor who wanted to make the activity of Ezra and Nehemiah appear contemporary transposed this part of the history to its present position. *Nehemiah* 9, the prayer of confession of Ezra, also fits badly as a continuation of chapter 8 and is a later addition. At any rate the biblical portrait of Ezra is not a contemporary record but, in my view, is Hellenistic in date and must be used with caution in any historical reconstruction of the period.

Biblical Tradition. Ezra's introduction, in *Ezra* 7:1–5, identifies him as a priest and gives him a pedigree back to Aaron. But he is especially known as "the scribe of the law of God." The account indicates that he was given a special commission by the Persian king, Artaxerxes, to promulgate the Law of Moses not only in Judah but in the whole of Syria-Palestine. He also received considerable monetary support for the cult in Jerusalem. Ezra set out from Babylon with five thousand companions and great treasure and arrived in Jerusalem safely five months later. Shortly after he returned to Jerusalem he discovered that many Jews had intermarried with non-Jews, and after much soul-searching he set about to dissolve all the mixed marriages. In the second year after his arrival, in the seventh month, at Sukkot, Ezra brought forth the Law and read it to the people in a great public ceremony (*Neh.* 8). This is now followed (in *Neh.* 9) by a fast on the twenty-fourth day of the seventh month, in which Ezra leads the people in a great confession of sins and a covenant renewal (*Neh.* 10) by which the people commit themselves to the support of the sanctuary, the observance of the Sabbath, and other laws of the Torah.

There are various layers in the biblical tradition concerning Ezra. The one that identifies Ezra as the scribe who brought the Law to the restored community in Jerusalem is clearly the oldest tradition. Many scholars believe that this tradition reflects the introduction of the Pentateuch into, and its formal acceptance by, the Jewish community in Jerusalem. For this reason the figure of Ezra represents a new era in which the community stands under the Law and its interpreters and becomes, in this view, a religion "of the book," so that it is often regarded as the beginning of Judaism. However, any notion of a radical discontinuity with the religion of the Jews in the late monarchy or exilic periods is quite unwarranted, since the Pentateuch itself embodies much from these periods.

Nevertheless, the mission of Ezra is now seen in the Bible through the eyes of the Chronicler, who considered his presentation of the Law as the climax of his history, and later Judaism did much to further enhance the significance of this event. Already within the biblical account the later levels of the Ezra tradition that portray him as a judge and reformer (*Ezr.* 9–10), or as an intercessor and covenant mediator (*Neh.* 9–10), cast him more and more in the image of a second Moses.

Historical Problems. The exact dating of Ezra's activity within the Persian period and especially his relationship to his near contemporary Nehemiah have long been matters of disagreement among scholars. The *Book of Ezra* dates the beginning of Ezra's activity to the seventh year, and Nehemiah to the twentieth year, of Artaxerxes. If these dates refer to the same king, then Ezra would be prior to Nehemiah, as the present biblical tradition suggests. But there is reason to believe that Ezra should be dated to the reign of Artaxerxes II (404–359 BCE) which would put him about 397 BCE, well after Nehemiah. Ezra's return seems to presuppose a revitalized Jerusalem community with protective walls (*Ezr.* 9:9), while Nehemiah seems to know nothing of the large band of exiles that returned with Ezra. It also seems most unlikely that Ezra waited thirteen years after his arrival before promulgating his law if this was his primary commission. Another possibility is to view Ezra as coming during Nehemiah's second term of office, in the thirty-seventh year of Artaxerxes I, but this involves a textual emendation for which there is little justification.

Another area of debate is how to understand the law book that Ezra brought to Jerusalem from the Babylonian exile. Was it a particular part of the Pentateuch, such as the so-called Priestly code, or was it a more complete form of the Torah, much as it is today? And just exactly what was the nature of Ezra's commission from the Persian court and the scope of his authority? The way in which one answers these questions greatly affects one's understanding of the history of the restoration and the development and interpretation of the Pentateuch.

The Apocalypse of Ezra. Also known as *4 Ezra*, the *Apocalypse of Ezra* is a Jewish work of about 100 CE that presents Ezra (also called Salathiel) as a prophet who experiences dreams and visions of an apocalyptic nature in the thirtieth year after the destruction of Jerusalem. In addition, just like Moses he hears the voice of God speaking from a thornbush and then withdraws from the people for forty days to receive a revelation from God. This revelation includes not only the Law of Moses that had been lost in the destruction of Jerusalem but also the complete twenty-four books of the Hebrew scriptures and seventy secret books for the "wise." Like Moses, Ezra also experienced an assumption to heaven.

How this earlier Ezra the prophet was thought to relate to the later Ezra the scribe is problematic. The common element is Ezra's association with the Law of Moses and his portrayal as a second Moses. This seems to have been carried to the point where in one form of the tradition, Ezra, like Moses, never got back to the land of Palestine. This extracanonical form of the tradition received great elaboration in the medieval period.

Ezra in Judaism, Christianity, and Islam. The Jewish *aggadah* regarded Ezra with great honor. He was not just a priest but the high priest and a second Moses. He was especially revered for restoring the Law of Moses, which had been forgotten, and for establishing the regular public reading of the Law. He is also credited with setting up schools for the study of the Law. The law that

Ezra brought to the people was not only the written Law of Moses but included the unwritten law as well. In addition, he is also credited with writing parts of *Chronicles* and the *Book of Psalms* and is identified by some as the prophet Malachi.

Following *4 Ezra* early Christian authors regarded Ezra as a prophet who under inspiration recovered all the ancient scriptures that had been destroyed by the Babylonian invasion—not just the Law of Moses. Some extracanonical works such as *Enoch* are also attributed to his prophetic recollection. Whether there were two Ezras, the prophet and the priest-scribe, or just one was a matter of debate.

The Qur'ān contains only one curious remark about Ezra, that the Jews believed him to be the son of God (surah 9:30). The basis for this statement is not clear and not reflected in any extant Jewish source.

BIBLIOGRAPHY

The many literary and historical problems associated with Ezra make the literature on this subject enormous and controversial. For the historical reconstructions of the times of Ezra and Nehemiah one should compare the histories of John Bright, *A History of Israel*, 3d ed. (Philadelphia, 1981); Siegfried Herrmann, *Geschichte Israels in alttestamentlicher Zeit*, 2d ed. (Munich, 1973), translated by John Bowden as *A History of Israel in Old Testament Times*, 2d ed. (Philadelphia, 1981); and Peter R. Ackroyd, *Israel under Babylon and Persia* (London, 1970).

For a treatment of Ezra's place in the religion of Israel and especially his relationship to the Law, compare the very influential but somewhat controversial treatment by Yeḥezkel Kaufmann, *Toledot ha-emunah ha-Yisre'elit*, vol. 4 (Tel Aviv, 1956), translated by Clarence W. Efroymson as *History of the Religion of Israel*, vol. 4, *From the Babylonian Captivity to the End of Prophecy* (New York, 1977), with the work of J. G. Vink et al., *The Priestly Code and Seven Other Studies*, "Oudtestamentische Studien," vol. 15 (Leiden, 1969).

Very helpful on matters of literary composition, text, and versions is the commentary by Jacob M. Myers in *Ezra, Nehemiah*, vol. 14 of the Anchor Bible (Garden City, N.Y., 1965).

For a review of recent scholarship and a comprehensive bibliography, see the article "Esra/Esraschriften" by Magne Saebo, in *Theologische Realenzyklopädie*, vol. 10 (New York, 1982).

JOHN VAN SETERS

F

FA-HSIEN (fl. 399–418), Chinese Buddhist monk, translator, and the earliest successful Chinese Buddhist pilgrim to India. Fa-hsien's family name was Kung; he was born in Wu-yang in P'ing-yang Prefecture (in Shansi Province). After being fully ordained at the age of twenty, Fa-hsien recognized that the Buddhist monastic rules (the Vinaya) available in China at the time were incomplete and confused and thus vowed to journey to India to search for Vinaya texts. After years of preparation he organized a party of five monks, who left Ch'ang-an in 399 and passed out of China through Ch'ien-kuei, Chang-yeh and Tun-huang (all in northwestern China). From Tun-huang they proceeded along the southern marches of the Tarim basin to the Central Asian kingdoms of Shan-shan, Agni, and Khotan, where they watched the religious procession of the Buddha's image. From there they traveled to Chakarka, crossed the Pamirs and Agzi, and finally arrived at the kingdom of Uḍḍiyāna in North India, via Darada and the Indus River valley. So long and arduous was their journey that it took three years for the Chinese pilgrims to reach North India from China.

Fa-hsien spent a summer retreat in Uḍḍiyāna then traveled to the south, passed through Suvastu, Gandhāra, Takṣaśīla (Taxila), and arrived at Puruṣapura. There, three members of the mission decided to return to China. Fa-hsien and the others continued the journey, traveling to Hilo and paying homage to the Buddha's shadow at Nagārhara. They crossed over the Lesser Snow Mountain, where Hui-ching, one of the three members of the party, died. Fa-hsien then traveled to Lakki, where he had the summer retreat in 403, after which he went on to Mathurā via Harana and Uccha. He passed the summer retreat in 404 at Śaṃkāśya. Turning southeastward, he then passed through Kanyakubja (Kanauj), Vaiśākha, the Jetavana grove at Śrāvastī, and the birthplace of the Buddha at the Lumbinī near Kapilavastu on the Indo-Nepal border. From there he traveled eastward to Rāmagrāma, Kuśinagara, Vaiśālī, and finally arrived at Pāṭaliputra, the capital of Magadha kingdom. After a short stay at the city, Fa-hsien went to the southeast. In Rājagṛha he performed a rite of worship at the top of Gṛdhrakūta. He worshiped the Bodhi Tree at Bodh Gayā, visited other places nearby, and returned to Pāṭaliputra. From there he went westward, made a pilgrimage to Vārāṇasī, the Mṛgadava, or the Deer Park at Sārnāth, and concluded the trip with a visit to Kauśāmbi.

Between the years 405 and 407, Fa-hsien stayed at the Mahāyāna monastery of Pāṭaliputra, concentrating on the study of the Sanskrit language and Buddhist scriptures. From the monastery, he obtained a collection of the widely observed monastic discipline of the Mahāsāṃghika school. He also obtained a condensed version of the monastic rules according to the Sarvāstivāda school along with several other texts, including the *Saṃyuktābhidharma-hṛdaya Śāstra* in six thousand verses, the *Mahāparinirvāṇa Sūtra* in two thousand five hundred verses, the *Vaipulya-parinirvāṇa Sūtra* in five thousand verses, and the Abhidharma collection of the Mahāsāṃghika school. Although most of these texts seem to have been copied by Fa-hsien himself, at least one was presented to him by a lay Buddhist named Chia-lo at the Mahāyāna monastery as a token of appreciation for Fa-hsien's journey to India.

After the completion of his study at Pāṭaliputra, Taocheng, the other remaining member of the mission, declared his intention to stay in India permanently, leaving Fa-hsien alone to complete his mission. In 407 he left Pāṭaliputra for Tāmraliptī via Champa. He remained at Tāmraliptī for two years (408–409), after which he traveled to Sri Lanka. He stayed on the island for two years, made pilgrimages to the holy places, and attended lectures delivered by an Indian monk. He also obtained additional scriptures there, including the Vinaya of the Mahīśāsaka school, the *Dīrghāgama*, the *Saṃyuktāgama*, and the *Tsa-tsang ching*, none of which was available in China. In 411 he embarked on a merchant ship and sailed for home with the Sanskrit manuscripts he had collected during the trip. Ninety days later, after being blown off course by a typhoon, the ship arrived at the kingdom of Yavadvīpa (South Sumatra island). The monk remained on the island for five months, then embarked on another ship for Kuang-chou (Canton). A month into the voyage another typhoon disrupted the journey. After nearly ninety days the ship landed at a place that the travelers later discovered was Lao-shan in Chang-kuang Prefecture (Shantung Peninsula). The year was 412. Eventually, Fa-hsien went to Chien-k'ang (Nanking) and began to translate the Sanskrit texts he had collected in India and Sri Lanka. He had traveled to approximately thirty kingdoms in fifteen years, and was the first Chinese Buddhist monk to successfully journey to India and return with Buddhist scriptures.

In 416, Fa-hsien was asked by his colleagues to write an autobiographical account of his journey. The resulting chronicle, known as *Fo-kuo chi* (A Record of the Buddhist Countries), is an important historical and religious document for South Asian history and for the Buddhist tradition. Five of Fa-hsien's translations are extant. All of them have been translated jointly by Fa-hsien and Buddhabhadra (d. 429), an Indian Buddhist missionary. Two of these translations are of the Vinaya of the Mahāsāṃghika school (T.D. nos. 1425 and 1427), two are Mahāyāna scriptures (T.D. nos. 376 and 745), and one is a Hīnayāna scripture (T.D. no. 7). According to one catalog, a translation bearing the title *Tsa o-pi-t'an hsin-lun* in thirteen fascicles is also ascribed to him and Buddhabhadra, but the book has been lost. Two other Sanskrit texts brought back to China by Fa-hsien have been translated into Chinese by Buddhajīva (T.D. no. 1421) and Gunabhadra (T.D. no. 99) respectively. Fa-hsien continued to translate until the time of his death in 418 at the Hsin Monastery of Ching-chou (in Hupei Province). His successful journey to India and his search for an authentic tradition of Buddhism remained a source of inspiration for later generations of Chinese Buddhists.

[*See also* Pilgrimage, *article on* Buddhist Pilgrimage in South and Southeast Asia.]

BIBLIOGRAPHY

The earliest translation of Fa-hsien's autobiographical account is the *Foé Koué Ki, ou Relation des royaumes bouddhiques: Voyages dans la tartarie, dans l'Afghanistan et dans l'Inde,* translated by Jean Pierre Abel Rémusat et al. (Paris, 1836). The French text was translated into English with additional notes by J. W. Laidley under the title *The Pilgrimage of Fa Hian* (Calcutta, 1848). James Legge's translation, *A Record of Buddhistic Kingdoms* (1886; reprint, New York, 1965), still stands as a useful reference and is easily available. H. A. Giles's retranslation, *The Travel of Fa-hsien, 399–414 A.D.* (1923; reprint, London, 1959), is good. Li Yung-hsi's version, *A Record of the Buddhist Countries* (Peking, 1957), is the most recent and readable translation. Fa-hsien's biography in the *Kao-seng chuan* has been translated by Robert Shih in his *Biographies des moines éminents (Kao seng tchouan) de Houei-kiao* (Louvain, 1968), pp. 108–115. A study of his translations and writing is found in Prabodh Chandra Bagchi's *Le canon bouddhique en Chine,* vol. 1 (Paris, 1927), pp. 347–348.

Jan Yün-hua

FAIRIES. *Fay,* the old word for "fairy," is thought to come from the Latin *fata,* which signifies the Fates, supernatural women who appear beside the cradle of a newborn infant to decide its future. The fairies invited to Sleeping Beauty's christening are an echo of this belief. During the Middle Ages *fairy* meant the state of enchantment and the land of enchanted beings as well as those who live in it.

Fairies are found under various names in many countries, but they are more typical of Europe and Asia than of the Americas and Africa. To some extent their social organization reflects the world of man. In *Irish Fairy and Folk Tales* (1893) the poet William Butler Yeats distinguished between trooping fairies and solitary fairies. The trooping fairies appear in medieval Arthurian legend and romance and are most popular in the literature of Elizabethan England; since that time stories about them have ceased to be written. They are handsome, aristocratic, and beautifully dressed, and they take part in the Fairy Ride. Like their human counterparts, they hunt and hawk, trotting in procession behind their king and queen, who ride white horses decorated with silver bells. Their fairy realm, which is centered on their royal court, is noted for the excellence of its music, dancing, and feasting as well as for the beauty of its women. The Irish Tuatha Dé Danann ("people of the goddess Danu") are trooping fairies; they are immortal and live in Tír na n'Og, the Land of Youth.

The nonaristocratic, solitary fairies are described as

ugly and often ominous and ill-natured. Some are engaged in trade, like the Irish leprechaun shoemaker, who is quite harmless. A third category of fairy comprises those who live in family groups. They work the land, hold their own markets, and visit human fairs.

Nature fairies are spirits of streams, lakes, and trees. The Russian *rusalki* are water nymphs, who take the form of young maidens. Dryads are tree spirits. So are oak men; hence there is a saying, "Fairy folks are in old oaks." In England, hawthorn is haunted by the fairies, especially if it grows near fairy hills, and the Gooseberry Wife, in the form of a great hairy caterpillar, stands guard over the fruit bushes.

Tutelary fairies, the family guardians and domestic spirits, look after the fortunes of a particular household. The Scottish MacLeods on the island of Skye were given a fairy flag by their supernatural guardian. Germans call their house spirit *der Kobold* ("gnome"), an unreliable creature whose name gives us our modern *cobalt.* (German miners called this slightly magnetic element after the famous sprite because they found it tiresome and difficult to use.) Danes have their *nis;* the French their *esprit follet;* the Spaniards their *duende;* and the Faeroese Islanders, in the North Atlantic, their *niagruisar.*

Russians call their domestic spirits *domovoi*s, after *dom* ("house"). Legend says that these creatures were rebellious spirits who opposed God and so were thrown down from heaven, falling on people's roofs and into their yards. They are amiable and live in the warmth near the hearth. Because it is considered important to please the *domovoi,* peasants leave egg pancakes for him on the threshing floor. When a peasant family moves, they put a piece of bread beside the stove in hopes that the *domovoi* will come with them. In his autobiography *Childhood* (1913), the Russian writer Maxim Gorky describes how his family moved from their house: his grandmother took an old shoe, held it under the stove, and called to the household spirit, asking him to ride in the shoe and bring the family good luck in their new home.

English brownies are also associated with the hearth. They are active at night and do work that the servants have neglected: cleaning and drawing water for the house, tending farm animals, reaping, mowing, threshing, and churning butter. Families can leave food, such as a bowl of cream or little cakes spread with honey for the brownies, but direct gifts, such as money or clothes, will drive the spirit away.

Domestic spirits can be very tiresome. A folktale well known all over Europe tells of a farmer so bothered by the pranks of a boggart (or mischievous brownie) that he decides to move. The family packs their household belongings and loads the cart. As they are leaving, a voice from inside the milk churn says, "Yes, we're moving!" It is the boggart. The family gives up and decides to stay, for what would be the point of moving if the creature was coming too? In other versions of the story the boggart immigrates with the family to the United States.

The most tragic tutelary fairy is the banshee, an Irish and Highland Scottish spirit of death. The word means a woman *(ban)* of the fairy folk (*sídh,* pronounced "shee"). This apparition materializes when someone is about to die. In Scotland the banshee is seen washing the doomed person's graveclothes or bloodstained garmets and can be heard wailing and lamenting, her eyes red with tears. Melusine, daughter of the fairy Pressina, became the banshee of the house of Lusignan in France. When the family was wiped out and its castle fell to the crown, she appeared, foretelling the deaths of the kings of France.

Some supernatural creatures are closely associated with a particular historical era or geographic area. The gnomes of Europe, for example, were a product of the ancient Hermetic and Neoplatonic doctrine from which medieval medicine and science derived. According to medieval thought, all mortal creatures are a blend of earth, air, fire, and water, and the four elemental beings are gnomes (who inhabit the earth), sylphs (who inhabit the air), salamanders (who inhabit fire), and nereids (who inhabit water). The *Oxford English Dictionary* suggests that the word *gnome* is an elision of the Latin *genomus* ("earth dweller"). Philippus Aureolus Paracelsus (1493–1541), the Swiss physician and alchemist, provides in his *De nymphus* the first description of gnomes as elemental beings of the earth. According to tradition, gnomes live underground and are treasure guardians. Also known as dwarfs, they are skilled metalworkers, supplying medieval knights with armor and weapons that they themselves forge. They are also often associated with mines.

The knockers are said to live in the tin mines of England's Cornwall. They are friendly creatures and will knock on the mine walls to indicate veins of ore. An anti-Semitic legend claims that they were the ghosts of Jews who had been sent to work the mines as a punishment for taking part in the Crucifixion. Richard, earl of Cornwall (1200–1272), is said to have put the Jews to work in the Cornish tin mines, and Robert Hunt, in his *Popular Romances of the West of England* (1865), claims that the tin mines were farmed out to the Jews in the thirteenth century. But Jewish merchants had very little connection with the tin trade, and no evidence supports these improbable suggestions.

Pixies are another group of fairies belonging to

English west-country tradition. They are found in Somerset, Devonshire, and Cornwall. Anna Eliza Bray first brought them to the attention of the public in a series of letters to the poet Robert Southey that were published under the title *The Borders of the Tavy and the Tamar* (1836). The chief characteristic of pixies is that they mislead travelers; as recently as 1961, a woman claimed to have been misled by pixies in a wood near Budleigh Salterton. Local tradition says that pixies are the souls of those who died before Christ was born or of unbaptized children.

Closely related to the pixie and its habit of leading travelers astray is the will-o'-the-wisp (Fr., *le feu follet;* Ger., *das Irrlicht*), also called jack-o'-lantern or *ignis fatuus* ("foolish fire"). This sprite appears in the folklore of many countries and is often an omen of death. In England the will-o'-the-wisp is also identified with the mischievous sprite Puck, or Robin Goodfellow. Traditional legends about this spirit who lures folks to their death in the bog may be an attempt to account for marsh gas, which emanates from rotting organic matter and is ghostly in appearance.

Other malevolent spirits are also linked with the environment. The malicious yarthkins of Lincolnshire, England, another damp area, disappeared when the fens were drained.

The English *goblin,* or *hobgoblin,* is a generic term for evil spirits. It is difficult to distinguish between goblins and imps, however. Originally *imp* referred to an offshoot or a cutting, but in its sense as a supernatural creature it means a small demon, an offshoot of Satan. In England the Puritans thought all fairy creatures were devils, and thus the preacher John Bunyan, in his famous book *Pilgrim's Progress* (1678), numbers the hobgoblin and the "foul fiend" among the forces of evil to be resisted.

Elves reached England from Norse mythology, where they were known as *huldre* folk, closely resembling fairies. The girl elves are very beautiful but they are hollow behind and have long cow's tails. Trolls are another Norse group of supernatural beings. Originally they were thought of as giant ogres, but in later Swedish and Danish tradition they become dwarfs who live in hills and caverns. Like the German dwarfs, they are fine craftsmen and treasure guardians, noted for their stupidity. In the Shetland Islands, north of Scotland, where Scandinavian influence is strong, these beings are called *trows.*

Not all mischievous, supernatural creatures are of ancient origin. The gremlin, a supernatural being who causes trouble for pilots and aircrews, dates from World War I. An explanation for human error, flight fatigue, and high-altitude pressures, the gremlin may originate from the Old English word *gremian* ("to vex").

The relationships that fairies enjoy with human beings has varied considerably. Some can be very helpful; such helpfulness is said to be how the MacCrimmons, the most distinguished Scottish pipers, learned their skill. As mentioned, guardian spirits look after the families in their care, and brownies do household chores. But they become malevolent if badly treated—or simply disappear. Anybody who spies on them is severely punished.

In folk tradition human beings are sometimes abducted by the fairies. Thomas the Rhymer (Thomas of Ercildoune), the poet and prophet, lived in thirteenth-century England. His tale is told in *The Ballad of True Thomas* and by Sir Walter Scott in *Minstrelsy of the Scottish Border* (1802). Legend says that Thomas received the gift of prophecy from the Queen of Elfland, who loved him and took him away to live with her for seven years.

Stories of fairy brides are common and usually end in tragedy. The lovely creature marries a mortal and imposes some taboo on him. When it is broken, the fairy bride returns to fairyland, deserting her husband and children. Seal-maidens and swan-maidens are usually captured against their will by the theft of their skin or feathers. As soon as they can retrieve the stolen item, they escape.

When a mortal visits fairyland, the result is often equally tragic. The visitor cannot escape and becomes the victim of the supernatural passage of time, whereby one day represents hundreds of years. King Herla was able to return home with his knights, but when they dismounted they crumbled into dust because they had been away for three hundred years.

Although fairies lead independent lives, there are many examples of their dependence on mortals. Narratives tell of midwives summoned to help a fairy in labor and of fairies anxious to possess human children. Stories of the theft of babies continue from the Middle Ages to the present time. Typically the fairies steal an unbaptized child and leave an ugly fairy baby in its place. If the changeling is surprised, it will speak, revealing its true identity; then it can be driven away. Various methods may be used to trick the spirit, such as serving him beer brewed in eggshells. In German tradition the creature would exclaim, "I am as old as the forests of Bohemia, and I've never seen beer brewed in an eggshell before."

These legends conceal much human suffering and cruelty to children. Malformed babies were put over a fire in order to pressure the fairies into returning the supposedly stolen child. Such cases have been recorded as late as the early twentieth century in Ireland. Until recently it was thought that a defect in a child resulted from a defect in the parents. Basically, changelings were sickly, backward, or deformed children. Simple people, unwilling to accept that such a child could be theirs, maintained that the fairies had stolen the real baby and left this wretched thing in its place.

Belief in faires thus has an aetiologic function: it provides an explanation for mysterious objects and events that we do not understand. The remains of earlier civilizations, which puzzled the uneducated in days gone by, are another obvious example. The ancient Pictish areas of Scotland contain the remains of brochs, round, hill-shaped farmhouses with stone walls and a turf covering. These structures are often referred to as fairy knowes. Burial mounds have also been linked with fairyland. Sudden, disabling illness, such as that caused by a stroke, was traditionally considered to be the result of an elf shot, a wound from one of the flint arrows that are found in low-lying areas, and many Anglo-Saxon charms meant to protect against such attacks have been preserved. Various other illnesses whose origin seemed puzzling centuries ago, such as a slipped disk, rheumatism, and anything that deforms the body, were attributed to invisible blows from the little creatures. Paralysis, skin disease, wasting illnesses such as tuberculosis, and animal disorders such as swine fever and brucellosis have all been blamed on the fairies.

Unusual topographical features are also sometimes attributed to fairies. Those curious, dark green circles that appear on grassy lawns and meadows, often surrounded by a circle of mushrooms, are known as fairy rings, and it is considered very unlucky to damage them in any way. They are in fact caused by *Marasmius oreades*, a type of fungus, but people believe that they are spots where the fairies dance.

Sometimes supernatural origins are attributed to exceptionally large or beautiful objects. There are various stories of a cup stolen from the fairies. The "Luck of Eden Hall" in Cumberland, England, is a lovely green glass goblet, a talisman that was supposed to preserve the Eden family's fortunes. Legend says that the goblet was snatched from the fairies by a servant; if it broke, the family would be destroyed. Eden Hall was pulled down in 1934, but the "Luck" is preserved in the Victoria and Albert Museum in London.

In the thirteenth-century Church of Saint Mary at Frensham in Surrey, England, stands a huge caldron, measuring one yard across. Local tradition says that it was borrowed from the fairies who lived on nearby Borough Hill and was never returned. Probably it was employed in parish feasts and celebrations and then this early usage was forgotten.

Sightings and eyewitness accounts of fairies are common. A striking example was provided by Robert Kirk (1644–1692), a folklorist who became the subject of a fairy tale. Kirk was a Gaelic scholar and a minister of the Scottish church. Evidently his parishioners disapproved of his researches in the supernatural, for when he died and his body was found lying beside a fairy knowe, rumor said that he was living with the fairies inside it. This legend is recorded by Sir Walter Scott in his *Letters on Demonology and Witchcraft* (1830). Kirk's own account of fairy beliefs in the Scottish Highlands, *The Secret Commonwealth of Elves, Fauns and Fairies*, was not published until 1815, long after his death. The brilliant and eccentric English painter and poet William Blake (1757–1827) claimed to have seen a fairy funeral. The body, he said, was laid out on a rose leaf and carried in procession by creatures the size and color of grasshoppers.

In Ireland, places once associated with fairies are pointed out and treated with great respect. To interfere with them is thought to bring bad luck. More than once new roads have been rerouted for such a reason. Recently a fairy bush was cut down in front of a Dutch-owned factory in Limerick. Dutch workmen performed the task because local workers refused. When the works closed not long after and well over a thousand jobs were lost, the disaster was blamed on the removal of the fairy bush.

Traditionally, the fairies dress in green. Green is their color, and even today, many people regard it as unlucky and will not wear it, although they no longer remember the reason.

Various theories have been put forward to explain the origins of the fairies. A British tradition suggests that fairies represent memories of an ancient Stone Age race. When the Celts arrived in England from central Europe in about 500 BCE, the earlier inhabitants were driven back into the hills and hid in caves. They lived underground and were so adept at hiding in the woods that they seemed to be invisible. The popular belief that iron provides protection from the fairies is in line with this view, for the Celts possessed iron weapons, whereas the earlier inhabitants used objects of bronze or stone. The many stories of fairies' borrowings and thefts also lend weight to this theory, for it was thought that these earlier inhabitants borrowed grain and implements, and one can easily imagine a conquered people in hiding, creeping anxiously about to see what they could steal or borrow from their conquerors.

Another view suggests that fairies originated as memories of ancient pagan gods and heroes. They are small in stature because their significance has been reduced. Still another theory sees fairies as personified spirits of nature. Modern supporters of this argument believe that spirits fertilize plants and care for flowers. But this explanation excludes other types of fairy, such as the family guardians and the fairy communities with their elaborate social organization. A fourth suggestion is that the fairies are ghosts. Certainly there are many connections between fairies and the realm of the dead: they live in burial mounds, and many are obviously ghosts and are described as such. None of these theories is entirely adequate, and the answer may well lie in a blend of them all, coupled with the natural desire to find an explanation for puzzling phenomena in the world around us.

[*See also* Celtic Religion; Germanic Religion; Slavic Religion; *and, for a general discussion of intermediate beings,* Demons.]

BIBLIOGRAPHY

Briggs, K. M. *The Anatomy of Puck.* London, 1959. An examination of fairy beliefs among Shakespeare's contemporaries and successors.

Briggs, K. M. *The Fairies in Tradition and Literature.* London, 1967. Provides an account of fairy traditions, traffic between humans and fairies, and the literary use of these beliefs.

Croker, Thomas Crofton. *Fairy Legends and Traditions of the South of Ireland.* 3 vols. London, 1825–1828. This work was enthusiastically received by the public of its day. Jacob and Wilhelm Grimm translated it into German, and Sir Walter Scott corresponded with the author. It remains a valuable contribution to the development of forklore studies.

Gardner, Edward L. *Fairies.* London, 1945. A book that claims to present photographs of real fairies.

Hunt, Robert. *Popular Romances of the West of England.* 2 vols. London, 1865. The fruits of a ten-month walking tour in Cornwall during 1829, when the author collected, as he put it, "every existing tale of its ancient people."

Keightley, Thomas. *The Fairy Mythology* (1828). 2 vols. in 1. New York, 1968. An early study of comparative folklore by an Irish writer with an interest in oral tradition.

Sikes, Wirt. *British Goblins.* London, 1880. A collection of Welsh material assembled by the U.S. Consul for Wales.

Venetia Newall

FAITH, in probably the best-known definition of it, is "the assurance of things hoped for, the conviction of things not seen." Although this definition itself comes from the Christian scriptures, specifically from the anonymous epistle to the Hebrews in the New Testament, it can, *mutatis mutandis,* be applied across a broad spectrum of religions and religious traditions. Whether or not the term *faith* appears in those traditions is, at least in part, a matter of how various terms are translated into modern Western languages. More importantly, however, *faith* is used, even in Judaism and Christianity (where it has been the most successfully domesticated), to cover an entire cluster of concepts that are related to one another but are by no means identical. If there is truth in the contention that *faith* is the abstract term with which to describe that attitude of the human mind and spirit of which prayer is the concrete expression, then one or more of these concepts may probably be said to play some part in every religious tradition, and in that sense at least, "faith" may likewise be said to appear there. Hence an enumeration of these discrete concepts, each of them in some way a synonym for *faith,* may serve to provide, if not a logical definition, then at any rate a cumulative description, of it.

Faith-as-Faithfulness. In its most fundamental meaning, faith has been defined as faithfulness, and as such, it has been taken as an attribute both of the divine and of believers in the divine. The Latin adjective *pius,* for example, was used in Vergil's *Aeneid* to describe *pius Aeneas* or *pius Achates,* but it also appeared there in such a phrase as *pia numina* to characterize the reciprocal fidelity that the gods manifested in their dealings with human beings; something of both senses, presumably, attached to the word when it became a standard part of the official title of the Roman emperor, most familiarly in the case of Antoninus Pius (r. 138–161 CE). *Pius* went on having both meanings also in postclassical Latin, as the usage of the "Dies Irae" attests. The reciprocity implied in the concept of faith when predicated of human social relations, where (as in the notion of "keeping faith" with someone) "faith" has become almost synonymous with "loyalty," has carried over likewise into its use for the divine-human relation. Wherever the gods were said to promise something in that relation, *faith* would seem to be an appropriate term for their keeping or fulfilling the promise. Conversely—and much more customarily—it was the appropriate term for the loyalty or "fealty" (that English word is indeed derived, via medieval French, from the Latin *fidelitas*) that the gods in turn rightly expected of mortals. In those religions in which the initiates received a mark on their body as a sign of their special bond with the divine, these marks have often been seen as a pledge and a reminder to those who wore them that they were expected to remain faithful to the terms of that special bond. The consequences of a breach of faith-as-faithfulness formed the basis for practices of discipline, punishment, and in most traditions possible reinstatement, though only after a period of purgation and testing (see "The Community of Faith," below). Even where the other connotations of "faith" discussed below have appeared to predominate, this emphasis on faith-as-faithfulness, both divine and human, has never been absent, pertaining as it does to the very concept of adhering to the practices, structures, obligations, or beliefs of any particular way of having faith. When it has been divorced from some or all of those other connotations, however, faith-as-faithfulness could all too easily be reduced to the formalism and external propriety that the prophets and critics in many religious traditions have attacked.

Faith-as-Obedience. Faith as faithfulness has expressed itself not only in loyalty but in obedience, yet obedience has meant even more than faithfulness. The precise content of such obedience has varied enormously with the content of what was perceived to have been the divine will or law. Obedience, therefore, carried both liturgical and moral connotations. An imperative to reenact, periodically or once in a lifetime, the acts of the divine model required the obedient and meticulous observance of the demands that those acts had placed upon the believer. Initiation into the faith involved learning the specific methods of such ritual observance, with rites of passage frequently serving as the occasion for such learning. Where the divine will was conceived of as having laid down rules not only for ritual actions but for ethics, the obedience of faith meant moral behavior in conformity with divine commands; thus in Hinduism, *dharma* as moral law required righteous conduct. Ordinarily there was no explicit antithesis between ethics and ritual action, which together were the content of authentic obedience, often enjoined in the same gnomic saying or story. But the declaration of the prophet Samuel in the Hebrew scriptures, "Has the Lord as great delight in burnt offerings and sacrifices, as in obeying the voice of the Lord? Behold, to obey is better than sacrifice, and to hearken than the fat of rams" (*1 Sm.* 15:22), articulated the awareness, which other religions have shared with Judaism, that faith-as-obedience was above all a compliance with the moral imperative. Presupposed in those words was the belief, central to Judaism, that the moral imperative had been made known in the historical revelation of the word of God to Moses, and through him to the people of Israel. But they have been no less applicable in those religious and philosophical traditions that have emphasized the inner imperative of conscience rather than the outer imperative of law as the norm of ethical action: here, too, faith has been above all obedience, in Immanuel Kant's formula, "the recognition of all our duties as divine commands." Even where faith has been defined primarily as trust or as worship or as creed (see below), obedience was inevitably a constitutive element of it. [*See* Obedience.]

Faith and Works. The definition of faith as obedience, and yet as somehow not reducible to obedience, points to the perennial and unavoidable problem of the relation between faith and works. On the one hand, even the most theocentric versions of faith have found themselves obliged to assert, often in self-defense against the charge that they were severing the moral nerve, that they were in fact reinforcing ethics precisely by their emphasis on its vertical dimension: it has been a universal conviction of believers, across religious boundaries, that "faith without works is dead." On the other hand, those religious systems that have appeared to outsiders, whether critical or friendly, to equate faith and works and to be indifferent to any considerations except the "purely" moral ones prove, upon closer examination, to have been no less sensitive to the dialectic between works and faith. Especially since the Enlightenment, Western critics of traditional supernaturalism have taken Confucianism as the ideal of a religion that eschewed metaphysical subtleties to concentrate on the one thing needful, and they have either criticized traditional Western religions for not conforming to that ideal or reinterpreted them in accordance with it. For in the *Analects* Confucius repeatedly professed ignorance about the mysteries of "Heaven" and avoided discussing the miraculous phenomena in which conventional faith had sought manifestations of supernatural power; even the question of personal immortality did not admit of a clear and definite answer. Rather, he concentrated his attention on works of piety and of service to others, preferring generosity to greed and virtue to success. All of this Confucius (like many other religious teachers) called "the way," but it is an unwarranted modern reductionism to see in this attitude a moralistic preoccupation with works alone, at the expense of "faith." For "Heaven," which he said had "infused the virtue that is in me," was the authentic source of the works themselves, as well as the ultimate foundation for the serenity that made the works possible. The faith of Confucius may have been less detailed than that of some teachers in its information about the ontological status of "Heaven" and similar speculative questions, but he knew and expressed a confidence in its providential care as the basis for the works with which he and his disciples were to serve the will of "Heaven."

Faith-as-Trust. Such a confidence in the providential care of "Heaven" underlies the definition of faith-as-trust. In the classic formulation of Martin Luther, "to 'have a god' is nothing else than to trust and believe him with our whole heart," since "it is the trust and faith of the heart alone that makes both God and an idol" *(Large Catechism)*. Many of the conventional metaphors for the divine in various traditions, from "rock" and "mountain" to "mother" or "father," have served as representations of the conviction that "the trust and faith of the heart" could appropriately be vested in such an object, and that the divine object would prove worthy of human trust. Conventional practices like divination and prayer may likewise be read as expressions of the belief that the divine will—if it could once be known, or perhaps even if it was mysterious and ultimately unknowable—deserved trust. The historic triad of faith, hope, and love (best known from the New Testament, but paralleled elsewhere) has made it necessary for expositors to clarify the distinction between faith and hope as they were both applied to the expectation of future blessings. However, the definition of faith-as-trust has been a way of focusing such expectation on the reliability of divine providence in both prosperity and failure: for good or ill, the ways of the divine will could be counted on, even though the details of their specific intent might not be discernible at any given moment. Such faith-as-trust even in the inscrutable goodness of the divine order presupposed a pattern of divine guidance in the past, which made it safe to conclude that there would be a continuity of such guidance into the future. Historically as well as psychologically, therefore, it is difficult to conceive of faith-as-trust in the absence of such a pattern, be it the outcome of the individual's own cumulative autobiography or of the history of the community to which the individual has come to belong (or of both). Once established on the basis of this pattern of divine guidance, faith-as-trust has implied that the vicissitudes of the moment could not, or at any rate should not, undermine the confidence that ultimately the object of that trust would be vindicated. As Johann Wolfgang von Goethe said in his autobiography, *Dichtung und Wahrheit*, "Faith is a profound sense of security in regard to both the present and the future; and this assurance springs from confidence." In the choruses of the Greek tragedians or in the reflections of the Muslim mystics or in the discourses of Job, the ambiguities and difficulties of such confidence in the face of concrete reality have served to deepen the understanding of trust and to transform Pollyanna-like optimism into mature faith-as-trust.

Faith-as-Dependence. This combination of mystery and reliability in the divine will, even after that will has made itself known, has introduced into the definition of faith the element of dependence and submission. For if obedience to the divine will was the completion of the circle of faith in the moral realm, dependence on the divine will was the way faith-as-trust affirmed the relation of human weakness to divine power. In those traditions in which the divine has been seen as creator and/or preserver, faith-as-dependence has been, in the first instance, an affirmation of the origin and derivation of humanity and of its world; in those traditions that have tended not to distinguish as sharply between "being" as applied to the divine and as applied to human beings, dependence has been the basis for identifying the locations of both the divine and the human within the "great chain of Being"; in those traditions that have emphasized the recurrence of patterns known to be embedded within the very structure of the cosmos, dependence has made it possible for the community and its individual members to participate, through myth and ritual, in such patterns; and in those traditions that have interpreted human history as the arena in which the will and way of the divine could above all be discerned, dependence has employed the recitation of the decisive events in that history to reinforce the sovereignty of God as the one who was active and knowable within, but always transcendent over, such saving and revelatory events. Thus in Islam (a term that is commonly translated into English as "submission," but that might perhaps as well be translated as "dependence"), the saying of the Qur'ān, "God causes whom he wills to err, and whom he wills he guides; and you shall assuredly be called to account for your doings," gave voice to the Prophet's conviction that the believer must depend on the divine will regardless of circumstances, but that such dependence did not preclude human accountability. In Islam, the Five Pillars of Faith were the specific moral and cultic duties for which every Muslim believer would be held accountable, yet the first two Pillars (the recitation of faith in the oneness of God and the daily prayers) were declarations of the paradoxical affirmation that God was not dependent on creatures or their performance of these duties but would be sovereign regardless. That paradox has been central to the definition of faith-as-dependence in many religious traditions, with theories ranging all the way from thoroughgoing determinism to apparent moralism (for example, to use the terms familiar to the Western tradition, all the way from Calvinism to Pelagianism) as efforts to come to terms with both poles of a dialectical truth.

Faith-as-Experience. In one way or another, each of these definitions of faith has been derived from faith-as-experience. For even the most transcendent notions of the mystery of the divine will have, by their very act of affirming the mysteriousness of that mystery, laid claim to an experience in which the individual believer or the community tradition has caught a glimpse of just how mysterious the divine could be. Although mystics and prophets—and, following their lead, historians and philosophers of religion—have often spoken of such experiences in isolation from the continuum of human consciousness, that is not, of course, how they have actually occurred. From the biographies of seers and saints it is obvious that these experiences often came in response and in reaction to specific moments of exaltation or depression, in feverish intensity or in the excitement and release of love and death. That inseparability of faith-as-experience from all the other experiences of life has persuaded some observers of the phenomenon to see it as in fact the sublimation and "supernatural" reinterpretation of an essentially "natural" event. Ludwig Feuerbach, both as historian and as philosopher, penetrated deeply into this aspect of faith-as-experience; and Freudian psychology has been especially successful in explaining religious experience in its relation to the totality and complexity of how the human mind has attempted to cope with all the data of its experience. But in opposition to the reductionism that has frequently been represented as the only acceptable conclusion from this quality of faith-as-experience, the philosophical interpretation of religion, systematized perhaps most effectively by Rudolf Otto, has sought to identify what was distinct about this experience even if it was not separate from other experience. Otto's formulation, which has since become all but canonical, is "the experience of the Holy." He called it "a category of interpretation and valuation peculiar to the sphere of religion," and declared that "there is no religion in which it does not live as the real innermost core, and without it no religion would be worthy of the name." Yet precisely because faith's experience of the holy has upon further reflection come to include the recognition of its inherent ineffability, the language of faith has drawn upon other experience—aesthetic, moral, intellectual—to be able to speak about the unspeakable at all.

The Community of Faith. In the sacred literatures of religious faith, faith-as-experience has often been described in highly individualistic terms: how the poet or prophet has come to know the holy in personal experience has dominated how he or she has described that experience for others, so that they in turn, one at a time, might also come to share in such an experience and duplicate it for themselves. Individualism of that kind underlay, for example, the recurring definition of religion as "what one does with one's solitariness." Except for passing moments of intense mystical rapture, however, such individualism has been shown to be illusory. And except for occasional glossolalia, the very language in which the individual has spoken about faith-as-experience has been derived from the history of the community, even when that language has been aimed against the present corruption of the community or when it has been directed toward the founding of a new and purer community. When examined in its total context, moreover, it becomes apparent that the individualized experience of faith has repeatedly taken place during or after corporate worship: the setting of the private vision has often been the temple itself; or when the vision has come in the solitude of the desert or in the privacy of the soul, it has come as a consequence of participation in the ritual of the temple or as a response to instruction in the lore of the community's tradition. Just as the distinction between the experience of faith and general human experience has engaged the interest of psychologists of religion, so sociologists of religion have probed the connection (in the formulas of Joachim Wach) between "religion and natural groups," as well as then the "specifically religious organization of society." The community of faith, as coextensive with the family or tribe, has conferred its authority on that social organization in marriage, war, and commerce, and has derived its sanctions from it in turn. Then exclusion from the believing community was identical with ostracism from the natural community. But with the more sophisticated identification of the specific nature of faith has come a distinction between the two, often through the emergence of an *ecclesiola in ecclesia* as a more precisely delineated community of faith or (using a pejorative word in a nonpejorative sense) a "sect."

Faith and Worship. The community of faith has always been a community of worship; in fact, worship has been far more explicitly a part of its definition than has faith. Western observers of "primitive" societies have sometimes been prevented from recognizing this, either (as in the case of some Christian missionaries) by too particularistic an understanding of worship or (as in the case of some modern anthropologists) by too reductionistic an understanding of ritual. One of the most important scholarly sources for the new and deeper recognition of faith-as-worship has been the investigation of the interrelation between myth and ritual: myth came to be read as the validation, in the deeds of the ancients or of the gods, of what the ritual now enjoined upon believers; and ritual acquired a new dimension by being understood as not merely outward ceremonial performed *ex opere operato* but as the repetition in the believers' actions of what the myth recited in words about the divine actions that had made the world and founded the community. Amid an infinite variety of ritual forms and liturgical prescriptions, therefore, worship has defined "faith." For example, the fourth and last of the Four Noble Truths of Buddhism as formulated by Gautama Buddha himself was the recognition of the methods by which the believer could overcome the inner yearning for pleasure out of which the misery of *dukkha* sprang. Similarly, the eighth and last part of the Eightfold Path of Buddhism consisted in proper meditation, which was inseparable from the first seven. Methodologically, the task of discovering the specifics of the faith expressing itself in a particular worship ritual continues to challenge the ingenuity of historians of religion, as is manifested by their disputes over the meaning of (to cite an example present in several traditions) the ritual of circumcision. Even the widely shared assumption that the ritual antedated the myth, which in turn antedated the theological explanation of both, must be modified by the repeatedly attested rise of new rituals out of the composition of the myth or after the adoption of the theological doctrine. Yet in the absence of any verifiable statistical data it does seem a safe generalization to suggest that, even more than faith-as-obedience to a moral imperative or commandment, faith-as-worship has defined faith for most of the human race through most of its history. Even the term *orthodoxy*, which has acquired the meaning "right doctrine" in most of the languages where it appears and which carries that meaning also when it is used in a secular sense for political or literary theories, really means "right worship," as the Russian translation of the word, *pravoslavie* ("the right way to celebrate"), demonstrates. [*See* Orthopraxy.]

Faith-as-Credo. Yet *orthodoxy* does mean primarily "right doctrine" now, and one of the definitions of "faith" is "credo" (which is the Latin for "I believe"). Because so much of the history and interpretation of world religions has been the work of Christian thinkers trained in the doctrinal theology of the several Christian churches, early scholarship in "comparative religion" regularly consisted of a review, doctrine by doctrine, of what the various religions were perceived as having taught. As often as not, such reviews were organized according to the schema of categories devised by Thomistic or orthodox Lutheran and Reformed systematic theologians, even, for example, in so sensitive a treatment as Karl Friedrich Nägelsbach's *Homeric Theology* (1840) and *Post-Homeric Theology* (1857). The artificiality and arbitrariness of imposing these categories from the outside on literary and religious traditions having an integrity of their own led later generations of scholars to employ greater caution in claiming to have discovered "doctrinal" meanings (in the sense in which Christian theology spoke of "doctrines") in non-Christian religions, even sometimes in postbiblical Judaism. Significantly, however, one outcome of the tensions that have arisen between various of those religions and modern thought (see "Faith and Knowledge" below) has been the development, within the traditions themselves and at the hands of their own faithful devotees, of something very like systematic doctrinal theology, which has included comparative judgments about their relation to other traditions and their "doctrines." As already suggested, nevertheless, the definition of faith-as-credo has been especially prominent in Western and Christian thought.

In medieval usage, for example, the Latin word *fides* must commonly be translated as "*the* faith" rather than simply as "faith," because it referred in the first instance to the content of what was believed *(fides quae creditur)* rather than to the act of believing *(fides qua creditur)*, and specifically to one of the orthodox creeds of the church, generally the Apostles' Creed or the Nicene Creed; once defined, orthodox doctrines were binding *de fide*, by the authority of the faith. To "have faith," then, meant first of all to "hold *the* faith" as this had been laid down in the apostolic "deposit of faith" and legislated by church fathers, councils, and popes. And even the repudiation of the medieval system by the Protestant Reformation, a major plank of which was Luther's elevation of faith-as-trust over the Roman Catholic faith-as-credo, still retained, and in some ways even intensified, the insistence on right doctrine, a knowledge of which and an assent to which were the necessary presupposition for a correct faith-as-trust.

Faith and Tradition. Acceptance of a "deposit of faith" has implied some notion of tradition as that which has been *traditum*, first "handed down" and then "handed on." Although the thinkers of the eighteenth-century Enlightenment drew a sharp distinction between "traditionary religion" and "natural religion," vastly preferring the latter to the former, it was in fact only the former that was to be found in the history of religion; eventually even the "natural religion" of the Enlightenment acquired a certain traditional content and was transmitted from one generation to the next by way of an intellectual tradition. "Traditionary religion," therefore, has defined itself and its faith on the basis of received tradition. The myth of how holy things have happened; the ritual of how holy acts were to be performed; the rules of conduct by which the faithful were expected to guide their lives; the structure through which the holy community was founded and governed; the doctrine by which the community gave an account of the myth and ritual—all these expressions of faith have been the subject and the content of the holy tradition. In all those religions that have ascribed normative status to a holy book, the question of faith-as-tradition has taken a special form, as they have sought to deal with the question of the relation between the revelation in the book, as given once and for all, and the continuing revelation in the tradition. Reformers in each of those groups have drawn an antithesis between the purity of the original scripture and the accretions of later tradition, which needed to be expunged, while defenders of tradition have posited a continuity between the scripture and the tradition, sometimes by characterizing them as "two sources of revelation" but sometimes by describing the ongoing tradition as the process through which the properly validated authorities had gradually made explicit the content of the faith already implicit in scripture. Thus a twentieth-century Russian Orthodox thinker, Vladimir Lossky, defined tradition as "the life of the Holy Spirit in the Church, communicating to each member of the Body of Christ the faculty of hearing, of receiving, of knowing the Truth in the Light which belongs to it, and not according to the natural light of human reason." By setting faith into the framework of such a theory of tradition, Lossky and his counterparts in other faiths (who could have used much of the same language, substituting other proper names) have sought to combine the static view of tradition as a "deposit of the faith" in the past with a dynamic view of tradition as "living faith" in the present and future. [*See* Tradition.]

Faith and Knowledge. Whether it has been interpreted as a second channel of revelation for faith or as the development of a truth already implicitly present in the original deposit of faith, tradition has been a way of knowing the truth. Faith, therefore, has been taken to be a species of knowledge, differing from ordinary knowledge by its superior claims: an arcane character, a transcendent content, privileged channels of communication, or divine certainty (or all of the above). So long as such claims remained publicly uncontested, faith could stand as objectively sure, even when subjectively the individual believer might question or doubt it. There is no reason to suppose that such existential questioning and doubting have ever been absent from the experience of faith, and plenty of reason to find evidence of their presence in the artifacts and literary remains of various religious faiths from the past. What has made the situation of religious faith in the present unique, however, is the gravity and the universality of the tension between faith and knowledge. One by one, each of the world faiths has been obliged to confront the competing truth claims not only of other faiths, as it had perhaps done before, but of other forms of knowledge that seemed to render any faith-as-knowledge, regardless of which faith was involved, superfluous or absurd. The identification of faith with accounts of miracles and similar wondrous events that a later generation has found to be, quite literally, incredible has undermined the authority of the faith itself. Orthodox methods of harmonizing away contradictions in the authoritative tradition through allegory or a theory of multiple meanings have not been able to withstand the pressures of the historical method of dealing with the tradition. The discovery or invention of alternate means of dealing with those crises of life and needs of society for which faith had served as the divinely prescribed cure relegated it to a secondary status as a superstitious nostrum still needed only by those who did not know any better. When Immanuel Kant said in his *Critique of Pure Reason* (1781) that he had "found it necessary to deny *knowledge* of God, freedom, and immortality in order to find a place for *faith*," he was speaking for believers in many traditions who have salvaged faith by making it invulnerable to the claims and counterclaims of knowledge; but in so doing, they have also brought into question most of the other functions of faith. At the same time, the very challenge of knowledge to faith has produced a clearer understanding both of faith's relation to other aspects of human experience and of its distinctive meaning and power.

[*See also* Doubt and Belief. *For further discussion of the tension between knowledge and faith, see* Physics and Religion *and* Knowledge and Ignorance.]

BIBLIOGRAPHY

Eliade, Mircea. *Patterns in Comparative Religion.* New York, 1958.

Feuerbach, Ludwig. *The Essence of Christianity.* Translated by George Eliot. London, 1854.

Freud, Sigmund. *The Future of an Illusion.* London, 1928.

Heiler, Friedrich. *Prayer: A Study in the History and Psychology of Religion.* Oxford, 1932.

Hügel, Friedrich von. *The Mystical Element of Religion.* 2 vols. London, 1961.

James, William. *The Varieties of Religious Experience.* New York, 1902.

Lossky, Vladimir. *In the Image and Likeness of God.* Scarsdale, N.Y., 1974.

Otto, Rudolf. *The Idea of the Holy.* New York, 1928.

Smith, Wilfred Cantwell. *Faith and Belief.* Princeton, 1979.

Söderblom, Nathan. *The Living God: Basal Forms of Personal Religion.* Oxford, 1933.

Wach, Joachim. *Sociology of Religion.* Chicago, 1944.

JAROSLAV PELIKAN

FAKHR AL-DĪN AL-RĀZĪ. *See* Rāzī, Fakhr al-Dīn al-.

FALASHAS. *See* Judaism, *article on* Judaism in Asia and Northeast Africa.

FALL, THE. The concept of the fall appears in myths, traditions, and religions of a great many peoples and presents a number of interrelated themes of primary importance in the history of religious thought. In general, the fall is to be thought of as an accident that arose after the creation or genesis of the world bearing consequences for the present human condition; this accident explains a new situation in the world that is recognized as a decline or degradation when contrasted to the original state of man and the cosmos. This fundamental conception of the fall takes different forms in different cultures and religions.

Perspectives on Myths of the Fall. The theme of the fall may be considered from the perspective of (1) historical time and its unfolding; (2) theogony; (3) cosmogony; and (4) anthropogony, which encompasses the creation of man and his present condition.

Historical time. Considered temporally, the fall takes place between *Urzeit* and *Endzeit*, between the beginning and the end of creation. Within historical time, it is very close to the beginnings of time conceived as a golden age in contrast to which the fall and its consequences represent a break or degradation. This temporal and historical conception of the fall can be found in various popular traditions as well as myths of the golden age and paradise lost.

Theogony. The theogonic aspect of the fall deals with the degradation of the divine and is found in the numerous myths concerning the origin of the gods, of their victory over chaos, or of the victory of the more recent forces of divinity over older ones. Coextensive with the creation, the fall as presented in theogony implies the identification of evil and chaos on the one hand and of salvation and creation on the other. This conception of the fall is found especially in Sumero-Akkadian theogonic myths that recount the victory of order over preexisting chaos; it is found also in the Egyptian myth of the battle between Seth and Horus. Strictly speaking, these theogonic myths are not true myths of the fall, but two of their recurrent themes justify their inclusion in a typology of myths of the fall. First, they emphasize the ritual celebration of the maintenance of the creation and cosmic order, as in the festival of Akitu in Babylon. Second, they present, through a variety of mythologies, the theme of the degradation of divinity that results from the fall of some portion of the divine substance into matter, body, or darkness. This theme is central to the three most important forms of religious dualism: Orphism, gnosticism, and Manichaeism.

Cosmogony. From the perspective of cosmogony, the fall is seen as an accident occurring after the genesis of the world that affects cosmic forces and explains the present condition of earth or the universe. Myths that tell of the progressive degradation of the universe and its destruction and re-creation in successive cosmic cycles exemplify this cosmogonic view of the fall. The flood is an important example of this type of fall, and numerous myths of the flood are found among religious traditions of the world.

Anthropogony. Anthropogony, however, offers the most important perspective on the fall. From this perspective, the contemporary human condition—a condition of degradation in contrast to that of the golden age of humanity—is explained as the consequence of a fall, a tragic event that bursts into human history. Around this event are clustered those myths and symbols that seek to explain the origins of illness and death and the tragic nature of the human condition after the fall.

From these four perspectives, it is possible to develop a typology through which the myriad myths of the fall in cultures throughout the world become comprehensible. Furthermore, these perspectives illuminate the fundamental aspect of the concept of the fall and the inherent meaning that emerges from these myths: the present human condition is explained by the accident that occurred after creation and ended the golden age.

Myths of the fall clearly show three essential elements: (1) the concept of a golden age in the beginning, (2) the accident that is a break or degradation of original harmony, (3) the explanation of the present human condition. From these three elements, it is possible to trace a historico-phenomenological picture of the traditions dealing with the fall. One final remark needs to be added, however, before proceeding to an analysis of this picture. An understanding of the complexity of the problems related to the concept of the fall must not lose sight of the intimate relationship of this concept with the problem of evil; any conception of the fall has implications concerning the origins of evil, as well as intimations of a possible overcoming of evil through a recovery of the state that existed previous to the fall. Thus a philosophical and ethical dimension is grafted onto, and is coextensive with, the idea of the fall and forms an important part of a hermeneutical approach that tries to come to terms with its relationship to guilt or fault. The scope of this article, however, does not permit us to envisage these other aspects of the fall.

Archaic Religions and Oral Traditions. The myth of an earthly paradise, where man is immortal, is an integral part of cosmogony and descriptions of the world's beginning in many cultures. That primordial man enjoys a bliss and freedom that he loses as the result of a fall is the dominant theme of this myth, a theme offering many variations.

The Jorai cosmogony of the autochthonous peoples of Indochina gives an idyllic description of original man.

Living with the god Oi Adei, man enjoyed a deathless existence in a paradise where he could fly like a bird and talk with plants and animals, where bundles of wicker grew on trees and shovels turned over the earth by themselves. Man had only to feed his tools; but he got drunk and did not do so, and the tools revolted. In the Sre cosmogony of Indochina, man had no need to work in the earthly paradise, since the god Ong Ndu had made him immortal; but when the primordial couple refused the god's command to dive into a well, they were punished for their disobedience by suffering, old age, and death.

The cosmogonies of Bantu speakers from the Mayombe region north of the Kongo River, the cradle of the old Kongo civilization, contain significant stories of the fall. In the Yombe tradition, man's golden age was brought to an end by Nzondo, a spirit whose magic also created the Zaire River after a flood. Nzondo drove men from their original home, dispersing them over the earth and setting in motion the chain of disasters that have since befallen the race.

In a Dogon myth from Mali, heaven and earth were originally very close to each other. But God separated them and made men mortal, after being disturbed by the noise of the women crushing millet. Similarly, in a myth from Cameroon and Burkina Faso (Upper Volta), the vault of heaven was originally within man's reach, but when a woman who touched the vault with a load of wood she was carrying on her head asked God to move it out of her way, he moved it so far that he abandoned mankind to death. These myths tell of a paradise lost; but they also stress the theme of God's rejection of a disobedient mankind, of his consigning man to death as punishment for a variety of sins, that is, for violating a divine prohibition, for lying or theft, for domestic rivalries, for lack of charity. Death is explained as divine punishment prompted by man's disobedience. Similar myths are found among the Diola in Senegal, the Nupe in Nigeria, the Bena Kanioka in Zaire, and the Anyi in the Ivory Coast.

Myths of the fall as fate, though less frequently encountered than those of the fall as punishment, are also significant in sub-Saharan Africa. These myths involve an archetypal badly delivered message—a divine message of immortality that reaches men either too late or in abridged or altered form. Here, the original separation of heaven and earth replaces the earthly paradise where God and man live together; from heaven, God sends messages to man on earth. In a Tsonga myth, a chameleon carries the message of eternal life, while the giant lizard Galagala carries the message of death. The lizard, moving faster, arrives first, and man so becomes mortal. In a Bete version of the same myth, from the Ivory Coast, the lizard advises the chameleon to walk slowly. Animals are always the messengers in these myths, and the message of mortality always arrives first. Other myths emphasize the change and deterioration of the message in the course of its transmission; myths of this sort are found among the Mossi in Burkina Faso, the Ashanti in Ghana, the Kabiye in Togo, and the Kikuyu in Kenya.

In Australia, the Aranda regard their totem ancestors as the heroic forgers of civilizations who gave form to the countryside, who allotted individual lives to men by creating separate embryos, who lived in a mythical golden age where they were untouched by the woes of contemporary mankind. These totem ancestors were immortal, and those among them who apparently died in battle in fact went to heaven, where they became *tjurungas*, sacred beings who were powerful and creative, traveling to and fro above or below the earth.

Exhausted when they completed their creative work, and seized by an overwhelming lassitude, these mythical ancestors sank into the earth. But before they disappeared they laid down, by some of their actions, the rudiments of death; thus, the first men knew both death and the pains of the human condition. The myth of the magpie Urbura explains the permanence of death. When the first mortal tried to leave his tomb, Urbura struck at him with her claws, thrust a spear through his neck, and nailed him to the ground, establishing forever man's mortal condition. [*See* Death.]

Common to myths of the fall and to nostalgia for a lost golden age is the view that the original human condition was a condition of paradise. [*See* Golden Age.] Heaven lay close to the earth, and man could go there merely by climbing a mountain, a tree, a ladder, or a vine (Eliade, 1960). Enjoying the friendship of both the gods and the animals—and speaking their language—man enjoyed a life that was immortal, free, spontaneous, and perfectly happy.

That this paradise was lost as the result of the fall is a second commonly held view. Often, the fall is an accident, as in Australia, where myths of the Aranda tribe merely record it. In various African traditions the accident is equated with sleep: the god had asked men to remain awake through the night to await a message from him, but when it arrived they were asleep. If sleep is understood as a symbol for death, the accident of sleep explains both man's precarious condition and the establishment of death.

The fall may also result from human failings. Once again, the most important documentation is found in sub-Saharan Africa. A Maasai myth known in both Africa and Madagascar tells of a package that men were given by God but forbidden to open; driven by curiosity, they opened it and let loose sickness and death. The divine prohibition takes other forms in other traditions. In a Pygmy story of central Africa, it is against looking at something; in a story of the Luba in Zaire, it forbids the eating of certain fruits; in a Lozi myth found in Zaire and Malawi, it prohibits the taking of wild game.

Sometimes mankind's fault is best understood anthropologically, as in myths describing theft or lying, or those that stress lack of charity, or the race's capacity for domestic violence, as in a Chiga myth from Uganda. The curiosity of the primordial couple who aspire to the secrets of the gods is a frequent mythical theme in Africa, where myths of the fall also emphasize the cohesiveness of individual and group (Thomas, 1982, pp. 32–48).

Ancient Civilizations. Important approaches to the theme of the fall are found in the great civilizations of antiquity. This section examines those myths and traditions found in the civilizations of Egypt, Sumer and Babylonia, ancient India, ancient Iran, and ancient Greece.

Egypt. Egyptian religious thought also shows an awareness of a golden age existing at the beginning. The study of archaic texts has prompted the hypothesis that this age was thought to have had two stages, the first of which was *Urzeit,* primordial time before the creation. The idea of a primordial time is expressed by such formulas as "that did not yet exist" *(nhprt)* or, in the wording of Pyramid Texts 1040 and 1043, "When the heavens did not yet exist . . . there existed neither death nor disorder." In contrast to this mythic primordial time is the time that follows it, the time of creation and of creator gods such as Re and Osiris (Otto, 1969, pp. 96–99).

Whatever the validity of this hypothesis, the time of creation, the *Schöpfungszeit,* was definitely considered a golden age. A variety of texts make it possible to assert this interpretation with certainty. "Law was established in their time. Justice (Maat) came down from heaven to earth in their age and united herself with those on the earth. There was an abundance on the earth; stomachs were full, and there was no lean year in the Two Lands. Wall did not collapse, thorn did not prick in the time of the primeval Gods" (Kákosy, 1964, p. 206). An inscription from the temple of Idfu speaks in the same way: "There was no sin on the earth. The crocodile did not seize prey, the serpent did not bite in the age of the primeval Gods." This golden age is depicted in other temple inscriptions and is found again in the Coffin Texts; it is, in fact, a very ancient doctrine in which myths of a golden age and fall are tied to the problem of death.

Three great Egyptian cosmogonies explain the creation of the world. In the Memphis theology, the word of the god Ptah created all things; at Heliopolis, the creation takes place with Re-Atum's separation of heaven and earth; at Hermopolis Magna, the creator is the god Thoth, who fashions an egg from which the sun, organizer of the cosmos, emerges. The Memphis theology makes it clear that, by putting the cosmos, the gods, and the gods' images and cults in place, Ptah established a definitive cosmic order in which Maat, the principle of order, replaced disorder (Pyramid Text 265.1775b).

The myth of the celestial cow, a myth of archaic origin, although known from a text of the New Kingdom, is the most important witness to the Egyptian doctrine of the fall. It tells of insults hurled by men at the god Re (variously called "silver-boned Re," "golden-limbed Re," "Re of the lapis lazuli hair") and of Re's attempt to determine their punishment in a secret council of the gods held in the Nun, or primordial chaos. From his throne, Re glared fixedly at the rebellious humans, as the gods had advised; immediately, his eye became the goddess Hathor, henceforth called Sechmut, the Powerful; she organized a massacre of the rebels as they fled into the desert. Re, however, preferred to save remaining mankind; ordering that pomegranates be brought to him, he extracted their juice, and at dawn carried the juice to the flooded area of man's impending extermination. There he determined to spare the human race; but he also withdrew to the highest place in heaven, and sat on the back of Nut, the vault of heaven transformed into a cow, assigning to Thoth the role of scribe and the task of civilizing mankind.

The *Book of Going Forth by Day* is another witness to the Egyptian doctrine of the fall. Chapter 17, alluding to Re's enemies, declares: "I was All when I was in the Nun, and I am Re. . . . When Re first appeared as king of all that he had created, when the uprisings of Shu did not yet exist, he was on the hill that is at Hermopolis and at that time the children of the fall at Hermopolis were delivered over to him." To this passage, which tells of the revolt against Re, correspond the lines at the beginning of chapter 175, which speak of the disorder created by the children of Nut: "O Thoth, what is to be done with the children of Nut? They have fomented war, they have provoked quarrels, they have caused disorder, they have massacred. . . . They have brought low that which was great in all that I created. Show strength, Thoth, says Atum. . . . Shorten their years, cut off their months. For they have secretly destroyed all that you created."

From such texts, it is clear that pharaonic Egypt was acquainted very early with a doctrine of a golden age, an age followed by the fall that explains the *Jetztzeit,* the present human condition of death and degradation.

Nevertheless, the Egyptian theology that viewed royalty as a divine continuation of Maat, the cosmic and moral order, had a paramount influence on three thousand years of Egyptian history under the pharaohs and the Ptolemies, and although each great historic era ended in a period of disorder, the disorder itself gave rise to the reestablishment of Egyptian society under renewed pharaonic rule. Life and survival were inseparable in Egypt, and the optimism running throughout Egyptian culture is made obvious by the absence of traditions dealing with great cosmic disasters such as the flood.

There was also, however, a darker side to Egyptian thought, one that does relate that evil, incarnate in the god Seth, existed before the creation of man. Hence some Egyptologists interpret the verses quoted above from chapter 175 of the *Book of Going Forth by Day,* referring to the children of Nut, as an allusion to a quarrel among the gods and evidence of a primordial sin that stood at the origin of the fall.

Sumer and Babylonia. The numerous Mesopotamian traditions dealing with the origins of the gods, the cosmos, and man go back to the Sumerian period, well before the third millennium BCE, and become completely intermixed over time with Sumerian, Akkadian, and Babylonian myths. Thus, it is possible to present these traditions coherently by selecting characteristic examples from these three groups of myths.

Samuel Noah Kramer (1981) finds the first document of the golden age in the Sumerian story called *Emmerkai and the Lord of Aratta.* The story speaks of "an earlier time," before the fall, when mankind lived in peace and harmony, without fear and without rival. During that time, before the creation of snake or scorpion, hyena or lion, wolf or wild dog, all peoples of the universe worshiped the same god, Enlil. But the gods brought about man's fall when Enki cast an evil spell and stole Enlil's empire.

The creation poem *Enuma elish,* which dates from 1100 BCE but actually goes back to the first Babylonian dynasty at the beginning of the second millennium, relates the genesis of the gods before it describes the genesis of the world or man, and shows that strife and murder existed among the gods from the moment of their creation. The younger gods banded together against their mother, Tiamat; they behaved riotously and spread fear throughout the dwelling places on high. The goddess Ea caused the god Apsu—who would himself have murdered the other gods, had his scheme not been betrayed—to fall into a deep sleep, then undressed him to take away his strength, and finally put him to death. The Atrahasis myth, dating from the reign of the Babylonian king Ammisadaqa (1646–1626 BCE), gives another version of these events, in which the gods declared war on Enlil and gathered in arms before his temple for the decisive battle.

In these two myths, evil is coextensive with the first generation of the gods, and disorder begins in the divine world itself when the younger gods kill their mother, Tiamat (who in any case had planned to murder them). From this perspective, the gods are responsible for evil, and order appears among them only with the advent of the god Marduk, the principle of an ordered divine world. Hence, man simply finds evil in the world; he is not the cause of it.

Both the Atrahasis myth and the poem *Enuma elish* show that the gods created man with the intention of imposing burdensome tasks upon him: food gathering, the building of waterways, dikes, canals, and so forth. In the Atrahasis text, the god Weilu is killed by the other gods, who then mix his flesh and blood with clay to make man, upon whom they immediately impose the gods' "basket" (i.e., work load); in a story dating from the seventeenth century BCE and found in a bilingual text from the reign of King Tiglath-pileser I (1114–1076), An, Enlil, and Enki kill the Alla gods and from their blood create mankind, which they also charge with tasks previously borne by the gods.

In these texts, and in many others that echo them, it is clear that Mesopotamian thought saw the human condition as one of total subordination to the gods, who were absolute masters of the world. This dualistic thought presents a humanity fashioned both from the blood of a murdered god and from mere clay, a humanity knowing no primordial fall but only a destiny of submission to the gods and subordination to divine power. The gods reserve a deathless, happy life for themselves, imposing on man a precarious existence that ends in death, itself a divine decision. The dead lead only a shadowy existence in the realm of the god Nergal.

Two ancient texts provide Akkadian and Babylonian versions of the Mesopotamian flood. The earlier, dating from the beginning of the third millennium, was found on a Sumerian tablet unearthed in the ruins of Nippur; the other is found in tablet 11 of the *Epic of Gilgamesh.*

The Sumerian tablet describes the creation of the world and man and the building of the first cities, including Eridu and Shuruppak. The rather fragmentary story of the flood tells of how the gods decided upon a deluge, from which only the pious king Ziusudra was spared. After the disaster, Ziusudra sacrificed an ox and a sheep to the sun god Utu and thereby reconciled the gods and man.

In the Babylonian version, from the *Epic of Gilgamesh,* the man saved from the flood was Utanapishtim, to whom the gods gave immortality. After the flood, the quarrel that had divided the gods started up again, and

Enlil, the lord of earth and sky who had been the cause of the flood, wanted to destroy its sole survivor; but Ea and Ishtar, protectors of mankind, intervened and Utanapishtim was saved.

In neither version of the flood does the question of man's responsibility for the cosmic disaster arise; as in Mesopotamian stories of man's creation, the stories of the flood deal only with theogony and with quarrels of the gods. The Atrahasis myth does indicate the gods' motive for the flood—the noise and disturbance produced by the ever-increasing number of humans—but this motive is analogous to that behind the gods' first quarrel. Thus, whatever the reason for the gods' displeasure with humanity, the human failings that appear at the time of the fall are simply part of a divinely ordained chaos. In the final analysis, myths of the fall in Sumero-Babylonian thought are intimately tied to theogonic and cosmogonic myths in which the fall, like everything else that happens, results from the will of the gods.

Ancient India. In India, which has experienced its past far more through myths than through historical interpretation of actual past events, the most important documents of mythic history are the Purāṇas, or "ancient tales." One part of the speculations of the *Vāyu Purāṇa* treats the four *yuga*s, or ages, of the world. The present age, the fourth *yuga*, is called the *kaliyuga*. The first age, named *kṛtayuga* or *satyayuga*, is described in the *Vāyu Purāṇa* as a golden age when Prajāpati created all things from a superabundance of light and intelligence.

During this *yuga*, a perfect age that lasted four thousand years (plus an additional four hundred for its dawn and dusk), all creatures lived in a state of spiritual perfection, doing as they pleased, free from heat and cold, fatigue and suffering, ignorant alike of justice and injustice. Possessing similar forms, their pleasures, their life span, and their ever-youthful bodies ensured a life of abundant happiness, joy, and light, knowing neither classes nor different ways of being. Whatever was sought after by the spirit sprang from the earth, and all enjoyed truth, forbearance, satisfaction, and contentment.

The *Vāyu Purāṇa* does not describe a fall, but simply a decline, from this golden age. The second age, *tretāyuga*, was still, at its beginning, part of the golden age; beings still lived without suffering, joyous and satisfied. With time, however, they became greedy; they laid waste the fruit trees and the honey that had fed them in ease. Afflicted now by wind, heat, and cold, men built houses, then villages and cities. Now too rains came, bringing streams, rivers, and rank vegetation. Mankind was divided into four classes: *brāhmaṇa*, *kṣatriya*, *vaiśya*, and *śūdra*; and, since men no longer fulfilled their duties, the *brāhmaṇa*s assigned specific functions to each class. The *brāhmaṇa*s were to make sacrifices on behalf of others, to read the Veda, to receive offerings; the *kṣatriya*s were to exercise power, make war, and dispense justice; the *vaiśya*s were to raise livestock or practice agriculture or commerce; the *śūdra*s were to practice the various trades. The *brāhmaṇa*s likewise introduced and named the four stages of life: first, the quest for knowledge, followed by domestic life, the retreat into the forest, and, finally, renunciation.

It is clear from the *Vāyu Purāṇa* that by the end of the second *yuga* the conditions of man and the cosmos were such that the golden age had been lost, the victim not of a fall in the usual sense but of a progressive decline, and of the negative effects of time. As differences appeared among them, men lost their original vitality, turning to passion, vice, and greed, and ceasing to carry out their duties faithfully. The *Vāyu Purāṇa* emphasizes the role of human responsibility in this cosmic and social decline. [*See* Ages of the World.]

From the sixth century BCE on, the idea of *karman*, specific to Hindu religious thought, was used to explain the decline of the human condition. Linked to the idea of *saṃsāra*, the incessant whirlpool of rebirths, the ethical idea of *karman*, gradually replacing older Vedic ritual notions, placed the human soul under the necessity of being reborn in animal, human, or divine forms. Thus man by his actions was made responsible for his decline and for the repercussions of that decline in the cosmos. Holding man accountable for his position in the universe, the law of the *karman* became a law of just retribution for actions.

The Indian idea of the flood, of "cosmic disaster," appears within a cyclical conception of time—a conception analogous to the idea of the *karman* involving the periodic destruction and rebirth of the cosmos. The oldest of numerous Indian versions of a cosmic fall in the form of a flood is that of the *Śatapatha Brāhmaṇa* 1.8.1; it presents the story of Manu, the first man and the survivor of the flood, in a typically Vedic context. Warned of the flood by a fish, Manu takes the fish under his protection and then is saved by it as the waters rise and carry away all other creatures. Left alone, Manu offers the *pāka* sacrifice, and, after a year, a woman—his daughter, called Iḍā, the offering—is born; through her Manu will create his posterity, the renewed humanity.

Ancient Iran. The Avesta preserves ancient Iran's memories of the golden age that existed in the beginning, during the reign of the first king, Yima (*Vendidad* 2.1–20, *Yasna* 9.4–5, *Yashts* 9.9, 13.130, 15.15, 17.29, 19.32). According to *Yasna* 9.4, Yima, the good shepherd, the most glorious of mortals ever born, looked benevolently on all creatures; his reign was one with neither drought nor heat nor cold, when food was always plentiful, and when men and animals lived without want or old age or death. The *Vendidad* (2.7) says that Ahura Mazdā brought Yima the two implements symbolizing a prosperous reign, a golden seal and a sword encrusted with gold. Yima also asked for a thousand-year reign of immortality in the world created by the Lord. For three hundred years after the creation, the world filled up with men and animals; then Yima, advancing in the path of the sun, smote the earth with his seal and pierced it with his sword, and the earth increased in size by a third; he did this again after six hundred winters, and again the earth became a third larger; when he had repeated this act yet again, the earth was enlarged to three times its original surface (*Vendidad* 2.7, 2.8–9, 2.10–11, 2.17–19). Thus ends the story of the paradise of Yima, a paradise that in a Pahlavi text, the *Dēnkard* 8.1.24, is compared to the highest heaven.

The Avestan text *Yashts* 19.34–38 describes the fall that marked the end of this felicity. When Yima began to take pleasure in false and deceitful speech, the *khvarenah*—the celestial light, the mark of divinity, the sign of the elect and of power—at once abandoned him. He thus lost the three marks of glory associated with the *khvarenah*, the marks of the priest, the warrior, and the agriculturalist-herdsman. Seen in the context of Indo-Iranian thought, the loss of these marks represents the loss of the three great Aryan functions of sovereignty, power, and fecundity. Confounded and distraught, Yima fell to earth and became mortal.

The cause of the fall, the "lie against the truth," is stressed in *Yashts* 19.34; this lie deprived Yima of his aura of light and delivered him over defenseless to the Evil Spirit, who hounded him with demons and forced him to flee. Yima actually made two mistakes: the first was "the lie and the error," or *druj*, condemned by the entire Mazdean tradition and still decried in Manichaeism, for Mani taught that lying and deceit constitute the evil that resides in matter and darkness; the second mistake was the offense to God caused by pride (Widengren, 1968, p. 72). Since, in this very ancient myth, Yima is the archetype of the cosmic king who holds sovereignty over the gods and men, the king of the three functions that correspond to the three classes of society, his fall will mark both the cosmos and the human condition.

Describing Yima's meeting with Ahura Mazdā, *Vendidad* 2.21–22 mentions hard winters of bitter cold and heavy snow; in *Bundahishn* 7, there is a story of what appears to be a flood; and al-Masʿūdī (d. 957) relates how, according to one tradition, the flood came during Yima's time. In the nineteenth century, scholars like C. P. Tiele, François Lenormant, and A. V. Rydberg saw an allusion to the flood in this evidence; but early in the twentieth century, Nathan Söderblom, in a lengthy discussion of the question, showed that it is impossible to know whether the devastating winters mentioned in these passages were considered part of a real past before they came to symbolize the end of the world later incorporated into Mazdean eschatology. Söderblom leaned toward a strictly eschatological meaning of the myth of the *vara* of Yima and the winter of Mahrkuska; more recently, Geo Widengren has observed that in the few traces of a flood linked to the myth of Yima two different themes have been combined: one of the golden age of Yima, the other of a period when the more fortunate of mankind took refuge in the *vara* because winters threatened their existence (Widengren, 1968, pp. 70–71). Going over the evidence once again, Mary Boyce still finds the narrative of the *vara* of Yima puzzling; but she argues that, since the editing of the *Vendidad* in the Parthian period is comparatively recent, the Avestan story very probably was contaminated by the Mesopotamian and biblical stories of the cosmic flood (Boyce, 1975, pp. 92–96).

Ancient Greece. The term *golden age* (Gr., *chruseon genos*) comes from the ancient Greek world. In *Works and Days*, Hesiod provided the myth of the Golden Age to which later Greek and Latin poets would return again and again, a myth of five races of men to which correspond five ages of the world: ages of gold, silver, and bronze, of heroes, and, finally, of iron. Created when Kronos reigned in the heavens, the race of gold lived as gods on the earth, perfectly happy and secure, sheltered from all woe, fatigue, pain, or illness. The earth gave forth abundantly all things that men desired, and although this first race of men was not immortal, its death was a mere going to sleep. This age of paradise, when men enjoyed the blessing and friendship of the gods, ended with the fall of Kronos; then Zeus made benevolent gods of these first men.

Plato elaborated on the conditions of this golden age in the *Politics* (271c,d–272a); in that age, he says, the gods were responsible for different parts of the cosmos, and demons served as shepherds for the various species and groups of animals; the earth's climate was always temperate, and everything was designed to serve men, who lived on fruit picked from trees. There were neither cities nor even women or children, since they were reborn from the earth without any memory of earlier lives.

Horace, Vergil, and Ovid later take up this theme, adapting it to the legendary history of Rome; thus Kronos will become Saturn and Latium will have the name Ansonia during the golden age—a time when, according to the Latin poets, springtime was perpetual, and, since lying and theft did not yet exist, houses had no doors.

Four races will follow that of the golden age. Extremely slow in coming to maturity, the silver race will lose the qualities of life that characterized the previous age. Although created by the Olympian gods, the men of this race could not refrain from foolish excesses, even refusing to sacrifice to the gods, and Zeus buried them, transforming them into the spirits of the underworld. He then created the fearless and warlike race of bronze, a race so given to violence that it destroyed itself and was followed in its turn by the race of heroes, heroes who founded famous cities, fought beneath the walls of Troy and Thebes, and ended their days in the Isles of the Blessed. At last came the present race of men, the race of iron, whose ephemeral and vulnerable existence is plagued by illness and want.

The myth of the races of man, which recalls the Indian myth of the four *yugas*, is, like it, a myth of decline rather than fall; like the text of the *Vāyu Purāṇa*, the Hesiodic text emphasizes progressive degeneration. Gradually mankind loses the virtues and qualities of the primordial period; its strength and endurance diminish, and finally it loses the longevity of the first age. Recent analyses of this myth have also laid stress on the evil pointed out by Hesiod: man's pride, the hubris that makes him refuse to sacrifice to the gods and to defy *dikē* ("justice").

In his *Theogony*, Hesiod describes the triumph of an ordered world over chaos and proclaims the sovereign power of Zeus, who imposes himself upon both the universe and the other Olympian gods, to whom he distributes functions and privileges. In *Works and Days*, before recounting the myth of the races of man, he tells the story of Pandora, the first woman, created by Zeus's command to bring punishment upon the human race. All the Olympians joined in making this special gift to man. Zeus sent her to the naive Epimetheus, who was seduced by her beauty and married her.

At pains to stress how men had originally enjoyed the earth free from troubles, weariness, or illness, Hesiod now relates that Pandora had barely arrived on earth when she was devoured by curiosity to learn the contents of the vase she had brought with her and lifted its lid, thus sending throughout the world all the present and future afflictions and woes of mankind, leaving only hope at the bottom of the vase when she replaced the lid. Henceforth, innumerable miseries will plague mankind, and thus, Hesiod concludes, none can escape the plan of Zeus (*Works and Days* 90–102, 105). In the myth of Pandora, the themes of hubris and fate come together, and the description of the fall shows the fundamental link between divine will and human fate.

Orpheus seems to be a figure of the archaic religious type that, in certain traditions, is thrown back to the earliest time; he stands in sharp contrast to the Olympian gods. Hesiod's theogony and cosmogony oppose an ordered world upon which Zeus has at last imposed himself to an earlier, primordial chaos; Orphic theogony, on the other hand, presents a primordial Eros, or Protogonos ("firstborn"), or Phanes ("light"), that itself creates night, Ouranos, Kronos, Zeus, and, finally, Dionysos.

Orphic anthropogony, in sources that date from later antiquity, recounts the myth of a Dionysos torn apart and cut to pieces by the Titans, who then divided the dead god among themselves and ate him. Zeus hurled lightning bolts at them as a punishment and killed them; he then created the present race of men from their ashes. Thus, men possess both the evil nature of the Titans and the divine nature of Dionysos whom the Titans had assimilated by eating him. The Neoplatonist Proclus talks of three races of men: the race of gold ruled by Phanes, the god of the beginning of things; the silver race over which Kronos was lord; and the Titanic race, created by Zeus from limbs of Titans whom he had punished for their crime. Plato himself had already referred to this race, Titanic in origin, who likewise refused to obey both laws and parents, refused to abide by oaths, and despised the gods. Both Diodorus Siculus and Firmicus Maternus repeat these basic elements of the Orphic myth; and the dualism of Orphic anthropogony, in which the story of the Titans is presented as an etiological myth accounting for the present human condition, has been further confirmed by the discovery, in 1962, of the fourth-century Dervani Papyrus.

Orphism explains the human condition through the dualistic myth of the exiled soul. Man is composed of a divine soul, daughter of heaven, and of an evil, Titanic nature; the tragedy of his condition comes from this mixture, itself the outcome of an earlier, prehuman crime. Evil is the legacy of an event that stands at the origin of man's mixed nature; it originates in the murder of Dionysos, but that murder signifies both the death of the god and the participation of his slayers in his divine nature. The original sin, the sin of the fall, is murder, and with the murder of Dionysos the soul experiences a brutal descent into a body that becomes its prison (see Ricoeur, 1960, pp. 264–279).

The myth of Deukalion and Pyrrha presents the Greek version of the flood, but the fragmentary Greek texts do not give Zeus's reasons for suppressing mankind. However, as Roman mythology disappeared, it absorbed Greek mythology (a phenomenon discussed by Georges

Dumézil, *La religion romaine archaïque,* 2d ed., Paris, 1974, pp. 63–75), and it is therefore legitimate to seek Zeus's reasons in Roman mythology, especially in Ovid's *Metamorphoses,* which provides a fuller account of the Greek version of the flood (*Metamorphoses* 1.230, 7.352–356). Taking up the Hesiodic theme of the ages of the world, Ovid emphasizes that men were progressively perverted by crime and lust. Zeus, before mankind's destruction, visited Lycaon, king of Arcadia, who served him a feast of human flesh; outraged and at the end of his patience, Zeus swept away all creatures, cities, almost the whole of earth itself, in the flood. Only one couple, Deukalion and his wife, Pyrrha, were saved, and from them Zeus re-created the race.

World Religions. Each of the world religions discussed in this section—gnosticism and Manichaeism, and the three great monotheisms, Judaism, Christianity, and Islam—lend great richness to the concept of the fall.

Gnosticism and Manichaeism. From the second century CE onward, gnosticism, a religious movement composed of a number of different sects, came to maturity throughout the Mediterranean world and in the Near East. The central element of gnostic metaphysical speculation is a dualistic doctrine according to which man possesses a divine spark that, although originating from on high, has fallen into matter, into body, which holds it prisoner in the lower world. The myth of the fall, therefore, is an integral part of gnostic teaching. Each gnostic sect offered salvation through its specific creed and rites of initiation into these dualistic mysteries. These constituted its particular gnosis. Understood only by adherents who were gradually initiated into it, the gnosis brought about an identity of the initiate with the means of his salvation and with divine substance.

Because it claims to possess the most perfect gnosis, Manichaeism holds a special place in the spectrum of gnostic thought. Its founder, Mani (216–277), taught that, as the transmitter of the gnosis, he was the greatest of the prophets and the ultimate revelation, sent by the Holy Spirit, after the trials and failures of his predecessors—most notably Zarathushtra, the Buddha, and Jesus—to establish the church of the end of time, the church of light, and to provide the definitive revelation that would enlighten all men. According to Mani, the soul, a spark detached from divine light and held prisoner by matter, must tear itself away from the darkness of the body in order to return to the realm of light where it had originated.

The Manichaean gnosis offers the clearest conception of the beginning, the middle, and the end, the three divisions of time. In the beginning, there existed two radically opposed natures, darkness and light, eternal and unborn principles. These two natures created two earths, two different realms. The realm of light is located on high, in a city of incomparable beauty, in the house of the Father of Greatness; the breath of the spirit breathes life and light throughout this realm, where all things exude blessing and peace. But beneath this realm, and separated from it by an impregnable border, lies the realm of darkness, the domain of matter and of demons, a realm governed by the Prince of Lies. Obviously, the Manichaean gnosis presents the golden age within a context of radical gnostic dualism.

In other forms of gnosis, dualism appears against a monistic background, since the world on high—everlasting, immutable, and incorruptible—is held to have existed before the lower world. Indeed, many gnostic writings speak of the Pleroma, of the world on high in all its plenitude, emanating from a being that is the source of all things. The gnostic Pleroma is the union of the Aeons that emanate from the All and constitute, with the First Father, the harmonious universe of peace and light.

The symbol of the fall is omnipresent in gnostic texts; indeed, the precosmic fall of a portion of the divine principle is the underlying reason for the genesis of the cosmos and man (Jonas, 1963). In the different metaphysical speculations that explain this fall, it is generally held that the divine principle descended voluntarily, and that guilt came into being as the Aeons turned toward the lower world. Turning toward matter by a burning desire to know it, the soul then sank into it and was swallowed up. Hence, the fall that gave birth to the cosmos also imprisoned the soul in matter.

In gnostic writings, important groups of symbols suggesting captivity describe the tragic fate of this dualistic, imprisoned soul. One group of symbols suggests pain or danger: violence, fear, and the wounds and bites of animals; another suggests the soul's forgetfulness: torpor, sleep, death, darkness, drunkenness, lack of conscience, ignorance. As a snake's bite causes an infection that debilitates the body, so the poison of darkness causes an infection of the soul that makes it lose awareness of its divine origin. In a frequently used image, the soul falls asleep in matter, and the gnostic message strives to awaken it; hence, gnosticism attaches great importance to its call. Also characteristic of gnostic writings are the images used by Valentinus when describing the behavior of Sophia ("wisdom") after she had fallen into error. The youngest Aeon of the Pleroma, Sophia was the cause of her own fall, through the passion that carried her away—the origin of a fall that brought about the lower world of the Demiurge, who created the material world.

A true religious genius endowed with uncommon

imagination, Mani brought together a number of Eastern cosmogonic myths and from them produced a synthesis in which the entire range of dualistic cosmogony, soteriology, and eschatology is included.

In the beginning, Mani taught, the Prince of Darkness, jealous and envious of the Father, hurled a war cry against the realm of light, signaling the beginning of a gigantic cosmic conflict. Primordial Man, the first emanation of the Father, marched against the forces of darkness, but he was wounded and defeated and fell among the archons (cosmic rulers). This was the fall, the moment when the living soul, the divine portion of Primordial Man, was engulfed by darkness; it was also the beginning of the second division of time, the middle, when divinity fell into matter and man's mixed nature became fixed. Henceforth, salvation became an imperious necessity. The liberation of Primordial Man from this fallen state is the prototype of the salvation of each soul; and the second emanation of the Father, the Living Spirit (also called the Friend of Light or the Great Architect), extends his right hand to Primordial Man and leads him back to the realm of light. But the fall has permanent consequences, since a part of the light remains captive in the lower realm.

The first moment of middle time, the moment of the fall, is followed by the moment of the creation and the freeing of another part of light, as part of the punishment of the archons. The Living Spirit chained down the archons and cut them to pieces; from their skins he made the vault of heaven, from their bones the mountains, from their flesh and excrement the earth, and from the light taken from them he created the sun, moon, and stars. When a Third Messenger descended from on high in the form of a luminous virgin, the semen of the archons excited by this apparition fell on the earth and produced trees and vegetation. Animals were next created, and finally the first couple was born, the work of demons. This couple was Adam and Eve, creatures of mixed nature whose posterity nonetheless carried with it the greater part of light.

The third moment of middle time is the moment of the messengers of the gnosis, the moment of true and divine hypostasis brought about by the fourth emanation of the Father, Jesus the Splendid, a transcendent, cosmic being, fifth Greatness of the Realm, the life and salvation of men. Messengers of the gnosis have followed one after another from Sethel, the son of Adam, to Jesus (here considered as a historical figure), who both announced and sent the final messenger, Mani. Hence, everything was made ready for the third division of time, the end, when all things will become as they had been at the beginning, and the total separation of the realms of darkness and light will be reestablished.

The Eastern myths of the fall brought together by Mani constitute one great myth of the fall and redemption of the divine soul. Each human soul is part of the divine soul that is partly imprisoned in bodies, partly in plants, trees, and earth; in all its imprisoned parts, that divine soul is the soul of the world and the third representation of Jesus, *Jesus patibilis*. In the great Manichaean myth of the fall is found the gnostic myth of the exiled soul; but, in contrast to most gnostic creeds, in Manichaeism the soul is not responsible for its fall and exile in the body, since that exile is a part of a greater, cosmic fall of light. To this cosmic myth of the fall corresponds the cosmic salvation by a gnosis accessible to individual souls in a church that is both the location and the means of individual salvation, a church charged with proclaiming the message of the fall and issuing the call to salvation, as well as awakening men's souls and initiating them into the dualistic mysteries.

Judaism. Central to the biblical message is the view that the creation of man and the cosmos is the work of a unique and transcendent God who freely willed and effected a creation that also marks the beginning of time.

Two different stories of the creation are given in *Genesis*. The Bible opens with the so-called sacerdotal account of the creation, "the work of six days" (*Gn.* 1:1–31, 2:1–3). In this cosmogony, primordial chaos is replaced by order through the creative power of God's word. The sacerdotal account emphasizes the transcendence of the creator God and presents his creative activity in an order of ascending importance; although the creation of the world and of animal and vegetable life are all deemed "good," the crowning work in the beginning is the creation of man.

The second, so-called Yahvistic, creation story (*Gn.* 2:4–25) does not talk of the creation of the earth and sky but rather of a desert made fertile by Yahveh; it stresses God's action, his fashioning the first man from clay and breathing the breath of life into his nostrils. It is in the Yahvistic story that God plants a garden in Eden, where man is the creature of unequaled importance, the rest of creation being made in relation to him. Together, the two stories of creation provide genetic explanations of important aspects of the human condition; in both, man occupies a privileged position in creation. The biblical stories stress that man is free and not controlled by fate.

In Hebrew, the word *gan*—*paradeisos* in Greek (related to the Iranian *paridaida*)—designates the place where, according to *Genesis* 2:8, God placed man. [*See*

Paradise.] The Yahvistic creation story speaks of an arid land on which Yahveh caused rain to fall, after which he took man and placed him in the garden of Eden, created especially for him. This paradise appears as an oasis in the Oriental desert, although its name is linked by some scholars to the Sumerian word *edin*, for which several Assyrologists read "plain" or "countryside." The word *paradeisos* adopted by the Greek Bible denotes the pleasure gardens and royal hunting lands of Iran and Asia Minor. For the Greek reader the word suggests a garden of fruits and fruit trees. Certainly the biblical garden is the archetype of all regions of luxuriant vegetation (*Gn.* 13:10, *Is.* 51:3, *Ez.* 31:8). [*See* Gardens.]

The text of *Genesis* 2:10–14, which mentions the four rivers flowing out of Eden, is clearly intended to locate the garden symbolically at the center of the cosmos; a story in Mesopotamian mythology also places a divine residence at the source of rivers. The biblical text seeks to establish a relationship between a divine garden and a human earth, thereby emphasizing the marvelous fertility of man's first home. The garden of Eden is also characterized by the presence of two special trees—the tree of life and the tree of the knowledge of good and evil (*Gn.* 2:16–17). The tree of life is part of a larger Mesopotamian group of symbols, known through a number of texts. The tree of the knowledge of good and evil, however, has no parallel in any other ancient text; it is specific to the Yahvistic story of creation and stresses the relationship between life and obedience to God.

Adam and Eve enjoy a life of paradise in the garden, living together in harmony and at peace with the animals, as in Mesopotamian myths of the golden age. Both the Yahvistic and the sacerdotal text stress man's privileged situation in Eden—his intimacy with God, his hope of immortality, suggested by the tree of life—and evoke the harmony that exists there, seen in man's relations with the rest of creation and his life of ease. The presence in Eden of the tree of the knowledge of good and evil shows that obedience to God is essential to maintaining this privileged situation. The biblical text emphasizes considerations that are absent in all other myths of the golden age—considerations of freedom, of moral choice in the face of good and evil. Through a choice of his own, man decides his standing before God and at the same time the direction of his destiny.

The testing of man in Eden is related to the problem of human freedom. In mythical language, *Genesis* 2–3 describes the situation of man in the world and in the face of God. The garden of Eden is the place where man lives in easy familiarity with God, but it is also the symbolic microcosm where he has been given mastery, and where he enjoys the free use of all other created things; thus the conquest and humanization of the world will become the condition of his vocation. The prohibition against eating from the tree of knowledge belongs to another order, for it deals with man's basic appreciation of the value of earthly things and of his situation before God (*Gn.* 3:5–6). It will bring about his fall from paradise.

The story of Eden stresses the primordial couple's disobedience to God and their expulsion from the garden, and it emphasizes that they lost the privileged status of Eden for themselves and for their descendants. Thus, their sin is presented as the prototype of that part of human sin that is universal. The essence of hubris is the desire to be like God; when this desire becomes action, the fall takes place and ushers in the woes of mankind. The Yahvistic document asserts both directly and symbolically that man's experience of evil had an absolute beginning, a beginning that coincides with the beginning of man's history, the history of freedom. Although the first exercise of that freedom resulted in disaster, through it man inaugurated the drama of choice that gives particular significance to his life and his relationship to God. Subsequent biblical books and apocryphal texts repeatedly return to these lessons of the fall (*Ez.* 28; *Dt.* 30:15–20; *Prv.* 3:2, 3:22, 6:15, 10:25; *Sir.* 37:3; *Wis.* 1:13–14, 10:1–2).

The editors of chapters 4–11 of *Genesis* saw in the fall of man in Eden not only the loss of paradise and the transformation of the human condition but also the source of a whole series of evils that subsequently beset mankind. Thus, at each stage in the rise of civilization and the institutionalization of the social developments that formed men's lives in antiquity, the biblical text notes humanity's corruption, variously described as fratricidal war, polygamy, desert warfare, or the division of nations and tongues (*Gn.* 4:8, 4:19, 4:23–24, 11:5–9). Since the fall, evil is born in the hearts of men and always remains at the heart of history, an inevitable force in human affairs.

The most important biblical event having the characteristics of a universal fall is the flood (*Gn.* 6:5–8:14). The story of Noah in the Bible reinforces elements of the *Epic of Gilgamesh*, but its editors have taken over and reinterpreted Mesopotamian themes in order to transform them into an episode in sacred history and to show the progressive degeneration of humanity that justifies the flood. In both its Yahvistic and its sacerdotal forms, the biblical story is very different from the Mesopotamian one. The latter sees in the flood simply the decree of gods annoyed with a despised humanity.

In the Bible, the memory of the flood serves as the prototype of God's judgment against a sinful mankind; man's situation as a responsible being is stressed, and humanity is not abandoned to the blows of blind destiny. In this myth of the universal fall, a new alliance is foreseen, in which *Urzeit* leads to *Endzeit*. [*See* Flood, The.]

Genesis 6:1–4 contains the story of the *benei Elohim* who take the daughters of men as wives. This unusual text presupposes an oral tradition and possibly other written texts. It appears as a preface to the flood and may be interpreted as further evidence of the sins that will provoke the flood, but it is also the starting point for numerous speculations about the fall of the angels. The rabbinical interpretation has seen in the *benei Elohim*, "the sons of God," angels who sinned with the daughters of men and were for that reason shut up in the depths of the earth; at the last judgment, they will be thrown into the fire.

Christianity. Allusions to man's fall appear throughout the New Testament, although the Gospels speak of it only in *Matthew* 19:4–6, *Mark* 10:6–8, and *John* 3:5 and 8:41–44. It was Paul who was especially interested in the relationship between the fall and sin. In chapters 1–3 of *Romans*, he asserts that no one can escape the domination of sin, and in chapter 7 he gives a lengthy description of the human condition in the earthly paradise, where as yet humans knew neither covetousness nor death, and contrasts this with the actual condition to which they have been reduced by sin and death. He asserts that the actual human condition comes from the first sin, the sin of Adam and Eve in the earthly paradise (*Rom.* 7:13–15); and in *1 Corinthians* 15:21–22, he opposes the first Adam, the author of death, to Christ, the second Adam, the author of life. In general, Paul sees in the story of Eden not only man's hereditary punishment of suffering and death but also his hereditary fallen state, a state of sin transmitted to all mankind.

Islam. The Qur'ān demonstrates the importance Islam attaches to the idea of God the creator, the all-powerful. God is the creator *(al-khāliq)*, the creator *par excellence (al-khallāq);* all things are created by virtue of the divine resolution that precedes their appearance. The Qur'ān describes a God who creates through his word, a word that is creative, eternal, and ever present (surahs 11:9 and 41:8–11).

God created man and called him *khalīfah*, vicar or viceroy (2:28). Adam, *khalīfat Allāh*, vicar of a God who had placed him at the center of the world, is the preeminent creature, although, made of mud and clay, he owes everything to God (15:26). Many verses of the Qur'ān stress the preeminent dignity of man; even the angels must bow down before him (2:32), and when the evil angel Iblīs refuses to do so, God damns him and Iblīs falls, followed by other angels (15:26–35, 17:63–67). The continuing work of creation is also stressed by the Qur'ān; since every man is made by God, the activity of God the creator is permanent.

God put Adam and his wife in the midst of a garden where they could take fruit from the trees, but he forbade them to approach one tree, under pain of falling among sinners (2:33). But the demon made Adam and his wife sin by eating fruit from that tree and thereby caused their expulsion from the place where God had placed them. God said to them, "Leave the garden. You are now enemies one of another, and on earth you will have only brief enjoyment, and brief lives" (2:34). The episodes in the Qur'ān concerning Adam are reminiscent of *Genesis:* his creation out of earth, his title of vicar, his temptation, fall, and expulsion from paradise. Only the episode of Iblīs is not found in the Bible.

Surah 7 mentions the story of the fall and punishment (7:21–24). Here it is the demon who suggests that man break the divine prohibition in order to obtain immortality. After Adam has sinned, God declares that henceforth men born of the first couple will be enemies one of another (2:34, 7:23, 20:21), and the Qur'ān relates the first fratricidal struggle, between two unnamed sons of Adam whom later Muslim authors call Qābīl and Hābīl.

Noah appears in the Qur'ān as a great prophet who opposes unbelievers (11:27–36, 23:23–26). He receives from God the command to build an ark in order to survive the flood; but, contrary to *Genesis*, which stresses the universal character of the flood, the Qur'ān appears to restrict divine punishment to Noah's own people, who had become impious. The Qur'ān treats their punishment as both a warning and a sign.

Conclusion. Reflection on the fall is a constant preoccupation of *homo religiosus*. In his "nostalgia for beginnings," he turns instinctively toward a primordial, sacred history, where he finds a golden age that corresponds to what man must have been in the beginning. He sees that man's present situation no longer corresponds to that of the golden age, and he strives to explain the accident that has taken place and the consequences of that accident, of that break with primordial harmony.

This article has sought to present the theme of the fall as it appears in the religious thought of the greater part of mankind, although it has been necessary to limit the discussion of myths of the fall to those that describe the fall in relation to a supposed golden age—an age that has haunted man's memory—and that locates man's fall and his present condition between *Urzeit* and *End-*

zeit. Most of our attention was given to myths of man's fall; but, when pertinent, myths of a cosmic fall, or of the fall of lesser deities, have also been considered.

Nostalgia for the beginning of things is clearly a permanent feature of mankind's collective memory, and representation of a golden age provides the archetype through which that nostalgia is repeatedly expressed. As can be seen by the study of various peoples and cultures, man has everywhere sought to explain his present condition through the contrast it provides to his supposed primordial condition; in light of that contrast, he has also classified and interpreted his mythical, historical, and symbolic heritage and related these to sacred history.

[*For further discussion of the fall and its consequences, see* Evil.]

BIBLIOGRAPHY

Baumann, Hermann. *Schöpfung und Urzeit des Menschen im Mythos der afrikanischen Völker.* Berlin, 1936.

Boyce, Mary. *A History of Zoroastrianism*, vol. 1. Leiden, 1975.

Dexinger, Ferdinand. *Sturz der Göttersöhne oder Engel vor der Sintflut.* Vienna, 1966.

Eliade, Mircea. *Patterns in Comparative Religion.* New York, 1958.

Eliade, Mircea. "Nostalgia for Paradise in the Primitive Traditions." In his *Myths, Dreams and Mysteries.* New York, 1960.

Feldmann, Joseph. *Paradies und Sündenfall.* Münster, 1913.

Frazer, James G. *Folk-lore in the Old Testament.* 3 vols. London, 1919.

Jonas, Hans. *The Gnostic Religion.* 2d rev. ed. Boston, 1963.

Kákosy, L. "Ideas about the Fallen State of the World in Egyptian Religion: Decline of the Golden Age." *Acta Orientalia* (Budapest) 17 (1964): 205–216.

Kramer, Samuel Noah. *History Begins at Sumer* (1957). 3d ed. Philadelphia, 1981.

Lambert, W. G., and A. R. Millard. *Atra-Ḫasīs: The Babylonian Story of the Flood.* Oxford, 1968.

Otto, Eberhard. "Das goldene Zeitalter in einem aegyptischen Text." In his *Religions en Egypte hellénistique et romaine.* Paris, 1969.

Ricoeur, Paul. *La symbolique du mal.* 2 vols. Paris, 1960. Translated as *The Symbolism of Evil* (Boston, 1967).

Söderblom, Nathan. *La vie future d'après le mazdéisme à la lumière des croyances parallèles dans les autres religions.* Paris, 1901.

Thomas, Louis-Vincent. *La mort africaine.* Paris, 1982.

Widengren, Geo. *Les religions de l'Iran.* Paris, 1968.

JULIEN RIES

Translated from French by Jeffrey Haight and Annie S. Mahler

FALSAFAH. The term *falsafah* is the arabized loan word from the Greek *philosophia*, "love of wisdom," and hence in its general sense simply means "philosophy." It is, however, also used (as it will be in this account) in a more specific sense as an abbreviation of the expression *al-falsafah al-islāmīyah*, "Islamic philosophy." Similarly, the general Arabic word for "philosophers," *falāsifah* (sg., *faylasūf*), is used more specifically as an abbreviation for the expression *al-falāsifah al-islāmīyūn*, "the Islamic philosophers."

Since for many Muslims, past and present, *falsafah* remains at best doctrinally suspect, the sense in which it will be referred to here as "Islamic" requires clarification. This term, as applied to *falsafah* and *falāsifah*, will first of all be used in a broad cultural sense, for *falsafah* was developed within an Islamic cultural milieu by men whose culture was Islamic. This cultural use of the term *Islamic* is implicit in medieval Arabic usage. Thus, for example, one famous intellectual who condemned some of the *falāsifah* as "infidels" nonetheless referred to them as "Islamic," while another included among the Islamic philosophers the Christians of Baghdad who wrote in Arabic. This latter example calls for a narrowing of the sense in which *Islamic* will be used, however, for in addition to being "Islamic" in the cultural sense, the *falāsifah* were "Islamic" in that they regarded themselves as Muslims, claiming that their conceptions of God and the world were consistent with the Qur'anic view. Most of them attempted to demonstrate the harmony between their respective philosophies and Islamic revelation, and whether such attempts proved convincing or not, they represent a characteristic feature of *falsafah*.

It should be stressed that while the *falāsifah* were theists, they were not theologians. For a proper understanding of *falsafah*, it must be distinguished from *kalām*, Islamic speculative theology. Both disciplines used reason in formulating their respective conceptions of God and his creation, but they differed in approach and motivation. The starting point of *kalām* was revelation. Reason was used in defending the revealed word and in interpreting the natural order in conformity with a Qur'anic view of creation. With *falsafah*, the starting point was reason; the motivation, the quest after "the true nature of things." The *falāsifah* maintained that this quest led them to a demonstrative proof of the existence of a first cause of the universe, which they claimed was identical with the God of the Qur'ān—a claim contested by the Islamic theologians, particularly those who followed the school of *kalām* of al-Ash'arī (d. 935). At issue between *falsafah* and *kalām* was not the question of God's existence; rather, the question was the nature of God.

Another difference between them was historical. *Ka-*

lām antedated *falsafah*; its beginnings are traceable to the period of the Umayyad caliphate (AH 41–132/661–750 CE) and more definitely, to the second half of the eighth century. Moreover, it arose out of religious and political conflicts within Islam. Although subject to foreign influences, particularly Greek thought, *kalām*'s modes of argument and perspectives remained to a great extent indigenous. *Falsafah*, on the other hand, was the direct result of a concerted effort to translate Greek science and philosophy into Arabic beginning early in the ninth century. The first Islamic philosopher, al-Kindī, it should be noted, died around 870.

Falsafah was thus rooted in Greek philosophy, or more accurately, Greek philosophy in its translated form. The *falāsifah* regarded themselves not only as guardians of the truths arrived at by the ancient Greek philosophers but also as participants in a continuous quest after truth: as al-Kindī expressed it, the attainment of truth is difficult and requires the cooperative efforts of generations past and present. Thus, the *falāsifah* did not simply accept ideas they received through the translations. They criticized, selected, and rejected; they made distinctions, refined and remolded concepts to formulate their own philosophies. But the conceptual building blocks, so to speak, of these philosophies remained Greek.

The Translation Movement. Although there are indications that some translations of Greek scientific works were made in the period of the Umayyad caliphate, the translation movement properly speaking took place during the caliphate of the Abbasids, who came to power in 750. Translations were undertaken sporadically just after the establishment of Abbasid rule but flourished in the ninth and tenth centuries. The ruler who gave this movement its real impetus was the caliph al-Ma'mūn, who ruled from 813 to 833, and his active sponsorship of the translation of Greek philosophy and science into Arabic was continued by his successors and by families attached to the caliphal court. The Bayt al-Ḥikmah (House of Wisdom), a center for scientific activity and translations that al-Ma'mūn built in Baghdad, symbolized this Abbasid sponsorship of the translation movement.

The motives for this concern with translations were varied. There were practical considerations, such as the need for medical and astronomical knowledge. There was also the probable motive of prestige: the Byzantines could boast of the Greek philosophical and scientific tradition, and the Abbasids likewise wanted to avail themselves of the intellectual treasures of the ancients. This was also a period of intellectual ferment and genuine interest in learning, and scholars were available to undertake the task of translation. In particular, within the Abbasid realm and close to the heart of their empire were the Syriac-speaking people, a culture within a culture who were themselves partly hellenized. The utilization of this rich intellectual resource by the intelligent leaders of the Islamic state seemed natural.

Apart from the Syriac-speaking scholars, who were mostly Nestorian and Jacobite Christians, there were scholars in the north Syrian city of Harran who also undertook translations. The Harranians adhered to the Sabian sect, a religion that included star worship but also had a Greek philosophical base. Among the Christian scholars, there were two traditions of scholarship. One was the tradition of the medical and philosophical school of Alexandria; members of this school seem to have moved in the Umayyad period to Antioch and then in the Abbasid period to Harran and finally to Baghdad. The other tradition was that of the medical school and hospital of the Nestorians of Jundīshāpūr in Persia. Originally a camp for Roman captives built in the third century CE by the Sasanid emperor Shāpūr I, Jundīshāpūr became a refuge for Nestorians after the deposition of their patriarch, Nestorius, at the Council of Ephesus in 431. The school flourished in Sasanid times, and although little is known about it in the Umayyad period, it became prominent under the Abbasids as well; from 765 to 870, its Bakhtīshū' family provided court physicians for the caliphs.

Among the early translators, mention must be made of Yaḥyā ibn al-Biṭrīq (d. 830?); Astat (Eustathius), about whom very little is known, but who made a translation of Aristotle's *Metaphysics*, a work known to al-Kindī; and Ibn Nā'imah al-Ḥimṣī (d. 835), who translated the very influential if apocryphal *Theology of Aristotle*. The best-known and most influential of the translators was the Nestorian physician and scholar Ḥunayn ibn Isḥāq (d. 873), who was known for his translations of medical works but who was responsible for translating logical and philosophical treatises as well. Unlike earlier and some later scholars, Ḥunayn knew Greek; he followed a system of collating Greek manuscripts before translating and undertook revision of earlier translations from the Syriac. He worked with a team of other translators, who included his son Isḥāq, his nephew Ḥubaysh, and 'Isā ibn Yaḥyā. Among the Harranians the most important translator was Thābit ibn Qurrah (d. 901), who also wrote a commentary on Aristotle's *Physics*. Later translators included Qusṭā ibn Lūqā (d. 912?), also noted for his treatise *The Difference between Soul and Spirit*, Abū 'Uthmān Sa'īd al-Dimashqī (d. 900), the logician Abū Bishr Mattā (d. 940), Yaḥyā ibn 'Adī (d. 974), Ibn Zur'ah (d. 1008), and Ibn al-Khammār (d. 1020).

The three ancient philosophers who conditioned the

rise and development of *falsafah* were Plato, Aristotle, and Plotinus. As with medieval western Europe, Aristotle was the most authoritative figure; his influence lay in the realms of logic, physics, and metaphysics. Plato, whose thought was known largely through the expositions of others, particularly the translated works of the physician Galen, had his greatest influence on the political philosophy of the *falāsifah*. Plotinus was likewise known indirectly, through two main works, the Neoplatonic *Theology of Aristotle*, a paraphrase of books 4, 5, and 6 of the *Enneads*, and the work based on Proclus known in Arabic as *Fī maḥḍ al-khayr* (On the Pure Good), which was translated into medieval Latin as the *Liber de causis*.

A substantial body of commentary, particularly on Aristotle, was also translated. Thus such commentators as Themistius, Simplicius, and Alexander of Aphrodisias were influential in the development of *falsafah*. There was knowledge of pre-Socratic philosophy and late Stoic philosophy and logic, and the translations also included a body of medical works, particularly those of Galen, and mathematical and scientific works such as Euclid's *Elements* and Ptolemy's *Almagest*.

Al-Kindī and al-Rāzī. The philosophical venture in medieval Islam was pioneered in different ways by two remarkable thinkers, Abū Yūsuf Yaʿqūb al-Kindī and the physician-philosopher Abū Bakr al-Rāzī (d. 926). Their philosophies, particularly in their doctrines on the world's creation and the nature of the Creator, differed radically from the thought of the major philosophers who succeeded them. As *falāsifah*, they were atypical; moreover, they differed radically from each other.

Ironically, al-Kindī was atypical because his philosophy conformed with fundamental, generally accepted Muslim beliefs. Thus he argued vigorously and at great length to prove that the world was created *ex nihilo* and at a finite moment of time in the past relative to the present. He also upheld the doctrine of bodily resurrection. At the same time, his writings were thoroughly philosophical in approach and spirit. "We must not," he insisted, "be ashamed of deeming truth good and of acquiring truth from wherever it comes, even if it comes from races remote from us and nations different from us" (*Rasāʾil al-Kindī al-falsafīyah*, ed. M. A. A. Abū Rīdah, Cairo, 1950, p. 103). Al-Kindī was born around the year 800 in Kufa. Little is known about his education except that he was associated with Christian translators and the caliphs who sponsored the translation movement. He alights on the philosophical scene quite unexpectedly, yet with full confidence, betraying none of the hesitancy of the novice. Like the Islamic philosophers who succeeded him, he was also a physician and a scientist, and the range of his learning was encyclopedic.

Of his numerous writings, only a few treatises, philosophical and scientific, have survived. Fortunately, these include the very important work *On First Philosophy*, a relatively long treatise consisting of four chapters. In the first, al-Kindī offers an introduction to philosophy, which he defines as "knowledge of things in their true nature, to the extent of man's capability." The chapter is also a justification and promotion of its pursuit: philosophy's ultimate concern, he argues, is the quest after "the True One," the supreme good, the cause of all things.

The chapters that follow constitute a remarkable piece of vigorous, sustained argument. Most of the second chapter is devoted to proving the creation of the world *ex nihilo* at a distant but finite past. The argument rests on a basic premise, the impossibility of an infinite magnitude. Al-Kindī begins by arguing that an infinite body is impossible. If we suppose the existence of such a body, he maintains, then theoretically it is possible to remove from it a finite part. What remains would also be infinite, but less than the original infinite by the amount of the finite body removed. The consequence would then be the existence of two unequal infinities, amounting, for al-Kindī, to a contradiction. But if a body must be finite, he then tries to show, time and motion must also be finite. The temporal existence of the world could not then go back to infinity; it must have a temporal beginning. Moreover, he argues, creation in time cannot simply mean that a static world (and hence a world outside time) was put into motion at some past finite moment relative to the present. A body by definition, he argues, must be in motion; a static world is a contradiction in terms. Hence not only did the world begin at a finite moment in the past, but it came into being out of nothing.

Having proved the doctrine of creation *ex nihilo* to his own satisfaction, al-Kindī then offers a proof for the existence of God, "the True One," and an investigation of the nature of this oneness. The Neoplatonic influences on this part of the treatise are very manifest, particularly in al-Kindī's exposition of the nature of divine oneness. The proof for God's existence is a causal one, based, however, on the phenomenon of plurality and unity in the world. The proof, given in a short version and a lengthy one, is quite elaborate. The fundamental point al-Kindī makes is that the unity that we experience in things and that is the cause of plurality does not belong essentially to things; it is a derivative, accidental unity. He then argues that it must derive ultimately from a being who is essentially one and the only being who is essentially one. This is the True One who bestows accidental unities on things. The giver of this unity is the giver of existence.

In this and other treatises, al-Kindī also makes statements about prophecy and the nature of revelation. These are not detailed statements, but the ones concerning prophecy are suggestive of the kind of developed theories we encounter later on in the thought of al-Fārābī and Ibn Sīnā (Avicenna). Thus, anticipating Ibn Sīnā, al-Kindī argues that prophetic knowledge is received "instantaneously," requiring neither intellectual exertion on the part of the prophet nor the disciplines of mathematics and logic. In conformity with generally accepted Islamic belief, al-Kindī maintains that the inimitability of the Qur'ān lies in the excellence of its literary expression, in the way it conveys divine truths directly and succinctly.

Although al-Kindī had followers, notably al-Sarakhsī (d. 899), properly speaking it cannot be said that he founded a school of philosophical thought. The same is true of the major *faylasūf* to succeed him, al-Rāzī. Abū Bakr Zakarīyā' al-Rāzī (Rhazes), one of the foremost physicians of medieval times, was born in 865 in the Persian town of Rayy, and he practiced medicine there as well as in Baghdad. Very few of his philosophical works have survived, and consequently, much of his philosophical thought has to be reconstructed from medieval Islamic accounts that are, for the most part, highly critical of his ideas.

In his cosmogony, al-Rāzī was greatly influenced by Plato's *Timaeus.* The world, he holds, was created at a finite moment in time, but not out of nothing. As with Plato, creation for al-Rāzī means the imposing of order on disorder. He subscribes to the doctrine of the five eternal principles: atomic matter, space, time, the world soul, and the Creator. The atoms, flitting about in disorder, are given order by God at a moment in time. The now-organized atoms allow the world soul to join matter and to become individuated by it, forming individual living beings. Just as this ordering of the atoms, that is, creation, came about at a finite moment of time in the past, the order will cease at a finite moment of time in the future when the five eternal principles revert to their original state. Al-Rāzī offers discussions of atomic matter, absolute space, and absolute time that are scientific in spirit and approach. But when it comes to explaining ultimates, namely, the reason for the world's creation, he resorts to myth, and his philosophy is noted for its myth of creation.

For al-Rāzī, creation poses two related questions: Why is it that the world was created at one particular moment of time and not at any other, and why was the world created at all? In answering the first, al-Rāzī holds that it is precisely because all the moments of time are similar that God's choice of one moment rather than another was utterly free. If the moments of time were not similar, then his choice of one moment rather than another would have been determined by "a giver of preponderance" (*murajjiḥ*) outside him. Hence it is because the Creator's will is utterly free that he arbitrarily chooses one moment for his creation to take place. It is in his answer to the second question that al-Rāzī gives us his famous myth.

The world soul became infatuated with matter and sought union with it. To achieve this union, the soul endeavored to give disorganized matter form. Matter, however, resisted this forming activity of the soul, leaving the latter in sorrow. God, being powerful and compassionate, then intervened to help the soul and introduced form, order to the material atoms; in other words, he created the world. In creating man, God endowed him with reason, an emanation of his very essence, so that the soul would awake from its bodily slumber and seek a return to its original eternal existence. This, for al-Rāzī, is salvation. At some finite moment in the future, all men's souls, awakened by philosophy, will shun the body. The individual souls then will reunite with the eternal world soul, and the atoms will resume their chaotic state for eternity.

Salvation, as defined by al-Rāzī, is possible only through philosophy. He thus maintains that there is no need for prophets. All men are capable of pursuing truth through reason. The fact that many do not pursue this rational course is not due to inability, but to willful choice. He further argues that it would also be unjust for the Creator to favor either one individual or one nation with prophethood. The mistaken belief that God has favored individuals and nations with prophets has caused nothing but strife, so that, al-Rāzī maintains, for the most part wars are caused by religion. If we add to this that al-Rāzī also subscribed to a theory of the transmigration of souls, one can see why his ideas did not find favor within Islam. Nonetheless, he helped the fermentation of philosophical ideas, and the responses to his philosophy constitute a body of intense argument, philosophical and theological.

Apart from the intrinsic interest of their philosophies, both al-Kindī and al-Rāzī showed in their respective ways how philosophizing is possible within medieval Islam, and thus they prepared the ground for the flowering of *falsafah* in medieval Islam.

Al-Fārābī and Ibn Sīnā. In the tenth and early eleventh centuries, Islamic philosophical thought was dominated by two intellectual giants, al-Fārābī (d. 950) and Ibn Sīnā (d. 1037). Their philosophies have much in common, but remain quite distinct. Al-Fārābī, born shortly after 870 in Transoxania, studied and taught in

Baghdad until 942. He studied logic with the Nestorian logician Yūḥannā ibn Ḥaylān (d. 910) and was associated with Abū Bishr Mattā ibn Yūnus, who was another renowned Nestorian logician. He also studied Arabic grammar with Ibn al-Sarrāj (d. 929), a leading grammarian of the period. In 942, for reasons not fully known, he left Baghdad for Syria, and he seems to have lived the remaining years of his life in relative seclusion in Damascus, where he died.

The foremost logician of his time, al-Fārābī wrote commentaries on Aristotle's *Organon* and on other works of Aristotle and other Greek writers. He was medieval Islam's greatest musical theorist and musicologist and is reputed to have been a skilled instrumentalist. He developed a Neoplatonic emanative scheme that greatly influenced the development of emanative systems by his Islamic successors. But perhaps above all else, he was the founder of a Platonic theory of the state that was adopted (with variations) by the major *falāsifah* who succeeded him. It should be noted, however, that his philosophical writings pose problems of dating and raise the question of whether they always reflect his real views.

For al-Fārābī, the world is an eternal emanation from God, forming a hierarchically ordered series of existents with the closest to him being the highest in rank. This highest existent is a first intelligence, overflowing directly from God. From it the emanative process continues in the form of dyads: the intelligence undergoes two acts of cognition, an act of knowing God and an act of self-knowledge, from which in turn proceed two existents, a second intelligence and a body—the outermost body of the universe. The second intelligence undergoes a similar act of knowing God and knowing itself, resulting in the emanation of a third intelligence and the sphere of the fixed stars. Successive intelligences repeat this cognitive process, causing the existence of the spheres of the planets, the sun, the moon, and finally, from the last of the intelligences, the Active Intellect, which is our world, the world of generation and corruption.

This entire cosmic order is rational and harmonious, with each sphere governed by an intelligence. Man in the world of generation and corruption, endowed with reason and free will, must actualize his potentialities and attain the highest good, happiness. This is achieved when in his way of life he emulates the rational cosmic order, but he can only do this in the society of others. Hence he must strive to form a society that is itself in tune with the rational cosmic order, a hierarchical society ruled by reason, where the various ranks actualize their potentialities in harmony.

In order to achieve this ideal political order, which al-Fārābī refers to as "virtuous," its first ruler must be both a philosopher and a prophet, an individual who receives the revealed law. Since this law is received from the Active Intellect in the form of images that symbolize universal philosophical knowledge or represent particular examples of it, revelation is the "imitation" of philosophy, a copy of it in images and symbols that the nonphilosopher can understand. Revelation and philosophy are thus in total harmony. Another necessary condition for achieving a virtuous political regime, however, is that the philosopher-ruler must be endowed with exceptional practical powers, for he must persuade, lead, and educate a majority of citizens incapable of philosophical understanding. In fact, he must not address the nonphilosophical majority in philosophical language.

Al-Fārābī's political philosophy is comprehensive, detailed, and subtle. It includes, for example, detailed discussion of the existence of nonvirtuous states, the majority of which he characterizes as "ignorant" because they are led by men who are ignorant of the true nature of happiness. While his view is certainly Platonic in its essentials, we meet in al-Fārābī a tendency toward universalism that is less perceptible in Plato. Thus al-Fārābī does not speak only of the virtuous "city" but also of a desirable nation consisting of virtuous "cities" and of a desirable world consisting of virtuous "nations." He also maintains that inasmuch as people in different parts of the world differ in language and in their symbols, it is quite possible that the differences among religions are merely differences in symbols, not in what is being symbolized.

It was on the foundations laid by al-Fārābī in logic, metaphysics, and political theory that his successor, the renowned Ibn Sīnā, built his imposing philosophical system. Born in 980 near Bukhara and largely self-taught, Ibn Sīnā was one of medieval Islam's leading physicians, an astronomer, and a scientist. He held positions as court physician, sometimes as vizier as well, in various Persian principalities until his death in 1037.

Of his numerous writings, mostly in Arabic, but some in Persian, two in particular were very influential in Europe, namely, the encyclopedic *Al-qānūn fī al-ṭibb* (Canon of Medicine) and his major philosophical work, the voluminous *Al-shifā'* (Healing). His writings include short mystical narratives and treatises where the language of symbolism is used. This mysticism, encountered in his writings, is not inconsistent with his "rationalism." The mystic's journey to God is the journey of the rational soul to the ultimate source of all reason. God, for Ibn Sīnā, is pure mind (*'aql maḥḍ*).

Ibn Sīnā's philosophical system is "rationalist." He maintains that in addition to the self-evident first principles of logic, not dependent on our sense perception of the external world, there are self-evident intuitive concepts, also not dependent on sense experience. These intuitive concepts include the "existent," the "thing," and the "necessary," the last with its correlates, the "possible" and the "impossible." A rational consideration of these concepts is sufficient to yield a demonstration of God's existence. In itself, an "existent" is either necessary or only possible. If it is necessary in itself, Ibn Sīnā then tries to show, it must be the only such existent, devoid of multiplicity and uncaused. If it is only possible in itself, he then argues, it must be necessitated by another existent, the latter by yet another, and so on, forming a chain that must be finite, having as its beginning the existent necessary in itself. Hence each alternative affirms the existent necessary in itself, which is God.

But what does it mean to say that every existent other than God is in itself only possible? This brings us to the distinction on which Ibn Sīnā's philosophy rests, the distinction between the quiddity or essence of the possible and its existence. From what a thing is, we cannot infer that it exists, because existence is not included in the definition of the possible existent. The quiddity considered in itself excludes not only existence, but unity and plurality, particularity and universality. From this concept of the quiddity considered in itself, Ibn Sīnā develops a theory of universals (where universality is something added to the quiddity as such) that is of intrinsic philosophical interest and one that had great influence on medieval Latin thought.

Although the existent, other than God, is in itself only possible, it is necessitated by another. Ibn Sīnā uses this concept of the possible in itself but necessary through another to transform al-Fārābī's dyadic emanative scheme into a triadic system. God, the existent necessary in himself, undergoes an eternal act of self-knowledge that necessitates the existence of a first intelligence, an existent in itself only possible, but necessary through another. This intelligence then undergoes three acts of cognition: knowledge of God, knowledge of itself as a necessitated being, and knowledge of itself as a possible being. These three acts produce three other existents respectively: another intelligence, a soul, and a body, the outermost body of the universe. This process is repeated by each successive intellect, giving existence to the various heavenly spheres, each with its soul and intelligence, until from the last of the celestial intelligences, the Active Intellect, the world of generation and corruption emanates.

The human rational soul, an emanation from the Active Intellect, is immaterial, becomes individuated when it joins the body, and retains its individuality as an immortal soul when it separates from the body after death. Good souls, untarnished by having succumbed in their earthly existence to animal passions, live an eternal life of bliss contemplating the celestial intelligences and God; bad souls live an eternal life of misery, being deprived from such contemplation yet forever seeking it. All theoretical knowledge is received from the Active Intellect. This knowledge consists of primary intelligibles, which are the self-evident logical truths and primitive concepts received by all people without the need of experience and learning. It also consists of the secondary intelligibles (received only by those capable of abstract thought), namely, deductions from the primary intelligible as well as more complex concepts. Normally the reception of these intelligibles from the Active Intellect requires preparatory activities of the soul such as sensation, memory, imagination, and cogitation and the learning processes associated with them. Only the prophets do not require these preparatory activities of the soul; they receive all or most of the secondary intelligibles directly and instantaneously, and this theoretical knowledge is then translated through the prophet's imaginative faculty into symbols and images that the nonphilosopher can understand. These constitute the revealed word, which is in total harmony with philosophy, and here Ibn Sīnā embraces al-Fārābī's doctrine that religion is the "imitation" of philosophy.

Ibn Sīnā thus believes in the oneness of God, the prophethood of Muḥammad, and the individual immortality of the soul. His philosophical interpretations of these beliefs, however, were found unacceptable by his chief critic, al-Ghazālī.

Al-Ghazālī's Critique of the Falāsifah. *Falsafah*, as represented by al-Fārābī and Ibn Sīnā, received its most severe rational criticism at the hands of Islam's great religious thinker, the lawyer, Ashʿarī theologian, and mystic Abū Ḥāmid al-Ghazālī (d. 1111). Tension between *kalām* and *falsafah* had existed prior to al-Ghazālī's critique of the *falāsifah*, although it was expressed in reciprocal, but on the whole, muted criticism. Underlying this tension were differences in starting point and ethos, which crystallized in irreconcilable metaphysical outlooks.

Kalām in its Ashʿarī form was atomic in its theory of matter and occasionalist in its interpretation of causal sequences. Accordingly, the temporal and transient conglomerates of atoms forming the physical world were not seen to interact causally with each other in reality. Causal efficacy resided with God; what appear to us as natural causes and effects are in reality concomitant events created directly by God. The uniform order of nature has no intrinsic necessity but is arbitrarily decreed by the divine will; the divine act is not the outcome of any necessity within the divine nature. Causal action proceeds only from a living, willing, powerful agent, not as the necessary consequence of an existent's nature or essence. By contrast, al-Fārābī and Ibn Sīnā embraced the Aristotelian theory of matter as potentially infinitely divisible. Moreover, Ibn Sīnā maintains quite explicitly that the world proceeds from God as the necessitated effect of God, the supreme cause of all other existents, and this doctrine seems implicit in al-Fārābī's emanative scheme as well. God, in his essence an eternally active, changeless cause, necessarily produces an eternal effect—the world.

It is the conflict between these two worldviews that al-Ghazālī makes explicit in his attack on philosophy. Between 1091 and 1095, while teaching Islamic law in Baghdad, he made a systematic study of *falsafah*, particularly that of Ibn Sīnā. It should be emphasized that al-Ghazālī was greatly impressed by Ibn Sīnā's logic and wrote a number of works explaining this logic to his fellow theologians and lawyers, urging them to adopt it. He considered this discipline doctrinally neutral, a mere tool of knowledge, nothing more, a view that he expresses in one of the four introductions to his incisive critique of al-Fārābī and Ibn Sīnā, *Tahāfut al-falāsifah* (The Incoherence of the Philosophers). In these introductions he asserts that his concern is only with those philosophical theories that contravene religious principle and that he will show how, contrary to their own claims, the *falāsifah* have failed to demonstrate such theories. Moreover, he states that in this work he will not adopt any particular doctrinal position, his task being only to refute, and it is true that in the *Tahāfut*, for the sake of arguing against the *falāsifah*, al-Ghazālī sometimes adopts non-Ashʿarī views. It can be shown, however, that for the most part the premises underlying his attack on *falsafah* remain Ashʿarī.

Al-Ghazālī directs logical arguments against twenty philosophical theories, seventeen of which he regards as heretical innovations and three as utter Islamic unbelief. His method is to present the opponents' position clearly, object to it, raise possible objections to his objection, answer these, and so on, until he is satisfied that the theory in question has been refuted. Thus, before condemning these theories, he strives to show on rational grounds either that they have been unproven or that they are outright inconsistent. The three theories he condemns as utterly irreligious are those of the world's pre-eternity, Ibn Sīnā's theory that God knows the particulars in the world of generation and corruption only in a universal way (which means that he does not know every individual in the terrestrial world), and the doctrine of the soul's individual immortality, which denies bodily resurrection.

The most detailed of his discussions is the first, in which he attacks the theory of the world's pre-eternity. The main thrust of his attack is that such a theory is based on the unproven premise that God's acts proceed by necessity, a premise that, in effect, denies the divine attribute of will. Further, Ibn Sīnā's theory that God knows terrestrial individuals only in a universal way is unproven and contrary to the Qur'anic pronouncements that God knows all things. The denial of bodily resurrection is also a denial of divine power, al-Ghazālī argues; bodily resurrection is not logically impossible, and what is logically possible is within God's power.

In the Seventeenth Discussion of the *Tahāfut*, al-Ghazālī argues for the possibility of certain kinds of miracles that are rejected as impossible by the *falāsifah*, who base their rejection on a theory of natural, necessary causal connection. Al-Ghazālī first tries to show that this theory is provable neither logically nor empirically—observation shows only concomitance, not necessary causal connection. In this he voices the Ashʿarī position that all change is caused directly by God and then suggests another possible causal theory, modifying the philosophers' theory to allow the possibility of the miracles the philosophers reject. In the *Tahāfut*, he declares that both these theories are possible, but in his *Iqtiṣād fī al-iʿtiqād* (Moderation in Belief), the theological work that complements the *Tahāfut*, he reaffirms the Ashʿarī occasionalist position as the only true one.

Al-Ghazālī's attack on *falsafah* put it on the defensive, more so than it had hitherto been. At the same time, his attack made *falsafah* better known, since in order to refute the *falāsifah*, al-Ghazālī had to explain them to the nonphilosophers. In the same way, he legitimized and popularized the study of Ibn Sīnā's logic, and this had the effect of making Greek modes of thinking accessible to the more traditional Muslims. Finally, his criticism evoked replies, the most important of which came from Islamic Spain.

Falsafah in Islamic Spain. In the intellectual history of Islamic Spain, or al-Andalus, as the Arabs called it, *falsafah* was a latecomer. A lone Andalusian *faylasūf*, Ibn Masarrah (d. 931), appeared relatively early, but he was a shadowy figure who made no real philosophical impact. The first major Andalusian *faylasūf* was Ibn Bājjah (Avempace, d. 1138), and he was followed by two major thinkers, Ibn Ṭufayl (d. 1185) and Ibn Rushd (Averroës) (d. 1198), the greatest of the Andalusian *falāsifah*. The late flowering of *falsafah* in Spain was partly due to its geographic remoteness from the centers where the translation movement took place. Scientific and philosophical ideas, however, did travel from the Islamic East to Spain, stimulating a very significant scientific and philosophical movement.

A number of Ibn Bājjah's philosophical treatises have survived, including his *Tadbīr al-mutawaḥḥid* (Governance of the Solitary), a major work in the tradition of al-Fārābī's metaphysical and political thought. It expands on a theme that appears in al-Fārābī almost in passing, namely that of the philosopher in a corrupt political state. Al-Fārābī had stated that such a philosopher should immigrate to a virtuous city, but that if no such city existed at the time, the philosopher would be "a stranger in the world, live poorly in it, death for him being better than life" (al-Fārābī, *Fuṣūl muntazaʿah,* ed. F. M. Najjār, Beirut, 1971, p. 95). Ibn Bājjah, however, argues that if no virtuous city exists at the time, the philosopher must isolate himself from society, associating with others only to ensure survival, and must devote himself to his inner intellectual and moral growth. Ibn Bājjah discusses psychology, epistemology, ethics, and metaphysics as he outlines the path the solitary philosopher must pursue to attain the highest good, the state of union with the Active Intellect. The philosopher's isolation, Ibn Bājjah admits, is "essentially" an evil, since man by nature is a social or political animal. Under the circumstances of the philosopher's having to live in a corrupt political regime, however, his isolation becomes "accidentally" a good.

Most of the writings of Ibn Bājjah's successor, Ibn Ṭufayl, physician, astronomer, and administrator at the court of the Almohad (al-Muwaḥḥid) dynasty then ruling al-Andalus, are lost. The notable exception is his masterly philosophical story, *Ḥayy ibn Yaqẓān,* written as an answer to a friend (real or fictitious) who asks Ibn Ṭufayl to divulge to him the secrets of Ibn Sīnā's mystical philosophy. In the introduction, which includes criticisms of al-Fārābī, al-Ghazālī, and Ibn Bājjah, Ibn Ṭufayl answers, in effect, that since the mystical experience is ineffable, he can only suggest to his friend the sort of thing its pursuit involves by narrating the story of Ḥayy.

Ḥayy ibn Yaqẓān (literally, "the living, son of the awake") is the name of the story's hero. In a lush equatorial island, uninhabited by humans, a baby boy, Ḥayy, comes on the scene. (The author gives two possible explanations for his being there.) A deer that had lost its young discovers the infant, suckles him, and rears him. Ḥayy then undergoes a process of self-education, learning how to clothe himself and fend for himself, but he continues to live with his mother, the deer. She eventually dies, and in his anguish, Ḥayy tries to bring her back to life by dissecting her, only to realize then that his real mother was spirit, not the material body that died. At this point his education takes a reflective turn: through observation and rational thought, he discovers that every event must have a cause, that an actual infinity of causes is impossible, and hence that there must be one cause of all existents, which is God. He now seeks knowledge of God, and through contemplation, asceticism, and spiritual exercises he achieves his goal: direct experiences of the divine and of the emanative chain of being descending from him. Meanwhile, on a nearby island, a community ruled by the revealed law, which is a replica of philosophical truth, there are two brothers named Salāmān and Absāl (or Āsāl) who have different attitudes toward scriptural language. Salāmān and the rest of the community accept it literally, being incapable of comprehending its inner meaning. Absāl, on the other hand, pursues its inner meaning. Finding no one on the island who understands his quest, he seeks seclusion on a deserted island, which turns out to be Ḥayy's abode. The two meet. Absāl teaches Ḥayy language and discovers that Ḥayy is an unusual philosophical mystic who, unaided, has attained the highest truth, of which Absāl's own religion gives symbolic expression. For his part, Ḥayy recognizes Absāl's religion to be true and believes in its prophet. Both return to Absāl's island, where Ḥayy endeavors to teach some of its religious citizens the inner meaning of their religion. In this he fails because they are incapable of understanding him. He then adjures them to forget everything he has told them and to continue to take their religion literally. He and Absāl leave for their deserted island to live their mystical existence to the end of their days.

This story, amenable to a variety of interpretations, gives dramatic illustration of two of al-Fārābī's principles: that religion is the "imitation" of philosophy, and that the nonphilosopher ought not be addressed in philosophical language.

It was Ibn Ṭufayl who introduced Ibn Rushd to the Almohad court. Born in 1126 in Cordova, Ibn Rushd was the son and grandson of noted Islamic judges. Trained in medicine, philosophy, and Islamic law, this most Aristotelian of the *falāsifah* was a noted Islamic lawyer and, according to medieval accounts, an authority on Arabic poetry. In 1169 he was appointed judge in Seville and in 1171, chief judge of Cordova. He then became attached to the Almohad court, serving its philosophical ruler Abū Yaʿqūb until the latter's death in 1184, and then his son, al-Manṣūr, for another ten years. Largely because of the opposition of conservative religious scholars, as it seems, al-Manṣūr exiled Ibn Rushd in 1194 but reinstated him soon afterward. The philosopher died in the service of this monarch in 1198.

Ibn Rushd is noted in the history of philosophy for his substantial body of commentaries, largely on Aristotle but also on other thinkers. These commentaries had great impact on medieval Latin philosophy as well as the philosophy of the Italian Renaissance. Although Ibn Rushd never set out to formulate a philosophical system of his own, from his commentaries, and perhaps more so from his philosophical reply to al-Ghazālī's criticism of *falsafah,* an Aristotelian philosophical view emerges, informed by Ibn Rushd's individual insights and stamped by his personality. The view is powerful and compelling.

Al-Ghazālī's attack on *falsafah* in his *Tahāfut,* although logically incisive, was theologically motivated. Moreover, his condemnation of al-Fārābī and Ibn Sīnā as "infidels" was a pronouncement in terms of Islamic law. Thus Ibn Rushd's reply to al-Ghazālī encompasses the legal, the theological, and the philosophical. The legal and theological replies are embodied in two main works that are relatively short, namely, the *Fasl al-maqāl* (Decisive Treatise) and the *Kashf ʿan manāhij al-adillah* (Expositions of the Methods of Proof); the philosophical reply to al-Ghazālī's *Tahāfut* is the *Tahāfut al-Tahāfut* (Incoherence of *The Incoherence*), a much larger book.

In the *Faṣl,* Ibn Rushd raises the general question of whether Islamic law commands, allows, or prohibits the study of philosophy. He answers that the law commands its study but that this command is incumbent only on the one class of scholars, the demonstrative class (i.e. scholars who understand and use Aristotle's demonstrative method in acquiring knowledge), capable of understanding philosophy; nonphilosophers must not pursue it. Ibn Rushd's position is essentially that of al-Fārābī, but it is now couched in Islamic legal language. The *Faṣl* also includes a theory of scriptural interpretation and a defense of the *falāsifah*'s three doctrines against al-Ghazālī's charge that they were irreligious. The *Kashf* complements the *Faṣl* but offers more specific criticisms of Ashʿarī theological principles.

In the *Tahāfut al-Tahāfut,* Ibn Rushd quotes almost all of al-Ghazālī's *Tahāfut,* commenting on it paragraph by paragraph. Although his main criticisms are directed against al-Ghazālī, at times he criticizes Ibn Sīnā, particularly for his Neoplatonism. Ibn Rushd's *Tahāfut* is a sober work of criticism that tracks down ambiguities, draws distinctions, reformulates positions, corrects misunderstandings, and offers analyses. It reasserts and defends an Aristotelian causal view, arguing incessantly against the Ashʿarī conception of divine causality and against their denial of natural causes.

Ibn Rushd's writings on the hereafter, however, pose the question of what he actually believes on this matter. His "technical" discussions of the question of the soul's immortality—whether in his commentaries on Aristotle or in those parts of the *Tahāfut* where he is highly critical of Ibn Sīnā's doctrine of the soul's individual immortality—leave no room for a theory of the soul's individual immortality, to say nothing of a doctrine of bodily resurrection. In the *Kashf,* however, he affirms a doctrine of individual immortality, whether this is confined to the soul or involves bodily resurrection. Again, at the end of the *Tahāfut* (where the discussion is not technical) he seems to affirm a doctrine of bodily resurrection. The indications are that in these conflicting statements he is practicing what he preaches as a follower of al-Fārābī's political thinking. In other words, he is addressing the philosophers philosophically and the nonphilosophers in language they can understand. He also seems to be protecting himself against charges of unbelief.

Falsafah did not end with Ibn Rushd. But the period from al-Kindī to Ibn Rushd witnessed some of its greatest practitioners and established a rich philosophical tradition on which later Islamic thinkers, men of originality and genius, were to build and enrich *falsafah* even more. The majority of these thinkers came from Persia and were in a real sense the spiritual descendants of Ibn Sīnā. But some came from other parts of the Islamic world—Spain and North Africa, for example.

Persia became noted for its mystical philosophy of illumination, *al-ishrāq.* The founder of this tradition was al-Suhrawardī (d. 1191), a contemporary of Ibn Rushd. The basic idea of his philosophy is that reality consists of light of varying degrees of intensity. Light, which for al-Suhrawardī is neither material nor definable, proceeds from the Light of lights *(nūr al-anwār),* God. Its emanation and diffusion at various levels constitute the created world. In this metaphysics of light and illumination, he harks back to the old religions of Persia. He is also noted for criticizing the Aristotelians for their rejection of the Platonic doctrine of eternal forms. From the thirteenth century onward, al-Suhrawardī was succeeded by a series of Persian philosophers who either adopted his doctrine of *al-ishrāq* or, like the philosopher-scientist Nāṣir al-Dīn al-Ṭūsī (d. 1274), were greatly influenced by it. Those who adopted it included such leading thinkers as Mīr Dāmād (d. 1631), Mullā Ṣadrā (d. 1640), and the latter's commentator, Sabzawārī (d. 1866), to name but a few.

Of al-Suhrawardī's successors, Mullā Ṣadrā is generally recognized as the most important and most original. Although he adopted al-Suhrawardī's metaphysics of illumination, he disagreed with him on a basic idea concerning the relation of essence to existence. Al-Suhrawardī had argued for the priority of essence over existence. Mullā Ṣadrā maintained the reverse, arguing for the priority and "primacy of existence" *(aṣālat al-wujūd).* By "existence," he meant real existence as distinct from the static concept of existence in the mind.

Real existence is grasped intuitively, the act of intuiting it being itself part of the flow of existence. The key idea governing his whole philosophy is that of existence as a dynamic process. This manifests itself in his theories of motion and time. Motion is not simply the rotation of forms over a static substratum, but is inherent in the substratum itself. Similarly, time is not merely the measure of motion: physical body has an inherent time dimension. There is an ever upward moving process of existence (to us imperceptible) that is irreversible, a manifestation of God's ceaseless creative impulse.

In Western Islam, philosophical mystical thought attained its heights with two thirteenth-century thinkers, both from Murcia, Spain. The first was the great philosophical mystic Ibn al-ʿArabī (d. 1240), noted for his doctrine of the unity of being *(waḥdat al-wujūd)*, which exerted a very great influence on Persian mystical thought. The second was Ibn Sabʿīn (d. 1270), a mystic-philosopher who expounded a doctrine of the unity of being in terms of Aristotle's concept of form. A much more empirical approach is encountered in the thought of the Tunisian-born historian-philosopher Ibn Khaldūn, one of Islam's most original minds. He served various Islamic rulers as ambassador, envoy, and chief judge. Combining a thorough legal, theological, and philosophical education with first-hand experience in politics, he utilized this background to write his universal history, best noted for its *muqaddimah* ("prolegomena"). It is in this *muqaddimah* that he sets forth his conception of history as a science concerned with the causal explanation for the rise, decline, and fall of civilizations and that he probed the rise and development of social institutions. In doing this, he gave us, in effect, a philosophy of history.

Both Ibn Khaldūn and Mullā Ṣadrā in their very different ways are examples of philosophers who broadened the dimensions of *falsafah*. They certainly made advances over the thought of their predecessors. But these were advances within a rich philosophical tradition whose first foundation stone was laid in the ninth century by al-Kindī.

[*See also* Isrāqīyah; Kalām; *and biographies of the principal figures mentioned herein.*]

BIBLIOGRAPHY

General Histories

Corbin, Henry. *Histoire de la philosophie islamique.* Paris, 1964.

Fakhry, Majid. *A History of Islamic Philosophy.* Rev. ed. New York, 1983.

Sharif, M. M., ed. *A History of Muslim Philosophy,* vol. 1. Wiesbaden, 1963.

Collections of Studies

Anawati, Georges C. *Études de philosophie musulmane.* Paris, 1974.

Hourani, G. F., ed. *Essays on Islamic Philosophy and Science.* Albany, N.Y., 1975.

Marmura, M. E., ed. *Islamic Theology and Philosophy: Studies in Honor of G. F. Hourani.* Albany, N.Y., 1984.

Morewedge, Parvis, ed. *Islamic Philosophical Theology.* Albany, N.Y., 1979.

Morewedge, Parvis, ed. *Islamic Philosophy and Mysticism.* Delmar, N.Y., 1981.

Stern, S. M., Albert Hourani, and Vivian Brown, eds. *Islamic Philosophy and the Classical Tradition.* Columbia, S.C., 1972.

Walzer, Richard. *Greek into Arabic: Essays on Islamic Philosophy.* Cambridge, Mass., 1962.

Translations

Fārābī, al-. *Alfarabi's Philosophy of Plato and Aristotle.* Translated by Muhsin Mahdi. New York, 1962.

Fārābī, al-. *Al-Farabi's Commentary and Short Treatise on Aristotle's De Interpretatione.* Translated by F. W. Zimmerman. London, 1981.

Hyman, Alfred, and James J. Walsh, eds. *Philosophy in the Middle Ages: The Christian, Islamic and Jewish Traditions.* New York, 1967. Includes translations of al-Fārābī, Avicenna, al-Ghazālī, and Averroës (pp. 20–235).

Ibn Rushd (Averroës). *Tahāfut al-Tahāfut.* Translated by S. Van Den Bergh as *The Incoherence of the Incoherence.* London, 1953.

Ibn Sīnā (Avicenna). *Avicenna's Philosophy.* Translated by Fazlur Rahman. London, 1952.

Ibn Sīnā. *The Life of Ibn Sīnā.* Edited and translated by William E. Gohlman. New York, 1967.

Kindī, al-. *Al-Kindī's Metaphysics.* Translated by Alfred L. Ivry. New York, 1963.

Lerner, Ralph, and Muhsin Madhi, eds. *Medieval Political Philosophy: A Source Book.* New York, 1963. Includes translations of al-Fārābī, Avicenna, Ibn Bājjah, Ibn Ṭufayl, and Averroës (pp. 21–190)

MICHAEL E. MARMURA

FALSIFICATION. *See* Logical Positivism *and* Doubt and Belief.

FAMILY is vitally important to most religious traditions in two closely interconnected ways: various ritual processes enacted by, to, and for the family help to create and sustain it as well as give it meaning, and it functions as an important symbol of deity. Historically and cross-culturally, family in various forms has (until the late twentieth century in postindustrialized cultures) been so basic to human existence as to be a universal symbol of ultimacy.

Definition. Exactly what constitutes family is not always clear. Some scholars equate family with household, another imprecise construct that variously includes all permanent members such as servants or else excludes unrelated householders. Further confusion results because most anthropologists posit two basic kinds of family: the nuclear family, consisting of mother, father, and unmarried children, and the extended family, typically including mother, father, all unmarried children, and one or more sons with their wives and children. Numerous complicated variations exist, including different polygynous arrangements in which two or more co-wives live under the same roof. A few domestic groupings, such as those of the Nayar of India, whose men never live with their wives, defy all categories. Nonetheless, family, in some variant, is considered universal.

Also confusing is the fact that all married people simultaneously belong to two different families. Family as seat of origination stresses ties of blood, whereas family as affiliation emphasizes bonds of marriage. To keep separate these two different kinds of family, some anthropologists designate the first as "kin" and the second as "family." Kin are those who share common ancestors, as do mother and child (in contrast to mother and father, who do not). Strictly speaking, although family incorporates kin, the reverse is not true since, excepting incestuous marriages, spouses usually are not blood relatives.

Consequently, family is basically a reconciliation of many different opposites: female and male, life and death, ascendants and descendants, kin and affines (relatives by marriage), biology and culture, freedom and servitude, corporation and individuality. The differing ways in which family contains these opposites represent diverse systems of order in which family roles are valued according to accepted local religiocultural belief and custom. Valuation of all members is almost never equal; therefore, family as a whole embodies and symbolizes order of a particular sort—hierarchy.

In its entirety this "natural" order of human relationships, presumed to have evolved out of earlier hominid bands of approximately thirty, has frequently been deified, with members typically reflecting family as experienced in a particular culture. Thus Kwoiam, the warrior hero of Mabuiag, an island off New Guinea, lives with his mother, her brother and sister, and his sister's son in a matrilineal "family" (technically, a kin system) that omits the father. Very different is the Homeric extended patriarchal family of Zeus and Hera, which includes variously begotten offspring. The smaller nuclear family is symbolized in various cultures, as for example the Egyptian Osiris, Isis, and Horus; the holy family of Christianity consisting of Joseph (or God the Father), Mary, and Jesus; and the holy triad of the Yurak Samoyed: Nyebye-haha, the mother deity; Wesako-haha, her spouse; and Nyu-haha, their son. Curious variants appear in the enneads (triple triads) so characteristic of dynastic Egypt.

In its smallest possible configuration (apart from the single individual sometimes defined as family in the postindustrialized West)—as husband and wife—family appears in almost all mythologies. Universally, tales of the *hieros gamos* tell of the sacred marriage of Heaven and Earth from whom humanity springs, as illustrated by the Zuni Awitelintsita, the fourfold-containing Mother Earth, and Apoyan Ta 'Chu, the all-covering Father Sky. Often such etiological stories of how the world came to be tell how one or more of the children produced by the union separate the pair, often forcibly, to form the realms of earth and sky. Such is the case in the Vedic account of Dyaus and Pṛthivī. [*See* Hieros Gamos.]

Ancestors. Probably no members so fully embody both the ritual and the symbolic significance of the traditional extended family as do ancestors. From the Paleolithic period to the present, many cultures have venerated ancestors to varying degrees, although Herbert Spencer's theory that ancestor worship stands behind all religious practice has been generally discarded. For example, almost all Native American tribes believe that spirits of tribal ancestors return to earth to warn, protect, and instruct the living, although only specially trained shamans are capable of seeing them.

Babylonian mythology and artifacts incorporate important motifs of ancestor veneration. The failed attempt of the hero Gilgamesh to escape mortality by visiting his ancestor Sitnapishtim, the Babylonian Noah who did escape it, indicates the salvific role hoped for from ancestors. Between the third millennium BCE or earlier, when sacrifices were offered to the departed kings Shulgi and Gudea, and about 2500 BCE, when Grimalsin of the second dynasty of Ur appears to have been deified while still living, two other important themes emerge: ancestor worship by actual descendants tends to merge with homage paid by a whole people to departed rulers or "fathers." Thus, in many cultures ancestors function variously as objects of domestic and state devotion, a situation that became pronounced in the Roman empire. Attribution of divine ancestry has been common for kings, as notably in post-Meiji Restoration Japan, where the emperor was officially proclaimed a direct descendant of the sun goddess Amaterasu Ōmikami. Such ancestry has even been assigned to whole peoples, as repeatedly shown in epic poetry.

So important are the honored ancestors in cultures such as those in China, Japan after Chinese contact (seventh century CE), and areas of Aryan influence, particularly India and Rome, that the traditional family often seems to exist more for their sake than for that of the living. This point indicates one theme present in the traditional family, its orientation toward death. Furthermore, because typically in these cultures ancestors collectively overpower and stifle the individuality now common in the Western world, ancestor veneration also highlights a second important theme: family as corporate entity strongly opposes the individuality of its members.

Emphasis on ancestors indicates that family is not only the matrix within which an individual enters life but also the means by which he (less commonly she) achieves a kind of immortality. Paradoxically, this denial of death that leads to ancestor veneration makes the family a kind of perpetual cult of the dead enacted by the living. [*See* Ancestors.]

Children. In contrast to dead family members, who are almost universally venerated, children are often treated ambivalently. Though desired in the abstract for perpetuating the family, children may be abused or even denied life, as in the ancient classical world. Hippocrates illustrates this point when he asks, "Which children should be raised?" The essentially universal theme of infanticide is clearly present in the biblical stories of Isaac and Moses, who were saved. To this day the practice continues sporadically for girls in parts of India and China, as historically had been the case almost worldwide.

The countertheme of life orientation surfaces most strongly in connection with those newborns elected to survive. Yet even here the tension of opposites is strained, for only some attain family membership. Commonly thought of as "natural," family construction is actually often highly artificial.

Birth, mating, and death, the three natural methods of creating, maintaining, and pruning families, are simultaneously both biological and socioreligious events. Successful delivery of a live baby does not guarantee the existence of a new family member. In many cultures, once a child is born (notably, in patriarchal Hellenic Greece or even contemporary China or India), the father must determine whether or not to keep it. Then it must be incorporated into the family. The contemporary Islamic Malays illustrate one variant of this once nearly universal practice: first, the father whispers into the infant's ear the Islamic call to prayer; next, a specially selected person touches certain objects to the baby's lips to guard against future lying and gossiping; then, forty-four days later, the father buries the placenta beneath a coconut palm seedling. These and other birth rituals help place the child in its familial and socioreligious context. Thus a new family member is "created" only in the most superficial way by its actual birth. Subsequent actions of family members, often other than the mother, bring the child fully into family life.

As a symbol of deity, the divine child appears in various traditions. [*See* Child.] Archaeological finds such as vase paintings and figurines depicting infancy themes and rituals place this concept at least as far back as the Neolithic and Chalcolithic periods (c. 7000–3500 BCE) in Old Europe (roughly, southeastern Europe from Czechoslovakia to the Aegean). Motifs of birth and maturing of the infant later took shape mythically and cultically in many variations that recount the passion of the young god of vegetation. Representative is the cult of the infant Dionysos, originally Boeotian and Cretan but subsequently almost universal in Greece, in which the infant Dionysos-Zagreus is dismembered. According to myth, the Titans lured the child with rattles, knucklebones, a top, a ball, and a mirror, then cut him to pieces, cooked him, and devoured him. In some versions he is resurrected by the earth mother, Rhea. This death and resurrection theme, common to the complex of images central to agrarian religion, finds in the child (or alternatively in the seed) an appropriate image of renewal.

Worship of the divine child was originally shared by or even predominantly directed to the mother goddess, as in the case of Ishtar, Astarte, and Cybele, whose son-consorts were of secondary importance. With time, however, the child, originally of either sex as suggested by numerous Sumerian female Marduks, ceases to be merely the child or sacrificial consort and becomes more and more an object of veneration in his own right. Christianity epitomizes this process whereby the divine child eclipses his mother.

In a very different form, images of the divine child as divine hero are also common in Native American mythology. This pattern is typified by the Haida story of Shining Heavens. One day a Haida woman was digging on the beach. Hearing a cry from a cockle shell, she uncovered it and found the baby Shining Heavens. She took him home and soon discovered his supernatural power, manifested in his ability to grow up almost immediately. This common motif of the wonder child who grows almost instantly from baby to strong youth or man is also illustrated by the Siouan Young Rabbit and the Algonquian Blood-Clot Boy. Sometimes the child-hero even makes plans in the womb, as do the Iroquoian twins Good Mind and Evil Mind. Such "unnatural" capabilities illustrate the power of godhead to transcend nature.

Such capability is even more apparent in the Vallabha and Caitanya sects of Hinduism, in which worship of the cowherd Kṛṣṇa as the divine child has been popular from at least 900 CE. In the spontaneity of his laughter, pranks, dancing, disobedience, and play, the child Kṛṣṇa symbolizes the unconditional nature of divinity. In such activity, engaged in for no purpose beyond sheer joy, the play of the child metaphorically expresses an aspect of divinity less easily rendered by "adult" personifications.

Mothers. So important is a woman's role as mother in most societies that the biblical Hebrews, for example, insisted that a wife who failed to bear children was obligated to provide her husband with a concubine (*Gn.* 16:2). According to popular Islamic tradition, the main duty of a woman is to obey and serve her husband respectfully; her second duty is to give him male heirs. In traditional China with its strong Confucian ethic, life was meaningless without sons. Without sons, a wife could count on a second wife essentially replacing her.

Theorists assume that the discovery of stockbreeding and planting taught humans about male reproductive capability. That means that for only about twelve thousand of the million years of hominid existence have humans understood paternity and reckoned male as well as female lineage. Thus was the ancient mother-child kin tie challenged by the familial tie. The nineteenth-century belief in mother right, espoused by J. J. Bachofen, Robert Stephen Briffault, Henry Maine, and others, whereby women were thought to have held social and political power during a prepatriarchal era, has long been invalidated; but current scholarship makes indisputable the existence of a practice of prehistoric mother worship in Europe and Asia Minor. [*See* Goddess Worship.]

Material evidence in the form of large numbers of "Venuses," often with exaggerated secondary sex characteristics and pregnant bellies, as exemplified by the well-known Venus of Willendorf, firmly roots the idea of divine motherhood in the Upper Paleolithic period in Eurasia (c. 22,000 BCE). By the time of the Neolithic and Chalcolithic periods (c. 7000–3500 BCE) in Old Europe and the Near East, the Great Mother, with her accumulated Paleolithic traits, is well established in the variant forms that generally characterize her in agricultural societies around the world. (In patrilineal totemic and patriarchal nomadic cultures she figures less prominently, as an adjunct to the dominant sky god.) Under various names she appears almost universally wherever agriculture develops—as Ishtar (Babylon and Assyria); Astarte (Canaan); Isis (Egypt); Cybele (Phrygia); Rhea, Gaia (pre-Hellenic Greece); Pṛthivī (Vedic India); Ti (ancient China); Pachamama (Inca); and so on.

In cultures such as those of Old Europe, pre-Hellenistic Greece, and pre-Vedic India (Harappa, Mohenjo-Daro), which were not dominated by nomadic pastoral peoples, motherhood is typically aligned with a concept seemingly opposed to it—that of virginity. But this belief reflects the archaic notion that birth results from parthenogenesis, an understandable belief for those unaware of the male role. Far from being a moralistic concept, as it subsequently became in patrilineal and patriarchal cultures, it originally reflected an understanding of woman as creator and powerful figure in her own right. [*See* Virgin Goddess.]

Earth and related vegetal phenomena such as grains are not the only natural elements associated with motherhood. Water, the medium from which humans originally emerge onto land, also functions this way, as with the ancient Mexican goddess of the waters, Chalchiuhtlicue, and the water mother common to the ancient Karelians and other Finno-Ugric peoples. Sometimes, as with the Japanese sun goddess Amaterasu, or the pre-Islamic mother of the heavens Allat, or the Egyptian sky goddess Nut, the traditional association of earth with motherhood and of sky with fatherhood are reversed; consequently, the predominant associations do not always hold, as when the concept "down," normally affiliated with earth and motherhood, attaches to a male chthonic deity. The variant son-consorts of the mother goddess, such as Adonis and Tammuz, reflect this phenomenon.

Various interconnected processes particularly affect the ways motherhood is represented in divinity and vice versa. Specialization tends to separate qualities originally mixed together in a single great goddess figure into different embodying images, as exemplified by the goddesses of the Homeric pantheon. Artemis and Aphrodite, for example, both lose their original fullness of personality to become mainly associated with the hunt and with erotic love, respectively. In this way motherhood, especially in Western cultures dominated by monotheism, has typically been strictly separated from all other potential and actual attributes of womanhood. Thus hunting, wisdom, sex, and war, all attributes of the undifferentiated goddess, come to appear totally divorced from each other.

A related process polarizes "good" and "bad" qualities into beneficient and terrible goddesses. Such terrible mothers of death and destruction as the Hindu Kālī, the Aztec Tlamatecuhtli, and the Greek Medusa typify this process. Such splitting dichotomizes the originally unified cycle of birth and death, in which Mother Earth gives birth (often quite literally, as in the Greek story of Erichthonius and in the many Native American myths that portray humanity emerging from the womb of the Earth) and later takes back her dead for burial (as in the Pueblo belief that Shipapu, the underworld, is also the womb of the earth goddess, Natya Ha 'Atse.) With polarization come goddesses of the underearth realm such as the Greek Persephone and the dread Sumero-Akkadian Ereshkigal, who are separate from beneficent counterparts such as Demeter and Ishtar.

In a variant process the single goddess multiplies, usually into a triad, as in the case of the Scandinavian Norns, the Greek Fates, or the strange *matres* and *matrones* figures from the Celtic and Germanic provinces of the Roman empire. Such trinitarian representations often involve different stages of motherhood, as in various ubiquitous virgin-mother-crone triads (the Hindu Pārvatī, Durgā, and Umā and the Celtic Macha, Morríghan, and Badhbh, for example).

Fathers. Next to ancestors and frequently amalgamated with them conceptually, fathers hold the greatest power in traditional patriarchal families, whether or not their fatherhood is biological. This paradox is logical when fatherhood is divided into three categories: the genetic father fertilizes the ovum; the genitor contributes to the child's growth in the womb, as when the Holy Ghost causes Mary to conceive through her ear; and the social father, known as the *pater,* dominates family life. Whether as genetic father, adoptive father, or maternal uncle, the *pater* supplies the child's social position.

In a patrifocal extended family the *pater,* as oldest living father in a direct line of descent, firmly heads the family hierarchy. This pattern was thoroughly worked out in the Roman family, where patriarchal power was so complete that, until he died, the father retained limitless authority over unmarried daughters and grown sons and their children. A married daughter customarily joined the household of her husband and so came under the authority of his father. Such extreme paternal power distinguished the Roman father from fathers in other societies in degree, but not in kind.

In contrast to motherhood, which results from pregnancy and childbirth, fatherhood is not immediately self-evident. Nor can fatherhood be as readily represented in images. Development and evolution of the concept are consequently less certain and less easy to follow. Almost everywhere, the most archaic manifestation of divine fatherhood is the "high god" located in the sky. [*See* Sky.] Typically this "father" is originally a creator whose traits include goodness, age (eternity), and remoteness from the world of human affairs. So transcendent is he that he often abdicates his role of creator, handing it over to a successor-demiurge. Consequently, he is seldom reverenced in cult and may even disappear entirely. [*See* Deus Otiosus.] Representative examples are the Australian All-Father deities Baiame, worshiped by the Kamilaroi, and Bunjil (of the Kulin tribes); the Andamanese Puluga; numerous African father gods such as Nzambi of the Bantu-speaking peoples and Nyan Kupon of the Tshis. Existence of a sky god of this sort is evident from Neolithic times on and may well go back to Paleolithic times, but hard material evidence to prove it is currently insufficient. Aside from images suggesting the bull-roarers universally associated with father gods, no images comparable to the Paleolithic Venuses have been discovered.

The fatherhood of such archaic deities is often less specifically biological than creative, as reflected by the terms *Bawai* and *Apap,* applied respectively by the African Chawai and Teso, which convey the fatherhood of God relative to creation. In this sense the supreme being is a "father" whether or not he creates in the well-known *hieros gamos* of Mother Earth and Father Sky or through powers entirely his, as Baiami does. [*See* Supreme Beings.]

By contrast, in many less archaic mythological and ritualized conceptions, divine fatherhood is unmistakably biological. Here the archaic mating of Mother Earth and Father Sky, originally an abstract description of creation, becomes far more concrete. The sovereign father is typically eclipsed by his son, as is the Greek Ouranos by Kronos, the Australian Baiami by Grogoragally, the Tiv Awondo by the Sun. Thus, one theme typically connected to divine fatherhood in most mythologies is the generational conflict of fathers and sons. As the archaic father god recedes, the son who replaces him, even as he himself achieves fatherhood, seldom attains the stature of his own progenitor. This is indicated by his characteristic shift from sky god variously to solar or weather god (as when the weather god Zeus replaces Kronos) or agricultural deity (as when the Babylonian Marduk, both a solar and a vegetation deity, eventually supplants the Sumerian great triad of sky gods Anu, Enlil, and Ea), all of which lack the majestic connotations universally ascribed to the sky.

Particularly in the Chalcolithic cultures of the Near East (e.g., Sumer, Babylonia), where worship of the Paleolithic goddess developed strongly into the historic period, this shift is apparent. Here earth as mother, rather than sky as father, typically symbolizes the supreme being, rendering fatherhood a less exalted concept. The god is father solely as fecundator, being more often lover than spouse. Such vegetation gods as Adonis, Tammuz, and their myriad counterparts function this way.

In marked contrast to this biological, often chthonic, fatherhood is the refinement of sky-oriented fatherhood apparent in the monotheistic religions—Judaism, Christianity, and Islam—and in dualistic Zoroastrianism, all of which developed out of patriarchal nomadic herding societies that retained more of the archaic religion than did their matrilineal agricultural counterparts. The biblical Yahveh, for example, is thought to have emerged from the celestial West Semitic deity known as Ya, Yami, or Yahu.

One of the attributes frequently credited to father-gods in almost all patriarchal cultures is that of giving birth: the biblical God creates life without aid from a female deity; Zeus produces Athena from his brow and gestates Dionysos in his thigh; the Scandinavian giant Ymir and the Aboriginal Australian Great Father, Kakora, both give birth from their armpits; and the Egyptian Khepri variously spits and masturbates to produce Shu and Tefnut, respectively.

In ritual, too, fathers often mimic the maternal role. Particularly among various Australian Aboriginal groups, initiation rites for boys, frequently reveal the fathers of a tribe functioning as male mothers, as they ritually mimic menstruation and "giving birth" to the young male initiates. Such sexual crossing over introduces into the concept of fatherhood several conflicting themes. Variously, fatherhood is as self-contained as motherhood in its parthenogenetic form; or it projects a "maternal" nurturing quality far different from the remoteness of the archaic sky god; or sometimes it deemphasizes sexual differentiation by blurring, a theme explicit in fertility figures such as Marduk, whose sex changes. These are just some of the ways in which concepts of fatherhood and divine fathers have developed their complexity worldwide.

Siblings. Symbolically, relationships between siblings are almost as central to religion and mythology as those between parents and children. This is partly because brothers and sisters are frequently also spouses, like Zeus and Hera, especially in creation myths, making the theme of incest a common universal mythologem. Almost universally, cross twins (those of opposite sex) are believed to have been the first humans from whom all others descend.

The first couple of the ancient Egyptian ennead were the twins Shu and Tefnut; the second were the brother and sister Geb and Nut, the father and mother of the Osirian gods. The Vedic twins Yama and Yami and the Norse Askr and Embla functioned similarly.

Some idea of the possible meanings of sibling "marriage," whether of twins or not, is evident from the Japanese myth of Amaterasu Ōmikami, the Heaven-Illuminating Goddess, and her brother Susano-o no Mikoto, the Valiant-Swift-Impetuous Hero. The rule of the universe was divided between these two: the realm of light, including heaven and earth, was presided over wisely by the sun goddess, while the ocean and the domain of hidden things was ruled widely by her stormy brother. In consequence of her brother's evil behavior, Amaterasu hid in a cave, plunging the entire world into darkness. When she emerged, light triumphed over dark, and her brother was banished to a remote region.

Most variants of this rivalry show the siblings as two brothers, often twins, as in the ancient Persian Zoroastrian myth of the twins Ōhrmazd ("light") and Ahriman ("darkness") or in the Iroquoian myth of Ioskeha, the creator and preserver, and Tawiskara, the deadly winter god. Unlike the Iroquoian pair, however, the Persian dyad, representing the principles of good and evil, respectively, set the stage for a dualistic system of thought in which both principles are equal.

Often sibling rivalry incorporates the theme of fratricide, as in the case of the Egyptian Seth who kills Osiris or the Greek brothers Ismenos and Kaanthos through whom fratricide was first introduced into the world. This common theme dramatizes the invidious distinction most cultures make between elder brothers and all other children. An Australian creation myth about two brothers traveling together at the beginning of time vividly dramatizes this distinction. When the elder brother desires a wife, he operates on his sibling, making him into a woman. The younger brother-turned-wife simply continues in the subordinate position he had occupied all along, making clear the equivalent impotence of younger brothers and wives.

All these sibling tales ring changes on certain important familial themes. Battling twins represent identity altering into difference; fighting sisters and brothers depict familial opposition; cohabiting sisters and brothers embody familial unity; and battling brothers symbolize the struggle between equality and hierarchy, as brotherhood gives way to the rights of the elder brother, the patriarch-to-be. [*See also* Twins.]

Servants. Of all the traditional family members, none so emphasizes the way family functions as both example and symbol of a hierarchical order as does the servant, the hired or enslaved person contributing to family life and economics in both agrarian and commercial settings. Particularly in its most extreme form, as slavery, servitude emphasizes the hierarchical nature of the traditional family. In ancient Hawaiian culture, for instance, one outcast social group, the *kauwa,* were designated to serve the chiefs and touch them directly. They alone were exempt from the *kapu* ("taboo") that prohibited touching the chiefs on pain of death. Yet these *kauwa* were themselves untouchable: it was not proper to eat with them or sleep close to them. At the death of their masters, they were buried alive, often as sacrificial atonement for *kapu* violations committed by others. While extreme, this example, like others involving Indian untouchable servants, American black slaves, and Middle Eastern eunuchs, clearly embodies the themes of scapegoating, sacrifice, and hierarchy common to families in general.

Certain religious traditions overtly take up the themes implicit in servitude, stressing them as positive rather than negative attributes, as in the cases of Hanuman, the perfect Hindu servant, and Christ, understood as fulfilling the promise of the servant poems of "Second Isaiah." Others simply portray servitude as an institution as natural to divinity as to humanity: in Japanese mythology, for example, the fox functions as the messenger of the god of harvests, Inari, much as Hermes serves the Greek Olympians. Among the Haida of the Northwest Coast, Old-Woman-under-the-Fire serves as messenger of the supernaturals, going between this world and that of the spirits. Servitude, exemplifying a humility appropriate to worshipers, characterizes many traditions; thus the Vedic Hindus feel like slaves in the presence of Varuṇa (*Ṛgveda* 1.25.1).

[*For a discussion of the symbolic meaning and orientation of the dwelling place, see* Home; *for discussions of rituals that center in the home, see* Domestic Observances.]

BIBLIOGRAPHY

Besides canonical scriptures, the most useful primary texts for students of the family are the ancient religio-legal codes developed by most literate cultures. Representative is the *Institutes of Hindu Law, or The Ordinances of Menu, according to the Gloss of Culluca; Comprising the Indian System of Duties, Religious and Civil,* translated from the original Sanskrit by William Jones (1794; 2d ed., London, 1876); the ordinances cover a wide range of family-related topics, including divorce, remarriage, status of wives, and the like. An excellent compendium of various issues of concern to contemporary students of family is the Spring 1977 issue of *Daedalus,* which ranges from articles on specific cultures to family policy issues in the United States to the study of the history of the family.

Of the hundreds of recent works on family studies, *Household and Family in Past Time,* edited by Peter Laslett with the assistance of Richard Wall (Cambridge, 1972), is most representative of the controversial demographic approach. In this work Laslett presents his provocative, ground-breaking argument that the nuclear family preceded the industrial revolution and hence was causative rather than resultant. Also representative of the new demographic scholarship on family is Michael Mitterauer and Reinhard Seider's *The European Family: Patriarchy to Partnership from the Middle Ages to the Present* (Chicago, 1977). For those who wish to pursue the historical aspects of family in depth, particularly by looking at small numbers of people in very precisely documented areas, the *Journal of Family History* (Worcester, Mass., 1796–) presents the most recent work.

Among numerous excellent sources of information on the mother goddess, two stand out for their lucidity: E. O. James's *The Cult of the Mother-Goddess: An Archaeological and Documentary Study* (New York, 1959) and Marija Gimbutas's *The Goddesses and Gods of Old Europe, 6500–3500 B.C.: Myths and Cult Images* (Berkeley, 1982). Somewhat more difficult to trace for lack of early material evidence and fewer books devoted exclusively to the subject is the concept of the father god. Helpful sources include E. O. James's *The Worship of the Sky-God: A Comparative Study in Semitic and Indo-European Religion* (London, 1963); Wilhelm Schmidt's *The Origin and Growth of Religion: Facts and Theories* (1931; New York, 1972), considered by many the *locus classicus* for its topic; and Mircea Eliade's *Patterns in Comparative Religion* (New York, 1958), in which see especially chapter 2, "The Sky and Sky Gods," and chapter 3, "The Sun and Sun-Worship." A helpful discussion of Kṛṣṇa as divine child appears in David Kinsley's *The Sword and the Flute: Kali and Kṛṣṇa, Dark Visions of the Terrible and the Sublime in Hindu Mythology* (Berkeley, 1975). Much useful information on siblings appears in Donald J. Ward's *The Divine Twins: An Indo-European Myth in Germanic Tradition* (Berkeley, 1968).

KATHRYN ALLEN RABUZZI

FANG-SHIH.

The *fang-shih* ("masters of esoteric techniques"), also called "magicians" and "immortalists," were important contributors to the development of religious Taoism. They were experimental philosophers and occult technicians who, in the course of their observations of nature and search for physical immortality, created a body of prescientific knowledge that formed the basis of Chinese medicine, pharmacology, chemistry, astrology, divination, and physiological alchemy. A major part of this knowledge was later incorporated into the Taoist religion.

The origin and precise meaning of the term *fang-shih* are far from certain; but by the second century BCE the term was used to refer to a group of practitioners of various esoteric arts who were generally outside the literati mainstream. These practitioners apparently maintained their own texts and lore and transmitted their knowledge from master to disciple, yet they have never been regarded as constituting a distinct philosophical school. While early historians respected the arcane skills of the *fang-shih,* they did not in general hold them in very high regard because these abilities were often used to strive for power both inside and outside the existing political structure. The *fang-shih* were most influential in China during a period of roughly six hundred years beginning in the third century BCE.

While in later times they came from various areas on the periphery of the empire, the *fang-shih* were first associated with the coastal states of Ch'i and Yen (now Shantung), and it is here in about 330 BCE that we hear of them encouraging local rulers to set out to sea in search of the holy immortals *(hsien)* who possessed the potions of immortality. Though their exact relationship to the Naturalist school first systematized by Tsou Yen (340–270 BCE) remains unclear, we know that they took the ideas of this school as the philosophical basis for their observations of nature and their various experimental techniques. According to this Naturalist philosophy, all phenomena are infused by one of the Five Phases *(wu-hsing)* of Energy *(ch'i)*, namely, Earth, Fire, Water, Wood, and Metal. Phenomena infused with the same phase of energy influence and resonate with one another, and these phases themselves spontaneously transform according to their own inherent laws, and so influence all things from the succession of seasons to the succession of dynasties.

When the first emperor of China, Ch'in Shih-huang-ti, united the country in 221 BCE, *fang-shih* from Ch'i and Yen flocked to his court. Their influence there is clearly attested to by the historical records. The emperor believed that he had come to power because the energetic phase of water had gained ascendancy in the world, and so he adopted water as the symbol of his reign. He also sent expeditions to search for P'eng-lai, the Isle of the Immortals, and was himself devoted to the quest for immortality.

In the succeeding century and a half, the cult of immortality flourished, and its principal proponents, the *fang-shih*, were influential among the ruling elite. Their power reached its zenith under Han Wu-ti (140–87 BCE), who appointed a number of them court officials when they promised to contact the immortals and to provide him with their secrets of avoiding death. On the advice of these esoteric masters, the emperor undertook expeditions both to the eastern seacoast and to the sacred K'un-lun mountains in the west in quest of these secrets. He also reinstated ancient sacrifices to the spirits, the most important of which were the *feng* and *shan* sacrifices on Mount T'ai. According to the *fang-shih*, the *feng* and *shan* sacrifices had last been performed by their patron and ancestor, the Yellow Emperor (Huang-ti), who thereupon had achieved immortality. The ultimate failure of these endeavors was discouraging to Emperor Wu, and after his reign the influence of these esoteric masters declined considerably on a national scale.

On the local level, however, the *fang-shih* were still powerful at the courts of a number of vassal states. The most notable was the state of Huai-nan, whose ruler, Liu An, was sponsor and editor of the important philosophical compendium the *Huai-nan–tzu*. Liu An died in 122 BCE after his planned rebellion was discovered by imperial authorities, but according to legend, the *fang-shih* gave him and his family a potion of immortality and they all ascended to heaven to live forever. It is interesting to note that rulers of several other vassal states in which the esoteric masters were influential during the next two centuries also plotted (unsuccessful) rebellions and that a number of esoteric masters were associated with Wang Mang, who seized the reins of the empire for fifteen years early in the first century CE.

Probably because of their association with anti-imperial forces, the *fang-shih* were employed only sporadically in the service of the empire after the Wang Mang interregnum. Their aid was most often enlisted for divination about the future, and they were masters of various divination techniques ranging from the ancient use of tortoise shells to physiognomy, astrology, and the use of wind directions. However, many *fang-shih* withdrew from society and lived as hermits, patterning themselves on the immortals whom they admired so greatly.

The surviving records show the *fang-shih* to have been involved in a wide range of experiments aimed at lengthening life and avoiding death. Their experimentation with transmuting cinnabar to mercury and gold in the search for the potion of eternal life is regarded as the origin of Chinese alchemy and chemistry. Their creation of various plant and animal compounds for health and longevity is the basis of the long Chinese pharmacological and medical traditions. Their respiratory and gymnastic techniques, methods of dietary hygiene, and various "bedroom arts" are among the earliest examples of physiological alchemy. The *fang-shih* were also adept at shamanistic trance and at contacting and influencing spirits and demons.

Ultimately a large part of the knowledge and practices of the *fang-shih* found its way into the Taoist religion. It is therefore not surprising that the work regarded as the oldest source of this religion, the *T'ai-p'ing ching*, was probably authored by *fang-shih* and was presented to the imperial court by one in 140 CE. However, because the rise of Taoism as a religious and political force during the second century CE took place largely outside the purview of the official historians who are our main sources, the precise role of the *fang-shih* in the beginnings of the Taoist religion is difficult to clarify.

[*For an overview of the role of the* fang-shih *in the formation of Taoism, see* Taoism, *overview article. See also* Alchemy, *article on* Chinese Alchemy; Hsien; Yin-yang Wu-hsing; *and the biographies of Liu An and Tsou Yen.*]

BIBLIOGRAPHY

There are three Western-language sources devoted exclusively to the *fang-shih.* Ngo Van Xuyet's *Divination, magie et politique dans la Chine ancienne* (Paris, 1976) contains an accurate translation of all the *fang-shih* biographies in the *History of the Latter Han (Hou Han shu)* as well as excellent supporting material including a detailed discussion of the historical context of the biographies and appendices on the various esoteric techniques of the *fang-shih.* Kenneth J. DeWoskin has published one article and one book on the *fang-shih.* "A Source Guide to the Lives and Techniques of Han and Six Dynasties *Fang-Shih,*" *Society for the Study of Chinese Religion Bulletin* 9 (1981): 79–105, is a valuable list of biographical sources and makes an important attempt to define the *fang-shih* and delineate their activities. Many of the biographies listed in this article, and all of those translated in Ngo's work, are translated by DeWoskin in *Doctors, Diviners, and Magicians of Ancient China: Biographies of Fang-shih* (New York, 1983), which also contains a useful introduction. This work is the most comprehensive to date in the West but unfortunately fails to deal with the very thorny problem of the role of the *fang-shih* in the rise of the Taoist religion.

Information on the *fang-shih* can be found in a number of other works, the most valuable of which is Yü Ying-shih's "Life and Immortality in the Mind of Han China," *Harvard Journal of Asiatic Studies* 25 (1964–1965): 80–122. Anna K. Seidel's superb study *La divinisation de Lao-tseu dans le taoïsme des Han* (Paris, 1969) contains some useful information on the *fang-shih* and their relationship to the Yellow Emperor and to the Huang-Lao Taoists. The activities of the *fang-shih* under Ch'in Shih-huang-ti and Emperor Wu of the Han can be found in Burton Watson's translation of Ssu-ma Ch'ien's *Shih chi, Records of the Grand Historian of China,* vol. 2 (New York, 1963), pp. 13–69. There are also scattered references to the *fang-shih* in Joseph Needham's *Science and Civilization in China* (Cambridge, 1956–1976), especially volume 2, which contains an excellent discussion of the school of Naturalists, and volume 5, part 3, which discusses alchemy. Finally, for the relationship between the various streams of Taoism in the early Han and the *fang-shih,* see Holmes Welch's *Taoism: The Parting of the Way* (Boston, 1966).

HAROLD D. ROTH

FĀRĀBĪ, AL- (AH 258–339?/870–950? CE), more fully Abū Naṣr Muḥammad ibn Muḥammad ibn Tarkhān ibn Awzalagh (?); Arab philosopher and logician known in Arabic texts as Abū Naṣr or "the second teacher" (after Aristotle) and in Latin as Avennasar or Alfarabius.

Of his life little is really known. He was probably born in Transoxiana (western Turkistan) and is often believed to be of Turkish descent. He had deep intellectual contacts with Christians of different persuasions as well as with Muslims. According to al-Fārābī himself, he studied logic with the Nestorian Christian Yuḥannā ibn Haylān (who is otherwise rather unknown); this encounter took place either in Harran or in Baghdad. He worked with another Nestorian, the Aristotelian translator and commentator Abū Bishr Mattā ibn Yūnus (d. 940), and his most famous disciple was the Jacobite Christian translator, philosopher, and theologian Yaḥyā ibn 'Adī (d. 972?). In 942, after many years in Baghdad, the capital of the Sunnī caliphate, al-Fārābī joined the entourage of the Shī'ī Hamdanid ruler Sayf al-Dawlah and lived mainly in Aleppo and Damascus, where he died.

Al-Fārābī claimed that religion is merely an imaginative imitation of true philosophy, which must therefore be prior to it both logically and chronologically. True philosophy is the one handed down by Plato and Aristotle, who remain in fundamental agreement because they were both pursuing the same aim. The philosophical method is demonstration, which restricts philosophy to an intellectual elite. Religion, in this view, is a "popular" philosophy that translates philosophical concepts and truths into symbols and symbolic statements; its method is imaginative persuasion. As symbols are culturally determined, al-Fārābī envisioned a plurality of religions using different symbols for different cultures, and he believed that the value of a religion can be measured by the accuracy of its translation of the true philosophy into symbolic language and by the degree of cultural fitness of such a language.

Within al-Fārābī's framework, both philosophic illumination and its translation into symbols—which are forms of revelation—emanate from the Active Intellect, the tenth separate intelligence, which is symbolized in Islamic terms by the angel Gabriel, who communicated revelation to Muḥammad. In this way, al-Fārābī vests Plato's philosopher-king and lawgiver with the garb of a prophet.

Al-Fārābī's belief in the priority of philosophy over religion may have been influenced in part by the fact that Christians were usually not permitted to study Aristotle's *Logic* beyond the *Prior Analytics,* whereas al-Fārābī and other Arab philosophers did. The Muslim theologian al-Ghazālī (d. 1111), who defended Islamic orthodoxy in *The Incoherence of the Philosophers,* consistently took al-Fārābī as one of his two main targets.

BIBLIOGRAPHY

Al-Fārābī wrote, in Arabic, numerous philosophical books and epistles as well as an extensive treatise on music. Few of his works, unfortunately, have been translated into Western languages. The most interesting texts for his views on religion are *Fī mabādi' ārā' ahl al-madīnah al-fāḍilah,* which has been edited and translated by Richard Walzer as *Al-Farabi on the Perfect State* (Oxford, 1984); *Fuṣūl al-madanī,* which has been edited and translated by D. M. Dunlop as *Aphorisms of the*

Statesman (Cambridge, 1961); and *Fī taḥṣīl al-sa'ādah*, which has been translated by Muhsin Mahdi in *Alfarabi's Philosophy of Plato and Aristotle* (New York, 1962) as *The Attainment of Happiness*.

There is no really good book on al-Fārābī. The best article on his views on religion is Muhsin Mahdi's "Alfarabi on Philosophy and Religion," *Philosophical Forum*, n.s. 4 (Fall 1972): 5–25. One should also consult Erwin I. J. Rosenthal's contribution to the study of *Kitāb al-millah* (The Book of Religion), "Some Observations on al-Farabi's 'Kitab al-Milla,' " in *Dirāsāt falsafīyah muhdāh ilā al-Duktūr Ibrāhīm Madkūr*, edited by 'Uthmān Amīn (Cairo, 1974), and Muhsin Mahdi's "Remarks on Alfarabi's *Attainment of Happiness*," in *Essays on Islamic Philosophy and Science*, edited by George F. Hourani (Albany, N.Y., 1975). Herbert A. Davidson's "Alfarabi and Avicenna on the Active Intellect," *Viator: Medieval and Renaissance Studies* 3 (1972): 134–154, is a first-rate study of al-Fārābī's conception of the Active Intellect.

THÉRÈSE-ANNE DRUART

FAREL, GUILLAUME (1489–1565), early Protestant reformer of western Switzerland. Born in Gap in the Alps of southeastern France of a poor but noble family, Farel studied in Paris and there came under the influence of the Christian humanist Jacques Lefèvre. Through Lefèvre, Farel was introduced to Paul's epistles and to the doctrine of justification by faith alone. Lefèvre and his students left Paris for Meaux, where they had the support of Bishop Briçonnet, a mild reformer and also a student of Lefèvre, and of Marguerite of Navarre. Farel and others were authorized to preach in the surrounding territory. Neither Briçonnet nor Lefèvre saw a need to renounce Catholicism, and Farel's ideas and preaching were soon forbidden as too radical.

After leaving Meaux, Farel became acquainted with most of the leading reformers. In 1526 he settled in Aigle under the control of Bern, taking part in that city's religious reformation, and in 1529 he introduced the Reformation to Neuchatel. In 1532 he visited the Waldensians and was present at the synod when they adopted the principles of the Protestant Reformation and began their alignment with Reformed Protestantism.

Farel's most significant work for the future of Protestantism took place in Geneva, which he first visited in 1532. Opposition to the Reformation was strong, but Farel persisted under the protection of Bern. Geneva came to a full acceptance of the Reformation on Sunday, 21 May 1536.

Expelled, along with Calvin, in 1538 from Geneva, Farel returned to Neuchatel and devoted the last twenty-seven years of his life to building up this church. He continued his preaching missions in neighboring territories almost to the time of his death at sixty-seven in 1565. It remained for Calvin, whom Farel had compelled to serve the Reformation in Geneva, to make that city the center of Reformed Protestantism.

Farel's primary contribution was that of a preacher and advocate of the Reformation. He was an intense man of passionate conviction and a powerful preacher who commanded the attention of audiences and elicited opposition as well as conviction. He is best known for his work in Geneva and the support he gave to Calvin until the latter's death. As a writer, he left 350 to 400 letters that, together with those of other reformers, played an important part in the Reformation. He was also the author of various polemical and practical tracts. His liturgy, "The Manner Observed in Preaching When the People Are Assembled to Hear the Word of God," was, according to Bard Thompson in his *Liturgies of the Western Church*, the "first manual of evangelical worship in the French language." Farel's best and most important work was *Sommaire: C'est une brieve declaration d'aucuns lieux fort nécessaires a un chacun chrestien pour mettre sa confiance en Dieu et a ayder son prochain*, the first summary of the evangelical faith in the French language. It was published in six editions during Farel's lifetime; the last was corrected and completed in conformity with Calvinist theology.

BIBLIOGRAPHY

Guillaume Farel, 1489–1565: Biographie nouvelle écrite d'après les documents originaux (Paris, 1930) is an outstanding volume published by a committee of Farel scholars with many collaborators. Two English translations of lives of Farel by nineteenth-century biographers are available: Melchior Kirchhofer's *The Life of William Farel, the Swiss Reformer* (London, 1837) and Frances A. Bevan's *William Farel*, 5th ed. (London, 1880). An extended account of Farel's work can be found in Philip Schaff's *History of the Christian Church*, vol. 7, *Modern Christianity: The German Reformation and the Swiss Reformation* (1910; reprint, Grand Rapids, Mich., 1974) and in Williston Walker's biography, *John Calvin: The Organizer of Reformed Calvinism, 1509–1564* (1906; reprint, New York, 1969).

JOHN H. LEITH

FASTI. The *fasti* (from *fasti dies*, "the authorized days") were the calendars of the ancient Romans; painted on a white-washed surface or etched in marble, the *fasti* publicized a specific body of information. The character of the information as well as the extent of the community it addressed would vary; but whether the community was the entire Roman people or a more limited group, such as a college of priests or craftsmen, the *fasti* were meant to be posted in a public place (or, at an earlier period, to be read aloud in public). On them were listed the most important, constant elements and festivals of the religious life or even the names of the eponymous magistrates (whose names were given to the years they were in office) and those who were celebrating a triumph.

On the whole, the *fasti* of the Roman people were religious in nature, and, thus, their creation was associated with the college of the pontifices (or principal priests), although at some point this college lost its monopoly on the esoteric knowledge behind the *fasti.* The *fasti* of the liturgical year would set forth and determine the dates of the major public festivals and would assign a status to various days: a *fastus* day would be one on which citizens might bring suit in court and on which their secular activities had a mystical basis that was lacking on a *nefastus* day; a *comitialis* day was one on which the *comitia,* or assembly, of the Romans could meet; and so on. In a parallel manner, the consular and pretorian *fasti* listed the names of those in the highest offices and thus provided chronological points of reference, since, in daily life, the years did not bear a date but the names of consuls (or, in a college, the name of the president, *magister*) in charge; in dubious cases, it was possible to consult public lists. Finally, the triumphal *fasti* recorded the proofs of the *felicitas* ("happiness, prosperity") of the republic and bore witness to the *pax deorum* ("favor of the gods"), thus to some extent providing a positive counterbalance to the *annales maximi* ("chronicles of the chief high priest"), which apparently kept an account not only of magistracies but also of portents and other disquieting events. Publication of the triumphal *fasti* and the lists of catastrophes allowed the republic to exercise a kind of global control over the relations between the city and its gods and thus over its history. On a restricted scale, in a college of priests for example, the same body of information is found: a list of the eponyms of the city and of the college, followed by a list of notable events and, finally, the *fasti* of the liturgical year.

At one stage of historical development, the politico-religious *fasti* of the Roman people were kept secret. The religious festivals *(feriae)* were proclaimed only on the nones of the month by the king or, later, by the *rex sacrorum* (the priest who in the republican period carried out the religious duties that formerly belonged to the king). In 304 BCE Gnaeus Flavius posted in the Forum all the necessary data for the year and, in particular, the status of the various days.

In 189 BCE Marcus Fulvius Nobilior posted a calendar in which the festivals were accompanied by a commentary; from this time on, it became customary to fill out the *fasti* and provide them with a commentary. The most famous example of this is the *fasti* or calendar of Praeneste, which was annotated in letters of two sizes: large letters for the status of the days and the forty-five festivals, including the calends, nones, and ides, and small letters for the rites and the more recent or less important festivals. The basis of this differentiation is disputed. According to scholars following the German classicist Theodor Mommsen (1817–1903), these forty-five festivals represent the oldest calendar (to which they give the name Calendar of Numa). Others, following Otto Ernst Hartmann, maintain that, while these forty-five festivals are indeed ancient, the important point is that they are the essential ones; that is, they concern the people as a whole and are not movable. In any case, there is general agreement in dating the so-called Fasti of Numa to the mid-sixth century BCE. Its set of festivals, even if it does not include the movable festivals or those celebrated by only a part of the people, bears witness to a religious calendar that was common to all at the time when the city of Rome came into existence. Even if it was to some extent secret, it was nonetheless proclaimed in a public place, namely, the Capitol, and in circumstances in which every citizen could be present—that is, on the calends of the month an announcement was made of the day on which the nones would fall and on which the king would proclaim the festivals for that month. As such, the Calendar of Numa is an important witness to the political change that took place during that time.

[*See also* Calendars.]

BIBLIOGRAPHY

Dumézil, Georges. "Matralia, N ou NP." In his *Mythe et épopée,* vol. 3, *Histoires romaines.* Paris, 1973.

Michels, Agnes. *The Calendar of the Roman Republic.* Princeton, 1967.

Scullard, H. H. *Festivals and Ceremonies of the Roman Republic.* London, 1981.

JOHN SCHEID
Translated from French by Matthew J. O'Connell

FASTING, that is, complete or partial abstinence from nourishment, is an almost universal phenomenon within both Eastern and Western cultures. Although fasting has been and continues to be subscribed to for a variety of reasons, the present article deals with it as a phenomenon evoked for religious reasons, that is, by ideals or beliefs that consider it a necessary or advantageous practice leading to the initiation or maintenance of contact with divinity, or some supranatural or transcendent being.

Although the origins of fasting as a moral or religious discipline are obscure, the custom or practice of fasting is attested in many ancient cultures. The fact that it was in some cultures connected with rites of mourning has led some scholars to equate its origins with the custom whereby friends and relatives leave with the dead the food and drink that they (the living) would normally consume, so that the deceased might have nourishment in an afterlife.

Others consider fasting in earlier cultures to have arisen as a result of the discovery that it could induce a state of susceptibility to visions and dreams and hence give the practitioner direct access to a spiritual world. As such it became for some a discipline creating the proper state necessary for some degree of participation in divinity. It gradually became an integral part of a purity ritual with definite religious intent. In some of the more archaic religions fasting became part of the discipline ensuring both a defense against taboo powers and a means of obtaining *mana,* or sacred power.

Within certain Greco-Roman philosophical schools and religious fellowships (e.g., the Pythagorean), fasting, as one aspect of asceticism, was closely aligned to the belief that humanity had originally experienced a primordial state of perfection that was forfeited by a transgression. Through various ascetic practices such as fasting, poverty, and so forth, the individual could be restored to a state where communication and union with the divine was again made possible. Hence, in various religious traditions a return to a primordial state of innocence or bliss triggered a number of ascetical practices deemed necessary or advantageous in bringing about such return. For such groups the basic underlying assumption was that fasting was in some way conducive to initiating or maintaining contact with some divine power or powers. In some religious groups (for example, Judaism, Christianity, and Islam) fasting gradually became a standard way of expressing devotion and worship to a specific divine being.

Although it is difficult to pinpoint a specific rationale or motivation for an individual's or a group's fasting, in most cultures that ascribe to it at least three motivations are easily discernible: (1) preliminary to or preparatory for an important event or time in an individual's or a people's life; (2) as an act of penitence or purification; or (3) as an act of supplication.

Preparatory Fasting. In addition to the basic underlying assumption that fasting is an essential preparation for divine revelation or for some type of communing with the spiritual (what is above or beyond the natural for humans), many cultures believe that fasting is a prelude to important times in a person's life. It purifies or prepares the person (or group) for greater receptivity in communion with the spiritual. In the Greco-Roman mystery religions, for example, fasting was deemed an aid to enlightenment by a deity, and an initiate into most of these religions had to abstain from all or certain specified foods and drink in order to receive knowledge of the mysteries of the specific religion.

Within some of the mystery cults, fasting was incorporated as part of the ritual preparation for the incubation sleep that, by means of dreams, was to provide answers to specific questions and needs of the person. Dreams and visions were viewed as media through which spiritual or divine revelations were made manifest. Philostratus (c. 170–c. 245 CE), for example, presents the view that since the soul was influenced by diet, only by frugal living and the avoidance of meat and drink could the soul receive unconfused dreams (*Life of Apollonius* 2.37). Both Greek philosophers (e.g., Pythagoreans and Neoplatonists) and Hebrew prophets believed that fasting could produce trancelike states through which revelations would occur. Plutarch narrates how the priests of ancient Egypt abstained from meat and wine in order to receive and interpret divine revelations (*Isis and Osiris* 5–6), and Iamblichus tells how the prophetess fasted three days prior to giving an oracle (*Egyptian Mysteries* 3.7).

Among the Eastern traditions Hindu and Jain ascetics fasted while on pilgrimage and in preparation for certain festivals. Within classical Chinese religious practice, *chai,* or ritual fasting, preceded the time of sacrifices. By contrast, later Chinese religious thought, particularly Taoism, taught that "fasting of the heart" *(hsin-chai),* rather than bodily fasting, was more beneficial to arriving at "the Way" *(tao).* Confucianism followed the practice of Confucius in approving fasting as preparation for those times set aside for worship of ancestral spirits. Although the Buddha taught moderation rather than excessive fasting, many Buddhist monks and nuns adhered to the custom of eating only one meal per day, in the forenoon, and they were obliged to fast on days of new and full moon. Among modern-day Buddhists it is more common to fast and confess one's sins four times per month.

Within the Judaic tradition only one day of fasting was imposed by Mosaic law, Yom Kippur, the Day of Atonement (*Lv.* 16:29–34), but four additional days were added after the Babylonian exile (*Zec.* 8:19) to commemorate days on which disasters had occurred. The Hebrew scriptures set fasting within the context of being vigilant in the service of Yahveh (e.g., *Lv.* 16:29ff.; *Jgs.* 20:26), and it was considered important as a preliminary to prophecy (e.g., Moses fasted forty days on Sinai; Elijah fasted forty days as he journeyed to Horeb). Judaism allowed for individual voluntary fasts, and there is evidence that Mondays and Thursdays were set aside by some Jewish communities as special days of fasting. According to Tacitus, fasting had become so characteristic of the Jews of the first century that Augustus could boast that he fasted more seriously than a Jew (*Histories* 5.4).

Although formalized fasting was spoken against in the New Testament (*Mt.* 6:16–6:18), it eventually became the favorite ascetic practice of the desert dwellers and monastic men and women who saw it as a necessary measure to free the soul from worldly attachments and desires. Within the Christian tradition there gradually developed seasonal fasts such as the Lenten one of forty days preparatory to Easter; Rogation Days in spring in supplication for good crops; and Ember Days, days of prayer and fasting during each of the four seasons of the year. There were also weekly fasts on Wednesdays and Fridays and fasts prior to solemn occasions celebrating important moments in people's lives (e.g., baptism, ordination to priesthood, admission to knighthood, and reception of the Eucharist).

In the Islamic tradition Muslims continue to observe the ninth month, Ramaḍān, as one of rigorous fasting (*ṣawm*), during which days no liquid or food is allowed between dawn and sunset, as stipulated in the Qur'ān (2:180ff.). Some of the stricter Muslim groups fast each Monday and Thursday, and the Qur'ān recommends fasting as a penance during a pilgrimage, three days going and seven returning (2:193). Ṣūfīs recommend additional fasting for the purpose of communing with the divine, and the Shī'ī Muslims require fasting as one of the ways of commemorating the martyrdom of 'Alī, the son-in-law of the Prophet, and his two sons. [*See also* Ṣawm.]

Basic to the beliefs of many Native American tribes was the view that fasting was efficacious for receiving guidance from the Great Spirit. Generally, a brave was sent off into the wilderness on a fast in quest of such guidance, which was usually revealed through a personal vision. The young man's vision was often viewed as necessary for his future success in life, indicating a personal relationship between himself and his guardian spirit. Lakota braves, for example, were advised in their search for a vision of Wakantanka, the supreme being, to "walk in remote places, crying to Wakantanka, and neither eat nor drink for four days." Within many of the tribes there was a period of ritual fasting prior to a boy's reaching puberty and a girl's first menstrual period, considered times of growth into adulthood. In New South Wales, Australia, boys had to fast for two days at their *bora* ceremonies. In the Aztec culture the ritual training required of one who aspired to become a sacrificing priest included fasting as one form of abstinence. While fasting was often viewed as a disciplinary measure that would strengthen the body and character of the individual, prolonged fasting and other austerities were also undergone so that the individual might see or hear the guardian spirit who would remain with him or her for life.

Fasting as Penance or Purification. Ancient Egyptian and Babylonian customs included ritualized fasting as a form of penance that accompanied other expressions of sorrow for wrongdoing. Like people of later times, these nations viewed fasting as meritorious in atoning for faults and sins and thus turning away the wrath of the gods. In the *Book of Jonah*, for example, the Assyrians are depicted as covered with sackcloth, weeping, fasting, and praying to God for forgiveness (*Jon.* 3:5ff.).

For the Jews, fasting was an outward expression of inner penitence, and on various occasions a general fast was proclaimed as a public recognition of the sin of the people (*1 Sm.* 14:24, *1 Kgs.* 21:9, *Jer.* 36:9). Yom Kippur, the Day of Atonement, is such a day of fasting and praying for forgiveness of sins. But fasting is also viewed as a means of orienting the human spirit to something or someone greater. According to Philo Judaeus (25 BCE–50 CE), the Therapeutae, a group of Jewish contemplatives living in community, fasted as a means of purifying the spirit so that it could turn itself to more spiritual activities such as reading and study (*On the Contemplative Life*). The Essenes, a Jewish group who followed their "righteous teacher" into the wilderness at Qumran (c. 135 BCE–70 CE), in their *Manual of Discipline* prescribed fasting as one of the ways of purification, of preparing for the coming of the "end of days."

Although fasting as a means of atonement and purification is evident in other traditions, it was among the Christians that fasting became a predominant feature. Already in the first and second centuries it began to appear as one of the many ascetic practices that became widespread in the Middle Ages. With the rapid growth of ascetic movements that incorporated Greek dualism into their thought patterns, fasting became an important means of ridding the body of its attachment to material possessions and pleasures, thus freeing the person for attaining the higher good, the love for and imitation of Christ. The prevailing notion was that whereas food in moderation was a necessary good for maintaining health, abstention from food was particularly effective in controlling the balance between body and spirit. Like the Pythagoreans with their elaborate taboos on food (fourth to sixth century BCE), the early Christians saw such ascetic practices as fasting, praying, and almsgiving as means of reducing or eliminating the tension between the earthbound body and the divine, spiritual soul. Although it is true that for some individuals or groups fasting became an end in itself rather than a means to an end, most monastic manuals or rules warn the monastics to avoid excessive fasting, which could bring harm to both body and soul. Though the practice of fasting varied in different countries, most Christian manuals of instruction and worship began to regulate more strictly the times for obligatory fasts (cf. *Didachē* 7ff.; Justin Martyr, *1 Apology* 61). But it was with the growth of monastic communities in the fourth century that fasts began to be more universal.

Modern-day Christian denominations display a considerable diversity of opinion and practice in regard to fasting. For most Protestant denominations, except for some of the more evangelically oriented groups, fasting is left to the discretion of the individual. Although within the Roman Catholic and Greek Orthodox churches prescriptions still govern both individual and corporate practices, rigid fasting practices have been abolished. Roman Catholics still practice partial fasting and abstinence from meat on Ash Wednesday and Good Friday. Within the Greek Orthodox church fasting is usually one of the acts of purification preparing one for participation in the liturgical mysteries.

Although Buddhists generally favor restraint in taking food, and many consider fasting a non-Buddhist practice, it is listed as one of the thirteen Buddhist practices that can serve as an aid to leading a happy life, a means of purification *(dhutanga)*. Therefore, many Buddhist monks have the custom of eating only one meal a day, often eating only from the alms bowl and declining a second helping. For other Buddhists enlightenment was considered more easily attainable by renunciation of wrong ideas and views rather than by fasting. Within Jainism there is the belief that certain ascetic practices, like fasting, are purificatory in that they can remove the accumulation of *karman* that weighs down the life-monad. Fasting could therefore carry people upward along the path to liberation from *karman*. Within the Islamic tradition fasting is viewed as one of the "good works," one of the recognized duties of the devout Muslim, and is considered efficacious in pardoning an individual from all past sins (Tibrīzī, *Mishkāt al-maṣābīh* 7.7.1).

Within some of the Native American tribes, the practice of fasting was considered conducive to purifying the body prior to some great feat or challenge. The Cherokee Indians believed that prior to slaying an eagle the individual had to undergo a long period of prayer and fasting that purified the body, strengthening it for the necessary combat. Siouan-speaking Indians believed that before both hunting and war the body had to be purified through fasting for these noble tasks. Among the Incas, fasting from salt, chili peppers, meat, or *chicha* (beer made from maize) was one of the ways of preparing the body for an important event and also for a public form of penance.

Fasting as Supplication. Although it is difficult in many instances to distinguish clearly between fasting as a means of penitence and fasting as a means of supplication, within certain traditions the latter has widespread usage. Within Judaism, for example, fasting was one way of "bending the ear of Yahveh," of asking God to turn to the Jews in mercy and grant them the favor requested. Ahab, for example, fasted to avert the disaster predicted by Elijah (*1 Kgs.* 21:27–29, cf. *Nm.* 1:4, *2 Chr.* 20:3, *Jer.* 36:9). Since penitence and supplication were often dual motivational forces for fasting within Judaism, fasting emerged as both conciliatory and supplicatory. As in the Christian and Islamic traditions, the Jewish notion of fasting reflected an attitude of interior sorrow and conversion of heart. Within the Christian ascetic circles, fasting was viewed as one of the more meritorious acts, which exorcised demons and demonic temptation from the individual's consciousness. Therefore, fasting emerged within Christianity as a potent force in calling down God's mercy and aid in ridding the individual of temptations against "the world, the flesh, and the devil." Fasting was a means of calling God to the struggling Christians' side in order to be both strength and encouragement in the battle against sin. In the Qur'ān fasting as supplication to God is considered of merit only if one also abandons false words and deeds. Otherwise, God pays no heed to the supplication (see, e.g., surah 2:26).

Within other groups fasting was also viewed as meritorious in obtaining rewards from higher powers. In the Intichiuma ceremonies of the tribes in central Australia fasting was practiced to assure an increase in the totem food supply. Young Jain girls fasted as one means of requesting the higher power to give them a good husband and a happy married life. Fasting frequently accompanied or preceded the dance rituals of certain tribes who prayed for a renewal of fertility and a productive harvest from the earth (e.g., the Dakota Sun Dance; the Cheyenne New Life Lodge; the Ponca Sacred Dance, or Mystery Dance).

In summary, from earliest records to contemporary society, fasting has been a common religious practice, serving as both a prelude to and a means of deepening the experience of transcendence of the material or bodily state. The voluntary abstinence from nourishment has been for many an ideal means of expressing human dependence on a higher power, or a liberation from those things that stifle aspirations toward a "higher" form of existence. Fasting has often served as a sign and symbol of the human conversion toward something beyond the everyday, a turning toward the spiritual, the transcendent, the Great Spirit, God, and so on. In modern times the therapeutic value of fasting has been adopted as a good health practice that has often taken on the aspect of religious ritual.

[*See also* Asceticism.]

BIBLIOGRAPHY

Brandon, S. G. F., ed. *A Dictionary of Comparative Religion.* London, 1970.

MacCulloch, J. A., and A. J. Maclean. "Fasting." In *Encyclopaedia of Religion and Ethics,* edited by James Hastings, vol. 5. Edinburgh, 1912.

MacDermot, Violet. *The Cult of the Seer in the Ancient Middle East.* London, 1971.

Rogers, Eric N. *Fasting: The Phenomenon of Self-Denial.* Nashville, 1976.

Ryan, Thomas. *Fasting Rediscovered: A Guide to Health and Wholeness for Your Body-Spirit.* New York, 1981.

Underhill, Ruth M. *Red Man's America: A History of Indians in the United States.* Rev. ed. Chicago, 1971.

Wakefield, Gordon S., ed. *The Westminster Dictionary of Christian Spirituality.* London, 1983.

ROSEMARY RADER

FATE. Derived from the Latin *fatum* (something spoken, a prophetic declaration, an oracle, a divine determination), the term *fate* denotes the idea that everything in human lives, in society, and in the world itself takes place according to a set, immutable pattern. *Fatalism* is the term for man's submission to fate in resignation. Fate and fatalism should not be confused with the idea of determinism propagated by nineteenth-century philosophical positivism, which was convinced that science was on its way to uncovering the laws of all cause and effect relationships in the world. The assumption of determinism was that a complete set of scientific laws was within reach of the human mind, and that all of these would reside in the public domain and hence be transparent to inquiring reason. By contrast, the notion of fate, in whatever variation, language, or shade of meaning it occurs, always retains a basic element of mystery. Fate may be in the hands of some powerful, superhuman being; it may be superior to the gods; it may be accessible to some select individuals. But, quite differently from the case of philosophical determinism, vis-à-vis fate not only is a certain knowledge possible but also a certain "negotiation" with or even an aversion of fate's decrees.

There are no religious traditions in which a notion of fate is supreme, exclusive, and all-powerful, and precisely this fact sets limits to the effort to define fate in a universally valid manner once we have left the formal lines drawn so far. Only in psychological terms can we add some generalizations. The more problematic, and at the same time more fascinating issues arise when we confront the variety in cultures and historical eras.

Psychological Observations. In the intellectual mood of our age it is natural to think of the notion of fate first of all in psychological terms. Some generalizations can certainly be made, although they do not help a great deal in understanding fate in the ways in which it is presented in specific religious contexts.

The idea that a root cause of all religion is fear was already proposed in antiquity, and through the ages thinkers have tried to revive this idea, though with little success. With respect to fate and fatalism, however, the function of a psychological ambivalence in many human situations seems hard to deny. Especially in the case of fatalism, that is, the full surrender to fate, an attitude of defeat is in evidence in the belief that the future is as inevitable and fixed as the past. One's acts become acts of a higher power, and Freud's observations concerning a death wish as the ultimate motivation may be fully applicable in many instances. The ambivalence we are here referring to consists of the renunciation of one's own reason (hence also of one's own responsibility), and the hypothesis of a rational coherence of events in another order. An example, if not of fatalism per se, but of tendencies in this direction in the modern West after World War II is the wave of astrology in general literature, as a rubric in almost every newspaper, and as a way of filling up the empty space of an underlying uncertainty.

Examples of fatalism of a more grisly sort have also become familiar in the twentieth century. From World War II we know of suicidal Japanese torpedo attacks and of suicides in SS (Schutzstaffel) quarters during Hitler's regime in response to a notion of destiny *(Schicksal)* supposedly far beyond the value of individual human lives. In the 1980s, religiously inspired suicidal attacks on targets conceived as threats to Islam, especially in the cause of Shiism, became an almost regular feature in newspaper reports on the Near East.

The cluster of fear, escape from fear, and dismissal of one's responsibility as a fundamental cause in the formation of certain conceptions of religion and fate is not limited to the recent past. It is attested also in ancient civilizations. We may be quite certain that fear of rulers, wild animals, foes, disease, and everything that we would sum up under the term *nature* has had its influence on the formulation of religious ideas even in the earliest times. Samuel Noah Kramer (1963) has translated a few expressive lines from a Sumerian poet who obviously had meditated on a golden age as a time that contrasted with a fateful present. Most characteristically, he thought of that age as one without fear:

> Once upon a time, there was no snake,
> there was no scorpion,
> There was no hyena, there was no lion,
> There was no wild dog, no wolf,
> There was no fear, no terror,
> Man had no rival.
> (Kramer, 1963, p.262)

It would be hasty to conclude that the idea of fate could be fully explained as a projection of man's basic fears or uncertainties. The most striking problem militating against this explanation is that certain periods and cultures that knew many fears and reasons for fear have very little to tell us of fatalism.

Earliest Cultures. There is no evidence of any religiously central preoccupation with fate in cultures preceding the earliest civilizations based on the cultivation of cereals, nor can we demonstrate any special religiously significant place provided for notions of fate in hunting cultures. One looks in vain for a significant role or clear expression of "fate" in truly archaic or preliterate societies in general. Everything points to the relative comfort of a grain or rice-producing culture as a minimum condition for a religious articulation concerning fate.

Diffusion of Astrology. One complex of a fatalistic type, though certainly not among the earliest ones, has clearly passed beyond the borders of its land of origin and through many different language areas as well, and that is astrology. Two reasons may be given for its spread. [*See* Astrology.]

In the first place, it is possible to look upon man's endeavor to relate his celestial observations to the course of his own destiny as a special modification, under certain historical conditions, of the macrocosmic-microcosmic correspondence that seems to occur with the structure of human religious symbolization everywhere. Hence, in a sense, astrology is not an altogether new phenomenon but rather a transplantation within a common matrix, when it appears and is diffused in late antiquity, to be grafted onto existing cosmogonic and cosmological traditions.

Although astronomical calculation had risen to great heights in ancient Babylon, full-blown astrological systems were first produced in the Greek language of the Hellenistic period. Nevertheless, it is important to realize that astronomy in earlier antiquity was not what we would call an exact science distinct from religion and the humanities. Details such as the linkage of the five classical planets plus the sun and moon to different celestial spheres were accepted in all parts of the world that had any contact with the ancient Near East. In all probability, this diffusion of ideas began well before the Hellenistic age. Cosmological ideas among Siberian tribes as well as architectonic expressions as far east as the Borobudur temple on Java show the powerful influence of ancient Near Eastern discoveries. And here we come to the second reason why astrology passed so easily from one cultural area to others very different.

From the outset, that is, from the earliest astronomical and mathematical tables in Babylon onward, formulas tracing and predicting the course of the heavenly bodies had never taken the form of a scientific enterprise in isolation. Hence we find that in the ancient Near East this "science" is presented together with invocations of deities; the clay tablets and other writings with astronomical and calendrical data frequently show religious symbols at the same time. In Siberian and Mongolian shamanism, the shaman, the man (or woman) with expert knowledge and experience of the traffic between this and the otherworld, travels in his ecstatic journey from earth to heaven passing through the heavenly spheres in between, each as a rule represented by notches in the pole that he ascends. In India, the Vedic texts make frequent use of calendrical numbers, of months or days in the year, and equate them with ingredients necessary for traditional sacrifices and other rituals.

Thus each religious system did what was natural to it; rather than adding "scientific" information to its body of traditional lore, each appropriated the new discoveries as further revelations of religious reality and inserted them in the existing tradition as was fitting. That human life was intrinsically, harmoniously related to the cosmos was beyond doubt. The ground was well prepared for the waves of astrological influences that followed. As a result, the line separating astronomy from astrology is not easy to draw in the ancient and classical worlds. Astrology was accepted as a way to gain knowledge of details in the general macro-microcosmic harmony. Now it became possible to calculate the relation of a person to the course of the heavenly bodies on the basis of the time of that person's birth and the sign under which the birth had taken place. Hence, in principle, it became possible also to alter destiny. It is not difficult to see that astrology functions by and large in the same way in very different religious traditions and cultural areas. In Hinduism, the astrologer's counsel is taken very seriously, for example to determine the appropriate day for a wedding ceremony. In the world of Judaism and Christianity, astrology cannot boast of such integration in the religious tradition. However, wherever astrology functions, it remains based on the same principles of ancient science, and in that respect we may speak of a certain sameness, a homogeneity in the astrological complex throughout history.

Ancient and Classical Concerns. Wherever we have clear references to fate in religious documents, the expressions used show at once that we cannot speak of fate itself as one single concept, except with great reserve or within the brackets of special, formal, and external inquiries, such as logic, psychology, or sociology. Within the history of religions, the statements that can be made must depend on a clear recognition of the intentions that specific traditions exhibit. It is beyond the scope of one article to survey all religions, yet a number of different tendencies within their symbolic contexts can be indicated. The following points present some strands that show specific meanings of "fate." The points made below are heterogeneous in nature and should not be given undue weight. They are to be seen primarily as heuristic devices or views necessary for our understanding. They may, at most, be called "moments," in the sense of elements that now here, then there, are constituents of well-delineated notions of fate.

Fate relatively independent within a religious tradition. Not only moderns who consider themselves secularized, and in some measure "objective" in their views of religious traditions but also the ancients, among them the Greeks and Romans, have had difficulties in finding ways to define fate. The religious documents themselves show ambivalence. The documents show, however, that such ambivalence is not mere intellectual uncertainty but often an intentional compromise of distinct views, each of which is unassailable. In the case of fate, such necessary ambiguity is much easier to fathom than in most other symbolic complexes (e.g., sacrifices or forms of worship).

In the *Theogony*, Hesiod (eighth century BCE) collected and tried to classify ancient and even some pre-Homeric traditions. The Moirai, the goddesses of fate, together with some others, are called by Hesiod daughters of Night (*Theogony* 211–225), although he immediately adds that they punish transgressions of men and gods (217–222). When Zeus, the king of the gods, has firmly established his rule, the role of the Moirai (together with the Horae, that is, the three goddesses Eunomia, Dike, and Eirene) is that of dispensers of good and evil. Their function as goddesses of fate continues, however, in the new context, and in addition they are also called the honored daughters of Zeus. The ambivalence of their descent from Night and from the supreme god, whose veneration is certainly the major theme of Hesiod's *Theogony*, cannot be satisfactorily explained as a conflict of different traditions. It is, of course, possible that such supposed separate traditions existed, but then the major problem still remains: how could such very different pedigrees for the representations of fate have come about? The ambivalence is no doubt likely to be related to the nature of fate: on the one hand, there exists an origin of darkness, if not of uncanny supreme independence; on the other, the central god cannot be depicted as subordinate to fate but must be seen as in fact generating it.

In the famous epics of the classical traditions, we find this view confirmed in detail. Homer (eighth century BCE) presents a series of dramatic scenes in *Iliad* 16 that establish the case of a purposeful ambivalence. Under the guidance of Patroclus, the Danaans win a mighty victory over the Trojans. Patroclus himself kills several heroes in succession. Then the Trojan warrior Sarpedon attempts to turn the battle and attacks Patroclus, only to meet with death by his opponent's spear. However, before this fight ensues, Zeus looks down on the battlefield. He has good reason to be concerned, for Sarpedon is his son. Zeus asks his wife, Hera, whether he should remove Sarpedon from the scene of battle and thus preserve his life or allow him to be killed. Hera answers him with a moving argument. Mortals are doomed by fate. At the same time, Zeus can do as he pleases; however, once he takes action to save his son, every one of the gods might do the same for a son in battle, for each one loves his son. The best thing, she concludes, is to let Sarpedon be killed by Patroclus, then let him be sent back to his homeland in Lycia, where his family and friends can conduct a proper funeral. In this argument, a high point in the religion of the Olympians, Zeus remains supreme; yet in perfect harmony with his supremacy, fate is accepted.

The Roman poet Vergil (70–19 BCE) brings fate even closer to the supreme god in the story of Dido and Aeneas in the fourth chapter of the *Aeneid*. Aeneas, who according to Jupiter's plans must go to Italy to lay the foundations of the Roman state, is delayed in his journey through the charms of the love-stricken Dido. Juno, Jupiter's consort, contrives to have the two marry to make the relation legal. But Venus counsels Juno to inquire into Jupiter's plans. Jupiter, thus alerted, sends Mercury to Aeneas to remind him of his real goal: to establish rule over Italy. Thematically less subtle than Homer, Vergil leaves no doubt concerning the supremacy over destiny of the king of the gods. Even Venus, known for her truly fateful power, here victimizing Aeneas as much as Dido, is no match for Jupiter's determination of fate.

This purposeful ambivalence has early roots in the classical world. The classicist William Chase Greene, who studied the subject of fate extensively, attributes much to man's dependence since pre-Hellenic times on nature, expressed in Greece in the figure of Mother Earth, Gaia. Was she, on whom everything depended, identified with fate? Greene touches the heart of the matter in summarizing earlier classicists (notably Jane E. Harrison) and through his own study of texts by explaining that Gaia's way is the way of Dike. *Dikē* ("justice," but also "judgment" or "punishment") is a term akin to *fate*. In any event, the documents do not allow us to speak of an unambiguous identification. Often the texts speak also of Themis as a goddess; she is "the right tradition" and also "the right dispensation." It is true that she is sometimes identified with Gaia ("earth"). (The Titan goddess Gaia-Themis is the mother of Prometheus.) However, in the myths this goddess is not a supreme deity but rather the guardian of ancient sacred customs when their solidity is shaken.

Comparable to Themis, right tradition, *dharma*, in Hinduism occurs also as a divinity, the god Dharma. Typically, however, this god is not identified with any supreme deity; rather, he occurs in legends and myths as the embodied reminder of what should be done. In the epic *Mahābhārata*, the hero Yudhiṣṭhira is also known as Dharmarāja. He is the son of the god Dharma, and his name implies his justness as a ruler. This heroic character has been divinized and enjoys a cult in a number of minor, popular traditions in South India. However, the complexity of these cults involves also other divine and divinized characters who play significant roles in myth and ritual. Although *dharma*, right tradition, the maintenance of right tradition, and a hero/god are drawn together, this popular tradition also refrains from identifying any notion of fate with a divine power.

Much earlier, in the period of the Vedas and in Brahmanism (from c. 1200 to 600 BCE, but also in later texts), we find the term *ṛta*. It may be rendered as "truth," and in that sense it is commonly used in later times. Nevertheless, its earliest meaning, never completely lost later on, is rather closer to "cosmic balance." It is the power or function that preserves the world in its proper order. Its kinship to the general generic term *fate* is evident, but like all the others, this case too is preserved in its own mystery. Two deities, Mitra and Varuṇa, are called the guardians of *ṛta* in the Vedic texts but not its owners. No deity appropriates it, owns it, or is identical with it.

The Moirai in Greece, fate personified in three goddesses, are sometimes called by individual names: Clotho, who spins the thread of life; Lachesis, who measures it; and Atropos, who cuts it off. The symbolism of weaving is eloquent: a tapestry of life is created and by itself does not imply the design of a superior deity. Homer, as we have seen, does not identify Zeus with fate, but he speaks in several places of one single Moira, whose decisions are irrevocable, and to whom even the gods are subjected. Moira's inscrutable nature is not evil; indeed, a wholly evil divinity does not occur in Homer, unless it be the goddess Ate, but her role is not significant within the structure of Classical Greek religion.

The act of weaving (not only of cloth but also of baskets) has been a source of symbolism concerning fate in many places and times. [*See* Webs and Nets.] Urðr (Urd) in Old Norse literature is a personification of fate: a female figure, seated at a source under the world tree, determining destiny. Her name is related to the verb *verða*, akin to Latin *vertere* ("to turn"), especially the turning and twisting of the thread. Norse mythology has much to say about fate, including the inevitable destruction of the world (Ragnarǫk). Conceivably, our sources, which for the most part are very late, show a certain obsession with destiny under the impact of the changes bought about by Christianity.

In Germanic heroic poetry the role of goddesses of fate is largely played by the valkyries, nine in number. They are servants of Óðinn (Odin), and their name indicates their activity in war. The Old Norse term *valkyrja* refers to their task of selecting those to be slain in battle. According to the sagas, Óðinn will employ the valkyries in the final battle before Ragnarǫk. Thus in the Germanic world also we see a certain, no doubt purposeful, ambiguity regarding fate: those who determine fate are somehow independent and even beyond the gods, and nevertheless their activity jibes with the supreme god's will.

In Sanskrit literature, the most common word for fate is *daiva*, an adjectival form of *deva*, "god." It is "the divine" in a most general sense, for it refers to what is beyond human beings and human ken. A term that took on far greater significance in the sphere of fate in Indian religious history is the term *karman*. It owes its principal force to the context in which it first occurs in Vedic sacrificial texts. Vedic sacrificial proceedings, the heart of early Indian religious life as we know it from the texts, are a matter of acts that by definition could not be in vain; a ritual was an act *(karman) par excellence*. It is true that it is usually difficult to define its purpose, but this is a modern reader's problem. The texts agree that all power and in fact everything that we might want to cover with the word *religion* was concentrated in the act performed, whether by gods or men, that could not miss its mark.

In later Vedic texts (the *Upaniṣads*), in the Indian epics, and in Yoga literature, the meaning of the term *karman* absorbs the meaning of the manner in which life is determined by previous acts, or acts in a previous existence. In Buddhism finally, *karman* is the term used for the law of causality determining the cycle of *saṃsāra*, that is, the continuous flow of all finite existences. This meaning of *karman* has become the dominant meaning in virtually all Indian religious tradition. Obviously, this notion, in spite of its philosophical contexts and subtleties, can be understood as an expression of fate and fatalism. The religious center, however, from which its meaning derives and which is necessary for our understanding, is not immutable destiny itself, but the access in human existence toward *mokṣa* or *nirvāṇa*, that is, freedom from bondage to the law of *karman*. Notably, certain Indian religious traditions with archaic Indian roots, such as the *bhakti* cults of the South, are relatively unaffected by ideas concerning the law of *karman*. The loving devotion *(bhakti)* to a gracious god or goddess is so central and also so strongly supported by ancient local temple traditions as to make theories concerning laws of causality recede in significance.

Fate beyond the gods. In the Mediterranean world in late antiquity, ancient notions of fate do not disappear, but new views begin to prevail, at least in certain circles, and old notions are understood in a modified way. The new mood is the same that provided a ready acceptence of astrological ideas and of gnosticism. Tyche in Greece and Fortuna in Rome are goddesses who enjoyed worship, though their names do not seem to indicate much more than "chance," "fortune," and "good luck." Fortuna was invoked under several names, for example, Annonaria (referring to her function of providing food), Muliebris ("womanhood"), Primigenia ("she who is first born, the original one"), Virilis ("she who is strong and masculine"). Her greatest sanctuary was at Praeneste, of which the oldest part was built c. 200 BCE. She came to be identified with Tyche ("fate, chance"), and was a tutelary deity of the state in Hellenistic times. Her cult became very popular. [*See* Goddess Worship, *article on* Goddess Worship in the Hellenistic World.]

It is true that earlier times had had their deities of fate, as we have seen, whose names did not seem personal in the strict sense of the word. *Moira* and *daiva* are among the examples. Also the Greek term *anankē* may be mentioned here. It does not denote a deity but is a general word for "necessity," yet necessity of a more than physical nature; it is seen as the antithesis to freedom (and forms an important subject in Plato, e.g., in his *Timaeus*). *Anankē* preserved its mysterious, dreadful meaning throughout Greek history. Rather different, Moira was fate in person from the earliest times on, in spite of the clear, rather abstract etymology of the word. The name *Moira* is related to a verb of which the participial form *heimarmenē* meant, and continued to mean in later times, "fate" proper. However, the personification in the Hellenistic period of such deities as Fortuna is quite distinct. Her veneration is symptomatic of a certain obsession with "chance." Typically, the Roman poet and philosopher Lucretius (c. 96–55 BCE) begins his work *De rerum natura* (The Way Things Are) with an invocation of Venus, the classical goddess of love, who in that capacity is closely associated with "chance" and "fate." It is she who embodies control over all things, but Lucretius's poem makes a very strong case for chance (and in doing so, does not conceal his critique of all established religion.)

Specific epithets for several goddesses who enjoyed worship at the time, including Venus, all refer to the same fundamental concern with chance or fate. The epithets for Fortuna in popular use all amount to a transparent allegorical naming of the mysterious power that determines the course of nature and history. The great classical gods seem to recede to the background. In roughly the same period, and well into the Middle Ages, during the time in which Indian influences extended into Southeast Asia, the god Kāma ("love," in the sense of erotic love) came to be much celebrated.

Autonomous fate and divinities holding fate in their power. The eventual victory of Christianity over the Hellenistic religions signifies a change in the religious occupation with fate. "Fate" or "chance" as an independent or supreme force in the universe became a major enemy for many a Christian. One might even argue that a prevailing mood shifted from one extreme to another. In much later times, Western philosophers, such as Spinoza (1632–1677) and Hume (1711–1776), still felt it necessary to go to great lengths to refute Lucretius's rational reflections on chance. Generally, the biblically rooted religions, Judaism, Christianity, and Islam, looked askance at every semblance of a fate that could be ascertained apart from God.

Luther dismissed all the serious claims of astrology, since it had "neither principle nor proofs" (*Tischreden* 3.2834b, Weimar ed., 1914). Calvin's predestination, which is often mistaken for a form of determinism or fatalism, is in fact something very different, and Calvin took great pains, with all the philosophical means at his disposal, to explain man's ultimate destiny as God's decision, made within the mystery of God's eternity, inaccessible to man's inquiring mind (*Institutes* 3.21–23, 1559 ed.). [*See* Free Will and Predestination.] In contrast to the biblically rooted religions, it is striking that in Hinduism, which was not affected by these historical religious developments, astrology continued to flourish unabated, integrated in the Hindu religious structures themselves.

Before the emergence of the religion of Israel, there

occur in Mesopotamia eloquent expressions of the fate held in a god's hands. In the Akkadian creation epic known as *Enuma elish,* written down about 1000 BCE but much older in origin, we are told of the "tablets of fate" given to Marduk, the leading warrior and king of the gods. The presentation of these tablets is the seal of his sovereignty. He may be said to determine fate. At the same time, religious practice in the ancient Near East was multifarious, and a dogmatic definition of "god" and "fate" is not given. Among the terms for fate used are the early Sumerian *me* or *mu* and the Akkadian *shimtu* (pl., *shimatu*). *Shimatu,* "destinies," can somehow be manipulated; this is literally true according to our documents. The tablet of destinies *(tup-shimati)* is a cuneiform tablet; it controls the world, and the myths tell us that it could change hands. A lesser god, Anzu, once stole the tablet, thus endangering the order of the universe. Although the *Enuma elish* has destiny firmly planted in Marduk's power, a text (the *Exaltation of Inanna)* tells us of the goddess Inanna hanging the *me*s (destinies) on her head like jewels. On one occasion, Inanna tricked Enki (the Sumerian name of Ea, Marduk's father, who used to hold fate in his power) out of the destinies. One cannot do justice to the Babylonian notions concerning fate by explaining it, because of the highly developed art of divination, as a central item in a world of magic; divination was not a mere superstition but rather an attempt to understand and control reality (Buccellati, 1982). Furthermore, Mesopotamia never developed a cult of fate. The Mesopotamian notion of fate can perhaps best be seen as parallel to the notion of necessity *(anankē)* in Plato, and there is no reason to oppose the art of gaining knowledge concerning the laws controlling the universe to Greek philosophy as if the former were "more primitive" than the latter. In any event, a divine autonomy over destiny is a prevailing theme in ancient Mesopotamia, and this certainly differs from Plato's tendency to oppose *anankē* to God's *nous* ("mind") that created the world and man.

Historical continuations may be difficult to demonstrate in detail, yet in the Near East the world of Islam seems to have preserved some very ancient ideas concerning destiny. These ideas found their way into the text of the Qur'ān. Specific terms are set in human life: sex, happiness, misery, the amount of one's sustenance, and the time of death (a point especially emphasized for soldiers). Qur'ān 9:51 even states that nothing will happen to a man but what God has written down for him. Fate in God's hands here seems to come close to determinism. However, as in the ancient Near East of many centuries earlier, dogmatic consistency is not the issue. In Islamic teaching, beginning with the Qur'ān, rewards and punishments in this world as well as in the hereafter are far more significant, and their logical connection is not always immediately evident. In the history of Islam, theologians and lawyers have struggled with problems that arose from the text. Unjustly, many outsiders looking at Islam have considered all Muslims fatalists. God, the almighty, is at the same time the compassionate. The religious "inconsistency" here in the handling of fate is no more conducive to a seamless, monolithic conceptualization than representations of fate elsewhere.

In the religion of Israel, the basic pattern to be continued in Judaism, Christianity, and Islam had already clearly emerged. In the youngest of the biblically rooted religions, the most general tendency is to associate destiny with the will of God. Joseph and Daniel are the outstanding examples of dream readers, but their stories make it clear that they can look into the future through their art only under the inspiration of God. A complementary story of a man interested in necromancy who is not presented as a man of God is that of Saul consulting a woman of Endor, who conjures up the ghost of the dead Samuel (*1 Sm.* 28:8–25).

The problem of fate beyond God or gods. The theme of a destiny that is in harmony with a supreme divinity or ultimately dependent on that divinity's will is widespread, in spite of many variations, and yet some periods have seen inroads on this general rule. The clearest examples come from situations of great intellectual concern and from an overflow of mystical craving. The conception of a god can "dry up," as it were; it can become a pale, rational reflection in the history of a tradition. In the expression of great mystics such a development can be translated into a frightening reality, a horror that is too great to be endured. It would be too simple to suggest that the conceptualization of the idea of God causes mysticism, but as a historical factor, no doubt it plays a role. Not only in Jewish but also in Christian mysticism certain stark phrases and terms, though they certainly do not sum up the whole of the mystic's vision, may be understood in part as reactions to a world of abstract propositions. Among these are the *deus absconditus*; certain metaphorical, not to say euphemistic names in early Spanish Qabbalah, especially *Ein Sof;* "the dark night of the soul" of John of the Cross, 1542–1591; and "the abyss of the deity" of Johannes Tauler, 1300–1361. In the history of Buddhism, the tenacious process of negation in the meditations of Nāgārjuna (second century CE) may also serve as an example. In all these cases the traditional concepts are forced to yield a higher reality, a vision the tradition supposedly intended but had not disclosed hitherto. In the history of Islamic mysticism, such use and interpretation of and reaction to traditional concepts have often led to open conflict or to the seer's condemnation and execution (as in the famous case of al-Ḥallāj, d. 922).

There is a compelling reason to relate these trends in heterogeneous forms of mysticism to the subject of fate: in all instances something higher and more powerful than what tradition allowed or was capable of understanding is posited as absolute. The term *fate* falls short of the meaning of this highest element, which is often called ineffable. And yet, in intellectual circles that are not or not necessarily inclined toward mysticism, the desire to point to and name the power beyond what the tradition tolerates does occur. The Christian theologian Paul Tillich spoke of a "God who is Being itself," who as such would transcend "God who is *a* being." He intended this idea as a bulwark against any fatefulness of the sort that he thought threatened Greek religion in the form of a fate above Zeus, and he made his case with the help of the mystic vocabulary concerning God as ground and abyss of every being. In late antiquity, gnosticism's doctrines of salvation show patterns with very striking resemblances to a fate beyond God. The traditional image of God is rejected as in fact inferior to the real God, who is truly supreme, and who is the source of salvation. The person's self is instructed to consider itself ultimately as alien to the world as is the real, truly transcendent God. Thus, here also, something is posited beyond that which the tradition had declared supreme, and this something higher is that which really determines the world.

Other Themes of Fate. As stated before, the subject of fate cannot easily be isolated from its religious context, and the points made pertain only to some pronounced "moments" in expressions of fate. A few words should suffice here as a reminder of some traditions that show special aspects of destiny.

Rome. Practical, down-to-earth ways of handling fate occur nowhere so markedly as in ancient Roman religion. "Signs" are read to interpret the uncertainties of life, signs that are very common, such as sneezes or twitches of the eyelids, or signs that are completely beyond the reach of man, such as celestial phenomena or the flight of birds. [*See* Prodigia.] Messages *(omina)* can be deduced from all such signs. As a rule one has already set out on an enterprise, and then the signs are observed, and precisely this custom preserves a very practical human freedom. There seems to have existed a great certainty that the interpretations were of use to the actions undertaken. The Roman situation differs considerably from that of the Greeks, who exhibit a much more encompassing interest in the drama of the future. The Greek oracles, such as the famous oracle at Delphi, did not provide "yes" or "no" answers to an inquiry; rather, each oracular event was itself a mystery in need of interpretation. [*See* Oracles.] All major trends in Greece show a good deal of respect for the nature of fate, and nothing that might resemble a trivialization. Quite strikingly, Plato, in his last work, *Laws*, conceives a heavy penalty not only for those who are of the opinion that the gods can be caused to change their minds (10.909a). From the perspective not only of the Greeks but of most traditions with explicit concerns for fate, the Roman customs seem almost trivial in comparison.

China. The practicality in conceptions of fate in China differs markedly from ancient Roman customs. On a wider scale of comparison, the religions of China seem generally much less concerned with theory and very much down-to-earth. This difference is quite visible in expressions touching on fate and fatalism. Typically, the philosopher Wang Ch'ung (probably first century CE) compared the significance of a man to that of a flea or louse in the folds of the garment of the universe. The ultimate order of the world could not be affected by such a creature's doings. In Neo-Taoist literature, expressions with a fatalistic ring occasionally occur. The *Lieh-tzu*, written in the third century CE, contains a dialogue between Effort and Fate. At the moment when Fate seems all-powerful, Fate's reply to the question whether the way things are is indeed under its control is surprising: "Since I am called Fate, how can I have control? . . . [All things] come naturally and of themselves. How should I know anything about them?" (6.1a). Tao, the Way, shows its force in preventing Fate itself from reaching sovereignty. In Confucian tradition strict fatalism is difficult to detect. In ordinary life, however, Confucian scholars have as a rule declined to instruct any one who did not give them the respect they deserved, thereby leaving unwise decision-makers to their own "fate." This very practical "fatalism" is clearly only a by-product; it does not tell us much about the essentials of Confucius and Confucianism.

Iran. The very special place of ancient Iran in the general history of religions is also reflected in ideas concerning fate. Zoroastrianism conceived of a set period of duration of the world. In the end, the forces of good would triumph over those of evil. Man's life has its significance on the stage of this world drama. Both good and evil ulitmately follow the course of destiny. In later Zoroastrian orthodoxy, many identified fate with time; a system approaching determinism developed. In effect, all power of Ahriman, or Angra Mainyu (the evil spirit), as well as of Ōhrmazd, or Ahura Mazdā (the wise lord), was thus dissipated. This later period is commonly referred to as Zurvanism, after Zurwān, in whom Infinite Time is personalized and mythologized. (Zurvanites were the predominant sect in the third century BCE) The identification of fate and time has no prototype in other or earlier Iranian religion. One later text, known as the *Epistle of Tonsar* (probably end of sixth century CE) condemns both him who trusts exclusively in his own efforts and him who entrusts himself exclusively to fate. Manichaeism was strongly affected by Zoroastrian thought in its ideas about time, fate, good, and evil.

Fates of nations and empires. National fate should not be left unmentioned, since it cannot be separated from the subject of religion or pseudoreligion. China's "mandate of Heaven" was interwoven with the religious significance of kingship, and it was thought to determine the country's, and indeed, the world's lot. We have seen above that Jupiter decided the founding of Rome. In modern history, "manifest destiny," the American doctrine that gained great popularity in the nineteenth-century age of nationalism, held that it was the duty and fate of the Anglo-Saxon nations, more particularly the United States, to dominate the Western hemisphere. Closely related to "manifest destiny" is the appeal of the British poet laureate Rudyard Kipling in his poem *The White Man's Burden*, published in 1903. It calls on the white man to persevere through hardships in his heroic duty to protect, instruct, and lead to a truly civilized existence his "new-caught, sullen peoples / Half devil and half child." Equally fraught with pseudoreligious pathos is the *Schicksal* verbiage indulged in by the leaders of Nazi Germany.

Tenacity of Notions of Fate. The overwhelming complexity of notions of fate and their frames of reference should not prevent us from observing the force of certain underlying ideas over very long periods of time. Faithful to his theistic inheritance, the mathematician and philosopher Isaac Newton (1642–1727) interpreted his astronomical observations and calculations in terms of God's design. A rather recent Japanese religious movement, Tenrikyō (which came about late in the nineteenth century), is in most ways eclectic and has freely borrowed from theistic systems, yet its ideas concerning fate are in perfect harmony with prevailing popular Buddhist ideas of *karman*. Victorian and other faddish interest in astrology in the West should not blind one to the fact that rarely is there a serious interest in influencing one's individual future by means of astrology. Also worth noting is the fact that the interest in astrology in the modern West is limited to comparatively well-to-do circles in industrial societies.

Moreover, in moments of crisis that hit the individual, the charm of astrology tends to disappear, and earlier ideas of fate reemerge. This is not altogether surprising, as astrology was never accepted in dominant Western religious traditions. Everything points to the remarkable religious tenacity of deep-seated convictions touching on fate, destiny, chance, and other related problems. Even when certain rather conservative religious phenomena submerge or change, as for instance when funeral ceremonies are replaced by other means of disposing of the dead, basic assumptions about fate and image of fate seem hard to repress in social and private life. When occupying German authorities forced Jewish professors to step down, students in Amsterdam published in November 1940 a farewell message concluding: "In this heavy trial brought on you, we implore the Almighty to support you, Him in Whose hands your and our destiny lies, and Whose decisions rule the course of existence for all of us." More conspicuously than in the case of other symbolisms, individuals do not make up novel ideas concerning fate. Instead, old ideas dominant in a culture come to the surface from time to time. They may appear new and striking, yet on closer scrutiny they are rather like irrepressible sounds made when old strings vibrate anew.

[*See also* Chance.]

BIBLIOGRAPHY

Fatalistic Beliefs in Religion, Folklore, and Literature, edited by Helmer Ringgren (Stockholm, 1967), contains essays by specialists on religion, folklore, and literature. The basic work on early science and astronomy from which astrological systems derived is Otto Neugebauer's *The Exact Sciences in Antiquity*, 2d ed. (New York, 1969). Giorgio Buccellati's *A Primer of Ancient Mesopotamian Religion* (Malibu, 1982) pays special attention to a nonreductionistic interpretation of fate and to magic relating to fate. Samuel Noah Kramer's *The Sumerians: Their History, Culture, and Character* (Chicago, 1963) gives a sober yet vivid account of the earliest civilization, including its views of fate. Madeleine David's *Les dieux et le destin en Babylonie* (Paris, 1949) is a philologically based study, written with great philosophical sensitivity. Mary Boyce's *A History of Zoroastrianism* (London, 1961) is of special use for an inquiry into fate because of its treatment of Zurvanism. Fundamental to an understanding of the transformation and diffusion of ancient Near Eastern ideas to nonliterate cultures is Mircea Eliade's *Shamanism: Archaic Techniques of Ecstasy*, rev. & enl. ed. (New York, 1964).

William C. Greene's *Moira: Fate, Good and Evil in Greek Thought* (Cambridge, Mass., 1944) is an exhaustive study of fate in Greece. Jean Bayet's *Histoire politique et psychologique de la religion romaine* (1956; 2d ed., Paris, 1969) is of special importance for placing dealings with fate in their ordinary life surroundings. Rolfe Humphries's translation of Lucretius's *De rerum natura*, published as *The Way Things Are* (Bloomington, Ind., 1968), is the best translation of the most famous text on chance and related topics. Robert M. Grant's *Gnosticism: A Source Book of Heretical Writings from the Early Christian Period* (New York, 1961) is the most convenient collection of gnostic texts, with helpful indexes. Hans Jonas's *The Gnostic Religion*, 2d ed., rev. (Boston, 1963), interprets the world of late antiquity in which ideas and cults of fate flourished.

See Jan Gonda's *Die Religionen Indiens*, 2 vols. (Stuttgart, 1960–1963), for information concerning astronomically and astrologically inspired ideas in Hinduism. David Pingree is rendering the service for India that Otto Neugebauer rendered for the ancient Near East in a number of publications, notably his *The Yavanajātaka of Sphujidhvaja*, 2 vols. (Cambridge, Mass., 1978). *Karma and Rebirth in Classical Indian Traditions*, edited by Wendy Doniger O'Flaherty (Berkeley, 1980), contains excellent studies by specialists on the subject in India that is most relevant to the concept of *karman*.

Joseph Needham's *Science and Civilisation in China*, vol. 2, *History of Scientific Thought* (Cambridge, 1956), dealing with scientific thought on a large scale, presents astronomical and astrological ideas in China. Yang Ch'ing-k'un's *Religion in Chinese Society* (Berkeley, 1961) devotes special attention to Chinese attitudes toward fate in social life. *Sources of Chinese Tradition*, edited by Wm. Theodore de Bary et al. (New York, 1960), contains important documents, especially in part 3, showing notions of fate in specific settings.

KEES W. BOLLE

FĀṬIMAH BINT MUḤAMMAD

FĀṬIMAH BINT MUḤAMMAD (d. AH 11/633 CE), daughter of the prophet Muḥammad and his first wife, Khadījah, and the only direct source for the continuance of his bloodline.

Life. While the date of her birth is contested, most traditional sources place it between 609 and 614 CE. Although there is scant mention of Fāṭimah in early historical accounts of the period prior to the Hijrah ("emigration") from Mecca to Medina, note is made of her overwhelming grief at Khadījah's death. Fāṭimah herself becomes a figure of historical importance only with her marriage and subsequent motherhood.

Her marriage to ʿAlī ibn Abī Ṭālib, the son of Muḥammad's uncle and early protector, was evidently a less than felicitous match. Not only did this couple share the poverty of the community's early years of struggle in Medina, but there was discord between the two of them as well. Many *ḥadīth*s (traditions) speak in close and realistic detail of the Prophet's intervention on both counts. Offering financial and emotional support, he acted as arbitrator in disputes between his daughter and son-in-law. In one instance, the reports of which have become a proof-text for the Prophet's devotion to Fāṭimah, Muḥammad blocked ʿAlī's intention to take another wife.

Dissension also marked Fāṭimah's life in the days following her father's death. She found herself in conflict with the first caliph, Abū Bakr, on several grounds: politically she resented Abū Bakr's usurpation of her husband's blood right to leadership of the community, while the caliph's rejection of her claim to certain assets from the Prophet's estate led to an economic grievance as well. These conflicts were not, however, long-lived because Fāṭimah died within a year of her father's passing.

Legend. Fāṭimah's importance in later Islamic thought and devotion is out of all proportion to the paucity of historical detail with which the early sources treat her. Unlike ʿĀ'ishah, the Prophet's favored wife, she is infrequently mentioned as a transmitter in the *isnād*s of the standard *ḥadīth* collections, yet she eventually became the preeminent female figure in Muslim, particularly Shīʿī, piety. As the ultimate carnal link to the Prophet himself she has assured a great and enduring importance.

Although Fāṭimah is not mentioned by name in the Qur'ān, certain verses have been interpreted in a way which forms a basis for the subsequent hagiography. Surah 33:33, for example, contains the phrase "people of the house" *(ahl al-bayt)*, which Shīʿī commentators have restricted to five people: Muḥammad, ʿAlī, Fāṭimah, and their two sons, Ḥasan and Ḥusayn. The occasion of revelation sketched in numerous *ḥadīth*s portrays the Prophet enveloping the four in his cloak as he declares them to be "the people of my house." Some early Shīʿī interpreters of this verse, such as Muḥammad al-Ḥasan al-Ṭūsī (*Al-tibyan*, Najaf, 1957–1963, vol. 8, p. 339–341), extend the spiritual attribute of *ʿiṣmah* (impeccability, infallibility), which came to be applied to the Prophet and the imams, to Fāṭimah as well. In this tendency may be found seeds for the spiritual veneration of Fāṭimah and for the later development of her cult.

Likewise, Shīʿī exegesis of surah 3:61 associates Fāṭimah with the others of the *ahl al-bayt* in the famous challenge to mutual adjuration *(al-mubāhalah)* issued against the Christian delegation from Najrān. While there is some mention of this incident in the Sunnī *tafsīr* of al-Ṭabarī, it assumes central importance in Shīʿī commentaries of the classical period. Indeed, such Shīʿī discussions of whether Fāṭimah's two sons, Ḥasan and Ḥusayn, had reached the age of religious majority requisite to their full participation in this ceremony could perhaps be analyzed by modern scholars to refine the range of speculation on her birthdate. Commemoration of the *mubāhalah* in the last month of the Islamic year constitutes the principal Shīʿī feast in honor of Fāṭimah.

Fed by such Qur'anic interpretation, the veneration of Fāṭimah developed to the point that the Safavid theologian Muḥammad Bāqir Majlisī could offer a substantial catalog of material on the events of Fāṭimah's life, the divine blessings accorded her, and her own eschatological importance. In his Persian work entitled *Jalā al-ʿuyūn*, Majlisī discusses the epithets which have accrued to her, such as Umm Abīhā ("mother of her father"), Zahrā ("shining"), Batūl ("virgin"), and Maryam al-Kubrā ("Mary the Greater"). Evidence that this still-elusive figure continues to fascinate scholar and devotee alike may be found in such twentieth-century studies as those of Louis Massignon and Henri Lammens, as well as the more recent work of ʿAlī Sharīʿatī. This Western-educated Persian intellectual (d. 1977) found in Fāṭimah a role model with which to encourage nascent Muslim feminism. His work *Fāṭimah Fāṭimah ast* (Fāṭimah Is Fāṭimah) draws upon both history and hagiography to present Fāṭimah as a potent symbol of female authenticity and liberation.

BIBLIOGRAPHY

The only monograph of note on Fāṭimah in European languages is the early twentieth-century work by Henri Lammens, *Fāṭimah et les filles de Mahomet* (Rome, 1912). His far from sympathetic portrait is challenged by another French-speaking Orientalist, Louis Massignon, in a number of articles. Chief among these are "La mubāhala de Médine et l'hyperdulie de Fatima," *Annuaire de l'École des Hautes Études* (1943), and "La notion du vœu et la dévotion musulmane à Fāṭima," *Studi orientalistici in onore di Giorgio della Vida* (Rome, 1956), vol. 2, pp. 102–126. These have been reprinted in Massignon's *Opera minora* (Beirut, 1963), vol. 1. Massignon's work presents a transhistorical, highly spiritualized account of Fāṭimah as a kind of Islamic counterpart of the Virgin Mary in Christianity. An examination of the Qur'anic depiction of Mary in light of the Fāṭimah cult can be found in my own "Chosen of All Women: Mary and Fāṭimah in Qur'ānic Exegesis," *Islamochristiana* 7 (1981): 19–28. For an overview of both historical and legendary material on the Prophet's daughter, see Laura Veccia Vaglieri's entry, "Fāṭima," in *The Encyclopaedia of Islam*, new ed. (Leiden, 1960–).

JANE DAMMEN MCAULIFFE

FA-TSANG (643–712), also known as Hsien-shou; third patriarch and systematizer of the Hua-yen school, a Chinese Buddhist tradition centered around exegesis of the *Avataṃsaka Sūtra*. His surname, Kʿang, indicates that his family was originally from Samarkand in Central Asia. Fa-tsang was a son of Mi, a high-ranking army officer in the Tʿang dynasty. When he was sixteen years old he burned off one of his fingers as an offering to the Buddha before an Aśoka stupa in which relics of the Buddha were enshrined. After seeking without success for a satisfactory teacher, he entered Mount Tʿai-pei, where he studied Mahāyāna Buddhism in seclusion. Some years later, hearing that his parents were ill, he returned home to Chʿang-an, where Chih-yen (later reckoned the second Hua-yen patriarch) was lecturing on the *Hua-yen ching (Mahāvaipulya-buddhagaṇḍavyūha Sūtra)* at the Yün-hua Ssu. Yen Chao-yin, Fa-tsang's biographer, described the meeting of these two as a "smooth acceptance, like pouring water into a vessel, a harmonious condition compared to mingling milk and water." Subsequent to this encounter, Fa-tsang became Chih-yen's disciple.

In 668, when his master Chih-yen passed away, Fa-tsang was still a layman. When he was twenty-eight, Empress Wu Tse-tʿien built a new temple named Tʿai-yüan Ssu in memory of her mother, Yung-kuo. It was at this time that Fa-tsang was ordained and became a monk at this temple, probably at the empress's request. In 684, he met Divākara, a monk from middle India, at Hsi-tʿai-yüan Ssu and studied Śīlabhadra's and Jñānaprabha's *chiao-pʿan* (classification of Buddhist teachings). The next year he joined with Divākara for the translation of that portion of the *Gaṇḍavyūha* (an independent *sūtra* comprising the last chapter of the *Hua-yen ching*) that was missing from Buddhabhadra's translation of the text. He also frequently assisted such excellent translators as Devaprajñā, Śikṣānanda, and I-ching.

Fa-tsang is best known as the systematizer and propagator of Hua-yen Buddhism; he is said to have given more than thirty lectures on the *Hua-yen ching*. His principal works are (1) *Hua-yen ching chih-kuei* (The Essential Meaning of the *Hua-yen ching;* T.D. no. 1871); (2) *Hua-yen wu-chiao chang* (Outline of the Hua-yen Five Teachings Doctrine; T.D. no. 1866); (3) *Hua-yen ching tʿan-hsüan chi* (Plumbing the Profound Import of the *Hua-yen ching;* T.D. no. 1733); (4) *Ta-sheng chʿi-hsin-lun i-chi* (A Commentary on the *Awakening of Faith;* T.D. no. 1846); (5) *Pʿan-jo-hsin ching lüeh-shu* (A Brief Commentary on the *Prajñāpāramitāhṛdaya Sūtra;* T.D. no. 1712); (6) *Ju-leng-chʿieh hsin-hsüan i* (The Essential Meaning of the *Laṅkāvatāra Sūtra;* T.D. no. 1790); (7) *Fan-wan ching pʿu-sa chieh-pen shu* (A Commentary on the Bodhisattva Precepts in the *Brahmajāla Sūtra;* T.D. no. 1813); and (8) *Hua-yen ching chʿuan-chi* (On the Tradition of Study of the *Hua-yen ching;* T.D. no. 2073).

According to legend, Fa-tsang was a miracle worker who sought merit for the people. One of his miracles allegedly caused both Emperor Chung-tsung and his successor Jui-tsung to receive the *bodhisattva* precepts and provide government support to establish five temples for the propagation of Hua-yen Buddhism. When Fa-tsang died in November of 712, the emperor Hsüan-tsung bestowed upon him the honorary title of Hung-lu-chʿing, director of palace ceremonies.

Fa-tsang is credited with three major advances in Hua-yen doctrine. The first is his classification of Buddhist teachings in "five grades and ten qualities." Through this classification Fa-tsang tried to show that Hua-yen Buddhism should be regarded as the acme of

Buddhist teachings, superior even to the Fa-hsiang (Yogācāra) school newly imported by Hsüan-tsang. The second achievement is his advocacy of a doctrine known as *san-hsing t'ung-i-i* ("the original way of explaining the doctrine of the three kinds of existence"). Using this theory, he insisted that ultimate truth and deluded consciousness are not mutually exclusive and that consequently even deluded consciousness can penetrate into the very root of truth. Fa-tsang's third achievement is his clarification of the ultimate modality of *pratītya-samutpāda* ("dependent origination"). That is to say, Fa-tsang elaborated upon Chih-yen's philosophy of *fa-chieh yüan-ch'i* (*"pratītya-samutpāda* in the True Realm") so as to emphasize that matter was no different from the truth *(li-shih wu-ai)*. According to Fa-tsang, when seen from the viewpoint of the Buddha, all phenomena not only depend upon each other but also enter into each other infinitely *(shih-shih wu-ai)*.

[*See also* Hua-yen.]

BIBLIOGRAPHY

Chan, Wing-tsit. *A Source Book in Chinese Philosophy*. Princeton, 1963. Pages 406–424 include a brief survey of Hua-yen thought and translations of the *Chin-shih-tzu chang* (complete), attributed to Fa-tsang, and two chapters from his *Hua-yen i-hai po-men*.

Kamata Shigeo. *Chūgoku kegonshisōshi kenkyū*. Tokyo, 1965. In the chapter entitled "Bushūōchō ni okeru kegon shisō no keisei" the author discusses the political and intellectual background of Fa-tsang's thought.

Kimura Kiyotaka. "Hōzō no kegon kyōgaku." *Risō* 606 (1983): 64–86. Treats the role of Fa-tsang's understanding of *pratītya-samutpāda* in the history of the development of Hua-yen thought.

Yoshizu Yoshihide. "Hōzōden no kenkyū." *Komazawa daigaku bukkyōgakubu kenkyū kiyō* 37 (1983): 168–193. The most recent and comprehensive study of the life of Fa-tsang.

KIMURA KIYOTAKA

FAUST. In sixteenth-century Europe, Faust was reviled as a godless man who, as a consequence of making a pact with the Devil, met a gruesome yet appropriate fate. By the nineteenth century, he had become the archetypal Romantic hero; the term *Faustian*, coined by Oswald Spengler (1880–1936), was taken as a positive epithet to describe those tormented, defiant individuals who strive for more than is humanly possible. Whether condemned or condoned, Faust is the protagonist of an enduring story that embodies fundamental religious and philosophical questions about man's place in the universe, the nature of good and evil, and the limitations of human knowledge.

The Historical Faust. Between 1507 and 1540, numerous references appear in German diaries, letters, and records to an unsavory character with the last name of Faust. The picture that emerges is of a fairly well educated man: he may have been the Johann Faust listed in the matriculation records of the University of Heidelberg for 1509, or he may have been the Georg Faust who received a hostile reception at the University of Erfurt. In any event, he traveled extensively, and he was viewed with a mixture of fear and contempt by his contemporaries, who describe him variously as a magician, a necromancer, a charlatan, an astrologer, an alchemist, a braggart, a sodomite, a gourmand, and a drunkard. His evil reputation, enhanced by his boast of having made a pact with the Devil, is confirmed by references to his expulsion from various cities. According to contemporary accounts, Faust died mysteriously. Philipp Melanchthon (1497–1560) says he was strangled by the Devil in a rural inn in Württemberg on the day their pact fell due.

Origin of the Faust Legend. The development of the Faust legend began in 1540, shortly after contemporary references to his activities ceased. The legend, a by-product of the Reformation, originated in Lutheran circles as a reaction against Roman Catholicism and Renaissance magic and science. It illustrates the anti-intellectual strain within the Christian tradition that has errupted periodically in campaigns of censorship and denunciations of "forbidden" knowledge. Faust became a convenient symbol of deviant religious, scientific, and philosophical thought. He was identified with several of the most controversial thinkers of the sixteenth century: Paracelsus, Trithemius, and Agrippa.

Literary Treatment of the Faust Legend. The earliest printed collection of Faust stories, known as the *Spies Faustbuch*, was published by Johann Spies at Frankfurt in 1587. Enormously popular, it was reprinted eighteen times in the next ten years. Before the end of the century, translations appeared in English, Dutch, and French. The German text went through several revisions, the last of which, republished frequently in the eighteenth century, was probably known to Goethe.

The basic story presents Faust as a scholar whose intellectual arrogance prompts him to abandon the legitimate study of theology for the forbidden science of magic. In return for a specified number of years of power and knowledge, Faust sells his soul to the Devil. He performs astonishing magical feats, conjures up the dead, flies over the earth, and eventually captivates the most beautiful woman in the world, Helen of Troy, by whom he has a son. When the pact expires, he is carried off to Hell.

The two most famous literary treatments of the story are Christopher Marlowe's *The Tragicall History of Doctor Faustus* (1604) and Goethe's *Faust* (1808, 1832). Marlowe based his play on the English *Faustbook*. His version of the story is in the tradition of morality plays, but he adds the specifically Protestant theme that Faust's damnation was due to his despairing fatalism and his refusal to accept justification by faith.

The first recorded performance of Marlowe's play was in Graz, Austria, by a company of English players. The play became a staple of German puppet theater, where it was seen by both Lessing and Goethe as children. As adults, both used the Faust story in plays of their own. Faust's defiant attempt to transcend the limits of human existence appealed to both men and fit in with the repudiation of Enlightenment rationalism that characterized the *Sturm und Drang* movement to which they belonged.

Only fragments of Lessing's proposed Faust dramas exist, but Goethe's two-part drama is considered the greatest work of Germany's greatest poet. By emphasizing the tragic elements only hinted at in earlier versions and by making them the source of Faust's salvation rather than his damnation, Goethe transformed the story of a venal, vainglorious magician into that of an inspiring, tragic hero. In Goethe's drama, God has the last word in the prologue: striving and error go hand in hand ("Es irrt der Mensch, solang' er strebt"), but only those who dare to cultivate the divine spark within can hope to be saved ("Ein guter Mensch in seinem dunkel Drange / Ist sich des rechten Weges wohl bewusst").

The Faust story continued to be popular throughout the nineteenth and twentieth centuries. Among the many authors attracted to the legend were Lenau, Klinger, Chamisso, Grillparzer, Heine, de Nerval, Valéry, and Mann. Most of them, however, rejected Goethe's optimistic conclusion and stressed instead the danger inherent in Faust's insatiable thirst for knowledge.

BIBLIOGRAPHY

In *The Sources of the Faust Tradition* (Oxford, 1936), P. M. Palmer and R. P. More discuss the background to the Faust tradition and print many of the sources, together with the English *Faustbook* of 1592, several early Faust dramas and puppet plays, and the fragments of Lessing's Faust dramas. Another important book on the tradition's development is Frank Baron's *Doctor Faustus: From History to Legend* (Munich, 1978). E. M. Butler has made a wide-ranging study of the Faust legend in three books: *The Myth of the Magus* (Cambridge, 1948), *Ritual Magic* (Cambridge, 1949), and *The Fortunes of Faust* (Cambridge, 1952). Geneviève Bianquis surveys the literature in *Faust à travers quatre siècles*, 2d rev. ed. (Aubier, 1955). Lily B. Campbell discusses Marlowe's *Doctor Faustus* in the context of Reformation theology in "Dr. Faustus: A Case of Conscience," *Publications of the Modern Language Association of America* 67 (March 1952): 219–239.

ALLISON COUDERT

FEASTING. *See* Food; Seasonal Ceremonies; *and* Worship and Cultic Life.

FEET are multivalent symbols. In some mythologies the rays of the sun—as depicted, for example, in the figure of the swastika—are likened to feet. C. G. Jung finds the foot frequently phallic in significance; others believe it is sometimes a symbol of the soul, an idea rarely directly substantiated but indirectly confirmed when lameness is taken to symbolize some defect of the spirit, as in the cases of Hephaistos, Wieland the blacksmith, Mani, and Oedipus.

The heel of the foot is both suitable for and vulnerable to attack; it may dispatch a serpent or it may be the locus of a fatal wound (Achilles, Sigurd, and Kṛṣṇa). In the Hebrew scriptures, Jacob grasps Esau's heel in order to defeat him. In Celtic legend, Gwydion masters Arianrhod by grasping her foot.

Feet are also vulnerable because of their contact with the earth. Vital and sacred forces can be drained away through them. For this reason, the Aztec ruler Moctezuma II was carried on the shoulders of noblemen, and members of the royal family in Uganda were carried on the shoulders of men of the Buffalo clan. An emperor of Japan, it is said, would have been deprived of his office had his feet ever touched the earth. The Irish hero Oisín, who had lived in the Land of Youth for three hundred years, could remain young upon revisiting the land of his birth only if he did not touch his feet to the ground.

The foot is also a symbol of humility because it touches and is besmirched by the dust of the earth. Victory and subjection are represented by the conqueror placing his foot on the neck of the vanquished or using him as a footstool. Worshipers all over the ancient world removed their shoes before entering sanctuaries and temples, as Muslims, Hindus, and Jains do today before entering places of worship. Foot washing has commonly served as part of rites of purification.

Foot washing as an act of hospitality was also widespread throughout the ancient world. The Christian ritual of foot washing was derived from this practice, and especially from Jesus' washing his disciples' feet (*Jn.* 13:5). As such, the ritual does not focus on cleansing but on humility, and on the Christian ideals of willing service and penitence.

Footprints of divine or holy figures may symbolize the way to the truth, or the salvation offered by them. Footprints of both Viṣṇu and the Buddha appear all over India. Such physical evidence of the earthly presence of divinity is a way of picturing what is wholly transcendent. This is probably the intended symbolism in depictions of Christ's ascension, found especially in eleventh-century English art, where only the feet and part of the legs show at the top of the picture. On a carved medieval bench-end from Launcells in Cornwall, the feet of Christ are seen vanishing into clouds while footprints are left on a rock. Similarily, pilgrims to Palestine can see footprints in the Church of the Ascension on the Mount of Olives.

BIBLIOGRAPHY

There is no really adequate discussion of feet as a religious symbol. James G. Frazer in *The Golden Bough*, 3d ed., rev. & enl. (London, 1911-1915), discusses the taboo against touching the feet to the ground, but he focuses on the loss of power and on the earth as the agency of loss rather than on feet. For a more convenient and up-to-date source, see *The New Golden Bough*, the one-volume abridgment by Theodor H. Gaster (New York, 1959). On foot washing, see G. A. Frank Knight's article "Feet-Washing," in the *Encyclopaedia of Religion and Ethics*, edited by James Hastings, vol. 5 (Edinburgh, 1912), which discusses both secular and religious customs in great detail. Concerning Hephaistos and the "magical or shamanic lameness," consult *Hephaïstos, ou La légende du magicien* by Marie Delcourt (Paris, 1957).

ELAINE MAGALIS

FEINSTEIN, MOSHE (1895–1986), American Orthodox rabbi and Jewish legal authority. Born to a rabbinical family in Uzda, Belorussia, Feinstein prepared for a career in the rabbinate under the tutelage of his father, David Feinstein, and subsequently as a student in the leading Talmudic academies of that region. Upon his arrival in the United States in 1937, Feinstein became dean of the Talmudic academy Metivta Tiferet Jerusalem in New York, a position that he held until his death. He played a prominent role in both the Union of Orthodox Rabbis and Agudat Yisra'el, the world movement of Orthodox Jewry. [*See* Agudat Yisra'el.]

Feinstein enjoyed worldwide recognition by Orthodox rabbis and laity alike as a leading interpreter and decisor of Jewish law. His *responsa* (legal decisions) have been published in a work entitled *Iggerot Mosheh* (Letters of Moshe), which to date encompasses six volumes. Students of Jewish law have enthusiastically hailed the appearance of *Iggerot Mosheh* because it offers a Jewish legal perspective on numerous issues relating to contemporary scientific, technological, and sociological developments. The topics Feinstein covers include heart transplants, autopsies, brain death, experimentation with live human tissue, intrauterine devices, the use of electric blankets and transistor microphones on the Sabbath, adoption, life insurance, labor unions, and sex manuals. Thus, the subject matter of *Iggerot Mosheh* dramatizes Feinstein's concern to use the technical capability of Jewish law to address ongoing changes in social reality.

Moreover, a number of Feinstein's rulings reflect a creative and bold flexibility, particularly in the realm of Jewish family law. In one controversial decision, Feinstein permitted, with qualification, artificial insemination even from a donor other than the husband. In a series of rulings regarding the status of a marriage solemnized in either a civil or non-Orthodox ceremony, Feinstein permitted the subsequent remarriage of either spouse without the prior granting of a *geṭ*, a Jewish writ of divorce.

It would be inaccurate, however, to characterize Feinstein as a liberal interpreter of Jewish law. A staunchly traditionalist work, the *Iggerot Mosheh* contains numerous rulings of a conservative nature as well. In the final analysis, then, the Jewish legal process as reflected in the *Iggerot Mosheh* demonstrates both receptivity and resistance to changing sociocultural circumstances. Feinstein's profound and encyclopedic grasp of Jewish law and his legal creativity were coupled with an outstanding reputation for personal piety and selflessness. It is because of these qualities that his halakhic rulings are considered authoritative by a wide cross-section of Orthodox Jewry.

BIBLIOGRAPHY

Eisenstadt, Benzion. *Sefer dorot ha-Aḥaronim.* Brooklyn, N.Y., 1940. See volume 2, pages 191–192.

Kirschenbaum, Aaron. "Rabbi Moshe Feinstein's Responsa: A Major Halakhic Event." *Judaism* 15 (Summer 1966): 364–373.

Rackman, Emanuel. "Halakhic Progress: Rabbi Moshe Feinstein's *Igrot Moshe* on *Even Ha-Ezer.*" *Judaism* 13 (Summer 1964): 365–373.

Rand, Oscar Z., ed. *Toledot anshei shem.* New York, 1950. See page 98.

ROD M. GLOGOWER

FEMININE SACRALITY. Attributing gender to manifestations of sacred power in the world is a long-standing human practice. Generally such manifestations are said to be "feminine" when they function in ways analogous to women's most common modes of physiological and/or cultural activity. Hence, that which contains, as in a womb, is commonly considered feminine, particularly if the containment can be perceived as gestation—for example, the gestation of seeds in the earth. That which nurtures by providing food and shelter or spiritual sustenance, as a mother offers milk and refuge to her child, may also be considered feminine. That which changes may be feminine, especially if it changes periodically, as a woman's body changes through its monthly cycle, or swells in pregnancy with developing life, or replaces its own innocent smoothness in childhood with the voluptuous fullness of maturity, and later replaces this with the flaccidity of old age. Similarly, that which works changes on materials outside itself may be feminine, just as a woman's care changes her infant into a self-sufficient child, or as a woman's processing changes raw materials into food and clothing. Feminine symbols and divinities were especially prominent in the religious systems of ancient cultures; they continue to be important in agricultural societies and among some surviving hunting peoples.

Feminine Sacrality in Nature. Perhaps the best-known and most frequently cited forms of feminine sacrality have been those connected with that portion of the world at large which produces and reproduces itself without human intervention. Many peoples have experienced this "natural" world as a constellation of powers and realities that both limit humans and define their opportunities. Often such powers and realities in nature are perceived as female. In fact, the entire natural realm may be experienced as female: people in modern Western cultures acknowledge such an experience when they speak of "Mother Nature." But the experience of the feminine in nature is more commonly restricted to certain sectors.

The earth. "According to Basilus Valentinius, the earth . . . is not a dead body, but is inhabited by a spirit that is its life and soul. All created things, minerals included, draw their strength from the earth spirit. This spirit is life, . . . and it gives nourishment to all the living things it shelters in its womb" (C. G. Jung, *Psychology and Alchemy*, in *Collected Works*, vol. 12, Princeton, 1968, p. 342). The earth is a living organism, and the ultimate source of all other organisms that inhabit its crevices and surface. As such, it must be acknowledged as the ultimate womb and mother of us all.

A poet of ancient India celebrated the earth as "the mistress of that which was and shall be" and declared that "the earth is the mother, and I the earth's son"; she is the "womb of all," pouring forth milk for her offspring (*Atharvaveda* 12.1.1, 10, 12, 43). A poet of ancient Greece sang to her as "mother of all things, feeding upon her soil all that exists" (Homeric *Hymn to Earth*). The Oglala of the upper Great Plains in North America were solemnly instructed: "For the Earth is your Grandmother and Mother and she is sacred. Every step that is taken upon her should be as a prayer" (Brown, 1953, pp. 5–6). Thus they prayed: "O you, Grandmother, from whom all things come, and O you, Mother Earth, who bear and nourish all fruits, behold us and listen" (ibid., p. 133).

Where she is represented iconographically, the Earth takes the form of a buxom, mature woman. Hindu temple sculptors have portrayed her in this way in illustrations of the story of her rescue by a great boar who dives in pursuit when a demon carries her to the bottom of the ocean; she clings demurely to the boar's tusk as he rises from the waters. This boar is a form of Viṣṇu, great lord of the cosmic order; hence the Earth also appears beside Viṣṇu in temple images as his consort the goddess Bhū, "that which becomes." Buddhist art offers a more revealing portrayal; in scenes where the Buddha-to-be calls the Earth to attest to his generosity as he strives to repel the attack of the god of death and desire Māra, the goddess appears as torso only, rising from the ground. The lower portion of her body—her "womb"—must be understood as the earth itself, of which the humanized torso is just a temporary projection. Interestingly, this portrayal of the goddess Earth as torso only is also found in representations of Gaia, earth goddess of ancient Greece.

The Earth's motherhood is not to be taken as metaphor only, for throughout the world myths have asserted that humans and other creatures first emerged out of a womb in her depths. Anthropologist Bronislaw Malinowski's celebrated studies of the Trobriand Islands report that peoples of each village traced their ancestry to a sister and brother who had come out of a hole in the ground in that village's vicinity. In West Africa, the Ashanti likewise claimed that their ancestors had come from holes in the earth. One hundred and twenty versions of the emergence story have been recorded among native peoples of North America. The Oglala, for example, tell how the people were initially tricked into leaving their earth-womb as the result of a conspiracy between Inktomi, the trickster Spider, and Anukite, the double-faced Deer Woman, the paradigmatic Oglala seductress. Inktomi and Anukite enticed the people to the surface with gifts of meat and clothing and a promise of unending plenty, but then winter came, the buffalo grew scarce, and the people could no longer find their way back into the cave-womb. In the Southwest, the Navajo and Pueblo peoples have developed complex emergence myths which describe how the people evolved into higher and higher levels of refinement as they ascended through a succession of wombs before finally emerging on the face of the earth.

How are the offspring thus born of the Earth first engendered? The Earth does not necessarily require a partner to help her produce her children. Thus the Trobriand myths cited above make no mention of a genitor who fertilizes the great genetrix, nor were Trobriand males believed to fertilize Trobriand females: like the Earth from which they were descended, Trobriand women received the spirits of departed ancestors directly into their wombs and returned them to life as children. Hence both Earth and women accomplished a form of parthenogenesis—virgin birth. [*See* Virgin Birth.]

In other cultures, however, the Earth is paired with a male fecundator, usually Sky Father. Before the world that we know is created, she and he are a single entity, locked together in a lasting embrace. But then the embrace is broken and Earth and Sky separate, allowing light and motion to enter the intervening realm. Sometimes this separation is voluntary, as in the long cosmogonic narrative of the North American Zuni, where Earth Mother pushes Sky Father away after she becomes pregnant. Often the separation is accomplished by means of external force. In a version of this myth told by the Arawa tribe of New Zealand, the primeval parents Rangi and Papa are separated by their children, who have become weary of the darkness. After several fruitless attempts, the parents are finally shoved apart by their son Tane-mahuta, the "father of forests"—in other words, by a gigantic tree. In the Mediterranean world the act becomes still more violent: according to the Greek poet Hesiod, the primeval mother and father, Gaia and Ouranos are separated when their child Kronos castrates his father with a sickle.

If the Earth is a sacred mother, it follows that the act of tilling her is also potentially an act of violence. The violence implicit in gardening is vividly acknowledged in a myth from the island of Ceram in Indonesia. A pubescent maiden named Hainuwele is slain and dismembered as her people perform a spiral dance. When planted, the parts of her body yield the yams that are the islanders' chief staple food and gardening product. But her murder also brings death into the world: the violence that brings her people their all-important yams also costs them the paradisal life that had theretofore existed.

Repugnance about violating the Earth in order to seize her products can also be seen in a frequently cited speech by the American Indian prophet Smohalla. Told that his people should become farmers, Smohalla responded: "You ask me to plough the ground. Shall I take a knife and tear my mother's breast? Then when I die she will not take my bosom to rest. You ask me to dig for stone. Shall I dig under her skin for her bones? Then when I die I cannot enter her body to be born again. You ask me to cut grass and make hay and sell it and be rich like white men. But how dare I cut off my mother's hair?" (James Mooney, *Annual Report of the Bureau of American Ethnology,* vol. 14, Washington, D.C., 1896, p. 721). [*See* Earth.]

The cave as earth-womb. If humans are children of the Earth, born of the womb that is her depth, the significance of caves in religious belief and practice becomes apparent. [*See* Caves.] Frequently a people identifies some cave or grotto within its ancestral territory as its own place of origin. Thus, for example, the Oglala say that their ancestors emerged at Wind Cave in the Black Hills of South Dakota. The belief that caves are the original earth-wombs may have been responsible for the great cave sanctuaries of Paleolithic times in Europe. The sections of these caverns which bear splendid paintings of animals and the hunt are all difficult of access and located at a distance from the entrance. Hence some scholars have argued that these caverns may have been utilized for another sort of "birthing" from the earth—rituals of initiation such as those that even today often feature a symbolic return to the womb. In this case, the return would have been literal, as initiates worked their way laboriously back into the bowels of the Earth from which their ancestors had ascended.

Another sort of return to the Earth Mother is accomplished when humans encounter death. Hence it is not surprising that the land of the dead is often located in a cavern beneath the earth. In Vergil's *Aeneid,* the hero Aeneas descends to the land of the dead by means of a cave at Cumae, west of present-day Naples. The Greeks similarly located their Erebos or Tartaros in a subterranean region, as did the Hebrews their She'ol. Muslim texts portray the underworld as the great fiery crater Jahannam, into which the unrighteous were thrown after judgment. Dante borrowed from such concepts when he portrayed his Inferno as a fiery pit whose nadir is deep within the earth's bowels.

The feminine character of the caves or underworlds cited above is not defined sharply, although in the classical Mediterranean world a goddess (the Greek Persephone or Roman Proserpina) shared the throne of the dead with her consort (the Greek Hades or Roman Pluto). But in ancient Sumeria the netherworld's queen was a lone goddess, a widow, the dread Ereshkigal. Similarly the Germanic goddess Hel served as the underworld's sole ruler. In Japan, her counterpart was the primeval ancestress Izanagi, who became the first to die after giving birth to fire. Among the Maori of New Zealand, she was Hine-nui-te-po ("great goddess of darkness"), a former dawn maiden who fled to the underworld in shame after discovering that her husband was also her father.

Alternatively, a dread female may guard the underworld's entrance; she is often less woman than female monster. Perhaps the most interesting example is a figure prominent in myth and ritual of the island of Malekula in the New Hebrides archipelago. Malekulans say that the soul released by death is blown by the wind across the waters of death. On the farther side, by the underworld's entrance, the soul encounters the monstrous female Le-hev-hev. Before her on the sand is the design of a maze or labyrinth, half of which she erases as the soul approaches. The soul must restore the missing half of the drawing in order to enter the land of the dead; if it fails, the guardian devours it. Mastery of this labyrinth thus becomes a central feature of Malekulan initiation rites.

Feminine sacrality and the waters. It is instructive that the Malekulan myth perceives the journey of death not only as a passage into a female underworld but also as a voyage that crosses water. Waters appear often in stories of human descents into and emergences from subterranean regions. [*See* Water.] The Greek who entered the underworld of the dead had to cross the river Styx; called by Hesiod the "awful goddess hated by the other gods," the Styx was a branch of the ocean stream that coiled around the world (*Theogony* 12.775–778). According to Plato, the soul that returned to earth for rebirth had to cross and also drink from another river, Lethe, the stream of forgetfulness (*Republic* 10.620). Even during the twentieth century, in some regions of rural Europe souls of children were said to emerge not only from caves but also from grottoes, pools, and springs. Versions of the Native American emergence myth replace the usual cave of emergence with a lake, or have a subterranean flood drive the people to the surface.

But the waters are not merely an amniotic presence within the earth-womb; in cosmogonic accounts they may become as well the matrix from which the earth itself is born. Even the resolutely male-centered Judeo-Christian creation myth acknowledges their presence: in the beginning, the spirit of God hovered upon the face of the waters. In the ancient Near East, where this account originated, other stories of the world's beginning depict a gradual process of evolution from these primeval waters. According to the Babylonian creation epic *Enuma elish,* the waters alone existed in the beginning, for the sweet and potable waters, Apsu, that now lie beneath the earth were then commingled with the primal sea, Tiamat. As Apsu and Tiamat lay together, the early generations of the gods were born, culminating in the lord Ea. Then Apsu plotted to kill his own children, since their clamor disturbed him. But Ea overcame Apsu and established a dwelling place for himself upon Apsu. Thus occurred the first separation of the waters. The second followed when Tiamat, angered by the loss of her consort, gave birth to an army of monsters that attacked her divine children. But the latter found a new hero, Ea's son Marduk. Following a ferocious battle, Marduk slew Tiamat and split her body in a second separation of the waters. Half of that body was cast upward to become the waters of the sky. A gap in the epic's text prevents us from learning what happened to the other half, but presumably it became the rivers and ocean, while Ea's dwelling, the land, was extended as homes for other gods were added. Finally mankind was created, to serve the gods in their new shrines.

According to one Hindu version of the cosmogony, the world's source is a gigantic male who sleeps upon a serpent in the primal waters. A lotus or tree grows from his navel; both are symbols of the cosmos. Alternatively, an egg is born from the waters and then breaks apart; its two halves evolve into heaven and earth. In the Finnish epic *Kalevala,* a bird lays the cosmic egg on a knee that the Mother of Waters raises, so that the bird will have a place for her nest.

The waters that precede the birth of the earth become even more explicitly amniotic in the earth diver myths common in Siberia and on the west coast of North America. Here, in a gesture reminiscent of sexual intercourse, a male animal dives beneath the waters to secure a few scrapings of soil that will become the germ of the land. The land is then stretched out from a central point, just as an embryo develops outward from its navel. Often the diver in such stories is a duck or a turtle. In fact, the boar who rescues the Earth and takes her as consort in the Hindu story cited earlier is an alternative form of the Siberian earth diver transplanted onto Indian soil.

Just as the waters that give birth to the earth and/or nourish nascent life beneath her surface are often female, so also are the waters that flow over the earth's surface. India is perhaps the preeminent land of sacred female watercourses: all her rivers are goddesses, the first of them being Gaṅgā Mātā, or Mother Ganges. Female divinities guarded rivers in China, above all in the South; especially prominent in ancient times, they often had dragonlike characteristics. In ancient Mexico, all rivers belonged to the goddess Chalchihuitlicue ("jade skirt"). The face of the Mediterranean world was dotted by springs, pools, and streams inhabited by water nymphs or dryads. Similar lesser female divinities associated with local waters are found, with countless regional variations, across the Eurasian continent. Sometimes, like the little mermaid of Hans Christian Andersen's celebrated folk tale, they venture forth on the earth seeking human lovers or husbands; the child born of such a liaison may become a great king or hero.

Mounds, rocks, mountains. Rivers are not the only manifestation of the feminine upon the earth's surface; any protuberance or extension of the earth may be viewed as a special concentration of the feminine. Hence mounds are often associated with the feminine sacred and are honored as earth navels—places where the earth first rose above the waters. The famous *omphalos* ("navel") at Delphi, where the Pythia sat to receive visions of the future, was such a mound; appropriately, like the mound itself and the earth from which it erupted, the priestess-seer of the oracle was also female. Rocks may be symbols of female powers; in village shrines of South India, for example, small rocks or heaps of stones may represent the *ammas*, local goddesses who protect each village. When the goddess Cybele was moved to Rome from her original home in Anatolia, she too was represented by a sacred black stone. Again, a mountain or volcano may be the visible form of a goddess or her dwelling place or her birthplace; a good example is the Hawaiian volcano Kilauea, once venerated as home of the goddess Pele. [*See* Mountains *and* Stones.]

Vegetation. Sacred plants and vegetation divinities have been both male and female in the varied mythologies of the world. But plants are conspicuously connected to both the earth and the waters, hence they are often linked to female powers. Popular images of a goddess who is a source of life and fertility may show her seated under a tree or clinging to a branch with her hand; or her body may become the tree's trunk while its branches rise from her shoulders. Trees are often haunted by female spirits. Herbs may be female: a hymn of India's *Yajurveda* exclaims, "O herbs! O, you who are mothers! I hail you as goddesses!" (4.2.6). Sacred plants that grow in swamps are often female; India's lotus, closely associated with Lakṣmī, goddess of prosperity, is an excellent example. [*See* Lotus.]

Staple food plants, too, are sometimes manifestations or gifts or transformations of feminine sacred powers. We have already encountered this concept in the myth of the murdered maiden Hainuwele; the yam is the transformed maiden. In North America, a similar story is told about the origin of corn, which many Native Americans revere as Corn Mother. According to one version of the Corn Mother story, the goddess was killed and dragged along the ground to fertilize the land where the corn would emerge. An alternative version claims that the goddess gave the corn and its rites to the husband, who pursued her after she had run away from home.

Lady of the animals. Given the central role of the earth and the waters in crop production, it is not surprising that forms of feminine sacrality are often prominent among peoples who practice gardening and agriculture. Except for the earth mother, whose honor is widespread among all people who depend on her products, significant feminine powers are found less often among hunting peoples. Occasionally, however, one discovers a goddess among the category of divinities known as lords of the animals. Such divinities control the supply of animals essential to the hunting economy either by creating them, or by corralling and releasing them to produce scarcity and abundance, or by restoring them to life after they have been slain. One such lady of the animals is the ill-tempered Sedna of Inuit (Eskimo) legends. Deprived of her fingers and drowned by her father, this once-human maiden tends the seals at the bottom of the ocean. But the misdeeds of the Inuit foul her hair, which she cannot comb for lack of fingers. She then becomes angry and withholds the seals. She releases them only after a shaman descends to comb her matted hair for her. A far more positive figure is the White Buffalo Calf Woman of the Oglala Lakota. This divinity, who appears either as a white buffalo or as an extremely beautiful young woman, brought the sacred pipe to the Lakota and taught them how to use it to summon the Great Spirit. She is a prototype not only of the buffalo but also of Oglala women, who were initiated into womanhood at puberty by a rite in which they imitated the movements of a buffalo cow. [*See* Lady of the Animals.]

Darkness, night, and moon. We have noted that the earth's dark crevices are often perceived as the womb of an awesome feminine power. By extension, darkness of any kind may be perceived as female. Hence night becomes a female divinity, often of awesome power; according to the *Iliad*, even Zeus, king of the gods, dared not displease Night. She may replace the waters as preformal matrix in accounts of the birth of the cosmos: an Orphic myth recounts how Night laid a silver egg in the womb of Darkness; Eros, or Desire, was born from that egg and set the universe in motion. In most mythologies, however, Night is relegated to the background of dramatic action; her principal luminary, the Moon, receives far more attention. [*See* Moon.]

The Moon is perhaps most simply perceived as a complement to the Sun—as spouse, lover, or sibling. As the gentler of the two lights, the Moon is often, but not always, the female partner. Myths of marriage between the Sun and Moon are legion, as are etiological accounts explaining why they do not travel through the sky at the same time. The most common cause of their separation is some kind of falling-out. An African myth reports, for example, that the Moon tired of the Sun and took a lover, after she had born many children (the stars) to her husband; the Sun then divided his possessions with her and drove her and her children away from his home. A similar myth of the Oglala tells how the two were assigned to separate realms after the woman Face usurped the Moon's place beside her husband at a banquet.

Perhaps because she is so often a prototypal spouse, or because her body swells periodically, the Moon is closely linked to pregnancy and childbirth; hence lunar goddesses often preside over childbirth or protect married women during their childbearing years. Examples are Juno, a powerful goddess of ancient Italy who became queen of the Roman pantheon, and Mama Quilla, sister and wife and second in command to Inti, the sun god of the Inca empire. In many areas of the world, mothers will hold newborn babies up to the light of the moon, believing that this act will bring blessings upon the children. Even when portrayed as a masculine power, the moon retains its connection with childbearing; many peoples tell tales of women who were made pregnant by moonbeams.

But the moon is also cyclical, and the connection between the lunar and menstrual cycles has often been noted. The Mbuti (Pygmy) peoples of Africa call the menstrual blood *matu* ("moon maiden"), while the Iroquois of North America have maintained that all menstrual periods occur when the moon is new. Both the association with childbearing and this link to the menstrual cycle seem to generate a special bond between the moon and pubescent women. Hence the Ceramese story of Hainuwele—the maiden whose murder results in the first yams (see above)—has a striking variant in which the murder is preceded by a rape and the maiden becomes the moon. In this account the maiden Rabia is solicited in marriage by the sun-man Tuwale, but her parents substitute a dead pig for the maiden in the marriage bed. Tuwale then pursues his bride and claims her so violently that he forces her body into the ground. No one can extricate her; therefore, as she continues to sink, she asks her parents to substitute a pig for her and to perform a three-day funeral ritual: on the third night she will reappear, shining down upon them as a light from heaven.

The myth of Rabia points also to another aspect of lunar sacrality: its ties to cycles of death and regeneration. The moon constantly dies and is as constantly reborn. Thus the moon may be a source of immortality, or the home of a goddess who possesses some life-sustaining nectar. The Chinese say, for example, that the moon goddess Ch'ang-o was once a woman who stole the elixir of immortality from her husband; she then fled to the moon to escape her husband's anger. Women and children honored this goddess in one of China's three great annual festivals.

Finally, the lunar rhythms mark off the passage of time and so help to weave the tapestry that is human history. Thus the moon is linked to goddesses who determine human fate, such as the Greek Moirai or the Germanic Norns. Like the moon herself, such goddesses have often been portrayed as spinners and weavers; two of the Norns spun and twisted the thread of life, while the third broke it off. Lunar goddesses of fate were also commonly portrayed in triple form, corresponding to the waxing, full, and waning moon, as well as to past, present, and future or to youth, adulthood, and old age.

Sun and fire. But the sun, in its journeys through the sky, has also woven human time and cosmic rhythms. Hence the sun may also be a weaver, as is shown by Japanese tales of Amaterasu, one of the rare female solar divinities to become the focus of a significant cult. Amaterasu was the ancestress of Japan's imperial lineage; priestesses drawn from the imperial family served her shrine at Ise. According to the chronicles *Kojiki* and *Nihongi*, she was born from the right eye of the primal ancestor Izanami, as he cleansed himself in a river following an abortive attempt to rescue his consort Izanagi from the land of the dead. Amaterasu's most famous myth describes how she fled from the earth and secluded herself in a cave, from which she was coaxed by the sight of her own shining reflection in a mirror. Her flight had been precipitated when her obstreperous brother Susano-o polluted her sacred weaving hall by heaving into it a piebald colt that was skinned backward. One startled weaving maiden stabbed her genitals with a shuttle and died as a result; according to one version of the story, Amaterasu herself was the maiden thus injured.

Like the sun, fire is most commonly perceived as a masculine power, but there are noteworthy exceptions. In the ancient Mediterranean world, the hearth fire was a goddess (the Greek Hestia or Roman Vesta). In ancient Rome, this goddess had a special temple at which a perpetual fire burned. The priestesses who tended this fire were required to remain celibate; the loss of virginity and consequent polluting of the vestal fire incurred a penalty of death. The hearth fire was also a goddess among the Ainu people of Japan. This Old Goddess of the Hearth, named Fuji, like Japan's most famous volcano, was not only a means of cooking and the source of a family's warmth, but also a psychopomp, guiding souls of the dead back to the land of spirits from which they had come. Another apparent connection between the fire of the hearth and volcanic fires under the earth is found in one of the many Polynesian tales about the trickster Māui. Māui steals fire for the use of mankind from his ancestress Mahui-ike, who lives in the underworld and hoards the fire in her fingernails. Fire likewise emerges from a tellurian woman's body in the Japanese story (cited above) of the ancestress Izanagi, who dies as she gives birth to her fiery son.

Feminine Sacrality in Culture. In his massive study of feminine symbols and divinities entitled *The Great Mother* (1963), analytical psychologist Erich Neumann pointed to two fundamental aspects of feminine power that such symbols and divinities manifest: on the one hand this power is source, giving rise to the multiple forms of life, while on the other hand it is process, an agent of growth and transformation. We can recognize both aspects of the feminine in the manifestations in nature described in the preceding section. But it is the second, the transformative aspect, that becomes prominent as we examine the modes of feminine sacrality associated with cultural activities and institutions. For the production of culture itself is a process of transformation: that which comes to us "raw" from the natural realm is "cooked" and hence made fit for human consumption.

Feminine sacrality can enter at virtually any point in this transformative process. In rituals of initiation, for example, where initiates must leave one mode of human existence and enter into another, the transition may be accomplished by passing them through the womb of a female power. We have already noted the postulated relationship between this practice and the cave sanctuaries of western Europe. Both men and women may evoke feminine powers in rituals of this sort, although the ways in which they utilize them are likely to differ.

Gardening, weaving, baking and cooking, pottery. Certain transformative processes seem so inherently female that some cultures assign them predominantly, or even exclusively, to women. The fundamental premise seems to be that women, who bear life and nurture it into growth, are better attuned to the powers that achieve these transformations and hence better qualified to awaken and channel such powers.

Gardening is perhaps the simplest example of a process in which women work with a power construed as feminine to capture a segment of the wild natural world and tame it so that it can be appropriated by humans. In some societies, gardening is practiced only by women, particularly if alternative economic activities such as hunting give men a useful function. Among the North American Iroquois, for example, women were not only responsible for all the practical functions of gardening but also summoned and supervised all calendrical rites associated with gardening and "owned" all the songs whose themes were related to the food crops.

Weaving is another example of a transformative skill often located within the special province of women. We have seen how celestial powers that mark off time, such as the moon and the sun, are regarded as spinners and weavers of human destiny. Appropriately, women who shape human destiny on earth as they bear and nurture children may be accounted the appropriate masters of the mysteries of spinning and weaving. Moreover, the two processes may influence each other. Thus people of rural Sweden once believed that if a woman who had just finished weaving rode away carrying a stick that she had stuck in her web, she would become pregnant with a child whose sex was the same as the first person or animal that she met. And if her husband cut her web from its loom, and did so quickly and efficiently, his horses would deliver their foals with comparable facility. The transformative power of the weaver's web, and its ability to alter the world around it, also explain the many weaving enchantresses who populate the world's folklore. [*See* Textiles *and* Webs and Nets.]

Cooking and baking likewise tap the transformative powers characteristic of feminine sacrality and women. A striking illustration is found in the Navajo Kinaaldá ceremony, which marks a girl's achievement of adulthood following the appearance of her menses. During the ceremony the girl impersonates and becomes Changing Woman, a complex mythical being who empowers all growth and transformation in the cosmos. As a focal act of the long and taxing ritual, the girl and the women who sponsor her prepare an emormous corn cake. It is then baked in a pit in the earth for an entire night, during which time the girl and other participants must not fall asleep. On the following day, the cake is cut and the girl distributes it to the guests at the ceremony. Because many aspects of the ceremony test the girl's ability to function as a woman, we can assume that the cake is also a test. It tests her ability, as representative of Changing Woman, to take the corn that is sacred to the Navajo and transmute it into food.

The story of Changing Woman's own Kinaaldá claims that the cake represents Mother Earth. The cake is in fact born of the earth, a product of the corn and the pit in which it is cooked. Moreover, the transformative powers of cooking and baking are often linked to the earth, for the various pots, caldrons, and ovens in which these processes are accomplished are made of the clay and/or iron that constitute the earth's own substance. Thus pots, caldrons, and ovens are doubly feminine, both as extensions of the earth and as sources of nourishment. It is no wonder, then, that pottery-making is sometimes restricted to women, as, for example, among the Pueblo peoples of North America. Nor are we surprised to learn that pots can substitute for the earth or earth goddesses in myths and rituals. Thus a story of the Dinka in East Africa recounts how the Creator grew the first humans to full size in a pot after he had made them; the pot clearly represents the earth-womb. Rural people of South India may enshrine a pot to represent the village goddess, rather than the usual stone or image.

Spiritual transformations. Nor is the province of the feminine sacred restricted to material transformations. Processes of spiritual growth and transformation may also tap powers perceived as feminine.

Institutions offering spiritual nourishment and the promise of renewed life may be described through feminine metaphors. Thus the Christian church has been called the mother of Christ's flock, nourishing his children with her milk. Such maternal imagery is in part an extension of the metaphor in the New Testament *Letter to the Ephesians* that portrays the church as the "bride of Christ." For Jews, the life-giving bride is not the Jewish community itself, but the radiant Sabbath that arrives to restore it each week. "Come, my friend, to meet the bride; Let us receive the face of the Sabbath" begins a sixteenth-century song (by Shelomoh Alkabets) still sung at Friday-evening Sabbath services. Nor is this concept of the Sabbath bride merely a literary image; during medieval times in Europe, Jewish qabbalists used to dress in their best clothes on the Sabbath eve and go to the fields to welcome the incoming beloved. [*See* Shabbat.]

Alternatively, the knowledge, insight, or wisdom that brings spiritual maturation may be assigned a feminine gender and be portrayed iconographically by female images. In Hindu India, Sarasvatī, a goddess, is the patron of knowledge, honored especially by scholars and students. For Buddhists of the Mahāyāna tradition (which is also Indian in origin), the term for liberating insight—*prajñā*—is likewise feminine; its ultimate form *prajñāpāramitā* ("perfection of wisdom") is called the "Mother of Buddhas" and is portrayed in iconographic representations as a goddess. In writings of Hellenistic Judaism and of Greek Orthodox Christianity Sophia, or saving Wisdom, was at times identified as the female aspect of an androgynous God. [*See* Wisdom.]

The compassionate figure who intervenes to aid the needy struggler for salvation may likewise be female. The *bodhisattva* Kuan-yin of Pure Land Buddhist sects in China is an especially interesting example because her prototype, the Indian Avalokiteśvara, was male. This personification of the Mahāyāna virtue of compassion came to escort the faithful to paradise at the hour of death. But he or she also offered other, lesser varieties of salvation by extinguishing fires, stilling waves, calming storms, freeing those condemned to prison or slavery or execution, disarming enemies, blinding demons, or even bringing healthy babies to imploring women. Roman Catholic and Eastern Orthodox Christians are familiar with the compassionate intervening female in the form of the Virgin Mary.

The Dark Side of the Feminine Sacred. Thus far we have concentrated on positive aspects of feminine sacrality: its role in producing life and nourishing growth of all varieties. But already, in exploring concepts of the earth as feminine power, we have discovered a darker aspect. For this power who brings forth life also reabsorbs it into herself as the dread goddess who rules the subterranean land of the dead. Moreover, the terrible aspect of certain female deities is not merely a product of association with the bowels of a feminine earth; rather, it is the other side of the processes of growth and transformation that so many female deities represent. For life and growth inevitably entail death and decay, and misdirected spiritual striving readily deteriorates into madness.

Perhaps the most infamous of the deadly goddesses is Kālī, the Black Goddess of India, born from the wrath of her demon-slaying mother Durgā. Kālī's teeth are fangs; her tongue lolls forth from her devouring mouth like that of a wild dog or tiger. One of her many hands brandishes an upraised sword; another holds aloft a bowl of blood that is the sliced-off cap of a human skull. She wears a necklace of human heads and a skirt of lopped-off human arms; sometimes she stands or squats or dances on the lifeless body of her consort, the great lord Śiva. She is time and death, but also life, and may be adored as a loving mother. She is also the illusion inherent in life's pleasures, so that affirming her for what she is may sustain her worshiper on a liberating path.

Still more gruesome than Kālī was a trio reflecting the horrors implicit in the Aztec cult of war and human sacrifice. To recognize their role as the dark side of the same process that generates life, one must understand the Aztec presupposition that human sacrifice was necessary to replenish the swiftly waning vitality of the cosmos, and that war was also necessary to provide victims for the sacrifice. Coatlicue ("snake skirt") was mother to the war god Huitzilopochtli. She wears a skirt of writhing snakes from which she derives her name; her hands are the heads of serpents; and her feet have the claws of a predatory bird. She is headless; twin spurts of blood gush from her neck into the mouths of waiting rattlesnakes. Closely related to Coatlicue is

Cihuacoatl ("snake woman"), said to "preside over and personify the collective hunger of the gods for human victims" (Brundage, 1979, p. 170). She was also sometimes called the war god's mother, for she incited the wars over which Huitzilopochtli presided. In Aztec iconography, the lower jaw of her gaping mouth is that of a bare human skeleton. Her clothes and body are the chalky white of a heap of bleached bones. She prowls at night, braying and screaming insanely; on her back is the knife of sacrifice, swaddled like an Aztec baby. This knife is itself a transformation of the third terrible goddess, Itzpapalotl ("obsidian knife butterfly"). The knife is one of the fragments into which this goddess shattered after antagonistic gods cast her into a fire. Itzpapalotl wears a skirt fringed with knives and has the wings and tail of a bird; similarly, her hands and feet have a predatory bird's sharp talons.

Cihuacoatl sometimes was said to change into a beautiful young woman, seducing men who withered and died after they had had intercourse with her. She has counterparts in the sirens and seducers recurring in folk songs and legends throughout the world, since the seduction that lures men to madness or death is a common characteristic of the awful feminine sacred. Or the dreadful powers may be patrons of witches, like Hekate, the triple-headed goddess of ancient Greece, who also prowled the world with a pack of bitches in the dark of the night, hunting souls to take to her friend Persephone, queen of the dead.

Feminine Sacrality in Women. This same ambiguity of response to feminine sacrality—the recognition that it holds both constructive and destructive potential—is found in conceptions of the sacrality of ordinary women. Women themselves have been viewed as repositories of creative and transformative power throughout human history and within a wide variety of cultural contexts. We have already encountered this concept in the belief that women are better attuned than men to transformative procedures such as weaving and cooking. We shall explore further this concept of feminine powers linking women to other aspects of the cosmos in the next and final section of this entry. But let us first examine two different ways in which women's sacrality has been imagined.

According to one prominent conception, women are sacred under specific physiological circumstances: sacred power resides in the condition, rather than in the woman. For example, menstruation and childbirth often render a woman taboo and dangerous because she produces blood, an extremely potent substance. Pregnancy may likewise bring danger: in rural Taiwan, a pregnant woman is a threat to brides and children. Virginity evokes purity, hence virgins may be essential to certain ritual roles, such as cutting the sacred tree during the Lakota Sun Dance or tending the vestal fire in ancient Rome. Menopause may leave a woman with magical or curative powers; hence older women are subject to accusations of witchcraft, but may also be solicited for special ritual functions.

A different conception of women's sacrality perceives women as repositories of a single power that they manifest and channel throughout their lives. But this power becomes alternatively beneficent or destructive, depending on whether or not it is disciplined in an appropriate manner. For example, all women of Tamil Nadu in South India are understood to be vehicles for *śakti*, a natural energy essential to all action and prosperity. A married woman who controls her *śakti* by means of faithfulness to her husband is extremely auspicious. Considered a living incarnation of Lakṣmī, the goddess of good fortune, she blesses her family not only while she is alive, but even after her death. More capricious, but still beneficent, is the unmarried virgin whose *śakti* is an unrealized potential. Negative and potentially dangerous figures are widows, unmarried mothers, barren women, and women who die in pregnancy and childbirth. The awesome power of a disciplined *śakti* is most dramatically displayed in the Tamil epic *Cilappatikāram:* the faithful wife Kannagi, widowed by miscarried justice, destroys not only the king responsible for her suffering but also his capital city of Madurai.

No matter how conceived, women's sacrality is often acknowledged as having existed prior to the powers that men may hold or channel. A myth acknowledging this priority has been recorded in regions of the world as disparate as Africa, Australia, and Tierra del Fuego. Once upon a time, it says, women had control of the sacred symbols and rituals. But one day the men stole the symbols and rituals (according to some versions, because the women were abusing their tremendous power). An Australian version of the story points to the counterbalancing reserve of sacrality that compensates the women for their loss. When the Djanggawul sisters realize what has happened, they say: "We know everything. We have really lost nothing, for we remember it all, and we can let them have that small part. For aren't we still sacred, even if we have lost the bags? Haven't we still our uteri?" (Ronald M. Berndt, *Djanggawul,* New York, 1953, pp. 40–41).

Feminine Sacrality as Unifying Power with Multiple Manifestations. As we survey the wide variety of forms through which feminine sacrality has been manifested, we must remember that the powers called "sacred" and "feminine" are not always related to these forms in the same way. People who speak of the earth as their sacred mother sometimes intend this statement quite literally:

the earth itself is the awesome power that sustains them. But they may also be referring to a generative and transformative power that resides within the earth. The same is true of other manifestations. The moon may be a divinity, discrete and specific to the ever-changing orb that paces the night sky. Or a divinity may show herself (or himself) through the moon. This distinction between manifestation and power is reflected in the common assertion that the moon—or mountain or cave or spring—is the divinity's "home." Such an assertion leaves open the possibility that the divinity will have another or possibly many homes—that is to say, that the power which is the divinity may have many modes of manifestation. In fact, many of the great goddesses not explored in this article represent powers of birth, transformation, and death that show themselves in many different ways. The celebrated goddesses of the ancient Near East were all multiple-mode divinities of this order. The Egyptian Isis, for example, was the deified throne, which in turn extended and concentrated the power of the earth. But she was also known as the "mother of stars," or Night, while her tears produced the Nile's annual and fructifying flood. She could bring life out of death, and did so when she awoke her dead husband Osiris and secured from him the child Horus. Yet she also was death, as shown by her title "queen of the west," west being the direction of the underworld. She even became the compassionate savior who bestows wisdom and immortality upon the faithful, when the Greeks and Romans converted her cult into a mystery religion. Changing Woman of the Navajo, Durgā of India, and even the Virgin Mary of Christianity—all are feminine powers with multiple modes of expression.

In some cases even the divinity herself is understood to be a form of some more abstract energy that she shares with other manifestations. South India's multiple goddesses—Durgā, her extension Kālī, the many village "mothers"—are all modes of *śakti,* which, as we have seen, is also manifested not only in women but in all forces of increase and prosperity. [*See* Durgā Hinduism.] Moreover, this inherently female energy may iṇ turn be located within some overarching schema that juxtaposes it against a complementary energy identified as male. The Chinese *yin-yang* concept is a classic example. Here the *yin* predominates in everything that is dark, shaded, cool, wet, waning, bending, earthy, female, while *yang* is bright, hot, dry, waxing, stubborn and aggressive, heavenly, and male. Despite the high level of abstraction that has generated these concepts, we recognize in *yin* several components associated with feminine sacrality in many eras and cultures: the earth, the dark, the waters, changing, and dying.

More frequently, the concept of a common power remains unarticulated; only the network of symbols clustered together in myth or ritual reveals the presumption that they somehow share a common essence. Earth/waters/moon/women/root crops is one such cluster, often found in horticultural societies, which links together the sources and manifestations of growth and transformation. But the complex does not have to be the same in all cultures. Ethnographer Joseph Bastien has recorded a complex in Andean Bolivia that clusters women, river, wind, and rats—powers sharing the capacity to flow or erode and therefore to bring about change.

Thus, although common themes underlie the manifestations of feminine sacrality, these themes have been articulated in many different ways. Various powers of birth, growth, destruction, and transformation may be conceived as discrete and distinct from one another, or may be viewed as diffractions of a single central feminine energy. Feminine sacrality may be concrete, identical with the sector of the world that is its manifestation. Or it may be abstract, a power that shows itself through some concrete vehicle but still remains separate from the latter. It may be personal—a goddess, female spirit, or woman—or it may remain an impersonal creative/destructive force. It may be peripheral within a given religious tradition, one small, feminine segment of a great patriarchal system. Or it may be central, a focal conception generating major forms of community and practice. It may be the very center of a tradition, that which bestows its principal unity and coherence. Or it may be offset and balanced by some masculine power that is equivalently focal. Moreover, the juxtaposition of its symbols and hierophanies against others within a given system generates nuances of emphasis and implication that vary extensively from system to system. To examine the symbols, stories, and practices of feminine sacrality apart from their initial religious settings is therefore, inevitably, to distort and oversimplify them. To understand them fully, one must study them in context.

[*See also* Goddess Worship; *entries on specific goddesses; and* Women's Studies. Qabbalah *and* Tantrism *include discussion of feminine sacrality in Judaism and the religions of South Asia.*]

BIBLIOGRAPHY

The most comprehensive and provocative study of feminine sacrality continues to be Jungian psychologist Erich Neumann's *The Great Mother,* 2d ed. (1963; Princeton, 1974); the volume's large collection of plates is especially valuable. Neumann's data is embedded in a controversial theory of the evolution of human consciousness; hence the reader who seeks to use his work must remain critically alert. Two valuable collections of essays that update Neumann's information on goddesses are *Mother Worship,* edited by James J. Preston (Chapel Hill, N.C., 1982), and *The Book of the Goddess Past and Present,* edited by Carl Olson (New York, 1983); see also *The Divine Consort: Rādhā and the Goddesses of India,* edited by John Stratton Hawley and Donna M. Wulff (Berkeley, 1982), which covers only Indian materials. Extensive older literature is available on goddesses of the ancient Near East, Greece, and Rome, as well as Isis and the Virgin Mary.

Mircea Eliade's *Patterns in Comparative Religion* (New York, 1958) contains much valuable information about feminine symbolisms of the earth, waters, moon, vegetation, and gardening; his *Birth and Rebirth* (London, 1958), issued in the United States as *Rites and Symbols of Initiation* (1958; New York, 1975), offers significant insights into the role of feminine symbolism in initiation. Charles H. Long's *Alpha: The Myths of Creation* (New York, 1963) furnishes excellent examples of world-parent, earth-diver, and emergence myths, as well as an illuminating commentary. For a helpful survey of emergence myths in North America, see also Erminie Wheeler-Voegelin and Remedios W. Moore's "The Emergence Myth in North America," in *Studies in Folklore,* edited by W. Edson Richmond (Bloomington, Ind., 1957), pp. 66–91.

A singularly valuable resource for the study of goddesses who produce food crops from their bodies is Gudmund Hatt's "The Corn Mother in America and in Indonesia," *Anthropos* 46 (1951): 853–914. The original collection of variations on the Hainuwele motif is Adolf E. Jensen's *Hainuwele* (Frankfurt, 1939). Joseph Campbell offers a psychological interpretation of this motif and others related to it in *The Masks of God,* vol. 1, *Primitive Mythology* (New York, 1959); this book is generally a helpful source of materials on feminine powers in little-known traditions.

Although highly specialized, Steven G. Darian's *The Ganges in Myth and History* (Honolulu, 1978) and Edward H. Schafer's *The Divine Woman* (Berkeley, 1973) furnish interesting views of water-related divinities in India and China. Henry Whitehead's *The Village Gods of South India* (1916; 2d ed., rev. & enl., Delhi, 1976) is still an invaluable introduction to the cult of the local South Indian deities. For the White Buffalo Calf Woman of the Sioux, see Joseph Epes Brown's *The Sacred Pipe* (Norman, Okla., 1953); a broader survey of feminine powers among the Oglala Sioux is Marilyn M. N. Powers's "Oglala Women in Myth, Ritual and Reality" (Ph.D. diss., Rutgers University, 1984).

Materials on the transformative powers manifested through women's cultural activities are still sparse. But see K. R. V. Wikman's *Die Magie des Webens und des Webstuhls im Schwedischen Volksglauben* (Turku, 1920). The most complete source on the Navajo puberty ritual for girls is Charlotte Johnson Frisbie's *Kinaaldá* (Middletown, Conn., 1967). Neumann's *The Great Mother* (see above) remains the most comprehensive source on the role of feminine powers in spiritual transformations. But see also Joanna R. Macy's "Perfection of Wisdom," in *Beyond Androcentrism,* edited by Rita M. Gross (Missoula, Mont., 1977), pp. 315–334; the same volume contains an intriguing essay on the transformative powers of Sedna, the Inuit lady of the animals, by Gael Hodgkins (pp. 305–314).

The most readable analysis of the goddess Kālī is in David R. Kinsley's *The Sword and the Flute* (Berkeley, 1975). Burr C. Brundage offers a compact and fascinating sketch of the terrifying Aztec goddesses, as well as other, more benevolent deities, in *The Fifth Sun* (Austin, 1979). For the Malekulan monster Le-hev-hev, see John W. Layard's *Stone Men of Malekula* (London, 1942).

For the sacrality of women's physiological states, see Rita M. Gross's "Exclusion and Participation: The Role of Women in Aboriginal Australian Religion" (Ph.D. diss., University of Chicago, 1974). A summary of Gross's principal argument is in *Unspoken Worlds,* edited by Nancy A. Falk and Rita M. Gross (New York, 1980); the same volume contains articles on the women/gardening/vegetation ritual link among the Iroquois (Annemarie Shimony's "Women of Influence and Prestige among the Native American Iroquois") and the women/river/wind complex of the Bolivian Qollahuaya (Joseph W. Bastien's "Rosinta, Rats and River"). Carolyn Niethammer's *Daughters of the Earth* (New York, 1977) offers examples of responses to menstruation, childbirth, and postmenopausal women among Native Americans. Emily M. Ahern's "The Power and Pollution of Chinese Women" also documents perceptions of menstruation and childbirth; it is published in *Women in Chinese Society,* edited by Margery Wolf and Roxanne Witke (Stanford, Calif., 1975). Excellent information on the concept of *śakti* and its influence on perceptions of South Indian women can be found in *The Powers of Tamil Women,* edited by Susan S. Wadley (Syracuse, N.Y., 1980).

Sections on North America, Mexico, Oceania, Japan, India, Africa, and classical Greece and Rome in any good volume or series on world mythologies should yield a substantial selection of myths in which various types of female powers are prominent. Roslyn Poignant's *Oceanic Mythology* of the "Paul Hamlyn Series" (London, 1967) is an especially good example of this genre; Geoffrey Parrinder's *African Mythology* (London, 1967), from the same series, is also useful.

NANCY E. AUER FALK

FÉNELON, FRANÇOIS (1651–1715), French philosopher, theologian, and educator; Roman Catholic archbishop of Cambrai. Born in the Château de Fénelon in Périgord, François de Salignac de la Mothe Fénelon, an aristocrat by birth and upbringing, spent the first years of his education at home. After the death of his father in 1663, he was sent to study with the Jesuits at the University of Cahors; then, in 1665, he went to Paris, where he studied philosophy and theology at the College of Le Plessis. Finally, probably in 1672, he entered the Seminary of Saint-Sulpice to prepare for the priesthood.

Ordained at the age of twenty-four, Fénelon worked in the parish of Saint-Sulpice from 1675 to 1678. In

1678 he became superior of the Convent of New Catholics (a position he held until 1689), where he strengthened the faith of young women recently converted to the Catholic church. In August 1689 Louis XIV chose him to be private tutor to his grandson, the duke of Burgundy, a post Fénelon held until 1699. In 1693 he was elected a member of the French Academy and in 1695 was nominated archbishop of Cambrai. Fénelon spent the final years of his life as a successful administrator and zealous bishop.

Fénelon's writings concern pedagogy, literature, politics, philosophy, and theology. In his *Traité de l'éducation des filles* (1687), for example, foreshadowing Rousseau's *Émile,* we find his educational philosophy. His literary ability and political ideas are felicitously woven together in his *Les aventures de Télémaque* (1699), a mythological novel written for the instruction of the dauphin. Here allegory dissimulates the real import of his views. Fénelon depicts the confused ideal of a monarchy at once absolute, aristocratic, and urbane, while condemning indirectly the despotic and bellicose reign of Louis XIV. The views expressed in this novel redounded inevitably to his discredit in the eyes of the king and his loss of favor at court.

It is the controversy over Quietism, however, that has weighed most heavily on the memory of Fénelon, making it difficult to give an objective assessment of him. His undulating and generous nature had made him adopt the principle of the "dévotion idéale" professed by Madame Guyon (1648–1717), a mystic Fénelon had met and befriended in 1688: the soul, completely absorbed by the love of God, becomes indifferent to everything, even its own life and salvation. Feeling obliged, however, to justify himself before the public, Fénelon formally disowned the excesses and consequences of Quietism in his *L'explication des maximes des saints sur la vie intérieure* (1697). Nevertheless, in 1699 the Holy See decided to condemn twenty-three propositions extracted from this book. [*See* Quietism.]

Yet, with his aristocratic cast of mind and his poetic makeup, Fénelon exercised a strong influence on his contemporaries and left a mark on the history of spirituality. Original insofar as he adopted a scale of values that was personal to him, he provided a philosophical justification for his attitude toward spiritual matters by establishing as the basis of his spiritual system two notions directly connected with each other: pure love and indifference, the latter being the psychological state in which pure love is born.

Fénelon's life and works witness to the more human and subtle exigencies of French spirituality. He was aware of his own defects yet was too deeply committed to the world to have the courage to deny it. His troubled and sublime spirit needed more the experience of God and less the life of the intellect, more freedom for the soul, more spontaneity, and less dedication to the rewards of piety.

BIBLIOGRAPHY

There have been numerous editions of Fénelon's *Œuvres complètes:* Paris, 1810; Versailles, 1820–1830; Paris, 1835; Paris, 1851–1852; and Paris, 1854. For general information about Fénelon, the following two biographies are still useful: Paul Janet's *Fénelon* (Paris, 1892) and Élie Carcassonne's *Fénelon* (Paris, 1946). Janet's book has been translated into English and edited, with introduction, notes, and index, by Victor Leuliette as *Fénelon: His Life and Works* (Port Washington, N.Y., 1970). See also Carcassonne's *État présent des travaux sur Fénelon* (Paris, 1939). For informative articles on Fénelon, see A. Largent's "Fénelon," *Dictionnaire de théologie catholique,* vol. 5 (Paris, 1924), and Louis Cognet's "Fénelon," *Dictionnaire de spiritualité ascétique et mystique,* vol. 5 (Paris, 1964).

E. GERARD CARROLL

FERGHUS MAC ROICH. Tradition has it that Ferghus mac Roich was king of the Ulaidh, or Ulstermen, but was driven from his throne by Conchobhar mac Nessa, the king of Ulster, during the momentous events related by the epic *Táin Bó Cuailnge* (The Cattle Raid of Cuailnge) and other tales. Ferghus went into exile to Cruachain, the court of Ailill and Medhbh of Connacht, and this is why he and his companions were in the Connacht camp when Ailill and Medhbh made their famous incursion into Ulster. An alternative, and probably secondary, explanation for his absence from Ulster is provided by the Old Irish tale *Longes mac nUislenn* (The Exile of the Sons of Uisliu), which is really the story of the tragic heroine Deirdre: acting on Conchobhar's behalf, Ferghus offers to the Sons of Uisliu safe conduct back from their exile in Scotland, and when Conchobhar slays them despite these assurances, Ferghus wreaks carnage at Emhain Mhacha before going into exile himself.

Both elements of his name suggest physical power: *Ferghus* is a compound word meaning "manly vigor, excellence" and *Roich* (originally disyllabic *Roïch*) is the genitive of *ro-ech* ("great horse"). His virility was proverbial and measured in heptads: he ate seven times as much as an ordinary man and had the strength of seven hundred men; his nose, mouth, and penis were seven fingers in length, and his scrotum as large as a sack of flour; finally, he needed seven women to satisfy him when separated from his wife Flidhais, a goddess who ruled over the beasts of the forest. This is reminiscent of the description of Indra in the *Ṛgveda* (6.46.3) as *sa-*

hasramuṣka ("with the thousand testicles"), an epithet which, as Georges Dumézil remarks, alludes to the *supervirilité* which all peoples freely attribute to warriors and warrior gods (*Heur et malheur du guerrier*, Paris, 1969, p. 64). As late as the nineteenth century the famous Lia Fáil, the standing stone at Tara which in early times was reputed to cry out on contact with the man destined to be king, was known to local people as *bod Fhearghusa* ("the phallus of Ferghus"). It is particularly appropriate, therefore, that the much-mated Medhbh, queen and goddess of sovereignty, whose sexual capacity is a commonplace of the early literature, should have cuckolded her husband Ailill with Ferghus, as is recounted in *The Cattle Raid of Cuailnge.*

Ferghus had a famous sword called Caladhbholg (the Irish counterpart of the Welsh Caledvwlch, later to become the Escalibur of Arthurian romance), and with it he lopped off the tops of three hills in the province of Midhe when in the grip of his battle rage. According to T. F. O'Rahilly, this is the lightning sword of the great otherworld deity with whom he identifies Ferghus and other mythic-heroic figures (*Early Irish History and Mythology*, Dublin, 1946, p. 68). In several archaic genealogical poems a number of tributary peoples in the province of Munster are assigned descent from Ferghus, and it is clear that the substance of the tradition embodied in the Ulster saga of *The Cattle Raid of Cuailnge* was already familiar in the southern province in the early seventh century. The name *Ferghus* is borne by several pseudohistorical kings of Emhain Mhacha (the royal center of the province of Ulster), and one of these, Ferghus mac Leide, who is the hero of a submarine adventure, is very probably a doublet of Ferghus mac Roich.

BIBLIOGRAPHY

Further information on Ferghus can be found in Rudolf Thurneysen's *Die irische Helden- und Königsage bis zum siebzehnten Jahrhundert*, 2 vols. (Halle, 1921), the classic study of *Táin Bó Cuailnge.*

Proinsias Mac Cana

FESTIVALS.

See Seasonal Ceremonies; Worship and Cultic Life; *and entries under the names of particular festivals.*

FETISHISM.

The term *fetishism* derives from the Portuguese *feitiço*, which literally means "that which is made in order to make." The word *feitiço* appears to have been in use already in the fourteenth century. As applied to an object such as a basket, for instance, it could mean either that the basket was "made" (manufactured) or that it was bewitched *(encantado, feiticeiro).* When, during the fifteenth, sixteenth, and seventeenth centuries, Portuguese navigators and merchants sailing along the coasts of Africa (particularly the west coast) noticed the carved figurines made by Africans and used by them in their magico-religious cults, they accordingly described these figurines as *feitiços*, or as "having *feitiço.*" The French, who were soon competing with the Portuguese along the Guinea seaboard, translated the Portuguese word as *fétiche*, and in this form the word became current in those parts of Europe where French culture was most influential. Any carved or sculpted figure made in sub-Saharan Africa came to be known as a fetish. It is interesting to note that until very recently, Portuguese ethnographers used the term *fétiche* instead of *feitiço.*

In 1760, Charles de Brosses (1709–1777) published in Paris his *Du culte des dieux fétiches: Parallèle de l'ancienne religion de l'Égypte avec la religion actuelle de Nigritie,* in which he propounded the view that all religions had derived from fetishist cults. Later, this view was taken up by Auguste Comte (1798–1857) in his *Cours de philosophie positive,* when formulating the well-known and much-debated "law of the three stages" in the development of human intelligence: the theological (temporary and preparatory); the metaphysical (transitory); and the positive (normal). According to Comte, the first stage consists of three phases. One of these is fetishism, which endows all external objects with human forms of life and culminates in the worship of the celestial bodies. Comte further taught that primitive peoples believe in an intimate and exact correspondence between man and the world; hence their belief in fetishes, which are regarded as living creatures. For Comte, such a belief is a step forward in the evolution of the human mind from its animal-like torpor. The fetishist is a step closer to positivist science than is the theologian.

Comte's theories influenced the philosophical and socioethnological thought of his time. Opinion gradually changed, however, due to more extensive information and renewed attempts to explain peoples of non-European stock. In the end, African cults were seen to involve the worship of fetishes not as material objects but as objects housing forces akin to spiritual forces. The notion of fetishism was therefore replaced by those of animism, manism, animatism, totemism, and so forth, which began to be applied to the magico-religious practices of Africans and other so-called primitive peoples.

E. B. Tylor introduced the theory of animism, which describes the magico-religious belief that everything is endowed with soul *(anima)* or power (*mana*, from the

Melanesian languages). [*See* Animism and Animatism.] Tylor's interpretation of *mana* as energy, power, and so forth, was reinforced by Maurice Leenhardt in his study on the religion of the Melanesians (*Do Kamo,* Chicago 1979). Placide Tempels, writing about the Bantu-speaking peoples of Africa, preferred to speak of "life force" (*Bantu Philosophy,* Paris, 1952). It is interesting to note that these definitions are very close to that of the word *energy* used by Western scientists with differing meanings in physics, chemistry, biology, and so on. This is perhaps why Freud took animism to be the most complete religious system *(Totem and Taboo).* In his well-known essay "The Worship of Animals and Plants," John McLennan, taking theories about fetishism as his starting point, introduced his notion of totemism, asserting that it could be understood by means of a single formula: totemism = fetishism + exogamy + matrilinear descent. This was a mistaken view, however, due no doubt to McLennan's lack of data. Frazer, Spencer, Rivers, Reinah, Lang, and Durkheim have in turn all presented totemic hypotheses of their own. The death blow has been dealt to totemism by Claude Lévi-Strauss (*Totemism,* Boston, 1963). [*See* Totemism.]

Today it is possible to say that, as far as the language of anthropology is concerned, the word *fetishism* has been abolished for the description of religious practices. In ethnographic studies, however, it is not unusual to encounter the term *fetish* applied to figurines used in magico-religious cults. As Jean Pouillon has written, these are fetishes without fetishism.

Both Karl Marx and Sigmund Freud employed the notion of fetishism, giving it specific meanings of their own. For Marx, fetishism consists of attributing objective reality to nonexistent things. It is a process that grows out of alienation, one where man, when dominated by the products of his own labor, expresses his alienation by projecting ontological status onto idols (or ideas). Submitting himself in turn to these idols, he is in the end crushed by them. As an example, Marx refers to the "fetishism of goods." Freudian psychoanalysts use the terms *fetish* and *fetishism* in a similar fashion in their writings.

Marcel Mauss rejected the word *fetishism,* claiming that it was the result of a misunderstanding and was useless as a scientific concept. He argued that the notions of fetish and fetishism should be eliminated from sociological theories of African religions (particularly that of the Bantu-speaking peoples) and that they should be replaced by the concept of *nkiosi* (or *nkisi*), which is close to that of *mana.*

We have seen that the notion of fetishism derives from the term *feitiço,* which is to be found in historical sources dating back to the fifteenth century, when the Portuguese first came into contact with the west coast of Africa and spoke of the magico-religious practices of Bantu-speaking peoples, especially those of the Zaire or Kongo Basin. In fact, our present knowledge of these peoples confirms that their magico-religious practices contain much of what came to be known under the terms *fetishism, totemism* or *totemic reminiscences, animism, animatism, life force,* and even *euhemerism.* Most of these ethnic groups use a large number of natural and manufactured objects that could fall into the category of fetishes: diviners' implements (i.e., the figurines contained in the diviner's basket, most of which are carved from any one of a variety of materials); figurines sculpted in clay or in termite secretion; small dried trees or even parts of a tree, such as roots, twigs, leaves, branches, and fruit; coarsely sculpted tree trunks; small dolls clothed in net; miniature musical instruments or miniature agricultural or hunting implements; a large number of figurines carved in wood, bone, or ivory in the shape of human beings, animals or even abstract forms; horns, nails, or claws, or bits of human or animal skin; small tortoise shells; sacred rocks or minerals; crucifixes, medals, or images used in Christian cults; philters or magic substances and medicines. All these objects are believed to contain force and power and are capable of achieving that which is beyond the grasp of ordinary individuals. They are imbued with an underlying power that must be manipulated by human beings if it is to be put to use. This power is always connected with a spirit or genie embodying special qualities and can even be connected with an ancestor, located in either historical or mythic time. In certain cases, this power is the mythic ancestor himself, who for a time resides in the object.

Some of these objects possess propitiatory, repulsive, regressive, or otherwise "positive" functions, whereas others carry out the opposite "negative" functions. The latter category includes objects intended to cause harm or to protect against the evil spells of the *nganga* ("witch doctor"), who in such societies plays an important but ambiguous role. The *nganga* is a legendary figure, half man, half beast. He is often spoken of, but only rarely is anybody ever said to be a true *nganga.* Whenever a charge of witchcraft is leveled at a member of the group, such a charge is made timidly, and there is always difficulty in finding the culprit: so-and-so and so-and-so are said to have fetish or to possess a specific fetish (among certain Kasai ethnic groups, they are said to have *wanga*). Thus one may say that the *nganga* is a quasi-metaphysical, extraterrestrial, "supernatural" personage, who wields and captures the mysterious forces of the universe, possessing the power to unleash them at will, whenever he is asked to do so and most often with evil intent. In the mental makeup of the groups under consideration, the *nganga* is an ever-present being and force that acts even when not actually invoked; the figurine in which he resides need not even be handled and the user need not make his intention or desire clear. [*See* Witchcraft, *article on* African Witchcraft.]

Among the Chokwe (a Kasai people), for instance, the notion of *nganga* is paradoxical. Where evil spells are concerned, they say that the real culprit is not the *nganga* himself but the individual or group who invoked him, whether through threats, through either a nonverbalized or a conscious intention, through prayers or by any other means. This individual or group is made to bear full responsibility for invoking the *nganga* and to suffer the full weight of social sanctions.

The name *nganga* is connected with certain acoustic phenomena that are deemed inexplicable by these peoples: the sounds of the forest, the cries of certain night birds, the croaking of frogs, the hissing of snakes, and so forth, particularly if these unusual sounds occur in isolated or eerie spots. Everybody knows that the *nganga* has the power to turn himself into certain beasts and that he can, by direct or indirect means, either destabilize the social fabric or bring harmony to it. However, not everybody can gain access to the powers of the *nganga*. Only certain members of the group can do so: the medicine men, doctors, diviners, magicians, for example, who in most cases also prescribe and make the so-called fetishes. These persons are to a certain extent immune to the evil spells of the *nganga*, since in addition to undergoing specific initiation rites, they can also make use of processes that protect them against the occult powers; their immunity is not complete, however, for if they fail to follow the rules of the game, they can be harmed by their own fetishes.

In the foregoing examples, we detect two principles or attitudes in the magico-religious practices of the Bantu-speaking peoples, represented above all by those living in the Zaire-Kasai area: one belonging to the public domain and the other to the private domain of the witch doctors. Similarly, we should note two opposed functions connected with the power of the fetish: the positive and the negative, the public and the private—in a word, the good and the evil. In their attempts to define and signify the forces of this ambiguous power, these societies possess paired words such as *hamba* and *wanga* (among the Lunda Chokwe of the Kasai Basin, for instance) and *nkisi* and *ndoki* (among the Kongo and other peoples of the Zaire Basin). With regard to concrete representations of these forces, one of these principles can be and very often is turned into its opposite: this is achieved simply by placing a series of ingredients in the object, such as magic substances or philters. Thus, the Chokwe are able to transform a *hamba* figurine into *wanga* by making a small hole in the figurine and placing magical substances in it. Finally, we may say that the above two principles represent, at one and the same time, force, action, quality, and a concrete object, although one aspect may be less personalized and less ubiquitous than another.

In short, fetishism is not found in an absolute and exclusive form within the known magico-religious systems. Nevertheless, it is an extremely important component in our understanding of the behavior of the individuals and groups under consideration. Fetishism is signified by the fetish, a symbol of a "supernatural-divine" energy which can be harnessed and used. It would appear, therefore, that the sixteenth-century Portuguese were not altogether mistaken in applying the word *fetish* to the figurines used in the cults they encountered on the west coast of Africa.

[*See also* Images; Idolatry; *and the biographies of the principal scholars mentioned herein.*]

BIBLIOGRAPHY

Almada, André Alvares de. *Tratado breve dos rios de Guiné do Cabo-Verde dêsde o Rio Sanagá até aos baixos de Sant' Anna de todas as nações de negros que há na dita costa e dos seus costumes, armas, trajes, juramentos, e guerras, anno de 1594.* Porto (Oporto), 1841. Basic work for ethnographic knowledge of the Guinea coast (in the widest sense) at the end of the sixteenth century, written by a Coloured inhabitant of Cape Verde.

Brosses, Charles de. *Du culte des dieux fétiches: Parallèle de l'ancienne religion de l'Egypte avec la religion actuelle de Nigritie.* Paris, 1760. One of the first European works to try to widen the definition of *fetish* used by the Portuguese sailors of the African coast. Affirms that fetishism is a direct cult of the "object" or "thing," of an animal or element of the sky, of its power, of its force, and of its experience; that there is nothing symbolic in the relationship between the object and the believer; that the "fetish" is not the transformation of a spiritual or superior power. Brosses believes that fetishism is the cult of the beginnings of humanity, and so constitutes, in some way, an "infantile" or "childish" cult.

Comte, Auguste. *The Positive Philosophy of Auguste Comte* (1855). 2 vols. New York, 1970. Comte believes that positivism represents the final stage of humanity, following a theological stage and a metaphysical stage. The theological stage is characterized by fetishism.

Freud, Sigmund. "Unsuitable Substitutes for the Sexual Object: Fetishism" (1905) and "Fetishism" (1927). In *The Standard Edition of the Complete Psychological Works of Sigmund Freud,* translated by James Strachey, vol. 7, pp. 153–155, and vol. 21, pp. 149–157. London, 1953, 1961. For Freud, fetishism involves an individual attitude and is pathological in origin. For the psychopath, the fetish is a "substitute" for the penis or the clitoris.

Himmelheber, Hans. "Le système de la religion des Dan." In *Les religions africaines traditionnelles*, pp. 75–96. Paris, 1965. Attempts to define *fetish* and presents an important classification.

Lima, Mesquitela. *Fonctions sociologiques des figurines de culte hamba dans la société et dans la culture tshokwé (Angola)*. Luanda, 1971. Includes a systematic study of a large number of sculpted figures of the Chokwe ethnic group of northeast Angola (Kasai Basin), related to magico-religious cults and rites. The great majority of these figurines can be categorized as fetishes.

Lopes, Fernão. *Crónica del Rei Dom Joãom I de Boa Memória e dos reis de Portugal o decimo* (1443?). Lisbon, 1973. An account, written in a masterly style, of the accession to power of John I, first king of the second Portuguese dynasty, and of his reign (1385–1433).

Marx, Karl. *Capital: A Critique of Political Economy*, vol. 1, *The Process of Capitalist Production* (1867). New York, 1977. Marx tries to demonstrate that merchandise as value-object in a capitalist society possesses not only worldly value but also religious values, which lead to illusion and alienation. He denounces the "fetishism of values," since he believes that it is in the religious form of fetishism that the sacred is most thoroughly made objective. Such values have their own life, he says, not merely in practical terms but in religious terms. He thus affirms that fetishism is inseparable from the production of goods.

Mauss, Marcel. "Notes à l'essai sur 'L'art et le mythe.' " In *Oeuvres*, vol. 2, pp. 244–246. Paris, 1974. In making a critique of Wilhelm Wundt's *Völkerpsychologie* (Leipzig, 1900–1909), Mauss focuses on Wundt's conceptions of art and myth, giving at the same time a series of notes in which he raises the problem of fetishism, especially the religious concept of fetishism, an expression that he says should be banished from sociological terminology applied to African religions.

Philippart, L. *Le Bas-Congo*. 2d ed. Louvain, 1947. Albeit an ethnocentric work, chapter 3 deals in a reasonable way with the problem of *fétichisme* and *féticheurs* or *sorciers*.

Pouillon, Jean. "Fétiches sans fétichisme." *Nouvelle revue de psychanalyse* 2 (Autumn 1970): 135–147. Discusses fetishism in the thought of Marx, Freud, Hegel, and Mauss, agreeing with Mauss's theory that there can be *fétiches* without *fétichisme*.

Redinha, José. *Etnossociologia do nordeste de Angola*. Lisbon, 1958. Chapter 2, section 4, deals with the question of *feiticeiro*, *feitiço*, and *feiticismo* in northeast Angola, especially among the Chokwe ethnic group. Does not supply a precise definition of the *feiticeiro nganga*.

Zurara, Gomes Eanes de. *Crónica da tomada de Ceuta por el rei D. João I* (1450?). Lisbon, 1942. Vigorous narrative of the taking of the city of Ceuta by the Portuguese in 1415. Full of rich detail about the strategic, economic, and commercial importance of Ceuta in the context of Moorish power in the Maghreb and on the Iberian Peninsula. Recounts some customs of the city's residents.

Mesquitela Lima
Translated from Portuguese by Monica Varese Andrade

FEUERBACH, LUDWIG (1804–1872), German humanistic philosopher of religion and influential spokesman for the Young Hegelians. Born into a gifted Bavarian family, Ludwig Andreas Feuerbach studied theology at the University of Heidelberg before transferring to Berlin, where he became an enthusiastic convert to Hegelianism. In 1828 he completed his doctoral work at the University of Erlangen, where he remained as a docent until he was denied tenure, having been identified as the author of the anonymously published book *Thoughts on Death and Immortality*. In it he argued that the Christian doctrine of personal immortality was a form of egoism incompatible with a belief in the Absolute as infinite love. The book was especially offensive because of the sarcastic epigrams about pietistic Christianity appended to the text. Never again was he offered an academic position.

In 1837 Feuerbach married Bertha Low, and the income from a porcelain factory of which she was part owner supported him until it went bankrupt in 1860. Although in the early 1830s he contributed to the principal journal of the Young Hegelians, the *Hallische Jahrbücher für deutsche Wissenschaft und Kunst*, he shunned political activity and, except for a brief appearance in the Frankfurt Assembly in 1848, lived in studious seclusion in Bruckberg. He became famous in the early 1840s for his atheistic interpretation of religion in *The Essence of Christianity* (1841), as well as for his attacks on Hegelian philosophy in two monographs, *Vorläufige Thesen zur Reform der Philosophie* and *Grundsätze der Philosophie der Zukunft*, which influenced the young Karl Marx. Although Feuerbach returned again and again to the interpretation of religion, his later writings were relatively ignored. He maintained a prolific correspondence with friends all over Europe and America, and when the porcelain factory went bankrupt, he and his wife were sustained by the generosity of friends. When the social democratic press reported that he had suffered a stroke in 1870, contributions poured in from Europe and the United States. He died in Nuremberg in 1872.

Feuerbach's *Essence of Christianity* can best be understood against the background of his two fundamental criticisms of Hegel's speculative idealism. The first was of Hegel's basic tendency to treat abstract predicates—reason, thought, consciousness, and being—as entities.

For example, having established that thought was of the essence of humanity, Hegel then transformed this predicate into a metaphysical entity, a subject. Thus whatever truth there was in Hegel's thought could be appropriated by inverting once again the subject and the predicate, so as to make thinking and consciousness the predicates of existing individuals. The second criticism of Hegel concerned his preoccupation with thought in contrast to the actual sensuous existence of human beings. Hegel, together with classical philosophy generally, believed that the ultimate criteria of the real is its capability of being thought. For Feuerbach, the real is that which offers resistance to the entire sensuous being of the person—to sight, feeling, even love. Consequently, human existence is existence with others—it is communal.

Feuerbach's inversion of Hegel's basic metaphysical vision informs *The Essence of Christianity.* If Hegel regarded nature and history as the self-objectification of the Absolute, Feuerbach regarded God, the Absolute, as the reification of the essential predicates of human existence: reason, feeling, and love. The idea of God is the idea of the species characteristics of mankind involuntarily and unconsciously projected as an object of thought and worship. God is, so to speak, an acoustical illusion of consciousness. Hence the history of religions, of which Christianity is the culmination, is the childlike, collective dream of humanity in which it worships and contemplates its own essential nature. Just as Hegel argued that the Absolute must become reconciled with its alienated objectifications (the finite), so too Feuerbach argued that human well-being depends on the reappropriation of the real content contained in the alienated idea of God. The inner meaning of Christian theology is anthropology.

The first part of *The Essence of Christianity* attempts to show that all the major Christian doctrines—especially those of God and the incarnation—can best be understood as anthropology. The second part is more negative, seeking to establish that Christian theology is full of contradictions if these human predicates are attributed to a single, metaphysical being.

Feuerbach's book is still regarded by many as one of the seminal works of the nineteenth century and the first comprehensive projection theory of religion. Religion is not dismissed merely as superstitious belief, but seen as a necessary stage in the development of human self-consciousness. Moreover, the book is the first systematic attempt to develop a body of principles for interpreting Christian doctrine in its entirety. Christian doctrines are profound insights when taken as anthropological truths, but a mass of contradictions when taken as objective theological propositions.

Feuerbach modified his theory of religion in a small book, *The Essence of Religion* (1845), which in turn was amplified in *Lectures on the Essence of Religion* (1848). In these books he emphasized the role of external nature in the development of the religious consciousness, as well as the causal role played by wishes, needs, instincts, and desires. The basic drive of the self to preserve and develop all its powers *(Egoismus)* is said to be the hidden subjective cause of religion, while nature, falsified by the imagination, is said to be its objective ground.

Feuerbach stated that his first and last thoughts were about religion, and he turned to it once again in *Theogonie,* first published in 1857 and again, with a slightly altered title, in 1866. This work attempts to explain morality, culture, and religion in terms of a basic drive for happiness *(Glückseligkeitstrieb),* with arguments drawn from classical Greek, Hebraic, and early Christian sources. The gods are said to be the reified wishes of mankind. Since all wishes are fraught with a haunting sense of their contingency and possible failure, the imagination seizes upon the idea of a being that is not subject to limitation and death. Although Feuerbach regarded this book as his finest, it has generally been ignored.

BIBLIOGRAPHY

A new critical edition of Feuerbach's works, *Gesammelte Werke,* 16 vols. (Berlin, 1967–), is under the editorship of Werner Schuffenhauer; indispensable for serious scholarship, it contains the textual variations of all editions of Feuerbach's major works. It supplants Wilhelm Bolin and Friedrich Jodl's edition, *Sämtliche Werke,* 10 vols. (Stuttgart, 1903–1911), which was reissued in facsimile in 1960–1964 under the editorship of H.-M. Sass. In the facsimile edition, two more volumes were added. The eleventh contains a photographic facsimile of Feuerbach's inauguration dissertation of 1828 (in Latin), his *Thoughts on Death and Immortality* (1830), and an extensive bibliography of all works on Feuerbach in German between 1833 and 1961. The twelve (double) volumes contain Sass's expanded edition of Bolin's *Selected Correspondence from and to Ludwig Feuerbach,* together with some of Bolin's memoirs.

Six of Feuerbach's works have been translated into English: (1) *Thoughts on Death and Immortality,* translated with introduction and notes by James A. Massey (Berkeley, 1980); (2) *The Essence of Christianity,* the famous translation by George Eliot of the second German edition (New York, 1957); (3) *The Essence of Faith according to Luther,* translated with a brief but suggestive introduction by Melvin Cherno (New York, 1967); (4) *Principles of the Philosophy of the Future* (Indianapolis, 1966), which contains a long introduction by the translator, Manfred H. Vogel, exploring Feuerbach's philosophy of religion and his relationship to Hegel; (5) *Lectures on the Essence of Religion* (New York, 1967), a translation by Ralph Manheim based on the Bolin-Jodl version of 1908 and not the text Feuerbach himself published; and (6) *The Essence of Religion* (New York, 1873), an abridged edition translated by Alexander Loos, long out of print.

Until the appearance of Marx W. Wartofsky's *Feuerbach* (New York, 1977), there was no major scholarly work in English. A useful introduction is Eugene Kamenka's *The Philosophy of Ludwig Feuerbach* (New York, 1970). In German there are many important books about Feuerbach. Still indispensable is Simon Rawidowicz's *Ludwig Feuerbachs Philosophie: Ursprung und Schicksal* (1931; reprint, Berlin, 1964).

VAN A. HARVEY

FICHTE, JOHANN GOTTLIEB (1762–1814), German Idealist philosopher and religious thinker. Usually remembered mainly for his part in the development of German Idealism from Kant to Hegel and for his contribution to the rise of German national consciousness, Fichte is also an important figure in European religious thought at the end of the Enlightenment. Born in Rammenau (Lausitz), he enrolled in the University of Jena as a student of theology when he was eighteen. During his studies and a subsequent period as a private tutor in Zurich, he was apparently unacquainted with Kant's philosophy and seems to have been a determinist who admired Spinoza. Returning to Leipzig in 1790, he began a study of Kant that led to his conversion to Kantian practical philosophy. His fragmentary "Aphorismen über Religion und Deismus," written at this time, reveals his concern with the tension between simple Christian piety and philosophical speculation.

A fateful turn in Fichte's life and career came in 1791, when he traveled to Königsberg to meet Kant. Hoping to attract the master's attention, Fichte set out to write his own letter of introduction in the form of a Kantian-style "critique of revelation." When financial hardship cut short his stay in Königsberg, Fichte asked Kant for a loan to finance his return to Leipzig but got instead an offer to arrange publication of Fichte's manuscript with Kant's own publisher. Delayed for a time by the Prussian state censor, Fichte's *Attempt at a Critique of All Revelation* made its debut at the Leipzig Easter Fair in 1792 under puzzling circumstances. The publisher, perhaps deliberately, omitted both the author's name and his signed preface. The book was widely assumed to be Kant's long-awaited work on religion and received laudatory reviews in the leading journals. When Kant announced the true authorship, Fichte became an important philosopher virtually overnight. The book appeared in a revised second edition the following year, with Fichte's name on the title page, and in 1794 he was appointed to a chair of philosophy in Jena.

Like Kant's *Religion within the Limits of Reason Alone* (published a year later), Fichte's *Critique of All Revelation* argues that a valid revelation must conform to the moral law, which is purely an internal concern of reason. Fichte maintains that a revelation in external nature is nevertheless possible because some men are so enmeshed in the sensuous that God can advance the moral law only by presenting it in sensuous terms. When Fichte published his own Idealist system in 1794, entitled *Wissenschaftslehre* (Science of Knowledge), he abandoned his explicit dependence on Kant's philosophy while claiming to remain loyal to its fundamental aims. By giving up the Kantian "thing-in-itself" *(Ding an sich)*, Fichte overcomes the duality of theoretical and practical, deriving all knowing from the activity of the transcendental ego *(das Ich)*. He thereby inaugurates the transformation of Kant's critical philosophy, which culminates in the absolute Idealism of Schelling and Hegel. Fichte's essay on the divine governance of the world, published in 1798, led to the famous Atheism Controversy, which resulted in the loss of his position in Jena and his move to Berlin. Fichte's religious position at this time could be more accurately described as ethical pantheism than as atheism, for he equated man's inner sense of the moral law with God's governance of the world. Convicted of teaching "atheism," he was dismissed from the University of Jena in 1799.

During the last period of his life in Berlin, Fichte developed his political and economic views in the *Speeches to the German Nation*, while continuing to revise and develop his *Wissenschaftslehre* in lectures and in print. Ironically, the man who lost his position for being an atheist moved in an increasingly mystical and theosophical direction in his later years.

Fichte died in 1814 of a fever caught from his wife, who was nursing victims of an epidemic. His writings exerted a continuing influence not only on philosophers but also on theologians, including Friedrich Schleiermacher. Fichte stands as a Janus figure between the religious rationalism of the Enlightenment, which he embraced in his youth, and the new currents of Idealist and Romantic thought, to which he contributed original impulses.

BIBLIOGRAPHY

Works by Fichte. The standard and most accessible edition of Fichte's works is *Johann Gottlieb Fichte's sämmtliche Werke*, 8 vols., edited by J. H. Fichte (1845–1846; reprint, Berlin 1971); the writings on religion make up volume 5. A critical edition is being published as the *J. G. Fichte-Gesamtausgabe der Bayerischen Akademie der Wissenschaften*, edited by Reinhard Lauth and Hans Jacob (Stuttgart, 1964–). I have translated *Versuch einer Kritik aller Offenbarung*, 2d ed. (Königsberg, 1793), as *Attempt at a Critique of All Revelation* (Cambridge, 1978), with an introduction and a bibliography of primary and secondary works.

Works about Fichte. An insightful discussion of Fichte's importance for Christian thought is contained in volume 4 of Emanuel Hirsch's *Geschichte der neuern evangelischen Theologie,* 5 vols. (Gütersloh, 1949). Wolfgang Ritzel traces the development of Fichte's religious thought through his entire career in *Fichtes Religionsphilosophie,* "Forschungen zur Kirchen- und Geistesgeschichte," vol. 5 (Stuttgart, 1956).

GARRETT GREEN

FICINO, MARSILIO (1433–1499), the most eminent philosopher of the Renaissance. Ficino employed Neoplatonism, the characteristic form of Renaissance philosophy, as a support for Christianity. Cosimo de' Medici, impressed with Ficino's precosity, gave him the opportunity to learn Greek and presented him with his country house at Florence, the Villa Careggi, where Ficino presided over his "Platonic academy."

Ficino edited the complete works of Plato, translated Plato's *Dialogues,* wrote a commentary on the *Symposium,* and edited and translated various works of Neoplatonists such as Plotinus (the *Enneads*), Proclus, Iamblichus, Porphyry, and Dionysius the Areopagite. He also translated from Greek to Latin various second- and third-century mystical and gnostic texts *(Poimandres)* ascribed to Hermes Trismegistos.

In 1473, after an extended period of melancholy, Ficino became a priest. His own best-known works are *On the Christian Religion* and *Platonic Theology,* the latter an elaborate statement of his christianized Neoplatonic philosophy. Ficino's "pious philosophy" or "learned religion" presupposed an epistemology of poesy and faith. Divine poetry and allegory serve as a veil for true religion, for the rhapsodic and the mystical express religious truth, which cannot be expressed by simple intellectual formulas. A religious syncretist and universalist, Ficino believed that truth has been transmitted through a long tradition from the ancient philosophers and that wisdom has been revealed in many forms. Plato and the Neoplatonists, he believed, encompassed in their thought all the elements of the "ancient philosophy of the gentiles." Ficino envisioned everything within the cosmos as a great hierarchy of being. The One (God) is the absolute and uncontradicted original essence prior to the plurality of finite things, the ultimate unity of all things. The lesser orders are brought into being by emanations proceeding from the One. The way of ascent to the eternal One moves from bodies, through qualities, souls, and heavenly intelligences, with man at the center of this great chain of being, for he is bound to the world of matter by his body and linked to the realm of the spirit by his soul. Man is assured of his own divinity, since God is immanent in him through emanation. Ficino added a Christian patina to this Neoplatonic theodicy by identifying the demiurge, or intermediary, between the One and the subdivided spiritual and material world with the divine Logos, Christ, through whom the world was made and who "became flesh and dwelt among us." The church through dogma and sacrament keeps man in touch with the spiritual world. Someday man's immortal soul, freed from the prison house of the body, will enjoy the beatific vision of God without mediation.

All parts of the universe, Ficino taught in his treatise *On Light,* are held together by bonds of sympathetic love. The highest form of love, Platonic love, moves the true lover to love another for the sake of God. This love guides man in his choice of good over evil and of the beautiful over the unlovely. Ficino's close association of goodness and truth with beauty appealed to the aesthetic sense of the Renaissance and influenced literature and art as well as philosophy and theology.

BIBLIOGRAPHY

Ficino's works have been published as *Opera omnia* (1576), 2 vols. (Turin, 1959), and *Supplementum Ficinianum,* 2 vols., edited by Paul O. Kristeller (Florence, 1937). See also *The Letters of Marsilio Ficino,* 3 vols. (London, 1975–1981). On his thought, the most comprehensive study available in English is Kristeller's *The Philosophy of Marsilio Ficino* (1943; reprint, Gloucester, Mass., 1964). For a brief introduction to his thought, one may turn to Kristeller's *Eight Philosophers of the Italian Renaissance* (Stanford, Calif., 1964), pp. 37–53, and *The Renaissance Philosophy of Man,* edited by Ernst Cassirer et al. (Chicago, 1948), pp. 185–212. For the larger picture of Neoplatonism and its influence, see Nesca A. Robb's *Neoplatonism of the Italian Renaissance* (1935; reprint, New York, 1968).

LEWIS W. SPITZ

FIDES. The Roman goddess Fides is the personification of an idea that in itself is secular: the idea of "confidence" *(fides)* and, especially (in a more derivative sense of *fides*), the "good faith" or "trustworthiness" that inspires confidence. Fides made her appearance in the Roman pantheon in the third century BCE, about 250, when a temple was dedicated to her by A. Atilius Calatinus. This temple stood on the Capitol, directly next to the temple of Jupiter. But there must have been an earlier sanctuary of Fides (tradition says the cult was established by Numa, the second king of Rome), and the temple built by Calatinus was probably erected on the same site.

The site of the temple of Fides, next to that of Jupiter, is indicative of her origin, for everything points to her having emerged from the supreme deity by a process of hypostatization. In this light, it is easy to understand why Jupiter is guarantor, not only with Fides but also with Dius Fidius, of the observance of oaths and compacts *(federa)*. In fact, Dius Fidius, as "patron of good faith," is a first, archaic hypostatization of Jupiter. He is the god of oaths taken *sub divo*, that is, "in the open air." His temple, open to the sky, was located on the Quirinal, where it was situated on the *Capitolium vetus* ("old Capitol," or place of headship), next to the *sacellum Iovis, Iunonis, Minervae* ("chapel of Jupiter, Juno, Minerva"). Fides, for her part, appears in the wake of Jupiter Capitolinus. Her powers are broader and more flexible than those of Dius Fidius and include in particular the guaranteeing both of secrets and of the virtue (the interior disposition) of trustworthiness.

The goddess was honored by a special ritual: each year some *flamines* (priests) journeyed to her temple in solemn fashion, riding in a covered cart. The sacrificing priest—the *flamen* of Jupiter—celebrated the cult with his right hand wrapped in a piece of white material. The right hand was shielded in this way because it was considered as consecrated when used to swear fidelity. For this reason it was liable to the wrath of heaven if the fidelity was violated. Mucius Scaevola, who lost his right hand after swearing a false oath, is a mythical illustration of this belief. The rite of the veiled hand is also attested in Umbria in connection with the god Fisu Sakio, who closely resembles Dius Fidius. At Rome, too, it was the *fidius* aspect of Jupiter that was honored in this way in the person of Fides.

The temple of Fides stood on the *area Capitolina* (the level top of the Capitoline Hill), probably right against its southern edge. Its importance was considerable, since the goddess was patroness of all agreements entered into with a gesture of the right hand. From her commanding position, visible from many points in Rome, she also stood as guarantor of political accords and economic contracts; she encouraged the trustworthiness of citizens toward one another as well as that of the Roman people toward other nations. Her religious function was to procure confidence, credit, and hence often, albeit indirectly, wealth for her trustworthy disciples. (Her temple stood immediately next to that of Ops, a goddess of fertility and plenty.)

The cult of the goddess Fides, suspended during a good part of the first century BCE, was probably restored by the emperor Augustus. Treaties and military documents were posted on the wall of her temple at least until the end of the first century CE. The many representations of Fides on coins minted after that date show that her influence extended well beyond the first century of the common era.

BIBLIOGRAPHY

Dumézil, Georges. "Credo et fides." In his *Idées romaines*, pp. 48–59. Paris, 1969.

Freyburger, Gérard. "Vénus et Fides." In *Hommages à Robert Schilling*, edited by Hubert Zehnacker and Gustave Hentz, pp. 101–108. Paris, 1983.

Lombardi, Luigi. *Dalla "fides" alla "bona fides."* Milan, 1961. See especially pages 147–162.

Piccaluga, Giulia. "Fides nella religione romana di età imperiale." In *Aufstieg und Niedergang der römischen Welt*, vol. 2.17.2, pp. 703–735. Berlin and New York, 1981.

GÉRARD FREYBURGER
Translated from French by Matthew J. O'Connell

FILARET OF MOSCOW (1782–1867), metropolitan of Moscow, Russian Orthodox church leader. Filaret was born into the clerical "caste." He became a monk in 1808 and was ordained a priest in the following year. By 1812 he was rector of the Saint Petersburg Theological Academy. He became archbishop of Moscow (1821), then metropolitan of Moscow (1826); he served in the latter office until he died. Meanwhile Filaret had become a member of the Holy Synod (1819), the governing body of the Russian Orthodox church. Whether active participant or (from 1842) estranged consultant, he was to dominate its work for almost half a century. In the process he was able to demonstrate that the church need not be as subservient to the state as successive lay procurators-general of the synod expected it to be.

Filaret was barred from participation in the deliberations of the synod after 1842 largely because of the ban imposed on a privately circulated translation of the Old Testament. This translation was held suspect for two reasons: it was made from the Hebrew, rather than the Septuagint (considered normative by the Orthodox church), and it was made into modern Russian. Filaret had early been a proponent of exactly such a translation, and he had participated in the Russian Bible Society's work on the New Testament and *Psalms* (published 1818–1823). This work, discouraged after 1824, was not resumed until 1858. The publication of a complete (and, until the late twentieth century, standard) Russian translation of the Bible was begun in the year after Filaret's death. But it was associated with his name.

Filaret also supported the pioneer translation into Russian of patristic literature. This translation had an impact far beyond the boundaries of those academic centers in which it was undertaken. The freshly uncovered wisdom of the Fathers was to inform and transmute the thought, even the piety, of the Russian church and to rescue it from its previous "Babylonian captivity" to Western theological patterns. Filaret himself was prominent among the beneficiaries of this rescue operation.

Filaret gave much thought to the reform of theological schooling and stressed that Russian Orthodox scholarship should "develop its own models in the true spirit of the apostolic church." He produced a standard text, *Longer Catechism* (1823, revised 1839), to help the clergy with its work. Of more lasting importance were his carefully considered sermons, which mark him as an exceptionally subtle theologian, always willing to have his personal and profound experience tempered by Orthodox tradition.

Filaret's posthumous publications include a vast range of memoranda, opinions, and correspondence. They show him to have been a statesman as well as a hierarch of the church. They also demonstrate his curious mixture of determined liberalism with cautious conservatism. He was ill at ease with "democratic principles." But whatever his limitations in the secular sphere, he reinvigorated the Russian church at every level of its life and, in the fullest sense, reoriented it.

BIBLIOGRAPHY

A rich Russian-language bibliography is provided in Georgii V. Florovskii's *Puti russkogo bogosloviia* (Paris, 1937). Among Filaret's variously collected works should be mentioned his sermons: *Slova i rechi*, 7th ed., 5 vols. (Moscow, 1873-1885). Some of these appeared in English translation as *Select Sermons by the Late Metropolitan of Moscow, Philaret* (London, 1873). Others appeared in French, notably those translated by A. Serpinet as *Choix de sermons et discours de son Eminence Mgr Philarète*, 3 vols. (Paris, 1866). Less revealing is Filaret's *Longer Catechism*, translated by R. W. Blackmore in *The Doctrine of the Russian Church* (1845; Willits, Calif., 1973). No full-length study of Filaret has appeared in English, though the publication of R. L. Nichol's dissertation on him, "Metropolitan Filaret of Moscow and the Awakening of Orthodoxy" (University of Washington, 1972), is projected.

SERGEI HACKEL

FILIDH. The *filidh* were one of the great Irish priestly classes, etymologically the "seeing" druids (cf. Welsh *gweled*, Breton *gwelout*, "to see"). Functionally, the *filidh* was the equivalent of the Gaulish bard. But there were also Irish bards, whose function was wholly or partially usurped or assumed by the *filidh*. The Laws, the earliest recorded Irish tradition, treats the bard as an inferior. However, this change in status probably goes back to the period of christianization and its aftermath.

Originally the *filidh* was a soothsayer, and in this capacity his functions included writing *(ogham)*. He carved his spells on the wood of yews and possessed formidable magical powers. However, the christianization of Ireland had two consequences for all members of the priestly class. First, it abolished or caused the disappearance of the majority of doctrines, all rites of sacrifice, and most procedures of divination (for they were linked to sacrifice): the druid, as such, no longer had a *raison d'être*. Second, it radically altered the purpose of writing, which became didactic and pedagogical rather than magical and religious. Writing now was essential to the transmission of traditional knowledge.

The legal reforms brought about by christianization thus limited the religious role (divination and prophecy) of the *filidh*, but considerably broadened his literary function (storytelling, genealogy, courtly poetry, official records). At the same time, the designation *druid* was frequently replaced by or confused with *filidh*. Hence the *filidh* became preponderant in Ireland.

Medieval texts give a number of specializations of the *filidh*: *sencha* (historian, antiquarian, genealogist, panegyrist); *brithem* (judge, jurist, lawmaker, arbitrator); *scelaige* (storyteller); *cainte* (satirist); *liaig* (leech, who used the three forms of medicine: magical, bloodletting, and herbal); *cruitire* (harpist); and *deogbaire* (cupbearer). To this list should be added the functions of architect and ambassador, for which there exist examples without specific names.

The Irish *filidh* followed an apprenticeship of twelve years, during which time he studied law, genealogy, poetry, and all matters pertaining to specialization, as well as a considerable number of stories in prose and in verse (up to 350 long stories and 150 short ones). These tales were meant to be told in the course of the royal evenings. Neither their composition nor their recitation was free-form. On the contrary, the *filidh* adhered to strict rules and obligations regarding choice of poetic meter and subject matter. Like the Celts of antiquity, the writers of medieval Ireland knew no personal fantasy or imagination.

Hierarchy was strict and depended upon the scope of knowledge, from the doctor who could recite hundreds of stories to the apprentice who contented himself with seven stories and lowly pieces to be recited at banquets. Thanks to insular texts, scholars know the details of this hierarchy:

> Seven times fifty stories for the *ollam*,
> Three times fifty and the half of fifty
> for the *anruth*,
> Eighty for the *cli*,
> Sixty for the *cana*,
> Fifty for the *dos*,
> Forty for the *mac fuirmid*,

Thirty for the *fochloc*,
Twenty for the *drisac*,
Ten stories for the *taman*,
Seven stories for the *oblaire*.

As to the nature and form of the tales, they were like Irish literature as it appears in its most archaic state, with prose and verse interspersed. The versified fragments are the fixed, immutable part of the narrative, and the prose is a commentary enlarged or developed at the discretion of the teller.

BIBLIOGRAPHY

Le Roux, Françoise, and Christian-J. Guyonvarc'h. "Les druides." *Celticum* (Rennes), no. 14 (1982).

Le Roux, Françoise, and Christian-J. Guyonvarc'h. "La civilisation celtique." *Celticum* (Rennes), no. 24 (1983).

FRANÇOISE LE ROUX AND CHRISTIAN-J. GUYONVARC'H
Translated from French by Erica Meltzer

FILM. *See* Cinema and Religion.

FINNIC RELIGIONS.

Finno-Ugric languages are spoken by more than a dozen peoples and tribes scattered widely across northern and eastern Europe. The living environments and histories of the various peoples differ greatly. Thus their religious traditions have also developed in different directions, although they do have certain age-old features in common.

Languages and Peoples. The Finnic languages, like the Ugric and Samoyed languages, are branches of the Uralic language family. Judging from lexical research and archaeological finds, people speaking Uralic languages lived on the northern slopes of the Ural Mountains from around 6000 to 4000 BCE. Expansion to the west began in the hunting and fishing culture of the Neolithic period, and by the third millennium BCE there were Finno-Ugrians living in the region of the Urals and also along the Kama River and the middle reaches of the Volga. These latter areas remained centers of Finnic culture right up to the historical era. Archaeologists today link the Stone Age and Bronze Age cultures along the Volga and the Kama with the emergence of the Finno-Permian and Finno-Volgan peoples.

As a result of the expansion of Volosovo culture in the Volga region, the Finno-Volgan people, who engaged in primitive farming, spread across wide areas of eastern Europe around 1500 BCE, finally reaching the Baltic region and Finland. Even earlier (c. 3000 BCE), hunters thought to be Finno-Ugrians had found their way to Fennoscandia. The rock paintings with their predominance of elk motifs and various objects of these Stone Age people have been interpreted as elements of animal ceremonialism and shamanism.

There are signs of more extensive migration connected with the spread of the Volosovo culture. Settlement in the Baltic and Finnish regions became established, and when the linguistic ties with the Volga Finns were severed in about 500 BCE the Balto-Finnic group of languages emerged. When the Meri and the Muroma living in the region between the lands of the Baltic Finns and the Volga Finns gradually merged with the Slavs, who infiltrated the area from around 400 to 600 CE, the Finnic peoples gradually divided into the three main categories known in historic times: the Permians, the Volga Finns, and the Baltic Finns.

In the ninth century the Permians divided into two separate groups: the Komi (Zyrians, 326,700 in 1979), with their subgroup the Permiaks (150,800), and the Udmurts (Votiaks, 713,700). The Volga Finns include the Mari (Cheremis, 622,000) and one of the largest Finnic peoples, the Mordvins (1,191,800). A group culturally distinct from the other peoples in the Baltic area are the Saami (Lapps, 40,000). The largest and most developed of the Finnic peoples are the Finns (4.75 million) living on the northern side of the Gulf of Finland and the Estonians (1,019,900) on the southern side. Representing the eastern Baltic Finns are the Karelians (138,400), the Ingrians, and the Votes, who, like the Livonians living in Latvia, are merging with the dominant population of the region. [*See the map accompanying* Southern Siberian Religions.]

Differences in living conditions and natural environment are clearly reflected in the belief traditions of different peoples. The Saami of the Arctic region preserved a tradition reminiscent of the shamanism of the Samoyeds and Ob-Ugrians until the eighteenth century. Among the Komi, the Karelians, and the Finns, the woodland farmers and hunters in the coniferous forests in the north, primitive hunting rites held a position of importance. On the other hand the calendrical rites and spirit systems of the more southern peoples, who concentrated on farming and cattle breeding, were linked with events in the farming year and were intended to ensure success.

The influence of neighboring peoples on the development of the Finnic religions was considerable. Among the Baltic Finns there are traces of ancient Indo-European loans, as well as of Baltic and Germanic influences. The tradition of the Karelians and the Finnic peoples living farther to the east has a marked Slavic stamp. The Bulgar realm that emerged around the middle Volga and lower Kama subjugated the Udmurts and the Mari in the ninth century. The subsequent Tatar domination that followed the Mongol conquests from the thirteenth to the sixteenth century increased the Turkic influence.

The world religions adopted by the ruling nations molded the autochthonous religions of the Finnic peoples in different ways. When the Bulgars converted to Islam in 922, the Mari and Udmurts were forced to follow suit. The Islamic influence was reinforced by Tatar power, and the Mordvins also came into contact with this tradition, although Islam was not able to destroy the ethnic religion.

The Baltic Finnic tribes within the political and cultural constellation of Novgorod came under the influence of Orthodox Christianity in the twelfth century. At about the same time the first people in western Finland were baptized by Roman Catholics from Sweden. Novgorod's trading partners the Komi came into contact with Christianity as early as the twelfth century and were finally converted in the fourteenth century by Stephen of Perm. The Udmurts, on the other hand, strongly resisted baptism, the first known occurrence of which did not take place until the mid-sixteenth century. Even in the early twentieth century certain eastern Udmurt groups had still preserved their ethnic religion. Like the Udmurts, the Mari also adhered to their own religion, even though efforts to convert them were intensified in the eighteenth century. At the beginning of the twentieth century many of the eastern Mari were still not baptized. In 1551, with the downfall of the Kazan khanate that had dominated the region, the conversion of the Mordvins to Christianity began, leading to major unrest and migration. Missionary work was established in the 1740s by Anna, regent of Russia; over the course of several centuries, Christianity, seasoned with popular Russian religion, took root among the Mordvins.

Many of the old concepts and rites of the autochthonous Finnic religions were preserved within the Orthodox church. But the introduction of Lutheranism, which reached the western regions of the Baltic in the mid-sixteenth century, led to the systematic elimination of folk religious phenomena.

Mythology. The epic poetry and incantations of the Baltic Finns and the Mordvins have retained the old mythic themes that relate the origins of the world, of natural phenomena, and of culture.

The origin of the world. One version of the widely known cosmogonic myth is given in the Balto-Finnic epic *Maailman synty* (Origin of the World). A giant bird lays eggs on a hummock in the sea; the eggs break as they roll into the sea and become the sun, the moon, and the stars. Even more well known than this account is the Finnic variant of the perennial earth-diver motif. According to this myth, the creator, drifting in the primeval sea, orders either a waterfowl, the Devil in the form of a bird, or the first human being to dive into the sea for mud from the bottom, from which he molds the earth. Also related to the origins of the world are the tales of how the lights in the sky were set free. Two versions of this myth are known in Finland: in one the lights of heaven are found in the Pohjola, the "dark north," the abode of disease and the dead; in the other they are found in the belly of a giant fish.

The Finnic people have known two myths describing the origin of man. The Volga Finnic story of man's creation is part of the tradition that spread in eastern Europe. God creates man out of clay and leaves a hairless dog to guard him. The Devil blights man with his spit, having promised the dog a hairy coat in order to reach man. Another story reminiscent of the Asian myth of the origin of man has been preserved in Finnish-Karelian poetry: a tree stump rises from the sea, it splits in half, and two boys step from it. In the Finnish-Karelian area the creator hero at the time the world was born is Väinämöinen, the hero of epic poetry. As he floats in the primeval sea he digs fish hollows and forms the rocks and skerries. The canopy of the heavens is forged by the smith Ilmarinen, who also discovered iron and, with Väinämöinen, fire. [*See* Ilmarinen *and* Väinämöinen.]

Cosmography. The cosmographic concepts of the Finnic peoples display a combination of beliefs common in northern Eurasia on the one hand and widespread concepts typical of the high cultures of the south on the other. According to the Udmurts the world consists of three parts: heaven, the abode of Inmar, the god of the sky; the middle world, inhabited by man; and the underworld, the realm of the dead. This tripartite division is also encountered among the other Finnic peoples. The extremes of the earth, encompassed by the canopy of the sky, are most often described as a circle. In the Finnish and Saami traditions there are also signs of the theory that the sky is supported by a giant pillar through the center of the earth. The sky is attached to this pillar by a nail, the North Star. The Saami also had a name for the North Star that suggests that it was linked to the cosmic pillar. The center of the earth was further marked by the world mountain or world tree.

Also part of the world tree mythology is the story preserved in Finnish incantations of the felling of a giant oak. The tip of the oak covers the sun and the moon and prevents the movement of the clouds. A lengthy search for a man to fell the tree is conducted in vain until a diminutive man finally appears as savior. The Erzä Mordvins have also told of an enormous birch tree growing in the center of the earth; its tip and root each have three branches and it covers the sun with its foliage.

The water surrounding the world has been described by the Mordvins as a vast sea whose waters flow into a bottomless chasm. The Baltic Finns place this chasm in the far north. According to Mordvin tradition, the earth, floating in the sea, is supported by three fish whose movements shake the earth.

There are several parallel concepts of the underworld. The established farmers share the belief in the family burial ground as the village of the dead. Here the dead were thought to live a life comparable to that on earth. The Finns also shared the concept common among the northern hunting peoples of a distant realm of the dead. The river of Tuonela, the underworld, corresponding to the cosmic river, divides the realm of the dead from the abode of the living. The description of this river as fiery, rushing, and fraught with objects to torment the sinful bears the mark of Christian visionary literature. Most Saami believed that their dead inhabited the bottoms of lakes, but those in the western regions, like the ancient Scandinavians, held that the dead resided within mountains.

Supranormal Beings. Despite the fact that many researchers have regarded the cult of the dead as the oldest and only phenomenon of autochthonous culture that all the Finnic peoples have in common, many features of the various spirit systems are quite similar. The various directions taken by the individual groups were caused by differences in natural conditions, the influence of neighboring belief traditions, and the nature and extent of beliefs assimilated from Islam and Christianity. New formations and borrowings further enriched the already numerous body of spirits and gods. The overall view is obstructed by the wealth of parallel names; similar beings are sometimes called by different names in different dialect areas. Confusion and the merging of once separate beings further obscure the picture. Furthermore, there were no clear concepts of the nature of many beings by the time tradition began to be recorded. A good example of this is the list of "gods" of the Karelians and the Häme people (a tribe in western Finland) given in the preface to Michael Agricola's Psalter of 1551. In addition to the high gods, the list includes various guardian spirits, spirits of the dead, and figures descended from the saints.

The gods of the sky. The sky god clearly has a special status as the highest and mightiest deity. Although among the Volga Finns a variety of attendant deities were subject to the sky god, the original Finnic pantheon was not arranged hierarchically. Etymologically, most of the names for the sky god derive from some word meaning "sky": the Udmurt *Inmar* and the Komi *Jen* have the same root, meaning both "sky" and "god"; the Finnish *Ilmarinen*, the name of the god of the storm and the weather, is derived from the word *ilma*, "air" or "weather." The name of the Mari sky god, *Jumo*, is etymologically related to the Estonian *Jumal* and the Finnish *Jumala*, all of which derive from words that originally meant "sky."

The Mordvin term meaning "god of the sky," *škaj pavas* or *škaj pas*, was derived in a slightly different way. The word *pavas* or *pas* ("god"), of Iranian origin, has been attached to the word *škaj*, meaning "giver of birth, creator." Like the Tatars who assimilated with Islam, the Mordvins, Udmurts, and Mari called the sky god "great."

The Udmurt Inmar was above all the god of farming, as attested by the functions of "inseminating" and "maintaining," that are attributed to him and by the fact that sacrifices to him were made chiefly in the fields. Originally the time for worship was in the spring. Later, Inmar became generalized into a monotheistic god appealed to in all needs of life, under the influence of the neighboring high religions. A similar development also took place among the Volga Finns. According to the Mordvins, the sky god had a wife and children. Although he is visualized as a remote being living behind an iron fence, a living person is chosen to represent him in ritual situations. Notions of the sky god as a father farming the land are also found among the Mari. The various assistant spirits acting as intermediaries between Jumo and man are of Turco-Tatar origin.

The Permians and the Volga Finns turned to the god of the sky for their everyday needs. The supreme god was the general patron of life. A similar role is ascribed to the Finnish Ukko, who is similar to the Scandinavian god of thunder, Thor. Ukko's attributes are a golden hammer, a club, and a sword. Ukko, thought to be the giver of rain, was worshiped during the spring sowing rites and in summer whenever drought threatened. In the incantation poetry that emerged in the Middle Ages, the nature of Ukko, influenced by the Christian concept of God, became that of a universal lord, a supreme god in heaven whose help was entreated in the event of any misfortune. [*See* Ukko.]

The Saami name for the sky god, *Veralden Olmai* (also *Maylmen Olmai*), is of Scandinavian origin. His cult symbol is the image of the cosmic pillar. Reindeer bulls or other animals were sacrificed to Veralden Olmai to ensure that he would not let the world collapse; sacrifices were also made to him during eclipses of the sun and the moon.

Other gods of nature. The higher gods of nature are difficult to distinguish from the various spirits of nature. These have been called not only by a general name meaning "a god," but also by names including the concept "father" or "mother," sometimes used to designate spirits. In addition to the god of the sky the Permians and Volga Finns worshiped the great gods of nature in their sacred groves. In principle, sacrifices were made to the mightiest gods of nature during joint family and village rites, whereas lesser spirits were conciliated in greater privacy, in the areas within their power.

Concepts of the gods of nature are vague in that on the one hand natural phenomena were worshiped as such, yet on the other hand they were sometimes thought of as individual functioning beings as well. The gods of nature probably were originally natural phenomena conceived of as animate beings, although many of them experienced later development; for example, as a result of the assimilation of beliefs of the world religions, the gods of nature became divine beings capable of breaking away from their original natural elements.

The Mordvins and the Mari honored such natural phenomena as the sun, the moon, thunder, lightning, and clouds as gods. The earth mother, the most prominent nature deity, was of great importance to the Permians and Volga Finns. The Mordvins say, "First we bow to the god of the sky, then to the earth mother." The Udmurts also worshiped the earth god or earth giver in cults dedicated to the god of the sky. The merging of Inmar and the earth giver that is occasionally encountered is a later development. The concept of a divine couple consisting of the sky god and the earth mother, one begetting, the other giving birth, has its roots in the high religions of the ancient Near East.

The supreme gods of the Saami have features in common with the gods of both the Scandinavians and the eastern Uralic peoples. In the western regions the name of the god of thunder, *Horagalles*, is reminiscent of that of the Scandinavian god of thunder, *Þórr (Thor)*. The name of the thunder god of the eastern Saami, *Tiermes*, is of the same etymological origin as *Torem*, the name of the Mansi sky god. The Balto-Finnic gods of nature have to a great extent become obscured, merged with cults of the saints and various guardian spirits.

Guardian spirits. The tradition of beliefs among the Finnic peoples includes a vast number of spirits who rule over a particular place or phenomenon. These spirits are the rulers of natural elements (such as fire or wind), natural areas (the forest or water), or various cultural domains (dwelling places, cattle sheds, and so on); people come into contact with them on entering the spirit's domain.

The distinctions between the different spirits are not all that clear. The Mari, for example, venerate a water mother (Wüt-awa) who could be approached wherever there was even a little water, as well as a spirit of water in human form inhabiting deep water. Similarly the Mordvin water mother (Ved-ava), the general spirit of water, reflects the concept of the animate nature of water. In addition to the water mother, the Mordvins have local spirits of lakes and rivers.

The nature of the guardian spirit tradition varies greatly according to ecological factors. Thus the Saami spirits are above all the guardians of nature. In addition to the spirits of nature and the elements, homage is paid to the guardian spirits of animal species. This type of lord of the animals is also found in the regions of eastern and northern Finland, where hunting was an important secondary occupation. Among the Finns the general protector of game was Tapio, the guardian spirit of the forest. The spirits associated with buildings and cultural domains are especially varied in the stable farming villages of the Volga Finns, the Udmurts, and the southern Baltic Finns.

At the most archaic level are beliefs surrounding the spirits of nature. Sometimes these spirits take on human form. The Mari, for example, recognize both forest and water spirits in human form. One typical feature is, however, the fact that the form varies. The spirits of nature are indifferent to man, taking action only when disturbed.

The spirits of cultural domains, such as the house, the cowshed, the stable, the barn, and the sauna, are also often in human form. Although some spirits have special names, they are, like the spirits of nature, most often called by a two-part name. The first part refers to the spirit's field or domain, the second is a word of respect more generally attributed to a spirit: *mother, father, old man,* or *lord, mistress,* or *keeper.* The household-spirit tradition is connected to the cult of the dead in that some former member of the family may become the household spirit. Keepers of their own realm, the spirits of the cultural domains watch over social intercourse, human behavior, and the well-being of their masters.

Ancestors. The beliefs of the Permians, Volga Finns, and eastern Baltic Finns concerning the dead have much in common. The dead were buried in family graves, where newcomers were welcomed by those already there. The family was an entity consisting of both living and the dead members. Although the dead were feared, their care was vital to the well-being of the living members of the family. Two factors were emphasized in the treatment of the dead: assisting the dead to join the community of ancestors by performing the appropriate rites, and conciliating the family ancestors through constant remembrance.

The soul of the departed was thought to linger in the home for some time after death; according to Udmurt belief this period lasted for forty days. Thus the rites conducted between the moment of death and the burial were characterized by measures honoring the deceased to ensure that he was not offended. This meant, for example, keeping watch through the night on which the death occurred, avoiding the use of the name of the departed, singing laments, and so on. During the burial ceremonies the dead were transferred to the community of ancestors and were provided for both spiritually and materially. The amount of clothes, food, and utensils placed in the grave varied. The basic idea was nevertheless to ensure the deceased a chance of living in the other world a life similar to that he had lived on earth. The Udmurts, Mari, and Ingrians placed the deceased person's favorite objects in the grave, saying, "Here is your share, this is all you will get." Although the deceased was able to take some of his possessions with him, he had to leave happiness and prosperity to his relatives who remained. The same idea lay behind the animal sacrifices made at the grave. Attached to the return from the grave were rites whose aim was the prevention of the return of the deceased, such as sweeping over footprints, scattering ashes, and so on.

Memorial ceremonies were held both for the recently departed and in honor of all family ancestors. The graveyard was visited, and the dead were feasted at home. The Udmurts and Volga Finns elected a representative of the deceased to attend the memorial ceremonies following a death, and at this time he might be asked about life beyond the grave.

Memorial feasts in honor of all the family ancestors were an annual event. Like the Russians, the Karelians held these feasts in the spring and autumn, but the ceremonies differed from those of their Russian counterparts. At the graveyard, all the ancestors were called by name to attend a feast prepared in advance at which each ancestor had his own appointed place. In western Finland the Kekri (or Köyri) festival in honor of the ancestors was held in the autumn. Feasting the dead and taking them to the sauna were part of the ceremonies.

If the deceased was not accompanied to the abode of the family ancestors, he would haunt the living. In Finland, a number of ghosts have been known by special names. Certain names (such as Ihtiriekko) indicate that the soul of the deceased, in the form of a bird, was believed to haunt the living.

Cultic Life. The nature of cultic life has varied greatly according to the living conditions and occupations of different peoples. Its vitality has depended on how strong each culture was within the sphere of influence of the world religions.

Sacred groves. The Permians, Volga Finns, and Baltic Finns all had sacred groves marked by one or more trees that were meeting places for larger cult communities. A spring or a special stone might also be the symbol of a cultic site.

Sacred groves that functioned as the meeting places for wider sacrificial circles vanished from western Finland soon after the introduction of Christianity. In 1229 Pope Gregory IX issued a bull granting the church the right to seize and destroy the *hiisi* groves of the Finns. In eastern Finland, Lutheran priests were still destroying groves that had served as sacrificial sites in the eighteenth century. The only established cultic sites that remained in existence longer than the groves of inland Finland were those known only within particular families. As they pressed further into the wilds of the forest as they cleared agricultural land, the farming families founded places of sacrifice near their dwellings. Gifts for the deceased and different spirits were brought to the foot of the sacrificial tree on special days. Reminiscent of the single sacrificial stones of the forest farmers were the Saami *seita*s, either natural stones or carved tree stumps. They were usually situated in hunting terrain or along the deer trails, however.

The Karelians, Ingrians, and Votes retained communal fenced sacrificial sites longer than did the Finns and the Estonians, that is, until the early twentieth century, because the Orthodox church adapted the old sacrificial festivals to the cult of the saints. Either sacrifices were made in the yard surrounding the Orthodox chapel on saints' days, or separate groves were dedicated for Christian purposes. There are two types of sacrificial groves among the Udmurts: *lud* groves that were the scenes of major sacrificial festivals within the family, and joint groves consisting of a sacrificial circle *(mer)* embracing a tribe or a group of families within a village. Both types were located within the forest. There was only one entrance to the tribal *lud;* sometimes there was a small building within it. The master of the *lud,* a frightening spirit in Tatar dress, was worshiped in the family *lud.* But at the larger places of worship in the mother villages, Inmar and the various gods and spirits of nature were more approachable.

The enclosed *keremet* groves of the Mordvins and Mari were reminiscent of the Udmurt *lud*s. Like the *lud* master, the *keremet* was honored by the name *sultan* or *saltan.* Like the hero cults of the Udmurts and the Volga

Finns (e.g., Mardan, the founder of eleven Udmurt villages; T'ušta'n, the hero prince of the Mordvins; and the Old Man of Nemda Mountain, the ancient military leader of the Mari), the *keremet* worship is probably a Turco-Tatar influence. The Mari also had groves dedicated to Jumo, his assistants, and the gods of nature. Among the Mordvins the great enclosed groves began to vanish earlier than among the Mari. Cultic sites were located in gorges or in pockets of forest close to villages, and in many villages they were marked by a spring.

Home sanctuaries. In the Russian Orthodox Balto-Finnic region the center of the home cult was the back corner of the cottage. On a shelf in this corner were images of the saints. The Karelian icon shelf derives from the same source as the Udmurt *kuala* and Mari *kudo.*

The Udmurt *kuala* was a simple log cabin used as a storehouse. In the center was a fireplace surrounded by stones, and on the far wall, at a man's height, was a shelf on which were placed the sacrificial offerings and, sometimes, a sacrificial box made of bast. The sacrificial box was connected with the family benefactor *voršud,* an offering box that the son fetched from his father's home in the course of special rites. According to early sources the *voršud* formerly contained wooden or clay dolls that were worshiped. It may be assumed that the dolls kept in the sacrificial box were images of the domestic spirits. The strict ties of kinship of the *kuala* cult and certain features reminiscent of the ancestor cult suggest that the guardian spirits of the home were originally notable family ancestors.

The center of the Cheremis *kudo* cult was a simple building similar to the Udmurt *kuala.* It is likewise known that wooden dolls were kept in a little box on a corner shelf in the *kudo.* Sacrificial and cult object boxes have also been reported among the Balto-Finnic peoples.

Cult practices. Large numbers of rites and ceremonies were celebrated annually among all the Finnic peoples. The great sacrificial festivals in honor of the god of the sky and other gods of nature were, however, retained only among the Udmurts and Cheremis who had not been baptized and who had sacred groves common to several villages.

There are several descriptions of great Udmurt sacrificial festivals celebrated in the Viatka region during the nineteenth century. After the seed had been sown in the spring, men and women from as many as fifteen villages would come together to make sacrifices to Inmar and the earth gods. During the festivals, which lasted many days, a foal was sacrificed to Inmar to guarantee a good harvest; in addition, an ox was sacrificed to the earth god, a white calf was sacrificed to the god of the corn, and poultry was sacrificed to other beings. Sacred swans were set free and bore Inmar a message of the feast. The great sacrificial festivals shared by several Mari villages fell into two categories according to the direction of worship. There were separate groves for worship looking "upward" to the god of the sky and certain gods of nature, while worship directed "downward" to the gods of the earth took place at other cultic sites.

The great sacrificial circles of the Mordvins vanished early. Joint village festivals were held according to the Orthodox calendar. Probably of ancient standing were the sheep or ox sacrifices made around Easter and Pentecost, when the sky god as well as the Orthodox saints were asked to grant protection and favorable weather. The Mordvin cult tradition also included a host of rites of Russian origin, such as the Bratšina festival, held by families in the house where the group's cult symbol, a large wax candle, was kept. The Baba-ozks ("offering of the women") was a festival for married women, during which the women prayed for health and fortune and dedicated nectar and porridge to the "mother of the gods."

The ceremonies conducted by the Baltic Finns to promote farming and livestock were, like those of the Mordvins, attached to the cult of the saints and holidays of the Christian calendar. However, as late as the nineteenth century there were still reports from inland Finland of a beer festival (Ukon Vakat) at which the god of thunder was entreated to send rain to make the crops grow. According to sixteenth century reports, this festival might also include sexual rites aiming at increasing fertility.

The most archaic tradition of hunting festivals is represented by the bear ceremonies of the Finns and Saami. These have counterparts in northern Siberia and America. The rituals surrounding the killing of the bear and the subsequent feast are connected to a myth revealing the origin of the bear that is also found among the Ob-Ugrians. An ancient form of animal ceremonialism is the preservation of the bear's bones and the fastening of its skull to a pine tree that belonged to the guardian of the bears. The aim of returning the bones and the soul hidden among them was to assure the continuation of the species.

Within the sphere of Orthodox Christianity, the rites of passage in human life partly observed the traditional models, and they were partly conducted by the church. Until the twentieth century, the rites conducted to solve various crises, cases of theft, to banish disease, and so on belonged to the realm of the expert in folk belief, the seer.

Cultic authorities. Only the Saami retained the ancient shamanic tradition of the Finnic peoples. Among other groups, the specialist in autochthonous religion was the seer, who in addition to incantations and divining did resort to various trance techniques. Although seers were usually men, a woman could also possess the necessary skills. With the exception of the Mordvins, conducting sacrifices and prayers was, however, above all the task of men. Responsibility for the observance of the annual festivals within the home and family lay with the head of the family. Some person acquainted with ceremony would act as the sacrificial priest in larger cult communities. The sacrificial priests at the great festivals of the Udmurts and the Mari were often chosen by a seer. The post of guard to the *kuala, lud,* and other such sacred places and groves was either passed down within a family or was granted on the seer's advice. Those with the best command of tradition would sing laments and act as the masters of ceremony at weddings. Apart from being a seer, singing laments and acting as psychopomp, that is, accompanying the deceased to the other world, was the most important public role of women.

Cultural Change. Primitive folk religion rapidly vanished among most of the Finnic peoples at the beginning of the twentieth century. The real watershed in the Balto-Finnic region was World War II, before which it was possible to collect material in many fields of autochthonous religion. The rapid processes of cultural change among the small Finnic peoples in the Soviet Union have wiped away the traditional belief systems. The types of folk belief that have lived on longest in Finland are the seer tradition and belief in the spirits of the dead.

[*See also* Finno-Ugric Religions, *overview article;* Mari and Mordvin Religion; *and* Saami Religion.]

BIBLIOGRAPHY

The oldest general treatise on Finnic religions is *Suomen suvun pakanallinen jumalanpalvelus* by Julius Krohn (Helsinki, 1894). The merit of the work lies in the list of early Russian sources included in the bibliography. More reliable than this and based partly on the author's own fieldwork is Uno Harva's discourse on Finno-Ugric mythology in *The Mythology of All Races,* vol. 4, *Finno-Ugric, Siberian* (1927; reprint, New York, 1964). More recent general treatises include Ivar Paulson's "Die Religionen der finnischen Völker," in *Die Religionen Nordeurasiens und der amerikanischen Arktis,* edited by Paulson, Åke Hultkrantz, and Karl Jettmar (Stuttgart, 1962), pp. 145–303, and Lauri Honko's "Religionen der finnisch-ugrischen Völker," in *Handbuch der Religionsgeschichte,* edited by Jes Peter Asmussen and Jørgen Laessøe, vol. 1 (Göttingen, 1971), pp. 173–224. Both contain a selected bibliography of the main monographs.

In the early decades of the twentieth century Finnish and Hungarian researchers made field trips among the Permians and the Volga Finns. Descriptions of the folk religion of the Zyrians (Komi), Votiaks (Udmurts), Mordvins, and Cheremis (Mari) as well as folk poetry texts are published in many volumes of the series "Memoires de la Société Finno-Ougrienne" (Helsinki, 1890–). Notable collections of material also include Ödön Beke's *Tscheremissische Texte zur Religion und Volkskunde* (Oslo, 1931), a publication of the Oslo Etnografiske Museum.

The most important study of the religion of the Permian peoples is *Permalaisten uskonto* (Porvoo, 1914) by Uno Holmberg (Uno Harva as of 1928), although it concentrates almost entirely on Votiak (Udmurt) religion. Field research was also conducted among the Votiaks by Albert Hämäläinen and is reported in his "Der vorsud-mudor Kult der Wotjaken," *Eurasia Septentrionalis Antiqua* 6 (1961). Of the articles on Zyrian (Komi) religion, D. R. Fuchs's "Beiträge zur Kenntnis des Volksglaubens der Syrjänen," *Finnisch-ugrische Forschungen* 16 (1923–1924): 237–274, is outstanding.

The main monographs on the Volga peoples are those by Uno Holmberg (Harva): *Die Religion der Tscheremissen,* "Folklore Fellows Communications," no. 61 (Helsinki, 1926), and *Die religiösen Vorstellungen der Mordwinen,* "Folklore Fellows Communications," no. 142 (Helsinki, 1952). The work on the religion of the Cheremis (Mari) contains descriptions of rites observed by Harva and authentic photographs of sacrificial festivals.

The extensive literature on Finnish folk religion includes Uno Harva's general treatise *Suomalaisten muinaisusko* (Porvoo, 1948) and Lauri Honko's systematic account of Finnish mythology, "Finnische Mythologie," in *Wörterbuch der Mythologie,* edited by H. W. Haussig, vol. 2 (Stuttgart, 1973), pp. 261–271. Martti Haavio's *Väinämöinen, Eternal Sage,* "Folklore Fellows Communications," no. 144 (Helsinki, 1952), deals with central mythical themes, and his *Heilige Heine in Ingermanland,* "Folklore Fellows Communications," no. 189 (Helsinki, 1963), examines the sacred groves of the Baltic Finns and the cults attached to them. The most important work on the guardian spirit tradition of the Baltic Finns is Lauri Honko's *Geisterglaube in Ingermanland,* "Folklore Fellows Communications," no. 185 (Helsinki, 1962).

Estonian mythology and folk religion have been dealt with by Matthias J. Eisen in *Estnische Mythologie* (Leipzig, 1925) and by Oskar Loorits in *Grundzüge des estnischen Volksglaubens,* 3 vols., "Skrifter utgivna av Kungliga Gustav Adolfs Akademien for Folklivsforskning," vol. 18 (Lund, 1949–1960). Loorits also published a thorough treatise on the folk religion of the Livonians, *Liivi rahva usund,* 3 vols. (Tartu, 1926–1928).

A broad description of the religion of the Lapps (Saami) is given in Uno Holmberg's *Lappalaisten uskonto* (Porvoo, 1915) and T. I. Itkonen's *Heidnische Religion und späterer Aberglaube bei den finnischen Lappen,* "Memoires de la Société Finno-Ougrienne," vol. 87 (Helsinki, 1946).

Among the main works on comparative research into the special features of religion are Uno Holmberg's *Der Baum des Lebens* (Helsinki, 1923), in the series "Acta Academiae Scientiarum Fennicae"; Ivar Paulson's *Die primitiven Seelenvorstellungen der nordeurasischen Völker* (Stockholm, 1958), a publication of the Ethnographical Museum of Sweden; and Gustav Ränk's

Die heilige Hinterecke im Hauskult der Völker Nordosteuropas und Nordasiens, "Folklore Fellows Communications," no. 137 (Helsinki, 1949).

ANNA-LEENA SIIKALA
Translated from Finnish by Susan Sinisalo

FINNO-UGRIC RELIGIONS. [*This entry consists of two articles.* An Overview *treats the methodological problems raised in generalizing about Finno-Ugric peoples and proposes various morphologies for understanding their religious life.* History of Study *reviews the work of modern scholars who have contributed to the field.*]

An Overview

The Finno-Ugric peoples constitute a family of scattered nations and populations in northeastern and central Europe in an area that reaches from northernmost Scandinavia and Finland to western Siberia and from the Volga-Kama Basin to Hungary. They speak fifteen cognate languages, which, together with four Samoyed languages, form the Uralic family of languages. It is mainly the linguistic affinity that links these peoples and cultures; the cultural and religious affinities between them are more difficult to ascertain, spanning as they do considerable geographical distance and over five thousand years of history. An "original" Finno-Ugric religion thus remains hypothetical, but the religious beliefs and practices of the Finno-Ugric peoples provide an interesting test case for comparative methodology in the history of religions.

Genealogy of Languages, Peoples, and Cultures. Theories of linguistic descent are usually based on the concept of a protolanguage and its subsequent differentiation. The real development, however, more probably consisted of complex processes of multiple integration into and differentiation from cognate languages, with the interpenetration of noncognate languages in a given region also playing a role. According to the generally accepted chronology, the Uralic protofamily began to split up into Finno-Ugric and Samoyed protolanguages around 4000 BCE. Today, the Samoyed languages are spoken by some thirty-five thousand people living on the shores of the Arctic Ocean and along the banks of rivers flowing into it between the Taimyr and Kanin peninsulas. The early Uralic and Finno-Ugric settlements were presumably located in the south, somewhere between the Ural Mountains and the middle reaches of the Volga River. After the differentiation of the Ugric branch around 3000 BCE, and its subsequent division into the Ob-Ugric and what later became the Hungarian branch, the rest of the Finno-Ugrians either stayed near the Volga and developed into the Mari (Cheremis) and Mordvin peoples of today or moved to the north or the northwest. The northern group, the Permian settlement, persisted over two millennia and became divided only a little over one thousand years ago into the Komi (Zyrians), living in the region between the upper reaches of the western Dvina River, the Kama, and the Pechora; and the Udmurts (Votiaks), living between the Kama and Viatka rivers. The northwestern group reached the eastern shores of the Baltic Sea and developed into what we now know as Saami (Lapps), Finns, Karelians, Ingrians, Votes, Veps, Estonians, and Livonians. The development was far from unilinear and regular, as is shown by the fact that contemporary linguistic groups within the Ugric branch range from fourteen million Hungarians to small populations of Mansi (Voguls) and Khanty (Ostiaks) in the northern Ural Mountains and along the Ob River. Similarly, among close to five million Finns and one million Estonians we find traces of almost extinct Votes and Livonians. (See figure 1.) [*See also map accompanying* Southern Siberian Religions.]

Finno-Ugrians once inhabited most of northeast Europe; it was relatively late that the Slavic expansion changed the picture. Another impact was made by the Turco-Tatar tribes and by the Bulgar empire in the Middle Ages, which particularly affected the culture of the southeastern Mari and Udmurts. Western influence was strongest in the Baltic sphere, where early loanwords were adopted from the Balts and Germanic people during the first millennium BCE. Some remote groups of Finno-Ugrians were able to preserve their autochthonous religious traditions fairly late, until the nineteenth and early twentieth centuries, because the Christian discipline of the Eastern Orthodox church was rather ineffective or permissive; in western Finland, for instance, Roman Catholicism and, later, Lutheranism abolished religious phenomena that survived in the Orthodox east (eastern Finland, Karelia, Ingria). Among the southeastern Finno-Ugrians the traditions of their Islamic neighbors left marks on the folk religion.

Since the history of Christian missions is fairly long (it began in the twelfth century among the Finns and in the fourteenth century among the Komi, for example, and trade relations with christianized cultures existed much earlier), it must be assumed that the survival of early folk belief, myth, and ritual among the Finno-Ugrians is partly an example of the coexistence of great and little traditions. The same people who were devout Christians could also perform ancient rites and hold beliefs that did not necessarily contradict Christian doctrine because they were so skillfully adapted and integrated into each other. Indigenous religion began to

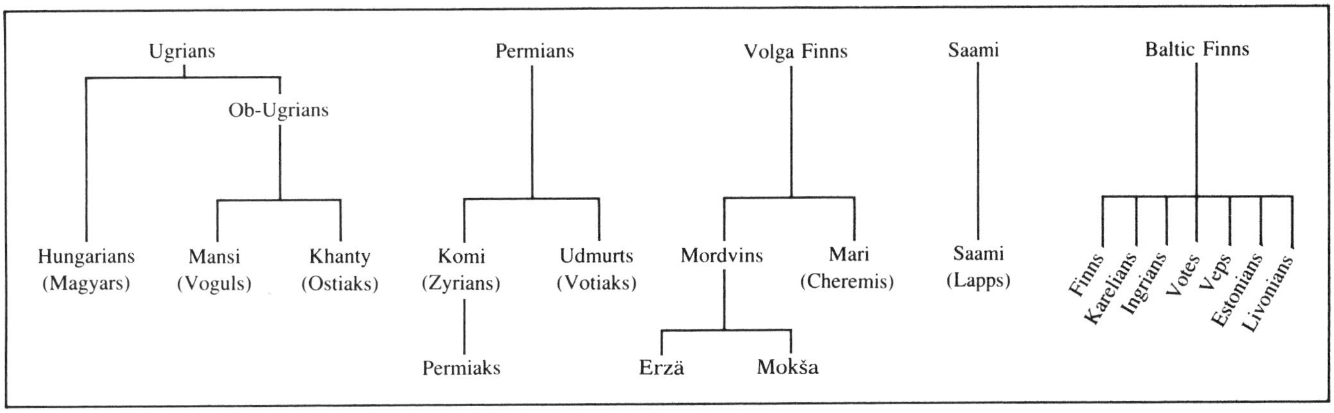

FIGURE 1. *Finno-Ugric Peoples*

adopt Christian elements before formal missionizing took place, and long after it had established its position as the official religion, the Christian religion found itself in a symbiosis with pagan belief and custom, at least at the level of folk religiosity.

Methods of Comparison. The development of and variation in the religions of the Finno-Ugrians must be seen as an interplay of phenomenological, ecological, and historical aspects. At the phenomenological level the question is: Are there any typically Finno-Ugric contributions to the phenomenology of religious universals? The wide natural-geographical and cultural-historical scale, ranging from mobile hunting and fishing communities in the Arctic north to stable farming and cattle-breeding societies in the south and from remote pockets of religious tradition to the crossroads of Byzantine and Roman influence, permits one to examine the relative importance of linguistic continuity in cultural variation. To reconstruct a true proto-Finno-Ugric religion may be impossible, as the religious systems have changed so many times, but some structural or systematic elements may be discerned, irrespective of whether they belong to a vertical tradition. There are similarities in cosmological belief, in the system of spirits, and in ancestor worship that may not occur as frequently among non-Finno-Ugrians. From the phenomenological point of view, however, dissimilarities may turn out to be as important as similarities, and in the area of language we must remember the existence of superstrate and substrate area of traditions, that is, the language of a population may change although the traditional content is retained. Under Slavic linguistic form we may find substrata of Finno-Ugric tradition, especially in the north of Russia.

Ecological comparisons may help to explain similarities that are not based on historical contact and interaction between cultures. Ecological comparison often turns out to be regional: similar trends become discernible among all or most cultures in a given zone, regardless of linguistic affinities. There are different "ecologies" to be observed: those that are based on the natural environment, those that are dependent upon the socio-cultural development or stage of development in the societies to be compared, and those that refer to the morphology of the religious tradition itself. Finno-Ugric material provides interesting points of departure for attempts to understand the extent to which physical environment, the stage of societal development, and the morphology of the tradition may interact with each other or with linguistic or regional factors.

The third and most common level of comparison has been the historical one. This does not mean that early historical sources and archaeological findings in the field of Finno-Ugric religion are abundant and illuminating. On the contrary, they are rather scanty and problematic. Most historical assumptions must be based on the evidence of relatively late documents of tradition. The assumption usually is unidirectional: one culture has borrowed beliefs or rituals from another. Interaction in cultural contact or dissimilar functions of similar traits (or similar functions of dissimilar traits) in different tradition systems are rarely discussed. In spite of this, quite interesting evidence of early historically connected strata in Finno-Ugric religious tradition has been dectected, as for instance in the case of bear killing and the bear feast of the Ob-Ugrians, Karelians, and Saami. There are also phenomena that can only be explained historically, such as the revival of dirge ceremonies in Russian and Karelian areas due to the sufferings caused by World War II.

Morphology. One way to organize the Finno-Ugric religious traditions is by the occupations of hunting and fishing, cattle breeding and nomadism, and agriculture and subordinate handicraft industries. These forms of subsistence do not normally occur alone, however, but in various combinations. It is the skillful combination of numerous different sources of livelihood and the calendar cycle based on these that characterizes most Finno-Ugric groups and their religious tradition. Three calendar systems contribute to the formation of the cycle: the calendars of nature, of human work, and of the church (saints' days etc.). The cycle requires new roles of the individual and the re-creating of different social worlds of the community; specialists exist, but the division of labor rarely allows specialists of one domain only. The calendrical cycle is crucial for the cohesion of society and its communal economic activity.

Another important organizing factor of ritual life is the life cycle from birth to death and the accompanying rites of passage. Through these it is possible to express and legitimize changes of social status, and reinforce the prevailing social structure. The early Finno-Ugric communities do not seem to have developed elaborate ceremonies of initiation—even the shamanic initiation did not involve large audiences—but the idea of initiation can be seen in small rituals such as the wrapping of a newborn child in his father's sweaty shirt, bringing "tooth money" to the new child (Karelia), dressing the bride, guiding the deceased to their relatives in the otherworld, and so on. Weddings and funerals, along with feasts of the agricultural year, comprise the most developed ritual dramas.

Religion of hunters and fisherman. True hunting communities survived longest in the Arctic and sub-Arctic zones, but traces of their mythology and rites continue to survive in various combined economies where hunting or fishing played a subsidiary role. The Finno-Ugric materials demonstrate a very special sensitivity to and knowledge of nature. In the world of the hunter, who generally works alone, animals, plants, and rocks possess a character of their own and must be addressed properly. The hunter sees himself as an interloper on someone else's territory; the animals and features of the forest communicate promises, warnings, and threats. It is not enough for the hunter to know about the best fishing and hunting places and seasons. He must also know about the being who rules over the forest and its inhabitants, the forest master or mistress; he must understand the ways of the "lord of the animals" who determines the movement and fate of all the living creatures in the forest and of the special guardian spirits that watch over particular animal species. The territorial aspect is also important, in that different formations of nature possess their own local spirits. No less important is the annual cycle, especially the beginning and the end of a season, which came to be marked by saints' days.

The most venerated animal was the bear, seen by the Saami and Ob-Ugrians as their totemic ancestor and as the son of the sky god by the Ob-Ugrians and Finns. Several myths that recount either the marriage between the first bear and a human girl or the heavenly origin of the bear and its descent to earth, and relate how it was slain and returned home to the celestial father after special ceremonies, seem to be of common Finno-Ugric origin. These myths were recited in bear ceremonies, during both the killing and the feast itself, events that abound in dramatic and verbal elements. Among the Ob-Ugrians we find the bear ceremony developed into real theater; hundreds of ritual and semiprofane plays and dances could be performed during the feast, which lasted many days. The totemic element is apparent in the Ob-Ugric moiety system, which consists of the *mós* (the heavenly people, hunters, who eat raw meat) and the *por* (the underground people, wizards, who eat cooked meat); these phratries observe different norms concerning bear hunting. Although the bear is the object of rites and veneration among most of the northern peoples of Asia and America, there are few ritual dramas comparable to the bear ceremonies of the Ob-Ugrians, Finns, and Saami. Even during the course of the more normal hunting of game, the verbal component, prayers, spells, and songs, is well developed among the Finno-Ugrians. The spirits are usually designated by compounds such as "forest-man," "forest-father," or "forest-master." The system of "fathers" and/or "mothers" of territories, places, buildings, and so on was very common.

Religion of cattle breeders and nomads. Cattle breeding is an important subsidiary means of livelihood especially among the Finno-Ugrians of the north, where agriculture is constantly threatened by the climate. The religious profile of cattle breeders is not as clearcut as that of the hunters and farmers; it also appears in symbiosis with the beliefs of those who practice agriculture. As a means of subsistence, nomadism is also subsidiary, not only to agriculture but also to hunting. When the flocks of wild reindeer grew thin, the Arctic hunter of both Fennoscandia and the Kanin Peninsula developed reindeer herding, which in some places, such as Sweden, led to full domestication and a dairy economy. Only the reindeer was capable of finding its food even under the snow, and it soon became an indispensable draft and slaughter animal. Another area of wide-scale herding is the Hungarian plains, where the swampy land was unsuitable for farming but provided excellent pasture.

The yearly cycle of the cattle breeder is roughly divided into two halves, the indoor and the outdoor period; only in Hungary is there some outdoor herding all year round. In the winter horses and cows are under the rule of the owner/cattle breeder and his or her supranormal counterpart, the stable or cowhouse spirit. In the summer the herdsman, often an employee, takes over and the supranormal guardianship is transferred to the forest spirit or other spirits in the landscape. The cattle owner and herdsman observe numerous rituals, which tend to accumulate at the beginning and the end of a season; minor prayers and offerings that relate to such events as imminent danger or bad weather are also performed during the season.

In the Balto-Finnic areas, Saint George's Day (23 April) marked the sending of the cattle to pasture; the ritual had to be performed even if it was too cold for outdoor herding. The animals were encircled by people who walked around the flock carrying an icon of Saint George, an ax, burning coal, gunpowder, churchyard dirt, quicksilver, a hymnal, and a bear's tooth, among other items. Magic signs were drawn on the animals, doorposts, or the cattle's intended route. Food offerings were brought to the forest spirit, and an egg was thrown over the flock. The cattle owner asked the herdsman, the victorious dragon-slayer Saint George, and the forest mistress to join forces to protect the cattle against bears, wolves, and other dangers.

In October the cattle were taken indoors; the autumnal season was brought to an end by slaughtering a sheep or cow around Michaelmas (29 September) or All Saints' Day (1 November). This was the first "New Year" festival, during which dead relatives visited one's home, and, in northern Karelia, the myth of the slaying of the Great Ox was sung. Many southern Finno-Ugric peoples combine their cattle breeding cult with summer feasts and offerings organized primarily as part of the agricultural cycle. In long prayers presented on these occasions cow luck, horse luck, and so on is asked from numerous gods of the sky and the earth.

Religion of farmers. The society and religion of hunters and cattle breeders is competitive; among the latter, especially, the rites are directed against fellows and neighbors. Even if the principle of "limited good" (one's success means another's loss and vice versa, because the sum of good is constant) is valid also in agriculture, the atmosphere is clearly more social and collective than in cattle husbandry. This social atmosphere is very clearly expressed in the great rural ritual feasts of the southern Finno-Ugric peoples, the Mordvins, the Mari, and the Udmurts. The traditions of the last two groups derive to a large extent from their Turco-Tatar neighbors, whereas the Mordvins have adopted more from the Russians; all three have utilized Finno-Ugric and other traditions of their particular region in creating their agricultural cycles. A broad social approach, in which success is sought not only for the individual or his family but for the whole village or a larger population, especially the poor and disabled, prevails in the long prayer recitations performed in connection with animal and food offerings to dozens of gods and spirits. A Mari prayer from the Kazan area lists what is valued in the following order: family, cattle, corn, bees, money, and long life and great happiness. Another value often stressed in prayer is "harmony," that is, avoidance of quarrels and disruptive feelings, seen as a condition to be met before addressing the gods.

The central mythologems of the farmer are the earth and the sky. These parts of the cosmos or their personifications alternately are manifest in the prayers and rites. Earth is above all the female progenitor, Mother Earth; as such, she sometimes is represented as the generic Corn Mother, and sometimes as the mother or guardian of a particular kind of grain or of a particular field. The sky god is closely associated with weather, rain, wind, and storm. Thought of as male, he begets the earth. The myth of *hieros gamos,* the matrimony of heaven and earth, has been preserved in epic poetry and in connection with rainmaking rituals of the Balto-Finnic area. Importance is also attached to the patron saints of agriculture, among whom Elijah and the saints Peter and Nicholas are the most central. Various feasts may be observed during midsummer, the period of growth, when the working routines are laid still and the crops are at the mercy of the weather, insects, forest animals, and other natural factors. The Finno-Ugric farmer's worldview is oriented toward peace and harmony, every kind of growth and fertility, personal health, social good, and avoidance of misfortune. The farmer enumerates all the gods in order to avoid offending any of them, and bows to them all; a Mari or Udmurt bows "upward," sacrificing a white animal to the sky, and "downward," sacrificing a black animal to the ancestors, thus placing himself in the middle of a three-storied universe.

Cosmology. Two well-known myths of the origin of the world are found among Finno-Ugric peoples, those of the earth diver and of the world egg. In the diver myth, God orders the Devil (originally a water bird) to bring earth from the botton of the primeval sea; at the third attempt, he succeeds but tries to hide some of the earth in his mouth. When God scatters sand and the earth begins to grow, the deceit is unmasked; from the earth found in the cheek of the Devil, the mountains and hills are formed. The myth is known from the Ob River to Finland and to the Mordvins in the Volga area. The eastern Finnish variant contains an interesting introduction: God stands on a golden statue in the sea and orders his reflection in the water to rise; this reflection becomes the Devil. The global distribution of the world-egg myth is equatorial, but its northernmost occurrence is found in Finland and Estonia. A water bird or an eagle makes a nest on the knee of the creator (Väinämöinen), who is floating in the sea. It lays an egg, which rolls into the water, and pieces of it become the earth, the sky, the moon, and the stars. Myths concerning the creation of man are found in various forms among the Mansi, Volga Finns, and Karelians; the Karelian version typifies the basic scenario: a hummock rises from the sea, a tree stump on it splits open, and the first human couple steps forth.

Cosmogonic myths function as powerful protomyths: the origin of any phenomenon must be linked to the central cosmographic symbols, and various etiological continuations to these basic myths are therefore abundant. According to the cosmography of the Finno-Ugrians, a stream encircles the world, which is covered by the canopy of the heavens, the central point of which is the North Star (the "nail of the sky" on which the sky rotates); this star is sometimes associated with the world pole that supports the sky. A world tree—often the tree of life—and a world mountain rise at the center of the universe; there is a world omphalos deep in the center of the earth and a corresponding abyss of the sea that swallows ships. On the backs of three fish rest the foundations of the earth; the movements of these fish cause floods and earthquakes. Another possible cause of the destruction of the world is that the world pole collapses and the heavens—sometimes described as seven- or nine-storied—tumble down.

Much of this symbolism is well known in other parts of the world, but some details may be exclusively Finno-Ugric. An example is the belief that the sun, moon, and stars are found on the branches of the world tree, usually a great oak. Cosmographic symbols also occur frequently in contexts outside the rituals, in folk poetry.

Sanctuaries and Offerings. The home sanctuary of the Udmurts is called the *kuala*. It is a small log cabin in the corner of a square building formation that constitutes the house. In the back corner of the *kuala* is a shelf, on which are branches of deciduous trees and conifers, and above them is a *voršud*, an empty box with a lid. This is a family shrine for weekly offerings, but if the master of the house is the head of a large family, children may come from afar on certain days to worship here. A new *kuala* can only be founded with earth and ashes from the father's *kuala*. It is believed that in former times the *voršud* was not empty but contained effigies of spirits. Until relatively recent times the mobile Ob-Ugric hunters have carried their spirit effigies in a special sleigh when migrating.

Another Udmurt sanctuary is the *lud*—a fenced-off area in an isolated place in the woods. In the middle is a table for offerings that are made by the family to dispel diseases, to mark calendric observances, and so on. In addition, there are fenced-off sanctuaries for the offerings of the village; these sanctuaries are sometimes situated near the corn fields. Somewhat similar arrangements are found among the Volga Finns (the *keremet* of the ancestors) and in the Balto-Finnic area where, when slash-and-burn agriculture spread into virgin land and distances grew between pioneering families, village groves were replaced by sacrificial stones (with gouged cups on the surface) and sacred family trees near the dwellings.

Among the nomadic, reindeer-breeding and fishing Saami, the *seita* was a place for sacrifices; it was a cave, a tree stump, or a stone, often clearly visible because of its peculiar (natural) shape, usually chosen near difficult places along a reindeer trail or at some good fishing spot. Offerings were made to enhance the safety of reindeer, good fishing, and so on. Many a sanctuary was only temporary, used for one or two offerings only, and founded mainly to mark a good hunting or fishing ground and to guarantee future luck by giving the first piece of game to the gods.

Shamans and Other Mediators. Religious professionalism is rare among the Finno-Ugrians. The cults and rites discussed above were conducted by those in occupational roles, in some instances as head of a family or working team. Ancestor worship, the predominant cultic form, tends to support this kind of arrangement. Religious performance then becomes part and parcel of working routines and role performance in general.

There is, however, at least one important exception: the shaman. According to general scholarly opinion, the early stratum of Finno-Ugric religion must have contained shamanism, in spite of the fact that pure shamanism has been documented only in the far north among the Saami and Samoyeds. Indirect evidence supporting this hypothesis takes the form of similar oral traditions and officiants (from the Finnish *tietäjä* to the Hungarian *táltós)*, who experience "verbal ecstasy" and display comparable shamanic symbols in their outfits. It has been argued that the Finno-Ugric shamans were many things, including diviners, healers, priests, and experts in various technical skills. They held the highest authority on crisis rites and defended the society against malevolent forces by exercising countermagic and performing rites of propitiation. Their interpretation became the guideline in times of uncertainty. Cult priests like the Udmurt *tuno* or the Mari *kart* may represent relatively late specialization under the impact of foreign culture, whereas the designation for shaman that is found from Finland (Finn., *noita*; Saami, *noaide*) to the Ob River (Mansi, *ńajt*) speaks for a more original stratum (the term has many interesting parallels in these languages). Ancient Finnish folk poetry, Hungarian fairy tales, and other such material have been interpreted as carriers of shamanic motifs, and even if some assumptions prove faulty, the general picture is likely to persist. Another question is whether old Scandinavian tradition also includes a similar stratum and whether other European parallels should be considered. The fact remains that until the late nineteenth and early twentieth centuries the Finnish and Karelian *tietäjä* fulfilled many functions and used many techniques and expressions reminiscent of shamanism.

To balance the picture one should perhaps mention the female counterpart of the *tietäjä*, the lamenter (Finn., *itkijä*), who with her ecstatic performance was able to set the entire audience at a funeral or a memorial feast in the socially proper mood and prepared a catharsis from uncertainty and grief for her community. Lamenting was customary in the rites of departure (conscription, weddings, funerals) and the lamenter became a kind of psychopomp who with her intensive empathy and metaphorical language guided the helpless object of the rite. This tradition lived with the indirect support of the Russian Orthodox church much longer than most traditions discussed above and is still practiced in certain parts of Soviet Karelia.

[*For more specific discussions of the religious systems of Finno-Ugric people, see* Finnic Religions; Hungarian Religion; Khanty and Mansi Religion; Mari and Mordvin Religion; *and* Saami Religion.]

BIBLIOGRAPHY

A comprehensive presentation of Finno-Ugric mythology by Uno Holmberg (later, Harva) can be found in *The Mythology of All Races*, vol. 4 (1927; reprint, New York, 1964). Numerous monographs on the religion of the Finno-Ugric peoples have been published in the series "Folklore Fellows' Communications" (Helsinki, 1910–). More recent works are Ivar Paulson's "Die Religionen der finnischen Völker," in *Die Religionen Nordeurasiens und der amerikanischen Arktis*, edited by Paulson, Åke Hultkrantz, and Karl Jettmar (Stuttgart, 1962), pp. 145–303, and my "Religionen der finnisch-ugrischen Völker," in *Handbuch der Religionsgeschichte*, edited by Jes Peter Asmussen and Jørgen Laessøe, vol. 1 (Göttingen, 1971), pp. 173–224. Senni Timonen, Keith Bosley, Michael Branch, and I are currently assembling a collection of Finno-Ugric ritual texts that will be published in their original languages and in translation, with commentaries, in *The Great Bear: Folk Poetry in the Finno-Ugrian Languages* (forthcoming). Additional references to basic Finno-Ugric sources can be found in the bibliographies of all these works.

LAURI HONKO

History of Study

The life and customs of peoples inhabiting the northern regions of Europe concerned even the earliest historiographers, such as Herodotus and Tacitus. Nevertheless, the first genuinely valid data regarding peoples of the Finno-Ugric language family can be found only much later, in the works of writers living in the fifteenth to seventeenth centuries: Mathias de Miechow, Sigismundus Herberstein, Michael Agricola, Alessandro Guagnino, Nicolaes Witsen, Joannus Schefferus, Nicolaie Spatarul, and Adam Olearius, among others. The information conveyed by these writers has proved to be a valuable contribution not only to social history but to the history of religions as well.

Foundations of Eighteenth-Century Study. The eighteenth century was a time of great journeys and discoveries and of the publication of travel literature based upon eyewitness accounts. At this time the peoples of northern Eurasia and Siberia became objects of genuine scientific interest. Several authors of travel accounts, namely Y. E. Ides, D. G. Messerschmidt, P. J. Strahlenberg, J. G. Gmelin, and J. G. Georgi, made interesting observations not only about the languages of northern Eurasian peoples but also about their religious cults, and these writings established the basis for the eventual recognition of Finno-Ugric as a language family. Two German scholars, Johann Eberhard Fischer (1697–1771), who was a member of the Russian tsar's academy, and August Ludwig von Schlözer (1735–1809) played especially important roles in this discovery by summarizing in their work the available information concerning Finno-Ugric peoples: Fischer in *Sibirische Geschichte* (1768) and von Schlözer in *Allgemeine Nordische Geschichte* (Halle, 1771). In Hungary Finno-Ugric comparative linguistic research was initiated by the study *Demonstratio: Idioma Ungarorum et Lapponum idem esse* (Proof that the Languages of the Hungarians and the Saami are the Same; 1770), by Janos Sajnovics (1733–1785), and the study *Affinitas linguae Hungaricae cum linguis fennicae originis* (Relationship of the Hungarian Language to Languages of Finnic Origin; 1779), by Samuel Gyarmathi (1751–1830). Thus the first Finno-Ugric studies were written simultaneously with, and not independently of, studies in Indo-European comparative linguistics. Progress in Finno-Ugric studies was slower because as the Finno-Ugric peoples of Europe (Finns, Estonians, and Hungarians) live far from one another, their scholars too lived in scientific isolation.

Nevertheless, both the Finns and the Hungarians completed their first mythological summaries in the last decades of the eighteenth century. In Finland, Henrik Gabriel Porthan (1739–1804), professor of rhetoric at the University of Turku, advocated the publication of Erik Christian Lencquist's doctoral dissertation, entitled *De superstitione veterum Fennorum theoretica et practica* (Superstition in Belief and Practice among the Ancient Finns; Turku, 1782), which was based upon original collected data, and a few years later Porthan supported as well the publication by Christfrid Ganander (1741–1790) of a dictionary of mythology (*Mythologia Fennica;* Turku, 1789). The latter, a slender volume, provides an alphabetical listing of Finnish and Saami (Lapp) mythological terms and concepts. Daniel Cornides (1732–1787) lectured on ancient Hungarian religion at the University of Göttingen in 1785; basing his arguments on medieval chronicles, he compared the remains of ancient pagan Hungarian religion with elements of the ancient Jewish, Greek, and Scythian religions. Later, in his short study *Commentatio de religione veterum Hungarorum* (Vienna, 1791), he even compared ancient Hungarian religion to Persian religion.

Nineteenth-Century National Mythologies. During the first decades of the nineteeth century, there was a romantic interest in folk traditions everywhere in Europe and especially in Germany. Under the stimulus of Indo-European comparative linguistics and mythological research, the collection of folk poetry and the exploration of the folk narrative tradition began. [*See* Indo-European Religions, *article on* History of Study.] Two seminal works of the period were published during the year 1835. The first was *Deutsche Mythologie* (Göttingen, 1835) by Jacob Grimm (1785–1863), which subsequently served as a model for reconstructing the mythologies of several peoples, among them the Finns, the Estonians, the Saami, and the Hungarians. The other, the *Kalevala* (Helsinki, 1835) of Elias Lönnrot (1802–1884), contributed to the study of Finnish mythology by compiling folk poetry and ancient epic songs. The second, enlarged, and final edition of the *Kalevala* was published in 1849; it contained 22,759 lines in all. European readers at large became acquainted with it through a German translation published in 1852. [*See the biography of Lönnrot.*] The discovery that the Finns, a people small in number, produced heroic epic poetry comparable with the Homeric epics profoundly impressed the scholars of other Finno-Ugric nations as well. Thus, as early as the 1840s Reinhold Kreutzwald (1803–1882) began collecting Estonian epic songs about Kalevi-poeg, a folk hero of exceptional strength. While the first prototext of about twelve thousand lines was completed by 1853, the reconstructed epic itself, entitled *Kalevi poeg: Üks ennemuistene Eesti jut: Kaheskümnes laulus* (Kalevi-poeg: An Ancient Estonian Legend in Twenty Songs) was published considerably later (Kuopio, Finland, 1862), and in Estonian, even though it appeared in Finland. Meanwhile Kreutzwald had also worked on reconstructing Estonian national mythology, and he published a study of it, "Über den Charakter der estnischen Mythologie," in the journal *Verhandlungen der Gelehrten Estnischen Gesellschaft zu Dorpat* 2 (1850).

The romantic quest for related peoples and an ancient, common land of origin (where the forebears of related peoples lived together) prompted scholars of the mid-nineteenth century to undertake long journeys of exploration. Mathias Aleksanteri Castrén (1813–1852), for example, collected valuable material during his repeated Siberian travels and described his research in *Reiseerinnerungen aus den Jahren 1838–1844: Nordische Reisen und Forschungen* (Travel Recollections 1838–1844: Nordic Travel and Research; Saint Petersburg, 1833). Castrén's lectures on Finnic mythology, given during the last year of his life, were published in translation from Swedish under the title *Vorlesungen über die finnische Mythologie* (Saint Petersburg, 1853). At the same time, the Hungarian Antal Reguly (1819–1859) went on a research trip among the Ob-Ugrians and presented the results of his research in his study entitled *Ethnographisch-geographische Karte des nördlichen Uralgebietes* (Ethnogeographical Map of the Northern Ural Region; Saint Petersburg, 1846). Only some two decades later did Pál Hunfalvy (1810–1891), one of the founders of Finno-Ugric comparative linguistics, publish Reguly's collection, which contained valuable folk literature—primarily texts of Mansi (Vogul) heroic epics—in a book entitled *A vogul föld és nép* (The Vogul Land and its People; Pest, 1864).

For the sake of proper chronology, one must mention the first comprehensive collection of Hungarian mythology (*Magyar Mythologia,* Pest, 1854), published during the romantic era of reform after the Hungarian revolt against Austria (1848–1849). Its author, Arnold Ipolyi (1823–1886), a learned Roman Catholic bishop, had already collected original folk tales, legends, and folk beliefs of the region. At the same time he was intimately familiar with the contemporary scholarly literature dealing with comparative mythology. As he points out, his work was greatly influenced by the mythological studies of Jakob Grimm, G. F. Creuzer, and Joseph von Görres, but he also quoted and was familiar with the above-mentioned Finnish studies by Lencquist, Ganander, and Castrén. Ipolyi's study, more than five hundred pages long, is a genuine comparative-mythological survey, though its assertions should today be looked upon from a critical distance. A few years later, Ferenc Kállay (1790–1861) compiled another work, albeit more modest, about the religion of the pre-Christian Hungarians (*A pogány magyarok vallása,* Pest,

1861), in which he described the major figures of ancient Hungarian mythology. For the one thousandth anniversary of the Magyar conquest of Hungary, Kabos Kandra (1843–1905) prepared the third edition of *Magyar Mythologia* (1897; reprint, San Francisco, 1978). Although Kandra was in a position to build upon the findings of contemporary Finno-Ugric linguistics, his work is basically the last romantic attempt at reconstructing the system of Hungarian mythology. While the most important text among the materials used for purposes of comparison is the *Kalevala*, the *Mythologia* also depends on quotations from the studies and text collections of Bernát Munkácsi (1860–1937). Munkácsi's fieldwork among the Udmurts (Votiaks) and Mansi (Voguls) took place in the second half of the 1880s. He published his own and Antal Reguly's findings in four thick volumes, with copious notes on mythology, entitled *Vogul Népköltési Gyüjtemény* (Vogul Folklore Collection; 4 vols., Budapest, 1892–1902). He also published studies on comparative mythology in Hungarian and German.

While there are quite early and finely detailed descriptions at our disposal concerning the ancient religion of the Saami, for example, Joannus Schefferus's *Lapponica . . . de origine, superstitione, sacris magicis* (1673; reprint, Uppsala, 1956), the first real reconstruction and description of Saami mythology *(Lappisk Mythologi)* was published as late as 1871 by Jens Andreas Friis (1821–1896).

As the ethnic minorities of tsarist Russia began increasing in national self-awareness during the last decades of the nineteenth century, they also began collecting texts of folklore. One should mention Serafim Patkanov (1856–1888), who did research among the southern groups of Khanty (Ostiaks), and Ivan Nikolaevich Smirnov (1856–1904), a professor of the University of Kazan, Russia, who collected valuable material among the Finno-Ugric peoples of Perm and along the Volga. Smirnov published several books on his findings: *Cheremisy* (Kazan, 1889), *Votiaki* (Kazan, 1890), and *Permiaki* (Kazan, 1891). Several chapters in these volumes are devoted to the gods and religious customs of Finno-Ugric peoples living by the Volga, and they serve as useful source material for comparative research.

Twentieth-Century Comparative Research. During the decades around the turn of the century, the most important feature of Finno-Ugric studies was scientifically planned fieldwork. For the most part it was carried out by well-trained linguists, who in the process also recorded much material valuable for folklorists and students of mythology. In this context one should mention the research of the Hungarian József Pápay (1873–1931) and the Finns Heikki Paasonen (1869–1919), Yrjö Wichmann (1868–1932), Kai Donner (1888–1935), and Artturi Kannisto (1874–1943). Their authentic text collections made it possible to reconstruct the belief systems of certain Finno-Ugric peoples and consequently to prepare comprehensive comparative studies. Since, unlike research on Indo-European mythology, Finno-Ugric comparative mythological research is based almost entirely on folkloric material, it was logical first to describe the mythology of particular peoples as accurately as the circumstances would allow. In 1908 Kaarle Krohn (1863–1933) and Aladár Bán (1871–1960) published *A finnugor népek pogány istentisztelete* (Pre-Christian God Worship of the Finno-Ugric Peoples); together with Bán's supplement, this work essentially became the first Finno-Ugric comparative religious study. The book is based on the lectures of Julius Krohn (1835–1888), held at the University of Helsinki in 1884. In the first chapter the authors review the history of research, the sources, and scholarly literature, and in subsequent chapters they discuss sacred places of sacrifice, sacred images, activities of shamans, and actual sacrificial rituals. What renders this volume valuable even today is the use it makes of contemporary Russian scientific literature that is now not readily available.

The second major summary of the religious beliefs of the Finno-Ugric peoples (*Die Religion der Jugra-Völker*, Porvoo, Finland, 1922–1927), a three-volume study, was written by Kustaa Fredrik Karjalainen (1871–1919). This monumental work was based upon the complete literature available at the time and was combined with the author's original research. It remains the most detailed overview of the religious beliefs of Finno-Ugric peoples to date. At the end of the 1920s, Uno Holmberg (later Harva, 1882–1949) published yet another summary, "Finno-Ugric Mythology" in the fourth volume of *The Mythology of All Races* (1927; reprint, New York, 1964). Here Holmberg methodically reviews beliefs in the soul, the cult of the dead, hunting magic, and veneration of nature spirits (spirits of stones, water, forest, and fire), of home spirits, of the lord of the sky, and of heroes revered as gods; and finally he devotes a separate chapter to the description of sacrifices and the examination of questions concerning shamanism characteristic of Finno-Ugric peoples.

In 1931 there appeared in the Soviet Union, where the majority of Finno-Ugric peoples live today, a collection of texts about the religious beliefs of the Soviet peoples *(Religioznye verovaniia narodov SSSR)*. The sole value of this two-volume collection lies in the fact that it quotes passages from older Russian publications; for many decades following its publication, the monopoly of Marxist critiques of religion practically halted mythological research in that country. After World War II encyclopedic handbooks began to be published elsewhere, and generally summaries of research appeared every ten years or so. Of these, the overview written by Ivar Paulson (1922–1966) should be mentioned; it provides a phenomenological synthesis of the religions of northern Eurasian hunting nations and utilizes the new ethnographic and archaeological data. Paulson's study was published in the third volume of *Die Religion der Menschheit* (Stuttgart, 1962). A second modern overview, written by Lauri Honko, was published in the first volume of *Das Handbuch der Religionsgeschichte* (Göttingen, 1971). Later, in a shortened English version entitled "Finno-Ugric Religion," written for the *Encyclopaedia Britannica* (1974), Honko made this observation: "Today there is general agreement that a hypothetical reconstruction representing the 'original religion' of a single language family is virtually impossible."

The most recent study can be found in the second volume of the encyclopedic undertaking of Soviet researchers on myths of the peoples of the world (*Mify narodov mira*, Moscow, 1982). In this summary entry the authors, V. Ia. Petrukhin and E. A. Kelimskii, do not even attempt to provide a comprehensive picture, but instead they discuss the mythologies of different peoples separately. This fact signals a dual problem of Finno-Ugric scholarship. First, the field of Finno-Ugric research has lacked a scholar of the stature of, say, Georges Dumézil, which is a pity, insofar as it is also probable that the material itself has unique features (for example, its system of gods, which is not as strictly hierarchical as that in Indo-European mythology—a distinction perhaps reflecting the different structures of society prevalent among Indo-European and Finno-Ugric peoples). In addition, certain Finno-Ugric languages are quite distantly related, and not all scholars can easily peruse the full collection of folkloric texts constituting the basic sources. Despite the difficulties, a few exceptional monographs have been produced that, though not aiming at a reconstruction of the whole system, nevertheless enable us to engage in comparative studies of certain topics. These topics include, for example, lower-order spirits, totemism, and the cult of idols (see J. Haekel, "Idolkult und Dualsystem bei den Ugriern," *Archiv für Völkerkunde* 1, 1946, pp. 95–163); hunting rituals and the bear cult (C. M. Edsman, *Bärenfest*, Tübingen, 1957); and concepts of the soul of the northern Eurasian peoples (Ivar Paulson, *Die primitiven Seelenvorstellungender nordeurasischen Völker*, Stockholm, 1958).

Recent Developments. In the last few decades, especially in the Soviet Union, some surprising new results have been gained in certain areas, primarily as a result of an effort to involve other sciences in comparative mythological research and thus to revivify its methodological tools. Soviet researchers have thus turned to archaeology, which is "materialistic," and to the cataloging of decorative art objects, which are seen as products of the mythological consciousness of ancient peoples. A characteristic monograph of these times is S. V. Ivanov's gigantic work about the folk arts of the peoples of Siberia, a work that for the most part reviews museum collections assembled around the turn of the twentieth century (*Materialy po izobrazitel'nomu iskusstvu narodov Sibiri XIX–nachalo XX. V.*, Moscow, 1954). This rich study, which contains both Finno-Ugric and other material, becomes especially interesting when read together with the study by Dmitrii K. Zelenin (1878–1954) of Siberian idol cults and beliefs in spirits (*Le culte des idoles en Siberie*, Paris, 1952).

At present, archaeologists are able to contribute most significantly to the reconstruction of ancient beliefs, and thus of Finno-Ugric mythology, by interpreting the highly diverse physical evidence. A few of the valuable works containing such analyses are Vanda Mosinskaia's *Drevniaia skulptura Urala i Zapadnoi Sibiri* (Ancient Sculptures of the Ural and Western Siberia, Moscow, 1976); L. A. Golubeva's *Zoomorfnye ukrasheniia finnougrov* (Finno-Ugric Zoomorphic Decorative Art, Moscow, 1979); and L. S. Gribova's *The Animal Style as One of the Components of Social-Ideological System of Totemism and Stage in the Development of Fine Arts* (Syktyvkar, U.S.S.R., 1980). Soviet archaeologists can be credited with the discovery of another important source group, that is, petroglyphs, or rock art. During the last decades, remains of rock art have been extensively uncovered (mostly in the form of engravings) in northern Eurasia. In this discovery Aleksandr P. Okladnikov (1908–1981) had a particularly outstanding role; together with his co-workers he published a series of monographs that contained more than ten thousand Siberian rock drawings and included valuable notes on the history of religions. His major contribution to Finno-Ugric research, written with A. I. Martinov, is *Sokrovishcha tomskikh pisamits* (Treasures of Petroglyphs around Tomsk; Moscow, 1972).

Aleksandr Zolotarev (1907–1943) began his research in the 1930s, under the influence of Marxist conceptions of ancient history and society, but his study of the mythology of ancient society, *Rodovoi stroi i pervobytnaia mifologiia* (Tribal System and Ancient Mythology; Moscow, 1964), could be published only after his death. In this study, Zolotarev bases his arguments upon a large body of source materials and shows that the dualistic cosmological myths and the dualistic societies of Siberian peoples reflected one another; basically this recognition resembles Georges Dumézil's position. Zolotarev arranged his materials within a firm theoretical framework. Because of his recognition of the system of dual oppositions, he can be considered a forerunner of structuralism, though his work is unknown to the West.

The introduction by Soviet scholars of structuralist and semiotic methods to mythological analyses at the beginning of the 1970s proved to be a methodological turning point. These scholars were independent of the western European (primarily French) structuralists in that they formed their own theories, basing them on their structuralist predecessors—for example, Roman Jakobson, Ol'ga Freidenberg, Vladimir Propp, and Mikhail Bakhtin. Their most important contention was that mythology is explicable as a system of signs and that it is one of the texts or codes of a culture (see V. V. Ivanov and V. N. Toporov, "Towards the Description of Ket Semiotic Systems," *Semiotica* 9, 1973; E. M. Meletinsky, "Typological Analysis of the Paleo-Asiatic Raven Myths," *Acta Ethnographica* 22, 1973). In the description of the Finno-Ugric, or, according to more recent terminology, the Uralic mythological system, I was the first to employ this method. The hierarchy of the gods can now be described with the aid of dual oppositions functioning as distinctive features (Hoppál, 1976), and consequently mythological structures clarified through semantic characteristics can be compared more accurately than before (Toporov, 1974).

Another new development in the research is the fact that in studying certain topics, some scholars have moved outside the narrow Finno-Ugric confines and are analyzing particular topics within a wider Uralian or even Eurasian context, as in, for example, the investigation of the question of a supposed ancient Eurasian mother cult, or of the problematics of shamanism. The examination of shamanism has an especially old tradition among Hungarian scholars; it might be worthwhile to remind the reader that Géza Róheim (1891–1955), the founder of psychoanalytic anthropology, devoted an interesting chapter to the question of Ob-Ugrian shamanism in his study *Hungarian and Vogul Mythology* (Locust Valley, N.Y., 1954). Another study of this subject was written by Vilmos Diószegi (1923–1972), who explored the residues of shamanism in recent Hungarian folklore in *A sámánhit emlékei a magyar népi müveltségben* (Budapest, 1958). Two further studies on the question of Siberian shamanism have been published: *The Rite Technique of the Siberian Shaman* (1978) by Anna-Leena Siikala; and *Obriad i fol'klor v sibirskom shamanizme* (Ritual and Folklore in Siberian Shamanism; Moscow, 1984) by E. S. Novik, who analyzes the syntagmatic structure of shamanic ritual and of narrative folklore.

In summary one could say that, because Finno-Ugric peoples are generally not numerous, and—more important—because most of them constitute ethnic minorities within the Soviet Union, their search for common roots and mythology, expressed in the language of folklore, has been a way of establishing their own identity and of buttressing their national self-consciousness. For these reasons we can expect Finno-Ugric mythology and folklore to remain of interest for a long time to come. Apart from this sociopolitical consideration, naturally, the strictly scientific-philological aspects are no less compelling, a fact that renders the prospect of comparative Finno-Ugric mythological research in the future exceptionally interesting in terms of methodology as well, precisely because of the still insufficiently clarified relations among Finno-Ugric peoples, because of their divergent lines of cultural progress, and because of their varied relations with neighboring peoples.

BIBLIOGRAPHY

Chernetsov, V. N. "Concepts of the Soul among the Ob Ugrians." In *Studies in Siberian Shamanism*, edited by Henry N. Michael, pp. 3–45. Toronto, 1963. One of the fundamental studies by the father of Finno-Ugric archaeology, based upon his own collection.

Corradi, Carla. *Le divinita femminili nella mitologia ugro-finnica*. Parma, 1982. A modern summary on female divinity.

Diószegi, Vilmos. *A pogány magyarok hitvilága*. Budapest, 1967. A reconstruction of the old Hungarian pagan mythological worldview in terms of shamanism.

Diószegi, Vilmos, and Mihály Hoppál, eds. *Shamanism in Siberia*. Budapest, 1978. A collection of studies on different aspects of shamanism.

Dömötör, Tekla. *Hungarian Folk Beliefs*. Budapest and Bloomington, Ind., 1983. The most recent outline of the Hungarian folk belief system.

Ferdinandy, Michael de. "Die Mythologie der Ungarn." In *Wörterbuch der Mythologie*, edited by H. W. Haussig, vol. 1., pp. 211–259. Stuttgart, 1965. Since the study lists historical legends from medieval chronicles as its mythological sources, it is somewhat romantic in its outlook. However, it contains rich material.

Haavio, Martti. *Suomalainen mytologia*. Porvoo, Finland, 1967. The most detailed account of Finnish mythology to date which lists the gods and provides much material for comparative purposes, but one should read it with critical distance.

Hajdú, Peter, ed. *Ancient Cultures of the Uralian Peoples*. Budapest, 1976. This study discusses the history of Uralic languages and the folklore, mythology, and folk poetry of Uralic peoples. The articles in it summarize the results of the most recent research.

Holmberg (Harva), Uno. "Finno-Ugric Mythology." In *Mythology of All Races*, vol. 4. Boston, 1927. To date the most detailed summary of the ancient religious beliefs of the Finno-Ugric peoples.

Hoppál, Mihály. "Folk Beliefs and Shamanism among the

Uralic Peoples." In *Ancient Cultures of the Uralian Peoples,* edited by Peter Hajdú, pp. 215–242. Budapest, 1976. An outline and a semiotic description of beliefs and mythological worldview of the Finno-Ugric peoples, with special references to the main features of shamanism.

Hoppál, Mihály, ed. *Shamanism in Eurasia.* 2 vols. Göttingen, 1984. Based on a symposium on various aspects of Eurasian shamanism.

Kannisto, Artturi. *Materialen zur Mythologie der Wogulen: Gesammelt von Artturi Kannisto.* Helsinki, 1958. One of the best and most credible mythological text collections of the Ob-Ugrians.

Karsten, Rafael. *The Religion of the Samek: Ancient Beliefs and Cults of the Scandinavian and Finnish Lapps.* Leiden, 1955. An overview of the gods of Saami mythology, shamanism, religious sacrifices, and cult of the dead. A very thorough work.

Kuusi, Matti, Keith Bosley, and Michael Branch, eds. *Finnish Folk Poetry—Epic: An Anthology in Finnish and English.* Helsinki, 1977. The volume contains the authentic texts of the original folksingers' versions of the *Kalevala* with numerous and thorough notes.

Loorits, Oskar. *Grundzuge des Estnischen Volksglaubens,* vols. 1–3. Lund, 1949–1957. The most complete overview of Estonian folk superstitions to date with abundant original texts and details.

Paulson, Ivar. *The Old Estonian Folk Religion.* Bloomington, Ind., 1971. A system reconstructed on the basis of Estonian folk beliefs, published after the author's death, probably unfinished.

Toporov, V. N. "On the Typological Similarity of Mythological Structures among the Ket and Neighbouring Peoples." *Semiotica* 10 (1974): 19–42.

MIHÁLY HOPPÁL
Translated from Hungarian by Timea Szell

FIQH. *See* Uṣūl al-Fiqh.

FIRE, with its warmth and light, fulfills a vital requirement of human life. Yet the same element can wreak sheer destruction. Both the positive and negative functions are united in fire's role as an instrument of melting, refinement, and purification.

In a religious context, fire has, through its widely varying character, come to play a very large role in cult, myth, and symbolic speech. The abundance of variations is great in different religions, cultures, and epochs and is partly universal to all mankind and partly historically conditioned, particularly in the Indo-European context.

The presentation that follows is, for the most part, based on a thematic rather than a chronological or regional outline. It can only give examples and intimations. The relatively detailed bibliography is intended to supplement what is here only touched upon.

Ancient Origins. Some elements of fire worship and the use of fire in ritual and in symbolism are rooted in and develop out of the practical experiences of human beings. History can be divided between a fireless age and an age when fire came into use. We may postulate that fire was first collected from natural conflagrations, lightning, or spontaneous combustion (250,000 years ago); then produced and kindled by percussion or friction (50,000 years ago); and domesticated (10,000 years ago). Methods for maintaining and transporting fire survived from older times, so that it was seldom necessary to kindle fresh fire. Conversely, life and fire were so intimately connected that widespread custom dictated that the household fire be extinguished when someone died.

The development of hearths, altars, and stoves as well as the collection of fuel of different kinds was influenced by both practical and ritual considerations. Borrowing fire from one's neighbor was still common during later times and the keeping of a public or national fire may be explained in the same way. Charlemagne issued an edict that a fire should be kept burning in every inhabited house. The ringing of bells when evening fell, designated as *curfew* ("cover fire," i.e., as a signal to bank the fire in the hearth), persisted in Europe up to the eighteenth century. Making the fire was a woman's affair, as woman, hearth, and home were linked together in a complex of concepts related to warmth, cooking, and light.

Fire has also been widely used to keep dangerous animals away, to flush out forest game, to clear forests, and to harden implements (such as spear points). Cremation of the dead was common in the Bronze and Iron ages and has remained a widespread practice throughout the world in traditions other than Judaism, Christianity, and Islam.

In religious ritual a basic distinction is made between the purer "perpetual fire" and the "new fire" that is kindled with great conscientiousness and awe. The different origins of fire, whether drilled from wood or sparked by lightning from heaven, are reflected in myths in which the fire sticks represent male and female or where the fire is brought from above by a bird (e.g., the Vedic *śyena,* or falcon) or stolen by a human thief. The name *Prometheus,* usually translated as "the prudent," or "he with foresight," is likely to be related to the Sanskrit word *math,* "to steal, rob, take away," a verb that since ancient times has been confounded with *manth,* "to stir, churn; to produce fire by rapidly whirling a dry stick in another dry stick."

The torch races in connection with religious festivals in ancient Greece were probably modeled on the image of Prometheus's theft. In the case of Euchidas, who in 479 BCE ran naked from Plataea to the altar of Apollo at Delphi to take the sacred fire, the reason for the run is explicitly stated: it was for kindling the new fire in places where the old one had been polluted by the Persian barbarians. As the torch race usually was run in relays, Plato can speak symbolically of parents "handing over life like a torch" when they give birth and feed children. The same language is used in Buddhism to describe rebirth without substantial transmigration: it occurs as when a flame is lit from another flame without any fire being transferred (Staal, 1983, pp. 77–88).

Just as every home had its hearth, so, too, in Greco-Roman antiquity every community had its public fire, which was not allowed to expire. In the Greek city-states it burned in the *prutaneion*, the city hall; in Rome a special round temple by the Forum Romanum was dedicated to the fire goddess Vesta. There the fire was tended by the six Vestals. On the altar in ancient Hebrew sanctuaries fire continuously burned (*Lv.* 6:13). The "eternal light" or "continually wakeful lamp" found in Jewish synagogues and in Christian churches correspond to a certain degree to the "perpetual fire" of antiquity but with a completely spiritualized interpretation: they constitute symbols of God's presence (Simons, 1949, pp. 67ff., 107ff.). However, analogies to this wholly spiritual function are not lacking outside Judaism and Christianity, for example, the "fire of Ahura Mazdā (Ōhrmazd)" in ancient Iran.

Both the eternal flame and the new fire are well known in African tribal religions and in Inca, Maya, and North American Indian beliefs (Freise, 1969). In fact, the perpetual fire and the new fire alike belong as much to the present as to history. The lighting of the most sacred fire, *ātash bahrām,* of which there are eight among today's Parsis in India, is a tremendously complicated ceremony. The ceremony is simpler for the village temple fire *(ātash ādarān)*. The hearth fire *(ātash dādgāh),* which is of a lower dignity, requires special rites when it is lighted anew (Duchesne-Guillemin, 1962, p. 83). The custom of making a "willfire" *(nödeld)* in the ancient way, with a fire drill, when cattle have fallen sick, has persisted in the Nordic countries into the twentieth century. Annual fires, originally meant to promote warmth, light, and fertility, are still lighted today (Charrière, 1978). The Roman Catholic new fire and candle blessing during Easter Vigil, with its thoroughly Christian symbolism, is a living ecclesiastical custom based in part on folk tradition. Similar ceremonies involving the kindling of the flame in the Church of the Holy Sepulcher in Jerusalem, from early Christian times to today, have become widely known. New modern fire rituals without any traditional religious background have also sprung up. The flame that is lit for the Olympic Games has since 1936 been kindled from a fire in the temple grove of ancient Olympia, from whence a torch relay starts. Beneath the Arc de Triomphe in Paris burns the eternal flame on the grave of the Unknown Soldier.

Indo-Iranian Fire Worship. The fire god Agni is invoked in about two hundred of the 1,028 hymns of the *Ṛgveda*, coming second only to Indra. [*See* Agni.] He is closely connected with the element fire, although in time he takes on more anthropomorphic traits. Agni is "brilliant, golden, has flaming hair and beard, three or seven tongues; his face is light, his eyes shine, he has sharp teeth, he makes a cracking noise and leaves a black trail behind" (Staal, 1983, p. 73). He loves clarified butter as an oblation, but he eats or destroys everything: wood, forests, demons, and enemies. Agni is old but at the same time eternally young, fertile, and life-giving. He is born from the kindling sticks, from the lightning and the sun on high, but also from the celestial waters (i.e., the clouds), and from terrestrial plants and woods, themselves born from water. The contrasting elements of fire and water are combined, too, in the rising and setting of the sun in the eastern and western oceans, respectively, and in the male, heavenly generative heat entering the female earthly waters.

As the domestic fire, Agni watches and lights the home. He is the friendly guest and chief of the clan; at the same time he is the domestic priest and the sacrificer to the gods. He delivers offerings to the gods, but he also lets the gods descend to earth to share them. The wise and omniscient seer Agni is the messenger between gods and men. He has relations with all of them and is, together with Soma, the main deity of Vedic ritual.

In later Hinduism, Agni becomes a minor deity, represented in mythology as a seducer of women and an adulterer, the symbol of sexual fire. But he is also the heat, or *tapas*, of ascetic practice (Blair, 1961).

Besides the more complicated ritual sacrifices of the priests in Vedic times, there was also the simple "fire-offering" (Agnihotra), which consisted of a daily oblation to the domestic and sacrificial fires. The oblation was composed chiefly of milk, oil, and sour gruel and was performed by the householder every morning and evening. Oblations into the fire are still common in India, whereas the keeping of the three sacred fires is confined to brahman homes.

Among scholars there has been lively discussion of the original meaning of the Agnihotra. As a matter of fact, the ritual formulas are not directed to any one deity but simply establish the fact that the light of the sun is the fire; as H. W. Bodewitz (1976, p. 3) points out, the Agnihotra is "not a daily homage to Agni . . . but a transference of the sun (the heated milk) into Agni," a procedure that maintains the cosmic process of sunset and sunrise.

The so-called Vedic nomads (i.e., people speaking an Indo-European language and coming from Inner Asia to the Indian subcontinent around 1500 BCE), introduced fire worship to their new homelands. Right up to the present day, the "spirit," "virgin," or "mother" of fire has been invoked in prayers and has received offerings from the Altaic peoples in Siberia (Roux, 1976). Likewise, the female Hestia and Vesta, in ancient Greece and Rome respectively, were offered parts of the daily meals. There are traces of the same worship of a female fire deity in Scandinavian folk customs of more recent times (Wikman, 1929).

A nomadic background of fire rituals also probably lies behind the fire cult of ancient Iran, where fire temples were built as late as the fourth century BCE and became common religious centers only during the Sasanid dynasty (226–650 CE). The Iranians called the divinity of fire Ātar and made offerings to it thrice daily at the prayer times, sunrise, noon, and sunset. The offering consisted of clean, dry fuel and incense (e.g., the dried leaves of herbs). In addition, whenever the family had meat to cook, a small portion of animal fat was poured into the flames on the hearth, so they blazed up and thus showed their new strength.

Along with an offering to water, fire worship was included in the Yasna, the daily sacrifice performed by the priests without any gifts but originally using the blood of slaughtered domestic animals. According to the ancient Iranian creation myth, the gods created fire on the seventh day, not only the visible fire in its various forms, but also the invisible one that, as an unseen, vital force, pervades the whole animate creation (Boyce, 1979, pp. 4ff., 12).

In the doctrine of Zarathushtra (Zoroaster), fire is under the protection of Asha Vahishta ("best truth, best righteousness"), one of the seven Amesha Spentas ("holy immortals") who keep the world in order. During the five daily prayers, the believer looks at the symbol of righteousness, the hearth fire. Among the seven obligatory festivals, the last one, Nō Rūz (Pers., "new day"), is dedicated to Asha Vahishta and fire. The fire cannot be used to burn rubbish; it must be kept clean, and cooking in it has to be done with the utmost care (Boyce, 1979, pp. 23, 33, 44).

Under the Achaemenids (539–331 BCE), the priests elevated the fire before which the king prayed, so that he had to face a raised stand in his palace, furnished with a three-tiered base and an inverted three-tiered top. The fire symbolized both the king's Zoroastrian faith and his sovereign rule. The new worship of fire in temples, which was probably introduced to counteract the Near Eastern cult of the mother goddess, utilized similar stands. In principle they remained, like the dynastic fire of each new king, the traditional hearth fire with traditional offerings. Because of the building of such "places of fire" or "houses of fire" the Zoroastrians were called "fire worshipers." Darius III (r. 336–330) had embers from the fire that the Persians called sacred and eternal carried before his troops. The fires of the more important temples, created through complicated rites, were called "fire of Verethragna," thus associating them with the deity of victory. The fires of the lesser sanctuaries, kindled from the hearth fires by members of the various social classes, were labeled "fire of fires."

In contrast to the traditional hearth, where the offerings served a practical purpose in maintaining the fire, the new sacred fires had no worldly use but employed a large priesthood (Boyce, 1979, pp. 50ff., 57ff., 60, 62ff.).

During Sasanid times, the building of a new fire temple was connected with coronations or important events in the nation's life and constituted an especially meritorious act. The king was also able to give donations to already existing temples, or could, like the nation's men of power and commoners alike, make pilgrimages to shrines. Such shrines, sometimes bearing the names of their founders, were categorized into different ranks; the top three categories were probably connected with the priests, warriors, and peasants. A compilation of archaeological and literary evidence has so far indicated the locations of 136 Iranian fire temples (Schippman, 1971).

Biblical Conceptions. The ambiguous character of fire appears very clearly in the Hebrew scriptures (Old Testament), where it is described as a manifestation of divine glory or a sign of God's actions and presence. It functions as an instrument of purification, ordeal, destruction, or punishment. The word *fire* is often used in a concrete sense, but it may also have figurative significance. The theophanic use of fire is well documented throughout the Hebrew scriptures, from Mosaic Yahvism onward. The perpetual flame on the altar in *Leviticus* 6:13 belongs to the postexilic period and might have been influenced by Zoroastrian fire worship. Fire also appears as a weapon of God, called "fire from heaven," "lightning," and "devouring fire." These expressions for the wrath of God have extrabiblical parallels as well.

Some illustrations of these general statements follow: "The glory of the Lord looked to the Israelites as a devouring fire" (*Ex.* 24:17); "by night Yahveh guided them as a pillar of fire" (*Ex.* 13:21f.); "and the angel of the Lord appeared to Moses in the flame of a burning bush" (*Ex.* 3:2); "The fire of the Lord consumed the offering" (*1 Kgs.* 18:38). He protects his chosen people against both water and fire—"Walk through fire and you will not be scorched" (*Is.* 43:2)—as the three men in the blazing furnace could confirm, (*Dn.* 3); Yahveh makes flames of fire his servants (*Ps.* 104:4). Paradise is guarded by the cherubim and a sword whirling and flashing fire (*Gn.* 3:24), and Elijah is carried up to heaven in a chariot of fire drawn by horses of fire (*2 Kgs.* 2:11). From before the Ancient of Days and his flaming throne a river of fire streams out (*Dn.* 7:10). The evil gossip of a scoundrel is like a burning fire (*Prv.* 16:27).

On the other hand, the fire of love, as in *Luke* 24:32 ("our hearts on fire"), has a positive meaning in the New Testament. There fire and, even more so, light appear as heavenly attributes. But the fire will also test the worth of each man's work (*1 Cor.* 3:13), and the eternal fire is ready for the devil and his angels (*Mt.* 25:41). A world conflagration is mentioned in the New Testament (2 *Pt.* 3:10).

In postbiblical times, fire symbolism, (e.g., the pillar of fire) played a great role among ascetic anchorites in the Syrian and Egyptian deserts. Fire and light are not only godly attributes; they are also regarded as manifestations of holiness. As in later mysticism, such apparitions are believed to be signs of transfiguration or deification that may be seen by the illuminated eye. Fire and light phenomena are related to corresponding biblical descriptions and interpreted as revelations of the transcendent world (Edsman, 1940, p. 158; Edsman, 1974; *Dictionnaire de spiritualité*, 1932; Ricard, 1979; *Reallexikon für Antike und Christentum*).

Cosmology and Anthropology. Besides the three sacrificial fires, Vedic India knew five fires of differing origins. These five proceed from (1) the celestial world, from which the elixir of immortality, soma, comes; (2) the storm *(parjanya)*, which gives rise to rain; (3) the earth *(pṛthivī)*, which bestows food upon us; (4) man *(puruṣa)*, who gives sperm; (5) woman *(yoṣā)*, who carries the embryo. In a slightly different order and formulation, this division into five appears in ancient Iran, where it can be found already in the Avesta as (1) the fire that shines before the Lord; (2) the fire that is found in the bodies of men and animals; (3) the fire that is hidden in plants; (4) the fire battles in the clouds with the thunder demon Spenjagrya; and (5) the fire that is used in daily work, that is, the hearth fire.

Therefore, according to the Indo-Iranian view, fire is everywhere present in the cosmos. [*See also* Tapas.] The lightning brings forth the rain, which is put to use by the plants. From these, one can extract fire by rubbing two branches against one another. Both animals and man nourish themselves on plants, turning them into body heat or life force. The interpretation of "the fire that shines before the Lord" is uncertain, but it probably has to do with the fire altars.

In Iran, this pervasive fire- or life-fluid had a special name, indicating its emission from the sun, that is, *khvarenah* ("the radiance of light"). According to another view, this radiance dwells in water, which is vital to life, and rises from water into plants, animals, and men, among whom it especially locates in the head. From the head it shines forth as a nimbus (Collinet-Guérin, 1961), the origin of the saintly halo in Buddhism, Christianity, and Islam (Duchesne-Guillemin, 1962, pp. 92ff.; 1970, pp. 636f.).

Indo-Iranian cosmology sheds light on various seemingly contradictory notions about the changing role of fire in classical antiquity and the late Roman period. The Ionian natural philosophers spoke of an original substance from which all other substances came, and Heraclitus identified fire as the basic element. The Stoics shared the latter belief and asserted that the world's constantly recurring cycles begin and end with fire, *ekpurōsis*, the world conflagration. They also made a distinction between the celestial or "reasonable" fire and the earthly, dark, or burning fire. In Greek mythology, on the other hand, the same fire destroys and renews.

According to the beliefs of the late Roman period, the soul was an immortal spark that, after death, returned to the world of fire and light where it really belonged. The Stoics explained that this world existed on the moon. In these heavenly territories they also placed the Elysian Fields of the Blessed. Caesar Julianus, who deserted Christianity in favor of Neoplatonism, held a similar view, that dead Caesars held their feasts in this place. Philosophically stated, the soul first regains its strength when it arrives in the ethereal sphere that corresponds to its true nature; the ethereal fire renews.

The philosophers of late Roman antiquity were further of the opinion that the soul's fire-nature was darkened and tainted by earthly existence. Thus it had to be purified during its journey through space. In the initiation rites of the mysteries, such purification was acted out by the initiate (Edsman, 1949, pp. 205 ff.; Delcourt, 1965; Cremer, 1969).

Purification and Ordeal. Even before Zarathusthra, ordeals by fire were practiced in Indo-Iranian territories. An accused person could prove his innocence by passing unharmed between two blazing piles of wood. Or molten copper could be poured on his bare breast to test his innocence. In the later Sasanid period, a Persian high priest is said to have actually undergone such a fiery ordeal successfully, in this case to vindicate his faith (Boyce, 1979, pp. 9, 118). As early as the Avesta, a coming ordeal by fire is spoken of in connection with the Last Judgment. In later sources we are told that the deity of friendship and healing, Airyaman, together with Ātar, will send a fiery river flowing out of the melted metal in the mountains and over the earth. All mankind will have to pass through this river. "For him who is righteous it will seem like warm milk, and for him who is wicked, it will seem as if he is walking in the flesh through molten metal" (*Greater Bundahishn* 34:18f., quoted in Boyce, p. 28). Through this world conflagration, all evil is destroyed and the whole universe is transfigured.

This fiery stream also occurs in Jewish, Christian, and gnostic sources from *Daniel* 7:10 in the second century BCE onward. But in this literature it also comes to figure in visions of the fate of the individual soul immediately after death. The Alexandrian church teacher Origen (third century) expresses this eschatological idea in various ways when he comments on different scripture passages: Jesus, standing in a flaming river, will baptize with fire those who would enter paradise and who have already received the baptism of water and spirit (*Lk.* 3:16). In other connections, Origen underlines the fact that all men must pass through this river, even Peter and Paul. The Syrian church father Ephraem (fourth century) describes the different ways in which the fire reacts to the righteous and to sinners: for the former, it calms down; for the latter, it blazes up (Edsman, 1940, pp. 1ff., 124).

Fire walking, an almost universal phenomenon, sometimes has the character of an ordeal. But it is joined with so many notions and so many different cults that it is very difficult to find a common explanation for this phenomenon (Price, 1936). This ceremony has attracted great attention in a Greek Orthodox milieu in present-day northern Greece (Antoniades, 1954) and in Bulgaria (Šarankov, 1980) during recent decades.

Immortality and Rejuvenation. In ancient India, cremation came to be thought of as a transition to immortality. The Indian fire god Agni, himself immortal, confers immortality and guides the deceased to the celestial world. Cremation is actually man's third birth. The first birth is man's entry into this world, and the second takes place through Agnicayana, the fire altar ritual, which bestows on the sacrificer a celestial identity. The funeral pyre has become the symbol of divine life in India to such a great extent that ascetics voluntarily ascend it. The immolation of widows has a corresponding belief as its background. Holy suicide by fire, Agnipravesá, was already described in the old Indian epic the *Rāmāyaṇa*: the ascetic Śarabhaṅga, who has nothing more to gain from terrestrial life, wishes to leave his limbs like the snake wriggling out of its old skin. He lights a fire, sacrifices butter while uttering the appropriate formulas, and steps into the fire. It then consumes his hair, his old skin, bones, flesh and blood. A youth, the fire's counterpart, arises shining and wanders through the world of the gods to the highest heaven (3.5.37ff.).

A similar passage in the *Rāmāyaṇa* describes the female ascetic Śabarī, who, like a flaming fire, goes into heaven (3.74.33ff.). The Greek historians of Alexander's conquests confirm that Agnipravesá is not only a feature of the miraculous happenings in hero tales. They describe how, in fact, the Indian ascetic Kalanos, in front of Alexander and the Greek army, ascended the pyre. They also tell of a similar act by an Indian in Athens.

Voluntary death through self-immolation is also known in Buddhism, where it is known by a term meaning "to abandon the body, to lose the body." It is cited in the Chinese translation of the much-read *Saddharmapuṇḍarīka Sūtra* (Sutra of the Lotus of the Wonderful Law; chap. 22, concerning Bhaiṣajyarāja). Death through fire has been chosen for moral, devotional, or political reasons. But it has also occasionally been regarded as promoting rebirth into a higher existence as a *bodhisattva*, an incipient Buddha, or admittance to the "paradise" of the Buddha Amitāba known as Sukhāvatī, the Pure Land in the western quarter of our universe.

Buddhist suicides in Vietnam in the 1960s were enacted against a similar background; for this reason—unlike the suicides of their Western imitators—they do not constitute purely political protest actions.

The Demeter hymn, recited at the ancient Greek pre-Christian mysteries in Eleusis, tells the tale of the goddess Demeter's visit to a palace. Disguised, she enters service as wet-nurse to the princeling Demophon. In the night, the goddess holds the little prince in the fire in order to make him immortal. But Demeter is prevented by the terrified queen from fulfilling her purpose and angrily takes her leave. It is also related that Scylla, the sea monster slain by Herakles, is reawakened to life by being burned with torches by its father, Phorcys. Even better known is the story of Herakles' own death on the pyre. Such a death frees him not only from the poisoned mantle of Nessus but also confers immortality upon him among the gods of Olympus and wins him a wife, the goddess of youth herself, Hebe.

The story of the death of the hero on the pyre is probably an etiological myth originating in the custom of celebrating an annual fire festival, similar to the later

European bonfires kindled especially during Lent and on Saint John's Day. Archaeological discoveries on Mount Oite include offerings of animals and figures of human beings. In the Herakles myth, the notion that the flames are a means of making the hero immortal belongs to a later period. Through Stoic influence the story has developed into a prototype of heroic and imperial apotheosis.

The legend about the phoenix, the wonderful bird that renewed itself in fire, was already used in the second century after Christ as an argument for Christian resurrection. The later Christian poet Dracontius (fifth century CE) argues in the following way: the non-Christian who believes that the phoenix is reborn out of its own ashes has no grounds for reproach against the Christian who holds the same belief about the decayed body. And life can be rekindled, just as a slaked fire can flare up again, or, to use Dracontius's own words, "The phoenix's perfect youth God renews with fire."

Fairy tales and legends, too, often deal with the theme of renewal or rejuvenation through fire. To the extent that the pyre serves as the means of re-creation, there is a direct dependence on Indian belief and ritual. During the era of the Crusades, such tales of Indian origin spread to Europe.

The apparatus of rejuvenation can also include a furnace. In the folk legend of the Master of All Masters, which has medieval roots, Jesus Christ, disguised as an apprentice smith, rejuvenates an old woman by reforging her. When the smith himself tries to repeat the miracle, he fails, and what results instead is the first monkey. In a modern, exotic form, rejuvenation through fire occurs in H. Rider Haggard's fantasy novel *She*, where the beautiful heroine's bath of fire does not, in the end, succeed.

[*See also* Light and Darkness.]

BIBLIOGRAPHY

General References. Most of the basic reference books in religious studies include articles on fire and related topics. In the *Dictionnaire de spiritualité ascétique et mystique, doctrine et histoire* (Paris, 1932), for example, see "Feu," "Lumière," and "Lumineux"; in the *Reallexikon für Antike und Christentum* (Stuttgart, 1950–), see "Demeter," "Deus internus," "Divinatio," "Dornstrauch," "Dynamis," "Elementum," "Engel," "Epiphanie," "Erneuerung," "Feuersäule," "Gloria," and "Gottesschau." The *Theological Dictionary of the Old Testament*, edited by G. Johannes Botterweck and Helmer Ringgren, vol. 1 (Grand Rapids, Mich., 1974), includes "Esh [Fire]" by Jan Bergman et al. The *Theological Dictionary of the New Testament*, edited by Gerhard Kittel, vol. 6 (Grand Rapids, Mich., 1976), includes "Pur [Fire]" by Friedrich Lang, and the index volume (10.2) lists thirty-four references, mainly to articles on Bible passages, that supplement the principal entry. My own article "Feuer," in *Die Religion in Geschichte und Gegenwart*, 3d ed., vol. 2 (Tübingen, 1958), includes bibliographic references not reproduced here.

Specialized Studies

Antoniades, Anne Gault. *The Anastenaria: Thracian Firewalking Festival*. Athens, 1954.

Blair, Chauncey J. *Heat in the Rig Veda and Atharva Veda*. New Haven, 1961. A collection of passages where the root *tap* and derivatives occur, followed by a systematic survey of heat against enemies, heat of the body, heat and the cosmos, and heat and the gods.

Bodewitz, H. W. *The Daily Evening and Morning Offering (Agnihotra) according to the Brāhmaṇas*. Leiden, 1976.

Boyce, Mary. *Zoroastrians: Their Religious Beliefs and Practices*. London, 1979. A chronological discussion, from the oldest times to the present.

Charrière, G. "Feux, bûchers et autodafés bien de chez nous." *Revue de l'histoire des religions* 194 (January 1978): 23–64.

Collinet-Guérin, Marthe. *Histoire du nimbe, des origines aux temps modernes*. Paris, 1961.

Cremer, Friedrich W. *Die chaldäischen Orakel und Jamblich de mysteriis*. Meisenheim am Glan, 1969.

Delcourt, Marie. *Pyrrhos et Pyrrha: Recherches sur les valeurs du feu dans les légendes helléniques*. Paris, 1965.

Duchesne-Guillemin, Jacques. *La religion de l'Iran ancien*. Paris, 1962. Translated as *Religion of Ancient Iran* (Bombay, 1973).

Duchesne-Guillemin, Jacques. "Fire in Iran and in Greece." *East and West* 13 (June–September 1962):198–206.

Duchesne-Guillemin, Jacques. "Heraclitus and Iran." *History of Religions* 3 (Summer 1963): 34–49.

Duchesne-Guillemin, Jacques. "L'Iran antique et Zorâstre." In *Histoire des religions*, edited by Henri-Charles Puech, vol. 1, pp. 625–694. Paris, 1970.

Edsman, Carl-Martin. *Le baptême de feu*. Uppsala, 1940.

Edsman, Carl-Martin. *Ignis divinus: Le feu comme moyen de rajeunissement et d'immortalité; Contes, légendes, mythes et rites*. Lund, 1949.

Edsman, Carl-Martin. " 'Le buisson ardent': Contribution nordique à la mystique de la lumière." In *Mélanges d'histoire des religions offerts à Henri-Charles Puech*, pp. 591–600. Paris, 1974. See also Antoine Guillaumont's contribution to this collection, "Le baptême de feu chez les messaliens" (pp. 517–523).

Freise, Reinhilde. *Studie zum Feuer in Vorstellungswelt und Praktiken der Indianer des südwestlichen Nordamerika*. Tübingen,1969.

Goldberg, Arnold M. *Untersuchungen über die Vorstellung von der Schekhinah in der frühen rabbinischen Literatur (Talmud und Midrash)*. Berlin, 1969.

Graz, Louis. *Le feu dans l'Iliade et l'Odyssée*. Paris, 1965.

Jan Yün-hua. "Buddhist Self-immolation in Medieval China." *History of Religions* 4 (Winter 1965): 243–268.

Kirfel, Willibald. *Die fünf Elemente, insbesondere Wasser und Feuer: Ihre Bedeutung für den Ursprung altindischer und altmediterraner Heilkunde*. Walldorf-Hessen, 1951.

Laughlin, John Charles Hugh. "A Study of the Motif of Holy Fire in the Old Testament." Ph.D. diss., Southern Baptist Theological Seminary, 1975.

Maurach, Gregor. *Coelum empyreum: Versuch einer Begriffsgeschichte*. Wiesbaden, 1968.

Pax, Elpidius. *Epiphaneia: Ein religionsgeschichtlicher Beitrag zur biblischen Theologie*. Munich, 1955.

Price, Harry. *A Report on Two Experimental Fire-Walks*. London, 1936. Includes a bibliography.

Ricard, Robert. "Saint Jean de la Croix et l'image de la 'bûche enflammée': Contribution a l'étude d'un thème symbolique." *Lettres romanes* 33 (February 1979): 73–85.

Roux, Jean-Paul. "Fonctions chamaniques et valeurs du feu chez les peuples altaïques." *Revue de l'histoire des religions* 189 (January 1976): 67–101. A critical survey of the existing material by a specialist in the field.

Šarankov, Emanuil. *Feuergehen: Psychologisch-physiologische und historisch-geographische Untersuchung des Nestinarentums in Bulgarien*. Stuttgart, 1980.

Schippmann, Klaus. *Die iranischen Feuerheiligtümer*. Berlin, 1971.

Simons, Lyda Maria Regina. *Flamma aeterna: Studie over de betekenis van het eeuwige vuur in de cultus van de Hellenistisch-Romeinse oudheid*. Amsterdam, 1949.

Speyer, Wolfgang. "Die Zeugungskraft des himmlishen Feuers in Antike und Urchristentum." *Antike und Abendland* 24 (1978): 57–75.

Staal, Frits, ed. *Agni: The Vedic Ritual of the Fire Altar*. 2 vols. Berkeley, 1983. Describes in detail the 1975 performance of the Agnicayana ritual, with a general introduction on Agni and fire. A standard work.

Wikman, K. R. V. "Eldborgs skål." *Budkavlen* 8 (1929): 198–214.

CARL-MARTIN EDSMAN
Translated from Swedish by David Mel Paul and Margareta Paul

FISH. Inherent in fish symbolism is the sacred power of the abyss, the reciprocities of life and death. Paleolithic fish figurines have been found with the spiral of creativity carved on one side and the labyrinth of death on the other, evincing the spiritual world of early man in which fish represented propagating and perishing, killing and consuming, life renewed and sustained.

In the ancient Near East and the Mediterranean world, fish were associated with the great goddesses, archetypal images of femininity, love, and fertility. Astarte was worshiped in the form of a fish; Atargatis named her son Ichthys, Sacred Fish. In ancient Greece, Rome, and Scandinavia, the goddesses Aphrodite, Venus, and Frigg were assimilated to fish, and on Friday, the day sacred to them, fish were eaten as a way of participating in their fecundity. In many parts of the world—India, Greenland, Samoa, and Brazil—virgins were thought to be made pregnant by the gift of a fish, while a "fishing dance" was a common fertility rite in the women's societies of Africa. The dual nature of the symbol was manifested, and fish were regarded as unclean, wherever the goddess was characterized as libidinous and devouring. Fish gods were venerated as creators and vivifiers among Sumero-Semitic peoples and represented phallic power. An Assyrian seal of about 700 BCE depicts "Fish Gods Fertilizing the Tree of Life." Babylonian seals bear the image of a great fish with a vase from which fish stream.

A ubiquitous food in much of the world, fish are a universal motif of plenty. They are an emblem of abundance and good augury on Buddhist altars and are cited as one of the five boons in the Tantric text *Vāmācāris*.

At ritual meals in the temples of Babylon, fish was the sacred food of the priests. In Judaism, fish was regarded as the food of the blessed in Paradise and was eaten at the Sabbath meal. The old Jewish Passover was in the month of Adar, the Fish, and the traditional symbol of the national restoration that is to come with the advent of the Messiah is the great fish on which the righteous will feast. Sabbath utensils and the chalice of benediction are often decorated with images of fish.

Sacred fish occur in Syrian and Iranian myths. Throughout the dynastic period in Egypt, they were regarded as the manifestation or abode of a god. Hapi, father of the gods, was "Lord of the Fishes," and a fish denoted the phallus of the dismembered god Osiris. An attribute of the sea god Poseidon (or Neptune), fish were associated with lunar power, and when represented with an ax, as in Crete, designated both lunar and solar power. Pisces, the twelfth sign of the Zodiac, is a pair of parallel fishes pointing in opposite directions, symbolizing spiritual and temporal power, the upper and lower worlds, past and future, involution and evolution, the ending of one cycle and the beginning of another. A pair of fishes on Chinese Bronze Age vessels signifies creative power. The Japanese believed that the world was supported by a mighty fish. Among the primitive societies of Oceania, Africa, and North and South America, fish were sacred totemic figures, emblematic of the power of the clan. Peruvian Indians believed that the original fish had engendered all others; they worshiped the species that was caught in the greatest numbers. Sea gods riding on a fish signified freedom; shown on the footprint of the Buddha, a fish meant emancipation from attachment and desire.

A corollary of the fish as blessing is its assimilation to a savior. The alchemical sign for *Salvator mundi* is a fish. The Hindu god Viṣṇu, transformed into a fish by Brahmā, recovered the Vedas from the Flood, saved mankind, and started a new race. Christ was symbolized by the fish, as seen in carved inscriptions in the catacombs of Rome; in Greek, the initial letters of "Jesus Christ, Son of God, Savior" form the Greek word *ichthus* ("fish"). The depiction of Jesus standing in water confirms the metaphor of a fish drawn from the deep to bring salvation to mankind. The feeding of the multitude by the miraculous multiplication of the loaves and fishes is the prototype of the Eucharist; the fish, like the bread, symbolizes the body of the Lord. The concept of Christ as both sacrificed and sacrificer is inherent in the Mass. Three fish with one head, or three intertwined fish—found in the iconography of ancient Mesopotamia, Egypt, India, and Persia, and even down to modern times—is a universal symbol for unity in trinity, and came to represent Christian baptism. Christ's disciples and the newly baptized were denoted by the sign of a fish, and a neophyte in fish garb is depicted on early Christian lamps. In Christian mortuary painting, on pagan sarcophagi, and in representations of Chinese feasts of the dead, fish relate to resurrection and regeneration.

The experience of entering the belly of a whale or big fish, as in the Jonah story, is equated to a religious idea that informed the initiatory mysteries and rituals of death and of rebirth through newfound wisdom. Variants of this transition symbol are found worldwide, from the initiation rites of Oceania, West Africa, Lapland, and Finland to the North American Indian tale of Hiawatha, who was swallowed by the King of Fishes.

Fishing symbolizes both looking for souls and looking into the soul, that is, drawing the treasure of wisdom from the sea of the unknown. The Babylonians considered the sea the source of wisdom, and a mystic fisherman called "Warden of the Fish" is represented on a seal of the second millennium BCE. The mythical hero Ea-Oannes, half man, half fish, rose from the waters to bring culture and wisdom to mankind. The figure evolved into a fish god, Lord of the Deeps, whose priests wore fish skins and a fish headdress and whose image was ultimately transmuted into the miter of Christian bishops. The name *Orpheus* derives from a term for "fish," and one of the figures on an Orphic sacramental bowl of the third or fourth century BCE shows Orpheus as a fisher of men, with a fish and pole at his feet. The Celtic god Nodon was a fisher-god, and the Welsh god Bran the Blessed was called "Fisher of Men." His counterpart is the Grail King whom Parsifal found fishing as he waited for his deliverer. According to Augustine, Christ's exhortation "Follow me, and I will make you fishers of men" implied that the world is a sea of fish to be converted. For the tenth-century Ṣūfī mystic Niffari, the sea of spiritual experience through which the mystic passes on his journey to God is full of strange and frightening fish.

Many forms of sea life embody specific religious symbols. The dolphin was regarded as a divine intermediary between the upper and lower worlds; as a guide to departed souls, he was depicted on Greek vases bearing warriors to the Isles of the Blest. The dolphin as psychopomp, or guide of the souls of the dead, is also represented in Christian art. The octupus was a favorite motif in the ceramic arts of ancient Crete, allied to the spiritual in symbolizing the mystic center and the unfolding of creation. In the Celtic legend of Finn, the hero eats the Salmon of Wisdom, which endows him with the foreknowledge of the gods. The European Stella Maris, or starfish, is a symbol of the Virgin Mary and the Holy Spirit.

BIBLIOGRAPHY

Baum, Julius. "Symbolic Representations of the Eucharist." In *The Mysteries*, vol. 2 of *Papers from the Eranos Yearbooks*, edited by Joseph Campbell. New York, 1956. A close analysis of the symbolic acts of Christ represented in the rite of the Eucharist, based on fish iconography on sarcophagi and artifacts in sacramental chapels.

Campbell, Joseph. *The Masks of God*, vol. 4, *Creative Mythology*, New York, 1968. A survey of the mystic fisherman symbolism in Orphic, Babylonian, and Christian artifacts, correlating the symbols of the mystagogue, Orpheus the Fisherman, and the Fisher King of the Grail legend.

Lengyel, Lancelot. *Le secret des Celtes*. Paris, 1969. The fish as symbol of wisdom in the Celtic legend of the hero Finn and his acquisition of supernatural knowledge by consuming the Salmon of Wisdom.

Neumann, Erich. *The Origins and History of Consciousness*. New York, 1954. Includes an account of the predominance of female deities in early fish cults and of culture heroes that rise from the waters, half fish, half man, to bring revelation and wisdom to humankind.

Zimmer, Heinrich. *Philosophies of India* (1951). Edited by Joseph Campbell. Reprint, Princeton, 1969. In his summary of the *śāstra* of the Science of Wealth, the author examines the Indian doctrine of *Matsya-nyāya*, or the law of the fishes, in which fish symbolize the breeding force of the sea—life abundant, self-sustaining, and self-consuming.

ANN DUNNIGAN

FLACIUS, MATTHIAS (1520–1575), known as Matthias Flacius Illyricus, Italo-Croatian scholar and polemicist, a creative, fiery theological leader of the late Lutheran Reformation. Born in Albona, Istria, Flacius was trained in the humanist schools of Venice under the influence of his uncle, the Franciscan provincial Baldo Luperino, who was sympathetic to Lutheranism. Flacius studied at Tübingen before moving to Wittenberg, where Luther's intervention in a personal religious crisis confirmed Flacius as his passionately committed disciple. The defeat of Lutheran princes in the Smalcald War ended Flacius's career as a Hebrew instructor at Wittenberg and propelled him into the leadership of the Gnesio-Lutheran party, formed by Luther's more radical disciples in opposition to the imposition of the Augsburg Interim (1548) and the compromise settlement worked out by other Lutheran leaders, the Leipzig Interim (1548). Flacius's historical and liturgical research, as well as his biblical, lay-oriented argumentation, led him to criticize both settlements, attacking the Leipzig Interim as a betrayal of Luther's Reformation. As a private scholar at the center of resistance to both interims, Magdeburg (1548–1557); as a professor and counselor at Jena (1557–1561); and later as a consultant and private scholar in Regensburg, Antwerp, and Strassburg, Flacius provided theological leadership and inspired controversy.

Among his major contributions are his pioneering work in Protestant biblical hermeneutics, which climaxed in *Clavis scripturae sacrae* (1567), and in Protestant historiography, which culminated in his own *Catalogus testium veritatis* (1556) and in the *Magdeburg Centuries*, composed by members of a research team that he helped organize and manage.

According to his modern biographer, Oliver K. Olson, Flacius's theology can be described negatively as a program of "de-hellenization," that is, a turning away from Platonism and Aristotle, and positively as an insistent prophetic witness to correct biblical teaching *(pura doctrina)*. That witness led him to fight for the independence of the church from the state and to reject many aspects of medieval ecclesiastical custom and polity. Above all, it led him to defend Luther's doctrine of salvation by God's grace through faith in Christ in controversies with other Protestant theologians, especially his formidable antagonist Philipp Melanchthon. These controversies concerned, most importantly, the role of good works in salvation and the role of the human will in conversion. In the controversy over human will Flacius defined original sin as the formal substance of the fallen sinner, who, he argued, is the image of Satan. This position was misinterpreted even by some fellow Gnesio-Lutherans and contributed to his alienation from most of his contemporaries at the end of his life, when agents of leading Lutheran princes prevented him from finding a permanent home.

Flacius's ardent polemics in defense of Luther's message at a time when it was seriously menaced by political and ideological forces contributed much to its preservation, and his intellectual contributions in liturgics, hermeneutics, church history, and dogmatics greatly enriched Protestant orthodoxy.

BIBLIOGRAPHY

Oliver K. Olson provides a superb overview of Flacius's thought and life and a sketch of his forthcoming two-volume biography, as well as an extensive bibliography, in his essay "Matthias Flacius Illyricus, 1520–1575," in *Shapers of Religious Traditions in Germany, Switzerland, and Poland, 1560–1600*, edited by Jill Raitt (New Haven, 1981), pp. 1–17. The classic treatment of the subject to date is Wilhelm Preger's *Matthias Flacius Illyricus und seine Zeit*, 2 vols. in 1 (Erlangen, 1859–1861). In addition to Olson's articles and dissertation, contemporary studies of Flacius include Günter Moldaenke's *Schriftverständnis und Schriftdeutung im Zeitalter der Reformation*, vol. 1, *Matthias Flacius Illyricus* (Stuttgart, 1936), and Lauri Haikola's *Gesetz und Evangelium bei Matthias Flacius Illyricus* (Lund, 1952).

ROBERT KOLB

FLAMEN

FLAMEN. A flamen was a Roman priest who, unlike other priests, served a particular deity exclusively. Cicero (*De legibus* 2.20) used this criterion to contrast the flamens with the pontiffs.

Among the attempts to explain the semantics of *flamen*, the most plausible is found in the connection made with the Sanskrit *brahman*, "sacrificer" (Dumézil, 1970), by reason of the frequent concordance of politico-religious terms between the Indo-Iranian and the Italo-Celtic cultures. The ancients were reduced to reliance upon popular etymologies: thus the scholar Varro (*De lingua Latina* 5.84) seeks to derive *flamines* from *filamines*, arguing that the flamens wore a band of wool *(filum)* on their heads.

The *flamines* constituted a group of fifteen, the three *flamines maiores* ("greater priests") and the twelve *flamines minores* ("lesser priests"). The names of the three *flamines maiores* corresponded to the archaic triad Jupiter-Mars-Quirinus, and each of the three was named after the god he served: *flamen Dialis, flamen Martialis, flamen Quirinalis*. The three *flamines maiores* had to be patricians, and they alone of the flamens belonged to the pontifical college. In the priestly hierarchy they ranked after the *rex* ("king") and before the *pontifex maximus*.

Of the twelve *flamines minores*, only ten are known to us by name. The list of them, with their corresponding divinities, is as follows. The first four were the *flamen Portunalis*, serving Portunus; the *flamen Carmentalis*, serving Carmenta; the *flamen Cerialis*, serving Ceres; the *flamen Volcanalis*, serving Vulcan. According to Ennius (cited by Varro, *De lingua Latina* 7.45), the last six were in this order: the *flamen Volturnalis*, serving Voltunus; the *flamen Palatualis*, serving Palatua; the *flamen Furinalis*, serving Fur(r)ina; the *flamen Floralis*, serving

Flora; the *flamen Falacer,* serving Falacer; and the *flamen Pomonalis,* serving Pomona. Some of these names appeared obscure even to the ancients, as for instance *Furrina* and *Falacer* (Varro, *De lingua Latina* 5.84). Indeed, most of these offices were obsolete.

Nevertheless, the three *flamines maiores,* believed to have been created by King Numa Pompilius (Livy, 1.20.2), attested to the ancient importance of their institution. Once a year they went together in a chariot to the *sacrarium* of Fides ("faith"; Livy, 1.21.4). This was an eloquent symbol of the need for loyal cooperation among the three orders of society. However, the *flamen Dialis* stood out by virtue of a special dignity (*dignatio;* Festus, ed. Lindsay, 1913, p. 144 L.). He was paired with the *rex,* in the sense that from the beginning he handled the king's religious obligations in order to allow him to fulfill his political, judicial, and military responsibilities. The *flamen Dialis* was entirely consecrated to Jupiter night and day; in other words, for him every day was sacred. Thus he was forbidden to observe any labor and accordingly was preceded by heralds (*praecia;* Festus, op. cit., p. 250 L.) who halted all activity along the flamen's path. Various taboos stressed the exclusiveness of this consecration to Jupiter (Gellius, 10.15). Since the priesthood ruled out all political activity, the position appeared fossilized and anachronistic. The post remained vacant for seventy-five years, from 87 BCE until its reestablishment by Augustus in 11 BCE.

BIBLIOGRAPHY

Dumézil, Georges. *Archaic Roman Religion.* 2 vols. Translated by Philip Krapp. Chicago, 1970.

Dumézil, Georges. *Fêtes romaines d'été et d'automne.* Paris, 1975. See pages 32–37. A brilliant interpretation of Furrina and the Furrinalia.

Samter, E. "Flamines." In *Real-encyclopädie der klassischen Altertum wissenschaft,* vol. 6. Stuttgart, 1909.

Schilling, Robert. *La religion romaine de Vénus.* 2d ed. Paris, 1982. See pages 43–44 on the *venenatum* of the *flaminica* and pages 129–130 on the *flamen Dialis* and the Vinalia (wine festivals).

Wissowa, Georg. *Religion und Kultus der Römer.* 2d ed. Munich, 1912. See especially pages 504–507.

ROBERT SCHILLING
Translated from French by Paul C. Duggan

FLAVIUS JOSEPHUS. *See* Josephus Flavius.

FLIGHT. The image of a human being escaping the bonds of earthly life to float and soar about the skies unencumbered and free appears in religious myths, mystical tracts, ritual dramas, and imaginative expressions around the world, from the most archaic to the most contemporary of cultures. While of course their specific historical circumstances and motivations vary, one still feels that in some ways the imagination of the Paleolithic cave dweller who painted the figure of a man with a bird's head on the walls of the caves at Lascaux is not so different from the imagination that created the ancient Greek story of Icarus yearning to fly to the sun or that of the poets of Vedic India who sang praises of the long-haired ascetic who "flies through the air, looking on all shapes below, the friend to all the gods" (*Ṛgveda* 10.136.4). Perhaps, too, this imagination is not so different in the end from that which helped lift the Wright brothers into the air above Kitty Hawk.

Accounts of human flight are at times quite dramatic, as in the neo-Hebraic text the *Apocalypse of Moses,* which tells of Moses' ascension into the various heavens, each one inhabited by frightening and dreadful angels who breathe fire and lightning and whose sweat flows into a mighty burning river. Other tales of flight convey a mood of peacefulness, as in the nineteenth-century accounts of Sister Mary of Jesus Crucified, a Carmelite nun who floated about the yard of her nunnery for hours at a time, sometimes perching softly in the treetops like a bird. Some accounts are quite charming, like the medieval Sanskrit text that tells neophyte yogins that a person trying to master the art of levitation may have some difficulty at first and so will bounce across the ground like a jumping frog, but after increased practice will fly about with ease (see *Yogatattva Upaniṣad* 53–55).

Rituals as well as myths also frequently include references to or enactment of aerial travel. Alchemists and Taoist priests in ancient China, for example, clothed themselves with feathered wings while performing various religious ceremonies so that they might fly about the skies with the immortals. Similarly, at one point in the Vedic Vājapeya rite the priest and the ritual's patron are instructed to climb the sacrificial pillar, at the top of which they spread their arms as if flapping their wings and proclaim, "We have come to the heavens, to the gods we have come! We have become immortal" (*Taittirīya Saṃhitā* 1.7.9). The Vedic ritual system as a whole is often described in ornithological terms. The performance of the Agnicayana (fire ritual), for example, revolves around the construction of an altar in the shape of a bird, suggesting that the ritual transports its oblations to the heavens the way a bird soars through the skies.

Dimensions of Magical Flight. Scholars have offered a variety of theories regarding the origin and meaning of humanity's fascination with magical flight. Some, such as Arthur Maurice Hocart, an anthropologist, have seen in this theme remnants of an archaic solar worship and reverence for the king (who was felt to be the sun, or the son of the sun), who was always carried about on the shoulders of his subjects and thus "flew" everywhere he went. Others, such as Geo Widengren, a scholar of Near Eastern religions, have seen in myths and rituals involving flight distinct elements of religious ideologies based on divine kingship; the protagonist exemplifying such ideologies (originally the king, but later also a prophet or savior) is said to ascend to the realm of the high god in order to receive the sanction to rule the earthly community below. Some theorists feel that the theme represents elements of initiation and rites of passage: the flight typifies the state of being in which the initiate stands between the old and the new modes of existence. Some psychologists, especially those influenced by the theories of Sigmund Freud, have argued that the desire to fly is really a subliminal desire for sexual power, and that the feelings accompanying such an experience are repressed aspects of sexual arousal. Students of other disciplines in the social sciences maintain that magical flight expresses a person's search for a legitimation of authority over other people, or a wish to be free of personal limitations.

There is no doubt that to fly is to have power, and some theorists have held that the search for power is the central motivation common to all religious experience and expression. Whether or not this means, however, that themes of magical flight in religious myths and rituals derive from specific modes of power (such as royal prestige, prophetic influence, personal gratification, or existential autonomy) will remain open to debate. The issue is complicated by the fact that many types of persons—sovereigns, saints, visionaries, magicians, priests, ascetics, mystics, lovers, philosophers—have been said to undergo such uplifting experiences. Since the 1950s Mircea Eliade has argued that it would be a mistake to conclude that the mythic theme of magical flight derives from only one source, or that it reflects only one stage in human cultural or personal development. According to Eliade, magical flight and its related symbolism (learning the language of birds, the cultivation of ecstasy, rapturous mystical images, and so on) reflect an experience of abolishing everday ways of knowing the world, the desire for which is expressed in images of transcendence and freedom. Eliade further maintains that this desire is, in fact, constitutive of humanity itself. If this interpretation is correct, then symbols of magical flight not only derive from a moment in human history but also reveal a structure of human consciousness, an existential dimension to the human imagination that "must be ranked among the specific marks of man" (Eliade, 1960, p. 106).

The point is well taken. Studies in the history of religions have repeatedly emphasized that *Homo sapiens* is *homo symbolicus*, defined in part by the ability to make and be moved by symbols, especially symbols of various extraordinary modes of being. Nearly a century ago James G. Frazer and Julius von Negelein, among others, noted that religions from around the world have used the image of the bird to signify the human soul, suggesting that celestial and aerial symbols often represent sublime emotions and spiritual ideals. One might recognize such themes in Augustine's account in his *Confessions* of his experience at Ostia when he and his mother, both radiant with spiritual love, soar up to the heavens from where the celestial bodies shine onto the earth. One finds similar themes in traditional Islamic accounts of Muḥammad's Miʿrāj, in which the Prophet ascends through the seven heavens of the vertical cosmos to learn sacred lessons from his predecessors in the prophetic lineage who now live in each heaven and draw near to the throne of Allāh. This ascension has become a mythic and poetic paradigm for the practices and ideals of Ṣūfī mysticism. Tales of a person's flight through the skies frequently include an emotional tone of longing to be free of the bonds that tie humanity to the ways of the world. A similar longing perhaps enlivened the imagination of the Hebrew psalmist who sang, "Oh that I had wings like a dove! for then I would fly away and be at rest" (*Ps.* 55:6).

Protagonists who fly through the air do so for more than emotional and mystical reasons. They may assert their ability to rise above the laws of the physical world and thus to gain control over what may be experienced as an oppressive universe. This may be inferred from the South Asian use of such Sanskrit terms as *kaivalya* ("autonomy") to describe one of the goals of yogic practice, which is marked by such autonomous acts as flying through the air (see Patañjali's *Yoga Sūtra*, chap. 4 and its commentaries). Similarly, the Theravāda Buddhist tradition teaches that an adept monk can fly cross-legged through the atmosphere "like a bird in flight" (see *Majjhima Nikāya* 1.33, etc.).

At other times, the world is understood to reflect the beauty and wisdom of the divine plan; to fly about it, then, is to see more of it than is normally possible. This may be part of what the Persian Ṣūfī Farīd al-Dīn ʿAṭṭār longed to do when, in his epic poem *The Conference of Birds*, he expresses a wish to fly through the air to all regions of the earth in order "to enjoy all beauties."

At other times, people may want to fly in order to see

into the future (movement through vertical space is often associated with movement through time); to escort dead people to their new lives in the unknown world; to obtain valuable medicinal or cultic knowledge from various spiritual beings; or to locate souls that have become lost in the different layers of the universe. While the religious specialist most adept at such divination is the shaman of north-central Asia, the ecstatic experience characterized by such flights appears throughout the world.

The ability to fly through the air therefore often includes an ethical or normative dimension, for the protagonist who can travel to the future, as well as to other worlds, can see what kinds of lives people on earth can expect to have in other realms after they die. Subsequent to such a flight, the aerial traveler can return to earth to tell people how to act so that they may live in the more comfortable or prestigious afterworlds. Such is the case, for example, in the Zoroastrian tale told in the *Ardā Virāz Nāmag,* in which the priest Virāf falls into an ecstatic sleep after drinking a cup of mang and travels through the heavens and hells that are the respective postmortal homes of the pious and the infidel members of the priestly community. Having gained this knowledge, he then returns to his colleagues on earth and tells them what he has learned so that they can adjust their religious practices accordingly.

Types of Magical Flight. The various scenarios in the world's myths and rituals involving extraordinary aerial flight are so numerous that one could distinguish any number of forms and interpret their individual meanings in an equal number of ways. To arrive at a universal typology of flight, then, is to generalize in a way that might make even thoroughgoing structuralists somewhat wary. The following schema is intended to be comprehensive, but does not pretend to include all variations.

Autonomous this-worldly flight (levitation). Hagiographies from religious traditions around the world often include depictions of various saints, mediators, devotees, and other exemplary figures who are able at certain times to float up off the ground without visible assistance and without injury. Sometimes these experiences are intentional and desirable, as is implied in a lesson from the *Yogatattva Upaniṣad* (117): "Thrusting the tongue into the back of the throat and focusing one's eyes on the spot between the eyebrows, one sits in the posture in which one gains the power to float up into the air." At other times, these experiences seem to catch the community by surprise, as in a story about Alphonsus Liguori, who, while giving a sermon one day, offered himself to an image of the Virgin and, stretching out his arms (like a bird?), floated several feet off the platform, whereupon the two thousand people listening were amazed and filled with admiration. While most traditional hagiographies express wonder at such events, many also include implicit or explicit criticism of people who willingly drift about in the air in front of others, since such behavior is either physically dangerous or distracting to the normal person's religious concentration or constitutes an arrogant display of spiritual authority. The Ṣūfī tradition, for example, criticizes those who undertake a magical levitation in order to enact a miracle or gain a vision, for to do so is comparable to making the pilgrimage to Mecca merely for the sake of business or pleasure.

The Bollandists' *Acta Sanctorum* uses such descriptive terms as *a terra levabatur* ("raised above the surface of the earth"), *corporalite elevatus est* ("he or she was elevated bodily"), and *raptus* ("taken up") to describe those events in Roman Catholic history in which a person is reported to have floated up off the ground while deep in prayer, during moments of deep emotion, or while performing devotions. Since the classical period in India, Sanskrit texts have used such technical terms as *laghuman* ("lightness"), *utkramaṇa* ("stepping upward"), and *gauravahīnatā* ("gravity destroying") to describe the power a yogin gains as he learns to meditate properly. Islam distinguishes two types of mystics, those who are passively "drawn upward" *(majdhūb)* and those who actively stride *(sālik)* upward through the spheres by their own arduous reflection and effort. But such technical terms, among any number of others from the literatures of the world's religions, seem too specialized for comparative use. The English and French word *levitation* has been used since the nineteenth century by European hagiographers to describe such events in their respective traditions. While the term seems somewhat clumsy, it might suit the comparativist who has recognized such themes in other religions as well.

Levitations may be intentional or unintentional, repeated or unique, momentary or long-lasting. They may take the person over an extensive geography or they may involve rising just an inch or two above the ground. In any case, the adept remains independent of external assistance and, while he may be said to alter the physical laws of the world, he never leaves the physical structure of the cosmos.

Although levitations are often depicted as strange and astounding events that arrest people's attention and thrill the storytellers, they are of themselves rarely if ever soteriologically transformative and do not constitute an ultimately valuable experience. Rather, tales of levitation mark the esteem that the particular tradition holds for the central figure, or they serve as a means by which the tradition recognizes those specific practices and attitudes (spiritual integrity, strength of will, loving purity and devotion, self-discipline, obedience to the divine, etc.) that it holds to be most valuable.

Dependent this-worldly flight. To the category of dependent magical flights belong those instances in which a person is lifted up off the ground by a flying animal, spirit, or divine creature of some sort and is escorted through the skies over a wide area of the earth and sometimes at great height. These flights are similar to autonomous levitations in that the protagonists never leave the realm of the atmosphere and thus remain within the worldly cosmos, the realm of human activity and community. They differ from levitations in that the protagonists are dependent on another being or outside agent to bring them into the skies.

Sometimes these flights allow a hero to escape in a horizontal direction and at great speed from a situation of great anxiety or terror, often from death personified. Accordingly, the emotional tone of such stories is fervent and fearful. Folklorists have used the German term *magische Flucht* to describe such a flight from a frightening predicament and have found the theme in cultures all over the world. Eliade has noted that "it is important to distinguish one essential element [in such horizontal high-speed flights]: the desperate effort to be rid of a monstrous presence, to free oneself" (Eliade, 1960, p. 104).

At other times, this-worldly flights escorted by a supernatural being reflect less frightening feelings and signify less anxious situations. Sometimes they bring the central character to a new and highly desirable land or a more satisfying life in a distant earthly paradise. Sometimes they free him from the drudgery of daily chores long enough to add new wonder to his understanding of the world. Sometimes they show him the superiority of his religious tradition over another, for to fly over the heads of the followers of another tradition is to be better than they are.

In general, tales of escorted this-worldly flights either express a notion that escape or existential change is possible no matter how bleak things look, or help the members of the religious community reaffirm the worthiness of their tradition and encourage people from other traditions to become part of their own. As such, many tales of an escorted this-worldly flight serve conversion as well as self-affirming functions.

Otherworldly flights (ascensions). A third general category of magical flights involves a protagonist's journey to dimensions or levels of the sacred cosmos other than the earthly one. These journeys may be solitary and autonomous or they may be guided by supernatural beings. In either case, otherworldly flights, or ascensions, necessarily involve a radical transformation of one's being, a change in ontological status so powerful that one moves from one mode of existence to another. This transformation is typically depicted as being of ultimate value and is considered soteriologically efficacious. Such experiences reward specific people for their commitment to religious practices, their transformative state of mind, or their embodiment of respected personality traits. The central axis of these aerial journeys tends to be a vertical one, although there are instances of horizontal travels to other worlds as well. Whereas stories of the *magische Flucht* type of this-worldly flight evoke emotions of release, freedom, safety, or personal power, narratives of ascent evoke emotions arising from the transcendence of this world and a concurrent disjunction with normal reality and personal existential situations. If this-worldly flight gets one out of the grasp of something horrible or above the heads of everybody else in the world, ascension gets one out of the world altogether.

Myths of vertical travel to the heavens above the skies are often associated with the protagonist's previous or subsequent descent along the same axis to the hells or otherworlds below. Therefore, ascensions, like other religious forms of magical flight, often include divinatory and ethical elements. However, unlike levitations and this-worldly flights (which involve travel across the geographies of the terrestrial world), an ascension takes one beyond the dimensions of human space and history, since vertical movement is often synonymous with movement through, or the abolition of, time. Ascensions are typologically different from levitations and this-worldly flights in that ascensions often include apocalyptic or eschatological themes. Thus, although they appear in other traditions as well, it is in Zoroastrianism, apocalyptic Judaism, Christianity, and Islam that myths of ascension are most prevalent, for it is in these traditions that the end of history is most consistently associated with the ascension of a savior into the vertical heavens above the terrestrial realm.

Figures from the world's religions who ascend to other worlds—prophets, visionaries, saints, founders, perfected beings, and so on—sometimes return to earth with new power or knowledge that is of soteriological benefit to the community as a whole. Such an ascending and returning mediator might well function, then, as a shaman. In other instances, he or she remains in the sacred world above, never to return. Such a person might then serve as a model for others in their religious practices and attitudes, or as an example of a new and transformed being.

[*See also* Ascension; Magico-Religious Powers; *and*

Shamanism. *For further discussion of the symbolism of flight, see* Birds.]

BIBLIOGRAPHY

The best place to begin further reading on flight and flight symbolism is with three works by Mircea Eliade: *Myths, Dreams and Mysteries* (New York, 1960), pp. 99–122; *Patterns in Comparative Religion* (New York, 1958), pp. 102–108; and *Shamanism: Archaic Techniques of Ecstasy*, 2d ed., rev. & enl. (New York, 1964), pp. 190–198, 477–507, and elsewhere. As always, Eliade's works are useful for their extensive bibliographies as well as their typological insights.

Students interested in the varieties of magical flight (more specifically, varieties of the *magische Flucht* of this essay's typology) in the world's folktales should look to Stith Thompson's *Motif-Index of Folk Literature*, 2d ed., rev. & enl., 6 vols. (Bloomington, Ind., and Helsinki, 1955–1958). Sample motifs include the following: D670, Magic Flight; E372, Soul in Form of Bird; F61, Person Wafted to Sky; F62, Bird Carries Person to or from Upper World; F1021, Extraordinary Flights through the Air. Folklorists would also want to see Antti Aarne's *Verzeichnis der Märchentypen*, translated and enlarged by Stith Thompson as *The Types of the Folk-Tale* (1928; reprint, New York, 1971), entries 313–314, "The Magic Flight," or Aarne's *Die magische Flucht* (Helsinki, 1930).

Those who wish to find traditional accounts of levitations, magical flights, and ascensions in the lives of Christian saints have no better place to turn than the *Acta Sanctorum*, a mammoth collection (64 volumes) of hagiographies edited by the Bollandists in a project that was begun in the seventeenth century by Johannes Bollandus and was carried on by Godefridus Henschenius and subsequent editors from the Society of Jesus in Belgium (Brussels, 1643–1931). A less imposing collection, and one centering exclusively on aerial events in the lives of the saints, is Olivier LeRoy's pedantic yet still somewhat amused *Levitation: An Examination of the Evidence and Explanations* (London, 1928). For accounts of celestial travel, usually by the soul after death, in antiquity, see Josef Kroll's *Die Himmelfarht der Seele in der Antike* (Cologne, 1931). A recent work that in a way complements LeRoy and Kroll is Ioan P. Culianu's "Le vol magique dans l'antiquité tardive," *Revue de l'histoire des religions* 198 (January–March 1981): 57–66; a short study of instances in late antiquity when people who are supposed to be able to fly fail to do so.

For views of the soul as a bird, see James G. Frazer's *The Golden Bough*, part 2, *Taboo and the Perils of the Soul*, 3d ed., rev. & enl. (London, 1911), or Julius von Negelein's "Seele als Vogel," *Globus* 74 (1901): 357–361, 381–384. Arthur Maurice Hocart's notion that magical flight derives from an ancient solar worship appears in his "Flying through the Air," *Indian Quarterly* (1923): 28–31 (also in *Indian Antiquary* 52 (1923): 80–82. Readers will find Geo Widengren's ideas on divine kingship and the aerial motif in his *The Ascension of the Apostle and the Heavenly Book (King and Savior III)* (Uppsala, 1950) and *Muḥammed, the Apostle of God, and His Ascension* (Uppsala, 1955).

For a study of Zoroastrian notions of ascension, see Martin Haug's *Über das Ardâi Vîrâf nâmeh* (Munich, 1870). For a collection and discussion of Jewish, Christian, gnostic, Greek, Roman, and Persian apocalyptic tales of ascension, see *Apocalypse: The Morphology of a Genre*, edited by John J. Collins, special issue of *Semeia* 14 (1975).

William K. Mahony

FLOOD, THE.

FLOOD, THE. Many peoples relate that floods accompany the end of a world. According to one Egyptian text, our world will disappear in the Nun, the divine water where the first god was formed (*The Book of Going Forth by Day* 175). For the Aztec and the Maya, the universe goes through several eras, separated from each other by the invasion of waves. India has successive creations, in which everything is abolished by a vast expanse of water; this water then constitutes the ocean from which the next creation will arise (*Mahābhārata* 3.188.80, 3.189.42).

Several tales associate men with this universal drama. The god Faro of the Bambara holds back the waters that will one day submerge the earth, to make way for the future world; warned of this occurrence, men must arm themselves with objects that will ensure their salvation. Iranian texts evoke the snows and floods that will cover the world at the end of a cosmic millennium; in anticipation of this crisis, Yima brings together a number of men in a hidden domain; they will survive and ensure the rebirth of humanity in the next millennium (*Vendidad* 2.22–41). A famous tale from the *Mahābhārata* makes Manu, the very symbol of man, the sole survivor of the flood; it is he who, through his spiritual austerities, will become the author of the new creation (*Śathapatha Brāhmaṇa* 1.8.1–6; *Mahābhārata* 3.190.2–56; *Bhāgavata Purāṇa* 8.24).

The most numerous narratives, however, deal with another sort of flood. They are more limited and find the full sense of their meaning in the history of mankind. They constitute one of its major expressions; for mankind, there is an antediluvian and a postdiluvian world.

The Antecedents of the Flood; Its Causes. Blunders sometimes characterize the beginning of a cosmogony, for example, the first union and first births of the Japanese deities Izanagi and Izanami, in the *Kojiki*. In an Indonesian myth, divine patriarchs came down one day from the heavens to the earth that was emerging from the waters. The first of them perched himself on the southern extremity and unbalanced it, so that it was inundated by the waves. The second placed himself at the other extremity as a counterbalance, but it folded up; the northern part plunged into the waves while the middle rose up. It was not until the last two patriarchs settled down in the central region that the earth recovered its flatness and stability.

In an equally awkward way, the gods began several times to create humanity on several occasions; floods are one of the means that they used to destroy the unfortunate results of their initial endeavors. After creating the heavens and the earth in darkness, say the Quechua peoples of South America, the god Viracocha made human beings too big; he turned some into statues and destroyed the rest with a flood. In the *Popul Vuh*, the sacred book of the Maya, we see formative or progenitor spirits create the first animated mannequins. These lived and procreated, but "this was only a trial, an attempt at humanity." They disappeared in the course of a complex series of events, in a vast inundation (*Popol Vuh* 3–4). Instead of annihilating an imperfect humanity, sometimes the creator god tries to improve it; he eliminates the defective humans by use of a flood. When everything seemed to be complete, say the Desána of South America, a number of plagues overcame the world, and evil beings ravaged men. Seeing the suffering of those he had created, Sun brought on a flood that drowned all the living, and then a fire that burned everything. There were survivors, however, and the god had them brought up.

In most of the myths, the flood occurs after a more complex series of events in which human behavior plays a decisive role, although men are not necessarily at fault. In one Philippine story, the god of the sky causes a flood to destroy humanity because it was becoming too numerous. In a Mesopotamian myth, the growth of humanity is accompanied by a perturbation that tires out the gods; to destroy it, they unleash several catastrophes, the last of which is a flood (Lambert and Millard, 1969). Usually, however, men commit some characteristic error. They refuse to give a god what he asks of them, show almost no compassion for the unfortunate, take to evil, or disobey religious and moral laws. In *Genesis*, it is because of the evil in men that God wished to wipe them out (*Gn.* 6:1–7, 6:17).

The Survivors. In myths where the flood is supposed to destroy the original, defective mankind, sometimes the latter disappears completely. In other cases, there are one or more survivors.

The tales in our possession do not state what all the qualities are that earned the survivors this privilege. The more explicit stories, however, attribute particular traits to them. The Greek Deukalion was a son of the god Prometheus (Lucian, *De dea Syria* 12ff.). A close relationship joins Atrahasis or Utanapishtim to the Mesopotamian god of waters, the sage Enki-Ea (*Epic of Gilgamesh*, tablet 11; Lambert and Millard, 1969). Furthermore, they themselves seem to possess an eminent wisdom. The merits of the survivors are more evident elsewhere. Alone among men, they give the gods what they ask. In Hindu myth, Manu is a great *ṛṣi*. A lengthy practice of asceticism raises him above his fellow mortals; he is able to recognize and save the divine being who, in the form of a fish, requests his protection. The biblical Noah by contrast is the only just man in an evil mankind.

The Postdiluvian World. We have seen that when the flood destroys a world and all of humanity, it sometimes precedes the creation of a new universe. It appears to separate two successive eras within a cyclical time. On this point, however, matters are not always clear. Although the Egyptian Nun, into which the world will disappear, is identical to the primordial waters, it is not clear that another world will ever emerge from it. A Carib myth says that men will one day disappear with the entire universe, which does not seem to leave any hope of a new beginning; a flood that has already taken place to punish men's evil simply warns them of the final catastrophe, for which they will also be to blame.

What happens when floods are linked more specifically to the fate of mortals? In some cases, we know that the gods, after completely destroying the original mankind, create another one; in other cases, the survivors themselves must ensure the survival of the human race.

This is not always a matter of course. When only one person escapes death, a miracle is needed to give him offspring. In a Jivaroan myth, we see the solitary man plant a part of his own flesh in the earth; from this a woman is born, with whom he couples. Other South American Indians relate that the woman came from bamboo. After the destruction of the world in Hindu myth, Manu feels the desire for posterity. He gives himself over to ascetic practices and offers a sacrifice. In the year that follows, a woman is born, approaches him, and says, "I am your daughter." He begets upon her the race of his descendants by practicing more spiritual austerities.

Things are less unusual when either a couple or numerous individuals escape death; in this case the conditions of natural procreation are fulfilled. However, we observe that the salvation of the survivors is in itself a marvel; in many cases, they owe their survival to divine intervention. In Australian Aboriginal myth, only the ancestors survive the flood: by eliminating their evil descendants, the inundation permits a return to origins, from which mankind will be able to start anew. Many myths attribute qualities to the survivors that set them apart: their descendants will be the products of a process of selection. In short, even when the present humanity issues from antediluvian mankind, it constitutes a second race.

Thus, in the history of mankind, just as it sometimes happens in the history of the cosmos, a destructive flood precedes a sort of new creation. The story of *Genesis* is a good example; Yahveh repeats to Noah's family the words he had spoken to Adam and Eve: "Be fecund, multiply on the earth and rule it" (*Gn.* 9:1ff.; cf. 1:28). But this new beginning is unique; once we are on the scale of humanity, we are no longer in cyclical time. This is evident in the biblical concept: the flood takes place within a linear history that goes from an absolute beginning to a definitive end.

The Position of Postdiluvian Humanity. When the flood is supposed to correct the effects of an initial blunder, it fulfills a positive function and is part of progress. In this case, however, it must be noted that the second race is imperfect; it commits errors and undergoes many vicissitudes. In Quechua myth, the new men ignore Viracocha and do not venerate him. This is why the god causes a fire to fall from the heavens, which burns the earth; only those who beg for mercy are spared. The position such myths ascribe to present-day mankind is similar to that found in the other types of stories.

The flood sometimes appears to be a part of a more general degradation. On the original earth, say the Guaraní of Paraguay, men lived close to the gods. Then incest unleashed a series of events, after which the flood wiped out humanity. A new earth was then created, the land of evil reserved for men. This pessimistic viewpoint is not common. More typically the flood follows a period of degradation and puts an end to it.

In all types of the myth, the new humanity exhibits traits that distinguish it from the old. Not only is it civilized, but many tales associate the flood with the origins of civilization itself. Viracocha teaches the rudiments of civilization to the second Quechua race he has just created, and the *Popul Vuh* relates how Maya civilization developed during the second humanity. In a myth of the Desána of Colombia, the sun god sends his daughter among the survivors of the flood to teach them the rules of living. Similarly, after a flood and other catastrophes, in a myth of the Fali of Chad and Sudan, the high god makes an ark descend from the heavens with the rain. This ark contains the symbol of all plant species, of wild and domesticated animals, and of the metals and tools of the smithy. Even in the pessimistic Guaraní myth, the man who survives the flood makes manioc, maize, and sweet potatoes appear.

In other narratives, the culture hero and the being who saves men from the flood are one and the same. We see this dual role in stories told among African peoples and among American Indians. In Greek myth, Prometheus is not only the hero who gives fire to men and teaches them the arts of civilization; it is also he who teaches Deukalion how to escape the flood.

Several peoples undoubtedly knew of the existence of an antediluvian civilization. The Mesopotamians list the kings prior to the cataclysm, while the Hebrews tell the story of the men who, compelled to work, have succeeded each other on the earth up to Noah. But in these cases too, the flood is associated with the history of civilization. Ea, the god who saves Utanapishtim, had been the protector of the wise men of old, to whom Utanapishtim himself could be related; Gilgamesh, who met him, transmitted an antediluvian wisdom to men. The survivor of the Sumerian flood, Atrahasis, takes "the master craftsmen" with him in his ark. Noah is "the farmer." After the flood, his family receives moral laws: this is when homicide is clearly prohibited, when meat as well as plants are offered as food to mankind, and when the rules of slaughter are prescribed.

In addition, mankind finds itself in a new position vis-à-vis the gods. According to the Guaraní myth, before the flood men lived with the gods on earth; on the second earth, they are alone. For many Australian peoples, the flood coincides with the withdrawal of the "*dema* deity," who abandons earth for a celestial dwelling. In the biblical tale itself, the flood is the culmination of events that begin with the expulsion of Adam and Eve from Paradise; it follows the murder by Cain and other occurrences. In mentioning these misfortunes Yahveh repents for having created humanity.

The Greek myths make a correlation between this rupture and the origin of civilization. The events that include the flood give rise to both of them. Prior to them, men received everything that was necessary for their subsistence from the gods and did not have to work at all. Separated from the gods, they must now toil in order to live, but they have learned the arts that will let them provide for their own needs.

The separation that accompanies the flood is not absolute, however. At the end of the inundation, we see a new sort of relation flourishing between men and gods. Those who beg mercy of Viracocha while he burns them acknowledge his divinity, whereas before they had neglected him. The procedures of the cult of the *dema* deities are defined after their separation, at the end of the Australian floods. Furthermore, the aurora borealis then becomes a sign for mankind of the *demas*' disposition. The daughter whose birth is brought about by Manu's spiritual austerities bears the name of a ritual offering and also symbolizes it. By committing the act that unleashes the entire process of separation between men and gods—the unequal allotment of a bovine—Prometheus makes a gesture to which the ritual of the great Greek sacrifices will refer: by bringing fire to mortals he gives them the instrument necessary for the burning of victims. At the end of the flood, his surviving son, Deukalion, celebrates the first sacrifice, and several traditions see in him the founder of cults. When the Mesopotamian flood has ended, Utanapishtim makes a sacrifice whose ritual is described in detail by the myth. Similarly, "Noah built an altar to the Lord, and took of every clean animal and of every clean bird, and offered burnt offerings on the altar" (*Gn.* 8:20). In addition, Yahveh makes an agreement with him that encompasses all of mankind to come, and of which the rainbow will remain a sign visible to the eyes of men.

The Forms of the Flood and the Function of the Diluvial Waters. The flood is not the only catastrophe with which the gods threaten to wipe out mankind. As the Egyptian wise men supposedly told Solon, "Men were destroyed and will be destroyed again in many ways; fire and water were the instruments of the most serious destructions" (Plato, *Timaeus* 22c). In some tales the flood itself is associated with other scourges, especially the burning of the earth. In the epic of Atrahasis it follows a plague and terrible droughts. Nevertheless, the myths return to the image of destruction by water, with particular frequency.

The diluvial waters are not just any water. As we have seen, the water into which the world disappears at the end of its existence coincides with the primordial water. The earth that the Indonesian patriarch unbalanced is an insular earth, located in the original ocean whose waves invade it.

If the flood takes the form of rain, as is often the case, this rain comes from the heavenly waters and can be accompanied by a brutal ascent of underground waters as well. "Nergal tears the beams from the heaven, Ninurta makes it unlock its dams . . . the foundations of the earth are broken like a shattered jar," we read in the *Epic of Gilgamesh*. *Genesis* continues: "All the fountains of the great deep burst forth and the windows of the heavens were opened" (*Gn.* 7:11). The Greek poet Nonnus (early fifth century CE) expresses the same notion. The world is thus submerged by the waters that surround it on all sides. According to some myths, these cosmic waters are the very same primordial waters that were thrown back to the periphery of the universe at the creation.

The diluvial waves thus possess the virtues of water in all their original vigor. [See *Water*.] It is not only that they can be destructive, as when at the end of the world they reduce everything to a state of original indifferentiation. They are also capable of fulfilling an amniotic function, when a new creation succeeds this annihilation. Perhaps their cathartic nature can be seen in their elimination of the bad elements of the human race. Their generative strength is manifested in the marvelous rebirth and proliferation of a purified humanity. They can, finally, play a role in the immortalization of heroes who have lived through the flood and survived. The brother and sister whose incestuous union provoked the flood of the Guaraní myth went into the water, in animal form, and were deified. The Mesopotamian survivors, Utanapishtim and his wife, also became immortal.

Conclusion. The influence peoples have exercised over each other in the course of history is not enough to explain why myths of the flood are present on every continent. In order to account for this, some authors have supposed that everywhere men preserve the memory of distant prehistoric catastrophes that destroyed the universe or vast regions of the earth. Such an explanation strikes me as misguided. For it to be pertinent, we would have to be able to explain in similar fashion the other mythic scourges that have imperiled humanity: the burning of the earth, for example, or the rage of a goddess in the form of a lion, as in an Egyptian myth about the destruction of men.

By resorting to this type of explanation, we also neglect the very thing that makes the flood so significant: the return of the world to its original state, in the case of cosmic destructions, and, in the case of destructions that have a special impact on mankind, the idea of an original intimacy between men and gods, the idea of their separation, and, finally, the belief that a relationship unites them despite this separation. Mythic thought uses the narrative to express these basic intuitions and elaborate on them. Commonplace occurrences, such as epidemics, ravishing fires, droughts or floods, the fear of wild animals, furnish it with vehicles for this purpose. Among such vehicles, the symbolic richness of water confers a special status to the image of the flood.

BIBLIOGRAPHY

Eliade, Mircea. "The Waters and Water Symbolism." In his *Patterns in Comparative Religion*, pp. 188–215. New York, 1958.

Gerland, Georg. *Der Mythus der Sintflut*. Bonn, 1912.

Ginzberg, Louis. *The Legends of the Jews*, vol. 1 (1909). Translated by Henrietta Szold et al. Reprint, Philadelphia, 1937. See pages 145–167.

Keeler, Clyde E. *Secrets of the Cuna Earthmother: A Comparative Study of Ancient Religion*. New York, 1960. See pages 59–82.

Lambert, W. G., and A. R. Millard. *Atra-Ḫasīs: The Babylonian Story of the Flood*. Oxford, 1969.

Müller, Werner. "Die altesten amerikanschen Sintfluterzählun-

gen." Ph.D. diss., Rheinische Friedrich-Wilhelms-Universität Bonn, 1930.
Osborne, Harold. *South American Mythology*. Feltham, England, 1968. See pages 100–105.
Pratt, Jane Abbott. *Consciousness and Sacrifice: An Interpretation of Two Episodes in the Indian Myth of Manu*. New York, 1967. See pages 3–33.
Robinson, Roland, et al. *Aboriginal Myths and Legends*. Melbourne, 1966.
Usener, Hermann. *Die Sintflutsagen*. Bonn, 1899.
Villas Boas, Orlando, and Claudio Villas Boas. *Xingu: The Indians, Their Myths*. Edited by Kenneth S. Breecher. New York, 1970.

JEAN RUDHARDT
Translated from French by Erica Meltzer

FLORENSKII, PAVEL (1882–1943/1950s?), Russian Orthodox priest and theologian. Florenskii was born in Evlakh, Azerbaijan, in Transcaucasian Russia. His engineer father was Russian, perhaps half-Georgian; his mother was Armenian. Religion did not play more than a cultural role in the Florenskii family. Young Florenskii was a child prodigy during his elementary school years in Tiflis (present-day Tbilisi), Georgia. He was sent to study mathematics at Moscow University, where he also became intensely interested in philosophy. At the university he studied with the famous Sergei Trubetskoi and L. M. Lopatin, falling under their religious influence. At this time, with his friends V. F. Ern and A. V. Elchaninov, who was to become a famous émigré Russian Orthodox priest in Western Europe after the Russian Revolution, Florenskii founded the utopian Christian Brotherhood of Battle, an organization that worked for social reforms in Russia and a new church-state policy that would give freedom to the church along the lines of the theocratic philosophy of the sophiologist Vladimir Solov'ev. Upon graduation from the university, Florenskii gave up a research fellowship in mathematics to enter the Moscow Theological Academy on the advice of his spiritual guide, Bishop Antonii Florensov. After completing his studies at the academy in 1908, Florenskii was elected to the academy's faculty of the history of philosophy. He married Anna Mikhailovna Giatsintova on 17 August 1910 and was ordained a priest of the Russian Orthodox church on 24 April 1911.

As a priest, Florenskii never held a formal pastorate, although he served in one of the chapels at the Saint Sergius Trinity Monastery (at present-day Zagorsk), where the Moscow Theological Academy was located, and he was always eager for pastoral work. His good friend Sergei Bulgakov, who returned to Christianity through Florenskii's ministry and became a famous Russian Orthodox archpriest and theologian, testified in his memoirs to the pastoral zeal of his spiritual guide. So also did the renowned, although very different, philosophers N. O. Lossky and Vasilii Rozanov, who also recovered their religious faith through his ministry, both the latter, however, would come to express serious doubts about their mentor's philosophical vision.

Florenskii wrote only one book of theology, the highly debated and generally considered epoch-making collection of twelve essays on theodicy entitled *Stolp i utverzhdenie istiny* (The Pillar and Bulwark of the Truth). Published in 1914 in a special typeface selected especially by the author, the book consists of more than eight hundred pages, with more than four hundred footnotes and commentaries touching upon virtually every area of human study: theology, philosophy, philology, history, mathematics, medicine, art, the various sciences, and even the occult. It is written in the form of intimate letters to a friend which Nikolai Berdiaev, among others, criticized for its pretentious aesthetical and lyrical stylization. The chapters, each introduced by a literary vignette, bear such titles as "Doubt," "Friendship," "Triunity," "Sophia," "The Comforter," "Light of Truth," "Contradiction," "Sin," and "Gehenna."

The Pillar and Bulwark of the Truth is not a systematic work. Its controlling intuition is expressed in its opening sentence: "Living religious experience [is] the sole legitimate method for understanding [religious, and certainly Christian] dogma." The author's fundamental claim is that ultimate truth, which is religious, comes from the liturgical, spiritual, and ecclesial experience of the whole person within the community of faith and worship of the Orthodox church; this experience fundamentally is the gracious realization by creatures of the indwelling divine life of the trinitarian godhead: Father, Son, and Holy Spirit. Following such thinkers as Solov'ev, Aleksei Khomiakov, and Ivan Kireevskii, and interpreting the theology of the Eastern Christian church fathers and the liturgical hymnography and iconography of the Orthodox tradition in their light, Florenskii forges a magnificent, and extremely complex, worldview. At the heart of Florenskii's worldview lies the experience of free and joyous communion in truth, love, and beauty. This communion is perfected by all creatures made in the image of the uncreated Trinity of divine persons. The eternal being and life of the Trinity provides the archetypal structure for human existence and fulfillment.

The work that formed the basis for *The Pillar and Bulwark of the Truth* was accepted by the Moscow Theological Academy as an orthodox expression of the faith of the Russian church, albeit in highly individualistic and idiosyncratic form, and Florenskii was granted his doctoral degree after its presentation. However, careful analyses of the finished and published product, accomplished almost exclusively outside of Russia after the Revolution, have questioned the work on virtually every point. Classical Orthodox theologians and scholars such as Vladimir Lossky and Georges Florovsky have rejected it as an expression of church dogmatics, and philosophers such as Nikolai Berdiaev have faulted its philosophical argumentation. So also have philosophical interpreters such as Vasilii Zenkovskii and N. O. Lossky, the latter of whom, as we have seen, was greatly influenced in his return to Christianity by Florenskii. In all cases, however, the brilliance of the gifted thinker, the fundamental correctness of his guiding intuition, and his rejection of a rationalist approach to religious and specifically Christian thinking, indeed, to any truly metaphysical reflections on the ultimate nature of things, have been applauded by all who have had the courage to labor through his prodigious creation.

After the Bolshevik Revolution of 1917 Florenskii was inducted by the regime into scientific service, often embarrassing the new rulers by appearing at scientific conferences and classes in his priestly cassock, wearing the cross. He worked for the Highest State Technical-Artistic Studios and the Commission for the Electrification of Soviet Russia. A member of the Academy of Sciences and editor of the Soviet *Technical Encyclopedia,* he was honored for several important scientific discoveries, one of which had to do with the refining of oil. He also wrote standard textbooks for Soviet schools. At the same time, he preached against the excesses of the regime whose fundamental worldview was contrary to his own. It is believed that Florenskii was imprisoned permanently during the Stalinist terror in 1933. According to Soviet records, he died in 1943, but other sources indicate that he may have survived into the 1950s. In 1956 the Soviet government formally rehabilitated the memory of the man who was called by many critics of his work the "Russian Leonardo da Vinci."

BIBLIOGRAPHY

Pavel Florenskii's major work, *Stolp i utverzhdenie istiny* (The Pillar and Bulwark of the Truth), was originally published in Moscow in 1914. A limited reprint was made in Berlin in 1929. Translations into French (Lausanne, 1975) and Italian (Milan, 1974) also exist. An English version of the fifth letter on the Holy Spirit, entitled "The Comforter," appears in Alexander Schmemann's *Ultimate Questions: An Anthology of Modern Russian Religious Thought* (New York, 1965). Essays on the life and work of Florenskii may be found in N. O. Lossky's *History of Russian Philosophy* (New York, 1951) and Vasilii V. Zenkovskii's *A History of Russian Philosophy,* translated by George L. Kline (New York, 1953). The only book in English on Florenskii, which contains complete bibliographical information in all languages, is Robert Slesinski's *Pavel Florensky: A Metaphysics of Love* (Crestwood, N.Y., 1984).

THOMAS HOPKO

FLOWERS. The blossom, or reproductive part, of trees, shrubs, and other flora is known as the flower. This part of a growing plant takes on very special and often sacred meanings in every culture and religion of the world. The symbolism of flowers is often determined by a flower's natural properties: its color and smell, where it grows, and the length of its blooming period. While each kind of flower may be assigned a special meaning, flowers in general symbolize beauty and the transitory nature of life. Flowers are often used to represent the cycle of life and are an important part of rituals and ceremonies that celebrate birth, marriage, death, and the promise of regeneration. Flowers also serve as offerings or as a means of communicating with a deity or other sacred being. They are frequently sacred gifts bestowed as signs of welcome or in celebration of victory. Flowers represent certain deities and are associated with cultural beliefs regarding heaven or the afterlife.

It is not just the bloom of a plant that holds these special meanings. Several different plants may be combined to create a "flower" for sacred purposes. In some societies other parts of a living plant may be referred to as a "flower." In Japan, maple leaves are considered to be flowers even though they are not the bloom of the maple tree. And even sea coral was treated as a flower in nineteenth-century Christianity in the United States and was believed to represent heavenly love. Palms and evergreens are often included in the general category of flowers and are used in sacred contexts.

Flowers are used to teach general religious principles. The Japanese myth *Mr. Butterfly and His Flowers* teaches that all creatures are destined to become Buddhas. In this story a hermit is visited by a number of women who are actually the spirits of the flowers from his garden, which he had left behind in his search for enlightenment. These flowers, as spirits of women, had come to share his Buddhist attainment because flowers too are on the path to enlightenment.

The art of flower arrangement in Japan is called *ikebana* ("living flowers") and has spiritual significance. The word for flower is *hana* and includes blossoms, branches, foliage of trees, as well as individual flowers and grasses. The art of arranging these "flowers" expresses the Buddhist ideals of content, calm, and piety. Religious spirit, restraint, serene disposition, and respect for mankind are qualities the flower arranger must possess as he strives to portray the growth cycle of the plant from bud to maturity. The Taoist concepts of *in* (Chin., *yin:* female, passive, earth, moon, darkness, coolness, silence) and *yō* (Chin., *yang:* male, heaven, sun, action, power) must also be combined in the flower arrangement.

The lotus is used in many cultures to stand for the ideal of purity and perfection. The plant grows in muddy water and yet remains pure. The flower itself is most frequently believed to symbolize the oneness of Buddhist instruction and enlightenment. [*See* Lotus.]

Flowers and Deities. Flowers are connected to the sacred realm through their association with gods and goddesses. Flora, the Roman goddess of springtime and flowers, brings beauty and fragrance to blossoms, sweetness to honey, and aroma to wine. The Aztec god Xochipilli Cinteotl was one of thirteen day lords. He was the prince of flowers—the god of beauty, love, happiness, and youth. His female twin Xochiquetzal ("flower feather") was also the goddess of love. The Hindu love god, Kāma, is represented riding a parrot with a bow and arrow made of flowers. Ko-no-hana-sakura-hime ("the lady who causes trees to bloom") is a supernatural being of Japan, a fairy represented by the cherry blossom. The Japanese *tennyo* (like the Indian *devatās*) are female deities of the sky. They play music and scatter flowers and the aroma of celestial perfume. The *tennyo* surround pious Buddhists like angels, they appear as decorations in Buddhist temples, and some have their own shrines. The *tennyo* may be identified with Shintō goddesses. In Zoroastrianism, thirty different species of flowers are associated with the thirty *yazatas*, or deities, that preside over the thirty days of the month.

Flowers may be created through the actions of gods. Almost every culture credits the presence of all forms of life, including flowers, to the sacred realm. The ancient Greek and Roman religions include several tales of creation. Jupiter, wishing to render Hercules immortal, placed him at the breast of the sleeping Juno. Some drops of her milk fell to the earth from which sprang the white lily.

The Muslims consider the rose a sacred plant that had sprung from the drops of perspiration that fell from the prophet during his heavenly journey. Among the Indian cultures of Latin America the geranium is believed to have grown from drops of Christ's blood that fell as he ran from Satan. And the lily of the valley is called "Our Lady's Tears," because this plant grew from the tears the Virgin Mary shed at the cross of Christ.

Flowers are also associated with the birth or creation of deities. Ancient Egyptian religion described the fixed stars in the heavens as gods or souls, and also as fields of heavenly flowers and plants, believed to be the dwelling place of the blessed dead. It was from these fields of flowers and souls that the gods were created. Ancient Egyptians also believed that the sun was born every day from a blue lotus in the celestial ocean. In Asia the lotus is the flower on which Brahmā alighted when he sprang from the navel of Viṣṇu. From this beginning Brahmā ordered the existence of all worlds.

Flowers and deities together may protect human birth. In China the *bodhisattva* Kuan-yin is known as "the lady who brings children." Sitting on a lotus flower and holding a child in her arms, she is a goddess of fertility and aids in the treatment of all sickness. Her image is found in most homes. Kishimojin (Hariti) is a female divinity of Japan who was converted by the Buddha. She is the protector of children and women in childbirth. This goddess is portrayed standing with a baby at her breast and holding the flower of happiness.

Important symbolism is attached to flowers through their appearance with a sacred being. Many times this connection arises because of particular characteristics of the flower or the season of the year in which the bloom appears and the relation of this blossoming to the religious calendar of the culture. Artists have depicted the angel Gabriel coming to Mary with a spray of lilies in his hand to announce that she will be the mother of Christ. Many flowers are connected to Mary. These flowers all stand for virginity and purity: the annunciation lily, the flowering almond, the madonna lily, the gillyflower, the snow drop, and the rose. The thorns of the rose allude to the suffering of Mary as the mother of Christ. Christ's crown of thorns is believed to have been formed from the acanthus, bramble, or rose-briar. The hawthorn is also believed to be a symbol of Jesus, because it blooms at Christmastime. Because the Easter lily blooms at Eastertide, it is a symbol of Christ's resurrection.

Flowers and Rituals. Flowers as a link between man and the deities are presented as offerings to the sacred world, as food for the gods, or even as a reward from the gods. Deities may be appeased and worshiped through the singing of hymns, the anointing of images, the use of lights and incense, and through the offering of foods and flowers. In India flowers are said to have dropped from heaven to express the joy of the gods.

The religions of Latin America are a mixture of sixteenth-century Catholicism and native Indian religions. In many areas the seven most important saint's days are celebrated in festivals lasting three days. The first day of the festival is spent renewing flower decorations and offerings for house and church altars. The flowers used on this day, and throughout the year, are important offerings to the saints and to God. The last day of the festival falls on the saint's day as declared in the Roman Catholic calendar.

Among the Sherpas of Nepal, the high gods have achieved salvation and bliss and are utterly fulfilled and self-contained. Following traditional Buddhist beliefs, these gods have obtained enlightenment partly through conquering the delights of the senses. The high gods are unconcerned with man and must be drawn down to aid mankind through a complex ritual involving sacred offerings. The god is "trapped" or seduced by the various offerings, each designed to appeal to one of the senses. The flower used in this ritual tempts the god to use his sense of smell.

Rites of passage. A rite of passage is a vehicle for transforming an individual, or a group of individuals, from one way of being to another through a series of culturally recognized stages. [*See* Rites of Passage.] In most cultures, these transitions are marked or given meaning through the ritual use of flowers.

The earliest evidence for the use of flowers in a rite of passage is connected with a Neanderthal burial in the Shanidar Cave in Iraq. This burial site dates from 60,000 years ago and reveals that the Neanderthals covered the body of the deceased with at least eight species of flowers.

The association of flowers with rituals of death occurs all over the world. The Greeks and Romans covered the dead and their graves with flowers. The souls of dying Buddhists in Japan are carried upward on a lotus, and the gravestones in cemeteries may rest on carved lotuses. Lotus leaves are also constructed out of gold or silver paper and are carried at Japanese funerals. Tahitians leave bouquets wrapped in ferns by the body after death and then pour floral perfume over the corpse to ease its passage into the sacred afterlife.

In Zorastrianism, the "rite of flowers" is performed by two priests; it invokes the blessings of the sacred and includes vows to the deceased. The priests conduct a complicated exchange of flowers accompanied by prayers and gestures. These flower exchanges symbolize the exchange of life between this world and the world after death. The ritual is also concerned with good and evil and the importance of good thoughts, words, and deeds.

Flowers are used in marriage rituals as an expression of fertility, virginity, purity, and to represent the sacred union of the bride and groom. Christian weddings in the United States include flowers for the altar, a bridal bouquet that represents the bride's fertility and the children that will result from the marriage, and flowers for virtually all the ritual participants. A Roman Catholic bride often lays her bridal bouquet at the foot of a statue of the Virgin Mary at the conclusion of the wedding ceremony as a dedication of her virginity to the mother of Christ.

The marriage ceremony of Java is a syncretism of Hinduism, Islam, and folk religion. This ceremony is completed only when the bride and groom exchange the *kembang majang* ("blossoming flowers") that represent their virginity. These "flowers" are large composite plants. The stems are from a banana tree trunk, the "blossom" consists of leaves, and the entire "flower" is wrapped in coconut branches.

Flowers and the afterlife or paradise. Not only are flowers used to express cultural beliefs about the changes in the life cycle, but they are also connected to ideas of life after death and paradise. Chinese Buddhists believe that at the hour of death the Buddha will appear to them, and their souls will be placed in a lotus. The souls will remain there until they are cleansed of all impurities, and then they will go to the Land of Extreme Felicity in the West, a paradise of all delights where showers of blossoms fall to the ground. The Aztec paradise was located above the ninth heaven and was called Xochitlicacan, the "place of flowers." The Huichol Indians of northwest Mexico call their paradise Wirikúta, a land of many flowers and much water. It is there that the ancient ones dwell, the ancestors and deities of the Huichol. These ancestor deities are called *neyeteurixa*, from *yeteurixa*, a thistle plant that flowers and then becomes the dry burrs found in the everyday world. Through the ingestion of peyote, or the five-petaled "flower," these Indians are able to journey to Wirikúta and to meet and join their ancestors amid the flowers of paradise.

Supernatural Powers of Flowers. Flowers are believed to possess powers that arise from their connection to the sacred realm. Greek and Roman religion held the amaranth as a sacred flower and associated it with immortality. In Switzerland it is believed that if this flower is worn on Ascension Day, it will render the wearer invisible. The peony is valued for medicinal properties and is named in celebration of Apollo, who as Paeon healed the wounds received by the gods in the Trojan War.

The Maya Indians of Zinacantan perform an illness-curing ceremony called "he enters in the flowers." This ritual includes visits to the ancestor/deity mountain shrines that surround the city of Zinacantan, as well as a ceremonial circuit of the sacred Roman Catholic churches within the town itself. This ceremonial circuit is called "great vision," referring to the number of gods visited during the ceremony, or "big flower," named for the large number of flowers necessary for the success of the procession. These flowers include not only the blooms of plants but also the sacred tips of evergreen trees. These tips are considered to be natural crosses, and two are erected alongside a permanent wooden cross to form the *calvario,* or calvary. This re-creation of the three crosses present at Christ's crucifixion is necessary for many rituals, including curing ceremonies.

Perfume, the Essence of Flowers. Flowers may also be present at sacred times in the form of incense or perfume. The aroma of the blooms is believed to reach into the sacred sphere. [*See* Incense.]

The people of Mayotte in the Comoro Islands have two religious systems that exist side by side. The public and male religion is Islam, while the religion of the private domestic sphere of women is a complex system of possession by spirits. Flowers, and especially the perfume made from them, are used to celebrate the sacred in both realms. The flowers are selected for their fragrance, not for their color or form. The cologne made from these flowers is used to mark and give meaning to several occasions: the onset of puberty in women, rituals of curing, and the anointing of the bride and groom during and after their wedding, as well as of the other major participants in the marriage ceremony. Every household keeps a supply of cologne and generously sprinkles the fragrance on body and clothing on all major holidays and Fridays at the weekly mosque service. Cologne is also offered to the mullahs at family rituals, especially during *mawlid* celebrations of the month of the Prophet's birth. Perfume contacts and pleases the sacred and enables prayers to travel more quickly.

The Zoroastrian Dhup-sarvi ("ceremony of the perfumes") involves the use of fragrant flowers, flower water, and other perfumes. These are passed out to the people, who are assembled to honor the dead, and they symbolize the fragrance and joyful nature of the path that righteous souls take to the afterworld.

The meanings attached to flowers, indeed the definition of *flower* itself, vary from culture to culture. The religious significance of these blooms is a very important part of the definition of *flower* for most societies. There is power in all life, especially in this form of nature that almost universally stands for beauty, purity, and the transitory nature of life.

[*See also* Gardens *and* Paradise.]

BIBLIOGRAPHY

One of the best examples of the nineteenth-century use of flowers by Christians is Andrew Joseph Ambauen's *The Floral Apostles, or, What the Flowers Say to Thinking Man* (Milwaukee, Wis., 1900). The use and meaning of flowers in religious practices, especially the historical development of their role in ritual, is well described by Jacques Duchesne-Guillemin in *Symbols and Values in Zoroastrianism: Their Survival and Renewal* (New York, 1966). For an excellent description of the Nyingmawa (Rñiṅ-ma-pa) sect of Tibetan Buddhist beliefs and practices, see Sherry Ortner's *Sherpas through Their Rituals* (New York, 1978). This book is primarily concerned with the underlying beliefs of hospitality that shape the lives of the Sherpas of Nepal and includes a consideration of flowers and their religious significance. The use of flowers as offerings to Mayan gods and Catholic saints is explored by Evon Z. Vogt in *Zinacantan: A Maya Community in the Highlands of Chiapas* (Cambridge, Mass., 1969). This is an extensive study of the Tzotzil-speaking Indians of Guatemala and includes a thorough description of the importance of flowers in ritual. Clifford Geertz's seminal work *The Religion of Java* (New York, 1960) describes the syncretism of Hindu, Islamic, and folk beliefs that constitute Javanese religion. He includes in this work an excellent consideration of flowers as part of the life-cycle rituals and in other religious celebrations. Michael Lambek presents a fascinating account of the importance of flowers and perfume among the people of Mayotte in the Comoro Islands in his *Human Spirits: A Cultural Account of Trance in Mayotte* (New York, 1981). Flowers and the perfume made from flower petals are essential ingredients for the two religious belief systems among the Mayotte: Islam and a native folk religion that centers around trance and possession by spirits. Barbara G. Myerhoff describes two different types of "flowers" in her consideration of Huichol Indian culture. In her book *Peyote Hunt: The Sacred Journey of the Huichol Indians* (Ithaca, N.Y., 1974), flowers represent the Huichol ancestor/deities in paradise and refer to the peyote, the five-petaled flower that enables the contemporary Huichol to journey to this paradise.

PAMELA R. FRESE

FLOW EXPERIENCE. All major world religions, as well as most sects and tribal cults, are said to produce on occasion, among their faithful, states of ecstasy or altered states of consciousness. Such experiences constitute for many believers one of the main attractions of religion, if not a proof of its ability to mediate the supernatural. In cults and sects such experiences are often induced by chemical substances ingested in ritual contexts; by fasting; by various hypnotic trances; or by what Émile Durkheim called "collective effervescence," a condition engineered by rhythmic music, dance, and ritual movements.

Remnants of such direct sensory means for inducing altered experiential states can still be found in the major religions. The use of music, chanting, lighting, and scent in liturgy and of fasting and ritual feasting clearly derive from earlier methods for producing ecstasy. But the great religious traditions have become gradually less dependent on sensory means, while at the same time they have developed the ability to induce ecstasy through cognitive disciplines. Prayer, meditation, *satori, samādhi,* despite the tremendous variety of cultural differences represented in their settings, are all mechanisms for providing a sense of mystic union with a sacred, transcendent force.

Is the ecstasy reported in religious practices and rituals unique to religion, or is it a species of a broader genus of experiential states? At least since the writings of William James, psychologists have supported the latter hypothesis. It is assumed that there is no qualitative difference between the unusual states of consciousness occasionally experienced in religious contexts and analogous states reported in a variety of secular contexts. The task for the scholar is to describe the experiential state precisely, and to explain why it occurs in the context of religious practice.

Perhaps the state of consciousness that most closely resembles accounts of religious ecstasy is the "flow experience," so named because many people have used the word *flow* in describing it. This subjective state has been reportedly experienced by creative artists when working, by athletes at the height of competition, by surgeons while performing difficult operations, and by ordinary people in the midst of their most satisfying activities. In other words, states of optimal experience in a wide variety of context, including meditation, prayer, and mystical union, are described in terms of very similar subjective parameters. The subsequent experience is "ecstatic" in that it is characterized by a sense of clarity and enjoyment that stands out from the blurred background of everyday routine.

The flow experience is characterized by the following phenomenological dimensions:

1. a narrowing of the focus of consciousness on a clearly delimited stimulus field;
2. exclusion from one's awareness of irrelevant immediate stimuli, memories of past events, and contemplation of the future; hence a focusing on the unfolding present;
3. merging of action and awareness, also described as absence of doubt and critical reflection about one's current activity;
4. awareness of clear goals and unambiguous feedback, so that one knows one's standing with reference to the goals;
5. lack of concern regarding one's ability to control the situation;
6. loss of self-consciousness, which in turn may lead to a sense of transcendence of ego boundaries and of union with a larger, transpersonal system.

When these conditions are present in consciousness, the experience is usually interpreted by the individual as being enjoyable and autotelic (worth seeking for its own sake). Activities available in everyday life form a continuum in terms of their capacity to induce flow. At the lowest level are "microflow" activities such as doodling, pacing, or smoking, which provide fleeting experiences of ordered existence. At the other extreme are "deep flow" activities that provide relatively lasting and totally absorbing experiences, as in creative endeavors, complex symbolic or religious thought, or the heights of physical performance.

Whether an activity is capable of providing flow depends in large part on the kind and degree of challenges (opportunities of action) that it makes available, and on the actor's skill (capacity to relate to them). When these two are in balance, flow occurs. If challenges overshadow skills, anxiety ensues; if skills are greater than the opportunities for using them, boredom follows. The complexity of a flow experience—or its ability to provide deep flow—is a function of the extent of challenges the activity presents and of the actor's skills. Games, spectacles, and rituals are structured so as to provide the maximum of flow experience.

Religious action-systems present a wide variety of opportunities for action, ranging from microflow-like repetitive physical rituals (e.g., the spinning of Tibetan prayer wheels) to the purely cognitive sequences of doctrinal exegesis. Religions occasionally are able to transform a person's entire life activity into a unified action-system with clear and congruent goals. It might be argued, for instance, that the religion of the early Puritans was an all-embracing flow activity that focused the consciousness of believers on the necessity of attaining salvation and prescribed a productive vocation as a means for attaining *certitudo salutis.* In this process Puritanism had to exclude many pleasurable experiences from the consciousness of the faithful, but within the limitations of its goals and rules it provided an all-embracing and enjoyable field of action.

In general, however, flow experiences—religious ones included—are liminal in terms of the dominant patterns of consciousness required by social existence. Prayer, ritual, meditation, or the reading of sacred texts establishes interludes of flow in a stream of consciousness that otherwise tends to be structured either too loosely or too rigidly. These activities are occasionally able to provide concrete experiences of a mode of existence more conducive to the expression of individual potentials than the socially restricted historical reality is capable of doing.

[*See also* Consciousness, States of; Ecstasy; *and* Religious Experience.]

BIBLIOGRAPHY

Crook, John H. *The Evolution of Human Consciousness.* London and New York, 1980.

Csikszentmihalyi, Mihaly. *Beyond Boredom and Anxiety: The Experience of Play in Work and Games.* San Francisco, 1975.

Csikszentmihalyi, Mihaly. "Toward a Psychology of Optimal Experience." In *Review of Personality and Social Psychology,* vol. 3, edited by Ladd Wheeler, pp. 13–36. Beverly Hills, Calif., 1982.

James, William. *The Varieties of Religious Experience* (1902). New York, 1963.

Laski, Marghanita. *Ecstasy: A Study of Some Secular and Religious Experiences* (1962). Reprint, Westport, Conn., 1968.

Turner, Victor. "Liminal to Liminoid, in Play, Flow, and Ritual: An Essay in Comparative Symbology." *Rice University Studies* 60 (Summer 1974): 53–92. Reprinted in Turner's collection of essays entitled *From Ritual to Theatre: The Human Seriousness of Play* (New York, 1982), pp. 20–60.

MIHALY CSIKSZENTMIHALYI

FOLK DANCE. *See* Dance, *article on* Popular and Folk Dance.

FOLKLORE. The Latin word *superstitio,* which lives on in the vocabulary of the educated, bears witness to the antiquity of interest in folklore of a religious kind. *Superstition* still conveys a negative attitude that sought to eradicate beliefs and practices not in keeping with the official religion; the pejorative connotation confirms this interpretation. [*See* Superstition.]

Historical Survey. Tacitus applied the word *superstition* to the spreading Christianity of his day, and it has retained its negative overtones down to our own time. The struggle against such superstitions was a constant concern of the clergy, and the canons of the councils provide numerous testimonies that not only demonstrate the continued existence of superstitions through the ages but also help to establish an approximative chronology. The decrees of tribunals, especially during the Middle Ages, are evidence of the tenacity of superstition in popular practice as well as the negative view always taken by the upper classes. The bitterest attack on superstition was launched during the eighteenth century by the practitioners of Enlightenment philosophy, who were utterly convinced that they had nothing to learn from the people and that they simply had to inculcate their own scientific principles.

This outlook changed with the Romantic movement, however. The new attitude toward popular culture can be traced to the Italian philosopher Giambattista Vico, whose ideas were to provide the basis for ethnology and the science of folklore. In his *New Science* (1725), Vico boldly assumed the trustworthiness of general ideas that had been brought into existence independently by different peoples. "Uniform ideas originating among entire peoples unknown to each other must have a common ground of truth." And it is this substantial element of truth that has ensured the permanence of such ideas: "Vulgar traditions must have had public grounds of truth, in virtue of which they came into being and were preserved by entire peoples over long periods of time." Consequently, "the fables were true and trustworthy histories of the customs of the most ancient peoples of Greece." Since Vico, the historical content of myths, "superstitions," and popular poetry has been acknowledged, and this broadened vision has led to what might be called an integral humanism, since the whole of the human race—primal man and civilized man, classical culture and popular culture—has gradually become part of a now unbounded field of study.

The first steps in the study of religious folklore were taken by the Grimm brothers, Jakob and Wilhelm. As early as 1811, in the preface to their *Altdänische Heldenlieder,* they identify as a distinctive mark of popular poetry the fact that it "manifests the image of God," which is the same everywhere:

> The divine spirit of poetry is the same among all peoples, and it has one and the same source. This is why we see similarities appearing everywhere; there is an antecedent correspondence, a hidden kinship, the originating principle of which has been lost but which nonetheless suggests a common ancestry. Finally, there is an analogous development, despite the fact that external conditions and differences varied.

The enthusiasm of the Grimm brothers betrays the typical Romantic exaltation that ends in the introduction of the sacred into the scientific study of popular traditions. In the preface to the third volume of their *Kinder- und Hausmärchen* they show the kinship between ancient myths and modern-day fairy tales. They claim that this filiation is evident: Brynhild has become Sleeping Beauty, Gudrun has become Cinderella, and so on. European fairy tales are therefore direct descendants of the ancient myths, but only after an intervening process of desacralization by means of which the myths have been emptied of their explanatory nucleus in the interests of a more developed mentality and thus have become simply stories for an idle hour. The Grimm brothers subsequently introduced the idea of evolution into the science of folklore and repeated their views on the dominant role of the sacred in ancient times and on the decline of this role as the modern age drew near. The popular traditions of all peoples contain inherited elements that the skill of the folklorist should bring to light. The concept of evolution was to become the key idea of ethnological study. [*See* Evolutionism.] Adalbert Kuhn, a disciple of the Grimms, attempted to apply it by analogy with the relation between Sanskrit and the Indo-European languages and postulated a filiation between the mythologies of the European peoples and the mythology of ancient India. This line of thought proved erroneous, however, because folkloric creations are governed by other, less rigorous laws.

The contribution of E. B. Tylor, especially his *Primitive Culture* (1871), broadened the vision of folklorists even further. This book established the existence of a popular culture that would serve as the initial reference point. Tylor brought out the two characteristic phenomena that prevail in the movement of popular culture: the survival and revival of inherited components. The first of these two terms designates the passive aspect of the process; the second, the active side, or the creativity of the popular strata of society. Set in the context of the economic and social environment, the two aspects together explain the psychic mechanism at work in tradition. The development generally takes the form of an ascent, although Tylor also envisaged the possibility of the opposite, a degeneration that would reverse the ascent; we are reminded here of the pattern of *corsi e ricorsi* (advances and retrogressions) discovered by Vico.

The evolution that took place in the agrarian world was to be copiously illuminated by Wilhelm Mannhardt in his *Wald- und Feldkulte* (1875), in which he compares the agrarian beliefs and practices of the European and especially the Germanic peoples with those of Greek and Latin antiquity. The errors of his predecessors showed him the correct method to follow. He established the necessity of distinguishing among the types found in each constitutive part of a contributory custom or belief and of conducting a comparative study of them while always examining each testimony in the context into which it was incorporated. In this way, relations of filiation became clearer, and it could be seen whether there was question of a more or less ancestral heritage or, on the contrary, of a borrowing that required explanation. The analogy with the distribution of geological strata suggested itself spontaneously, and Mannhardt made use of it in order to distinguish more clearly between inherited and borrowed elements.

James G. Frazer continued Mannhardt's studies in *The Golden Bough* (2 vols., 1890), which he gradually expanded into twelve volumes in the third edition of 1911–1915. This edition included all the forms attested to both in classical antiquity and in the traditions of every known people. *The Golden Bough* is a real "bible for modern times," presenting the successive manifestations of a cult or belief among primitives, then among the ancient Mediterranean peoples, and finally in the popular traditions of the civilized peoples of Europe. The development is traced with a magisterial hand, and the reader sees the often dramatic road traveled by the human race in gaining an understanding of its destiny. According to Frazer, the prime mover in this evolutionary process that began in prehistory was magic with its two components—imitation and contact—that were often intermingled, while its negative side took shape in taboos.

Arnold van Gennep's work *Les rites de passage* (1909) sketched the ancestral mechanism at work in the transitional phases of the human cycle as well as in other seasonal and territorial customs. His central idea is that a transition cannot be abrupt (it would then be cataclysmic) but must develop gradually in three steps: separation from the previous stage (preliminal rites), waiting (liminal rites), and incorporation into the new stage (postliminal rites).

Among later contributions mention must be made of R. R. Marett's *The Interpretation of Survivals* (1914), in which the author emphasizes the lively contemporary attraction that survivals have: beliefs do not survive by reason of a purely mechanical process of transmission, but because they fit in with a mentality that renders them plausible and therefore necessary to the contemporary world. This idea was germinally present in Tylor's concept of revival, and it had been developed about 1900 by Henri Hubert and Marcel Mauss in their *Étude sommaire de la représentation du temps dans la religion et la magie*, in which they contrast the fates of beliefs: some die, others are rejuvenated.

The progress of recent studies in the history of religions, especially those of Mircea Eliade, has shed further light on the world of religious folklore. At the present time it is clear that insofar as a contemporary mentality has an archaic structure it can generate equally "primitive" representations, with fossils living on in the traditional repertory alongside recent creations inspired by new advances in civilization. We need only recall the beliefs generated by the appearance of the railroad train in more or less backward countries, where it was regarded as the work of the devil but, at the same time, as a work that the devil rejected for the rocky heights that are his favorite domain.

Folkloric Customs. Generally speaking, customs, and the beliefs that contribute to them, offer the most disconcerting examples of the evolutionary process. They are so permeated by the popular mentality that they produce an abundance of forms, with the same action acquiring contrary meanings (sometimes even in the same locality), while different actions may take on the same meaning.

Annual cycles. Annually recurring customs highlight the succession of the seasons. Deriving from this succession are various meanings that establish fixed reference points in a rhythm without which life would be unthinkable. [*See* Seasonal Ceremonies.]

The New Year. The most important annual festival is the New Year. The further back we go toward prehistoric times, the more complex and richer in meaning this festival becomes. [*See* New Year Festivals.] The New Year was celebrated either at the beginning of agricultural activity, that is, at the beginning of spring, which varies according to climate, or at the end of the agricultural year, when it became a celebration of the entire harvest. In comparatively recent times, the festival lasted for several days and involved the participation of the entire village. Its primary purpose was to ensure the overall prosperity of the coming year: a rich harvest, the birth of many animals, human health and strength, and, in the final analysis, the most complete satisfaction of all desires. In consequence, every ritual action and word was meant as an encomium, with a view to obtaining the best effects imaginable. The comprehensive character of the festival was intensified by the participation of the dead, whose souls shared in the universal joy of the living. This participation of the dead has continued down to our own time almost everywhere in Europe, although it is most clearly observed in eastern Europe, especially at Christmas.

In the early centuries, Christmas was celebrated on the same day as Epiphany. In the Carolingian period, however, the New Year was designated to begin on Christmas Day (the separation of the two holidays dates only from the sixteenth to seventeenth centuries). This development led to a contamination and superposition of characteristics in varying degrees, depending on the influence exercised by the Christian church. In countries in which the church was stronger, Christmas absorbed almost all the attributes of New Year's Day. This confusion then colored the entire twelve-day period between Christmas (25 December) and Epiphany (6 January). In European countries this period clearly retained the ancient features of the Roman calendar, especially those of the Saturnalia and the *Calendae Januaris*, as mediated through the church, which was content to give them a more or less Christian veneer, since it was impossible to eliminate them entirely. As a result, the twelve-day interval kept its ancient negative character as a time during which the devil was thought to come into his own: it was a period of idleness that evidently functioned as a waiting period during the transition from the old year to the new. The dominant feature of the celebratory banquets was opulence: tables were laden with food and drink, especially at the banquets organized for the entire community and that still bore the influence of the ancient *epulum publicum*, attested especially for the Saturnalia. Through the law of imitation, abundance at these banquets was to ensure abundance during the following year.

Certain ritual actions of prehistoric origin were intended to preserve the cosmic order during this critical period of transition when the sun seemed threatened with extinction. The fire that had to be kept burning through the night and fed with oak logs (a relic of the ancient cult of the sun) was meant to strengthen the light of the sun by imitation. But most of the ritual actions were intended to ensure an abundance in every area of domestic life: the ashes of the Yule log (the *calendae*), for example, were scattered in the kitchen gardens and at the roots of fruit trees so that the crop might be more abundant; bits of ritual cake as well as the straw that was spread in the house were fed to the domestic animals to ensure their well-being and fecundity. In human beings the same propitiatory effect was also obtained by ritual blows with a budding branch and especially by good wishes expressed in song. Other actions had an apotropaic purpose: various noises, especially of little drums and bells or gunshots, were meant to frighten and drive away malicious spirits as well as the souls of the dead when the time granted them for remaining with the living had expired. Noises also had the function of adding to the display; this second meaning gradually gained in importance, while the first faded from consciousness.

In general, virtually everything people did during these days functioned as an omen, that is, was meant to serve as a model for similar actions during the coming year. The element of display was increased by various masked processions (usually men masked as she-bears, she-goats, storks, etc.), which were extremely archaic in character, doubtless being inherited from the prehistoric period. The main purpose of these displays was to ensure a luxuriant vegetation. The ritual often displayed remnants of an ancient scenario in which the participants mimed the death and resurrection of a god in animal form, thus also ensuring the vigor of fields and flocks. In western Europe the masked processions were held during Carnival, which marked the beginning of spring, while in eastern Europe they were held on Christmas, New Year's Day, or Epiphany, and often during the entire critical twelve-day period. There were also processions of young people who carried a plow—either a real one attached to oxen, or a miniature one—with which they dug or pretended to dig a furrow. This action was intended to induce an abundant harvest by means of imitative magic. In many instances, the act of plowing was accompanied by a verse narrative, in rare cases a sung one, which surveyed all the phases of the agricultural cycle from plowing to removing bread from the oven, all on a grandiose scale.

In central and especially in eastern Europe we may still encounter processions of children who utter good wishes by means of songs or recited stories, sometimes accompanying these with strokes from the ritual branch to reinforce the message. In the case of children's processions the effectiveness of the wish is associated with the supposed innocence of childhood. More vivid are the adolescents and adults (mingled without distinction of age in archaic regions), whose hats and caps are decorated with ivy or something else signifying spring, and who wish each household well by singing the great variety of Christmas songs that have most clearly retained the aspect of omen. That such songs continue the Roman repertory for the New Year festival is shown by the folk etymology of the Romanian *corinda*, based on *calendae* (cf. Slavic *koleda*).

According to their purpose, these songs are divided into categories for different age groups (children, young men and women [these are the most numerous], married people, wives with children, the widowed, old people), occupations (herders, fishers, masons, priests, mayors), and special situations (e.g., people possessing many domestic animals, beekeepers), or according to different phases of the custom (entering a house, receiving gifts, leaving the house; dawn, midday, or evening; at the end of a procession through the village). In certain areas of Romania and the Ukraine there are also Christmas songs of mourning for those who died during the previous year, and for the seriously ill. These songs contrast with the overflowing joy of the ritual in general, but are in keeping with the funereal note struck in the archaic New Year festival, which was also a festival of the dead. As a result of this functional diversity, the repertory is extremely rich, especially among the Romanians and Ukrainians, and yields as many as three hundred types. Wishes are expressed in two ways in these songs: directly, with the wish for good health and gladness, and indirectly, through epic paraphrases in the verses of the song, which is adapted to the particular status of the addressee. [*See* Winter Solstice Songs.]

Vegetation and harvest. Other periodically recurring customs are almost always meant to ensure the abundance of the vegetation, which is sometimes fused with human destiny itself. Ritual cradling and rocking, practiced in Europe at the beginning of spring, usually on the Feast of Saint George but sometimes on Easter or Pentecost, seeks to guarantee full strength through propitiatory contact with the greening of the trees. In eastern Europe this purpose has been further specified along erotic lines, an aspect emphasized, for example, in the ritual songs used among the Balkan Slavs. Other practices aim at lending vigor to the vegetation with the help of ritual water and fire. More widespread are practices intended to secure rain. The best known of these, *pirpiruna* (also *papaloga, dodola*), is probably a relic of a cult of the Balto-Slavic god Perun (Pērkons), but in its present form it is simply an act of imitative magic. In the procession the dominant figure is a young girl adorned with sheaves of leaves. While she summons the rain, in order that the granaries may be filled to overflowing with wheat and maize, the mistress of the house literally pours water over her. In some areas of central Europe this custom has been associated with the wild man, a young fellow dressed in foliage and other kinds of vegetation believed to induce an abundance of plant life. This custom is to be found today in western Europe. In the countries of southeastern Europe there is the parallel custom of the *caloïan (scaloïan),* which probably springs from the cult of the vegetation god (Osiris, Attis, Adonis, Dionysos) and had its counterpart in the twenty-four clay dolls, called *argei,* that the Romans threw into the Tiber during droughts. The folkloric scenario has preserved its ancient character since the custom repeats the death and resurrection of a doll that is buried in order to ensure abundant vegetation. Sometimes two dolls are made, one representing the father of the sun and the other, the mother of the rain. The ceremony is accompanied by a lament combined with invocation to solicit abundant rain through the intervention of the buried doll. Since the lament is only effective if accompanied by weeping, young girls elicit tears by artificial means if necessary. [*See* Tears.]

During the summer, the harvest becomes the workers' main preoccupation. Concern for the yield of the coming year takes concrete form in the special role allotted to the last, or the best, ears of grain. According to a widespread belief, the spirit that protects the fields seeks refuge in these ears at harvest time. Because the propitiatory effect is based on magic by contact, the ears are kept in the barn or in the house next to the icons. Grains from these ears are mixed with the seeds for future crops. The power of the ritual sheaf is increased by water from the time it is put together in the field until it reaches the owner's home. Sometimes the assembling of the ritual sheaf is accompanied by the sacrifice of an animal, usually a cock. Among the Romanians of Transylvania the transferal of the ritual sheaf is accompanied by a solemn song in which the singers tell of their great joy at an abundant harvest that guarantees them an untroubled life.

During the fall of the year the most outstanding practices have to do with the cult of the deceased. The most frequent scenario finds villagers gathering near a crossroads where they light a fire for their dead to return to and warm themselves. To welcome them, the villagers put out fruits and especially nuts. The villagers encircle the fire, sometimes in a dance, and at the end everyone jumps through the flames in an act of purification. [*See* Fire.]

Life cycles and the rites of passage. The way that the human cycle is integrated into the annual cycle shows the close relationship of the two. Human beings are dependent on cosmic conditions, but the reverse is also true. Since people can perform deeds that have cosmic consequences by way of magical analogy, it follows that they can influence the forces of the universe in a direction favorable to themselves. As a result, the influence exercised by the two cycles can be exerted in either direction depending on the needs of the moment. [*See* Rites of Passage.]

Birth. The beliefs and practices associated with birth, for example, ensure the carrying out of the rites of passage and especially of apotropaic rites. Because a newborn child and its mother are exposed to many dangers, special precautions are needed. Among the most widely feared dangers are the fairies who endeavor to steal the child and replace it with another who is deformed (a changeling). The name of the newborn is kept a secret lest the child be exposed to the harmful effects of spells. The rites of passage begin with the laying of the child on the ground; this is an echo of the cult of Mother Earth and represents the first step in the transition, namely, the separation of the child from its mother, while baptism, the final step, incorporates the child into the family and community. The custom of planting a fruit tree at the birth of a child functions as an omen and derives from an ancient dendrolatric cult that is still alive in many parts of Europe, although its original meaning has been lost.

Weddings. Marriage introduces the main stage of the human cycle, and it is for this reason that weddings are celebrated so fully in peasant societies. In archaic cultures the entire community took part in the wedding, which would last for several days. With increasing urban influence, however, the scale and length of the celebration were curtailed. It is possible to see the evolution not only of the external elements but also of the ritual actions themselves. Thus certain practices have lost their ancient ritual meaning and have taken on a modern meaning. Having lost every trace of magic, they have become merely ceremonial, that is, entirely secular. In the process of secularization, an action sometimes gains in breadth; for example, the gunshots, which at one time certainly had an apotropaic purpose, have become simply an element of display and therefore more numerous. The extent of the wedding also has been influenced by economic conditions. Poverty sometimes requires what people speak of as "a nighttime wedding," in which the celebration is limited to an evening party. Wedding gifts have also been modernized, and in place of the traditional domestic animals, clothing, food, and so on, money has come to be preferred, sometimes to the point of being the only gift.

In general, weddings have retained their communal character, although on a reduced scale. Rites of passage play the chief role in the scenario, but apotropaic and propitiatory rites also have an important place. Among the rites of passage, dances with a ritual (or more recently, a semiritual) function have pride of place. The young man to be married says farewell to his age group at a dance held in his home on the eve of the wedding, and sometimes the bride-to-be does the same in her parents' house. In like manner, the passage into the family circle, including the godparents, is marked by special round dances, while in some Balkan areas the newly married woman is conducted to the hearth of her new home, the actions performed being echoes of the ancient cult of the hearth gods. In many parts of central and eastern Europe the incorporation of the newly married woman into the village community is sealed by a dance in which all the participants, including the women, take part in turn.

In addition to ritual dances, there are songs sung during the principal actions in the nuptial scenario. The songs in widest use are those sung to the bride as she is dressed or as she leaves her father's house. Thematically the songs fall into two categories. Some are satirical, making jokes about the new wife's fears; the erotic allusions are sometimes only too clear. Other songs are full of sadness, contrasting the untroubled life the bride had enjoyed in her parent's house with the hard life she will have with her husband, a life not without its brutalities. Both types of songs attempt to teach a lesson, but from divergent points of view: the one derives from an archaic mentality that is disappearing, while the other, basically lyrical in character, is gradually spreading.

The propitiatory rites are more numerous since they must ensure above all the procreation of children. The fertility of the newly married woman is promoted by actions whose meaning is evident: she takes a child in her arms (or else they give her a doll made for this purpose); the young couple must eat a roasted fowl or cakes that have the power to render them fruitful. Certain rites are meant to strengthen conjugal unity: the young couple must enter the house while tied together with a halter or a napkin: they must eat with the same spoon, or both eat a single egg. In the past the nuptial veil, red in color and used to cover the couple, clearly had an apotropaic purpose. Later, however, it was reserved for the young woman only, whom it concealed from evil forces, while under the influence of the church its color was changed to white as a sign of purity.

In the nuptial rites the bride plays the chief part, since she is provided with several ritual attributes, some of which have lost their meaning but are still practiced out of fear of the unknown. In some places, a meeting with the bride or groom is thought to be fatal, bringing death, while in other places everyone hastens to look at the bride because the sight prevents afflictions of the eyes. It is almost always the bride's prerogative to use purificatory water; she sprinkles the assembly with it as though she were a priestess. In some parts of Romania the bride dons her wedding dress near branches from an apple tree, an act that increases her procreative ability as well as the fruitfulness of the apple tree (the magic flows in both directions).

Funerals. Among the customs connected with death, those that predominate in backward areas are rites of incorporation into the otherworld, but these are giving way to rites of separation and apotropaic rites in response to urban influence. [*See* Funeral Rites.] Actions that are apotropaic in intent are proving more tenacious, and measures taken to keep the dead person from becoming a ghost are held in strict respect even among the more educated classes. A series of actions seeks to facilitate separation from the living. The most widespread is the breaking of the pot containing the water with which the corpse has been washed. As a way of preventing the dead person's return there is the strange custom of having the coffin leave the house by an opening other than the door. In traditional areas this opening is expressly cut for the purpose, the intention being that the dead person should have no way of returning to the house of the relatives. Ritual stopping-places on the way to the cemetery have the same purpose and have been taken over into the Byzantine rite. In order to facilitate the incorporation of the dead into the community of the deceased, funeral meats are prepared for their sustenance on the journey. The dead are also given ritual money, which has several meanings but was originally meant to symbolize their total wealth. Such preparations are based on the ancient idea that the dead continue to live the same kind of life in the otherworld as they did when alive, but under different conditions, so that they will need a spouse, servants, cooking pots, and animals, which at one time were sacrificed during the funeral rites. Following the custom of the "death-marriage," which has survived in Europe, young women are dressed as spouses in order that the deceased male may be accepted into the world of the dead. Ritual meals, which are repeated at set times in accordance with the prescriptions of the church, are intended to aid the dead person. This is particularly so in those areas in which a material representation of the otherworld still has a strong hold on minds.

The dead are also helped to leave the living by means of funeral laments, which are poetical and musical compositions that have evolved from their very dramatic ancestral form in the direction of a rather temperate lyricism. The origin of these laments has not been satisfactorily explained, but it presupposes the idea, no longer held by Christians, that the dead have the ability to perceive their immediate surroundings. According to ancient beliefs a dead person has several souls, one of which is inseparable from the body. For this reason, among archaic collectivities the laments used to be accompanied by violent actions: the scratching of the face to make blood flow, the pulling out of hair, and so on, in order that the dead might be convinced of the deep love their relatives had for them. These violent gestures gradually disappeared, but the bitter cries continued, while the laments turned into funeral songs of an increasingly lyrical kind and finally disappeared altogether in more advanced regions. They are still in use in eastern Europe, as well as in southern Italy and southern Spain, but they occur only sporadically in the Scandinavian countries. This distribution makes it clear that they are in an inevitable decline. Almost always sung by women, the laments combine traditional motifs, which have acquired a set form in verse, and improvised verses that explain the actual circumstances surrounding the death.

Certain more formal, less improvisatory songs are always sung by a semiprofessional group of women and only at certain points in the scenario of the funeral; they are to be found only in southwestern Romania and southeastern Spain. The most widespread types are the "dawn song" (in Andalucía *los auroros,* but only for dead children), and the "song of the fir tree" for unmarried men. The fir tree symbolizes the husband or wife of the deceased. The "dawn song" provides directions to be followed during the journey to the otherworld and is a guidebook to the rites of incorporation among the dead. These ritual songs, which seem to be of Mediterranean origin, are probably a continuation of the ancient solemn laments reserved for kings, princes, and heroes who had distinguished themselves in war. Here and there in Europe are found the vestiges of funeral dances on the occasion of ritual commemorations. In northeastern Yugoslavia and southwestern Romania the dances on these occasions are round dances from the ordinary repertory, the funereal note being added simply by the lighted candles that the dancers hold. Since dancing is best able to express joy, it is meant here to show the joy caused by the return of the dead for these funeral commemorations. This function can be seen more clearly among the Mari (Cheremis). Someone who resembles the deceased dons the decease clothing, which has been kept specifically for this purpose, and dances to the music of bagpipes in the presence of the kneeling assembly. In places where this belief has disappeared, the funeral dance serves simply as a commemoration, as do the words of the ritual prayers.

Magic and Other Types of Custom. Spells are completely subordinated to magic. Their recitation is surrounded by a series of prescriptions, some prohibitory (taboos), others propitiatory, often varying within the same community, depending on the magical powers of the interpreters. Since taboos limit the spread of spells, people learn them furtively, but these limitations actually intensify the mystery surrounding spells and augment their effectiveness. Spells are the most individualistic and highly personal type of folklore. Their composition is therefore capricious, and they are the loosest of all the folkloric types. They are most always recited by a single woman, occasionally by a single man. The interpreter has a repertory of motifs, that is, of ideas in verse form which she combines according to her improvisational bent. A spell may be short, containing only a few verses, or very long, extending to several hundred verses.

According to the internal agency at work, spells are of two thematic groups: those that invoke the intervention of a demiurge and others that rely solely on the magical power of the word and accompanying factors (gestures, objects, special places and days). The first group is made up of prayers that are very difficult to distinguish structurally from prayers in the strict sense, especially those that invoke the saints of the church. The prayer character is confirmed by the capacity for adaptation to the dominant beliefs of the age; thus the figures most invoked in Europe are the Blessed Virgin, God (Jesus), and Saint Peter, less frequently the healer saints. Nevertheless a conservatism can be seen in the persistent invocation of other "pagan" demiurges: the sun for illnesses attributed to it and for certain love spells; the moon for other love spells; fairies for certain illnesses; and some plants, such as mandrake and enchanter's nightshade, for their miraculous powers. Special kinds of water (consecrated, for example) are invoked because of their purificatory powers, and at times fire, which has the same purificatory power or can be turned into an obedient agent of magic. Sometimes the saints are said to collaborate with these prehistoric demiurges, and some spells have supposedly been taught by the Blessed Virgin or even by God himself. [*See* Spells.]

Fantasy. Ritual implications also have been detected in other folklore that today have a purely secular character. Thus tales of fantasy are used not only for amusement but also to obtain an advantage. Among some Siberian peoples, hunters tell stories to amuse the lord of the animals, who will then send plenty of game as a reward. In the northern part of the Ural Mountains, fishermen tell stories in order to gain a large number of fish. Among the Latvians and Estonians the telling of stories during the autumn months is supposed to make the pigs grow fat for Christmas. Among the northern Romanians stories supposedly have other marvelous effects: if a herder can tell a different story (about a hundred stories) each evening during the time in which the ewes are first in heat and then carrying, the first lamb born will be extraordinary, with power to foretell everything that will happen to its master. In that same part of the world, stories are considered to have an apotropaic power; hence the custom in isolated homes of telling three stories each evening while making the rounds of the dwelling to prevent evil spirits from gaining entrance. It was for this reason that strangers would pay for their hospitality by telling stories. But storytelling can also have negative effects. Among the Ukrainians, Latvians, and Estonians it is forbidden to tell stories during the period when the ewes, and sometimes the cows, are carrying. This phenomenon is another confirmation of how evolution can give the same beliefs completely opposite meanings. These facts when taken together make plausible the hypothesis that stories of fantasy used to play a propitiatory role in initiation rites, while by analogy a hero's feats of valor could affect the listener.

We know nothing of a comparable role for the epic lays recited at public festivals. It seems, however, that the heroic ballad was closely connected with the cult of the ancestors and served a commemorative ritual function within it; that this would have been the case at least in the very distant past is suggested by the *Odyssey,* in which the blind bard at the court of Alcinous, king of the Phaeacians, sings a ballad of the fatal quarrel between Achilles and Odysseus simply for the amusement of the hearers and without any cultic implication.

Riddles and children's folklore. Disagreement about the ritual origin of the riddle has highlighted its role in rites of initiation and passage. [*See* Paradox and Riddles.] In some small tribes outside of Europe young men about to be married are tested to see if they possess certain knowledge that has been condensed into the enigmatic form of the riddle. Among European peoples this custom has long since disappeared, but the memory of it has been kept in the nuptial song used among the Romanians of western Transylvania. A procession following the groom enters the courtyard of the bride and there engages in a dialogue, with the bride's group asking questions, often in the form of riddles from the common repertory, and the other group giving the answers for the groom.

Folklore among children is richer in ritual elements. Studies have shown how their repertory retains elements that have passed out of use among adults, while some folkloric production becomes the prerogative of children because of their innocence. In addition to these categories, the repertory of children contains songs (which are sometimes only recited and not sung) that have an evident magical tinge. There are, for example, the invocations addressed to various small creatures: the snail, the hedgehog, the stork, the ladybird, the butterfly. And, above all, songs addressed to the sun bidding it shine again, to the new moon, which supposedly has beneficent powers, or to the rain bidding it go away. Also very widespread is the spell sung when a child loses its first tooth and asks for one of steel, or the spell for healing a sty. Other regional repertories contain spells having similar powers. Through the inherent naiveté that allows children to maintain a profound belief in the efficacy of these spells, prehistoric man lives on even in the modern world.

[*See also the biographies of the scholars mentioned herein. For discussion of folklore in specific traditions, see both* Folk Religion *and* Popular Christian Religiosity. *See also* Popular Religion.]

BIBLIOGRAPHY

The best introduction to religious folklore is Arnold van Gennep's *The Rites of Passage* (1909; Chicago, 1960). A wide-ranging survey of customs is given by Paul Sartori in *Sitte und Brauch*, vol. 1, *Die Hauptstufen des Menschendaseins;* vol. 2, *Leben und Arbeit daheim und draussen;* and vol. 3, *Zeiten und Feste des Jahres* (Leipzig, 1910–1914); each volume has an extensive bibliography arranged according to themes and countries. On the agrarian customs of the European peoples, see Wilhelm Mannhardt's classic study, *Wald- und Feldkulte,* 2 vols. (1905; Darmstadt, 1963). Then there is James G. Frazer's great work, *The Golden Bough*, 3d ed., rev. & enl. 12 vols. (London, 1911–1915); the abridged edition (London, 1922) has been translated into many languages.

To these may be added Waldermar Liungman's *Traditionswanderungen: Euphrat-Rhein,* 2 vols. (Helsinki, 1937–1938), which endeavors to show the migration of annually recurring customs that had their origin in ancient Mesopotamia. Petru Caraman's *Obrzęd Koldowania u Slowian i u Rumanow* (Cracow, 1933) compares Christmas customs among all the Slavic peoples, the Romanians, and the modern Greeks and argues for the Romanian origin of the ritual songs for Christmas and the New Year (a Romanian translation of the book is in press).

In addition to the books of van Gennep and Sartori cited above, other inclusive studies of customs in the human life cycle may be mentioned: Edward A. Westermarck's *The History of Human Marriage*, 5th ed., 3 vols. (1921; reprint, New York, 1971), and Johannes Piprek's excellent monograph, *Slawische Brautwerbungs- und Hochzeitsgebräuche* (Stuttgart, 1914). Valuable information, along with an extensive bibliography, can also be found in Alexander H. Krappe's *The Science of Folklore* (London, 1962) and Adolf Bach's *Die deutsche Volkskunde* (Heidelberg, 1960). The only history of Europe concerned with folklore, Giuseppe Cocchiara's *Storia del folklore in Europa* (Turin, 1954), has an extensive bibliography. See also my *Folclor Românesc: Momente şi Sinteze*, 2 vols. (Bucharest, 1981–1983).

OVIDIU BÎRLEA
Translated from French by Matthew J. O'Connell

FOLK RELIGION. [*This entry explores the religious complexes of peasant and rural societies insofar as they differ from mainstream religious traditions. It consists of four articles:*

An Overview
Folk Buddhism
Folk Judaism
Folk Islam

For a similar view of Christianity, see Popular Christian Religiosity.]

An Overview

Peasant populations (i.e., sedentary agricultural groups forming part of larger, more complex societies) have probably existed since 6000 BCE in southwestern Asia, since 3100 BCE in Egypt, and since 1500 BCE in southeastern Mexico. Unlike agricultural entrepreneurs who are active economic agents or semisubsistence cultivators practicing ritual exchange and barter, peasants are farmers whose surpluses are redistributed to urban centers by more powerful groups. In practice it is not always easy to decide who actually is or is not a peasant, especially in the case of farmers who hold factory jobs, modern European family farmers, contemporary North American small farmers, or cash crop slash-and-burn cultivators of South America and Africa. For the purposes of this article, this term applies to past and present-day sedentary cultivators and pastoralists of Asia, North Africa, southern Europe, and Latin America, and historically to sedentary cultivators in northern Europe and North America as well.

Because sedentary farming emerged independently at different times and in different parts of the world, taking radically different forms (including short-term fallowing with animal-drawn plows, alpine pastoralism, and permanent cultivation by means of hydraulic systems), the search for an original, universal religion based on agriculture seems doomed to wishful speculation. Attempts nevertheless have been made, concentrating on such notions as matriarchy, Earth Mother goddesses, and moon worship.

Yet peasant societies do, by definition, have features in common that set the requirements and limits on the kinds of religion that will serve their members: (1) peasants depend on a particular ecosystem; (2) most live in similar social environments (household-based, on dispersed farms or in small settlements); and (3) they depend on the larger society for which they produce food. Their religion usually provides them with ways to deal with the local natural and social world, as well as the wider social, economic, and political network of which they are a part.

To manage the ecosystem, peasants, like other people, mark the cycles of nature, day and night, the lunar cycle, the solar year, the life cycles of animals and plants—all hold particular importance for cultivators. Many peasant cultures have rituals and routines for transitions relating to equinoxes, planting, germination, and harvest. And because landscape and climate vary widely, peasants tend to establish locally distinct sacred places, times, and divinities. Whether it is at a spring, cave, mountaintop, riverbank, or a special tree, peasants come to pay homage to their divinities according to the calendar, and in times of crisis to seek solutions to such major agricultural threats as drought, hail, and insect plagues.

In terms of social relationships, peasant life is characterized by endemic disputes among households over such matters as inheritance, property boundaries, and irrigation; and yet as cultivators, peasants must normally undertake a certain amount of cooperative work with their neighbors (such as harvesting, herding, and maintaining roads and irrigation ditches), as well as provide mutual aid in time of crisis. To a lesser extent, these tensions and dependencies apply also between adjacent settlements, particularly when pasture or water rights are involved. In this context, religious devotion can facilitate the unity of households within a settlement (mutual fealty to a common divinity) and solidarity between settlements (worship at common shrines). On the other hand, religions also provide the source, pretext, or rallying cry for chronic and intractable conflict between settlements. With regard to patterns of authority and division of labor, the role of religion (through divine models of hierarchy, justice, and emotion) appears to be much the same in peasant as in nonpeasant societies.

Because the household is the critical social and economic unit, peasants pay special attention to consecrating the identity of household members at birth, the alliance of household economic units through marriage, and the reorganization of the household at death. In many peasant societies, elaborate care for the souls of deceased household members corresponds to the idea that the social personality of the house or farm endures beyond the lives of any particular inhabitants. Consequently, there are reasons why this relationship of religion and identity should be stronger with peasants than with others.

As a local phenomenon, peasant religion only rarely can be studied well from a distance, or by relying on surveys or written sources (aside from the rare documents of oral testimony). The ways that it consecrates relationships with nature, society, and identity must be lived to be understood. Context is crucial, for it gives meaning, often of a particularly local variety, to religious behavior that might otherwise appear to be universal.

Indeed, for most people, not just peasants, beliefs are more acted out (in the sense of worship or ritual) than they are thought out. Only when challenged are such beliefs formulated or declared by any but the religious specialist or exceptional devotee. Much of the study of religion as lived, therefore, is the study of that which is taken for granted, that which goes without saying. As a result students of peasant religion have adopted some of the methods used by anthropologists in studying tribal societies; they have stayed for extended periods in rural communities, paying special attention to public religious acts, local interpretation, individual biography, and the range of opinion and doubt.

But the religion of peasants does not address only local agricultural and human concerns, for by definition peasants are only specialists in a wider network of trade and power in which, given the vulnerability of agricultural life, they generally find themselves in a subordinate position. One of the vital tasks of government is to ensure an adequate food supply for its cities; peasant societies are geared for this purpose, for which they are both protected and exploited. Not coincidentally, there is always a major component of religion in peasant society that is held in common with city dwellers and that generally extends to even wider intersocietal or international exchange systems as well. Such religions include divine beings, sacred sites, rituals, and usually church organizations, all of which are common to peasant and nonpeasant alike.

One therefore can no more speak of a radical separateness of peasant religion than one can speak of a radical separateness of peasant society. Peasant religion is an integral part of wider religions, which provides a common frame of reference in the cosmic and ethical sense, a framework that sets the terms for regular social and economic interaction. Indeed, since peasants often do not experience the specifically agricultural features of their religion as something distinctly different or apart, it is usually incorrect to speak of peasant "religion" in any sense other than religiosity, for peasants are almost always Christians, Muslims, Jews, Buddhists, or of some other religion that transcends their immediate arena.

The presence in peasant society of religious specialists trained in a broader social context provides a neverending source of new techniques, ideas, and images, which the peasant society may adapt for specifically local purposes. And much of what anthropologists following Robert Redfield have called the "little tradition" of the peasantry is what survived of a "great tradition" in the countryside long after it was rejected or forgotten by urban theologians and administrators.

Because of the long-term stability of the peasants' physical and social landscape, some aspects of their religions have had a remarkable and perhaps misleading permanence, although the peasants themselves and the greater political and religious systems affecting them have undergone many changes. For example, present-day cult paintings and statues throughout the world contain elements from earlier, now extinct religions; places of veneration are located at the same kinds of sites as earlier devotions; and in many areas, vows and votive offerings have not essentially changed in over two thousand years.

Such apparent permanence, however, is often superficial, masking major changes in attitude and identity. Say that one finds that a given group of peasants who are self-confessed, practicing Muslims also leave offerings to images of cows, contrary to the teachings of the Qu'rān. It would be a distortion to think of them as covert pagans. For empirical studies have broadened our notion of religion to include both what believers profess and what they actually do and feel. Thus Islamic religion, for instance, can only be fully understood as the sum of the religious acts and beliefs of Muslims. Or, put another way, major world religions are, in practice, coalitions or mosaics of widely differing local adaptations that share a common core of beliefs, rituals, and organization.

While peasant religion may be composed of what may appear to be different kinds of elements and survivals from different traditions, in practice these elements usually form an indivisible, functional whole for believers. Where the notion of survivals exists among peasants themselves, it is often the result of church efforts to stigmatize nonapproved behavior as superstitious, or because of the spread of findings of early folklorists bent on unraveling the different strands of peasant religion according to "high" or "low" origin. More recent scholarship has concentrated on seeing how these strands work together as a whole.

A problem facing students of peasant or folk religion has been finding something with which it can be compared. One tack has been to treat it as "popular" religion and to compare it with the prescribed norms of the larger church or doctrine, much as the "little" tradition is compared to the "great." But such comparisons have not always proved fruitful, for they involve comparing two very different things—on the one hand, a religion as lived and, on the other, a set of norms that hardly represents a way of life and that, in fact, may not be lived strictly by any kind of person, peasant or nonpeasant.

A refinement on this method has involved observation of the practical impingement of the institutions of a central religion on the religious life of peasants—the extent to which peasant religion is effectively regulated, updated, and revised from without. For Europe, this has been done through longitudinal studies using fieldwork, church visitation, and government records.

An alternate approach compares the peasant religion to that of lay nonpeasants in the larger society, as in Clifford Geertz's studies in Java. But as yet, there is a general lack of qualitative knowledge of urban or nonpeasant lay religiosity, and it is difficult to be sure that the religion of peasants, apart from its attention to the natural landscape, was in a given time and society fundamentally different from that of urban laypersons. At least for some places and times, a distinction between peasant and nonpeasant religiosity has not proved particularly revealing.

For when studied with care and sufficient evidence, peasant religiosity has been found to share many of the characteristics hitherto considered the domain of the "civilized." For instance, peasant religion is not necessarily homogeneous. Even when there is a single religion practiced, there is likely to be a wide range of doubt, opinion, and speculation, whether in a thirteenth-century French village or a twentieth-century Chinese hamlet. Nor is peasant religion particularly fixed or stable. Throughout history peasants have converted, have been converted, or have attempted to convert from one religion to another. And peasants are not invariably and instinctively religious. There are areas where peasant religious indifference has long been common, and recently entire age and gender groups have been known to abandon religion enthusiastically under militantly atheist governments.

Indeed, radical changes in the world political economy over the past 150 years have affected the terms in which peasant religion can be studied. Urban and rural industrialization, as well as the growth of the service sector, has brought an increased homogeneity in peasant and urban lifestyles. As a result of socialist, communist, and anarchist movements, active, militant disbelief is an overt or latent presence in rural areas. Seasonal migrations to the cities, increased visiting in the cities with relatives, peasant participation in the international work force, and the tremendous growth in literacy, as well as the spread of radio and television, have all helped to diffuse new religious styles and cults more rapidly among the peasantry.

In most places this broadening of horizons has made peasants more aware of their "otherness" in religious matters, so that it is they themselves who internalize behavioral distinctions proposed by the dominant culture. Some scholars refer to this process as "biculturalism": acting in different ways at different levels (the local and the metropolitan), clearly distinguishing between the two, and segregating behavior appropriately.

As a corollary to this bicultural insecurity, there is intense religious and political competition for the allegiance of the peasants whose religion has been devalued or rendered impractical. There exists a global religious competition, in keeping with the global economy in which peasants are now involved, in which the competitors are missionaries, again both religious and political. Among Peru's Altiplano peasantry one finds several lifestyles based on models and aid from American and European religious organizations. Indeed, some of the class/clan factionalism that unitary religions once served to ease is now expressed with rival religions from the wider world.

Yet it is not that peasants must choose only from the great religions; on the contrary, as the anthropologist Eric Wolf has pointed out, there have been many instances of peasant religious innovation, through creative imitation or the inspiration of visionaries and prophets. Some have taken the form of millenarian movements, others as radical purification sects. (Some religiously innovative groups, such as the Mormons and the Mennonites, created peasants as much as they were created by them.) And as tribespeople become peasants in African nation-states, new sects and cults spring up that speak to the new conditions, most of which, true to form, are not just local but national or international in scope.

In the context of the nation-state, peasant religion is quite easily politicized. Two overlapping factors are at work. First, human-divine relations serve to consecrate and are thereby tied up with personal identities in the family, village, and nation. Second, the year-in, year-out give-and-take that characterizes peasant devotions to divine figures accumulate great emotional power. Both the investment of identity and the emotional power are generally located in divinities with relatively bounded territories of grace, presenting a permanent temptation to governments, political parties, and to the churches themselves. And if effective channels of political action are blocked, as in much of Latin America and Eastern Europe, the local religion, its shrines, divine protectors, and priests, can become symbols for the entire peasant way of life. Thus through religion, peasant discontent finds a charismatic expression. By the same token, in the face of powerful states like modern China, early modern Spain, or Spanish-occupied Mexico, in which the government is all-pervasive, private religious acts and beliefs provide some peasants with a margin of independent identity and action, a buffer against the politicization of private life.

Often peasant religion is mobilized or exploited by nonpeasant leaders. In the nineteenth and twentieth centuries, literary romanticists, folklorists, and nationalists alike have seen in local peasant religion a source of indigenous virtue, the survival of an earlier local culture and identity in the face of foreign domination. In Ireland, Brittany, Poland, the Basque country, Greece, Yugoslavia, Armenia, the Baltic states, as well as in many of Europe's colonial empires worldwide, independence and autonomy movements have fed on an exaltation of peasant religion that on a superficial level involves a kind of ruralization of the urban elite. An extreme but symptomatic example is Mohandas Gandhi's religious transformation from lawyer to peasant.

This type of idealization represents the obverse of metropolitan religious doctrines that long held much of peasant religiosity to be pagan superstition, an attitude shared by enlightened secularizers as well. For both clergy and sophisticates, peasant religion has represented an "other" against which both orthodoxy and civilization could be measured.

These seemingly contradictory points of view, by their emphasis on tradition, survivals, and stability, all draw attention to peasant religion's past rather than its dynamics of change or its present roles. Idealization and stigmatization both tend to attribute an integrity and homogeneity to this religion that it rarely possesses, and simplify a more complex, perhaps less manageable reality.

[*See also* Agriculture *and* Popular Religion. *For addi-*

tional clarification of the study of peasant societies, see Indo-European Religions, *article on* History of Study; Dance, *article on* Popular and Folk Dance; *and* Anthropology, Ethnology, and Religion.]

BIBLIOGRAPHY

The search for universal features of the religion of cultivators in keeping with the framework theory of religious evolution, as exemplified by the work of James G. Frazer and Wilhelm Schmidt, is reviewed by Mircea Eliade in his *Patterns in Comparative Religion* (New York, 1958).

A persuasive exposition of general characteristics of peasant life from an anthropological viewpoint is provided in Eric Wolf's *Peasants* (Englewood Cliffs, N.J., 1966), following on Robert Redfield's *Peasant Society and Culture* (Chicago, 1956). A model study by Clifford Geertz, *The Religion of Java* (Glencoe, Ill., 1960), compares the religion of peasants with that of merchants and nobles, all under the wide mantle of Islam. For Buddhism, Stanley J. Tambiah in *Buddhism and the Spirit Cults in North-East Thailand* (Cambridge, 1970) shows how in practice the elements of different religious traditions function as a whole in the religion of a village. For the contemporary religion of European peasantry, I describe Catholicism in northern Spain in its relation to the landscape and social relations in *Person and God in a Spanish Valley* (New York, 1972), and Lucy Rushton admirably relates Greek Orthodox theology to personal life in "Religion and Identity in a Rural Greek Community" (Ph.D. diss., University of Sussex, 1983).

In the last two decades many excellent historical studies of religion as practiced have been published, many of which deal in part with peasants. Much of the early work on popular religion in Europe is discussed in F. Bolgiani's "Religione Popolare," *Augustinianum* 21 (1981): 7–75, with ample bibliographic notes. Richard F. Gombrich in *Precept and Practice: Traditional Buddhism in the Rural Highlands of Ceylon* (Oxford, 1971) argues against the notion of popular religion, as does Jean-Claude Schmitt in " 'Religion populaire' et culture folklorique," *Annales: Économies, sociétés, civilisations* 31 (September–October 1976): 941–953. Unusual ethnographic information about peasant religion in the Friuli region of northeast Italy, gathered in the context of diocesan investigations, is provided by Carlo Ginzburg in *I Benandanti: Richerche sulla stregoneria e culti agrari tra Cinquecento e Seicento* (Turin, 1966), translated by John Tedeschi and Anne C. Tedeschi as *The Night Battles: Witchcraft and Agrarian Cults in the Sixteenth and Seventeenth Centuries* (Baltimore, 1983). Emmanuel Le Roy Ladurie's *Montaillou: The Promised Land of Error* (New York, 1978) describes in detail village Catholicism in the Pyrenees and the villagers' conversion to Cathar beliefs. Similarly rich in detail, although not about a single community, is Keith Thomas's *Religion and the Decline of Magic: Studies in Popular Beliefs in Sixteenth and Seventeenth Century England* (New York, 1971). Nancy M. Farriss's *Maya Society under Colonial Rule: The Collective Enterprise of Survival* (Princeton, 1984) and Victoria Reifler Bricker's *The Indian Christ, the Indian King: The Historical Substrate of Maya Myth and Ritual* (Austin, 1981) are outstanding historical studies of religious syncretism in the Yucatan, building on a long line of distinguished ethnographies. Peter Brown, in his elegant *The Cult of the Saints: Its Rise and Function in Latin Christianity* (Chicago, 1981), challenges a radical distinction between peasant and nonpeasant religion in the Mediterranean, as I do in *Local Religion in Sixteenth Century Spain* (Princeton, 1981).

Peasant millennial movements are studied in *Millennial Dreams in Action*, edited by Sylvia L. Thrupp (New York, 1970). Charles Tilly's *The Vendée* (Cambridge, Mass., 1964) asks important questions about the social and economic roots of a peasant uprising in the name of religion. And the ways the religions of China have provided the peasantry with a certain defense against the state are discussed by Ann Anagost in her "Hegemony and the Improvisation of Resistance: Political Culture and Popular Practice in Contemporary China" (Ph.D. diss., University of Michigan, 1985).

WILLIAM A. CHRISTIAN, JR.

Folk Buddhism

Religious traditions are, by their very nature, complex. On the one hand, they symbolize the highest aspirations of the human mind and spirit; on the other, they sanctify and give meaning to the most ordinary and commonplace human needs and activities. The complexity of religion and its functions have been analyzed in various ways. There has been a tendency, however, to distinguish between those aspects created by and appropriate to the educated elites, for example, priests and rulers, and those that help the uneducated, common folk cope with the uncertainties and exigencies of life. Scholars have sometimes referred to this distinction as obtaining between "great" and "little" traditions or between "elite" and "folk" traditions. It must be kept in mind that these formal distinctions do justice neither to the multiplexity of religious traditions nor to the organic unity that characterizes them, even though such categories may serve a useful analytical function.

"Folk" Buddhism may be understood as a persistent, complex, and syncretic dimension of the Buddhist tradition characterized by beliefs and practices dominated by magical intent and fashioned with the purpose of helping people cope with the uncertainties and exigencies of life. Its varied expressions emerge along the wide spectrum between the normative Buddhist ideal represented quintessentially but not exclusively by the Buddha and the concept of *nirvāṇa*, and the indigenous magical-animistic and shamanistic traditions of the given culture in which Buddhism becomes institutionalized. Consequently, some aspects of folk Buddhism (e.g., the figure of the Buddha, the person of the monk, and the practice of meditation) appear to be closely affiliated with the normative ideals of Buddhism, while others are barely distinguishable from native, non-

Buddhist religious forms. Folk Buddhist institutional structures, religious practices and practitioners, and oral and written literatures reflect this variation.

Buddhism has had a folk or popular dimension since its inception. Early Buddhist scriptures challenge the view of a "golden age" of pure monastic practice dedicated to the pursuit of *nirvāṇa* unencumbered and undisturbed by the needs and expectations of a simple, uneducated laity. That the Buddha and his followers were supported by laypersons for reasons of material gain and magical protection, as well as for spiritual benefit, cannot be denied. Even meditation, the *sine qua non* of monastic practice, was perceived as leading not only to equanimity and enlightenment but also to the acquisition of magical power. The *Mahāvagga* of the Theravāda Vinaya Piṭaka depicts the Buddha not simply as an enlightened teacher, but as a yogin who wins followers through his magic. Moreover, although the source is later commentary, it is significant that the future Buddha, just prior to his enlightenment, was said to have been offered food by a woman who mistook him for a tree deity. In general, Buddhist scriptures readily intermesh doctrinal exposition with magical and animistic figures and elements ranging from *deva*s (gods) to *mantra*s (sacred utterances).

To be sure, folk Buddhism became a more dominant aspect of Buddhist institutional and cultural life as the religion grew in size and cultural significance throughout Asia. In India, Aśoka's strong support of the Buddhist monastic order in the third century BCE proved to be crucial to its growth and diffusion, and the appropriation of folk elements from different cultures was a means by which Buddhism spread and accommodated itself to the cultures of Asia from at least the beginning of the common era. Indigenous folk religions, therefore, were the major media through which Buddhism became a popular religion not only in India, but in Southeast, Central, and East Asia as well. The fact remains, nevertheless, that the folk element within Buddhism has been a part of the tradition since its inception, and has persisted in different forms to the present.

Folk Buddhism has several different facets that reflect various modes of interaction between normative, doctrinal-institutional Buddhism and native religio-cultural traditions. In some cases, the normative Buddhist tradition made only inconsequential adjustments; in others, Buddhism emerged as a thinly veiled animism. The major ingredient of folk Buddhism is usually referred to as animism or magical-animism, that is, the belief in benevolent and malevolent supernatural powers and the attempt to avoid them or to enlist their aid. These powers range from spirits of the living and the deceased to deities of regional or even national jurisdiction associated with non-Buddhist (e.g., Brahmanic) pantheons. The dialectical relationship between Buddhism and indigenous animism such as the Bon of Tibet led to the parochialization of Buddhism, but also changed the face of those native traditions encountered in Tibet, Korea, Japan, and elsewhere. For example, Shintō, rooted in an autochthonous animism, developed in Japan in competition with the more sophisticated traditions of Chinese Buddhism, just as religious Taoism in China institutionalized, at least in part, in response to Indian Buddhist influence.

The complex nature of folk Buddhism can be analyzed in various ways, but the method should do justice to its common or generic elements as well as the uniqueness of distinctive religio-cultural environments. Folk Buddhism as an essentially syncretistic phenomenon can be seen in terms of three types or modes of interaction between Buddhist and non-Buddhist elements: appropriation, adaptation, and transformation. These categories are intended to characterize particular historical instances as well as describe general types. Although they have overlapping qualities, they point to the variety within folk Buddhist belief and practice as well.

Appropriation. In many cases, folk Buddhism merely appropriated and subordinated indigenous symbols, beliefs, and practices with very little change in meaning. This is particularly true in the incorporation of a wide range of supernatural beings and powers into the Buddhist system. Generally speaking, these supernaturals, whether gods or spirits, malevolent or benevolent, were subordinated to the dominant Buddhist symbols and motifs. Most often they played a protective role, standing guard at a sacred Buddhist precinct, be it temple or *maṇḍala*, or functioned in an appropriately subordinate way in relationship to the Buddha. In Sri Lanka, for example, a kind of divine pantheon evolved, a hierarchy of gods and spirits ranging from the most localized guardian spirits of village and field to the suzerainty of regional gods the likes of Skanda and Viṣṇu with the entire structure under the sway of the Buddha. In Tibet the gods of the everyday world *('jig rten pa)* became protectors of the *dharma*, obeying the commands of the great teachers. While they are so numerous and indeterminate as to defy a fixed ordering, they generally are divided according to the traditional Indian tripartite cosmology of heaven, earth, and the intermediate realm. In Burma the indigenous *nat* spirits are incorporated into Burmese Buddhism as *deva*s. Thagya Min, for instance, is assimilated into Sakka (the Brahmanic Indra), and resides in Tāvatiṃsa Heaven as king of the *deva*s, but is also said to be ruler of the "thirty-seven *nat*s." [*See* Nats.] In Thailand various supernaturals including *devatā*, *cao*, and *phī* have a complex relationship to Thai Buddhism involving linkage, hierarchy, and instances of both opposition and complementarity. In Japan, Buddhism absorbed native Japanese deities or *kami*. In many cases the *kami* are taken as manifestations of Buddhas or *bodhisattva*s (the theory of *honjisuijaku*), although a uniform set correspondence did not develop. [*See* Honjisuijaku.] A similar story can be told for Buddhism in China, Korea, and other parts of Asia. While the specific list of supernaturals appropriated into the Buddhist system varies from culture to culture, these beings represent a hierarchy of powers and suzerainties dependent on, under the authority of, or even in tension with, Buddhist figures, symbols, and motifs.

These supernaturals have been assimilated into the Buddhist cultus as well as into Asian Buddhist worldviews; they are amalgamated into orthodox ritual activity or become a distinct ritual subset. Throughout Buddhist Asia the guardian spirits of a temple precinct, such as the *phī* in Thailand or the *kami* in Japan, may be propitiated prior to an auspicious ceremonial event. In Tibet, Tantric ritual has provided a framework for customary religious practices in which Tibetan deities exist side by side with Indian Buddhist ones. In Sri Lanka, devout Sinhala Buddhists paying respects to the Buddha at the famous sanctuary of Lankatileke outside of Kandy will make offerings before images of the Hindu deities enshrined in *devale*s around the perimeter of the building. In Thailand, Brahmanic deities (e.g., Viṣṇu) may be invoked during a customary Buddhist ritual, and offerings are made to the guardians of the four quarters as part of the New Year celebration at a Buddhist monastery *(wat)*.

Of special significance in folk Buddhism have been the belief in the soul (the existence of which is scarcely maintained in scripture), or spirit element(s), of the individual, and various rituals associated with this belief, especially life-crisis or life-transition rites. The role of Buddhism in the conduct of mortuary and death anniversary rites for the souls of the dead in China, Korea, and Japan is well known. In Japan, the Obon festival celebrated in the seventh month honors the return of the souls of the dead. Graves at Buddhist temples will be cleaned in preparation for the spirits' return, and the household altar *(butsudan)* will be decorated with flowers, lanterns, and offerings of fruit. In Burma, mortuary rituals are performed to prevent the soul of the deceased from remaining in its former haunts and causing trouble. In Thailand, soul-calling *(riag khwan)* rites are performed at life-transition times such as weddings and even as part of ordination into the monkhood.

Adaptation. In assimilating indigenous magical-animistic and shamanistic religious beliefs and practices, Buddhism itself has changed. This process of adaptation and parochialization has been part of the Buddhist tradition from its outset: the Buddha as teacher but also miracle-worker, meditation as the vehicle for the attainment of insight and supernatural powers, the monk as *nirvāṇa*-seeker and magician. In the Theravāda traditions of Sri Lanka and Southeast Asia the miraculous power of the Buddha is attested to not only in supernatural feats of magical flight, prognostication, and the like, but also in the cult of Buddha relics and Buddha images that typifies ritual practice in this region. The Mahāyāna and Tantryāna traditions elaborated the salvific function of the Buddha through the proliferation of Buddhas and *bodhisattva*s. In China, Tao-an (312–385) popularized Buddhism by promoting Maitreya as a savior Buddha, the god of Tuṣita Heaven, an earthly paradise accessible to all. Hui-yüan (334–416) did for Amitābha Buddha and his Pure Land (Sukhāvatī) what Tao-an did for Maitreya and Tuṣita Heaven. Both Maitreyism and Amidism became fundamental to folk Buddhism. In Japan, one of the specific adaptations was the assimilation of popular elements into the figure of the *bodhisattva* Jizō (Skt., Kṣitigarbha), who thereby came to occupy an even more important place than did his Chinese counterpart, Ti-tsang. Not only does Jizō deliver souls from hell, but he also helps women in childbirth and, like Kannon (Chin., Kuan-yin), another popular savior, is seen as the giver of healthy children and a guide to the Western Paradise of Amida. [*See* Celestial Buddhas and Bodhisattvas; Kṣitigarbha; *and* Avalokiteśvara.]

The supernormal powers associated with meditation adepts has a close association with shamanism. Monks have become famous for their skills as alchemists, for their ability to communicate with the spirit world, and for their prognostication of future events, activities that conflict with the Vinaya. The biographies of such Tantric adepts as Padmasambhava and Mi-la-ras-pa attest to this type of parochialization, and even the lives of the Ch'an (Zen) patriarchs are not exempt from supernatural hagiographic elaboration. [*See also* Mahāsiddhas.] In Sri Lanka, ascetic monks are revered not only for their piety but for their magical prowess as well, and in Thailand a significant cult of monk-saints has developed. Popular magazines attest to their extraordinary deeds, their advice is sought for everything from lottery numbers to military ventures, and their amulets are worn for protection against danger and disease. [*See* Arhat.]

Transformation. Buddhism appropriated magical-animistic and shamanistic religious forms and adapted its own beliefs and practices to this type of cultural milieu. The degree to which assimilation and adaptation has occurred has led to profound transformations of the tradition. While decisive turns in the development of Buddhism have taken various forms, popular sectarian movements have provided one of the most fruitful contexts for this kind of transmutation. Examples abound throughout Buddhist Asia. In Burma and Thailand messianic Buddhist groups emerged in the modern period centered around charismatic leaders often claiming to be Maitreya Buddha. In China, Buddhist sectarian groups led by "rebel monks" split off from monasteries in the Northern Wei kingdom (386–535) as early as the fifth century. The best known is the White Lotus movement, a complex of rebel eschatologies active from the twelfth to the nineteenth century. Other major sects include the Maitreya, White Cloud, and Lo, or Wu-wei. These groups were lay-based, heterodox, and syncretistic, and were often politically militant. The White Lotus sect developed its own texts, a married clergy, hereditary leadership, and by the mid-fourteenth century a full-blown eschatology derived from both the Maitreyan tradition and Manichaeism. By the late sixteenth century the principal deity of the White Lotus groups was a mother goddess. Eventually, by the late nineteenth century, the Buddhist elements were so extenuated that they had become congregational folk religion rather than a distinctive form of folk Buddhism. [*See* Millenarianism, *article on* Chinese Millenarian Movements.]

In Japan as early as the Heian period (794–1185) holy men *(hijiri)* developed a folk Buddhism outside the orthodox ecclesiastical system. [*See* Hijiri.] In the tenth and eleventh centuries Amida *hijiri* and Nembutsu *hijiri*, preeminent among whom was Kōya, a layman of the Tendai sect, taught universal salvation through the repetition of the Nembutsu (the formulaic recitation of the name of Amida Buddha). The Nembutsu came to be seen as a powerful form of protection against the spirits of the dead and evil spirits *(goryō)* and a means to release them into Amida's paradise. [*See* Nembutsu.] While the founders of the orthodox Pure Land sects, Hōnen and Shinran, rejected the animistic and magical aspects of the Nembutsu, the attitudes of the common folk did not substantially change. The Amida *mantra* was considered a causally effective means to attain the Pure Land after death as well as a magical spell for sending evil spirits to Amida. Popular sectarianism has continued to develop into the contemporary period. Some of the so-called new religions *(shinkō shūkyō)* in Japan represent a unique form of folk Buddhism. Arising in the nineteenth and twentieth centuries in a period of political and social crisis, these religions, which developed around strong, charismatic leaders, are syncretistic and often utilize magical ritual practices. Two of the best known are Risshō Kōseikai and Sōka Gakkai. Both are indebted to the *Lotus Sutra*-Nichiren tradition. Through its political wing, Sōka Gakkai has become a sometimes militant force in Japanese politics. [*See* New Religions, *article on* New Religions in Japan.]

The Buddhist encounter with folk religion, which has taken the forms of appropriation, adaptation, and transformation, has not occurred without conflict. In Southeast Asia stories abound of the Buddha's encounter with indigenous supernatural beings who are only eventually subdued and made to vow their allegiance to the *dhamma*. Other heroic figures exemplify a similar pattern. Especially noteworthy is Padmasambhava's propagation of the *dharma* in Tibet. The key to his success, in contrast to the previous failure of the great teacher Śāntirakṣita, was Padmasambhava's magical prowess in subduing the powerful Tibetan deities. Such conflict may be mirrored in Buddhist ritual as well as in myth and legend. In northern Thailand, for example, offerings of buffalo meat to the guardian spirits *(phī)* of Chiang Mai are made as part of the New Year celebration; however, this ritual activity has no formal connection with the elaborate ceremonies occurring at Buddhist sanctuaries in the area.

The practitioners of folk Buddhism likewise present a great diversity. Those most closely tied to the autochthonous animism may be likened to shamans, for they function in a shaman-like manner. They have the power to enter into the realm of the supernaturals, an act often symbolized by magical flight; they may also become possessed by supernatural beings or function as a medium between the supernatural and human realms, and have the knowledge to enlist or ward off their power. In Tibet, *mdos* rituals are performed by wandering lamas (Tib., *bla mas*) or exorcists *(sṅags pa)* for protection against dangers, hindrances, injuries, illness, and obstacles caused by evil powers. The person who carries out exorcistic rituals *(gto)* must be an expert in meditating on his *yi dam* or tutelary divinity. The *yamabushi* or mountain ascetics of Japan, while affiliated with the Tendai and Shingon sects, perform exorcisms and function as village magicians. The Chinese shaman *(wu)*, who exorcised spirits of evil and illness and danced and chanted to ward off disasters, influenced the popular conception of the charismatic leadership of folk Buddhist sects in China. Often, lay Buddhists are the principal practitioners of the folk traditions, especially because many of the magical practices associated with folk Buddhism are either forbidden or discouraged by the orthodox Vinaya. In the Esoteric schools of Buddhism (e.g., Shingon), as well as in sectarian movements, the differentiation between mainstream beliefs and practices and those of the folk dimension are more difficult to perceive. Even in the Theravāda countries of

Southeast Asia, however, actual monastic custom and practice may be far removed from the strict ideal of monastic discipline, which discourages fortune telling, alchemy, and the like.

The texts of folk Buddhism also reflect the ways in which the normative tradition has appropriated, adapted, and been transformed by indigenous folk religion. An important genre of folk literature is the miraculous tale, often purporting to be an episode from the life of the Buddha or a famous Buddhist figure such as Maudgalyāyana or Vimalakīrti. Included in this literary genre are the Jātakas, which are themselves examples of the appropriation of folktales, mythic accounts of heavens and hells (e.g., *Petavatthu*), legendary elements in chronicles, lives of the saints in various Buddhist traditions, and vernacular collections such as the Chinese *pien-wen* (texts of marvelous events). Other texts, such as the *paritta* (scriptural passages which, when chanted, are said to have apotropaic power) in the Theravāda tradition, function in a magical manner in Buddhist ritual, even though the content reflects the highest ethical and spiritual ideals of the normative tradition. The *Bar do thos grol* (Tibetan Book of the Dead), although at the center of the Tantric technique of liberation, certainly incorporates shamanistic elements. Another type of folk Buddhist literature includes those texts specifically related to the practice of astrology, fortune telling, and animistic rituals.

In the final analysis, folk Buddhism should not be seen as a later degeneration of the normative Buddhist ideal. Rather, it is a complex dimension of the tradition, present from its origin, that has provided the tradition with much of its vitality and variation from culture to culture.

[*See also* Priesthood, *article on* Buddhist Priesthood; Chinese Religion, *article on* Popular Religion; Japanese Religion, *article on* Popular Religion; *and* Worship and Cultic Life, *articles on Buddhist cultic life.*]

BIBLIOGRAPHY

In recent years studies of folk or popular Buddhism have been greatly enhanced by the work of anthropologists, especially those working in Southeast Asia. These descriptive and analytic studies provide an important complement to the work of cultural historians and historians of religion. Notable of mention for the Theravāda Buddhist cultures are the works of Stanley J. Tambiah, in particular his *Buddhism and the Spirit Cults in North-East Thailand* (Cambridge, 1970). While this work is a micro-study, like many anthropologists Tambiah offers a more comprehensive interpretation of the religious system in northeast Thailand. Tambiah's structuralist-functionalist approach contrasts with the social-psychological perspective (as found, for instance, in the works of Abram Kardiner) of Melford E. Spiro's *Buddhism and Society: A Great Tradition and Its Burmese Vicissitudes*, 2d ed. (Berkeley, 1982). A dominant theme in anthropological studies is the nature of the interrelationship between the folk or "little" tradition and the "great" tradition. In various ways this theme is addressed in Michael M. Ames's "Magical-animism and Buddhism: A Structural Analysis of the Sinhalese Religious System," in *Religion in South Asia*, edited by Edward B. Harper (Seattle, 1964), pp. 21–52; Gananath Obeyesekere's "The Great Tradition and the Little in the Perspective of Sinhalese Buddhism," *Journal of Asian Studies* 22 (February 1963): 139–153; Manning Nash's *The Golden Road to Modernity: Village Life in Contemporary Burma* (New York, 1965); and A. Thomas Kirsch's "Complexity in the Thai Religious System: An Interpretation," *Journal of Asian Studies* 36 (February 1977): 241–266. This theme figures in studies of the religious systems in Central and East Asia as well. See, for example, J. H. Kamstra's *Encounter or Syncretism: The Initial Growth of Japanese Buddhism* (Leiden, 1967), Alicia Matsunaga's *The Buddhist Philosophy of Assimilation: The Historical Development of the Honji-Suijaku Theory* (Rutland, Vt., and Tokyo, 1969), and Christoph von Fürer-Haimendorf's *Morals and Merit: A Study of Values and Social Controls in South Asian Societies* (London, 1967).

Popular Buddhist millenarian movements constitute another theme addressed by recent studies of folk Buddhism. For Southeast Asia, E. Michael Mendelson's "The King of the Weaving Mountain," *Journal of the Royal Central Asian Society* 48 (July–October 1961): 229–237, and Charles F. Keyes's "Millennialism, Theravāda Buddhism, and Thai Society," *Journal of Asian Studies* 36 (February 1977): 283–302, are particularly noteworthy. For China, Daniel L. Overmeyer's *Folk Buddhist Religion: Dissenting Sects in Late Traditional China* (Cambridge, Mass., 1976) is definitive.

Studies dealing with folk Buddhism that do not take a particular thematic perspective abound. Francis L. K. Hsu's *Under the Ancestors' Shadow; Chinese Culture and Personality* (New York, 1948) treats Chinese popular religion and the ancestral cult. H. Byron Earhart's *A Religious Study of the Mount Haguro Sect of Shugendō* (Tokyo, 1970) deals with the Shugendō sect, a popular movement combining Esoteric Buddhism with Japanese folk religious beliefs. René de Nebesky-Wojkowitz's *Oracles and Demons of Tibet: The Cult and Iconography of the Tibetan Protective Deities* (The Hague, 1956) treats popular Tibetan protective deities. For folk Buddhism in Japan, see also Hori Ichirō's *Folk Religion in Japan; Continuity and Change*, edited and translated by Joseph M. Kitagawa and Alan L. Miller (Chicago, 1968).

DONALD K. SWEARER

Folk Judaism

In the course of its millennial history, biblical and Jewish folk religion has found its expression in beliefs in male and female deities other than God; in angels, devils, demons, ghosts, and spirits; in saints and holy men; in the "evil eye" and other baleful influences; and in rites and practices such as magic, witchcraft, divination, and the use of amulets, charms, and talismans. Manifestations of Jewish folk religion were found from earliest biblical times and continued to appear, until in the nineteenth century it waned in those European countries in which the Jews came under the influence of the Enlightenment. In the Middle Eastern Jewish communities folk religion retained its vitality until 1948, after which the people of these communities were largely transplanted to Israel.

Biblical Period. In a few cases the biblical authors refer to folk beliefs and rites without condemnation. These "naive" references pertain mostly to cosmic origins or to the early history of mankind, the Hebrew patriarchs, and the people of Israel. Thus *Genesis* 6:1–4 clearly reflects a folk belief in the existence of "sons of God"; *Isaiah* 14:12–15, in a rebellious angel who was cast down into the nether world; and various passages in *Isaiah, Psalms,* and *Job,* in sea dragons and other monsters who dared to oppose God. *Terafim,* small household gods taken by Rachel from her father's house (*Gn.* 31:19, 31:30–35), and larger versions of the same kept by Saul's daughter Michal (the wife of David) in her chambers (*1 Sm.* 19:13, 19:16), are clear examples of folk belief.

In sharp contrast to these uncritical mentions of folk religion are the condemnatory references to the popular (as well as institutional) worship of gods other than Yahveh contained in the historical and prophetic writings of the Bible. But these scornful references are, at the same time, also testimonies to the popular worship in Israel of several male and female deities (such as Baal, Kemosh, Milcom, Asherah, Astarte, and the Queen of Heaven) from the time of the Judges to the destruction of Israel and Judah in 722 and 587/6 BCE and even later (see *Jer.* 44:15–19). These biblical data are supplemented by archaeological discoveries of small figurines of goddesses (Asherah, Astarte) in many excavated Israelite homes from the biblical period all over the country.

Demons. With reference to demons the biblical evidence shows a similar duality. On the one hand, there are prohibitions of witchcraft and all trafficking with, or consultation of, demons, ghosts, and spirits, which practices are considered capital sins punishable by death (*Ex.* 22:17, *Dt.* 18:10–12), and historical notes tell of the attempted extermination by royal decree of "those that divined by a ghost or familiar spirit" (*1 Sm.* 28:3). On the other, there is ample testimony to the belief, shared by the Yahvist historians and prophets with the common folk, in the existence of demons and their power to harm men's bodies and minds (*Gn.* 32:25ff.; *Lv.* 16:10; *Is.* 13:21, 34:14; *1 Sm.* 16:15, 16:23; *1 Kgs.* 22:22–23; *Ps.* 91:5–6). Israelite folk religion seems to have made room for species of demons *(shedim, se'irim),* as well as individual demons, for example ʿAz'azel. Most of the latter are known from the religions of the neighboring peoples as gods, thus, for example, Lilith, Mavet ("death"), and Reshef ("pestilence"). From the late biblical and apocryphal literature are known the devil-like demons called Saṭan, Masṭemah, Belial (Beliyyaʿal), Asmodeus (Ashmed'ai), while both in the New Testament and in rabbinic literature demons are referred to as "unclean" or "evil spirits." In the three synoptic gospels the prince of demons has the name Beelzebul (Baʿal Zebub). These demons, generic and individual, are all reflections of Jewish folk belief.

Magic and divination. The Bible repeatedly condemns action taken to influence the mysterious forces of nature and the spirits. *Deuteronomy* 18:10–11 decrees, "There shall not be found among you any one that . . . useth divination, a soothsayer, or an enchanter, or a sorcerer, or a charmer, or one that consulteth a ghost or a familiar spirit, or a necromancer." *Exodus* 22:17 rules explicitly, "Thou shalt not suffer a sorceress to live" (cf. *Lv.* 20:27). Passages such as these indicate that the biblical authors shared with the common people the belief in the reality and efficacy of magic, but, in contrast with the common folk, condemned it as an act of unfaithfulness to God (cf. *Dt.* 18:12–13).

Recognizing the assurance divination provided, biblical legislation, while outlawing it in the form practiced by the Canaanites, supplied a substitute for it in the mantic activity of prophets, whose legitimacy, it states, would be proven by subsequent events (*Dt.* 18:14–22). The people, it seems, turned to the prophets primarily in order to profit from their mantic powers (*1 Sm.* 9:6; *1 Kgs.* 14:1ff., 22:5ff.; *2 Kgs.* 3:11). Divination included the questioning of the Urim and Tummim (*1 Sm.* 23:9–12), consultation of the *terafim* (*Jgs.* 17:5, 18:14; *Hos.* 3:4; *Ez.* 21:26; *Zec.* 10:2), the use of goblets (*Gn.* 44:5), arrows (*Ez.* 21:26), spoken words (*Gn.* 24:14, *1 Sm.* 14:9–10, cf. v. 12), and the interpretation of the liver (*Ez.* 21:26), stars (*Is.* 47:13, *Jer.* 10:2), and dreams (*1 Sm.* 28:6). The hold diviners had over the people is best illustrated by the story about King Saul: he "cut them off the land," but when in trouble sought out one of those who remained (*1 Sm.* 28:3–25). [*See* Prophecy, *article on* Biblical Prophecy.]

The persistence into the first century BCE of magic as a part of popular religion is attested by *2 Maccabees* 12:40, which tells about the Jewish warriors who wore under their tunics amulets *(hieromata)* taken from the idols of Yavneh. This practice was condemned by the author because of the pagan derivation of the amulets. On the other hand, in *Tobit,* an apocryphal book of the first century BCE, a method of exorcising a demon from a possessed person with the help of fumigation is described as having been taught by the angel Raphael, that is, as a religiously orthodox act.

Talmudic Period. After the Babylonian exile, Jewish folk religion found its expression, partly under the impact of Babylonian, Persian, and, later, Hellenistic influences, in a proliferation of angels, demons (some of whom had figured already in the Bible), evil spirits, the evil eye, and so on, and in practices aiming at the invocation of beneficial superhuman powers and the propitiation of, or protection against, those with evil intentions. While in the Jerusalem (Palestinian) Talmud only three categories of demons *(mazziqim, shedim,* and *ruḥot)* are mentioned, demonology is more prominent in the Palestinian *midrashim.* However, it is the Babylonian Talmud (completed c. 500 CE) that is the richest source for Jewish folk religion in general and demonology in particular. [*See* Talmud.]

For Talmudic Judaism the number of demons was legion. Ashmed'ai was their king, while their queen, Iggrat the daughter of Maḥalat, went about with a retinue of 180,000 "angels of destruction" (B.T., *Pes.* 112b). The Talmudic sages fought valiantly, not against the popular belief in demons, but against the demons themselves. Thus Ḥanina' ben Dosa' and Abbaye succeeded in restricting the activities of Iggrat to certain times and places. Other sages conducted conversations with demons. Most dangerous was the female demon Lilith, who seduced men at night and strangled babes, and who could be kept away only by means of protective charms. [*See* Lilith.]

Since both Talmuds and the *midrashim* record the sayings, rulings, and acts of the sages, and not of the common folk, our knowledge of folk religion is largely confined to its reflection in the recorded words and deeds of the rabbis, and it is on them that we must base our conclusions as to the religious beliefs and acts of the simple people. Thus, for example, the Mishnah (*San.* 6.4) and the Jerusalem Talmud (*San.* 6.9, 23c) tell about the leading first century BCE Palestinian sage and head of the Sanhedrin, Shim'on ben Sheṭaḥ, that he had eighty witches hanged in the port city of Ashqelon. Such a report is, of course, evidence of the existence of a belief in witches among both the people and their spiritual leaders.

Occasional references in the Mishnah and Talmud indicate that *kishshuf,* witchcraft, was widespread, especially among women (*Sot.* 9.13, *Avot.* 2.7; B.T., *San.* 67a), despite the fact that it was a capital offense (*San.* 7.4, 7.11; B.T., *San.* 67b), punishable by stoning. Persons accused of witchcraft were frequently brought before the judges, who therefore were required to have a thorough familiarity with the workings of magic (B.T., *San.* 17a). They also had certain criteria by which they were able to differentiate between witchcraft and mere trickery (B.T., *San.* 67b).

Of several sages it is reported that they themselves practiced and taught magic (B.T., *San.* 67b–68a), as did the daughters of at least one of them (B.T., *Giṭ.* 45a). Some women engaged in faith healing (B.T., *Soṭ.* 22a, cf. Rashi). One of the pious men of the first century BCE, Ḥoni the Circle Maker, practiced rain magic (*Ta'an.* 3.8). The use of incantations and the recitation of magic formulas for curative purposes was widespread (B.T., *Shab.* 67a).

As for amulets (sg., *qamei'a),* in Talmudic times two kinds were in vogue: those written on and those containing roots and leaves. They were dispensed by physicians to cure ailments, and also used by people for protection against the evil eye and demons, and to make women conceive (*Kel.* 23.1, *Shab.* 6.2; B.T., *Shab.* 61a–b, *Pes.* 111b; J.T., *Shab.* 6, 8b top; *Gn. Rab.* 45; *Nm. Rab.* 12; et al.). (Whether the biblical *duda'im* [mandrakes] found by Reuben in the field were ingested by the sterile Rachel or used by her as an amulet is not clear. See *Gn.* 30:14–15, 30:22–23.) An amulet was usually put around the neck of a child soon after its birth (B.T., *Qid.* 73b), which custom has remained alive until modern times in Middle Eastern Jewish communities. Amulets that had proven their efficacy were allowed to be worn outside the home even on the Sabbath, although on that rest day the carrying of all objects was prohibited (*Shab.* 6.2).

Divination *(niḥush)* continued in the Talmudic period as an integral part of popular religion, despite rabbinic prohibition and its punishment by flogging. The influence of Jewish and Babylonian folk religion on the Babylonian amoraim (Talmudic sages of the third to fifth centuries) can be seen in the permission they gave to use *simanim* (signs or omens) in trying to foretell the future. Very popular in Talmudic times was the divinatory use of biblical verses randomly recited by children (B.T., *Ḥag.* 15a–b, *Ḥul.* 95b). There were so few people who refrained from practicing some kind of divination that those who did were considered more meritorious than the ministering angels (B.T., *Ned.* 32a).

Middle Ages and Later Times. The medieval development of Qabbalah constituted a favorable environment for the further proliferation of the belief in demons. Folk belief and the teachings of Qabbalah mutually reinforced each other. The sexual seduction of humans by demons was considered an imminent danger, resulting in the birth of additional demons. Many illnesses were believed to be the result of spirit possession, and consequently the exorcism of spirits (dybbuks) became an important method of popular medicine. While the exorcists seem to have been men only, the persons considered possessed were mostly women. Childlessness—generally considered the wife's "fault"—gave rise to a wide variety of folk cures, including the ingestion of substances of animal origin prohibited by *halakhah* (traditional Jewish law).

Much of medieval Jewish folk religion expressed itself in rites and ceremonies performed at the three major stages of human life: birth (including circumcision), marriage, and death. On these occasions the demons were believed to be especially aggressive and dangerous, and the protection of the principals as well as the attendants was a major concern that gave rise to numerous folk rites.

Features of folk religion are also present at the celebrations of the official Jewish holy days, despite repeated attempts by rabbinical authorities to suppress them. The Tashlikh rite (the symbolic casting of one's sins into water on Ro'sh ha-Shanah, the Jewish New Year) and the Kapparah (the symbolic transference of one's sins onto a hen or a cock on the eve of Yom Kippur) are two examples of practices that Jewish folk religion introduced into the High Holy Days celebrations over the objection of the rabbis.

Of special interest for the historian of religion is the extent to which Jewish folk religion succeeded in being accepted by the leading Jewish religious authorities, who, by including numerous folk beliefs and customs into their halakhic codes, made them part of official Judaism. The *Shulḥan 'arukh,* the law code that governs Jewish traditional life to this day, contains rulings that show that its author, the Sefardi Yosef Karo (1488–1575), and his chief annotator, the Ashkenazi Mosheh Isserles (1525–1572), believed in the power of the evil eye to harm a person even in the synagogue, in the efficacy of amulets, in the influence of the stars on human life, in omens, in incantations to subdue demons and dangerous animals, in the magic prevention or cure of illness, in consulting the dead and the demons, and so on.

The veneration of saintly men and, more rarely, women, expressed mainly in visits to their tombs with appropriate offerings in the hope of obtaining various benefits, has been an integral part of Jewish folk religion, especially in Islamic countries, for centuries. Occasionally the same Jewish or Muslim saint has been venerated by both Jews and Muslims. [*See* Pilgrimage, *article on* Contemporary Jewish Pilgrimage.]

Although several leading medieval rabbinical authorities (including Moses Maimonides, 1135/8–1204) objected to the use of amulets, charms, and magic remedies, their popularity could not be checked, and after the expulsion of the Jews from Spain in 1492 they spread to eastern Europe. Prepared by rabbis, healers, or holy men for a fee, they were believed to save the wearer or user from all types of harm; to cure his (or her) ailments; to protect him from demons; and to provide good luck, health, and many other kinds of benefits. The amulets, widely used especially in the Middle East down to recent times, whether written on paper or made of silver, brass, tin, or iron, are often decorated with magic triangles and squares, the Magen David (Shield of David), or menorahs. The metal amulets typically have the shape of a circle, a square, a rectangle, a shield, a hand (the most frequent shape), and, rarely, a foot. They are inscribed with divine and angelic names, brief quotations from the Bible, and magic combinations of letters or obscure words. Often the amulet states the name of the person for whom it was prepared and the name of his or her mother.

In the seventeenth and eighteenth centuries in central and eastern Europe a magician who prepared such amulets was called *Ba'al Shem,* that is, "Master of the Name," because he was an expert in the use of holy names for magico-religious purposes. The founder of Hasidism, Yisra'el ben Eli'ezer, known as the Besht (acronym of Ba'al Shem Ṭov), was, in his early years, such a provider of amulets. [*See the biography of the Besht.*] The popular belief in the efficacy of amulets was so strong that numerous rabbis openly supported their use and wrote treatises in their defense. While practically all the Hasidic *rebeyim* (as the miracle-working saintly leaders were known) were men, at least occasionally women functioned in the same capacity. [*See* Hasidism, *overview article.*]

Divination continued to be a widespread practice among the Jews down to modern times. More recent methods resorted to include the lighting of candles, the observation of shadows, opening the Bible at random, casting lots, gazing at a polished surface, incantations, and consulting with the dead. The interpretation of omens developed into a veritable folk science to which frequent references are found in medieval and later rabbinic literature. It also led to a literary genre of its own in Hebrew, *sifrei goralot,* "books of lots," which contain instructions and rules for the predictive use of names of animals, birds, the twelve tribes, the twelve signs of the Zodiac, cosmic phenomena, the twenty-two letters of the Hebrew alphabet, and so on. These books, which, as a rule, are of southern European or Middle Eastern origin, are the counterpart in the field of divination to the even richer assortment of books on charms and magic remedies, some of which were composed or reprinted as late as the twentieth century. [*For discussion of the manipulation and interpretation of the letters of the Hebrew alphabet, see* Alphabets.]

Modern Period. The spread of the Haskalah (Jewish Enlightenment) in the nineteenth century resulted in a decline of both Jewish folk religion and Jewish orthodoxy. By the second half of the twentieth century folk religion remained a significant element only in the culture of a diminishing sector of unsecularized ultraconservative Jews. Those of Middle Eastern extraction transplanted into Israel colorful customs connected with the life cycle and the ritual calendar, as well as features such as the Moroccan Maimuna feast that commemorates the death of Maimonides and the veneration of other saints, similar to the long-established Lag ba-'Omer festivities at the tomb of the second-century tanna Shim'on bar Yoḥ'ai in Meron. In Israeli *kibbutsim* and in some circles in the Unites States, attempts are being made to endow traditional religious ceremonies (such as the Passover Seder) with contemporary religious, social, and political relevance. In the United States, outside Orthodox circles, traditional Jewish folk religion is largely moribund, but the transformation of the synagogue into a "center" of social, educational, cultural, and charitable activities and the proliferation of men's clubs, sisterhoods, youth groups, and *ḥavurot* (egalitarian religious fellowships) can be interpreted as a new departure in the realm of folk Judaism. Manifestations such as these can be taken as indications that folk religion, which has always been a significant aspect of Jewish religious life, is still alive and can be expected to produce as yet unforeseeable developments.

BIBLIOGRAPHY

There is no single book dealing with the whole field of Jewish folk religion, or even with Jewish folk religion in one particular period. There are, however, numerous studies on specific aspects of Jewish folk religion in each of the major historical periods of Judaism.

Biblical Period. Several of the standard histories of biblical Hebrew religion discuss such elements in it as folk belief, folk custom, and magic. See also Reginald C. Thompson's *Semitic Magic: Its Origins and Development* (London, 1908); Alfred Guillaume's *Prophecy and Divination among the Hebrews and Other Semites* (London, 1938); James G. Frazer's *Folk-Lore in the Old Testament*, 3 vols. (London, 1919); and S. H. Hooke's *The Origins of Early Semitic Ritual* (Oxford, 1938).

Talmudic Period. There is no study on Talmudic folk religion in general, but several books deal with Talmudic magic and other aspects of Talmudic folk belief. See Gideon Brecher's *Das Transcendentale, Magie, und magische Heilarten im Talmud* (Vienna, 1850), mainly of historical interest as a pioneering study; Ludwig Blau's *Das altjüdische Zauberwesen* (Strasbourg, 1898), still very valuable; Samuel Daiches's *Babylonian Oil Magic in the Talmud and Later Jewish Literature* (Oxford, 1913); *Sefer ha-razim*, edited by Mordechai Margalioth (Jerusalem, 1969); and my *Man and Temple in Ancient Jewish Myth and Ritual* (1947; 2d ed., New York, 1967).

Middle Ages and Later Times. The subject most thoroughly researched within the general field of medieval and later Jewish folk religion is magic. See in particular *The Sword of Moses: An Ancient Book of Magic*, edited by Moses Gaster (London, 1896), and Gaster's *Studies and Texts in Folklore, Magic, Medieval Romance, Hebrew Apocrypha, and Samaritan Archaeology*, 3 vols. (1925–1928; reprint, New York, 1971); Hermann Gollancz's *Book of the Key of Solomon*, in Hebrew and English (Oxford, 1914); Joshua Trachtenberg's *Jewish Magic and Superstition* (1939; reprint, New York, 1982); H. J. Zimmels's *Magicians, Theologians and Doctors* (London, 1952).

Special Subjects. Among the books dealing with special subjects within the general field of Jewish folk religion the following should be mentioned: Michael L. Rodkinson's *History of Amulets, Charms, and Talismans* (New York, 1893); Theodore Schrire's *Hebrew Amulets* (London, 1966); reprinted as *Hebrew Magic Amulets* (New York, 1982); Angelo S. Rappoport's *The Folklore of the Jews* (London, 1937); my *On Jewish Folklore* (Detroit, 1983); and Michael Molho's *Usos y costumbres de los Sefardíes de Salónica* (Madrid, 1950).

Much material on Jewish folk religion is contained in the journals devoted to Jewish folklore and folk life: *Mitteilungen zur jüdischen Volkskunde* (Berlin, 1898–1929) and *Jahrbuch für jüdische Volkskunde* (Berlin, 1923–1925), both edited by Max Grunwald; *Edoth: A Quarterly for Folklore and Ethnology* (in Hebrew and English), edited by myself and Joseph J. Rivlin (Jerusalem, 1945–1948); and *Yeda'-'Am*, edited by Yom-Ṭov Levinsky (Tel Aviv, 1948–).

RAPHAEL PATAI

Folk Islam

A number of factors make the presentation of folk religion in Islamic countries difficult within the framework of a brief article. One is that Islam, the youngest of the three monotheistic faiths, has retained many pagan features, and such features, although of a distinctly "folk" character, have become part and parcel of official Islam. Second, down to modern times, Muslim peoples have been characterized by greater reliance on the spoken, rather than the written word, which meant that even the officially sanctioned beliefs, doctrines, and practices of Islam reached the masses by means of oral transmission and thus tended to be colored by "folk" features; that is to say, as is often the case, the differences between official and folk religion have been blurred. Third, the proliferation of Muslim sects, schools of jurisprudence (*madhhabs*), dervish and other religious orders, and fraternities created a favorable atmosphere for the mixing together of officially prescribed elements of religion with folk features either barely tolerated by the religious leadership or even proscribed by them, although in vain. Fourth, Islam absorbed much from the religions it displaced, especially on its peripheries (in Central, South, and Southeast Asia, and in sub-Saharan Africa), and many of these exogenous features have survived within an Islamic framework without being clearly differentiated from official Islam or being recognized as elements of folk religion. Fifth, in Islam, which is a men's religion *par excellence*, with an almost total exclusion of women from the official forms and observances of worship, the women have developed and maintained religious practices of their own that are suffused with folk features. Finally, in Muslim lands it is frequently difficult to establish a clear distinction between religion and other aspects of private and social life. It has often been said that Islam is not merely a religion but a total way of life, and the same holds true for folk religion, which is practically indistinguishable from folk life in the broadest sense of the term. While manifestations of folk religion often contradict official Muslim monotheism, the simple people remain unaware of such contradictions, and the religious authorities who are aware of them in most cases tolerate, even if only grudgingly, the ineradicable popular beliefs and practices. Leaving aside these problematic issues, the discussion that follows will consider aspects of popular belief and practice in various Muslim lands.

Beliefs in Supernatural Beings apart from God. Belief in such beings, usually termed *jinn*, going back to pre-Islamic Arabia, was endorsed by the Qur'ān and accepted in official Islam. In folk belief the world is densely populated by *jinn* and other kinds of demons (*ghūl*s, *ʿifrīt*s, *shayṭān*s), most of whom are inimical and hence dangerous to humans. Their world duplicates the human one: there are male and female, as well as Muslim, Jewish, Christian, and pagan *jinn*. They are, as a rule, invisible but can assume animal or human form, and humans even run the risk of inadvertently marrying a *jinnī*. The *jinn* can cause epidemics, madness (*majnūn*, literally "*jinn*-possessed," is the Arabic word for "mad"), pain, seizures, and fits. Women in childbirth, newborn infants, brides, and bridegrooms are in particular danger of being harmed by *jinn*, whose favorite haunts are water, the fireplace, thresholds, latrines, and bathhouses. They love darkness and are afraid of light (cf. *Gn.* 32:27), salt, iron, certain herbs, and the sacred words of the Qur'ān. As a protection against them one should always say the Basmalah ("In the name of God") before eating or undertaking anything important.

Veneration of Saints and Holy People, and Their Barakah. As a counterweight to the omnipresent *jinn*, Muslim folk religion puts its trust in saints *(awlīyā'*; sg., *walī)* and prophets *(anbiyā'*; sg., *nabī)*, whose tombs are places of pilgrimage and great gatherings, especially on their birthdays and anniversaries of their deaths. The saints and prophets, whose tombs are found almost everywhere in Muslim lands, range from Adam and Eve (the latter's grave is pointed out in Jidda, the Saudi Arabian seaport), to pious people who have died within living memory. Folk belief has it that the saints, while alive, were endowed with *barakah*, a beneficent supernatural potential or virtue, and that this force emanates from their tombs, so that a visit to a saint's shrine can benefit the supplicant. *Barakah* can also be contained in diverse objects, such as grain or olive trees, can be transferred from one object to another, and can be destroyed by something or someone unclean.

Of special interest are the instances in which such features of folk religion have supplanted, with the acquiescence of the religious authorities, the official Muslim rites. Thus the duty of performing the *ḥajj*, or pilgrimage to Mecca, which is the fourth "pillar" of Islam, is in many Muslim communities replaced by *ziyārāt* ("visits") to the shrines of locally venerated saints. In general, in the life of the Muslim masses the visitation and veneration of such local saints' tombs, or of famous tomb-sanctuaries such as those of Mashhad, Karbala, and Najaf in Shīʿī Islam, play a much more important role than the *ḥajj* to Mecca, and this despite the disapproval expressed in the *fiqh*, official Islamic jurisprudence. The annual *mawlid*s ("birthday celebrations") of saints are the greatest folk holidays known in Islamic lands, surpassed only by the Shīʿī public mourning, with self-flagellation and ecstatic self-laceration, on the anniversary of the death of Ḥusayn ʿĀshūrā', on the tenth day of the month of Muḥarram. Related to these observances is the practice of visiting graves in general, a folk custom approved by Muslim theologians as a religious exercise. [*See* Mawlid *and* ʿĀshūrā'.]

The Evil Eye and Protection against It. The belief in the evil eye (Arab., *ʿayn*, "eye") that can cause untold harm was inherited by Islam from pagan Arabia, Talmudic Judaism, and other pre-Islamic sources. Numerous Arabic proverbs, such as "Most men die victims of the evil eye," or "The evil eye empties the houses and fills the graves," testify to the prevalence of this belief and to the general fear of "the eye." Some people consciously use the power of the evil eye that they possess, while others may cause harm involuntarily, by a staring glance. Those believed most likely to have the evil eye are old sterile women and the unmarried, as well as people with blue or deep-set eyes, with eyebrows that meet, or those who are misshapen or have some other reason to be envious. The persons who most attract the evil eye—that is, who are in the greatest danger of being harmed by it—are the same as those who can most easily be hurt by demons: small children (especially boys), pregnant women, brides and bridegrooms, participants in feasts and celebrations, and, in general, persons whose beauty, success, or other distinctions make them objects of envy. The evil eye can be repelled by a very large number of preventive or curative measures: gestures (with the five fingers spread out), spoken formulas, fumigations, the use of fire, salt, horn, metal, the wearing of amulets (often hand-shaped), tattoo marks, jewels, the application of blue color, the symbols of the number five, and so forth.

The Use of Amulets, Charms, and Magic Cures. These have a wide application in addition to the warding off of the evil eye. Closest to the realm of religion is the wearing of a piece of paper or parchment inscribed with a passage from the Qur'ān; often such a written amulet is encased in a decorated leather or metal capsule and hung around the neck. In many cases the inscription contains the names of God and/or angels. Other amulets or talismans (Arab., *ṭilsam;* pl., *ṭalāsim*) consist of small metal plates, up to three by four inches in size, in the form of a hand, a disk, a square, or a rectangle, or with an undulating outline, and engraved with magic names, words whose meaning is unknown, or magic letters, or numbers arranged in a grid among others. The amulets are prepared by members of religious orders, dervishes, shaykhs, and other persons having saintly reputations. In order to be truly effective, the amulet must be prepared, against payment, directly for the person who wants to wear it. The purposes for which the amulets are used run the entire gamut of human fears and desires: protection against demons, the evil eye, illness, accidents, enemy attacks, misfortunes and mishaps, or financial losses, and, on the positive side, for success in love, in childbirth, in travels, in dealings with persons of power, and other undertakings. In many places, soon after their birth, infants are provided with amulets (called *tamā'im;* sg., *tamīmah*) for their protection, and outside of cosmopolitan cities one rarely sees children without amulets around their necks.

Magic, Witchcraft, Exorcism. The belief in demons has its corollary in magic *(siḥr),* which, according to the Qur'ān (2:96), was taught to humankind by the angels Hārūt and Mārūt. Although magic was prohibited under penalty of death, it remained widespread in all Muslim lands and was reinforced by the folk practices of those peoples who were forcibly converted to Islam and yet retained many of their old beliefs and rites. Magic constitutes an important part in the folk religion of Muslim women, and in Muslim folk belief in general magic is associated especially with women, Jews, and blacks. Written spells are often in Hebrew or contain Hebrew words, and Jews are considered greater adepts at magic than Muslims. Strong African influences are present in the *zār* cult, which is widespread among women, especially in the Muslim societies of northeast Africa, and which aims at controlling and exorcising spirits that take possession of humans (almost exclusively women) and cause them suffering. A great variety of magical incantations is used for purposes such as casting magic spells upon others or protecting people against magic and witchcraft, against demons, against the evil eye, and so forth.

Divination, Omens, and Signs. The traditional and frequently repeated dictum, "There is no divination *(kihānah)* after the prophecy," meaning that once Muḥammad had accomplished his prophetic mission, divination no longer had any place in the life of Muslims, is reminiscent of the biblical commandment that prohibits divination and enjoins instead belief in, and obedience to, the words of prophets (*Dt.* 18:10–15). However, as in biblical Israel, such admonitions went unheeded in Islam. Recourse to divination remained an integral part of folk religion in the Islamic countries, to such an extent that it forced Muslim religious scholars to pay attention to it and to try to legitimize it as a branch, albeit the lowest, of prophetic practice. In fact, medieval Muslim scholars carefully classified the divinatory practices into a great number of categories, all of which together were termed *'ilm al-ghayb* ("the science of the hidden"). A special branch of divination is dream interpretation *(ta'bīr),* which is as much a part of folk life today as it was in the days of the biblical Joseph.

Rites of Passage and the Annual Cycle. As in every folk culture, a vast number of Muslim folk beliefs and practices cluster around the three great stations of human life: birth, marriage, and death. At these junctures the principals as well as the attendants are believed to be especially vulnerable to attacks by evil spirits and the evil eye, and for this reason special efforts are made to protect them, through the use of water, fire, salt, iron, henna, amulets, incantations, concoctions, fumigations, sacrifices, symbolic acts, and so forth. Some of the rites defy Islamic law: the shaving of part of a child's head and leaving another part unshaven, for example, is practiced all over the Muslim world despite its prohibition by Muḥammad. The circumcision of boys, on the other hand, although not prescribed by the Qur'ān, is performed unfailingly in all Muslim communities before the boys reach adulthood, often as a group ceremony and accompanied by lavish public festivities. In many Muslim lands girls, too, are circumcised—although only one Muslim school of jurisprudence, the Shāfiʿī, considers it obligatory—in a quiet, almost clandestine, observance. Female circumcision (clitoridectomy) is still practiced, for example, in southern Arabia, southern Iraq, Egypt, and Sudan. The ceremonies of marriage, death, burial, and mourning are complex rituals that last for days, often for a full week, and occasion the performance of numerous folk rites. The cycle of the year, especially in agricultural communities, is also marked by many manifestations of folk religion that introduce color and excitement into folk life.

[*See also* Domestic Observances, *article on* Muslim Practices; Islamic Religious Year; *and* Rites of Passage, *article on* Muslim Rites.]

BIBLIOGRAPHY

In contrast to official Islam, which has been the subject of numerous excellent and systematical studies, there is not a single book dealing with the total field of folk religion in Muslim countries. There are, however, several fine studies dealing with certain aspects of Islamic folk religion, or with folk religion in individual Muslim countries. Among these the pride of place belongs to Edward A. Westermarck's *Marriage Ceremonies in Morocco* (1914; reprint, London, 1972) and *Ritual and Belief in Morocco* (1926; reprint, New Hyde Park, N.Y., 1968). His *Pagan Survivals in Mohammedan Civilization* (London, 1933) is more general but less thorough. Very valuable is Edmond Doutté's *Magie et religion dans l'Afrique du Nord* (Algiers, 1909), which, like Westermarck's books, deals with Morocco. Folk customs and beliefs in neighboring Algeria are discussed in Joseph Desparmet's *Coutumes, institutions, croyances des indigènes de l'Algérie*, 2d ed. (Algiers, 1913), and *Ethnographie traditionnelle de la Mettidja: Le mal magique* (Algiers, 1932). Folk religion in Arab Palestine is sketched in Samuel Ives Curtiss's *Primitive Semitic Religion Today* (New York, 1902) and figures prominently in Taufik Canaan's *Mohammedan Saints and Sanctuaries in Palestine* (London, 1927) and in Hilma Granqvist's *Birth and Childhood among the Arabs* (1947; reprint, New York, 1975), *Child Problems among the Arabs* (Helsinki, 1950), and *Muslim Death and Burial* (Helsinki, 1965). A discussion of Islam in India is contained in Jaʿfar Sharīf's *Islam in India, or the Qānūn-i-Islam*, translated by G. A. Herklots and edited by William Crooke (1921; reprint, London, 1972). A thorough study of Persian beliefs and customs is Henri Massé's *Croyances et coutumes persanes*, 2 vols. (Paris, 1938). The two classics on the survival of pre-Islamic religion in Islam are Julius Wellhausen's *Reste arabischen Heidentums*, 2d ed. (Berlin, 1897), and William Robertson Smith's *Lectures on the Religion of the Semites*, 2d ed. (1894; reprint, New York, 1969). Specific aspects of Islamic folk religion are covered in John Porter Brown's still very valuable *The Dervishes, or Oriental Spiritualism* (London, 1868), and in Toufic Fahd's *La divination arabe* (Leiden, 1966). Much information is contained in articles in the first edition of *The Encyclopaedia of Islam* (Leiden, 1931–1934) and in the new edition (Leiden, 1960–), found under Arabic titles such as *ʿayn*, *ghūl*, and *siḥr*.

Raphael Patai

FOMHOIRE. In all Irish mythology and folklore, the Fomhoire are a race of evil spirits. They merge, on the one hand, with the demons of Christianity and, on the other, with the Scandinavian invaders who oppressed and despoiled medieval Ireland. They are represented consistently as horrible beings—malicious, deformed, black, and diabolical. Their specific trait is singleness: they have only one eye, one arm, one leg. This trait of physical ugliness has been accentuated in the Christian transmission of the legends.

The principal text treating the Fomhoire is the long narrative the *Second Battle of Magh Tuiredh*, which recounts their defeat and expulsion from Ireland by the Tuatha Dé Danann. The problem of the Fomhoire is not resolved by their defeat, however, because actually they are spirits inherent in the land of Ireland: they never needed to arrive or to take possession of it.

The Fomhoire have strong genealogical and familial, even political, ties to the Tuatha Dé Danann that indicate a common origin. This origin is explicit in the name of their shared Fomorian ancestor: *Delbaeth* ("undifferentiated form"), one of the very rare indigenous Celtic expressions for the original chaos. The two central figures of the struggle between these groups have influence in both camps: Bres, the wicked interim king of the Tuatha Dé Danann, who is son of Eriu, a daughter of the Tuatha Dé Danann, and of the Fomorian Delbaeth; and Lugh, first god of the Irish pantheon and chief of the Tuatha Dé Danann, also of mixed parentage. Lugh slays his grandfather, the cyclopean giant Balar, and liberates Ireland from oppression by the Fomhoire.

The name *Fomhoire* has usually been interpreted in two different ways: as a compound of *fo* ("under") and *-moire* ("sea") or in relation to the root *mor* ("nightmare"). Though they express characteristics of the Fomhoire, these etymologies are not accurate. They do not take into account the alternation of *b* and *m*, frequent in Irish as in all Celtic languages, an alternation rendered more frequent from a very early date by the aspiration of both these consonants when in internal position. *Fomhoire* is an alternative form of *fobhar* ("spirit, specter"), and is undoubtedly a recent name, influenced by Christianity, for a very archaic mythic concept related to the Vedic *deva* and *asura*.

BIBLIOGRAPHY

For further information, see Christian-J. Guyonvarc'h's *Textes mythologiques irlandais*, vol. 1 (Rennes, 1980.)

FRANÇOISE LE ROUX AND CHRISTIAN-J. GUYONVARC'H
Translated from French by Erica Meltzer

FON AND EWE RELIGION. The Ewe and Fon, related linguistically and culturally, live along the coast and in the hinterland of Benin (formerly Dahomey), Togo, and eastern Ghana in West Africa. They number some three million; depend on fishing, intensive farming, and crafts (especially weaving); and live mostly in towns and large villages.

Europeans in contact with the Fon of Dahomey late in the seventeenth century left an exotic and exaggerated picture of kings, wealth, women soldiers ("Amazons"), brutal human sacrifice, and slave trading; such a picture has fallen into disrepute. Today the seat of the royal family is still centered in the towns of Abomey and Kana, which differ somewhat in both social organization and religion from the hinterland. The people today are organized into dispersed patrilineal clans in each of which the oldest living man is said to be "between the two worlds" of the living and the dead. There was traditionally a complex hierarchical organization from the compound to village chief to king. The kingdom has now lost its former political prerogatives but still retains many traditional ceremonies required by worship of the royal ancestors.

The Ewe of Togo and Ghana, historically representing the outposts of Fon civilization, share a sense of identity and history of migration (ultimately from Ọyọ in Nigeria) that is commemorated annually. The northern inland Ewe lack centralized political authority and have localized clans, while the coastal groups (known as Anlo Ewe) have a tradition of weak kingship, dispersed clans, and ancestral shrines that are of central importance in the religious life of the community. In each Ewe lineage there is a carved wooden stool, which is the locus of the cult of the lineage diety. During rituals this stool is the place to which ancestral spirits may temporarily be summoned.

Fon. The ancestral cult, believed to be necessary for the perpetuation of the clan, is the focal point of Fon social organization and of much religious activity. Funeral ceremonies for dead adults are concluded three years after their death so that their souls are not lost to the clan. Every decade or so the ancestors are "established," that is, they are deified as *tovodu* (family gods) by a rite in which a local group head must name all the dead group members from the most recently dead back to the earliest. At this rite an ancestral shrine *(dexoxo)* is built. There, the *tovodu* are annually "fed" and honored with dancing and praise songs. The individual who is seen as the human founder of a clan is also a deified ancestor; because of this status, the founder is worshiped by a cult of priests and initiates who do not necessarily belong to that particular clan. Royal clan members, however, may worship only their own ancestral deities and cannot be cult-initiates of "public" pantheons of gods; ancestral worship is their only form of religious affiliation.

More powerful than the *tovodu* are the spirits of those who lived so long ago that their names are no longer known by their descendants: these ancestors, personified by Dambada Hwedo, are important because a "forgotten" ancestor is angry and dangerous. Also in the *tovodu* category are the spirits of twins, of children born after twins, and of malformed and aborted children. These last spirits are considered very powerful as they guard the rivers over which the spirits of the dead must pass to reach the other world. Furthermore, the world of the dead reflects that of the living, with local rank there being established by priority of birth in the land of the living.

The Fon have a number of variant cosmologies, and some disagreement exists concerning the identities of the various deities. Some say that the world was created by one god, Nana Buluku, both male and female, who gave birth to twins named Mawu and Lisa; the first, female, was given command of the night, and the second, male, was associated with the day. Opinion varies as to the identifying characteristics and even the relationship between the twins, whose names are often merged together in everyday speech as though they were a single deity, Mawu-Lisa. In addition to being siblings, Mawu and Lisa are also spouses. [*See* Mawu-Lisa.] Other public gods who represent the forces of nature that affect all humans alike include Sagbata, the earth deity who watches over the fields and waters of the earth and punishes offenders with smallpox, and Sogbo, or Xevioso, the thunder and sea god who sends fertilizing rains but also punishes with his "ax," the thunderbolt. Under each of these is a pantheon of named deities *(vodu)* ranked according to their birth order, each with differing tasks. Worship of each pantheon of these gods is in the hands of an associated priesthood. None of these three pantheons of deities has universal worship.

No single god is all-powerful, not even Mawu who is the parent of the others and controls life and death. The "writing" of Mawu is called Fa, the destiny of the universe. A highly specialized system of divination (derived from the Yoruba), administered by officials known as *bokono,* permits humans to know what destiny has been decreed for them. Only the divine trickster Legba, who is the youngest son of Mawu, can change a person's destiny. His worship is universal (unlike that of the other major divinities) and individual, with neither priests nor cult houses. Other forms of divination are practiced, including mirror-gazing and the study of entrails. Finally, most widespread of all forms of divination are magical charms *(gbo)* of many and various kinds. These are said to be given to man by Legba and Sagbata, and especially by the *aziza,* small hairy creatures who live in anthills and silk-cotton trees *(Eriondendron anfractuosum).*

Ewe. The Ewe share many aspects of culture, religion, and art with the Fon and indeed occasionally travel to Benin to obtain shrines and spiritual aid. They share many gods, including Mawu, the remote creator god associated with the sky, and Torgbi-nyigbla, the head of the nature gods *(tro)* associated with war and thunder (and thus with Xevioso). Similar, too, are the practice of Afa divination and the Legba cult, including both *dulegba* and *alegba* (town and individual protective deities). There is, however, ambiguous usage among the Ewe of such key terms as *vodu, dulegba, tro,* and *dzo* (amulets), which are often confused. Most of these deities come from outside Eweland and each is thought of as a discrete entity; this inconsistent usage probably reflects differences in the history of migration and introduction of the cults.

Religious Change. Vast numbers of slaves were taken from the Fon-Ewe coast to the New World and they took many aspects of their religion with them. Syncretized with Catholicism in Haiti, Brazil, Cuba, and Jamaica, Fon and Ewe religions contributed important influences to the formation of many cults in the New World, including Voodoo *(vodoun)* and the cult of Shango, among others.

Christian missionaries have worked among the Fon and Ewe since the mid-nineteenth century. Today the vast majority of people declare themselves to be Christian, although most Ewe are involved in both Christian and traditional religious practices. In the north, reportedly, many rites of passage are now abandoned; traditional funerals, especially in the south, however, are still very important.

BIBLIOGRAPHY

The standard work on Fon religion is Melville J. Herskovits's *Dahomey: An Ancient West African Kingdom,* 2 vols. (New York, 1938); on the Ewe there are several early accounts, mostly very patchy and superficial, summarized by Madeline Manoukian in *The Ewe-speaking People of Togoland and the Gold Coast* (London, 1952). More recent works include D. K. Fiawoo's "The Influence of Contemporary Social Changes on the Magico-Religious Concepts and Organization of the Southern Ewe-speaking Peoples of Ghana" (Ph.D. diss., University of Edinburgh, 1958) and my "Mystical Protection among the Anlo Ewe," *African Arts* 15 (August 1982): 60–66, 90.

MICHELLE GILBERT

FOOD. Historians of religion and cultural anthropologists face an extraordinarily diffcult task when they attempt to analyze food customs on a worldwide basis. This is because dietary laws, food taboos, and the religious and social environments that have molded them are as varied as the human race itself.

Though there are no universal food customs or food taboos, such things are part of the daily life of every society. [*See* Taboo.] Both nonliterate and highly advanced societies have placed restrictions on what their members may or may not eat and on the circumstances in which certain types of nourishment may be taken. Foods that are thus singled out take on a symbolic significance they would not otherwise possess. In many instances, religious observances are such an integral part of daily life that they cannot be distinguished from purely social proprieties.

Food Taboos. Many salient features of a group's religious beliefs come into sharper focus when specific food taboos are studied.

Judaism. The Jewish religion has a well-defined and long-established body of dietary laws. Most are found in the Pentateuch, in *Leviticus, Deuteronomy, Genesis,* and *Exodus.* Others come from rabbinic teachings that over a period of time acquired the force of religious law.

When the Jews were definitively exiled from Palestine by the Romans in the first century CE, their identity was immediately placed in jeopardy. It was all but inevitable that the Jews would respond to this danger by strengthening their interpretation of their distinctive dietary laws. [*See* Kashrut.] It was at this point in their history that the ritual slaughter of animals became mandatory; the flesh of animals had to be presoaked and then salted to draw off any blood that remained, for blood was a symbol of life, and life belonged to God. Dairy and meat products were separated, both in preparation and eating. Rabbinic Judaism stipulated that these two kinds of foods be prepared and eaten with entirely separate sets of utensils. To ensure that wine too was kosher, it had to be made by Jews. There were no restrictions on fruits and vegetables.

Specifically, Jewish dietary laws, among many other things, permit the eating of fish that have both fins and scales. Animals that chew the cud and have cloven feet may also be consumed. Pork is excluded from Jewish diets because swine have cloven feet but do not chew the cud.

In an effort to defend this proscription against pork on rational grounds, great moment has been made of hygiene and the well-known danger of contracting trichinosis from undercooked pork. What seems to be overlooked or ignored is the fact that parasitic diseases were not identified until the nineteenth century and that dietary laws have been part and parcel of Jewish observances for over two millennia. Ritual avoidance of certain foods can sometimes, of course, be beneficial to health. But incidental benefits do not explain the existence of the taboos themselves. Moreover, if hygiene and health are in fact the *raison d'être* of Jewish dietary laws, why do perfectly wholesome foods also fall into the category of proscribed foods?

For many observant Jews, no rational justification of their dietary laws is needed. The mere fact that Yahveh has so ordained is a totally sufficient reason unto itself.

It should be noted that followers of Reform Judaism (a religious movement that began early in the nineteenth century) have abandoned many traditional Jewish practices, including the observance of dietary laws. Declaring religious faith and ethics to be the sole criteria of authentic Judaism, they have dispensed with dietary laws as anachronistic.

Hasidic Jews, on the other hand, have adopted dietary laws that in several ways are more stringent than those observed by Orthodox Jews. In doing so, they provide additional evidence that food customs serve to distinguish and separate members even of the same religious group. Hasidic food customs thus symbolize something more than mere Jewishness. They call attention to the special character of the Ḥasidim, or "pious ones."

The notion of clean and unclean is also fundamental to Jewish dietary laws. Before approaching the altar to perform the Temple sacrifices, priests cleansed themselves through ritual ablutions and were often the only persons permitted to consume the sacrificial offerings. Cleanliness based on food regulations set them apart; it also created classes among other segments of the Jewish community including the Levites, Nazirites, and soldiers.

Islam. Islamic dietary laws, as spelled out in the Qur'ān, clearly reflect many elements of the Mosaic law. Muslims are forbidden, for example, to consume blood and pork. They may not consume food that has been offered to idols or the flesh of animals that have been found dead. Animals must be slaughtered according to a ritual that calls for the cutting of the windpipe, carotid arteries, and gullet; while performing these duties the butcher invokes the name of God. No Muslim may partake of alcoholic beverages, but he remains free of sin if he is forced to eat forbidden foods. Though Islamic dietary laws apply to all Muslims, they do not distinguish social classes as they do in certain other religions.

Hinduism. In a discussion of food taboos, the caste system of India offers the best example of the relationship between food customs and social systems. In India there are so many rules of pollution and purity that any search for coherence must be found in a complete investigation of Indian social, economic, and religious life. Food in relation to pollution must be considered in terms of its production, preparation, and eating; all play an important role in protecting the boundaries of the caste system.

One of the most important elements of Hindu ritual is clarified butter, ghee. During a marriage ceremony, for instance, the principals—bride, groom, and priests—face a ritual fire that is periodically fed by butter spooned onto the flames. Butter, as a symbol of purity, is also used by Hindus to bathe religious statues.

Food prepared with ghee is reserved for the highest class, the brahmans. The food must not be tasted by the cook because of the danger of touching the fingers to the lips, thereby losing the condition of purity. Saliva is extremely defiling, even one's own.

Christianity. When we turn to the Christian cultures, one of the most striking features of dietary laws is their virtual nonexistence. This curious fact leads us to a brief survey of the early history of Christianity. Because the first disciples of Jesus were good Jews, they observed the Mosaic dietary laws. But when Paul began his mission to the gentiles, new ethnic frontiers were breached. The universality of Christianity deprived it of cultural identity, and that in turn left no single cultural frame of reference to give form to dietary laws, as had been the case with Judaism and other religions. Mark quotes Jesus as saying: "Nothing that goes into a man from outside can pollute him" (*Mk.* 7:15). Mark then proceeded to editorialize when he remarked that Jesus declared all food to be clean. This also seems to be the significance of Peter's vision about killing and eating unclean animals (*Acts* 10:9–16). While it is true that certain restrictions on food were reaffirmed in *Acts* 15:20, many exegetes contend that the affirmation was nothing more than a desire to avoid scandalizing Judaic Christians. With the exception of the Coptic rite, all Christian dietary laws were moribund by the end of the second century. Abstention from meat on Friday was never more than a disciplinary law in the Roman Catholic church.

Modern Research. In an attempt to make sense out of the bewildering array of food customs that have been documented in both ancient and modern societies at all stages of their development, scholars have traveled many different roads in order to discover common elements that would justify the organization of food customs into intelligible categories that could then be discussed as distinct units.

An investigation of food customs, however, may reveal that many taboos do not seem to be rational. There is, to be sure, a reason for each taboo, but the reason often has little or nothing to do with intellectual considerations. In any such investigation, it is important that conclusions drawn not even be presumed to apply to peoples in like circumstances, because food customs involve many factors that come into play in certain societies but not in others.

Many anthropologists consider social identity to be a powerful factor in preserving a given society's dietary laws. Such customs set peoples apart; they foster group unity; they protect identities. While this is true in certain cases, the larger question persists: is the desire to remain separate and distinctive, especially in the case of a minority group that must struggle to prevent assimilation into a larger group, an adequate explanation for the existence of food taboos? Or is the desire to retain one's identity merely a powerful motive for observing customs that have more ancient origins? Or, perhaps, is the preservation of a group's identity simply a by-product of such observances? These and similar questions still beg definitive answers.

In *Purity and Danger* (1966), Mary Douglas focuses on spiritual pollution in a thought-provoking analysis of food taboos. Religions, she says, have an interest in providing their adherents with a sense of identity. This is accomplished through symbolic activities that are related to concrete aspects of social behavior. Among the most fundamental and important of these is eating—the production, preparation, and consumption of food. Douglas then suggests that food taboos are best understood in the context of spiritual pollution.

That any given food can have a spiritually polluting quality independent of a cultural context does not seem to be based on an objective fact. This means that spiritual defilement cannot be understood apart from a system of ideas that, in effect, creates a specific universe for each society. Cleanliness, in this context, becomes an attribute of anything that contributes to the order of that universe. [*See* Purification.] Douglas then introduces the word *dirt* to signify anything that is at odds with that order and its established relationships. Whatever disrupts that order creates chaos; it is spiritually polluting and unclean. It is "dirt" and therefore taboo. When this hypothesis is applied to Judaism, the law of Moses is seen as dividing the universe of the Jews into three types of creatures: those whose natural environment is either land, sea, or sky (see *Lv.* 12). Creatures that do not meet the stipulated requirements of their respective categories are taboo.

Though broad outlines of this theory are easy to grasp, the hypothesis ought to be tested by applying the categories to each element of various dietary laws. The theory stands or falls on the validity of its application. Special taboos either fit the pattern or raise doubts about its legitimacy.

Holiness is another term that assumes great importance in Douglas's vocabulary. She notes that each injunction to observe the Mosaic law is prefaced by a command to be holy. The root meaning of the Hebrew word for "holiness," an attribute of Yahveh, is "to set apart."

God's blessing, Douglas explains, creates and preserves order, and this assures that man's affairs will prosper. If man observes God's law, is faithful to his commandments, and observes the covenant, dangers recede and prosperity ensues. When God's blessing is withdrawn, man is under a curse and confusion reigns. Man must consequently foster holiness in his own life to become godlike—whole, complete, perfect. The law required the Temple priest to be holy and enjoined worshipers to present offerings that were without blemish—be they lambs, pigeons, turtledoves, or cereals. Dietary laws thus embody the notion of holiness by designating persons, places, and things as sacred, set apart, whole, or blemish-free. Anything that falls short of perfection is defective and therefore unclean. It is, in Douglas's expression, "dirt." Because awareness of imperfections means a concomitant awareness of the perfection and purity of Yahveh, dietary laws serve as constant reminders of his holiness. Every meal becomes an indirect encounter with God.

One of the implications of Douglas's theory is that each group or society must be studied separately. First, it must be determined how each group has constructed its universe and according to what norms and principles. Confirmation of the theory would then depend on the degree and manner in which food customs, work, sex, and other human activities reflect that universe.

Some anthropologists have linked food taboos to ecology. Their argument is most persuasive when applied to tribes living in lands where food is scarce and wildlife dangerous. To assure an adequate supply of scarce foods, hunter-gatherer societies have invested these foods with a symbolic significance that sets them apart and restricts their use. Though this theory may be applicable to certain nomadic societies, it does not apply to the vast majority of peoples and their food taboos.

The notion of social identity has also been viewed as a means of avoiding contamination from one's "pagan neighbors." This interpretation was inspired by studies of minority groups fearful of losing their identities and of religious communities living in environments where several cults were vying with one another for broader acceptance. In such situations, religious observances, including dietary practices, were tantamount to public confessions of faith.

The Israelites found themselves in just such a predicament. Some scholars, accordingly, affirm that the Israelites viewed pork as abhorrent and unclean because pigs were worshiped by their "pagan neighbors," the Egyptians and the Canaanites. History, to be sure, confirms that the Israelites sedulously shunned certain Canaanite practices, but it also bears witness to the fact that the Jews took a benign view of other Canaanite rituals and apparently felt no compunction about adopting them. Could it be that the Israelites instinctively turned away from some of the practices of their neighbors and embraced others, on the basis of established Jewish thought? If so, Mary Douglas's case is strengthened.

Food taboos have also been analyzed in terms of psychology. Writers who approach the subject in this manner speculate that food is a symbol of sexuality and identity because nursing brings the infant and mother together in their first intimate contact. This view suggests that an infant derives not only its attitude toward food from its mother but also, as a direct consequence, broader attitudes such as those regarding money and wealth and the willingness or reluctance to share these things with others. Much has been made of the infant-mother relationship. It is the most intimate of all human relationships and exists in every society at every stage of development. For that very reason it cannot explain the immense variety and selectivity of food taboos that have flourished in every society from time immemorial. It is also appropriate to ask what it was that molded a mother's view of the world in the first place.

Claude Lévi-Strauss has looked at the structure of human thought and related it to the structure of human society. Using linguistic analysis as a model, he has affirmed that the cooking of food can be viewed as a kind of language because it expresses thoughts and ideas that can be clearly understood by those who are attentive to what is being "said." The categories represented in food taboos help people perceive their worlds in terms of polarities that exist in the structure of the mind. Categories thus aid in maintaining such binary divisions as nature/culture and animal/man. Lévi-Strauss finds it unnecessary to examine each food taboo in great detail, concentrating instead on the basic relationships that he contends exist among their constituent elements. In time, he believes, all cultures will be found to have similar structures.

Two eminent and influential scholars who stressed the importance of fieldwork during the first half of the twentieth century were A. R. Radcliffe-Brown and Bronislaw Malinowski. Representing what has become known as the functional approach to social anthropology, they were chiefly concerned with the connections they believed tie various social institutions to one another. For them, food serves a social function and indicates a person's place in his community.

Radcliffe-Brown cites the example of the Andaman Islanders, whose most important social activity is the acquisition of food. For these people, food is also the instrument that unites their society, preserves their traditions, and instills in the young the society's value system. The social importance of food is communicated to impressionable boys and girls through initiation rites and food taboos that become less restrictive as the children mature. These children are thus incorporated into a society with strong food traditions that reflect social values.

Africa provides further evidence of the functional role of food in certain societies. In Ghana, for example, village women usually eat with the children rather than with their husbands. In cases where dowries are substantial and the norms of inheritance are well defined, however, women of high social status tend to eat with men of equal status and partake of the same cuisine. Audrey I. Richards notes that even the cooking of porridge can have functional significance inasmuch as it can be a normal way of expressing the correct relationship between a woman and various male relatives.

The functional approach places more emphasis on social meanings of food regulations than on religious meanings. Food transactions are looked upon as expressions of social relations, as in marriage transfers. This functional point of view is applied not only to food customs but also to the production and distribution of food.

Another approach to food customs has been offered by A. E. Crawley. A student of primitive religions and marriage, he developed a special interest in the relationship between food customs and sex and perceived "spiritual dangers" in sexual relations. The linkage between sex and food customs is exemplified by the Bantu-speaking Lele of Africa. During a Lele woman's monthly period she neither cooks for her husband nor pokes the coals of the fire lest he fall ill. After sexual intercourse, the wife must cleanse her husband and then wash herself before cooking. To do otherwise would jeopardize her husband's virility. Among the

Bemba of central Africa, children are protected from death that could result, it is believed, from contact with a cooking fire that had been contaminated by a person who had failed to perform ritual purification after engaging in sex. Moreover, a Jewish dietary law reads: "You shall not boil a kid in its mother's milk." This injunction has also led certain scholars to develop relationships between food taboos and sex. As stated above, in some cultures there appear to be hints of just such relationships. It is almost as if, in the quotation cited above, the law were prohibiting culinary incest.

While there are other interesting parallels between sex and food taboos, a truly satisfying elucidation of dietary customs would require that very broad sociocultural considerations be included.

Anthropologists have also studied societies at various levels of social and technological development. Horizontal analysis serves practical ends, even though the categories thus created are somewhat arbitrary and do not always reflect the complexity of the real world. Even so, comparing different groups at the same relative stage of development, or studying the same group at progressive stages of its own development, has been rewarding. Research has revealed, for example, that hunter-gatherer societies have much in common, whether they live in desert regions, the Arctic, India, or Africa. Anthropologists place such nomads on the lowest rung of the ladder of social sophistication. It may be thought that these small unstable communities, often living precarious lives amidst scarcity and danger, would utilize all available food to the maximum. But such peoples also have food taboos that exclude or restrict the use of certain foods. The Alaska Inuit (Eskimo), for instance, draw a distinction between land and sea foods that is reminiscent of Jewish dietary laws regarding meat and dairy products. The Inuit are taught that these restrictions cannot be disregarded with impunity, for to do so is to court misfortune.

A higher stage of development is reached when a group takes up permanent residence on land over which it exercises exclusive rights. At that stage, initiation rites welcoming children into the adult community become more elaborate and are celebrated with feasts and the exchange of gifts of food. The acquisition and distribution of food becomes one of the strongest bonds uniting these communities.

When an individual or group begins to exercise political or economic control over several communities, chiefdoms or principalities evolve. During this stage of a community's history, food is gathered and stored for use during festivals, religious celebrations, and periods of famine. To ensure adequate food reserves, chiefs characteristically resort to intimidation by warning that dire consequences await those who disregard the food taboos. A fisherman, for example, might well believe that his future well-being depends on turning over a portion of his catch to those in charge of the community.

Food and Sacrifice. There is a vast body of literature on the origins and meaning of sacrifice and the role it has played in human history. [*See* Sacrifice.] The objects of sacrifice have been almost anything that seemed appropriate, notably the first fruits of the land. Cereal offerings were common to many cultures because they were the staple of the diet and thus fitting symbols of man's gratitude to the gods for their beneficence. It is not surprising, therefore, that peoples of all races have felt the need to offer sacrifices to their respective deities as providers of life-sustaining foods.

Animals of all types have also been sacrificed according to rites dictated by individual cultures. The proper preparation of the sacrifice was often an integral part of the prescribed ritual.

In a quite different way, however, Christianity has perpetuated the ancient tradition of celebrating sacrifice. The eucharistic meal consists of bread and wine. These foods commemorate the Last Supper, which anticipated the death and resurrection of Jesus. In the setting of a Passover meal, Jesus declared the bread and wine to be his body and blood. Jesus said: "This is my blood, drink all of it." These words were in direct conflict with the Old Covenant, which strictly forbade the consumption of blood. Another example of food used in Christian rituals is salt, which was placed on the tongue of the one about to be baptized to signify wisdom.

In some religions, it was unthinkable that the gods could be in need of food offerings. This fundamental tenet of faith was confirmed through burnt offerings. Because nothing but ashes remained after the offering was consumed by fire, the sacrifice became invisible and symbolic.

This ritual possibly led to the sacrificial meal, during which the cultic community consumed food in the presence of the deity. By admitting man to his table, the god became bound to the community in a special relationship. The eating of foods sacrificed by members of a different cult was an unspeakable abomination. In ancient religions most of the ordinary functions of worship were summed up in sacrificial meals. A part of the meal often signified the whole, so that breaking bread together or sharing salt became synonymous with brotherhood and alliance. Communal meals thus came to have both religious and human dimensions.

Funerary offerings constitute another major category

of sacrifices. Providing food for the dead is a very ancient practice followed by a wide variety of peoples even in remote areas of the world. Concern for the welfare of the dead is based on the belief that the soul needs nourishment until it reaches its final resting place. The obligation to make such offerings is especially incumbent upon the heirs of the deceased, but it also extends to other relatives. Food could be left on top of the grave, placed in pottery that is buried in the ground, or even put into the mouths of the deceased. The Greeks and Romans made much of libations and used funnels to convey wine from the surface of the earth to the grave below. By long-established tradition, food has a key role in such rites of passage as birth, marriage, and initiation into the adult community. The identity and role of each member of the community is confirmed by such ceremonies, which by their very nature unite the group and contribute to its continuity and preservation.

Fasting. Just as the sacrificial meal expresses thanksgiving and unity with the deity, so fasting indicates such things as repentance, petition, and passage to a new status in life. One of the most universal of religious practices, fasting is even in modern times commonly associated with asceticism. [*See* Fasting.] It is widely considered to be a means of attaining grace. Shamans fast in order to see visions. For centuries Roman Catholics fasted during the penitential season of Lent and at other shorter periods during the liturgical year.

Under the influence of the great religions of India, abstinence became a way of life for many people and total abstention from meat highly meritorious. Complete abstention from fermented beverages is a basic tenet of many religious beliefs and applies in some cases to all adherents, in others only to priests and holy men.

For Muslims, fasting is so important during Ramaḍān that it constitutes the fourth of the five pillars of Islam. Muslims may not eat or drink from sunrise to sunset during the entire month of Ramaḍān. Those who are sick or traveling are supposed to fast an equal number of days at some other time. [*See* Ṣawm.]

Myths about the Origin and Role of Foods. Social anthropologists have also gathered abundant evidence of myths that, in sometimes different ways, account for the origins of certain foods, notably tubers and cereals, by linking their existence to ancestral deities known collectively as *dema*. For instance, the inhabitants of Ceram, an island in the Indonesian archipelago, tell the story of a quasi-divine young girl whose body produced tubers after it was cut up and buried. These tubers are believed to harbor a divine substance that is transmitted to those who eat them.

A belief among the Ojibwa Indians of North America bears a striking resemblance to that just mentioned. The Great Spirit, according to the Ojibwa, dispatched a celestial being to Earth. After fighting with an impoverished Indian, the sky visitor died and was buried. Maize, a staple of the Indians' diet, later began to grow on the grave site. For this reason the Indians revere corn as a divine gift.

In Tongan mythology, Eel was condemned to death for allegedly causing the pregnancy of a virgin who shared his Samoan bathing pool. Villagers who planted Eel's severed head, as he had requested, testified that the coconut tree first appeared on that very spot. Another Polynesian myth affirms that the breadfruit tree emerged from the plot where a woman had buried the head of her husband.

Variations of this death-produces-food theme have been found in numerous mythologies. Some speak of a child or man who consented to be immolated so that his body might produce food plants of one sort or another. In a similar vein, Peruvians believe that a divine force ensures the growth and fertility of all food plants. For that reason they use maize stalks to fashion effigies in honor of the Mother of Maize.

In many of these myths, death becomes a source of new life and of life-sustaining foods. Myths that focus on divinities also serve to establish a continuity between the primordial world and the present world of human beings.

The deaths of divine beings, it is also believed, created a need for food. Man can both satisfy a basic human need and participate in the existence of divinities by eating foods provided by deities.

Hsi Wang Mu, the Chinese Queen Mother of the West, figures in myths that associate immortality with certain foods. According to Taoist beliefs, Hsi Wang Mu presides over a female fairyland called Hsi Hua. In this realm is a garden celebrated for its rare flowers and exotic birds, that produces *p'an t'ao*, the flat peach of immortality. During the Ming dynasty, a *p'an t'ao* stone was reportedly discovered among treasure acquired by earlier Yüan dynasty rulers. Ten engraved characters identified the stone as coming from the *p'an t'ao* that Hsi Wang Mu had given to a Han dynasty emperor some fifteen centuries earlier.

The *Epic of Gilgamesh* describes the renowned Mesopotamian hero's relentless search for immortality. With the help of Utanapishtim he succeeds in locating a plant that was said to frustrate death by restoring youth to one who ate it. Gilgamesh's hopes, however, were dashed when a serpent stole the precious plant.

The practice of cannibalism, which existed at one time or another in virtually every part of the world, most commonly involved specific human organs rather than the indiscriminate eating of human flesh. [*See* Cannibalism.] In many instances, cannibalism was the concluding act of ritual murders or an essential element of sorcery. (This latter practice suggests another broad field of inquiry: the role of food in the context of magic.) Those who consumed the flesh of slain enemies commonly believed they could absorb the manly qualities of their victims. Aboriginal Australians are known to have feasted on the bodies of deceased relatives as an act of respect. It should be noted, however, that although some closely related ethnic groups sometimes practiced cannibalism, others thought it an abomination.

Food also plays an important role in myths of the netherworld. In Greek mythology, for example, Hades attempted to induce his wife Persephone to eat a pomegranate so that it would be impossible for her ever to leave his domain. He failed, but because Persephone had eaten a single pomegranate seed, she was destined to live in the underworld for part of every year. Similar myths documented in New Caledonia, New Guinea, and other regions recall the conflict between Mot, the Semitic god of the dead and infertility, and his archenemy Baal, the god of springs, sky, and fertility.

The sense of taste appears to play a relatively minor role in most myths about food, but it becomes a powerful religious metaphor during the Jewish feast of Passover. Bitter herbs are eaten during the Seder meal to remind Jews that their ancestors endured "bitter lives" while slaves of the Egyptian pharaohs. The *Psalms* of the Old Testament also use this metaphor in recommending that we "taste and see that the Lord is good" (34:8) and later, in remarking that the Lord's words taste as sweet as honey (119:103).

From all that has been said, one fact stands out in bold relief: food in religious life is a subject of immense proportions. The study of food in India alone, for example, would tax any ordinary scholar's endurance, because the food customs and taboos there are inextricably tied to notions of purity and contamination, the caste system, religion, sex, and even economics. Tribal societies and the countries of East Asia are also fertile fields awaiting further investigation.

[*For a discussion of the relationship between food acquisition and religious symbolism, see* Agriculture. *See also entries on specific foods:* Salt; Bread; Leaven; *and* Beverages.]

BIBLIOGRAPHY

André, Jacques. *L'alimentation et la cuisine à Rome.* Paris, 1961. Food customs in ancient Rome.

Campbell, Joseph. *The Masks of God,* vol. 1, *Primitive Mythology.* New York, 1959. Food myths of planters and hunters are discussed in this important work.

Chang, K. C., ed. *Food in Chinese Culture: Anthropological and Historical Perspectives.* New Haven, 1977. Indispensable for an insight into the importance and complexity of Chinese food customs.

Darby, William, Paul Ghalioungui, and Louis Grivetti. *Food: The Gift of Osiris.* 2 vols. London, 1977. Contains illustrations from ancient Egypt and summaries of different foods of the time.

Douglas, Mary. *Purity and Danger: An Analysis of Concepts of Pollution and Taboo.* New York, 1966. An excellent study of how food customs mirror the ordered patterning of a society. Douglas's approach applies equally to secular and to religious life, both primitive and modern.

Eliade, Mircea. *Patterns in Comparative Religion.* New York, 1958. Chapter 8 of this classic deals with "Vegetation: Rites and Symbols of Regeneration" and chapter 9 with "Agriculture and Fertility Cults."

Goody, Jack. *Cooking, Cuisine and Class: A Study in Comparative Sociology.* Cambridge, 1982. Begins with a summary of the advances made by anthropologists and sociologists in their study of food customs. Compares differences in African and Eurasian cuisine as reflections of their different societal structures.

Kilgallen, John J. "All Food Is Clean." *The Bible Today* 19 (July 1981): 259–263. Discussion of the texts in the New Testament that led to the abrogation of the Mosaic dietary laws for Christians.

Lévi-Strauss, Claude. *Tristes tropiques* (1955). 2d ed., rev. Paris, 1968. Published in English under the same title (New York, 1974).

Lévi-Strauss, Claude. *Mythologiques.* 4 vols. Paris, 1964–1971. See particularly volumes 1, 2, and 4, published in English as *The Raw and the Cooked* (New York, 1969), *From Honey to Ashes* (New York, 1973), and *The Naked Man* (New York, 1981). Lévi-Strauss offers complex analyses of tribal myths, many of which deal with food.

Prakash, Om. *Food and Drinks in Ancient India: From Earliest Times to c. 1200 A.D.* Delhi, 1961. Contains lists of types of food in different eras with some commentary about practices. The primary sources are cited in Sanskrit.

Simoons, Frederick. *Eat Not This Flesh: Food Avoidances in the Old World.* Madison, Wis., 1961. A popular treatment of the subject.

Soler, Jean. "Semiotics of Food in the Bible." In *Food and Drink in History,* edited by Robert Forster and Orest Ranum, pp. 126–138. Baltimore, 1979. A structuralist approach to the dietary laws in the Hebrew Bible. A clear and convincing article similar to the work of Mary Douglas.

Tannahill, Reay. *Food in History.* New York, 1973. A popular treatment of the subject but useful for its bibliography.

JAMES E. LATHAM

FOOLS, HOLY. *See* Clowns; *see also* Humor and Satire. *Discussion of holy fools in specific traditions can be found in articles under* Drama.

FORTUNA was the Latin and perhaps Sabine goddess of the incalculable element in life. Her name is derived from the Latin word *fors* ("luck"). In Rome Fortuna was extraneous to the oldest stratum of cults traditionally connected with King Numa Pompilius. She was considered the special patron and friend of King Servius Tullius, who was credited with the building of the two oldest temples to her in Rome. One, in the Forum Boarium, was associated with the temple of Mater Matuta; the other, on the right side of the Tiber, was specifically known as Fanum Fortis Fortunae. Two other temples were dedicated in 293 BCE and 17 CE. Fortuna appealed to the lower classes of Roman society and in particular to slaves: she was considered a benefactor rather than a menace. Some forms of her cult appealed to special categories of persons. The cult put emphasis on fertility or on success in certain endeavors. Fortuna Muliebris, whose sanctuary was immediately outside Rome on the Via Latina, was worshiped by married women and played a part in the legend of Coriolanus. On 1 April Fortuna Virilis, associated with Venus, was worshiped by women with prayers and ritual baths in men's bathhouses. A special cult of Fortuna Virgo is doubtful. Fortuna Equestris received a temple in 173 BCE after a victory of the Roman cavalry, whereas a temple to "Fortune of this day" (Fortuna Huiusce Dies) celebrated the victory by Q. Lutatius Catulus at Vercellae in 101 BCE. Chapels and altars to Fortuna Bona, Fortuna Mala, Fortuna Dubia, Fortuna Publica, and others multiplied, along with dedications to the Fortuna of certain localities. These minor monuments took more notice of the negative aspects of Fortuna. Later imperial temples in Rome and elsewhere connect Fortuna, always positively, with the emperors (Fortuna Augusta, Fortuna Redux).

The sanctuary of Fortuna Primigenia at Praeneste (modern-day Palestrina) presented Fortuna as *filia primigenia* (first daughter of Jupiter?), a most unusual notion in a Latin context. Indo-European, Etruscan, or Greek influence has been suggested. Cicero adds to the confusion by describing the Fortuna of Praeneste as Jupiter's nurse (*De divinatione* 2.85). The building, excavated by Italian archaeologists, belongs to approximately the second century BCE, but the cult itself, famous for its oracle, is certainly much older. After a period of friction with Roman authorities, the cult of Fortuna Primigenia was introduced from Praeneste to Rome toward the end of the Second Punic War. It became very popular. The first temple to Fortuna Primigenia on the Quirinal was soon followed by two other temples on the same hill. Another famous center of the cult of Fortuna with an oracle was in Antium (Horace, *Carmina* 1.35). Here, for unexplained reasons, the worship was to two Fortunas.

The diffusion of the cult of Fortuna in Italy and in the Latin West was influenced by the corresponding Greek cult of Tyche. This is evident in the iconography of Fortuna, who is often represented, like Tyche, as a standing woman with a rudder in her right hand and a cornucopia in her left hand. Like Tyche, Fortuna was in some cases depicted with several attributes of Isis. The interference of Tyche is also clear in literary texts (for instance, in works by Horace and Seneca) that try to clarify the nature of Fortuna. Goddess Fortuna was occasionally identified with Nemesis and associated with Felicitas and Bonus Eventus. In Pompeii she is included among the *penates*.

BIBLIOGRAPHY

Champeaux, Jacqueline. *Fortuna,* vol. 1. Rome, 1982. Reviewed by Gerhard Radke in *Gnomon* 56 (1984): 419–426.

Fasolo, Furio, and Giorgio Gullini. *Il santuario della Fortuna Primigenia a Palestrina.* Rome, 1953.

Kajanto, Iiro. "Fortuna." In *Aufstieg und Niedergang der römischen Welt,* vol. 2.17.1, pp. 502–558. Berlin and New York, 1981.

Otto, Walter F. "Fortuna." In *Real-Encyclopädie der classischen Altertumswissenschaft,* vol. 13, cols. 12–42. Stuttgart, 1910.

Radke, Gerhard. *Die Götter Altitaliens.* Münster, 1965. See pages 132–134.

Wissowa, Georg. *Religion und Kultus der Römer.* 2d ed. Munich, 1912. See pages 256–258.

ARNALDO MOMIGLIANO

FORTUNE. *See* Chance *and* Fate.

FOUCHER, ALFRED (1865–1952), French Indologist, specialist in Buddhist archaeology. Alfred C. A. Foucher studied in Paris, under the guidance of Sylvain Lévi, and in India (1895–1897), where he combined philosophical training at the Sanskrit College of Banaras with "militant" archaeology through extensive pilgrimages to several places of historical interest.

Foucher was a pioneer in the area of religious archaeology with his study of the relation between artistic representations and their doctrinal and literary background. His field of predilection was the area known as Gandhara (roughly, those portions of Afghanistan and Pakistan between the Hindu Kush mountains and the Indus River), where the Indian and Greek worlds had been in contact at around the beginning of the common era. The publication of Foucher's *L'art gréco-bouddhique du Gandhâra: Étude sur les origines de l'influence clas-*

sique dans l'art bouddhique de l'Inde et de l'Extrême-Orient extended over half a century and comprised three volumes: volume 1, *Introduction; Les édifices; Les bas-reliefs* (1905); volume 2, *Images* (1922); and volume 3, *Additions et corrections; index* (1951). Though criticized for some of its conclusions regarding chronology and style, this work remains the most accurate sourcebook on early Buddhist iconography.

Foucher's interest in Gandhara received a new impulse when Afghanistan opened its frontiers to archaeological investigation. Foucher, who was then working at the Archaeological Survey of India (1919–1921), was immediately *à pied d'œuvre* as the first director of the Délégation Archéologique Française en Afghanistan (1921–1925). In Afghanistan, as previously in Northwest India, his habit of methodically following the itinerary of Hsüan-tsang, his natural gift for observation, and his archaeological insight led Foucher to remarkable discoveries in Haḍḍa, Kāpiśī-Bēgrām, Bamian, Balkh, and the Lampaka-Laghmān region. [*For information concerning Hsüan-tsang's travels, see the biography of Hsüan-tsang.*] The gist of these discoveries is expressed in a work accomplished with the collaboration of his wife, Eugénie Bazin-Foucher, *La vieille route de l'Inde de Bactres à Taxila* (2 vols., 1942–1947). Foucher also collaborated with John Marshall in editing the three huge volumes of *The Monuments of Sanchi* (1939), a work focused on the main Buddhist site of central India.

The clear-sightedness of Foucher as an archaeologist was no doubt the result of his deep penetration of the Indian tradition. Foucher, who used old texts as guides in his archaeological researches, in turn used monuments for a better understanding of Buddhism and especially of its founder, Śākyamuni Buddha. Foucher's best-known book, *La vie du Bouddha* (1949; English trans., 1963) is, significantly, subtitled *D'après les textes et les monuments de l'Inde.* Foucher was aware of all the difficulties of such a biography. In 1894 he had translated from German into French Hermann Oldenberg's study of the Buddha's life (*Le Bouddha, sa vie, sa doctrine, sa communauté*, 2d ed., 1903), which remains the best "positive" history of the Buddha following the Pali sources. At the same time, Foucher was much in contact with Émile Senart, who had proposed a mythical interpretation of the life of the Buddha. In the 1930s, Foucher had also witnessed the brilliant attempt at a new interpretation of Buddhism through archaeology and sociology made by his young contemporary Paul Mus. It was only at the end of his life that Foucher's own biography of the Buddha came to maturation. This book shows the geographical (centers of pilgrimages) and historical (superposition of hagiographical patterns) influences on the tales surrounding Śākyamuni. It remains the most satisfactory approach toward the personality of the historical Buddha as he has been seen through the Asian tradition.

Though deeply original in his method and his achievements, Foucher cannot be isolated from a golden age of French philological studies of which he is a typical representative. Even if different in spirit, his *La vie du Bouddha* recalls the much earlier *Vie de Jésus* (1863) by Foucher's fellow Breton, Ernest Renan. Foucher's systematic inventory of architectural remains and iconographical documents as an approach to an understanding of Buddhism has a parallel in the encyclopedic research on Christian symbolism done by his contemporary Émile Mâle.

Besides his already mentioned sojourns in India and Afghanistan, Foucher lived for a time in French Indochina (1901 and 1905–1907), where he succeeded his friend Louis Finot as the director of the École Française d'Extrême-Orient, and in Japan (1925–1926), where he established with Sylvain Lévi the Maison Franco-Japonaise.

BIBLIOGRAPHY

In addition to the writings mentioned above, Foucher's *The Beginnings of Buddhist Art and Other Essays in Indian and Central-Asian Archaeology* (London, 1917) should be noted. Although outdated, it remains a testimony to his exactitude, clarity, and elegance. For bibliographic data, see Shinshō Hanayama's *Bibliography on Buddhism* (Tokyo, 1961); *Bibliographie bouddhique*, 32 vols., compiled by Marcelle Lalou (Paris, 1928–1967); and Henri Deydier's *Contribution à l'étude de l'art du Gandhâra* (Paris, 1950). A biographical sketch of Foucher can be found in Alfred Merlin's "Notice sur la vie et les travaux de M. Alfred Foucher," in *Académie des Inscriptions et Belles Lettres: Comptes rendus* (Paris, 1954), pp. 457–469.

HUBERT DURT

FOUNDATION RITES comprise a number of customs, magical practices, and beliefs having to do with the erection of small private buildings (particularly houses) and certain large public edifices (churches, schools, castles, mills, gates, and cities) or with the repair of dikes. These customs, practices, and beliefs are reflected in popular legends, tales, and songs that, in turn, supplement our information about certain details of construction rituals and, more important, about the prominence of construction rites in the cultural life of peoples throughout history. On the other hand, the legends, tales, and songs perpetuate the construction rites. By virtue of their etiological character, they claim to tell the truth and are believed. Thus, to their literary function is added that of rite.

It seems that the attention of scholars was attracted to the building customs themselves later than to their folkloric and literary by-products. A southeastern European ballad referring to the sacrifice of a woman in the foundation of a building has enjoyed the privileged attention of scholars ever since the first half of the nineteenth century. Yet customs pertaining to the erection of structures acquired the importance they have for scholars today only toward the end of the last century. For some time, research into southeastern European songs was carried on separately from research concerning the rituals that had generated them; only rarely did anyone notice their resemblance to construction legends, and almost never were they thought of in connection with tales about deceiving the Devil. Only in recent decades has it been understood that these are all really aspects of the same phenomenon and that they must be researched together.

Ethnologists and folklorists, archaeologists and historians of religions have all contributed to an immense literature examining construction rites from antiquity to the present day. Some authors have brought to light proofs of such practices by the Canaanites, Phoenicians, and Carthaginians as early as 2000 BCE; testimonies to their practice are found in the Hebrew scriptures as well as in Herodotus and Vitruvius. At the same time, field-workers are constantly adding data about more recent phases of building rites in various regions of the world. Yet there still exists a great disparity in the amount of information on these rites from different areas. For this reason I shall refer more frequently to those regions that are better represented in specialized studies.

To achieve greater clarity in the maze of this rich material, we must distinguish between small private buildings and large public ones. These two categories differ as to purpose, size, and difficulty of construction; hence the number and function of the rites also differ. Furthermore, we must also distinguish archaeological documents, which inform us about building rites in a distant past, both from ethnological material, which as a rule reflects the customs of today, and also from folkloric material (legends, tales, and songs), which present the specific circumstances in which buildings—especially public ones—may have been erected. Thus, the folkloric material occupies an intermediate position: in contrast to the archaeological evidence, it has a literary character, while in distinction from the ethnological material, it refers to a more or less remote past. Nevertheless, like archaeological documents, folklore can claim to reflect truth and therefore to constitute history; whereas, as with the ethnological material, its having afforded a model of behavior in rural regions means that it has served to maintain customs and perpetuate their viability.

The Construction of a House. Since in a rural milieu almost every family builds a house, construction rites hold a great importance in everyday life. In the hierarchy of folk customs, they are situated among the so-called rites of passage, immediately after those of birth, marriage, and burial.

Selecting the site. As we know, the magical mentality created a mythical geography. That is why the first concern of the potential housebuilder is that the place he has in mind be "clean," that is, that it not be in the possession of mythical beings whose invisible world lies in surrounding nature, and who might not be agreeable to the erection of a house on that spot. There are very few places not occupied by mythical beings on which man can build without risking their wrath. Such places the one who wishes to build must identify. The Romanians and the Letts, for example, preferred to build their houses on locations where coins had been found, or beside a road on which a house already stood where life was happy; but in the latter case, the wall would have to be built a meter higher, to ensure the new family's prosperity.

In contrast, boundary strips, ditches, fallow fields, marshes, grounds on which hemp is grown, or soil containing roots of trees (especially elders)—places, that is, in the possession of unclean spirits—are rejected by the Romanians. Sites that have served as roads, especially crossroads, are rejected by the Ukrainians and Russians, because these are places where spells are cast. Ukrainians, Livonians, and Romanians also avoid places where people have been buried, especially unbaptized children, since these could appear in the house as ghosts.

Rejected likewise is any site on which some misfortune has occurred (such as a murder, suicide, or fire), one on which domestic animals have been killed, one bought with stolen money, or one that has been cursed. According to the beliefs of the American Indians, Melanesians, Papuans, Letts, Ukrainians, and Romanians, the whole troubled history of such sites could be repeated by those living in the new house. As we can see, the magico-religious plane here encounters the historical; or more precisely, history acquires magical qualities that become transmissible.

The magical cleanness of a place must be carefully verified. The Siberian Russians, South Slavs, and Romanians cast ordinary or fancy bread on the spot where they intend to build. They build only if the bread falls in the direction of the hearth site. Russians, Ruthenians,

Romanians, and Serbo-Croatians fix the corners of the future house by placing four slices of bread (or glasses of water or brandy, or other edibles) on the ground, and they decide to build there only if these remain untouched overnight. In some African regions chickens are used in the same way. On the other hand, in Nyasaland (modern Malawi), if the flour left out remains untouched, it is a sign that the spirit of the place, Muzimos, is not agreeable to the occupation of the site. Baltic Slavs, Romanians, and Serbo-Croatians place four stones or pieces of bark where they want the corners of the future house to be; if insects and worms collect underneath, the spot is favorable.

The selection of the building site cannot be made by just anyone; lest his actions prejudice the destiny of the family that will live there, the one who selects the site must be a man free from physical defects, the eldest son, and married only once. Among the Romanians and South Slavs, he taps on the ground with a stick and listens to the reply. In India, however, the master builder pounds a stake cut from a khadira tree into the ground at a spot indicated by an astrologer, driving it into the head of the mythical snake that supports the earth; this prevents earthquakes.

In the case of the Romanians, materials to be used in the new building are selected with care; in no event are materials used from an old house in which misfortune has occurred. The beams must be cut in the forest under a full moon, if the family is to have prosperity in all things. Even the masons must be chosen carefully, because their defects could be transmitted to the residents of the house. It is essential that the masons not be childless. Fiddlers play while the masons and the owner settle on wages. Moreover masons, like smiths, are considered possessors of professional secrets and manipulators of magical powers, and therefore must be well disposed all the while they are working. They are given the best food and drink, so they will have no reason to curse the house or bewitch it.

Laying the first stone. The laying of the first stone in the foundation has a determining importance for the destiny of the building and the family. The laying of the stone must be done while taking into account the magical sensitivity of time, especially the phases of the moon. The Ukrainians do not begin a building project on a Friday, Saturday, or Sunday; the Letts begin only when the wind is from the north or the moon is full; and some African peoples prefer the moon to be in one of its quarters. The beginning must be made with all involved parties feeling well disposed. Before the laying of the first stone, the owner, the workers, and the neighbors gather together, drink freely, and wish one another success in the new enterprise. With the help of a bunch of basil sanctified at Epiphany, the place and the participants are sprinkled with holy water to obtain the necessary magical cleanness.

Under the foundation stone—sometimes under the future threshold of the house—elements of animal, vegetable, and mineral origin are placed. To ensure a plentiful supply of agricultural products, Romanians deposit fresh grains of the most important cereals, while the East Slavs, Germans, and Dutch put in foods of all sorts. In order to have a good atmosphere in the new house, bottles of liquor and cooking oil are included. The Belgians deposit a branch of cowberry. Various flowers and sugar assure that life in the new dwelling place will "blossom," grains of pepper ensure procreation and banish unclean spirits, and garlic removes possible evil spells cast by enemies and keeps vampires at a distance. As for minerals, salt will cancel out spells, and among the Chinese, Russians, Ruthenians, Ukrainians, Poles, Germans, French, Italians, Serbo-Croatians, Romanians, and Albanians, coins will bring luck and health. Gold or silver coins, minted in the year the construction began and depicting the head of a ruler, will cause money never to be lacking in the house and at the same time ensure the strength of the walls, since they also represent a payment to the so-called genius of the place.

Sacrifice. The coins deposited under a foundation stone are also a substitute for the head of a person, which, according to folk belief, must be sacrificed in the foundation of any building. This is an indirect, tacit agreement between the human occupants and the genius of the place; without the fulfillment of the agreement, the genius might not consent to the house's erection but might cause what was built in the day to collapse in the night, frustrating forever the work of the craftsmen. Thus the spirit of the place claims as his due reward the sacrifice of a human being. However, it is man's nature to try to free himself from such burdens (indeed, the obligation to sacrifice a human being at the foundation of every building can be compared to the expiation of original sin), so instead he offers as little as possible. Thus in place of people, either animals, birds, or insects are sacrificed: fish, cats, dogs, wolves, doves, sparrows, swallows, bats, mice, moles, hedgehogs, cockchafers, lizards, frogs, pigs, sheep, goats, lambs, kids, rams, cattle, horses, buffalo, bulls, and so on. The commonest objects of sacrifice, however, are fowls—young chickens, hens, and roosters. The great variety of creatures sacrificed corresponds to the wide distribution of the practice: it is in fact universal.

These are the sacrifices recorded by ethnologists in the nineteenth and twentieth centuries. Archaeologists, however, tell of human skeletons discovered in the foundations of buildings, beginning in antiquity, while popular legends describe such human sacrifices, especially in the foundations of monuments particularly admired for their size and beauty. This millennial practice has not survived into our time as such. Even in this century, however, the walling-up of substitutes for human sacrificial victims has been attested: the shadow or "stature" of a person (measured in secret with a green rod or a thread, which was then deposited in the foundation), or even a photograph. The secrecy surrounding the walling-up of the substitutes for the human body transports the rite into the realm of black magic and sorcery, and thus, in part, alienates it from its original character, since the shadow, measurement, or photograph was stolen and could constitute a weapon of revenge. Nevertheless, their inclusion in a foundation had the same effects: the walls were erected with success while the person died within forty days after the performance of the rite.

The practice of immolating substitutes seems to be limited to the Balkan Peninsula and Romania, a region in which the old custom of sacrificing persons in foundations underwent numerous adaptations and modernizations, including those indicated here. Mircea Eliade (1972) states that in this region pre-Indo-European and Paleo-Indo-European cultural elements have been preserved exceptionally well. Here also there developed a "cosmic Christianity" that cannot be found in the cultures of other regions. The building sacrifice probably has deeper roots in southeastern Europe, and the people there continued to believe longer in the old rite—a phenomenon to which the ballad of the walled-in woman must also have contributed. In any event, the enclosure of the shadow, measurement, or photograph of a person is probably the last sure testimony to the sacrifice of human beings in a remote past. Whereas other peoples moved directly from the sacrifice of persons to that of barnyard fowls and animals in general, the southeastern European peoples created intermediate forms, thereby enriching the building rites and prolonging their existence in the region.

Entering the new house. Let us next consider the rites performed at the termination of construction and upon moving into the new home. Sensitivity to magical time grows as the construction of the house nears its end, because completion and occupation of the house constitute a gesture of final appropriation—the withdrawal of the building from the power of the spirit of the place, and its coming under the protection of the spirit of the house. On the other hand, the completion of the house, like its beginning, can indicate the destiny of the family or individual persons who will inhabit the new home. This, therefore, is sufficient reason for the conclusion of the work to constitute a moment of frenzy like the one at the beginning of construction. Among the Romanians, this phase starts with the erection of the frame of the roof, to whose highest point a young tree adorned with flowers and colored ribbons is fastened. (Would this be a sign of the victory of man over the powers of the earth? Or have we to do here with a way of keeping at a distance the powers that could be detrimental to the new edifice or the person who will reside there?) To this tree is attached a bottle of liquor for each member of the family. The master builder tastes from every bottle, dedicating it to one of the family members, pronounces good wishes, and throws the bottle to the ground. If the bottle breaks, it is a sign that the person in whose name it was thrown will not have a happy fate in the new house.

On the other hand, the completion of the construction is also the moment when the owner of the new house ought to indemnify the powers of the place. The payment the man would be obliged to give to these powers is the head of a human being. He will receive the right to occupy the new structure only on condition that someone from his family be sacrificed. That is why, among the Poles and Romanians, the last stone is never placed in the wall, so that payment can be postponed indefinitely.

The occupation of the house is a moment of maximum tension, and consequently, it is preceded by numerous magical practices. The Slovenes and Romanians offer the house for one night to a beggar or transient, or else they rent it out for a time. In Yorubaland, slaves are sent to sleep in the new house, while in Calabar, the house is first occupied by a priest. The White Russians put various animals in the house to sleep there on six consecutive nights: first a hen and a rooster, then a goose or a male and female cat, then a piglet, a sheep, a cow, and a horse; only if nothing has happened to the animals do the owners sleep in the house on the seventh night. Here the most frequently recorded custom is the enclosure of a rooster in the new house for a night; as is well known, the rooster has the power, by virtue of his dread crowing, of driving out any unclean powers that might not want to quit the place. According to some, the rooster would attract to itself the evil intended to fall upon the family, and for this reason the cock is not sacrificed but is allowed to die of old age. In other instances, a hen or rooster is decapitated on the threshold of the new house, so that the blood flows on it; or, rarely, the fowl's body is put into a jar and buried beneath the hearth of the house. The object is to avoid human sacrifice. The French carry a decapitated young chicken through every room of the new house, as evidence of the sacrifice.

In order for life to be abundant, but also to achieve a reconciliation with the demonic powers, agricultural products are brought into the new house: bread, wine, and so forth, then salt, money, or a crucifix. In Sicily people shout: "May poverty go far away! May wealth come to me!" In Ireland prayers are made in every corner of the bedroom. The move, however, cannot be made at just any time. Generally a Monday is preferred when the moon is full; in any event, the move cannot be made at the new moon on a Friday. Some peoples prefer Wednesday, Thursday, or Saturday. The priest holds a special ceremony, and another festivity is organized, attended like a baptism or a wedding by relatives, neighbors, and friends, and ending in dancing.

A number of objects used in the old house (such as the broom, distaff, reel, oven rake, icons) are left there, because they are symbols of poverty from which the departing occupant wishes to distance himself. The first things done in the new house likewise have a great importance for the integrity of the family. The first fire—"live fire" or fire produced by use of a tinder box—is made by an old man or a foreigner, lest some young member of the family die. The first whitewashing is never done by a young girl, lest she die. For the first week the family sleeps with the lamp lit, and the first dream in the new house will surely come true.

The Erection of Large Public Structures and the Repair of Dikes. Up to this point we have utilized mainly information collected by ethnologists, and have learned about construction rites beginning from about 1800, that is, from the inception of ethnology. But since we are treating one of the oldest myths of mankind, the question arises: what were construction rites like before the beginning of the nineteenth century, and what means have we for covering those several millennia of human culture before ethnology appeared as a science? Certainly we cannot know all the phases in the development of building rites, if they were recorded in a relatively systematic way only in the modern world, precisely when their impoverishment had begun. No matter how important those few references to the subject in ancient and medieval sources are, they prove only the existence of building rites, not the stages through which they have passed. While interesting but sparse information is furnished by archaeology, the richest documentary source consists of legends, tales, and songs. Legends are not lacking from antiquity (about the founding of Rome, Antioch, and Ancyra, when living men may have been sacrificed), or from the Middle Ages (the legend of Merlin, noted in the ninth century), to say nothing of the sixteenth to twentieth centuries, which abound in all sorts of documents and publications. But do these legends tell the truth?

Tricking the Devil. The multitude of legends known in the specialized literature refer to various aspects of the erection of public buildings (and rarely also to some private buildings). There are legends telling how walls erected in the day fell down at night (among the Finns, Baltic Slavs, and Germans). Popular imagination often has attempted to explain who constructed churches, walled cities, and so forth; in Europe their erection was attributed to giants, dwarfs, and fairies. At other times an explanation was sought for the fact that some churches were never finished, while near them were great piles of stone—hence the anecdotal tales about the tricking of the Devil. At a certain point the builder cannot continue the work for lack of money, so he enters into a compact with a stranger (the Devil), who promises to finish the structure before the first cockcrow. The stranger will not claim any payment if his name is guessed or if he fails to put the last stone in place before the time stated; otherwise, he demands that the first being to enter the church (or cross the bridge) belong to him. Nearly always the Devil is tricked: sometimes his name is guessed; at other times a cat or dog, rather than a human being, enters the church (or crosses the bridge) first, and the Devil must be content with that. Or, according to other tales, the roosters are awakened early, at the very moment when the Devil flies up with the last load of stones—which he then abandons beside the walls in order to save his own skin. Thus the work remains unfinished, and the pile of stones becomes proof that the Devil was surprised by the crowing of the roosters. Rarely is the son of the builder or the daughter of the king offered as a sacrifice according to the terms of the contract. All these stories occur with great frequency in northern and central Europe, where they have vied with those about the walled-in sacrifice that will concern us below.

Human sacrifice. Sometimes the legends relate that the master builder kills his apprentice, because the latter has built a church more beautiful than the one he himself erected. In a smaller group of legends, the masons, stranded on the rooftop, make wings of wood and try to fly, then fall to their death on the threshold of the very edifice they had raised with their own hands, sometimes with the sacrifice of a human being in the foundation (a church or city tower in Romania and the U.S.S.R.).

A very rich group of legends explains why some buildings—especially churches—were built on a particular spot. The legends show how the site was chosen by the throwing of an ax, a hammer, or a bow (Germans, Romanians). At other times it is said that it was there that a tree, thrown in the water, came to rest, thus determining a suitable site for a church (Swedes, Baltic Slavs);

or that a crucifix was found there (Germans, Baltic Slavs), or an icon or a statue (Finns, Germans, Romanians); or that snow fell there in midsummer (Germans, Baltic Slavs, Romanians); or that the site was indicated by birds (Finns, Swedes, northern Germans) or by an unidentified voice (Swedes, Finns, Germans, Belgians, Romanians). Other traditions say that on that spot oxen or cattle were standing (Germans, Baltic Slavs, Belgians, Dutch), or that a monastery was erected on old ruins or on places known only to cattle herders (Romanians).

The largest group of legends concerns a walled-in sacrifice—the sacrifice of a person in the foundation. To a certain extent, these legends reproduce customs regarding the construction of houses; they fall into three categories:

1. *The walling-in of certain objects:* bottles of wine, prayer books (Germans); gold and precious stones (Mexico); or coins (Germans, French, Belgians, Italians, South Slavs). Some of these objects may have a ritual function other than that of a walled-in sacrifice.
2. *The walling-in of birds and animals:* a swallow (Lithuanians, Romanians); rams or he-goats (Senegal, South Slavs, Romanians); sheep (Ghanaians, Albanians, South Slavs); horses (Germans, Danes); a wolf (Moroccans); dogs (Flemish, Germans, Letts); a cat (French, Belgians, Germans, Romanians); or fowls (French, South Slavs, Romanians).
3. *The walling-in of people* (in the case of gates, city walls, palaces, churches, and mills—at numerous locations in Asia, Africa, and Europe): the builder (French, Letts); a fool (British); a sorcerer (Austrians); a beggar (Germans); a poor sinner (Germans, Mordvinians); a prisoner (Germans, Scots, Mexicans); a black man (Palestinians); a brahman (Indian); one who volunteers freely (Chinese, Japanese, Letts, French); one whose name is found in a miraculous way (Chinese); one born under certain constellations (Burmese); pairs of men (South Slavs, French, Germans, Transcaucasians); girls, or boys and girls (Venezuela, Borneo); a virgin girl (Germans, Letts, Estonians, Gruzinians, Armenians, Indians); the only sister of seven brothers, or the only daughter of an old man or of the master builder (U.S.S.R., India, Kurdistan); a child—sometimes a sick child—(numerous examples of castles, churches, bridges, city walls, dikes, and tunnels among the South Slavs, Romanians, Germans, and French); an illegitimate child sold by its own mother, or a child sold and walled in by its own father (castles, walls of cities, watchtowers, and mills among the Germans and French); children sealed in coffins or in stone cradles (Germans); a suckling child, bought, who speaks at the moment of his sacrifice (castles, city walls or gates, towers, churches, dikes, and bridges among the Germans); the only child of a widow (castles among the Armenians); a child, the walling in of whom fails (Swedes, Germans, Celts, South Slavs); a woman (churches, castles, dikes, towers, and bridges in the U.S.S.R., Sweden, Great Britain, Yugoslavia, and Romania); the brothers who became saints, Collum Cille and Oran (churches in Great Britain); the shadow, measurement, or photograph of a person (schools, churches, mills, cellars, sanatoriums, railway tunnels, and bridges in Romania, Yugoslavia, Albania, and Greece). To the ancient legends mentioned above referring to human sacrifice in the foundation of cities, a few modern ones can be added: Novgorod (also called Detinets) in the U.S.S.R. and Einbeck in West Germany, at the founding of which children were put into the walls.

A somewhat separate category is the material referring to dikes, which originates in regions subject to flooding. With a few exceptions, legends of this kind do not describe the construction of the dikes, but their repair. A crack appears in the wall of the dike, threatening the community, and it cannot be plugged until a child is sacrificed whose name is discovered in a miraculous way; elsewhere a trap is prepared with food as bait, and a child is attracted to it, falling into the crack (Japan, China, Germany).

Folk ballads and songs. The enormous mass of construction rites has also led to the creation of folk ballads and songs on the same theme. These describe the fate of a child walled in at the founding of a castle (Gruzinians, Mordvinians, Abhazians), or the wife of the principal mason (Greeks, Albanians, Bulgars, Serbo-Croatians, Romanians, and Magyars in Romania). The song about the mason's wife is a ballad of rare beauty, perhaps the most impressive in world folklore. It tells about the building of a bridge, castle, or monastery whose foundations keep collapsing. From an old man, a mythical being, or a dream, the masters learn that they will not be able to erect the structure until they sacrifice a human being in the foundation. They wall in the wife of the chief master builder (the mother of a suckling child), after which the walls become miraculously strong. Thus the masters are able to build the most beautiful structure ever erected. The sacrifice of the woman confers strength on the walls and imparts a soul to the new architectural work. Through this extraordinary song, the peoples of southeastern Europe have ennobled their construction rites, creating out of a horrible, barbaric ritual an artistic product of surpassing beauty.

It is evident, then, that the soil in which the popular legends, tales, and songs grew is that of the rites pertaining to the construction of a house. Indeed, these rites encompass an endless series of beliefs, magical practices, and customs, and possess a character more complex than the legends, tales, and songs. In other words, the latter are merely a selection drawn from the construction rites, treating only those rites having a deeper significance. Although less rich, they play a very important role within the context of the building rites, since they possess a great power to impress.

Conclusion. Each of these architectural works—house, church, monastery, bridge, walled town, castle, dike, and so forth—possesses individual symbolic value. What they have in common, however, is the achievement of man through sacrifice: the incorporation of the soul of the sacrificial victim in the new structure.

The rites of construction for a house—seemingly, the product of paleo-cultivators—deserve more detailed analysis. Here, however, we cannot but note that between man and mythical beings there exists a kind of communication, a magical language: man tries to verify the magical cleanness of the place, wants to find out the attitude of the mythical beings, and succeeds in receiving their response. Between the mythical world and the real world there exist channels through which questions can be asked and answers received. The malice of the mythical beings can be assuaged through sacrifice or other magical means. At the same time, history acquires mythical qualities: it is fixed on a certain spot, from which troubles or joys radiate. Evil and good are personified; they persist, but can be approached with the help of magical means.

More important, if the rite is respected—that is, if the site is chosen by a man without physical or moral defects; if the timbers used in the structure are cut in the full moon; if the masons are free of defects and well treated during the time of the work; if the construction is begun in accordance with tradition; if a festival is organized to create the joyous atmosphere necessary to any work of creation (dance, too, has a magical function here); and finally if, beneath the foundation or the threshold, or at the termination of the work, a being is offered to the genius of the place—in fine, if all the rites for the occupation of the house are respected, then the house becomes sacred like a temple. The purity of the new edifice is conducive to health and a good disposition, to increase in all things, to children, and so on. Being sacred, the new house is situated at the center of the world and is transformed into an *imago mundi,* as Mircea Eliade (1972, p. 184) expresses it. Its sacredness permits the reestablishment of earth's communications with the heavens and regains that which was lost, or could have been lost, forever.

[*For further discussion of this topic, see* Architecture; *see also* Sacred Space *and* Sacrifice.]

BIBLIOGRAPHY

This article is based upon my work *Meşterul Manole: Contribuţie la studiul unei teme de folclor european* (Bucharest, 1973), the bibliography of which contains almost six hundred items. One of the oldest studies on this theme is that of Richard Andree, *Ethnographische Parallelen und Vergleiche* (Stuttgart, 1878), which summarizes much of the ethnological research up to that time. A deepening of the historical perspective is achieved in Felix Liebrecht's *Zur Volkskunde: Alte und neue Aufsätze* (Heilbronn, 1897), which brings to light information about Greek and Roman antiquity and the Middle Ages. A fundamental contribution is Paul Sartori's study "Über das Bauopfer," *Zeitschrift für Ethnologie* 30 (1898): 1–54, completed by the author in *Sitte und Brauch,* vol. 2, *Leben und Arbeit daheim und draussen* (Leipzig, 1911). Important, and in some respects richer, but even so uneven, is the work of Kurt Klusemann, *Das Bauopfer: Eine ethnographisch-prähistorisch-linguistische Studie* (Graz, 1919). The first author to approach the theme from both the ethnographic and also the historico-religious and philosophical viewpoint is Mircea Eliade in *Comentarii la legenda Meşterul Manole* (Bucharest, 1943). He takes it up again several times, especially in *Zalmoxis, the Vanishing God* (Chicago, 1972). Written from a similar perspective is Giuseppe Cocchiara's "Il ponte di Arta: I sacrifici nella letteratura popolare e nella storia del pensiero magico-religoso," in his *Il paese di Cuccagna* (Turin, 1956), pp. 84–125. To be counted as an erudite but chaotic work is Lewis D. Burdick's *Foundation Rites, with Some Kindred Ceremonies* (New York, 1901). For the spirit of the builders, Lauri Honko's monograph, *Geisterglaube in Ingermanland* (Helsinki, 1962), is important, despite the fact that it deals with a small geographic region.

Ion Taloş
Translated from Romanian by Mac Linscott Ricketts

FOUNTAIN. The word *fountain* derives from the Latin *fons,* meaning "source." As physical phenomena serving as the material basis of hierophanies (appearances of the divine), fountains may be described as the flowing of pressurized water up and out through an aperture from some hidden depth below the earth's surface. As hierophanies, they manifest locally the flowing of diverse creative, re-creative, or transformative potentialities from depths beyond the ordinary or profane plane of existence. There is no single sort of potentiality attributed in common to all sacred fountains in the world's religions, but a number of potentialities are severally attributed to them, for example, healing powers, oracular powers, rejuvenating powers, and so forth.

Likewise, no single divinity is regarded as a manifestation common to all fountains; the various named and nameless gods, spirits, and nymphs of fountains are particular to individual instances. Furthermore, sacred significance is attributed seemingly no less to man-made than to naturally occurring fountains.

The typical attributes of fountains reflect diverse metaphoric images expressive of the principal water potentiality, the cosmogonic; cosmogonic water is viewed as pristine, as formless, as eternal, as receptive, as living, as chaotic. For example, the creative power of fountains can be understood as one manifestation of the world-creating power itself, and the water of fountains as homologous to the cosmogonic water from which creation arises and into which it dissolves, like the Babylonian waters of Apsu or the Vedic watery source of all things and all existence.

Some fountains are sacred as sources of divine power. In times of drought, for example, the priest of the god Zeus Lykaios in Arcadia cast an oak branch into the mountainside spring, activating the spring's power to make rain.

Again, some fountains restore to an original or pristine condition those who bathe in them or drink from their waters. It was thought, for instance, that when the goddess Hera or the members of her cult bathed in the Nauplian spring, they became virginal again. The pristine state is homologous to the virginal aspect of the cosmogonic waters before the creative act. Thus, fountains of youth manifest a forever self-renewing potentiality for creation. In Brahmanic legend the fountain of youth typically renews power or vigor, but it does not bestow immortality. However, in other legends immortality is granted. In the Greek romance of Alexander by Pseudo-Callisthenes, Alexander's cook accidentally discovers a fountain that bestows immortal life. In Islamic folklore, the figure Khidr is mentioned as the only being who gained immortality by drinking from the fountain of life, which represents the principle of eternal existence.

Some fountains function as principles or causes of life itself. For example, in the prophet Ezekiel's vision of Yahveh's regenerated Temple, a spring flows out from under the Temple. Its waters cause perpetually bearing fruit trees to spring up at once along its banks. This water demonstrates two additional potentialities attributed to certain sacred fountains, namely, healing and fructifying powers. "Fish will be very plentiful, for wherever the water goes it brings health, and life teems wherever the river flows" (*Ez.* 47:1–12).

In Babylonian religious thought, Apsu, the water of creation, is called "house of wisdom," or the house of Ea, god of wisdom. Wisdom, supernatural insight, oracular vision, and poetic inspiration are other typical attributes of various sacred fountains. For example, the gods in Germanic mythology determine the world's fate beside the Spring of Mímir, and the Germanic tribes had "springs of justice" where justice was meted out. Among the Romans, the priestess of Carmentis sang of the newborn child's destiny after drinking from a spring, and likewise the Greek priestess of Apollo at Delphi delivered oracles after drinking from the Castalian Spring. The Greek muses, goddesses of inspiration, were originally nymphs connected with springs.

Finally, the dissolving power of a fountain's water, its chaotic quality, is the typical attribute manifested by both those fountains having the positive potential for sacred cleansing and also those bringing insanity or terrible loss. The Greek term *numpholēptos,* meaning "insane, senseless, beside oneself with fright," is related to the poetic word for water, *numphē.* Similarly, in Germanic folklore the female spirits of certain springs stole children or seduced their human lovers to destruction.

BIBLIOGRAPHY

Jones, Francis T. D. *The Holy Wells of Wales.* Cardiff, 1954.

Kristensen, W. Brede. *The Meaning of Religion.* The Hague, 1960.

RICHARD W. THURN

FOUR NOBLE TRUTHS. All strands of the Buddhist tradition recognize in the Four Noble Truths (Skt., *catvāry āryasatyānī;* Pali, *cattāri ariyasaccāni*) one of the earliest formulations of the salvific insight gained by the Buddha on the occasion of his enlightenment. For the Theravāda tradition, the discourse on the Four Truths constitutes part of the first sermon of the Buddha, the *Dhammacakkappavattana Sutta,* delivered in the Deer Park near Banaras to his five original disciples. The standard formulaic enumeration of the Four Truths as found in this discourse is as follows:

> This, monks, is the noble truth of *dukkha* ["suffering"]: birth is *dukkha,* old age is *dukkha,* disease is *dukkha,* dying is *dukkha,* association with what is not dear is *dukkha,* separation from what is dear is *dukkha,* not getting that which is wished for is *dukkha;* in brief, the five groups of grasping [i.e., the five *khandhas*; Skt., *skandhas*] are *dukkha.*
>
> And this, monks, is the noble truth of the uprising [*samudaya*] of *dukkha:* this craving, which is characterized by repeated existence, accompanied by passion for joys, delighting in this and that; that is to say, craving for sensual desires, craving for existence, craving for cessation of existence.

And this, monks, is the noble truth of the cessation [*nirodha*] of *dukkha:* complete dispassion and cessation of craving, abandonment, rejection, release of it, without attachment to it.

And this, monks, is the noble truth of the path [*magga*] leading to the cessation of *dukkha;* just this Noble Eightfold Way; that is to say, proper view, proper intention, proper speech, proper action, proper livelihood, proper effort, proper mindfulness, proper concentration.

(*Saṃyutta Nikāya* 5.420ff.)

These Four Noble Truths (formulaically, *dukkha, samudaya, nirodha, magga*) constitute a "middle way" between rigorous asceticism and sensual indulgence. The twin foci of truths are craving (Skt., *tṛṣṇā;* Pali, *taṇhā)* and ignorance *(avidyā)*, craving to hold that which is impermanent, grasping for substantiality where there is no abiding substance, and not knowing that this orientation inevitably yields unsatisfactoriness (Pali, *dukkha;* Skt., *duḥkha*). Hence the twin foci draw attention to the fundamental cause *(samudaya)* of *dukkha,* and meditation on *dukkha* leads to a discernment that craving and ignorance are its matrix.

The Eightfold Path, the fourth of the Four Noble Truths, provides a means especially adapted to lead one into salvific insight, a way conforming completely to the Buddha's own salvific realization. In this sense, the Eightfold Path is the proper mode of religious living, one that subsumes ethics into soteriology.

Although some uncertainty remains among scholars as to whether the passage quoted above indeed represents the earliest formulation of the Buddha's teaching, in the early phase of the Buddhist tradition in India (the so-called Hīnayāna phase) the Four Noble Truths played a major role in shaping the fundamental orientation to religious living on the part of Buddhists. Early Buddhist schools in India differed in their interpretations of the Four Noble Truths, but uniformly regarded its underlying thematic structure as one informed by metaphors of healing: symptom-disease, diagnosis-cause, elimination of cause, treatment or remedy. With the rise of the Mahāyāna tradition the Four Noble Truths became less central as a fundamental statement of the life situation and one's mode of engagement in a soteriological process, but continued to be revered as a fundamental part of the Buddha's early teachings.

Theravāda Interpretations. The Theravāda Buddhist tradition is prevalent in contemporary Sri Lanka, Burma, and Thailand. For at least two millennia it has regarded the Four Truths as constitutive of its central soteriological doctrine. As a result, considerable effort has been expended in the tradition on its exegesis. In an extended discussion on the Four Noble Truths, Buddhaghosa, in his fifth century CE classic, *Visuddhimagga* (The Path of Purity), comments at one point on the meaning of the term *sacca* ("truth"):

For those who examine [truth] closely with the eye of salvific wisdom [*paññā*], it is not distorted, like an illusion, equivocated, like a mirage, and of an undiscoverable inherent nature, like the self among sectarians, but, rather, it is the pasture of noble gnosis [*ñāṇa*] by means of its actual, undistorted, authentic condition. Just like [the characteristics of] fire, like the nature of the world, the actual undistorted, authentic condition is to be understood as the meaning of truth. (*Visuddhimagga* 16.24)

Among the many interpretations offered by Buddhaghosa for the existence of four, and only four, truths is the Buddha's realization that the evolution of suffering, its cause, the devolution of suffering, and *its* cause are fully comprehensive of an analysis of the human condition and the way to liberation through it. (See *Visuddhimagga* 16.27.) Other analyses of the Four Truths suggest that the first Truth relates to the basis of craving; the second, to craving itself; the third, to the cessation of craving; and the fourth, to the means to the cessation of craving. Similarly, the Truths may be viewed as pertaining, respectively, to the sense of attachment, delight in attachment, removal of attachment, and the means to the removal of attachment. (See *Visuddhimagga* 16.27–28.) According to the *Dhammacakkappavattana Sutta,* the practitioner is to cultivate a fourfold awareness of the Four Truths in which *dukkha* is to be fully understood; the origin of *dukkha,* abandoned; *nirodha,* realized; and *magga,* cultivated. The Theravāda commentarial tradition has maintained that the soteriological moment arises in the simultaneity of this fourfold awareness. (See *Visuddhimagga* 22.92.)

Although the tradition continued to elaborate analyses of the Four Truths arranged according to various numerical configurations (most frequently with the number sixteen), it has held to the conviction that when the Truths are fully penetrated and soteriologically known it is by one knowledge, through a single penetration, and at one instant. This knowledge of the Four Truths, they aver, is in and of itself salvific.

The Theravāda has continued to interpret the Eightfold Path as comprising three basic elements deemed integral to religious living at its fullest: *sīla* (Skt., *śīla*), or moral virtue; *samādhi,* or meditative concentration; and *paññā* (Skt., *prajñā*), or salvific wisdom. Proper view and intention are classed as salvific wisdom; proper speech, action, and livelihood are classed as expressions of moral virtue; and proper effort, mindfulness, and concentration are classed as forms of meditative concentration.

Finally, the tradition has utilized the notion of "emptiness" (Pali, *suññatā;* Skt., *śūnyatā*) in the analysis of the Four Noble Truths. Buddhaghosa wrote:

> In the highest sense, all the truths are to be understood as empty because of the absence of an experiencer, a doer, someone extinguished, and a goer. Hence this is said:
>
> For there is only suffering, no one who suffers,
> No doer, only the doing is found,
> Extinction there is, no extinguished man,
> There is the path, no goer is found.
>
> Or alternatively,
>
> The first pair are empty
> Of stableness, beauty, pleasure, self;
> Empty of self is the deathless state.
> Without stableness, pleasure, self is the path.
> Such, regarding them, is emptiness [*suññatā*].
> (*Visuddhimagga* 16.90)

Mahāyāna Interpretations. Although the Theravāda tradition applied the notion of "emptiness" in negating permanence, abiding happiness, and substantiality as legitimate descriptions of sentient life, it is within the Mahāyāna that one finds emptiness as a designation of reality in the highest sense. As part of the general critique of "substantiality" carried out by the Prajñāpāramitā literature, even the Four Truths are declared void of real existence. In this analysis, suffering, the origin of suffering, the cessation of suffering, and the path to the cessation of suffering are themselves "empty."

In the *Saddharmapuṇḍarīka Sūtra* (Lotus Sutra), the old standard formulas of the epithets of the Buddha and characteristics of *dharma* are repeated for the Tathāgata Candrasūryapradīpa and his preaching, but the Four Noble Truths are only mentioned by title—there is no elaboration. The *Saddharmapuṇḍarīka* proclaims that such teaching is taken up and absorbed into the one comprehensive and central soteriological message (i.e., the "single vehicle"; *ekayāna*) of the *sūtra.*

Although the Four Noble Truths are not featured in their earlier formulation in many Mahāyāna texts, the basic theme nonetheless persists: life is awry, craving and ignorance are the cause, one's life can be changed, and a way or means that brings this about is available. For example, the verse text of Śāntideva's *Bodhicaryāvatāra* does not contain the complete formula of the Four Noble Truths. Prajñākaramati, a commentator on this great text, even points to the one verse (chap. 9, verse 41) where he finds a contrast clearly presented between the Four Noble Truths and the "teaching of emptiness." Yet even though a fundamental shift in the understanding of the path to liberation has taken place in this and other Mahāyāna texts, the underlying assessment as to the cause of suffering, that is, the basic thematic structure of the Four Truths, remains unchanged.

In the *Madhyamakakārikā,* Nāgārjuna provides an incisive, penetrating analysis of the Four Noble Truths. He maintains that *duḥkha,* which evolves from the interplay of the constituents of individuality and the objects of perception, can no longer be seen as having any fundamental ontological status, even in *saṃsāra,* the fleeting "whirl" of repeated existence. The same is true, for that matter, of *saṃsāra* itself, or even of *nirvāṇa:* all is emptiness *(śūnyatā).*

Thus, the older-formulated Eightfold Path, which provided the remedy for the dis-ease *(duḥkha)* of undisciplined and uninformed human existence, yielded with this shift in worldview to another formulation of the soteriological process, to another religious orientation that is also to be cultivated—the *bodhisattva* path. Although the ontological interpretation of the Four Noble Truths underwent change in the cumulative development of the Buddhist tradition, as in the case of the great Chinese Buddhist thinker Chih-i (538–597), the fundamental theme that the inadequacy of human life results from craving and ignorance, which can be eradicated by following the path to enlightenment taught by the Buddha, has continued.

[*See also* Eightfold Path *and* Soteriology, *article on* Buddhist Soteriology.]

BIBLIOGRAPHY

The text of the *Dhammacakkappavattana Sutta* is available in English translation in *Saṃyutta Nikāya: The Book of Kindred Sayings* (1917–1930), translated by C. A. F. Rhys Davids and F. L. Woodward (London, 1950–1956). For the *Visuddhimagga,* see the reliable translation by Bhikku Ñyāṇamoli, *The Path of Purification,* 2d ed. (Colombo, 1964). A related text, Upatissa's *Vimuttimagga,* has been translated from the Chinese as *The Path of Freedom* by N. R. M. Ehara, Soma Thera, and Kheminda Thera (Kandy, 1977). For an overview and analysis of the Four Truths from a Theravāda perspective, see Walpola Rahula's *What the Buddha Taught,* rev. ed. (New York, 1974).

JOHN ROSS CARTER

FOX, GEORGE (1624–1691), chief founder and early leader of the Quakers, a popular movement without clergy, ritual, or sacraments, gathered from among English Puritan Separatists. Despite frequent imprisonments, he traveled throughout Britain, North America, and northern Europe, calling hearers to experience directly the Spirit of God, met as "the Light of Christ" or "Truth" within each person. Those who were open and obedient to the Light he called upon to gather as "Children of Light" and to bear witness to God's power, which was to conquer the world without outward violence in "the Lamb's War." Fox also gave structure to gatherings, or Meetings of Friends, and wrote 270 tracts and 400 "epistles."

Fox was the son of a Puritan weaver of Fenny Drayton in Leicestershire. As a young man he was apprenticed as a cobbler and shepherd; his sensitivity to temptations caused him intense strain, which in 1643 drove him away from his family and then from a series of prominent Puritan clergy and congregations whom he had sought out in the Midlands and in London. By contacts with Separatist and Baptist groups, and perhaps also among Ranters and Familists, he acquired beliefs about the inward nature of heaven, the Last Judgment, the sacraments, and Christ's "heavenly body." He experienced in 1646 and 1647 a series of "openings," or insights, into the Bible, much of which he knew by heart: namely, that true ministers are not made at universities; that Christ within "can speak to thy condition"; that Christ too experienced and conquered temptation; that the source of temptation is the evil within human hearts. Notably, Fox saw evil in his own heart, where "there was an ocean of darkness and death, but an infinite ocean of light and love, which flowed over the ocean of darkness."

Having faced his dark impulses, he called others to "the witness of God within them," which would "judge and guide them"—not into a vicarious righteousness but into a total purging and obedience. When he began preaching in the Midlands he was jailed at Derby in 1650–1651 for blasphemy, having glimpsed perfect holiness as he "was come up in spirit through the flaming sword into the paradise of God." He refused a captaincy in Oliver Cromwell's army, since he "lived in the virtue of that life and power that took away the occasion of all wars." In 1651 he preached through northern Yorkshire, winning his chief colleagues, Nayler, Dewsbury, Farnworth, and Aldam. In 1652 he went northwest by way of Pendle Hill, where he had a vision of "a great people to be gathered," and he went on to win to his cause several groups of Separatists who met on Firbank Fell and in villages around the English Lake District. Swarthmoor Hall, home of Margaret Fell and her family, became the center for a mass movement throughout the poorly served moorland parishes of Westmorland and Cumberland, despite jailings and mob violence in several towns. In 1654, a "valiant sixty" of the newly won Quaker men and women, mainly yeomen farmers, spread out on foot throughout Britain as "publishers of Truth," announcing "the Day of the Lord." Fox recalled them that winter to plan their further work and to have them agree to report their travels to Swarthmoor. In 1655 Fox was sent as a prisoner to London, which had already become a Quaker center through casual contacts and earlier missions. Freed by Oliver Cromwell, Fox talked sympathetically with him, attempting without success to persuade him to end the parish system.

While traveling through southern England to Lands End, Fox was jailed in Launceston's "Doomsdale" dungeon for a harsh winter, during which his colleague James Nayler let some women disciples stir up a breach between the two leaders and stage in Nayler's honor a reenactment of Palm Sunday at Bristol. Nayler was tried for blasphemy before Parliament and savagely punished, but this episode, offending England's growing conservatism from 1656 through 1658, cast a shadow over the Quakers. To rally them, Fox encouraged older Quakers to visit the struggling Meetings already gathered for weekly worship in silence, while younger Friends carried the Quaker message overseas to Ireland, continental Europe, and the American colonies. Fox was mainly near London as the Puritan Commonwealth fell apart, and he went through weeks of doubt and exhaustion when the Quakers were asked by a radical Puritan government to provide Commissioners of Militia to protect twenty years' gains in justice and freedom. Fox's warning against reliance on arms became a standard to which Quakers could point after the returning Royalists in 1660 accused Friends of plotting rebellion against Charles II. Fox also organized weekly meetings of Quaker men and women leaders in London and wrote piecemeal his only long theological book, *The Great Mistery* (1659). Between and after two more long imprisonments for refusing the Oath of Allegiance (and all oaths) and defying the 1664 Conventicle Act, Fox again visited Quaker Meetings throughout England and Ireland to set up a network of men's and women's Monthly and Quarterly Meetings for local groups and for counties. At Bristol on 17 October 1669 he married Margaret Fell, eleven years a widow; though his letters to her were curiously formal, he began to express to her the affection and humor others had loved in him.

After the 1670 Second Conventicle Act, when Fox and thousands of "Nonconformists" to the Anglican church were again arrested, the Indulgence of 1672 freed him to sail with twelve other Quakers to visit Quaker groups in the American colonies. They proclaimed their Christian orthodoxy to the governor of Barbados and gathered into regular Meetings the Friends of Jamaica and Chesapeake Bay and later those in New England and Virginia. Guided by Indians through the forests of New Jersey, Fox would urge Quakers to colonize there in 1675. Returning to England in June 1673, Fox was again imprisoned and seriously ill at Worcester in December. Later, recovering his health slowly at Swarthmoor Hall, Fox dictated to Margaret's son-in-law Thomas Lower the text of his *Journal*. In 1677 Fox traveled with William Penn and Robert Barclay to visit small Quaker groups in Holland and northwestern Germany. Fox revisited Holland in 1684 but spent most of his last years in or near London, where he died on 13 January 1691. Penn witnessed that "abruptly and brokenly as sometimes his sentences would fall from him . . . it showed that God had sent him, that he had nothing of man's wit or wisdom, so that he was an original, being no man's copy. He had an extraordinary gift in opening the Scriptures. But above all the most awful, living, reverent frame was his in prayer."

BIBLIOGRAPHY

Works by Fox

A Battle-Dor for Teachers and Professors to Learn Singular and Plural (1660). Written with John Stubs and Benjamin Furly. Reprint, Menston, England, 1968. Shows that "thee & thou," as used by Quakers to all individuals, was true grammar in forty languages.

Catechism. London, 1657. Lessons for children.

Doctrinals (originally, *Gospel Truth Demonstrated*). London, 1706. Ninety-nine of his 252 previously printed tracts.

Epistles. London, 1698. Four hundred letters, twenty-nine previously printed.

George Fox's Book of Miracles. Cambridge, 1973. Henry Cadbury's careful reconstruction of a lost Fox manuscript.

The Great Mistery of the Great Whore Unfolded. London, 1659. Refutes anti-Quaker tracts by Puritans, Baptists, and others.

Journal. Edited by Thomas Ellwood, with a preface by William Penn. London, 1694. Repeatedly reprinted in abridged form with prefaces by Rufus Jones, Henry Cadbury, et al.; currently available from Friends United Press (Richmond, Ind., 1983).

The Works of George Fox. 8 vols. Philadelphia, 1831. Reproduces first editions of Fox's works uncritically.

Works about Fox

Benson, Lewis. *Catholic Quakerism*. Philadelphia, 1968. Presents Fox's ethic.

Braithwaite, William C. *The Beginnings of Quakerism* (1912). Rev. ed. Cambridge, 1955. Presents historical facts and settings of Fox's life.

Braithwaite, William C. *The Second Period of Quakerism* (1919). Revised by Henry Cadbury. Cambridge, 1961.

HUGH BARBOUR

FOXES. The fox has enjoyed immense popularity as a character in the fables of many cultures, from those of Aesop to those of "Uncle Remus" to Leoš Janáček's opera *The Cunning Little Vixen*. It was once believed in Wales and Germany that witches assume the form of foxes. In fact, foxes were sometimes burned in the midsummer fires.

In the mythology of the North American Indians the fox as a male animal character is well known for its craftiness and slyness. Especially among the California Indians the fox plays a prominent role in trickster and other tales. In many instances Fox is a trickster's companion, and at times he deceives Coyote and eats the food that Coyote has procured for himself. The fox also appears as a female animal in a cycle of fox tales widespread among the North American Indians. A poor man, living alone, comes home at night to find his house in order and his dinner on the fire. He discovers that every morning a vixen comes to his hut, sheds her skin, and becomes a woman. Having stolen the skin, he makes her his wife. They live in happiness for many years until she discovers the skin, puts it on, and runs away. This scenario of the "mysterious housekeeper" is also found among the Inuit (Eskimo) in Greenland and Labrador, as well as among the Koriak of northeastern Siberia.

In Inner Asia, among the Buriats, the fox is known as a guide to the land of the dead; when the hero Mumonto lifts up a large black stone and shouts "Come here," a fox appears in the opening under the stone and says, "Hold fast to my tail."

Chinese folklore is rich in the motif of the fox who transforms itself into an attractive woman and seduces young men. Foxes are capable of this transformation through the study of Chinese classics or through erotic tricks. Foxes who study the classics acquire first the power to become humans, then immortals, and finally gods. In many stories, young foxes are depicted as sitting in a circle, listening to an old white fox at the center expounding the classics. Foxes can assume human form, if at first only briefly, through the absorption and accumulation of the *semen virile* of a male sex partner; by seducing humans, usually young men, foxes steal life essence and add it to their own. For example, an ambitious young man who has retired to a deserted cottage or temple to prepare for the state examinations is visited at dusk by a beautiful young woman who becomes his mistress. Her erotic skill is such that he becomes exhausted and dies. Fox-women sometimes sincerely love their human paramours and help them with their studies, but they seldom return the life essence they have stolen. Occasionally, the parents or friends become aware of the situation in time and call in either a shaman or a Taoist specially trained in fox exorcism and drive her away.

Folk belief in the fox is still alive in Japan; the fox is considered to be most skillful of animals in transforming itself into human form, often female. It is feared as a wicked animal that haunts and possesses people. But, at the same time, the fox is respected as the messenger of *inari*, the beneficent rice goddess Uka no Mitama, of Shintō religion.

BIBLIOGRAPHY

On the fox in the East Asian spiritual world, there is much useful material in Marinus W. de Visser's "The Fox and the Badger in Japanese Folklore," *Transactions of Asiatic Society of Japan* 36, pt. 3 (1908): 1–159. Gudmund Hatt discusses the fox as a mysterious housekeeper in his *Asiatic Influences in American Folklore* (Copenhagen, 1949), pp. 96ff.

MANABU WAIDA

FRANCISCANS is the common designation for various groups professing to live according to the ideals of Francis of Assisi (1181/2–1226). [*See the biography of Francis.*] About 1205 Francis withdrew from society to adopt the austere life of a penitent. His vocation received a decisive focus in 1208 when he was struck by the gospel text in which Jesus charged his apostles with their preaching mission (*Mt.* 10). This passage became a key element in what Francis called his "life according to the gospel," characterized by the attempt "to follow the teaching and footsteps of our Lord Jesus Christ" by living in lowliness and poverty, preaching a message of radical conversion of life by word and example. Within Francis's lifetime, his followers had organized into three distinct but related orders: the Friars Minor; the cloistered nuns commonly called the Poor Clares; and the lay Order of Penance, later known as the Third Order. Although they differed in their manner of expression, all were based on Francis's vision of a gospel way of life. The concrete implications of this ideal have led to bitter dissension in the course of Franciscan history.

The Friars Minor, who received initial papal approval in 1210, were originally itinerant preachers, supporting themselves by whatever trade they knew, living in poverty without fixed residences. However, they underwent a rapid transformation between 1220 and 1260. First of all, the phenomenal growth of the order—by 1221 there were about five thousand friars—demanded more complex internal structures. At the same time, the papacy recognized in the Franciscan movement a potent instrument of reform and increasingly intervened to oversee and channel its growth. The attitude of Francis himself toward these changes, already apparent in the definitive 1223 version of his rule, has long been debated by historians. In any case, whether this development is viewed as a betrayal or a natural evolution, by midcentury the life of the friars was increasingly focused on the organized pastoral ministry of the church, especially preaching and the hearing of confessions. To support these apostolic tasks, the original rigorous observance of poverty was relaxed by several papal interventions. The training schools of the order in such centers as Paris and Oxford produced some of the greatest masters of Scholastic theology, such as Bonaventure, John Duns Scotus, and William of Ockham.

Within the order, however, there was substantial resistance to these new orientations. Toward the end of the thirteenth century, various minority factions known collectively as the Spirituals, standing for the literal observance of the rule, refused to submit to the modifications of absolute poverty accepted by the majority of friars. This increasingly bitter struggle led eventually to outright persecution of the Spirituals, culminating in a decision by John XXII in 1323 to brand as heretical the opinion that Christ and his apostles had lived in absolute poverty. The Friars Minor thus gradually conformed to the practice of common ownership of property that was usual among members of other religious orders.

During the latter part of the fourteenth century, however, a certain reaction set in, with small groups of friars receiving permission to retire to remote houses to live a more primitive form of Franciscan life. This movement, known as the Observant reform, gained momentum during the next century under such leaders as Bernardino of Siena, ultimately achieving a quasi-autonomous status within the order. Relations between the friars who accepted this reform and those who did not, known as the Conventuals, grew increasingly tense, until Leo X finally split them into two separate orders in 1517. The zeal for reform refused to be contained, however, and in the course of the sixteenth century even stricter parties appeared. The largest of these, the Capuchins, played a prominent role in the Counter-Reformation as popular preachers among the lower classes; they were granted complete independence in 1619. Other groups—the Discalced, the Recollects, and the Reformed—attained a large degree of autonomy within the Observant branch. Despite this continual fragmentation, the Franciscans continued to prosper after the Reformation. Although they lost some of their intellectual preeminence, they exercised a notable role as missionaries during the Spanish, Portuguese, and French colonial periods. By 1760, they had reached their peak, numbering 135,000 friars in all branches.

The friars, especially the Conventuals, suffered greatly in the secularizing epoch in Europe and Latin America during and after the French Revolution. However, a revival did occur in the latter part of the nineteenth century, spurred on by research into early Franciscan sources. Also, under papal initiative, the various

Observant groups were reunited in 1897, to be referred to simply as Friars Minor. Since 1965, the whole order has been in a period of renewal and transition in the wake of the Second Vatican Council, emphasizing a return to the charisma of Francis. In 1983 there were about 20,100 Friars Minor, 11,900 Capuchins, and 4,100 Conventuals. There is also a small community of friars in the Anglican church.

The Poor Clares, sometimes referred to as the Second Order, dates from 1212, when Clare, of a noble Assisi family, received the habit from Francis. Although Clare and her followers soon came to devote themselves to a cloistered life of prayer and penance, they did not escape the disputes of the friars over the practice of poverty. The primitive rule of 1219 was modified in 1247, although Clare fought for and received a stricter version shortly before her death in 1253. Because each convent of Poor Clares is largely autonomous, practices have varied greatly. A reform, analogous to the Observance among the friars, was begun by Colette of Corbie in the fourteenth century. In 1983 there were more than 800 convents of Poor Clares, chiefly in Spain and Italy, with 19,200 nuns.

Francis can be called the founder of the Third Order only in an analogous sense. His preaching of radical conversion moved many of his hearers to reform their lives, and so he sought to prescribe for these individuals ways of life appropriate to their respective social conditions. Some became hermits, while others continued living in their own homes, joining existing orders of lay penitents. These confraternities developed stronger relationships with the friars over the course of the century. This Order of Penance was characterized by a simple way of life, cooperative works of charity, and the refusal to bear arms or take oaths. The tertiaries were a potent religious and social force in late medieval society. In the latter part of the thirteenth century some of these Franciscan penitents began living together in communities, eventually binding themselves under vows. The rule of this Third Order Regular received its final form in 1521. During the nineteenth century there was a veritable explosion of congregations of women following this rule, devoted to teaching, nursing, and other charitable activities. In 1980 there were over 270 distinct congregations of Franciscan sisters with approximately 138,000 members and in 1983 about 1,500 male members of the Third Order Regular. Meanwhile, the secular Franciscan fraternities continued to expand, but with a different emphasis after the Reformation period. Although their charitable activities continued, their countercultural way of life increasingly conformed to societal norms; they numbered over 1,200,000 in 1983. After Vatican II both branches of the Third Order revised their rules of life, attempting to return to their original spirit and function.

BIBLIOGRAPHY

The best available general survey of the entire Franciscan movement is Lazaro Iriarte de Aspurz's *Franciscan History: The Three Orders of St. Francis of Assisi* (Chicago, 1983). For the medieval period, J. R. H. Moorman's solid if unadventurous study, *History of the Franciscan Order: From Its Origins to the Year 1517* (Oxford, 1968), remains the standard treatment. However, it should be balanced by Kajetan Esser's *Origins of the Franciscan Order* (Chicago, 1970), which is fundamental for understanding the early friars. The period from 1220 to 1260, so critical in the history of the order, has been illumined by Rosalind B. Brooke's stimulating *Early Franciscan Government: Elias to Bonaventure,* "Cambridge Studies in Medieval Life and Thought," n.s. vol. 7 (Cambridge, 1959), as well as by Lawrence C. Landini's *The Causes of the Clericalization of the Order of Friars Minor, 1209–1260* (Chicago, 1968). Malcolm D. Lambert's *Franciscan Poverty: The Doctrine of the Absolute Poverty of Christ and the Apostles in the Franciscan Order, 1210–1323* (London, 1961) is an indispensable guide through that complicated and acrimonious debate. An extensive research bibliography to Franciscan spirituality and history has been compiled by Raphael Brown in *St. Francis of Assisi: Omnibus of Sources,* 4th rev. ed., edited by Marion A. Habig (Chicago, 1983).

DOMINIC V. MONTI, O.F.M.

FRANCIS OF ASSISI (Giovanni Francesco Bernardone, 1181/2–1226), Christian saint and founder of the Franciscans. John was Francis's baptismal name, but a fondness for France on the part of his merchant father and an acknowledgment of the national origin of his mother prompted the parents to call him Francis. Endowed with a jovial disposition and the means to pamper it, Francis enjoyed the good life of his times; this life was, however, interrupted when his hometown warred with neighboring Perugia. Inducted, imprisoned, and then released, Francis returned home with his military ambitions dampened. A business career with his father held no attraction.

Francis's conversion was the culmination of a period of prayerful reflection in a local grotto, an encounter with a leper, an invitation from God to repair Assisi's abandoned chapel of San Damiano, and Francis's study of *Matthew* 10, which imparted to him a sense of irreversible dedication to the kingdom of God. Within a few months (by April 1208) others asked to share his life, and thus a brotherhood was born.

In 1209 Francis journeyed to Rome to seek papal approval for the brotherhood. After some hesitation, Innocent III gave verbal assent to the rule authored by Francis, who then returned to Assisi and remained at the chapel of the Portiuncula; from there the brothers, two by two, preached gospel renewal. Intent on extending this preaching, Francis departed for Syria, but bad weather hampered the venture. Later a more successful journey took him to meet the sultan in Damietta. In 1212 Francis offered the religious habit to the young noblewoman Clare, and quickly other young women from Assisi sought to share her way of life at San Damiano, forming the order known as the Poor Clares. In 1215 the Fourth Lateran Council promulgated reforms championed in his preaching.

In 1220 Francis resigned his post as head of the Franciscans. Still, with over five thousand brothers, his involvement continued. After reworking his rule, Francis submitted it to Pope Honorius III in 1223, and it received written approval. That same year Francis presented a living Christmas crèche at Greccio, which encouraged the popularity of that custom in subsequent centuries. At Alverna he received the stigmata (the wounds of Christ crucified), thereby reflecting outwardly that which he interiorly imitated.

Though suffering serious illness in his last years, Francis composed his intensely joyful "Canticle of Brother Sun." The closing strophe addresses "Sister Death," whom he welcomed on 3 October 1226. Within two years Francis was proclaimed a saint. In 1939 he was officially offered to Italy as its patron; in 1979 he was recognized by Pope John Paul II as the patron saint of ecology.

As Francis's brotherhood increased in size, his work encompassed the nurturing of followers including the Poor Clares and the Secular Franciscans (lay men and women who wished to follow Francis). Franciscans were not committed to one particular work but engaged in whatever labors their travel and presence brought them. Francis's work and thought indicate a living, ecclesial faith that seeks to be for and with the poor.

Central to every aspect of his life was Francis's experience of the trinitarian God. He wanted to reveal the Father to all by imitating the Son through the inspiration of the Holy Spirit. Like his Lord, he was eager to make his way back to the Father and to summon all creation to accompany him on that painful but peaceful journey. An adult innocence aided him in transcending the spirit-matter dichotomy, making him a sublime example of both the spirituality of matter and the materialization of spirit.

Francis embraced voluntary poverty because he wanted to imitate his Lord, who had made himself poor (*2 Cor.* 8:9). In this poverty Francis found a freedom that fostered fraternity. The poor, in their more evident dependence on God, reminded Francis of the mystery of divine sympathy and of each creature's intrinsic poverty. In the spirit of poverty he urged his brothers to renounce their desire to dominate, and though called to minister to all, to favor labor among the lepers and farmhands.

Aware that the Roman Catholic church was capable of taming the gospel, Francis persisted in the belief that Christ was to be found in this institution, especially in the Eucharist. He sought a cardinal protector for the Franciscan order and acknowledged the pontiff to be the final arbiter in spiritual matters. Although Francis's relations with the Curia Romana may have weakened his project, the majority of scholars submit that his relation to the hierarchy was loyal, challenging, and constructive.

Movements for peace and for the marginalized have in Francis a ready patron. He sent his brothers out, not against but among the Saracens, and he required that all his followers (lay included) not bear arms. His pursuit of Lady Poverty inspires those of every age who seek simplicity. His fondness for animals and nature has deepened humanity's understanding of the interrelatedness of all creation grounded in a creator whose richness it reflects.

Francis managed to steer a course that avoided the excesses of feudal authority and of the bourgeois pursuit of money. In his rule he taught his followers to use only that which was needed, to own nothing, and to renounce any desire to dominate; he insisted that authority for the *minores* (those who wished to lead a biblically inspired simple life) meant fraternal service. The church, although initially cautious, soon adopted some of his insights for its own apostolic strategy; between 1218 and 1226 six papal bulls were issued relating to aspects of his vision. The Holy See recognized that the manner of his preaching touched the lives of the people; it also gave the vernacular a new respectability and provided themes for artists such as Cimabue and Giotto. Though no intellectual, Francis's emphasis on humanity inspired the deeply incarnational systems of Bonaventure and of Duns Scotus.

Francis's legacy to the Christian tradition was a revitalized gospel that clearly perceived many forms of brotherhood: with superiors—once, having been denied by a bishop the right to preach in his diocese, Francis exited, paused, reentered, and resubmitted his petition successfully; with strangers—in his rule of 1221 he calls for a simple, nonpolemical style of missionary presence; with the underclass—when a brother asked if it were proper to feed some robbers, he responded affirmatively, for in every person he saw a possible thief and in every thief a possible brother or sister; with nature—he urged his brothers when establishing the boundaries of their shelters not to build walls but to plant hedges. The movement founded by Francis offered the church a new form of gospel commitment. It combined a contemplative life with an apostolic work that was mobile, diverse, and urban. Although it was a consecrated life, it was not removed from daily concerns.

[*See also* Franciscans.]

BIBLIOGRAPHY

Kajetan Esser, the scholar most responsible for the critical texts of Francis's writings, discusses 181 manuscripts in his *Opuscula Sancti Francisci Assisiensis* (Rome, 1978) and his *Rule and Testament of St. Francis* (Chicago, 1977). The excellent *Francis and Clare: The Complete Works* (New York, 1982), edited by Regis J. Armstrong and Ignatius Brady, offers a list for the first time in English of Francis's authentic writings (twenty-eight in all) and inauthentic writings (including the popular "Peace Prayer"). The most practical single volume for primary sources remains *St. Francis of Assisi: Writings and Early Biographies, English Omnibus of the Sources* (Chicago, 1973), edited by Marion A. Habig. It includes lives of Francis by Celano and by Bonaventure, *The Little Flowers of Saint Francis* (a treasure of fourteenth-century popular literature), and an extensive bibliography, though not always reliably translated. Classic biographies include Omer Englebert's astute *Saint Francis of Assisi* (Chicago, 1965), and Father Cuthbert of Brighton's accurate *Life of St. Francis of Assisi* (London, 1912). Paul Sabatier's *Life of St. Francis of Assisi* (London, 1894) is provocative. Of the more than sixty modern biographies, G. K. Chesterton in *St. Francis of Assisi* (London, 1923) captures his heart and Nikos Kazantzakis in *Saint Francis: A Novel* (New York, 1962) presents a poet. A former mayor of Assisi, Arnaldo Fortini, in his *Francis of Assisi* (New York, 1981), offers an invaluable historical appendix. Anglican bishop J. R. H. Moorman presents, in his new edition of *Saint Francis of Assisi* (London, 1976), a precise historical life. Leonardo Boff characterizes Francis, in *Saint Francis* (New York, 1982), as a model for human liberation.

RAYMOND J. BUCHER, O.F.M.

FRANCKE, AUGUST HERMANN (1663–1727), after Spener the major spokesman for early Lutheran Pietism, born in the Hanseatic city of Lübeck on 22 March 1663. Both his father and his maternal grandfather were prominent jurists, and young August was more or less expected to take up a learned career. Because the Francke household was pervaded by the piety of Johann Arndt (1555–1621), it was quite natural for August to prepare himself for the Lutheran ministry. Accordingly, he studied at Erfurt and Kiel, and finally received his master of arts degree from the University of Leipzig. For religious reasons he refused further academic preparation, though much of his time continued to be spent in private study. Thus he emerged from his student career superbly prepared not only in philosophy, theology, and biblical studies but with considerable competence in Latin, Greek, Hebrew, Italian, French, and English, besides his native German.

As the result of an experience of a conscious religious awakening (1687), Francke joined the circle of Spener's followers and eventually became the leader of the Spenerian renewal movement of continental Protestantism. The University of Halle, to the faculty of which he was appointed in 1691, quickly became the intellectual center of Lutheran Pietism. His pioneer work in establishing an imposing array of educational and charitable institutions attracted much attention in Europe. His extensive system of connections included a large segment of European nobility as well as several European courts. The periodic reports of his work, such as *Segensvolle Fußstapfen* (translated into English in 1706 under the title *Liber Pietatis Hallensis)*, spurred educational, charitable, missionary, and ecumenical impulses not only on the continent but in England and in the English colonies of North America. Under Francke's guidance the Canstein Bible Institute, begun in 1710, satisfied the ever-increasing need for cheap Bibles and devotional aids. The theological works issuing from Francke's pen and from Halle were a major factor in substituting biblical for dogmatic theology and ethically oriented concerns for purely theological discourses in Protestant pulpits. At the zenith of his career Francke was widely respected as an innovative pastor, theologian, educator, organizer of charitable institutions, promoter of domestic and foreign missions, and advocate of a new vision of ecumenical cooperation.

BIBLIOGRAPHY

Important for Francke study is still D. Gustav Kramer's *August Hermann Francke*, 2 vols. (Halle, 1880–1882), though dated in many respects. The best biography is the scholarly, very appreciative study by Erich Beyreuther, *August Hermann Francke, 1663–1727* (Marburg, 1956). For Francke's theology, Erhard Peschke's *Studien zur Theologie August Hermann Franckes*, 2 vols. (Berlin, 1964–1966) is indispensable. Peschke also edited a selection of Francke's works titled *Streitschriften* (New York, 1981). Available in English are Gary Stattler's *God's Glory and the Neighbor's Good: A Brief Introduction to the Life and Writings of August Hermann Francke* (Chicago, 1982) and a small selection of Francke's writings in Peter C. Erb's *The Pietists: Selected Writings* (Ramsey, N.J., 1983).

F. ERNEST STOEFFLER

FRANKEL, ZACHARIAS (1801–1875), the founder, in Germany, of Historical Judaism, the forerunner of Conservative Judaism in America. A member of the first generation of modern rabbis, Frankel fashioned a multifaceted career as pulpit rabbi, spokesman for political emancipation, critic of radical religious reform, editor, head of the first modern rabbinical seminary, and historian of Jewish law.

Frankel was born in Prague, then still the largest Jewish community in Europe, into a financially comfortable family with a distinguished lineage of rabbinic and communal leaders. His education combined traditional immersion in Jewish texts with systematic exposure to secular studies in a manner that was still far from typical. In 1830 he received his doctorate from the University of Pest and in 1831 acquired the post of district rabbi of Litoměřice, becoming the first Bohemian rabbi to hold a doctorate. His advocacy of changes in the synagogue service, the education of the young, and the training and role of the rabbi brought him, in 1836, an invitation from the government of Saxony to occupy the pulpit in Dresden as chief rabbi of the realm. Despite several subsequent offers from the much larger and rapidly growing Jewish community of Berlin, Frankel stayed in Dresden until 1854, when he was called to become the first director of the new rabbinical and teachers' seminary in Breslau. By 1879, four years after his death, the seminary had instructed some 272 students and had placed nearly 120 teachers, preachers, and rabbis in the most important Jewish communities in Europe.

A self-styled moderate reformer in matters of religion, Frankel formulated his program of "positive, historical Judaism" in the 1840s to stem the rising tide of radical religious reform. Against the Reform movement's unbounded rationalism, Frankel defended Judaism's legal character, the sanctity of historical experience, and the authority of current practice. The term *positive* pointed to prescribed ritual behavior *(halakhah)* as the dominant means for the expression of religious sentiment in Judaism, while the term *historical* designated its nonlegal realm, sanctified by time and suffering.

What gives Frankel's definition its dynamic quality is the role of the people. Genuine reform evolves organically from below and not by fiat from above. It is for this reason that Frankel repudiated the innovations of the three rabbinical conferences of the 1840s; whether dictated by political considerations or the canons of reason, their measures did violence to prevailing sentiment and practice.

On a popular level Frankel tried, as author and editor, to deepen Jews' loyalty to the past by offering them a brand of heroic history that stressed cultural achievement. As a scholar Frankel was the preeminent modern rabbinist of his generation, and he devoted a prolific career to introducing the concept of the development of Jewish law over time. Using the method as well as the ideology of Friedrich C. Savigny's *geschichtliche Rechtswissenschaft,* Frankel tried to recover and analyze the stages of legal evolution, from Alexandrian exegeses of scripture to medieval rabbinic *responsa.* In the process he left enduring contributions to the modern study of the Mishnah and the Palestinian Talmud.

Frankel's undogmatic research on the Mishnah challenged the traditional image of the ancient rabbis as transmitters rather than creators of the oral law and provoked a bitter assault in 1861 from the Neo-Orthodox camp of Samson Raphael Hirsch. Growing religious polarization served to clarify denominational lines and forced Frankel to occupy the middle ground.

Two institutions created by Frankel embodied, amplified, and disseminated his vision of Historical Judaism. *Die Monatsschrift für Geschichte und Wissenschaft des Judentums,* which he edited for eighteen taxing years (1851–1868), provided its readers with a balance of high-level popularization and critical scholarship, setting the standard for all later nineteenth-century journals of Jewish studies. Similarly, the Breslau seminary, which he led for twenty-one years, transformed rabbinic education by integrating modern scholarship with traditional piety and requiring its graduates to be both spiritual leaders and practitioners of *Wissenschaft.*

BIBLIOGRAPHY

Brann, Marcus, ed. *Zacharias Frankel: Gedenkblätter zu seinem hundertsten Geburtstage.* Breslau, 1901.

Heinemann, Isaac. "The Idea of the Jewish Theological Seminary Seventy-Five Years Ago and Today." In *Das Breslauer Seminar,* edited by Guido Kisch, pp. 85–100. Tübingen, 1963.

Rabinowitz, Saul Pinchas. *R. Zekharyah Frankel* (in Hebrew). Warsaw, 1898.

Schorsch, Ismar. "Zacharias Frankel and the European Origins of Conservative Judaism." *Judaism* 30 (Summer 1981): 344–354.

ISMAR SCHORSCH

FRANKFORT, HENRI (1897–1954), archaeologist and historian of religion. Frankfort began his studies at the University of Amsterdam, where he studied history, but he transferred to the University of London in order to work under Flinders Petrie in Egyptian archaeology. He always preferred, however, to designate himself as a historian.

In 1922, Frankfort became a member of Petrie's expedition to Egypt, and from 1924 to 1925, he studied at the British School of Archaeology in Athens. He obtained his M.A. from the University of London in 1924 and his Ph.D. from the University of Leiden in 1927. From 1925 to 1929 he served as director of the excavations of the Egypt Exploration Society at Tell al-ʿAmarna, Abydos, and Erment. In 1929 he accepted the directorship of the Iraq expedition of the University of Chicago's Oriental Institute, which he held until 1937, when excavations were discontinued. In 1932, Frankfort was appointed research professor of Oriental archaeology at the Oriental Institute and associate professor of the ancient Near East at the University of Amsterdam. He served as acting chairman of the Department of Near Eastern Languages and Literatures at the University of Chicago during World War II. In 1949 he accepted the post of director of the Warburg Institute in London and was appointed professor of the history of preclassical antiquity at the University of London.

Frankfort's first major work, *Studies in Early Pottery in the Near East* (1924–1927), was of fundamental importance for Near Eastern archaeology. He was the first to classify and date ancient Near Eastern ceramics and thus to make it a basic means of periodization and relative dating. Of similarly fundamental importance was his later study of cylinder seals, for which he identified characteristic features for successive periods, thereby establishing a relative dating system for this important and very numerous class of objects. The resulting study, *Cylinder Seals: A Documentary Essay on the Art and Religion of the Ancient Near East* (1939), is not only important to archaeologists but also presents the student of religion with a wealth of data on mythology and ritual.

The results of the various expeditions directed by Frankfort in Egypt and Iraq were published in a series of preliminary and final reports, partly by Frankfort alone, and partly by him and members of the staff. Among the former, the valuable volumes *Sculpture of the Third Millennium B.C. from Tel Asmar and Khafajah* (1939), *More Sculpture from the Diyala Region* (1943), and *Stratified Cylinder Seals from the Diyala Region* (1955) should be mentioned. Of more general purview are the important studies *Archaeology and the Sumerian Problem* (1932) and *The Birth of Civilization in the Near East* (1951). An overview of ancient Near Eastern archaeology is given in his *The Art and Architecture of the Ancient Orient* (1954).

Of special interest to historians of religion is *The Intellectual Adventure of Ancient Man* (1946), which was later reissued under the title *Before Philosophy* (1963). The lecture series on which this book is based was organized by Frankfort, and he and his wife contributed the introductory and concluding chapters, "Myth and Reality," a penetrating and clear analysis of the logic of mythopoeic thought, and "The Emancipation of Thought from Myth," which traces the road from mythical to genuinely philosophical thought. During the time that Frankfort initiated and contributed to these lectures, he finished the two larger studies, *Ancient Egyptian Religion: An Interpretation* (2d ed., 1949), and the influential *Kingship and the Gods: A Study of Ancient Near Eastern Religion as the Integration of Society and Nature* (1948). Frankfort's method of approach is that of phenomenology of religion, which respects the religious commitment and values reflected in the data studied. The aim of the latter work is well expressed in the subtitle, and the treatment of both Egyptian and Mesopotamian materials, with attention both to their characteristic similarities and to their differences, lends depth to the study. Frankfort was deeply aware that an understanding of religious data can be gained only in terms of the general culture in which the religion in question is embedded and from which the specific meanings of its symbols are derived. This position is given its most complete methodological statement in his Frazer Lecture of 1951, published as *The Problem of Similarity in Ancient Near Eastern Religions* (1951), where he argues cogently against a comparative method that would emphasize general similarities and neglect specific differences, for it is the latter that hold the true clues to understanding: "Once again, then, our danger lies in the similarities themselves, for it is—as always—the cultural context which holds the secret of their significance."

BIBLIOGRAPHY

In addition to works cited in the text, see Frankfort's lectures published in the *Journal of the Warburg and Courtauld Institutes:* "State Festivals in Egypt and Mesopotamia" (vol. 15, 1952, pp. 1–12), "The Dying God" (vol. 21, 1958, pp. 141–151), "Heresy in a Theocratic State" (vol. 21, 1958, pp. 152–161), and "The Archetype in Analytical Psychology and the History of Religion" (vol. 21, 1958, pp. 166–178). For an obituary notice written by Pinhas Delongaz and me, see "Henri Frankfort, 24 II 1897–16 VII 1954," *Journal of Near Eastern Studies* 14 (1955): 1–3; this piece is followed by a bibliography compiled by J. Vindenaess.

THORKILD JACOBSEN

FRASHŌKERETI. The Avestan term *Frashōkereti* ("making wonderful" or "rehabilitation" of existence) corresponds to *Frashgird,* the Middle Persian term for the Last Judgment, or final day of humanity's existence. The Avestan term derives from the expression "to make existence splendid." The concept is eschatological and soteriological and, already present in the *Gāthās,* is at the basis of Zoroastrian doctrine. With this concept Zarathushtra (Zoroaster) abolished the archaic ideology of the cosmic cycle and of the eternal return modeled on atemporal archetypes, proclaiming the expectation of, and hope for, an *eschaton.* He thus introduced a linear conception of cosmic time, an innovation in religious thought that had an enormous influence on humanity's subsequent spiritual history. According to his doctrine, the final event will be completed not because of a cosmogonic ritual but by the will of the creator: the resurrection of the body and last judgment are essential and significant aspects of the Frashōkereti.

In the *Gāthās* the Frashōkereti is felt to be near, but later Zoroastrianism developed an eschatological doctrine situating it further off in time, within the concept of a Great Year divided into three periods, each a millennium in length and each beginning with the coming of a Saoshyant, a savior born of the seed of Zarathushtra. The last of these will be the Saoshyant *par excellence,* the maker of the final Frashōkereti.

The Frashōkereti is described in one of the hymns of the Avesta (*Yashts* 19). It declares that *druj,* the "lie," the principle or deity of evil, will be brought down; the *daiva* Aēshma, "fury," will be destroyed by a bloody mace; the *daiva* Aka Manah ("bad thought") will be overcome; hunger and thirst will be defeated; and the great god of evil, Angra Mainyu, deprived of his power, will be driven to flight.

The Pahlavi literature of the ninth and tenth centuries CE furnishes further details. The Frashgird will be announced by positive signs: the abolition of meat as a food for man and its gradual replacement by an increasingly spiritual diet, without milk, water, or plants; the progressive fading of concupiscence; and so forth. Finally, after the resurrection of the body and after a test by molten metal, through which all, both just and unjust, must pass, there will take place a great, eschatological sacrifice of a bull. Its fat, mixed with white *haoma,* will make the drink of immortality for all men.

BIBLIOGRAPHY

Bailey, H. W. *Zoroastrian Problems in the Ninth-Century Books* (1943). Reprint, Oxford, 1971.

Duchesne-Guillemin, Jacques. *La religion de l'Iran ancient.* Paris, 1962.

Gnoli, Gherardo. "Questioni sull'interpretazione della dottrina gathica." *Annali dell'Instituto Universitario Orientale di Napoli,* n.s. 21 (1971): 341–370.

Humbach, Helmut, ed. and trans. *Die Gathas des Zarathustra.* Heidelberg, 1959.

Lommel, Herman. *Die Religion Zarathustras nach dem Awesta dargestellt.* Tübingen, 1930.

Molé, Marijan. *Culte, mythe et cosmologie dans l'Iran ancien.* Paris, 1963.

Nyberg, H. S. *Irans forntida religioner.* Stockholm, 1937. Translated as *Die Religionen des alten Iran* (1938; 2d ed., Osnabrück, 1966).

Zaehner, R. C. *The Dawn and Twilight of Zoroastrianism.* London, 1961.

GHERARDO GNOLI
Translated from Italian by Roger DeGaris

FRAVASHIS, beneficent and protective guardian spirits whose services must be secured by means of ritual offerings, are an essential element of the religious structure of Zoroastrianism. They play an important role in the frequency of rainfall and are responsible for guaranteeing the prosperity and preservation of the family. As the spirits of the dead, they are the protagonists in a great feast held on the last night of the year. They are thought to preexist human beings and to survive them.

The *fravashis* do not appear in the *Gāthās.* In the Avesta, the first mention of them occurs in the *Yasna Haptanhāiti,* and an entire hymn (*Yashts* 13) is dedicated to them.

The conception of the *fravashi* has all the characteristics of an archaic, pre-Zoroastrian belief that was later absorbed and adapted by the tradition. Examples of these characteristics include their identification with the spirits of the dead (Söderblom, 1899, pp. 229–260, 373–418) and their warlike nature.

As the spirits of the dead the *fravashis* have often been compared to the Roman *manes* or to the Indian *pitaraḥ;* as warlike beings, they have been compared with the Germanic valkyries or to the Indian Maruts, the company of celestial warriors. In particular, in the context of the Indo-European tripartite ideology, the *fravashis* are seen as a Zoroastrian substitute for the Maruts (Dumézil, 1953); both are linked to the concepts and ethics of the Aryan *Männerbund.* Most likely, Zoroastrianism absorbed this ancient concept, typical of a warrior society, through its ties to the cult of the dead and reinterpreted the *fravashis* as combatants for the rule of Ahura Mazdā. We find such a zoroastrianization in the myth told in the third chapter of the *Bundahishn* (Book of Primordial Creation), which relates that the *fravashis* chose to be incarnated in material bodies in order to fight Ahriman and the evil powers instead of remaining peacefully in the celestial world.

The etymology of the word *fravashi* is uncertain. Originally it may have been used to designate the spirit of a deceased hero who was endowed with **vṛti,* "valor" (Bailey, 1943, pp. 107ff.); or it may have expressed the theological concept, fundamental to Zoroastrianism, of choice, **fra-vṛti* (Lommel, 1930, pp. 151, 159–163) or that of the profession of faith (Hoffmann, 1979, p. 91; Schlerath, 1980, pp. 207ff.).

BIBLIOGRAPHY

Bailey, H.W. *Zoroastrian Problems in the Ninth-Century Books* (1943). Oxford, 1971.

Duchesne-Guillemin, Jacques. "L'homme dans la religion iranienne." In *Anthropologie religieuse,* edited by C. Jouco Bleeker, pp. 93–107. Leiden, 1955.

Dumézil, Georges. "Víṣṇu et les Marút à travers la réforme zoroastrienne." *Journal asiatique* 241 (1953): 1–25.

Gnoli, Gherardo. "Le fravaši e l'immortalità." In *La mort, les morts dans les sociétés anciennes,* edited by Gherardo Gnoli and Jean-Pierre Vernant, pp. 339–347. Paris, 1982.

Hoffmann, Karl. "Das Avesta in der Persis." In *Prolegomena to the Sources of the History of Pre-Islamic Central Asia,* edited by János Harmatta, pp. 89–93. Budapest, 1979.

Lommel, Herman. *Die Religion Zarathustras nach dem Awesta dargestellt.* Tübingen, 1930.

Malandra, William W. "The 'Fravaši Yašt.'" Ph.D. diss., University of Pennsylvania, 1971.

Nyberg, H. S. *Irans forntida religioner.* Stockholm, 1937. Translated as *Die Religionen des alten Iran* (1938; 2d ed., Osnabrück, 1966).

Schlerath, Bernfried. "Indo-Iranisch *var- 'wählen.'" *Studien zur Indologie und Iranistik* (*Festschrift Paul Thieme*) 5–6 (1980): 199–208.

Söderblom, Nathan. "Les Fravashis: Étude sur les traces dans le mazdéisme d'une ancienne conception sur la survivance des morts." *Revue de l'histoire des religions* 39 (1899): 229–260, 373–418.

GHERARDO GNOLI
Translated from Italian by Roger DeGaris

FRAZER, JAMES G. (1854–1941), British anthropologist and historian of religion. James George Frazer, the eldest of four children, was born in preindustrial Glasgow, the son of a successful pharmacist. His parents were devout members of the Free Church of Scotland, a conservative sect that in the 1840s had broken away from the (Established) Church of Scotland on matters of church governance. Accordingly Frazer was raised in an atmosphere of deep piety, which, be it noted, he later said that he did not find oppressive.

Frazer early showed academic promise and entered the University of Glasgow at the then not unusually early age of fifteen. There, he writes in a genial memoir composed at the end of his life, three important things occurred: he conceived his lifelong love of the classics, he came to see that the world is governed by a system of unvarying natural laws, and he painlessly lost the religious faith of his childhood.

Frazer did brilliantly at Glasgow but soon realized that although Scottish education gave him a broader background than an English one would have, its standards were not as high. After taking his degree at Glasgow he therefore matriculated at Trinity College, Cambridge, in 1874 for a second baccalaureate. He took second place in the classical tripos of 1878. A dissertation on Platonic epistemology gained him a fellowship at Trinity in 1879, which after three renewals was granted for life; he was a fellow of Trinity for more than sixty years.

In 1896 Frazer married Mrs. Elizabeth (Lilly) Grove, a French widow with two children who had become a writer out of economic necessity. She wrote an early and important volume on the history of the dance, along with many playlets in French for schoolroom use. She soon became convinced that the academic world was overlooking her husband's merits and strove mightily to advance his career (he was the stereotype of a research scholar, unworldly and shy). She also arranged for his work to be translated into French, which meant that Frazer was very well known in France after the war. Frazer was knighted in 1914, became a fellow of the Royal Society in 1920, and was awarded the Order of Merit in 1925.

Frazer's first scholarly writing, from which his interest in anthropology can be said to date, came about through his friendship with William Robertson Smith (1847–1894), the eminent Scottish theologian and comparative Semiticist. More than any other person, Smith was responsible for disseminating the results of German biblical scholarship in Great Britain at the end of the century. For his pains he became the defendant in the last significant heresy trials in Great Britain. Although he was exonerated, Smith had become too notorious for provincial Scotland and therefore accepted an appointment in Cambridge. [*See the biography of Smith.*] Among his many other activities, he was editor of the ninth edition of the *Encyclopaedia Britannica* and as such was always looking for likely contributors. Meeting his countryman Frazer at Trinity, Smith soon set him to work. Because in those days encyclopedias were brought out a volume at a time, and because the volumes through the letter *O* had already appeared, Frazer was assigned articles beginning with *P* and subsequent letters. Thus it was that he came to write the important entries "Taboo" and "Totem," which launched him into the then sparsely populated field of anthropology.

In 1889 Frazer wrote to the publisher George Macmillan offering him a manuscript on magic, folklore, and religion in the ancient world. Macmillan accepted *The Golden Bough,* and it was published in two volumes in the following year. It was generally well received, the reviewers noting Frazer's impressive erudition and stylistic gifts. As soon as he had brought out the first edition, Frazer began preparing an enlarged second edition, which duly appeared in three volumes in 1900. The third and final edition, in twelve volumes, came out from 1911 to 1915. It is this massive version that Frazer himself abridged in 1922; he produced a thirteenth volume, *Aftermath,* in 1936.

The Golden Bough merits special attention because it remains Frazer's best-known work, but it hardly exhausts his contribution to the historical and anthropological study of ancient and "primitive" religion. In 1898 he published *Pausanias's Description of Greece*—a translation of Pausanias's report of his travels—accompanied by five volumes of commentary, maps, and plates, all of which represented fifteen years of work. Pausanias, who in the second century CE prepared this guidebook to his country, was especially curious about religion and inquired ceaselessly about artifacts and rituals that had survived in the countryside but were no longer extant in Athens. Pausanias's record is frequently the only surviving witness of many phenomena of ancient Greek folk religion. His travels constituted an ideal text for Frazer, permitting him to use his classical as well as his comparative anthropological knowledge.

Among Frazer's other major productions in the history of religion are *Lectures on the Early History of the Kingship* (1905); *Totemism and Exogamy* (1910), which gave Freud much data as well as the idea for a title (*Totem and Taboo*, 1911); *Folk-Lore in the Old Testament*, (1918), which arose out of Frazer's study of Hebrew; and an edition of Ovid's *Fasti* (1929). The *Fasti* is a narrative poem organized around the cycle of the Roman holidays, and, like *Pausanias*, it gave Frazer an opportunity to employ the whole of his considerable scholarly equipment.

The Golden Bough was noteworthy because it offered something that had not been done before in English: a treatment from the philosophical, evolutionary point of view, delivered in sonorous and untechnical language, of the beliefs and behavior of the ancient Greeks and Romans as if they were those of "primitives." By the end of the nineteenth century, the classical world had lost much of the privileged status it had enjoyed since the Renaissance as the origin and repository of the greatest that had ever been thought and said. Indeed eighteenth- and nineteenth-century classical historiography was largely demythologizing in its impulse. But because of the centrality maintained by the classics in the educational curriculum and thus in the training and habit of mind of the governing classes in Great Britain, it came as a shock to a cultured reader when Frazer insisted on the ways in which life and thought in classical antiquity strongly resembled, overall and in detail, those of the "primitives" (or "savages") who had become well known to Europeans as a result of the imperialist expansion of the eighteenth and especially the nineteenth century.

Although many scholars have disagreed with some or all of it, the argument of *The Golden Bough* may fairly be said by now to have become part of the basis of modern culture (at least on the level of metaphor), and many educated people who employ its argument are unaware of its origins. Briefly, the work purports to be an explanation of a curious ritual combat that ancient sources tell us took place in classical times in the town of Aricia outside Rome. In a grove at Nemi a "priest" stood guard at all times, awaiting a challenger to his supremacy. The rule of the place was that any runaway slave who managed to reach the grove would gain his freedom if he succeeded in killing its guardian; with such success, however, came the obligation to assume the role of priest, and to kill or be killed in turn. In Frazer's view, this combat cannot be understood solely or wholly in terms of Roman religion; instead its elements must be analyzed comparatively (by adducing examples of analogous behavior from other "primitive" societies). He asserts that the guardian of the grove was a priest-king, who, like all such in primitive societies, literally incarnated the well-being of the community and thus had to be kept alive and well at all costs. This leads to a discussion of the strategies, both actual and symbolic (such as taboo, magic, sacrifice, and scapegoats), that such communities undertook to keep the king from weakness or death. At the heart of the work is a lengthy analysis of the complex of myth and ritual in the religions of the ancient eastern Mediterranean, all of which turn on death and resurrection and whose themes are often played out in seasonal combats and other fertility ceremonies. The main rites discussed are those of Attis, Adonis, Osiris, and Dionysos, all of whom Frazer understands as divine protagonists in the same, ubiquitous, recurrent vegetational drama.

The actual goings-on in the grove at Nemi are, Frazer finally admits, merely pretexts, for he is in fact interested in something more important: nothing less than the laws that describe the workings of the "primitive mind," which by definition is less well developed than our own. Although this mind is inaccessible to us directly, it may be studied nevertheless, by adopting (from the work of the pioneering German folklorist Wilhelm Mannhardt) "the law of similarity": when customs are similar in different societies, we may then infer that the motives of the people performing them are also similar. This follows from the then generally accepted idea (advanced by E. B. Tylor) that the human race has evolved in a uniform fashion, mentally as well as physically. Further, because in Frazer's view the mentality of the primitive "Aryan" was still extant in that of the modern European peasantry since the peasantry still participated in a mental universe untouched by modern thought, it was therefore appropriate to compare the behavior of these so-called modern primitives (peasants and underdeveloped tribal societies) with that of historical societies of the ancient world in order to extract laws of primitive mental functioning.

Finally, however, Frazer was interested in even bigger

game than primitive epistemology. For although in his survey of the dying-and-reviving gods of the eastern Mediterranean Frazer never mentions the name of Jesus, only the slowest of his readers could have failed to make the comparison between the pagan rites that result from an imperfect (because irrational) understanding of the universe and contemporary Christianity. Frazer employed the "objective," scientific comparative method as a weapon to finally dispatch Christianity as an outworn relic of misunderstanding, credulity, and superstition. There can be no doubt that his subliminal message was successfully delivered: the many uses of Frazerian arguments and images in the literature and cultural analysis of the post–World War I period (the most well-known of which is T. S. Eliot's *The Waste Land*) are ample testimony to that. (In addition, the Frazer papers in the library of Trinity College, Cambridge, contain many unsolicited letters from readers, educated and otherwise, that thank Frazer for having finally dispelled the veil of illusion from before their eyes as to the "real" nature of Christianity.)

As time has passed, Frazer's affinities are increasingly seen to be with those polymath scholars who, periodically since the Renaissance, have had the vision and industry to attempt a description and interpretation of the entire phenomenon of religion. Living when and where he did conferred several advantages on him. First, only by the end of the nineteenth century had European imperialism gone far enough to open up virtually the entire tribal world. Thus Frazer's was the first generation for which the data existed to permit a credible, anthropologically based worldwide conspectus of religious behavior. Second, the triumph of Darwinism automatically promoted as self-evidently correct any explanatory model that was based on evolutionary premises. If mind had developed in a linear fashion, as Frazer (and Tylor) believed, then a rigid, uniform progression from magic through religion to positive science seemed a plausible description of the pathway toward understanding that humanity had in fact taken.

From our point of view, however, viewing Frazer as we do from the other side of a gulf produced by a nightmarish century and by seventy years of anthropological fieldwork and much greater philosophical and methodological sophistication, he seems himself to be a relic of a habit of thought that, if not exactly primitive, then is at least of long ago and far away. His extreme empiricism and antitheoretical inclination made him a victim, finally, of his mountains of data. At the same time, he could never have presented such a stirring picture of the long evolutionary struggle of humanity toward self-understanding had he not been so willing to use simple categories under which to organize his data.

Frazer's professional descendants are many and various, as are their evaluations of his work. For English-speaking anthropologists, he is seen mainly as a horrible example of the "armchair school" of anthropology that was swept away by the advent of fieldwork. Historians of religion hold him in higher esteem, probably because the comparative method (of which his work is the greatest exemplar) is still in guarded use in that discipline. Finally, his name stands highest among literary critics and cultural historians, to whose field he made no explicit contribution.

It may be most reasonable to situate Frazer in a grand tradition—one that understands religion humanistically and therefore regards it as a perennially appropriate subject for discourse with the educated reader—that has been eclipsed in our day as a result of the aspirations to scientific status of anthropology. One may see him, then, despite his obvious limitations, as a scholar whose vision and literary gifts ensure him a permanent place in the ranks of those who have expanded the modern idea of our mysterious past.

BIBLIOGRAPHY

For further biographical information, see my *J. G. Frazer: His Life and Work* (Cambridge, 1987). Two memoirs by Robert Angus Downie, *James George Frazer* (London, 1940) and *Frazer and the Golden Bough* (London, 1970), are sketchy. Theodore Besterman's *A Bibliography of Sir James Frazer, O.M.* (London, 1934) offers a useful guide to Frazer's complex oeuvre. E. O. James's obituary notice in the *Dictionary of National Biography, 1941–1950* (supp. 3), R. R. Marett's in the *Proceedings of the British Academy* 27 (1941): 377–492, and H. J. Fleure's in the *Obituary Notices of Fellows of the Royal Society* 3 (1941): 897–914, are helpful. See also Bronislaw Malinowski's "Sir James George Frazer: A Biographical Appreciation," in his *A Scientific Theory of Culture and Other Essays* (Chapel Hill, N.C., 1944), pp. 177–221.

ROBERT ACKERMAN

FREEMASONS. A system of moral teachings and a set of fraternal organizations that practice these teachings, Freemasonry cannot properly be called a "secret society," though secrecy is both practiced as a device for instruction during initiation into its rites and used as a symbol. In some instances, the names of members and the existence of the society itself have been withheld from political authorities because of Freemasonry's historical association with political movements in Italy, Spain, and Latin America. As modern fraternal orders, however, Masonic lodges and related organizations have been more open to public scrutiny, and membership is in almost all cases publicly displayed.

History. The history of Freemasonry is shrouded in legend and ambiguity. This historical obscurity stems from the institution's use of legendary history in its rituals and ceremonies, and from the fragmentariness of the records of the early Masonic organizations. Few historians have undertaken a comprehensive study of Freemasonry's history and cultural significance. However, in recent years, both social historians and historians of ideas have sought to understand the significance of Masonic development as an institution and a set of philosophical symbols.

The origin of Freemasonry can be traced to periodic gatherings of operative stonemasons engaged in the building of churches and cathedrals in England. The earliest manuscripts associated with the work and moral symbolism of these stonemasons date from the late fourteenth century. The most noted of these manuscripts is the so-called *Regius Manuscript* (c. 1390). This and similar documents make up the "Gothic Constitutions" that trace the legendary history of the craft of masonry back to the Flood or to the building of the Egyptian pyramids or Solomon's Temple. This collection also contains specific moral responsibilities that are enjoined upon members as apprentices, fellow-craftsmen (or journeymen), and master masons. It is probable that secrecy as a device for teaching and as a symbol dates from this period, when knowledge of the building techniques of individual master masons was restricted to guild members.

The historian of ideas Frances A. Yates claims that during the seventeenth century Freemasonry merged with Elizabethan courtly philosophy and continental, particularly German, Rosicrucianism (*Giordano Bruno and the Hermetic Tradition*, 1964). Elizabethan philosophy was associated with such figures as John Dee, Robert Fludd, Thomas Vaughan, and Giordano Bruno. It was Neoplatonic in character, and evoked the memory of the legendary Hermes Trismegistos, understood in the seventeenth century to be a pre-Christian prophet of Christianity. Rosicrucianism was, according to Yates, a self-conscious reform movement that bore the imprint of classical and Renaissance humanism. The impact of these two movements upon the stonemasons' tradition was twofold: (1) it transformed the working tools of the operatives into a system of symbols for personal morality and transformation through initiation, and (2) it projected the Masonic motif, and subsequently the Masonic institutional organization, into the nonoperative arena of eighteenth-century world affairs. The Masonic initiation in 1646 of the antiquarian Elias Ashmole recommends Yates's interpretation of this period.

Freemasonry as an institution can be dated from the formation of the first national Masonic organization, the "Grand Lodge" of England, which resulted from the combining of four small lodges of nonoperative masons at the Goose and Gridiron alehouse, London, on 24 June 1717. From this time, a general narrative history of Freemasonry can be pieced together from journals, minutes, and newspaper accounts. The order attracted royal patronage, and several members of the Royal Society became members of the Masonic fraternity. Notable among these members was John Theophilus Desaguliers, an Anglican priest of Huguenot ancestry who became the order's third elected Grand Master.

The introduction of the order into France in the early eighteenth century signified the transition of the institution from a largely nonpolitical organization into a body that was closely identified with the Enlightenment concepts of deism and equality. The ritual and symbolism of the craft tradition were soon embellished into a system of *hautes grades*, or high degrees, which altered noticeably the character of the fraternity. The higher degrees were later grouped into two main rites, or systems: the Scottish, which was derived from the French *hautes grades*, and the York, which was the result of a commingling of English and American ceremonials. Several rites of numerous degrees were erected and a new knightly or chivalric motif was added to the earlier craft or stonemason tradition. The rites of the Freemasons in continental Europe incorporated the legends of the Knights Templar, the Teutonic Knights, and Knights Hospitaler of Saint John (or Knights of Malta). These Masonic bodies became avidly anticlerical and advocates of political and social reform.

British Freemasonry, organized into separate Irish, Scottish, and English grand lodges, remained nonpartisan during the political-religious disputes of the eighteenth century, but removed any requirement that its initiates be Christians with the adoption of the *Constitutions of 1723*, revised in 1738 by Scots Presbyterian minister James Anderson. Largely as a result of British imperial expansion, lodges of Freemasons were established in North America, India, and the West Indies.

During the late eighteenth century a schism occurred within English-speaking Freemasonry that signaled the development of a general class distinction among Masons between the "Antients" and the "Moderns." Further, this division led to the addition of the Holy Royal Arch to the basic three-degree system of English Freemasonry, which comprises Entered Apprentices, Fellow Craftsmen, and Master Masons. While not of the highly imaginative character of continental *hautes grades*, the Royal Arch provided Freemasons with a degree that proposed to impart the ineffable name of deity to the degree's recipient. This degree was incorporated into the British Masonic system when the two rival "Antient" and "Modern" grand lodges merged under the grand mastership of Augustus Frederick, Duke of Sussex, son of George III. The Royal Arch, essentially an "Antient" invention, won wide acceptance throughout the Masonic fraternity in the nineteenth century.

Freemasonry in the nineteenth and twentieth centuries continued to develop along the lines established by the differing English and French models. English, Irish, and Scottish Freemasonry shaped the fraternity and its teachings in Canada, the United States, the West Indies, India, and much of Africa. The impact of the French tradition, with its anticlerical, rationalistic, and politicized emphasis, was more deeply felt in Austro-Hungary, Spain, Portugal, Italy, and Latin America. By 1877, communication between these two groups had virtually ceased. This separation was formalized when the Grand Orient of France removed the requirement that its initiates declare a belief in the existence of God as the "Great Architect of the Universe." In English-speaking areas, Freemasonry has in general prospered as a support to constituted government and organized religion. One notable exception is the anti-Masonic episode in the United States. The alleged abduction and murder of William Morgan of Batavia, New York, in 1829 caused a widespread reaction against Freemasonry throughout the country. Other secret societies, including Phi Beta Kappa, were affected, largely as a reaction against the perceived influence of political and social elites. An interesting result of this movement was its precipitating the first American political party convention, that of the Anti-Masonic party in 1832.

Masonic Teachings. Since the origin of Freemasonry as a speculative system, Masonic teachings have remained remarkably consistent. Despite there being no demonstrable, historical tie between Freemasonry in the seventeenth century and the medieval operative stonemasons, the teachings of Freemasonry have been linked to medieval and even to biblical sagas, notably the accounts in *1 Kings* and *2 Chronicles* of the building of the Solomonic Temple. Two other strata—the Hermetic-Rosicrucian and the Enlightenment rationalistic-deistic—are superimposed upon the biblical and medieval traditions within the superstructure of Masonic degrees. All Masonic degrees are related to the transformation of the human personality from a state of primitive darkness to a higher level of human consciousness. Mozart's opera *Die Zauberflöte* is in many ways a prototype of Masonic ceremonial.

Because Freemasonry has transposed a system of moral and noetic teaching upon a graded institutional structure, it has frequently been deemed both a threat to confessional and orthodox religion and a religion itself. The basis for such assumptions is the fraternity's use of symbols that describe the change of personal moral character and human awareness by stages, or degrees. These degrees have been interpreted as a plan for spiritual redemption. A study of the basic ceremonials and teachings, however, suggests that the goal of Masonic initiation is not redemption but rather a shift in the initiate's perception toward the betterment of his personal moral character. The lack of central authority and the multitude of Masonic degrees and ceremonials make it impossible to state unequivocally that Freemasonry is religious in any final or conclusive sense. Since Clement XII's encyclical *In eminenti* in 1738, the Roman Catholic church has proscribed Masonic affiliation. The identification of many major southern European and Latin American revolutionary leaders—such as Benso, Garibaldi, Bolívar, O'Higgins, and Martí y Pérez—with Masonic lodges evoked further condemnation by the nineteenth-century Roman Catholic church. More recently, the Lutheran Church–Missouri Synod, U.S.A., and the General Conference of the Methodist Church in England and Wales have legislated claims that Freemasonry is a system of faith and morals outside of the magisterium of the church.

Protestant opposition to Freemasonry stems from the elements of deism and Hermetic Rosicrucianism in Masonic rituals and is thus more theological in tone. Confessional churches and churches with strong traditions of scholastic orthodoxy, such as Lutheranism, have deemed the humanistic and Neoplatonic elements in Masonic philosophy to be inconsistent with Christian teaching. Churches that have maintained a less exclusive understanding of revelation have been more tolerant of Freemasonry's belief in a universal brotherhood of man under the fatherhood of God.

Freemasonry has a worldwide membership of approximately six million people. It is governed by independent national grand lodges, except in the United States, Canada, and Australia, where grand lodges are organized by state or province. While Freemasonry is racially mixed, there are independent, largely black, grand lodges. The largest of these black lodges is traced to Prince Hall, a freed slave in eighteenth-century Massachusetts. Numerous appendant and collateral bodies, such as the Ancient Arabic Order, Nobles of the Mystic Shrine, and the Order of the Eastern Star are associated with the grand lodges.

[*See also* Rosicrucians *and* Esotericism.]

BIBLIOGRAPHY

Chailley, Jacques. *The Magic Flute: Masonic Opera.* New York, 1971.

Dumenil, Lynn. *Freemasonry and American Culture, 1880–1930.* Princeton, 1984.

Gould, Robert Freke. *History of Freemasonry.* London, 1886–1887.
Horne, Alex. *Sources of Masonic Symbolism.* Trenton, N.J., 1981.
Jacob, Margaret C. *The Radical Enlightenment: Pantheists, Freemasons and Republicans.* Boston, 1981.
Lipson, Dorothy Ann. *Freemasonry in Federalist Connecticut.* Princeton, 1977.
Pound, Roscoe. *Masonic Addresses and Writings.* New York, 1953.
Stubbs, James W. *The United Grand Lodge of England, 1717–1967.* Oxford, 1967.
Yates, Frances A. *The Rosicrucian Enlightenment.* London, 1972.

William H. Stemper, Jr.

FREE WILL AND DETERMINISM. Free will is a moral, religious, and social concept that is central to philosophy and most religions. It has been argued that the basis of freedom lies in the contingency of natural events. Though this line of reasoning has been by and large abandoned, for freedom to exist at all the concept of strict universal causality will have to be suspended, at least in the moral sphere. Another line of thought sees the foundation of freedom in spirituality: the soul, as immaterial, is not subject to the deterministic laws of nature. Whatever the explanation, belief in free will amounts to the conviction that, as individuals, human beings are endowed with the capacity for choice of action, for decision among alternatives, and specifically that, given an innate moral sense, man can freely discern good and evil and choose the good, though he often does not. Determinism is the philosophical view that, given certain initial conditions, everything that ensues is bound to happen as it does and in no other possible way; thus nothing in nature is contingent, nor is there any room for human freedom. The partisans of a "hard" determinism hold that none of our actions is free, but only appear to be so; consequently, moral responsibility is an illusion as well; "soft" determinists, or compatibilists, believe that while our actions are indeed caused, we are nevertheless free, since causality does not compel our will. [*See* Cosmic Law *and* Soteriology.]

Philosophical Interpretations. In Greek antiquity the idea of free will was clearly derived from the difference between free individuals and slaves, in modern times from the political structures of rising democratic electoral systems. A whole lineage of philosophers tried to reconcile the idea of determinism, the theological one in particular, with that of free will as uninhibited intentional action. Early Greek thought regarded free will as the denial of all intrinsic limitations upon the pursuit of voluntary goals. Plato shows in the *Republic* that social structures and moral conventions can be masterminded and manipulated at will. Both Socrates and Plato shifted the locus of freedom from the power to affect external events to the inner exercise of will and conviction. For Aristotle the power of free will lies in the capacity of thought to harmonize itself not only with God but with the good and the good life (*On Interpretation,* chap. 9). To be free meant to be rational. According to Augustine of Hippo *(On Free Will),* God's foreknowledge of events does not curtail the capacity to choose and indeed the necessity of doing so, since God's knowledge of eternity is somewhat akin to that of a ubiquitous present. The will is certainly free and there is no reason to believe that God's knowledge of the object of the will should impair its freedom in any way. Man's freedom is to love God and act upon his own will. In accordance with the same line of argument, Boethius *(On the Consolation of Philosophy)* defined eternity as "the simultaneous and complete possession of infinite life." Thomas Aquinas similarly held that God's eternal vision could in no way cause our actions (*Summa theologiae* 1.14.13).

Modern philosophers struggled with the dilemma of divine foreknowledge and human freedom by redefining the latter, for instance, as "lack of constraint" (Hobbes); others, for example, Descartes, emphasized the infinity of the will in espousing the true and rejecting the false even though human understanding may be limited. Spinoza conceived of man's free will as self-determination; Leibniz, as a form of uncaused spontaneity, which was later to be equated with "freedom from indifference." It followed from these views that God could never be blamed for man's errors. Yet this concept of a mind causally undetermined, inexplicably free, was found unsatisfactory and was replaced by Locke's concept of preference as cause (opposed to the previous idea about the irrelevance of judgments to our will), and by Hume's argument that a free action is one that could have been avoided. For Kant, determinism is phenomenal and freedom is noumenal, since the pure practical reason upon which man freely acts lies outside the realm of causation and makes up the essence and autonomy of moral life. Hegel and his left-wing followers looked upon freedom and necessity as two sides of the same coin, two ideas dialectically interconnected through "knowledge" or "understanding": freedom is necessity understood. Other nineteenth century idealists, called libertarians, tended to postulate a special entity, the "self," which uses the body as a causal instrument while being itself immune to causation. The materialists, to the contrary, had favored since antiquity an almost total subordination of freedom to the necessary or contingent play of natural and social forces outside of both individual and divine control. [*See* Existentialism; Materialism; *and* Naturalism.]

Religious Interpretations. The essential presupposition of most major religions is that humans are born with freedom of choice. Free will is the capacity to choose among courses of action, objectives, things, desires, and so forth, and also to assume full moral responsibility for them. For the will to be free it is therefore necessary that there be no direct coercion, serious compulsion, or distortion of truth (for example, through propaganda or brainwashing) and also that alternatives for choice be at hand. A variety of conditions in society will allow for a variety of beliefs and the free exercise of human choice. Classically, this idea is defined as the absence of obstacles to the realization of various freedoms; it has a negative aspect, *freedom from* (want, fear, et al.), and a positive one, *freedom for* (worship, creativity, symbolic acts of speech, et al.). Religious freedom, including, but not reducible to, freedom of worship, illustrates the inseparability of these aspects, being at the same time freedom from spiritual coercion (for example, forcibly inculcated atheism, active proselytism) and freedom for the consciousness to believe, the individual to practice, and the community to exercise the rules of conduct and rituals of its own tradition. [*See* Conscience; Morality and Religion; *and* Natural Law.]

The principle of determinism, which claims that the states of the universe, including human volition, are to be rigidly deduced from previous causes, and that nothing could be other than it is or was, is a negation of free will. To the extent that they involve moral responsibility, all religions must recognize that man is a free agent. However, the presupposition of monotheistic religions that the one God is not only omnipotent but also omniscient seems to annul the power of free decision in man, which leads to the contradiction of man being held responsible for some courses of action for which he is actually not responsible.

Most religions have sought a theological solution to this dilemma. In Hinduism, even though the blame for evil is usually cast upon the god who causes man's imperfections and thus dooms him to downfall, man is still held morally responsible for his woes, as he is for corrupting other human beings; parents are considered morally responsible for their children's—even physical—constitution. A concept present across the board in Asian religions, from Jainism and Brahmanism to Buddhism, Sikkhism, Parsi, and animistic religions, is *karman,* which mainly points to action and reaction in the long series of reincarnations but is erroneously understood sometimes as rigid universal determinism, fate, or even retributive justice. Actually *karman* encompasses the unity and interrelatedness of all phenomena, their fundamental contingency, and the acts or rituals *(karman)* capable of destroying the bonds of transmigration. Under the law of *karman* an individual is essentially free to accept or to attempt to change the chain of cosmic events. There are many oscillations (from myth to myth and scripture to scripture) and ambiguities concerning the status of the individual in the cosmos: on the one hand, he might be considered as a passive entity subject to the laws of the universe, now weakened and contaminated, now strengthened and purified, by the flow of events; on the other hand, he enjoys a certain amount of spontaneous freedom. In any case, the goodness to which one should aspire is the integration and the harmony of ambivalent features rather than their dissociation. This is what makes the Hindu concept of free will radically different from the Judeo-Christian one. [*See* Karman.]

There are two main concepts designating freedom in Indian philosophy: the one is *svāraj* (self-rule), which appears already in the *Chāndogya Upaniṣad* and has definite social, political, and moral connotations; the other is *mokṣa,* which has the psychological and metaphysical connotations of deliverance, emancipation, and release. There is both a tension and a synthesis between the two, out of which the real notion of freedom in Hinduism emerges. *Mokṣa* is, however, the ultimate goal of Hindu religion. It is freedom from *karman* and bondage, which in turn is freedom from ignorance, a freedom to be attained not after death but here and now through physical and mental discipline. Biological and social freedom is a necessary yet not sufficient condition for its achievement. [*See* Mokṣa.]

In Judaism, man is born free because he is created in the image of God (who is free). Also, it is God's goodness that is reflected in man's freedom. The faithful are to abolish completely their will in favor of God's. Yet, according to the teachings of the Bible, man's obligations flow from two sources: divine law and the voice of inner conscience. In the Talmud, the *mitsvot* appear as absolute prescriptions, that is, decrees to be followed by man. Jewish philosophers, nevertheless, and particularly those influenced by Hellenism (e.g., Philo Judaeus and Josephus Flavius), insist on the heteronomous nature of the *mitsvot,* which are also an explicit expression of natural law. Judaism offers little evidence for the idea that events in the life of an individual might have been "fated" (in the Greek sense of *moira*); yet the major collective occurrences in the life of the people of Israel were commanded and predetermined by God. As lord of history and judge, God both rules over nature and determines the end result of human deeds and conflicts. God may sometimes be portrayed in the Hebrew scriptures (*Is.* 34:17) as a caster of lots. In the rabbinical period, the belief emerged that God did predetermine major events such as the dates of birth, death, and marriage in the individual's life. Outside of these, however, there was no predetermination. Nothing could abolish the free will and therefore the moral responsibility of the person. [*See* Israelite Law.]

Islam holds the belief that major events are fated and decreed by God; this allows one to affirm the underlying uniformity and rationality of the universe. The concept of fate, however, was borrowed from pre-Islamic Arabic literature, especially from poetry that was not necessarily religious. It became subordinated in Islam to a divine predestination that by itself does not preclude the actual freedom of the individual's will. More and more, Islamic theologians shun the attribute of fatalism bestowed upon the Muslim religion. "Fate" is often a label given after the fact; to say that something is fated is to give an easy and weak explanation to an otherwise inexplicable event. The argument is that while in God's mind everything is determined in advance, the active believer is wholly ignorant of this determination and therefore enjoys fully the freedom to choose. [*See* Fate.]

Christianity is among the major religions that emphasize the freedom of man to the last consequence. Even the existence of evil in face of the omnipotence of God is justified in terms of the supremacy of man's essential freedom to adopt his own goals and to choose his own course of action. The controversy between Augustine of Hippo and Pelagius as early as the fifth century set the scene for what was to be an ongoing theological debate in Western Christianity. To Augustine's almost exclusive emphasis on indwelling grace, Pelagius, a British monk who lived in Africa and was condemned for heresy by two synods, opposed the notion that the human, unassisted free will acts in a sovereign way in bringing about or jeopardizing man's salvation. In the sixteenth century, Erasmus of Rotterdam defended the church doctrine of free will against Martin Luther's aggressive denial of it and Luther's affirmation of man's complete dependence upon God's grace. Protestant theology with Zwingli, Wyclif, Calvin, and their followers steadily upheld the soteriological and metaphysical doctrine of predestination. [*See* Pelagianism *and* Theodicy.]

In Mādhyamika Buddhism, freedom from pain, which implies a complete, blissful regeneration of man, is achieved by the elimination of all conceptual constructions at their very roots: the duality between "is" and "is-not." The spiritual discipline of attaining enlightenment or achieving Buddhahood through the resolution of the painful conflict between the private and the social good is conducive to wisdom, *prajñā*, which is itself liberating. To achieve freedom is mainly a negative process consisting in the elimination of hindrances that obscure the real, such as attachment, aversion, and all mental fictional constructions. *Śūnyatā* as the intellectual intuition of voidness is equated with freedom. [*See* Prajñā *and* Śūnyam and Śūnyatā.]

Avowedly the relationship between free will and determinism is one of paradox, that is, of mutual implication and repulsion occurring simultaneously. This paradox can more or less be dissolved by relegating free will to the realms of spiritual awareness, psychologically lived reality, and practical (moral) action; whereas determinism and predestination would belong to the actual ontological and existential givenness of things and events in the world. Attempts at solving this paradox have led some theistic process philosophers and theologians (e.g., Charles Hartshorne) to want to weaken the divine attributes of omniscience and omnipotence. It is not God's unsurpassable power but his monopoly on it that is denied. This should allow for openness and indeterminacy in the future in which man's options can be exercised freely. The present stage of the philosophical discussion of free will and determinism in relation to both cosmology and individual existence involves sophisticated epistemological arguments from the theory of explanation, causality, the symmetry of past and future, and the theory of human action.

[*See also* Free Will and Predestination. *For further elaboration of ideas about free will and determinism, see also the biographies of the philosophers and religious thinkers mentioned herein.*]

BIBLIOGRAPHY

Campbell, Charles Arthur. *Selfhood and Godhood.* London, 1957.

Hartshorne, Charles. *A Natural Theology of Our Time.* LaSalle, Ill., 1967.

James, William. *The Will to Believe.* New York, 1921.

Kant, Immanuel. *Critique of Practical Reason.* Translated by Lewis Beek. Chicago, 1949.

Morgenbesser, Sidney and James Walsh, eds. *Free Will.* Englewood Cliffs, N.J., 1962.

Murti, T. R. V. *The Central Philosophy of Buddhism.* 2d ed. London, 1955. See especially pp. 261–269.

Ryle, Gilbert. *The Concept of Mind* (1949). Reprint, Chicago, 1984.

Schopenhauer, Arthur. *Essay on the Freedom of the Will.* Translated by Konstantin Kolenda. Indianapolis, 1960.

Spinoza, Barukh. *Ethics.* Translated by William Hale White. New York, 1949.

Winter, Ernst, ed. *Discourse on Free Will: Selections from Erasmus and Luther.* New York, 1961.

Zagzebski, Linda. "Divine Foreknowledge and Human Free Will." *Religious Studies* 3 (1985): 279–298.

Ileana Marcoulesco

FREE WILL AND PREDESTINATION. [*This entry consists of three articles that deal with the theological issue of human freedom and divine omnipotence:*

An Overview
Christian Concepts
Islamic Concept

The first article surveys issues of free will and predestination in various religious traditions. The companion pieces focus on two religions, Christianity and Islam, in whose theological systems questions of free will and predestination have particular importance.]

An Overview

Free will and predestination constitute a polarity in many of the religions of the world: is salvation determined by a divine choice or is it a matter of personal self-determination? *Free will* in this article does not refer to the general philosophical problem of the will's freedom but to the specific meaning and function of willing and self-determination in the process of salvation. Some religious thinkers have sharply distinguished between the will's freedom in the material and civil affairs of life and its freedom or unfreedom with regard to the spiritual life, and it is with the latter that this article is concerned.

At least two ways of thinking about the freedom of the will in spiritual matters have been common: free will as a freedom of choice, whereby one does freely what one has also had the power to choose to do, and free will as the absence of compulsion, whereby one willingly does what one does without actively choosing what is done. The latter has been described as voluntary necessity. In the first of these meanings of freedom, freedom seems incompatible with divine determination; in the second, it does not, and is opposed not to causality but to constraint.

Predestination as it is treated in this article is separated from the general consideration of providence, determinism, and fate, and refers only to the voluntary divine choice of certain groups or individuals for salvation. Sometimes predestination is considered as a part of divine providence, namely, that aspect of the divine determination of all things that refers to the supernatural end of souls, as opposed to the determination of persons with regard to all else or of the natural order. But predestination is to be sharply distinguished from some forms of determinism and from fatalism, which do not necessarily involve the theistic concept of a personal deity making conscious choices. *Determinism* may mean any one of a number of systems claiming that all events cannot occur otherwise than they do, sometimes without reference to deity. *Fate* suggests an impersonal determining force that may even transcend the gods. [*See* Fate.]

The terms *election* and *reprobation* have meanings related to predestination. [*See* Election.] One traditional use of these terms considers predestination the larger divine act, which encompasses the separate decrees of election (predestination to salvation) and reprobation (predestination to damnation). *Reprobation*, however, is seldom used now, and *election* is more commonly simply substituted for *predestination*, because it seems more positive in its connotations. In biblical studies, *election* has been the preferred term for referring to divine choice.

Predestination has been considered not inevitably contradictory to free will. Sometimes both are held together as paradoxical, yet complementary, aspects of truth; but more classically, free will is understood not as freedom of choice but as voluntary necessity. That is, where freedom means the absence of compulsion, necessary acts determined by God nonetheless can be freely done. Almost all predestinarian theologies have therefore maintained that the predestined will acts freely and with consequent responsibility for its actions, even though it lacks the power to choose its actions. In this sense of freedom, even the decree of reprobation has been seen as compatible with responsibility and not as entailing a divine compulsion to do evil. This compatibility of free will and predestination has historically been a commonplace of Augustinian and Calvinistic theology in Christianity, and of Islamic theology through its doctrine of acquisition. Even such a materialistic determinist as Thomas Hobbes thought that necessary acts were entirely voluntary and therefore responsible acts. It is this that sharply distinguishes predestination from fatalism, which may entail compulsion to act in a certain way. Roman Catholic theology refers to any predestinarian doctrine that proceeds without reference to the will's freedom as the error of predestinarianism. Only in rare cases in Christian and Islamic theology has that way of understanding predestination appeared.

Occurrence in the History of Religions. The issue of free will and predestination in relation to salvation arises in those religions that believe in a personal, omnipotent God, and thus has appeared mainly in Judaism, Christianity, and Islam. But it has also occurred in ancient Greece and India among certain groups that have had a similar religious understanding.

Ancient Greece. Ancient Greek monotheism, centering on the figure of Zeus, came near to personal theism in Stoicism, particularly among the later Stoics who believed in immortality. They considered Zeus a universal mind and will determining all things, including the virtue by which good men resigned themselves to the inevitable; through this providence elect souls triumphed over the sufferings of earthly existence.

Judaism. In Judaism, the Deuteronomic tradition especially accents Yahveh's choice of Israel as his people. In the Hebrew scriptures, the stories of Moses, Samuel, Isaiah, and Jeremiah show God's choice of particular persons to fulfill special offices. But this election, whether of persons or of the group, is grounded by the Hebrew scriptures in the divine initiative, not in the chosen object, and involves special tasks and responsibilities more than special privileges. The will's freedom of choice in obeying God's commandments is clearly asserted in many passages of the Hebrew scriptures, as, for example, in *Deuteronomy* 30:15–20. The apocryphal book of *Ben Sira* asserts that God does not lead persons astray but created them with the freedom not to sin (15:11–17).

Josephus Flavius, in describing the Pharisees to his Hellenistic audience, said that they considered all events predetermined but still did not deprive the human will of involvement in decisions about virtue and vice. The Sadducees he described as rejecting determinism altogether (*Jewish Antiquities* 13.171–173; *Jewish War*, 2.162–166). The Essenes were the most predestinarian of the Jewish groups, if the Qumran texts are to be attributed to them. The Qumran literature teaches that God created the spirits of men to be cast in the lots of either good or evil and that salvation is divinely initiated and based on God's choice. Nonetheless, the Essenes also maintained human accountability for evil. Elsewhere in the Judaism of the Hellenistic age, Philo Judaeus upheld the will's complete freedom.

Rabbinic literature taught both God's foresight and providence directing all things and human freedom of choice with respect to the doing of good or evil. A saying of Aʿqiva' ben Yosef juxtaposes them: "All is foreseen and yet freedom is granted" (*Avot* 3:15). Some rabbinic sayings suggest that everything about a person's life is determined by God except for the soul's obedience to God (B.T., *Ber.* 33b, *Meg.* 25a, *Nid.* 16b). This matter did not become a serious question for Jewish thinkers until contact with Islamic speculations in the tenth century, when Saʿadyah Gaon took up the problem. He and all the medieval Jewish philosophers maintained the will's freedom of choice. But Maimonides alluded to the view of "uninformed" Jews that God decrees that an individual will be either good or evil when the infant is being formed in the womb (*Mishneh Torah*, Repentance 5.2).

Christianity. Predestination has had a more central place in Christian thought. The theme of predestination to salvation appears strongly in the Pauline literature, especially the *Letter to the Romans*. For Paul, predestination results from the divine initiative and is grounded in grace, so that no one may boast of being saved by his own efforts. Paul also speaks of God's hardening of the hearts of unbelievers (*Rom.* 9:18). [*See* Justification.]

In spite of the numerous New Testament references to predestination, patristic writers, especially the Greek fathers, tended to ignore the theme before Augustine of Hippo. This was probably partly the result of the early church's struggle with the fatalistic determinism of the gnostics. Augustine, writing against the Pelagians, taught that God predestined to salvation some out of the mass of sinners, passing by the rest and thus leaving them to just condemnation for the sins they willingly committed. Augustine thought that the will was unable to do the good that God commanded unless aided by grace. [*See* Grace.] To do evil willingly was a slavery to sin from which grace rescued those whom God had chosen. Augustine had many medieval followers in this doctrine, including Gottschalk in the ninth century, who stated the doctrine in an extreme fashion, and Thomas Bradwardine in the fourteenth century, who opposed those he considered his Pelagian contemporaries. Thomas Aquinas was also a predestinarian, but he treated the doctrine in the context of God's providence as a whole. On the other hand, such medieval scholastics as John Duns Scotus and William of Ockham sought to reconcile God's prescience with human freedom of choice.

In the Renaissance and Reformation there was a revival of predestinarian thinking. Lorenzo Valla was the main representative of determinism among Renaissance philosophers, while almost all of the major Protestant reformers found the doctrine of predestination useful in their insistence upon the primacy of divine grace in salvation. Luther (and Lutheranism, in the Formula of Concord) soon backed away from the extreme predestinarian teaching of his early *Bondage of the Will* and taught only election to life, with the possibility of falling from grace. The Reformed churches, following their teachers Ulrich Zwingli, Martin Bucer, John Calvin, and Peter Martyr Vermigli, gave the doctrine an important role in the defense of grace in salvation and also taught double predestination, but still insisted on the freedom of the will, which they understood in the Augustinian sense of voluntary necessity. Later scholastic Reformed theologians, such as Theodore Beza, William Perkins, and Franciscus Turrentinus, gave the doctrine of predestination a central role in their theological systems. An important eighteenth-century defense of the Reformed view of predestination and the freedom of the will came from Jonathan Edwards in colonial Massachusetts. The Church of England adopted the predestinarian theology of the Reformers in its Thirty-nine Articles and in the first century of its existence generally taught the Reformed view of the matter.

The Roman Catholic theology of the same period, especially that of the Jesuits, stressed human responsibility in the process of salvation, with Luis de Molina maintaining the position of "congruism," that is, of grace as efficacious according as the will cooperates with it. Countering this was a revival of Augustinian theology, represented by the Spanish Dominican Domingo Bañez and by Cornelis Jansen in the Netherlands. The Jansenists in France, including Blaise Pascal, considered the Jesuits Pelagian. Predestination has not been an important theme in more modern Roman Catholic theology, and Catholic treatments of Augustine tend to focus on other aspects of his thought.

In the later history of Protestantism, emphasis upon predestination has generally declined, and freedom of choice in salvation has frequently been asserted. From the beginning, few of the Anabaptists were predestinarian. Some of the early Protestant reformers, including Heinrich Bullinger and Andreas Bibliander, were cautious in their treatment of predestination, and the Dutch Reformed theologian Jacobus Arminius (1560–1609) asserted that God predestined to salvation those whom he foresaw would believe. This assertion of the will's freedom of choice in salvation came to be known as Arminianism and gained ground among English Protestants throughout the seventeenth century. In the next century John Wesley adopted it as the theology of Methodism, and it generally made headway among evangelicals who wanted to be able to make straightforward appeals for conversions. Thus its avowal by the nineteenth-century American evangelist Charles G. Finney influenced many in the formally Calvinistic Presbyterian and Congregationalist denominations, although his contemporary, the Princeton theologian Charles Hodge, continued to uphold double predestination in its scholastic form. The liberal Protestant theology of the nineteenth and early twentieth century usually rejected any form of predestinarian theology. But in the twentieth century, two Reformed theologians, Emil Brunner and Karl Barth, have attempted reformulations of predestination while abandoning its more unpalatable features.

Islam. Free will and predestination have been important issues in Islamic thought. Basic to Muḥammad's religious experience was a sense of God's power, majesty, and judgment. The Qur'ān exhorts submission before the divine sovereignty and declares even that "God leads astray whom he pleases and guides whom he pleases" (surah 74:34). But the Qur'ān also presupposes choice on the part of persons who have been summoned by revelation. Early in the history of Islam, the predestinarian emphasis was reinforced by a general Arab cultural belief in fate, and some Muslims thought that God permitted Satan's irresistible incitement to evil. But one of the first groups of Islamic philosophers, the Muʿtazilah, argued that, however much other events were determined beforehand, there was a free human choice of good or evil. Later Muslim theologians, emphatically teaching predestination, nonetheless tried to reconcile it with free will through varying interpretations of the doctrine of acquisition. According to this doctrine, man is regarded as voluntarily willing his actions and thus "acquiring" them, even though God has created these acts so that they occur by necessity. Such a viewpoint has many parallels with Augustinianism, and generally Islam is no more fatalistic than is Christianity.

Hinduism. The main traditions of Hinduism and Buddhism do not posit a personal deity with an omnipotent will, and thus the polarity of free will and predestination in relation to the salvation of souls has not been so prominent as in Judaism, Christianity, and Islam. The doctrine of *karman* can constitute a kind of determinism whereby an individual's lot in life is determined by his behavior in past lives, but the doctrine can also imply that a soul is in charge of its future destiny; its modern proponents therefore sometimes consider the doctrine to imply freedom more than fatalism. But in either case, *karman* is usually seen not as the willing of a personal deity but as the workings of an impersonal force.

However, some schools of Hinduism maintain personal theism and an omnipotent God and consequently wrestle with the problem of free will and predestination. For example, the Vaiṣṇava sect of Madhva (1238–1317) believed that Viṣṇu predestined some souls to blessedness and others to damnation, simply for his good pleasure and not because of the merits or demerits of the souls themselves. A more cautious theology of predestination appeared in the interpretation of the Vedanta by Rāmānuja (fl. c. 1100). He taught that the souls of some persons were led to repentance by a divine initiative, but he also held that the choice of good or evil nonetheless included personal acts performed by means of a God-given freedom. Rāmānuja's followers divided over the extent to which divine power controlled souls. The Tengalai, or "cat school," taught that God's irresistible grace saves some souls the way the mother cat carries her young by the nape of the neck, while the Vadagalai, or "monkey school," taught that God's grace and the human will cooperate in salvation the way the infant monkey clings to the mother.

As a Phenomenon of Religious Experience. The notion of the freedom of the will in relation to salvation arises out of the everyday experience of free choice and personal responsibility. There seems to be a human need to feel in control of one's life. Modern experience has been especially characterized by a sense of autonomy, and this has abetted the assumption of the will's freedom of choice with reference to salvation.

Belief in predestination, on the other hand, represents and abstracts from the experience of creatureliness before the majesty of the divine. It was Friedrich Schleiermacher (1768–1834) who first looked at predestination as a transcript of subjective piety, concluding that it was an element in the religious person's consciousness of dependence upon God. Following Schleiermacher, Rudolf Otto attempted a phenomenology of the "creature feeling" that he thought lay behind the doctrine of predestination. As Otto interpreted it, the idea of predestination was rooted not in speculative thought but in religious self-abasement, the "annulment of personal strength and claims and achievements in the presence of the transcendent," and thus was "an immediate and pure expression of the actual religious experience of grace." The one who receives grace feels that nothing has merited this favor, and that it is not a result of his own effort, resolve, or achievement. Rather, grace is a force that has grasped, impelled, and led him. Predestination is thus a numinous experience of awe in the face of the *mysterium tremendum*.

Besides being rooted in the human sense of createdness and of grace, predestination as a religious phenomenon also depends on a sense of trust and confidence in the reliability of the divine and in its power to complete what has been begun in the creature. Such belief in an ordered world and rejection of the sheer fortuitousness of things is an important element of much religious consciousness and leads to a sense of assurance about God's purpose and about one's own spiritual security. Ernst Troeltsch thought that it was in the interest of the assurance of salvation that predestination became such a central doctrine in Protestant theology.

Belief in predestination may also be regarded as arising from the search for a purely spiritual religion, for it has the effect of stripping away all concrete mediation and leaving the soul alone before God. It was this that led Max Weber to consider belief in predestination as functionally related to the process of the elimination of magic from the world. This aspect of predestinarian religion has been greatly attractive to religious reformers, for the doctrine can become a means to sweep away much accumulation of religiosity.

Another aspect of belief in predestination as a matter of religious experience is that it has had the effect, not (as might be supposed) of giving rise to fatalistic acquiescence, but of energizing the will for the fulfillment of divinely assigned tasks. Thus Calvinist theologians spoke of predestination as election to holiness.

As a Problem of Religious Thought. While beliefs concerning free will and predestination may be rooted in religious experience, they are also connected to certain intellectual concerns and puzzlements. One motive for such reflection has been the simple observation that some believe while others do not—is this fact the consequence of personal freedom of choice or of divine predetermination?

Reflection on divine omnipotence has led to the inference that the divine choice must be the determining factor in salvation. If some things were excepted from the general principle that all things occur by virtue of a divine causality, then God would seem to lack the efficacy to bring his purposes to fruition. Even the bare acknowledgment of divine foreknowledge seems to entail determinism, for if God knows what will happen from eternity, it must necessarily happen in that way or else his knowledge would be rendered erroneous. And though it may be argued that God foresees actual human choices, nonetheless when the time for those choices arrives, they cannot be other than they are; this is precisely what identifies an event as predetermined. Opponents of this viewpoint have maintained, however, that foresight is not a cause and that therefore a foreseen event need not be a determined one.

Still, the doctrine of predestination has probably been rooted primarily not in this kind of consideration but in the theological need to maintain the gratuitousness of salvation. To connect this with predestination effectively rules out any possibility of human merit.

Theologies that have asserted the will's freedom of choice in salvation have, on the other hand, focused on different theological needs, primarily those of preserving human responsibility in the process of salvation and God's goodness and justice in the governing of his creation. If salvation is entirely God's gift, how can those left out be held responsible? In the modern period, the Augustinian definition of freedom as absence of constraint has not been widely persuasive, in spite of the fact that many elements of contemporary thought, especially in relation to heredity, have provided some basis for considering human freedom in this way.

The problem of theodicy, in Christian thought in particular, seems almost inevitably to rely on the assumption of human freedom of choice in salvation. [*See* Theodicy.] Even the Puritan poet John Milton, in seeking to "justify the ways of God to man," fell back upon an assertion of such freedom.

Several considerations may be brought forward in religious thought in order, if not exactly to solve, then at least to extenuate this problem. One approach is simply to acquiesce to the polarity of free will and predestination as a paradox. Another consideration is Augustine's argument that God exists not in time but in the qualitatively different state of eternity. Thus since for God there is no past or future, there is no priority of time for his foresight or decree in relation to the events of salvation; priority is implied only by our inadequate language. A further Augustinian consideration is that, since the evil of an evil act is a deficiency of being, it requires no divine causality at all. Evil is only a falling away from the good (and from freedom) and hence needs no positive causality.

[*For related discussion from a philosophical perspective, see* Free Will and Determinism.]

BIBLIOGRAPHY

There are several useful introductions to the subject: C. H. Ratschow, Erich Dinkler, E. Kähler, and Wolfhart Pannenberg's "Prädestination," in *Die Religion in Geschichte und Gegenwart*, 3d ed. (Tübingen, 1957–1965), and Henri Rondet and Karl Rahner's "Predestination," in *Sacramentum Mundi: An Encyclopedia of Theology*, edited by Karl Rahner (New York, 1968–1970), both of which give an extensive bibliography in several languages; Giorgio Tourn's *La predestinazione nella Bibbia e nella storia* (Turin, 1978); and Vernon J. Bourke's *Will in Western Thought: An Historico-Critical Survey* (New York, 1964).

Rudolf Otto's *The Idea of the Holy* (1923), 2d ed. (London, 1950), offers a classic phenomenological analysis of the problem. Discussion of the general historical significance of predestination appears in my *Puritans and Predestination* (Chapel Hill, N.C., 1982), pp. 191–196. For the Bible and ancient Judaism, see Harold H. Rowley's *The Biblical Doctrine of Election* (London, 1950), Eugene H. Merrill's *Qumran and Predestination* (Leiden, 1975), and George Foot Moore's "Fate and Free Will in the Jewish Philosophies according to Josephus," *Harvard Theological Review* 22 (October 1929): 371–389. Two rather traditional Christian theological investigations of the problem, the first Protestant and the second Roman Catholic, are Gaston Deluz's *Prédestination et liberté* (Paris, 1942) and M. John Farrelly's *Predestination, Grace, and Free Will* (Westminster, Md., 1964). For Indian thought, see Sarvepalli Radhakrishnan's *Indian Philosophy*, 2d ed., 2 vols. (London, 1927–1931), pp. 659–721, 731–751, and Rudolf Otto's *Die Gnadenreligion Indiens und das Christentum* (Gotha, 1930), translated by Frank H. Foster as *India's Religion of Grace and Christianity* (New York, 1930). The standard work on this subject for Islam is W. Montgomery Watt's *Free Will and Predestination in Early Islam* (London, 1948).

DEWEY D. WALLACE, JR.

Christian Concepts

Christian theologians—and eventually the creeds of the churches—have formulated concepts of free will and predestination to explain the respective roles of divine and human agency in the accomplishment of salvation. The notion of predestination introduces the matter of time order in affirming that God makes a decision or decree concerning those who would be saved by Christ *prior* to any action that they might choose to take during their lifetime in relation to their own salvation. Following Augustine and Paul, theologians and the creeds have usually maintained that God's decision occurs "before the foundation of the world."

Contrary to a widely held opinion, Calvinists have not been the only Christians to believe in predestination. Moreover, no tradition has denied free will in all senses of the term. On the contrary, all mainstream Christian traditions have in some way affirmed both free will and predestination, though they have often meant very different things by these concepts and have given them different roles in relation to each other. In recent times, churches have tended to mute their references to predestination, allowing secular discourse to debate the question in a new form as freedom and determinism. [*See* Free Will and Determinism.]

The Issues and the Scriptures. That the question arises—and that it persists—may be attributed to the human experience of being able to choose responsibly among real options while simultaneously being overwhelmed by forces apparently beyond human decision. Christians have used the doctrines of free will and predestination as means of expressing these contrary experiences—on the one hand, the certitude of salvation as God's act; on the other hand, the human responsibility to believe and do what is right. [*See also* Atonement, *article on* Christian Concepts; Grace; Justification; *and* Merit, *article on* Christian Concepts.]

Christians have related these two concepts to many others, including God's sovereignty and grace, divine foreknowledge of future human acts, divine election in relation to human merits, eternity and time, causation, and the process of salvation. They have raised periodic warnings against trying to penetrate the mystery of salvation, against impugning the justice or the mercy of God, and against making God the author of evil.

Advocates of all positions have appealed to the scriptures, even though the scriptures do not contain doctrines or concepts of free will and predestination, nor even these words. The Latin term *praedestinatione* derives from the creation of an abstract noun from the translation of the Greek verb *proorizō*, which refers to deciding or setting limits on something beforehand. The word occurs six times in four passages in the New Testament: *Acts of the Apostles* 4:28, *Romans* 8:28–30, *1 Corinthians* 2:7, and *Ephesians* 1:3–14. The King James translation renders the *Romans* passage this way: "For whom he did foreknow, he also did predestinate to be conformed to the image of his Son. . . . Moreover whom he did predestinate, them he also called. . . ." In constructing the concept, theologians had to piece passages together logically, and the way they did this led to differences. Commonly they linked *proorizō* with a time metaphor from *Ephesians* 1 about God "choosing us" "before the foundation of the world." This they augmented with Paul's references in *Romans* 9 to Old Testament passages about God's "hardening the heart of Pharaoh" and choosing Jacob instead of Esau even before these twins were conceived. Over the ages through this process of turning verbs and metaphors into nouns and concepts theologians have built a logical edifice of considerable magnitude; the process has passed through four phases so far.

From Scripture to Early Augustine. Paul's writings formed the basis of all future treatments. For three hundred years after Paul, theologians were content to produce commentaries on the pertinent passages. Following the lead of Clement of Alexandria (fl. c. AD 200), however, they interpreted *proorizō* as depending upon *proginōskō* (foreknow)—those whom God foreknew would believe he decided upon beforehand to save. Their chief concern was to combat the concept of fatalism and affirm that humans are free to do what is righteous. Thus Origen fought the gnostics toward the middle of the third century, and Augustine wrote *On Free Will* against the Manichaeans (c. 397). Origen asserted that humans were created with free will in the sense "that it is our own doing whether we live rightly or not, and that we are not compelled, either by those causes which come to us from without, or, as some think, by the presence of fate."

Augustine through the 1400s. Augustine changed his emphasis as a result of a challenge from Pelagius, who sought to defend human free will against Augustine's apparent denial of it in his *Confessions* (400): "Grant us what you [God] command, and command us what you will." In numerous treatises written over the succeeding two decades against Pelagius and those later called semi-Pelagians, Augustine gradually created the doctrine of predestination and set the standard to which virtually all subsequent discussions have related. He states that God created humans with the free will to choose between good and evil. By choosing evil they lost their free will to do God's will completely and thereafter needed God's grace to be saved and to live righteously. In *On the Predestination of the Saints* (428–429) Augustine claimed that the gift of grace is prepared by God's prior decision from eternity to predestine some to salvation and that grace comes as the effect of that predestination. God supremely predestined Christ to be the Son of God and called all those predestined for salvation to be members of Christ's body. Those so elected do indeed choose by their free will to believe, but since they are the elect, their "will is prepared by the Lord." In Augustine's view, none of this depends on divine foreknowledge of future human merits. In the *City of God* (413–426) he claims that God has "a plan whereby he might complete the fixed number of citizens predestined in his wisdom, even out of the condemned human race." God decides on the plan in eternity (an everlasting present) and foreknows in one sweeping vision the whole of time (the course of the past, present, and future). In *Enchiridion* (421) Augustine taught what came to be called "double predestination," that God not only in his mercy predestines some to salvation but in his justice predestines the rest to damnation or reprobation.

A succession of church councils culminating in the Council of Orange (529) elevated Augustine's position to the status of orthodoxy. Thereafter the view not quite accurately attributed to the Pelagians—that original sin has no power to keep humans from using their free will to gain their own salvation—was deemed unacceptable. The Council of Quiercy (853), responding to the concept of double predestination as elaborated by Gottschalk (848), declared that view unacceptable as well. The council held that while God surely preelects some to salvation, he merely leaves the remainder of humanity in their freely chosen sin with its predestined consequence of eternal punishment.

In the period roughly between 1050 and 1450, numerous theologians worked in Augustine's lineage to construct logical definitions of free will or predestination. They include Anselm of Canterbury (d. 1109), Peter Lombard (d. 1160), Duns Scotus (d. 1308), William of Ockham (d. 1349?), John Wyclif (d. 1384), Lorenzo Valla (d. 1457), and others. In his *Summa theologiae* (1266–1273), Thomas Aquinas gathered and elaborated a great array of logical distinctions to explain the concepts of free will and predestination: sufficient and efficient grace, habitual and actual grace, operating and cooperating grace, unconditional and conditional necessity, antecedent and consequent will, primary and secondary cause, and so on. Predestination was "the planned sending of a rational creature to the end which is eternal life." It "presupposes election, and election [presupposes] love." Thomas believed that his logic would show that none of this impairs free will.

Reformation through the 1800s. The rupture of Christendom called the Reformation led to a proliferation of positions roughly analogous to the pluralism of ecclesiastical traditions produced after the 1520s. A brief statement by Martin Luther (1520) that appeared to deny free will prompted Desiderius Erasmus to write

On the Freedom of the Will (1524) in the hope of settling the matter simply. Instead of a resolution, however, this initiated a controversy lasting four hundred years. By the time it ended, theologians in virtually all traditions had attempted definitions of the nature of free will and predestination, and every major church tradition had built some statement into its creed.

Erasmus picked up a concept that Thomas and others had used about cooperating grace and brought the analogous concept of cooperating will or assisting will into the discussion. Erasmus asserts that the will of God "preveniently moves the [human] will to will." Yet, humans do indeed will and achieve something. He concludes that *Philippians* 2:12–16 "certainly teaches that both humans and God work." Luther retorted with *On the Bondage of the Will* (1525), denying any possibility of cooperation between God and human will. The term *free will*, he claims, applies only to God or to the "lower choices" that humans make about everyday matters. All matters pertaining to salvation "depend on the work of God alone," the only power able to free the will from bondage to sin. Luther adopted Augustine's position on predestination. The Lutheran Formula of Concord (1576) states: "The predestination or eternal election of God extends only to the good and beloved children of God, and this is the cause of their salvation." Concerning the nonelect, the formula urges caution when speaking of reprobation.

Caution had become necessary, the Lutherans thought, because of John Calvin's views. In his *Romans* (1540) and *Institutes of the Christian Religion*, Calvin adopted Augustine's views and followed Luther in rejecting the notion of divine and human cooperation in salvation. By the final edition of the *Institutes* (1559), however, he defines predestination expansively to include double predestination: "By predestination we mean the eternal decree of God, by which he determined with himself whatever he wished to happen with regard to every person. All are not created on equal terms, but some are preordained to eternal life, others to eternal damnation." A succession of Reformed creeds like the French Reformed Confession (1559), the Scots Confession (1560), the Belgic Confession (1561), and the Second Helvetic Confession (1566) adopted Calvin's teachings, except those about the nonelect. On this point they urged caution or, like the Belgic Confession, affirmed that God was "just, in leaving others in the fall and perdition wherein they have involved themselves." Of the Reformed creeds, only the Westminster Confession (1647) adopted double predestination. The Canons of Dordt (1619) condemned the formulation presented by Jacobus Arminius and the Remonstrants' creed (1610) concerning God's assisting or cooperating grace. Arminius had characterized predestination as God's eternal decree, by which he determines to save through Christ "those who, through the grace of the Holy Spirit, shall believe on this his Son Jesus" and who by cooperating grace are enabled to persevere to the end. Many generations later Jonathan Edwards wrote his *Freedom of the Will* (1754) against the Arminians. The mainstream of the Baptist tradition sided with the Calvinists against the Arminians in adopting the New Hampshire Confession (1833) and the Louisville Abstract of Principle (1859).

In the Anglican tradition, the Thirty-nine Articles of the Church of England (1563, 1571) followed Calvin on both free will (article 10) and predestination (article 17), but not on double predestination. However, the Irish Articles (1615), written by James Ussher, even included double predestination. Anglican theologians, from Richard Hooker (1590s) to J. B. Mozley (author of *Predestination*, 1855) sought various ways to affirm both predestination and free will.

The Council of Trent treated the matter for the Roman Catholic tradition in its Decree on Justification (1547). The decree spoke of God's prevenient grace and associated it with predestination. But the council took issue with Luther and Calvin, declaring that God disposes people "through his quickening and assisting grace, to convert themselves to their own justification, by freely assenting to and cooperating with that grace." Certitude about being among the predestined came only when salvation was complete for those who persevered to the end. The Jesuit Luis de Molina expanded upon Trent in his *Concordia* (1588), in which he presents the concept of the concurrence of assisting grace with free will. Predestination, for Molina, depends on a *scientia media* by which God, when preordaining some to salvation, takes into account how each person would use free will in all possible circumstances. Cornelis Jansen wrote *Augustinus* (1640) to combat Molina, Trent, and the logical distinctions devised by Thomas Aquinas and the Thomists. He proposed a revival of Augustine's views in order to defeat any suggestion of concurrence and cooperation between divine and human will. A papal bull condemned Jansenism in 1653.

For the Eastern Orthodox tradition, the Russian Orthodox Confession (1643) and the Confession of Jerusalem (1673) responded to the Lutherans, Calvinists, and Trent by reaffirming the pre-Augustinian belief that God predestines some to glory and others to condemnation solely because "he foreknew the one would make a right use of their free will and the other a wrong." They affirmed synergism, the working together of God's prevenient grace and human free will throughout a lifetime of perseverance.

In 1784, John Wesley, founder of what became the Methodist tradition, prepared the Articles of Religion, a revision of the Anglican Thirty-nine Articles. In them he omits reference to predestination but retains the article on free will that attributes the will to believe to "the grace of God by Christ preventing [i.e., going before] us." In 1774, Wesley himself had affirmed predestination in the form of what he called conditional election, God's eternal choice of some to be saved, based on foreknowledge of their future belief. He contended that unconditional election not based on such foreknowledge is really the same thing as double predestination.

The Twentieth Century. In the twentieth century, theologians as diverse as William Temple (Anglican), Karl Rahner (Roman Catholic), Karl Barth and G. C. Berkouwer (Reformed), and Wolfhart Pannenberg (Lutheran) have given attention to the concepts of free will and predestination. Church statements from Vatican II and the Lutheran-Roman Catholic dialogue in the United States to the Synod of the Christian Reformed Church have referred to both. In 1920, Max Weber pronounced predestination to be the cardinal doctrine of Calvinism. Still, many Christian thinkers have let the subject drop, in keeping with the declaration by the World Conference on Faith and Order (1937) that theories about how the truths of God's grace and human free will might be reconciled are not part of the Christian faith. As Christians have become more appreciative of metaphor and time, and more wary of logical abstraction, secular philosophers have filled the void with their own concepts of freedom and necessity, free will and determinism.

[*See also the biographies of the Christian thinkers mentioned herein.*]

BIBLIOGRAPHY

Most of the original writings by the thinkers mentioned herein are readily available. The texts of the church creeds are in Philip Schaff's *Creeds of Christendom*, 6th ed., 3 vols. (1919; reprint, Grand Rapids, Mich., 1983), and *Creeds of the Churches*, 3d rev. ed., edited by John H. Leith (Atlanta, 1982). Worthy surveys of the doctrines are Réginald Garrigou-Lagrange's *Predestination* (Saint Louis, 1939); M. John Farrelly's *Predestination, Grace, and Free Will* (Westminster, Md., 1964); and Henri Rondet's *The Grace of Christ* (Westminster, Md., 1967). The many books on specific thinkers or traditions are easily located in subject indexes. Of these, especially good are J. Patout Burns's *The Development of Augustine's Doctrine of Operative Grace* (Paris, 1980); Richard A. Muller's *Christ and the Decree: Christology and Predestination in Reformed Theology from Calvin to Perkins* (Durham, N.C., 1984); and Nigel Abercrombie's *The Origins of Jansenism* (Oxford, 1936).

C. T. McIntire

Islamic Concept

Free will and predestination has been a prominent topic in Islamic religious thinking. For Muslims, the basis of the discussion is found in the Qur'ān and to a lesser extent in *ḥadīth* (reports about Muḥammad often called "traditions"), but these were influenced in turn by pre-Islamic Arab beliefs.

Predestination in Pre-Islamic Arabia. Something is known of the outlook of the pre-Islamic Arabs from what has been preserved of their poetry. In this we find a strong belief that much of human life, especially misfortune, is determined by time *(dahr, zamān)*. It has sometimes been thought that time here is the same as fate, but since the same determination of human life is sometimes attributed to "the days" or even "the nights," the idea of time must be uppermost. Time here is not something to be worshiped, but rather a natural fact, not unlike "the course of events."

In particular it was believed that a person's *ajal*, his term or the date of his death, was determined or predetermined. If he was destined to die on a certain day, he would die then, no matter what he did. It was also believed that a person's *rizq*, "provision" or "sustenance," that is, food, was also determined. This fatalistic attitude helped the nomads to survive in the harsh conditions of desert life. In the Arabian deserts the regularities of nature experienced elsewhere tended to be replaced by irregularities. If someone tried to take precautions against all eventualities, he would become a nervous wreck, but a readiness to accept whatever happened fatalistically reduced anxiety and thus was an aid to survival. It is to be noted, however, that in the belief of the nomads it is the outcome of human actions which is determined, not the actions themselves.

Predestination in the Qur'ān. The belief of the pre-Islamic Arabs in the control of events by time is described in the Qur'ān (surah 45:24): "There is only our present life; we die and we live, and time [*dahr*] alone destroys us." The conception of the *ajal*, or term of life, also occurs several times, but it is God who both fixes the *ajal* beforehand and then brings about the person's death: "He is the one who created you from clay, and then fixed an *ajal*" (6:2); "God will not defer [the death of] any person when his *ajal* comes" (63:11). There is thus a sense in which God takes over the functions of time; indeed, there is a *ḥadīth* which reports that the Messenger of God said that God said, "The sons of Adam insult *dahr*, but I am *dahr*." There are also several passages in the Qur'ān in which it is stated or implied that man's fate is not merely determined by God beforehand but also written down: "No misfortune has happened either in respect of the land or of yourselves but it was in a book before we [God] brought it about" (57:22). A clear statement of the uselessness of trying to avoid what has been predetermined is given in a passage about those who criticized Muḥammad's decision, when attacked in Medina by the Meccans, to go out to Mount Uḥud to fight: "If you had been in your houses, those for whom killing was written down would have sallied out to the places of their falling" (3:154). The Qur'ān also speaks of God as the source of man's *rizq* or provision: "He lavishes *rizq* on whom he wills, or stints it" (30:37); this was doubtless a reflection of the common experience in desert life that one tribe might have plenty while a neighboring tribe was starving.

Just as the pre-Islamic Arab did not believe that his acts were predetermined, but only their outcome, so this seems to be all that is implied by the Qur'anic statements about *ajal* and similar matters. All Muslims hold that human freedom in some sense and human responsibility in acting are implied in the Qur'anic teaching that God judges mortals on the Last Day and that their good and bad deeds are weighed in balances. Human freedom is not necessarily contradicted by such verses as: "Do not say of anything, I am doing that tomorrow, without [adding], If God wills" (18:23ff.); " . . . to him of you who wills to go straight; but you will not [so] will, unless God wills" (81:28ff.). Such verses may be understood as expressing God's control of the outcome of acts. There is a stronger case, however, for doubting whether an individual of his own free choice becomes a believer or an unbeliever. Many verses speak of God guiding and aiding people or of leading them astray and abandoning them: "If God wills to guide anyone, he enlarges his breast for Islam" (6:125); "He leads astray whom he wills and guides whom he wills" (16:93), so that those whom he guides become believers and those whom he leads astray become unbelievers. Other verses, however, assert that this guiding or leading astray is, as it were, in recompense for what the people in question have done previously: "Those who do not believe in God's signs, God does not guide" (16:104); "He leads astray none but the wrongdoers" (2:26). The phrase "leading astray" might be compared with God's "hardening of the heart" of Pharaoh and others in the Bible.

Umayyad Apologetic and Qadarī Opposition. Most modern students of Islamic history have tended to suppose that the Umayyad dynasty, which ruled from AH 41 to 132 (661–750 CE), was not very religious. This view is based, however, on the acceptance of pro-Abbasid, anti-Umayyad propaganda and is not borne out by documents of the Umayyad period such as the poems of Jarīr and al-Farazdaq. In these it becomes clear that the Umayyads, besides justifying their rule on traditional Arab lines, had a theological defense of their legitimacy: they held that the caliphate had been bestowed on them by God in the same way as the Qur'ān (2:30) described the bestowing of a caliphate on Adam. This meant taking the word *khalīfah*, or caliph, in the sense of "deputy" rather than of "successor," which it can also mean, and from this they argued that to oppose their decisions was to oppose God.

It was because of this theological position of the Umayyads that some of their opponents adopted what came to be known as the Qadarī heresy. This includes various slightly different formulations, all asserting human free will in some form. One version held that a person's good acts came from God and his bad acts from himself. From this it would follow that the bad acts of an Umayyad caliph were from himself and not from God, and thus a good Muslim could oppose such acts without making himself an unbeliever. The first to subscribe to the Qadarī heresy is usually said to have been Ma'bad al-Juhanī, who participated in an armed revolt which began in 701, and who was executed three years later upon the collapse of the revolt. Many of the participants in this revolt, however, were not among the Qadarīyah. Another person frequently mentioned as holding Qadarī views was Ghaylān al-Dimashqī. For a time he was a government official and was friendly with more than one caliph, but his political program, while including Qadarī ideas, went beyond it; in 730 the caliph Hishām became suspicious of the program and had Ghaylān executed. For the next twenty years there are many references to Qadarī opponents of the Umayyad regime, especially in Syria. After the replacement of the Umayyad dynasty by the Abbasid in 750, the Qadarī movement lost much of its political *raison d'être*, and either faded out or was absorbed into the rationalist Mu'tazilī movement. [*See* Mu'tazilah.]

Earlier scholars attributed the belief in free will to Christian influence; Ghaylān was indeed of Coptic origin, while Ma'bad was said to have derived his views from a Christian. From what has just been said, however, it would appear that the doctrine of free will was brought into Islamic discussions, not primarily because it was held to be true, but because it served a useful purpose in internal Islamic political discussions.

Ḥasan al-Baṣrī. The most important name connected with these theological questions is that of Ḥasan al-Baṣrī (d. 728). From his own lifetime or shortly afterward scholars debated whether he was a Qadarī or not, and both views were vigorously asserted. Distinguished Western scholars earlier in this century continued the debate. In 1933, however, there was published a long *risālah*, or epistle, written for the caliph 'Abd al-Malik by Ḥasan in defense of his views on this topic. From this treatise it is possible to give an account of what he believed. The Qur'ān is central for him and is the source of his arguments. Against the predestinarians who quoted verses about God's leading astray he replies with other verses which imply that those led astray were already wrongdoers and had in some form chosen evil. He also contends that the fact that God knows that some people will disbelieve is only descriptive; that is, he knows that by their own free choice they will disbelieve, but his knowledge does not predetermine their unbelief. He holds that the verse quoted above about misfortunes being in a book (57:22) applies only to wealth and material things, and not to belief or unbelief, obedience or disobedience. He further holds that when the Qur'ān speaks of someone acting or willing, he really does so, and his acts are not predetermined. He takes verse 33:38 to mean, "God's command [*amr*] is a determination [*qadar*] determined," and then argues that God determines human behavior only by commanding certain acts and prohibiting others. In this way, he can maintain that God creates only good, and that evil comes from human beings or from Satan.

Politically Ḥasan al-Baṣrī was critical of the Umayyads. The later scholar Ibn Qutaybah (d. 889) thought him a Qadarī in some respects and told how some of his friends would say to him, "These princes [the Umayyads] shed the blood of Muslims and seize their goods and then say, 'Our acts are only according to God's determination [*qadar*].'" To this Ḥasan would reply, "The enemies of God lie." Ḥasan's remark must be understood in the light of his identification of God's determination with his command, but the Umayyads were doubtless taking *qadar* in the traditional sense of prior effective determination. Despite his critical attitude Ḥasan resolutely refused to join any insurrection against the Umayyads and urged his friends and disciples to do likewise. In view of all these facts, Ḥasan's position might fairly be described as moderately Qadarī.

Predestination in the Ḥadīth (Traditions). Western scholars formerly thought that all *ḥadīth* were predestinarian and saw in this the reason why Ḥasan al-Baṣrī based his arguments on the Qur'ān and not on *ḥadīth*. There are indeed a few *ḥadīth* which express an opposite view; but the most likely reason for the absence of *ḥadīth* from Ḥasan's arguments is that at the time he was writing they were not regarded as having the authority later ascribed to them, and perhaps were not widely known and circulated. Had they been generally regarded as authoritative, he would surely have had some argument against them. It was the jurist al-Shāfi'ī, about a century after Ḥasan, who gave *ḥadīth* an assured place in Islamic thought as one of the "roots of law," and by his time, the study of *ḥadīth* had become much more extensive.

It will suffice here to mention some of the best-known predestinarian *ḥadīth*. One was the report that the Prophet had said, "The first thing God created was the pen; then he said to it, 'Write all that will happen until the Last Day.'" Another group of sayings of the Prophet speaks of an angel being entrusted with the child in the womb and asking God to determine whether it is male or female, whether it is to be fortunate or unfortunate, what is its *rizq* and what its *ajal*. Again, in connection with the act of a Muslim fighter at the Battle of Uḥud, who took his own life when his battle wounds became unbearable, the Prophet is reported to have said, "One man will work the works of the people of Paradise until he is only an arm's length from it, and then the book will overtake him, and he will work the works of the people of Hell and enter it," while in the case of another man the reverse will happen. Associated with such *ḥadīth* were some reported remarks by early Muslims to the effect that, if one wants to avoid hell, one must believe that God determines both good and bad, and that what reaches one could not have missed one, and what misses one could not have reached one.

It will be noticed that these predestinarian *ḥadīth* to some extent reflect pre-Islamic attitudes.

The Move Away from Qadarī Thought. In the last half-century of the Umayyad period it seems likely that many of the religious scholars who were critical of the rulers were also sympathetic with at least a moderately Qadarī view, while those who supported the rulers inclined to predestinarian views. Among such views, however, two levels may be distinguished: (1) the belief that what happens to someone is predetermined, but not his own acts; (2) the belief that both what happens to him and his own acts are predetermined. At a later period emphasis came to be placed less on God's predetermination of happenings and acts than on his present control of them.

Although something of the old pre-Islamic Arab predestinarianism was still strong among many Muslims and, because associated with God, felt to be part of Islam, it was difficult to express this sentiment under the Umayyads without seeming to approve all their actions. With the coming of the Abbasids, however, all this was altered. Belief in human free will lost most of its political relevance, and the expression of predestinarian views no longer suggested approval of an unjust government. Although those Qadarīyah who were primarily political were located chiefly in Syria, the main academic discussions took place in Basra among the followers and disciples of Ḥasan al-Baṣrī, where two opposing trends can be discerned, one toward more libertarian views, the other toward predestinarianism. Just as in pre-Islamic times belief in a predetermined *ajal* and similar matters helped to reduce anxiety, so the belief that God was in control of all events and that no disaster could happen to one except by his will relieved anxiety and gave confidence. The trend toward predestinarianism grew stronger not only in Basra but throughout the Islamic world, and some form of belief in God's control of events became an article in Sunnī creeds.

As this happened and as Qadarī views came to be regarded as heretical, there was a rewriting of history. Those with strong predestinarian or determinist views were unhappy to think that many great earlier scholars, their intellectual predecessors, had been tainted with heresy. They therefore emphasized the role of Ma'bad al-Juhamī and Ghaylān al-Dimashqī in the origination and spread of Qadarī ideas, since these were men who had been rebels and also under foreign influence. A little later stories were spread to discredit one particular member of Ḥasan's circle, 'Amr ibn 'Ubayd, and to suggest that he was worse than his contemporaries: besides being the leader of the libertarians among Ḥasan's followers, he had been elevated to the position of a founding father of the Mu'tazilah.

The Arabic name of the sect, Qadarīyah, itself bears witness to the struggle between the two trends among religious scholars generally. Like most early names of sects it is a nickname, but the curious point is that it is those who hold that the *qadar* is man's and not God's who are called "*qadar*-people." Texts now published show that there was a time when each side in the dispute called the other "Qadarī." In his book on sectarian views, al-Ash'arī (d. 935) mentions that his own party has been called "Qadarī," but continues, "the Qadarī is he who affirms that the *qadar* is his own and not his Lord's, and that he himself determines his acts and not his Creator." There was no Qadarīyah, properly speaking, after the Umayyad period, but some scholars used the name as an offensive nickname for the Mu'tazilah.

Even in the heyday of the Qadarīyah there was never a single clearly defined Qadarī sect. What made one a Qadarī was one article of belief, either that defined by al-Ash'arī or something like it, but this belief could be combined with a variety of beliefs on other matters. When the Abbasids came to power, many continued to believe in human free will but at the same time had views on the new political problems, and it was chiefly on the basis of these other views that sectarian names were bestowed. As a result the name *Qadarī* gradually died out and after the first half-century of the Abbasid period is hardly found except as an alternative to *Mu'tazilī.*

Mu'tazilah and Ash'arīyah. By the time of the caliph al-Ma'mūn (r. 813–833), the Mu'tazilah had defined their sect as based on five principles, of which free will was only one. At the same time, some of the leading Mu'tazilah had important positions at the caliphal court. Just after 847, however, official policy changed abruptly; the Mu'tazilah fell from favor, while the government abandoned their doctrine of the createdness of the Qur'ān and on that and other points supported the central Sunnī position. The Mu'tazilah are chiefly remembered as the group which first developed the discipline of *kalām,* that is, the use of Greek philosophical concepts and methods of argument. Gradually, however, some scholars realized that *kalām* could be used also to defend more generally acceptable doctrines than those of the Mu'tazilah. The creation of a nonheretical Sunnī *kalām* is traditionally attributed to al-Ash'arī, but it is now realized that in this he had several predecessors. Most of our information, however, is about the debates between Mu'tazilah and Ash'arīyah.

Within the discipline of *kalām* the discussions about free will took a new direction and were chiefly concerned with God's control of human acts in the present. This did not imply abandoning the belief that God had predetermined these acts, since it could be held that in controlling them in the present he was acting in accordance with his foreknowledge of what he had predetermined. The Ash'arī view was that God created human acts by creating in the agent at the moment of action the power to do the particular act. The Mu'tazilah agreed that the act came about through a power created by God, but held that this power was created by God before the act and was a power to do either this act or its opposite. In this way they left a place for the agent's choice.

The Mu'tazilah also argued that, if God sent people to hell as punishment for predetermined acts for which they were not responsible, he would be acting unjustly, and this was unthinkable. The Ash'arīyah met this argument with the formula that human acts are God's creation and the agent's "acquisition" *(kasb);* this term could also be translated as "making one's own" or "having credited to one." In effect the Ash'arīyah were saying that, although the act is God's creation, it is also in some unspecified way the human agent's act. Other scholars, even Sunnī theologians like the Māturīdīyah, found the term obscure and unsatisfactory and called the Ash'arīyah "determinists" *(mujbirah);* but *kasb* continued to have its place in this prominent theological school, and fresh generations of scholars introduced new subtleties. Among the Shī'ah, Zaydī views were very close to those of the Mu'tazilah, but those of most Imāmīyah (Ithnā 'Asharīyah, or Twelvers) and

Ismāʿīlīyah were not dissimilar. At the same time, they accepted God's "decree" and "determination" *(qaḍā', qadar)*, while interpreting these in various ways.

Recent interpreters of Islamic belief, such as Muḥammad ʿAbduh (d. 1905) and Muhammad Iqbal (d. 1938), have insisted on human freedom of choice while retaining a belief in divine predestination, but they have not attempted to reconcile the concepts with any depth.

[*See also* Kalām *and* Ashʿarīyah.]

BIBLIOGRAPHY

A general account of the Qadarī thinkers and their opponents will be found in my work *The Formative Period of Islamic Thought* (Edinburgh, 1973)—in which see especially pages 82–118, 232–242, and 315—and more briefly in my *Islamic Philosophy and Theology*, 2d enl. ed. (Edinburgh, 1985). My earlier *Free Will and Predestination in Early Islam* (London, 1948) has greater detail but requires correction in the light of later works. Since 1973 Josef van Ess has published several important documents and discussions, notably, *Zwischen Ḥadīṯ und Theologie: Studien zum Entstehen prädestinatianischer Überlieferung* (Berlin, 1975), *Anfänge muslimischer Theologie: Zwei antiqadaritische Traktate aus dem ersten Jahrhundert der Hiǧra* (Beirut, 1977), and the article "Ḳadariyya," in *The Encyclopaedia of Islam*, new ed. (Leiden, 1960–). His earlier *Traditionistische Polemik gegen ʿAmr b. ʿUbaid* (Beirut, 1967) is also of interest. An idea of how al-Ashʿarī argued against the Muʿtazilah may be gained from the translations in *The Theology of al-Ashʿarī* by Richard J. McCarthy (Beirut, 1953) and *Al-Ašʿarī's Al-Ibānah* by Walter C. Klein (New Haven, 1940).

W. MONTGOMERY WATT

FRENZY. The English word *frenzy* comes through the Latin *phrenesis* from the Greek *phrēn*, meaning the midriff, the heart, the upper part of the body, the diaphragm, the lungs or pericardium—that is, that part of the body held responsible for passions and thought. The ultimate derivation of the word is from the Indo-European **gwhren-*, meaning the diaphragm, the seat of intellect, understanding, and thought. The term will be used in this entry in its restricted sense, to refer not to mental derangement, madness, or folly generally but to a seizure of violent agitation or wild excitement, to uncontrollable rage or to delirious fury.

Although "frenzy" is not an established category in religious studies, the term occurs frequently in the description of a number of religious states and activities, and its occurrence is often interpreted in religious terms. It is related to such categories as "enthusiasm," "mania," "fury," "inspiration," "intoxication," "spirit possession," and "ecstasy," and, like these states, it is characterized by a certain spontaneity, an autonomy, as if beyond the control of the individual, as if coming from without or from deep within him. In the *Phaedrus* (244ff.), Plato distinguishes several types of frenzy *(mania)* that impart gifts to man: the frenzy of the seer who reveals the future; that of the consecrated mystic who absolves man from sin; that of the poet possessed by the Muses; and that of the philosopher. In common parlance, however, *frenzy* usually has an aggressive connotation.

Three manifestations of frenzy will be considered here: frenzy as the result of combat (furor), frenzy as a symptom of certain culturally specific psychotic syndromes (amok), and frenzy as a stage of trance understood as spirit possession. The juxtaposition of these three manifestations of frenzy should not be considered synthetic. The term *frenzy* should, in my opinion, be used descriptively in specific contexts and not isolated as a separate and separable category of religious experience.

Furor. It has been reported in both legend and history that in the heat of battle certain warriors enter into a delirious fury, attacking anyone in their reach. Moroccan Arabs recount, for example, that Sīdinā ʿAlī, the prophet Muḥammad's son-in-law, whom they regard as the ideal warrior, was once in combat with the Jews. Blood flowed up to his stirrups, so great was his prowess. When he had killed all of the Jews, he turned on his own people and would have slaughtered them too, had not one of them, a beggar, asked him for a crust of bread (*barakah*, lit., "blessing"). This request cooled down his frenzy *(ḥashimīyah)*, for he knew that only an Arab was fool enough to beg from him in his state. Roman legend has it that after one of the Horatii had defeated three enemy brothers, the Curiatii, he turned in furor on his sister, who, in mourning for one of them, had revealed the "feminine" weakness of a lover's grief.

In an analogous Celtic tale, Cú Chulainn, the hero of the Ulster legend, while still a child defeated the three sons of Nechta, the enemy of his people, and returned to his capital still in a frenzy. There he spurned the queen, who tried to divert him by making crude sexual advances. As he was momentarily distracted, his men seized him and threw him into a vat of cold water to cool him down. From then on Cú Chulainn kept his furor in reserve for battle. Georges Dumézil suggests that this tale of initiatory combat relates to the domestication of savage frenzy—the ideal of prehistoric Italic, Celtic, and Germanic warriors—and its submission to legionary discipline. To the psychoanalytically oriented, the tale is concerned with the conversion into disciplined military aggression of the warrior's uncontrolled rage toward his mother, or toward women more generally, and, by extension, toward his own weakness symbolized by women.

Amok. There are a number of culture-bound reactive syndromes, the so-called ethnopsychoses, that involve frenzied behavior. The best known of these "hypereridic rage reactions" is amok, which occurs primarily in Malaysia and Indonesia. The *pengamok*, the person who runs amok, usually suffers from neurasthenia, chronic illness, or a loss of a sense of social order and, with time, comes to experience an increasingly threatening external pressure that frightens or enrages him. Suddenly, as if to escape this pressure, he runs wild, attacking people, animals, and objects around him, even himself. He then falls into a stupor and awakes depressed and without any memory of his having run amok. Amok has occurred among warriors dedicated to self-sacrifice, and it has been explained as an escape from the pervasive Malay-Indonesian sense of fatalism and concern for propriety *(alus)*. As the occurrence of amok peaked in the nineteenth century, with Western contact, it has been regarded as a transitional reaction to modernization.

Similar hypereridic reactions have been reported elsewhere, for example, in New Guinea (wild-man behavior, *negi negi, lulu*), in Malawi *(misala)*, and in Puerto Rico *(mal de pelea)*. Just as frenzied behavior occurs in certain hypermanic disorders, so it occurs in other culture-bound reactive syndromes. Ainu women of northern Japan afflicted with *imu* burst out aggressively or flee in panic after seeing a snake and then, within minutes, fall into catalepsy, echo those about them, and execute orders automatically. Inuit (Eskimos) suffering from *piblotko*, or Arctic hysteria, tear off their clothing, run around, throw things, and imitate animals. Northern Algonquian-speaking Indians of Canada who are possessed of a *windigo* spirit are overcome with a frenzied craving for human flesh and are said to pounce on men, women, and children and devour them ravenously. Frenzied behavior is often interpreted as spirit possession or as the result of sorcery.

Spirit Possession. Frenzy has often been associated with spirit possession. The herdsman's description of the Bacchantes, worshiping Dionysos, in Euripides' *The Bacchae* (ll. 677–774) is a classic example. Having himself escaped attack, the herdsman watches as the possessed women attack the villagers' grazing cattle.

> And then
> you could have seen a single woman with bare hands
> tear a fat calf, still bellowing with fright,
> in two, while others clawed the heifers to pieces.
> There were ribs and cloven hooves scattered everywhere,
> and scraps smeared with blood hung from the fir trees.
> And bulls, their raging fury gathered in their horns,
> lowered their heads to charge, then fell, stumbling
> to the earth, pulled down by hordes of women
> and stripped of flesh and skin more quickly, sire,
> than you could blink your royal eyes. Then,
> carried by their own speed, they flew like birds
> across the spreading fields along Asopus' stream
> where most of all the ground is good for harvesting.
> Like invaders they swooped on Hysiae
> and on Erythrae in the foothills of Cithaeron.
> Everything in sight they pillaged and destroyed.
> They snatched the children from their homes. And when
> they piled their plunder on their backs, it stayed in place,
> untied. Nothing, neither bronze nor iron,
> fell to the dark earth. Flames flickered
> in their curls and did not burn them.
> (*The Bacchae*, trans. Arrowsmith, ll. 736–758)

Euripides' description has become a model in Western discourse for literary descriptions of Dionysian worship (e.g., Thomas Mann's in *Death in Venice*) and indeed for scientific description of the frenzy of the spirit possessed.

In many exorcistic rites the spirit-possessed moves from a gentle, "dreamy," somnambulistic trance into a frenzied one in which he or she loses all control of behavior. Thus, in Balinese folk dramas *(sanghyangs)* an entranced dancer will imitate, say, a pig, lumbering about on all fours, grunting and groveling, and then suddenly, often on provocation from the audience, he will fall into frenzy, darting, leaping, thrashing about, wallowing uncontrollably in the mud, shaking in convulsions, and struggling against those who try to pin him down. Doused with water, he grows quiet. The frenzied stage of trance possession is usually followed by torpor and exhaustion. Such frenzies, as in *The Bacchae*, seem to be facilitated by group participation and excitement.

[*See also* Spirit Possession; Medicine, *article on* Medicine and Religion in Tribal Cultures; Berserkers; *and* Omophagia. *For related concepts, see* Enthusiasm *and* Ecstasy.]

BIBLIOGRAPHY

Belo, Jane. *Trance in Bali*. New York, 1960. A detailed description of trance (including frenzy) in Bali.

Crapanzano, Vincent. *The Hamadsha: An Essay in Moroccan Ethnopsychiatry*. Berkeley, 1973. Discusses the frenzied state of spirit possession among Moroccan Arabs.

Dumézil, Georges. *The Destiny of the Warrior*. Translated by Alf Hiltebeitel. Chicago, 1970. Discusses furor in Indo-European thought.

Euripides. *The Bacchae*. Translated by William Arrowsmith. In *The Complete Greek Tragedies*, edited by David Grene and Richmond Lattimore, vol. 4, *Euripedes*, pp. 543–608. Chicago, 1959. Contains an exemplary description of frenzy.

Murphy, H. B. M. "History and Evolution of Syndromes: The Striking Case of *Latah* and *Amok*." In *Psychopathology: Contributions from the Social, Behavioral, and Biological Sci-*

ences, edited by Muriel Hammer et al., pp. 33–55. New York, 1973. One of the few historical studies of amok.

Pfeiffer, Wolfgang M. *Transkulturelle Psychiatrie.* Stuttgart, 1971. A good discussion of amok and other ethnic psychoses.

Yap, Pow Meng. "The Culture-Bound Reaction Syndromes." In *Mental Health Research in Asia and the Pacific,* edited by William Caudill and Tsung-yi Lin. Honolulu, 1969. General discussion of ethnopsychoses, including amok.

VINCENT CRAPANZANO

FREUD, SIGMUND (1856–1939), originator of psychoanalysis, a method of treating those mental disorders commonly designated as the neuroses. Psychoanalysis began as a method of healing, but became also a psychological theory of personality or mind and a general theory of culture—of morality, group life, society, history, art, and religion. When treating his patients, Freud found it necessary to emphasize their unconscious feelings and thoughts, which, precisely because they were unacknowledged, created symptoms. Freud believed that dreams and dream symbolism were keys to his patients' unconscious thinking, and also to their symptoms. It was therefore inevitable that his method of treatment would generate theoretical concepts important for understanding the human mind, and that these in turn would lead him to psychological conclusions about the cultural meanings of the symbols found in religious myths, beliefs, and rituals. Freud's psychoanalytic theory is widely accepted by scholars in many different fields, and Freud is commonly ranked with Karl Marx, Max Weber, Friedrich Nietzsche, and Émile Durkheim as one of the architects of the modern world. But scholars of religion also acknowledge that Freud has made a lasting contribution to their understanding of the religious thought and life of humankind.

Life and Principal Works. Freud's personal beginnings contain little to suggest his later achievements. Born into a large Jewish family of modest means in Freiberg, Moravia (now Pribor, Czechoslovakia), he was four when his father, a wool merchant, moved the family to Vienna, where Freud spent all but the last year of his life. As a youth, he received an excellent education that emphasized both classics and science. For a while he contemplated a career in law or in politics, but finally decided upon scientific work and attended medical school at the University of Vienna, from which he graduated in 1881. A year later he became engaged to Martha Bernays, whom he subsequently married.

Partly for financial reasons and partly on account of official anti-Semitism (it was customary for the university to pass over Jewish candidates for research positions), Freud shifted his career goals to the medical practice of psychiatry. He became interested in hysterical patients, and began to collaborate with the eminent Viennese physician Josef Breuer.

Freud and Breuer discovered that the symptoms of hysterical patients diminished as they were encouraged to talk about the intense feelings they held toward those close to them. Freud also noticed that dreams were included in these reports, and he began to evolve his theory that both dreams and hysterical symptoms disguised deeply felt and deeply feared thoughts and feelings. At the end of his period of collaboration with Breuer, Freud began to write his first and most famous book, *The Interpretation of Dreams* (1900). This work contained the essence of all his major ideas about the neuroses, about dreams, and about psychoanalytic treatment—and also the essence of his theory that religious symbols and myths are modeled upon dreams.

In the 1910s and 1920s, Freud's reputation grew. New patients came, and he continued to publish papers and to gather students about him. Many of these men and women underwent psychoanalysis with Freud, and studied his ideas. Among the more eminent were the Swiss psychiatrist Carl Gustav Jung and the socialist Alfred Adler. In 1908 the first international congress in psychoanalysis was held in Salzburg, and in 1909 Freud and Jung gave lectures at Clark University in Massachusetts. The most important of Freud's many publications during these decades were *Introductory Lectures on Psychoanalysis* (1915), which explained psychoanalytic theory and practice to a lay audience; *Group Psychology and the Analysis of the Ego* (1921), in which Freud analyzed the psychological forces beneath the group behavior of armies and churches; and *The Ego and the Id* (1923), a theoretical treatise on the fundamental psychological structures of the human mind.

Although Freud throughout his life created new works of psychological observation and interpretation, which brought him ever greater recognition, the 1920s produced a major shift in his person and thought, one whose effects persisted to his death. The aftermath of World War I, the death of a beloved daughter, and the discovery of a cancerous growth in his jaw, all forced upon him a reflective and resigned attitude, which in turn fueled his most profound studies of culture and religion. Taking up arms in the time-honored conflict between science and religion, Freud asserted (in *The Future of an Illusion,* 1927) that psychoanalysis was but the latest and most compelling scientific argument against the consolations of religion. Three years later, in *Civilization and Its Discontents,* he addressed the oppressive quality of contemporary social life, arguing that society itself carried within it the mechanisms that created neurotic conflict. In his last major work, *Moses and Monotheism* (1939), written in sections over the 1930s, Freud returned to his own Jewish origins and searched for a positive estimate of that religion, arguing—paradoxically—that Western monotheism was an ascetic force that supported the renunciations required by scientific endeavors.

When the Nazis persecuted the adherents of psychoanalysis and forced Freud to leave his home, he fled to London, where—aged, ill, persecuted, and famous—he died on the eve of World War II.

Psychoanalytic Theory. While Freud's psychoanalysis is really a threefold discipline—clinical treatment of neurotic conflict, general theory of personality, and theory of culture and religion—it is important to realize that he generalized from the first to the second and from both to the third. Therefore, all expositions of his thought about religion should begin with the psychoanalytic method and its clinical context, usually referred to as the analytic situation.

Two concepts form the foundation of the analytic situation, the unconscious and childhood. All deliberate, intentional, and conscious life, for the healthy adult and the neurotic alike, is constantly subject to influence by an unconscious dimension of feeling, willing, and intending. Freud often referred to the unconscious as a portion of mental life split off from, and existing alongside of, the system of conscious mental processes. This separation first occurs during the years of childhood. Because of the prolonged and at times virtually total dependency of the infant upon caretakers, some of the strong feelings of love, hate, envy, and jealousy—in short, portions of all the fundamental wishes and fears of living and being—are forgotten or forced out of awareness. These thoughts and feelings, which Freud described as repressed, live on in the normal activities of the adult, making their appearance symbolically in dreams, slips of the tongue, jokes, and love relationships. The normal adult is capable of introspection and self-analysis when unconscious wishes and thoughts press for attention.

However, under conditions of stress produced by the various tasks and responsibilities of living, even the healthy adult can falter. In such cases, the mental organization of the person returns to earlier patterns of regulation, a process known as regression, and neurotic symptoms (for example, phobias or irrational fears, obsessional ideas, or compulsive acts) serve to defend against the return. Because persons in this condition can no longer control portions of their behavior, psychoanalytic treatment is helpful for them. In the analytic situation the patient allows his or her thoughts and feelings, and especially dreams, to flow freely (in "free association") without moral or intellectual control and in doing so forms an intense, irrational, emotional bond with the doctor. Freud called this bond "transference." Because the transference relation embodies old and forgotten childhood memories, the doctor can interpret the bond in the light of dreams and fantasies, gradually bringing the repressed wishes back under the control of conscious life.

Theory of Culture and Religion. Contrary to much opinion on the subject, Freud recognized religion as a complex phenomenon, and his estimate of it was both appreciative and skeptical. He was more interested in religion than he was in any other manifestation of culture. He rarely approached religion in the abstract, instead always seeing it in the context of culture as a whole—the social arrangements and systems of symbols that integrate a community of people. Understood as a system of authoritative beliefs about the world, which includes moral guides and the consoling sense of specialness that authoritativeness confers, religion is the historical force that energizes the forms assumed by culture. Freud therefore wrote about art, humor, morality, fairy tales, legends, myths, and rituals, without always attempting to make sharp distinctions among them.

The key to Freud's appreciative stance toward religion lies in his psychology of myth and in particular in his theory that myths are to be understood after the fashion of dreams, although they are collective rather than individual dreams. By noting parallels between dreams and myths, Freud transformed the model of dream interpretation into a tool for research into the psychological character of culture. Both dreams and myths, he felt, are imaginative structures composed of symbols organized along a narrative line. Both are produced by unconscious forces, for myths as well as dreams are experienced as given to individuals, rather than as being created by them. As such, both display mechanisms of symbol formation, whereby figures in dreams and myths take on shifting roles and significances. Both are therefore creative activities of the human mind.

But Freud also observed that dreams expressed the wishes, desires, and fantasies of his patients and were closely related to their motives and intentions. He concluded that myths are collective or group fantasies. Behind the apparent diversity of human societies and cultures there persist certain primordial or typical human situations—the conflicts between parents and children and between the children themselves, conflicts surrounding perennial human issues such as sexuality, death, envy, gratitude, hate, and love. Because these psychological constants or universals are shared by all people, and because they are so pervasive, powerful, and threatening, they are repressed to some degree by everyone, but they reappear for all to see in the myths of each society. A myth, then, represents the shared unconscious wishes of a group, and the psychological interpretation of myth discloses the nature of these wishes.

For example, in fairy tales a king and queen can represent shared unconscious ideas and fears about fathers and mothers, just as princes and princesses represent those held by sons and daughters. A witch can symbolize a hateful, unempathic mother, and a savage monster may suggest aggressive wishes too powerful for individual consciousness or an individual dream to support. Of the world religions, Freud was especially interested in Judaism and Christianity. The idea of God the Father in Judaism represents shared unconscious wishes for a totally powerful and morally perfect group father. Christianity's devotion to Jesus Christ, the Son of God, expresses the Western preoccupation with the anxiety sons experience in relation to their fathers. Catholicism's adoration of the Virgin discloses an intense idealization of motherhood, which Protestant families subsequently rejected. The omnipresence of explicitly sexual themes in the myths of Indian religions contrasts with their absence in Western religious traditions, whose asceticism betrays anxiety over bodily desires.

Freud's skeptical attitude toward religion derived from his training in physiology, neurology, and medicine, which emphasized causality, energy, and rigorous objectivity. But these scientific ideas also served a moral purpose for Freud. He believed that the most profound unconscious human wish was for a grandiose sense of specialness, which he called "narcissism," and that both science and psychoanalysis could reduce or modify this narcissism, or self-love. On the other hand, religion indulged and encouraged self-love by conferring upon people the illusion that they were special or privileged by virtue of their relation to an all-powerful and all-loving god. Freud cited the Western discovery that the earth revolved around the sun. As a result of that scientific insight, people could no longer think of themselves as central points in a divine drama. The theory of evolution deprived people of the wish to see themselves as special beings created by an omnipotent god. And Freud believed that his own discovery of the unconscious shattered the grandiose belief in the supreme capacities of human reason. Each scientific discovery was a blow to human narcissism and to the religious doctrine that supported it. Freud concluded that belief in an all-powerful divine being with whom one had a special relationship forestalled, rather than facilitated, new knowledge about the world—for in each case religious leaders had mounted the strongest objections to these discoveries.

Contribution to the Study of Religion. Because of Freud's appreciation of the power of religious symbols, and despite his skeptical stance toward religion, his theories exercised an important influence upon the religious thought of post–World War II Europe and, especially, America. By this time his ideas had become widely acknowledged, and the leaders of religious communities wanted to use them and to respond to his challenge. In particular, Paul Tillich and Mircea Eliade deserve mention here.

Paul Tillich was convinced that an overly rational society had cut the Christian faith off from its historic depths and from its role as a shaper of culture. He hailed the secular Freud's concept of the unconscious roots of religious reality as an attempt to restore what he called a depth dimension to human reason and cultural life. Even Freud's skeptical side Tillich incorporated into theology, arguing that modern churches had become authoritarian and oppressive to human depth, and that Freud's objections to religion were in this sense well founded. Tillich likened Freud to a biblical prophet whose attacks on the idolatry of the faithful were mounted in the service of a deeper, more transcendent reality.

Alongside Tillich's theological analyses of culture, a second movement emerged, led by the renowned historian of religions Mircea Eliade. Like Tillich, Eliade believed that contemporary culture was excessively rational and technological and that a renewal of a religious kind was essential. But unlike Tillich, Eliade turned to primitive religions and to Eastern traditions and myths to renew the life of modern man. Eliade wrote that Freud's view of myth as an unconscious imaginative structure and the links he had built between dreams and myths would enrich the dry, technical tones of modern life, and that both could be used to reinstate a religious view of humanity. In fact, Eliade described the history of religions as a metapsychoanalysis, by which he meant that religion added a dimension to the foundations supplied by Freud.

Yet neither Tillich nor Eliade could tolerate Freud's skepticism, his view that once the unconscious meaning of a religious myth was disclosed, then the consoling sense of specialness that belief conferred would necessarily be given up in the interest of a broader psychological self-understanding. The task of advancing this thought was left to the sociologist Philip Rieff, who devised the term "psychological man," to describe a new type of person in modern society, one who had accepted Freud's interpretations and had accordingly adopted a psychological rather than a religious ethic. Rieff's view called attention to the roles of religion and psychoanalysis as competing social forces in Western history, a focus ignored by Tillich and Eliade, who had centered their efforts on the more speculative aspects of Freud's theories of religion.

BIBLIOGRAPHY

Freud's psychological writings have been collected for the English-language reader in *The Standard Edition of the Complete Psychological Writings of Sigmund Freud*, 24 vols., translated from German under the general editorship of James Strachey (London, 1953–1974). Each of Freud's publications in this definitive edition is prefaced by valuable information regarding date of composition and of first publication, relevant biographical details, and a short discussion of its leading ideas in relation to Freud's thought as a whole.

The best single book on Freud's life, social circumstances, and major ideas is Ernest Jones's major study *The Life and Work of Sigmund Freud*, edited and abridged by Lionel Trilling and Stephen Marcus (New York, 1961). Philip Rieff's careful, thorough, and clearly written book *Freud: The Mind of the Moralist* (1959; 3d ed., Chicago, 1979) remains the best overall discussion of Freud's social, philosophical, and religious ideas. Rieff also analyzes the impact of psychoanalysis upon both the Western religious heritage and contemporary society. An excellent illustration of the use of Freud's approach to dream symbolism to interpret social and cultural symbols is Bruno Bettelheim's *The Uses of Enchantment: The Meaning and Importance of Fairy Tales* (New York, 1977). The best theological discussion of Freud's theory of religious experience is to be found in Paul Tillich's *The Courage to Be* (New Haven, 1952). The many implications of psychoanalysis for the historical study of religion are clearly stated by Mircea Eliade in *Myths, Dreams and Mysteries* (New York, 1960).

PETER HOMANS

FREYJA, the daughter of Njǫrðr and sister of Freyr, is the main Germanic goddess in the Vanic group. She was originally born in the land of the Vanir of Njǫrðr and his anonymous sister-wife. It is not stated explicitly how she came to the world of Æsir, but she may have entered Ásgarðr in the guise of the seeress Gullveig (*Vǫluspá*, ss. 21–22), whose features fit the personage of Freyja particularly well since Freyja taught the Æsir magic *(seiðr)* and has a reputation for greed, especially as far as jewels are concerned. Freyja is the goddess men invoke in matters of love, and she is often called upon for that purpose. She is the wife of Óðr, a rather obscure deity whose name derives from the same root as *Óðinn* (Germanic, **wōð-*, presumably meaning "inspired mental activity"). According to Snorri Sturluson (*Gylfaginning*, chap. 35), Freyja bore Óðr a daughter, Hnoss ("jewel"), although the marriage was apparently not a happy one. Óðr disappeared on long journeys, and she wept tears of "red gold" in his absence. She also looked for him in many countries and assumed various names in her wanderings. It is said that she was as dignified as Óðinn's wife Frigg, and Snorri Sturluson claims (with a correct etymological connection) that distinguished Scandinavian ladies are called *fróvor* (the plural of Old Norse *frú[a]*) with reference to her name (*Glyfaginning*, chap. 24).

Freyja's personality is complex: she is said to enjoy "love poetry," but the Old Norse term *mansǫngr* in Snorri's text refers to an erotic genre that was forbidden in Iceland under threat of *skóggangr* ("banishment into the woods"; Ström, 1975, p. 151). Her lustfulness is often stressed, not only by Loki, who denounces her as incestuous and grossly promiscuous (*Lokasenna*, ss. 30 and 32), but also in other contexts, such as the *Hyndluljóð* (ss. 30–31), where she is described as "running through the night in heat like [the goat] Heiðrún." Her unfaithfulness to her husband is accentuated as well: "Under your apron still others have crept" (Hollander, 1962, p. 135). A story in the late thirteenth-century *Flateyarbók*, the *Sǫrlaþáttr*, tells how she slept with four dwarfs in order to obtain the famous necklace Brísingamen, which they had forged. Such behavior is, however, in keeping with the personality of a fertility goddess. Freyja's association with the cat in late Norse tradition—her chariot is pulled by cats—is another hint at her lasciviousness, since the cat was considered by Norsemen to be a most lascivious animal. In the case of Freyja, the feline is the equivalent of the lions and panthers associated with such ancient Near Eastern fertility goddesses as the Dea Syria or Cybele.

Freyja often appears as a pawn in the shady negotiations between the Æsir and the giants: when the giant Þrymr gets hold of Þórr's hammer, Mjǫllnir, the Æsir are ready to exchange Freyja for it—but upon her stern refusal, Þórr, disguised as Freyja, goes instead to retrieve Mjǫllnir. In the episode of the master builder of Ásgarðr, the Æsir are willing to surrender Freyja, together with the sun and the moon, provided the contractor completes the work by the summer solstice (*Gylfaginning* chap. 42), though in the *Vǫluspá* (st. 25) it sounds as if she had already been surrendered to the giant. Myths like these, however, are fraught with symbolic meaning: apparently, the giants intend to plunge the world into eternal cold and darkness. The *hrímþursar* ("frost giants") threaten eternal winter, sterility, and darkness, all of which northern people were in constant fear of.

Freyja has many features in common with her

brother Freyr: like him, she rides a boar with shining golden bristles made especially for her by the dwarfs; it is called Hildisvíni ("battle swine"). Pigs are sacred to her as they are to Freyr, and Freyja is even nicknamed Sýr ("sow"), a shape she may have taken on occasion.

The cult of Freyja was widely dispersed over Scandinavia, according to the testimony of Nordic place-names, though it is not always easy to determine whether the toponyms refer to Freyr or to Freyja (de Vries, 1957, pp. 308–310). The greatest concentration seems to be along the west coast of Norway and in the Swedish Uppland, and the name of the deity is connected with terms meaning "lake," "grove," and "hill," as well as "field" or "meadow" or, more specifically, "sanctuary."

Freyja also goes under such other names as *Hǫrn*, a term often occurring in skaldic kennings for "woman" and related to the Old Norse term *hǫrr* ("flax" or "linen"); it also occurs in a few place-names and points to the worship of the goddess as deity of the flax harvest in eastern Sweden (de Vries, 1957, p. 331). As Mardǫll she appears in kennings for "gold" such as *Mardallar tár* ("Mardǫll's tears") She is also known as Gefn, a name derived from the verb *gefa* ("give") and referring to the concept of the fertility goddess as the generous dispenser of wealth, goods, and well-being. This term is also preserved in the name of the Matronae Gabiae, or Dea Garmangabis, in Roman times in the Rhineland. Freyja has therefore been connected with Gefjon, who plowed Sjælland away from the Swedish mainland with the help of her four sons (*Gylfaginning*, chap. 1). There are indeed some striking parallels between Freyja and Gefjon, as suggested by Loki's reference (*Lokasenna*, st. 20) to Gefjon's seduction of a "fair-haired lad" (possibly Heimdallr) who gave her a necklace (presumably Brísingamen) in exchange for her favors. Though the Eddic literature treats them as separate deities, Gefjon can hardly be anything but a local incarnation of the omnipresent fertility goddess. Another possible hypostasis of Freyja is the beautiful Menglǫð (lit., "glad about her necklace"), who lives in the company of nine maidens with salutiferous names on top of the Lyfjaberg (the "mount of [magical] healing herbs"), surrounded by a wall of flickering flames (de Vries, 1957, pp. 328–329; cf. *Fjǫlsvinnsmál*, ss. 31–38).

BIBLIOGRAPHY

Hollander, Lee M. *The Poetic Edda.* 2d rev. ed. Austin, 1962.

Holtsmark, Anne, and Jon Helgason, eds. *Snorri Sturluson Edda: Gylfaginning og prosafortellingene av skáldskaparmál.* Copenhagen, 1950.

Turville-Petre, E. O. G. *Myth and Religion of the North: The Religion of Ancient Scandinavia.* New York, 1964.

Vries, Jan de. *Altgermanische Religionsgeschichte*, vol. 2. 2d rev. ed. Berlin, 1957.

EDGAR C. POLOMÉ

FREYR, the son of Njǫrðr, is the main fertility god of ancient Scandinavia. People invoked him for peace and good crops, and he bestowed wealth upon them (*Gylfaginning*, chap. 24). He made women happy and freed captives (*Lokasenna*, st. 37). Though considered a lord of peace—his legendary reign in Sweden is characterized by Snorri Sturluson as the prosperous "peace of Fróði" (*Ynglingasaga*, chap. 10)—he also appears as a courageous warrior, and his name occurs frequently in kennings for *warrior*. He is represented as the ancestor of the Swedish kings under the name *Yngvi* (the eponym of the royal family of the *Ynglingar*), a name also associated with *Ing* (Germanic, *Ingw[az]) in the Old English Runic Poem and the eponym of the Germanic tribal group the Inguaeones.

Among Freyr's prized possessions is the ship Skíðblaðnir (*Grímnismál*, st. 44), which skillful dwarfs made for him; it can be folded up and carried in a pouch, but when needed, it can carry the whole company of the Æsir, weapons and all, and always sails with a favorable wind (*Gylfaginning*, chap. 43). The motif of the wonderful boat, which also occurs in the Celtic tradition, is particularly significant because of the close association of ships with fertility cults, from their representation on Scandinavian Bronze Age rock carvings to the medieval rites described by Jakob Grimm (1835). [*See also* Boats.] Another important present from the dwarfs is Freyr's golden wild boar, Gullinbyrsti ("gold bristle") or Sliðrugtanni ("razor tooth"), who runs faster than a horse and shines brightly at night.

Freyr is not involved in many myths; probably the best known is from the *Poetic Edda: Skírnismál* (The Lay of Skirnir), the story of the wooing of Gerðr (daughter of the giant Gymir) by Freyr's servant, Skírnir, on behalf of his master. The *Ynglingasaga* mentions Gerðr as Freyr's wife and indicates that they had a son, Fjǫlnir. Elsewhere (*Lokasenna*, st. 42), Loki accuses Freyr of having acquired Gerðr with gold and by surrendering his sword. The Eddic narrative itself is rather strange. Seeing the beautiful giantess from the promontory overlooking all the world, Freyr falls deeply in love with her. Pining away for want of her affection he sends Skírnir to woo her. The journey to the home of Gymir is hazardous, and Skírnir manages to reach it only because Freyr's horse, which he is riding, can jump over the circles of flames protecting Gymir's property. At the gate, Skírnir finds savage dogs and a shepherd sitting on a mound, who tells him he must be either doomed or dead to have come so far. Skírnir is nevertheless greeted by Gerðr, who offers him mead. As he begins his plea for her love on behalf of Freyr, he tries to entice her with presents—the apples of eternal youth, the magic armring (Draupnir), and Freyr's invincible sword—but he meets with refusal. Switching from blandishments to threats, Skírnir ominously warns Gerðr that she will be exiled and will waste away, ugly and desolate and plagued by lust, for having incurred the wrath of the Æsir; worse still, he will deliver her by magic to a three-headed fiend from hell, to quench her thirst with "stalings of stinking goats" (Hollander, 1962, p. 72). Scared by these woeful prospects, Gerðr gives in and promises to meet Freyr after nine nights in a "trysting glade" called Barri.

The couple Freyr-Gerðr has been identified with effigies found on gold plates from the Viking age in Jæderen, Denmark: they show a man and a woman facing each other; she holds an object that could be a branch with leaves and a flower, and the man touches her cheek or her breast with his hand in an obvious gesture of endearment. The clear erotic elements in this depiction seem to be entirely in keeping with the obvious sexual connotations of fertility cults. Adam of Bremen, depicting the triad of gods worshiped in the temple at Uppsala in eleventh-century Sweden, describes Freyr as endowed with a huge sex organ, and he adds that all kinds of "lewd practices that remain better unmentioned" accompanied the ceremonies of Freyr's cult. Freyr's sexual mores are also illustrated by his euhemeristic correspondent, the Swedish king Frø (Saxo Grammaticus, bk. 9, sec. 251), who had the wives of his dead enemies taken to a house of ill repute and raped publicly. The story of Gunnar Helming tells of a Norwegian refugee who took the place of Freyr's effigy, which was destroyed in a storm while it was being ceremoniously conveyed in a chariot to bring fertility to the fields. There is indication here that priestesses served the god; since, in this case, a priestess was impregnated by the substitute "Freyr," and her pregnancy was interpreted by the peasantry as a good omen for their harvest, it has been assumed that such episodes might reflect an early tradition of sacral prostitution in connection with Freyr's cult. [*See also* Hierodouleia.]

Little is known directly about the worship of Freyr, but it held a prominent place in Sweden, where he was the principal god as well as the divine ancestor of the royal house. Toponymy supplies strong evidence of the spread of his cult: place-names incorporating *Freyr* are quite numerous in Sweden, especially in the agricultural area of Svealand. Similarly, the god's name combines with words for fields, meadows, and so on in the agricultural regions of Norway, and it appears in a few places in eastern and southeastern Iceland as well. Here, the traditional elements preserved in the *Hrafnkellssaga* attest to the persistence of the veneration of Freyr: a chieftain called Hrafnkell was allegedly a "priest of Freyr" (Old Icelandic, *Freysgoði*), to whom he had dedicated a stallion; when someone desecrated the horse by riding it in spite of Hrafnkell's stern warnings, the latter killed the culprit. However, Hrafnkell's enemies captured the stallion and pushed him over a cliff after covering his head with a bag—as if his slaughterers were afraid of the power in his eyes. The desecration of horses belonging to Freyr is also attributed to Ólaf Tryggvason, who destroyed a sanctuary of the god in Norway.

The horse is not the only animal closely associated with Freyr: in the important annual sacrifice dedicated to him in Sweden—the Frøblot, allegedly established by Hading[us] (Saxo Grammaticus, bk. 1, sec. 29)—black bovines are offered up (the typical victims for chthonic deities). Several other sources relate the solemn offering of a bull or an ox to Freyr. The boar was also considered suitable for sacrifice to Freyr, particularly at Yuletide, a critical time of the year when the forces of fertility needed to be stimulated. Even human beings were slaughtered to please Freyr: Saxo Grammaticus (bk. 3, sec. 67) states that King Frø, "a viceroy of gods," instituted these sacrifices in Uppsala; Adam of Bremen reports that sometimes up to seventy-two bodies of men, horses, and dogs would hang together there in a grove near the temple.

The rationale for these sacrifices was presumably concern for good crops; this is confirmed by the story of Freyr's death as related in the *Ynglingasaga* (chap. 10). When "King Freyr" succumbed to long illness, he was secretly buried, and people were made to believe he was still alive. For three years their tribute—first of gold, then of silver, and ultimately of copper coins—was poured into Freyr's funeral mound, and good seasons and peace endured. This story has often been compared to the occultation of the Thracian god Zalmoxis, but as Mircea Eliade has shown (1972, pp. 47–48), this comparison has to be dismissed.

Besides Skírnir, Freyr has two other "servants" who only appear episodically in the *Lokasenna* (ss. 43–46): Byggvir, presumably "grain of barley," as suggested by the reference to the quern in stanza 44, and Beyla, whose name Georges Dumézil (1973, pp. 102–105) interprets as a diminutive of the Germanic word for "bee" in spite of insuperable phonological difficulties; this would make these figures symbolic of beer and mead, the inebriating beverages used in libation rituals and other ceremonial activities. However, it may be more correct to connect Beyla with the Old Norse term *baula* ("cow"), and to see the couple as representatives of the two aspects of Freyr's functional domain: agriculture and animal husbandry.

BIBLIOGRAPHY

Dumézil, Georges. *Gods of the Ancient Northmen.* Berkeley, 1973.

Eliade, Mircea. *Zalmoxis, the Vanishing God: Comparative Studies in the Religion and Folklore of Dacia and Eastern Europe.* Chicago, 1972.

Grimm, Jakob. *Deutsche Mythologie.* Göttingen, 1835. Translated from the fourth edition and edited by James Steven Stallybras as *Teutonic Mythology,* 4 vols. (1966; reprint, Gloucester, Mass., 1976).

Hollander, Lee M. *The Poetic Edda.* 2d rev. ed. Austin, 1962.

Holtsmark, Anne, and Jon Helgason, eds. *Snorri Sturluson Edda: Gylfaginning og prosafortellingene av skáldskaparmál.* Copenhagen, 1950.

Vries, Jan de. *Altgermanische Religionsgeschichte,* vol. 2. 2d rev. ed. Berlin, 1957.

EDGAR C. POLOMÉ

FRICK, HEINRICH (1893–1952), German religious thinker. The term *religious thinker* characterizes Frick as a scholar who endeavors to combine two potentially conflicting attitudes: Christian theological piety and the ability to analyze in a religio-historical way his own religion and the religions of others.

Born in Darmstadt, Hesse, Frick during his childhood belonged to Bible youth groups. He studied Protestant theology and Arabic in Giessen and Tübingen. He received his licentiate in theology in 1917 from the University of Giessen and joined the Lutheran ministry in Darmstadt. In 1918 he earned his doctorate, also at Giessen; his thesis was *Ghazālīs Selbstbiographie: Ein Vergleich mit Augustins Konfessionen* (Al-Ghazālī's *Autobiography:* A Comparison with Augustine's *Confessions;* 1919). Frick began his academic career in 1919 as privatdocent in *Religionswissenschaft* and missiology at the Technische Hochschule, Darmstadt. He moved to the University of Giessen in 1921, from which he was called to Marburg as successor to Rudolf Otto, whose professorship in systematic theology was, for Frick, extended to include *Religionswissenschaft* and missiology. In addition, he became director of the Religionskundliche Sammlung, a collection of religious materials from many religions of the world that had been founded by Otto in 1927.

Frick's bibliography contains more than 150 items, most of them articles, reports, prefaces, lectures, speeches, sermons, and statements. Of his few books, only one pertains to *Religionswissenschaft* proper, that is, *Vergleichende Religionswissenschaft* (Comparative Study of Religions; 1928). Here he lucidly develops his typology of religions, analyzing parallels between historical-religions of different origin, as well as their respective "peculiarities." He concludes his argument by presenting three fundamental typological phenomena as essentially characteristic of religion: the Catholic-Protestant dissension (religio-historical); the polarity of mystical and believing piety (religio-psychological); and, crucial to the "quality" a religion has, the alternative of symbolization in space or time (religio-philosophical). The book aims at demonstrating that comparative religion is an "indispensable branch of effective theology" (p. 134), in that it proves the necessity of choice between several religious possibilities and offers empirical arguments for a "clear answer to the question why we cling to the gospel in spite of all the parallels and in spite of all the attractions in non-Christian religion" (p. 132).

This theological intention did not prevent Frick from developing, here and in other publications, points of comparison between religions that have since been generally accepted. It was an approach he had already adopted in his thesis comparing al-Ghazālī with Augustine and again in his reviews and articles on special problems, for example, "Der Begriff des Prophetischen in Islamkunde und Theologie" (The Concept of the Prophetic in Islamic Studies and Theology), in *Festschrift P. Kahle* (1935); in his programmatic writings, for example, *Das Evangelium und die Religionen* (The Gospel and Religion, 1933); and in his article "Christliche Grundbegriffe in ihrer Besonderheit gegenueber Fremdreligionen" (Fundamental Christian Ideas in Comparison with Other Religions), *Evangelische Missionzeitschrift* (1944): 193–205, 225–233.

Motivated by a lifelong sensitivity to secularistic tendencies and the "crisis of religion," Frick summed up his views on *Religionswissenschaft* near the end of his life in two lectures on *Religionsphaenomenologie* (1950) and *Religionswissenschaft* (1951). Casting doubt on the moral right of neutrality in the field of *Religionswissenschaft* at a time when modern man had become more and more irreligious, Frick called upon his colleagues to search for a synthesis of the venerable religio-cultural traditions and modernity. In his opinion the "most important task of present *Religionswissenschaft* and related fields in all the scholarly faculties is to fulfill its modest but irremissible part in this."

BIBLIOGRAPHY

Neubauer, Reinhard. "Heinrich Frick, 1893–1952: Theologe." In *Marburger Gelehrte in der ersten Hälfte des 20. Jahrhunderts,* edited by Ingeborg Schnack, pp. 75–90. Marburg, 1977.

Neumann, Käthe. "Bibliographie Heinrich Frick." *Theologische Literaturzeitung* 78 (1953): 440–442. A complete list of his publications is available at Religionskundliche Sammlung, Philipps-Universität Marburg.

Röhr, Heinz. "Der Einfluss der Religionswissenschaft auf die Missionstheorie Heinrich Fricks." Ph.D. diss., Marburg University, 1959.

MARTIN KRAATZ

FRIENDS, SOCIETY OF. *See* Quakers.

FROBENIUS, LEO (1873–1938), German ethnologist and philosopher of culture. Leo Viktor Frobenius was born 29 July 1873 in Berlin, where he spent his early years. Even in his youth he devoted himself enthusiastically to the investigation of African cultures, collecting all available written and pictorial material that dealt with particular ethnological motifs. (Later, these materials became the matrix for an Africa archive that Frobenius assembled.) Despite the fact that he never received a high school diploma and did not complete a university program, Frobenius achieved extraordinary success in his scientific pursuits.

Stimulated by the work of Heinrich Schurtz (whom Frobenius claimed as his teacher), Friedrich Ratzel, and Richard Andrée, Frobenius was responsible for introducing a new way of scientific thinking into the field of ethnology. His new concept, hinging on the term *Kulturkreis* ("culture circle"), first appeared in his 1898 work *Der Ursprung der afrikanischen Kulturen* (The Origin of African Civilization). Unlike other scholars, who put the term to one-dimensional uses, Frobenius developed the concept of *Kulturkreis* into an all-encompassing cultural morphology. His method involved the notion that individual elements of culture should be investigated according to their placement within the organic whole of which they are parts. According to Frobenius, this method provides a way for understanding the complex, historical nature of cultures.

Frobenius's primary concern was for the investigator's recognition of the essence of culture in general. Frobenius found that cultures display "biological" characteristics similar to those of living organisms. He drew parallels between a culture's stages and the elements of an organic life cycle, using terms such as *Ergriffenheit* ("emotion," by which Frobenius meant to signify a culture's youth), *Ausdruck* ("expression," or a culture's maturity), and *Anwendung* ("utilization," its old age). Every culture, argued Frobenius, possesses laws that determine its process independently of the individual human beings who participate in the culture. He labeled this inherent power with the Greek word *paideuma* ("what is acquired by learning") and devoted an entire book, *Paideuma: Umrisse einer Kultur- und Seelenlehre* (Outline of a Theory of Culture and Spirit; 1921), to this theme. *Paideuma* is also the title of a periodical, established by Frobenius in 1938 and still being published, devoted to the problem of cultural morphology. Although the philosophy of culture espoused by Frobenius has been disputed, he is still considered an ethnological field-researcher of the first order.

Frobenius went on twelve research expeditions to various parts of Africa to document the lives of tribal peoples. In addition, he studied the most important rock-painting sites of both northern and southern Africa. The results of his ethnological researches were presented in a work entitled *Und Afrika sprach,* 3 vols. (1912–1913; translated as *The Voice of Africa,* 2 vols., 1913). He also published a series of twelve volumes of folk tales and poems under the general title *Atlantis* between 1921 and 1928; these have proved to be particularly rich source materials for historians of religions. He summarized his research in *Kulturgeschichte Afrikas* (1933).

Frobenius's impact upon the world outside his professional field is demonstrated by the fact that the Senegalese politician and poet Leopold Senghor has credited Frobenius with helping to foster a revitalization of self-awareness among present-day Africans. The materials collected on Frobenius's many expeditions were brought together in 1922 to be housed at the newly founded Institute for Cultural Morphology in Munich. In 1925 the institute was removed to Frankfurt, where Frobenius received an honorary lectureship in the department of ethnology and cultural studies at the university. In 1934 he was appointed director of the Municipal Ethnological Museum in Frankfurt. Shortly after his sixty-fifth birthday, Frobenius died at his residence on Lake Maggiore in Italy.

[*See also* Kulturkreiselehre.]

BIBLIOGRAPHY

For bibliographical data, see Heinz Wieschoff's article "Das Schrifttum von Leo Frobenius," in *Leo Frobenius, Ein Lebenswerk aus der Zeit der Kulturwende,* edited by Walter J. Otto (Leipzig, 1933), pp. 163–170; *Afrika Rundschau* (1938), pp. 119–121; and Jacques Waardenburg's *Classical Approaches to the Study of Religion,* vol. 2 (The Hague, 1974), p. 82. For biographical information, see Helmut Petri's article "Leo Frobenius und die historische Ethnologie," *Saeculum* 4 (1953): 45–60.

OTTO ZERRIES

Translated from German by John Maressa

FROGS AND TOADS. The frog or toad is a lunar animal *par excellence.* Its shape or behavior is reminiscent of the moon; it swells and shrinks, submerges under water but emerges again, and hides under the ground in winter but reappears in spring. The frog lives according to the lunar rhythm. In fact, a great many myths speak of a frog in the moon. According to the Chinese, the moon has not only an evergreen cassia tree and a rabbit but also a frog inside it. Thus the *T'ien wen* section of the *Ch'u-tzu* (fourth or third century BCE) asks: "What is the peculiar virtue of the moon, the brightness of the night, which causes it to grow once more after its death? What does it advantage to keep a frog in its belly?"

The frog, then, is naturally associated with all sorts of aquatic elements such as water, rain, ocean, and flood. Frogs are said to croak incessantly before it rains, or to announce or bring rain by croaking. They are usually mentioned in the innumerable rites for inducing rain. North American Indians see in the moon the primeval toad, which contained all the waters and caused the flood by discharging them over the earth. According to the Kurnai of southeastern Australia, once upon a time all the waters were swallowed by a huge frog; the other animals tried in vain to make him laugh until the eel danced about, twisting itself into the most ridiculous contortions, whereupon the frog burst into laughter and the waters rushed out of his mouth and produced the flood. The frog sometimes plays a part in the precosmogonic period when there is nothing but water. A Huron myth narrates how several animals descended in vain into the primeval waters, until the toad returned successfully with a little soil in its mouth; the soil was placed on the back of the tortoise, and the miraculous growth of the land then began.

Significantly, the frog is also associated with the principles of evil and death. According to Altaic beliefs, the creation of man and woman by the god Ülgen was marred by the devil Erlik. Consequently, the god decided to destroy them, but changed his mind when a frog proposed that mankind exist under the curse of mortality. In Iranian mythology the frog appears as a symbol or embodiment of the evil spirit or the most important of its creatures. In Inner Asian cosmogonic myths—apparently colored by Iranian influence—frogs are among those animals that, together with lizards, worms, and mice, come out of the hole made in the earth by the satanic figure. In Africa the frog emerges sometimes as the messenger of death. At the time of beginning, say the Ekoi of Nigeria, the duck was charged by God with a message of immortality to mankind, whereas the frog was given a message of death. The frog got to the earth first, delivered his message, and thus brought death to humankind.

BIBLIOGRAPHY

There is much useful material in volume 2 of Robert Briffault's *The Mothers: A Study of the Origins of Sentiments and Institutions*, 3 vols. (1927; reprint, New York, 1969), pp. 634ff. Mircea Eliade has discussed frog symbolism in *Patterns in Comparative Religion* (New York, 1958), pp. 160ff. See also Lutz Röhrich's "Hund, Pferd, Kröte und Schlange als symbolische Leitgestalten in Volksglauben und Sage," *Zeitschrift für Religions- und Geistesgeschichte* 3 (1951): 69–76.

MANABU WAIDA

FUJIWARA SEIKA (1561–1619), Japanese Confucian scholar of the early Tokugawa period. Once regarded as the founder of Tokugawa Neo-Confucianism, Fujiwara Seika is today understood increasingly as a transitional figure in the development of an intellectually self-contained Confucianism out of the Zen-flavored Confucianism that flourished in the Gozan Zen temples of the Muromachi period.

Seika was a twelfth-generation descendant of the thirteenth-century court poet Fujiwara no Teika, but his immediate forebears were small local lords in the Harima area (present-day Hyōgo Prefecture). A younger son, at the age of seven or eight he was sent to study at a Zen temple in the area where, it so happened, the priests were interested in Confucianism. When he was eighteen, his father and elder brother were killed in battle, and the family's ancestral lands were lost. Through the mediation of two uncles who were priests at important Zen temples in Kyoto, Seika, who had taken refuge in the capital, became a priest at the major Zen center of Shōkokuji. There, as was common practice, he pursued the study of Confucian texts as an adjunct to his training as a Zen priest. Gradually he formed a deeper commitment to Confucianism, and in his mid-thirties he left the temple and devoted himself to the study of Confucianism.

In 1596, at the age of thirty-five, Seika attempted to go to China to study Confucianism with an authentic master. The attempt was unsuccessful, but he was able to broaden and deepen his understanding of Confucianism through contact with Korean scholars captured by Japanese troops during Toyotomi Hideyoshi's invasion of Korea and brought back to Japan. At his urging, the captive scholars were set to copying out the Four Books and the Five Classics, while he punctuated the copied text in Japanese according to the Sung and Ming Neo-Confucian commentaries. Individual classics had been punctuated previously by Japanese scholars using the

Neo-Confucian interpretations, but this was the first instance in which one person systematically punctuated all the central texts of Confucianism. Seika's plan to make his punctuated edition available in published form went unrealized, but the plan itself and his comprehensive rather than piecemeal approach to the basic Confucian texts stand as landmarks in the history of Confucianism in Japan.

In other ways, too, Seika took steps to establish Confucianism as a self-sufficient intellectual tradition independent of Buddhism. For some time after leaving Shōkokuji Seika continued to dress as a priest, but in 1600 he formally manifested the shift in his intellectual allegiance by adopting a style of dress patterned after that of the Chinese scholar-official class. The same year he lectured on Chinese historical works before Tokugawa Ieyasu, founder of the Tokugawa shogunate, and engaged the Zen monks present in a debate over the respective merits of the Confucian and Buddhist approaches to life. Seika refused an invitation to serve Ieyasu on a permanent basis, but he maintained informal ties as a scholar with a number of daimyo.

Although Seika took action that contributed to the development of Confucianism as a public teaching (in contrast to the "secret transmission" tradition of medieval scholarship) institutionally independent of Buddhism, his writings on Confucianism reveal lingering traces of Zen ideas. Seika objected to the otherworldly orientation of Buddhism, but his emphasis on "stilling the mind" so as to allow it to return to its original state of good reflects the influence of the Zen concept of enlightenment and of the views of late Ming scholars such as Lin Ch'ao-en, who had attempted a fusion of Zen, Confucian, and Taoist teachings. For this Seika was criticized by later Confucian scholars, including his disciple Hayashi Razan.

[*See also* Confucianism in Japan.]

BIBLIOGRAPHY

Abe Yoshio. *Nihon Shushigaku to Chōsen.* Tokyo, 1965. An important reevaluation of the formation of Tokugawa Neo-Confucianism that treats major thinkers individually and stresses the connections between Korean Confucianism and early Tokugawa thought.

Ishida Ichirō. "Hayashi Razan: Muromachi jidai ni okeru Zenju itchi to Fujiwara Seika-Hayashi Razan no shisō." In *Edo no shisōka tachi,* edited by Sagara Tōru et al., vol.1. Tokyo, 1979. A recent study that challenges earlier assumptions about the discontinuity between medieval and Tokugawa thought and instead attempts to trace the stages of development from the Zen-oriented Confucianism of the Muromachi period to the independent Confucianism of the Tokugawa period.

KATE WILDMAN NAKAI

FULANI RELIGION. *See* Fulbe Religion.

FULBE RELIGION. The Fulbe are groups of pastoralists, semi-pastoralists, farmers, and city dwellers who constitute large minorities in the Sahelian countries stretching from the Atlantic Ocean to the Red Sea (Mauritania, Senegal, Gambia, Guinea, Mali, Burkina Faso, Niger, Nigeria, Chad, Cameroon, and Sudan). Also called Fulani, Fellata, and Peul, these people have played a significant role in West African history and attracted the attention of European observers of African societies. While almost all are Muslim today, they possess a strong cattle-herding tradition that antedates their Islamic allegiance.

The Fulbe speak Fulfulde (also called Pulār), a language of the West Atlantic branch of Niger-Congo languages. The northern section of the West Atlantic branch includes Wolof, Serer, and Fulfulde, which are the dominant languages of Senegal but were in earlier times spoken farther north, in today's Mauritania. The early Fulbe probably left some of the rock paintings of cattle and herders in the area that gradually became the Sahara. In the last millennium largely nomadic Fulbe have progressively migrated from this location to the east, as far as Cameroon and Chad. In recent centuries they have spread into the Sudan. Until the eighteenth century most of these Fulbe maintained a pastoral lifestyle and had relatively little attachment to Islam.

The intensive islamization of the Fulbe since the eighteenth century makes it difficult to recapture pre-Islamic Fulbe religion. However, the Malian Fulbe intellectual Amadou Hampaté Ba and the French ethnographer Germaine Dieterlen, who recorded an initiation text from a Senegalese informant and made a French translation and commentary entitled *Koumen* (1961), have provided a very suggestive statement. Koumen, the initiation ceremony, consists of twelve "chapters," or "clearings," in which the first human herder acquires knowledge of cattle and the world. The world is governed by the eternal and all-powerful God. God designates Canaba, who usually takes the form of a serpent, to be the guardian of cattle, and Koumen to be Canaba's herder. It is Koumen, often in the form of a child, and his wife Foroforondu who actually provide instruction to the novice Sile (a local variation of Sulayman or Solomon). At the end of the story Sile becomes the first *silatigi,* master of the bush and pastoral life. The story reveals the close ties among men, cattle, land, and vegetation—the trees, vines, and creeping plants that supply the staffs, cords, calabashes, and other vital instruments, as well as the shrines where Sile must demonstrate his attachment to God and the numerous spirits that populate the universe. A rich symbolism of color and number runs throughout the text. Yellow, red, black, and white correlate respectively with fire, air, water, and earth; with east, west, south, and north; and finally with the four original lineages of the Fulbe: Jal or Jallo, Bâ, Sō, and Bari. Sile gradually learns to read the symbolism and to use the configuration of cattle of different coats to divine the proper course of action.

While the Koumen ritual is quite specific to the Fulbe, many of its features recall the religious beliefs and practices of other people living in the region of Senegal and Mali. The *silatigi* resembles a priest-king. His progress in understanding parallels the learning process that takes place in other initiations. The serpent Canaba recalls the importance of serpents in Soninke and Mandinka symbolism, and his path down the Niger River repeats the trajectory of Mande creation myths. The story also suggests the importance of military leadership, the social stratification characteristic of the Western Sudan, and through the evocation of Solomon, the influence of the Jewish, Islamic, and Christian heritage. A blacksmith who is a member of an artisan caste aids Sile in his initiation. Sile is expected to demonstrate *pulaaku,* the Fulbe code of honor, shame, and restraint. This code is often defined in contrast to the behavior of slaves, who do not have an affinity for cattle and do not know how to act in general. The slave is seen to be crude, naive, irresponsible, and dark in color; he or she resembles the other "black," non-Fulbe populations of West Africa. *Pulaaku* resembles the codes of a number of other stratified societies in West Africa who distinguish sharply between the conduct that one may expect of the noble and free strata and the behavior that one must tolerate from slaves and the people of "caste"—the hereditary corporations of blacksmiths and other trades. In general, *pulaaku* and the whole ritual of Koumen are consistent with pastoral Fulbe custom across the Sahelian zone. In the present state of knowledge they can be considered representative of pre-Islamic Fulbe beliefs and practices.

Until the eighteenth century the Fulbe were not in the forefront of forming states or practicing Islam in the western and central Sudanic region. The Timbuktu scholars who wrote the chronicles called the *Ta'rīkh al-Fattāsh* and *Ta'rīkh al-Sudān* in the sixteenth and seventeenth centuries regarded some Fulbe as the enemies of Islam, agriculture, commerce, and cities. Beginning in the eighteenth century Fulbe in several locations took the lead in establishing specifically Islamic states and societies. They used the process of *jihād,* or war against unbelievers, to reverse regimes that they considered pagan or nominally Muslim, appoint leaders who were knowledgeable in the faith, and erect educational and judicial systems in which Islamic law would be learned and practiced. While they failed to implement all of their ideal, they did spur, for the first time, the permanent development of an Islamic culture in the countryside outside of the capitals and commercial centers. The leaders in this process were scholars and sedentary Fulbe who were already at some distance from the predominantly pastoral pre-Islamic tradition. Over time they developed new genealogies where the four original Fulbe lineages were all descended from 'Uqba, usually identified with 'Uqba ibn Nāfi', the Arab conqueror of much of North Africa in the seventh century CE. This origin is widely accepted by Fulbe of all persuasions today.

The first two of these Islamic revolutions occurred in the eighteenth century in the two Fūtas, regions fairly close to the Atlantic Ocean. The leaders in Fūta Jalon, the mountainous zone of Guinea, created an elaborate system of Islamic instruction in Fulfulde as well as Arabic. The Fulfulde system, based on a modified Arabic alphabet, was designed to reach the women, pastoralists, and others who were unlikely to acquire the ability to read and write for themselves. The people of Fūta Tōro, the middle valley of the Senegal River, became known as the "Tokolor," a word that served to distinguish them from the Fulbe who were less committed to the establishment of an Islamic state and culture.

The most important revolution occurred in Hausaland, or northern Nigeria. In the early 1800s Usuman dan Fodio, his brother 'Abdullāh, and his son Muhammadu Bello launched the *jihād* against the ruling class of the Hausa state of Gobir. Dan Fodio's students and allies then carried the campaign against other states and established new settlements beyond Hausaland. By 1812 a vast new confederation had emerged with its principal center at Sokoto, in northwest Nigeria. Dan Fodio and his associates wrote a large number of influential treatises that became the standard texts for the practice and spread of the faith in the western and central Sudan. [*See the biography of Dan Fodio.*] The last revolution occurred in the middle delta of the Niger River, between the towns of Segu and Timbuktu and created the caliphate of Hamdullāhi around 1820. The movement led by 'Umar Tāl put an end to this regime in 1862. [*See the biography of 'Umar Tāl.*]

Fulbe scholars also played an important role in spreading the Qādirīyah and Tijānīyah Islamic orders, which could be practiced in the countryside, away from the large mosques, schools, and courts of the towns. One can say that the Fulbe supplied the most important agents of islamization in West Africa in the nineteenth century.

Many Fulbe have remained relatively marginal to these processes of state formation and islamization. Despite devastating droughts in the 1980s, they have tried to sustain their pastoral economy and lifestyle in the regions of West Africa that are more suited to grazing than to agriculture. For all public purposes they are Muslim; they observe the obligations incumbent on all members of the faith. In their family life and relationship to cattle, they observe the customs and values reflected in the Koumen ceremony.

BIBLIOGRAPHY

The classic statement of Fulbe values is in Amadou Hampaté Ba and Germaine Dieterlen's *Koumen: Texte initiatique des pasteur peul* (Paris, 1961). A useful English statement on the Fulbe is Paul Riesman's *Freedom in Fulani Social Life: An Introspective Ethnography* (Chicago, 1977). Marguerite Dupire has provided a detailed study of the social organization of the pastoral Fulbe in *Organisation sociale des Peul: Étude d'ethnographie comparée* (Paris, 1970). The dualism of many contemporary Fulbe is well described in Derrick J. Stenning's *Savannah Nomads* (Oxford, 1959), while the similarities of myth and ritual in the western Sudan are explicated in two articles by Germaine Dieterlen in the *Journal de la Société des Africanistes*, "Myth et organisation sociale au Soudan Français," vol. 25, nos. 1–2 (1955): 39–76 and "Mythe et organisation sociale en Afrique occidentale," vol. 29, nos. 1–2 (1959): 119–138. For a useful summary of the Fulbe's role in the state-formation process of recent centuries, see my *The Holy War of Umar Tal: The Western Sudan in the Mid-Nineteenth Century* (Oxford, 1985), esp. chap. 2.

DAVID ROBINSON

FUNCTIONALISM is the analytical tendency within the social sciences—most notably, sociology and social anthropology—which exhibits a particular interest in the functions of social or cultural phenomena. In its most traditional form, functionalism has claimed that all items and activities in a system should be explained in reference to their objective consequences for the system as a whole. Thus the pivotal meaning of *function* is the objective consequence of an activity or phenomenon for the system of which it is a part. A secondary—but nonetheless significant—meaning of *function* in social science is similar to the use of the term in mathematics. When it is stated that x is a function of y, it is meant that x varies in direct proportion to variation in y. In social science this perspective on the concept of function has to do with interrelatedness. The dominant and the secondary meanings are linked as follows. The notion of function as consequence for the state of the system suggests that all phenomena in the system are considered, at least initially, as being relevant to the system's persistence. It is then but a small move to the postulate that all phenomena in a system are interrelated and that a change in one aspect will have implications for all others and for the system as a whole.

The Early French School. The functional analysis of religion played quite an important part in the development of the functional orientation in social science as a whole. Of more immediate relevance, however, is the fact that the functional analysis of religion has also played a very significant part in the development of the sociology and anthropology of religion. The functional orientation has a long history, but it was during the French Enlightenment of the eighteenth century that the seeds were fully sown for the explicit crystallization of sociological functionalism in the second half of the nineteenth century. Many eighteenth-century French philosophers and protosociologists were interested in the possibility of a form of society which would operate according to principles of rationality and enlightenment, without what they saw as the impediments of religious dogma and clerical predominance. On the other hand, many of these thinkers were also concerned with what could take the place of religious faith and practice in a prospective rational-secular society. Thus one of the earliest and most influential of the Enlightenment philosophers, Jean-Jacques Rousseau (1712–1778), maintained that a society needed a civil religion—a religion concerned not with the traditional matters of faith and practice in relation to a supernatural being or realm but rather with the generation and maintenance of involvement in, and respect for, the society as such. He, like a number of his contemporaries, was well aware that religion had, among other things, traditionally performed significant functions of legitimation. In fact, at the end of the eighteenth century the leaders of the French Revolution made a great effort to replace traditional Catholic symbols and rituals with "secular-religious" ones.

The awareness of crucial links between religion and politics grew in a period when, in many parts of Europe, there was a widespread challenge to the intrinsic validity of religious belief and the traditional church (above all in predominantly Catholic countries). Yet despite the conviction that traditional religion had had deleterious consequences for society, it was affirmed that the functions supposedly performed by religion still had to be met. One particularly significant version of that perspective was provided in France by Claude Henri, Comte de Saint-Simon (1760–1825), who maintained that religion was a society's most significant political institution. That idea was later developed by Alexis de Tocqueville (1805–1859), who studied the relationship between religion and democracy. Tocqueville's particular interest was in the prospects for democracy in France, given the predominance there of Catholicism and the conviction of many intellectuals that democracy and religion were incompatible. Tocqueville tried to show that American evangelical Protestantism fostered the American democratic spirit. In so doing, he sought to disprove the claim that religion necessarily inhibited or disrupted democracy, and subsequently argued that, with modification, Catholicism could support democracy in France.

While Tocqueville did not argue explicitly in terms of what came to be called functionalism, he helped crystallize the sociological view that religion performs vital social functions. In the case of Saint-Simon, however, the functional orientation had been somewhat more explicit. After having celebrated the emergent industrial order and noted its antipathy to religion, Saint-Simon concluded that a "New Christianity" was necessary to provide commitment and vitality to the new industrial type of society. With Saint-Simon's protégé, Auguste Comte (1798–1857), an even more calculated functional orientation appears. Often spoken of as the father of sociology, Comte advocated a secular science of society, to be based on a "positive" philosophy that had been made possible by the epochal demise of theological and metaphysical modes of thought. Sociology should become the cognitive keystone of modern societies. Sociology and sociology-based ethics were to take the place of religion. However, late in life Comte—in parallel with Saint-Simon—restructured his views and argued that a "religion of humanity" was required in order to guarantee commitment to and respect for society. In that regard Comte made elaborate proposals for France concerning festivals, rituals, functionaries, and symbols for the religion of humanity.

Spencer. It was the work of the English philosopher Herbert Spencer (1820–1903) that gave the concept of function and the functional orientation in sociology their first fully explicit renderings. Spencer argued that societies are organisms and that one should conceive of the former in the same terms as the latter. Thus he articulated the two main principles outlined earlier: the interrelatedness of all items in a system (most importantly the whole society) and the referring of items within a system to the functioning of the system as a whole. Spencer was, moreover, an evolutionist, which at that time implied, among other things, a belief that as societies progressed to an advanced evolutionary condition, they relied less and less on religious thought and practice. For Spencer, the main institutions of an advanced society were incompatible with religion, while the society as a whole operated increasingly in terms of contractual relationships among individuals (although Spencer did believe that the evolutionary engine was driven by a mysterious force which gave purposeful direction to societal change).

Durkheim. Unlike Saint-Simon and Comte, Spencer never showed signs of retreating from his own views concerning the (unproblematic) demise of religion. And it is in terms of this difference between Spencer and Saint-Simon that the seminal work of the French sociologist Émile Durkheim (1858–1917) can best be approached. Durkheim's work was based partly on a rejection of Spencer's highly secular conception of modern societies, even though it maintained some features of Spencer's methodological functionalism. At the same time, Durkheim was taken with the ways in which Saint-Simon and Comte had come to appreciate the functional significance of religion. He believed, however, that they had erred in first seeing society as bereft of religion and then attempting to add religion to it. What Durkheim sought, most elaborately in *The Elementary Forms of the Religious Life* (1912), was a way in which to ground religion in society itself.

In his early methodological work Durkheim argued that the sociologist should work with two basic explanatory concepts: function and cause. *Function* had to do with the general needs of the societal organism which a social phenomenon served, while *cause* referred to those features of society which more directly facilitated a phenomenon. Durkheim was eager to dissociate himself from those who closely related function to ends or purposes. He insisted that there is no mysterious final cause of societal patterns or change and that one should not think of function as having to do with the intentions lying behind the establishment of institutions. (On the latter point Durkheim argued that social phenomena do not generally exist for the useful results which they produce.) In his early writing on the forms of social solidarity, Durkheim reacted to Spencer by maintaining that all contractual relationships must be based on *pre*contractual elements of society. His interest in religion developed largely in the attempt to comprehend precisely what those precontractual elements are. From the outset, Durkheim had been concerned with the issue of morality in modern societies. While seeking a sociological understanding of the foundations of morality, he endeavored to show that, for moral principles to have social weight, they must be more than logically persuasive. Durkheim contended that the principles of moral reason adumbrated by Immanuel Kant in the eighteenth century could be socially operative only insofar as they were socially imperative. He wanted to know, in other words, on what the obligatory character of morals rest.

Durkheim eventually reached the full-fledged conclusion that the primary function of religion lay in its distinction between the sacred and the profane. Religion, said Durkheim, has to do with sacred things. It is "the serious life." Religion is crucial in providing individuals with freedom from unchecked desire, in highlighting the moral character of the collectivity, and in binding individuals together within the latter. Durkheim is often interpreted as having simply emphasized the positive, integrative functions of religion. That was indeed a significant aspect of his theory of religion (which was at the same time a theory of society), yet Durkheim was also deeply concerned with the social sources, the causes, of religious belief and practice, as well as with the larger ramifications of religion in human life. Although Durkheim's work was almost certainly the most vital contribution to the functionalist orientation in sociology and to the functionalist analysis of religion in sociology and social anthropology, his ideas were developed in specific reference to what he perceived as a moral crisis in modern societies. This is true even though his major work on religion referred mostly to the primitive religious life of Australian Aborigines and even though he was greatly inspired by the writing of the French historian Fustel de Çoulanges on religion in ancient Rome and Greece and by that of the Scotsman W. Robertson Smith on ancient Semitic religion.

Since, in terms of Durkheim's own definition of religion as involving the distinction between the sacred and the profane (rather than being defined, more narrowly, as belief in supernatural beings), religion had been ubiquitous in all civilizations, Durkheim concluded that it must have been functionally essential to all societies. Yet he was acutely aware that traditional religious faith had become increasingly fragile. In articulating his own theory of religion, Durkheim emphasized at the outset that religion, in contrast to magic, is fundamentally a collective phenomenon and that, in religion, ritual is as important as belief. In those terms he set about showing how, at least in primitive societies, the basic categories of religious belief are established and maintained through the collective experience of social structure. In religious ritual individuals experience acutely a dependence upon society; indeed, religious worship can be thought of as the celebration of that dependence. In his most radical terms, Durkheim suggested that the real object of religious worship is society, not God. His main point, however, was that it is from our experience of society that we obtain the sense of something transcendent and authoritative. Yet Durkheim denied that he was making a judgment about the intrinsic validity of religious belief. Rather, he concentrated upon showing both the social conditions and the social functions of religion. As far as modern societies are concerned, Durkheim asserted that there is now a need for new religious forms which would perform the same kind of function as traditional religion but in a less spiritualistic way. In the tradition of Rousseau, Durkheim argued the need for new forms of civil religion and saw religion as critical in the periodic regeneration of societies.

Malinowski and Radcliffe-Brown. Durkheim's writing had a great effect on those social anthropologists of the 1920s and 1930s who sought to redirect anthropological inquiry away from speculatory evolutionism toward more analytically rigorous fieldwork. The two major figures in that regard were the Polish-born Bronislaw Malinowski (1884–1942) and the British-born Arthur Radcliffe-Brown (1881–1955), both of whom employed functional orientations in the study of primitive societies, including the religious aspects thereof. Malinowski's functionalism centered upon two claims: first, that any particular society is a unique, functioning whole, and, second, that the social arrangements and cultural forms obtaining in a society have functional significance in relation to the psychological needs of individuals. Thus in spite of his interest in the functional interrelatedness of social institutions and practices, Malinowski saw their most fundamental functional significance in their meeting the psychological needs of individuals. In contrast, Radcliffe-Brown took a more self-consciously Durkheimian position. He advocated a systematic science of society, involving comparative analysis of the structural patterns of societies with respect both to their overall cohesiveness and to the functional requirements of societies as systemic wholes. Both Malinowski and Radcliffe-Brown wrote about religion in their respective functional terms.

Parsons and His Critics. Among those sociologists and anthropologists of religion who have written entirely within the twentieth century, the most prolific analyst of religion was the American Talcott Parsons (1902–1978). Deeply, but by no means only, influenced by Durkheim, Parsons in the 1950s acquired the reputation of being the functionalist *par excellence.* From Durkheim, Parsons took the basic idea that religion is a universal feature of human life. However, he expressed strong reservations concerning Durkheim's attempt to talk not merely about the functional significance of religion but also about its social-structural bases. In the latter regard, said Parsons, Durkheim was often a reductionist, in the sense of reducing religion to society. In contrast, Parsons himself considered religion to be the pivotal aspect of the realm of cultural values, beliefs, and symbols. According to Parsons, patterns of culture operate in varying degrees of independence from social structure and certainly cannot be reduced to the latter. Culture provides meaning, general morality, expressive symbols, and basic beliefs to systems of social action and to individuals. Religion also relates systems of human action to what Parsons called "ultimate reality." He maintained that questions concerning the ultimate boundary of human action and interaction constitute a universal attribute of human life. Parsons's attempt to establish what for a long time he called a structural-functional form of general sociological theory has met with considerable criticism from the late 1940s onward. One of Parsons's most influential critics has been the American sociologist Robert Merton (b. 1910), who has attempted to systematize functional analysis so as to overcome what he has regarded as its weaknesses. Religion has figured strongly in his discussion.

Merton argues that many functionalists have singled out the integrative functions of religion—mainly in reference to certain primitive societies—while neglecting its potentially disintegrative consequences, or dysfunctions. They have also, he maintains, confused two issues: whether what is indispensable to society is the phenomenon, such as religious belief, or only the function supposedly met by such a phenomenon. Merton emphasizes the dangers of viewing the phenomenon itself as indispensable and suggests that sociologists develop a clear conception of functional alternatives. As an example of such an alternative, he proposes that the positive functions of religion might well be provided by something other than religion in its conventional sense (e.g., secular ideology).

Merton also raises the question as to whether functionalism is—as many of its critics have charged—inherently conservative. His conclusion is that it is not. Even though the main modern tradition of antireligion—Marxism—regards religion as a consequence of an economically exploitative society, it also looks upon religion as performing integrative functions in precommunist societies. Religion, in Marxist perspective, inhibits social change. Thus functional analysis can be used from both conservative and radical standpoints. Indeed, since the 1960s a clear strand of Marxist functionalism has concerned itself with the persistence of capitalist societies and the function religion plays in that persistence.

Issues arising from the long debate about the functional form of analysis have been central to the controversy concerning the degree to which the modern world is characterized by secularization. For the most part, functionalists have resisted the thesis of extensive secularization, on the grounds that the functions performed by religion are essential to all societies. Thus Parsons tended to argue that even though a society may manifest ostensibly atheistic sentiments, it is still subject to the functional imperative of relating to ultimate reality. It was the hallmark of Parsons's approach to religion (and here he followed Durkheim) that we should not be overly constrained by the particular, substantive forms that religion has taken historically. In contrast to Spencer, Parsons argued that religion does not lose significance as human society evolves; rather, religion takes on increasingly general forms as societies become more differentiated and complex.

Recent Functionalist Theoreticians. A particularly radical type of functionalism has been proposed by the German sociologist Niklas Luhmann (b. 1927). Luhmann argues that religion can no longer provide an overarching set of integrative values to a society. Unlike Parsons, who maintained that religious values and beliefs become more general but still remain overarching as societal evolution proceeds, Luhmann insists that the social differentiation central to societal evolution has now gone so far that religion is but one subsystem among many. Religion is now "free" to concentrate on its primary function of answering purely religious—as opposed to social, economic, political, and scientific—questions.

Some of Luhmann's ideas overlap with those of the British sociologist Bryan Wilson, an adamant proponent of the secularization thesis. Wilson's argument hinges upon his claim that the historically latent functions of religion—*latent* is Merton's term for hidden, unrecognized functions—have become increasingly manifest (i.e., consciously recognized) and are now fulfilled by other social agencies, while historically manifest functions of religion—those providing guidelines for salvation—have been undermined. The main process which has both undermined the manifest and made manifest the latent functions of religion is the supplanting of communities by rationally organized, impersonal, and functionally specialized societies.

Conclusion. Even though functional analysis has been a frequent target of hostile critique, it has been continuously pivotal in the sociological and anthropological analysis of religion. And while there have undoubtedly been phases of crude functionalism—expressed in bland statements concerning the universality of religion and its beneficial consequences, as well as attempts to reduce religion to its societal consequences—it is nonetheless impossible to address the topic of religion in social-scientific terms without careful attention to its functional significance vis-à-vis other aspects of human life. Indeed, that perspective has pervaded modern consciousness, in the sense that religion is increasingly discussed and assessed in relation to its consequences for individuals and societies.

BIBLIOGRAPHY

The classic work in the tradition of functionalism is Émile Durkheim's *The Elementary Forms of the Religious Life* (1915; reprint, New York, 1965). An important discussion of functional analysis, with particular reference to religion, appears in Robert K. Merton's *Social Theory and Social Structure* (New York, 1968), pp. 73–138. Anthony F. C. Wallace's *Religion: An Anthropological View* (New York, 1966) contains an extended discussion of the functions of religion in several types of society. A flexible functionalist theory of religion is offered in J. Milton Yinger's *The Scientific Study of Religion* (New York, 1970). Relevant discussions of the history of the sociology of religion and of functionalist approaches are contained in my book *The Sociological Interpretation of Religion* (New York, 1970). Much of Talcott Parsons's theory of religion is found in his study *The Evolution of Societies* (Englewood Cliffs, N.J., 1977). For a lengthy discussion of Parsons's work on religion, with an extensive bibliography, see *Sociological Analysis* 43 (Winter 1982), a special issue edited by me. A functionalist interpretation of religion in the modern world is provided by Bryan R. Wilson in his *Religion in Sociological Perspective* (Oxford, 1982), while the radically functionalist theory of Niklas Luhmann is presented in his *Funktion der Religion* (Frankfurt, 1982). Analyses of civil religion in the tradition initiated by Rousseau, with reference also to Tocqueville, are provided in neofunctionalist terms by Robert N. Bellah and Phillip E. Hammond in their *Varieties of Civil Religion* (San Francisco, 1980).

ROLAND ROBERTSON

FUNDAMENTAL CHRISTIANITY. *See* Evangelical and Fundamental Christianity.

FUNERAL RITES. Death is not only a biological occurrence leaving the corpse as a residue that must be administered to; it is also, and more importantly, a sociocultural fundamental because of the beliefs and representations it gives rise to and the attitudes and rituals it brings about. It is of course understood that rites are the immediate extension of beliefs, and that funeral rites, in particular, are the conscious cultural forms of one of our most ancient, universal, and unconscious impulses: the need to overcome the distress of death and dying.

We will here take the word *rite* in its anthropological sense; that is, in a larger sense, quite apart from liturgical or theological concerns. A rite, then, is a ceremony in which behaviors, gestures and postures, words or songs uttered, and objects handled, manufactured, destroyed, or consumed are supposed to possess virtues or powers or to produce specific effects. Centered on the mortal remains or its substitute, then on whatever survives of those—material traces or souvenir relics—funeral rites may reveal three finalities. First, it is believed that they preside over the future of the departed, over both the metamorphosis of the corpse and the destiny of the person, whenever death is defined as transition, passage, or deliverance. Second, they attend to the surviving close kin, mourners who must be consoled and reassured. Finally, they participate in the revitalization of the group that has been disturbed by the death of one of its own. Very often in traditional societies, in Africa and more often in Asia (notably in China), the funeral rites are presented as a theater of renewal, with acted parts, mimes, dancers, musicians, and even clowns.

Funeral rites are so important that the presence of the participants becomes a strict obligation, particularly in traditional societies. In traditional Africa, funeral rites are the most resistant to the pressure of acculturation. A function of the rite essential to the social group is easily seen; after all, numerous psychiatrists affirm that many problems derive from the guilt arising when one hurries over obsequies or comes out of mourning too soon.

Chief Moments in Funeral Rites

Funeral rites may comprise numerous ceremonies. The Toraja of Sulawesi (Celebes) see four fundamental stages. During the first, the deceased is said to be ill: washed, dressed, and adorned, he may be nurtured for as long as a year. Then comes the first festivity, lasting from five to seven days, with sacrifices, lamentations, songs, and dances; this marks the difficult passage from life to death and ends with a provisional interment inside the house. During the following intermediary period, these festivities increase. Finally the ultimate ceremony is performed, requiring several months of preparation during which winding-sheets, cenotaphs, and, most notably, an effigy (the famous *tau-tau*) are employed, not without ostentation; it concludes with the burial and the installation of the deceased in the beyond.

The succession of funerary acts sometimes takes on a bureaucratic tone, particularly in Chinese Taoism, where the main part of the rite is devoted to drawing up documents and contracts with the gods. Especially noteworthy are the consultation of cosmic forces in order to determine propitious days and places for the rites; the *kung-te*, or acquisition of merits for the deceased; the *p'u-tu*, or offerings for wandering souls; and the ritual for liberating the soul.

Nevertheless, to determine the chief moments of funerals, anthropologists use the formulation, however incorrect, of the double funeral, which implies rites of separation followed by intervals varying from a few weeks to several years, followed by rites of integration that put an end to the mourning.

Separation Rites. In most traditional societies, the passage from decay to mineralization dictates the two chief moments in the funerary ritual. The first funeral, or separation rite, is for the purpose of "killing the dead," as the Mossi of Burkina Faso say—in other words, killing what remains alive in the dead person by breaking the emotional bonds that unite him to the community. While the corpse decays, simultaneously corrupt and corrupting, it is terribly vulnerable and dangerous. Two attitudes, contradictory yet complementary, orient the conduct of the living toward the dead: solicitude and rejection, shown in a symbolic or realistic manner according to points of view that vary with each ethnic group.

Solicitude begins immediately after death, tinged with commiseration and fear: the dead person is given food, gongs are sounded to scare away evil spirits, the corpse is washed and purified, and its evolutions are watched, especially if the body lies in state for a long time (from three to twelve days among the Miao of Southeast Asia). It is dressed, its natural orifices are stopped, and, most important, the wake is organized. This can be the occasion for big reunions and a large-scale ritual. For the Maori of New Zealand it is an intensely dramatic ceremony, the key moment of the funeral rite, accompanied by songs, cries, lamentations, elegies, and more or less generous meals, depending on the fortune of the deceased. To multiple meals the Inca of Peru added games of dice with very complex symbolism. The outcome of the game was supposed to orient the soul of the deceased so as to help him attain heaven. The dead person participated by influencing the manner in which the dice fell, thereby revealing whether he was well or ill disposed toward the player. The deceased's possessions were divided according to the results.

When respectful solicitude has soothed the dead, rejection asserts itself. Once the last homages are rendered, the deceased is invited to rejoin his ancestors or to prepare for his afterlife (metamorphoses, reincarnation, sojourn with God, etc.). To overcome his hesitation, a number of methods are used: one may tie him down securely or mutilate him (poke his eyes out, break his legs); lose him by returning suddenly from the cemetery by a detour; or arrange to deposit him at the foot of a mountain or on the far side of a river he cannot cross. In compensation, sometimes an effigy remains at home as a substitute for him, or he may be promised an annual invitation. Because the decaying of the corpse constitutes a risk that its double will prowl in the village, the relatives submit to the constraints of mourning, which puts them outside the social circuit. The specific purpose of these interdictions is to separate all those contaminated by the corpse's decay. Curiously enough, in India the Toda have a single term, *kedr,* which simultaneously designates the corpse, the state of mourning, and the interval between the first and second funerals. A statement made by a dying Maori chief to his son likewise clarifies the problem: "For three years your person must be sacred and you must remain separated from your tribe . . . for all this time my hands will be gathering the earth and my mouth will be constantly eating worms . . . then when my head falls on my body, awake me from my sleep, show my face the light of day, and you shall be *noa* [free]" (Hertz, 1970, p. 33). Therefore, when mineralization, whether natural or artifically accelerated, sets in, it is a sign that the deceased has fulfilled his posthumous destiny. He has passed the initiatory tests imposed on him; he has rejoined the ancestors or the gods; or perhaps he is ready for metempsychosis or reincarnation.

Rites of Integration and the Cessation of Mourning. In almost all traditional societies, double funerals are held. After a delay varying from a few weeks to ten years, according to the ethnic group and the resources at the family's disposal, a final ceremony takes place that confirms the deceased in his new destiny and confers on his remains a definitive status. Like the integration of the dead person, this ritual consecrates the reintegration of the mourners into the group: order is reestablished and interdictions are lifted. As a rule, the bones are exhumed and then treated in different ways according to local traditions: washed, dried, sometimes covered with ocher, they are preserved as visible relics, placed in containers, buried again, or even pulverized and mixed with ritual beverages. In sub-Saharan Africa, the latter custom is quite prevalent, especially among Bantu-speaking peoples. Among the Bamileke of Cameroon, the inheritance of skulls according to rigorous rules symbolically secures the collective memory and the continuity of the clam. In Madagascar the Famadihana (which has been wrongly translated as "turning over the corpses") gives way to costly festivities: when a family decides to celebrate the cult of its dead, they proceed from opening the tombs and changing the winding-sheets to rewrapping and reburial with great ceremony, before an audience in a state of great jollity. For two days songs, dances, music, processions, and festivities punctuate the ritual manipulations.

In Borneo, the Olo Nyadju give themselves up to analogous states on the occasion of Tiwah. Along with some degree of fasting, the majority of Indonesian ethnic groups do the same thing. This bone cult, which is generally referred to as an ancestor cult, flourishes among the American Indians, in China, and elsewhere, and still has its equivalent in Europe. There is hardly any difference between the old Chinese who carefully brushes his ancestor's bones and the skeleton washer of Neapolitan cemeteries who, two years after the burial, when the corpse has dried out, washes the bones in front of the families before putting them in a marble urn. In the French provinces, the custom of the anniversary meal and mass is clearly a response to the same fantasies of reestablishing order.

Indeed, the ritual of secondary obsequies ending in definitive burial has a twofold justification in the imagination. First of all, the transfer of the bones to another place completes the purification process. It is as if the earth has been corrupted by the decaying body, necessitating the removal of the purified bones to an unsullied location. Second, although the provisional inhumation is always individual, the final burial is very often collective. Such is the custom of the Goajiro Indians in Venezuala: three years after death, the bones are sorted and dried, then exposed during a funeral wake. They are then transferred into a large urn, where the remains of all the dead from the matriclan or the matrilineage are gathered together. Thus, communal reunion of the sublimated remains follows the isolation of impure decay.

On the other hand, Western ossuaries, by virtue of their anonymous character, have hardly any impact on an individualistic society. At the very most, as "display cases" they provide the "exposition of the bones" as an aid to meditation. "Let us come to the charnelhouse, Christians; let us see the skeletons of our brothers," says a Breton song. In any case, if inhumation in a common ditch is judged shocking and infamous by us, the collective ossuary does not scandalize anyone. In fact, it can be seen as a solution to the problem of cemetery space and an orientation for a new cult of the dead. The possibility has even been raised of reintegrating the sacred into cemeteries in the form of an "ossuary-necrology" that would reassemble the community of the dead and make the living sensitive to the bonds uniting them to the past.

With the second funeral, therefore, the fate of the deceased has been settled. To borrow the vivid language of the Mossi of Burkina Faso, the ritual of integration "makes the dead live again." From then on, grief no longer has reason to exist. The marginal period has permitted the mourning work to be finished. But, in any case, is not ritualization, like elegance, a way of charming anguish? At this stage, interdictions are always relaxed. After undergoing purifying baths and multiple reparation sacrifices, the mourners are reintegrated into the group. Thanks to the symbolic support of the bone, life on every level henceforth reasserts all its rights—both the life of the metamorphosed deceased and the life of the group from which he emerged. Once the decaying flesh and the signs of death have disappeared, the imperishable vestige is left with its charge of symbols. Funeral rites thus have the capacity "to reduce any object at all to significance, let it pass over to the other side of the gulf" (Maertens, 1979, p. 236). This can be clearly seen in the following set of processes: decay → mineralization; excluded mourners → reintegrated mourners; oversignificant corpse → hypersignificant remains.

In Vietnam, ritual constitutes what is called the "transfer of life": while the body is buried in a tomb defined according to the rules of geomancy, the soul, set on a tablet that itself is enclosed in a box covered with a red and gold case, becomes the protective ancestor that one venerates and prays to at the family altar.

A qualifying remark must be inserted: the conditions of death (place, moment, means) orient the meaning of the rite. The evil dead person, for example, can be deprived of a funeral, or may have the right to only a truncated or clandestine funeral; he will never become an ancestor or know happiness. Status, age, and sex also play a determining role in the elaboration of ceremonies.

Some Key Rites

Only a few fundamental rites concerning the good death will be considered, because of their quasi-universality and the depth of the fantasies that they express.

Attendance at Death, Certification of Death, and Interrogation. If to die far away from home or to die a violent death is usually equivalent to a bad death in traditional societies, it is not only because uncertainty is alarming but also, and more importantly, because the dying cannot be helped. Mothering, making secure, and taking charge of the dying person, who is consoled, caressed, and helped to die for the same reason he was helped to be born, is a universal constant. This attitude has a religious aspect. To take only one example, we know the importance to elderly and very sick people of the Christian last sacraments, including the purifying aspersion that evokes baptism and redemption through the Passion and the Resurrection, as well as the profession of faith and, when possible, the Eucharist. As for the anointing of the sick, let us recall that this new ritual, although it abandons the expiatory aspect and gives only a circumstantial role to the effacement of sin, nevertheless insists on help by grace.

It is important to make sure that the deceased is really dead. Besides interpreting tangible signs like the stopping of the breath and the heart, one can call on the diviner, the priest, or the doctor. There are also other ways of making sure: right after the death of a Chinese, one of his close kin climbs the roof of the house to "call back his soul"; if it does not return, there is no doubt about his death. While for the Toraja of Sulawesi the deceased is not dead but only ill (as noted), among the Tibetans and the Miao (Hmong) the deceased must be informed that he is really dead because he doesn't know that he is: "The illness fell on the rocks and the rocks could not bear it. Then it slid into the grass, but the grass could not carry it. And that is why, O Dead One, the illness has come to you. The earth could not bear the illness, so the illness reached your soul. That is why you have found death" (Georges, 1982, p. 183). Then, with great kindness and consideration, they explain to him what he needs for the great journey: bamboos to communicate with the survivors or the gods, the "wooden house" (coffin), the hemp shoes, alcohol, food, and the cock that will show him the way. The announcement of the death also obeys precise rules. Women's lamentations punctuated by cries, drums, and bells, as well as symbolic formulas and the sending of messengers, are the most frequent practices.

In traditional societies, another notable belief is that the corpse is simultaneously alive and dead. It no longer has a voice, but in its fashion it speaks. No one hesitates to question it in order to learn why it died or, sometimes, its desires concerning the transmission of its possessions; only little children and fools escape this rite, because "they don't know what they say." Among the Diola of Senegal, the dead person, tied to a bier, is supported by four men, and people take turns asking it questions. If the corpse moves forward when questioned, the response is positive; if it moves backward, it is negative; if it wavers in the same place, it is indicating hesitation. Among the Somba of Benin, "no" is expressed by a rocking from left to right, and "yes" by a rocking from back to front. For the Senufo of the Ivory Coast, leaning to the left indicates the deceased's agreement, and leaning to the right, his disagreement. It sometimes happens that the dead person bears down on one of those present in order to demand that questions be put to him (the Diola) or requires that the carriers be changed in order to pursue the rite (the Lobi of Burkina Faso). Substitute objects sometimes replace the corpse at the time of the interrogation, on condition that they participate in its vital forces. An assegai with the hair of the deceased is an adequate substitute for the Boni of Guyana, while a tree trunk containing his nails and body hairs suffices for the Bete of the Ivory Coast. If the death was willed by God or the ancestors, a frequent occurrence among the Ẹgba of Benin and the Orokawa of New Guinea, the group feels reassured. But if it resulted from a crime, witchcraft, or violation of a taboo, the fault must be immediately atoned for and the guilty punished. In its way, by its voiceless word the corpse plays an important role in social regulation.

Laying Out the Dead: Purification and Mothering Rituals. The funeral rite proper begins with the laying out of the corpse, which, in its essential aspect, is equivalent to an authentic purification, a symbolic prelude to rebirth. A holy task among the Jews and especially in Islam, it is a matter of divine obligation, thus of *'ibādāt*, involving a relationship with God and not just a social function. Laying out the corpse is universal and rigorously codified in ancient societies. In the West Indies, especially in the Antilles and in Haiti, this ritual is reminiscent of that of the midwife. Death, like birth, demands a certain ceremonial that is no less than the "transitory reintegration in the indistinct," to borrow Mircea Eliade's expression. By placing, for example, a vat of water underneath the couch where the corpse is lying, one symbolically reestablishes the sources of life (amniotic fluid). One is again assured that the soul, which has just left the body, will not disappear into nothingness, and that the deceased, thus purified, will be reborn in another world.

Among the Agni-Bora of the Ivory Coast, there is a similarity between the grooming of the newborn baby and the grooming of the deceased: holding the naked body on their knees, old women wash it with three successive rinses, perfume it, and dress it. For the baby, the rite is always accompanied by singing; the washing is done from the head to the feet with the right hand. In the case of the deceased, however, the rite is executed in silence with the left hand, and proceeds from the feet to the head. This is because birth is an arrival, and rebirth a departure. In the European countryside the laying out is still the work of the "woman who helps" (the midwife), who is also the "woman who does the dead." The laying out of the dead is again an act of mothering.

Among the Miao, the deceased is rubbed with a warm towel without being undressed; then is dressed in new clothing finished off with a richly decorated kimono. The head is wrapped in a turban, and—an important detail—the feet are shod in felt or leather shoes with curled tips, like those sold by the Chinese. Sometimes the duty of one of the relatives is to make these shoes. The dead must depart with good shoes for the trip about to be undertaken. A harquebusier comes up to the deceased and forewarns deferentially: "Now we are going to fire a few shots that will accompany and protect you for the whole length of your trip. Don't be afraid."

Display of the Deceased: The Corpse Detained. Aside from punitive exhibition (desecration of the corpse) in the case of a bad death, when a devalued dead person is deprived of a funeral, the display of the corpse reflects the noblest intentions (valorization of the corpse).

In traditional societies, where death is a public affair involving the whole community, display of the corpse is almost a general rule. It is stretched out on a mat, on a funeral bed, or in a coffin, placed in the mortuary in a special case or in the open air, or suspended at the top of a tree or on a scaffold in the middle of the village square. Sometimes it even presides over its own funeral. The presentation varies according to places and beliefs, but most often it is done in state, with all the symbols that recall the deceased's social function. In Senegal, the dead Diola appears much as if he were alive, but with his most beautiful clothes, his bow and arrows if he was a good hunter, his farming implements and sheaves of rice if he was a good farmer. The horns of cows he sacrificed during his life and heads of cattle are exhibited to emphasize his wealth. The ostentatious display of belongings is frequent. Sometimes the dead person is displayed in the midst of his herd, as among the Karamojong of Uganda and certain Indians of North America. The length of time for displaying the dead and his goods may vary according to his wealth: among the Dayak of Borneo, it ranges from one to six years. Another custom, peculiar to the Sioux, is to suspend the head and tail of the dead person's horse on the same scaffold on which he is exposed. Display of the dead seems to serve a double function: to show the dead that he is being rendered the homage due him by offering him to view in his best light, and to show him as a model of the role he played in the group. The dead person is glorified as having accomplished his mission, and the aura with which he is endowed is reflected on the collectivity, which thus reaffirms the identity and cohesion it so needs upon losing one of its members.

In southern Sulawesi, the Toraja still use the effigy, or *tau-tau*, especially for the deceased of high rank. This figure, made of breadfruit wood according to strict rules, must resemble the deceased as much as possible (same sex, height, face), though often with improvements. Dressed in the dead person's clothing and adorned with jewels, necklaces, and bracelets, it is the object of numerous rites whereby it is in turn animated and made to die, wept over and consecrated. At the end of a very long ceremony, the corpse, swathed in its winding-sheets, is raised on a platform below which is placed the *tau-tau*. Both then preside over the buffalo sacrifices and receive their part of the offerings. Finally, when the corpse goes back to the sepulcher for the last time, its representative is permanently exhibited as near as possible to the tomb. For the Toraja, the effigy becomes more than a ritual object associated with death; it is, if not the deceased, at least its visible double.

In the West today, the embalmed corpse lies in state in funeral homes. It is still a matter of rendering homage to one no longer alive, and of facilitating the mourning work by conserving a better image of the departed: the mortician's work spares the dead person the stigma of death for a time and gives the impression that he is sleeping in peace. The essential thing is that the dead person should be present, recognizable to his family (to a certain extent, a disfigured corpse is tantamount to an absent one). The certainty of his death can be borne more easily than the uncertainty surrounding his absence and silence.

In this respect, wakes have a soothing value, supposedly for the departed and certainly for the survivors. The sacred and the profane are mixed. In Spain, rosaries and responses are recited. People speak of the deceased, because to speak of him is to be with him again. And if sometimes the conversation turns to funny stories, this does not imply a lack of respect for the dead but a pleasant relationship with him. At one extreme, these wakes are almost feast days. Perhaps this is because in some villages, like the Aragonese village of Leciñena, the immediate neighbors cook the celebrated *tortas*, a kind of brioche made only on feast days (the Feast of the Virgin, a marriage) and for a death wake.

When there are mourners, especially female ones, display of the dead facilitates the sincere and organized expression of emotions through praise of the departed, invitations to return among the living (visits, possession, reincarnation), reproaches or invectives concerning his cruelty in leaving his close kin, and advice for his posthumous destiny. This is how the rhapsodist addresses the deceased Miao after the ritual offering of the cock: "Take it and eat. Henceforth you will have the cock's soul with you. Follow it. Hurry and look for the silk suit you wore at birth. You will find it hidden under the earth [an allusion to the placenta of the newborn, which is always carefully buried near the house in which he was born]. Now leave" (Georges, 1982, p. 187). Again dressed in his silk garment and guided by the cock, the soul of the dead person then sets out on the long journey the singer is chanting about. Finally, before the final farewells, the dead person may be transported into the village and the fields, visiting for the last time the places where he lived, and communing with himself before the altars where he made sacrifices.

Food Given to the Dead and in Homage to the Dead. We will mention only briefly the offering of victuals to the dead, whether during the funeral or at the moment of burial. To help the deceased on his long journey, the Aztec burned food with him—usually a fat little dog with a tawny coat—to help him cross the rivers on his infernal route. This rite, common to almost all cultures, corresponds to a widespread belief: the offerings are the indispensable viaticum that permits the dead to survive the transitory journey into the world of the ancestors. The sacrifices offered simultaneously play the same role, albeit symbolically.

Better yet is the common meal that accompanies funerals almost everywhere. A practical necessity justifies it: those who have come to honor the dead and console the close kin must be fed. The importance of the feast is often such that it takes on the dimensions of a potlatch: in numerous ethnic groups, brief rites are initiated at the time of death, and the funeral services are deferred until sufficient reserves of rice, palm wine, and cattle have been set out. In the view of traditional mythologies, it is a communal event in which the dead person participates: a seat, plate, or part of the food (often the best) is reserved for him, or a descendant represents him, or the table is set in the presence of the corpse—diverse customs showing an intention to intensify the relationship with the deceased and to persuade the group that he is not completely dead. In Western societies, the funeral meal is a means of appeasing grief by reinforcing the bonds that unite the living in the absence of the dead. The meal following the death is like a birth for the talkative and hungry community of the living, which has been wounded, split up, and interrupted by the death.

But all these reasons are valid only on an obvious level. On the symbolic level, the funeral meal is a way of retaining the dead person, and on these grounds, it is a substitute for the cannibalistic meal. In Haiti, the funeral meal is appropriately termed a *mangé-mort,* just as in Quebec, where the expression *manger le mort* is still in use. In fact, the manducation of the corpse is connected to a universal fantasy that psychoanalysts neatly term "the exquisite corpse" (an expression borrowed from surrealist poetry). Obeying the pleasure principle, the fantasy mechanism of the exquisite corpse responds to the trauma of loss through the desire for incorporation of the lost object. Amorous fusion with the other is then achieved in an exaltation that, in the real world, would perhaps be secret. The dead person is fixed and assimilated in his best features; he who devours him makes him his own in spite of all taboos. In this connection, let us recall a strange Mexican custom that does not even disguise the necrophagic intention. On the Day of the Dead, an extraordinary commercial activity mobilizes the whole population: superb confections are sold that represent the skulls and skeletons of the dead, ravishing or burlesque in appearance, with first names engraved in order to help the customers make their choices.

Controlling Decay

Decay is the justification for all funeral rites. Everything is brought into play in order to tame it (display of the corpse), hide it (winding-sheets, the sarcophagus), forbid it absolutely (embalming and mummification, incineration, cannibalistic ingestion), retard it (corporal attentions), or accelerate it (towers of silence; see below). A profound need underlies all these approaches to decay: to stabilize the deceased in an indestructible medium—a stage marking the reconciliation of the community with his death. These remains—mummy, relic, ashes, or bones—all civilizations, without exception, persist in preserving.

Tamed or Accelerated Decay. Conditions of exposure may eventually accelerate the mineralization of the corpse. Sunlight and even moonlight, as well as a smoky fire, are believed to contribute, but the body is sometimes also offered to birds of prey and other carnivores, or to ants. In the Tibetan tradition, corpses were torn apart by the *ragyapas* ("dismemberers") and thrown to the dogs, so that the bones would be stripped much faster. But the most spectacular example is given us by the towers of silence built in the seventeenth century, particularly in Iran by the Zoroastrians. According to the sacred texts of the *Zand,* the corpse is the essence of impurity. It is therefore out of the question to pollute "the things belonging to the good creation" by carrying out the final burial of a decomposing body. Hence the custom of exposing the body in a remote location known to be frequented by carnivorous animals. Vultures, in particular, are the purifiers that disencumber the dead person of rotting flesh, the medium of demonic infection. From this came the practice, which spread little by little, of building towers of rock especially designed to isolate corpses and avoid their contaminating presence during the purification process. The interior of the "tower of silence," or *dakhma,* consists of a platform inclined toward a central pit. Cells *(pāvis)* hollowed out in three concentric circles receive the corpses—men in the outer zone, women in the middle zone, and children toward the central pit. In this case, in which the custom of second obsequies no longer takes the symbolic form of the commemorative meal, the dried bones are thrown down twice a year into the depths of the pit. There, under the combined effect of the sun and the lime that is spread there, the bones are transformed into dust. The pit branches into four canals for the evacuation of rainwater, which is received and purified in four subterreanean pits where carbon and sand clarify it. Formerly, the remains were removed periodically, to be kept in an ossuary: cleansed of all impurities, they testified that the soul was ready for the final ceremonies. [*See* Dakhma.]

Decomposition Accepted but Hidden. Obviously, the cemetery is a place where remains are preserved and concealed. The feminine and maternal valence of the earth responds to a universal fantasy: "Naked I came out of the maternal womb; naked I shall return there" (*Jb.* 1:21). In African cosmogonic thought, burial in Mother Earth, the source of fertility and dwelling place of the ancestors, takes on a quasi-metaphysical significance. The same symbolism serves for other forms of interment, such as the deposit of the corpse in grottos or in funeral jars that evoke the uterine cavity. The earth is indeed the place *par excellence* for transformations. Not only does one plow seeds into it at the time of sowing, but it is also a mediator in all rites of passage: the corpse is entrusted to it at the time of the funeral, as are neophytes' nail clippings, hair, and other fleshly remains from initiation rites and the placenta and umbilical cord at birth. Burial can also, in a sense, transform the land. Thus the Hebrews did not begin to bury their dead until as a people they became sedentary; burial is always connected to the ownership of land, that is, to the appropriation of a "promised land," without doubt, a way of salvation.

One could go on forever describing the infinite variety of types of cemeteries (mass burial sites or scattered individual crypts, as in Madagascar; at the heart of the village or far-flung) and types of tombs (simple ditches to elaborate mausoleums to modern, efficient columbaria for cremated bodies). In many systems of burial the distinction between social classes is still, as it were, heavily felt.

The corpse's position in the tomb is no less variable: seated; stretched out on its back or side; in the fetal position; even on its stomach, as was once the case in our own culture for adulterous women; or standing, in the manner of some military men or heroes of the American West. The orientation of the body can also be important. For some emigrant groups, it is toward the country of birth. For populations that traditionally ascribe birth to sunrise and death to sunset, the deceased must have his head to the east in order to be in position for rebirth. On the other hand, medieval Christians who wanted to be buried facing the direction from which salvation came placed the head toward the west so that the deceased could face Jerusalem. Similarly, Muslims are buried on their right side, turned toward Mecca.

The necropolis does not exist in India or Nepal since ashes are thrown into the sacred rivers, nor is it commonly of importance in sub-Saharan Africa. But where it does exist, the cemetery is still a symbol charged with emotion, sometimes arousing fear and melancholy, sometimes calm and reflection. In this regard one must praise Islamic wisdom, by which the very texture and functions of the cemetery maintain a state of relative osmosis between the living and the dead. The cemetery *(maqbarah)* is often designated by the more euphemistic term *rawḍah* ("garden"). Certainly, its ground has often been consecrated to that use by a pious tradition, but it is not closed. The dead rest there on the bare ground in a simple winding-sheet, thus returning to the elements. In both senses of the term, it is open to nature. But it is open to society, too. The belief prevails that bonds exist with the bodies of the deceased before the Last Judgment and that for the living to visit the tombs is a praiseworthy act and, what is more, a deed that will be considered in their favor then. The cemetery is also a traditional place to go for a walk: women often meet there on Fridays.

Prohibited Decay. Setting aside the still rare phenomenon of cryogenation (in which the deceased wait in liquid nitrogen until the time when people will know how to restore them to life), there are three common forms of prohibited decay.

Cannibalism, decay, and mineralization. Robert Hertz (1970) has emphasized the particular function of cannibalism that spares the dead person the horror of a slow and ignoble decomposition and brings the bones almost immediately to their final state. This is obviously true for endocannibalism, when it is practiced on revered dead persons. There is no doubt that the purpose of cannibalism is to prohibit rotting. On the one hand, consumption of the flesh occurs as soon as possible after death, and, since the flesh is usually cooked, putrefaction does not begin in the course of consumption. On the other hand, inquiries among populations with a tradition of cannibalism clearly reveal the finality of the act: "In this way, we knew where he [the dead] was and his flesh would not rot," said the Australian Turrbals (Hertz, 1970, p. 24, n. 1). This is also the view expressed by the Merina, according to a historical Malagasy document of the last century: "Our kinsman is dead; what shall we do with his body, for he was a man we loved?" Some answered, "Since he is dead, let us not bury him but let us eat him, because it would be sad to see him rotting in the ground." (ibid., p. 28).

Cannibalism promotes mineralization, but intentions toward the corpse in this regard differ according to whether endocannibalism or exocannibalism is involved.

Endocannibalism refers us back to the traditional scheme of the double funeral: on the first occasion, the dead person is buried in the earth or, similarly, in the belly, where human digestion prepares its accelerated passage to mineralization; on the second occasion, the remaining bones are handled with respect and receive the final obsequies. The destruction resulting from the manducation is only a mutation of forms that symbolically achieve a kind of conservation: incorporation. In a sense, ingestion could be interpreted as embalming transferred to the oral register. As for exocannibalism, however, the situation is different, at least concerning the treatment of the remains. The cannibal feast undoubtedly implies incorporation and, by its reference to myths of origin, it can take the form of a veritable primitive mass in which the bread and wine are really flesh and blood. But whereas the vital force animating the enemy's corpse is assimilated, his bones and uneaten parts may be abandoned or held up to ridicule. The Ocaina Indians of the Peruvian Amazon suspend the enemy's penis from a necklace worn by the victor's spouse; the mummified hands are used as spoons, the bones as flutes, and the painted and exposed skull serves as a ritual bell. [*See* Cannibalism.]

The cremated corpse. According to many mythologies, the purifying fire is above all liberating. In Bali, as long as the fire has not reduced the corpse to ashes, the dead person is impure; he continues to wait, his spirit not yet separated from his body. According to many beliefs, fire is the promise of regeneration and rebirth. [*See* Fire.] Through fire, a superior level of existence can be attained. According to Greek mythology, Herakles stretched himself out on the pyre of Mount Oeta, while Zeus announced to the other gods that Herakles was about to become their equal: the fire would relieve him of his human part, immortalize him, and make him divine. The same theme is found in the Upaniṣads, the classic texts of Hinduism. It is therefore not the impurity of the corpse that is implicated in the cremation ritual, but the impurity of the body and the human condition. Ashes are the proof of that impurity; if the body were perfect, it would burn without ashes.

The destiny of the remains varies. In Japan, the bones are traditionally divided between two containers, one of which is buried at the place of cremation and the other in the natal village of the deceased. In Thailand, part of the remains are collected in an urn kept at home, while the remainder is buried at the foot of the pyre, kept in a reliquary monument, or even thrown into a river. In India, custom formerly demanded that the ashes be deposited in a tomb. Later a rule was imposed that still persists today: since fire is the son of the waters, funeral rites should summon first one and then the other. Also, the ashes and noncalcinated bones are sprinkled with water, and cow's milk and coconut milk as well, before being thrown into the Ganges, the sacred river that flows from Śiva's hair. The same procedure is followed in Nepal and in Thailand, where other sacred rivers conduct the deceased downstream toward his celestial residence. In Bali, the remains are thrown into the sea after having been meticulously sorted by the relatives, washed in sacred water, arranged on white linen, and inserted into a dried coconut adorned with flowers. Finally, there is the particular case of the Yanoama Indians of Venezuela, who crush the remaining bones after the incineration of their warriors, in order to consume them mixed with game dishes or beverages in the course of a communal meal.

Cremation can be assimilated to all other modes of provisional burial, and people who burn their dead conform in many respects to the classic scheme of the double funeral, but with different means and a shortened duration. The first funeral, corresponding to the ritual of the exclusion of the dead, soothes the corpse and leads it to a purification that can be accomplished only by the process of decay. Those who cremate the dead find the equivalent of the first funeral in the rites that accompany the handling of the body during the generally short period between death and combustion on the pyre. The second obsequies, which concern the charred and purified remains, correspond to the rites of integration of the dead in his status in the beyond, while mourning is lifted for the survivors.

Preservation of bodies. Egyptian embalming practices are famous. The long, difficult techniques only make sense, however, in the framework of the osirification ritual that makes the dead person a god through assimilation with Osiris. Before, during, and after the technical manipulations, an extremely complicated ceremony took place, which undoubtedly explains the long duration of the treatment and the great number of participants. Invocations, readings, and prayers punctuated each act of the embalmers, whose very gestures were strictly regulated. Afterlife was not possible unless the liturgy was observed in its minutest details. "You will not cease living; you will not cease to be young, for always and forever," cried the priest at the end of the embalming. Then the last ceremony could be performed: the opening of the mouth. In the purification tent or at the entrance to the tomb, the gestures of the officiating priest were accompanied by aspersions, offerings, and sacrifices, fumigations with incense, and magico-religious formulas. With the end of his adz the priest touched the dead person's face in order to reintroduce the vital energy.

In addition, mummies discovered in South America and the testimony of Spanish chroniclers affirm that the Inca, for example, embalmed their dead. The technical success of their mummies seems not to have been as spectacular as that of the Egyptian mummies, especially if one remembers that the Inca empire occurred relatively close to our own time (at the end of our Middle Ages). The body was treated with different ingredients (honey, resin, and herbs) and painted with *roucou* (a vegetable dye); the viscera, preliminarily removed, were prepared and kept separate in a receptacle. The dry climate and the burial methods (a hole in a rocky wall, or a funeral jar) were favorable for preservation. Like the pharaohs, the sovereigns were the objects of particular care. An illustrated story from the sixteenth century, whose author, Huaman Poma, was of Inca origin, recounts the royal funeral ritual: the embalmed Inca, adorned with his emblems, lay in state for a month; at his sides were placed women and servants, likewise embalmed, to serve him in the other world. Although the techniques were rudimentary, there is good reason to assume that a very precise ritual was used to increase efficacity. Thus, the funeral offerings deposited next to the body appeased the maleficent spirits that caused decomposition. Indeed, since the life principle (the *aya*) remained in all parts of the corpse, rotting involved the destruction of the individual. On the other hand, if the body was preserved, the spirit of the dead could be reincarnated in a descendant. This belief in a second birth appears to explain the fetal position of corpses found in tombs and funeral jars.

Whatever the modalities, we can agree with Robert Hertz that it is legitimate "to consider mummification as a particular case derived from provisional interment" (Hertz, 1970, p. 20). If the interval separating death from final burial corresponds to the duration necessary for mineralization or desiccation, then a symmetry exists between the Egyptian rite and that of certain archaic ethnic groups. It is only when the embalming is concluded "that the body, having become imperishable, will be conducted to the tomb, that the soul will leave for the country of Ialou, and that the mourning of the survivors will come to an end." The waiting period, that is, the time necessary to achieve mineralization, can be reduced only by a manipulative intervention; it has not changed meaning at all, even if in this case the corpse is the equivalent of the body in its apparent totality (a mummy) or in part (a trophy head), rather than the residue of bones and ashes.

Conclusion

I have, as it were, painted a composite picture of funeral rites, in which it can be seen that they border on the *stricto sensu* sphere of the sacred. It may in fact be argued that, thanks to rites—those of former times especially, and to a lesser degree those of today—everything is brought into play in order to put death (even if accepted) at a distance, and eventually to make fun of it or tame it by permitting the community, when it feels concerned, to pull itself together. This is why funeral rites can shift the drama of dying from the plane of the real to that of the imaginary (by displacements and metonymy, symbols and metaphors), and it is in this that their efficacity resides. To reorganize the society disturbed by death and to console the survivors even while the deceased is being served and his destiny oriented—these are the two fundamental aims of funeral customs. In all regions, then, such rites are simultaneously defined first as liturgical drama with its places and scenes, its actors and their scripts, and also as individual or collective therapies (one might recall Nasser's moving funeral). In this respect, traditional cultures have inexhaustible resources of rich symbolism that the modern world has forgotten.

Indeed, modern life, especially in an urban milieu, entails multiple mutations that are probably irreversible on the level of ritual, and perhaps disquieting for the psychic equilibrium of our contemporaries. Many practices are simplified or omitted: the wake is impossible at the hospital or in tiny apartments, condolences and corteges are practically eliminated. Consider, for example, today's laying out of the dead: for the impurity of former times, the pretext of hygiene is substituted; for respect for the corpse as subject, obsession with or horror of the corpse as object; for family deference, the anonymity of an indifferent wage. In the same way, the signs of mourning have fallen into disuse—we have passed from "mourning clothes in twenty-four hours" to twenty-four hours of mourning!—and it is unseemly to show one's sorrow. People care less and less about the deceased, who sink into the anonymity of the forgotten; fewer and fewer masses are said for the repose of their souls, while the scattering of ashes eliminates the only possible physical support for a cult of the dead. If, at least on the imaginary plane, rites once primarily concerned the deceased, today they primarily concern the survivors. Thus, to take only one example, the new Roman Catholic ritual of anointing the sick tends to deritualize and desacralize death itself as an essential mutation. It is truly the disappearance of death, considered as a passage, that is witnessed by others.

Without a doubt, man today is condemning himself to a dangerous cultural void concerning rites and their symbols. We may well ask if our funerals, expedited in the "strictest intimacy," do not dangerously deprive us of a ritual that would help us to live.

[*See also* Rites of Passage *and* Ancestors. *For symbols and myths associated with funeral rites, see* Bones; Ashes; Tombs; *and* Death.]

BIBLIOGRAPHY

Ariès, Philippe. *Western Attitudes toward Death: From the Middle Ages to the Present.* Translated by Patricia Ranum. Baltimore, 1974.

Ariès, Philippe. *Essais sur l'histoire de la mort en Occident.* Paris, 1975.

Gennep, Arnold van. *Rites of Passage.* Translated by Monika B. Vizedom and Gabrielle L. Caffee. Chicago, 1960. See chapter 8.

Gennep, Arnold van. "Du berceau à la tombe." In *Manuel de folklore français contemporain,* edited by Arnold van Gennep, vol. 1, pp. 111–373. Paris, 1976.

Georges, Elaine. *Voyages de la mort.* Paris, 1982.

Guiart, Jean, ed. *Les hommes et la mort: Rituels funéraires à travers le monde.* Paris, 1979.

Hertz, Robert. "Contribution à une étude sur la représentation collective de la mort." In *Sociologie religieuse et folklore,* edited by Robert Hertz. Paris, 1970.

Maertens, Jean-Thierry. *Le masque et le miroir.* Paris, 1978.

Maertens, Jean-Thierry. *Le jeu du mort.* Paris, 1979.

Thomas, Louis-Vincent. *Anthropologie de la mort.* Paris, 1975.

Thomas, Louis-Vincent. *Le cadavre.* Brussels, 1980.

Thomas, Louis-Vincent. *La mort africaine.* Paris, 1982.

Thomas, Louis-Vincent. *Rites du mort: Pour la paix des vivants.* Paris, 1985.

Urbain, Jean-Didier. *La société de conservation.* Paris, 1978.

Walter, Jean-Jacques. *Psychanalyse des rites.* Paris, 1977.

LOUIS-VINCENT THOMAS
Translated from French by Kristine Anderson

FUSTEL DE COULANGES, N. D. (1830–1889), French historian, best known as author of *La cité antique* (1864). Numa Denis Fustel de Coulanges would perhaps be surprised to find himself the subject of an entry in this encyclopedia. He entered the École Normale Supérieure in Paris in 1850, and chafed under the strictly conventional classical education imposed by the regime of Napoléon III; if the revolutionary movements of 1848 left him with a lasting fear of civil war and violence, as expressed above all in his thesis on Polybius's approval of the Roman conquest of Greece (1858), the counterreaction engendered his equally persistent anticlericalism.

Fustel taught in Strasbourg from 1861 to 1870, then in Paris at the Sorbonne and the École Normale, of which he was director from 1880 to 1883. He saw himself as a scientific historian, examining evidence systematically and without preconceptions. Throughout his life, the main target of his critical scrutiny was the belief that primitive society was democratic. In *La cité antique* Fustel criticized the view that the concept of personal liberty was born in the ancient city-state and that in early Greek and Roman society there was no private ownership of land. Later, in the first volume of his *Histoire des institutions politiques de l'ancienne France* (1875), Fustel asserted that the determining influence in French history did not come from the Frankish invaders but from the Roman legacy in Gaul; finally, in his book *Recherches sur quelques problèmes de l'histoire* (1885), he argued that the primitive, democratic village community, which held land in common, could not be found even in Germany.

Fustel's reputation as a founding father of the sociology of religion is based largely on his assertion that religious ideas could have a decisive effect in the formulation of a society's social and economic structure. In *La cité antique* Fustel argues that the practice of worshiping ancestors determined the form of the family and the patrilineal form of lineage *(gens)* that grew out of it. The private ownership of land was derived from ancestor worship. A man was buried in the fields he had farmed, and since his descendants were obliged to care for his tomb they could not allow the land that contained it to pass out of the family. Religion tied culture and social structure to nature. To care for family tombs was natural and needed no explanation (or so it seemed to Fustel and his contemporaries, though the cemetery had only recently become a place of pilgrimage in their own time). At more complex levels of social organization religion was linked to nature in a different way: people worshiped gods who were believed to control physical forces and whose rites could be shared by a wide circle.

Pagan religion thus followed the contours of social organization. The paganism of the Gauls merged easily into that of the Romans as the Gauls became latinized. Fustel dismisses druidism as a brief interlude; he viewed the druids as professional religious specialists whose doctrines and practices did not arise naturally from social life. The power of the druids had been based on a close alliance with the native political elite who turned away from them after the Roman conquest.

Fustel's treatment of Christianity is more complex. Early Christianity, he thought, was truly democratic in its organization. With its incorporation into the empire, the structure of the church became more hierarchical, mirroring the structure of political society. Fustel became somewhat torn between his dislike of priestly hierarchy and his desire to see the church as the vehicle by which Roman social organization was preserved and transmitted to medieval France. Because it was separate from the state and grew up initially without official recognition, the church constituted an alternative source of authority on which the conception of the individual's rights against the state could be based; but contraposition to the state also turned the church into a political organization. In his early *Mémoire sur l'île de Chio* (1856) Fustel showed how the opposition between the Roman Catholic and the Greek Orthodox churches became the focus of hostility between Greeks and Franks.

Émile Durkheim and the structural-functionalists followed and extended Fustel's insight into the relation between religion and social structure. Much more recently, Louis Dumont has revived his idea of a link between Christianity and individualism in his *Essais sur l'individualisme* (1983). Fustel's complex attitude toward the priesthood and his interest in the relation between church and state form part of a chapter of nineteenth-century intellectual history that has yet to be written.

BIBLIOGRAPHY

The most recent English edition of *The Ancient City* (Baltimore, 1980) contains an introduction by Arnaldo Momigliano and myself. A new French edition, with an introduction by François Hartog, was published in Paris in 1984. Fustel's other work on religion is to be found in the *Histoire des institutions politiques de l'ancienne France*, 6 vols. (Paris, 1888–1893), *Nouvelles recherches sur quelques problèmes de l'histoire* (Paris, 1891), and *Questions historiques* (Paris, 1893); all were edited posthumously by Camille Jullian. Jane Herrick's *The Historical Thought of Fustel de Coulanges* (Washington, D.C., 1954) contains useful material of Fustel's attitude to religion. Further bibliography and information on Fustel's intellectual background can be found in Arnaldo Momigliano's "*The Ancient City* of Fustel de Coulanges," in his *Essays in Ancient and Modern Historiography* (Oxford, 1977), pp. 325–343.

S. C. HUMPHREYS

FYLGJUR are fetches and guardian spirits in Old Norse literary tradition. The term apparently derives from the Old Norse verb *fylgja* ("to accompany"), but it is homonymous with and perhaps identical to the word for "afterbirth, placenta." The singular noun *fylgja* denotes two distinct groups: fetches in animal form and guardian spirits in female form.

Fylgjur in animal form are most often wolves or bears, but many other animals are attested, such as oxen, boars, and such birds as eagles, falcons, and hawks. These figures appear to people primarily in dreams and warn of impending death, danger, or some future event. Frequently the *fylgja* is that of the doomed or threatened man's enemy.

These conceptions appear to reflect notions, common in Norse and later Scandinavian tradition, of the soul operating out of the body. In their textual context they must be viewed as part of a broader tradition of portents and dreams, but the animal form of the *fylgjur* may relate to the phenomena of the werewolf and the man-bear. [*See* Therianthropism.] The emphasis on beasts of battle suggests the cult of Óðinn, the most important shape-changer of Scandinavian myth and religion. Óðinn was known for his ability to send his soul out from his body and for sending his companion ravens out into the world as scouts. The animal form of Óðinn's berserkers may also be relevant. [*See* Berserkers.]

The female *fylgjur* share many features with *dísir* and *hamingjur* and more distantly with *landvættir,* Norns, and valkyries; there is little terminological consistency. Unlike the animal *fylgjur,* they are not the alter egos of individuals. Their actions are to some extent comparable to those of the animal *fylgjur,* in that they sometimes appear in dreams and portend death or foretell the future, but they generally act in sympathy with a central individual rather than in enmity, giving counsel, good fortune, or aid in battle. These *fylgjur* may attach to a single family or an entire family. They may be related to the cult of the *matronae,* attested from the Roman period in Germany.

BIBLIOGRAPHY

A full treatment of the literary evidence is provided in Else Mundal's *Fylgjemotiva i norrøn litteratur* (Oslo, 1974). Helpful for the larger context are Dag Strömbäck's *Tidrande och diserna* (Lund, 1949) and Folke Ström's *Diser, norner, valkyrjor* (Stockholm, 1954). E. O. G. Turville-Petre's "Liggja fylgjur þínar til Íslands," originally published in 1940 and reprinted in his *Nine Norse Studies* (London, 1972), distinguishes between the primarily concrete *fylgja* and the primarily abstract *hamingja.*

JOHN LINDOW

G

GADJERI. The name *Gadjeri (Gadjari, Kadjeri)* is known over a wide area of northern Australia. It means "old woman," implying status and not necessarily age. Gadjeri is also the "sacred mother," or "mother of us all," and the theme of birth, death, and rebirth is pervasive throughout all of the myths concerning her. She symbolizes the productive qualities of the earth—of all natural resources, including human beings. But it is people, and not natural species, who came from her uterus in the creative era of the Dreaming. Among a number of language groups from the Roper River westward, she is called Kunapipi (or Gunabibi), which means "uterus," "penis incision" (and, by extension, "vagina"), and "emergence" (referring to rebirth). In that same area she is also called Mumuna or Mumunga, a bull-roarer that, when swung, is her voice. In the northwest, on the Daly River and at Port Keats, as in the central-west part of the Northern Territory, she is also a bull-roarer named Kalwadi, although the term *Gadjeri* is more generally used; at Port Keats her local name is Mutjingga ("old woman"). In the southeastern Kimberley and southward into the Western Desert, she is known as Ganabuda. Mostly the Mother is a single mythic being, but in some cultural areas she may be identified with two females of equivalent characteristics, while the term *Ganabuda* may refer to a mythic group of women.

Gadjeri is often associated with two or more of her daughters, the Munga-munga, or Manga-manga, who play an important role in the mythic constellations of men and women in both secret-sacred and open-sacred ritual activities. The Munga-munga are sometimes referred to as the Kaleri-kalering, a name also used for a group of mythic men. The Mother's husband is Lightning or Rainbow Snake. [*See* Rainbow Snake.]

Baldwin Spencer (1914, pp. 162, 164, 213–218) first mentioned the term *Kunapipi* as the name of a bull-roarer used by people living in the areas of the Katherine and Roper rivers. The myth he recorded relates to a "big man" named Kunapipi who carries about with him woven bags containing spirit children. At one place he removes male children and places them on grass in an enclosed area surrounded by a raised mound. [*See* Djanggawul.] After decorating them as circumcision novices, he divides the children into two groups (moieties) and into subsection categories and gives them "totemic" affiliations—instituting present-day social organization. He also carries out circumcision and subincision rituals that attract visitors from outlying areas. When the rituals are over he kills and eats some of the visitors, then vomits their bones—not whole bodies, as he had expected. Two men who escape from him go in search of their relatives, and together they all return to kill Kunapipi. When they cut open his belly, they find two of his "own children," who are recovered alive. Spencer recounts an additional myth relating to a woman whose Dreaming is Kunapipi and who possesses a Kunapipi bull-roarer: she too is responsible for leaving spirit children at particular places. Together with a number of other women of the same mythic affiliation, she performs rituals. These are observed by a mythic man who sees that the women have a bull-roarer and takes it from them. As a result, the women lose their power to carry out this form of secret-sacred ritual.

Actually, Spencer seems not to have been referring to

Kunapipi as a male at all, but as a female. In the Alawa language group, Gadjeri is said to have emerged from the sea to rest on a sandbank at the mouth of the Roper River (Berndt, 1951, p. 188) and then to have proceeded upstream. In one Mara version, Gadjeri, as Mumuna, eats men who were enticed to her camp by her daughters, the Munga-munga. She swallows them whole but vomits their bones; she had expected them to emerge whole and to be be revived. This happens on a number of occasions with different men, each time without success. Eventually, she is killed by relatives of the men she has eaten (Berndt, 1951, pp. 148–152). A crucial point here is the one made by the Aborigines who told this myth: "They didn't come out like we do, they came out half and half." That is, in Kunapipi ritual men enter the sacred ground, which is the Mother's uterus, and leave it reborn. The myth here emphasizes not cannibalism but the dangerous nature of this ritual experience.

When the Kunapipi cycle entered eastern Arnhem Land, it was adapted to local mythology (see Warner, 1958, pp. 290–311; Berndt, 1951, pp. 18–32ff.). [*See* Wawalag.] In western Arnhem Land, two mythic Nagugur men, smeared with blood and grease, are credited with bringing the Kunapipi ritual complex. As they travel about the country they carry with them a Rainbow Snake (Ngalyod, in female form) wrapped in paper bark. In the rituals carried out in this area, a trench *(ganala)* symbolizes the Mother's uterus and is identified with Ngalyod; snake designs are incised on its inner walls (Berndt and Berndt, 1970, pp. 122–123, 138–142).

W. E. H. Stanner (1960, pp. 249, 260–266) gives a Murinbata (Port Keats) version of the Old Woman, or Mutjingga, myth. She swallows children whose mothers have left them for her to look after. Once the mothers return, they find the children missing and search without success; two men, Left Hand and Right Hand, eventually find Mutjingga hidden under the water. When she emerges, they kill her, open her belly, and remove the children, still alive, from her womb. They clean them, rub them with red ocher, and give them headbands, which signify that an initiation ritual has taken place. Although the myth differs from the Mara account in content, it is symbolically the same. Stanner, however, interpreted it as pointing to a "wrongful turning of life"; to him, the killing of Mutjingga was a kind of "immemorial misdirection" which applied to human affairs, and living men were committed to its consequences (see Berndt and Berndt, 1970, pp. 229, 233–234). Evidence from other cultures does not support the contention that "a primordial tragedy" took place in the myth. On the contrary, its format is consistent with that of other Kunapipi versions: it concerns the symbolism of ritual death and rebirth. Mutjingga is also linked in myth, but not in ritual, with Kunmanggur (Rainbow Snake), whom Stanner (1961, pp. 240–258) regarded as "the Father," complementing Mutjingga as "the Mother." In Port Keats, Kunmanggur dies in order to ensure that fire is available to human beings.

This pervasive theme of birth, death, and rebirth receives constant emphasis in the central-western Northern Territory Gadjeri. In drawings, for instance, the Mother is depicted with men and women "flowing from" her into a "ring place" (the sacred ground). She may also be shown as a composite structure of poles and bushes, decorated with meandering designs of feather down and ocher and wearing a pearl-shell pubic covering suspended from a hair waistband (see Berndt and Berndt, 1946, pp. 71–73). Furthermore, unlike many other deities or mythic beings, she does not change shape: she is not manifested directly through a natural species. Human birth is transferred to the nonhuman dimension through divine intervention, made possible through human ritual: that is, human ritual releases the Mother's power to make species-renewal possible. The central-western Gadjeri complex is quite close to the mainstream Kunapipi cultic perspective of the Roper River, except that the Mother's death is mentioned only obliquely in the central-western interpretation. For example, in regard to subincision, which is an integral part of her ritual, it is said that the blood which results from the regular opening of the penis incision is symbolic of that shed by the Mother when she was killed. But blood is also life-giving, and through this the Mother lives on spiritually and physically in her daughters, the Munga-munga.

In the northern and central-west areas of the Northern Territory, Gadjeri is ritually dominant, with or without the presence of the Rainbow Snake. In the fringes of the Western Desert her rituals focus mainly on other mythic beings. The Walbiri are a case in point. Their major mythic beings are the male Mamandabari pair. While this mythic constellation is classified under a Gadjeri heading and called "Big Sunday" (Meggitt, 1966, pp. 3ff.), and its ritual paraphernalia and symbolism are specific to Gadjeri, there is no reference either to the Mother or to her daughters. She is treated almost as a presiding deity who stands some distance away from ritual performance. The Mamandabari are similar to the two mythic Nagugur (of western Arnhem Land) who act as intermediaries. But what the Nagugur do is carried out in the name of Kunapipi, and this is not the case with the Mamandabari. Nevertheless, an important clue to the relationship between the Walbiri and Mara Kunapipi versions is to be found in a number of songs they hold in common (Meggitt, 1966, pp. 26-27).

In the southeastern Kimberley, Gadjeri is represented by the Ganabuda group of women, who are included in several of the mythic and ritual Dingari cycles. These Dingari are made up of an accretion of myths that are not necessarily woven into an integrated pattern. In them, the Ganabuda move from one site to another, either following or preceding a group of Dingari men who are concerned with initiating novices (see Berndt, 1970, pp. 216-247). In one excerpt, the Munga-munga walk ahead of the Ganabuda women, who are burdened with sacred *daragu* boards. During the course of their travels, they encounter a mythic man, who is astonished to see not only what they are carrying but also that they are swinging bull-roarers—because the men had none of these things. At night he sneaks up and steals their power, which resides under the armpits of the Ganabuda. In that way, men obtained ritual power.

In another excerpt, Dingari men sit within their ring place while the Ganabuda remain some distance away in their own camp. The women discover that some young men (novices) are among the older men. They meet some of the young men and have intercourse with them. When the older men find out about this, they become angry. They light a bush fire, which sweeps across the countryside, burning many of the young men to death. The Ganabuda escape the fire by submerging themselves in a lake. When the fire has passed by, they discover what has happened. Overwhelmed by grief and anger, they go in search of the older men and kill some of them in revenge.

Again, this last mythic incident represents, symbolically, a typical initiatory sequence: removal of novices from the authority of their "mothers," their seclusion from women (that is, their ritual death, expressed in their mythic death by fire), and the grief of the women at the loss of the young men (the women take revenge on the older men). In short, the Mara myth provides us with a glimpse of the Kunapipi Mother who has not perfected the ritual process of death and rebirth. She must therefore die in order to live spiritually in the form of her emblematic representation. In the Mutjingga myth the process is taken a step further, with the removal of the children alive from her womb. The central-western Northern Territory example gives assurance that Gadjeri has perfected the ritual process of death and rebirth: she is the epitome of all physical and spiritual renewal.

The Ganabuda mythology, on the other hand, poses a paradox which is not so easily explained. The answer lies in the nature of Western Desert mythology and ritual, which, although it emphasizes seasonal renewal and the growth of all species, also underlines the essential unpredictability of natural phenomena and the vulnerability of human beings. Gadjeri's womb is still fertile, but there are still many dangers associated with the ritual (and human) implementation of her life-giving power.

BIBLIOGRAPHY

Berndt, Ronald M. *Kunapipi: A Study of an Australian Aboriginal Religious Cult.* Melbourne, 1951. A study of the Kunapipi cult and ritual, focusing especially on northeastern Arnhem Land; includes songs of some of the major cycles, with interpretations, and dreams reported by participants.

Berndt, Ronald M. "Traditional Morality as Expressed through the Medium of an Australian Aboriginal Religion." In *Australian Aboriginal Anthropology*, edited by Ronald M. Berndt, pp. 216–247. Nedlands, Australia, 1970. This article contains an analysis and interpretation of the Ganabuda mythology and ritual relating to the southeastern Kimberley.

Berndt, Ronald M, and Catherine H. Berndt. Review of *The Eternal Ones of the Dream*, by Géza Róheim. *Oceania* 17 (1946): 67–78. Includes material on Gadjeri, with some illustrations.

Berndt, Ronald M., and Catherine H. Berndt. *Man, Land and Myth in North Australia: The Gunwinggu People.* Sydney, 1970. A study of Gunwinggu society and culture, which covers material on religious myth and ritual, including the western Arnhem Land Kunapipi.

Meggitt, M. J. *Gadjari among the Walbiri Aborigines of Central Australia.* Sydney, 1966. A detailed study of the Gadjeri cult that has been adapted to a fringe Desert sociocultural perspective.

Stanner, W. E. H. "On Aboriginal Religion." *Oceania* 30 (1960): 245–278 and 31 (1961): 233–258. Focuses on the Port Keats area, but in general terms is analytic and interpretative.

Spencer, Baldwin. *Native Tribes of the Northern Territory of Australia.* London, 1914. A classic sourcebook that, although unsystematic in the recording of Aboriginal material, provides clues to a number of features of religious belief.

Warner, William Lloyd. *A Black Civilization: A Study of an Australian Tribe* (1937). New York, 1958. This important study of north-central coastal Arnhem Land society and culture contains empirical material on the Kunapipi (Gunabibi) in that area, and an analysis in relation to other local religious constellations.

Ronald M. Berndt

GALEN (130?–200? CE, or later), Greek physician and philosopher. The last and greatest medical scientist of antiquity, Galen exercised an unparalleled influence on the development of medicine. Galen was born in Pergamum (modern Bergama, Turkey), an important city in western Asia Minor, the only son of Nikon, an architect and geometer. He was educated by his father until the age of fourteen, when he began to attend lectures in philosophy. When Galen was sixteen his father decided that he should become a physician and thereafter spared no expense in his education. After studying under prominent medical teachers in Pergamum, Galen traveled to Smyrna in western Asia Minor, Corinth in Greece, and Alexandria in Egypt, to study medicine.

At the age of twenty-eight he returned to Pergamum, where he was appointed physician to the school of gladiators. This position provided him with broad medical experience that laid the foundation of his later career. In 161 Galen left Pergamum for Rome, where he quickly established a reputation as a successful physician and made many prominent acquaintances. He returned to Pergamum in 166, claiming as the reason the envy of his colleagues, but more probably to escape a severe plague. Shortly after his return, however, he was summoned by the emperor Marcus Aurelius to Aquileia (at the head of the Adriatic), where he was engaged in preparations for war against the Germans. Galen followed the emperor to Rome in 169 and avoided further military service by gaining appointment as physician to the emperor's son Commodus. His position gave him the leisure to pursue medical research, writing, and lecturing, which he did with great success. Not much is known of Galen's later career. He continued to attend Commodus after he ascended the throne in 180 as well as Septimius Severus, who became emperor in 193. The date of Galen's death is uncertain. One source states that he died at the age of seventy, which would be about 200 CE. However, according to Arab biographers, he lived to be over eighty, which would place his death later than 210.

Galen was one of the most prolific authors of classical antiquity. He wrote over four hundred treatises. Many of his works have been lost, including a large number of his philosophical treatises that were destroyed in a fire in the Temple of Peace at Rome in 191. Nearly 140 works in Greek that have survived either in whole or in part are attributed to Galen. Some are of doubtful genuineness and others are spurious. Still other works, while lost in Greek, are extant in Latin and Arabic translations. His writings are extremely diverse and include works on anatomy, pathology, therapeutics, hygiene, dietetics, pharmacy, grammar, ethics, and logic, as well as commentaries on Hippocrates and Aristotle. Most of his extant works deal with medicine. Galen wrote clear Attic Greek, but he was prolix and diffuse and his works are not easy to read. Moreover, he was vain, tactless, and quarrelsome, and his writings are often characterized by a polemical tone.

Galen was a brilliant student of anatomy. His exactness in dissecting primates and other animals (from which he drew inferences for human anatomy) was unequaled in the ancient world. His understanding of the human body and medicine followed traditional lines. He admired Hippocrates, whom he regarded as the repository of medical wisdom, and he claimed merely to reproduce his doctrines. Thus he accepted humoral pathology, which viewed health as the product of an equilibrium of the four humors. The basic principle of life for Galen was the *pneuma* ("spirit"), which he thought responsible for many vital processes. Galen's medical theory is deeply indebted to philosophy, the study of which he believed was essential to the education of a physician. He did not follow exclusively the teachings of any one philosophical school, though he was deeply influenced by Aristotle. As an eclectic, he borrowed freely from most philosophical schools with the exception of the Skeptics and Epicureans, whose doctrines he opposed.

Galen's writings reveal a strong teleological emphasis. He believed that everything had been made by the Creator (or Demiurge) for a divine purpose and that the entire creation bears witness to his benevolence. In his treatise *On the Usefulness of the Parts of the Human Body* he expresses the belief that true piety lies in recognizing and explaining the wisdom, power, and excellence of the Creator rather than in offering a multitude of sacrifices. He accepted the Aristotelian principle that nature does nothing in vain and he attempted to show that every organ was designed to serve a particular function. In the minutest detail the human body exhibits its divine design.

Although Galen believed in one god, his depiction of him as a divine craftsman was drawn not from Judeo-Christian sources, but from Plato's *Timaeus*, as was his argument from design. He criticized Moses for holding (in the account of creation in *Genesis*) the doctrine of *creatio ex nihilo* and the belief that nature was created as an act of God's sovereign will. Galen was acquainted with both Jews and Christians and he refers several times in his philosophical and medical works to their beliefs. He was the first pagan writer to treat Christianity with respect as a philosophy rather than, like most educated Romans, as a superstitious sect. He admired Christians for their contempt of death, sexual purity, self-control in regard to food and drink, and their pursuit of justice: in all of which he regarded them as not inferior to pagan philosophers. He criticized Christians and Jews, however, for their refusal to base their doctrines on reason rather than solely on faith and revealed authority. A group of Roman Christians in Asia Minor, led by Theodotus of Byzantium, attempted in the late second century to present Christianity in philosophical terms. They are said to have admired Galen and it is likely that they were influenced by his philosophical works. They taught an adoptionist Christology, and for this and other heresies they were excommunicated by church authorities.

Galen enjoyed an enviable reputation in his own time both as a physician and as a philosopher. Soon after his death he came to be recognized as the greatest of all medical authorities. His eclecticism, which permitted him to take what was best from all medical sects, his claim to reproduce the ideas of Hippocrates, the encyclopedic comprehensiveness of his medical works, and his greatness as a scientist were largely responsible for his influence. Because his writings were voluminous they were summarized in handbooks, synopses, and medical encyclopedias. The pre-Galenic medical sects gradually disappeared and were replaced by an all-embracing Galenic system that united medicine and philosophy and came to dominate medicine for over a millennium. As anatomical and physiological research ceased in late antiquity, medicine became increasingly scholastic and was taught from a selection of Galen's works.

Galen's direct influence was initially greater in the Byzantine East, where his ideas were relayed by medical encyclopedias, than in the Latin West. In the ninth century many of his works were collected and translated into Arabic and Syriac by Ḥunayn ibn Isḥāq, a Nestorian Arab physician, and his school. In the course of the eleventh century they were translated from Arabic into Latin and Hebrew and came to dominate medicine in the West just as they had dominated Byzantine and Arabic medicine. The authority of Galen was regarded as second only to that of Aristotle. Although a pagan, he appealed equally to Jews, Muslims, and Christians, who found his teleology and monotheism compatible with their own faiths. The appearance of his collected Greek works in the sixteenth century spurred new interest in Galen and led to a revival of medical experimentation. It was during the Renaissance that his reputation reached its apex, but it soon began to be challenged by new discoveries, particularly in the fields of anatomy and physiology. Nevertheless, ideas championed by Galen (particularly humoral pathology) continued to influence medical theory until the nineteenth century.

BIBLIOGRAPHY

The only complete edition of Galen, with Latin translation, remains C. G. Kühn's *Claudii Galeni Opera Omnia*, 20 vols. (1821–1833; reprint, Hildesheim, 1964–1965). While the text is unreliable, Kühn's edition is still useful in the absence of critical editions of most of Galen's works. Several of Galen's treatises have been translated into English. See in particular *Galen on the Usefulness of the Parts of the Body*, 2 vols., translated and edited by Margaret T. May (Ithaca, N.Y., 1968). A representative selection of extracts from Galen's writings is found in *Greek Medicine*, edited and translated by Arthur John Brock (London, 1929), pp. 130–244.

The only comprehensive account in English of Galen's life and work is George Sarton's *Galen of Pergamon* (Lawrence, Kans., 1954); it is, however, brief and not wholly satisfactory. For an extensive discussion of Galen's theology and his attitudes to Christians and Jews, see Richard Walzer's *Galen on Jews and Christians* (Oxford, 1949). On the influence of Galen on medical thought, see Owsei Temkin's *Galenism: Rise and Decline of a Medical Philosophy* (Ithaca, N.Y., 1973).

GARY B. FERNGREN

GALILEO GALILEI (1564–1642), Italian scientist considered to be the father of modern science. Born at Pisa, Galileo received some of his early schooling there. He then was sent to the ancient Camaldolese monastery at Vallombroso, where, attracted by the quiet and studious life, he joined the order as a novice. His father, however, wished him to study medicine and took him to Florence, where Galileo continued his studies with the Camaldolese monks until he matriculated at the University of Pisa in 1581. During his student years at Pisa, Galileo is said to have made his celebrated observation of the sanctuary lamp swinging like a pendulum from the cathedral ceiling and to have thereby discovered that the time taken for a swing was independent of the size of the arc, a fact that he used later for measuring time in his astronomical studies.

Finding that his talents for mathematics and philosophy were increasingly being recognized, Galileo gave up his medical studies and left the university in 1585, without a degree, to begin lecturing at the Florentine academy. There he published an account of his invention of the hydrostatic balance (1586) and then an essay on the center of gravity in solid bodies (1588), which won him a lectureship at Pisa. In 1592 he was appointed professor of mathematics at the renowned University of Padua, where he remained for eighteen years. There, in 1604, he published his laws of motion of falling bodies in his book *De motu*.

In 1597 Galileo wrote to Johannes Kepler that he had been a Copernican "for several years." Having heard in Venice of the newly invented telescope, Galileo immediately constructed one of his own and in 1610 announced many astronomical discoveries. These included his discovery that the Milky Way is made up of innumerable stars and his observation of the satellites of Jupiter. He also made observations of sunspots and of the phases of Venus. Thus he vastly expanded astronomical knowledge and challenged the established natural philosophy, which was based on Aristotelian ideas that had been reconciled with Christian doctrine by Thomas Aquinas. Shortly after the publication of these discoveries, Galileo was appointed philosopher and mathematician to the grand duke of Tuscany.

In 1613, Galileo's *Letters on Sunspots* was published. Its preface claimed that Galileo had been the first to observe sunspots, an assertion that generated bitter resentment among some Jesuit scholars (who had an arguable claim to priority of observation) and that eventually had serious consequences for Galileo. In this book, he first stated in print his unequivocal acceptance of Copernican astronomy, challenging a basic postulate of the Aristotelian view by insisting that all celestial phenomena should be interpreted in terms of terrestrial analogies. Furthermore, Galileo wished to make science independent of philosophy by his assertions that the essence of things cannot be known and that science should concern itself only with the properties of things and with observed events. It was the philosophers rather than the theologians who were the early opponents of the Copernican system and, insofar as he supported it, of Galileo's work. No doubt they were also put off by Galileo's extremely high opinion of himself, and they exploited personal jealousies and resentments against him and tried to enlist the aid of theologians in condemning both Copernican ideas and Galileo's advocacy of them.

Not until 1616, seventy-three years after the publication of Copernicus's *De revolutionibus orbium coelestium* (On the Revolution of the Heavenly Spheres), did the Theological Consultors of the Holy Office declare it "false and contrary to Holy Scripture" and recommend that Copernicus's book be "suspended until corrected." Cardinal Roberto Bellarmino had earlier written to Galileo warning him to confine himself to the realm of hypothesis until demonstrative proof could be produced. When Galileo went to Rome to defend his position, he was officially cautioned neither to hold nor to defend the Copernican ideas. And Galileo, good Catholic that he was (and remained), agreed.

Throughout, Galileo maintained that the purpose of scripture is not to teach natural philosophy and that issues of faith and issues of science should be kept separate and should be settled on different grounds. He quoted Tertullian approvingly: "We conclude that God is known first through nature, and then again, more particularly, by doctrine; by nature in his works, and by doctrine in his revealed word." He also cited Cardinal Césare Baronio, a contemporary, who had quipped, "The Bible tells us how to go to Heaven, not how the heavens go."

The appearance of the great comets in 1618 stirred up much controversy, which Galileo joined by writing his *Discourse on Comets,* annoying the philosophers still further because of his anti-Aristotelian bias. In 1623, Galileo published *The Assayer,* which he dedicated to Urban VIII, the new pope, who was much more favorably disposed toward intellectuals and their work than his predecessor had been. In 1624, Galileo visited Rome and had six audiences with the pope. In 1632, Galileo published his *Dialogue on the Two Great World Systems.* Having intended this book to be "a most ample confirmation" of the Copernican opinion, Galileo in effect had ignored the spirit of the instructions given him by the church in 1616. Neverthless, during the trial that followed the publication of the *Dialogue,* Galileo maintained that he had obeyed the instructions to the letter.

Galileo's trial in 1633 marked the beginning of what has since become a cliché—namely, the idea that science and religion must inevitably be in conflict. Also, Galileo is often seen as science's first martyr in the perennial battle between the church and the spirit of free inquiry. There is no question that the church took a wrong position (contrary to its own tradition in such matters as established by Augustine and Thomas Aquinas); this much was acknowledged by a statement made by John Paul II in 1979, and it was underscored by the Vatican's publication, in 1984, of all documents from its archives relating to Galileo's trial. However, a considerable amount of blame for Galileo's persecution must also fall on the philosophers. Indeed, the decree of sentence issued by the Holy Office was signed by only seven of the ten cardinal-judges.

Unlike innumerable martyrs who have accepted torture or even death for the sake of their convictions, Galileo chose, most unheroically, to abjure his beliefs. (The myth that he, on leaving the tribunal, stamped his foot and said, "Yet it [i.e., the earth] does move," was invented by Giuseppe Baretti in 1757 and has no basis in fact.) Galileo's sentence was then commuted; there was no formal imprisonment. He was allowed to move back to his country estate near Florence, where he resumed his writing. His *Discourses Concerning Two New Sciences,* regarded by many as his greatest scientific contribution, was published in 1638.

[*For further discussion of the Copernican revolution in astronomy, see the biography of Copernicus. For the life and work of Galileo's principal antagonist, see the biography of Bellarmino.*]

BIBLIOGRAPHY

The best scientific biography of Galileo, tracing the historical development of his thought, is Stillman Drake's *Galileo at Work* (Chicago, 1978). A knowledgeable presentation of Galileo's philosophy is Ludovico Geymonat's *Galileo Galilei: A Biography and Inquiry into His Philosophy of Science* (New York, 1965). For Galileo's theological views and accounts of his trial, the following three books are indispensable: Giorgio de Santillana's *The Crime of Galileo* (New York, 1955), Jerome J. Langford's *Galileo, Science and the Church* (Ann Arbor, 1971), and Stillman Drake's *Galileo* (New York, 1980). The play by Bertolt Brecht, *Galileo* (New York, 1966), is tendentious and historically unreliable. Galileo's own views and remarks concerning the relationship between science and religion are scattered throughout his many letters and other writings. Among these the most important are his *Letter to the Grand Duchess Christina* (1615) and *The Assayer* (1623); both of these have been translated by Stillman Drake and are published in his *Discoveries and Opinions of Galileo* (Garden City, N.Y., 1957). The latest, and perhaps the final, effort made by the Roman Catholic church to repair its wrong decision in the case of Galileo is represented by the publication, by the Pontifical Academy of Sciences, of *I documenti del processo di Galileo Galilei* (Rome, 1984), which contains transcriptions of documents relating to Galileo's trial that had been held in the Vatican archives.

RAVI RAVINDRA

GALLICANISM. The political dominance of the papacy during a period of the high Middle Ages was necessarily a temporary phenomenon. In central Europe the political fragmentation that followed Charlemagne's attempt at imperial restoration was not reversed by the efforts of successive German dynasties to establish hegemony and to extend their power beyond the Alps. But in western Europe, territories were consolidated that would ultimately become national states. Their growth in size and complexity, together with developments in secular education, favored the employment of laity rather than ecclesiastics in public office. As the opportunity to build larger state units increased, so did the state's determination to assert its power over agencies within its territory. On the international level this would limit the papacy's capacity to intervene in temporal conflicts; within states, it led to a tightening of lay control over the church's tangible assets.

These changes in the relations of power inevitably brought conflict. In England tensions between crown and church are visible in the twelfth century; in France the harangue of King Philip IV (the Fair) before the first meeting of the Estates General in 1302 is a dramatic statement of the rights of the crown over against the church. In the aftermath of the schism that split the papacy between popes and antipopes, Charles VI spoke of "the traditional liberties of the French church." The fifteenth- and sixteenth-century Spanish monarchy combined centralization with control of the church, and the popes surrendered many ancient prerogatives. In some countries the process of realignment of power culminated in the total control of the church during the Protestant Reformation; in other countries it could promote or retard Catholic reformation. In Roman Catholic countries the doctrine of the state's ascendancy over the church received a variety of names: Gallicanism in France, Febronianism in the German states, cameralism or Josephism in the Habsburg lands, and regalism in Mediterranean countries.

Generically, this swing back to lay dominance in public affairs was a corollary of the growth of modern state power. An early formulation in a decree of the French king Charles VII—the Pragmatic Sanction of Bourges, 1438—contains the major elements that subsequently would be emphasized first, the supremacy of the king over the pope in the temporal affairs of the French church, with a rejection of the pope's right to intervene in these matters; second, the supremacy of regularly convened general councils over the papacy; and third, the cooperation of the crown and the episcopacy in settling French ecclesiastical issues.

Since the boundary between temporal and spiritual is never unambiguous, and since various interest groups interpreted these "Gallican liberties" to meet their specific needs, it is proper to distinguish several Gallicanisms. Royal Gallicanism sought the extension of state power over ecclesiastical appointments and properties, generally through negotiation. Academic Gallicanism usually enlisted a majority of Sorbonne doctors, who strongly defended the independence of the church and the dignity of the papacy but saw the need for some limitations to papal power. The episcopal Gallicanism of the bishops insisted on the control of their dioceses while accepting the crown's full temporal sovereignty in church affairs and the pope's full sovereignty in spiritual matters. Finally, the parliamentary Gallicanism of the superior courts claimed that the Pragmatic Sanction represented the constitution of the French church and that they were its guardians and interpreters; hence no papal document or agent could enter France without prior approval of the Parlement of Paris, which could also declare its jurisdiction over all church issues *(appel comme d'abus)*.

The classic statement of Gallicanism appeared in a conflict between King Louis XIV and Pope Innocent XI involving royal financial control over vacant dioceses. The assembly of the French clergy in 1682 sought to reestablish peace by clearly defining the respective powers of pope, king, and bishops. The Four Gallican Articles, drawn up by the very orthodox bishop Jacques Bénigne Bossuet of Meaux, were intended to be conciliatory. In substance they declared that (1) kings are not subject to any ecclesiastical power in temporal matters;

(2) the reservations of the Council of Constance (1414–1418) on the spiritual supremacy of the pope still apply; (3) the pope is obliged to heed the customs and canons of the Gallican church in the exercise of his functions; and (4) the pope is supreme in matters of faith, but his decisions are not final unless they are confirmed by the judgment of the episcopacy. Although the popes ignored these decrees, Gallicanism retained considerable influence in eighteenth-century France and was generally taught in the seminaries. The Civil Constitution of the Clergy (1790), so decisive in fixing the religious pattern of the French Revolution, had a strong Gallican flavor, as did the seventy-seven Organic Articles unilaterally appended to the Concordat of 1801 by Napoleon.

The clearest example of parliamentary Gallicanism was its use by the Jesuits' Jansenist enemies, who employed it skillfully in securing the suppression of the Society of Jesus in France in 1764. Although many factors contributed to this condemnation, it could not have happened without the strong Gallican—and hence anti-Jesuit—orientation of the judicial bodies.

Gallicanism reached the flood tide of its political influence in the Revolutionary and Napoleonic eras; thereafter its strength ebbed. The sufferings and occasionally the heroism of the popes during this prolonged crisis evoked wide sympathy, not exclusively among the Roman Catholic populations. The disappearance or weakening of the Old Regime monarchs, who had been friendly to Catholicism while striving to control it, created a new political atmosphere in which isolated or persecuted Catholics turned to the papacy for protection. Improvements in communications and other features of modernization assisted. Nearly everywhere in the nineteenth century, ultramontanism, the antithesis of Gallicanism, triumphed. It is ironic that during the century when European nationalism reached its culmination, official Catholicism moved toward greater accent on its international features. Although the early stages of the modern national state system favored the development of Gallicanism, the maturation of the national state saw its virtual disappearance.

[*See also* Ultramontanism. *For broader discussion of church-state issues, see* Church and State.]

BIBLIOGRAPHY

Martimort, A.-G. *Le gallicanisme de Bossuet.* Paris, 1953. Traces the development of Gallican ideas among the bishops, the magistrates, and the ministers of the crown. The best account available of the Extraordinary Assembly of the Clergy of France, 1681–1682.

Martimort, A.-G. *Le gallicanisme.* Paris, 1973. The best introduction to this complicated topic, with the most up-to-date bibliography currently in print. Although brief, it covers an immense span, from Phillip II to the First Vatican Council, with particular attention to the late medieval period. Chapter 7 is useful for its distinctions among the types of Gallicanism.

Martin, Victor. *Les origines du gallicanisme.* 2 vols. Paris, 1939. Martin apparently intended to encompasss the whole movement but ended his work after reaching the Pragmatic Sanction of Bourges. It is an immense mobilization of sources for the earlier period, with an exhaustive index.

Rothkrug, Lionel. *Opposition to Louis XIV: The Political and Social Origins of the French Enlightenment.* Princeton, 1965. A broad perspective on seventeenth-century conflicts. Chapter 1, "The Intellectual and Religious Opposition to Reform," includes a useful sketch of Gallicanism.

Van Kley, Dale. *The Jansenists and the Expulsion of the Jesuits from France, 1757–1765.* New Haven, 1975. The best explanation in English of the use made by the Jansenists of the Gallican attitudes of the Parlements. Particularly helpful in distinguishing the varied forms Gallicanism assumed in the eighteenth century. And it makes an exciting story.

JOSEPH N. MOODY

GAMALIEL OF YAVNEH. *See* Gamli'el of Yavneh.

GAMALIEL THE ELDER. *See* Gamli'el the Elder.

GAMBLING. The religious significance of gambling is, in effect, twofold. Many religious traditions, especially the great religions, in their works of legislation and codification, promote as their orthodox norm a prohibition against, or at least discouragement of, gambling. On the other hand, in many cultures gambling takes on religious significance in connection with myths and rituals.

This twofold simplification, however, addresses gambling only insofar as it takes on overt religious significance. No discussion of gambling would be complete, however, without acknowledging its covert religious significance, particularly in cultures that prohibit it or, having adopted a secularized attitude, look upon it as something nonreligious or merely "cultural." Although beyond the main focus of this essay, it is evident that much of what goes on in the name of secular, cultural, or even legalized gambling is both enhanced by the flaunting or circumvention of traditional prohibitions and heightened by ritualized procedures too numerous to mention, by special "sacred" and "liminal" times (the American Superbowl) and places (casinos in remote or international spots), and by a cast of mythological characters and aspirations (the cool, passionate, roving, or desperate gambler; the jackpot winner).

In definitional terms, religious gambling is not easily

separated from games and divination. Since gambling cannot be discussed without reference to games, I shall speak of games only where they are the focus of wages and stakes. As for divination, the use in certain cases of similar implements (lots, bones, dice) and the occurrence of similar attitudes to unseen forces are not sufficient to support the frequently aired view that gambling derives from divination (Tylor, 1871). One does not, in fact, need implements or games at all to gamble. I shall, however, refer to the drawing of lots and other forms of divination where their use is similar or related to that of gambling practices.

Gambling in Traditional Cultures. Unless one adopts a diffusionist perspective and attempts to derive all forms of gambling from ancient Near Eastern or other Asian prototypes, the prevalence of gambling rites and myths in archaic cultures strongly suggests that the origins of religious gambling are irretrievable. Archaeologists have suggested that the painted pebbles found in the Mas d'Azil caves in the Pyrenees, from the Mesolithic period, are gambling implements. The earliest known dice and board game is that found in the Sumerian royal tombs at Ur, from about 2600 BCE. Gambling can only be assumed here, as with Indus Valley dice from about 2000 BCE and Egyptian (1990–1780 BCE), Cretan (1800–1650 BCE), and Palestinian (c. sixteenth century BCE) finds, some of which resemble cribbage boards. Evidence of ball games and gaming boards from Mesoamerican cultures, of types that continue to be played in that area today, is also traceable to about 1500 BCE. And *Ṛgveda* 10.34 gives us our first gambler's lament in its "Hymn to Gambling" (c. 1200 BCE).

The games of ancient cultures appear not only to be similar to those found in recent and contemporary field contexts but to have had in some cases—such as the Mesoamerican—remarkable continuity from past to present. As the religious significance of gambling is clearly more in a state of living "expression" than belated "application" (Jensen, 1963, pp. 59–64) in contemporary tribal cultures, such cultures present the best evidence for understanding the religious dimensions of gambling in general.

Unfortunately, ethnographic discussion of "sacred" gambling is uneven. We have sufficient documentation to be confident that it is found on all continents and probably among most, if not all, tribal communities. Many games and implements have been described and collected from around the world, but few studies have examined the cultural and religious significance of gambling at the field level in any detailed way. The only thorough field research on gambling seems to be Geertz's study of the Balinese cockfight, and in that situation its rather covert religious significance is tied in with the Balinese version of popular Hinduism (Geertz, 1973). Nonetheless, Geertz's findings and insights are illuminating with respect to a wider view of religious gambling.

Generally, one finds two models for understanding the archaic religious significance of gambling: Geertz's notion of "deep play," a consuming passionate involvement drawing on deeply ingrained cultural codes and strategies, and the pervasively cited notion that gambling games draw on "cosmic symbolism," or have "cosmic significance." Since Geertz mentions calendrical and cosmological ideas that bear upon the choice and placement of cocks (p. 427), it is evident that the two approaches are not antithetical. In fact, the "cosmic significance" clearly lends itself to the "deepening" of the play.

The cosmological significance of gambling games was maintained by Culin, author of several monumental works on games. In his book on North American Indian games, he summarizes the common pattern of references to gambling games in the origin myths of numerous tribes:

> They usually consist of a series of contests in which the demiurge, the first man, the culture hero, overcomes some opponent, a foe of the human race, by exercise of superior cunning, skill, or magic. Comparison of these myths . . . discloses the primal gamblers as those curious children, the divine Twins, the miraculous offspring of the Sun. . . . They live in the east and the west; they rule night and day, winter and summer. They are the morning and evening stars. Their virgin mother, who appears also as their sister and wife, is constantly spoken of as their grandmother, and is the Moon, or the Earth, the Spider Woman, the embodiment of the feminine principle in nature. Always contending, they are the original patrons of play, and their games are now played by men. (Culin, 1907, p. 32)

In Culin's Zuni example, the emblems of the Twin War Gods, their weapons, are classified fourfold in accord with the four directions and are interchangeable with their gaming implements. Thus, for example, stick dice are arrows, shafts, or miniature bows (ibid., p. 33). A correlation between dice and weapons is also made in the Hindu *Mahābhārata* epic.

It is not, in fact, difficult to advance the principle that every game, ancient or modern, creates a miniature cosmos, its arena, rules, apparatus, and players comprising a unique spatiotemporal world that reflects and symbolizes aspects of known and accepted cosmological structures. This is as true of Monopoly, football, or cricket as it is of more traditional games such as snakes and ladders, which in its Indian context symbolized a difficult ascent to heaven (Grunfeld, 1975, pp. 131–133). There are many examples from American Indian cultures of counting boards, playing boards, and ball-game courts having "gateways" or quadrants that correspond to the four directions; to the alternating seasons; to the equinoctial points; to tribal divisions such as men versus women, married women versus single women, old men versus young men; and to moiety divisions identified with heaven and earth, changes in the seasons, or other cosmological referents (Culin, 1907, pp. 34–208 passim). In his careful study of the Mesoamerican ball game, Humphrey (1979) thus allows that "there seems to be no question" that it "was based on a kind of cosmic symbolism." He suggests that the movement of the ball represented the course of heavenly bodies through dualistically conceived upper and lower worlds, the two sides thus enacting the struggle between light and darkness, summer and winter, life and death. The ancient Chinese game of pitchpot (see Yang, 1969, pp. 138–165) may rely on cosmological notions of the pot (or, sometimes, the gourd) as a container of the world and symbol of primal chaos. Also striking in this connection is the ancient Aztec board game of *patolli,* which has evident formal similarities with the South Asian game of *pachisi.* Arguments over whether the similarities are due to diffusion or independent use of similar cosmological structures have remained unresolved since the late nineteenth century. In any case, Beck (1982, pp. 199–205) has argued cogently for the cosmological significance of *pachisi.* The pieces move around the four-armed board, representing the world quarters, in a way that follows the reverse (counterclockwise) movement of the sun through the houses of the zodiac. The four-sided dice are identified with the four Indian ages (*yugas*). The goal of returning to the center thus suggests a triumph over spatiotemporal conditions.

Geertz's discussion of the Balinese cockfight draws its concept of deep play from Jeremy Bentham (1748–1832), the English economist and philosopher, who uses the term to refer to situations in which stakes are so high that participation is irrational. At the cockfight, two kinds of bets are made: even-money center bets between the two cock owners and their allied supporters, and side bets on odds made among the assembled crowd. As a rule, the larger the center bets, the more even are the odds reached in the crowd. Interest and "depth" are thus enhanced by making the outcome appear as unpredictable as possible. But the size of the center bet also "deepens" the stakes for the cock owners. For the stakes here are not just material, but are matters of honor, esteem, status, and, also, delight in bringing oblique affront to the opponent. Except for addicted gamblers, who are drawn—usually to their ruin—to the small center bet and long odds matches, real status remains largely unaffected, since victories and losses tend to balance out. But the deep play at status reversals and reclamations of status is real enough in its psychological and social impact. Only men play, while on the periphery of the cockfight, roulette and other gambling games of sheer chance are operated by concessionaires for women, children, the poor, and others who find themselves excluded.

"Deep-play" cockfighting is thus for "the solid citizenry" and resembles an *"affaire d'honneur"* (Geertz, 1973, pp. 435–436). Moreover, it pits not merely individuals against each other, but corporate groups—most notably, whole villages and patriarchal descent groups. Support money for the central bet comes from other members of the group, and even side-betting against the cock of one's group is considered disloyal. The cock owners thus have not only their own status at stake, but their status within their respective groups and that of the groups themselves.

All of this is displayed "in a medium of feathers, blood, crowds, and money" (ibid., p. 444) that arouses the deepest passions but is rounded off with furtive payments that affirm a cultivated embarrassment at such personal identification with the world of demonic and animal violence. For the cockfight is also, fundamentally, an encounter with the demonic: "a blood sacrifice offered, with the appropriate chants and oblations, to the demons in order to pacify their ravenous, cannibal hunger" (ibid., p. 420). The fights are regularly performed in connection with temple festivals and as collective responses to such natural evils as illness, crop failure, and volcanic eruptions.

A correlation between status—in the largest sense—and deep-play gambling can certainly be found. The importance of status is reflected in the fact that gambling is frequently the province of kings, heroes, and aristocrats: the models of what comes down to us as the genteel bettor. Humphrey (1979, pp. 141–146) has applied Geertz's categories to the aristocratic patronage of the Mesoamerican ball game. But still better confirmation for such an analysis comes from descriptions of the North American Huron Indian dice games collected by Culin (1907, pp. 105–110). Sacrificial offerings of tobacco to the spirits of the game precede the action. Sometimes whole townships and even tribes contend. In one eight-day game between townships, every inhabitant of each party threw the dice at least once. Players with lucky dreams were sought out for the casting:

> At this game they hazard all they possess, and many do not leave off till they are almost stripped quite naked and till they have lost all they have in their cabins. Some have been known to stake their liberty for a time. . . . The players appear like people possessed, and the spectators are not more calm. They all make a thousand contortions, talk to the

> bones [i.e., throw the dice], load the spirits of the adverse party with imprecations. . . . They quarrel and fight, which never happens among [them] but on these occasions and in drunkenness. (ibid., pp. 105–106)

Women and girls play the same game, but only separately and under inferior conditions: with different numbers of dice, and throwing by hand on a blanket rather than with a dice box or basket as the men do (ibid., p. 107).

Gambling on one's freedom is an ultimate status wager and is a type of bet instanced in many cultures. Another suggestive feature of deep play that emerges here is the significance of "stripping," for being willing to gamble all one possesses may both literally and figuratively involve such an outcome. Loss of status is thus potentially far more than just loss of face. As Geertz remarks, there is both a literal and a metaphoric significance—sustained by the Balinese language as in the English—to the Balinese cockfighter's identification with his cock (Geertz, 1973, pp. 417–418). I shall note important recurrences of this gambling-stripping correlation, which has a wide range of effects, from deep humiliation to eroticism. Obviously, strip poker is a "secular" example of the latter orientation.

Ritualized gambling thus seems to rely on both its cosmological significance and its character as deep play. The forces of chance draw the contestants into deep involvement in a context that allows for both the regulated breakdown and the creative redefinition of the structural roles by which society and cosmos operate—a context that the games reflect. The games thus have the character of liminal passage rites, or ordeals (Humphrey, 1979, p. 144), as well as of reiterations of the cosmogony, the reestablishment of cosmos out of chaos. Such initiatory and cosmogonic overtones have been detected in the dice match that concluded the ancient Indian sacrifice of royal consecration, or *rājasūya*. In playing dice on even terms with members of different castes, the king overcomes the forces of chance, chaos, and confusion by his triumph (Heesterman, 1957, pp. 140–157). As is often the case in ritual gambling, the game is rigged to assure the desired outcome. But the important point is that the participants submit to the principles of the game. Similar initiatory and cosmogonic overtones are found in contexts where gambling is performed for the sick, over the dead, or at turning points in the seasons (for examples, see Culin, 1907, pp. 108–115; Hartland, 1924–1927, pp. 168–169; Jensen, 1963, p. 60).

Prohibitions on Gambling. The principles by which different religions have denounced or prohibited gambling are revealing on two fronts. First, they reflect the axiomatic theological and cultural values operative in the respective traditions. Second, they often provide theologically and culturally attuned indications of what it is that is so appealing about what they seek to oppose. Not surprisingly, cosmological significance and deep-play involvement are among the condemned attractions.

In *Isaiah* 65:11–12, gambling is thus one of the ways by which Israel provokes the Lord: "[You] who set up a table for Fortune and fill cups of mixed wine for Destiny, I will destine you to the sword." Gad (Fortune) and Meni (Destiny) were gods of fortune, possibly of Syrian or Phoenician origin. The polemic against gambling is thus made in the same terms as that against idolatry, which in turn is a polemic against involvement in false cosmologies ruled by false gods. The context also suggests that such gambling was, at least to the mind of the prophet, one of the alluring vices of acculturation besetting Israel. This attitude persists in Talmudic and rabbinic prohibitions against a variety of games, from the Greek Olympics to cards and chess, which Jews regarded themselves as having adopted from their neighbors. But it is particularly those games that involve gambling that are singled out for condemnation. The Mishnah declares twice that dice players and pigeon racers are disqualified from appearing as witnesses in a court of justice (*R. ha-Sh.* 1.8; *San.* 3.3), and the medieval Sefardic philosopher Mosheh ben Maimon (Maimonides, 1135/8–1204) extends the ban to include those who play chess for money (Commentary on *Sanhedrin* 3.3). This disqualification rests on the principle that gamblers are guilty of facilitating acts of robbery and are thus, in effect, criminals. Curiously, gamblers are similarly disqualified in Hindu law books, joined to thieves, assassins, and other dangerous characters for being "incompetent on account of their depravity" and persons in whom no truth can be found (*Nārada Smṛti* 1.159, 1.178; *Bṛhaspati Dharmaśāstra* 7.30).

The passage from *Isaiah* also introduces another strain of condemnation: using the same Hebrew root in two words, Yahveh "destines" to the sword those who tempt "Destiny." Such a scene is, in fact, played out in another passage from *Isaiah,* where the *rabshakeh* (field marshal) of the Assyrian king Sennacherib challenges Israel to a wager over horses, and to an additional (though implied) theological wager—expressed by boasts referring to Yahveh as a fallible god like those of the surrounding nations—that Yahveh cannot deliver Israel. The wager over the horses is ignored, but the arrogant theological presumption of the affront to the Lord results in the salvation of Jerusalem and Sennacherib's death by the sword (*Is.* 36–37).

If gambling was denounced in the Bible, however, the

casting of lots was not. The throwing of lots with the Urim and Tummim (Yes and No), articles kept in the priest's apron, was accepted as a means of discerning the divine will. Thus Saul was chosen by lot to be king (*1 Sm.* 10:20–21); rural priests were chosen by lot to serve in Jerusalem (*1 Chr.* 24–25); and Matthias was selected by lot to become Judas's successor as the twelfth apostle (*Acts* 1:26). In these instances, the casting of lots cannot be called gambling. But it is also evident that Israel knew of the use of lots for gambling, though the references suggest that it was only other nations that so employed them. In *Joel* 3:1–3, Yahveh speaks of bringing judgment upon the nations for "having divided up my land" and "cast lots for my people." And in *Psalms* 22:16–18, the psalmist, seeing himself dead, describes the "company of evildoers" who "divide my garments among them, and for my raiment cast lots." It is this latter passage that is taken in *John* 19:23–24 as a prophecy of the scene at Jesus' crucifixion, where the Roman soldiers divide up the crucified Christ's garments and gamble for his seamless tunic. Here the symbolism of stripping and gambling accentuates the deepest humiliation and suffering (see *Mk.* 15:16–20, 25; *Mt.* 27:28–29, 36).

Early Christian canon law condemned gambling in no uncertain terms. Two of the so-called Apostolic Canons (41, 42) prohibited both laity and clergy, under pain of excommunication, from engaging in games of chance. And at the Council of Elvira (AD 306), the seventy-ninth canon decreed a year's banishment from communion for anyone guilty of gambling. But restrictions of later councils were directed toward the clergy, and only certain games (especially cards and dice) were forbidden (Slater, 1909, pp. 375–376). Such relaxing of restrictions on lay gambling has facilitated church sponsorship of bingo and lottery games in fund-raising efforts. The same is true in Orthodox churches.

Christian condemnations of gambling gather their fullest force in Puritan writings. According to the doctrine of predestination, since every action is foreordained, matters of so-called chance are in the hands of God alone. To invoke God in the name of fortune is to offend him "by making him the assistant in idle pleasures" (Knappen, 1939, p. 439). Similarly, man is but a steward of his goods, which ultimately belong to God. Thus he must not wager what is truly God's (Paton, 1924, p. 166). Furthermore, losers at gambling tend to express themselves in curses.

A rather practical Islamic stance is expressed in the Qur'ān when Muḥammad discourages wine and a form of gambling with arrows in which the loser pays for a young camel that is slaughtered and given to the poor: "In both there is sin and profit to men; but the sin of both is greater than the profit of the same" (Palmer, 1880, p. 32).

The Hindu law books are full of cautionary remarks on gambling. As noted already, gamblers are judged incompetent witnesses in matters of law. There are statements that gambling makes one impure, and that the wealth obtained by gambling is tainted. Most significant, however, is a passage from the *Laws of Manu* concerning the duties of kings: of the royal vices, ten are born of pleasure and eight of anger, and all end in misery; of the ten that "spring from love of pleasure," the most pernicious are drinking, dice, women, and hunting (7.45–50). This list of four vices recurs in the *Mahābhārata* (3.14.7) in the mouth of the divine Kṛṣṇa when he denounces the epic's famous dice match. Kṛṣṇa adds that gambling is the worst "desire-born" vice of all. Thus we seem to have here a condemnation of gambling as deep play. This correlation between gambling and desire takes us to the very heart of the Indian meditation on gambling, for actions born of desire are binding to this world. Yet in Hindu terms it is also the things of desire—including the four just mentioned—that draw man to the divine. Thus, whereas Kṛṣṇa here warns of gambling's dangers, when he reveals his "supernal manifestations" in the *Bhagavadgītā* he claims to be identical with the game of dice itself: "I am the gambling of rogues" (10.36).

Buddhist tradition sustains the same critique of gambling without such accent on the ambiguity. In the sixteenth chapter of the *Parabhava Sutta,* the Buddha includes addiction to women, strong drink, and dice as one of eleven combinations of means whereby men are brought to loss. The text contrasts these eleven roads to ruin with the one path to victory: loving the *dhamma,* the Buddha's teaching. Elsewhere, monks are warned that numerous games and spectacles—including combats between elephants, horses, buffalo, bulls, goats, rams, and cocks; various board games; chariot racing; and dicing—are addictive distractions and detrimental to virtue (*Tevijja Sutta, Majjhima Sīlam* 2–4).

Gambling Gods, Demons, and Heroes. Yet even the gods—not to mention their demonic adversaries—are wont to gamble. Yahveh makes an implied wager with Satan that Job will remain blameless and upright when deprived of all he has (*Jb.* 1:6–12). In Christian traditions, the devil continues to gamble for the human soul, as in Stephen Vincent Benét's story *The Devil and Daniel Webster* (1937). In Tibet, an annual ceremony was performed in which a priest representing a grand lama played dice with a man dressed as a demonic ghost king. With fixed dice, the priest won, chasing the demon away and confirming the truth of the teaching (Waddell, 1895, p. 512). In India, the two lowest of the four dice throws are demonic. Thus in the epic story of Nala and Damayantī, one demon (Dvāpara) enters the dice, and the other (Kali) "possesses" the hero, dooming him to lose all he has won (*Mahābhārata* 3.55–56). But the Hindu gods play anyway, and are even, as we have seen, identified with gambling. This is true not only of Kṛṣṇa but, more decisively, of Śiva, who is from very early times the lord of gamblers, and who plays dice in classical myths with his wife Pārvatī.

As noted, Indian dice are named after the four ages (*yugas*), which "roll" four by four a thousand times within the larger time unit of the *kalpa*. The dice play of the divine couple thus represents the continuity of the universe and their absorption with and within it. This "deep play" is one expression of the theological concept of *līlā*, literally "divine play" or "divine sport." The game's disruption holds the implication of the end of the universe (the *mahāpralaya*), while its resumption holds the implication of the re-creation (the cosmogony). But insofar as the game is associated with the rise and fall of the *yugas*, it is played ritually at liminal temporal junctures in which the continuity of the universe is imperiled. Śiva and Pārvatī thus provide the mythic model for those who play dice ritually at the festival of Dīwali (Dīpāvali), which marks a traditional new year. And it is at the mythic juncture of the Dvāparayuga and the Kaliyuga that the great dice match of the *Mahābhārata* occurs.

One of the most important themes that unites the dice play of Śiva and Pārvatī with the dice match of the *Mahābhārata* is that of stripping. The stakes for which Śiva and Pārvatī play are their clothes and ornaments. When Śiva loses his loincloth, he gets angry, goes off naked, or refuses to pay up. Pārvatī points out that he never wins, except by cheating (O'Flaherty, 1973, pp. 204, 223, 247). Thus it never comes to pass that both of them are reduced to nakedness, which would imply their merger as Śiva and Śakti, Puruṣa and Prakṛti, at the *mahāpralaya*. What is striking about the dice match in the *Mahābhārata* is that after the five Pāṇḍava brothers have gambled away everything, even their freedom and their wife-in-common, Draupadī, the culminating act is the attempt by the winners (the Kauravas) to disrobe the heroine in front of her husbands and the whole assembly. As Draupadī is an incarnation of the Goddess, the miraculous intervention by Kṛṣṇa that prevents her stripping is a sign that the dissolution of the universe will not occur in untimely fashion during the intra-*yuga* period in which the story is set.

We see, then, that divine gambling involves persistent encounters with the demonic. Hindu materials carry this theme to great depths, accentuating a continuum between demonic possession and divine rapture. In South Indian *terukkūttu* ("street-drama") folk plays that enact the epic story, the attempts by the Kaurava Duḥśāsana to disrobe Draupadī result in his demonic possession, while Draupadī at the same time experiences the most sublime *bhakti* ("divine love"). On the divine-demonic turf of gambling, in fact, no hero can hope to win without recourse to the powers that hold the demonic in check. The hero is thus the one who is willing to take the risk, even against the seemingly highest odds. It is striking how many epics include episodes of gambling, and even more striking how frequently the "good" hero loses, awaiting final triumph or vindication elsewhere. This occurs not only in the *Mahābhārata* but in Indian folk epics as well. In the Tamil folk epic *The Elder Brother's Story*, the twin brothers play six games of dice with Viṣṇu at intervals preceding dramatic turns of fortune, the last of which is their death (Beck, 1982, p. 143). In the Telegu epic *The Heroes of Palnāḍu*, a cockfight wager divides irreparably the two camps of half brothers, and a game of tops and a dice match between another set of younger brothers in the heroic camp foreshadow the events that lead to their death. In recent years, actual cockfights have been outlawed at the festivals at which these stories are recited (Roghair, 1982, pp. 30 and 62–295 passim). In the Tibetan epic of Ge-sar of Ling, the hero repeatedly plays *mōs* (see Waddell, 1895, pp. 465–474), a game of divination using colored pebbles, before his adventures. Here the lots fall out in the divine hero's favor. In the Mwindo epic of the Nyanga people of the Congo Republic, the hero Mwindo plays *wiki*, a gambling game with seeds. Mwindo plays in the underworld against the supreme divinity of fire, first losing everything and then winning it back, in an effort to reclaim his antagonistic father from the underworld with a view toward their reconciliation.

Yet there is another dimension to the stance of the heroic gambler that figures, at least metaphorically, in all the great religions of faith: that of the person who may lose everything, or be stripped like Job or Draupadī, but will not gamble away salvation. In positive terms, this is the wager that God exists, the famous wager that Pascal set forth with such precision in his *Pensées* (1670):

> But here there is an infinity of infinitely happy life to be won, one chance of winning against a finite number of chances of losing. That leaves no choice; wherever there is infinity, and where there are not infinite chances of losing against that of winning, there is no room for hesitation. You must give everything. And thus, since you are obliged to play, you must be renouncing reason if you hoard your life rather than risk it for an infinite gain, just as likely to occur as a loss amounting to nothing. (Krailsheimer, 1966, p. 151)

Pascal is thus at pains to show that the central bet, as in the Balinese cockfight, is for even money.

[*See* Chance *for a discussion of the cosmological framework of gambling. See also* Divination *and* Games.]

BIBLIOGRAPHY

A good bibliography, mainly on the history and legislation of European and American gambling, is found in Stephen Powell's *A Gambling Bibliography, Based on the Collection, University of Nevada, Las Vegas* (Las Vegas, 1972). Valuable encyclopedia articles include those by J. L. Paton on "Gambling," E. Sidney Hartland on "Games," and G. Margoulith on "Games (Hebrew and Jewish)," in the *Encyclopaedia of Religion and Ethics,* edited by James Hastings, vol. 6 (Edinburgh, 1913); T. Slater's "Gambling," in *Catholic Encyclopedia,* vol. 6 (New York, 1909); and R. F. Schnell's "Games OT," in *The Interpreter's Dictionary of the Bible,* edited by George Arthur Buttrick (New York, 1962).

For theoretical discussion, see Edward Burnett Tylor's *Primitive Culture,* vol. 1, *The Origins of Culture* (1871; reprint, New York, 1958), pp. 78–83, emphasizing diffusion and divination, and Charles John Erasmus's "Patolli, Pachisi, and the Limitation of Possibilities," *Southwestern Journal of Anthropology* 6 (1950): 369–387, which evaluates Tylor's views and various opposing views (including those of Robert Stewart Culin). On "play" in different aspects, see Adolf E. Jensen's *Myth and Cult among Primitive Peoples,* translated by Marianna Tax Choldin and Wolfgang Weissleder (Chicago, 1963), pp. 59–64, and, especially, Clifford Geertz's *The Interpretation of Cultures: Selected Essays* (New York, 1973), pp. 412–453, on the Balinese cockfight. Recent proceedings of the Association for the Anthropological Study of Play (ATASP) are worth consulting, especially for the following: Bernard Mergen's "Reisman Redux: Football as Work, Play, Ritual and Metaphor" and Robert L. Humphrey's "Suggestions for a Cognitive Study of the Mesoamerican Ball Game," in *Play as Context* (ATASP Proceedings, 1979), edited by Alyce Taylor Cheska (West Point, N.Y., 1981), and Pierre Ventur's "Mopan Maya Dice Games from the Southern Peten," in *Play and Culture* (ATASP Proceedings, 1980), edited by Helen B. Schwartzman (West Point, N.Y., 1980).

On documentation, see Frederic V. Grunfeld's *Games of the World* (New York, 1975), for informed discussion with illustrations. On American Indian games, see the classic study by Robert Stewart Culin, *Games of the North American Indians,* "Bureau of American Ethnology Report," no. 24 (1907; reprint, Washington, D.C., 1973). See also Rafael Karsten's "Ceremonial Games of the South American Indians" (in English), *Societas Scientarum Fennica: Commentationes Humanarum Litterarum,* vol. 3, pt. 2 (Helsinki, 1930); Jan C. Heesterman's *The Ancient Indian Royal Consecration* (The Hague, 1957); Lien-Sheng Yang's *Excursions in Sinology* (Cambridge, Mass., 1969); L. Austune Waddell's *The Buddhism of Tibet, or Lamaism* (1895; reprint, Cambridge, 1958). On prohibitions of gambling, see the articles by Hartland, Paton, and Slater mentioned above; M. M. Knappen's *Tudor Puritanism* (Chicago, 1939); and *The Qur'an,* translated by E. H. Palmer in "Sacred Books of the East," vol. 6 (1880; reprint, Delhi, 1970).

On gambling in myths and epics, see Wendy Doniger O'Flaherty's *Asceticism and Eroticism in the Mythology of Śiva* (Oxford, 1973); Brenda E. F. Beck's *The Three Twins: The Telling of a South Indian Folk Epic* (Bloomington, Ind., 1982); Gene H. Roghair's *The Epic of Palnāḍu: A Study and Translation of Palnāṭi Vīrula Katha* (Oxford, 1982); Alexandra David-Neel's *The Superhuman Life of Gesar of Ling,* translated by Violet Sydney, rev. ed. (London, 1959); and Daniel P. Biebuyck and Kohombo C. Mateene's *The Mwindo Epic* (Berkeley, 1969). On Pascal's wager, see Blaise Pascal's *Pensées,* translated by A. J. Krailsheimer (Harmondsworth, 1966).

ALF HILTEBEITEL

GAMES are analytically distinguished from other forms of contest by being framed as "play" and from other forms of play by their competitive format and the institutional—public, systematic, and jural—character of their rules. The American anthropologist Gregory Bateson (1972, pp. 177–193) has described the universal semantic process by which behaviors are framed as play. Conventionalized signals create a "metamessage" that instructs players not to take the behaviors they engage in as denoting what those behaviors would denote in other, nonplay, contexts. In this sense, game actions are "untrue." A nip is not a bite, a bullfight is not a hunt, a checkmate is not a regicide, a soccer match is not a war, a wrestling bout or footrace is not a cosmogony or theogony, regardless of overt similarities in the words, objects, gestures, emotional states, or social categories of persons involved. The framing of contests as play makes them self-referential in several ways, shifting attributed motivation to intrinsic enjoyment and sociability, turning means into ends in themselves, and understanding extrinsic outcomes as "mere" contingencies. [*See* Play.]

Yet, paradoxically, as Bateson and many other theorists of play have noted, the prior and consensual assertion of untruth, in the sense of disconnection from standard meanings, makes assertions of truthful correspondences between the worlds of nonplay and play possible, likely, and even predominant over a discourse of "set-apartness." Like other play forms, games are about boundaries and the boundaries between boundaries. Games create, in the phrases of the English psychoanalyst D. W. Winnicott (1971), a world of "transitional objects," a realm of the "not-not-true." Freedom from denotation makes rich freedom for connotation, for human individuals and groups to re-represent their lives to themselves in "experimental" ways. Alternative or virtual realities, including those asserted by religion, can thus be tested against what the phenomenologist Alfred Schutz termed "the paramount realities of everyday life."

Play in Culture: The Religious Character of Games. Contest and representation are basic aspects of play, argued the Dutch historian Johan Huizinga in his manifesto *Homo Ludens,* and they may "unite in such a way that the game 'represents' a contest or else becomes a contest for the best representation of something" (1955, p. 13). The materials of games are drawn from the sociocultural world and at the same time stand in figurative relations—metaphoric, analogical, symbolic—with it. "The more profound, double sense of 'social game,'" said the German sociologist Georg Simmel, "is not only that the game is played in a society (as its external medium) but that, with its help, people actually 'play' 'society,'" including the society of the gods (1950, p. 50). Particularly where enjoyment, competition, and gambling supply strong motivations to attend to the progress and outcome of games, this setting of the empirical world in juxtaposition with "another" world can lead to an interrogation of their relationship sufficient to involve ultimate epistemological questions and functional necessities of human existence. On this general ground, the appearance of game forms in the religious mythologies and cults of various peoples has been explained by writers and scholars, some of whom have gone on to find in the ludic process a mode of transcendence and, therefore, an essential aspect of the religious imagination itself.

Among Western humanists, Huizinga has perhaps been the boldest in this regard. In *Homo Ludens,* he argued for "the identity of play and ritual" and even claimed, on the authority of Plato, that the sacred can be comprised in the category of play (pp. 18–19). "God alone is worthy of supreme seriousness," so Huizinga translated Plato (*Laws* 7.803), "but man is made God's plaything, and that is the best part of him. . . . What then is the right way of living? Life must be lived as play, playing certain games, making sacrifices, singing and dancing, and then a man will be able to propitiate the gods, and defend himself against his enemies, and win the contest." Whether Plato really meant to identify "play and holiness" so thoroughly can be disputed. Moreover, as the final clause of Huizinga's reading of Plato suggests, classicists have found reason to doubt that the "for-their-own-sake" character Huizinga believed crucial to "true play and games" was really present or developed in classical Greek ideology.

From the famous stadium games to the isomorphic agonistic ethos and format in other cultural domains, elements that together comprise what historians and sociologists from Jakob Burckhardt (1898–1902) to Alvin W. Gouldner (1965) have styled the "Greek contest system," functional requirements, inextricably civic and religious, do not appear to have been culturally "bracketed off" as contingencies in the classical world, as they have been in that stream of European thought that Huizinga so well represented. In Greek mythology and theology, in notable contrast to Christianity, the gods themselves played games, chartered the games of human beings, and intervened in them as "co-players." In athletic games—as the poetry of Pindar makes evocatively plain—individual fate, the polity, and the divine world found a preferential idiom of communication in archaic and classical Greek culture, such that an *axis mundi,* in the sense discussed by Mircea Eliade, could be created in the person of the victorious athlete.

The Olympic games, the Delphic oracle, and Homeric poetry emerged together in the eighth century BCE as pan-Hellenic institutions, just as the segmentary and rivalrous city-state was arising as the dominant form of social organization within the Greek world. Relations among these key institutions are apparent in the traditions of the ancient Olympic games. Homeric theology and hero cults came to inform the charter myths of the games at Olympia, and a famous oracle at Delphi (where crown games were also celebrated) "renewed" the sanction from Zeus, to whose worship the Olympic festival was devoted. The great games gave rise to practices seeking to distinguish Greek from non-Greek (*barbaroi* were not to compete at Olympia) and to mediate between Greek mythic and human time. Though its significance is much debated, the reckoning of dates according to the formula "in the second year of the Olympiad in which so-and-so won the *stade*" provided Greece with her main calendar of historical time beyond city-state and regional limitations.

One mythic tradition ascribes the foundation of the Olympic games to Idean Herakles, another to Pelops's victory over King Oenomaus in a chariot race for the latter's daughter Hippodamia ("horse woman"). Here, as in the related story of Atalanta in the Greek corpus and in other Indo-European contexts, comparative mythologists such as James G. Frazer, Georges Dumézil, Eliade, and Bernard Jeu have recognized a repeated pattern associating sacred marriage *(hieros gamos),* an implicit theogony (often of newer gods over older ones), the acquisition of transforming technology (fire, the horse, metallurgy, the chariot), the domestication of invader kings ("Dorians" in the Greek case), and the athletic race that embodies, mediates, and "resolves" these generative contests between vigorous and dying god-kings, male and female, earth and heaven, nature and culture, cosmos and history.

Games transform ambiguous, perturbed, or disputed potentials and conditions into certain outcomes, and this is one reason for their widespread association, in myth or in practice, with such ritualized natural and social transitions as seasonal cycles, birth, initiation, marriage, funerals, and warfare. Furthermore, games necessarily incorporate a dialectic between hierarchy and equality, two central organizing principles of human social arrangements and cognitive functioning. From an (at least asserted or presumed) equality before the rules of the game results a ranked hierarchy of outcomes. Societies and theologies differ in the relative valuation placed on hierarchy and equality in human and divine affairs and, thus, differentially emphasize one or the other pole in games. Yet for all known social types, games appear, in the expression of the French anthropologist Claude Lévi-Strauss, to be "good to think with" and, as the present-day Olympic games forcefully illustrate, may permit highly diverse and rivalrous social formations to compete cooperatively. If games have been seen as "the moral equivalent of war," it is because warfare and other means of political and ideological domination, including religion, have their moral dimensions.

Ingomar Weiler (1981) finds the "contest system" not limited to Greece but widespread in the ancient Mediterranean world, and scholars like Huizinga emphasize parallels to the Greek and Roman materials in non-Western warrior-states. In the Hindu *Mahābhārata,* the world is conceived as a game of dice between Śiva and his queen (8.2368, 8.2381), and a dice match for the kingdom sets off the conflict between the Kauravas and the Pāṇḍavas that organizes the epic. "I am the dicing of tricksters," says Kṛṣṇa in the *Bhagavadgītā* (10.36), and forms of *līlā,* or sacred play, are widely associated with this god and his worship. According to Marcel Granet (1930), the Chinese cosmic duality of *yin* and *yang* replayed important social dualisms; festal, magical competitions of many sorts were both the central agencies for regenerating life in the early "tribal" period and a means by which the later transformation to state institutions was accomplished. The Spanish philosopher Ortega y Gasset likewise argued for the "sportive origin of the state" out of primitive institutions of ritual contest involving both cosmological and social sanctions.

The ethnology of nonliterate "primitive" societies provided further rich material for such humanistic speculations. In his elaborate compendium *Games of the North American Indians,* Stewart Culin observed the common occurrence of game motifs in the origin myths of a wide variety of linguistically and culturally unrelated tribes. The complementarity in rivalry of the "divine twins"—associated with oppositions between night and day, winter and summer, east and west, morning and evening stars, consanguinal and affinal kin—or of a demiurgic First Man or First Woman with monsters, nature, or each other is a widespread motif. In folklore, culture-creating heroes—Coyote, Raven, or Spider—are frequently trickster beings whose fondness for games, as with other supernaturals, is both a source of their power and a means by which they can be manipulated for human moral or material purposes. As to adult human games, which he divided into those of "chance" and those of "dexterity," Culin concluded that "In general, [they] appear to be played ceremonially, as pleasing to the gods, with the object of securing fertility, causing rain, giving and prolonging life, expelling demons, or curing sickness" (Culin, 1975, p. 34).

Theories regarding the "Desacralization" of Games. This stress on the religious character of games in the cultures of exotic or prestigiously ancestral "others" was generated by and contributed to those broader evolutionist trends of European thought variously styled "rationalization," "modernization," and "secularization." Huizinga and other philosophers of history, while seeking to show the essential unity of humankind in play, nevertheless saw games as becoming progressively "secularized" through "universal cultural history." British classicists, most notably Jane E. Harrison, proposed the view that games—like such other forms of cultural expression as theater, dance, music, and poetry—had separated from an original religious ritual matrix in the primitive and ancient worlds. Where games were seen to retain magical or religious elements, such as peasant Shrovetide football matches in the "folk cultures" of early modern France and England or the grand *sumō* tournaments of Shintō Japan or the various martial arts competitions in monastic communities of the Near and Far East, these were interpreted as backward "survivals" of an archaic past in "fossil" social structures still partially attuned in cult to cosmological and agricultural rhythms. Such views fit well with the nineteenth-century development of Western social science, centered around a purported evolutionary passage—"of potentially universal significance," as Max Weber put it—from "traditional" to "modern" societies under the impact of the industrial revolution and modern science. From important means by which communities represented their ultimate concerns to themselves and engaged in imitative worship, games became associated, in such Western eyes, with the sphere of secular leisure, recreation, mass entertainment: "mere games" of undoubted commercial or social value but of little sacred or spiritual significance.

While still very influential, the "modernization" point of view has been criticized as Eurocentric and imperialist. Moreover, social history has shown that in the West itself religion has not regularly and inevitably declined and that the cultural history of forms like games has not followed any simple unilinear pattern. As symbolized by the emperor Theodosius's suppression of the Olympic games as a "pagan rite," early Christianity did indeed oppose itself to Greek (and certainly Roman) traditions of public games, save in the appropriation of athletics as an ascetic metaphor by canonical writers like the apostle Paul. A centuries-long tradition culminating in continental and English "puritanism" did seek to suppress games, gambling, and other forms of folk amusement as "works of the devil" that turned the Christian away from sober religious duty, the social predominance of the churches, and disciplined labor. Through much of the twentieth century, religious leaders and sociologists alike have attributed declining church attendance, where it has occurred, in part to the increasing popularity of sports events and other kinds of mass recreation on the Sabbath.

Yet contrary trends are everywhere in evidence. In the Middle Ages, the church may have turned against the cult of the body in athletic games, but it attached itself to the medieval tournament. In the contemporary *palio* horse race of Siena, Italy, which dates back to the eleventh century, the cult of the Virgin Mary and priestly blessings of the rival *contrade* are central features of the ritual contest. In nineteenth-century England, devout Anglican schoolmasters and Christian socialists, like Thomas Hughes and Charles Kingsley, played the central role in elaborating the ideology of "muscular Christianity," that combination of athletic games, virility, fair play, courage, and defense of the weak associated with a new *imitatio Christi,* on the one side, and with English colonialism, on the other. Many contemporary English soccer clubs are descended from church organizations, and missionaries in the British Empire sought not only to suppress the indigenous games of conquered peoples, particularly those with overt sexual and magical content, but to replace them with cricket, soccer, hockey, and running as "schools of Christian character." Upon decolonization in "new nations"—as East African long-distance running, Trobriand and Caribbean cricket, and Indian field hockey indicate—these game forms have often been retained, but transformed to reaccommodate indigenous cultural values or to serve "civil" or "national" religion, whether in the form of an explicit cult of the state or a more diffuse "functional equivalent" of traditional religious institutions. In dialectical concert with enduring ludic forms bent to "nativist" purposes—West African wrestling, Native American running (see Nabokov, 1981), central Asian *buzkashi,* Japanese *sumō,* or the Balinese cockfight made famous by the anthropologist Clifford Geertz (1972)—such transformations of imposed forms illustrate the inadequacies of any unilineal or evolutionary theory of world history and the place of games within it. Again in the Judeo-Christian context, home of such theories, present-day developments—from a skiing pope, decorated with the Olympic Order, to the incipient interlock between the directorates of the World Council of Churches and the International Olympic Committee, to the widespread activity of Christian athletes in domestic and foreign missionizing—further illustrate the labile relations between religion and games. Nor are such relations limited to practical and institutional exigencies. The recent "theology of play" movement in Christian religious circles (see Moltmann, 1972), with its rebellious attempt to reshape the image of the deity and its arguments that in the freedom and joy of games and festivity humans achieve a foretaste of the kingdom of heaven, suggests how the potentials for transcendence in play must ever draw religion into a dialogue with ludic form and experience. Even religions whose orthodox or mainstream versions may find less explicit place for play in their theophanies, cults, and ethics—Judaism, Christianity, and Islam, perhaps in contrast to Hinduism, Buddhism, and many tribal religions—must preoccupy themselves with what comparative religionist David L. Miller (1970, p. 14) calls "the game game," that effort to discover, articulate, and conform to an "ultimate reality" that sets a limit to divine and human manipulation.

Games and Social Life. Dissatisfaction with evolutionist or modernization perspectives has led to closer attention by theorists to the types and internal properties of games. The French sociologist of religion Roger Caillois suggested in *Man, Play, and Games* (1961) that games can be usefully placed along a continuum from *paidia* (relatively unstructured, spontaneous, labile forms typified by many children's games) to those of *ludus* (more conventionalized, jural, and elaborated forms). All true games, however, minimally involve specification of a goal for action, delimitations of space and time, selection of some subset of possibilities in a total action field as relevant and permissible (the "moves" of the game), rules for the initial apportioning of resources and roles and their reapportioning in the course of play, and criteria for evaluating the outcomes (success or failure, winning or losing). By selectively emphasizing features of this core structure of games, a number of classification schemes have been generated to reveal dominant metaphysical assumptions and to model theoretically how individuals and groups "play society."

Like most continental game theorists, Caillois focused on the experiential aspects of game types. Seeking not merely a sociology of games but a "sociology derived from games," Caillois subsumed all games under four categories: agon (competition), alea (chance), mimicry (simulation), and ilinx (vertigo). This scheme is helpful in parsing the religious functions associated with types of games: cosmological, eschatological, moral contests; divination; imitative magic and ceremonial; altered states of consciousness. But it has generated little insight of a truly comparative nature. Actual games contain combinations of these aspects—all games are in some sense competitive, for example—and all religions accommodate these functions. The insights of psychoanalysis, which sees in play and games the disguised representation of unconscious conflicts and a compulsion to repeat "primitive" traumas so as to master them, have been limited by inattention to cultural context and to the complexity and variety of game forms. Continental structuralism of the psychological sort associated with Piaget finds an important place for children's games in characterizing mental development, and the anthropological sort associated with Lévi-Strauss (1966, pp. 30–33) has revealed much of the symbolic "logic of the concrete" that connects games to myth, ritual, and kinship. Yet in the search for universal structures of mind these theories also overlook social and historical context, and their contributions have been largely methodological.

British and North American social scientists, on the other hand, have largely focused on the strategic and role-playing aspects of games, exploring them from the functional standpoint of social integration, decision making, and value transmission. "Game theory" in the social and information sciences has produced taxonomies of rational calculation and strategic choice among individual actors seeking to maximize their payoffs in the face of uncertainty and limited resources. Critics, however, have found "game theory" to be a fundamental misnomer, since play, under its aspects of intrinsic motivation and Batesonian framing, is missing or unaccounted for in such understandings of social action. "Game theory" has contributed little to the analysis of specifically religious institutions.

Social psychologists have focused on the role playing and socialization features of games to construct fundamental questions about the organization of the self itself. George Herbert Mead pointed to the youngster's ability to play a single position in a baseball game while articulating that role with all of the others on the field as a sign of and a means toward development of a "reflexive self," incorporating the expectations of others in the context of the "generalized other" represented by the total game. Erving Goffman (1967, 1974) still further stressed the aspects of role-playing, mimicry, dissimulation, and the "rules for breaking the rules" in building an explicit theory from the now popular metaphorical utterance, "social life is a game." The human self is seen by Goffman to be endlessly preoccupied with "the arts of impression management," ludic yet ever-watchful to define situations so as to prevent embarrassment to oneself and others. [*See* Reflexivity.] Like formal "game theory," social psychologies built from the model of games have contributed less to the understanding of social institutions per se, including religious ones, than they have to understanding individual and small-group processes of negotiation. At the same time, such theories do implicitly challenge authoritative ontologies and conventional understandings of divine affairs in Western cultures.

While games undoubtedly serve to reproduce or to rebel against dominant social structures and ideologies, they have been seen by recent anthropologists as speculative enterprises as well, means by which human communities discover their dominant values in the first place and formulate alternatives to them. Victor Turner—who like Huizinga saw cultural life as a process of passage from institutional structure to ludic, "antistructural" recombination, to the incrustations of structure once again—extended analysis of religious ritual to understand play forms in this way (1974). Clifford Geertz (1972), who sees the interpretation of experiences as in and of itself a human necessity, argues that the Balinese cockfight is a form of "social metacommentary," a "story the Balinese tell about themselves," a function likewise ascribed to religious ritual. Other anthropologists (Don Handelman and I, for example) find it important to stress the differences between games and ritual as collective hermeneutics. On the Batesonian level of metacommunication, ritual does seem to be framed differently from play. Ritual asserts *a priori* that all statements within it are true and not untrue and creates a world of "let us believe" rather than of "let us make believe."

Such distinctions make it possible to recognize complex performance types that incorporate both rite and game, like the *palio* or the Olympics, and depend for their power on moving actors and audiences back and forth from frame to frame. Then too, activities are reframed through the course of a people's history. Alexander Lesser (1978) has shown how the Pawnee hand game passed from a form of amusement to a religious salvation ritual and back again between 1865 and 1930, a process reminiscent of athletics in nineteenth-century England. What is discovered as possible (or impossible) in play and given organized display in games may be asserted by ritual as undeniable. Whether this is the essential relation between games and religion we will not know until greater conceptual clarity and theoretical sophistication are brought to bear on the vast new findings in the ethnology and social history of games, such that a ludic equivalent to Max Weber's comparative "economic ethics of the world religions" is achieved.

[*See also* Gambling *and* Martial Arts.]

BIBLIOGRAPHY

The charter discussion of the Greek "agonistic" system is found in Jakob Burckhardt's *Griechische Kulturgeschichte*, 4 vols. (Berlin, 1898–1902), translated by Palmer Hilty in abridged form as *History of Greek Culture* (New York, 1963). On the classical world, see also Alvin W. Gouldner's *Enter Plato* (New York, 1965). In the soundest scholarly guide to athletic games in the ancient Mediterranean world, *Sport bei den Völkern der alten Welt* (Darmstadt, 1981), Ingomar Weiler argues against the uniqueness of Greece in this area, a position taken by Johan Huizinga as well. Huizinga's *Homo Ludens* (Boston, 1955) remains the essential manifesto on the role of play in culture, including relationships between games and religion. Victor Turner extends his discussion of religious ritual to include the role of play in culture in "Liminal to Liminoid, in Play, Flow and Ritual," *Rice University Studies* 60 (Summer 1974): 53–92.

Roger Caillois presents a taxonomy of games, intended both to refine Huizinga's insights and to organize cross-cultural material in more useful fashion, in *Man, Play, and Games* (New York, 1961). Among ethnological compendia on games in "primitive" societies, Stewart Culin's *Games of the North American Indians* (1907; Washington, D.C., 1975) has been the most widely cited. On running as practiced by Native Americans, see Peter Nabokov's *Indian Running* (Santa Barbara, Calif., 1981). Anthropological case studies of special value include Alexander Lesser's *The Pawnee Ghost Dance Hand Game* (Madison, Wis., 1978) and Clifford Geertz's "Deep Play: Notes on the Balinese Cock Fight," *Daedalus* 101 (1972): 1–38. On China, see Marcel Granet's *Chinese Civilization* (London, 1930).

David L. Miller's *Gods and Games* (New York, 1973) is indicative of the Christian "theology of play" movement and contains valuable discussions of the role of games in contemporary existential, linguistic, and mathematical philosophy. Also see Jürgen Moltmann's *Theology of Play* (New York, 1972).

Gregory Bateson's fundamental contribution to understanding play and games as forms of metacommunication is contained in "A Theory of Play and Fantasy," in his *Steps to an Ecology of Mind* (New York, 1972). Erving Goffman develops the view of social life as a game in several works, including *Interaction Ritual* (Garden City, N.Y., 1967) and *Frame Analysis* (New York, 1974). Also see Georg Simmel's discussion on social reality as play in *The Sociology of Georg Simmel*, translated and edited by Kurt H. Wolff (Glencoe, Ill., 1950). On the role of play in human development, see D. W. Winnicott's *Playing and Reality* (London, 1971). Claude Lévi-Strauss's discussion of the different logics of games and rituals is found in his *The Savage Mind* (Chicago, 1966). Don Handelman considers related problems in his "Play and Ritual: Complementary Forms of Metacommunication" in *It's a Funny Thing, Humour*, edited by A. J. Chapman and H. Foot (London, 1977), pp. 135–192. Complex performance forms joining games and rites are the subject of my "Olympic Games and the Theory of Spectacle in Modern Societies," in *Rite, Drama, Festival, Spectacle* (Philadelphia, 1984), pp. 241–280.

JOHN J. MACALOON

GAMLI'EL OF YAVNEH, also known as Gamli'el II; Palestinian tanna. Gamli'el was rabbi, patriarch *(nasi')*, and head of the academy at Yavneh in the late first and early second century. In contrast to contemporary authorities, who either bear no title or, more often, are referred to by the title *rabbi*, Gamli'el was accorded the apparently honorific title *rabban*, which he shares with other leaders of the patriarchal house (see *Avot* 1.16, 1.18). His traditions are recorded in the Mishnah and related texts.

Gamli'el bore major responsibility for the centralization of rabbinical authority at Yavneh following the war with the Romans in 66–70. Succeeding the apparent founder of that academy, Yoḥanan ben Zakk'ai, Gamli'el was in a position to guide the rabbinical effort in the reconstruction of a nation that had seen its spiritual center in the Jerusalem Temple destroyed, a nation that lacked clear leadership. To address this challenge, Gamli'el supported the religious ascendency of the Yavneh academy and the political and religious authority of a Sanhedrin reconstituted under his leadership. [*See* Sanhedrin.] He was later believed to have had a hereditary claim on the patriarchate.

It it reported that Gamli'el sometimes conducted this campaign in an undiplomatic manner, but he won the support of contemporary rabbinical authorities. To assure a centralized authority, he insisted on the power of his court to fix the calendar for all of Jewry, to ensure the consistency of observance. To similar ends he demanded that individuals bow to the decision of the collective rabbinate in disputes, an insistence that in one instance is believed to have led to the ban on Eli'ezer ben Hyrcanus (B.T., *B.M.* 59b) and in another caused Yehoshu'a ben Ḥananyah to transgress what by his reckoning was Yom Kippur (*R. ha-Sh.* 2.8–9). Nevertheless, he is described as declaring that this demand was not to assure his own honor, but to assure that "disputes not be multiplied in Israel" (B.T., *B.M.* 59b).

In response to the vacuum left in the wake of the Temple's destruction, tradition bears witness to Gamli'el's activity in establishing ritual and prayer norms. His academy formalized the eighteen-benediction prayer (Shemoneh 'Esreh) that has been employed in various forms to this day. Perhaps to facilitate its acceptance as the core of Jewish daily worship, he allowed formal representatives to recite the prayer for untutored individuals. In addition, Gamli'el contributed significantly to the formulation of a post-Temple Passover Seder.

Appropriately to the image of patriarch, Gamli'el is described as having had extensive exchanges with "philosophers" and others outside the Judaic tradition. Gamli'el's son Shim'on reports that "in my father's house five hundred [children] studied Greek wisdom . . . because they were close to the authorities" (B.T., *Soṭ.* 49b; Tosefta, *Soṭ.* 15.8). We are told that Roman authorities were sympathetic to Gamli'el and the Judaism that he taught, and that Gamli'el occasionally reciprocated their sympathy.

Gamli'el's status is enhanced by the stories of his extensive travels, including a trip to Rome. He is also described as wealthy and spoiled, and his relationship with his righteous slave, Tabi, is legendary.

Gamli'el was apparently a person of great piety and sensitivity. He was strict with himself, even when lenient with others, and he refused to excuse himself from his responsibilities to heaven for even one moment. To alleviate the immense burden put upon surviving relatives who had to see to the burial of their deceased, Gamli'el had himself buried in simple shrouds, a practice followed by Jews to this day.

Gamli'el's traditions are outstanding for the relatively high proportion that are set down in narrative form. This is probably connected to his patriarchal authority at a crucial period in history. He came to serve as a model for the rabbinic community. Also notable is the absence of significant contributions to criminal statutes, reflecting perhaps the diminished authority of the early patriarchate in this area.

[*See also* Tannaim.]

BIBLIOGRAPHY

The most comprehensive review of Gamli'el's traditions is Shammai Kanter's *Rabban Gamaliel II, the Legal Traditions* (Chico, Calif., 1980). On Gamli'el's deposition from leadership of the Yavnean academy, an event central to his struggle for authority, see Robert Goldenberg's "The Deposition of Rabban Gamaliel II: An Examination of the Sources," *Journal of Jewish Studies* 23 (Autumn 1972): 167–190. For a biography that also examines the nonlegal traditions, see "Gamali'el ben Shim'on ha-neherag" in Aaron Hyman's *Toledot tanna'im ve-amora'im* (1910; reprint, Jerusalem, 1964).

DAVID KRAEMER

GAMLI'EL THE ELDER (fl. first half of the first century CE), properly Rabban ("our teacher") Gamli'el the Elder; the first Jewish teacher with this title. Gamli'el was a son or grandson of Hillel and likewise was regarded in rabbinic tradition as a *nasi'* (head of the court). He is designated "the Elder" in Talmudic literature apparently to distinguish him from Gamli'el of Yavneh (Gamli'el II) with whom he is often confused, and he is referred to as a Pharisee and "teacher of the Law" in *Acts of the Apostles* (5:34). [*See* Pharisees.]

Gamli'el appears frequently in tannaitic sources, where his various *taqqanot* (enactments) are recorded. The following examples from Mishnah *Giṭṭin* (4.2–3) were considered "for the general welfare":

1. A man who wishes to invalidate a divorce document that he has already sent to his wife must convene a court in her town rather than elsewhere. Otherwise she may mistakenly believe the document is still valid and remarry.
2. Both parties to a divorce are required to use all of the names by which they are known when signing the document.
3. All witnesses to the delivery of the document must sign it.

These *taqqanot* were especially intended to benefit women. Similarly, Gamli'el permitted a woman to remarry based on the testimony of one witness to the death of her husband, rather than the two generally required by Jewish law (*Yev.* 16.7). Of special interest are the letters that Gamli'el is reported to have dictated on the steps of the Temple (Tosefta *San.* 2.6 and parallels). Those sent to "our brethren" in the upper and lower south (Daroma) and in the upper and lower Galilee contained reminders pertaining to tithes. Another directed to "our brethren" in Babylonia and Media and to all other exiles of Israel announced the leap year. [*See* Jewish Religious Year.] It was said (*Soṭ.* 9.15) that "when Rabban Gamli'el the Elder died, the glory of the Torah ceased and purity and abstinence perished."

In *Acts* (5:34ff.), Gamli'el (Gamaliel) pleads with his fellow members of the Sanhedrin to free the apostles. Elsewhere in *Acts* (22:3), Paul states that he was brought up "at the feet of" Gamli'el. Christian legend later regarded Gamli'el as a Christian.

BIBLIOGRAPHY

The references to Rabban Gamli'el the Elder in Talmudic literature are collected and analyzed in volumes 1 (pp. 341–376) and 3 (pp. 272f., 314f.) of Jacob Neusner's *The Rabbinic Traditions about the Pharisees before 70*, 3 vols. (Leiden, 1971). Neusner questions Gamli'el's association with Beit Hillel and regards him as more of a "public official" and leader within the Pharisees than a "sectarian authority" of that party. A discussion of Gamli'el and some of the earlier assessments of him appears in Alexander Guttmann's *Rabbinic Judaism in the Making: A Chapter in the History of the Halakhah from Ezra to Judah I* (Detroit, 1970), pp. 177–182. Information on Gamli'el in the Christian tradition can be found in volume 2 (pp. 367ff.) of

Emil Schürer's *The History of the Jewish People in the Age of Jesus Christ, 175 B.C.–A.D. 135* (1901–1909), a new English version revised and edited by Géza Vermès, Fergus Millar, and Matthew Black (Edinburgh, 1979). Morton S. Enslin questions whether Paul actually "sat at Gamaliel's feet" and if so how much rabbinic training he received, in "Paul and Gamaliel," *Journal of Religion* 7 (July 1927): 360–375.

STUART S. MILLER

GĀṆAPATYAS are a sect of Hindus who regard Gaṇeśa (Gaṇapati) as their supreme object of devotion. They view Gaṇeśa, the elephant-faced son of Śiva and Pārvatī, as the form of ultimate reality *(brahman)* that is accessible to the senses, the mind, and (through devotional practices) the heart. Most Hindus worship Gaṇeśa along with other deities because he is the god who overcomes obstacles and makes rites and other undertakings effective. Gāṇapatyas share this view but extend it to make Gaṇeśa their central deity, either as their family or clan patron-god *(kuladevatā)* or their personal lord *(iṣṭadevatā)*. Devotion in the first case tends to be more formal and take place during specific ceremonies and festivals, while the second form of devotion is more likely to be personal, informal, and intense.

Although Gāṇapatyas may be found in many parts of India and from many castes, the sect has found its most articulated cultic expression in western India, in the Marathi-speaking region of Maharashtra, among high-caste Hindus. The sect rose to prominence in the region between the seventeenth and nineteenth centuries CE, during the rule of the Marathas. Gaṇeśa worship is also important in South India, where a number of temples are dedicated to him.

Gāṇapatya groups first appeared between the sixth and ninth centuries CE, and worshiped their deity in various forms according to the prevailing Brahmanic and Tantric practices. Two Sanskrit Purāṇas, the *Gaṇeśa* and the *Mudgala*, date from the twelfth and fourteenth centuries CE, respectively. These Purāṇas recount and celebrate the myths of Gaṇeśa's triumphs over demons on behalf of the gods and his devotees. They also include instructions for ritual performance and hymns of praise. Since the seventeenth century there has been a steady flow of devotional literature in both Sanskrit and Marathi.

In Maharashtra, devotion to Gaṇeśa has centered around eight shrines (*aṣṭavināyakas*) clustering around the city of Poona (Pune) and the nearby village of Cincvad, and associated with Gaṇeśa's most famous devotee, Morayā Gosāvī (d. 1651). For the past three centuries Cincvad has served as the administrative center for the sect in the region. The Gāṇapatya tradition enjoyed the patronage of Hindu, and at times Muslim, kings. The brahman Peshwas, the hereditary rulers of the Maratha empire after the death of its founder, Śivajī, contributed substantially to the construction of shrines and financing of rituals during the eighteenth and early nineteenth centuries. That patronage continued for a while under British rule, but gradually diminished and has been replaced by contributions from the faithful. As Gaṇeśa's popularity among the masses of Hindus has increased in contemporary times, the Gāṇapatya shrines have prospered.

The sect regards Morayā Gosāvī as its spiritual progenitor. Tradition holds that Morayā migrated from southern India to the Gaṇeśa shrine at Moragaon (70 kilometers southeast of Poona), where he experienced a series of visions of Gaṇeśa. In one vision Gaṇeśa told him that he would incarnate himself in his devotee and remain in his lineage for seven generations. Morayā Gosāvī's own religious charisma and the tradition of living deities in the shrine at Cincvad contributed largely to its religious significance in the region. In 1651 Morayā Gosāvī underwent *jīvansamādhi*, or entombment while alive, in a chamber beneath the shrine, and thereby passed out of visible existence. Devotees believe he attained release *(mokṣa)* from rebirth and that his presence continues to endow the shrine with sacred significance. Several of Morayā Gosāvī's descendants are likewise enshrined at Cincvad. Devotees come there both to honor the image of Gaṇeśa and receive its auspicious sight *(darśana)*, and to worship the shrines of Morayā Gosāvī and his descendants.

Twice each year the priests at Cincvad, along with thousands of devotees, take an image of Gaṇeśa from this shrine to the temple at Moragaon, where Morayā Gośavī received his visions, about a hundred kilometers to the southeast. The second annual pilgrimage coincides with the intensely popular Gaṇeśa festival that is celebrated particularly in the towns and cities of Maharashtra in August and September.

Many Gāṇapatyas make periodic pilgrimages to receive the auspicious viewing of Gaṇeśa at his eight shrines. Devotees maintain that it is particularly salutary to visit all eight shrines in a single pilgrimage.

[*See also* Gaṇeśa *and* Marathi Religions.]

BIBLIOGRAPHY

The works by Gāṇapatyas remain almost entirely untranslated into Western languages. Part of the *Gaṇeśa Purāṇa* has been translated and edited by Kiyoshi Yoroi in *Gaṇeśagītā: A Study, Translation with Notes, and a Condensed Rendering of the Commentary of Nilakaṇṭha* (The Hague, 1968). The most complete collection of Gāṇapatya literature and lore in Marathi is Amarendra L. Gadgil's *Śrī Gaṇeś Koś* (Poona, India, 1968). A survey of the Gāṇapatyas in the context of the myth and ritual traditions of Gaṇeśa can be found in my book *Gaṇeśa: Lord of Obstacles, Lord of Beginnings* (New York, 1985). Excellent discussions of the sect and its political significance appear in G. S. Ghurye's *Gods and Men* (Bombay, 1962) and in Laurence W. Preston's "Subregional Religious Centres in the History of Maharashtra: The Sites Sacred to Ganesh," in *Images of Maharashtra: A Regional Profile of India*, edited by N. K. Wagle (Toronto, 1980).

PAUL B. COURTRIGHT

GANDHI, MOHANDAS (1869–1948), political leader, social reformer, and religious visionary of modern India. Although Gandhi initially achieved public notice as a leader of India's nationalist movement and as a champion of nonviolent techniques for resolving conflicts, he was also a religious innovator who did much to encourage the growth of a reformed, liberal Hinduism in India. In the West, Gandhi is venerated by many who seek an intercultural and socially conscious religion and see him as the representative of a universal faith.

Religious Influences on Gandhi. Mohandas Karamchand Gandhi was born into a *bania* (merchant caste) family in a religiously pluralistic area of western India—the Kathiawar Peninsula in the state of Gujarat. His parents were Vaiṣṇava Hindus who followed the Vallabhācārya tradition of loving devotion to Lord Kṛṣṇa. His father, Karamchand Uttamchand, the chief administrative officer of a princely state, was not a very religious man, but his mother, Putalibai, became a follower of the region's popular Prānāmi cult. This group was founded in the eighteenth century by Mehraj Thakore, known as Prāṇanāth ("master of the life force"), and was influenced by Islam. Prāṇanāth rejected all images of God and, like the famous fifteenth-century Hindu saint Narsinh Mehta, who came from the same region, advocated a direct link with the divine, unmediated by priests and ritual. This Protestant form of Hinduism seems to have been accepted by Gandhi as normative throughout his life.

Other enduring religious influences from Gandhi's childhood came from the Jains and Muslims who frequented the family household. Gandhi's closest childhood friend, Mehtab, was a Muslim, and his spiritual mentor, Raychandbhai, was a Jain. Early contacts with Christian street evangelists in his home town of Porbandar, however, left Gandhi unimpressed.

When Gandhi went to London to study law at the age of nineteen he encountered forms of Christianity of quite a different sort. Respecting vows made to his mother, Gandhi sought meatless fare at a vegetarian restaurant, where his fellow diners were a motly mix of Theosophists, Fabian Socialists, and Christian visionaries who were followers of Tolstoi. These esoteric and socialist forms of Western spirtuality made a deep impression on Gandhi and encouraged him to look for parallels in the Hindu tradition.

When, in 1893, Gandhi settled in South Africa as a lawyer (initially serving in a Muslim firm), he was impressed by a Trappist monastery he visited near Durban. He soon set up a series of ashrams (religious retreat centers) supported by Hermann Kallenbach, a South African architect of Jewish background, whom Gandhi had met through Theosophical circles. Gandhi named one of his communities Tolstoi Farm in honor of the Christian utopian with whom he had developed a lively correspondence. While in South Africa Gandhi first met C. F. Andrews, the Anglican missionary to India who had become an emissary of Indian nationalist leaders and who eventually became Gandhi's lifelong friend and confidant. It was through Andrews that Gandhi met the Indian poet Rabindranath Tagore in 1915, after Gandhi had returned to India to join the growing nationalist movement. Tagore, following the practice of Theosophists in South Africa, designated Gandhi a *mahātma*, or "great soul." [*See also the biography of Tagore.*]

Gandhi's Religious Thought. Although the influences on Gandhi's religious thought are varied—from the Sermon on the Mount to the *Bhagavadgītā*—his ideas are surprisingly consistent. Gandhi considered them to be Hindu, and in fact, they are all firmly rooted in the Indian religious tradition. His main ideas include the following.

1. *Satya* ("truth"). Gandhi equated truth with God, implying that morality and spirituality are ultimately the same. This concept is the bedrock of Gandhi's approach to conflict, *satyāgraha*, which requires a fighter to "hold firmly to truth." While Gandhi did not further define the term, he regarded the rule of *ahiṃsā* as the litmus test that would determine where truth could be found.
2. *Ahiṃsā* ("nonviolence"). This ancient Indian concept prohibiting physical violence was broadened by Gandhi to include any form of coercion or denigration. For Gandhi, *ahiṃsā* was a moral stance involving love for and the affirmation of all life.
3. *Tapasya* ("renunciation"). Gandhi's asceticism was, in Max Weber's terms, "worldly" and not removed from social and political involvements. To Gandhi, *tapasya* meant not only the traditional requirements of simplicity and purity in personal habits but also

the willingness of a fighter to shoulder the burden of suffering in a conflict.

4. *Swaraj* ("self-rule"). This term was often used during India's struggle for independence to signify freedom from the British, but Gandhi used it more broadly to refer to an ideal of personal integrity. He regarded *swaraj* as a worthy goal for the moral strivings of individuals and nations alike, linking it to the notion of finding one's inner self.

In addition to these concepts, Gandhi affirmed the traditional Hindu notions of *karman* and *dharma*. Even though Gandhi never systematized these ideas, when taken together they form a coherent theological position. Gandhi's copious writings are almost entirely in the form of letters and short essays in the newspapers and journals he published. These writings and the accounts of Gandhi's life show that he had very little interest in what is sometimes regarded as emblematic of Hinduism: its colorful anthropomorphic deities and its reliance upon the rituals performed by Brahmanic priests.

It is not his rejection of these elements of Hindu culture that makes Gandhi innovative, however, for they are also omitted by the leaders of many other sects and movements in modern India. What is distinctive about Gandhi's Hinduism is his emphasis on social ethics as an integral part of the faith, a shift of emphasis that carries with it many conceptual changes as well. Gandhi's innovations include the use of the concept of truth as a basis for moral and political action, the equation of nonviolence with the Christian notion of selfless love, the broadening of the concept of *karmayoga* to include social service and political action, the redefinition of untouchability and the elevation of untouchables' tasks, and the hope for a more perfect world even in this present age of darkness *(kaliyuga)*.

Gandhi's religious practices, like his ideas, combined both social and spiritual elements. In addition to his daily prayers, consisting of a simple service of readings and silent contemplation, he regarded his daily practice of spinning cotton as a form of mediation and his campaigns for social reform as sacrifices more efficacious than those made by priests at the altar. After Gandhi retired from politics in 1933, he took as his central theme the campaign for the uplift of untouchables, whom he called *harijans* ("people of God"). Other concerns included the protection of cows, moral education, and the reconciliation of Hindus and Muslims. The latter was especially important to Gandhi during the turmoil precipitated by India's independence, when the subcontinent was divided along religious lines. It was opposition to Gandhi's cries for religious tolerance that led to his assassination, on 30 January 1948, by a fanatical member of the Hindu right wing.

Gandhi's Legacy. Since Gandhi's death, neither Indian society nor Hindu belief has been restructured along Gandhian lines, but the Gandhian approach has been kept alive in India through the Sarvodaya movement, for which Vinoba Bhave has provided the spiritual leadership, and Jayaprakash Narayan the political. Gandhi has provided the inspiration for religious and social activists in other parts of the world as well. These include Martin Luther King, Jr., and Joan Baez in the United States, E. M. Schumacher in England, Danilo Dolci in Sicily, Albert Luthuli in South Africa, Lanza del Vasto in France, and A. T. Ariyaratna in Sri Lanka. [*See the biographies of Bhave and King.*]

Over the years, the image of Gandhi has loomed larger than life, and he is popularly portrayed as an international saint. This canonization of Gandhi began in the West with the writings of an American Unitarian pastor, John Haynes Holmes, who in 1921 proclaimed Gandhi "the greatest man in the world today." It continues in an unabated flow of homiletic writings and films, including David Attenborough's *Gandhi*, one of the most widely seen motion pictures in history. At the core of this Gandhian hagiography lies the enduring and appealing image of a man who was able to achieve a significant religious goal: the ability to live simultaneously a life of moral action and spiritual fulfillment. For that reason Gandhi continues to serve as an inspiration for a humane and socially engaged form of religion in India and throughout the world.

[*See also* Ahiṃsā.]

BIBLIOGRAPHY

Gandhi's own writings are assembled in his *Collected Works*, 89 vols. (Delhi, 1958–1983). Many briefer anthologies are available, however, including *The Gandhi Reader*, edited by Homer Jack (New York, 1961). A reliable biography is to be found in Geoffrey Ashe's *Gandhi* (New York, 1969). The religious ideas of Gandhi are best explored in Margaret Chatterjee's *Gandhi's Religious Thought* (Notre Dame, Ind., 1983) and Raghavan Iyer's *The Moral and Political Thought of Mahatma Gandhi* (New York, 1973). The concept of *satyāgraha* is explicated and put into comparative perspective in Joan Bondurant's *Conquest of Violence: The Gandhian Philosophy of Conflict*, rev. ed. (Berkeley, 1965), and my *Fighting with Gandhi* (San Francisco, 1984). Gandhi's saintly politics are described in Lloyd I. Rudolph and Susanne Hoeber Rudolph's *Gandhi: The Traditional Roots of Charisma* (Chicago, 1983), and his image as a universal saint is discussed in my essay "St. Gandhi," in *Saints and Virtues*, edited by John Stratton Hawley (Berkeley, 1986).

MARK JUERGENSMEYER

GAṆEŚA ("lord of the group") is the elephant-headed Hindu deity. Also called Vināyaka ("leader"), Gajānana ("elephant-faced"), Gaṇādhipa ("lord of the group"), Ekadanta ("one-tusked"), Lambodara ("potbellied"), Vighnarāja ("lord of obstacles"), and Siddhadāta ("giver of success"), he is the son of Śiva and Pārvatī, and leader of Śiva's group of attendants (*gaṇas*). His special province within the Hindu pantheon is to remove and create obstacles to various undertakings. His images are found both in temples dedicated exclusively to him and, more frequently, as doorway guardians of temples to other deities, especially Śiva and Pārvatī. Gaṇeśa enjoys widespread devotion from Hindus of various sectarian affiliations and ranks. Hindus who regard him as their principal deity of devotion are called Gāṇapatyas; they are located primarily in southern and western India.

Gaṇeśa's historical origins are obscure. Early Vedic literatures refer to a Gaṇapati ("lord of the group") and to Hastimukha ("elephant-faced"), and devotees regard these references as evidence for Gaṇeśa's Vedic roots. It is more likely that these epithets refer to Bṛhaspati, Indra, or Śiva. Numismatic evidence suggests that Gaṇeśa originated in the first century CE. Sculptural evidence places his entry into the Hindu pantheon about four centuries later. Literarily and iconographically, Gaṇeśa is well established in myth and cult by the fifth century within the general framework of Śaivism, although he receives worship by Hindus of various devotional and sectarian orientations for his general role as the overcomer of obstacles.

Gaṇeśa's mythology centers on several themes: his birth, beheading and restoration, lordship over the *gaṇas*, associations with demons, and powers as creator and remover of obstacles. Stories in the Purāṇas and vernacular folklore traditions tell of occasions when Pārvatī created Gaṇeśa out of the substance, sometimes called *mala* ("dirt") or *lepa* ("rubbing"), rubbed off the surface of her body and formed into the shape of a handsome youth. Once, while Śiva was absent and deep in meditation, Pārvatī commanded this young man to guard her private quarters from all intruders. When Śiva returned and sought entry into Pārvatī's presence, the young man barred the door. During the battle that followed, Śiva beheaded the youth. Pārvatī became angry and demanded that Śiva restore him at once. Śiva sent out his group of attendants (*gaṇas*) to find the first available head, which happened to belong to an elephant. Śiva restored the youth with the elephant's head and gave him command over his group of *gaṇas*, thus naming him Gaṇapati or Gaṇeśa, Lord of the Group. Śiva also told all gods and brahmans that Gaṇeśa must be worshiped first before all other undertakings, ritual or otherwise, or else their efforts would come to ruin.

Gaṇeśa is also called Vināyaka, meaning "leader." The early Dharmasūtra literature, predating the above-mentioned myths of Gaṇeśa, describes rituals prescribed to ward off *vināyakas*, evil demons who possess their victims and cause them to act in strange and inauspicious ways. Gaṇeśa's dwarfish torso resembles the iconography of these *vināyakas*. Some scholars have suggested that Gaṇeśa may originally have been a member of this class of demons but gradually achieved brahmanical recognition and gained admittance into its pantheon as the son of Śiva and Pārvatī.

In receiving the head of the elephant, Gaṇeśa also takes on some of the symbolism associated with elephants in Indian culture. Elephant motifs frequently are found at the bases of temples, appearing to hold up the massive edifices. Elephants guard the doors of temples and serve as the vehicles for deities and royalty. Gaṇeśa also serves in these protective capacities as the remover and placer of obstacles.

[*For the worship of Gaṇeśa, see* Gāṇapatyas. *For further discussion of the god's mythic form, see* Elephants.]

BIBLIOGRAPHY

Courtright, Paul B. *Gaṇeśa: Lord of Obstacles, Lord of Beginnings.* New York, 1985. A detailed survey of the myths and rituals surrounding the figures of Gaṇeśa in classical Sanskrit sources and contemporary western India (Maharashtra).

Getty, Alice. *Gaṇeśa: A Monograph on the Elephant-Faced God.* Oxford, 1936. A study of the myth and iconography of Gaṇeśa in India, Southeast Asia, and East Asia.

PAUL B. COURTRIGHT

GANGES RIVER. The Ganges (Gaṅgā), considered the holiest of India's rivers, is 1,560 miles long. Rising at Gangotri in the Himalayas, this great river flows through the North Indian plain and into the Bay of Bengal. To Hindus, the Ganges is the archetype of all sacred waters; she is a goddess, Mother Gaṅgā (Gaṅgā Mātā), representative of the life-giving maternal waters of the ancient Vedic hymns; above all, she is the symbol *par excellence* of purity and the purifying power of the sacred. These affective and symbolic values of the Ganges hold true for all Hindus, irrespective of sectarian differences.

Celebration of the Goddess-River. According to Hindu belief, the Ganges purifies all that she touches. Her entire course is a pilgrimage route for the faithful. Millions of Hindus visit the preeminent *tīrthas* ("crossings," places of pilgrimage) that mark her path: the source at Gangotri; Hardwar (also called Gaṅgādvāra, "gateway of the Ganges"), where the river enters the plain;

Prayāg (present-day Allahabad), where she joins both the holy Yamunā (Jumna) and the mythical river Sarasvatī, thus earning the name Triveṇī ("river of three currents"); Kāśī (Banaras), abode of the god Śiva and the holiest city of the Hindus; and Gangasagar, where the Ganges enters the sea. Pilgrims go to these places to bathe in the Ganges, to drink her water, to worship the river, and to chant her holy name. Especially in Banaras, many come to cremate their kin, to deposit the ashes of the dead in the river, or to perform religious rites for their ancestors. Some come to spend their last days on the banks of the river, to die there and thus "cross over" the ocean of birth and death. Holy men, widows, and others who have dedicated themselves to the contemplative life live in numbers in the sacred places along the Ganges. They in turn attract millions who congregate at periodic festivals and fairs, the greatest of which is the Kumbha Melā, celebrated every twelve years in Prayāg. All who come to the Ganges come in the firm belief that bathing in this river, even the mere sight of Mother Gaṅgā, will cleanse them of their sins, taking them a step nearer to final release *(mokṣa)*. Those who cannot make the trip can partake of the river's sacred water from the sealed jars that pilgrims carry home. Ganges water is given to participants and guests at weddings, as well as to the sick and the dying; it validates Hindu oaths; and in an ancient daily rite, every devout Hindu invokes the Ganges, along with the other sacred rivers, to be present in the water in which he bathes. The purifying powers of the Ganges are great indeed.

The Ganges in Mythology and Iconography. The Vedic Aryans celebrated the Indus, not the Ganges, and her tributaries as their "seven sacred rivers." It is in the epics *Mahābhārata* and *Rāmāyaṇa* (roughly fourth century BCE), which reflect Aryan settlement in the Ganges Plain, that the Ganges takes her place at the head of seven holy rivers that are now geographically spread over all of India. The principal myths of the Ganges are found in the epics and the Purāṇas (mythological texts that include the lore of sacred places), and in Sanskrit hymns of praise such as the *Gaṅgālaharī* (The Waves of the Ganges) by the seventeenth-century poet Jagannātha. The central myth of the Ganges is the story of her descent *(avatāra, avataraṇa)* from heaven to earth, a story narrated with variations in several texts (*Rāmāyaṇa*, "Bāla Kāṇḍa" 38–44; *Mahābhārata* 3.104–108; *Skanda Purāṇa*, "Kāśī Khaṇḍa" 30). In response to the great and steadfast penance of King Bhagīratha, the sky-river Ganges agreed to descend to earth in order to purify the ashes of the sixty thousand sons of Bhagīratha's ancestor Sagara, who had been burned by the wrath of a sage (Kapila) whom they had offended. The great ascetic god Śiva caught the falling stream in his matted hair in order to soften the blow on earth; the Ganges followed Bhagīratha to the sea, whence she flowed into the netherworld to fulfill her mission. This myth explains several of the Ganges's names, including Bhāgīrathī ("she who descended at Bhagīratha's request") and Tripathagāminī ("she who flows through the three worlds"). The descent of the Ganges is the subject of a famous seventh-century rock sculpture at Mahabalipuram in South India.

In the Vaiṣṇava version of the descent myth, the Ganges is said to have descended when Viṣṇu, as Trivikrama who measured heaven and earth, pierced the vault of heaven with his upraised foot. The association of the river with both great gods of Hinduism points to the universality of the Ganges in Hinduism. In minor myths the river is portrayed as the mother of the *Mahābhārata* hero Bhīṣma and the mother of Skanda-Kārttikeya, who was born from Śiva's seed flung into the Ganges.

The Ganges' most sustained association is with the god Śiva himself. Not only does she flow through his hair, she is considered to be his wife, along with Pārvatī, the other daughter of the god of the Himalaya, Himavat. As powerful river and goddess-consort, the Ganges is *śakti*, the feminine energy of the universe, and the female aspect of the androgynous Śiva. Like Śiva and the ambrosial moon on his head, the Ganges—whose life-sustaining ambrosial waters flow from the realm of the moon—is connected with both life and death.

The themes of purification, life, and death that appear in the myths and rites associated with the Ganges are also expressed in her iconography, especially in the representation of the Gaṅgā and Yamunā as goddesses carved on either side of the entrances of Hindu temples of the medieval period (roughly from the fifth to the eleventh century CE). Ancient symbols of fertility (trees, vegetation, overflowing pots, the female herself) appear in these images; yet the Ganges rides on a *makara* ("crocodile"), who represents the dangers of death as well as the abundance of life. As "goddess of the threshold" the Ganges no doubt initiates, purifies, and blesses with worldly prosperity the devotee who enters the sacred realm of the temple; at the same time, in the esoteric symbolism of Yoga and Tantra, the river-goddess is said to represent *iḍā*, one of the *nāḍī*s (subtle channels) through which one's energy is activated in order to achieve the supreme realization of the self—final release from worldly existence. However, in the last analysis, for the average Hindu it is not a matter of esoteric interpretation but of simple faith—reinforced by popular texts—that the goddess-river Ganges is the most accessible and powerful agent of salvation available to him in the *kaliyuga,* the present dark and degraded age of mankind.

[*For further discussion of the sacred geography of the Ganges, see* Banaras *and* Kumbha Melā. *See also* Śiva.]

BIBLIOGRAPHY

Diana L. Eck's essay entitled "Gaṅgā: The Goddess in Hindu Sacred Geography," in *The Divine Consort: Rādhā and the Goddesses of India,* edited by John Stratton Hawley and Donna M. Wulff (Berkeley, 1982), pp. 166–183, is the best introduction to the religious significance of the Ganges in Hinduism. The same author has a good discussion of the Ganges in the context of Kāśī, the holy city of the Hindus, in chapter 5 of *Banaras: City of Light* (New York, 1982). Spectacular visual images of the Ganges and the life along her banks, accompanied by a highly informative and readable introductory text, may be found in *Ganga: Sacred River of India,* photographs by Raghubir Singh, introduction by Eric Newby (Hong Kong, 1974). Steven G. Darian's *The Ganges in Myth and History* (Honolulu, 1978) is a solid, well-written, well-illustrated historical study of the many dimensions of the Ganges. Finally, Heinrich von Stietencron's *Gaṅgā und Yamunā: Zur symbolischen Bedeutung der Flussgöttinnen an indischen Tempeln* (Wiesbaden, 1972) is an excellent scholarly work on the symbolism of the iconography of the great river-goddesses in Hinduism.

Indira Viswanathan Peterson

GANJIN (Chin., Chien-chen; 688–763), Buddhist Vinaya master from China who introduced procedures for ordaining Buddhist clergy into Japan and who established the Risshū, or Vinaya school, of Buddhism there. Ganjin's birthplace was Yang-chou, a prosperous shipping town in eastern China. There he underwent tonsure at a local temple in 701. Four years later he received the *bodhisattva* precepts, a set of vows administered as a sign of devotion to Mahāyāna Buddhist principles.

At the age of nineteen, Ganjin traveled to China's traditional capitals of Lo-yang and Ch'ang-an to study at the major centers of Buddhist learning. His primary field of training was Vinaya, the ancient rules and procedures governing the life and behavior of Buddhist priests and nuns. Interest in the Vinaya had peaked in China a century earlier, and a formal school, the Lü-tsung, was established to preserve and promote clerical practices based on the *Ssu-fen-lü* (T.D. no. 1428), the version of the Vinaya inherited from the Dharmaguptaka school of India. This Vinaya, which lists 250 precepts for priests and 348 for nuns, was Hīnayāna in origin, but it became the basis for ordination and clerical discipline in the overwhelmingly Mahāyāna schools of China and Japan. Ganjin himself took the 250 precepts at the time of his full ordination in 708, a year after his arrival in Ch'ang-an. In 713, at the age of twenty-five, he returned to Yang-chou and began his own career as a Vinaya master. Over the next thirty years Ganjin distinguished himself as one of the most eminent Buddhist teachers in central China. He is said to have ordained more than 40,000 priests during his career and to have conducted formal lectures on the Vinaya on 130 occasions.

In 733 the Japanese imperial court sent two Buddhist priests, Eiei and Fushō, to China to enlist Vinaya masters to administer ordinations in Japan. There was great concern in Japan that all the ordinations performed up to that time were not valid, since the requisite number of duly ordained priests prescribed by the Vinaya had never been present to officiate. The Japanese felt it important to rectify this breach. Authentic ordination, they believed, made the clergy legitimate heirs of the Buddha's teachings and endowed them with religious and worldly power to act in behalf of Buddhism. Eiei and Fushō first succeeded in recruiting a young Vinaya master named Tao-hsüan from Lo-yang. He arrived in Japan in 736, but was hampered in conducting ordinations for lack of the required number of ordained participants. In 742 they went to Yang-chou to seek Ganjin's assistance. He too was sympathetic, and he resolved to travel to Japan himself to oversee ordinations. But the path leading Ganjin to Japan was long and treacherous, involving five unsuccessful voyages thwarted by pirates, shipwreck, and arrest by civil authorities. During the course of these events Ganjin lost his eyesight and Eiei lost his life. Finally, in 753, on his sixth attempt, Ganjin reached the shores of Japan accompanied by twenty-four disciples whose participation would validate ordination ceremonies. Ganjin was sixty-five years old at the time.

In early 754 Ganjin and his entourage were welcomed into the Japanese capital of Nara with great fanfare. Within weeks he set up a temporary ordination platform at the Tōdaiji, the imperial temple in the capital, and performed the first proper ordination on Japanese soil. The following year he established a permanent ordination platform at the Tōdaiji, all according to the meticulous specifications of the Vinaya tradition in China. The establishment of specific locations for ordination had the effect of tightening control over the clergy, since entrance into the priesthood could be regulated by those overseeing ordination. This centralizing of authority, as well as the Vinaya's emphasis on strict discipline, suited the government's desire to harness Buddhism for its own interests. Ganjin, as the preeminent figure in this ordination process, was named to the Sōgō council, the ecclesiastical body responsible to the government for Buddhism's activities. He served in this capacity from 756 until his resignation in 758. A year later Ganjin was granted land on which to build his own temple. He constructed the Tōshōdaiji and spent the remaining four years of his life there instructing priests in the intricacies of the Vinaya. These followers formed the core of the Risshū in Japan. Ganjin died at the Tōshōdaiji in 763 at the age of seventy-five. His great contribution to Japan was the institution of ordination procedures and the delineation of clerical discipline. This model of discipline was later challenged by Saichō, who sought to substitute the *bodhisattva* vows of Mahāyāna for the clerical precepts of Hīnayāna. Nonetheless, Ganjin's system persisted alongside Saichō's as the traditional path of ordination in early Japanese Buddhism.

[*See also* Vinaya *and the biography of Saichō.*]

BIBLIOGRAPHY

The most important work in Western languages on Ganjin is a French study by Takakusu Junjirō, "Le voyage de Kanshin en Orient, 742–754," *Bulletin de l'École Française d'Extrême-Orient* 28 (1928): 1–41 and 29 (1929): 47–62. This is a translation of a biography written in 779 by the Japanese scholar Mabito Genkai entitled *Tō Daiwajō Tōsei den* (T.D. no. 2089). In Japanese there are numerous studies of Ganjin, including Ishida Mizumaro's *Ganjin: Sono shisō to shōgai* (Tokyo, 1958) and Ando Kōsei's *Ganjin Wajō*, "Jinbutsu sōsho," no. 146 (Tokyo, 1967).

James C. Dobbins

GARDENS. The gardens of the world, like the religions of the world, may be divided into West and East, with the line between them running somewhere through the subcontinent of India. In the West, men seek to conquer nature, and minds run to extremes: the day of judgment, the triumph of the good, and the annihilation of evil. In the East, they try to accommodate themselves to nature and to reconcile its dualisms. These differences find expression in the formal gardening of the West and in the landscape gardening of the East. [*See also* Nature.]

The West. The religions which inherited the traditions of the Old Testament, namely, Islam and Christianity, came straight out of the desert. Their scriptures concentrated upon the life-giving properties of water, the virtues of the green leaf, and the restfulness of shade. A man was blessed by being told he would be "like a watered garden" (*Is.* 58:11) and cursed with the prospect of becoming "as a garden that hath no water" (*Is.* 1:30). Wells and fountains quickened the green leaf. Green became the color of Islam itself, and Christians believed in the green herb for medicinal remedy. The trees that water brought to life provided both nourishment and shade, and in seventeenth-century England Andrew Marvell envisaged paradise as "a green thought in a green shade." The God-fearing dwelt "mid shades and fountains," while a just king, as the Mughal emperor Akbar said when he invaded Kashmir in 1585 CE, enabled his subjects to sit in the shade of tranquillity. Above all, the influence of the desert environment appeared in the way in which, in the West, the garden was seen as an oasis, in stark contrast to the wilderness outside. The sense of the faith, or of the church, as an enclosure, a refuge from a hostile environment, was paramount (though there was also another, more puritanical tradition, in which the roles were reversed, and the garden, with its luxury, appeared as the scene of temptation, while the wilderness appeared as the true garden).

Gardeners, inspired by the supposition of a Garden of Eden at the beginning of history, aimed to re-create the conditions thought to have existed in the original garden by providing a mild climate and a never-failing supply of flowers and fruit. The gardener brought order out of chaos, and gardens were laid out in regular patterns, with right angles and straight lines to extend man's dominion over fallen nature. Both the original Garden of Eden and the future Heaven were commonly conceived of as formal gardens. The tradition that Eden was watered by four rivers led Muslim gardeners from Persia to Spain tenaciously to reproduce the *chahār bāgh*, a rectangular enclosure divided into four quarters by two streams crossing at right angles. It was an approach which combined easily with secular and humanist ideas, derived from the classical civilizations of Persia, Greece, and Rome, of the regular pattern as the triumph of human intelligence and of abstract principles of mathematics and law. The same layout was to be found in medieval Christian monasteries and in Renaissance gardens alike, and already by the fifteenth century it was not always easy to be sure whether religious or secular symbolism predominated.

In the West, every plant was enriched with spiritual symbolism. The violet genuflected, and the branches of an orchard bowed toward God. The trees opened their arms in the gesture of the prayer of supplication. Muslims believed that the rose had been created from a drop of perspiration which fell from the Prophet's forehead as he was carried up into Heaven. The rosebush prayed standing upright, and Muslims and Christians agreed that the fragrant flowers budding among its thorns represented God's mercy emerging from his wrath. The cypress (woven into so many carpets) stood both for mortality, because it did not sprout when cut, and for everlasting life, because it was evergreen. In both Islam and Christianity the symbolism extended to the tradition that, as Rābiʿah al-ʿAdawīyah (d. 801 CE) put it, "the real gardens and flowers are within." It was only when a man's stonelike nature had been broken down into dust by affliction that his heart could become a garden blessed by rain, and roses grow out of him. [*See* Flowers.]

Thus far the early symbolism of the garden in Islam ran parallel to that in Christianity, though the Muslim Paradise, with its *ḥūrīs*, its green brocades, and its non-intoxicating wines, was painted in more literal detail than the Christian Heaven. Where Christian tradition diverged from Islam was in the identification of the garden with specific occasions in the life of Christ. The "garden enclosed" of the *Song of Songs* was interpreted to refer to the Virgin Mary, whose womb was an oasis so select that none but the Holy Spirit could enter in. Adam had been a gardener. Through Adam death came into the world. Christ, who had conquered death in the Resurrection, therefore made his first post-Resurrection appearance dressed in a gardener's clothes.

The East. In China and Japan, early responses to nature were characterized by belief in spirits. Both the awesome mountains and the streams which issued from them were possessed by spirits, and were thought, therefore, to be every bit as alive as plants, animals, and men themselves. Pious villagers made pilgrimages to the mountains, and the returned pilgrim, wishing to convey what he had seen, invented the landscape garden. This was designed with two objectives in mind: to raise man's understanding to the level of the cosmos and, simultaneously, to bring the cosmos within the compass of human experience.

The first objective of landscape gardening was achieved largely through the priority accorded in Chinese gardens to rocks and pools or streams. Up to a point this art of *shan-shui* represented the physical geography of the region, that is, the mountains of Central Asia and the seas of the eastern coast. Beyond that point, in Taoist philosophy, it stood for the skeleton of the whole earth and the arteries which nourished it. To the Buddhist it furnished a lesson in time. The flowers opened and were blown in a month. The seasons revolved. But the rocks, which decayed according to a different time scale, appeared unchanged. Contemplating the rocks, men conceived of the present as a moving infinity. The symbolism was as varied and extensible as the clouds which gathered round the mountain peaks. The selection of rocks for the landscape garden was a matter for the connoisseur, and the garden was laid out by professional geomancers, who read the spiritual contours of the site according to the science of *feng-shui*. [*See* Geomancy.]

The second objective was achieved by allowing everything in this garden cosmos to appear as though affected by the dualistic forces which beset men themselves. The garden contained both friendly and unfriendly spirits. But threatening spirits were not persecuted as they might have been in the West: they were either left undisturbed (for example, by not digging the ground too deeply) or frustrated (as in the case of the demons who traveled in straight lines, by constructing zigzag bridges). Everything in the universe was split into two parts. The Chinese spoke of the *yin* and the *yang*, the Japanese of the *in* and the *yō*. *Yin* was female, passive, and weak; *yang* was male, active, and virile. In China, mountains were male, pools female; hence a mountain stood for intelligence, a lake for feeling. In Japan the more stylized gardens sometimes contained both male and female rocks—five erect, four recumbent. In both countries there were to be found together with the rocks and streams a feeling for youth and a feeling for age, a feeling for growth and a feeling for decay. It became a tradition that the trunk of the tree upon which the "youthful" plum blossom hung should resemble an old man's body, crooked and bent. Flowers were esteemed to be "as lovely in their withering as in their first florescence," and the samurai were compared to the blossom of the cherry—having a short life and an exquisite end. The *Yüan-yeh* (a treatise on gardening, dating from the end of the Ming period) records how "when a remarkable tree was about to bloom," people moved their beds outdoors in order that they might be able to observe how the flowers upon a tree developed "from childhood to maturity and finally faded and died."

Nowhere is the contrast between East and West more apparent than in their respective attitudes to night and moonlight. In the West day was connected symbolically with good, night with evil. The creatures which moved by night, such as bats, owls, and foxes, were repellent, ominous, or crafty, and the moon was contemned as a second-rate luminary. In China, on the other hand, day and night were accorded equal status and pavillions were built and furnished for the contemplation of the moon. Chinese poets sang of the moonlight "washing its soul" in the garden pool, and the *Yüan-yeh* encouraged the reader to look forward to the day when he might even "dig in the moon on the top of a mountain."

In such a garden a man recognized a picture of his own life. The cedar, resisting the storm, represented the beholder's own struggle with adversity. The symbolism attaching to individual plants related to the qualities expected of a human being, and the chrysanthemum, for example, which braved the autumn frosts, was admired for its courage. Death itself was held in proportion in a continuous cycle of decay and regrowth. Chinese gardening did much to ease mankind into contentment with its lot. But the peoples of the East did sometimes dream of an alternative to life as they knew it. Taoists spoke of the Blessed Isles of the Eastern Sea, and many Buddhists have believed in a land, presided over by the Buddha Amida (Skt., Amitābha), where lotus flowers holding the souls of the faithful bloom upon the waters of a brilliant lake—concepts for which there have been parallels in the West. More often than not, however, Buddhists have thought in terms of *nirvāṇa*, or a release from the cycle of reincarnation, and for this there is no Western equivalent. The Indian youth of the *Matsya Purāṇa* (c. 500 CE), who had passed through lives by the thousand and who had in his time been a beast of prey, a domestic animal, grass, shrubs, creepers, and trees, looked forward not to a better world but to release from self. In China the highest aspiration open to a landscape gardener would have been to imitate the Hang painter Wu-tao-tzu, who is said to have entered into the scene he had created, merged with his masterpiece, and been seen no more.

[*See also* Paradise *and* Flowers.]

BIBLIOGRAPHY

Very few books on gardening acknowledge the importance of religious symbolism. Among those which do, the best general history remains Marie Luise Gothein's *A History of Garden Art*, 2 vols. (1928; New York, 1966). Numerous aspects of Islamic gardening are touched on in *The Islamic Garden*, edited by Elizabeth B. Macdougall and Richard Ettinghausen (Washington, D.C., 1976). The most perceptive of recent works on medieval Christian gardening (and cooking) is Teresa McLean's *Medieval English Gardens* (London, 1981). For a view into the "garden enclosed" of the *Song of Songs*, see Stanley N. Stewart's study *The Enclosed Garden: The Tradition and the Image in Seventeenth-Century Poetry* (Madison, Wis., 1966). For a discussion of some effects of the discovery of America on gardeners' attempts to re-create the Garden of Eden, see my book *The Garden of Eden: The Botanic Garden and the Re-Creation of Paradise* (New Haven, 1981). The distinctive features of the successive periods of Japanese gardening are best conveyed in Teiji Ito's *The Japanese Garden: An Approach to Nature* (New Haven, 1972). Chinese gardening ideals are delightfully portrayed in Dorothy Graham's *Chinese Gardens* (London, 1938). Osvald Siren's study *China and Gardens of Europe of the Eighteenth Century* (New York, 1950) winningly discusses the significance of Chinese influences in the adoption of the landscape garden in Europe.

JOHN PREST

GATEWAYS. *See* Portals.

GAUḌAPĀDA, Indian philosopher and reputed *parama-guru* ("teacher's teacher") of Śaṅkara. Information about Gauḍapāda is scant and has been subject to scholarly controversy. In what is now regarded as a fantastic thesis, Max von Walleser professed in his *Der ältere Vedanta: Geschichte, Kritik und Lehre* (Heidelberg, 1910) that Gauḍapāda never existed at all. However, both V. Bhattacharya (1943) and T. M. P. Mahadevan (1969) have argued convincingly that Gauḍapāda was a real person, the author of what is called *Āgama Śāstra* or *Gauḍapādīyakārikā*, or simply *Māṇḍukyakārikā*.

The name *Gauḍa* indicates that he must have come from Gauḍadesá ("Gauḍa country"), or Bengal. On the authority of the *Śārīrakamīmāṃsābhāṣya-vārttika* of Bālakṛṣṇānanda Sarasvatī (seventeenth century CE), we know that in the country of Kurukṣetra (north of present-day Delhi), near the Hīrāvatī River, there lived a group of people who had migrated from Bengal (and hence were called Gauḍas); the most eminent among them was one Gauḍapāda. Exactly when Gauḍapāda lived has also been a matter of controversy. Some scholars place him in the fifth century CE, but this theory contradicts the traditional belief that he was Śaṅkara's teacher's teacher, for Śaṅkara is generally assumed to have flourished somewhere between 788 and 820 CE. Another asumption is that Gauḍapāda was a contemporary of Apollonius of Tyana, who traveled to India in the first century CE. This, however, is highly conjectural, and would place Gauḍapāda at an earlier, and even less likely date.

According to Ānandagiri (a pupil of Śaṅkara), Gauḍapāda lived the final part of his life in Badarikāśrama, the holy residence of Nara-Nārāyaṇa, and spent his time in deep meditation on the lord (Nārāyaṇa-Kṛṣṇa). Greatly pleased with Gauḍapāda, the lord thus revealed to him an insight into the quintessence of Upaniṣadic wisdom, which he recorded in his *Māṇḍukya-kārikā*. Commenting on Gauḍapāda's *Āgama-Śāstra*, a certain Śaṅkara (perhaps identical with the great Śaṅkara) remarked that nondualism had been recovered from the Vedas by Gauḍapāda in order to refute the dualism of the Sāṃkhya masters.

The *Āgama Śāstra* is divided into four *prakaraṇas*, or chapters. It is regarded as a commentary on the brief, enigmatic Upaniṣad called *Māṇḍukya*. Only in the first chapter are the *mantras* of the *Māṇḍukya* discussed. Then the author goes on to establish the Advaita ("nondual") doctrine by arguing against the dualists, such as the Sāṃkhya philosophers, and the pluralists, such as the Nyāya philosophers. His doctrine is called the *ajātivāda*, or the "theory of nonorigination." The paradox of permanence and change is invoked to show that causation or origination of new things is unintelligible. The

Sāṃkhya philosophers who say that the cause persists in, and is identical with, the effect *(satkāryavāda)*, and the Nyāya philosophers who say that the cause creates the effect, which was nonexistent before *(asatkāryavāda)*, oppose each other and both, thereby, are refuted; this then points toward the truth of the view of nonorigination, that is, that nothing can originate. Creation is only an illusion; the diversity of the world has only a dreamlike existence, for the ultimate reality is a nondifferential unity.

It is believed that Gauḍapāda was strongly influenced by Buddhism, especially by the Yogācāra school. It has even been suggested that the *Āgama Śāstra* is actually a Buddhist text. But while the influence of Buddhist doctrines and arguments upon Gauḍapāda is undeniable, it would be wrong to conclude that he was a Buddhist. The fourth chapter of the *Āgama Śāstra* undoubtedly includes much Buddhist material. But it is still safe to conclude that Gauḍapāda was an early Vedāntin who must have influenced Śaṅkara in the development of his celebrated nondualism.

[*See also* Sāṃkhya; Nyāya; *and the biography of Śaṅkara.*]

BIBLIOGRAPHY

Bhattacharya, Vidhushekhara. *The Āgamaśāstra of Gauḍapāda.* Calcutta, 1943. An indispensable sourcebook containing edited text, annotated translation, and introduction.

Mahadevan, T. M. P. *Gauḍapāda: A Study in Early Advaita.* Madras, 1969.

Bimal Krishna Matilal

GAUTAMA. *See* Buddha.

GEIGER, ABRAHAM (1810–1874), rabbi, foremost exponent and ideologue of Reform Judaism in nineteenth-century Germany and outstanding scholar of *Wissenschaft des Judentums* (the modern scholarly study of Judaism). Geiger was born in Frankfurt, where he received a distinguished, traditional Talmudic education. He was also attracted to secular studies and in 1833 received his doctorate from the University of Bonn for a work entitled *Was hat Mohammed aus dem Judenthume aufgenommen* (What Did Muḥammad Take from Judaism?), a study that measured Judaism's influence on early Islam. In 1832 Geiger became rabbi in Wiesbaden, and there he set out to rescue Judaism from medieval rabbinic forms that he regarded as rigid, unaesthetic, and unappealing to Jews of contemporary cultural sensibilities. He did this by initiating reforms in the synagogue service and by calling, in 1837, for a conference of Reform rabbis in Wiesbaden. Moreover, he hoped to show how the academic study of the Jewish past could be enlisted as an aid in the causes of Jewish political emancipation and religious reform through the publication of the *Wissenschaftliche Zeitschrift für jüdische Theologie* (1835–1847).

Geiger became embroiled in controversy in 1838 when the Breslau Jewish community selected him as *dayyan* (religious judge) and assistant rabbi over the strong protests of the Breslau Orthodox rabbi, Solomon Tiktin. Indeed, because of this opposition, Geiger could not accept the position until 1840. Upon Tiktin's death in 1843 Geiger became rabbi of the city. There he continued his activities on behalf of Reform, playing an active role in the Reform rabbinical conferences of 1845 and 1846, held respectively in Frankfurt and Breslau.

Geiger's undiminished commitment to the academic study of Judaism and his belief in the need for a modern rabbinical seminary to train rabbis in the spirit of modern Western culture and *Wissenschaft des Judentums* led, in 1854, to the creation of the Jüdisch-Theologisches Seminar in Breslau. Geiger was bitterly disappointed, though, when the board of the seminary decided to appoint as principal the more conservative Zacharias Frankel instead of himself. It was not until 1872, two years after Geiger had come to Berlin as a Reform rabbi to the community, that his dream of directing a modern rabbinical seminary came to fruition. For in that year the Hochschule für die Wissenschaft des Judentums was established, with Geiger at its head. He remained director of this center for the training of Liberal rabbis until his death.

Geiger's scholarship was prodigious and profound. His most influential work, *Urschrift und Uebersetzungen der Bibel . . .* (The Original Text and Translations of the Bible . . . ; 1857), advocated the methodology of biblical criticism, and a host of other scholarly and polemical articles and books displays his broad knowledge of all facets of Jewish history and culture. These publications reveal his determination to make Judaism an integral part of Western culture and indicate both his theological bent and his ability to employ historical and philological studies in the cause of religious reform.

Geiger's work, carried out in the context of *Religionswissenschaft,* pointed to the evolutionary nature of the Jewish religion and, under the influence of Schleiermacher, allowed him to focus on the inwardness of the Jewish religious spirit. Having thereby mitigated the force of tradition, Geiger was able, in terms borrowed from Hegel, to view Judaism as a universal religion identified with the self-actualization of the Absolute. He therefore downplayed nationalistic elements in the Jewish past, denied them any validity in the present, and justified Jewish separateness in the modern world by speaking of Judaism's theological uniqueness and spiritual mission. Nevertheless, Geiger, unlike his more radical colleague Samuel Holdheim, represented a moderate approach to Reform. He refused to serve a Reform congregation that separated itself from the general Jewish community, he observed Jewish dietary laws, and he urged the retention of traditional Jewish laws of marriage and divorce. In addition, he favored the observance of the second day of the festivals and, like his more conservative peer Frankel, spoke of "positive-historical" elements in Judaism.

BIBLIOGRAPHY

The best English introduction to Geiger's life and writings appears in *Abraham Geiger and Liberal Judaism*, compiled and edited by Max Wiener and translated by Ernst J. Schlochauer (Philadelphia, 1962). David Philipson's *The Reform Movement in Judaism* (New York, 1967) also contains a great deal of information about Geiger's career and thought. Geiger's own views of Judaism are summarized in a series of lectures he delivered in Frankfurt that have been translated by Charles Newburgh as *Judaism and Its History* (New York, 1911). Jakob J. Petuchowski provides interesting insights into Geiger's approach to Judaism and contrasts him with Samuel Holdheim in the article "Abraham Geiger and Samuel Holdheim: Their Differences in Germany and Repercussions in America," *Leo Baeck Institute Yearbook* 22 (1977): 139–159. Finally, Petuchowski has edited a series of essays by several eminent scholars on the meaning and significance of Geiger's career and scholarship in a work entitled *New Perspectives on Abraham Geiger* (Cincinnati, 1975).

DAVID ELLENSON

GELUGPA. *See* Dge-lugs-pa.

GE MYTHOLOGY. Before Brazilian expansion diminished their territories, the widely scattered, generally independent and isolated groups that speak languages of the Ge family occupied a large expanse of the Brazilian interior, from approximately 2° to 28° south latitude, and from 42° to 58° west longitude. They are usually grouped into three branches on the basis of linguistic similarities: the northern Ge (the Kayapó, Suyá, Apinagé, and the various Timbirá groups in the Brazilian states of Pará, Mato Grosso, Goiás, and Maranhão), the central Ge (the Xavante and Xerente, in the states of Mato Grosso and Goiás), and the southern Ge (the Kaingán and Xokleng, in the states of São Paulo, Santa Catarina, and Rio Grande do Sul).

In addition to their language affiliation, the Ge-speaking groups share a tendency to occupy savanna or upland regions away from rivers, to live in relatively large semipermanent villages, and to subsist on extensive hunting and collecting and some degree of horticulture. Compared with other lowland groups in South America, the Ge have a fairly simple material culture and very complex forms of social organization involving moieties, clans, and name-based groups. Their rites of passage are long and elaborate. Several non-Ge-speaking groups on the Brazilian central plateau also have some of these traits. Among the most important of these are the Boróro and Karajá.

The French anthropologist Claude Lévi-Strauss has convincingly demonstrated that similarities among the myths of the Americas do exist. Ge mythology is, however, significantly different in content and emphasis from that of other large language families in lowland South America (the Tupi, Arawak, Carib, and Tucanoan). The complexity of Ge and Boróro social organization, the elaborateness of their rites of passage, and the apparently secular nature of many of their narratives have challenged scholars to explain the importance of their myths. Lévi-Strauss uses Ge and Boróro myths as a point of departure in his four-volume *Mythologiques* (1964–1971; translated as *Introduction to a Science of Mythology*, 1969–1981), and some of his most careful critics have used those myths to discuss his work or to investigate the sociological context of myths in general. Ge mythology thus occupies an important place in the study of South American mythology both because of the challenges the narratives themselves present and because of the ways a number of distinguished scholars have confronted them.

Narrative Styles. Most anthropologists who write about lowland South American mythology use the word *myth* to refer to any narrative, be it cosmogonic, historical, or apparently anecdotal, since genre distinctions are difficult to establish for cosmologies that have no deities. The Ge have many different styles of oratory, formal speech, and song; the narration of myths constitutes only a small part of this repertoire. The word *myth* covers a number of distinct narrative styles, which vary from the relatively fixed chanted texts of some Xokleng myths to fairly flexible narrative forms that closely resemble the European folktale in style and content. The definitions of genre differ from group to group. Among the Xavante, story, history, and dreams are apparently equated; other groups separate events of the distant past from those of the more recent past and again from the experience of dreams.

With the exception of some ritualized performances among the southern Ge, myths are neither secret nor restricted as to the time or place they may be told. They are often recounted at night, by men or women, to children or adults, and mix adventure, humor, ethics, and cosmogony in a way that delights the audience regardless of its age. The narrator imitates sounds and the voices of the characters with considerable musicality, and his or her gestures often add dramatic impact. Many myths have parts that are sung. Questions are often interjected by the audience, and in response the narrator may expand upon some point or another.

Ge myths published in collections are almost exclusively in the third person, but in performance they are not restricted to that format. Performance style varies greatly, which reflects the difference between an oral narrative and a written text. Many performances are almost entirely in dialogue form with a minimum of narrative explanation; the context is largely implicit, and the narrator presumes the audience has previous knowledge of the story. Members of the society have heard the stories from birth, and any given performance is an ephemeral event and so not preserved.

Content and Setting. Compared with the mythology of the other major language groups in Brazil, Ge mythology exhibits in its subject matter little elaboration of the spirit world, an absence of genealogical myths about ancestors, and little cosmological complexity. Here Ge cosmology must be distinguished from Ge mythology. Ethnographies of the Ge societies report beliefs in several types of spirits, in an afterlife in a village of the dead, and in shamans who travel to the sky. Ge mythology, however, rarely describes either these beliefs or their origins.

One of the difficulties scholars have had in interpreting Ge myths is their apparent unrelatedness to other aspects of society, including the elaborate Ge ceremonial life. Some South American societies explain the present by referring to the way the ancestors behaved; but among Ge speakers myths rarely make direct reference to the present in their description of events that involve ethical dilemmas and social processes central to the society. No detailed native exegesis of the stories has been reported; the Ge rarely use a myth to interpret anything other than the narrative itself.

Ge mythology generally focuses on the relationships between the social world of human beings and the natural domain of the animal and the monstrous. The main actors are humans, animals, and beings that are both human and animal. The setting is usually the village and surrounding jungle, although some myths relate a visit to the sky or to a level below the surface of the earth. Because the subject of the myths is the tension between correct social behavior and incorrect or animal-like behavior, rather than the establishment of a given character as a deity or ancestor, the actors of one myth very rarely appear in another. Recurrent features are not individuals but rather relationships (brothers-in-law, siblings, parents and children, formal friends), settings (the villages or the forest), and animals (deer, jaguars, tapirs, wild pigs). All these appear regularly in the myths. An exception to this singularity of character is a series of stories about Sun and Moon found among the northern and central Ge.

Transformation Myths. The central event in a Ge myth is usually a transformation, involving, for example, the change of a continuity into discontinuity, as in the origin of night and death; or the acquisition of an object that transforms society, such as fire, garden crops, and ceremonies that humans are said to have obtained from animals.

The origin of fire. A good example of a transformation myth is that of the origin of fire, versions of which have been collected from most Ge communities. Lévi-Strauss (1969) and Turner (1980) have analyzed it extensively. The following version was recorded among the Suyá; for the complete version, see Wilbert (1984).

> A long time ago the Suyá ate meat warmed in the sun because they had no fire. One day a man takes his young brother-in-law into the forest to look for fledgling macaws to take back to the village, where they will be raised for their feathers. The two walk a long way. The man sets a pole against a rock ledge, and the boy climbs up to look at a nest. When the man asks the boy what the young birds in the nest look like (i.e., whether they have enough feathers to survive in the village), the boy shouts down, "They look like your wife's pubic hair." (This insulting response is a very funny moment for Suyá audiences, who always laugh heartily and repeat the question and response several times for effect. The exact incident that results in the boy's being left in the nest varies among the different Ge groups.)
>
> Angered, the man throws aside the pole and leaves the boy up in the nest, where he grows very thin and is gradually covered with bird excrement. After some time a jaguar comes walking by. Seeing the boy's shadow, the animal pounces on it several times, then looks up and sees the boy. The boy tells the jaguar of his difficulty, and the jaguar asks him to throw down the fledglings. The boy does so, and the jaguar gobbles them up. Then it puts the pole against the cliff and tells the boy to descend. Although terrified, the boy finally climbs down and goes with the jaguar to its house.
>
> When they arrive, the boy sees a fire for the first time. It is burning on a single huge log. The jaguar gives the boy roasted meat to eat. A threatening female jaguar arrives. (The degree of threat varies among the different Ge groups.) The jaguar gives the boy more meat and shows him the way home. When he arrives at the village, he tells the men that the jaguar has fire. They decide to take it from the jaguar.
>
> Taking the form of different animal species, the men go to the jaguars' camp where they find the jaguars asleep. They place hot beeswax on the eyes and paws of the jaguars, which then run screaming into the jungle. The men-animals

pick up the fire log and run with it back to the village, in the style of a burity-palm log relay race.

First a rhea carries the fire log, then a deer, then a wild pig, then a tapir. The frog wants to carry the log and in spite of objections is allowed to do so. The log is so hot the frog runs with it to the water and drops it in. The fire goes out. "The fire is dead!" everyone shouts in consternation. Then the toucan, the curassow, and other birds run up, their head and neck feathers bright red because they have been swallowing the live coals that have fallen from the log. They vomit the coals onto the ashes, and the fire starts up again. The tapir picks up the log again and runs with it all the way to the village. When they arrive, the men return to human form and divide the fire among all the houses. Ever since then the Suyá have eaten roasted meat.

The origin of the Savanna Deer ceremony. The myth of the man who is turned into a savanna deer by a jealous rival, representative of another type of transformation story, is cited as the origin myth of a ceremony still performed today by the Suyá; for the complete version, see Wilbert (1984).

Once, before the Suyá had learned the Savanna Deer ceremony, they were painting and preparing for a Mouse ceremony. In this ceremony the adult men take a few young women for collective sexual relations. While some of the men leap, dance, and sing, others choose the women who will take part in this activity, and take them to the men's ceremonial camp.

One man is very possessive about his young wife. To prevent her from being taken as a sex partner for the ceremony, he sings standing next to her in the house. He does not leave her to sing in the men's house. Another man wants to have sexual relations with the woman and is angered by the husband's attentiveness. The angry man is a witch who can transform people or kill them. He decides to transform the woman's husband.

The husband begins to sweat as he dances. His dance cape sticks to his head and will not come off. He tries to pull it off, but it has grown on and has begun to stick to his neck and back as well. "Hey!" he shouts, "I am being transformed into something bad!" He leaves his wife and goes to the men's house, where he sings all night along with the other caped singers.

The next morning the singers' sisters strip them of their capes, and so the men stop dancing and singing, but the husband keeps on (he cannot stop, for his cape will not come off). The men shout at him to stop singing. He keeps dancing and singing. Suddenly he rushes off into the forest, still singing. Later his relatives go off to find him, and after several days they find him near a lake, his body bent over. The rattles tied to his legs have begun to turn into hooves. Antlers fan out above his head. He is singing. (Here the narrator usually sings the song the man-deer is supposed to have been singing.)

The men who find him listen to his song. One man tells the others, "Listen and learn our companion's song," and they sit and listen. (Here the narrator usually sings the rest of the man-deer's song.)

Then the husband becomes a forest deer. He still lives there at the lake. People have seen him there recently. Today the Suyá sing his songs in the Savanna Deer ceremony.

The Analysis of Ge Mythology. Early collections of Ge myths were usually appended to ethnographic accounts of the societies, with little commentary. With the appearance of Lévi-Strauss's *Mythologiques,* however, scholarly interest in Ge mythology increased dramatically. These four volumes have engendered tremendous controversy, but they nonetheless provide an entirely new perspective on the mythology and cosmology of the Americas.

Lévi-Strauss argues that certain empirical categories, such as raw and cooked, fresh and decayed, and noisy and silent, are conceptual tools that the native populations of the Americas use to elaborate abstract ideas and to combine these ideas in the form of propositions. Amerindian mythology is thus a kind of philosophical speculation about the universe and its processes, but one that uses principles quite foreign to Western philosophy. These propositions are best discovered through an analysis that treats myths as elements of a nearly infinite body of partial statements, rather than through an analysis that isolates individual narratives. According to Lévi-Strauss, myths should be interpreted only through other myths, to establish similarities or differences. He further argues that the myths of one society can be interpreted through the myths of surrounding societies, or even through those of distant societies on the same or another continent.

Lévi-Strauss's work must be evaluated in two distinct ways. First, one must consider his comparative method. While the debate on structural analysis in anthropology and literature is extensive, much of the criticism of *Mythologiques* has centered on Lévi-Strauss's removal of myths from the contexts of the societies in which they are told, and on his preferring instead to compare them with the myths of very different societies. Lévi-Strauss (1981), writing in defense of his method of analyzing the native cosmologies of the Americas as a whole (rather than what he claims are individual manifestations, i.e., the myths of a particular society), defines his objective as being that of attempting to understand the workings of the human mind in general.

Second, one must consider whether those categories that Lévi-Strauss highlights as central to cosmologies across the Americas actually are important to specific societies. There is general agreement that they are, and some of the categories delineated by Lévi-Strauss have even proved to be keys to the analyses of the cosmologies of groups about which Lévi-Strauss had no information whatsoever. There is no doubt that the study of South American societies has been revolutionized by Lévi-Strauss's analyses of myth.

Although Lévi-Strauss's work is highly suggestive, his analyses do not answer the questions social anthropologists usually pose about myths: why is it that a given people tells a given story and how does the mythology relate to other aspects of the society? Few anthropologists are satisfied with analyses that treat myth, religion, and cosmology as isolated phenomena. An alternative tradition of interpreting Ge myths derives from the founders of sociological and anthropological theory: Karl Marx, Max Weber, Émile Durkheim, and their followers. A number of important works have examined the relationship between Ge myths and other features of Ge-speaking societies. These authors often use some version of a structural method derived from Lévi-Strauss, but they employ it to quite different ends. They either analyze a myth of a single Ge society or compare a myth found in different groups to show how variations in the myth are paralleled by variations in specific features of the social organization. In this way they support the argument that myths and social processes are related in particular ways.

The most systematic and challenging of these alternative analyses is the work of the American anthropologist Terence Turner (1977, 1980), who combines his reanalysis of a Kayapó myth of the origin of fire with an extensive critique of Lévi-Straussian structuralism. Turner shows that every event, object, and relationship in the fire myth has particular relevance to specific features of Kayapó social organization, social processes, and cosmology. He argues that, for the Kayapó, the telling of myths plays an important part in their understanding of their lives.

Other analysts have related myth to general ethical propositions (Lukesch, 1976), to issues of domestic authority (DaMatta, 1973), to messianic movements, and to the ways in which the Ge societies have confronted conflict and contact with Brazilian society. All these analyses take into account the social, political, and ethical contexts of which Ge myths are always a part, and they have considerably advanced our understanding of the role of myths in tribal societies.

The two very different traditions of scholarship I have described—the study of myths as logical propositions using categories found throughout the Americas and the study of myths within their specific social context—have stimulated the study of Ge narrative itself and have also resulted in the increasingly careful collection and greater availability of adequate texts. With improved recording technology, greater interest in the performative aspects of verbal art, and the contributions of missionaries who are themselves specialists in textual exegesis, there has been a vast improvement in the accuracy of published narratives. While early collections of myths were usually narrative summaries derived from dictation in Portuguese, more recent works have included exact transcriptions of longer Portuguese versions, careful transcriptions of recordings made in the native languages, collections recorded and translated by the Indians themselves, and bilingual publications designed for use as primers by the groups who tell the myths. These improved collections will allow specialists and nonspecialists alike to better understand the myths and evaluate analyses of them.

BIBLIOGRAPHY

The outstanding English source for Ge myths is Johannes Wilbert's *Folk Literature of the Gê Indians*, 2 vols. (Los Angeles, 1979, 1984). In addition to assembling and translating the major published collections, Wilbert has indexed the 362 narratives using the Stith Thompson folk-literature motif index, which may aid comparative work. Texts collected and translated by Indians at a Salesian mission appear in Bartolomeu Giaccaria and Adalberto Heide's *Jeronomo Xavante conta mitos e lendas* and *Jeronomo Xavante sonha contos e sonhos* (both, Campo Grande, Brazil, 1975). Anton Lukesch presents an analysis of the major propositions of Kayapó mythology in *Mythos und Leben der Kayapo* (Vienna, 1968), translated as *Mito e vida dos índios Caiapós* (São Paulo, 1976). For ethnographic background on the Ge, see Curt Nimuendajú's *The Eastern Timbira* (Berkeley, 1946) and David Maybury-Lewis's edited volume *Dialectical Societies: The Gê and Bororo of Central Brazil* (Cambridge, Mass., 1979). Nimuendajú gives a detailed description of a single society, and Maybury-Lewis provides a good background on the sociological issues among the northern and central Ge. Claude Lévi-Strauss's four volumes on Amerindian mythology, published originally in French (Paris, 1964–1971), have been translated into English as *The Raw and the Cooked* (1969), *From Honey to Ashes* (1973), *The Origin of Table Manners* (1978), and *The Naked Man* (1981). My own *Nature and Society in Central Brazil: The Suya Indians of Mato Grosso* (Cambridge, Mass., 1981) demonstrates that many of the ideas and categories Lévi-Strauss discovered through the analysis of Ge mythology are indeed to be found in other aspects of the cosmology, social organization, and values of the Suyá, one of the northern Ge groups. For a critique of Lévi-Straussian structuralism and a reanalysis of one of the Ge myths, see Terence S. Turner's "Narrative Structure and Mythopoesis: A Critique and Reformulation of Structuralist Concepts of Myth, Narrative and Poetics," *Arethusa* 10 (Spring 1977): 103–163; and "Le dénicheur d'oiseaux en contexte," *Anthropologie et sociétés* 4 (1980): 85–115. Roberto DaMatta's "Mito e autoridade domestica," in his *Ensaios de antropologia estrutural* (Petrópolis, Brazil, 1973), is an excellent example of how the analysis of a single myth common to two societies can reveal differences in their social organization.

Anthony Seeger

GENDER ROLES of certain ritualists—priests, shamans, curers, diviners, oracles, seers, and prophets, among others—may express altered sexuality in certain tribes or ethnic groups. As transvestites, some ritualists use dress to affect an appearance of gender change but keep up many, if not most, of the activities of their biological sex. As transsexuals, others almost completely change gender in role and behavior. Gender-changed religious persons may live in celibacy, or they may express sexuality in marriage, promiscuity, or some other form of active sex life. Scant information in literary sources provides little clue to personal or cultural distinctions between transvestites and transsexuals. For this essay, however, it is more important to stress the importance and meaning of gender changes in religion than it is to determine clinical definitions.

Gender change, laden with religious meaning, almost always occurs through a supernatural calling in visions or dreams. Permanent change is seldom, if ever, imposed on an infant for religious reasons at birth. More commonly, it occurs in adolescence or adulthood and is at times accompanied by illness or spirit possession. Thus, when someone takes up permanent gender change, he or she appears to contain supernatural powers strong enough to affect the fertility, health, and welfare of an entire group. If not caused through spirit possession, gender change in a religious context usually takes place with ritual to mark its importance for the community. Awe inevitably surrounds the changed person's apparent ability to contact and control supernatural realms.

This essay distinguishes between lifelong and occasional gender change. Occasional gender change occurs within calendrical, fertility, or life-change rites (rites of passage), curing ceremonies, or other events happening within a set time. Such temporary change in gender role often comically or aggressively highlights values or conflicts in a group's attitudes and beliefs toward sex. These dramas usually occur in an anticipated ritual form, though their content often produces great spontaneity and excitement.

This essay will explore instead attitudes and beliefs in selected cultural settings toward lifelong gender change of key ritualists. Here attitudes are defined as emotions or feelings about gender change (fear, respect, ridicule, distrust, and so forth), while beliefs mean the conviction of truth or the perceived reality of some fact (for example, that many gender-changed ritualists may be not only curers but also witches).

Certainly groups exist whose gender-changed members do not assume sacred roles. At this point, however, it lies beyond the scope of this essay, if not of social science itself, to predict which attitudes and beliefs infuse gender-changed roles with religious meaning and which remain secular. The purpose here is to show *how* gender change, attitudes, and beliefs mutually affect one another and not *why* gender change originated for religious worship.

Research shows that no one theory, indeed perhaps no theory at all, can account for the complex manifestation of such behavior. Therefore this essay, aside from refuting theories about the cause of gender change, will also explore religious attitudes and beliefs about it in selected diverse cultural settings: medieval Christianity, American Indian religions, and the religion of a New Guinean people.

Within its limited goal, this essay will show that, while theories may not hold up, certain somewhat consistent attitudes and beliefs emerge. Research shows that people may value sacred gender-changed ritualists as religious commodities, public resources, or a public good. Such gender-changed ritualists have, in effect, turned their altered sexuality over to the community. This sexuality becomes a form of potent abstract ritual property available to augment spiritual or supernatural advantage.

Aspects of Gender Role. The purpose here is in part to examine what we do and do not know about gender change and in part to refute certain false assumptions made regarding the religious aspects of lifelong gender change. Some of these assumptions begin with the biological and social understanding of gender role itself.

Gender change as biology. Although beliefs or perceived "facts" about gender might seem to be very clear, determining biological gender may become a confusing issue. Patricia A. Jacobs (1966) states that anatomically there are two genders, male and female, with a very rare occurrence of hermaphrodites: persons born with ambiguous genitalia or, even more rarely, with truly mixed male and female chromosomes. Some writers have erroneously labeled as "hermaphrodites" persons who strive to become in all aspects a member of the opposite sex (transsexuals) and those who dress and act like the opposite sex (transvestites) but do not wish to change their biological sex and do not give up all biologically sex-related activities.

Cultures respond very differently to hermaphrodites. According to anthropologist Willard Williams Hill (1935), in "The Status of the Hermaphrodite and Transvestite in the Navaho Culture," the Navajo of the American Southwest welcomed hermaphrodites along with transvestites as wealth-bringers to the tribe. On the other hand, classical scholar Marie Delcourt (1961) states that the ancient Greeks put hermaphrodites to death. Anthropologist Fitz John Porter Poole reports that the modern-day Bimin-Kuskusmin of Papua New Guinea destroy boys with only one testis or with one that has obviously not descended into the scrotum (an anomalous monorchid), but accord the pseudohermaphrodite special ritual privileges. [*See* Androgynes.]

Gender change in the social context. Just as cultures define the biology of gender change differently, so they define differently the attitudes toward transsexualism, transvestism, and other cultural manifestations of gender change. Attitude differences occur among cultures and among individuals within the same culture. Waldemar Bogoraz, the noted ethnologist of Siberian peoples, stated in *The Chukchee* (1904–1909) that gender-changed shamans among the Chukchi were privately ridiculed by fellow tribesfolk but feared as possible witches and so were publicly respected for their great magical powers.

Depictions of human figures displaying both male and female genitals may also indicate varying attitudes toward altered sexuality. Those divided vertically (bilaterally) often express an ideal of totality, fullness, or political and social unity. Such a depiction of Louis XIV may be found in an essay by A. J. Busst (1967).

Depictions divided horizontally (laterally) most often express attitudes of sexual fertility and eroticism, as the genitals are then explicitly functional. Marie Delcourt illustrates this form of gender change throughout her *Hermaphrodite* (1961).

Religious attitudes and gender roles. Religious sanctions, along with other rules and regulations, define and control behavior and attitudes attached to gender assignments based on anatomy at birth. Thus, each culture's environment, values, and experiences influence both perceived "facts" about gender formation as well as feelings toward gender roles. Religious thinking attributes different mystical powers, spiritual worth, and purity or pollution to each gender or gender-changed person. Margaret Mead in her study *Male and Female* (1967), Sherry B. Ortner and Harriet Whitehead (1981), and Michelle Zimbalist Rosaldo and Louise Lamphere (1974) all sensitively address the cultural and social processes by which people attach values and definitions to gender in both social and religious contexts. If the contextual definition of gender role varies widely, is it possible to arrive at any theories that account for gender-changed roles?

Brief Review of Explanations and Theories. Social scientists have made several heroic but unsuccessful attempts to draft encompassing theories applicable to all cases known throughout the world. Most of these theories remain unproved for four reasons: assumptions in which cultural variables cannot be tested; an arbitrary selection of variables to which they compare gender-change behavior; difficulty in establishing a logical basis for gender change; or inability to account for exceptions. Further, most of them concern only male-to-female gender change and do not readily apply to female-to-male gender change. The theories and counterarguments can be summarized as follows.

1. James G. Frazer, in *Adonis, Attis, Osiris* (1914), volumes 5 and 6 of the third edition of *The Golden Bough*, postulates that the gender change of male ritual leaders stems from the worship of goddesses by matrilineal kin groups. Male ritual leaders, he says, obeyed divine orders from these goddesses to act like women or to assume a female role or feminine gender. Arguments against Frazer's postulation include the following: a proliferation of goddesses for matrilineal kin organizations has never been established; groups worship deities of both sexes, no matter which form of organization prevails; gender change in roles and behavior has not been correlated with any particular form of kinship organization. Frazer does not explain why goddesses should be more likely to cause gender change as opposed, for example, to masculine, bisexual, or asexual gods. Further, he does not explain why deities should be isolated as prime motivators for gender change, as opposed to other elements selected from religions or other aspects of social, economic, and/or ecological settings.

2. Hermann Baumann, in *Das doppelte Geschlecht* (Dual Sexuality; 1955), links forms of gender to complexity of religious beliefs. He associates transvestites in "archaic agricultural societies" with mythological twins and androgynous souls, and androgynous priests with "older high cultures" and androgynous high gods. There are a number of problems with Baumann's theory. First, his patterns of diffusion and evolution patterns for religion rely on highly debatable evidence. Like Frazer, he fails to explain why beliefs about gods and souls should have been isolated from other social and religious variables in conjunction with the institution of gender-changed figures. In the end, diffusionary arguments do not provide adequate analysis of the gender-changed figures within the cultural-religious context. Scholars have challenged Baumann's interpretation of his sources (see Gisela Bleibtreu-Ehrenberg, discussed below). In his arguments he has vastly underrepresented native North America with its manifold, varying, and religiously active gender-changed ritualists, the berdaches. It should be noted that Italo Signorini, in "Transvestism and Institutionalized Homosexuality in North America" (1972), finds novel and worthwhile arguments in Baumann's work but does not elaborate on their value.

3. Gisela Bleibtreu-Ehrenberg, in "Homosexualität und Transvestition im Schamanismus" (Homosexuality and Transvestism in Shamanism; 1970), after completely dismissing Baumann's work for both misused sources and illogical arguments, claims that transvestism is most commonly found in cultures with "possession-shamans" who are inherently predisposed to identify with a female deity. But the same question must be posed here as for Frazer and Baumann: why isolate deities in explaining transvestism? Why select certain female deities out of any pantheon in which gods can have many attributes? Bleibtreu-Ehrenberg also furthers an erroneous theory that the berdache chose his/her lot to avoid the dangers and pressures of warfare and the aggressive male ideal of certain American Indian groups. This theory has been advanced by Jeannette Mirsky in "The Dakota" (1937) and is repeated by Royal Hassrick in *The Sioux: Life and Customs of a Warrior Society* (1964) and by Donald G. Forgey in "The Institution of Berdache among the North American Plains Indians" (1975). Charles Callender and Lee M. Kochems, in "The North American Berdache" (1983), provide ample evidence that men had the option to live as "unsuccessful" males in American Indian groups without having to change gender behavior. The berdache was often an outstanding craftsperson, conversationalist, and ritual leader; such behavior did not conform to the role of the despised, outcast coward. Furthermore, such a theory cannot account for the berdache in less warlike tribes or for the female berdache, the woman who behaved like a male and participated in warfare and other male pursuits, including the visions and powers of the male religious domain.

4. Robert L. Munroe, John W. M. Whiting, and Donald J. Halley propose in "Institutionalized Male Transvestism and Sex Distinctions" (1969) that societies with "minimal sex distinctions" tolerate institutionalized male transvestism more than societies with "maximal sex distinctions." The authors do not explain why they selected seven categories from the total range of sex distinctions manifested among humans. Most important, their assumption that men in societies with minimal sex distinctions would find it easy to change gender has no basis in fact. To say that one society "felt" a change in these distinctions more than another presumes a more intimate knowledge of emotional responses than anthropologists can claim today. Ethnographic evidence strongly shows that no matter how rigid or lax the sex distinctions, all groups show clear, definite, at times proscribed, and always culturally value-laden attitudes toward transvestites and/or gender-changed behavior. These authors also do not account for the strong religious component in assigning roles to gender-changed males in their survey.

As was noted earlier, seeking relatively simple causes for the complex ritual behavior and religious attitudes of groups toward gender change leads to dubious results. One must ask again if it is possible to explore how gender-changed persons appear in human thought and how their sexuality becomes a community resource, a contribution to the public good.

Case Studies of Ritual Gender Change. To make cross-cultural surveys of the magnitude suggested above defies any controlled comparison possible today. Every caution advised by noted social anthropologist E. E. Evans-Pritchard (1965) applies to this especially difficult topic. For this reason, examples cited in this essay are drawn from some of the better-documented ethnological and historical sources.

Gender change and devout female Christians. Although the Bible makes a clear statement about sexually appropriate dress, people have applied its words to their own life settings. *Deuteronomy* 22:5 states: "The woman shall not wear that which pertaineth unto a man, neither shall a man put on a woman's garment; for all that do so are abominations unto the Lord thy God." Strictly adhering to this admonition, a devout member of a Christian sect in the United States refused to wear protective overalls to ward against dangerous chemicals in her factory work. A freedom-of-religion law enabled her to retailor the trousers into a long skirt. For her, religious teaching clearly determined the boundaries of her gender-role behavior and dress code.

Deuteronomy notwithstanding, historian Vern L. Bullough (1974, 1980) reveals that certain legendary female saints of the early Middle Ages dressed and lived as ascetic monks, shunning the worldly ways of either sex. Pelagia of Antioch, a dancing girl and prostitute who was converted to Christianity, lived in male garb until her true sex was discovered after her death. Another devout woman, Margarita, fled the bridal chamber to become Pelagius the monk and eventually the prior of a monastery. Expelled for allegedly fathering the doorkeeper's child, she kept secret her true identity and died alone as a hermit, at which time her innocence was recognized. A similar accusation of alleged paternity, followed by later reinstatement to holiness, befell the female ascetic monk Marina (Marinus). These and other examples lead Bullough to conclude that certain women strove to achieve the superior moral and spiritual status accorded to Christian men of this epoch. The church evidently did not disparage this gender-changed behavior.

Bullough notes in contrast that not one transvestite male saint is known. Men would not gain in sanctity by dressing like women, who were considered to be of lower status and less sexually continent; in this belief system, male transvestism could serve only lewd purposes.

Delcourt (1961) suggests that these early legends may have prompted Joan of Arc (c. 1412–1431) to wear male clothing when obeying the voices of saints Margaret, Catherine, and Michael; Bullough (1974, 1980) agrees. Joan, however, took up the sword and, unlike the earlier women, competed in the male secular, political sphere. Yvonne Lanhers (1974) suggests that Joan's major heresy may have been bypassing the authority of the church to heed her voices directly and become the mouthpiece of God to save France from the English. For this alone she could have been repudiated, no matter what her attire. Her soldier's uniform gave her notoriety, though, and became one of the major charges against her as a witch and a heretic.

Thus devout Christian women responded with different behavior to a clear gender-based biblical dress code (and, by implication, behavior). The twentieth-century Christian woman cited earlier refused to accept the relatively lax sex distinctions in the dress of her time. On the other hand, the saints of the early Middle Ages overrode inflexible sex distinctions by adopting male religious garb (presumably distinct from ordinary male clothing), and Joan of Arc emphasized her unique status in the eyes of the French by wearing a colorful male uniform but answering to the title "Maid."

Joan and the twentieth-century woman used their dress to stand apart from their contemporaries, thus heightening their link with their God. In contrast, early medieval saints took up transvestism to increase sanctity by disguise. Attitudes toward their gender change could arise only after their deaths, since they lived their altered sexuality in complete secrecy. Joan and the twentieth-century woman stressed the importance of gender change to affect religious belief, whereas the early saints took up gender change to conform to a prevailing attitude.

Is it possible that where beliefs and attitudes undergo change or mutual conflict, as in Joan's case, the gender change may heighten the alarm and reluctance of others to face changes in these religious beliefs and attitudes?

Bullough (1980) states that Joan competed with men in social status and was therefore destroyed. Yet status alone cannot account for Joan's ostracism, for the earlier transvestite female saints could have been decried upon discovery of their true sex at death. The social settings for the two types of gender-changed behavior were quite different.

Early Christians had to establish their faith, defending and defining it in opposition to rival pagan religions. Early Christian saints exerted individual willpower to reinforce religious, social, and sexual order through their disguised gender. Heroines of this era affirmed the teaching of the church that attributed more spiritual worth to men than to women. In their disguise, these holy women did not challenge the gender hierarchy as Joan did, but instead spurned social and political power precisely as did other humble hermits and monks. Once their disguises were revealed at death, their contemporaries saw them as having transcended their intrinsically less pure femininity, affirming both the beliefs and attitudes of early Christians.

When Joan, however, exerted individual will to counteract the established religious, social, and sexual order to express her religious beliefs, she left herself vulnerable to those ready to blame a sexually perverted witch for every misfortune, illness, or abnormality. Such "perverts" included heretics or challengers of the religious establishment, according to Hugh R. Trevor-Roper (1967).

Joan could not prove that her political quest or her male attire served saintly rather than satanic purposes and met her death as a result. Beliefs about social hierarchies were changing, but attitudes toward the appropriate dress and sexuality of Christian women were not. Hence the unease that Joan stirred in her enemies. The modern factory worker who exerted individual will to express religious beliefs in a secular workplace won her right with no social threat to her community. If anything, she was returning to an earlier, stricter Christian belief system, despite current attitudes about attire and saintliness. In each of the Christian lives, the transvestism (or rejection of it) startled and amazed contemporaries. What then of the institution of transvestism found among numerous American Indian tribes?

The berdache. In "The North American Berdache" (1983), Charles Callender and Lee M. Kochems tabulate the widespread accounts of the berdache as an institution in tribal America. Traditionally, the berdache (etymology unknown) was a ritual leader, a sacred figure, and in some cases, a shaman. The berdache practiced degrees of transvestism, and usually, but not always, enacted some form of gender-changed behavior.

Some were homosexual, others apparently were not. Some lived with wives, fathered children, and fought in battle.

Harriet Whitehead also discusses the berdache cross-culturally in "The Bow and the Burden Strap: A New Look at Institutionalized Homosexuality in Native North America" (in Ortner and Whitehead, 1981, pp. 80–115). She examines this role from the cultural, ecological, and economic view, rather than from that of religious function. Her focus would be useful in further studies to examine the berdache in a full social context.

Another perspective, from James Steel Thayer in "The Berdache of the Northern Plains: A Socioreligious Perspective" (1980), applies the ideas of Mary Douglas's *Purity and Danger* (1966) to the lives of the male (but not female) berdache of the northern Plains. Douglas states that creative powers and forces are unleashed when boundaries of conceptual categories (such as gender categories) are crossed, confused, or in some way threatened. Thus in cultures where gender-changed ritualists perpetuate sexual confusion in a social and religious context, they become dangerous, fearsome, and sacred. Such ideas would have greater applicability to the berdache if any of the early historical or anthropological accounts provided substantial information about the religious duties and powers the berdache could claim.

What we know of his or her religious obligations and powers is scant, but it appears that the berdache mediated between the sexes (among the Cheyenne) or between human and supernatural realms as a shaman (among the so-called Sioux). While some modern writers have alleged that the Sioux berdache was a ridiculed outcast (see Callender and Kochems 1983, 461–462), anthropologist William K. Powers emphatically denies this, asserting that non-Indian values have altered what was once the *wakan,* or holy status, of the berdache. The berdache, then, is an example of Douglas's idea that confusing a category such as gender can enrich as well as threaten.

Indians usually heeded a calling in a dream or vision quest to become a berdache. Thayer (1980) likens the berdache to other sacred and eccentric roles elicited in visions: sacred clowns, love magic makers, and/or shamans, among other ritualists. (For further ethnographic information, see in particular James Owen Dorsey, *A Study of Siouan Cults,* 1890; Clark Wissler, *Societies and Ceremonial Associations in the Oglala Division of the Teton-Dakota,* 1916; and William K. Powers, *Oglala Religion,* 1977. The last is a thoughtful modern reevaluation of the earlier ethnographic works.) In addition, the berdache was often reputed to be the finest at handicrafts, the hardest worker among women, and the most skilled healer.

According to Claude E. Schaeffer's "The Kutenai Female Berdache: Courrier, Guide, Prophetess, and Warrior" (1965), an article with much historical detail and insight, the female berdache first assumed her masculinized role and then gained a reputation for strength of spirit to match her strength of body and character. Such also is Schaeffer's description of the Crow female chief. Again, deficient historical and religious detail prevent us from fully weighing the sacred role of the female berdache among her people, although her existence appears to be well documented.

So far, no author has analyzed the role of the berdache in the full context of cultic and shamanic behavior, so as to help explain how gender change reflected religious notions associated with sexuality, fertility, and tribal well-being. Most interesting perhaps is the parallel between the great religious power of elderly, no longer fertile women and the nonchildbearing, nonfemale berdache.

Whether male or female, what is universal to this gender-change behavior is the very act of transforming a basic biological given into a heightened sexual ambiguity. The berdache usually turned his/her sexual definition into a spiritual power, which in turn was usually regarded as a form of valuable community property. Berdache sexuality left the individual domain and entered the realm of the public good.

Other important gender changes. Gender change for the public good radiates from shamans in Siberia to their villages. All shamans, whether male or female, create special communicating powers with the supernatural world, mediating between humans and the invisible forces. According to Mircea Eliade's encompassing work *Shamanism: Archaic Techniques of Ecstasy* (1964), shamans effect the merging of opposites like the human and supernatural realms. For Eliade, male shamans wearing women's clothes and/or behaving like women unite the opposites of male and female. A high incidence has been recorded among the Siberian Chukchi by Bogoraz (1904–1907) and among the Yukagir by Waldemar Jochelson (1926). Among the Chukchi, Bogoraz also cited females dressing and acting like males.

In Indonesia, male ritualists and guardians of sacred objects lived and dressed as women among the Land and Sea Dayaks. *Ngaju Religion* (1946), by anthropologist Hans Schärer, describes how ritual transvestites called *basir* were chosen to speak for the divinities and unite such important cosmic opposites as earth/sky, land/water, left/right, and male/female.

But what of the woman who, for the good of her kin,

is transformed by the village into an asexual, androgynous, and powerful ritualist, as happens among the Bimin-Kuskusmin of Papua New Guinea?

A gender-changed female ritualist among the Bimin-Kuskusmin. Here a case study by anthropologist Fitz John Porter Poole (1981) contributes to the relatively scant literature about female gender change. That so many more men than women are reported in the literature may reflect a social fact or merely an accident of reporting. But more important than description, the Poole case adds a depth of researched information and profound thought that can be a guide for carefully reasoned future study.

One basic difference exists between this androgynous woman and the other gender-changed ritualists, whether the Indonesian *basir* or the Plains Indian berdache. No dream or vision calls her to her post; instead, her male and female ritual clan leaders recruit and transform her to fulfill this role. As with the early Christian saints, her new gender enforces an ideal of controlled asceticism rather than uncontrolled sexuality. As in the case of the berdache, the role is an accepted institution, but, more than that, it is vital to maintaining ritual, religious, and social life amid these people of New Guinea.

Poole examines bodily substances in analyzing this sacred woman *(waneng aiyem ser)* who is called a "male mother" *(auk kunum imok).* Ritually androgynous and highly sacred, two "male mothers" are found in nearly all clans of the Bimin-Kuskusmin of Papua New Guinea. These clans trace membership through fathers to a common ancestor. Patrilineages, also traced through males, form each larger clan. The Bimin-Kuskusmin believe that, like all other humans, the male mother combines male and female substances in her body. The male substances are strong, hard, and internal, whereas the female are weak, soft, and external, the first to decompose at death. Unlike other women, however, especially nonpatrilineal wives who are "uncontrolled," dangerous, and immoral, the no-longer-married, postmenopausal male mother can no longer pollute men through their loss of semen in sex or through her own loss of menstrual fluids. She embodies to the highest degree the positive spirit bond of the patrilineage, which men share with their patrilineal sisters, whose menstrual blood and fertility (unlike that of their nonpatrilineal wives) they control.

The male mother is initiated into her role only by the other clan male mother through a series of rites that symbolically remove all vestiges of her menstrual blood. She learns some, but not all, male sacred lore, being forbidden access to the deepest wisdoms. Upon her death, as her skull is placed in the male cult house, men break a hole in the skull so that it can fill up with the male lore once denied her. In life she receives a male name and a sacred name and may wear some, but not all, male regalia. She enjoys certain male foods and privileges forbidden to other women but remains isolated from normal life, since she may easily be polluted by nonsacred people, both male and female.

In the same way that she ritually controls and balances male and female substances, she helps to control ritually the increase of the patrilineage protecting the children born, reared, and exposed to the blood pollution of their biological nonpatrilineal mothers. She enables children not yet "pure" enough to become pure, and she helps expel murderous nonpatrilineal wife-witches from their lives. These wives are so evil that even their own patrilineal brothers cannot control them.

The male mother functions as a patrilineal male in domains where ordinary men would suffer dire pollution, such as during the birth of a patrilineal brother's child or at menarche, which is highly polluting to all males and females. She also serves as a patrilineal female during sacred men's rituals, where ordinary women would be strictly forbidden. As male initiates crawl beneath her legs, the male mothers symbolically give birth to them. Each male mother is dressed for the part as the transvestite figure of the hermaphroditic god-ancestors. At this male initiation, boys are "born" into the adult world without the contaminating blood shed by the mother in biological birth.

Thus whatever men dare not and women cannot do, the male mother does, so that the patrilineage may increase with offspring not contaminated by their nonpatrilineal mothers. The sterile, nonpolluting male mother represents all that Bimin-Kuskusmin men wish to control in women but cannot control if they wish also to procreate, since they cannot marry their sisters. Where menstrual blood, semen, or other bodily substances would pollute, the male mother can ritually mediate and neutralize the dangerous pollutants. In his analysis, Poole shows that beliefs and attitudes toward gender flow in ritual expression, as do the substances of the body.

At one point Poole refers to the male mother as an "artifact." Indeed, the sexually transformed are often associated with important artifacts: the Plains berdache with the splendid crafts from his or her hands, which are guided by the spirits; the *basir* with sacred cult objects; the Navajo hermaphrodite with wealth and money for his or her family. Thus for some groups gender change becomes a form of religious wealth, a source of power, a scarce and precious resource to control and "spend" wisely. Like all scarce resources, the source must be renewed when it is diminished through pollution or ritual use. For others, this resource (like uranium) may be as dangerous as it is beneficial, as transvestism was for Joan of Arc.

Conclusion. The female ritualist of the Bimin-Kuskusmin gives her sexuality to the common good, as did saints and the berdache. Is it possible that, where the ritualist reinforces existing attitudes and beliefs, the gender change may become a beneficial institution, as for the Cheyenne, Sioux, Navajo, and other tribes with the berdache, the Land and Sea Dayaks, and the Bimin-Kuskusmin? Is it possible that, where the ritualist enters into the embroilments of social or religious change, altered sexuality may become a threat?

Among the Siberian Chukchi, for example, attitudes reflect ridicule and mockery of the transvestite shaman, but beliefs hold him or her to be spiritually very powerful. Unlike the Bimin-Kuskusmin male mother, however, the transvestite does not integrate clans or stabilize marriages. In fact, this shaman removes intergroup marriage as a source of Chukchi social integration by "marrying" a member of the same biological sex: the transvestite shaman does not receive a woman in exchange from another group because he/she takes a male partner.

Is it possible to speculate further that gender change as an established institution is more likely to be linked to wealth and sacred objects than is gender change as an agent of conflictive change, where association with material abundance becomes less evident? This question can be answered only with more information on gender change than is currently available. Detailed studies like Poole's, showing how the community interacts with the gender-changed ritualist, need to be written. Greater attention must now be paid to the powers and responsibilities of gender-changed ritualists and to their rites of worship. The value placed on their spirituality must be understood as compared to that of other ritualists in the community.

Too often, especially in the past, the gender-changed person has been singled out as an anomaly. Yet such gender change often in fact represents a range of sexual alternatives permitted, if not expected, by the attitudes and beliefs of the religion in question. These attitudes and beliefs require full exploration, so that assumptions made about individual cases rest on the fullest evidence possible.

BIBLIOGRAPHY

Literature abounds with references to gender-changed males and females who perform important religious functions for their communities. With few exceptions, until recently only a few authors have examined such ritual leaders in full religious context, outlining in detail their obligations and responsibilities. Information on cultural attitudes and behavior toward gender ambiguity in a religious context is also sketchy, usually outlined in broad descriptions, with no clear indication from the author as to sources or the method of interpreting the information. Most of the works listed below are cited without comment, since they provide only descriptions. Other major works have been examined critically in the text of the article. Annotations have been added when an important work has not received comment in the text above.

Baumann, Hermann. *Das doppelte Geschlecht.* Berlin, 1955.

Bleibtreu-Ehrenberg, Gisela. "Homosexualität und Transvestition im Schamanismus." *Anthropos* 65 (1970): 189–228.

Bogoraz, Waldemar. *The Chukchee.* Leiden, 1904–1909.

Bogoraz, Waldemar. *Chukchee Mythology.* Leiden, 1910. The range of gender change for supernatural reasons is not explored in the full context of gender roles. Critical comments aside, this ethnography must be carefully read by any serious scholar examining gender change in the religious context.

Bullough, Vern L. "Transvestites in the Middle Ages." *American Journal of Sociology* 79 (May 1974): 1381–1394.

Bullough, Vern L. *Sexual Variance in Society and History.* Chicago, 1980.

Busst, A. J. "The Image of the Androgyne in the Nineteenth Century." In *Romance Mythologies,* edited by Theodore Fletcher. London, 1967.

Callender, Charles, and Lee M. Kochems. "The North American Berdache." *Current Anthropology* 24 (August–October 1983): 443–470. The authors provide a rich compilation of detail as well as a thoughtful analysis of the berdache's complex social, sexual, and religious role.

Delcourt, Marie. *Hermaphrodite: Myths and Rites of the Bisexual Figure in Classical Antiquity.* Translated by Jennifer Nicholson. London, 1961.

Douglas, Mary. *Purity and Danger.* New York, 1966.

Eliade, Mircea. *Shamanism: Archaic Techniques of Ecstasy.* Rev. & enl. ed. New York, 1964.

Evans-Pritchard, E. E. "The Comparative Method in Social Anthropology." In *The Position of Women in Primitive Societies and Other Essays in Social Anthropology,* edited by E. E. Evans-Pritchard, pp. 13–36. New York, 1965.

Forgey, Donald G. "The Institution of Berdache among the North American Plains Indians." *Journal of Sex Research* 11 (1975): 1–15.

Hassrick, Royal B. *The Sioux: Life and Customs of a Warrior Society.* Norman, Okla., 1964.

Hill, Willard Williams. "The Status of the Hermaphrodite and Transvestite in Navaho Culture." *American Anthropologist* 37 (1935): 273–279.

Jacobs, Patricia A. "Abnormalities of the Sex Chromosomes in Man." *Advances in Reproductive Physiology* 1 (1966): 61–69.

Jochelson, Waldemar. *The Yukaghir and the Yukaghirized Tungus* (1926). New York, 1975.

Lanhers, Yvonne. "Joan of Arc." In *Encyclopaedia Britannica (Macropaedia),* 15th ed. Chicago, 1974.

Mead, Margaret. *Sex and Temperament in Three Primitive Societies.* London, 1935.

Mirsky, Jeannette. "The Dakota." In *Cooperation and Competition among Primitive Peoples,* edited by Margaret Mead, pp. 382–427. New York, 1937.

Munroe, Robert L., John W. M. Whiting, and David H. Hally. "Institutionalized male Transvestism and Sex Distinctions." *American Anthropologist* 71 (1969): 87–91.

Ortner, Sherry B., and Harriet Whitehead, eds. *Sexual Meanings: The Cultural Construction of Gender of Sexuality.* Cambridge, 1981.

Poole, Fitz John Porter. "Transforming 'Natural' Woman: Female Ritual Leaders and Gender Ideology among Bimin-Kuskusmin." In *Sexual Meanings: The Cultural Construction of Gender and Sexuality,* edited by Sherry B. Ortner and Harriet Whitehead, pp. 116–165. Cambridge, 1981.

Rosaldo, Michelle Zimbalist, and Louise Lamphere, eds. *Women, Culture, and Society.* Stanford, Calif., 1974.

Schaeffer, Claude E. "The Kutenai Female Berdache: Courier, Guide, Prophetess, and Warrior." *Ethnohistory* 12 (Summer 1965): 193–236. This work makes outstanding use of primary sources in its thorough coverage of the topic.

Schärer, Hans. *Ngaju Religion: The Conception of God among a South Borneo People* (1946). Translated by Rodney Needham. The Hague, 1963.

Signorini, Italo. "Transvestism and Institutionalized Homosexuality in North America." In *Atti del XL Congresso Internazionale degli Americanisti,* vol. 2 Genoa, 1972.

Thayer, James S. "The Berdache of the Northern Plains: A Socioreligious Perspective." *Journal of Anthropological Research* 36 (1980): 287–293.

Trevor-Roper, Hugh R. "The European Witch Craze of the Sixteenth and Seventeenth Centuries." In his *The Crisis of the Seventeenth Century: Religion, the Reformation, and Social Change,* pp. 90–192. New York, 1967.

PRISCILLA RACHUN LINN

GENEALOGY. As formal structure, genealogy is foremost an intellectual discipline. Its concern is with recording and putting into systematic order the histories of families, differentiating them by rules of descent and allocating to each a share of those enduring human valuables that consist of privileges and honors, titles and powers. Although grounded in myth and circumscribed by tradition and, thus, seemingly a rote and rigid subject, genealogy is to be understood rather as a product of informed speculative reasoning about metaphysical, specifically ontological, matters. Its subject matter goes beyond the listing of pedigrees. It identifies and differentiates the forces and generative sources that give shape to and regulate the entire universe of life. From its cosmological concepts, it draws implications for human conduct and for the structure of the social order. Most directly, genealogies connect human families with their mythical origins, joining them as kinfolk within the universal community of gods, spirits, and other forms of life.

Principles of Genealogy. The genealogical discipline exercises a controlling influence upon everyday life, for it is the source of the morality and of the principles of systematic order that bind systems of descent into clans, lineages, and similar groupings. Among tribal societies especially, the genealogical order frequently dictates all social relations. In early and more complex traditional societies, where only royalty and related families come within its scope, the genealogical system acts as the focus of authority. In sum, for preindustrial societies the genealogical discipline is unitary and unifying, joining the social and the religious forms by demonstrating that society is an extension of the mythical era of original creations. From this unitary perspective, the gods, spirits, and ancestral beings who brought human beings into existence are themselves drawn into the human sphere. In more recent times, genealogical interest has been reduced. Stripped of its religious and cosmological associations, genealogy serves, at most, the general purpose of celebrating ethnicity.

The general model for making genealogical distinctions is drawn from nature. This is most clearly exemplified in totemic systems, whose family lines are represented as descended from animals or other distinctive natural forms. Each line of descent appears as a species and therefore stands as one among all the other natural varieties of life. In nontotemic systems, the special qualities attributed to particular human ancestors serve the same purpose of distinguishing the lines of descent. Thus, human founders of clans and lineages are held to be the primary sources of the vigor and continuity of their descendants, as are totemic ancestors. In both systems, the natural species exemplify the traits of continuity and social immortality that human societies seek through their own genealogies.

As a process, differentiation appears as the signifier of forces that promote growth and development. The natural evolution commonly depicted in creation myths begins with relatively amorphous beings and proceeds systematically to final stages of specificity. This understanding of the natural direction of life underlies the metaphoric assumption that takes the contrast between the chaotic and the structured in ritual and myth to be analogous to the contrast between the deathlike and the vigorous in social life. Accordingly, genealogical systems—the primary promulgators of differentiation—are impelled to drive toward singularity, to single out families and persons for special distinction as principal bearers of vital powers.

Essentially, all the systematic modes of differentiation upon which genealogical systems are constructed express some concept of generative powers. The rules of primogeniture and of relative seniority of descent generally concern the special nature of powers presumed to lie in primacy, that is, in the original conditions that generated forms and natural processes. The rules of descent by gender (matriliny, patriliny, bilaterality) stem from the distinctive generative powers of femininity and masculinity. The rules governing direct and collateral lines reflect closeness to the central sources, and those that differentiate between long and short genealogies involve issues of inherent longevity. Each mode of descent has the added significance of being the appropriate mode of transmission of powers, and each member of a genealogical chain has stature as a designated and graded conveyor.

In substance, the characteristic modes of genealogical transmission impose a powerful order upon social structures. They regulate marriage and other social relations, and they determine the formal lines of social divisions and the character of dependency in subordinate branches. In keeping with the general idea of a genealogical system as an organism that grows and branches, lineages are quite commonly envisioned as vegetative.

The social and cosmological implications of genealogical differentiation are realized most fully in lineage structures. In contrast to clans, which only imply and therefore generalize their putative connections to founders, lineages depend upon true pedigrees, upon the real chain of names and their sequences, and often upon the sequences of outstanding events that demonstrate the potency and special quality of the names. Genealogical traditions and related rituals evoke, reanimate, and, in some sense, reincarnate ancestors. Remembering the long line of ancestors by name (in Polynesia, as far back as ninety-nine generations) is an act of piety that, even in tribal societies, imposes the technical requirement of creating the scholarly and priestly craft of official genealogist for royal and noble lines.

Aristocracy, understood as a social system in which a singular descent line has come forward as the focus of generative powers, may take shape among clans as well as among lineages, drawing upon their common genealogical rules. But it is the specificity of the lineage and its greater adeptness for drawing fine distinctions that endow royalty with the extra degree of moral authority for governing. The lineage is so much the social instrument of royalty that it readily becomes its own characteristic form of organization. Even among tribal societies, among whom organic unities are the common norm, it is not exceptional for chiefly lines to be the exclusive protagonists of the lineage system, and for all others to fall into a binlike category of relatively generalized descent. The Kwakiutl and some Polynesians, who are discussed below, illustrate what are, in effect, the social fractures in a system of descent.

It may seem paradoxical that lineages, although they are buttressed by deeply held human convictions about the binding powers of common descent, should, in fact, promote, as a matter of principle, countertenets of antagonisms, oppositions, and structural divisions. Yet, these forms of divisiveness are not accidental but are the complements of systems that transmit singular powers. Powers must demonstrate efficacy; efficacy invites contention. As a consequence, aristocratic lineages must sustain themselves, not by their genealogical authority alone, but by the abilities of their actual rulers to balance sometimes conflicting claims of birth and force.

Systems of Genealogy. Thus, their orderly premises notwithstanding, genealogical systems are variable. They are subject to the vicissitudes of history that ultimately erode the most formidable structures, as well as to the variability that is allowed by their rules and to the ambiguities of situation that disturb any social order. One cannot hope to describe the varieties of genealogical systems encyclopedically. The following examples from tribal societies and from ancient and more recent civilizations are not necessarily the most characteristic, but they call attention to special features that pertain to the general nature of genealogies.

The Cubeo. The Cubeo, Tropical Forest Indians of the Colombian Vaupés, exemplify genealogical aristocracy as developed within the constraints of a subsistence economy. Even within the meager material setting of slash-burn root horticulture, supplemented by fishing and hunting, the rudimentary form of aristocracy exhibited by the Cubeo resembles, in many formal respects, the hierarchical structures and the patterns of dominance and subordination of the more complex civilizations, indicating that aristocracy may be less a product of material than of genealogical factors. Cubeo society is an organization of ranked, exogamic, and patrilineal sibs (clans), who are joined together in a confraternity (phratry) for what are largely ritual purposes. The sibs exchange wives with those of similar rank in a corresponding phratry. The rank of the sibs was preordained and revealed in the order of birth from an underground dwelling that brought into being the first set of fraternal ancestors, the founders of sibs. The names of their descendants have entered into the genealogies of the sibs, to be inherited in alternate generations by the grandchildren. The personal names, like "souls," carry the immortality of the descent lines and, the Cubeo believe, promote the growth of the children who bear them.

The names are but one of four elements that enter into the substance of the genealogies. The others are sacred trumpets and flutes that bear the names and represent the original ancestors; the life souls that are apportioned to each of the sibs; and, finally, the figure of a sacred anaconda, in whose elongated form the sibs are imagined as ranked segments extending from the head to the tail. The anaconda symbolizes the animal nature of human beings and their kinship with the animal world. These four elements characterize the Cubeo genealogical structure as a complex conveyor of vital forces that ensure their ethnic continuity and are therefore central to their religious and ritual purposes, namely, to maintain connections with founding ancestors. "When we remember our ancestors," the Cubeo proclaim, "we bring them to life." For them, the act of recreating the ancestors in memory is comparable to the original creation, when the Creator willed people into existence by means of his own imaginative thought.

The correspondence of the hierarchical order of the sibs to the order in which the first ancestors emerged is also, in essential respects, a memorial to the circumstances of their origins; they are designated by genealogical relations as older brother/younger brother, and as grandparent/grandchild; by an original distribution of ritual powers, as chiefs, priests, shamans, warriors, and servants; and, by their place as segments of the body of the sacred anaconda, they are assigned a fixed order of residence along the rivers they occupy. The highest ranks, corresponding to the head of the anaconda, live toward the mouth of the river; the servants, toward the source. Thus the genealogical system—recapitulating in each generation the generative conditions of origins as an action of creative remembering—encompasses the main areas of Cubeo social and religious existence.

The Kwakiutl. A similar genealogical system, but one notable for the unusual significance it attaches to hereditary personal names, prevails among the Kwakiutl Indians of Vancouver Island. The qualities commonly attributed to personal names imply the presence in them of spiritual or magical powers, a "name soul," as, for example, among the Inuit (Eskimo). The Kwakiutl seem to have elevated the concept of name soul to a high level of concreteness, thereby bringing to the surface a mystical attribute of names that in other cases exists only by implication. Their treatment of names suggests how pedigrees may indeed constitute a great chain of being.

In Kwakiutl genealogies, each personal name stands for a desirable attribute of being, ordinarily a special power, and the ensemble of ancestral names covers the range of attributes and powers that govern life and death and control valued possessions. Even as it is a specified segment of the patterned mosaic of life forces, each name also has existence as a being, as a spiritual personage who is attached to and yet may have an existence apart from its bearer. The bearer is no ordinary being either, having been set apart and sanctified in having met the genealogical qualifications of seniority. Among the Kwakiutl tribes, which once numbered in the tens of thousands, only a very small number of personal names are of this type; all others are scorned as "made-up." The real names are the exclusive property of a nobility of chiefs, the secular and religious leaders. The remainder are the names of commoners, people who cannot claim descent from mythical ancestors.

The chiefly or spiritual names possess an autonomy congruent with their character as ancestral incarnations, and, as such, they impose their natures upon those who bear them. Under certain circumstances they stand apart entirely. Thus, a chief who possesses several names, some belonging to different divisions of the tribe, might engage in ritual transactions with his distant name as though it were another person. He might present this name with gifts, or, under other circumstances, go through a sham marriage with a name attached for this purpose to his arm, for example. Kwakiutl genealogies are histories of the acquisition and descent of all such names and of their intrinsic properties. Chanted at all important ceremonial events, the family history is a repository of its accumulated powers and capacities. [*See* Names and Naming.]

Polynesian societies. Cubeo and Kwakiutl genealogical systems are noteworthy examples of aristocracy that is deeply enlaced in mythological and shamanistic conceptions and, therefore, politically undeveloped. Polynesian societies offer contrasting examples. Perhaps because their religions are more fully theistic and relatively free of these other associations, the Polynesians were able to move in another direction. Upon similar genealogical principles, and upon an equally undifferentiated economy, Polynesian societies produced such relatively modern institutions as socioeconomic stratification and centralized territorial states. Thus, the capability of a genealogical system to evolve or to elaborate a new social order is never a function of rules of descent alone. New patterns emerge when genealogical rules are joined to an appropriate religious doctrine. In Polynesia, that doctrine has been based upon a concept of *mana,* a force that animates all of nature and characterizes the energetic properties of all substance. [*See*

Preanimism.] In principle, *mana* descends from the gods to the human generations in measured proportions as defined by the genealogical rules. Senior lines are richly endowed with *mana* and are energized and hence ennobled by it; the junior descent lines are left behind as the weakly endowed commoners.

Conceptualized as an efficient force manifested objectively in results—on the battlefield, in the fields of production, in the perfection of craft skills, in personal charisma, in the efficacious management of religious rituals—*mana* is not automatically and indisputably the gift of inheritance. Its possessor has also to demonstrate worthiness by standing up to challenge. Nevertheless, although the conviction that the powers that animate and bestow efficacy move by the generative forces of genealogical rules may yield to the acid test of actual events, it is never abondoned. When lower ranks win royal power by force, as they occasionally do, from time to time, they are still obliged to discover genealogical authority for their new office. Genealogical guilds guard the sanctity of royal and noble pedigrees.

Polynesian societies differ in the way each has managed to sustain the shifting balances between the genealogical and the pragmatic. The Maori of New Zealand exemplify relatively close adherence to traditional genealogical criteria. The Samoans, the Easter Islanders, and the Mangaians demonstrate a greater flexibility in following the traditional rules of descent. The emergent states and stratified societies of Tonga, Tahiti, and Hawaii, for example, reveal a seemingly typical developmental cycle that moves from traditionalism to greater openness and, finally, to the consolidation of hereditary rule, but within the framework of a markedly restructured social order.

Major civilizations. The histories of major civilizations—those of classical Greece, Japan, or England, to take but three examples—show their genealogical life as comparable, in many respects, with that in tribal societies. Hesiod assembled from the body of Homeric mythology a genealogical order of the gods that allotted to each of them appropriate honors, titles, and cosmological functions, and described "how the gods and men sprang from one source." Theogony emerges as one aspect of cosmogony. The gods, men, and the fully differentiated natural order evolve in these genealogical tales within a turbulent atmosphere, in a setting of disputes for power among contending forces, very much as they do in tribal creation myths. The patterns set by the gods, the immortals, in their evolution define the courses of human history.

The genealogists of archaic and preliterate Japan assembled from ancient myths a comparable cosmogony. Heaven and Earth, initially formed from Chaos, after several generations produced the god Izanagi and the goddess Izanami, who gave birth first to the islands of Japan, then to other gods, and, finally, after many generations and much social disorder, to men. The first mikado was granted sovereignty by the sun goddess and, as a link in the succession of the gods, became the center of the national religious cult. Similarly, each distinguished family or clan also claimed its derived divinity from other gods and from ancestral association with emperors. The Japanese chronicles of hereditary titles authenticated the social and religious organization.

Christianity, in principle, breaks with the tenet of the traditional genealogical order that claims divine descent, but it leaves essentially untouched the issues of sanctity and an even deeper concern with singularity and inequality. Even the egalitarian Quakers in England succumbed to the temptation of differentiating major from minor family lines. As for English royalty, it had found in the Roman Catholic church, itself the heir to the political institutions of the Roman empire, the questionable but powerful bases for claiming the "divine right of kings" as an authority for absolute power. The Glorious Revolution of 1688 set that thesis to rest, and later monarchs settled for the moderate option of divine approval.

Through the long course of English history, the constant principle of monarchy, starting with the Celtic rule of the fourth century BCE, is one of singular descent from divinely graced or otherwise extraordinary leaders. Except for kinship with the royal house, no other fixed principles for succession to the throne, as for example primogeniture, were established in England before the thirteenth century. As is common in such systems, genealogical authority fostered social unity when it was strong and wars for succession when it was weak. Social and cultural unity has been the aim and, to a considerable extent, the accomplishment of the genealogical order—which achieved its apotheosis in aristocracy—until relatively recent times.

Nongenealogical Succession. Tibetan Buddhism, or Lamaism, illustrates the contrary qualities of a dynastic order from which genealogical succession has been totally banished. In the fifteenth century, the monastery of Dge-lugs-pa (Gelugpa), a celibate order and the original seat of the Dalai Lama dynasty, promulgated a doctrine of successive reincarnations as the mode of accession to divine authority. They believed that the Dalai Lama would be reborn in some infant unrelated and unknown to him, and that through this reincarnation, he would continue his work of enlightenment. Discovered after an exhaustive search that brought to light his divine traits and evidence of an earlier existence, the new Dalai Lama was trained for his post during an interim regency. [*See* Dalai Lama.] The Tibetan doctrine set aside traditional considerations of individuality and family distinction so that the divine presence, a manifestation of the Buddha, would appear directly, albeit in human form. However, whatever forcefulness this system gained through directness of access to the religious source was at least partly dissipated by the dispersal of its constituencies. Unaffiliated to a systematic line of succession, Lamaist adherents were free to join any one of numerous monasteries, each of which was headed by an abbot, himself the incarnation of a lesser lama.

BIBLIOGRAPHY

The late Meyer Fortes was perhaps the most original and perceptive of anthropological authorities on genealogical issues. His *Kinship and the Social Order: The Legacy of Lewis Henry Morgan* (Chicago, 1969), a central work on the subject, is a most useful summary and refinement of his position with a rich bibliography of theoretical and ethnographic sources. For the Cubeo, the only work thus far is my *The Cubeo: Indians of the Northwest Amazon*, rev. ed. (Urbana, Ill., 1979), based on field work. Two exceptional studies on Barasana Indians, also of the Colombian Vaupés, that examine genealogical conceptions from structuralist and symbolist perspectives are Christine Hugh-Jones's *From the Milk River: Spatial and Temporal Processes in Northwest Amazonia* (Cambridge, 1979) and Stephen Hugh-Jones's *The Palm and the Pleiades: Initiation and Cosmology in Northwest Amazonia* (Cambridge, 1979). Taken together, the bibliographies in these three works are close to all-inclusive for this region. The best single-volume access to the very extensive literature on the Kwakiutl from the writings of Franz Boas and his native collaborator, George Hunt, is Boas's difficult but authoritative study, *The Social Organization and the Secret Societies of the Kwakiutl Indians* (1895; reprint, New York, 1970). A recent and useful interpretation of Kwakiutl culture and society that draws upon much of the Boas and Hunt texts is my *The Mouth of Heaven: An Introduction to Kwakiutl Religious Thought* (New York, 1975), which includes a bibliography of the published Boas field studies. There is no better introduction to the nature of Polynesian societies than the writings of one of Polynesia's native sons, Te Rangi Hiroa (Sir Peter Buck), of Maori descent and one-time director of the Bernice P. Bishop Museum at Honolulu. His greatest work is *The Coming of the Maori* (Wellington, 1952), an intimate yet anthropologically professional study. My *Ancient Polynesian Society* (Chicago, 1970) focuses more directly on genealogical issues since it is a study of variations in the forms of Polynesian aristocracy.

On the subject of the genealogies of the Greek gods, the principal sources are Hesiod's *Theogony* and *Works and Days*, conveniently available in the English translation by Hugh G. Evelyn-White in his *The Homeric Hymns and Homerica* (Cambridge, Mass., 1967). As background on the ancient period, M. I. Finley's *The Ancient Greeks* (New York, 1977) is both authoritative and succinct. For Japanese sources, the general work of choice is George B. Sansom's familiar classic, *Japan: A Short Cultural History*, rev. ed. (New York, 1962), to be used, however, in conjunction with the source book on the Japanese genealogical and historical chronicles, as compiled by Ryusaku Tsunoda, Wm. Theodore de Bary, and Donald Keene, *Sources of Japanese Tradition*, 2 vols. (New York, 1958). On the genealogies of the royal lines of England, G. M. Trevelyan's *History of England*, new illust. ed. (London, 1973), the *Oxford History of England*, especially volume 3, and Austin Lane Poole's *Domesday Book to Magna Carta, 1087–1216* (Oxford, 1955), are particularly noteworthy for their historical insights.

IRVING GOLDMAN

GENESIA. The Genesia was a Greek festival at which ancestors were commemorated. In ancient Greece, sacrifices at the graveside on the third, ninth, and thirtieth day after the funeral helped the bereaved to come to terms with their loss. After these initial commemorative rituals, the dead were also remembered at a yearly festival, the Genesia, or "festival of the fathers (or ancestors)." Contrary to what the name may suggest, this festival does not imply Greek ancestor worship: the family dead were to be remembered, but they were not expected to intervene in the lives of their descendants. Writing in the fifth century BCE, Herodotus (4.26) stated that the festival was "known to all the Greeks," but detailed information is available only about the Genesia at Athens.

In the early Archaic period (800–600 BCE), the Athenian Genesia was celebrated by individual aristocratic families on dates unknown to us, but it seems that around 590 BCE the reformer Solon (630?–560? BCE) fixed the date on the fifth of the month Boedromion (early September). The reason for this particular day is obscure, but the intention of the reform seems clear. In many Greek cities in the Archaic period, lawgivers restricted the public character of great aristocratic funerals. Funeral meals and games were occasions for impressive displays of aristocratic wealth and power, and in the later Archaic period these demonstrations became more and more an obstacle to the development of democracy. The institution of a yearly commemorative festival on a fixed day prevented the aristocrats from inviting relatives and friends other than those who had ancestors buried in the same cemetery. As Athens turned more democratic in the course of the fifth century BCE the commemoration of ancestors, which was mainly an aristocratic activity, must have become less acceptable, and by the end of the Classical period (c. 400 BCE) the Genesia seems to have fallen into oblivion.

BIBLIOGRAPHY

The standard study of the festival is Felix Jacoby's "Genesia: A Forgotten Festival of the Dead," *Classical Quarterly* 38 (1944): 65–75, reprinted in Jacoby's *Abhandlungen zur griechischen Geschichtsschreibung* (Leiden, 1956), pp. 243–259. This account is modified, with regard to some of the details, by Sarah C. Humphreys in *The Family, Women, and Death* (London, 1983), pp. 87–88.

JAN BREMMER

GENGHIS KHAN. *See* Chinggis Khan.

GENNEP, ARNOLD VAN (1873–1957), French anthropologist. Arnold van Gennep was born in Ludwigsburg, Germany, his father a descendant of French emigrants. When van Gennep was six, his parents divorced, and his mother returned to France with him. Several years later she married a doctor who had a summer practice at a spa in the French province of Savoy. Van Gennep's attachment to this region, which he considered his adopted homeland, dates from these years. He was to travel through Savoy, village by village, collecting ethnographic and folkloric materials.

He had a diversified and original university education at the École Pratique des Hautes Études and the École des Langues Orientales in Paris; his studies included general linguistics, ancient and modern Arabic, Egyptology, Islamic studies, and studies of the religions of primitive peoples. He possessed a rare gift for learning languages. For seven years he was in charge of translation at the Ministry of Agriculture in Paris, but he gave up this post, the only one that the French government ever offered him, in order to devote himself to his personal research. From 1912 to 1915, he taught ethnology at the University of Neuchâtel in Switzerland. After being expelled for having expressed doubts concerning Swiss claims to total neutrality during World War I, he made his living by the publication of numerous articles and periodic reports, lecturing, and commissioned translations.

His voluminous production can be divided into two periods separated by his most important work, *Les rites de passage* (1909). The concept that he discovered here permitted him, during the second part of his life, to devote himself entirely to the ethnography and folklore of France. In the first part he had been occupied with the problems posed by the English school of anthropology, concerning totemism, taboo, the original forms of religion and society, and the relationships between myth and rite. But he had approached these anthropological commonplaces with a certain originality. For example, in his study, based on documents collected in Madagascar, of the problems of taboo, he not only sees the expression of religious institutions and attitudes but also emphasizes the social effects of taboo, which creates, maintains, or transforms the order of nature, and which consolidates the bonds between a single clan's members, between animal and human members of a clan, between ancestors and descendants, and between men and gods. Taboo, he believed, is both a social and religious institution. The appearance of his work *L'état actuel du problème totémique* (1920), which purported to be a provisory summation of works on totemism, was in reality, as Claude Lévi-Strauss says, the "swan song" of speculations on totemism. The personal theoretical position of van Gennep in this work is pre-functionalist: totemism has as its function to maintain the existing cohesion of the social group and to assure its continuity, which the totem symbolically represents.

Van Gennep's main contribution remains the idea of "rites of passage," which he put forward and developed in the book of that title. By *rite of passage* he means any ceremony that accompanies the passage from one state to another and from one world, whether cosmic or social, to another. Each rite of passage includes three necessary stages: separation, boundary, and reaggregation (or the preliminal, the liminal, and the postliminal). Van Gennep also introduced other important ideas. By emphasizing "ceremonial sequence," van Gennep demonstrates the importance of the process of "unfolding" in rituals and in the relations that exist between rituals. He also introduces the concept of the "pivoting" of the sacred—that is, the idea that the sacred is not an absolute but rather an alternating value, an indication of the alternating situations in which an individual finds himself. Every individual, in the course of his life, passes through alternations of sacred and profane, and the rites of passage function to neutralize for the social group the harmful effects of the imbalances produced by these alternations.

Van Gennep was a nonconformist with regard to his ideas, which obliged him to live at the periphery of academic institutions. His most original contribution in the field of anthropology was to show profound connections between the social and religious spheres.

[*See also* Rites of Passage, *overview article.*]

BIBLIOGRAPHY

Belmont, Nicole. *Arnold Van Gennep: The Creator of French Ethnography.* Translated by Derek Coltman. Chicago, 1978.

Gennep, Arnold van. *Manuel de folklore français contemporain.* 9 vols. Paris, 1937–1958.

Gennep, Arnold van. *The Rites of Passage.* Translated by Monika B. Vizedom and Gabrielle L. Caffee. Chicago, 1960.

Gennep, Ketty van. *Bibliographie des œuvres d'Arnold van Gennep.* Paris, 1964.

NICOLE BELMONT
Translated from French by Roger Norton

GENSHIN (942–1017), also known by the title Eshin Sōzu; Japanese Buddhist priest of the Tendai sect and patriarch of Japanese Pure Land Buddhism. Genshin was born in the village of Taima in Yamato Province (modern Nara Prefecture) to a family of provincial gentry named Urabe. By his mid-teens he had entered the Tendai priesthood and had become a disciple of Ryōgen (Jie Daishi, 912–985), one of the most eminent clerics of the age. Little is known of Genshin's early career except that he presided at an important Tendai ceremony in 973 and five years later, when he was thirty-six, wrote a learned treatise on Buddhist metaphysics *(abhidharma),* the *Immyōronsho shisōi ryakuchūshaku.*

Shortly thereafter, Genshin's interests seem to have changed. In 981 he wrote a work on a Pure Land Buddhist theme, the *Amida Butsu byakugō kambō* (Contemplation upon Amida Buddha's Wisdom-Eye), and in 985 he completed the work for which he is chiefly known, the *Ōjōyōshū* (Essentials of Pure Land Rebirth). The *Essentials* was one of the first works on a Pure Land theme to have been composed in Japan. It signaled not only a shift in Genshin's interests but also the beginning of a transition in the history of Japanese Buddhism. In this work Genshin quotes 654 passages from some 160 Buddhist scriptures on the most important themes of Pure Land Buddhism—on the sufferings of the six paths of transmigration and especially the torments of hell, on the pleasures and advantages of Amida (Skt., Amitābha) Buddha's Pure Land, and on the way to achieve transmigratory rebirth into Amida's Pure Land, the cultivation of *nembutsu* (reflection on the Buddha). This latter subject is treated in voluminous detail. There are descriptions of methods of difficult, meditative *nembutsu* (*kannen nembutsu,* envisualizing Amida's form and meditating on his essence), of easy, invocational *nembutsu* (*shōmyō nembutsu,* calling on the name of Amida Buddha in deep devotion), of *nembutsu* for ninety-day sessions, and of *nembutsu* for the hour of death. The faith that should accompany *nembutsu* and abundant confirmation of its efficacy and merits are set out as well. Throughout the work, Genshin repeatedly deplores the sufferings of this world and urges his readers, whether they be rich or poor, laity or clergy, to seek emancipation through reliance on the compassion of Amida Buddha. The *Essentials* became one of the most popular works on a Buddhist theme in the history of Japanese literature.

In the year following the completion of the *Essentials,* Genshin and other Pure Land devotees, both clergy and laymen, formed a devotional society called the Nujugo Zammai-e (Nembutsu Samādhi Society of Twenty-five). Genshin's *Essentials of Pure Land Rebirth* no doubt served as an inspiration and guide to the devotional exercises of this society.

In Genshin's life and works can be seen the beginning of a shift in Japan from elite, monastic Buddhism to popular, devotional Buddhism. The *Essentials* itself is an attempt to reconcile these two types of faith. It teaches, for example, that meditative *nembutsu* is the highest form of spiritual cultivation, because it can bring about enlightenment in the present life, but that simple invocational *nembutsu* is excellent also, especially for laypeople and sinners, because it can result in rebirth in the next life into Amida Buddha's Pure Land and eventual enlightenment there. Thus Genshin's major significance lies in his contribution to the growth of a Pure Land movement in Japan.

For the common people, he vividly depicted the Pure Land Buddhist worldview of painful transmigration in this world versus the bliss of Amida's Western Pure Land, instilling a fear of the former and deep longing for the latter. To the intelligentsia and clergy, he introduced the vast literature of continental Pure Land Buddhism and an elaborate structure of Pure Land, especially *nembutsu,* theory and practice. For all Japanese, he offered the possibility of salvation based only on sincere devotion and simple *nembutsu* practice. Genshin's teachings were a major inspiration for Hōnen (1133–1212), founder of the Jōdoshū sect of Japanese Buddhism, and Genshin is considered one of the seven patriarchs of the Jōdo Shinshū sect.

[*See also* Nien-fo *and* Buddhism, *article on* Buddhism in Japan.]

BIBLIOGRAPHY

Major works of Genshin, in addition to the *Ōjōyōshū,* include the *Ichijō yōketsu* (Essentials of the One Vehicle) and *Kanjin ryakuyōshū* (Essentials of Esoteric Contemplation). For his complete works, see *Eshin Sōzu zenshū,* 5 vols. (Sakamoto, Japan, 1927–1928).

Works on Genshin in English are few. My study *The Teachings Essential for Rebirth: A Study of Genshin's Ōjōyōshū* (Tokyo, 1973) gives an outline of the development of Pure Land thought up to Genshin and an analysis of the *nembutsu* theory and practice of the *Ōjōyōshū.* In Japanese, Ishida Mizumaro's *Kanashiki mono no sukui: Ōjōyōshū* (Tokyo, 1967) summarizes Genshin's life and the Pure Land teachings of the *Ōjōyōshū.*

Ishida has also edited the *Ōjōyōshū* and translated it into modern Japanese in his *Ōjōyōshū: Nihon Jōdokyō no yoake,* 2 vols. (Tokyo, 1963–1964).

Allan A. Andrews

GEOGRAPHY.

A deeply rooted aspect of human behavior, the ordering of space is an activity that consists of establishing differences between places in terms of varied functions and degrees of meaning. [*See* Sacred Space.] Among peoples of diverse religious traditions, the most significant places are identified with special spiritual presences, qualities that set certain locales apart from ordinary, profane space. Charged with supernatural power, sacred places function as fixed points of reference and positions of orientation in the surrounding world. With the passage of time, sacred places become invested with accumulations of mythical and historical meanings in complex layers of cultural memory. When joined by paths, processional ways, or great routes of pilgrimage, sacred places form networks that may embrace local village or tribal lands, large nations, or vast regions of the globe occupied by major civilizations. These networks form sacred geographies—webs of religious meaning imposed upon the land—where natural features and man-made symbols establish communication between the earthly and the spiritual, embodying collective values and shared norms of conduct. Sacred geographies form a unifying ground, a lasting source of remembrance and renewal for the most important aspects of individual and communal life in many cultural traditions.

The creation of sacred geographies is behavior partly anterior to the development of culture, for it stems from the marking, exploitation, and defense of territories that join humankind to the larger animal kingdom. But the articulation of landscapes with symbolic imagery and the way in which such landscapes are made to reflect layers of mythology and history also correspond to patterns of thought and complex ways of recording meaningful events that seem peculiar to humankind. The widely different ways in which sacred geographies have been organized show how man has sought to grasp the perceived world and how he has explained his place within the cosmic schema. An examination of sacred geographies thus points to patterns of environmental cognition and ordering and to the wide range of spatial definitions that have evolved in response to different cultural needs, historical circumstances, and ecological possibilities.

This article focuses on four examples of sacred geography. They correspond to the symbolic landscapes of peoples of strikingly different social and cultural complexities who inhabit regions of varied ecologies. The first example is from the Australian Aborigines, whose gathering and hunting life in an austere desert environment was connected to systems of sacred places embedded within nature and unmarked by monumental art or architecture. These places, arranged in certain patterns within tribal territories, were thought to have been established by ancestral heroes in the Dreaming—the time of first creation. The second example is from the Maya Indian community of Zinacantan in southern Mexico, a farming people whose culture stems from an ancient native heritage. These Indians have evolved a pattern of centralization in their sacred geography that echoes similar structures among other peoples of sedentary farming life. The third example is from imperial China, where ancient beliefs concerning the worship of earth, water, and sky were expressed at great mountain shrines and in the sacred precincts of the imperial capital. In China, we find the creation of a sacred geography closely tied to the concerns of a powerfully centralized state. The last example touches upon the sacred geography of medieval Europe. Though politically disunited, the peoples of Europe followed routes of pilgrimage to the periphery of Christendom and held Jerusalem, the Sacred City, to be the center of their world. [*See* Center of the World.]

Aboriginal Australia. The Australian Aborigines are counted among the oldest human races. Their ancestors migrated from Southeast Asia perhaps thirty thousand years ago, when land bridges between New Guinea and Australia were almost certainly exposed. Throughout the millennia the Aborigines pursued an austere gathering and hunting life that was admirably adapted to their barren habitat. The Neolithic agricultural revolution never reached these isolated lands, where nomadic bands traveled within well-defined tribal territories, following seasonal rhythms in the unending search for food. But the inhabitants did not perceive the natural environment in economic terms alone; it was also seen as a storehouse of memory, replete with supernatural meanings. The flat, seemingly featureless terrain contained an invisible, magical domain in which hills, rocks, water holes, and groves were charged with sacred powers and mythical associations. Though apparently obeying the randomness of nature, such features were seen as well in terms of a specific order; people expressed their connection to them through pictographs, rock alignments, wooden sculptures, caches for totemic objects, and ceremonial places designed according to prescribed rules of organization.

The sacred sites of the Aborigines marked places

where events in the Dreaming took place. This concept, which is central to Aboriginal cosmogony, concerns a time when heroes and heroines wandered over a land where there were no hills, water holes, or living things. The paths and camping places of these heroes are sacred places described in myths. The ancestral heroes also brought fire to the people as well as the laws by which men live; many such heroes eventually transformed themselves into trees, boulders, and other natural features, thus creating the landscape that exists at present. A symbolic order that related to the time of origins and the travels of creators, rather than the cardinal directions, was called into being. In these austere settings, no sharp divisions were made between animals, plants, inanimate objects, and mankind. The ancestral heroes were not distant entities but integral components of the land, and they were made part of the experience of daily life through religious reenactments of events of the Dreaming. Joined by a network of sacred places, the land itself became symbolic, affirming a coherence of the physical and mythological domains. Among the Aborigines, sacred geography was the source of authority as well as the source of tribal identity. The latter was based on a title to the land that went back to the time of first creation.

Zinacantan. Conquest, colonialism, and the advances of industrial civilization have often spelled destruction or major alteration for traditional religions. In North America, forcible removal of Indian populations from old homelands frequently meant social disintegration for those whose religious sense of belonging to a specific landscape had been destroyed. But colonial cultures have also often produced a range of creative adaptations, as subjected peoples evolved syncretistic religions in which ancient sacred geographies continued to play traditional functions. Latin America, among Indian communities in former Spanish possessions from the Rio Grande Valley in New Mexico to the Bolivian Andes of South America, is especially rich in such instances.

Among many examples that could be discussed, the community of Zinacantan in the high, forested mountain country of Chiapas, southern Mexico, is particularly well documented. The inhabitants are a Maya people, ultimately descended from those who built city-states in southern Mexico, Guatemala, and the Yucatán Peninsula during the first centuries CE. Today, these farming people live in hamlets dispersed throughout the hills, around a civic and religious center that consists of a church, school, and administrative buildings.

The visible sacred geography of Zinacantan incorporates mountains, caves, water holes, and man-made crosses erected at shrine sites at determined locations around the civic and religious center. Mountains have important economic meaning in the life of Zinacantan, but certain peaks are also considered to be homes of ancestral deities who live within. These ancestors control the mists and vapors that rise to form rain clouds on the peaks; they are able to direct the rain clouds over the community. Crosses, placed on pathways around the mountains surrounding the Zinacantan center, were borrowed by the Indians from the symbolic forms of Spanish Christianity. But the crosses are not seen in Christian terms; they are perceived as spiritual openings for communication with ancestral beings. Cave shrines are also places for communication with Yahval Balamil, the earth lord, who dwells beneath the surface of the land; he may also be reached through prayers in caves, at sinkholes, and at springs throughout the Zinacantan domain. Sacrificial offerings are regularly made, especially at the sites of cross shrines. They are most often performed by people walking on ceremonial circuits around the whole community. Shamans are the main ritualists, performing prayers and making offerings on behalf of patients. Processions of other worshipers may also follow ceremonial circuits, usually moving in counterclockwise direction. The village church and its Christian images are also frequently included in the processional itineraries. The circuits around Zinacantan are a way of establishing boundaries, a way of saying "This is our sacred center, through which the holy river flows and around which our ancestral gods are watching over us." Circuits are replicated on many levels around individual fields, houses, or other objects, symbolically establishing property rights as well as marking social spaces in the Zinacantan world. The community and land at Zinacantan are infused with the sense of being whole and sacred; sacred geography places the living community in an intimate religious bond with its natural setting and with the ancestors and gods that dwell within that setting.

Imperial China. The sacred geographies of tribes or small agrarian communities are usually encompassed by paths or roadways within relatively restricted zones. But the development of ancient empires embracing vast regions and diverse populations posed different problems of spatial symbolism. For rulers, the problem was to create symbolic orders that might tend to unify such disparate domains and polities. Great ritual centers were designed to communicate the religious and political concerns of state organizations. The symbolic structure of such places expressed the idea of a sacred geography in microcosm, through the use of monumental art and architecture.

In China, where continuity of religious themes has been maintained over millennia, imperial ritual was especially focused on two outstanding places. The first was a sacred mountain, T'ai Shan, the central and most important of five sacred mountains associated with the cardinal directions and center. The worship of mountains has an ancient history in China, attested by early texts that describe peaks and the appropriate rites to be celebrated there. Some were local shrines affecting small areas, but others were majestic sovereigns that extended their influence over immense regions. These old beliefs surrounded T'ai Shan, and the sacred place gradually was invested with imperial monuments throughout the centuries. In effect, the mountain became a symbol of the cosmos and the state. The mountain was given royal title during the T'ang dynasty in 725 CE, inaugurating a practice followed by successive emperors. These honorific names underlined the conception of the mountain as a producer of life forces. It was identified with rain clouds and fertility and figured as an object of worship in spring rites of planting and at the fall harvest season. It was also seen as a symbol of stability and permanence and as a preventer of droughts, floods, and earthquakes. Indeed, it was a divinity with a sacred force that could be touched by prayers and sacrifice.

Just as the mountain was a symbol of order in the natural environment, so did the emperor personify the social and moral order. A close relationship developed between ruler and mountain, for the emperor was the pivot between society and nature. But both the emperor and the mountain were subordinate to Heaven, for it was through the mandate of Heaven that all harmony and validation derived. These relationships were spelled out in the elaborate system of monuments with which T'ai Shan was equipped. At the summit, an open circular platform was constructed for the Feng sacrifices, which consisted of burnt offerings to the heavens. Below, toward the base of the mountain, a polygonal open altar was constructed for the Shan sacrifices in honor of the earth. Between these key altars were a host of subsidiary temples dedicated to lesser nature divinities, ancestral heroes, and various miraculous saints and hermits. There were also commemorative monuments to various emperors, a school, a library, a Confucian temple, and many other sacred places scattered among the crags and groves. The whole site was simultaneously a symbol of the land, the empire, and the cosmos—a great unifying topographic icon.

The symbolic order that governed T'ai Shan also informed the cosmic imagery of ritual centers within the imperial capital. In Beijing, sacred enclosures featured open platform altars to the sky and earth, with subordinate temples to the sun, moon, and agriculture, each with its own complement of satellite monuments, altars, and secondary buildings. The Chinese love of order, hierarchy, and classification governed the orientation and symbolic ornament of the temples, with their gleaming white marble and carved imagery of mountains, clouds, water, and earthly or celestial dragons. These cosmic figures expressed the notion of a sacred geography in abstract form, becoming universal symbols. The magnificent altars, with their surrounding concourses and processional paths, formed the setting for imperial rites where the emperor offered sacrificial covenants to heaven and earth. The sacrifices expressed a complementary relationship to one another. The mysterious, limitless heights of heaven and the regular movements of the celestial bodies symbolized Heaven's regulative power to keep the universe in stable order and to produce the proper succession of seasons. This power was especially important to an agricultural people, and through sacrificial acts the emperors expressed the harmony of a well-ordered society within the universal schema.

Medieval Europe. The sacred geographies of the Far East and among the Indian peoples of the Americas tend to express a correspondence between man and nature and to be arranged in patterns of centralization. By contrast, the sacred geography of medieval Europe did not focus on a single European capital but was cast instead as a vast network that ran through many lands, leading to pilgrimage cities at the extremities of Christendom. From central and southern France, pilgrimage routes ran south over the Pyrenees, converging on a road that led across northern Spain to Santiago de Compostela, the tomb of the apostle James. Another route threaded down the Italian Peninsula to Rome. There, amid the ruins of antiquity, the pilgrim might meditate upon the early saints and martyrs and visit the old Lateran—the Mother Church and seat of the earthly Vicar of Christ. But the most perilous of routes led farther south to the port of Brindisi, and from there by ship across the Mediterranean, to the most distant, mysterious, and sacred of all goals, the city of Jerusalem.

The physical realities of this complex geography were translated in terms of a mythological hierarchy on thirteenth-century maps. These charts reveal a vision in which the horizontal surface of the earth was shown as a flat disc, with Jerusalem, the Holy City, marked clearly at the center. The outline of the Mediterranean Basin was summarily drawn, as were the features of Europe. Peripheral and unknown regions were shown to be the realms of bizarre or fabled races, sometimes held at bay behind great walled enclosures. On a vertical axis above Jerusalem, the Savior presided over the celestial sphere, while ferocious demons patrolled the infernal regions below. Such imagery was not primarily meant to illustrate an actual, material geography but rather a spiritual landscape whose central earthly icon, Jerusalem, could be interpreted on different levels. It was the Holy City of Palestine, the goal of pilgrims and crusaders; a symbol of the church; a metaphor for the Christian soul; and an analogy for the heavenly Jerusalem, the final Promised Land. [*See* Jerusalem.]

Such patterns were repeated in microcosm throughout Christendom in the art and architecture of cathedrals. In France, where these buildings reached their highest expression, sculpture, architecture, and stained glass formed a symbolic code to show the order of nature, to represent an abstract of history, and to summarize spiritual values. Within the soaring naves of the great cathedrals, at once mysterious and secure against the outside world, the assembled congregation saw the mirror of creation. Yet, like the maps, these buildings represented an essentially interior world, expressing the aims and aspirations of the innermost consciousness of the community. Such sacred places, joined in the larger network of routes to distant centers of faith, formed a sacred geography of a tradition that denied the physical world to emphasize instead theological, conceptual, and belief-oriented values that urged man to rise up, away from the earth, above animals, plants, and inanimate objects, toward a transcendent God.

Conclusion. This article summarizes the structure of four sacred geographies in societies that range from the level of tribal bands to complex civilizations. In all cases, sacred geographies have the functions of creating a sense of place and of creating a certain order in the world. Through the use of symbols, networks of meaning are imposed upon the land; such spatial orders clarify the difference between places by illustrating what is thought to be significant in the perceived world. These symbols may be natural features, such as mountains, lakes, or rivers; they may be pictographs or markings; or they may be elaborate works of art and architecture accompanied by writing. In the context of a landscape, such symbolic systems communicate the difference between sacred and profane space and answer the universal theme of establishing connections between a population and a time and place of origin.

Beyond such essential functions, sacred geographies are as varied as religions. These differences are the result of specific cultural and historical factors as well as geographical conditions. The circumstances of a wandering life in an isolated region; the need to form or unify a state organization; the pattern of an early chain of missions or military conquests; the lasting prestige and sacred quality of an ancient civic and religious center—these and countless other factors may determine how sacred geographies are shaped. By incorporating the imagery of history and related information, sacred geographies make visible a cultural or ethnic domain and signal territorial possession.

The study of sacred geography is especially important in understanding the processes of cultural history, particularly among peoples whose traditions are not documented in writing or whose traditions may be recorded in partly deciphered hieroglyphic texts and figural imagery. In Africa, Oceania, and the Americas, where the native spiritual and intellectual heritage was largely transmitted orally, major archaeological sites must be decoded without textual sources, and early European reports of contact are colored by an Indo-European outlook. Among these peoples, the broad patterns of sacred geography provide indispensable insight on the role of religious thought and symbolism in the evolution of civilization.

[*See also* Cosmology; *for discussion of the symbolic and religious interpretations of specific geographical phenomena, see* Mountains; Rivers; Lakes; Oceans; Deserts; *and* Gardens.]

BIBLIOGRAPHY

Bastien, Joseph W. *Mountain of the Condor.* Saint Paul, 1978.

Berndt, Ronald M., and E. S. Phillips, eds. *The Australian Aboriginal Heritage.* Sydney, 1973.

Campbell, Tony. *Early Maps.* New York, 1981.

Chavannes, Édouard. *Le T'ai Chan: Essai de monographie d'un culte chinois.* Paris, 1910.

Combaz, Gisbert. *Les temples impériaux de la Chine.* Brussels, 1912.

Harrington, John Peabody. *The Ethnogeography of the Tewa Indians.* Twenty-ninth Annual Report of the Bureau of American Ethnology, 1907–1908. Washington, D.C., 1908.

Hiatt, L. R. "Local Organization among the Australian Aborigines." *Oceania* 32 (June 1962): 267–286.

Hiatt, L. R. "Ownership and Use of Land among the Australian Aborigines." In *Man the Hunter,* edited by Richard B. Lee and Irven DeVore, pp. 99–102. Chicago, 1968.

Sirén, Osvald. *The Imperial Palaces of Peking.* 3 vols. Paris, 1926.

Stanner, William E. H. "Aboriginal Territorial Organization: Estate, Range, Domain and Regime." *Oceania* 36 (September 1965): 1–26.

Townsend, Richard F. "Pyramid and Sacred Mountain." In *Ethnoastronomy and Archaeoastronomy in the American Tropics,* edited by Anthony F. Aveni and Gary Urton, pp. 37–62. New York, 1982.

Turner, Victor, and Edith Turner. *Image and Pilgrimage in Christian Culture.* New York, 1978.

Vogt, Evon Z. *Zinacantan: A Maya Community in the Highlands of Chiapas.* Cambridge, Mass., 1969.

Wheatley, Paul. *The Pivot of the Four Quarters: A Preliminary Enquiry into the Origins and Character of the Ancient Chinese City.* Chicago, 1971.

RICHARD F. TOWNSEND

GEOMANCY is a form of divination based on the interpretation of figures or patterns drawn on the ground or other flat surface by means of sand or similar granular materials. The term is also used for the interpretation of geographic features. Among the Chinese, in particular, this practice of geomancy is rooted in traditional philosophic conceptions of the relationship that exists between human beings and the vital forces of their environment and the need to achieve a harmonious balance between the two to ensure well-being.

The Western form of geomancy, widespread in the Arab world, was also of importance in medieval Europe, where it was closely linked with alchemy and astrology. Geomancy of this kind is likely to have originated in the ancient Near East and may also have been developed further by Greek mathematical speculations. In the eighth and ninth centuries, during the period of Arab cultural florescence and expansion, it became systematized and was then widely distributed from its center to Byzantium and across North Africa and into Spain. From Spain it was also probably spread along a second route into Christian Europe. From Egypt and North Africa, geomancy was carried south with Islam and then even beyond, so that it is now found both in West Africa (for example, among the Yoruba of Nigeria) and in East Africa, including Madagascar.

The Arab system called *ram'l* ("sand") is based on complex mathematical calculations and involves conceptions of an orderly universe. Its numerical order provides the underlying framework for all other Western systems of geomancy. The fundamental common feature of geomancy is a pattern of binary oppositions of markings grouped into sixteen combinations of four positions. In both the Arab system and that of medieval Europe *(ars punctatoria)*, points or lines were drawn on sand in a pattern based on chance. In the Yoruba system (Ifa), which has been particularly well described, markings are based on the casting of palm kernels or cowrie shells according to prescribed procedures. For each of the resulting figures, from among a total of 256 possible combinations and permutations there is a set of verses that the diviner *(babalawo)* will have memorized to interpret the pattern and to apply to the case at hand. In general, the aim of this practice is not to divine future events but to discover the supernatural causes of present situations and their remedies.

In the European system the sixteen figures are related to astronomical signs of the planets and the zodiac; the scheme also includes four elements and four qualities. Although various authors have offered divergent interpretations of this system, its basic structure is remarkably constant and has been integrated into different philosophical conceptions with striking flexibility.

The system of medieval European geomancy appears to have had a brief revival in the occultism of the nineteenth century. The African systems are still viable, and forms of the Yoruba practice, in particular, have even been discovered in the Americas, notably in Cuba and Brazil.

Less complex systems of geomancy, apparently unrelated to those of the West, are to be found in Tibet in the form of "stone divination" and "pebble divination." These systems each have their own sets of rules, recorded in manuals. They are quite distinct from those discussed above.

The term *geomancy* is also used to refer to *feng-shui* ("winds and waters"), the traditional Chinese technique for determining propitious locations for towns, dwellings, and tombs. This system, which is still in very widespread use, concerns the distribution over the earth, by winds and water currents, of various terrestrial and atmospheric emanations that are believed to exert important influences on people. In addition to being a system of calculations for establishing favorable sites, geomancy is also a method for discerning the causes of human illness and suffering. Geomancers may claim that these causes lie in the negative influences on people of badly placed residences or of the unfortunate positioning of the tombs of ancestors, who consequently send illness and misfortune to their descendants as expressions of anger. Moreover, a given dwelling or tomb, which was originally well placed, may, in time, have its geomantic position shifted as a result of changes in the area, such as new constructions that produce an alteration in the balance of positive and negative currents. A geomancer will not only divine such causes but will also seek to remedy the situation by recommending reburial at a better spot, changing the position of a tomb, or urging the building of a wall or other structure to modify the direction of the currents. Because of the belief that illness may be due to such influences, geomancers must be included in any list of traditional Chinese diagnosticians and medical practitioners.

[*See also* Divination.]

BIBLIOGRAPHY

Bascom, William R. *Ifa Divination.* Bloomington, Ind., 1969.

Bascom, William R. *Sixteen Cowries: Yoruba Divination from Africa to the New World.* Bloomington, Ind., 1980.

Caslant, Eugène. *Traité élémentaire de géomancie.* Paris. 1935.

Ekvall, Robert B. *Religious Observances in Tibet.* Chicago, 1964.

Granet, Marcel. *The Religion of the Chinese People.* Translated by Maurice Freedman. New York, 1975.

Jaulin, Robert. *La géomancie: Analyse formelle.* Paris, 1966.

ERIKA BOURGUIGNON

GEOMETRY. During the last two millennia BCE, the period that produced most of our religious texts, geometry (lit., "earth measurement," from Greek *gaia, gē,* "the earth," and *metrein,* "to measure") was essentially a "geometrical algebra" with a focus on number. Problematic allusions to number and space, which abound in sacred texts, are presumably inspired by this early mathematical protoscience. During the much later development of Christianity and Islam, Euclidean geometry—based, so it seemed, on irrefutable deductive logic built from definitions, postulates, and theorems—became the rational paradigm for all sciences, including theology. The discovery of other geometries in the last two centuries has brought the realization that Euclidean geometry is merely a special case within a wider realm. Efforts to rid mathematics of its logical paradoxes have taught us that perfect consistency and certainty are unattainable in rational thought. These developments, together with a new awareness of the complexity of physical space and a better understanding of how culture shapes perceptions, have dramatically altered our philosophical dogmatism, making ancient and Eastern modes of thought more congenial to the modern West and contributing to the problems of contemporary religion.

Neolithic Cultures (6000–3500 BCE). In southeastern Europe and the Near East, Neolithic peoples decorated the surfaces of cult objects with geometric motifs—circles, ovals, parallel lines, chevrons, triangles, squares, meanders, and spirals. These abstract designs came to abound in the folk arts of most of the cultures of the globe, seemingly irrespective of time, of the degree of civilization attained, or of concomitant skill in the realistic depiction of natural objects such as animals, human faces, leaves, and landscapes. Creation myths inherited from Mesopotamia and Egypt of the third and second millennia BCE and later from Palestine, China, and Greece, as well as those recorded in modern times in the Americas, Africa, and Oceania show that the act of divine creation is universally conceived as an ordering, a shaping and selection that brings a world, a cosmos, into being. During the Neolithic period, the abstract geometrical motifs that ornament dress, vessels, walls, and other artifacts found in the earliest shrines and villages were expressions of an intuitive identification of order with the sacred and a consequent mobilization of aesthetic feeling in control of design.

In *A History of Mathematics* (1968), Carl B. Boyer observes that pottery, weaving, and basketry, from the time of their Neolithic origins, "show instances of congruences and symmetry, which are in essence parts of elementary geometry." To Boyer, "simple sequences in design"—such as translations, rotations, and reflections (see figure 1)—"suggest a sort of applied group theory, as well as propositions in geometry and arithmetic." Formal propositions did not appear, however, until the Greeks initiated them in the fifth and fourth centuries BCE. Group theory was not developed until the last two centuries; only recently has it been extended to cover the geometric symmetries in space that were already a concern in Palestinian stoneware, for instance, as early as 10,000 BCE. The oldest mathematical texts, dating from circa 1900 to 1600 BCE, show that geometry developed historically as "the science of dimensional order," in close alliance with arithmetic and algebra, although "the 'spaciness' of space and the 'numerosity' of number are essentially different things" (Alfred North Whitehead, *An Introduction to Mathematics,* 1911).

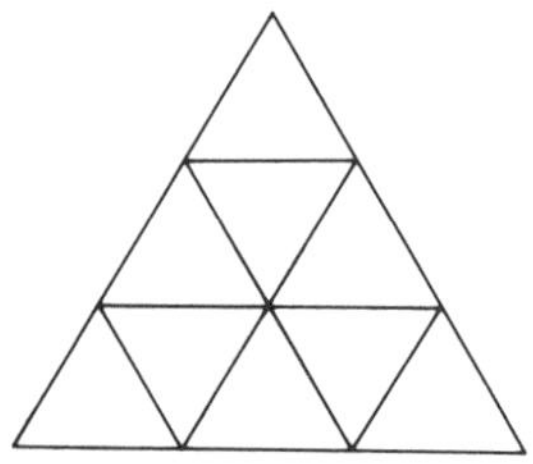

FIGURE 1. *Geometric Symmetry.* Simple design sequences, such as appear on Neolithic pottery, weaving, and basketry, suggest applied knowledge of propositions in geometry and arithmetic.

"There is a direct correlation between complexity of weaving and sophistication of arithmetic understanding," Walter A. Fairservis notes in *The Threshold of Civilization* (1975). In a settlement like that at Çatal Hüyük in central Turkey, occupied before 6500 BCE, the frame posts of the houses are filled in with sunbaked bricks made from molds, furnishing strong economic motivation for knowing precisely "how many bricks were necessary for each wall"; hence, "counting and notation were very much a part of the cultural scene." Far cruder artifacts—sequences of notches incised in bone, studied by Alexander Marshack (1972)—suggest "systems of lunar and other notation" that push the origins of arithmetic far back into Paleolithic times, twenty-five thousand and more years ago. Modern archaeologists and anthropologists are thus producing alternative theories to those of Herodotus (fifth century BCE), who believed geometry began in Egypt, motivated by the necessity of reestablishing boundaries after the annual Nile floods, and by Aristotle (fourth century BCE), who also assumed an origin in Egypt, but because "there the priestly caste was allowed to be at leisure."

Ancient Egypt. Chief sources of our knowledge of early Egyptian geometry are the Moscow Papyrus (c. 1890 BCE) and the Rhind Papyrus (c. 1650 BCE). The emphasis here is always on calculation, so that their geometry "turns out to have been mainly a branch of applied arithmetic" (Boyer, 1968). The concept of geometric similarity is applied to triangles, and there is a rudimentary trigonometry. There is a good approximation to π in the formula that computes the area of a circle by constructing a square on eight-ninths of its diameter (see figure 2). In addition, the Egyptians knew the formulas for elementary volumes and correctly calculated the volume of a truncated pyramid.

Modern scholars, however, are disappointed to find so little cause for the high estimation in which the Greeks later held Egyptian science. Our respect for the organizational and engineering skills required for the building of palaces, canals, and pyramids, for example, is tempered by the realization that such civic projects entail little more then what Otto Neugebauer (1969) calls "elementary household arithmetic which no mathematician would call mathematics." Neugebauer concludes: "Ancient science was the product of a very few men; and these few happened not to be Egyptian." Of far greater interest is what was happening in Babylon.

Babylon. Several hundred baked-clay tablets about the size of the palm of the hand, incised with neatly crowded rows of cuneiform inscriptions, give us more information about the mathematical sciences in Babylon circa 1900 to 1600 BCE than we possess for any other place or time preceding the *Elements* of Euclid, circa 320 BCE. Standard tables of multiplication of reciprocals and a place value notation on base sixty facilitated computation at a level Neugebauer compares with that of Europe in the early Renaissance, more than three thousand years later.

Babylonian geometry, like that of Egypt, was still "applied algebra or arithmetic in which numbers are attached to figures" (see figure 3). The ratio between the side and diagonal of a square (i.e., the square root of two) was computed correctly to about one part in a million (see figure 4). Ratios between the areas of a pentagon, hexagon, and heptagon and those of squares built on one side were closely approximated, as was the value of π. A geometric concept of similarity is applied to circles, and perhaps also to triangles. An angle inscribed in a semicircle is known to be a right angle (see figure 5). The Pythagorean theorem (which holds that the square on the hypotenuse of a right triangle is equal to the sum of the squares on the other two sides) was understood in all its generality a thousand years before Pythagoras. One tablet, known as Plimpton 322, develops a set of fifteen "Pythagorean triplets" (three numbers defining right triangles, such as 3,4,5) in a sequence in which acute angles vary by approximately one degree. This "prototrigonometry," unsuspected un-

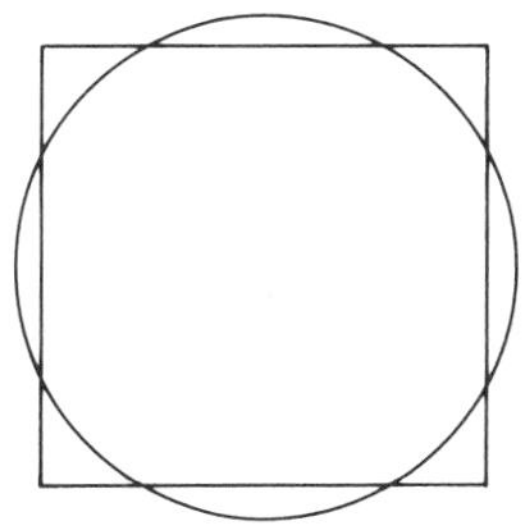

FIGURE 2. *Geometrical Algebra.* Ancient Egyptians approximated the area of a circle by a square with sides eight-ninths of its diameter. Attention is on the numerical answer.

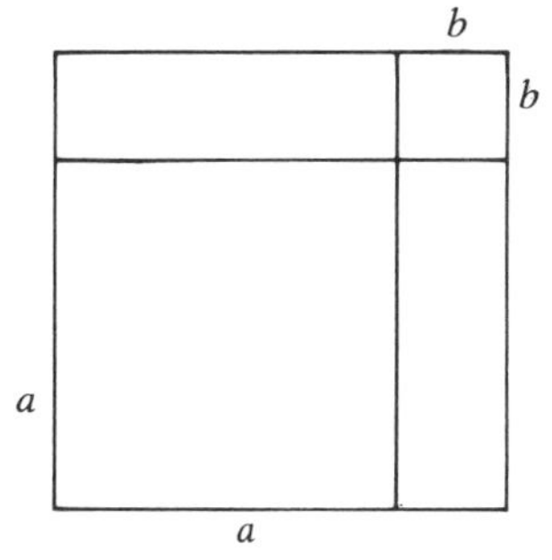

FIGURE 3. *Geometrical Algebra.* The binomial $(a + b)^2 = a^2 + 2ab + b^2$ can be visualized as a problem in geometry.

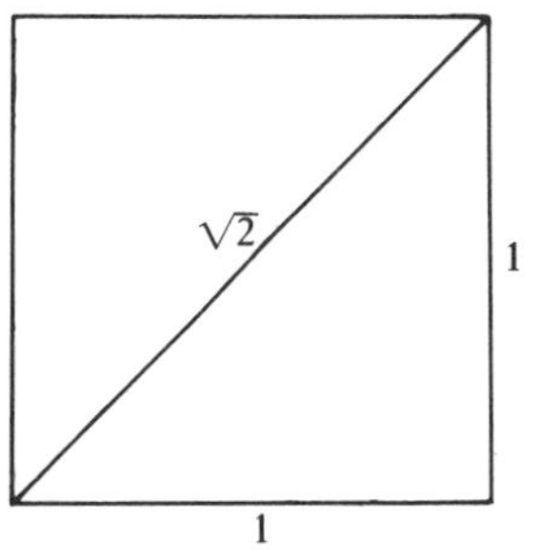

FIGURE 4. *Geometrical Algebra.* The square root of 2 can be visualized as the diagonal of a square.

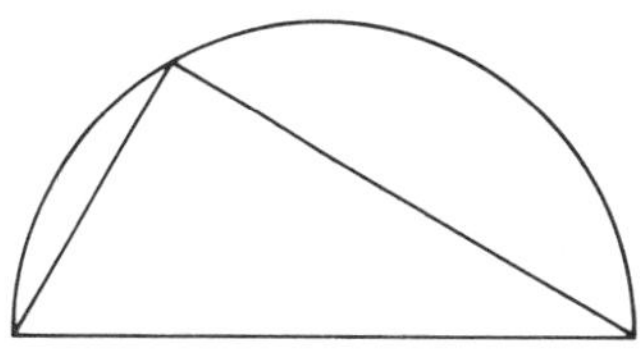

FIGURE 5. *Geometry of the Plane.* A triangle inscribed in a semicircle is a right triangle.

til the tablet was translated in this century, is one of the most astonishing mathematical achievements of the ancient world. It demonstrates empirical knowledge of a general formula:

Assuming integers p and q with $p > q$, and taking $p = 2$ and $q = 1$, the 3,4,5 triplet emerges as follows:

SIDE	SIDE	HYPOTENUSE
$2pq$	$p^2 - q^2$	$p^2 + q^2$
$2(2 \times 1) = 4$	$4 - 1 = 3$	$4 + 1 = 5$

It was from the Babylonians, rather than from the Egyptians, that the Greeks inherited the fund of empirical insights that they transformed into an exact science. The example just cited—in which the ratio of the musical octave, 2:1, is transformed into the Pythagorean triplet 3,4,5—is the foundation of Plato's cosmogony, and it may turn out to be one of our most important clues to the numerology of the ancient world.

Greek Transformation of Egyptian and Babylonian Knowledge. We are still trying to unravel the story of how the Greeks, in less than three centuries (600–300 BCE), transformed geometry—inherited essentially as an art of making arithmetical relations visible—into a science based on definitions, postulates, and theorems (and appealing therefore to an invisible *logos*). Material inherited from Egypt and Babylon through Thales (c. 585 BCE), and Pythagoras (c. 550 BCE) was riddled with confusion between exactness and approximation. A new "dialectical" spirit arose with Parmenides (c. 475 BCE) and his followers. Precise definition, always elusive, was the new goal that Socrates (d. 399 BCE) applied to moral and ethical questions by appealing to "harmonic" examples from the Pythagorean geometry of the vibrating string. Plato's affection for dialectics and his emphasis on abstraction bore unexpected fruit in Aristotle's rejection of his teacher's Pythagorean methods: "Dialectics is merely critical where philosophy claims to know (*Metaphysics* 1004b). Aristotelian "first philosophy" developed a new syllogistic rigor in the generation after Theaetetus (c. 414–c. 369 BCE) and Eudoxus (c. 400–c. 350 BCE), who changed the method and enlarged the scope of mathematics. Another generation later, Euclid's *Elements* completed the mathematical transformation so successfully that the only traces of earlier Greek mathematics that survive must be gleaned from his work. Little else was deemed worth copying.

For our understanding of geometrical symbolism in ancient religions, the Greek transformation has almost no meaning. Although Christianity and Islam are historically young enough to have been affected by the transformation, their holy books show virtually no influence of the new Greek science. (A possible notable exception is the opening line of the *Gospel of John:* "In the beginning was the Logos.") Plato, the first author in history whose works have survived intact, made an extended commentary on the mathematical bias in his philosophy and offers the richest insight into the intentionality that inserted so many mathematical elements in ancient mythology. The musical geometry at the heart of his mathematics was common to both East and West; its simplest pragmatic formula is found in China.

Harmonic Cosmology in China and Greece. The natural, or counting, numbers (1, 2, 3, . . . , infinity) are a primordial image of order. Developed systematically into Pythagorean triplets, they lead to a prototrigonometry of the plane. Applied systematically to the geometry of a vibrating string, they link the magical realm of tone with the numbers that measure the world. To use our economical modern concepts, the octave ratio 1:2 becomes the cyclic module (Plato's matrix, or "universal mother") in which the even numbers are "modular activities" (doubling and halving merely produce further "octave identities") and the odd numbers are "modular residues" (meaning that they define new pitches within the octave matrix). To build a scale, the simplest procedure is to follow the old Chinese rule of adding or subtracting one-third (from any reference pipe or string length). This is the geometrical analogue of the musical procedure of tuning by ear: a subtraction of one-third correlates with the musical interval of an ascending perfect fifth (3:2); an addition of one-third correlates with the descending perfect fourth (4:3). To avoid fractions in the arithmetic, the reference length must contain one factor of three for every "tone child" to be generated. The Chinese pentatonic (five-tone) scale must therefore be generated from $3^4 = 81$.

Tone	C		G		D		A		E
Number	81		54		72		48		64
Operation		$-\frac{1}{3}$		$+\frac{1}{3}$		$-\frac{1}{3}$		$+\frac{1}{3}$	

Rearranged into scale order, this number sequence has a reciprocal "twin" that defines frequency ratios:

Tone	C	D	E	G	A
Length ratio	81	72	64	54	48
Frequency	64	72	81	96	108

Both Chinese and Greek cosmology are projections from this tonal geometry, reducible to continued operations with the prime number 3. Note that the defining operation started on $3^4 = 9^2 = 81$. Ancient China was conceived as 1/81 part of the whole world, that is, as 1/9 of one of the nine "great continents." China was also considered to be divided into nine provinces, so that each Chinese province was 1/729 of the whole world; now $3^6 = 9^3 = 729$ is the base for the same tuning calculation when it is extended through seven tones for the complete diatonic scale, also standard in China in the

Tetractys		Algebraic value	Arithmetic example
point	o	( )	1
line	o o	a b	2 3
plane	o o o	a^2 ab b^2	4 6 9
solid	o o o o	a^3 a^2b ab^2 b^3	8 12 18 27

FIGURE 6. *The Pythagorean Holy Tetractys.* Note the modern algebraic formula and the Pythagorean arithmetic example in smallest integers.

fifth century BCE. At about the same time, Philolaus, a Greek Pythagorean philosopher, conceived the year as made up of "729 days and nights," a number that would seem to come from nowhere but such a musical cosmology. Plato linked the seven tones in this set to the sun, moon, and five planets; later, Ptolemy (second century CE) linked the scale to the zodiac.

The numbers 64 and 81, on which the alternate scale progressions commence, and the number 108, largest in the set of pentatonic frequency values, are immortalized in various ways. In China there are 64 hexagrams in the *I ching* divination text. The numbers $8^2 = 64$ and $9^2 = 81$ have been the favored squares on which to construct the Hindu fire altar since Vedic times (c. 1500 BCE). The number 108, upper limit in the set, is the number of beads in the Buddhist rosary. The tuning pattern itself has recently been discovered (but without numbers) on an Old Babylonian cuneiform tablet from circa 1800 BCE.

The set of twelve consecutive tones generated by the above procedure constitutes a chromatic scale. In ancient China each of the twelve tones in turn became the tonic of the standard pentatonic scale for a particular calendric period. Throughout Chinese history, the bureau of standards remained wedded to a tonal geometry: the length of a pitch pipe (an end-blown hollow tube) sounding the reference tone determined the standard foot measure for the regime; the measures of grain that the body of the pipe could contain became the standards for both weights and volumes. Each new regime established a new reference pitch; today we have the records of dozens of successive changes in the bureau of standards as the reference pitch oscillated over the range of about the interval of a sixth.

Unless one knows the musical procedure, the Taoist formula for the creation of the world sounds mystical: "The Tao [the Way] produced one, the one produced two, the two produced three, and the three produced the ten thousand things [everything]." The creation myth related by Plato in the *Timaeus* similarly develops the world's harmonical soul and body from the numbers 1, 2, and 3. Pythagoreans frankly announced that, to them, "All is number," and Aristotle quotes them as saying, "The world and all that is in it is determined by the number three." Plutarch describes planetary distances in the Philolaus system as "a geometrical progression with three as the common ratio." For eight hundred years Greek astronomers toyed with variations on this planetary tuning. Johannes Kepler discovered his laws of planetary motion (c. 1600 CE) while still looking for the right tones to associate with each celestial body. East and West, the "geometry" of heaven and earth was musical and profoundly trinitarian while astronomy was being gestated.

The Greek view of this tonal-planetary geometry points in the direction of a more abstract mathematical system. The Pythagorean "holy tetractys" was a pebble pattern symbolizing continuing geometric progression from a point through a line and a plane to the "solid" dimension (see figure 6). Plato takes advantage of the double meanings of integers (both as whole numbers and as reciprocal fractions) to generate the material for a seven-tone scale at the cube dimension ($3^3 = 27$; see figure 7). Nicomachus (fl. c. 100 CE), writing an introduction to Plato, simplifies the double view of the multiplication table for 2×3 up to the limit of $3^6 = 9^3 =$

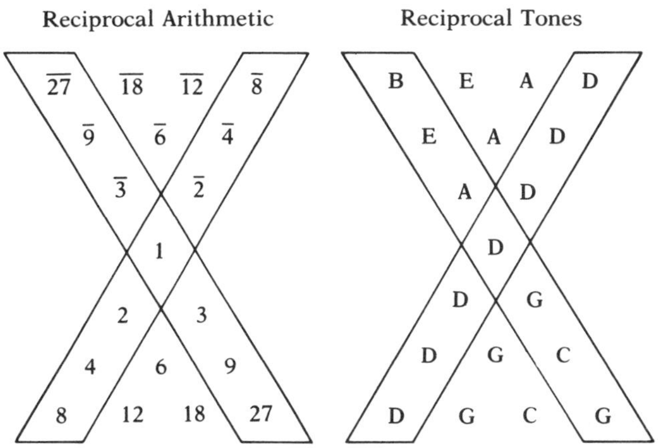

FIGURE 7. *Plato's Timaeus Cross (X).* This pattern reveals at a glance the Platonic theorem that between square numbers there is one geometric mean and between cube numbers there are two. The result is continuing geometric progression in every direction around the center. This construction is a stage in the process by which Plato develops the cubes of 2 and 3 into the model "world soul." Arithmetic doubles are known as octave equivalences to a musician and as modular identities to a mathematician.

1	2	4	8	16	32	64	=	F
	3	6	12	24	48	96	=	C
		9	18	36	72	144	=	G
			27	54	108	216	=	D
				81	162	324	=	A
					243	486	=	E
						729	=	B

FIGURE 8. *Nicomachus's Triangle.* Nicomachus presents Plato's reciprocal material in figure 7 in the form of a multiplication table for 2×3, extended to $3^6 = 9^3 = 729$ to avoid fractions. Note that he describes the numbers written out from left to right rather than arranged in the form of the Greek letter chi (X) that Plato specified.

729 (see figure 8). Stones, musical tones, planets, numbers, and geometry are all parts of one vast Pythagorean synthesis, replete with symbolic cross-references and a supporting mythology. An exasperated Aristotle mocked it; Euclid made it obsolete.

The problem of "excess and deficiency" with which a musician wrestles in adjusting the geometry of the string by ear had its arithmetical analogue in the ancient problem of making approximations between the areas of a circle and square and the volumes of a sphere and cube. Thus harmonics was a paradigm for an ethics of moderation; "nothing too much," the Greek ideal, had its counterpart in Confucian concepts of morality and behavior. Thousands of years earlier, the Egyptians had conceived the scales of Maat as the "great balance" on which the heart of the deceased was figuratively weighed to test its fitness for immortality. Thus the wisdom literature of the ancient world shows remarkable parallels between cultures.

The historical record is so fragmented, however, that interpretation of geometric symbols remains speculative. Modern studies in the neurophysiology of vision and in related psychological inferences suggest that schematic, geometric relations play decisive roles. The universal acceptance of the octave ratio 1:2 is further evidence of human psychophysical norms that could generate correspondence between cultures that were never in contact. While we can neither fully document the paths of cultural diffusion nor even claim that diffusion is necessary, we cannot entirely rid ourselves of suspicion that there was a great deal more diffusion than we can prove.

Problems in Ancient Geometric Symbols. It is easy to imagine that the ancient stone circles that abound in Europe and America linked people to events in the sky—that the twenty-eight poles arranged in a circle for the lodge of the Arapaho Indians' Sun Dance, for instance, may correspond to twenty-eight lunar mansions; that the twelve sections of the Crow tribe's lodge for that ceremony may allude to the months of the year; and that other cultures possessed similar symbols of earth, sky, and calendar (Burckhardt, 1976). But many familiar symbols are more puzzling. Why, for instance, did the Pythagoreans take a five-pointed star (see figure 9) as their special symbol? Is it because each line cuts two others in "mean and extreme ratio" (meaning that the whole lines is to the longer segment as the longer is to the shorter) so that the figure symbolizes both "continuing geometric progression" (the world's "best bonds," for Plato) and a victory over the "darkness" of the irrational? Could the Hindu "drum of Śiva" (see figure 10)—with its inverted triangles and the interlocked triangles of the star-hexagon (see figure 11), prevalent in Indian and Semitic cultures—be related to the Pythagorean symbols in figures 6 and 7?

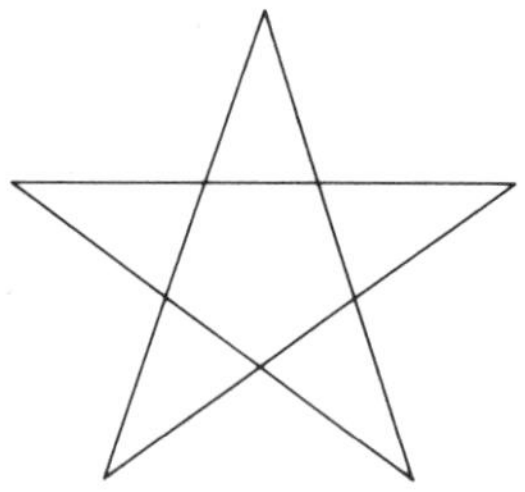

FIGURE 9. *Pythagorean Symbol.* Each line cuts two others in "mean and extreme" ratio.

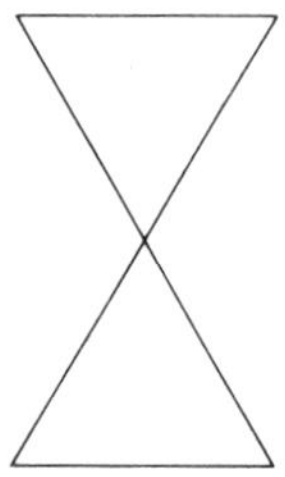

FIGURE 10. *The Drum of Śiva.* Note the hourglass shape attributed to Mount Meru, and compare with Plato's *Timaeus* pattern in figure 7.

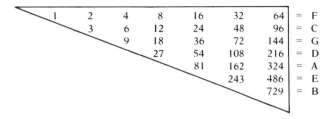

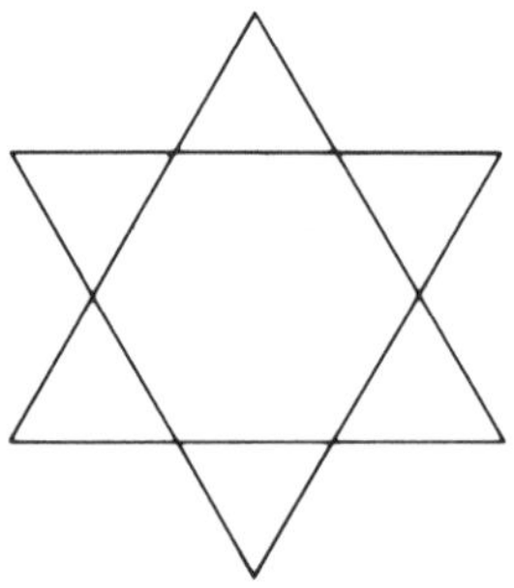

FIGURE 11. *Star Hexagon.* Indian and Semitic symbol.

Number of Syllables		Total number of variations
	1	
1	1 1	$2 = 2^1$
2	1 2 1	$4 = 2^2$
3	1 3 3 1	$8 = 2^3$
4	1 4 6 4 1	$16 = 2^4$
5	1 5 10 10 5 1	$32 = 2^5$
6	1 6 15 20 15 6 1	$64 = 2^6$

FIGURE 12. *Pascal's Triangle.* Known to Piṅgala (c. 200 BCE) as "Mount Meru," the Hindu and Buddhist holy mountain.

The so-called Pascal triangle (see figure 12), containing the coefficients for the expansion of the binomial $(a+b)^{2,3,4,5,6}$ was known to Piṅgala (c. 200 BCE) as Mount Meru, the Hindu-Buddhist holy mountain. Piṅgala interpreted this triangle as showing the possible variations of meter built from monosyllables, disyllables, trisyllables, and so on. Could this "Mount Meru" be related to the holy mountains of other Eastern religions? Is the Pythagorean tetractys simply the Greek form of older holy mountains? Is it significant that the Sumerian symbol for mountain is a triangular pile of bricks (see figure 13), aligned in a pattern Pythagoreans found useful for numbers? Is the hourglass shape of the later Buddhist holy mountain simply a geometric variation of the "drum of Śiva"?

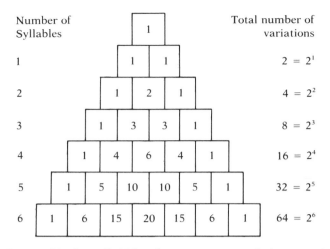

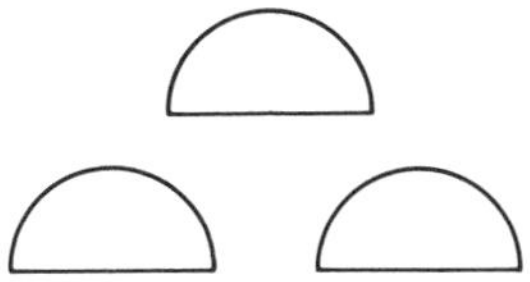

FIGURE 13. *Sumerian Symbol for a Mountain.* The triangular arrangement is the pattern that Pythagoreans found useful for numbers.

Translation of the ancient Babylonian mathematical texts now makes clear that the computational sophistication achieved four thousand years ago was so great that the sacred texts of all peoples must be studied with new alertness for evidence of rational—and not merely poetic—inspiration. The old Sumerian-Babylonian gods possessed straightforward numerical "nicknames" (used for scribal shorthand) in sexagesimal (base sixty) notation; the three great gods—Anu-An, whose numerical epithet was 60 (written as a large 1), Ea-Enki, associated with 40, and Enlil, associated with 50—are functional equivalents of Plato's 3,4,5 Pythagorean genetic triad. Could some of our ancient religious mythology turn out to be mathematical allegory?

It seems curious that the ancient Greek altar at Delphi is built on cubic dimensions, as are the chapel of the Egyptian goddess Leto that Herodotus saw in the city of Buto, the Vedic fire altar, the Holy of Holies in Solomon's temple, and the ancient Sumerian ark (first to "rescue a remnant of mankind from the flood"). The name of the most sacred Islamic shrine, the Ka'bah at Mecca, literally means "cube," and the city of New Jerusalem in the *Book of Revelation* is also measured in such dimensions. All of these cubic consonances between our religions suggest that poetic religious imagination has had a geometrical, "protoscientific" component for a very long time.

Geometry since Euclid. The thirteen books of Euclid's *Elements* culminate in a treatment of the five regular, or Platonic solids—tetrahedon, cube, octahedron, dodecahedron, and icosahedron—each with uniform sides and angles and all capable, when replicated, of closely packing three-dimensional, abstract space. Euclid mastered the transformational symmetries of these "rigid" bodies.

In the third century BCE Archimedes did important work on the area of the surface of a sphere and of a cylinder and on their respective volumes, and Apollonius carried the study of conic sections (ellipse, parabola, and hyperbola) to its highest development. Later Greek authors made further advances in geometry, but the great wave of development that had begun scarcely four hundred years earlier was spent.

Later Hindu talent has been mainly arithmetic and algebraic; theorems on the areas and diagonals of quadrilaterals in a circle were contributed by Brahmagupta (c. 628 CE). Important Arab contributions to the solution of cubic equations by the method of intersecting conics were summarized by 'Omar Khayyām (c. 1100 CE). European development has been rapid since Kepler's time; it was Kepler who introduced the concepts of the infinitely great and the infinitely small, which Euclid had carefully excised from consideration. The invention of analytic geometry by Pierre de Fermat and René Descartes in the seventeenth century led to a new integration of geometry and algebra.

The contributions of Euclid's *Elements* to the invention and development of the physical sciences during all these centuries is inestimable. His kind of logical, geometrical argument is the basis for Archimedes' formalization of the laws of the lever; for the Greek development of astronomy as a physical science (by Hipparchus, Ptolemy, and others); for Galileo's work on the dynamics of the inclined plane; for Kepler's laws of planetary motion; for Newton's laws of planetary gravitational dynamics; and for an endless host of related physical sciences. Euclidean geometry, still being improved today, has thus been one of the Western world's most powerful engines of progress. The *Elements* has been "the most influential textbook of all times" (Boyer, 1968), and it was long assumed to be as certain a guide to geometry as the Bible to absolute truth. God, it was confidently asserted, is a geometer.

During the nineteenth century, which Boyer calls the "golden age of geometry," this almost-perfected world of traditional, Euclidean-inspired mathematical physics exploded with a creative energy, leading to a crisis in the very foundations of mathematics. For example, one of the several new geometries that appeared, projective geometry, has nothing to do with measurement. Several "non-Euclidean" geometries, by N. I. Lobachevskii, Wolfgang Bolyai, and G. F. B. Riemann, omit Euclid's famous sixth postulate concerning parallel lines, always somewhat suspect, to create equally logical geometries of even wider generality.

In our century, the favored status of Euclidean geometry has evaporated. There are no longer any assumptions that command universal assent, no systems of logic powerful enough to validate themselves even in mathematics. Mathematics has thus lost some of its certainty even while multiplying its powers. Einstein's notion of "space-time," with its curvatures and paradoxes, has relegated Euclidean geometry to the role of a convenient tool for certain of our intuitions within a severely limited local space. Space perception itself has been proved culturally biased; intuition can be taught new tricks. Space has also multiplied its hallowed three dimensions beyond any possibility of imagining; today the number of its dimensions is the number of independent variables in our formulas.

With the shattering of mathematical certainty and the ending of our idolatry of Euclidean rationalism, Western scientists in particular have felt a new attraction to the philosophical skepticism of Vedic poets and to Taoist and Buddhist feeling for how the world behaves. The ancient worldview was created in imagination; today imagination is still proving more powerful than logic. In the ferment of this present age, mathematics and physics are committed, perhaps more clearly than ever—but as an act of faith rather than of reason—to the primordial affection for symmetry, guided less by reason than by aesthetic feeling for elegance and beauty.

[*See also* Numbers; Circle; *and* Quaternity. *For a more general discussion of the religious interpretations of space, see* Sacred Space.]

BIBLIOGRAPHY

For a basic textbook in Euclidean geometry and in the various non-Euclidean modern geometries, see H. S. M. Coxeter's *Introduction to Geometry* (1961; reprint, New York, 1969), notable for the elegant compression it achieves by rigorous pursuit of symmetry and of the "group" of transformations this includes. The history of geometry is set within the wider context of the whole of mathematics and the contributions of nations and individuals treated with great fairness in Carl B. Boyer's *A History of Mathematics* (New York, 1968). On the early period, Otto Neugebauer's *The Exact Sciences in Antiquity*, 2d ed. (New York, 1969), has become a classic. The transformation of Egyptian and Babylonian empirical knowledge into Greek science is studied in B. L. van der Waerden's *Science Awakening*, translated by Arnold Dresden (New York, 1963). Richard J. Gillings's *Mathematics in the Time of the Pharaohs* (Cambridge, Mass., 1972) is an effort to balance the somewhat negative views of mathematicians toward Egyptian science.

A splendidly illustrated study of Paleolithic stone and bone counting records is Alexander Marshack's *The Roots of Civilization* (New York, 1972). Neolithic symmetry in pottery and weaving designs is richly illustrated in Marija Gimbutas's *The Goddesses and Gods of Old Europe, 6500–3500 B.C.* (Berkeley, 1982). Modern concepts of symmetry are formalized, with great respect toward ancient craftsmen who explored it intuitively, in Hermann Weyl's *Symmetry* (Princeton, 1952).

Applications of traditional geometry to religious art and architecture can be found in Robert Lawlor's *Sacred Geometry: Philosophy and Practice* (New York, 1982) and Titus Burckhardt's *Art of Islam: Language and Meaning*, translated by J. Peter Hobson (London, 1976). A stone-by-stone analysis of the geometry employed by the several builders of a great cathedral is masterfully displayed in John James's *The Contractors of Chartres*, 2 vols. (Beckenham, Kent, 1980).

For a development of the tonal-geometrical symbolism hidden in ancient religious and philsophical texts, see my books *The Myth of Invariance* (New York, 1976), *The Pythagorean Plato* (Stony Brook, N.Y., 1978), and *Meditations through the Quran* (York Beach, Maine, 1981).

ERNEST G. MCCLAIN

GERMANIC RELIGION. The systematic study of Germanic mythology began with the publication in 1835 of Jakob Grimm's *Deutsche Mythologie* (Teutonic Mythology). Born out of the interest of Romanticism for the Germanic past, Grimm's work presented a rich collection of materials and well-organized data, but his etymologies and interpretations are now largely rejected. Moreover, he was convinced that the Scandinavian material represented the common heritage of all the Germanic tribes, whereas later studies by philologists like Karl Müllenhoff led to the recognition of the separateness of the Scandinavian sources.

The nineteenth century witnessed various trends in the interpretation of myth. Everything was claimed to pertain to natural phenomena: Max Müller connected all myths with the cycle of the sun, while Adalbert Kuhn looked for meteorological interpretations in the thunder and the storm. Wilhelm Mannhardt overemphasized agricultural rites, whereas original animism, with its spirits and demons, was postulated under the influence of the British school (as by E. B. Tylor), and myths were interpreted as "dreams" (as suggested by Andrew Lang).

Things changed toward the end of the century when there was a growing interest in folklore. Several scholars devoted monographs to major divine figures, such as the sky god (Rudolf Much), or focused on religion and ethical and spiritual concepts (Vilhelm Grönbech). Other studies were devoted to the Germanic system of values, to fate, and to the concept of the "holy" (Walter Baetke), while still others, following in the footsteps of Sophus Bugge, looked for adaptations of Christian models.

In the twentieth century, the crowning of decades of research was Jan de Vries's magisterial *Altgermanische Religionsgeschichte,* first published in 1935–1937. In its thoroughly revised second edition (1956–1957) it summarizes the research of the "historic" school (Karl Helm), as well as the new comparative method illustrated by the work of Georges Dumézil, and takes into account the work of folklorists, toponymists, and others.

Germanic Culture. The earliest Germanic culture that archaeologists identify as such is the so-called Jastorf culture, a cultural province of northern Europe in the early Iron Age (c. 600 BCE), covering present-day Holstein, Jutland, northeast Saxony, and western Mecklenburg. From the linguistic point of view, however, the Germanic people constitute an archaic branch of the Indo-European family. At the time they entered into history, their closest neighbors were the Celts in Gaul, as Germanic tribes had spread south toward the Rhine and the wooded hills of southern Germany. To the east their neighbors were the Balts and the Scythians and Sarmatians, Iranian tribes that roamed the plains of Russia. To the north, they were in contact with Lapps and with Finns. Most of the information we have about them from early times comes from classical authors such as Caesar and Tacitus. Although they were primarily pastoralists, they also practiced agriculture. Their cattle were rather puny and could not entirely be depended upon for a livelihood; hunting provided an additional supply of meat. Their social organization was originally geared toward egalitarian communalism, but as contact with the Roman empire changed economic conditions, a more diversified society developed in which wealth and rank tended to prevail, although, nominally, power still rested in the hands of the Þing (Thing), the popular assembly, of all free men able to carry arms. The information from Roman sources about Germanic religion is scanty, but whatever we have indicates a continuity through the centuries.

Sources. The sources of our knowledge of Germanic religion are of different kinds. Archaeology provides us with information about funeral rites and sacrificial offerings; monuments from the Roman period bear inscriptions with the names of Germanic deities; classical writers refer to Germanic gods under their *interpretatio Romana,* and later Christian authors mention them by name as they describe their abhorred cults or the actions taken by kings or evangelizing saints against their worship. Also, a large number of Bronze Age rock carvings in southern Scandinavia are often included in the earliest documentation; these have to be interpreted with specific reservations, as the sets of pictures they present are particularly complex, mixing numerous symbols of various kinds: ships, chariots, men plowing, people reveling to the sound of lurs and other musical instruments, worshipers carrying solar disks, imprints of feet and hands, and what not. To isolate one figure among those such as the "spear god," for example, because of its larger size, and identifying it further with Óðinn (Odin) because the latter had a wondrous spear called Gungnir, is, to say the least, conjectural. We cannot altogether dismiss the testimony of these engravings, but they must be interpreted with caution, since it cannot be formally ascertained that the agriculturists (or, farther north, the hunters) who produced them actually represented a proto-Germanic culture.

The age of migration and the following period, when the Germanic kingdoms became established in western Europe, yield only meager documents on the religion of the people who precipitated the downfall of the Roman empire. As mentioned above, they consist essentially of references to the antipagan actions of kings and the church in literary sources, chronicles, hagiography, legal texts, instructions to priests, and such. A few charms and spells have survived, as well as runic inscriptions, which provide some clues about particular aspects of popular religion and superstition. [*See* Runes.] The bulk of our information comes, however, from texts of the Viking age that were preserved in later manuscripts and from the maintenance of the Germanic mythological tradition in skaldic poetry, which led to the compilation of valuable sources like Snorri Sturluson's *Skáld-*

skaparmál (Poetic Diction). [*See* Eddas.] Sturluson's *Gylfaginning* (The Deluding of Gylfi) reads like a synopsis of the lays of the *Poetic Edda*, and in the *Heimskringla*, which records the lives of kings of Norway, he euhemerizes the major gods as mythical sovereigns of early Scandinavia, as Saxo Grammaticus does for Denmark in his *History of the Danes*. [*See the biographies of Snorri and Saxo.*] Moreover, descriptions of life in Iceland, Norway, and Sweden contain numerous details on religious practices and specific forms of worship, as well as on the shift from paganism to Christianity. Although, again, the sagas have to be used with caution as a source of information on early Scandinavian belief and rites, they contain a good deal of valuable data not available anywhere else, such as the detailed description of the temple of Þórr (Thor) at Hofstaðir in the *Eyrbyggjasaga*. [*See* Sagas.] The gods and their cults have also left their mark in the numerous toponyms attesting to the vitality of their worship in specific areas at the time of the settlement.

The Creation Myth. In the *Prose Edda*, Snorri Sturluson gives a complete description of creation that combines a number of older sources, which are not always consistent with each other. The major Eddic poems used by Snorri are the *Vafþrúðnismál* and *Grímnismál* (the lays of Vafþrúðnir and Grímnir), which more or less duplicate each other, and the *Vǫluspá* (Prophecy of the Seeress); but he also derives some details from sources lost to us and adds some deductions of his own. Quoting the *Vǫluspá* (st. 3), Snorri stresses that at the beginning of time there was nothing but a great void called Ginnungagap, a void filled with powerful magic forces (the term *ginnung* is related to Old Norse *ginnregin*, "the supreme gods," and runic *ginArunAR*, "runes endowed with magic power"). In the *Vǫluspá*, the text reads: "When Ymir lived, in earliest times, there was neither sand, nor sea, nor chill waves," whereas Snorri says, "In the beginning not anything existed, there was no sand, nor sea, nor cooling waves." It is probable that Snorri's version reflects the older tradition, because the idea of an empty space and a world of mere potentiality preceding creation seems to belong to the ancestral heritage of the Germanic people since it finds an uncanny parallel in the well-known cosmogonic hymn of the *Ṛgveda:* "There was neither nonbeing nor being; nor was there space nor the sky above" (10.129). The same idea is expressed in Old Norse by the phrase "Jǫrð fannz œva né upphiminn" ("Earth was unknown and heaven above"), an old poetic image paralleled in Old High German in the ninth-century Prayer of Wessobrunn: "Dat ero ni was noh ufhimil" ("There was neither earth nor sky above"), as well as in the Old English formula "Eorðan . . . and upheofon."

Long before the earth was formed there existed Niflheimr, the dark misty world of death. In Niflheimr was a well called Hvergelmir (lit., "resounding kettle," from *hverr*, "kettle," and *-gelmir*, related to *galmr*, "roaring"), from which eleven rivers flowed. In the south lay the blazing hot world of Múspell over which the giant Surtr ("black") held sway. The occurrence of the Old High German word *mūspilli* in a tenth-century Bavarian eschatological poem, where it designates the universal fire at the end of the world, indicates that the concept reflects an old Germanic tradition.

The rivers whipped by showers pouring out of Niflheimr froze and layer after layer of ice piled up in Ginnungagap. However, sparks and glowing embers flying out of Múspell met the hoarfrost and the ice, and from the slush and heat life emerged in the shape of an anthropomorphic primeval being who received the name of Ymir, or Aurgelmir. From this primal giant sprang the dreadful brood of the frost giants, whom he engendered by sweating a male and a female from under his left arm and begetting a son from one of his legs with the other.

Obviously, Snorri has merged two traditions here that the *Vafþrúðnismál* keeps separate: in stanza 21, Ymir is named as the giant involved in the formation of the world, but in stanzas 29–35, Vafþrúðnir, the oldest living giant, explains to Óðinn that the genealogy of the giants begins with Aurgelmir, who fathered Þruðgelmir, who fathered Bergelmir, who fathered Vafþrúðnir himself.

No direct source is available for the account of the origin of the gods that Snorri gives us next in the *Gylfaginning:* the melting rime has taken the shape of a cow, Auðhumla, whose name contains Old Norse *auðr* ("riches"), and another term connected with the English dialect word *hummel* or *humble* ("hornless cow"), presumably designating a "rich hornless cow." This cow feeds Ymir with the milk flowing from her udders, a tradition paralleling that of the primeval cow in Indo-Iranian mythology. Auðhumla gets her own food by licking the salty ice blocks, but in doing so, she gives shape to another primal being, Búri, who begets a son, Borr. Borr marries Bestla, the daughter of the giant Bǫlþorn (literally, "evil thorn," a term still used in the Jutland dialect [*bøltorn*] to designate a "scrappy, violent person"). Borr and his wife have three sons: Óðinn, Vili, and Vé.

When the three divine brothers kill the giant Ymir, the flow of blood gushing from his wounds drowns all the frost giants *(hrímþursar)*, except Bergelmir, who escapes mysteriously with his family to continue the race. Now the three gods set about building the earth. The body of Ymir is carried into the middle of the great void; his blood forms the sea and the lakes, his flesh the earth, and his skull the sky (with a dwarf at each corner, as if to uphold it), his hair the trees, his brain the clouds, his bones the mountains, and so on. Sparks flying from Múspell form the stars and heavenly bodies, and the gods order their movements, determining the divisions of time.

The earth was circular, surrounded by a vast ocean. In the middle of the earth the gods established Miðgarðr, a residence for mankind, strengthened by a fence made from the eyebrows of Ymir, and they gave land on the shore for the giants to settle down. The next task of the gods was the creation of man, which is related in the myth of Askr and Embla (*Vǫluspá* 17–18). Finally, they built Ásgarðr, their own residence.

Comments on the Creation Myth. A number of elements of the Eddic creation myth point to very old traditions. For example, the cow is a typical fertility symbol, and Auðhumla reminds us of the celestial cow in Middle Eastern and South Asian myths. Further, in the myth of Ymir, two motifs have apparently merged: the engenderment of primeval beings (in this case, giants) and the creation of the world from parts of his body.

The idea of an ancestral progenitor is already found in the Latin sources: Tacitus, in the second chapter of his *Germania,* tells about Tuisto, born from the earth, who begets Mannus, the common ancestor of the Germanic tribes. The names are quite revealing: Tuisto is connected with the numeral "two" and designates a bisexual being (Ger., *Zwitter*), an androgynous ancestor as one might assume Ymir could have been. Ymir has parallels in Indo-Iranian mythology, where the Old Indic Yama (Av., Yima, "twin") is supposed to have had incestuous relations with his twin sister. As for *Mannus,* not only does it obviously correspond to our word for *man,* but it also has striking parallels in India, where Manu is the ancestor of man, and in ancient Phrygia, where the ancestor of the Phrygians is Mánēs.

The three main Germanic tribes, which derive their names from the alleged sons of Mannus, show in at least two cases similar clear associations with deities. The Inguaeones are definitely linked with the minor god Ing, the male counterpart of the mother goddess; his name is preserved in Old English runic poems and in proper names like *Ingwine* ("friend of Ing") in *Beowulf,* and he is considered the ancestor of the dynasty of the Ynglingar in Sweden. The (H)erminones derive their name from Germanic **ermina-/*ermuna-* ("mighty, lofty"), a common divine epithet similar to Old Norse *Jǫrmunr* for Óðinn or (H)irmin for the Saxon god corresponding to Mars, according to Widukind (cf. the Saxon symbol of the *axis mundi,* Irminsul, described as "universalis columna"), also found in the compound *irmingot* ("mighty god") in the Old High German *Hildebrandslied.* The Istaevones are not related to any specific deity, but their name is perhaps connected with Gothic *aistan* ("honor, worship").

The idea of dismembering a giant to create the world is found also in Middle Eastern and other traditions. [*See* Dismemberment.] An Iranian myth as preserved in Manichaeism is the closest to that of Ymir as it equates the giant's skin with the sky, his flesh with the earth, his bones with the mountains, his hair with plants, and his blood with the sea. There can hardly be any question of mutual influence, diffusion, or borrowing from a common source. Taking into consideration the Puruṣa myth in the *Ṛgveda* (10.90), which explains similarly the origin of the world and society through the sacrifice of primal man and the projection of his bodily parts into the macrocosm, it cannot be doubted that we are actually dealing with an old Indo-European myth. Recently, Bruce Lincoln has elaborated the complex data about creation in various Indo-European traditions into a coherent scenario in which the first priest, *Manu-, kills his twin brother, *Yemo-, the first king, thus performing the first sacrifice. As a result of this act the world is created, and *Manu- fashions the earth and heavens as well as the three social classes from his brother's body. The female bovine that appears in the European version of the myth originally fed and cared for the twins before the creative act. Against this background, many of the archaic elements in the Germanic tradition appear in a new and broader light.

The Image of the Germanic Mythical World. Man lives in the center of the universe; the major Germanic traditions concur in calling his dwelling place Midgard ("the central abode"; Goth., Midjungards; OHG; Mittilgart; OE, Middangeard; ON, Miðgarðr). But the center is also the place where the gods built their residence, Ásgarðr. It is described as spacious, with numerous dwellings, surrounded by a beautiful green pasture, Iðavǫllr, and by a palisade built by a giant. Outside is Útgarðr, the dangerous world of demons, giants (in Jǫtunheimr), and other frightening creatures.

Germanic myth evinces a real fear of this no-man's-land outside the settlement, and the idea of the frontier is there all the time, with the gods serving to ward off dangers from the wild. The islanders and the people along the shore believe that a universal ocean surrounds the earth, with an unfathomable abyss at the horizon and a huge snake curling at the edge to hold the world together. The serpent is called Miðgarðsormr or Jǫrmungandr; according to Snorri Sturluson, this monstrous ophidian bit its tail—a concept that does not occur in the Germanic poetry but is quite common in Eastern religions and was introduced in Scandinavia by medieval Christian scholarship. The symbol (similar to the *ouroboros* in Jungian psychology) may be borrowed, but the concept is old, as the name *Jǫrmungandr* shows: this term is connected with *jǫrmungrund* (used in *Grímnismál* 20 for "earth"); the term *gandr* means literally "magic wand"; *jǫrmun-* (also a name of Óðinn) is an adjective meaning "great, powerful, lofty"; the compound *eormengrund* also appears in *Beowulf* 859.

When the gods go out into the world, it seems that the universal ocean does not exist for them, since they are always moving on solid ground in all directions. The north and the east are particularly dangerous abodes of demons; the south will not play any important role until the end of time (actually, historical events tend to give the south, the seat of advanced cultures, a favorable connotation). In the west lies the big sea. The old Germanic tradition of ship burials—letting loose the vessel of the dead, aflame, on the ocean—implies the concept of a world of the dead beyond the sea, a view perhaps borrowed from the Celts, as suggested by the Irish legends about the "islands of the blessed." This concept is also reflected in the image of Naglfar, the ship of death that sails from the world of the demons at Ragnarǫk (the end of time).

For the Germanic people in Norway Útgarðr must have been represented by the high mountains and the arctic territories to the north. The road is over land; Skírnir rides to Útgarðr on Freyr's horse (*Skírnismál* 10), and Þórr's adventures always take him eastward. There are the realms of Hymir, who lives at the "end of the world"; of Þrymr and Hrymr (*Vǫluspá* 49); and the "iron forest" *(iarnviðr)*, where the brood of demons is born (*Vǫluspá* 39). There is a great river at the border of Miðgarðr, with a boatman, Hárbarðr, to take people over. The frost giants *(hrímþursar)* live in the north; there is Jǫtunheimr where Loki will seek refuge. But the north is mainly the world of the dead, Nástrandir, (*Vǫluspá* 38). As Snorri Sturluson states: "Helvegr liggr niðr ok norðr" ("The way to Hel lies beneath and north"). Stone Age graves, with their northward orientation, confirm this view. Similarly, in the Scandinavian house, the main seat, called *ǫndvegi* ("way of the spirit") and supposed to be the seat of the ancestor, is located to the north. Furthermore, in magical rites, water flowing northward is related to the kingdom of death.

Another concept of the world of the dead situates it in the "netherworld," the dark hall of Hel (which is not a place of punishment). The term *Hel* ("hiding") applies to both the place and its ruler in Old Norse. The belief in this underworld seems to be common to all Germanic cultures. In 915, a poet celebrating the victory of the Saxons over the Franks wonders whether there will be enough room in "hell" for all those that fell in the battle. An elaborate description of the place is given in the Eddic sources: the approaches are protected by terribly noisy rivers, such as Valglaumir, Gjǫll, and Sliðr, which according to *Vǫluspá* 35 "is filled with swords and knives." This picture is apparently influenced by Christian visionary literature; *Grímnismál* 27 also mentions the river Geirvimul ("swarming with spears"). There is a bridge over Gjǫll, guarded by the maiden Móðguðr. The Greek hellhound Kerberos also has his parallel in Eddic tradition. The realm of Hel is surrounded by a fence (Helgrind or Nágrind), the gates of which open only for the dead. Hermóðr has to jump this barrier to get access to the goddess of the netherworld. In *Vafþrúðnismál* 43, the giant says that he has seen all the worlds, and he mentions Niflhel, lying "beneath the nine worlds he saw." Snorri describes Niflhel in even darker colors, interpreting it as "the lowest world where the wicked go"—similar to the Christian concept of Hell.

The sky is the abode of the gods in the later conception of the Germanic people, which transfers Ásgarðr to heaven. There, the gods' residences bear names like *Himinbjǫrg* ("protection of heaven"), for the hall of Heimdallr, the watchman of the gods, located at the rim of the sky (where the celestial outlook Hliðskjálf is also located). Valhǫll is a typical example of the shift. Originally, it was a subterraneous hall for warriors killed in combat; later connected with Óðinn, it becomes the heavenly residence of his heroic retinue, the *einherjar.* It is a huge palace with 540 rooms, each with a single door so large that eight hundred warriors exit through it to go and fight (*Grímnismál* 23–24). Over the gate and gable a wolf and an eagle are mounted, according to tradition, just as Charlemagne is said to have had an eagle nailed on his palace.

Like the netherworld, the sky is linked with the world by a bridge, this one guarded by Heimdallr; it is called Bilrǫst ("wavering road," i.e., the rainbow) or Bifrǫst ("shivering road"). In *Grímnismál* 29, the "bridge of the gods" *(ásbrú)* is "ablaze with flames." Here , the concept may represent a different cosmological view, symbolizing the Milky Way, which the forces of evil from Múspell will walk at the twilight of the world, and which, in many religious systems, is described as the "path of the souls."

The cosmic tree. The ash tree Yggdrasill, where the gods sit in council every day, rises to the sky, and its branches spread over the entire world. It is supported by three roots: one stretches to the world of the dead (Hel), another to the world of the frost giants, and the third to the world of men. At the foot of the tree are several springs: the spring of the goddess of fate, Urðr

(*Vǫluspá* 19) and the wells of Mímir (*Vǫluspá* 28) and Hvergelmir (*Grímnismál* 26). Snorri Sturluson has tried to relate these three springs to the three roots, but it may be there was only one well, known under different names according to its symbolic functions; that is, as the source of wisdom (Mímir), of fate (Urðr), or of the rivers of world (Hvergelmir). According to the Eddic poet, a clear vivifying liquid called *aurr* drips down continuously from the tree (*Vǫluspá* 19).

There are a number of animals associated with the cosmic tree: Snorri mentions an eagle in the branches of the ash, and between its eyes a hawk called Veðrfǫlnir ("faded by the weather"); a squirrel called Ratatoskr leaps up and down the tree, conveying words of abuse exchanged between the eagle and the monstrous, corpse-devouring Niðhǫggr (one of the many snakes gnawing at the roots of the tree). Four deer gambol about the branches, eating the shoots.

The symbolism of the tree is extremely important, as it is mirrored in other traditions. In ancient Babylonia, for example, a cosmic tree, Kiskanu, grew in a holy place; radiant with shining lapis lazuli (symbolizing the starry night), it stretched toward the primeval waters *(apsu)*. This was the dwelling place of Ea, the god of fertility and "skills" (agriculture, arts and crafts, writing, etc.), and his mother, Bau, the goddess of plenty (flocks and crops), rested there as well. Pictures of the tree sometimes show it surrounded by goats or with a bird poised on it. In ancient India, the universe is symbolized by an inverted tree, with its roots in the sky and its branches spreading over the earth, representing the downpouring of the sun's rays. Yggdrasill has sometimes been compared with the tree of life in the Hebrew scriptures, but this comparison is unsatisfactory. There is no proof of any Judeo-Christian element in the concept of Yggdrasill. The presence of the eagle and the snake, however, reminds us of the cosmological motif found in Indian mythology, where the combat of Garuḍa with the reptile symbolizes the struggle between light and darkness (the eagle is a sun bird, whereas the snake belongs to the underworld).

Yggdrasill is always green. According to the testimony of Adam of Bremen in his *History of the Bishops of Hamburg*, it is represented near the temple in Uppsala by a gigantic evergreen tree. What kind of tree is it? "Nobody knows," says Adam. The *Vǫluspá* describes it as an ash, which definitely reflects the western Scandinavian tradition, but it has been assumed in eastern Scandinavia that it could be a yew. The yew was venerated in Gaul, and classical writers mention its importance in Germania as well. The name *Yggdrasill* itself is ambiguous. The second element, the Old Norse term *drasill*, is a poetic word for "horse," but the first element might be either *Yggr*, a name for Óðinn (i.e., "Óðinn's horse"), or the adjective *yggr* ("frightening"); in either case, the dreadful mount appears to represent the gallows. Somewhat less plausible is an identification of *ygg-* with the Old Norse term *ýr* ("yew").

Aurr, the liquid dripping from the tree, can be compared with the streaming milk and honey in the Semitic myths of Paradise and with *amṛta*, the Old Indic beverage of immortality identified with mead *(madhu)*. In *Vǫluspá* 27, the tree is described as *heiðvanr;* the clear liquid *(heiðr)* it secretes must be the "sap of life." The same term *heið-* appears in the name of the goat Heiðrún, whose udders fill every day with mead the caldrons for Óðinn's retinue (the *einherjar*) while she feeds on the leaves of Læráðr, another name for Yggdrasill. Moreover, one can compare the honeydew it spreads with that spread by the Aśvins.

The cosmic tree is also an *axis mundi;* it props up the sky like the central pole of a tent, which sustains the whole roof. [*See* Axis Mundi.] The idea of propping up the sky was definitely part of the Germanic heritage, as is shown by the Irminsūl (or Saxon "idol") destroyed by Charlemagne in 772 and described by medieval historians such as Rudolf of Fulda as a huge tree trunk—"universalis columna, quasi sustinens omnia." Shamanistic elements are also linked with the cosmic tree. In certain rituals the shaman travels through nine worlds during his ecstasy; notches on the poles mark his ascent on the "mast of the world tent." Similarly, *Vǫluspá* 2 refers to these nine worlds in connection with the world tree, and Óðinn's acquisition of the runes (*Hávamál* 138ff.) is also reminiscent of shamanic initiation.

The end of the world. The destruction of the world hangs over the gods and man as a permanent threat. *Ragnarǫk* ("fate of the gods") has been misinterpreted as *ragnarøkkr* ("twilight of the gods"); another name for the former is *aldar rǫk* ("the fate of mankind"). The Old Norse term *rǫk* means "course of events, destiny, fate." The Germanic apocalyptic vision of the end of time appears essentially in the *Vǫluspá*, presumably written during the wane of paganism (end of the ninth or beginning of the tenth century). As Jan de Vries has indicated, the anonymous poet must have been a pious man, still convinced that sufficient faith in paganism persisted to promote a rebirth, but one who borrowed too much from Christianity to be considered a truly pagan seer. It is therefore difficult to assess how much of his worldview is genuinely Germanic heritage and how much his vision of the future and his yearning for a "brave new world" free of strife and lies is shaped by Christian influences.

The prelude to the final catastrophe is the murder of Baldr, but the elements of decay appear to have been present in the world from the start: as depicted in the *Grímnismál,* with "the hart browsing above, its bole rotting, and Níðhǫggr gnawing beneath" (st. 36), the cosmic tree Yggdrasill is weakened more than mankind suspects. Initially, however, the gods appear to enjoy an idyllic life in the shining plain of Iðavǫllr, where they relax playing checkers after building shrines and making gold jewels, until three giant maidens come and disturb the serenity of this garden of delight. These are the Nornir, who usher in uncontrollable fate into the Germanic world. From the moment of their arrival events appear to take their inescapable course. Tension grows between the two godly "tribes"—the Æsir and the Vanir; the strife worsens into a war when the seeress Gullveig brings the corruption of greed, lust, and witchcraft into Ásgarðr. Peace is temporarily restored and hostages are exchanged, but the age of innocence is gone. The gods can no longer be trusted; they break their most solemn promises or, at least, resort to trickery to avoid fulfilling them. Then comes the worst, the treacherous killing of Baldr by the throwing of the mistletoe, the missile in the hand of his blind brother Hǫðr, guided by the perfidious Loki. Punishment follows for the criminal, but the fateful action has triggered the chain of events that will culminate in ultimate disaster, with one horrible scene following upon another.

The seeress describes the river of the netherworld, full of sharp blades, and the shore of death with Hel's hall, whose walls are "clad with coiling snakes." Through the river wade perjurers, murderers, and adulterers, and the serpent Níðhǫggr feeds on corpses along its banks. She also describes the evil brood of Fenrir in the Iron Woods to the east, the wolves that will devour the sun and the moon. The sun grows dim, the weather "woe-bringing"; a horribly long winter will bring famine, as described in *Vafþrúðnismál* 44. The final doom is heralded by a couple of obscure stanzas in which three roosters crow to call up the fighters—giants, Óðinn's warriors in Valhǫll, and the dead in Hel's realm—for the last combat. Now the forces of evil break loose: the hellhound Garmr breaks its fetters, and in the world of men, fratricidal struggles erupt everywhere; the bonds of kinship are disregarded ("woe's in the world, much wantonness"), and no respect for human life remains. Heimdallr, the watchman of the gods, blows his horn, the cosmic tree Yggdrasill shakes in its roots, the world serpent "wallows in giant rage," and the ship of death, Naglfar, breaks her moorings. All the forces of destruction move in: Loki leads the "witless hordes" of giants; Surtr, the lord of Múspelheimr, arrives from the south with the fire demons that will put the world ablaze. The mountains totter, heaven is rent apart, and men tread the path of Hel. In the final clash the gods meet their fates: Óðinn is slaughtered by the Fenriswolf but avenged by his son Víðarr; Þórr meets his archfoe, the earth-girding serpent, and they kill each other; Freyr dies in single combat with Surtr. The sun turns dark, the stars fall from the sky, and the blazing earth sinks into the sea.

But this gloomy doomsday picture does not mean that all is lost: the earth, which was originally lifted from the primeval waters by Óðinn and his brothers, reemerges from the deep into which it had sunk, purified and regenerated. A new breed of gods meet again in the green pastures and take up the game of checkers that their "fathers" had played. Baldr and Hǫðr are reborn to dwell in perfect harmony in the divine halls, and henceforth, guiltless men will live forever in a gold-roofed abode called Gimlé. A mighty unnamed deity will reign over all, but evil has not been completely eradicated, for Níðhǫggr, the awful dragon carrying corpses in its pinions, is still roaming over the plains.

The *Vǫluspá,* whose description of the fate of the gods has been presented here, does not constitute our only source about Ragnarǫk, nor does it strictly reflect popular beliefs about the end of time. The Eddic poems, such as the *Vafþrúðnismál,* often contain divergent versions of certain episodes, and Snorri Sturluson, who gave a detailed account of the same events in the *Gylfaginning,* quotes from all the sources available to him. Thus, describing the tragic end of Óðinn and the way his son Víðarr avenged him, Snorri prefers the cruder and more primitive version of the *Vafþrúðnismál,* in which Víðarr, wearing a shoe made of all the leather pared off from men's shoes at the toes and heel since the beginning of time, pulls apart the jaws of the monstrous wolf. The uncanny similarity between the action of Víðarr and that of Lugh in the Irish tradition of the Second Battle of Magh Tuiredh, along with the association of the Celtic god Lug(us) with cobblers, may indicate that this strange reference to the origin of Víðarr's footwear reflects a very old, no longer well-understood tradition associating this Germanic deity with the shoemakers. Therefore, the *Vǫluspá* version, which states that Víðarr "hews the son of Hveðrungr to the heart," presumably represents a younger form of the story. In any event, there was a widespread intimation of the impending catastrophe affecting the gods in the Scandinavian world. This is widely demonstrated by numerous references in skaldic poetry. Thus, in a poem commissioned by the widow of Eirik Bloodax (killed in England in 954), the hero is assumed to have been called to Valhǫll by Óðinn, who needed him for the threatening final conflict, as the poet indicates: "The grey wolf [Fenrir] was glaring at the dwellings of the gods, ready to jump." Similarly, Eyvindr Skáldaspillir, celebrating Hákon the Good (d. 960), stated about him: "Unfettered will fare the Fenriswolf and ravage the / realm of men ere that cometh a kingly prince as / good to stand in his stead" (*Hákonarmál* 20; trans. Hollander, *Heimskringla,* Austin, 1964, p. 127).

The Creation of Man. The Germanic myth of the creation of man appears in two versions, in the *Vǫluspá* and in Snorri Sturluson's *Gylfaginning.* In both cases three deities are involved; in the former, the Æsir, in the latter, the sons of Borr. Walking along the shore, the gods find two tree trunks, which they "animate" and endow with a number of qualities (see table 1). Parallels for this Germanic myth have been sought, but no convincing comparison has emerged. Hesiod mentions that Zeus created a race of men from ash trees. This corresponds to the Germanic name for the first man: Askr ("ash tree"). There is correspondence also with an Indic tale in which a sculptor, a goldsmith, a weaver, and a priest, traveling together, whittle a piece of sandalwood into the shape of a pretty woman. The sculptor shapes it, the weaver dresses it, the goldsmith adorns it with jewels, the priest breathes life into it through his incantations.

The basic ideas in these myths are the same—a human being is fashioned out of a piece of wood—but the elaboration of the theme is totally different. In the Indic tale, giving life is the crowning act of the long process of shaping a human being; in the Scandinavian myth, the triad of gods creates the primordial being right away. What characterizes the Eddic account is the unity of the creative act by direct divine intervention in spite of the distribution of the human qualities by three different gods. It is interesting therefore to examine how these gifts relate to the nature and function of the deities involved.

In the *Gylfaginning,* the gods in question are the sons of Borr: Óðinn, Vili, and Vé, the same group that created the world by "sacrificing" the primal giant Ymir. Since Vili and Vé are little more than hypostases of Óðinn, the whole process of creation is ascribed to that supreme god (perhaps an effort to reduce the triad of gods to one under Christian influence).

TABLE 1. *Qualities Conferred upon Man*

VǪLUSPÁ	GYLFAGINNING
Life's breath/soul (Óðinn)	Spirit and life
Feeling/sense (Hœnir)	Understanding, power of movement
Craft, bearing, color/being, blooming hue (Lóðurr)	Form, speech, hearing, sight

The *Vǫluspá* version of man's creation undoubtedly represents an older tradition. That man would receive the breath of life from Óðinn is in keeping with Óðinn's position as sovereign god, meting out life-giving power (ON, *ǫnd,* "breath"; the translation "soul" has Christian implications that the Old Norse term acquired only later). Óðinn's name (Germanic, *Wōðan[az]) derives from a root meaning "to blow" and includes the connotation "life-giving power" in some of its derivations; it is cognate to Old Irish *fáith* ("seer, prophet") and Latin *vates* ("soothsayer"). Óðinn is indeed the inspired god, the prince of the poets, the master of the divinatory runes, the wielder of awesome magical powers. The Germanic stem of his name, **wōð-,* also appears in German as *Wut* ("rage"). Adam of Bremen thus correctly interpreted Óðinn's name as "furor" when describing the pagan gods in the temple at Uppsala. In Old Norse, *óðr,* usually translated "mind, reason, understanding, sense," is the gift of Hœnir according to *Vǫluspá* 18. But *óðr* is also used as an adjective meaning "mad, furious, vehement; eager, impatient," all of which point to either strong emotional stress or lack of control of the power of reasoning. The inspired cerebral activity expressed by **wōð-* can indeed verge on ecstasy; thus, the name of the "poets' mead," *óðrœrir,* literally means "rousing to the point of ecstasy."

Actually, *Vǫluspá* 18 is the only context in which *óðr* is assumed to have the meaning "intelligence, mind, reason," and the main reason for ascribing this meaning to it here is the parallel text by Snorri where the second god endows man with *vit* and *hrœring* ("wit and movement"), with special focus on *vit* ("intelligence"). However, *hrœring* need not apply only to physical movement. It occurs in compounds and phrases pointing clearly to emotions, so that Snorri's use of *vit* in association with *hrœring* may well indicate specifically the movements of the mind that the Old Norse term *óðr* expresses in the *Vǫluspá.*

This misinterpretation of *óðr* is also ascribable to the fact that Hœnir is often described as a wise god; his name is supposed to be derived from a root meaning "to make keen, to sharpen," so that he would be the god who sharpens the mind. Dumézil calls him "the patron of the deep, invisible part of intelligence." This view is based on two events. First, when Þjazi, in the shape of an eagle, requests of Hœnir a full share of the meal of the gods, Hœnir does not answer, but cannot help breathing heavily with anger. Second, whenever he attends the Þing of the gods as chief of the Vanir and fails to get Mímir's advice, Hœnir does not take a stand, but merely states "Let others decide!" Dumézil considers Hœnir's refusal to commit himself the only wise attitude under the circumstances and contrasts it with Loki's rashness, which turns into disaster when he tries to beat Þjazi with a stick after the giant snatches four pieces of meat from the gods. In the case of the Þing, Dumézil suggests that Mímir and Hœnir represent complementary symbolizations of our thought processes: Mímir represents the "collective consciousness" on which we rely for decision making and without which individual thought (i.e., Hœnir) is worthless. Ingenious as it is, Dumézil's explanation is far from convincing; all the texts show Hœnir as unable to act on his own, and while that may not make him "weak of wits," as various scholars have suggested, it hardly makes him a "god of reflective thought." He is rather the instrument of divine inspiration, the one who utters the message conveyed by another's wisdom. He remains silent in the absence of Mímir (his source of inspiration) at the Þing; therefore, he is described as the most fearful of all gods (because he cannot act without being advised). After Ragnarǫk, he will function as priest, consulting the oracles (i.e., interpreting the signs given by an outside power, again as the vehicle of divine inspiration). It is also in this capacity that he is instrumental in endowing man with "inspired mental activity" *(óðr);* thus some scholars have also considered him a hypostasis of Óðinn.

The third god in the divine triad, Lóðurr, is more difficult to define functionally: he is hardly known outside this context (elsewhere, he is described simply as a friend of Óðinn, an association he shares with quite a few gods in the Scandinavian pantheon). Because in other contexts Óðinn and Hœnir appear closely associated with Loki, scholars have also attempted to equate Lóðurr with Loki (as a god of fire) on the basis of etymological speculations, but the arguments advanced to back up this hypothesis have all proved untenable. The identification of Lóðurr with the term *logaþore* occurring together with the name *Wodan* and *Wigiþonar* in the runic inscription on the Fibula of Nordendorf (first half of the seventh century) is also disputable: *logaþore* is presumably to be compared with the Old English word *logðor* or *logeðer* ("wily, crafty"), applying to magicians.

This connection with magic, with the connotation of plotting mischief, could fit the personality of Óðinn fairly well, so that Lóðurr might just be another hypostasis of this god. But before overriding the etymological difficulties connected with this view, it is advisable to examine more closely the gifts bestowed by Lóðurr upon the primal human couple: according to the text, he gives them *lá, læti,* and *litir góðir.* The last of these means "good colors," implying good health and also physical beauty, which was considered a sign of noble ancestry among the Germanic people. (Thus, it is his handsome appearance that distinguishes Beowulf from his companions, and the Anglo-Saxon poet uses for this peerless appearance the very same term that Snorri uses to qualify the gift of the third deity.) *Læti* means "noise, voice; gestures, attitude" and refers specifically to manners in other contexts. Since Snorri specifies speech, hearing, and sight as ascribable to the intervention of the third deity in shaping the first human couple, it is obvious that this attribution of the major sensory perceptions by this god represents a different tradition from that of the Eddic poem.

The term *lá* is problematic because its etymological connections are difficult to assess: the translation that is often given—"blood"—rests on a disputable interpretation of a skaldic line. In another poetic context the term is associated with the adjective *sǫlr* ("pale"), suggesting the interpretation "sallow-complexioned." This would imply that *lá* means "look, mien." Lóðurr would then have given man his mien and good complexion (i.e., his physical appearance). The only corroboration for this interpretation is provided by the Tocharian term *lek* ("appearance, mien"), derived from the same Indo-European root. An alternate solution would be to interpret *lá* as "hair" (from the Germanic **lawō,* "cutting"), showing the same semantic development as the Sanskrit cognate *lava-* ("cutting, wool, hair").

The importance of hair as the most significant feature of human appearance is abundantly illustrated in the Germanic tradition. Hair was sacred: freely growing hair hanging on the shoulders was characteristic of priests, kings, and women; hair was the vehicle of the *hamingja* ("the soul; happiness"). In the Lex Salica, cutting a girl's hair without her parents' permission entailed a higher fine than seducing a female servant of the king. Cutting the hair was a rite of passage marking the accession to adulthood, and Tacitus reports that the young Chatti warriors would neither cut their hair nor shave their beard until they had killed their first enemy. Moreover, in the sagas, the fine presence of the heroes is always suggested by associating their complexion with a particular shade of hair. Thus, the Eddic line could well be interpreted as "Lóðurr gave hair and fair complexion to man."

If, then, Óðinn and Hœnir bestow essentially spiritual qualities upon man, whereas Lóðurr provides him with his physical aspect, Lóðurr must be a god presiding over the physical aspects of life, closer to nature than the lofty Æsir; in other words, he must be a Vanic deity, connected with the old Germanic fertility cult. His name may be connected with the Old Norse term *lóð* ("produce of the land"). Swedish toponymy indicates the occurrence of a **Ludhgodha* as the Germanic hypostasis of the Great Goddess of fertility. The male counterpart, **Loþverr,* could survive in *Lóðurr* as naming a divinity of generation and growth and protector of the ethnic community, like the Latin correspondent *Liber,* with which the name *Lóðurr* (from **Loþverr*) would be cognate.

The War of the Æsir and the Vanir. The Germanic gods are divided into two groups, the Æsir and the Vanir. Following the medieval practice of "etymologizing," Snorri Sturluson associated the name of the Æsir with Asia, an interpretation that does not appear to reflect any serious tradition. The historian of the Goths, Jordanes (sixth century CE), cites a Gothic term, *ansis* (or *anses*), glossed as "semigods," that also occurs in anthroponyms like the Gothic *Ansila,* the Burgundian *Ansemundos,* the Langobardic *Ansegranus,* and the Old High German names *Ansgar* and *Anshelm.* Together with the Old Norse term *áss,* these words derive from the Germanic term **ansuz,* designating some type of deity. The feminine form preserved in the southern Germanic inscriptional divine name *Vihansa* might refer to a war goddess if **wīh-* alternates with **wīg-* ("combat"; OHG, *wīg;* OE, *wīg;* ON, *víg*). The Æsir, however, appear as ruling gods, which makes it more plausible to associate their name with the Hittite term *hashshush* ("king") than to compare it with the Old Indic prefix *asu-* ("breath of life"), as is usually suggested.

As for *Vanir,* the term has been connected with the Old Norse term *vinr* ("friend"), with *Venus,* the Latin name for the goddess of love, and with the Sanskrit term *vánas-* ("lust"), an etymology most suitable for fertility gods. *Vanir* has also been related to the Sanskrit term *vánam* ("water"; cf. the latinized [Slavic] ethnic name *Veneti,* meaning "people of the waters"), an interpretation made doubtful by the fact that the Vanir are hardly aquatic deities. Whatever role the other gods (e.g., Þórr) may have played in promoting fertility, it remains the specific domain of the Vanir.

Though the Vanir live in peace with the Æsir, this was not always the case. At the dawn of time, a bitter war was fought between the two groups, which Snorri Sturluson reports (with varying details) in two distinct works, the *Ynglingasaga* and the *Skáldskaparmál.* The former is an euhemeristic narration of the early life of the Æsir in "Asia" (ON, Ásaland, Ásaheimr) where their main city was Ásgarðr and their neighbors, the Vanir, lived in Vanaland or Vanaheimr, in the vicinity of the Tanais, the classical name for the river Don.

According to Snorri, Óðinn leads his army against the Vanir, but they resist vigorously. The two sides are alternately victorious, and they loot each other's territory until they grow tired of fighting and conclude a peace that puts them on equal footing. They exchange hostages: the Vanir Njǫrðr and his son Freyr are transferred to the world of the Æsir, who, in turn, deliver Mímir and Hœnir to the Vanir. As Mímir is very wise, the Vanir reciprocate by sending "the cleverest among them"—Kvasir—to the Æsir. In the *Skáldskaparmál,* however, Snorri claims that Kvasir was created from the saliva of the Vanir and the Æsir when they spat into the communal caldron at the conclusion of the peace. Other evidence linking Kvasir's blood to the "mead of poetry" suggests that this second version is closer to the original.

The *Poetic Edda* describes the war between the Æsir and the Vanir in rather allusive terms (*Vǫluspá* 21–24), but since the theme was well known to any Scandinavian, the poem did not need to be explicit. The object of the poet is not to teach but to enliven the tale for his listeners. In the *Vafþrúðnismál* (st. 39), Njǫrðr is said to have been born in Vanaheimr, but to have been given away as a hostage—information that the *Lokasenna* (Loki's Mocking; st. 34) further confirms. The statement of the seeress in the *Vǫluspá* raises numerous problems. (Scholars disagree on the place of the stanzas in the poem as a whole and on their correct sequence, as well as on the interpretation of several terms and phrases in the text.)

The *vǫlva* ("seeress") remembers the first war in the world when they pierced Gullveig "from all sides with spears." The Old Norse phrase *geirum studdu* actually means "they propped her up" (so that she could not fall). Burning her three times did not destroy her; she was reborn every time. They called her Heiðr ("bright"); she was a seeress skilled in prophecy, in giving power to magic wands (ON, *gānda*), and in casting spells (ON, *seiðr*), sometimes in a trance, as a reading in the *Hauksbók* suggests.

According to stanza 23 of the *Vǫluspá,* "all the gods" *(regin ǫll)* gather in counsel: should they pay tribute or should "all the gods" (here written *goðin ǫll*) receive the tribute? The meaning of the text is very disputable. In line 6, *afráð gjalda* has been translated as "suffer a defeat" by R. C. Boer, as "avenge the evil" by Ernst A. Kock. Here, only the Æsir are concerned, but what difference is there between *regin ǫll* in line 1 and *goðin ǫll* in line 7? Does the former also apply to the Æsir only, or does it refer to the Æsir and the Vanir together? In line 8, *gildi eiga* has been translated "share a common meal" by Boer, as "receive a tribute" by Kock. In his recent translation of the *Vǫluspá,* Paul Schach prefers to maintain the ambiguity: "Then all the ruling powers *(regin ǫll)* . . . took counsel as to whether the Æsir should suffer great loss or whether all the gods *(goðin ǫll)* should receive redress" ("Some Thoughts on *Vǫluspá,*" in *Edda: A Collection of Essays,* ed. Glendinning and Bersason, Winnipeg, 1983, p. 95).

In stanza 24 Óðinn throws his spear in the enemy's camp in the ritual gesture to open the hostilities, thus dedicating the enemies to the war god and to death. The Vanir resort to magic rather than to military prowess to shatter the walls of Ásgarðr, and initially at least they seem to have been victorious: "They gained the field."

How is this to be interpreted? Stanzas 21–22 allude to the causes of the divine war, namely the appearance of Gullveig in Óðinn's hall and her triple rebirth as a witch practicing evil magic *(seiðr)*. Stanza 23, if it stands where it should, indicates that the gods first tried to negotiate, but that they were uncertain as to whether the Æsir alone should bear the loss and pay tribute *(afráð gjalda)* to the Vanir, or whether all the gods should receive compensation for the damage done. If stanza 23 is placed after 24, the sequence agrees closely with the story as related in the *Ynglingasaga:* the Æsir and the Vanir have fought with varying success, and both are tired of war. They agree to settle their differences, and ultimately each party will receive tribute (the second solution in stanza 23) in an exchange of hostages.

Who was Gullveig, so brutally assaulted and tortured by the Æsir? The name *Gullveig* occurs only in this context. It is a compound of the Old Norse terms *gull* ("gold") and *veig*, which presumably means "power" (it occurs frequently as second component of Scandinavian feminine names, e.g., *Solveig*). *Veig* was also commonly used in poetry to designate a strong drink. According to *Alvíssmál* 34, for example, it was the name the Æsir gave to beer. Thus *Gullveig* means literally the "power" or "drunkenness of gold," in other words, the madness and corruption engendered by this precious metal.

On the other hand, the name *Heiðr*, also given to Gullveig, applies to witches elsewhere as well, for example, the seeress Heiðr in the *Landnámabók*. Identical in meaning to the adjective *heiðr* ("shining"), the name perfectly fits the dazzlingly enticing "witch" who incarnates the "power or drunkenness of gold." She must have been one of the Vanir since they are the gods of wealth and control that evil form of magic called *seiðr*. Turville-Petre is therefore presumably right in identifying her with Freyja, the Vanadís or foremost goddess, among the Vanir. Indeed, it is obvious that Freyja was well established in the realm of the Æsir, though it is not stated that she went there as a hostage after the war. She was truly a goddess of gold: according to a kenning of skaldic poetry she weeps tears of gold; the names of her two daughters, *Hnoss* and *Gersimi*, both signify "jewel"; and she is the jealous owner of the celebrated Brising Necklace. She is also referred to as a lusty, seductive woman who, according to Loki, has slept with all the gods, including her own brother Freyr (*Lokasenna* 30–32). Moreover, she is a witch (ON, *fordœða*) and controls the *seiðr*—a Vanic practice the Æsir (in particular Óðinn) learn from her. There is no account of how she came to Ásgarðr, but if her identification with Gullveig is correct, she would have caused the outbreak of the war, which would suggest that the Vanir purposely sent her out to the realm of the Æsir to corrupt them with greed, lust, and witchcraft. Attempts by the Æsir to eliminate her have remained unsuccessful: she still lives there.

The Myth of Baldr. The story of Baldr's fate is probably the most moving and most controversial of all the Germanic myths. In this story, best known in Snorri Sturluson's rendition in the *Gylfaginning*, Óðinn's resplendent son Baldr is plagued by evil dreams of impending death. To protect against any danger his mother, Frigg, exacts an oath from everything in the world not to harm him, but neglects the puny mistletoe. Jealous of the attention Baldr receives in the games of the gods, Loki, in the disguise of a woman, wheedles the secret of Baldr's invulnerability out of his mother. He then persuades Baldr's blind brother, Hǫðr, who has been prevented by his infirmity from any participation in the sportive tossing of objects at Baldr, to throw a dart of mistletoe. Under Loki's guidance the missile hits Baldr and kills him. The gods are dumbfounded, and while preparations for Baldr's ship burial are in progress, they send out Hermóðr on Óðinn's horse to the kingdom of Hel to entreat the goddess of the netherworld for the release of the unfortunate god. Meanwhile, Baldr's wife, Nanna, dies of grief and her body is carried onto the ship Hringhorni ("curved prow"), where she joins her husband on the funeral pyre. As for Hermóðr, he returns with the message that Baldr will be released only on the condition that "everything in the world, both dead and alive, weeps for him." Immediately the Æsir dispatch messengers all over the universe to request everyone and everything to weep Baldr out of Hel's clutches. Even the stones and the metals participate in the universal grief, but a giantess called Þǫkk says she has no use for Baldr; as far as she is concerned, Hel can keep him! This is again Loki in disguise, and thus he succeeds in preventing the return of Baldr, who will only come back after Ragnarǫk.

The Pantheon. The earliest written testimony we have about the religion of the Germanic peoples is a statement by Julius Caesar in the sixth book of his *Gallic Wars* indicating that they worshiped the sun, the moon, and Vulcan, which is generally taken to mean "the fire." While there is no trace of a moon cult in the Germanic territories, archaeological and other evidence confirm the early existence of a widespread solar cult. Similarly, the role of the fire in cult and ritual seems to have been rather limited in historical times. Thus, the statement of Caesar apparently applies to an archaic state of things and is partly inaccurate. On the contrary, the data supplied some 150 years later by Tacitus provide a fairly accurate picture of what must have been the structure of the Germanic pantheon in his time (end of the first century CE).

The main god is Mercury, whose Latin name, *Mercurius*, is a Roman interpretation of the Germanic name **Wōðan[az]*, as also appears from the loan translation of Latin *Mercurii dies* into the Germanic **Wōðanizdag[az]* (Eng., *Wednesday*; Du., *woensdag*). Mercury is flanked by Mars and Hercules, the former representing the Germanic god *Tīw[az], whose name is preserved in *Tuesday* (OE, **Tīwesdæġ;* Lat., *Martis dies*), whereas the latter is usually interpreted as representing the Germanic champion of the gods, *Þun[a]r[az], though, as thunder god, he is also equated with Jupiter in the *interpretatio Romana*, as is shown by the Latin name *Jovis dies* (Eng., *Thursday*; Ger., *Donnerstag;* Du., *donderdag;* Germanic, **Þnriz-dag[az]*). As Mercury/*Wōðan[az] is the only Germanic god credited by Tacitus with receiving human sacrifice, many scholars assume that the *regnator omnium deus* ("god reigning over all") venerated by the Suevian tribe of the Semnones in their sacred grove and honored as their ethnic ancestor with regular human sacrifices must be the same deity, though perhaps Allan Lund is right in claiming that he must have been worshiped as an eponymous founder under the name **Semno*.

In another context (*Germania* 2), Tacitus provides similar information about the divine ancestors of the three major Germanic groups of tribes. They are descended from the three sons of Mannus (lit., "man"), himself the son of the god Tuisto, apparently a bisexual born from the earth. While the deity who engendered the Inguaeones, a tribe from the North Sea region, can readily be identified, it is not possible to identify the divine ancestors of the (H)erminones, whose territory extended from the lower Elbe southward into Bohemia, or of the Istaevones of the Weser-Rhine area. The most one can say about the prefix **Ist-* (in the name *Istaevones*) is that it is presumably related to the Gothic term *aistan* ("be awed"), while **ermin-* (in (H)erminones) is a Germanic adjective meaning "mighty, august" and applying both to deities and to other things and beings. *Jǫrmunr* is a name for Óðinn, which appears also in the compounds *Jǫrmungandr* (designating the cosmic serpent) and *jǫrmungrund* ("earth"). In Old High German, *irmin-* connotes "universal" in the compounds *irmindeot* and *irmingot,* found in the *Hildebrandslied.* In Old Saxon, Irminsūl is the cosmic pillar that supports the whole universe and is associated by the chroniclers with Mars/*Tīw[az]. In the case of *Ingw[az], the eponymic deity of the Inguaeones, an Old English runic poem indicates that he was venerated in southern Scandinavia (indeed, the Danes are called "Ingwine" in *Beowulf* 1044, 1319), and his association with Freyr is illustrated by the Old Norse compound *Yngvifreyr* (Germanic, **Ingwja-fraujaz*). Though little information is provided about his cult he is undoubtedly associated with fertility, and if the chariot that followed across the sea according to the runic poem is the "death chariot," he might well be the "god who dies"—in other words, a typically vernal fertility god.

Tacitus also refers to other locally worshiped Germanic deities such as Nerthus, Mother Earth, for whom the Inguaeonic people hold a yearly pageant during which they celebrate the powers of fertility that she incarnates, or the divine twins whom he calls Alcis (Germanic, *Alhīz) and equates with the Roman twins Castor and Pollux. In both cases he supplies a few details about cult and ritual, specifying, for example, that Nerthus shrouds herself in mystery: she remains hidden in a curtained chariot during her peregrinations among her worshipers; only her priest can approach her, and after the completion of her ceremonial journey she is bathed in a secret lake, but all those who officiate in this lustration rite are drowned afterward to maintain the "sacred ignorance" about her. Similarly, Tacitus indicates that the priests of the Dioscuri among the eastern Germanic Naharvales wear feminine attire, presumably referring also to their long hair, a feature closely associated with the Germanic divine twins. Moreover, he points out that these deities are not represented by any image or statue, which corroborates his general statement about the aniconic character of Germanic religion—"[They] do not think it proper to portray gods with any kind of human countenance" (*Germania* 9)—but is at least partly contradicted by the archaeological finds of some roughly hewn stakes offering a rudimentary anthropomorphic representation of the gods.

In the *Annals,* Tacitus refers to other Germanic deities, such as Tamfana, whose sanctuary was an important center of cultural activities in the territory of the Marsi (between the Lippe and the Ruhr rivers). Her "temple" was allegedly leveled by the Romans during the celebration of an autumnal festival in 4 CE. Its very existence contradicts Tacitus's statement in the *Germania* that the Germanic people "refuse to confine their gods within walls" and the contention that worship generally took place alfresco and in the woods, as with the Frisian goddess, Baduhenna, near whose sacred grove a Roman detachment was massacred.

In the Roman period, inscriptional material provides further data on the deities venerated by the Germanic people (within the boundaries of the empire), such as Nehalennia, whose sanctuary near Domburg in Sjæland has yielded an abundance of altars and statues. She was worshiped mainly by seamen and traders, mostly natives of the northwestern provinces of the empire, who dedicated the monuments to the goddess in return for the help received from her. Her attributes (cornucopias, specific fruits, dog, etc.) characterize her as a fertility goddess with strong chthonic overtones, but she apparently also shares the patronage of navigation with Isis, whose presence Tacitus mentions "among part of the Suevians" (presumably the Hermunduri, who were in close contact with the Roman province of Noricum where the cult of Isis had been integrated with that of the national goddess Noreia).

Important also are the *matres,* or *matronae,* documented by votive stones with dedicatory inscriptions found mainly in the territory of the Ubii on the left side of the Rhine in the second and third centuries CE. Their worshipers belonged essentially to the lower classes but also included some high officeholders in the Roman administration and army. They were invoked for protection against danger and catastrophes or for the prosperity of the family, and were described as bestowing their blessings generously, as such epithets as *Gabiae* ("givers"), *Friagabis* ("generous donors"), and *Arvagastiae* ("hospitable ones") indicate. As they often appear in groups of three and seem to be associated with the fate and welfare of man, they have been compared with the Nornir, especially since one stone carries the inscription "Matrib[us] Parc[is]," referring directly to the *interpretatio Romana* of the three deities of fate.

The picture that emerges from the data of the Roman period can be summarized as follows:

- The sovereign god, *Wōđan[az] (identified with Mercury), may have taken over the prominent place originally occupied by the old Indo-European sky god *Deiwos (Germanic, *Tīwaz; ON, Týr), who has still preserved a sufficiently prominent position among certain tribes, such as the Chatti, for the spoils of the enemy to be dedicated to him and *Wōđan[az] jointly.
- The divine champion, Þun[a]r[az], is identified with the thunder god (Hercules/Jupiter).
- The divine twins, *Alhiz, identified with Castor and Pollux, were venerated locally, especially among the eastern Germanic tribes.
- The fertility deities were worshiped regionally and had associated functions such as the protection of navigation or the determination of man's fate; they include Nehalennia, the *matres* or *matronae,* Nerthus, and *Ingw[az].

Although poorly documented, the Migration and post-Migration periods show an apparent continuity in this system:

- *Wōđan[az] remains the supreme god and is honored as the ancestor of royal lineages; there is also some evidence of his connection with magic. *Tīw[az], on the contrary, recedes to the background, but is perhaps to be identified with the tribal god of the Saxons, whose name occurs together with *Woden* and *Thunaer* in the abjuration formulation the Saxons had to pronounce with their baptismal vows during the forcible conversion campaign conducted by Charlemagne. The name *Saxnote* is, however, ambiguous: it can either mean "sword companion" or describe him as a "sacrificial" god. While the former interpretation ties in with the statement in the chronicles about the cult of "Mars" among the Saxons and could be connected with the presence of the cosmic pillar Irminsūl in their main sanctuary (a reference to *Tīw[az]'s original function as sky god), the latter would make more plausible Dumézil's suggestion that the triad Thunaer-Woden-Saxnote in the Saxon document corresponds to the Scandinavian trinity Þórr-Óðinn-Freyr in the Uppsala temple. Saxnote would indeed be a god of the tribal community, just as Freyr is *folkvaldi* ("leader of the people"); like Freyr, the *blótgoð Svía* ("sacrificial god of the Swedes"), Saxnote would receive sacrifice.
- *Þun[a]r[az], the thunder god, progressively gains prominence as the divine representative of the warrior class.
- Though there is no direct evidence of a cult of the divine twins, their functional role is euhemerized in the figures of the twin founding heroes of various Germanic groups, such as Hengist and Horsa for the early Saxons in Great Britain, Raos and Raptos for the Vandalic Hasdingi, and Ibor and Aio for the Winnili (Lombards). The names *Hengist* and *Horsa* (related respectively to German *Hengst,* "stallion," and English *horse*) remind us of the association of the divine twins with horses. In Greek they are referred to as *leukō pōlō* ("with white horses") and in ancient India they are known as the Aśvinau ("possessors of horses"). The names *Raos* and *Raptos* (related respectively to German *Rahe,* "yard," and English *rafter*) reflect the aniconic representation of the Dioscuri by beams, which occurred also in ancient Sparta, and in the shape of the Latin H or the Greek π. The Langobardic terms *Ibor* (presumably from Germanic **ebur-*, "boar") and *Aio* (Germanic, **agjo,* "edge, sharp side of a blade")

may refer to the sharp tusks of the wild boar, an animal also closely associated with the fertility deities Freyr and Freyja, with whose domain the divine twins also have direct links.

- Besides the already mentioned references to **Ingw*[*az*], a number of names of deities associated with fertility occur, such as *Erce,* a name apparently borrowed from Celtic and used to designate Mother Earth in an Old English charm; *Phol* (OHG, *Vol*), appearing together with *Wōden* and *Balder* in the Old High German Merseburg spell; *Friia* and *Frīg,* respectively, the Old High German and Old English names for the Germanic goddess identified with Venus, whose name survives in the German *Freitag* and the English *Friday.* The often assumed existence of a spring deity, *Austrō, from whose name the word *Easter* (Ger., *Ostern*) is supposedly derived, is, however, doubtful: it rests on an interpretation of the Old English term *Ēostrae* by Bede (672/3–735 CE) and has no backing either in cult or myth; it has recently been more convincingly explained as a Christian missionary term.
- There are also a few minor deities like Fosite, to whom an island was consecrated at the juncture of the Frisian and Danish territories. He is known merely through a reference in the life of Saint Willibrord, but his name shows a striking similarity to that of the Scandinavian god Forseti, whose specific function according to the *Grímnismál* is to settle all disputes; he is the son of Baldr and lives in Glitnir, a hall "propped with gold and shingled with shining silver" (st. 15). Forseti's name is transparent: it means "presiding [over the Þing]," but no satisfactory explanation can be given for the loss of the *r* in *Fosite,* so that the connection between Fosite and Forseti remains conjectural.

The situation becomes quite different in the Viking age when the blossoming of Scandinavian literature provides ample information about the pagan gods and the myths and cults of the Germanic North. Moreover, in their peregrinations, the Vikings carried with them their religious practices and beliefs, and reports from various sources attest to the prevalence of the worship of Þórr among them. This is also confirmed by onomastic studies that show very few names for Óðinn but an abundance of anthroponyms and toponyms containing the name *Þórr.* This situation should not, however, be misinterpreted: Óðinn is still the sovereign god, but he was the deity associated primarily with the nobility (the *jarls*), whereas Þórr was worshiped by the majority of the people (the "freemen," or *karls*).

The pantheon, then, can be sketched as follows in keeping with the Dumézilian trifunctional pattern:

1. Sovereignty is represented in its magical aspect by Óðinn, in its juridical aspect by Týr.
2. War and physical force are represented by Þórr.
3. Fertility and wealth are presented by Freyr, Freyja, and Njǫrðr.

Such a presentation, however, oversimplifies the picture of the Scandinavian system, which not only fails to show the characteristic slant toward the second (war) function, as Dumézil himself acknowledges, but ignores such complex figures as Heimdallr and Loki, who hardly fit into this neat matrix. Moreover, some very important functions of the major deities are not covered by the labels in the Dumézilian tripartite ideology. For example, Óðinn is essentially the god of "inspired cerebral activity" and therefore the patron of the poets, a role attested to by the myth in which he steals the valuable mead of poetry from the giant Suttungr and brings it to Ásgarðr. Further, though he manifests his sovereign power through potent magical interventions, he is definitely not the only one to wield magical powers: the Vanir use *seiðr,* which the Æsir deem despicable, but which Óðinn nevertheless is keen to learn from Freyja. Finally, Óðinn's capability to change shape is more than matched by the metamorphoses of Loki; it is also shared by certain giants such as Suttungr, who pursues Óðinn in the shape of an eagle when the latter flies away (also as an eagle) with his precious mead, or Þjazi, who also assumes the shape of an eagle to follow the deceitful trickster Loki flying away in Freyja's falcon coat with the goddess Iðunn, who had been changed into a nut.

As for the involvement with war, there is a basic difference between Óðinn's intervention in battles to give victory to whomever he chooses to favor and the direct participation in combat of the divine champion Þórr: the only time Óðinn personally takes to the battlefield is in his deadly encounter with the Fenriswolf at Ragnarǫk. On the other hand, it seems that the transfer of the Vanic gods as hostages to the realm of the Æsir made them partake of some of the latter's combative spirit, as when the peaceful Freyr, who having readily given up his sword to obtain the favors of a giant maiden he eagerly desired, faces the giant Beli without a weapon and kills him with a hart's horn. And while Óðinn collects half of the heroes who die on the battlefield to serve as his *einherjar* in Valhǫll, it is certainly striking that Freyja gets the other half.

As for fertility, it is well known that, as thunder god, Þórr was the protector of the peasant class, which depends on the weather for its crops, but he shares control of the atmosphere with Njǫrðr, who controls the path of the wind and, as sea god, counteracts the effects of the thunderstorms, quieting the sea and smothering the fire.

Heimdallr occupies a marginal position in the pantheon; it is not even clear to which group of gods he should be assigned. Apparently he offered up his *hljóð*, which was hidden as a pledge under the cosmic tree, Yggdrasill, as did Óðinn his eye. While Óðinn received exceptional vision in return, Heimdallr was gifted with extraordinary aural perception: "He can hear the grass grow on the earth and the wool on sheep." Therefore, it has been assumed that the Old Norse term *hljóð*—generally translated "horn" in this context (*Vǫluspá* 27), but usually meaning "silence; listening, hearing," also "music, noise"—must designate one of Heimdallr's ears. Offering up a body part in exchange for a major attribute is a characteristic feature of the most important Æsir, Óðinn and Týr. (The latter sacrificed his hand in order to guarantee a pledge that enabled the gods to fetter the ominous Fenriswolf, and in return, assumed the functions of protector of the Þing and the patronage of the law.) On the other hand, as guardian of the gods and watchman of Ásgarðr, Heimdallr assumes a military function, which would make him a second-function god in the Dumézilian system, like Þórr (with whom he shares the tendency to imbibe great quantities of mead). But the *Þrymskviða* (st. 15) describes him as a "foreknowing Van" who is able to "fathom the future." His affinity with the ram further complicates matters: was he originally a god of sheep breeders, as Freyr was a god of wheat growers and pig breeders?

Similarly, Loki is extremely difficult to classify. Originally a giant, he nevertheless played an important part in the decisions and activities of the gods. [*See* Tricksters.] Although primarily a mischievous trickster, Loki cannot be described as an "evil demon." He is restless and inventive, but also deceptive and unreliable. Although he frequently got the gods in trouble, he usually redeemed himself by ultimately solving the problem he created. Ultimately, however, he went too far, utterly outraging the whole divine world, and was condemned to be fettered until Ragnarǫk. Dumézil sees in him an "incarnation of impulsive intelligence," but this interpretation is disputable, the more so as it is partly based on an unacceptable contrast with the alleged "carefully weighed thought" of Hœnir, who, by himself, has actually no more wit than a barnyard rooster. There is no trace of any cult devoted to Loki, nor is he ever mentioned in place-names.

The minor deities are also problematic: some of them can in some way be integrated into the tripartite functional scheme, for example, Ullr, an archer god living in Ýdalir ("yew dales") in Ásgarðr, whose importance is made clear by Óðinn's statement in the *Grímnismál* (st. 42) that Ullr especially, among all the gods, will grant his blessing to he who "first quenches the fire." The most sacred oaths are sworn by Ullr's ring, and as a stepson of Þórr, he has close connections with the warriors. He was invoked by those engaged in single combat, and kennings describe the warrior as an "Ullr of battle." According to the evidence of place-names, he was the object of an extended cult in Norway and Sweden, where he was called Ullinn, but he seems to have been overshadowed by Þórr, Freyr, and Freyja. There is practically no trace of him in Danish toponymy, where the place-names containing Týr's name seem to be in complementary distribution with those containing Ullr's name in the north. This is rather significant in light of the story of Ullr's temporary usurpation of Óðinn's throne, as narrated by Saxo Grammaticus: Óðinn had committed a grievous breach of his royal majesty by assuming a feminine disguise; as a result of this disgrace he was replaced by Ullr, who reigned for ten years. When Óðinn was restored, Ullr (whose name, latinized into *Ollerus,* means "glory, brilliance") fled to Sweden but was killed afterward by Danes. In view of Ullr's connection with oath taking, Dumézil sees in this episode an illustration of the complementary nature of the two aspects of sovereignty, the inspired versus the majestic. The latter, with its juridical connotations, is illustrated by Saxo Grammaticus's second story of Óðinn's temporary ouster from power: in this case, Óðinn's fall is brought about by the misconduct of his wife, Frigg; he is replaced by a magician called Mithotyn, who introduces all kinds of innovations that the people dislike. As a result, they welcome Óðinn back while Mithotyn flees and is eventually killed on the island of Fyn. In this story, Dumézil has seen the contrast between the unitary and rather ill-defined religion of Óðinn and the analytic religion of Mithotyn (actually *Mitoð-inn, from Old Norse *mjǫtuðr,* "dispenser of fate," or, literally, "the measurer"), who introduces rules where there were none. As Dumézil puts it, "The lawyer replaces the inspired, and his very precision makes him hatable!" In other words, these stories are illustrations of the dichotomy of sovereignty according to the Dumézilian pattern.

Bragi is another lesser god about whom little is known. His name seems to be related to the Old Norse word *bragr,* which designates "poetic form," and he is described as the "foremost of poets," being in this way in competition with Óðinn as patron of poetry. In the *Lokasenna* (ss. 8–15) he bickers with Loki, who chides him for his lack of courage in combat. Obviously, his power is in speech, and his eloquence is strengthened by the magic of the runes carved on his tongue. Bragi is the husband of Iðunn, the guardian of the apples that ensure the eternal youth of the gods. The only myth relating to her tells about Loki delivering her with her apples to the giants and the ensuing catastrophe when all the deities in Ásgarðr grew old, hoary-headed, and weak. They summoned Loki before their council and compelled him to retrieve Iðunn and her apples. Accordingly, the mischievous trickster flew to Jǫtunheimr in the shape of a falcon to recover Iðunn and her precious possessions from the clutches of the giant Þjazi. The latter pursued Loki in the form of an eagle and was killed when he tried to fly into Ásgarðr. Though apples were not cultivated in Scandinavia until late in the Middle Ages, the theme of this story must be quite old, as the skald Þjóðólfr of Hvin refers to Iðunn and the "old-age medicine" of the gods in his poem *Haustlǫng,* written around the year 900. The motif of the giants wanting a goddess in addition to outrageous ransoms from the deities in Ásgarðr is again illustrated by the story of the "master builder" of the divine stronghold, who requests Freyja as payment for his work and demands the sun and the moon to boot, obviously intending to plunge the world into darkness and sterility if payment is not forthcoming.

Very little information is usually given about the goddesses. Frigg, Óðinn's wife, is the devoted mother of Baldr; she lives in Fensalir ("marshy halls"), attended by her confidant Fulla. Loki claims that she shared her sexual favors with her husband's brothers, Vili and Vé (*Lokasenna* 26); Saxo Grammaticus also refers to her loose morals, which trigger the episode with Mithotyn.

Jǫrð ("earth"), the mother of Þórr, is also known under the name of *Fjǫrgyn,* which may mean "goddess of the furrow" (cf. Frisian, *fŭrge;* Germanic, **furhō;* Old High German *fur[u]h,* German *Furche,* Old English *furh,* and English *furrow*). Her male counterpart is Fjorgynn, who is either the father or the lover of Frigg, called *Fjǫrgyns mær* in the *Lokasenna,* (st. 26). Fjorgynn's name, however, is related to the set of terms derived from the Indo-European term **perkw-* and associated with thunder, cragged mountains, and the oak tree. Among them are the Lithuanian name *Perkūnas* ("thunder"; cf. Slavic **Perunŭ*), the Gothic term *fairguni* ("mountain"; cf. Caesar's use of *Hercynia silva* for a wooded mountain range in ancient Germany), and the Latin word *quercus* ("oak"), as well as the Langobardic term *fereha aesculus* and the Old High German word *fereh-eih,* both of which designate a type of oak tree (cf. Old English *furh* and Old High German *for(a)ha,* "fir"). As Gregory Nagy has shown, these etymological links rest on the age-old perception of the predilection of lightning for rocky spots and oak trees and reflect the correlations established between them in Indo-European myth and tradition.

The goddess Gefjun is said to have torn away from Sweden a sizable chunk of land, which was dragged to the Danish island of Sjælland; to perform this deed she turned the four sons she had begotton in Jǫtunheimr into oxen and yoked them to the plow. Though she is mentioned as a separate deity in the *Lokasenna* (st. 20), she seems to be an alter ego of Freyja, who is also known as Gefn ("giver"), a name befitting a fertility goddess. Loki, indeed, reproaches Gefjun for having "lured to lust" Heimdallr, who gave her a precious jewel—presumably the mysterious "sea kidney" (ON, *hafnýra*) he had won in an epic battle with Loki—even before she "threw [her] thighs about him" (a behavior paralleling that of Freyja for the possession of the valuable Brising Necklace). How Snorri Sturluson can describe her in the *Gylfaginning* as a virgin, served by women who die unmarried, remains unexplained.

Sif, Þórr's wife and Ullr's mother by another male deity, plays a rather unobtrusive part in the society of the Æsir, but, though she is shy and retiring, Loki claimed to have enjoyed her favors (*Lokasenna* 54), and apparently Óðinn was aware of it, since, in the disguise of Hárbarðr, he warns Þórr about it: "With Sif someone sleeps in her bower" (*Hárbarðsljóð* 48). This explains why Loki dared to treat her like a whore (cutting off all her hair), since this was the treatment normally inflicted on adulteresses. Þórr, however, does not believe in the unfaithfulness of his wife and compels Loki to go to the dwarfs to obtain golden hair that will replace her lost locks. This story, then, accounts for the kenning "Sif's hair," meaning "gold."

In many cases it is questionable whether some names of deities quoted by Snorri Sturluson are more than local variants of the names of major gods, used largely to enhance the poetic expressions of the skalds. Thus we have no myths relating to such goddesses as Eir ("the best of physicians," according to the *Gylfaginning*) or to those specializing in bringing people to love, like Siǫfn, or who, like Lofn ("permission"), bring together those for whom marriage is apparently excluded.

[*For discussion of Germanic religion in a broader context, see* Indo-European Religions. *For more information about the deities, see* Freyja; Freyr; Heimdallr; Njorðr; Óðinn; Thor; *and* Týr. *On other mythic figures and topics, see* Álfar; Berserkers; Dvergar; Fylgjur; Jǫtnar; Landvættir; Loki; Valhǫll; *and* Valkyries.]

BIBLIOGRAPHY

On the Germanic pantheon, see E. O. G. Turville-Petre's general work *Myth and Religion of the North* (London, 1964) and Georges Dumézil's general study *Gods of the Ancient Northmen* (Berkeley, 1973). Other standard works on the topic include Jan de Vries's *Altgermanische Religionsgeschichte,* 2d ed., 2 vols. (Berlin, 1956–1957); R. L. M. Derolez's *Götter und Mythen der Germanen* (1959; Einsiedeln, Switzerland, 1963); and Régis Boyer's *La religion des Anciens Scandinaves* (Paris, 1981). Hilda R. Ellis Davidson's *Gods and Myths of Northern Europe* (Baltimore, 1964) is written for a wider public. A more controversial work is Åke V. Ström's *Germanische Religion*, "Die Religionen der Menschheit," vol. 19 (Stuttgart, 1975). A better summary, strongly influenced by Georges Dumézil, is Werner Betz's "Die altgermanische Religion," in Wolfgang Stammler's *Deutsche Philologie im Aufriss*, vol. 3 (Berlin, 1957). Succinct presentations are found in Lennart Ejerfeldt's contribution to the *Handbuch der Religionsgeschichte*, vol. 1, edited by Jes P. Asmussen and Jørgen Laessøe (Göttingen, 1971), pp. 277–342; and in Eduard Neumann and Helmut Voigt's entry in *Wörterbuch der Mythologie*, vol. 2 of *Das alte Europa*, edited by H. W. Haussig (Stuttgart, 1972).

On Tacitus, compare J. G. C. Anderson's *Cornelii Taciti De origine et situ Germanorum* (Oxford, 1961) and Rudolf Much's *Die Germania des Tacitus erläutert*, edited by Wolfgang Lange and Herbert Jankuhn (Heidelberg, 1967). On the sovereign gods, consult Georges Dumézil's *Les dieux souverains des Indo-Européens* (Paris, 1977). On the divine twins, compare Donald Ward's *The Divine Twins: An Indo-European Myth in Germanic Tradition* (Berkeley, 1968) and Georges Dumézil's *From Myth to Fiction: The Saga of Hadingus* (Chicago, 1973), esp. pp. 109–120.

Edgar C. Polomé

GERSHOM BEN YEHUDAH (c. 965–1028), German halakhist and Jewish communal leader. Despite the many uncertainties surrounding Gershom's life and historical role, it is clear that he was the central figure in the crystallization of Ashkenazic learning and communal organization in pre-Crusade Europe. A generation or two after his death Gershom was already termed Ma'or ha-Golah ("light of the exile"), a title reflecting the perception of both his spiritual stature and his historical impact.

Gershom's origins are not known, but it is likely that his immediate ancestry was French. He spent his adult life in Mainz, where in addition to writing commentaries on the Talmud and some liturgical poetry, he trained the men who were to be the mentors of Rashi. Gershom's personal life reflected the most painful experiences of medieval Jewish life: his son (and, according to one report, his wife as well) converted to Christianity. His poetry expresses the reality of persecution and the yearning for redemption.

Gershom's major contribution is revealed in his *responsa* and in the enactments *(taqqanot)* attributed to him. The *responsa* on questions of Jewish law are of course rooted in Talmudic literature, but they expose an original, decisive legal mind grappling with the central problems of his day. Some of his *responsa* dealt with Jews who converted to Christianity under duress, encouraging their return to Judaism by smoothing their path back to the community; others relaxed prohibitive regulations on Jewish-gentile commerce and empowered the community to govern more effectively by transferring to local communal leadership powers of compulsion that in Talmudic law are granted to central rabbinical courts. Matters of communal governance as well as issues of general social import were at the heart of the enactments attributed to Gershom.

The actual relationship between Gershom and the communities in whose name the enactments are also recorded is shrouded in obscurity, but present scholarly consensus sees Gershom as the central, driving figure behind this legislation. The enactments provide, *inter alia*, that the minority in a community must accept the authority of the majority, that taxes in dispute are to be paid before they are litigated, and that a defendant in a civil suit may be brought before a court in any community. These *taqqanot* were of great historical significance in legitimating community governance. Other enactments, such as those that prohibit marriage with more than one wife at the same time (permitted by both biblical and Talmudic law) and that forbid a husband to divorce his wife against her will, remain decisive for modern Jewish law and society. Both enactments reflect the status achieved by women in Gershom's society. While originally designed for the German communities of the Rhineland, they were gradually accepted by world Jewry.

BIBLIOGRAPHY

The most comprehensive discussion of Gershom's life and achievement is in Abraham Grossman's *Ḥakhmei Ashkenaz ha-ri'shonim* (Jerusalem, 1981), pp. 106–174. Louis Finkelstein, in *Jewish Self-Government in the Middle Ages* (1924; reprint, Westport, Conn., 1972), pp. 20–36, 111–139, presents the enactments attributed to Gershom in both the original Hebrew and in translation and discusses questions of authorship, provenance, and impact. Ze'ev W. Falk, in *Jewish Matrimonial Law in the Middle Ages* (Oxford, 1966), discusses the relationship between Gershom's enactments on monogamy and divorce and similar norms in Christian Europe.

Gerald J. Blidstein

GERSONIDES. *See* Levi ben Gershom

GESER (Tib., Ge-sar), or Geser Khan ("King Geser"), is a deity of the Mongols and Tibetans as well as the hero of a lengthy epic known in different versions from Lake Baikal to Bhutan and Sikkim and from Peking to Hunza in northern Pakistan. As an object of religious worship,

Geser's form is that of an equestrian deity showing the iconographic characteristics of an armed Central Asian warrior riding a horse and wearing a helmet and a cuirass.

Rooted in pre-Buddhist religion, Geser was ranged among the protective deities of Lamaist Buddhism. Geser's name and the epic associated with him seem to have entered Mongolian culture around 1600. The Mongols invoked him through prayer and sacrifice to grant fortune in war and hunting, to assure long life and good health, and to protect cattle and fruit as well as their state and religion.

In the nineteenth century Geser became identified with the Chinese god of war and protector of the Manchu dynasty, Kuan-ti, in whose honor numerous temples in Tibet and Mongolia were built. Geser's role as an oracular deity is the result of this association with Kuan-ti.

In Tibetan popular belief, Ge-sar is the divine hero-king who, as we know from his epic, descended in ancient times from heaven to the center of the world in order to restore order on earth, fighting against evil forces everywhere. He is still alive, protecting the good against all dangers. His help and advice are sought for all important endeavors, such as birth, marriage, travel, and business. To the faithful he is an incarnation of Avalokiteśvara, the Buddhist god of mercy and the patron deity of Tibet, also incarnate in the Dalai Lama, with whom Ge-sar becomes identical. To Buddhists in Tibet, Ge-sar will be the Buddhist king who victoriously leads the last and decisive battle against the barbarians, the Muslims. To the Tibetan Muslims, however, Ge-sar is the Antichrist who looses this battle against the Imam Mehdi and Jesus.

[*See also* Dalai Lama; Tibetan Religions, *overview article; and* Mongol Religions.]

BIBLIOGRAPHY

The classic study of the literary, historical, and religious aspects of the Ge-sar epic and its hero is Rolf A. Stein's *Recherches sur l'épopée et le barde au Tibet* (Paris, 1959), with an exhaustive bibliography. Geser Khan's role in Mongolian religion has been treated by Walther Heissig in *Die Religionen der Mongolei* (Stuttgart, 1970), translated by Geoffrey Samuel as *The Religions of Mongolia* (Berkeley, 1980). A summary of East Tibetan accounts from the Ge-sar cycle is given in Alexandra David-Neel's *La vie surhumaine de Guésar de Ling, le héros thibétain, racontée par les bardes de son pays* (Paris, 1931), translated with the collaboration of Violet Sydney as *The Superhuman Life of Gesar of Ling* (1933; rev. ed., London, 1959); the introduction, dealing with such topics as the historicity of Ge-sar's personality and Ge-sar as the "warrior messiah" of the Tibetans, is of special interest. English renderings of Ladakhi (West Tibetan) recensions of the epic have been published in *A Lower Ladakhi Version of the Kesar Saga*, translated and edited by A. H. Francke (Calcutta, 1905–1909).

KLAUS SAGASTER

GESTURES. *See* Postures and Gestures.

GETO-DACIAN RELIGION. The Getae and the Dacians were ancient Thracian peoples who lived in Moesia, on the northern plain of the river Danube, and in the Carpathian Mountains, approximately in the territory of modern-day Romania and the Moldavian Soviet Socialist Republic. Although the religion of the Getae and the Dacians escapes complete reconstruction, it forms, nevertheless, like the religion of the ancient Celts, one of the most interesting chapters in the history of Indo-European religions outside the Greco-Roman world. Despite the rationalistic tendency of some scholars to diminish the importance of religion among these peoples, evidence indicates that the foundation of the state consisting of the Getae and the Dacians was a result of theocratic ideas. These ideas stemmed from the worship of Zalmoxis, possibly an ancient religious reformer to whom the beginnings of Getic kingship are also related. Later on, Zalmoxis was divinized, a process that has frequent parallels in ancient Greece. [*See* Zalmoxis.]

As for the Dacians, testimonies explicitly relate their name to the Phrygian word *daos* ("wolf"). Paul Kretschmer's etymology, which derives *dakoi* from the Indo-European **dhawo-s* ("wolf"), has been supported by Vladimir Georgiev and has received an exhaustive historico-religious comment from Mircea Eliade (1972). Eliade claims that the Dacians, like several other Indo-European peoples, formed a *Männerbund* based on the idea of ritual lycanthropy. Young Dacian warriors were probably trained to imitate the behavior of ferocious wolves. This has nothing to do with the Getae's legendary contempt for death, however, as that was based on the Zalmoxean promise of immortality. In all probability the message of Zalmoxis referred to a paradise in which valiant warriors would survive after death in a state of perpetual happiness.

Greek evidence, starting with Herodotus, establishes a close relationship between Zalmoxis and Pythagoras. The set of religious ideas whose origin is attributed to Zalmoxis indeed presents resemblances with Pythagoreanism. Besides immortality, Zalmoxis is said to have also taught a highly praised form of psychosomatic medicine based on charms, whose purpose was to heal the soul together with the body. Plato gives a vivid and enthusiastic account of Zalmoxean medicine in the dialogue *Charmides* (156d–157c). This medical tradition was apparently long-lived: late in the third century CE forty-seven Dacian names of medicinal plants were inserted in the famous *Materia medica* of the Greek physician Dioscurides and in *De herbis,* attributed to Apuleius.

Zalmoxean Priesthood. The cult of Zalmoxis had strong connections with kingship. Plato, in fact, reports that Zalmoxis was king of the Getae (*Charmides* 156d), but Strabo (*Geography* 7.3–5) says that Zalmoxis was priest of the most important god of the Getae, that he became associated with kingship, and that he later was himself worshiped as a god; he was supposed to live in a cave on the sacred mountain Kōgaionon, where only the king and his messengers could visit him. Sacred priesthood continued down to Strabo's time (first century BCE). The sacred cave must have been the most ancient place where the god was worshiped and his priests dwelled. In Herodotus's time (fifth century BCE) a sanctuary of Zalmoxis must have existed, for Herodotus (*Histories* 4.95) relates the legend that Zalmoxis had had an underground chamber built and that he hid himself there for three years, after which he reappeared. Such a sanctuary, with a vast underground complex, has been found at Sarmizegetusa Regia (modern-day Grădiştea Muncelului, Romania).

Jordanes, the historian of the Goths, born in Moesia in the sixth century, mingled the traditions of the Goths with those of the Getae in order to give the former the prestige of an ancient and superior population. He composed a list of Zalmoxean priests from the epoch of Burebista (c. 80–44 BCE) to the time of the Dacian king Decebalus (d. 106 CE). The series opens with the well-known Decaeneus (Dicineus), Burebista's counselor, who may have decisively contributed to the latter's power and to the origin of his kingship. Decaeneus taught the Getae philosophy, physics, ethics, logic, and astronomy. In particular he introduced them to the secrets of astrology, planetary revolutions, phases of the moon, measurement of the sun's size, and cosmic revolutions. Jordanes's testimony has been too lightly dismissed in the past. Decaeneus actually taught the Getae cosmology, astrology, and astronomy as well as introducing them to one of the most intriguing of ancient calendars, whose mystery has not been yet convincingly explained. Decaeneus's successors were the priests Comosicus and Coryllus, both of them kings, the latter in Dacia. Probably this Coryllus (sometimes called Cocrilus or Scorilus) was the immediate predecessor of Decebalus, who was the last king of the Daco-Getae and was finally defeated by the Roman emperor Trajan in 106 CE.

This list of Zalmoxean priests seems to contradict a second list also furnished by Jordanes (*De origine actibusque Getarum* 39), according to which the king Zalmoxis came after Decaeneus. In fact, Jordanes is obviously not referring here to chronology; he says only that among the Getae the most important thinkers were first *(prius)* a certain Zeutas, then *(post etiam)* Decaeneus, and then again *(tertium)* Zalmoxis. One should infer from this that the predecessor of Decaeneus was Zeutas, not that Decaeneus was followed by Zalmoxis, who is simply the legendary founder of the Geto-Dacian priesthood; in fact, Decaeneus was followed by Comosicus. The name *Zeutas* is related to the southern Thracian name *Seuthes* and further to the Avestan term *haotar,* signifying an Iranian priest. Therefore, *zeutas* may simply be a generic term signifying Thracian priests.

Pythagorean Patterns. The geographer Strabo, quoting the Stoic philosopher Posidonius, was the first to give precious, but confused, information about the *ktistai* living in continence and abstinence, and the *abioi* (lit., "lifeless," i.e., strangers to normal life conditions) of whom Homer tells (*Iliad* 8.5–7). Strabo (7.3.5) also reports that Zalmoxis introduced vegetarianism among the Getae.

The Jewish historian Josephus Flavius (first century) compares the life of the ascetic Essenes with that of "those among the Dacians who are called *pleistoi*" (*Jewish Antiquities* 18.22). It seems that this text should be left without emendation. Following Posidonius and Strabo, the deep religious concern of the Geto-Dacians *(spoudē, theosebeia, pietas)* was a commonplace of antiquity.

The word *pleistoi* has received different interpretations, but it seems to be connected with the Thracian god Pleistoros (Herodotus, 9.119). Gheorghe Muşu has sought its etymology in the Indo-European root **ple(is),* meaning "to be full"; hence *pleistoi* would mean "bearers of fullness" (Muşu, in Vulpe, 1980). In a rather obscure article, Mihai Nasta has accepted the emendation *pleistois* in *polistais,* from *polizein,* meaning "to instruct in the spirit of the city [*polis*]; to polish" (Nasta, in Vulpe, 1980). The most probable etymology, however, is that proposed by Eugen Lozovan (1968), who reads *pleistoi* as a paronomasia of the Thracian **pleiskoi,* from the Indo-European **pleus-,* meaning "hair, lock." Hence, the *pleistoi* would be "hair bearers," that is, bearers, or wearers, of a woolen bonnet.

This explanation receives further confirmation from Jordanes (71), who reports that the headgear of the noble and wise priests of the Getae, called *pilleati,* was a tiara *(pilleus).* The rest of the people had no *pilleus;* thus they were *capillati,* or "bareheaded." Scholars have claimed that Jordanes's report was based on a misinterpretation of Dacian nobles as priests, since traditionally the *pilleus* was the distinctive sign of Geto-Dacian aristocracy. This observation is wholly irrelevant, however, since Geto-Dacian kingship had many of the characteristics of a theocracy, and the religious initiation of nobles was probably different from that of the common people. Thus, the *pilleati* could very well have been trained as priests. As often as not, Geto-Dacian high priesthood coincided with kingship.

The Calendar Temple at Sarmizegetusa Regia. In chapter 70 of his *De origine actibusque Getarum*, Jordanes presents a portrait of Getic warriors that has met only skepticism among modern scholars. According to Jordanes, the Getic warriors used the short time between battles to study the properties of plants and the secrets of the starry heavens. An astonishing confirmation of this picture has been provided by the decipherment of the meaning of the calendar temple discovered among the monumental ruins of Sarmizegetusa Regia, an impressive stronghold in the Carpathian Mountains that was the center of the Daco-Getic priesthood before the Roman conquest. The first hypotheses, put forward by D. M. Teodorescu, Constantin Daicoviciu, G. Charrière, and Hadrian Daicoviciu, have been recently replaced by an improved interpretation based on algorithms, proposed by Serban Bobancu, Cornel Samoilă, and Emil Poenaru (1980).

The calendar temple is composed of two circular sanctuaries made of pillars and slabs of stone and andesite and of wooden pillars plated with terra-cotta, disposed in regular patterns. The forms and materials correspond to different units of the Dacian calendar. According to the demonstration of Bobancu, Samoilă, and Poenaru, the Dacians used as their principal time measure a fluctuating week consisting of from 6 to 8 solar days. A Dacian year was composed of 47 such measures and had, accordingly, from 364 to 367 days. After one 13-year cycle the calendar needed a one-day correction, which was marked separately on a series of pillars indicating such cycles. After one "century" of 104 years, or 8 cycles of 13 years each, a new one-day correction was needed and marked. On a larger rectangular calendar, a 520-year time quantum could be measured, that is, a cycle of 5 Dacian centuries, after which a one-day correction was needed again. Besides the 104-year "centuries," the Dacian calendar also worked with 91-year "centuries," that is, 7 cycles of 13 years each.

Besides this "civilian" calendar, the Dacians also used a religious calendar, composed of 60 weeks of 6 days each. A 68-day correction, marked on a circle composed of 68 pillars, was exactly the astronomical operation needed after the passage of a 13-year cycle. Sophisticated and precise as it was, the Dacian calendar had a simple and effective method of use. After termination of each time quantum (week, year, 13-year cycle, 91-year and 104-year "centuries," 520-year period), a successive unit, represented by an architectural element (e.g., a pillar, a slab), was marked; this unit had another form and/or was made of a material different from that used for the preceding unit. The system of correspondences consists of distinguishing the different values of the circles of the sanctuaries and the different regular units of which each circle is composed. Once this is known, the whole pattern becomes predictable, and even a child or a modern scholar could be easily trained to keep the periodic marking.

Easy as it might seem in practice, such a calendar would be based on very complex mathematical principles. It would reach such a remarkable precision that after 2,275 years, corresponding to 175 cycles of 13 years, the time as given by the calendar would differ from the astronomical time by only 38.88 seconds. This is much too precise to be true.

The calendar temple at Sarmizegetusa Regia was not built before Decebalus, but it must have been based on a system discovered by Decaeneus. It provides perhaps a confirmation of Jordanes's characterization of the religious life of the Geto-Dacians.

BIBLIOGRAPHY

The written sources on the religion of the Geto-Dacians are contained in *Fontes historiae Dacoromanae*, 2 vols., edited by Virgil C. Popescu et al. (Bucharest, 1964–1970). On Thracian religion in general, Gawrill I. Kazarow's article, "Thrake (Religion)," in *Realencyclopädie der Altertumswissenschaft*, vol. 6 (Stuttgart, 1937), can still be profitably consulted, and an extensive bibliography can be found in Mircea Eliade's *Zalmoxis, the Vanishing God: Comparative Studies in the Religions and Folklore of Dacia and Eastern Europe* (Chicago, 1972).

For detailed study of the northern Thracians, the following works are recommended. In Romanian, Hadrian Daicoviciu's *Dacii*, 2d ed. (Bucharest, 1972), and I. I. Russu's article in *Anuarul Institutului de Studii Clasice* 5 (1944–1948): 61–137 are both essential works. Ion Horaţiu Crişan's *Burebista and His Time*, "Bibliotheca Historica Romaniae Monographs," no. 20 (Bucharest, 1978), translated into English from his second edition, is useful for its description of the old sanctuary at Sarmizegetusa Regia. Radu Vulpe's *Studia Thracologica*, in French, contains important articles on Burebista and Decaeneus, and the *Actes du Deuxième Congrès International de Thracologie*, vol. 3, *Linguistique, ethnologie, anthropologie*, edited by Vulpe (Bucharest, 1980), contains several interesting articles by Ioan Coman, Gheorghe Muşu, Mihai Nasta, and others. A still useful survey of some problems connected with the religion of the Geto-Dacians is Eugen Lozovan's "Dacia Sacra," *History of Religions* 7 (February 1968): 209–243. The best interpretation of the calendar temple at Sarmizegetusa Regia and a discussion of earlier hypotheses are presented by Serban Bobancu, Cornel Samoilă, and Emil Poenaru in *Caldendarul de la*

Sarmizegetusa Regia (Bucharest, 1980), which includes a useful English summary on pages 183–190.

IOAN PETRU CULIANU and CICERONE POGHIRC

GHAYBAH, the Arabic word for "concealment," in the sense of absence from human sight, is applied by various Shīʿī Muslim groups to the condition of one or another imam who disappeared rather than died and whose life is believed to have been prolonged (in a paradisial state or in God's presence) until his foreordained return as Mahdi (the Expected Deliverer) to initiate the eschatological drama concluding history.

Early History. The Qur'ān contrasts the invisible or hidden spiritual realm *(al-ghayb)* with the observable world of human experience. Drawing upon prototypes of such eschatological prophet figures as Moses and Jesus, the first generations of Muslims embraced the view that certain prophets were withdrawn by God from the eyes of mortals, among them Jesus, Idrīs (Enoch/Hermes), Ilyās (Elijah), and al-Khiḍr. The Qur'anic description of the crucifixion of Jesus (4:157–159) and legends of the bodily incorruptibility and the ascension and future return of a Mosaic-type prophet contributed to the focusing of such expectations on various members of the prophet Muḥammad's family. ʿAlī ibn Abī Ṭālib, the prophet's cousin and son-in-law, may have been the first given this honor by a small group of extremists among his partisans, the Sab'īyah, who refused to admit his death after his assassination in 661. After the martyrdom of Ḥusayn ibn ʿAlī at Karbala in 680, another son of ʿAlī, Muḥammad ibn al-Ḥanafīyah (d. 700?) became the center of millenarian hopes in the revolt of al-Mukhtār and the Kaysānīyah that occurred in 686 at Kufa in lower Iraq.

The Kaysānīyah drew an explicit parallel between a "docetic" understanding of the passion of Christ and the concealment and eventual return of their imam. Speculation about the concealment of the imam was tied to the doctrine of return *(al-rajʿah)* in terms of a this-worldly, bodily resurrection before the end time to accomplish eschatological vengeance upon the wicked and victory and justice for the righteous.

The Later Shīʿah. The early tendency of "stopping" at a certain claimant to the imamate who was seen to be in concealment and awaiting his near-return helped fragment the energies of the original Shīʿah. Historical circumstances determined the continuity of the Imāmīyah or Twelver Shīʿī line of imams until the death in 874 of the eleventh imam, al-Ḥasan al-ʿAskarī, whom tradition holds to have secretly fathered a son four years before his death, namely the twelfth or Hidden Imam, Muḥammad al-Mahdī. During the minor *ghaybah* from 874 to 941 this person's earthly existence and near-return was accepted by the Twelver communities, whose allegiance was given to at least four successive *safīrs*, or agents, the direct deputies of the Mahdi, especially in his juristic and financial functions. After 941 comes the era of the major *ghaybah*, in which the Twelver scholar-lawyers (*mujtahids* or *faqīhs*) collectively fulfill the functions of the imam's agents as an independently learned body of religious authorities. In the major *ghaybah* the Mahdi's concealment is seen as total and, though in earthly occultation, he is held to communicate to the faithful by virtue of his participation in the hierarchy of the invisible worlds. [*See* Shiism, *article on* Ithnā ʿAsharīyah.]

The early Ismāʿīlī Shīʿah eschewed the notion of a miraculous prolongation of life for the imam and emphasized a continuing line of succession to the imamate that included temporary or cyclical periods of concealment termed *satr*. They centralized the spiritual and cosmic role of the imam developed earlier by the radical Shīʿah. The Druze, however, maintain belief in the *ghaybah* of their founders, the Fatimid caliph al-Ḥākim and Hamzah. The two major branches of the Fatimid Ismāʿīlīyah both revere a living line of successive imams: for the Nizārī Ismāʿīlīyah he is the present Aga Khan, while the Mustaʿlī Ismāʿīlīyah or Bohoras hold that the present imams are in earthly concealment and are represented by a continuing line of *dāʿīs*, or agents acting as heads of the community. [*See* Shiism, *article on* Ismāʿīlīyah; Druze; *and* Aga Khan.]

For the Twelver Shīʿah, the need for a visible stand-in for the Hidden Imam, or Mahdi, has been assuaged by belief in his continuing efficacy and necessary suprahistorical role. Dream visions and transcendent appearances were occasions for the imam to momentarily break his concealment, while popular eschatology dwelt on the apocalyptic scenario of his triumphant return or the miraculous nature of his concealment. Shīʿī theosophical treatments expanded the cosmic role of the concealed imam and his presence in the spiritual realm of prophets and saints. Ṣūfī treatments of *ghaybah* have interiorized it by focusing on the complementary experience of *ḥaḍrah*, "presence" with the divine. Ṣūfīs revered the popular figures of prophetic longevity such as al-Khiḍr as well as the invisible yet active hierarchy of saints headed by the *quṭb*, or spiritual axis.

[*See also* Imamate *and* Messianism, *article on* Islamic Messianism.]

BIBLIOGRAPHY

For descriptions of the early views on *ghaybah*, consult Israel Friedlaender's "The Heterodoxies of the Shiites in the Presentation of Ibn Hazm," *Journal of the American Oriental Soci-*

ety 28 (1907): 1–80 and 29 (1908): 1–183. The Twelver doctrine of the concealment is well depicted by A. A. Sachedina in *Islamic Messianism* (Albany, N.Y., 1981), while the period of the minor *ghaybah* is treated in apologetic fashion by Jassim M. Hussain in *The Occultation of the Twelfth Imam* (London, 1982). Wilferd Madelung's articles, "Authority in the Twelver Shiism in the Absence of the Imam," in *La notion d'autorité au Moyen-Âge*, edited by George Makdisi et al. (Paris, 1982), pp. 163–174, and "Shiite Discussion on the Legality of the *kharāj*," in *Proceedings of the Ninth Congress of Arabic and Islamic Studies* (Leiden, 1981), pp. 193–202, deal with the claim of the Shīʿī scholars to deputyship of the Hidden Imam. The esoteric Shīʿī approach can be sampled in Henry Corbin's study, "Divine Epiphany and Spiritual Birth in Ismailian Gnosis," in *Man and Transformation*, vol. 5 of *Papers from the Eranos Yearbooks*, edited by Joseph Campbell (New York, 1964), pp. 69–160, first published in the *Eranos-Jahrbuch* 23 (1954): 141–249.

DOUGLAS S. CROW

GHAZĀLĪ, ABŪ ḤĀMID AL- (AH 450–505/1058–1111 CE), named Muḥammad ibn Muḥammad ibn Muḥammad; the distinguished Islamic jurist, theologian, and mystic who was given the honorific title Ḥujjat al-Islām (Arab., "the proof of Islam").

Life. Al-Ghazālī was born in the town of Ṭūs, near modern Mashhad (eastern Iran), and received his early education there. When he was about fifteen he went to the region of Gorgān (at the southeast corner of the Caspian Sea) to continue his studies. On the return journey, so the story goes, his notebooks were taken from him by robbers, and when he pleaded for their return they taunted him that he claimed to know what was in fact only in his notebooks; as a result of this incident he spent three years memorizing the material.

At the age of nineteen he went to Nishapur (about fifty miles to the west) to study at the important Niẓāmīyah college under ʿAbd al-Malik al-Juwaynī (d. 1085), known as Imām al-Ḥaramayn, one of the leading religious scholars of the period. Jurisprudence would be central in his studies, as in all Islamic higher education, but he was also initiated into Ashʿarī theology and perhaps encouraged to read the philosophy of al-Fārābī and Ibn Sīnā (Avicenna). He later helped with teaching and was recognized as a rising scholar. When al-Juwaynī died, the powerful vizier of the Seljuk sultans, Niẓām al-Mulk, invited him to join his court, which was in fact a camp that moved about, giving al-Ghazālī the opportunity to engage in discussions with other scholars.

In 1091, when he was about thirty-three, he was appointed to the main professorship at the Niẓāmīyah college in Baghdad, one of the leading positions in the Sunnī world; it can be assumed that the appointment was made by Niẓām al-Mulk, the founder of the colleges bearing his name. After just over four years, however, al-Ghazālī abandoned his professorship and adopted the life of an ascetic and mystic.

We know something of al-Ghazālī's personal history during these years in Baghdad from the autobiographical work he wrote when he was about fifty, entitled *Al-munqidh min al-ḍalāl* (The Deliverer from Error). This work is not conceived as an autobiography, however, but as a defense of his abandonment of the Baghdad professorship and of his subsequent return to teaching in Nishapur about a decade later. It is also not strictly chronological but was given a schematic form. In it, he describes his intellectual journey after the earliest years as containing a period of skepticism lasting "almost two months," when he doubted the possibility of attaining truth. Once he ceased to be completely skeptical, he set out on a search for truth among four "classes of seekers [of truth]," namely, the Ashʿarī theologians, the Neoplatonic philosophers, the Ismāʿīlīyah (whom he calls the party of *taʿlīm*, or authoritative instruction), and finally the Ṣūfīs, or mystics. He writes as if these were four successive stages in his journey, but in fact they must have overlapped; it is virtually certain that he gained some knowledge of mysticism during his early studies at Ṭūs and Nishapur. The period of skepticism, too, could only have come after he had some acquaintance with philosophy, since philosophical considerations were involved.

The first encounter, according to this scheme, was with the *mutakallimūn*, or rational theologians. These were, of course, the Ashʿarīyah, by whom he had been trained and among whom he is reckoned. In the *Munqidh* he complains that their reasoning is based on certain presuppositions and assumptions which they never try to justify, but which he cannot accept without some justification. In effect what happened was that he found in philosophy a way of justifying some of the bases of Ashʿarī theology. This can be seen in his principal work of Ashʿarī theology, *Al-iqtiṣād fī al-iʿtiqād* (The Golden Mean in Belief), where he introduces many philosophical arguments, including one for the existence of God. Until the end of his life he seems to have held that Ashʿarī theology was true so far as it went, and in his chief mystical work, *Iḥyāʾ ʿulūm al-dīn* (The Revival of the Religious Sciences), he includes an Ashʿarī creed of moderate length; this is known as *Al-risālah al-qudsīyah* (The Jerusalem Epistle) and was probably composed before his extensive study of philosophy.

The second encounter of his intellectual journey was with Greek philosophy and, in particular, the Arabic Neoplatonism of al-Fārābī and Ibn Sīnā. He had probably been introduced to philosophy by al-Juwaynī, but he began the intensive study of it early in his Baghdad professorship. Since philosophy, with other Greek sciences, was cultivated in institutions distinct from the colleges for Islamic jurisprudence and theology and was looked on with disapproval, al-Ghazālī had to study the books of the philosophers by himself. He describes how he devoted to this activity all the free time he had after lecturing to three hundred students and doing some writing. In less than two years he managed to gain such a thorough understanding of the various philosophical disciplines that his book, *Maqāṣid al-falāsifah* (The Views of the Philosophers), gives a clearer account of the teaching of Ibn Sīnā on logic, metaphysics, and physics than the works of the philosopher himself. After another year's reflection on these matters, al-Ghazālī wrote a powerful critique of the metaphysics or theology of the philosophers entitled *Tahāfut al-falāsifah* (The Inconsistency of the Philosophers). His argument against the philosophers is based on seventeen points on which he attacks their views as heretical and on three others on which he regards the philosophers as infidels. In discussing the seventeen points al-Ghazālī demonstrates the weaknesses of the philosophers' arguments for the existence of God, his unicity, and his incorporeality, and he rejects their view that God is a simple existent without quiddity and without attributes, their conception of his knowledge, and some of their assertions about the heavens and the human soul. The three points contrary to Islam are that there is no resurrection of bodies but only of spirits, that God knows universals but not particulars, and that the world has existed from eternity. Underlying the detailed arguments is his conviction that the philosophers are unable to give strict logical proofs of their metaphysical views. He therefore turned away from them also in his search for truth.

His third encounter was with a section of the Ismāʿīlīyah who held that true knowledge was to be gained from an infallible imam. It seems doubtful whether he seriously expected to gain much from such people. He did, however, study their views carefully, partly because the caliph of the day commanded him to write a refutation of them. He had little difficulty in showing that there were serious inadequacies in their teaching.

His final encounter was with Sufism; he had already realized that this mysticism entailed not only intellectual doctrines but also a way of life. After four years in Baghdad he felt himself so involved in the worldliness of his milieu that he was in danger of going to hell. The profound inner struggle he experienced led in 1095 to a psychosomatic illness. Dryness of the tongue prevented him from lecturing and even from eating, and the doctors could do nothing to alleviate the symptoms. After about six months he resolved to leave his professorship and adopt the life of a Ṣūfī. To avoid any attempts to stop him, he let it be known that he was setting out on the pilgrimage to Mecca. Actually he went only to Damascus, living there as a Ṣūfī for over a year, and then made the pilgrimage to Mecca in 1096. Some six months after that he was back in Baghdad and then seems to have made his way by stages back to his native Ṭūs. There he established a *khānāqāh* (hostel or convent), where some young disciples joined him in leading a communal Ṣūfī life. The genuineness of his conversion to Sufism has sometimes been questioned by Muslim scholars, and it has been suggested that he left his professorship because he was afraid his life was in danger on account of political involvements. To judge from his own account, however, religious considerations were uppermost in his mind.

The Muslim year 500 (which began on 2 September 1106 CE) marked the beginning of a new century. Muḥammad was reported to have said that God would send a "renewer" *(mujaddid)* of his religion at the beginning of each century, and various friends assured al-Ghazālī that he was the "renewer" for the sixth century. This induced him to take up an invitation from the vizier of the provincial governor in Nishapur to become the main professor in the Niẓāmīyah college there. He continued in this position for three or possibly four years and then returned to Ṭūs, probably because of ill health; he died there in 1111. His brother Aḥmad, himself a distinguished scholar, describes how on his last day, after ablutions, Abū Ḥāmid performed the dawn prayer and then, lying down on his bed facing Mecca, kissed his shroud, pressed it to his eyes with the words, "Obediently I enter into the presence of the King," and was dead before sunrise.

Works. Over four hundred titles of works ascribed to al-Ghazālī have been preserved, though some of these are different titles for the same work. At least seventy works are extant in manuscript; it is clear, however, that some of these, chiefly works of a mystical character, have been falsely attributed to al-Ghazālī, though in the case of one or two the inauthenticity is not universally admitted. Certain of these works are written from a standpoint close to that of the philosophers, and earlier scholars, regarding them as authentic, were led to suppose that before his death al-Ghazālī came to adopt the views he had previously attacked, or else that in addition to his publicly expressed views, he held esoteric views which he communicated only to a select few. Since about 1960, however, scholars have been aware of a manuscript written four years after his death, which bears a colophon stating that the short work it contains was completed by al-Ghazālī about a fortnight before he died. This work is *Iljām al-ʿawāmm ʿan ʿilm al-kalām* (The Restraining of the Common People from the Science of Theology), and in it he writes as a Shāfiʿī jurist who, at least up to a point, accepts Ashʿarī theology. It is also known that just over two years earlier he had completed a long and important work on the principles of jurisprudence, *Al-mustaṣfā* (The Choice Part, or Essentials); this was presumably one of the subjects on which he lectured at Nishapur. These facts make it inconceivable that at the end of his life al-Ghazālī adopted the heretical views he had previously denounced, and thus they strengthen the case for regarding as inauthentic works containing views which cannot be harmonized with what is expressed in books like the *Munqidh* and the *Iḥyā'*.

The genuine works of al-Ghazālī range over several fields. One of these is jurisprudence, which is dealt with in several early works, as well as in the much later *Mustaṣfā* mentioned above. These are the works most often referred to in connection with al-Ghazālī during the two centuries after his death. Most of these legal works were presumably written before he went to Baghdad. At Baghdad he turned to philosophy, producing the *Maqāṣid* and the *Tahāfut*, the exposition and critique of the Neoplatonic philosophers. About the same time, he wrote two small books on Aristotelian logic and a semiphilosophical work on ethics (which may, however, contain some interpolations). He also tells us that it was in Baghdad that he composed for the caliph al-Mustaẓhir the refutation of Ismāʿīlī thought known after the patron as the *Mustaẓhirī*. His exposition and philosophical defense of Ashʿarī doctrine in the *Iqtiṣād* must have been written either shortly before or shortly after leaving Baghdad.

For some time after that, al-Ghazālī's literary occupation seems to have been the composition of his greatest work, the *Iḥyā' ʿulūm al-dīn*. It consists of four "quarters," each divided into "books" or chapters; a complete English translation would probably contain at least two million words. The first quarter, entitled "the service of God," has books dealing with the creed, ritual purity, formal prayer *(ṣalāt)*, other types of prayer and devotion, almsgiving, fasting, and the pilgrimage. The second quarter deals with social customs as prescribed in the *sharīʿah* and has books on eating habits, marriage, acquiring goods, traveling, and the like; it concludes with a book presenting Muḥammad as an exemplar in social matters. The third quarter is about "things destructive," or vices, and, after two general books on "the mysteries of the heart" and how to control and educate it, gives counsel with regard to the various vices. The fourth quarter on "things leading to salvation" deals with the stages and aspects of the mystical life, such as penitence, patience, gratitude, renunciation, trust in God, and love for him. In most of the books al-Ghazālī begins with relevant quotations from the Qur'ān and the *ḥadīth* (anecdotes about Muḥammad, sometimes called traditions) and then proceeds to his own exposition. His overriding aim seems to be to show how the scrupulous observance of all the external acts prescribed by the *sharīʿah* contributes to the inner mystical life.

Al-Ghazālī presents a simpler version of the way of life to which the *Iḥyā'* points in *Bidāyat al-hidāyah* (The Beginning of Guidance). Other works of interest from his mystical period are an exposition of the ninety-nine names of God with the short title *Al-maqṣad al-asnā* (The Noblest Aim) and a discussion of light symbolism centered on the "light verse" of the Qur'ān (24:35) and entitled *Mishkāt al-anwār* (The Niche for Lights). There is also a Persian work, *Kīmiyā' al-saʿādah* (The Alchemy of Happiness), covering the same ground as the *Iḥyā'* but in about half the compass.

Among the works of doubtful authenticity is a refutation of Christianity with the title *Al-radd al-jamīl ʿalā ṣarīḥ al-injīl* (The Beautiful Refutation of the Evidence of the Gospel). Even if this is not by al-Ghazālī, it is of course an interesting document of roughly his period, and the same is true of the spurious mystical works.

The Achievements of al-Ghazālī: Philosophy, Theology, and Mysticism. At the present time it is still difficult to reach a balanced judgment on the achievement of al-Ghazālī. After the first translation of the *Munqidh* into a European language (French) was published in 1842, many European scholars found al-Ghazālī such an attractive figure that they paid much more attention to him than to any other Muslim thinker, and this fashion has been followed by Muslim scholars as well. His importance has thus tended to be exaggerated because of our relative ignorance of other writers. This ignorance is now rapidly decreasing, but care is still needed in making an assessment of al-Ghazālī.

Part of al-Ghazālī's aim in studying the various philosophical disciplines was to discover how far they were compatible with Islamic doctrine. He gave separate consideration to mathematics, logic, physics, metaphysics or theology *(ilāhīyāt)*, politics, and ethics. Metaphysics he criticized very severely in his *Tahāfut*, but most of the others he regarded as neutral in themselves, though liable to give less scholarly persons an unduly favorable opinion of the competence of the philosophers in every field of thought. He himself was very impressed by Aristotelian logic, especially the syllogism. He not only made use of logic in his own defense of doctrine but also wrote several books about it, in which he managed to commend it to his fellow-theologians as well as to expound its principles. From his time on, many theological treatises devote much space to philosophical preliminaries, and works on logic are written by theologians. The great positive achievement of al-Ghazālī here was to provide Islamic theology with a philosophical foundation.

It is more difficult to know how far his critique of philosophy led to its disappearance. Arabic Neoplatonic philosophy ceased to be cultivated in the East, though there was an important Persian tradition of theosophical philosophy, but there had been no philosopher of weight in the East since the death of Ibn Sīnā twenty years before al-Ghazālī was born. In the Islamic West philosophy following the Greek tradition continued until about 1200 and included a refutation of al-Ghazālī's *Tahāfut* by Ibn Rushd (Averroës), so that the decline in the West cannot be attributed to al-Ghazālī.

Sufism had been flourishing in the Islamic world for over two centuries. Many of the earliest Ṣūfīs had been chiefly interested in asceticism, but others had cultivated ecstatic experiences, and a few had become so "intoxicated" that they seemed to outsiders to claim unity with God. Such persons often also held that their mystical attainments freed them from duties such as ritual prayer. In al-Ghazālī's time, too, yet other Ṣūfīs were becoming interested in gnostic knowledge and developing theosophical doctrines. For these reasons many of the *ʿulamā'*, or religious scholars, were suspicious of all Sufism, despite the fact that some of their number practiced it in a moderate fashion without becoming either heretical in doctrine or antinomian in practice. Al-Ghazālī adopted the position of this latter group and, after his retirement from the professorship in Baghdad, spent much of his time in ascetical and mystical practices. The *khānaqāh* which he established at Ṭūs was probably not unlike a monastery of contemplatives. His great work the *Iḥyā'* provides both a theoretical justification of his position and a highly detailed elucidation of it which emphasized the deeper meaning of the external acts. In this way both by his writing and by his own life al-Ghazālī showed how a profound inner life can be combined with full observance of the *sharīʿah* and sound theological doctrine. The consequence of the life and work of al-Ghazālī was that religious scholars in the main stream of Sunnism had to look more favorably on the Ṣūfī movement, and this made it possible for ordinary Muslims to adopt moderate Ṣūfī practices.

BIBLIOGRAPHY

Two older books still have much of value, though they make use of works probably falsely attributed to al-Ghazālī: A. J. Wensinck's *La pensée de Ghazzālī* (Paris, 1940) and Margaret Smith's *Al-Ghazālī the Mystic* (London, 1944); the latter includes a full account of his life. My *Muslim Intellectual: A Study of al-Ghazali* (Edinburgh, 1963) looks at his life and thought in its intellectual context. In *La politique de Ġazālī* (Paris, 1970), Henri Laoust gives some account of his life as well as of his political thought. Hava Lazarus-Yafeh's *Studies in al-Ghazzali* (Jerusalem, 1975) includes among other things discussions of authenticity on the basis of linguistic criteria. The fullest account of all works ascribed to him, with extensive consideration of questions of authenticity, is Maurice Bouyges's *Essai de chronologie des œuvres de al-Ghazali*, edited by Michel Allard (Beirut, 1959). The following are a few of the numerous translations available: My *The Faith and Practice of al-Ghazālī* (London, 1953) has translations of the *Munqidh* and *Bidāyat al-hidāyah;* Richard J. McCarthy's *Freedom and Fulfillment* (Boston, 1980) has translations of the *Munqidh* and "other relevant works" with introduction and notes; William H. T. Gairdner's *Al-Ghazzālī's Mishkāt al-anwār* (The Niche for Lights; 1924; reprint, Lahore, 1952) is a translation with introduction of a mystical text; Muhammad A. Quasem's *The Jewels of the Qur'an: al Ghazali's Theory* (Bangi, Malaysia, 1977), a translation of *Jawāhir al-Qur'ān*, shows how the Qur'ān was understood and used by Ṣūfīs; Robert C. Stade's *Ninety-nine Names of God in Islam* (Ibadan, 1970) is the descriptive part of *Al-maqṣad al-asnā*.

A general overview of the *Iḥyā'* is given in G.-H. Bousquet's *Ghazali, Ih'ya ʿOuloum ed-dîn, ou vivification des sciences de la foi; analyse et index* (Paris, 1955). Translations of separate books include Nabih Amin Faris's *The Book of Knowledge* (book 1; Lahore, 1962); *The Foundations of the Articles of Faith* (book 2; Lahore, 1963); *The Mysteries of Purity* (book 3; Lahore, 1966); *The Mysteries of Almsgiving* (book 5; Lahore, 1974); *The Mysteries of Fasting* (book 6; Lahore, 1968); E. E. Calverley's *Worship in Islam* (book 4; 1925; reprint, Westport, Conn., 1981); Muhammad A. Quasem's *The Recitation and Interpretation of the Qur'an* (book 8; Selangor, Malaysia, 1979); D. B. Macdonald's "Emotional Religion in Islam as Affected by Music and Singing" (book 18), *Journal of the Royal Asiatic Society* (1901): 195–252, 705–748; and (1902): 1–28; Leon Zolondek's *Book XX of al-Ghazālī's Iḥyā'* (Leiden, 1963); and William McKane's *Al-Ghazali's Book of Fear and Hope* (book 33; Leiden, 1965).

W. MONTGOMERY WATT

GHOSE, AUROBINDO. *See* Aurobindo Ghose.

GHOST DANCE. The Ghost Dance was the major revivalist movement among nineteenth-century North American Indians. Dating from about 1870, it had its culmination in the 1890–1891 "messiah craze" of the Plains, which caused the last Indian war in the Dakotas. The name *Ghost Dance* refers to the ritual round-dances that were thought to imitate the dances of the dead and were performed to precipitate the renewal of the world and the return of the dead. There were other American Indian ceremonial dances that were called ghost dances—for instance, a ritual dance among the Iroquois. However, it was the messianic Ghost Dance of 1890 that attracted general attention because of its message and consequences. It has been considered prototypical of other revivalist movements among North American Indians, so much so that most later movements have been classified as "ghost dances" (La Barre, 1970).

History. Strictly speaking, there have been two Ghost Dances, closely connected with each other and almost identical in form and cultic performance.

The 1870 Ghost Dance. The Ghost Dance movement of 1870 was introduced on the Walker Lake Reservation in Nevada by a Northern Paiute Indian, Wodziwob ("gray hair," 1844–1918?). During a trance he was conveyed to the otherworld, where he learned that the dead were soon to return, that the disappearing game animals were to be restored, and that the old tribal life would come back again. In order to hasten this change, people had to perform round dances at night, without fires. This Ghost Dance lasted some few years among the Paiute, several middle and northern California tribes, and some Oregon Indians.

Wovoka and the Ghost Dance of 1890. One of Wodziwob's inspired adherents was Tävibo ("white man"), who despite his name was a full-blooded Northern Paiute. He had a son, Wovoka ("the cutter," 1856–1932). Wovoka lived in Mason Valley, Nevada, where he served as a farmhand to a white family named Wilson, and because of this association he went under the name of Jack Wilson. During an eclipse of the sun, probably in January 1889, he fell into a trance and was transported to the supreme being in the sky. In this vision the supreme being showed him the land of the dead and the happy life there, and promised that the living would have a reunion with the deceased, providing a series of rules were followed.

At this point our information divides. To the whites, Wovoka said that the reunion would take place in the otherworld if people behaved correctly (i.e., did not lie, steal, or fight) and performed the round dance. To the Indians, he announced the speedy coming of the dead (who would be guided by a cloudlike spirit that was interpreted as Jesus) as well as the return of game and a lasting peace with the whites. The round dance would more quickly bring about this change. The scene was to be on earth, not in the otherworld. It is obvious that, to the Indians, Wovoka presented the same message, in many ways, as Wodziwob.

The round dance was the same as well. It was conducted on four or five consecutive nights. Men and women danced together in a circle, interlacing their fingers and dancing round with shuffling side steps. The dance was exhausting, although not continuous, and no fainting spells or visions were reported.

This second Ghost Dance appeared when the Plains tribes had been subjugated and their old style of living was on the wane. The freedom-loving Plains Indians looked for an escape, and in their desperation they found it in the Ghost Dance. Emissaries were sent over to the "Messiah," Wovoka (who in fact had claimed only to be a prophet, not a messiah), and were instructed in his doctrine. However, the Plains delegates misinterpreted the message to mean that the whites would be driven off or exterminated. The Ghost Dance spread like fire among the Plains Indians, and in particular the Arapaho, Cheyenne, Lakota, Kiowa, and Caddo became staunch believers. Dancing songs expressed the wishes of the arrival of the dead and praised the Father above.

The Lakota added several new traits that were in line with their visionary and militant ethos: they became entranced while dancing; they pondered military action against the whites; and they covered their upper bodies with white "ghost shirts," decorated with spiritual emblems. The ghost shirt was supposed to protect the wearer magically against enemy bullets. It was probably patterned on Mormon garments worn by the Paiute for protection from bodily harm.

Although the Lakota plans for action were very vague, their frenetic dancing in the summer and fall of 1890 released countermeasures from the suspicious white authorities in the Dakotas, resulting in the so-called Ghost Dance Uprising. Highpoints of this development were the arrest and assassination of the famous Lakota leader Sitting Bull and the massacre at Wounded Knee at the end of December 1890, when Hotchkiss guns indiscriminately killed men, women, and children in Big Foot's camp.

After these catastrophic events, enthusiasm for the Ghost Dance ebbed. Some groups continued dancing, but their expectations of the coming of the dead were projected to a distant future. The last Ghost Dances were held in the 1950s, among Canadian Dakota and Wind River Shoshoni.

Three Main Roots. It is possible to find three main roots of the Ghost Dance: earlier religious movements stimulated by Christian missions, shamanic experiences, and indigenous rituals. Of these sources, the impact of earlier syncretic movements has been thoroughly analyzed, beginning with James Mooney's famous study (1896). The import of native religious development has been properly studied only relatively recently. Scholars have, of course, been aware of changes in the Indian's spiritual, cultural, and military background that may have triggered the outbreak of the

Ghost Dance. There is no unanimity of opinion, however, as to whether readjustment to a new sociopolitical situation or predominantly religious drives steered the development. The overwhelming majority of scholars, all of them anthropologists, favor the first view, whereas historians of religions prefer the latter.

The impetus for the Ghost Dance revivalism was the Indians' enforced contact with an expanding white civilization beginning in the 1860s. Because of growing white settlements, the white military takeover, and the introduction of white jurisdiction, there was no more room for the continuation of the old native existence, in particular for the hunters and gatherers of the West. Their independent cultures ceased rapidly, sometimes even abruptly, as on the Plains: the whole culture of the northern Plains tribes, built on hunting buffalo, collapsed when in 1883 the last herd of buffalo was exterminated. The Indians had to adjust to white man's culture and, in part, to his values, in order to survive. At the same time they drew on their past to mobilize a desperate spiritual resistance against the overwhelming white influence. In this reactive effort they combined Christian or Christian-derived elements with indigenous ideas and rituals to form a resistance ideology.

Earlier religious movements. The formation of mixed ("acculturated") ideologies is part of American Indian religious history since the beginning of European colonization: the restitutional ("nativistic") doctrines launched by the Tewa Indian Popé (1680–1692) and by Neolin, the so-called Delaware Prophet (around 1760), are among the better-known early instances. These prophets proposed an ethical and religious program. In many respects Neolin set the pattern for subsequent prophets, including those of the Ghost Dance: an inspired person who suffers from the ways of the white man enforced upon him and his people, who longs for a return to the good old Indian ways, and who experiences an ecstasy or similar state. In his vision he is brought to the Master of Life, from whom he obtains instructions about a right life. Provided this road is followed, he is told, the game will return, the whites will be driven away, and the old life will be restored. No wonder that such enchanting messages fostered Indian wars, like Pontiac's uprising, which was inspired by Neolin's prophecies.

While the messages of the prophets reflected a yearning for old value patterns, they were in fact deeply dependent on Christian missionary teachings. Exhortations to believers to refrain from liquor, adultery, lying, and murder and to show brotherly friendliness, even beyond tribal boundaries, reveal more or less Christian ethical precepts. Where the abandonment of traditional fetishes and rituals was propagated, as by the Shawnee prophet Tenskwatawa, Christian value judgments are easily recognizable. The very idea that the Supreme Being had to introduce the new religious program through revelation to a prophet also speaks of Christian influence. The hope for the day of salvation, or the coming liberation, implies a linear view of history and an eschatological goal, ideas that were never American Indian, but are thoroughly Christian.

Shamanic experiences. The second root of the Ghost Dance is shamanic experience. Although the instigators of the revivalist movements were prophets (i.e., ecstatics who had received their calling from God) and not shamans (i.e., vocational ecstatics acting on behalf of their fellowmen), the difference is a minor one, for shamans often receive their calling from spirits. There was definitely a Christian background to the Indian conception of the prophet, his reception of an eschatological message after a comatose experience, and his direct contact with a more or less christianized God. However, the pattern of spiritual communication is very much shamanic. Wovoka, for instance, was himself a medicine man, and fell repeatedly into self-induced trances. It was during these séances that he visited the otherworld and received his messages. Of course, the destination of his soul was the heaven of God, not the spirit land of the dead; these were two different realms in most Native American beliefs.

The Ghost Dance had its precursors in movements that crystallized around shamans. Leslie Spier (1935) retraced the Ghost Dance ideology to an older "Prophet Dance" founded on the intense relations of the living with the dead on the Northwest Coast and the Plateau. The Prophet Dance ideology contained such elements as a world cataclysm, renewal of the world, and the return of the dead. World renewal and the return of the dead could be hastened by the performance of the "dance of the dead." The Prophet Dance had its basis, according to Spier, in the periodic cataclysms (earthquakes) to which the region is subject and in the shamanic visits to the dead made to restore the lost soul of a sick person.

Round-dance ritual. The third main root of the Ghost Dance is, as Michael Hittman (1973) has observed, the indigenous round dance. The latter has been interpreted by some scholars as simply a dance for entertainment, but there is much evidence that the Basin round dance, performed around a pole or cedar tree, was a religious ceremony—the Father Dance, offered with thanksgivings to the Master of Life for food, rain, and health. In the Ghost Dance this old ceremony was given a new, eschatological meaning.

[*See also* North American Religions, *article on* Modern Movements; Shamanism, *article on* North American Shamanism; *and the biographies of Wovoka and Neolin.*]

BIBLIOGRAPHY

The classic in the field is still James Mooney's *The Ghost-Dance Religion and the Sioux Outbreak of 1890* (1896; reprint, Chicago, 1965). It is a reliable account of Mooney's field visits, just after the Lakota conflict, to a number of tribes that performed the Ghost Dance. Other general works, but less professional, are Paul Bailey's *Wovoka: The Indian Messiah* (Los Angeles, 1957) and David H. Miller's *Ghost Dance* (New York, 1959). In a wider setting of so-called crisis cults, the Ghost Dance religion has been discussed in, among other works, Weston La Barre's *The Ghost Dance* (Garden City, N.Y., 1970).

The discussion of the Ghost Dance has, in comparative works on prophetism, messianism, and millenarianism, concentrated on terminological, psychological, and acculturation problems, whereas the specialized works on the Ghost Dance have paid attention primarily to its origins. Pathbreaking has been Leslie Spier's *The Prophet Dance of the Northwest and Its Derivatives: The Source of the Ghost Dance* (Menasha, Wis., 1935). Spier's idea of an exclusively aboriginal origin of the Ghost Dance religion is today in doubt, but much of his work remains extremely useful.

The grounding of the 1890 Ghost Dance in Wodziwob's movement of the same name twenty years earlier has directed scholars' attention to the latter. The details of the 1870 movement have been excellently clarified in Cora Dubois's *The 1870 Ghost Dance* (Berkeley, 1939). A new orientation, which argues for the mutual independence of the 1870 and 1890 movements, is represented in Michael Hittman's "The 1870 Ghost Dance at the Walker River Reservation: A Reconstruction," *Ethnohistory* 20 (1973): 247–278.

The connection of the Ghost Dance with the Father Dance has been worked out in my book, *Belief and Worship in Native North America*, edited by Christopher Vessey (Syracuse, N.Y., 1981); see especially "The Changing Meaning of the Ghost Dance as Evidenced by the Wind River Shoshoni," pp. 264–281.

ÅKE HULTKRANTZ

GHOSTS.

In western Germanic languages words similar to the modern English *ghost* and the German *Geist* seem to be derived from roots indicating fury, wounding, or tearing in pieces. The spelling with *gh* in English appeared first in a work printed by William Caxton in the fifteenth century, influenced probably by a similar Flemish form. The term *ghost* has been used in various ways, to mean soul, spirit, breath, the immaterial part of man, moral nature, a good spirit, an evil spirit, and, in liturgical and dogmatic language, to designate the spirit of God as the "Holy Ghost." It has chiefly signified the soul of a deceased person appearing in a visible form, and hence has given rise to such phrases as *a ghost walking, raising a ghost,* or *laying a ghost.* It may be called "an apparition" or "a specter." In any case, the prevailing modern sense is that of a dead person manifesting its presence visibly to the living.

Other words are used to describe comparable phenomena, but with some differences. A fetch is, like the German *Doppelgänger,* the apparition of a living person. A wraith is an apparition or specter of a dead person or an immaterial appearance of someone living forewarning his own death. The Irish often speak of fetches, and the Scottish of wraiths. More generally, a phantom, from the Greek *phantasma,* is sometimes unreal or immaterial, an illusion or dream-image, a specter or ghost. A phantasm may be the same thing, but Edmund Gurney and others in *Phantasms of the Living* (1886) discussed as phantasms "all classes of cases where . . . the mind of one human being has affected the mind of another . . . by other means than through the recognized channels of sense" (vol. 1, p. 35). A poltergeist, from the German *poltern* ("to make noise") and *Geist* ("spirit") is regarded as a noisy spirit remarkable for throwing things about. Since the nineteenth century the French world *revenant* (lit., "one who comes back"), has been used in English to describe a being who returns from the dead.

The word *ghost* most commonly refers to a dead person who haunts or simply appears before the living, sometimes with a message or warning. The notion has been popular in literature. While Shakespeare wrote one play involving fairies and another involving witches, ghosts were an important feature in several of his works: Hamlet's father, Caesar, and Banquo all appear as ghosts. Hamlet's father—called a ghost, a spirit, an apparition, an illusion, and more than fantasy—expresses a belief in the activities of ghosts: "I am thy father's spirit; / Doom'd for a certain term to walk the night, / And for the day confin'd to fast in fires, / Till the foul crimes done in my days of nature / Are burnt and purg'd away" (1.5.9–13).

The Bible and the Qur'ān. The Hebrew scriptures have few references to ghosts. Isaiah attacked the practice of consulting "the mediums and the wizards who chirp and mutter" (*Is.* 8:19). This refers to the spiritualistic séance, forbidden but vividly illustrated in the story of the medium of Endor, consulted by Saul. She was said to raise up the dead prophet Samuel out of the earth, saying "An old man comes up, and he is covered with a robe" (*1 Sm.* 28:14). Samuel was not a haunting ghost, although he brought a fatal warning for Saul.

In Psalm 88:12 the grave is called the land of forgetfulness, and later Judas Maccabaeus makes sacrifices to free the dead from their sins (*2 Mc.* 12:45). In the apocryphal *Wisdom of Solomon* (17:15) lawless men are said to be troubled in their sleep by specters, apparitions, and phantoms. Otherwise ghosts are not mentioned except in the older translations where death is described as surrendering the spirit, "giving up the ghost."

In the New Testament there are also few references. When the disciples saw Jesus by night, on or by the sea, they were afraid, thinking him an apparition or ghost (*phantasma; Mark* 6:49; this is the only occurrence of this word in the New Testament). In one of Luke's accounts of the resurrection the disciples were terrified, supposing that they had seen a spirit *(pneuma)*, but Jesus assured them that this could not be so, for he had flesh and bones that a spirit had not (*Lk.* 24:37–39). Lazarus might be called a revenant, but he was not, strictly speaking, a ghost, since he came out of the grave alive (*Jn.* 11:44). Later Christian insistence upon the "resurrection of the flesh" *(sarx)*, as in the Apostles' Creed, also precluded "ghostly" survival and postulated instead a restoration of the full personality.

In developing Christian doctrine theologians discussed the nature of angels, good spirits, bad spirits, the resurrection of the dead, heaven, hell, and purgatory. But belief in ghosts and their possible return to earth was left indeterminate, neither accepted nor rejected. All Souls' Day, the commemoration of the faithful departed, has been universally celebrated in the Western church since the tenth century, and prayers at Mass request "to the souls of all thy servants a place of cool repose, the blessedness of quiet, the brightness of light . . . forgiveness and everlasting rest."

In practice many Christians have believed in ghosts and in haunted places, and this is said to have been particularly true among Germanic peoples. The survivors owed numerous duties to the departed, and unless honor and rituals were accorded, it was thought that the dead might return to take vengeance or reclaim their former property. Those who had died untimely or unnatural deaths, such as women in childbirth, might become wandering spirits. To this day stories are related in Europe about old monasteries or rectories where restless spirits are said to appear. Rituals of exorcism have been practiced, with restrictions, both to cast out evil spirits and to lay wandering ghosts to rest.

In the Islamic world the soul or self (Arab., *nafs;* cf. Heb. *nefesh*) was at first distinguished from the breath or wind (Arab., *rūḥ;* cf. Heb. *ruaḥ*), but the words came to be used interchangeably and are applied to the human spirit, angels, and genii *(jinn)*. Theologians teach that at death the soul goes to a first judgment and then remains in the grave until the final resurrection. Edward A. Westermarck stated in *Ritual and Belief in Morocco* (1926, vol. 2, p. 246) that while it was believed that dead saints might appear to the living and the dead might come to see their friends but remain invisible, "as to ordinary dead people I have been assured over and over again that the dead do not walk, and I remember how heartily my friends . . . laughed when I told them that many Christians believe in ghosts." However, the Moroccans believed that the dead would be angry if they were offended by anyone and would punish him, and if children did not visit the graves of their parents they would be cursed by them. The voices of some of the dead were thought to be audible in cemeteries, though only good people, children, and animals could hear them. If a person had been killed, the spot would be regarded as haunted, and passersby might hear him groan.

Among Berber-speaking tribes there were said to be more traces of the belief in apparitions of the dead than among Arabic-speaking Moroccans. Some of the Tuareg of the Sahara claimed that ghosts had been seen at night near cemeteries. In Egypt many stories have been told of apparitions of dead people, and Arabian bedouin believe that spirits of the wicked haunt the places of their burial and that the living should avoid passing cemeteries in the dark.

The *jinn* may be thought to haunt burial grounds and many other places, but they are fiery spirits and not dead people. Ghouls (Arab., *ghūl*) are monsters thought to haunt cemeteries and feed on dead bodies. An *'ifrīt* is mentioned in the Qur'ān (27:39) as "one of the *jinn,*" and in the *Thousand and One Nights*, in the story of the second shaykh, it is said that a benevolent Muslim woman "turned into an *'ifrītah,* a *jinnīyah.*" She changed her shape, saved her husband from drowning by carrying him on her shoulders, and told him that she had delivered him from death by the grace of God, since she believed in him and in his Prophet. In Egypt the word *'ifrīt* came to mean the ghost of a man who had been murdered or suffered a violent death.

Africa. In many parts of Africa ghosts are thought to appear to give warning or seek vengeance. Among the Ashanti of Ghana, a man who has committed suicide is called a wandering spirit, unable to find rest and refused entry into the land of spirits, roaming between this world and the next until his appointed time of death. If such a suicide is reborn, he will come back as a cruel man who might again suffer a bad end. At one time criminals who were executed had powerful charms tied on them to prevent their ghosts returning to harm the executioners. Some of the dead had their heads shaved and painted red, white, and black so that they would be recognized if they walked as ghosts.

The Ga of the Ghana coastline think that the spirit of

one who dies violently or prematurely wanders about for forty days as a ghost, angry at his early death and jealous of other people's pleasures. Those who go out late at night pursuing such pleasures may be pursued in turn by ghosts until they die of heart failure. Ghosts are said to be recognizable by their fiery breath and red mouths: red is the color of witches, fairies, and ghosts, but ghosts dislike white and may be kept away if one throws white cloths on the ground.

A common belief in the Ivory Coast is that the dead may return to their homes at night to steal children from their mothers' arms. Here and elsewhere widows must keep in mourning for months or years, often in rags, lest their dead husbands return and have sexual intercourse with them, which would have fatal results. Fishermen drowned at sea, hunters lost in the forest, people struck by lightning or burnt in fires, and others who die of diseases like smallpox or leprosy may not receive burial rites and so become ghosts, living in the "bad bush." Months after the death or disappearance, the family performs mourning ceremonies and lays the ghost to rest.

When infant mortality is high, a succession of dying children may be thought to be incarnations of the same child over and over again. The Yoruba of Nigeria call such babies "born to die" *(abiku),* and if one comes a third time and dies it is said that "there is no hoe" to bury it with. Marks are made on the body of the stillborn or dying baby to prevent the ghost from returning or to make the ghost recognizable.

In central Africa the Ila of Zambia think that some spirits are captured by witches and become their ghost-slaves, causing disease and sometimes possessing people. Like poltergeists, such ghosts reputedly attack people, knock burdens off their heads, or break axes and hoes. Ghosts are often thought to speak in unnatural ways, in guttural voices or twittering like birds, and some are said to be very small, with bodies reversed so that their faces are at the back of their heads. They appear in dreams, show anger at neglect, demand sacrifice, or cause sickness. Although stories are told that seem to imply that ghosts have objective or even physical existence, they are regarded as spiritual entities who only take the essence or heart of sacrifices.

In the region of Zaire the word *zumbi* is used for spirits of the dead and ghosts, and in Haiti it becomes *zombie,* a *revenant,* or one of the "living dead," whose soul has been eaten by a witch or whose corpse has been revived by a sorcerer for evil purposes.

South and East Asia. In popular Indian belief various words may be used for ghosts. The term *bhūta,* something that has been or has become, refers to the ghost of a dead person, one who has died a violent death or has not had a proper funeral ceremony, or it may apply generally to a good or evil spirit. In the *Bhagavadgītā* (9.25) the *bhūta* is a ghost or goblin, an inferior but not necessarily an evil being. A *preta* ("departed") is the spirit of a dead person before the obsequies are performed or an evil ghost; it also may be the spirit of a deformed person or of a child that died prematurely. A *yakṣa* is generally a benevolent spirit although sometimes classed with *piśācas* and other malignant spirits and ghosts; such terms are used loosely and often overlap.

Ghosts and demons in India are believed to haunt cemeteries or live in trees, appearing in ugly or beautiful forms and requiring food and blood. The special guardian against ghosts is the monkey god Hanuman, the "large-jawed"; his worshipers offer coconuts to him and pour oil and red lead over his images, taking some of the oil that drips off to mark their eyes as a protection. The lighting of lamps at the Dīvālī or Dīpāvali festival at the new year is also said to drive away ghosts and evil spirits.

Performance of Śrāddha funeral ceremonies is essential in India for the rest of the departed spirit, in order to provide food for it and to prevent it from becoming an evil spirit. Special Śrāddha is performed for those who died violently, as they would be likely to become haunting ghosts. Infants who die do not receive ordinary Śrāddha, but presents are given to brahmans on their behalf.

Buddhist dialogues discuss various states after death. In the *Milindapañha* (294) there are said to be four classes of ancestors *(peta),* only one of which lives on offerings from benefactors; the others feed on vomit, are tormented by hunger and thirst, or are consumed by craving. Any of these may be ghosts. In Sinhala another word *(holman)* indicates similar dangerous beings. These appear at night as naked white figures, especially in cemeteries, and sunset, midnight, and dawn are the most dangerous times for their activities. One of them, Mahasōnā, perhaps meaning "great cemetery," puts his hand on the backs of wanderers in graveyards at midnight, marks them with his imprint, and kills them with shock. *Peta* may be offered inferior food, as well as drugs or excrement, and if they act as troublesome poltergeists they are exorcized. Another term for ghostly creatures, *bhūtayā* ("has been") may be substituted for *peta* and other words for demons and harmful spirits.

Burmese Buddhists believe that although all beings pass on to rebirth, most go first to one of four "states of woe" as an animal, demon, ghost, or inhabitant of hell. Rebirth as a human being is an exception, one of "five rarities." Monks may be reborn as ghosts. One account of five heads of a monastery who died in quick succession attributed the premature deaths to the ghost of the original incumbent, who had owned the monastery personally and died before appointing a successor. Those who followed were usurpers, and as a ghost he caused their deaths. As a consequence the villagers decided to abandon that monastery and build a new one for the next abbot.

In Thailand the Indian word *preta* is used for the ghosts of the recently dead, who may have been condemned to hell or to wander the earth. Although not harmful to humans they may be disgusting and gigantic in appearance. Because of their tiny mouths they suffer from constant hunger and thirst. Relatives may transfer merit to the *pretas* by extra gifts to monks; some writers consider *pretas* to be the inversion of the Buddhist monk. Mural paintings in Buddhist temples of South Asia often depict both the joys of paradise and the sufferings of unhappy spirits.

In China a ghost *(kuei;* f., *yao)* was the spirit of someone who had died an unusual death, often as the result of crime. Ghosts of bandits were thought to linger near the place of their execution, and if a woman had a difficult labor it was attributed to her having passed near such a place during pregnancy and having offended one of the bandit ghosts. The ghost might try to oust the rightful soul during labor and be born as the woman's son.

Under Buddhist influence souls were thought to live in zones of formlessness until the time of rebirth. They were fed by surviving relatives, and if nobody cared for them they would haunt people. In the seventh month after death there was a great festival for "hungry souls," when the priests would recite texts not only for relatives but for the souls of strangers and those without anyone to care for them. Meals, models of houses, and paper money were dedicated to the dead and burned as offerings. Especially in southern China, paper boats, often with a host of deities aboard or with lanterns in the shape of lotus flowers, were set drifting down rivers to light the way for spirits and ghosts to cross the river of transmigration. If sickness or calamity afflicted the community, however, it was attributed to inadequate propitiation of ghosts.

In Japanese belief one category of the ancestral dead is that of wandering angry ghosts. Neglected ancestors may quickly change from benevolent beings to vicious, cursing tyrants, attacking their families in painful ways until proper food and potent texts are offered to them. There are also spirits with no particular affinity *(muenbotoke),* those who die childless or without kin to worship them, and they may attack any stranger whose weakness lays him open to spiritual possession.

The most dangerous ghosts are those of people who die violently, are murdered, or die in disgrace. They become angry spirits *(onryō)* requiring rituals for appeasement. In the literature of the eighth to the tenth century there are striking examples of these furious ghosts, such as the story of Prince Sawara. After horrifying starvation, exile, and death by poison, he was said to have brought a whole series of calamities on the country. And a minister who died in 903 in disgrace and exile was credited with a succession of natural disasters thanks to his furious ghost. In early times discontented ghosts were depicted in animal or natural form, but in later *nō* plays they appear as ordinary men and women who are finally revealed as ghosts in horned masks and long red wigs.

Notions of ghosts and spirits as restless, perhaps unburied or unavenged, beings with a message to convey or a task to fulfill abound in popular belief in many countries, although there may be little formal doctrine or orthodox teaching in the scriptures to support these ideas.

[*See* Soul *and* Afterlife.]

BIBLIOGRAPHY

The larger dictionaries provide examples of the ways in which *ghost* and similar words have been used, especially the complete or the "compact" edition of the *Oxford English Dictionary*, 2 vols. (Oxford, 1971). Biblical and ecclesiastical dictionaries rarely discuss ghosts, but the *Shorter Encyclopaedia of Islam* (1953; reprint, Leiden, 1974) has a useful article on the soul *(nafs).* Edward A. Westermarck's *Ritual and Belief in Morocco*, 2 vols. (1926; reprint, New Hyde Park, N.Y., 1968), is a treasury of popular beliefs. African beliefs have been collected in my *West African Psychology* (London, 1951). For Indian rituals Margaret S. Stevenson's *The Rites of the Twice-Born* (1920; reprint, New Delhi, 1971) is still valuable. There have been more recent studies of Buddhist countries: Richard F. Gombrich's *Precept and Practice* (Oxford, 1971) on Sri Lanka; Melford E. Spiro's *Buddhism and Society*, 2d ed. (Berkeley, 1982) on Burma; Stanley J. Tambiah's *Buddhism and the Spirit Cults in North-East Thailand* (Cambridge, 1970) on Thailand; and Carmen Blacker's *The Catalpa Bow* (London, 1975) on Japan.

GEOFFREY PARRINDER

GHOST THEORY. *See* Manism.

GIBBONS, JAMES (1834–1921), American Roman Catholic churchman, archbishop of Baltimore, cardinal. The fourth child and eldest son of immigrant parents, James Gibbons was born in Baltimore on 23 July 1834. After a sixteen-year (1837–1853) sojourn in Ballinrobe, County Mayo, Ireland, where he received his early education, Gibbons returned to the United States and settled in New Orleans. Acting on a long-held desire to seek ordination, he studied for the priesthood at Saint Charles College in Ellicott City, Maryland, and at Saint Mary's Seminary in Baltimore. He was ordained a priest for the archdiocese of Baltimore in 1861.

Gibbons's career in the parish ministry ended in 1865 when Archbishop Martin Spalding made him his secretary. Thereafter, Gibbons experienced a swift rise through the ranks of the hierarchy. In 1868 he was named the first vicar apostolic of North Carolina and elevated to the rank of bishop; in 1872 he became the bishop of Richmond, Virginia; in May 1877 he was named coadjutor archbishop of Baltimore with right of succession; and in October 1877 he became the archbishop of Baltimore upon the death of James R. Bayley.

In assuming leadership of the archdiocese of Baltimore, Gibbons found himself in a position of great importance and high visibility in the American Catholic church. As the oldest diocese in the United States and the see within whose boundaries the national capital fell, Baltimore and its bishops enjoyed a degree of ecclesiastical and political prestige that other dioceses and bishops did not possess. These factors, together with Gibbons's longevity, his elevation to the cardinalate (1886), his accessibility to public officials and his personal friendship with every president from Cleveland to Harding, his tactful and conciliatory mode of governing, his irenic attitude toward non-Catholics, and the phenomenal success of his catechetical *Faith of Our Fathers* (1876), combined to make him the outstanding American Catholic churchman of his time.

Although he is justly famous for his contributions to such intramural Catholic projects as the founding of the Catholic University of America (1889) and the establishment of the National Catholic War/Welfare Council (1917), Gibbons's place in American Catholic history is really the result of the use he made of the prestige of his office and his personal talents in addressing four major problems that confronted the American church between 1877 and 1921: immigration, industrialization, Nativism (the xenophobic reaction of Americans to immigrants), and Vatican apprehensions concerning American religious pluralism. Gibbons clearly saw that these four problems were interrelated, for all were concerned with the underlying problem of effecting some rapprochement between the Catholicism he loved and the American political and cultural life he revered. With his fellow americanizing bishops, John Ireland and John Keane, he sought both to assuage the fears of nervous Nativists and to insure the internal unity of the church by advocating a pragmatic policy of assimilation that urged immigrant Catholics to adopt the language and mores of the host culture. His program did not endear him to German-American Catholics, but, combined with his conspicuous patriotism during the Spanish-American War and World War I, and his writings in praise of the American political system, it did much to enhance both his and his church's reputation as bulwarks of patriotism.

The same desires to demonstrate the social utility of the chuch to the nation, to insure the internal health of the church, and to protect the church from detractors animated Gibbons's defense of the Knights of Labor before the Roman Curia. His advocacy of the Knights as well as his work to reconcile New York's socially-minded Father Edward McGlynn to the church earned him the reputation of a labor advocate comparable to Pope Leo XIII (1878–1903) and Cardinal Manning of Westminster in the universal church, and of a force for social peace at home.

While Gibbons enjoyed some measure of success in his attempts to demonstrate the compatibility of Catholicism and American life to non-Catholic Americans, the signal failure of his career was his inability to demonstrate the same either to conservative members of the American hierarchy or to Roman authorities who saw only a dangerous and corrosive indifferentism in the americanizers' praise of and accommodation to American mores. Leo XIII's condemnation of Americanism in 1899 *(Testem benevolentiae)* came as a stunning blow to Gibbons and his colleagues at the same time that it heartened the conservative followers of Archbishop Michael A. Corrigan of New York. In time, however, Gibbons's reputation in Rome was rehabilitated, and when he died in 1921 he was acknowledged by both his coreligionists and his fellow citizens to have been the dominant force in the American Catholic church.

BIBLIOGRAPHY

Browne, Henry J. *The Catholic Church and the Knights of Labor.* Washington, D.C., 1949. A narrative history of Catholicism's recognition of the rights of labor, with special attention to Gibbons's efforts to avert a papal condemnation of the Knights.

Cross, Robert D. *The Emergence of Liberal Catholicism in America.* Cambridge, Mass., 1958. Outlines the ideological position of the americanizers and the conservatives involved in the so-called battle of the prelates in the late nineteenth century.

Ellis, John Tracy. *The Life of James Cardinal Gibbons, Archbishop of Baltimore 1834–1921.* 2 vols. Milwaukee, 1952. The definitive biography of Gibbons.

Fogarty, Gerald P. *The Vatican and the American Hierarchy from 1870 to 1965.* Stuttgart, 1982. Examines the troubles encountered by the American hierarchy in dealing with a Curia that did not fully understand the American political system.

Gibbons, James. *A Retrospect of Fifty Years.* 2 vols. Baltimore,

1916. A collection of diary entries and articles written during Gibbons's episcopal career. Selections concerning the relationship of Catholicism and American life are especially helpful in understanding the man.

JOSEPH M. MCSHANE, S.J.

GIFT GIVING. The exchange of gifts is one of the most telling characteristics of human culture and, according to some authorities, may form the original basis of economics. From the religious perspective, gift giving has two primary aspects with many variations. First, gift giving is incorporated in a variety of ways within the religious customs and sanctions that regulate social behavior. Second, in the sense of offering, gift giving is an essential aspect of sacrifices ritually presented to a deity or deities. [*See* Sacrifice.] In both aspects the process of gift giving may involve distribution of the gift within the selected social group to which it is appropriate; it may also entail the destruction of all or part of the thing given, to signify its disappearance into the metaphysical realm.

The Potlatch as a Model for Gift Giving. With regard to the social aspect of gift giving, Marcel Mauss's *Essai sur le don* (Paris, 1925), translated as *The Gift* ([1954] 1967), shows gift giving to be the very means by which value can be taught and understood in a society, provoking humans to productivity but at the same time inspiring a sense of an intangible presence in the things distributed.

Mauss seems to regard the potlatch—an elaborate celebration entailing the lavish display and distribution of the host's possessions—as the most significant form of gift giving, possessing both religious significance and profound consequences for the development of economic systems. [*See* Potlatch.] The gifts associated with the potlatch, as practiced by the Kwakiutl Indians, include both tangible, useful materials, such as blankets, boats, and food, and an entirely symbolic article—the most valuable "prestation" of all (Mauss's term, signifying the repayment of an obligation)—namely, a hatchet-shaped copper plaque.

The potlatch originated along the rich coasts of the northwestern United States, western Canada, and Alaska. Many tribes in these regions adopted the potlatch, but the system appears in its most elaborate and well-recorded form among the Kwakiutl. (It has been greatly modified as native peoples have become increasingly assimilated into the dominant white culture.) Historically, the Kwakiutl were among the most thoroughly stratified tribes imaginable; they were fundamentally divided into two large groups, the *naqsala*, or nobility, and the *xamala*, or commoners. Every person, noble or common, belonged both to further-interrelated subgroups within the overall structure of tribes and to *numina*, or subdivisions, within the particular tribe. The nobles, and even the commoners, were identified within all the interlocking groups by discrete honorific titles and by a system of seating according to rank. In the formalized feasting that was the ritual setting for the act of prestation, this seating system had much to do with the way in which goods were distributed.

In one respect, the potlatch system might be thought of as a means of increasing one's capital through interest on loans, a process that requires brief explanation. One's status in the community was linked to the munificence with which one disposed of one's capital in the feasts. The capital consisted of what was regarded as valuable during a particular period: blankets, fish oil, food, shells, and slaves were such goods in premodern times. To cite an example, the list of gifts given in a potlatch in 1921 included the following items: Hudson Bay blankets, canoes, pool tables, bracelets, gaslights, violins, gasoline-powered boats, guitars, dresses, shawls, sweaters, shirts, oaken trunks, sewing machines, basins, glasses, washtubs, teapots, cups, bedsteads, bureaus, and sacks of flour and sugar (Rohner, 1970, p. 97). All of the items on this list were given to differentially ranked individuals. The pool tables, regarded as equivalent to the copper plaque (or "copper"), went to men of very high status. Glasses, washtubs, teapots, and cups went to women of various ranks. Thus, the distributor invested capital that gave him high status in the community and that was loaned, in a sense, in the expectation that all the items would be returned with interest at a future potlatch. Indeed, the interest was very precisely calculated; in the case of blankets, the return due at the end of one year was double the number of blankets given. The return of these loans (which were not solicited but had to be accepted, according to the system) was the occasion for the giving of new loans, much as it was the occasion for the potlatch feast. The purpose of the potlatch among the Kwakiutl was not to accumulate goods but to show one's ranked status in the community by the level of munificence one displayed. Some writers have compared the gift giving at the potlatch to a kind of warfare or war game in which the bestowal of extravagant gifts could inflict serious "wounds" on other participants.

Although it has not been commented on by leading writers, an analysis of the potlatch system reveals more than a few traits in common with the Hindu caste system, which likewise assigns rank during feasting in communal settings, and which includes a very large element of redistribution of economic resources. Indeed, those who ranked highest on the curve of potlatch status owned not only goods in quantity but sacred names that could be distributed only during the communal feast; moveover, the highest-ranking regarded themselves as an exclusive group and had only limited contact with those lower in the system. Similar elements can be found in the caste system, wherein the caste name, sometimes irrelevant to the actual work performed, is understood to define an inescapable social status—indeed, the bestowal of magical and sacred names is an almost universal phenomenon throughout the Hindu religious system. Of course this does not mean that the potlatch gift-giving system is the same as the caste system. But if Mauss's original insight is true, then the socially sanctioned distribution of gifts and other tokens of relationship, fraught with historical and structural significance as these things are, may be an irreducible element in human culture. The potlatch and caste systems are perhaps instances of a general principle. The universal relevance of these systems is clear, even in the apparent particularity of this description:

> The potlatch is more than a legal phenomenon; it is one of those phenomena we propose to call "total." It is religious, mythological and shamanistic because the chiefs taking part are incarnations of gods and ancestors, whose names they bear, whose dances they dance and whose spirits possess them. It is economic; and one has to assess the value, importance, causes and effects of transactions which are enormous even when reckoned by European standards. The potlatch is also a phenomenon of social morphology; the reunion of tribes, clans, families and nations produces great excitement. People fraternize but at the same time remain strangers; community of interest and opposition are revealed constantly in a great whirl of business. Finally, from the jural point of view, we have already noted the contractual forms and what we might call the human element of the contract, and the legal status of the contracting parties—as clans or families or with reference to rank or marital condition; and to this we now add that the material objects of the contracts have a virtue of their own which causes them to be given and compels the making of counter-gifts.
>
> (Mauss, 1967, pp. 36–37)

McKim Marriot's perhaps unscientifically conceived theory that the idea of pollution in the caste system implies a sort of contamination within invisible particles of matter that adhere to the distinct varieties of exchangeable substances was more conservatively conceptualized by Mauss, whose idea is that pollution is a sort of inversion of gift giving, for no matter what the degree of pollution there is some sort of giving involved, even if limited to the exchange of services; Mauss asserted that things given were still perceived to have links with the persons giving them. This characteristic of gifts would seem to be inescapable even in modern perceptions of their ultimate value, whether or not they are overtly sanctified by religion (as, for example, the blessed rings exchanged in a Christian wedding ceremony). After all, the caste system would have no power if it were not understood that everyone in the society exists of necessity in an intrinsic relation with everyone else. What is the basis of that relationship if not the exchange of goods and services?

Gifts for the Gods. In light of the foregoing conceptual framework and its implied universal applicability to social systems, it may be said that the characteristics of ritual gift giving very often provide a central element in religious life. What transpires at the social level, in the continuing drama of human relations, is reflected in the structure of the relationship between the human and the divine. Much of the ritual in world religions symbolically connects hierarchy with the distribution of gifts, an act that is so powerful in the social relationship itself. Furthermore, in everyday life a type of gift giving is used to express the fervor of certain sacred seasons. In those periods, the gift more nearly approximates a prestation without expectation of return, though there is still the sense that the value of the gift translates itself into the realm of the metaphysical.

Hinduism. In the way that gifts were offered to the gods, Hinduism divides into two periods, characterized by the offerings presented in the so-called Vedic sacrifice and by the apparently endless variety of offerings of the later Hindu temple cult with its corollaries in household and sectarian worship.

The gifts given to the gods in the Vedic sacrifice had relation to the organically perceived universe, which was, as the Upaniṣad says, "all food" (*Taittirīya Upaniṣad* 2.2). It appeared to the Vedic sacrificer that if the universe were to have the strength to keep running, certain foods had to be immolated on the Vedic fire altar. The ritual as it has come down to us today appears in several different forms. Great public rituals are now less common than before, although still performed on occasion. The numerous Brahmanic rituals, including the Saṇdhyā Vandana (the daily service) and those connected with domestic life, and others oriented toward the welfare of departed spirits, involved very simple offerings of ghee (clarified butter), water, grains, coconuts, and the like. In the Śrāddha ceremony for the dead, *piṇḍa* (rice balls) were believed to assuage the spirits. The more elaborate ceremonies in ancient times included animal sacrifices and the pressing of the *soma*, a type of intoxicant that was notably given to the god Indra to enable him to perform vigorously in his battle with Vṛtra, a cosmic monster. Horses and humans were slain in the sacrifices. The deities of the Vedic period had negative as well as positive traits; as in the context of other ritual systems, the offerings to the higher powers could bring benefits in reciprocation or ward off dangerous interventions. These are sometimes called the *do ut des* ("I give that you may give") and *do ut abeas* ("I give that you may go away") aspects of a ritual transaction.

In the period following 600 BCE, in the aftermath of the growing anthropomorphization of the deity (perhaps stimulated by the art and ritual of Buddhism and Jainism), the characteristic offerings in worship were likened to the food and gifts given to very exalted human beings. Thus, it has often been mentioned that the style of Hindu temple worship is patterned after the court life of ancient India. The deity is considered to be the most respectable and powerful associate of humanity, a visitor from another realm who condescends to dwell for a time within images in temples, and who can be approached with gifts, services, the arts, music, and literature. In fact, gifts from the whole realm of human creativity can be offered to him. Two examples will be illustrative. It has been observed that among the later Kṛṣṇaite sects of North India, that of the Vallabha Sampradāy (founded by Vallabhācārya, 1479–1531), whose fervent love of the child Kṛṣṇa results in a daylong ceremonial offering of food, is the most lavish in "ritualistic materialism," if one may call it that. On special holidays, such as Kṛṣṇa's birthday, a mountain of food is prepared by the devotees and brought to the shrine to be offered to the image. Whenever offered, the food becomes *prasāda,* a kind of sacrament imbued with the power of the deity (because touched by him in a spiritual sense) and given back to the worshipers for their own consumption. Money offerings are given for the *prasāda,* which is, in effect, sold. The receipts are used to maintain the temple property, the priestly class, and the like. On the other hand, some gift-giving ceremonies are not at all lavish; a simple ceremony performed in the household for family members and guests or for a ladies' association that meets regularly by turn in members' homes for worship may entail the preparation of a simple meal or sweets, first offered to the deity and then given to the participants in the ceremony.

On holidays, it is common throughout India to provide new clothing for family members, servants, and other dependents during the feast of Dīvālī (October–November). It is the time when merchant castes close out their books and the goddess Lakṣmī is implored for an abundance of profit in the coming year. Sweets are exchanged between close friends and business associates. As for other special occasions, perhaps the most oppressive practice of gift giving in Hinduism, likewise representative of an aspect of caste or subcaste behavior, is the system of exchanges between a bride's family and a groom's family, sometimes observed for a number of years both before and after the marriage proper. The prevailing custom places the burden upon the bride's family, and the demands are so excessive that responsible parents in the poorer classes are frequently forced into penury to provide a daughter with a husband. It is not unheard of for a father to commit suicide so that his insurance money can be used to pay off the resulting indebtedness.

Buddhism. There is a type of gift giving that is explicitly meant to relieve the needs of the poor and the destitute. Almsgiving, as this is called, likewise has a role to play in the economy of ascetic life, wherein monks and nuns live under some kind of vow of poverty and must therefore be supported by the actively working laity. Since Buddhism is a religion in which the monastic community (in its maintenance and perfecting of life in the Dharma) is the main focus, it follows that almsgiving will be a general practice among Buddhists.

Apart from this necessary form of gift giving, Buddhism teaches generosity, self-giving, and even gift giving as illustrative of different aspects of the way toward *nirvāṇa.* For example, the Jātaka stories that began to circulate early in the Buddhist period but were not completed before the fifth century CE demonstrate how the Buddha exemplified certain great lessons of life prior to his final emancipation. In his previous lives he was a *bodhisattva* and appeared in various embodiments. One of the Jātaka tales tells how the Buddha-to-be practiced the virtues leading to emancipation while in the body of a hare. He taught the other animals—the jackal, the otter, and the monkey—to give alms, keep the precepts, and observe fast days. In observing their rule, the hare instructed his disciples on a certain fast day to give as alms to any stranger who might visit them food that they had obtained in the course of their usual ways. He himself vowed—since hares live on vegetation alone—to offer his own body as food to any meat-eating stranger who might approach him on the fast day. A heavenly being, made aware of the hare's vow, came to earth disguised as a brahman and tested each of the animals in turn as to the sincerity of its vow to offer hospitality after its own kind. The hare in due course threw himself into the fire to provide the brahman's supper; but the heavenly being prevented the hare's being burned and, to commemorate his magnanimity, drew a likeness of his face on the moon to be admired thenceforth by all on earth.

Gift giving is also mentioned in one of the most famous works of the Mahāyāna tradition, the *Saddharmapuṇḍarīka Sūtra.* Therein the *bodhisattva* illustrates in numerous ways his vocation as savior of humanity, suffering in the endlessly repetitive world of *saṃsāra.*

The *bodhisattva* offers to deluded humanity the gift of a paradisiacal afterlife as an inducement to abandon the gross physical world. The paradises of the *bodhisattva,* particularly that of Amida Buddha in the West, are filled with jeweled trees, sparkling, diamantine sands, and enchanting birds and flowers, together with fountains and the like. This paradise is meant to provide a mediating position between the world of *saṃsāra* and the absolute state of *nirvāṇa.* The *bodhisattva* vows to take all beings together into that emancipated state. The Buddhist parables of the burning house and the prodigal son are parallel tales illustrating the means by which one might, through gifts, relieve one's obsession with the material world in favor of the higher world. Thus, the children in the burning house are offered gifts to induce them to leave the house and come outside. The kindly, concerned father is the figure of the *bodhisattva,* likewise offering an escape from the material world into paradise. In the story of the prodigal son, deluded humanity is represented by a wealthy father who finds his lost son after many years; the father tries to change his son's attitude toward himself by giving him gifts and positions of responsibility. This can be understood to refer to the training in spiritual life through which, with the *bodhisattva*'s help, the aspirant is brought into a state of awareness regarding the true nature of the world and the need for emancipation from it. Works in the Pali canon, such as the *Dakkhiṇāvibhaṅga Sutta* and the *Sigalovada Sutta,* give precise instructions for the giving of gifts to monks and the giving of gifts between the laity and in connection with the Buddhist holidays.

Chinese religion. Reading the colorful novel *The Golden Lotus,* which reflects life in the twelfth century, one gathers that in that period in China the well-positioned gift was the absolute essential for the improvement of one's social and economic position, for gaining preference at the court of the emperor, or for placating judges in the courts of law (see Egerton, 1972). Indeed, the novel affords a vivid object lesson on the ways in which bribes not only can move one up the ladder but also, as the companions of other vices, can bring one to one's doom, as is the case with the novel's hero, Ch'ing Hsi-men. It has sometimes been said of the Confucian doctrine that it not only attempted to inculcate a reasonable morality on the basis of equity between human beings, as expressed in the so-called Silver Rule ("Do not do unto others what you would not have them do unto you") but also came to terms with what was perceived to be the natural inequality between persons. Giving and receiving gifts within the hierarchical Chinese society was an inevitable aspect of rank differentiation. Those highest in rank received the most expensive and most numerous gifts. Analogously, the ceremonial life of the public cult involved the emperor's presenting gifts at the altar of Heaven within the so-called Forbidden City in Peking, both at the winter solstice and at other times. Precious stones and costly cloth were among the offerings. Lower-ranking officials throughout the empire offered their respective gifts to the gods, for example to the city god. This activity was consonant with the custom of making offerings at the shrines of the family ancestors. Gifts of incense and fruits were regularly presented before the ancestral tablets.

The rites offered to the spirits of Confucius and other sages included sacrifices of pigs and oxen; the great deities of the Taoist pantheon were given wine, cakes, and meat offerings. Indeed, it is not too farfetched to see the development of the Chinese cuisine in part as an outgrowth of the ritual life. Feasts were regularly a part of the offerings made by individuals in the Taoist and Buddhist temples. In the latter case, vegetarianism required the development of a special cuisine so that the proper foods could be offered to monks and others under similar vows.

Rituals for the departed often included the burning of effigies of material objects, such as imitation money or a tomb made of paper. In contemporary rituals even such modern accoutrements of life as refrigerators and cars may be constructed of paper and burned in the temple furnace with appropriate reverence under the axiom that the thing itself is less important than the thought behind it.

As already noted in the discussion of the potlatch and the Hindu caste system, sociological theory lends credence to the applicability of the potlatch as an analogue to many systems of social organization. Marcel Granet, in his *Danse et legendes de la Chine ancienne* (Paris, 1926), proposed a relationship between the potlatch and the prefeudal (early or pre-Shang) system of China, which was influential in the formation of Confucius's ideas of the ideal social order. This position has been recently reexamined in the work of Eugene Cooper, who argues convincingly for its validity, thus challenging recent anthropological theory that attempts to delimit the potlatch to Northwest Coast Amerindians (see "The Potlatch in Ancient China," *History of Religions* 22, 1982, pp. 103–128).

Judaism. Diaspora Judaism's theory of almsgiving and charity was built on a thoroughgoing moral system. The record of sacrifices in the Hebrew scriptures—offerings given to God according to the seasons and particular festivals and the day-to-day demands of ritual—has been preserved by some Jews in synagogue worship through recitations from *Exodus, Leviticus,* and *Numbers* in the Orthodox preliminary morning service contained in *Ha-siddur ha-shalem* (see Birnbaum, 1949). With the destruction in the Temple in 70 CE it was no longer possible to maintain the offerings in the prescribed setting; the Jewish community's concern with purity of food, however, dictated that there be a class of specialists in the ritual slaughter of animals (for food purposes if not for offering to God). With the establishment of the state of Israel, various groups, both Jewish and Christian (although there is considerable disagreement on the issue in Judaism), are making preparations for the rebuilding of the Temple in Jerusalem and for the reestablishment of ritual sacrifices. Of course other offerings besides animals were made as well; these included grain, oil, incense, and wine, and some vestige of them remains both in Sabbath observances in the Jewish home and in the Passover meal.

Of the popular holidays, two in particular are connected with gift giving within the family or among friends. The better known perhaps is the custom at Ḥanukkah of giving gifts (money and other things) to children on each of the eight nights of the festival. Much is made in contemporary Jewish discussion of the need to maintain some kind of distinction between this Jewish observance and the Christmas festival of Christians, particularly since both occur at approximately the same time of year. The playing of games of chance, which of course relate to the potential of gift giving for the redistribution of valuables within the social community, is also a part of the Ḥanukkah observance.

Purim, which commemorates the rescue of the Jews from the evil minister Hamman in the court of the king of Persia, is an occasion for exchanging food. The legend itself is told in the *Book of Esther,* which is read in the synagogue on the holiday in a mood of revelry compared sometimes to that of Carnival in Latin Christian countries. *Shalaḥ Manos* is the custom of sending gifts of food from house to house on Purim; the type of food given is food that can be eaten and drunk on the same day.

Christianity. Much as does the history of Buddhism, the history of Christianity reveals the development of a very elaborate system of gift giving for the maintenance of the institutions of the church, the clergy, and the monastic communities. [*See* Tithes.] During the earliest centuries of the church, persecutions were a constant threat, and the Christian community had to develop its own system of finances, since its survival was outside the concern of the state. From the time of Constantine (early fourth century) onward, the church received state recognition and was able to capitalize on its status to attract enormous endowments; with the advent of Muslim rulers in many Eastern Christian lands, however, the church was once again reduced to tense relations with the state. It survived in part through the generosity of the laity, and in part through official support, for even in Islamic lands the church was to a certain extent and at certain times patronized by the rulers. Gifts of lands and other wealth were given to the Church of the East (sometimes called Nestorian), which before the thirteenth century had spread into China and India. The Christian church of Kerala in South India received until modern times regular patronage from the Hindu rulers of the region. The right of the Christian community (and other religious communities) to receive gifts unencumbered by excessive government interference is an issue in the modern world. Specific exemptions from taxes and benefits for giving gifts are written into the laws to encourage the support of religious institutions.

The ritual life of Christianity is permeated with the idea of the gift and gift giving. The elements of the Eucharist, the bread and the wine, which are widely called the Holy Gifts, are offered to God as a "sacrifice," and according to some theologies they become the body and blood of Christ in an unbloody reproduction of the crucifixion. Other theologies describe these gifts as being received by God and sanctified to become the body and blood of Christ through the power of the Holy Spirit. The custom whereby the laity prepare and offer the bread and the wine of the Eucharist has been revived in some Christian bodies. In addition to the elements of the Eucharist and the paraphernalia that accompany it, such as chalices, monstrances, tabernacles of precious metal, and the like, the Christian churches have received uncountable offerings in the form not only of money but also of vestments, paintings, architecture, sculpture—gifts representing the full range of human creativity. These gifts still constitute a principal part of the heritage of Western civilization. Although sometimes limited by theological constraints, the Protestant churches have likewise encouraged gift giving through the arts. With the modern secularization of public life, however, the impetus to artistic creativity in connection with the religious gift-giving impulse seems to be under some constraint.

Caught somewhere between the sacred and the profane is the gift-giving extravaganza carried out, now virtually around the world, in the name of the infant Christ, who was born in Bethlehem and whose birth is widely celebrated on 25 December. The precedent for exchanging gifts on the Christian festival is based on the visit of the Wise Men from the East to the Christ Child, even though their time of arrival at Bethlehem is commemorated on 6 January. The date of Christmas was chosen, it is said, in order to attract the interest of the non-Christian masses of Europe who celebrated the winter solstice. [*See* Christmas.]

Islam. At least from what one gathers in reading the *ḥadīth*s, the Islamic idea of gift giving is but an extension of the underlying concept of alms, expressed in the two Arabic words *zakāt* and *ṣadaqah.* Perhaps because there are no sacrifices or sacraments in the usual religious sense in Islam—in other words, no way of transmuting a material object through a religious ceremony from the merely physical plane to a "new mode of being"—all events in Islamic religious practice tend to take on a moral overtone; righteousness is the primary goal of religious life. In general it appears that goodness in Islam is thought of as consequent upon obedience to the command of God to act in certain ways. Generosity may be expressed in a great number of actions that reflect the moral earnestness of a discipline enjoined by a higher power. The myriad customs and observances of Islamic law and tradition are further extensions of the original act of submission, which is a call to acknowledge faith in the one God. The prophet Muḥammad represents the ultimate degree of perfection in answering the call. Meditation on the minutiae of his life remains the source of the moral earnestness that is the characteristic of Islamic ethics.

In the realm of gift giving, the so-called poor tax, or *zakāt,* can be understood as a practical example for all types of giving. [*See* Zakāt.] Both in the Qur'ān and in the traditions of Muḥammad, the believer is constantly reminded that his days on earth are but a brief interlude, beyond which lies the state of bliss in Paradise, provided he has merited a reward in the afterlife. In the prostration of prayer, the believer is reminded that he is gazing into the pit of the grave where the two angels of Paradise or Hell will come to direct the soul to its intermediate state prior to the Last Judgment. The poor tax, especially as it impinges on human possessions, reflects this ascetic attitude toward the term of human existence; it is meant to make the Muslim believer deliver from his possessions a fixed amount annually—at the feasts of the end of Ramaḍān and during the *ḥajj*—for the relief of certain classes in Muslim society.

In the larger sense of sharing what one possesses, the term *ṣadaqah* is used, for example, in the *Mishkāt al-maṣābīḥ* (see Robson, 1963–1965). In book 12, *On Business Transactions,* several chapters are devoted to gifts. The Prophet encouraged the setting aside in "life tenancy" of lands whose produce would maintain certain charitable activities such as the provision of food for travelers. There are several references to gift giving within the family context in order to assure evenhandedness.

The problem of reciprocity in gift giving is addressed also in chapter 17, part 2, of the *Mishkāt al-maṣābīḥ,* wherein the Prophet is asked whether one must return equally for any gift received. His advice is to return equally if possible; if it is not possible, then an expression of sincere thanks and prayerful intercession will suffice. In general the Prophet encouraged gift giving between neighbors and among members of the community in order to stimulate mutual good feelings. Perfume was one of the Prophet's favorite gifts in this connection. Even today, when Muslims gather for prayer in the mosque, it is counted a righteous act for them to offer perfume from a small container to their fellow worshipers. To be clean and sweet-smelling is a gift to those with whom one associates, particularly at the time of prayer. It is also considered an act of gift giving to offer a smile rather than a dour look to a fellow human.

[*See also* Almsgiving; Hospitality; *and* Tithes. *For divine gift giving, see* Grace.]

BIBLIOGRAPHY

Birnbaum, Philip, ed. and trans. *Ha-Siddur ha-Shalem.* New York, 1949.

Burtt, Edwin A., ed. *The Teachings of the Compassionate Buddha.* New York, 1955.

Dumont, Louis. *Homo Hierarchicus.* Translated by Mark Sainsbury. Chicago, 1970.

Egerton, Clement, trans. *The Golden Lotus (Chin p'ing mei).* 4 vols. London, 1972.

Ferdon, Edwin N. *Early Tahiti as the Explorers Saw It, 1767–1797.* Tucson, 1981.

Kolenda, Pauline. *Caste in Contemporary India: Beyond Organic Solidarity.* Menlo Park, Calif., 1978.

Krause, Aurel. *The Tlingit Indians.* Seattle, 1956.

Mauss, Marcel. *The Gift: Forms and Functions of Exchange in Archaic Societies.* Translated by Ian Cunnison. Glencoe, Ill., 1954; reprint, New York, 1967.

Mayer, Adrian C. *Caste and Kinship in Central India.* Berkeley, 1960.

Robson, James, trans. *Mishkāt al-maṣābīḥ.* 4 vols. Lahore, 1963–1965.

Rohner, Ronald P., and Evelyn C. Rohner. *The Kwakiutl.* New York, 1970.

Rosman, Abraham, and Paula G. Rubel. *Feasting with Mine Enemy: Rank and Exchange among Northwest Coast Societies.* New York, 1971.

Siegel, Richard, et al., eds. *The Jewish Catalog.* Philadelphia, 1973.

Stryk, Lucien, ed. *World of the Buddha.* Garden City, N.Y., 1968.

Wouk, Herman. *This Is My God.* Garden City, N.Y., 1959.

Wu Ch'eng-en. *Monkey Subdues the White-Bone Demon.* Translated by Wang Hsing-pei. Peking, 1973.

CHARLES S. J. WHITE

GILGAMESH (c. 2650 BCE), ruler of the Sumerian city-state Uruk (biblical Erech). The evidence, though rather meager and indirect, supports the historical existence of Gilgamesh and places him in a period of intense intercity rivalries, lending credibility to the later tradition that made him the builder of the walls of Uruk and a rival of the ruler of Kish, a city to the north. His achievements, whatever they were, were such that he became the object of cult and the subject of legend.

Gilgamesh the God. About a century after his death, Gilgamesh appeared in a list of gods. He was probably first worshiped as a still-powerful priest-king, even in death, and as an enduring source of fertility. By about 2400 BCE, funerary offerings were being made to dead priests at a place called "the riverbank of Gilgamesh." By the third dynasty of Ur (c. 2100–2000 BCE), whose rulers legitimated themselves by making Gilgamesh and his father, Lugalbanda, another divinized ruler of Uruk, their ancestors, Gilgamesh was given a cult, declared brother and friend of the ruling kings, and called "king of the underworld," where he also served as judge. He was identified with Dumuzi (Tammuz), the annually dying and rising god, with Ningishzida, a tree god, or even, in the Assyro-Babylonian tradition, with the supreme god of the underworld, Nergal. The statue or figurines of Gilgamesh were present and invoked at burial rites, and in the sere month of Ab (July–August) they were associated with the cult of the spirits of the dead and with incantations to expel witches to the underworld.

Gilgamesh the Hero. The exploits of Gilgamesh undoubtedly lived on in the Sumerian oral tradition, especially at the court of Uruk. When the tradition was first committed to writing is not known. Five, perhaps six, compositions probably go back to the third dynasty of Ur. (1) *Gilgamesh and Huwawa* (c. 190–240 lines, three versions) tells how Gilgamesh, disturbed at the sight of dead bodies and determined to achieve the immortality of fame, sets out, together with his servant Enkidu and other retainers, to fight the monster Huwawa. The versions, reflecting oral variants, differ on how Huwawa was tricked and killed and what followed. (2) *Gilgamesh and the Bull of Heaven* (very poorly preserved) tells how the goddess Inanna, for reasons that are unclear, sent the Bull against Gilgamesh and Enkidu, who then probably slew it. (3) In *Gilgamesh, Enkidu, and the Netherworld* (c. 330 lines) Inanna gives Gilgamesh as a reward for certain services two objects of still-uncertain nature. These somehow become instruments for the oppression of Uruk and then fall into the underworld. Enkidu goes to fetch them back, but since he ignores Gilgamesh's warnings (not to call attention to himself or to distinguish himself as an alien) he must remain there. Eventually he appears before his master and answers his questions about the fate of various categories of underworld inhabitants. (4) The *Death of Gilgamesh* (very poorly preserved, c. 450 lines) seems to be concerned, in part at least, with Gilgamesh's resentment that he must die. (5) There is another fragment of what appears to belong to a distinct composition. (6) *Gilgamesh and Agga* (115 lines) tells of the conflict with the ruler of Kish.

Except for the last, the Sumerian works contain themes and tales that reappear in some form in the later Babylonian versions. However, comparison shows that with the exception of tablet 12, a late appendage, the Babylonian is never a translation of the Sumerian, and its dependence on the Sumerian, if any, is only as a highly selective and creative adaptation and transformation.

The Babylonian version seems to have been first put to writing in the Old Babylonian period (c. 1900–1600 BCE). Fragmentary though the evidence is, this version is probably all part of single composition, an epic of at least 1,000 lines, perhaps much longer. It has the unity of a central theme, man's mortality, and this limitation, as in the Sumerian tradition, Gilgamesh would at first transcend through the immortality of fame. But then—an innovation—Enkidu dies. Gilgamesh reacts by rejecting the conventional heroic ideal of the past, and he goes in search of the transcendence that belongs to the immortality reserved to the gods.

The Babylonian version also transforms the figure of Enkidu. In the Sumerian tradition he is the conventional courtier, the servant of his master, and so he is called. But in the Babylonian version he becomes a very close friend ("my friend whom I love so mightily"), perhaps a lover: note Gilgamesh's erotic dreams about Enkidu and the latter's anger at Gilgamesh's going—the interpretation is disputed—either to his (sacred?) bride or to the exercise of *ius primae noctis.* This intimacy turns Enkidu's death into a tragedy and makes its shattering effect on Gilgamesh plausible.

Enkidu is also transformed from someone physically undistinguished into a hairy savage born on the steppe and brought up with wild animals. The latter figure may ultimately reflect the myth and representations, going as far back as the early third millennium, of the Bull-man who fights the Naked Hero. But as described it belongs to the "hard primitivism" (Erwin Panofsky's term) found elsewhere in Sumerian and Babylonian (as well as classical) sources and their conception of primordial man as bestial. It introduces into the epic a sharp nature-culture contrast, and the epic, at least in its standard form, seems a muted celebration of the superiority of the latter, as of man over the animals. Enkidu's last words are a blessing of those responsible for his humanization. Since primordial man was also immortal man, Enkidu's grateful acceptance is in context most striking and, in its anticipation of the spirit of Gilgamesh's last words, is paradigmatic (see below).

Probably to be ascribed to the Old Babylonian version is the structuring of the narrative around three periods of six or seven days and seven nights, with each of which are associated a profound transformation of character and corresponding "rites of passage," especially washing and dressing: (1) Enkidu and the harlot make love *to* Enkidu the man = eating and drinking as a man, washing and anointing himself, putting on clothes; (2) Gilgamesh mourns over the body of Enkidu *to* Gilgamesh the anti-hero, anti-man, would-be god = the unwashed mourner, clothed in animal skins, outside the human community; (3) Gilgamesh sleeps before Utanapishtim *to* Gilgamesh resigned and accepting his humanity = washed and clothed as a man once more as he prepares to rejoin the human community.

The Old Babylonian version should perhaps also be read as a reflection of the ideological developments of the period that to some extent demythologized kingship and rejected the divinity that kings had been claiming for five centuries or so. Against this background the epic, beginning as it does with a hymn to Gilgamesh as the greatest of all kings, might be seen as an affirmation of the essential difference between gods and human kings, for the latter, even the greatest of them, even the son of a goddess, must perform the very human and undivine act of dying.

Except for one fragment, the evidence for the epic in the late second millennium comes from the periphery, where we also find Hittite and Hurrian, as well as Babylonian, versions. Unpublished tablets from ancient Emar in Syria indicate that the epic, with the probable exception of tablet 12, had assumed more or less final form by the thirteenth century BCE. The standard, originally eleven-tablet version, of which there continued to be oral and local variations, expanded the earlier tradition into a work of over three thousand lines. It is known mainly from the Nineveh recension on tablets of the seventh century BCE.

Most characteristic of the standard version is its strong didacticism. This is most evident in the new introduction and conclusion added to the earlier tradition. In contrast to the hymn with which the epic once began—a celebration of Gilgamesh's physical power and noble origins—the new lines emphasize not his strength but the range of his experience and knowledge, and the sufferings they cost him. By a tissue of allusions to a genre of pseudo-autobiography in which kings made lessons of their lives and recorded them for posterity, these lines also imply that Gilgamesh did the same. Based on and authenticated by this source, the epic, now addressing a reader ("thou") and intending to instruct him, becomes a part of wisdom literature.

Another addition, it is commonly agreed, is the story of the flood, which demonstrably draws on another myth. This "knowledge of days before the flood" does more than satisfy our curiosity about the remotest past. It also vividly illustrates a prominent theme of wisdom literature: the inscrutability of the gods. As told to Gilgamesh—but not in the source—the flood has no motivation; it happens simply because the gods want it to happen. Similarly, at the end of the story, equally inscrutable is the gentle grace of the high god Enlil's decision to grant immortality to the flood's survivors. "Who can understand the mind of the gods in heaven?" says the Babylonian sage.

The third addition, though this is less commonly agreed, is the story of the plant of life. Like the flood story, it reveals a secret of the gods. It also illustrates a wisdom theme complementing that of divine transcendence: human frailty.

Gilgamesh concludes that he should have turned back and left the boat at the shores of the waters of death. But this is not his final word. In urging the boatman to ascend the walls of Uruk, he brings us back to where we began and to a sense of human achievement. Man must die, but he can also build. This new understanding and appreciation of man the maker, so painfully acquired, explains why Gilgamesh returns to Uruk "weary but at peace." Acceptance of human limitations, insistence on human values—this is the teaching of the life of Gilgamesh.

Tablet 12, if intended to be an integral part of the epic, reaffirms, not very gracefully, the *lacrimae rerum*, the "tears of things." Its plangent litany of grief at the sad end of human life seems inappropriate and even churlish after tablets 1–11 and their affirmation of human values supporting a quiet resignation.

BIBLIOGRAPHY

The standard but badly outdated edition of the Babylonian Gilgamesh epic remains that of R. Campbell Thompson, *The Epic of Gilgamesh* (Oxford, 1930). More recent translations take account of a fuller and better-understood text. Most up-to-date is the German translation of Albert Schott, *Das Gilgamesch-Epos*, as revised by Wolfram von Soden (Stuttgart, 1966); and in English, the translations of E. A. Speiser and A. K. Grayson in *Ancient Near Eastern Texts relating to the Old Testament*, 3d ed., edited by J. B. Pritchard (Princeton, 1969), pp. 72–99, 503–507. The very important discovery that restores virtually the entire introduction was published by D. J. Wiseman, "A Gilgamesh Epic Fragment from Nimrud," *Iraq* 37 (1975): 157–163. Samuel Noah Kramer offers an ample description of the Sumerian tradition in *History Begins at Sumer*, 3d ed. (Philadelphia, 1981), pp. 30–35, 168–198, and some translations in Pritchard's *Ancient Near Eastern Texts,* pp. 44–52. Jeffrey H. Tigay has made a thorough investigation of the epic's development in *The Evolution of the Gilgamesh Epic* (Philadelphia, 1982). *Gilgameš et sa légende,* edited by Paul Garelli (Paris, 1960), a collection of articles in English, French, and German, is especially valuable for its very extensive bibliography, pp. 7–27. *Das Gilgamesch-Epos,* edited by Karl Oberhuber (Darmstadt, 1977), surveys the history of interpretation and presents a representative selection of articles from 1903 to 1964. Other important essays of interpretation, often quite different from the one outlined above, are: Mircea Eliade's *A History of Religious Ideas,* vol. 1, *From the Stone Age to the Eleusinian Mysteries* (Chicago, 1978), pp. 77–80; Thorkild Jacobsen's *The Treasures of Darkness: A History of Mesopotamian Religion* (New Haven, 1976), pp. 195–219; and Geoffrey Stephen Kirk's *Myth: Its Meaning and Functions in Ancient and Other Cultures* (Berkeley, 1970), pp. 132–152.

WILLIAM L. MORAN

GILSON, ÉTIENNE (1884–1978), historian of medieval philosophy, educator, lecturer, and author. Born in Paris, Gilson was a Christian believer and lifelong promoter and defender of the intellectual life of the church. He treasured his Roman Catholic schooling but discovered his love for philosophy in a secular *lycée* and at the positivistic Sorbonne. Convinced that before doing philosophy one had to learn what philosophy already existed, he entered upon a career of exact historical study, following the principled method that would mark all his work: to study the original writings of the great thinkers, to understand their thought within its historical context, and to present their teaching objectively.

Under competent Cartesian scholars Gilson concentrated on the modern classics but did his research on the medieval sources used by Descartes. While teaching in the *lycées* (1907–1913), he completed his dissertation on the scholastic texts utilized by Descartes for his doctrine of freedom. Following his doctorate (1913) he was appointed to teach at Lille, then (after World War I) at Strasbourg, and from 1921 on at Paris. In these national universities Gilson introduced regular study of the medieval theologian-philosophers. His courses on Thomas Aquinas, Augustine of Hippo, and Bonaventure were published and became standard tools for medieval scholars. Studies of other medieval authors provided the substance of his teaching for fifty years in Paris and at Toronto (in the research institute he founded there in 1929) and of his masterwork, *History of Christian Philosophy in the Middle Ages* (1955).

What is more significant, these studies led him to hold firmly to two controversial positions:

1. A distinct Christian philosophy is a matter of historical fact: it is the speculations of theologians about questions in principle accessible to natural reason.
2. The Thomism of Thomas Aquinas, rather than that of his interpreters, is the unique instance of a Christian philosophy that best mirrors Catholic thinking and that grounds the truths achieved by all other Christian philosophies. Thomism is the philosophy of a theologian and is characterized both by its metaphysics of being, which holds that what is real and intelligible is so by virtue of its act of existing, and by its theses on the integrity of human intelligence and on the realism and evidentiality of knowledge.

Although these are controversial theses, Gilson was so sure of his own position that in more than forty books and countless articles he rarely engaged in argument about them.

Gilson the historian brought the thought of the Middle Ages to the attention of twentieth-century scholars. Gilson the philosopher sparked in his European and North American audiences an active engagement in philosophical and theological issues that had long been dormant. In 1949 the French philosopher Jacques Maritain, remarking on the apostolic quality of Gilson's career, asserted that his championship of Christian intellectual issues in France had lent courage to and secured a hearing for the less hardy. There is little doubt that his promotion of the study of medieval thought and his outspoken defense of his convictions have been of lasting benefit not only to academic scholars but also to religious believers.

BIBLIOGRAPHY

Gilson's numerous works and the extensive writings about him are cited in Margaret McGrath's 1,210-item *Étienne Gilson: A Bibliography* (Toronto, 1982). Some major works by Gilson available in English are *The Spirit of Medieval Philosophy* (New York, 1936), an abridged version of *L'esprit de la philosophie médiévale,* 2 vols. (Paris, 1932); *The Christian Philosophy of St. Thomas Aquinas,* 5th ed. (New York, 1956); and *History of Christian Philosophy in the Middle Ages* (New York, 1955). The first of a number of appreciative symposia was that by Jacques Maritain and others, *Étienne Gilson: Philosophe de la Chrétienté* (Paris, 1949). The official biography was produced by a former student and colleague, Laurence K. Shook, *Étienne Gilson* (Toronto, 1984).

LINUS J. THRO, S.J.

GINĀN. A popularization of the Sanskrit word *jñan* ("contemplative knowledge"), the term *ginān* is used by the Nizārī Ismāʿīlīyah of Indo-Pakistan to refer to any one of the approximately eight hundred poems believed to have been composed by the Ismāʿīlī pirs or *dāʿīs* ("missionaries") between the thirteenth and early twentieth centuries. Composed in several Indian dialects and employing popular folk meters and indigenous musical modes, the *ginān*s vary considerably in length. The shortest ones consist of four to five verses, while longer ones, called *granth*s and distinguished by specific titles, may have well over a thousand verses. The *ginān*s are still sung and recited today as an integral part of religious ceremonies. Usually all members of the community who are present at such ceremonies participate in the recitation of the *ginān*s.

The *ginān*s, which often have several themes, may be classified into five major types according to the theme of greatest importance:

1. "Conversion" *ginān*s portraying Islam and specifically its Ismāʿīlī form as the completion of the Vaiṣṇava Hindu tradition, and also including accounts that give Ismāʿīlī dimensions to traditional figures of Hindu mythology as well as hagiographic accounts of the great Ismāʿīlī pirs (the *Das Avatar*, for example).
2. *Ginān*s dealing with a wide variety of eschatological and cosmological themes (such as *Brahmā Gāyatrī*).
3. Didactic *ginān*s imparting ethical and moral instruction for the conduct of worldly and religious life (such as *Moman Chetāmaṇī*).
4. *Ginān*s connected with mysticism, including guides for an individual's spiritual progress, literary expressions of the composers' mystical experiences, and petitions for spiritual union or vision (*Anaṅt Akhāḍo* and *Satveṇī*, for example).
5. *Ginān*s for recitation at certain religious rituals or at specific festivals such as the birthday of the Prophet or the Ismāʿīlī imam, Nawrūz (New Year), and so forth (*Nawrūznā din sohāmaṇā*, for example).

BIBLIOGRAPHY

Asani, Ali S. "The Ismāʿīlī *Ginān* Literature: Its Structure and Love Symbolism." In *Facets of Ismaili Studies.* Edited by Hermann Landolt. London, 1985.

Ivanov, Vladimir A. "Satpanth." In *Collectanea*, vol. 1, edited by Vladimir A. Ivanov, pp. 1–54. Leiden, 1948.

Nanji, Azim. *The Nizārī Ismāʿīlī Tradition in the Indo-Pakistan Subcontinent.* Delmar, N.Y., 1978.

ALI S. ASANI

GINZA. Among their many books, the gnostic Mandaeans of Iraq and Iran rank the voluminous *Ginza* ("treasure"), their "holy book," as the most important. It is studied by priests, and its presence is required at the performance of the major Mandaean rituals. In the seventh century of the common era, during the Islamic conquest, the Mandaeans assembled the *Ginza* in order to gain status as a "people of the book," allowed to resist conversion to Islam. The work, separated into *Right Ginza* and *Left Ginza*, contains a number of myths concerning the creation of the world and of human beings, descriptions of the human lot on earth, moral teachings, polemics against other faiths, and hymns. In Mandaeism generally, "right" and "left" are connected to the otherworldly and the earthly realms, respectively. However, in the case of the two parts of *Ginza*, the designations seem to contradict this pattern, for *Right Ginza* contains a great deal of cosmogonic and anthropogonic material, while the left part deals with the otherworldly fate of the soul.

Left Ginza, which has been called a "book of the dead," falls into three parts. *Left Ginza* 1.1–2 describe the death of Adam, who is reluctant to leave behind his body as well as his wife and children. Part 1.4 portrays the soul's journey through the purgatories *(matarata)* between earth and the Lightworld, the pristine upper world. The last two parts are composed of hymns for the soul rising to the Lightworld after the death of the body. The hymns of the twenty-eight sections of *Left Ginza* 2 concentrate on the complaints of the soul (here, *mana*, "vessel") in the earthly world. A helper is sent from the Lightworld to aid the soul. Some of the sixty-two *Left Ginza* 3 hymns are among the ritually used death-mass *(masiqta)* hymns, the oldest datable texts in Mandaeism (c. third century CE). Thus, these cultic texts testify to the antiquity of the *masiqta*, the "raising up" ceremony for the soul and the spirit at the death of the body.

In *Right Ginza*, helper figures command a central position. Two main envoys are Manda d-Hiia and Hibil, although a large tractate, *Right Ginza* 15, portrays several other messengers. In *Right Ginza* 5.1, Hibil descends to the underworld prior to the creation of the earth, in order to prevent an attack on the Lightworld by the powers of the underworld. He returns with Ruha, the spirit, the vital element necessary for human and earthly life. Extensive stories about the creation of the world and the human lot are found in *Right Ginza* 3 and 10. John the Baptist, the Mandaean prophet, expounds his teachings in *Right Ginza* 7. In view of the use of the Arabic form *Yaḥyā* for John in this text, it was probably written in the seventh century. Polemics against Judaism, Christianity, Islam, and other religions characterize *Right Ginza* 9.1, and moral instructions and warnings against surrender to evil powers recur in *Right*

Ginza 1, 2, 8, 13, 16, and 17. *Right Ginza* 18, written in the seventh century, is a Mandaean "history of the world" that ends in an apocalypse. This tractate closes *Right Ginza.*

Several European libraries possess *Ginza* manuscripts. The oldest, in the Bibliothèque Nationale in Paris, dates from 1560. In 1867, Heinrich Petermann published a largely useless edition and translation of *Ginza.* Mark Lidzbarski's 1925 version remains thus far the classical edition and translation. The new translation of *Ginza* undertaken by Kurt Rudolph will take into account the many discoveries of Mandaean texts and the advances made in studies on Mandaeism since Lidzbarski's time.

[*See also* Manda d-Hiia *and* Mandaean Religion.]

BIBLIOGRAPHY

The most reliable edition and translation of the Mandaean "holy book" was published in German under the editorship of Mark Lidzbarski as *Ginza: Der Schatz; oder, Das grosse Buch der Mandäer* (Göttingen, 1925; new edition in preparation by Kurt Rudolph). Representative *Ginza* material is included in *Gnosis: A Selection of Gnostic Texts,* vol. 2, *Coptic and Mandean Sources* (Oxford, 1974), edited by Werner Foerster. Kurt Rudolph's *Theogonie, Kosmogonie und Anthropogonie in den mandäischen Schriften* (Göttingen, 1965) offers a historical analysis of the traditions portrayed in the *Ginza* tractates. For his most recent view on *Ginza,* one may consult Rudolph's "Die mandäische Literatur," in *Zur Sprache und Literatur der Mandäer: Studia Mandaica I* (Berlin, 1976), edited by Rudolf Macuch.

JORUNN JACOBSEN BUCKLEY

GLASENAPP, HELMUTH VON (1891–1963),

German Indologist and historian of religions. Von Glasenapp's works, written from the 1930s to the early 1960s, have helped specialists and nonspecialists alike to understand more clearly the histories and fundamental teachings of the major religious systems of South Asia. A widely traveled, inquisitive, systematic, and astute scholar who approached his studies with the methods and intentions of *allgemeine Religionswissenschaft,* Otto Max Helmuth von Glasenapp stands as a notable figure in the development in Europe of both the sophisticated study of the religions of India and the comparative and historical study of religions as an academic discipline. His major books continue to be important reference works in these areas.

Born in Berlin, von Glasenapp enrolled at the University of Tübingen as a law student in 1910. During his first semester, however, he changed his field to Indology, having been influenced by Arthur Schopenhauer's philosophical works, many of which reflect South Asian religious and philosophical influences, and the more accurately informed and thorough studies of the religions of India by Hermann Oldenburg, Paul Deussen, and Richard Garbe (the last was his teacher at Tübingen). He stayed at Tübingen for four semesters before moving to Munich to study Sanskrit and Pali with Ernst Kuhn and Richard Simon. His interest in Jainism and in Indian philosophical systems was stimulated by Heinrich Lüders, Hermann Bechk, and Hermann Jacobi, all of whom he studied with in Berlin and Bonn from 1912 to 1914. He augmented these more specialized Indological pursuits with work in comparative studies under Karl Holl and Edvard Lehmann and in historical theology with Adolf von Harnack. He took his doctoral degree from Bonn in 1914 on the strength of his dissertation, *Die Lehre vom Karman in der Philosophie Jainas nach den Karmagranthas dargestellt* (published 1915), and received his habilitation at Bonn in 1918 after completing *Madhvas Philosophie des Vishnu-Glaubens* (1923).

In rapid succession over the next six years von Glasenapp published the important and influential *Der Hinduismus* (1922), *Der Jainismus* (1925), and *Brahma und Buddha: Die Religionen Indiens in ihrer geschichtlichen Entwickelung* (1926), revised and enlarged as *Die Religionen Indiens* (1943). In 1928 von Glasenapp was appointed professor of Indology at Königsberg, where he stayed until the end of World War II. Those years saw the publication of his *Der Buddhismus in Indien und im Fernen Osten* (1936) and *Buddhistische Mysterien* (1940), among other works.

In 1946 von Glasenapp returned to Tübingen to take up the professorship previously held by Richard Garbe, a position he held until 1959, during which time he published *Die Philosophie der Inder* (1949); *Die fünf grossen Religionen,* a work in two volumes (1951–1955), the first entitled *Die Religionen des ewigen Weltgesetzes* and the second *Islam und Christentum; Buddhismus und Gottesidee* (1954); *Kant und die Religionen des Ostens* (1954); and *Die Religionen der Menschheit, ihre Gegensätze und ihre Übereinstimmungen* (1954). He remained active after his retirement, bringing to print his *Glaube und Ritus der Hochreligionen in vergleichender Übersicht* (1960) and *Das Indienbild deutscher Denker* (1960). Helmuth von Glasenapp died in Tübingen on 25 June 1963, at the age of seventy-two.

BIBLIOGRAPHY

Readers interested in von Glasenapp's studies, travels, and personal observations on a variety of topics may fruitfully turn to his autobiography, *Meine Lebensreise: Menschen, Länder und Dinge, die ich sah* (Wiesbaden, 1964). A complete list of von Glasenapp's writings appears in Zoltán Károlyi's *Helmuth von Glasenapp: Bibliographie* (Wiesbaden, 1968), and a short list of his main works, many of which have not been mentioned in this article, can be found in Jacques Waardenburg's *Classical Approaches to the Study of Religion,* vol. 2, *Bibliography* (The Hague, 1974), pp. 89–91.

William K. Mahony

GLOSSOLALIA (from the Greek *glōssa,* "tongue, language," and *lalein,* "to talk") is a nonordinary speech behavior that is institutionalized as a religious ritual in numerous Western and non-Western religious communities. Its worldwide distribution attests to its antiquity, as does its mention in ancient documents. It is alluded to in the Hebrew scriptures and in the New Testament, as in the well-known narration in the *Acts of the Apostles* about events on the Day of the Pentecost. There are references to it in the Vedas (c. 1000 BCE), in Patañjali's *Yoga Sūtras,* and in Tibetan Tantric writings. Traces of it can be found in the litanies (*dhikr*s) of some orders of the Islamic Ṣūfī mystics.

Early ethnographic reports of glossolalia treated it with contempt, calling it "absurd nonsense, gibberish scarce worth recording," while Christian theologians tended to think of it as an exclusively Christian phenomenon, peculiar, according to some, to apostolic times. Modern-day forms of glossolalia were classed as abnormal psychological occurrences, possible evidence of schizophrenia or hysteria, because researchers observed it only in mental patients. The situation started to change when, as the result of interest renewed by the upsurge of the Pentecostal movement, field-workers began to examine glossolalia as a part of religious ritual. [*For further discussion, see* Pentecostal and Charismatic Christianity.]

In an article published in 1969, for instance, Virginia H. Hine reported on a comparative anthropological investigation of the Pentecostal movement in the United States, Mexico, Haiti, and Colombia, combining the use of questionnaires, interviews, and participant observation (*Journal for the Scientific Study of Religion* 8: 212–226). Her functional analysis showed glossolalia to be a component in the process of commitment to a movement, with implications for both personal and social change. This conclusion agrees in substance with numerous ethnographic reports from non-Western societies, where glossolalia often appears before or during the initiation of religious practitioners.

A few years before Hine's study, the pathology model of glossolalia was refuted by L. M. Vivier-van Etveldt (M.D. diss., University of the Witwatersrand, Johannesburg, 1960). He tested two carefully matched groups, one made up of members of a church that practiced glossolalia and the other made up of members of a traditional orthodox reformed church where such behavior was not accepted. A number of psychological tests, such as the Thematic Apperception Test (TAT) and the Personality Factor Test developed by James Cattell, indicated no inherent weakness in the neural organization of the glossolalists. On the contrary, they appeared to be less subject to suggestion and better adjusted than their conservative counterparts. By implication, this finding should put to rest the numerous allegations that shamans, who frequently utter glossolalia, are psychotic. The salient difference between a religious practitioner and a mental patient lies in the fact that the latter is unable to control his behavior ritually.

As to formal properties, glossolalia is a nonordinary speech event in the sense that it consists of nonsense syllables. In contrast with natural languages, its syllables and segments are not words; that is, they do not exhibit the attribution of meaning, and they are not strung together according to rules of grammar. For this reason, linguists reject the interpretation of glossolalia as xenoglossia (from the Greek *xenox,* "stranger," and *glōssa,* "language"), which claims that glossolalia is some foreign language that could be understood by another person who spoke it. William J. Samarin, a linguist working with English-speaking Christian groups, regards glossolalia instead as a type of pseudolanguage. In his 1972 article "Variation and Variables in Religious Glossolalia" (*Language in Society* 1: 121–130), he defines it as "unintelligible post-babbling speech that exhibits superficial phonological similarity to language without having consistent syntagmatic structure and that is not systematically derived from or related to known languages." He notes that glossolalia is repetitious and can be subdivided into macrosegments, which are comparable to sentences; microsegments, which are reminiscent of words; and sounds. There is also a pattern of stress and pitch. According to Samarin, speakers of English have an "English accent" in glossolalia; that is, their sounds are English speech sounds. He attributes these regularities to a particular style of discourse that practitioners assume by imitating certain preaching styles.

My own fieldwork and laboratory research have led me to somewhat different conclusions. As a psychological anthropologist and linguist I did participant observation in various English-, Spanish-, and Maya-speaking Pentecostal communities in the United States and Mexico as well as with the founder of a new religion in Japan. In addition, I compared tape recordings of non-Christian rituals from Africa, Borneo, Indonesia, and Japan. I found that when all features of glossolalia were taken into consideration—that is, its segmental structure (such as sounds, syllables, and phrases) and its suprasegmental elements (namely, rhythm, accent, and especially overall intonation)—they seemed cross-linguistically and cross-culturally identical. Laboratory tracings that used a level recorder, which registers changes in pressure density (in our case, intonation), confirmed these impressions at least in the case of intonation. This method is also suitable for distinguishing glossolalia from such other nonordinary speech events as sleep talking and talking during hypnotic regression (see my 1981 article "States of Consciousness: A Study of Soundtracks," *Journal of Mind and Behavior* 2: 209–219). The latter finding is important, because many ethnographic observers consider the behavior of which glossolalia is a part to be hypnotically induced, which in view of these results is in error.

Self-reporting by ethnographic consultants and observation of their behavior indicate the presence of a changed state of consciousness during glossolalia, ranging from minimal to quite intense. I therefore attribute the cross-cultural agreements in the features of glossolalia to these neurophysiological changes, collectively and popularly called trance, and I define glossolalia as a vocalization pattern, a speech automatism that is produced in the substratum of the trance and that reflects directly, in its segmental and suprasegmental structures, the neurophysiological processes present in this changed state of consciousness.

Put more simply, whatever takes place in the nervous system during a trance causes utterance to break down into phrases of equal length, provided we also include the pauses. That is, using a concept taken from music rather than linguistics, it causes the phrases to be divided into bars, each of which is accented on the first syllable, and it causes the bars to pulsate, to throb rhythmically in a sequence of consonant-vowel, consonant-vowel. And, I believe, the trance state is responsible for the haunting intonation of glossolalia; never varying, it rises to a peak at the end of the first third of the unit utterance and drops to a level much lower than that at the onset as it comes to a close.

The sounds of glossolalia do not necessarily reflect the inventory of the speaker's language, for they frequently include phones not found in a speaker's native tongue. English speakers, for instance, often use /a/ as a high central, unrounded vowel, the so-called continental sound, which does not occur in English, and Spanish speakers in Mexico may use /ö/ (the long, closed *o*, as in the German word *Öse*), which is not a Spanish vowel. In addition, shrieks as well as barking, whistling, grunting, growling, and many other so-called animal sounds have also been reported.

Although glossolalia is often described as a spontaneous outburst, it is, actually, a learned behavior, learned either unawarely or, sometimes, consciously. The fact that individual congregations with a stable membership tend to develop their own characteristic glossolalia "dialect" indicates that learning has occurred, and the many traditional forms in which glossolalia appears in non-Western societies are obviously taught. These include such conventions as speaking individually, in groups, and in the form of a dialogue, often heard in the Japanese new religions, and singing.

As the foregoing characterization of glossolalia indicates, we probably need to view trance as the primary behavior, on which vocalization is superimposed and into which the practitioner switches with the help of a large variety of stimuli, such as singing, dancing, clapping, and drumming. Present research suggests that this trance—a frenzy, rapture, ecstasy, or, in more neutral terms, an altered state of consciousness—involves a single, generalized neurophysiological process. Barbara W. Lex, a medical anthropologist, holds that what is involved is an alternation between two different arousals of the nervous system. This tunes the nervous system and releases tension, thus accounting for the beneficial effects of the experience. Observations of Christian and non-Western religious communities alike indicate that apparently anybody with a normal physical endowment is able to initiate this process and to switch into a trance. Differences in personality, treated extensively by early researchers, apparently do not enter into the picture.

An association between trance and glossolalia is now accepted by many researchers as a correct assumption (see, for instance, Williams, 1981). Thus, if we recognize trance as the primary, generating process of the features of glossolalia, we could then conclude that a vocalization consisting only of nonsense syllables, no matter how varied, may in fact represent a cultural convention and that other types of speech could also be uttered while the practitioner is in a trance, with the trance, of course, still expressing itself in some form or other. Field observation shows that this is indeed true. Nonsense syllables may occur in combination with words from the vernacular and/or a foreign language—such as "Come, Jesus" and "Hallelujah," which are often heard from American Pentecostals—without disturbing the accent pattern or intonation of the utterance, its trance features. In the circumpolar region, many shamans, among the Inuit (Eskimo), the Saami (Lapps), Chukchi, the Khanty (Ostiaks), the Yakuts, and the Evenki, use in their religious rituals secret languages that consist of a mixture of nonsense syllables and the vernacular. Just like a natural language, these secret trance dialects are taught by the master shamans to their neophytes.

From Africa, we have reports of a secret religious

trance language used exclusively by women. Bakweri women living on the slopes of Mount Cameroon speak a "mermaid language" in ritual context, which is taught to adolescent girls when they are ready for initiation. A girl's readiness is indicated by her "fainting," that is, experiencing a trance, and by her ability, while in this altered state of consciousness, to understand some of the mermaid language as it is spoken to her by a mature woman. No details of this language are known outside the tribe, for the male ethnographer was barred from learning it. (See Edwin Ardener, "Belief and the Problem of Women," in *The Interpretation of Ritual*, edited by J. S. La Fontaine, London, 1972, pp. 135–201.) It is probably a mixed form, for he mentions that scraps of the mermaid language are common currency even among Christian, educated, urban Bakweri women. This suggests that these "scraps" may have turned into words or that they were not originally nonsense syllables but had specific, assigned meanings.

When speaking in a trance, a practitioner may use no nonsense syllables at all, employing instead only the vernacular. If the principal pronouncement is in nonsense syllables, however, as, for instance, among Christians speaking in tongues or among the nomadic, reindeer-hunting Chukchi of Siberia, an "interpretation" may be provided. Such interpretations exhibit a distinct, trance-based rhythm and an intonation whose exactness cannot be reproduced in the ordinary state of consciousness. This is the same phenomenon exhibited in the many forms of "inspired," prophetic speeches, heard around the world, in which a scanning rhythm imparts a poetic quality to the utterance. In such speeches words are sometimes truncated, and rules of grammar violated, overridden by the exigencies of the trance. Even communicative intent may have to be altered. Thus the demons who spoke through the trance of a German university student, Anneliese Michel, could ask no questions because in spoken German the tone of an interrogative must rise at the end, while all trance utterances have a pronounced drop. (See my book about this case, *The Exorcism of Anneliese Michel*, New York, 1981.)

The case of Anneliese Michel brings up the question of what kinds of religious experience are commonly expressed by glossolalia. In her case, the experience was that of possession, and glossolalia was the voice, the "language," of the demons that she reported were possessing her. Possession is one of the most frequent ritual occasions for the use of glossolalia. In possession, an entity from the sacred dimension of reality is experienced as penetrating the respective person. In Christian contexts, the entity is most usually the Holy Spirit, and glossolalia is then felt to be its language. The Holy Spirit is experienced as power, not as personality, but other spirits—for instance, those of the dead of the Trobriand Islanders, ancestral spirits in Africa, and various spirits in Haitian Voodoo—have pronounced personality traits that are expressed in glossolalia. Western observers of possession may speak of role playing, but the experience is more that of being in the presence of a discrete being. The voice of the possessing being differs from that of the possessed practitioner. Anneliese Michel's demons spoke with a deep, raspy, male voice, and each one—there were six all told—exhibited distinct characteristics; Judas was brutal, for instance, and Nero effeminate. In Voodoo, female mediums are often possessed by male *lwa* (spirits), in which case a similar change in voice and, of course, in comportment takes place. In Umbanda, an Afro-Brazilian healing cult, possession by the child spirit will bring about an equally dramatic voice modification. Siberian shamans may be possessed by helpers in the form of animal spirits, and their speech then consists of animal voices, or "animal language." A similar change in language takes place when the shaman turns into an animal, which is a different experience, however.

According to a generally held belief, illness will result if a noxious being of the sacred dimension of reality possesses a person. Therefore, the harmful entity needs to be expelled, or exorcised. The method by which this is done depends on the tradition prevailing in the religious community in question. The ritual specialist carrying out the exorcism may merely recite a required formula while remaining in the ordinary state of consciousness—as was done for Anneliese Michel by a Catholic priest who spoke the exorcistic prayers from the *Rituale romanum*—or he may enter a trance and utter glossolalia, usually a mixed version, which is thought to influence the actions of demons. This happens in Tantric exorcistic rituals in Tibet, for instance, and during healing sessions among Buddhists of northern Thailand.

Communication by glossolalia is instituted not only with unfriendly beings, of course. On a tape recording made in Borneo a female healer can be heard calling her helping spirit. In the *zār* cult of Ethiopia, the shamans talk to the *zār*s (spirits) in a "secret language." The shamans of the Semai of Malaysia use glossolalia to invite the "nephews of the gods" to a feast, and the Yąnomamö Indians of Amazonia chant while in trance to their *hekura* demons, calling them to come live in their chests.

Quite generally, glossolalia cannot be considered a symbol. Rather, it is a medium of communication that directly informs both the participants and the onlookers of a ritual about the presence of and contact with the powers or the beings of the sacred dimension of reality—about the Holy Spirit who is baptizing a convert, perhaps, or about the appearance of any one of the multitude of entities that inhabit sacred realms.

[*For discussion in a broader context about various forms of related phenomena, see* Spirit Possession; Frenzy; *and* Enthusiasm. *For treatment of other kinds of religious language, see* Language, *article on* Sacred Language, *and* Chanting.]

BIBLIOGRAPHY

Three books came out simultaneously in 1972, each one discussing glossolalia from a different angle. My own work, *Speaking in Tongues: A Cross-Cultural Study of Glossolalia* (Chicago, 1972), provides a linguistic analysis of glossolalia and a descriptive study of the entire behavior; John P. Kildahl, in *The Psychology of Speaking in Tongues* (New York, 1972), takes up the relationship between personality variables and the practice of glossolalia; and William J. Samarin, in *Tongues of Men and Angels: The Religious Language of Pentecostalism* (New York, 1972), seeks to answer the question of why people speak in tongues by placing the behavior in social context. A comprehensive review of the research into glossolalia ten years later, including references to non-Western material, can be found in Cyril G. Williams's *Tongues of the Spirit: A Study of Pentecostal Glossolalia and Related Phenomena* (Cardiff, 1981). An anthology edited by Irving I. Zaretzky and Mark P. Leone, *Religious Movements in Contemporary America* (Princeton, 1974), gives a panoramic view of the multitude of religious movements in the United States, many of which use glossolalia. For a good description of glossolalia in a non-Western society, see Arkadii Federovich Anisimov's "The Shaman's Tent of the Evenks and the Origin of the Shamanistic Rite," translated from Russian by Dr. and Mrs. Stephen P. Dunn, in *Studies in Siberian Shamanism*, edited by Henry N. Michael (Toronto, 1963).

FELICITAS D. GOODMAN

GNOSTICISM. [*This entry consists of three articles:*
Gnosticism from Its Origins to the Middle Ages
Gnosticism from the Middle Ages to the Present
Gnosticism as a Christian Heresy
The first article is an overview of the gnostic movements that came into being during late Hellenism. This is followed by a discussion of related phenomena in the history of the West. The third piece discusses the view that defines gnosticism as a heretical form of Christianity.]

Gnosticism from Its Origins to the Middle Ages

Gnōsis (knowledge") is a Greek word of Indo-European origin, related to the English *know* and the Sanskrit *jñāna*. The term has long been used in comparative religion to indicate a current of antiquity that stressed awareness of the divine mysteries. This was held to be obtained either by direct experience of a revelation or by initiation into the secret, esoteric tradition of such revelations.

Pre-Christian Gnosis. The experience of gnosis was highly esteemed at the beginning of our era in various religious and philosophical circles of Aramaic and Greco-Roman civilization. It is a key word in the scrolls of the Jews of the Essene sect found at Qumran. In the canonical *Gospel of John*, Jesus is quoted as having said at the Last Supper: "This is [not "will be"] eternal life, that they know [not "believe in"] Thee [here and now], and know Jesus Christ, whom thou hast sent" (*Jn.* 17:3). Not even the prevailing philosophy of the time, so-called Middle Platonism, was completely beyond the influence of this general movement. Middle Platonism was primarily religious and otherworldly; it distinguished between discursive reasoning and intuition and taught the affinity of the soul with the godhead, basing these teachings on an oral tradition of the Platonic schools. The writings of Hermes Trismegistos ("thrice-greatest Hermes," identified with the Egyptian god Thoth) reflect the same atmosphere. [*See* Hermes Trismegistos.] These eighteen treatises, of which *Poimandres* and *Asclepius* are the most important, originate in the proverbial wisdom of ancient Egypt. A saying in a recently discovered Armenian collection attributed to Hermes Trismegistos is "He who knows himself, knows the All." The author of *Poimandres* expresses the same insight: "Let spiritual man know himself, then he will know that he is immortal and that Eros is the origin of death, and he will know the All." And to illustrate this saying the author tells the story of a divine being, Anthropos (Man), who becomes enamored of the world of (lower) nature and so falls into a material body. Most Hermetic treatises take up a short saying and expound on it in this manner. They also preserve the impact of Egyptian mythology. The ancient Egyptians spoke freely about sexual intercourse and about the homosexual behavior of their gods. The explicit sexual imagery of Egyptian mythology was adopted in a Hermetic prayer that addresses the spouse of God in the following words: "We know thee, womb pregnant by the phallus of the Father."

The idea of emanation was also prominent in Egyptian religion. Egyptian myth depicts the Nile as tears of the sun god Re. This concept too is found in Hermetic literature. On the other hand, the same writings show the influence of Greek philosophy; indeed, there was a Platonic school of Eudorus in Alexandria. And the impact of the biblical book of *Genesis* and that of Jewish mysticism are only too obvious. Christian influences, though, are completely absent from the so-called *Corpus Hermeticum*. The treatises in this group of works were all written around the beginning of the Christian era in Alexandria. They appear to be the scriptures of a school of mystics, a sort of lodge that practiced spiritualized sacraments such as "the bath of rebirth," a holy meal, and the kiss of peace.

Gnosticism. Ever since the congress on the origins of gnosticism held at Messina, Italy, in 1966, scholars have made a distinction between gnosis and gnosticism. *Gnosticism* is a modern term, not attested in antiquity. Even the substantive *gnostic* (Gr., *gnōstikos*, "knower"), found in patristic writings, was never used to indicate a general spiritual movement but was applied only to a single, particular sect. Today gnosticism is defined as a religion in its own right, whose myths state that the Unknown God is not the creator (demiurge, YHVH); that the world is an error, the consequence of a fall and split within the deity; and that man, spiritual man, is alien to the natural world and related to the deity and becomes conscious of his deepest Self when he hears the word of revelation. Not sin or guilt, but unconsciousness, is the cause of evil.

Until recent times the gnostic religion was almost exclusively known by reports of its opponents, ecclesiastical heresiologists such as Irenaeus (c. 180 CE), Hippolytus (c. 200), and Epiphanius (c. 350). Not until the eighteenth century were two primary sources, the Codex Askewianus (named for the physician A. Askew) and the Codex Brucianus (named after the Scottish explorer James Bruce), discovered in Egypt. These contained several Coptic gnostic writings: (1) *Two Books of Jeû* from the beginning of the third century; (2) book 4 of *Pistis Sophia* from about 225; and (3) *Pistis Sophia*, books 1, 2, and 3, from the second half of the third century. To these can now be added the writings found near Nag Hammadi in Upper Egypt in 1945. The stories told about the discovery are untrustworthy. The only certain fact is that, to date, about thirteen of the codices (books, not scrolls) comprising some fifty-two texts are preserved at the Coptic Museum in Old Cairo. They have been translated into English by a team under James M. Robinson (1977). Not all these writings are gnostic: the *Gospel of Thomas* (114 sayings attributed to Jesus) is encratitic; the *Thunder, Whole Mind* is Jewish; the *Acts of Peter and the Twelve Apostles* is Jewish-Christian; the *Prayer of Thanksgiving* is Hermetic; and the *Authoritative Teaching* is early Catholic (characterized by a monarchic episcopacy, a canon of holy writings, and a confession of faith). But the *Epistle of Eugnostos* and the *Apocryphon of John* lead us back very far, close to the sources of gnosticism in Alexandria.

Origins. The hypothesis once supported by Richard Reitzenstein, Geo Widengren, and Rudolf Bultmann that gnosticism is of Iranian origin has been abandoned; the alleged Iranian mystery of the "saved saviour" has been disproved. At present, many scholars are inclined to believe that gnosticism is built upon Hellenistic-Jewish foundations and can be traced to centers like Alexandria, which had a large Jewish population, much as the city of New York does today. Polemics in the writings of the Jewish philosopher Philo, who himself was an opponent of local heresies, make it clear that he knew Jewish groups that had already formulated certain basic elements of gnosticism, although a consistent system did not yet exist in pre-Christian times.

The divine Man. The prophet Ezekiel tells us in the first chapter of the biblical book that bears his name that in 593 BCE, dwelling in Babylonia, he beheld the personified Glory of the Lord, who would not abandon him even in exile. This figure, at once Light and Man, is described as having a form like the appearance of Adam, or "Man" (*Ez.* 1:26). This vision became a stock image of Jewish mysticism. As early as the second century BCE, the Jewish Alexandrian dramatist Ezekiel Tragicus alludes to the same figure in his Greek drama *Exodus*, fragmentarily preserved in the *Praeparatio evangelica* (9.29) of the Christian bishop Eusebius. In the play, Moses in a dream beholds a throne on top of Mount Sinai. Upon this throne sits Man (Gr., *ho phōs*) with a crown on his head and a scepter in his left hand. With his right hand he beckons Moses to the throne, presents him with a crown, and invites him to sit beside him on an adjacent throne. Thus is Moses enthroned at the right hand of God. A parallel passage is found in Palestinian Judaism: according to the founding father ʿAqiva' ben Yosef (early second century BCE), there are two thrones in heaven, one for God and one for David (B.T., *Ḥag.* 14a). This is the oldest extant reference to Adam Qadmon, who later became the central figure of qabbalistic literature. Somewhat later, in the *Book of Daniel*, written soon after 168 BCE, this same figure is called the Son of Man (i.e., "divine Man"). The same figure is found in the Gospels. In the Fourth Gospel, the Son of Man is referred to as the Glory of God, which comes from heaven, touches the earth for a moment, is incarnated in the man Jesus, and eventually returns to the heavenly realm. In the letters of Paul, the Glory is called the last Adam (comparable to Ezekiel's *kavod*), who is from heaven and should be distinguished from the first Adam of *Genesis* 1 and 2, who is from the earth. In the Hellenistic world this divine Man is identified with the Platonic idea of man.

Plato himself never says that there is such a thing as an "idea of man." In the dialogue *Parmenides* this philosopher ridicules the concept of an *eidos anthrōpou* (130c). Probably this passage reflects a debate of Platonists among themselves and with other schools. It would seem that the Skeptics denied the idea of man a separate existence because then empirical man and his idea would have something in common, and this would require a new idea, the "third man." In several Middle Platonic sources, however, the idea of man is supposed to exist. The translator of Ezekiel in the Septuagint identifies the figure of divine Man with the Platonic idea when he translates the phrase *demut ke-mar'eh adam* (*Ez.* 1:26) as *homoiōma hōs eidos anthrōpou,* a hellenizing quotation of Plato.

The same figure is to be found in the Hermetic *Poimandres,* clearly influenced by Alexandrian Jews. This writing relates how God generated a son to whom he delivered all creatures. The son is androgynous, equally Phos (Man, Adam, Light) and Zoe (Eve, Life). This being, who is still to be distinguished from the Logos, descends in order to create but falls in love with nature and assumes a material body. That is why human beings are both mortal and immortal. And yet the human body has the form of the original Man. This view is very Jewish and has parallels in rabbinical literature: not the soul but the human body was created after the image and likeness of God.

A next stage is reached in Philo's works. He never quotes *Ezekiel* 1:26 about the Glory of God resembling the form of a man, and yet he must have been familiar with mystical speculations about this divine figure. Philo calls *logos* "Man after his [God's] image" or "Man of God" and identifies the *logos* with the idea of man: incorporeal and neither male nor female. Yet he polemicizes against the concept that this heavenly Man was androgynous: "God made man," he says, "made him after the image of God. Male and female he made—now not 'him' but 'them' " (*Who Is the Heir* 164). Obviously, before Philo there must have been Jewish thinkers who claimed that the heavenly Man was androgynous. Such circles originated the Anthropos model of *gnōsis,* which is found in the doctrine of Saturninus (Antioch, c. 150). In his system, the female figure is completely absent. Our world is said to have been created by seven angels, the seven planets. Thereupon the Unknown God manifested his shining image, the Glory of the heavenly Man. The angels of creation tried to detain this Anthropos but were unable to do so; it returned to heaven at once. Thereupon the angels shaped a human body in the likeness of the heavenly Man. But this creature was unable to stand erect and slithered upon the earth like a worm. The heavenly Adam, having pity on the earthly Adam, sent to him the spark of life, the Spirit, which raised him up and made him live. It is this spark that at death hastens back to its spiritual home, whereas the body dissolves into its constituent elements.

Variations of the myth of Saturninus are found in quite a few of the writings from Nag Hammadi. Valentinus (c. 150) alludes to this myth when, in a preserved fragment, he states that the Adam of *Genesis* inspired awe in the angels who created him because he had been fashioned after the preexistent Anthropos. Mani (216–277) refers to the same story when he relates that in the beginning the Primal Man is sent out to combat the powers of darkness. This Archanthropos is overpowered and forced to leave "the Maiden who is his soul" embedded in matter. The entire world process is necessary to shape the Perfect Man so that the original state of androgyny (male and maiden at the same time) will be restored. All these speculations presuppose the god Man of *Ezekiel* 1:26. Moreover, it is possible that Paul was familiar with the same concept when he said that Christ was both the power *(dunamis)* and the wisdom *(sophia)* of God (*1 Cor.* 1:24).

Sophia. In the *Wisdom of Solomon,* part of the Greek and Roman Catholic Bible, written in Alexandria close to the beginning of the Christian era, personified wisdom, called Sophia, is said to be a holy spirit or the Holy Spirit, which penetrates the All. [*See* Sophia.] She is also referred to as the effluence of God's glory, an emanation of eternal light, and an immaculate mirror of God's activity. She is described as the beloved both of the wise man and of God, even more as the spouse of the Lord (*Wis.* 8:30).

In the *Thunder, Whole Mind,* from the same period and milieu, Sophia manifests herself as the wisdom of the Greeks and the *gnōsis* of the barbarians, the saint and the whore, the bridegroom and the bride. Over and over, she introduces these startling and paradoxical revelations with the formula "I am."

According to the eighth-century BCE inscriptions found near Hebron and in the Negev, the God of Israel had a foreign spouse, the Canaanite goddess Asherah. And in the fifth century BCE, Jewish soldiers garrisoned in Elephantine (near Aswān, Egypt) venerated another pagan fertility goddess called Anat Yahu, the wife of the Lord. Prophets and priests in Judaea did all they could to represent Yahveh as exclusively male and to delete all traces of the primeval matriarchy. But Wisdom survived as Ḥokhmah, especially in Alexandria. [*See* Ḥokhmah.]

This is the basis of the Sophia model of *gnōsis,* which finds expression in the teaching of the famous Samaritan Simon, who was attracted to and yet rejected by incipient Christianity (*Acts* 8). The Samaritans, the last survivors of the ten tribes of northern Israel, were and are heterodox Jews who keep the Law while rejecting the rest of the Bible. They transmit a certain tradition about Wisdom as the personal creator of the world. According to Simon, Wisdom, the spouse of the Lord, was also called Holy Spirit and God's first idea, the mother of all. She descended to the lower regions and gave birth to the angels by whom the world was created. She was overwhelmed and detained by these world powers that she might not return to her abode. She was even incarnated and reincarnated in human bodies, such as that of the Helen of Greek myth and poetry. Finally, she came to dwell as a whore in a brothel of Tyre in Phoenicia, where Simon, "the great power" of God, found and redeemed her. In the *Apocryphon of John* as well as in the school of Valentinus, this Sophia model has been combined with the Anthropos model. Both are pre-Christian in origin.

The Unknown God and the demiurge. The rabbis of the first Christian centuries complain repeatedly of the heretics *(minim)* who taught the existence of two gods. Dissident Jewish teachers believed that God had a representative, bearing his name Jao (the abbreviation of YHVH), who was therefore called Jaoel. According to this view, Jaoel sat upon a throne next to God's throne and was therefore called Metatron (a Greek loanword). In reality, however, Jaoel is nothing but an angel, the most important angel, the one who is called the angel of the Lord in the Hebrew Bible. Some dissident Jews called Magharians said that all anthropomorphisms in the Old Testament applied not to God himself but to this angel, who is also said to have created the world. In a Samaritan (i.e., heterodox Jewish) source called *Malef,* which is late but transmits earlier traditions, it is stated that the angel of the Lord formed the body of Adam from dust of the earth and that God breathed the breath of life into him.

Such views must have been known already to Philo of Alexandria, who polemicizes against them yet at the same time calls the Logos, who is instrumental in creation, both "a second god" and "archangel" on the one hand and "Lord" (YHVH) and "Name" (i.e., YHVH) on the other. Jewish gnostics such as Simon and Cerinthus affirm that the demiurge (identified with YHVH) was in fact this angel of the Lord, who had not yet rebelled against God. [*See* Demiurge.] In the *Apocryphon of John* the angel is called Saklas (Aramaic for "fool") because he does not know that there is a God greater than he. Valentinus, Marcion, and Apelles, who were familiar with the myth contained in the *Apocryphon of John,* all held that the demiurge was an angel. This is a typically Jewish concept. A non-Jew, when suffering under the misery of the world, would simply have declared that the *Genesis* story was a myth without truth; he could not have cared less about the origin of Jewish law. Only those who had been brought up to believe every word of the Bible and to cling to the faith that God is one, and who yet found reason to rebel against their inheritance, would have inclined toward the gnostic solution: God is one and the Bible reveals the truth, but anthropomorphisms such as the handicraft of a creative workman and personal lawgiving are to be attributed to a subordinate angel.

The god within. The biblical *Book of Genesis* relates that God blew the breath of life into the nose of Adam, transforming him into a living being (*Gn.* 2:7). Already in certain passages of the Old Testament (*Jb.* 34:13–15, *Ps.* 104:29–30), this breath is identified with the spirit of God. That is especially clear in the Dead Sea Scrolls: "I, the creature of dust, have known through the spirit, that Thou hast given me." The Alexandrian Jews have integrated and amplified this concept. They were familiar with Greek philosophy and knew that the Orphics, Plato, and the Stoics considered the human soul to be a part of the deity. They were influenced by the Stoic Posidonius (c. 100 BCE), according to whom "the daimon in us [the spirit] is akin to *and of the same nature* as the Daimon [God] who pervades the All." The oldest translators of the Septuagint rendered "breath" (Heb., *neshamah*) in *Genesis* 2:7 as "spirit" (Gr., *pneuma*). This variant is evidenced by the Old Latin Version *(spiritus)* translated from the Septuagint. Philo polemicizes against this particular translation because it deifies sinful man (*Allegorical Interpretation* 1; 13). And yet the Alexandrian *Wisdom of Solomon,* still included in every Roman Catholic Bible, declares explicitly that God's incorruptible *pneuma* is in all things (12:1). Most gnostics preserved this tendentious translation and made it the basis for their mythological speculations. It enabled them to tell how it came to pass that the Spirit sleeps in man and how it can be made conscious. So it is with Valentinus and Mani. Few people nowadays are aware that these mythologems presuppose a consensus of virtually all Greek philosophers and have a biblical foundation.

Jewish Gnosticism. The themes discussed above are the basic elements that contributed to the rise of a Jewish gnosticism, whose myth is contained in the *Apocryphon of John* and other related writings found at Nag Hammadi. The church father Irenaeus attributed this doctrine to the *gnōstikoi.* With this name he indicates not all those whom modern scholars call "gnostics" but only the adherents of a specific sect. It is misleading to call them Sethians (descendants of Seth, the son of Adam), as some scholars do nowadays. Notwithstanding its name, the *Apocryphon of John* (a disciple of Jesus) contains no Christian elements apart from the foreword and some minor interpolations. It can be summarized as follows: from the Unknown God (who exists beyond thought and name) and his spouse (who is his counterpart and mirror) issued the spiritual world. The last of the spiritual entities, Sophia, became wanton and brought forth a monster, the demiurge. He organized the zodiac and the seven planets. He proclaimed: "I am a jealous god, apart from me there is no other." Then a voice was heard, teaching him that above him existed the Unknown God and his spouse. Next, the "first Man in the form of a man" manifested himself to the lower angels. He is the Glory of *Ezekiel* 1:26. His reflection appears in the waters of chaos (cf. the mirror of the Anthropos in *Poimandres*). Thereupon the lower angels created the body of Adam after the image that they had seen, an imitation of the Man, who clearly serves as an ideal archetype for the human body. For a long time the body of Adam lay unable to move, for the seven planetary angels were unable to raise it up. Then Sophia caused the demiurge to breathe the *pneuma* he had inherited from her into the face of his creature. So begins a long struggle between the redeeming Sophia and the malicious demiurge, the struggle for and against the awakening of human spiritual consciousness.

Written in Alexandria about the beginning of the Christian era, the myth of the *Apocryphon of John*, a pivotal and seminal writing, combines the Anthropos model and the Sophia model. It is very complicated and confusing but had enormous influence in the Near East, where so many remnants of great religions survive today. (In the 1980s, for example, there were 420 Samaritans and 30,000 Nestorians.) Even today some 15,000 Mandaeans (the Aramaic term for gnostics) live in Iraq and Iran. Their religion features ablutions in streaming water and a funerary mass. When a Mandaean has died, a priest performs a complicated rite in order to return the soul to its heavenly abode, where it will receive a spiritual body. In this way, it is believed, the deceased is integrated into the so-called Secret Adam, the Glory, the divine body of God. This name confirms that, along with the Anthropos of *Poimandres* and the Adam Qadmon of later Jewish mysticism, this divine and heavenly figure is ultimately derived from the vision of the prophet Ezekiel. In Mandaean lore Sophia appears in degraded form as a mean and lewd creature called the Holy Spirit. The creation of the world is attributed to a lower demiurge. Ptahil, a pseudonym for the angel Gabriel (who, according to both the Mandaeans and the Magharians, is the angel who created the world).

The apostle Paul (or one of his pupils) maintains that Christ, who is for him the second Adam, is "the head of his Church, which is his body" (*Eph.* 1:22–23). The Christian is integrated into this body through baptism. Mandaean speculations about the Secret Adam may elucidate what Paul meant. In defining his view of the church as the mystical body of Christ, the apostle may be reflecting a familiarity with comparable Jewish and Hellenistic speculations about the *kavod* as the body of God. As a matter of fact, it has become clear from the verses of Ezekiel Tragicus that such ideas circulated in Alexandria long before the beginning of our era. They surfaced in Palestine toward the end of the first century CE in strictly Pharisaic circles that transmitted secret, esoteric traditions about the mystical journey of the sage through the seven heavenly places to behold the god Man on the throne of God. The author of the writing *Shi'ur Qoma*, the "measurement of the Body" of God, reports the enormous dimensions of the members of the Glory. The Orphics had taught that the cosmos was actually a divine body. Already early in Hellenistic Egypt similar speculations arose; these were the origin of the remarkable speculations of Palestinian rabbis concerning the mystical body of God. (These speculations ultimately led to the *Zohar*.) It is no coincidence that the Glory is called Geradamas (Arch-Adam) in some Nag Hammadi writings, Adam Qadmaia in Mandaean sources, and Adam Qadmon in medieval Jewish gnosticism.

In the ninth century several groups of Islamic gnostics arose in southern Iraq, where several other gnostic sects had found refuge during late antiquity and where the Mandaeans continue to live today. [*See* Mandaean Religion.] The best-known Islamic gnostics are the Ismā'īlīyah, of which the Aga Khan is the religious leader. [*See* Aga Khan.] Mythological themes central to their religion are (1) the cycles of the seven prophets; (2) the throne and the letters; (3) Kuni, the creative principle, who is feminine (a typical remythologizing of a monotheistic Father religion); (4) the higher Pentad; (5) the infatuation of the lower demiurge; (6) the seven planets and the twelve signs of the zodiac; (7) the divine Adam; and (8) the fall and ascent of the soul.

Since the discovery of the Nag Hammadi codices it has been established that these themes are best explained as transpositions into an Islamic terminology of the gnostic mythemes that are found in the *Apocryphon of John* and kindred documents of Jewish gnosticism.

Christian Gnosis. According to a reliable tradition, Barnabas, a missionary of the Jerusalem congregation, was the first to bring the gospel to Alexandria, a relatively easy journey. Egyptian Christianity is Judaic in origin, not gentile, and the great Egyptian gnostics seem all to have been of Jewish birth. The adherents of Basilides claimed: "We are no longer Jews and not yet Christians." The followers of Valentinus reported: "When we were Hebrews, we were orphans." Basilides and Valentinus both proclaimed a God beyond the Old Testament God, and both were familiar with the myth of the *Apocryphon of John,* which they christianized. The case of Marcion is similar: he was so well-informed about the Hebrew Bible and its flaws that his father, a bishop, may well be presumed to have been Jewish. Through a certain Cerdo, Marcion came to know an already existing gnostic system. Those who reject the god of the Old Testament obviously no longer hold to the Jewish faith, but nevertheless still belong ethnically to the Jewish people. Both Valentinus and Marcion went to Rome and were excommunicated there between 140 and 150. Basilides, who stayed in Alexandria, remained a respected schoolmaster there until his death. The Christians in Alexandria were divided among several synagogues and could afford to be tolerant, for a monarchic bishop did not yet exist and their faith was pluriform anyhow. Basilides, Valentinus, and Marcion were Christocentric and let themselves be influenced by the *Gospel of John* and the letters of Paul.

Marcion. When Marcion, a rich shipowner from Sinope in Pontus (on the Black Sea), was excommunicated, he organized an enormous alternative church that persisted for a long time, especially in the East (e.g., in Armenia). [*See* Marcion.] Marcion was a violin with one string, a religious genius with one overpowering idea: God, the Father of Jesus, was not the Hebrew YHVH. Like the gnostics, he distinguished between the Unknown God (whom he felt to be the only genuine God) and a lower divinity, the demiurge, who is responsible for creation and interacts with man. Above all, Marcion was fascinated by Paul's *Letter to the Galatians.* Following Paul, he contrasted the Law of the Old Testament and Israelite religion with the "gospel of forgiveness," which revealed the goodness of God.

Like his hero Paul, Marcion was overwhelmed by the unconditional and unwarranted love of God for poor creatures. This led him to deny the gnostic idea that man's inmost Self is related to the Godhead. For Marcion, man is nothing more than the creation of a cruel demiurge; the loving God who has rescued him, without any ulterior motive but simply out of a freely bestowed loving kindness, is totally alien to man, his nature, and his fate.

Until Augustine, no one understood Paul as well as Marcion; yet Marcion, the one genuine pupil, misunderstood Paul as well. Notwithstanding his dialectics, Paul never rejected the created world, sexuality, or the people of Israel, as did Marcion.

Basilides. Basilides was active as the leader of a school in Alexandria in the time of the emperors Hadrian (r. 117–138) and Antoninus Pius (r. 138–161). He seems to have been one of those many liberal Jews who had left behind the concept of a personal lord for belief in the Unknown God. Yet he was never excommunicated and remained a respected member of the church of Alexandria until his death.

Basilides must have known the earlier Alexandrian, pre-Christian myth contained in the *Apocryphon of John.* He too begins his cosmogony with the Unknown God, "the not-being God, who made a not-yet-being world out of nothing" by bringing forth a single germ of the All. This germ was the primeval chaos. From it in due time one element after another arose on high, while below there remained only the so-called third sonship, or the Spirit in the spiritual man.

When the time was right, Jesus was enlightened at his baptism in the river Jordan (a typically Jewish-Christian notion). He is considered to be the prototype of all spiritual men, who through his revealing word become conscious of their innermost being, the Spirit, and rise up to the spiritual realm.

When the entire third sonship has redeemed itself, God will take pity on the world, and he will allow the descent of "the great unconsciousness" upon the rest of mankind. Thereafter no one will have even an inkling that there was ever anything like the Spirit. Basilides foresees a godless and classless society.

Valentinus. The greatest gnostic of all times was the poet Valentinus. Despite his Latin name, he was a Greek born in the Nile Delta around the year 100 and educated in Alexandria. He and his followers did not separate from the church of Alexandria but created an academy for free research, which in turn formed a loose network of local groups within the institutional religion. Even among his opponents Valentinus became renowned for his eloquence and genius.

According to his own words, his views originated in a visionary experience in which he saw a newborn child. This vision inspired a "tragic myth," expressed by Valentinus in a psalm that described how the All emanates from the ground of being, called Depth, and his spouse, called Womb or Silence. Together they bring forth the Christ, or Logos, upon whom all aeons (half ideas, half angels) depend and through whom the All is coherent and connected. Through the revelation of Christ, Valentinus experienced the wholeness of the All, the fullness of being, and the nonentity "I and Thou" (known in Hinduism as *advaita*). Not dualism but duality is the underlying principle of reality, according to Valentinus: God himself is the transcendental unity of Depth and Silence; the aeons of the pleroma (spiritual world) are a diametrical union of the masculine, or creative, and the feminine, or receptive, principles; Christ and Sophia (Wisdom) are a couple (separated for a while on account of the trespass and fall of Sophia but in the end happily reunited). Man and his guardian angel, or transcendental counterpart, celebrate the mystical marriage of bride and bridegroom (the Ego and the Self). Polarity (Gr., *suzugia;* Lat., *coniunctio*) is characteristic of all things spiritual. On the basis of this metaphysical view, Valentinus and his followers valued both sex and marriage, at least for the pneumatics. A preserved fragment from the school of Valentinus gives the following interpretation of Jesus' statement in the *Gospel of John* that the Christian lives in the world but is not from it (*Jn.* 17:14–16): "Whosoever is *in* the world and has not loved a woman so as to become one with her, is not out of the Truth and will not attain the Truth; but he who is *from* the world and unites with a woman, will not attain the Truth, because he made sex out of concupiscence alone." The Valentinians permitted intercourse only between men and women who were able to experience it as a mystery and a sacrament, namely, those who were pneumatics. They forbade it between those whom they called "psychics" (Jews and Catholics) or "hylics" (materialists), because these two lower classes knew nothing but libido. As the only early Christian on record who spoke lovingly about sexual intercourse and womanhood, Valentinus must have been a great lover.

The Jung Codex. On 10 May 1952, at the behest of the Jung Institute in Zurich, I acquired one of the thirteen codices found at Nag Hammadi in 1945. In honor of the great psychiatrist who helped to put this manuscript at the disposal of competent scholars, it is called the Jung Codex. It contains five Valentinian writings:

1. The *Prayer of the Apostle Paul.*
2. The *Apocryphon of James* is a letter purporting to contain revelations of the risen Jesus, written by James, his brother. In reality, it contains Valentinian speculations grafted onto the root and fatness of the olive tree planted beside the waters of the Nile by Hebrew missionaries from Jerusalem (c. 160).
3. The *Gospel of Truth* is a meditation on the true eternal gospel proclaimed by Christ to awaken man's innermost being, the unconscious Spirit, probably written by Valentinus himself in about 150.
4. The *Epistle to Rheginos concerning the Resurrection* is adequate explanation of Paul's view on the subject: already, here and now, man anticipates eternal life, and after death he will receive an ethereal body.
5. The so-called *Tripartite Treatise* is a systematic and consistent exposition of the history of the All. It describes how the Spirit evolves through the inferno of a materialistic (pagan or "hylic") phase and the purgatory of a moral (Jewish and Catholic or "psychic") phase to the coming of Christ, who inaugurates the *paradiso* of final consummation, in which spiritual man becomes conscious of himself and of his identity with the Unknown God. The author, a leader of the Italic (Roman) school of Valentinianism, was most likely Heracleon (c. 170). It was against this shade of Valentinian gnosis that Plotinus, the Neoplatonic philosopher, wrote his pamphlet *Against the Gnostics* (c. 250).

Later Developments. Scholars have always admitted that Origen (c. 180–254), the greatest dogmatician of the Greek church, had much in common with the Valentinians: the spirits fall away from God and become souls before the creation of the world; the world purifies the soul; Jesus brings not only redemption to the faithful but also gnosis to the pneumatics. But whereas Valentinus was said to have taught predestination physics (the teaching that spiritual man was saved by nature), Origen on the contrary allegedly stressed free will. The *Tripartite Treatise* has undermined this apologetic position. There evil is no longer a tragic neurosis that befell Sophia but a free decision. Moreover, this writing is thoroughly optimistic: all is for the best in the best of all possible worlds, and providence educates mankind toward the realization of complete consciousness, as in Origen's soteriology. Some path led from the tragic view of Valentinus to the optimism of Heracleon, and from Heracleon to Origen was only one step more.

The Valentinians of Carthage spoke Latin, whereas the Christians in Rome spoke Greek. Translating their technical terms from Greek, the Valentinians coined Latin equivalents of *infinite, consubstantial, trinity, person,* and *substance.* These terms were eventually adopted by the Roman Catholic church. If ever there was a community that created a special language, it was the school of Valentinus at Carthage.

Mani. Gnosticism became a world religion when Mani (216–277) founded his alternative Christian church, which existed for more than a thousand years with adherents in lands from the Atlantic Ocean to the Pacific. [*See* Mani *and* Manichaeism.] From his fourth until his twenty-fifth year Mani was raised in a Jewish-Christian community of Baptists, followers of the prophet Elxai (c. 100). There he heard, first, that Jesus was "the true prophet," a manifestation of God's glory *(kavod)* who was first embodied in Adam, then revealed himself to the Old Testament patriarchs and was ultimately incarnated in the Messiah, Jesus. He also heard, second, that baptisms and ablutions were necessary for salvation and, third, that God was the origin of evil since Satan was the left hand of God. He modified the first belief, identifying himself as the seal of the prophets, who included the Buddha and Zarathushtra in the East and Jesus in the West. The second belief he rejected; in fact, he admitted no sacraments at all. Against the third belief he, being a cripple, rebelled with all his might. Evil, in Mani's view, did not originate in the world of light but had its source in a different principle, the world of darkness, matter, and concupiscence.

Influenced by encratitic asceticism of the Aramaic Christians of Asia, Mani rejected marriage and the consumption of alcohol and meat, and he designated among his followers an upper class of the elect who lived according to the Sermon on the Mount and a lower class of auditors who were allowed to have wives or concubines and to practice birth control. But very much in the spirit of Valentinus was Mani's primary religious experience. The basis of his entire myth, the encounter with his "twin" or transcendental Self, is gnostic, very much in the spirit of Valentinus: "I recognized him and understood that he was my Self from whom I had been separated." Mani encountered his spiritual Self at the age of twelve and encountered it a second time at the age of twenty-five. He felt constantly accompanied by his twin, and when he died a martyr in prison he was gazing at this familiar. The encounter with one's twin is central to the life of every Manichaean. The mystery of conjunction, the holy marriage of Ego and Self, is thereby democratized. To illustrate this process, Mani related a myth that is indebted to earlier gnostic movements. For Mani the world is in truth created by the Living Spirit, a manifestation of God, and not by a lower demiurge. But a split within the deity takes place when the archetypal Man loses in the battle against darkness, is thus overwhelmed, and abandons his soul as sparks of light dispersed throughout the material world and mankind. Man is contaminated in this way by concupiscence, an evil force from the world of darkness. The entire world system is devised to save these light elements and to restore man as Perfect Man in his original purity and integrity.

Augustine (354–430) was a Manichaean auditor for more than nine years before he became a Father of the Roman Catholic church. During that period he wrote a treatise (since lost), *On Beauty and Harmony*, in which he stated that the asexual mind was linked with a completely alien element of ire and concupiscence. As a heresy-hunter he later maintained that concupiscence was not created by God but was instead a consequence of the Fall. The assertion that the reproductive instinct is not a part of human nature does certainly have Manichaean overtones.

The Middle Ages. Manichaeism disappeared completely in the West and had no successors there: the term *medieval Manichee* is a misnomer. And yet Christianity during the Middle Ages both in Western and in Eastern Europe was not monolithically orthodox. Gnosticism flourished at that time. Such books as *Montaillou* by Emmanuce Leroy Ladurie and *The Name of the Rose* by Umberto Eco have drawn the attention of a large public of interested outsiders to the existence of dualistic sects such as the Cathari in southern France and northern Italy and the Bogomils (or "friends of God") in Yugoslavia and Bulgaria, because their views resemble those of the ancient gnostics. Indeed, their affiliation with ancient gnosticism, if somewhat complicated, is well established. [*See* Cathari.]

The Paulicians were typically Armenian sectarians who, persisting into modern times, turned up in 1837 in the village of Arh'wela (in Russian Armenia) with their holy book, the *Key of Truth* (eighth century). Two versions of their doctrine exist. According to one, Jesus was adopted to be the son of God. According to the second version, there are two gods; one is the Father in heaven, while the other is the creator of this world. This can be explained in the following way: Christianity was introduced to Armenia from Edessa at an early date, and Edessa owed its (adoptionist) Christology to Addai, the Jewish-Christian missionary from Jerusalem. When Roman Catholicism was established as the state church in 302 by Gregory the Illuminator, the Christians of Armenia were branded as heretics. Marcionites and gnostics had taken refuge in these marginal and mountainous regions. They united with the adoptionists to become one sect, the Paulicians, soon a warlike group. The emperors of Byzantium deported quite a few of them to the Balkans, especially to Bulgaria. It was there that the sect of the Bogomils originated, characterized by the belief that the devil (Satanael) created and rules this world. Their influence spread to the West, and from the beginning of the eleventh century gave rise to the church of the Cathari, which was strong in southern France and northern Italy. Thus gnosticism was never completely suppressed but survived into the Middle Ages.

Modern gnosis. The gnosis of modern times, launched by the shoemaker Jakob Boehme (c. 1600), was generated spontaneously as a result of direct experience. [*See* Theosophy.] It differs from ancient gnosticism in that it derives not only the light but also the darkness (not only good but also evil) from the ground of being. Inspired by Boehme is the influential gnosis of the English poet and artist William Blake (1757–1827), the only authentic gnostic of the entire Anglo-Saxon world. It is in the school of Boehme that the scholarly study of gnosticism has its roots, beginning with the *Impartial History of the Churches and Heresies* (1699) by Gotfrid Arnold. In this extremely learned work all heretics, including all gnostics, are represented as the true Christians—innocent and slandered lambs.

Ever since, the study of gnosticism has been an accepted academic subject in Germany, but in Germany alone. In his youth Goethe read Arnold's book and conceived his own gnostic system, as reported in his autobiography. Toward the end of his life Goethe recalled the love of his youth when he wrote the finale to *Faust*, the hierophany of "the Eternally Feminine," a version of the gnostic Sophia, the exclusive manifestation of the deity. Johann Lorenz von Mosheim and other great historians also took gnosis quite seriously. The brilliant August Neander, who belonged to the conservative reaction to the Enlightenment called the Great Awakening Revivalism *(Erweckungsbewegung)*, wrote his *Genetic Evolution of the Most Important Gnostic Systems* in 1818. Ferdinand Christian Baur, a prominent Hegelian, published his monumental *Christian Gnosis* in 1835, in which he defends the thesis that gnosis was a religious philosophy whose modern counterpart is the idealism of Schelling, Schleiermacher, and Hegel, all based upon the vision of Boehme. According to Baur, even German idealism was a form of gnosis. Yet when "the people of poets and thinkers" became, under Bismarck, a people of merchants and industrial workers, this wonderful empathy, this fantastic feel of gnosis, was almost completely lost.

Adolph von Harnack (1851–1930), the ideologue of Wilhelm's empire, defined gnosticism as the acute, and orthodoxy as the chronic, hellenization (i.e., rationalization) and hence alienation of Christianity. At the time it was difficult to appreciate the experience behind the gnostic symbols. Wilhelm Bousset, in his *Main Problems of Gnosis* (1907), described this religion as a museum of hoary and lifeless Oriental (Indian, Iranian, Babylonian) fossils. The same unimaginative approach led Richard Reitzenstein, Geo Widengren, and Rudolf Bultmann to postulate an Iranian mystery of salvation that never existed but was supposed to explain gnosticism, Manichaeism, and Christianity.

Existentialism and depth psychology were needed to rediscover the abysmal feelings that inspired the movement of gnosis. Hans Jonas (*The Gnostic Religion*, 1958) has depicted these feelings as dread, alienation, and an aversion to all worldly existence, as if the gnostics were followers of Heidegger. In the same vein are the writings of Kurt Rudolph, the expert on Mandaeism.

Under the influence of Carl Gustav Jung, I and other scholars (e.g., Henri-Charles Puech and Karl Kerényi) have interpreted the gnostic symbols as a mythical expression (i.e., projection) of self-experience. As a lone wolf, the Roman Catholic convert Erik Peterson suggested that the origins of gnosticism were not Iranian or Greek but Jewish. The gnostic writings from Nag Hammadi have shown Jung and Peterson to be in the right. At last the origins, development, and goal of this perennial philosophy have come to light.

BIBLIOGRAPHY

Jonas, Hans. *The Gnostic Religion: The Message of the Alien God and the Beginnings of Christianity.* 2d ed., rev. & enl. Boston, 1963.

Pagels, Elaine H. *The Gnostic Gospels.* New York, 1979.

Quispel, Gilles. *Gnostic Studies.* 2 vols. Istanbul, 1974–1975.

Robinson, James M., et al. *The Nag Hammadi Library in English.* San Francisco, 1977.

Rudolph, Kurt. *Gnosis.* San Francisco, 1983.

GILLES QUISPEL

Gnosticism from the Middle Ages to the Present

The existence of an underground gnostic tradition within Christianity, Judaism, and Islam, from the Middle Ages to the present, can be considered one of the near certainties of modern scholarship. Heretical Christian movements from Augustine to the eighteenth century fall into three different categories:

1. dualistic sects whose doctrines make use of gnostic and Manichaean mythological themes;
2. sects derived from Marcionism, which are not typically gnostic but which are dualistic, insofar as they make a distinction between a "just" divinity (that of the Old Testament) and a "good" divinity announced by Jesus Christ;
3. pauperistic movements (so called from Latin *pauper*, "poor"), which are fundamentally non-gnostic and nondualistic but which may be akin to the first two types of sects, insofar as they are strongly ascetic, encratic (i.e., rejecting marriage and sexual intercourse), antinomian (i.e., rejecting both worldly and religious institutions), anticlericalist, and sometimes vegetarian.

Furthermore, the doctrine of several medieval sects is a blending of a basic Marcionite lore with superimposed gnostic-Manichaean elements. The same situation faces us both in the two main trends of Islamic heresy (*zandaqa*), the *ghulāt* and the Ismāʿīlīyah, and in the late Jewish qabbalistic school of Isaac Luria. The history of gnostic ideas and imagery is not easy to follow, since it is basically a history of interactions between gnostic and merely Marcionite movements.

As the cradle of late medieval heresy was eastern Europe, the cradle of early medieval heresy was Armenia, where Marcionites, gnostics, and Manichaeans had sought refuge from the prosecutions of the church in the fourth and fifth centuries. The Paulicians, a sect founded by Constantine of Mananalis at the end of the seventh century, might have been based on Marcionite lore. Prosecuted by both Christians and Muslims, the Paulicians were nearly destroyed in the eighth century, but managed to become important again under the reformer Sergius Tychikos (d. 835). Nearly one hundred thousand of them were killed under the empress Theodora. The officer Karbeas, who was a Paulician, crossed the border to Arab Armenia and founded there, with five thousand followers, the cities of Tephrike (modern-day Divrigi) and Amara. Around 869, the Paulicians were about to send a mission to Thrace. One century later, the emperor John Tsimisces sent many of them to Philippopolis in Thrace, where they still were located in 1116.

The ideas of Priscillian of Avila in Spain, condemned in 385 as a sorcerer and a "Manichaean," are hardly known. His sect was Marcionite during the fifth and sixth centuries. Late Priscillianism and Paulicianism shared the following distinctive features: cosmological and anthropological dualism, encratism, docetism (according to which Christ's passion was not real), antinomianism. All these were consequences of Marcion's distinction of two gods, of which the evil one (i.e., the god of the Old Testament) was also the creator of the visible world.

Gnostic, Manichaean, and Jewish messianic ideas are likely to have influenced the first representatives of Shīʿī gnosis. Just as Simon Magus was the archheretic of Christian gnosis, the archheretic of Islamic *ghulūw* ("exaggeration") was a certain ʿAbdallāh ibn Sabaʾ, a Jew belonging to the adepts of the imam ʿAlī in the town Kufa in Iraq. Ibn Sabaʾ fostered, after ʿAlī's death, messianic expectations likely to be explained in the light of his Falasha background. Different sects of *ghulāt* ("extremists, exaggerators"), in which one or another descendant of ʿAlī was divinized and/or expected to come back as the Messiah long after he was dead, have been important among the Shīʿah from the early eighth century to the present. Their last remnants are, today, the Syrian Nuṣayrīyah, or ʿAlawīyūn. To the Kufic *ghulāt* belongs the book *Umm al-kitāb* (Mother of All Books; late eighth century), an apocalypse containing unequivocal gnostic motifs. Another apocalypse, in use among the Nuṣayrīyah, the *Kitāb al-aẓillah* (Book of Shadows), is equally based on gnostic mythology.

Ismāʿīlī gnosis, a distinct trend of *zandaqah,* was founded in the ninth century by a certain ʿAbdallāh of Ḥūzistān, perhaps a son of that Maimūn who was known to be a disciple of the Bardayṣan heresy. ʿAbdallāh, together with his acolyte al-Ahwāzī, fled to Syria, where an offshoot of the sect developed in the village of Salamīya. Al-Ḥusayn, the fourth descendant of ʿAbdallāh, went to North Africa and became the founder of the Fatimid dynasty. Al-Ahwāzī founded in Kufa, Iraq, a second branch of the sect known as the Qarāmiṭah after the name of a certain al-Aschʿat, surnamed Qarmaṭ, a disciple of al-Ahwāzī. The Qarāmiṭah of Iraq sent missions to Yemen, to countries bordering Yemen, and to Persia. The twelfth-century sect of the Assassins was a branch of the Qarāmiṭah. Today, different Ismāʿīlī sects are to be found in Syria, Lebanon, Yemen, and northwestern India. Among the most important are the Druze, a group dating from the early eleventh century that today lives in Syria, Lebanon, and Israel. The oldest writing of the Ismāʿīlīyah is *Kitāb al-kashf* (Book of Revelation). Its most ancient passages seem to have been composed at Salamīyah. The cosmogony of *Kitāb al-kashf* is based on the gnostic myth of the pride and ignorance of the demiurge, a theme resumed in the Druze treatise *Kashf al-ḥaqāʾiq* (Revelation of All Truths). The most important Ismāʿīlī thinker is the eleventh-century Iraqi Neoplatonist al-Kirmānī.

How might gnostic myths have reached the Ghulāt and the Ismāʿīlīyah? They were probably transmitted by the so-called *mawāli,* or "clients," from Kufa. The *mawāli* were foreigners converted to Islam after the conquest of Persia's capital, Seleucia-Ctesiphon (Arabic, al-Madāʾīn), and its transfer to Kufa under the Umayyads (637–638 CE). Among the *mawāli,* Jewish, Christian, Zoroastrian, gnostic, and Manichaean ideas were represented.

In the Christian world, a dualistic movement containing unequivocally gnostic elements burst forth in Bulgaria in the tenth century under the influence of the Paulician mission. This heresy was named after its founder, the priest Bogomil, active at the time of the emperor Peter (927–969). Cosmological and anthropological dualism, antinomianism, docetism, anticlericalism, encratism, asceticism, and vegetarianism characterized Bogomilism.

The basic creation myth of the Bogomils has an authentic gnostic flavor, but it derives in all probability from Inner Asian folklore. Similar myths occur elsewhere in dualistic religious contexts, such as in Persian Zurvanism. Bogomilism spread to Thrace and Asia Minor and reached the capital of the Byzantine empire in the eleventh century as an underground movement. At the beginning of the twelfth century, its leader in Constantinople was a doctor named Basilius. Some basic myths of the Byzantine strain of Bogomilism (the creation of Adam, the seduction of Eve) are unequivocally gnostic.

If twelfth-century Catharism was directly influenced by Bogomilism, earlier Western movements might have appeared either as a result of intermittent Bogomil influences or as a spontaneous revival of dualistic ideas. Religious groups sharing such beliefs as dualism, docetism, encratism, antinomianism, vegetarianism and anticlericalism were found and prosecuted during the eleventh century in towns throughout Europe: Orléans (1017–1022); Liège, Arras, Toulouse (1028); Monforte (northern Italy, 1028); Goslar (Saxony, 1052); Chalons-sur-Marne (1043–1062); Agen (1090). Of these sectarians, only those of Orléans, Liège, Arras, and Agen were certainly dualists. The European interviewers, who were not yet properly "inquisitors" (the Inquisition was established in 1227–1235), did not show the same forbearance as Alexius, emperor of Byzantium, who, in 1111, spent many days listening to the Bogomil Basilius before sending him to the hippodrome to be burned alive. If the heretics were not convinced within one morning to abjure their faith, they faced certain condemnation. Therefore, one should not expect from Western ecclesiastical historians such accurate descriptions of heretic doctrines as Eastern historians gave concerning the Byzantine Bogomils. Western sectarians of the eleventh century were, in most cases, so-called crypto-heretics who continued to go to church and to take sacraments. In some cases, they gladly accepted martyrdom after having been found guilty. Since vegetarianism was widespread among them, their refusal, for instance, to kill a chicken was considered sufficient cause for execution (as in Goslar in 1052), just as later the refusal of a young woman to have intercourse with the inquisitor was held to be sufficient evidence for condemning her as a Cathar.

Bogomilism spread westward as a mass movement in the middle of the twelfth century. Catharist churches were established in northern Italy and southern France. The churches grew, and a crusade was organized against them in 1208. A second crusade in 1227 resulted in the fall of Montségur (1244), the last stronghold of the Cathari. The movement declined, although it continued to face its prosecutors for about another century.

French and Italian Cathari were dependent on two mother churches in eastern Europe, a fact emphasized during the Council of Saint-Félix-de-Caraman (near Toulouse) when the priest Niketas, bishop of the Byzantine Bogomils, converted Italian and French Cathari from the Ordo Bulgariae to the Ordo Drugunthiae, to which he belonged. The Ecclesia Bulgariae, or Ordo Bulgariae, held a mitigated form of dualism, while the Ecclesia Drugunthiae (probably refering to Dragovitsa in Thrace, near Philippopoli) held a radical dualism. Italian Cathari were divided between the Ordo Bulgariae and the Ordo Drugunthiae. A third church existed in Italy, at Bagnolo San Vito, near Mantua, belonging to the Sclavini, or Sclavi ("Slavs"), a sect deriving from the Bogomil church of Bosnia.

Like the Bogomils, the Cathari professed cosmological and anthropological dualism, encratism, asceticism, antinomianism, anticlericalism, docetism, and vegetarianism. Their myths bore the incontestable imprint of Manichaeism, a fact that has not so far met with a convincing historical explanation.

Neither has the revival of gnostic myth in the qabbalistic school of Safad (Palestine) been explained historically. The founder of this school was Isaac Luria (1534–1572). Lurianic Qabbalah had two influential schools: the Palestinian one, represented by Ḥayyim Vital (1543–1620), and the Italian one, represented by Yisra'el Sarug (fl. 1590–1610). The fundamental doctrine of Lurianic Qabbalah was that of *tsimtsum*, or "contraction" of God within himself in order to free a zone outside himself, which is accordingly deprived of God and filled up with creation. Later in the process of creation, the spiritual "vessels" broke *(shevirat ha-kelim)* and were filled up with matter, while the "shells" *(qelippot)* fell in the void of creation. The mythologem of the broken vessels, found in the Valentinian treatise *The Gospel of Truth*, is an ancient gnostic tradition.

Lurianic Qabbalah was influential in Western thinking. The Lutheran qabbalist Friedrich Christoph Oetinger (1702–1782) was acquainted with the works of the Lurian adepts Ḥayyim Vital and 'Immanu'el H'ai Ricci ben Avraham (1688–1743). Oetinger took over, in his own works, the theory of *tsimtsum* and the Marcionite distinction between God's justice and bounty, a distinction that also played a role in Lurianic Qabbalah. According to Ernst Topitsch ("Marxismus und Gnosis," in *Sozialphilosophie zwischen Ideologie und Wissenschaft*, Neuwied-Berlin, 1966), Hegel's early writings were very much influenced by Oetinger's philosophy, and thus both Hegel and his materialist disciple Marx might be considered direct descendants of gnosticism. Yet the idea of a gnostic "devolution" is alien to Marx, who is a typical evolutionist. It is true that the proletarians are viewed as redeemers of the world and communist lore as a gnosis, but this analogy is not sufficient to make a gnostic of Marx.

Gnosis has left an indelible imprint on other products of Western culture, for instance on Goethe's *Faust*. During the nineteenth century, several Romantic poets seemed to reinvent gnostic myth, to describe a position that was no longer gnostic but was essentially nihilistic. These poets were P. B. Shelley (*Prometheus Unbound*, 1818–1819), Lord Byron (*Cain*, 1821), Giacomo Leopardi (*Ad Arimane*, 1833), Alphonse de Lamartine (*La *chute d'un ange,* 1837), Victor Hugo (*La fin de Satan,* 1854–1857), and Mihail Eminescu (*Muresanu* and *Demonism,* 1872). Apart from Leopardi, who was acquainted with ancient gnosticism, the other writers were compelled to invent mythologies that corresponded, sometimes in detail, with gnostic mythologies (this is especially true of Byron and Eminescu). Their desire to foster human liberation from the bonds of Christianity, especially as far as its Old Testament inheritance was concerned, stimulated these inventions. One way or another, each of these Romantics arrived at the Marcionite idea that the god of the Old Testament, who is also creator of this world, is an evil god who must be opposed. Only Shelley set against this evil god a sort of transcendent pleroma and a supreme and bounteous Father. Byron and the other poets eliminated this distinctive gnostic feature from their literary myths. For them, the world and man had become worthy of salvation from the clutches of the religious tyrant, and a sort of active nihilism was the way to reach that goal. This position of the Romantics was precisely the reverse of the gnostic position, insofar as the latter expressed a metaphysical denial of the world on behalf of transcendence, while the former expressed a nihilistic denial of transcendence on behalf of this world. Thus, while the mythological products of Romanticism were surprisingly akin to those of gnosticism, they were expressive of a completely different ideology.

In recent scholarship, the confusion between gnosticism and modern nihilism has grown. All sorts of philosophical and literary works were labeled as "gnostic" because of their nihilistic implications. Only in a few cases are analogies with gnosticism meaningful, for instance in the case of the philosopher Theodor W. Adorno, who reinvented several gnostic myths (e.g., the myth of the descent of the Great Ignorance upon the modern world in his *Minima Moralia* of 1944–1947; this myth was expressed in another form by the second-century gnostic Basilides).

Gnosticism has been a source of inspiration for a few modern writers, such as Anatole France (1844–1924), Aleksandr Blok (1880–1921), Albert Verwey (1865–1937), and Hermann Hesse (1877–1962). Social criticism took on gnostic accents in the novel *The Master and Margaretha* (1966) of the Russian writer Mikhail Bulgakov (1891–1940). The psychologist C. G. Jung (1875–1961) was very impressed by gnostic imagery and even produced in 1915–1916 a "gnostic" work, *Septem Sermones ad Mortuos,* inspired by Basilides' speculations.

In modern philosophy and literary criticism, the words *gnosis* and *gnostic* tend to be indiscriminately used to indicate the nihilistic character of a specific school of thought, the presence of a transcendental capacity in man, the emanationistic character of a system, or simply some "knowledge," esoteric or not. Such use of the word *gnosis* has little to do with gnosticism, which is characterized by dualism and extreme metaphysical nihilism. Even modern religious scholarship has not thus far come to agreement on the meaning of *gnosis* in its stricter sense. Louis Massignon and Henry Corbin, for instance, have enlarged the concept of "Islamic gnosis" to include many authors and trends of Islam that have nothing to do either with the *ghulāt* or with the Ismāʿīlīyah. Eric Voegelin, in *Science, Politics, and Gnosticism* (Chicago, 1960), defined gnosis broadly, both as a Christian heresy and as a perennial antinomian tendency worthy of condemnation. If gnosis was a *Weltreligion,* as Gilles Quispel asserts in *Gnosis als Weltreligion* (Zurich, 1951), this was due entirely to the historical continuity between gnosticism, Marcionism (sometimes considered a form of gnosticism), Manichaeism, Priscillianism, Paulicianism, the *ghulāt,* the Ismāʿīlīyah, Bogomilism, Catharism, and Lurianic Qabbalah.

Romantic mythology is nihilistic, not gnostic, and the history of modern nihilism has to be kept apart from the history of gnosticism. The same confusion between gnosis and nihilism occurs in the works of those authors who have tried to show, for instance, that existential philosophy or modern biology is "gnostic." The too liberal use of the words *gnosis* and *gnostic* can only bring these terms to semantic impoverishment, without any real profit for modern scholarship.

[*For discussion of Christian interpretations of some movements referred to in the foregoing article, see* Heresy, *article on* Christian Heresies; Marcionism; Manichaeism, *article on* Manichaeism and Christianity; Cathari; *and* Waldensians. *For Islamic interpretations, see* Shiism; Ismāʿīlīyah; Qarāmiṭah; ʿAlawīyūn; *and* Druze. *For Jewish interpretations, see* Qabbalah.]

BIBLIOGRAPHY

A somewhat dated but not unreliable survey of the history of heresy from Priscillianism and Paulicianism to Catharism is Ignaz von Döllinger's *Beiträge zur Sektengeschichte des Mittelalters,* vol. 1, *Geschichte der gnostisch-manichäischen Sekten im frühen Mittelalter* (1890; reprint, New York, 1960). Döllinger emphasizes the historical continuity between ancient gnosticism and medieval heresy but makes no distinctions between gnostic, Marcionite, and pauperistic trends. An up-to-date bibliography on this problem can be found in Giulia Sfameni Gasparro's "Sur l'histoire des influences du gnosticisme," in *Gnosis: Festschrift für Hans Jonas,* edited by Barbara Aland (Göttingen, 1978).

The most reliable monographs on Shīʿī gnosis are Heinz

Halm's *Kosmologie und Heilslehre der frühen Ismā'īlīya* (Wiesbaden, 1978) and *Die islamische Gnosis* (Munich, 1982).

On the history of medieval heresy, there is a succinct but useful general presentation by Malcolm Lambert, also containing the best bibliographical survey to date, *Medieval Heresy: Popular Movements from Bogomil to Hus* (London, 1976).

On Lurianic Qabbalah and its influence on the Shabbatean messianic movement of the seventeenth century, the best survey to date is Gershom Scholem's *Sabbatai Sevi: The Mystical Messiah, 1626–1676* (Princeton, 1973).

Gnosis und Politik, the proceedings of a symposium edited by Jacob Taubes (Paderborn, West Germany, 1984), is a well-documented collection of essays on several theories concerning gnosis and the history of modern ideas, from the beginning of the nineteenth century to date.

IOAN PETRU CULIANU

Gnosticism as a Christian Heresy

The pluralism of early Christianity in regional faith and praxis, as well as the shifting lines of authority within the first and second centuries, make it difficult to draw the sharp boundaries required to exclude a particular opinion or group as heretical. In *Against Heresies*, Irenaeus says that his predecessors were unable to refute the gnostics because they had inadequate knowledge of gnostic systems and because the gnostics appeared to say the same things as other Christians. Christian gnostics of the second century claimed to have the esoteric, spiritual interpretation of Christian scriptures, beliefs, and sacraments. Their orthodox opponents sought to prove that such persons were not Christians on the grounds that gnostic rites were occasions of immoral behavior, that their myths and doctrines were absurd, and that their intentions were destructive to true worship of God. In short, it appears that gnostics were defined as heretics by their opponents well before they stopped considering themselves to be spiritual members of the larger Christian community.

Three periods characterize the interaction of gnosticism and Christianity: (1) the late first century and early second century, in which the foundations of gnostic traditions were laid at the same time that the New Testament was being written; (2) the mid-second century to the early third century, the period of the great gnostic teachers and systems; and (3) the end of the second century into the fourth century, the period of the heresiological reaction against gnosticism.

The fluid boundaries of Christianity in the first period make it difficult to speak of gnosticism at that time as a heresy. Four types of tradition used in the second-century gnostic systems were developed in this period. First, there was a reinterpretation of *Genesis* that depicts the Jewish God as jealous and enslaving: freedom means escaping from bondage to that God. Second, there arose a tradition of Jesus' sayings as esoteric wisdom. Third, a soteriology of the soul's ascent to union with the divine from the popular forms of Platonism was adopted. And fourth, possibly, there was a mythical story of the descent of a divine being from the heavenly world to reveal that world as the true home of the soul. Each of the last three types of tradition lies behind conflicts or images in the New Testament writings.

Some scholars have argued that the incorporation of the sayings of Jesus into the gospel narrative of his life served to check the proliferation of sayings of the risen Lord uttered by Christian prophets. The soteriology of the soul's divinization through identification with wisdom has been seen behind the conflicts in *1 Corinthians*. Second-century gnostic writings use the same traditions from Philo that scholars invoke as parallel to *1 Corinthians*. The question of a first-century redeemer myth is debated in connection with the Johannine material. While the image of Jesus in the *Gospel of John* could have been developed out of existing metaphorical traditions and the structure of a gospel life of Jesus, the Johannine letters show that Johannine Christians were split over interpretation of the gospel. Both *1 John* and *2 John* condemn other Christians as heretics. Heretics deny the death of Jesus and may have held a docetic Christology. Though perhaps not based on the myth of a descending redeemer, the Johannine images contributed to second-century gnostic developments of that theme as applied to Jesus.

The second century brought fully developed gnostic systems from teachers who claimed that their systems represented the inner truth revealed by Jesus. During this period, the Greek originals of the Coptic treatises were collected at Nag Hammadi. From the orthodox side, Irenaeus's five books refuting the gnostics marked a decisive turn in Christian self-consciousness. These were followed by the antignostic writings of Hippolytus, Clement of Alexandria, Origen, Tertullian, and Epiphanius. Though Irenaeus may have drawn upon earlier antignostic writings, such as Justin's lost *Suntagma*, his work suggests a turn toward the systematic refutation of gnosticism. Rather than catalog sects and errors, Irenaeus turned to the refutation of gnostic systems using the rhetorical skills and *topoi* of philosophical debate. At the same time, he sought to provide a theoretical explication of orthodox Christian belief that would answer arguments advanced by gnostic teachers. He apparently had considerable information about Valentinian speculation, as well as some of the earlier sources of Valentinian mythology.

Like the other heresiologists, Irenaeus attacked Marcion as well as gnosticism. Marcion provided an easier target to identify as a "heresy" because he rejected the Old Testament and established a Christian canon consisting of edited versions of *Luke* and the Pauline letters. Marcion was concerned to set the boundaries between himself and the larger Christian community in a way that the gnostic teachers who claimed to provide the spiritual interpretation of Christianity were not. Irenaeus provided two guidelines for drawing the boundary that would exclude gnostic teachers from the Christian community. The first is reflected in the *regula fidei* of his *Against Heresies* (1.10.3), which gives topics about which legitimate theological speculation is possible and consequently rules out much of the cosmological speculation of the gnostic teachers. The second guideline is Irenaeus's rejection of gnostic allegorization of scripture. He insists that biblical passages must mean what they appear to mean and that they must be interpreted within their contexts. In book five, Irenaeus argues that the gnostics failed to support their claims for a spiritual resurrection in *1 Corinthians* 1:50 because they ignored the eschatological dimensions of the verses that follow.

The heresiologist's concern to draw boundaries between orthodox Christianity and gnostic teachings ran counter to the practice of second-century gnostics. Several of the Nag Hammadi treatises were apparently composed with the opposite aim. Writings such as the *Gospel of Truth* and the *Tripartite Tractate* drew explicit connections between gnostic teaching and both the teaching practice and the sacramental practice of the larger Christian community. Other gnostic writings fell within the developing patterns of ascetic Christianity in Syria and Egypt (e.g., *Gospel of Thomas, Book of Thomas the Contender, Dialogue of the Savior*). The ascetic tradition tended to reject the common Christian assumption that baptism provides a quality of sinlessness adequate to salvation and to insist that only rigorous separation from the body and its passions will lead to salvation. Such ascetic groups did, of course, draw sharp boundaries between themselves and the larger world of believers, but the preservation of the Nag Hammadi codices among Egyptian monks suggests that the division between ascetic and nonascetic Christians may have been stronger than that between "heretic" and "orthodox," even into the fourth century in some areas.

Other gnostic writings show that the efforts of heresiologists to draw boundaries against gnostics resulted in repressive measures from the orthodox side and increasing separation by gnostics (cf. *Apocalypse of Peter, Second Treatise of the Great Seth*). The *Testimony of Truth*, apparently written in third-century Alexandria, not only contains explicit attacks on the beliefs of orthodox Christians but also attacks other gnostic sects and teachers like Valentinus, Isidore, and Basilides. The author of this gnostic work considers other, nonascetic gnostics as heretics. However, the author still holds to something of the nonpolemical stance that had characterized earlier gnostic teachers, saying that the true teacher avoids disputes and makes himself equal to everyone. Another example of the effectiveness of the orthodox polemic in defining gnostics as heretics is found in what appears to be a gnostic community rule that calls for charity and love among the gnostic brethren as a sign of the truth of their claims over against the disunity of the orthodox in *Interpretation of Knowledge.* This call reverses one of Irenaeus's polemical points that the multiplicity and disunity of gnostic sects condemn their teaching when contrasted with the worldwide unity of the church.

Some scholars think that this third period, in which the gnostics were effectively isolated as "heretic" by orthodox polemic, led to a significant shift within gnostic circles. Gnosticism began to become dechristianized, to identify more with the non-Christian, esoteric, and hermetic elements within its traditions. Gnostics became members of an independent esoteric sect, moved toward the more congenial Mandaean or Manichaean circles, existed on the fringes of Alexandrian Neoplatonism in groups that emphasized thaumaturgy, or joined the monks in the Egyptian desert, where they found a kindred spirit in the combination of asceticism and Origenist mysticism. Those associated with Manichaeism or Origenism would continue to find themselves among the ranks of heretical Christians. The rest were no longer within the Christian sphere of influence.

[*See* Manichaeism; Neoplatonism; Marcionism; *and the biographies of Clement of Alexandria, Irenaeus, Origen, Philo, and Tertullian.*]

BIBLIOGRAPHY

Anyone interested in gnosticism should obtain the English translation of the Nag Hammadi codices edited by James M. Robinson, *The Nag Hammadi Library in English* (San Francisco, 1977). Another book that studies the structure and the apologetics of the gnostic dialogues from the Nag Hammadi collection is my *The Gnostic Dialogue: The Early Church and the Crisis of Gnosticism* (New York, 1980). The only other reliable treatments of the new material and its significance for the interaction of gnosticism and early Christianity are scholarly writings. Three volumes, containing papers by leading scholars in German, French, and English, provide important treatments of the subject: *Gnosis: Festschrift für Hans Jonas*, edited by Barbara Aland (Göttingen, 1978); *The Rediscovery of Gnosticism,* vol. 1, *The School of Valentinus,* and vol. 2, *Sethian Gnosticism,* edited by Bentley Layton (Leiden, 1980–1981).

The best study of the gnostic polemic against orthodox Christianity is Klaus Koschorke's *Die Polemik der Gnostiker gegen das kirchliche Christentum* (Leiden, 1978).

PHEME PERKINS

GOATS. *See* Sheep and Goats.

GOBLET D'ALVIELLA, EUGÈNE (1846–1925), Belgian historian of religions, jurist, politician, and grand master of Freemasonry (which means, in Belgium, that one is anticlerical). Count Goblet d'Alviella was the first professor of history of religions at the Université Libre (i.e., "free thinking") of Brussels, of which he was rector from 1896 to 1898. He was militant as a freethinker in trying to have the teaching of religion in schools replaced by that of the science of religion.

Goblet d'Alviella divided the study of religions into three disciplines: "hierography," "hierology," and "hierosophy." Hierography describes the development of each of the known religions. Hierology, by comparing religions, tries to formulate laws of evolution of religious phenomena; it thus "makes up for the paucity of information, in any given race or society, about the history of a belief or an institution, by appealing to the environment or period." Hierology is purely factual, while hierosophy is a philosophical attempt at classifying the various conceptions of man's relations with "superhuman beings."

Although lacking special philological training, Goblet d'Alviella studied, in hierography, various domains: Egyptian religion, Mithraism, Greek religion, Christianity, and Hinduism. In hierology, his most notable work was *La migration des symboles* (1891), in which he studied the forms, meanings, and migrations of such religious symbols as the swastika, the sacred tree, and the winged disk. The winged disk, for instance, originated in Egypt as a symbol of the sun and was adopted by the Syrians, the Hittites, the Assyrians, and the Persians, with additions and transformations in both form and meaning. In hierosophy Goblet d'Alviella studied Rationalist churches, the belief in immortality, the Buddhist catechism, progress, syncretism, and the crisis of religion.

BIBLIOGRAPHY

A large number of Goblet d'Alviella's articles are reprinted in book form under the title *Croyances, rites, institutions,* 3 vols. (Paris, 1911). Three of his works exist in English translation: *Contemporary Evolution of Religious Thought in England, America, and India* (New York, 1886); *The Migration of Symbols* (London, 1894); and his Hibbert Lectures of 1891, *Lectures on the Origin and Growth of the Conception of God as Illustrated by Anthropology and History* (London, 1892). A good summary of Goblet d'Alviella's work can be found in the article by Julien Ries in the *Dictionnaire des religions* (Paris, 1984).

JACQUES DUCHESNE-GUILLEMIN